Practicing American Politics

BASIC EDITION

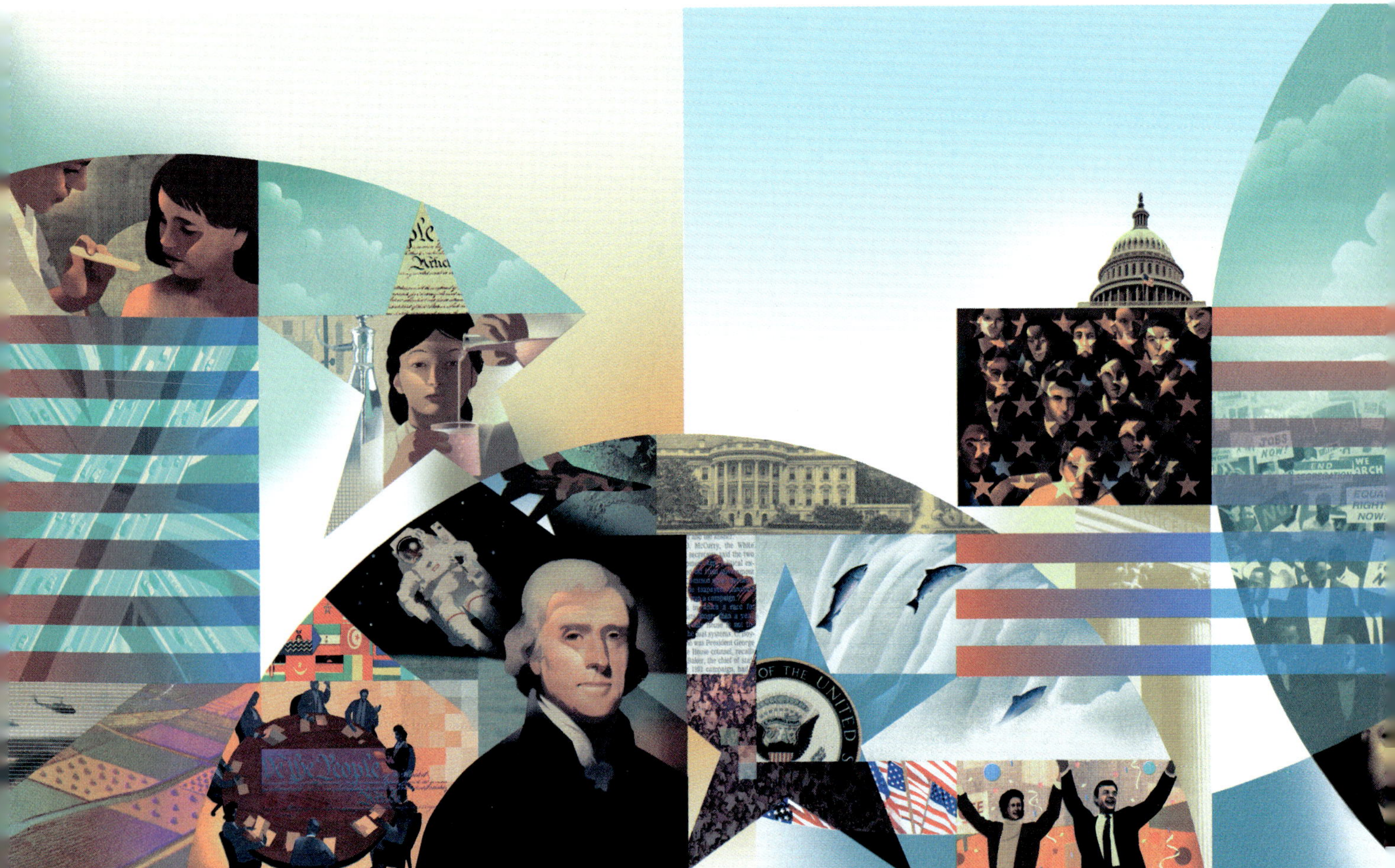
JOBS NOW!

BASIC EDITION

Practicing American Politics

An Introduction to Government

David V. Edwards **Alessandra Lippucci**

University of Texas, Austin

Worth Publishers

Practicing American Politics, Basic Edition

Copyright © 1998 by Worth Publishers

All rights reserved

Manufactured in the United States of America

Library of Congress Catalog Card Number: 97-62007

ISBN: 1-57259-533-7

Printing: 1 2 3 4 5   01 00 99 98

Executive Editor: Catherine Woods

Development Editors: Jane Tufts, Susan Seuling

Copy Editors: Ann Hofstra Grogg, Nancy Fleming

Design: Malcolm Grear Designers

Art Director: George Touloumes

Production Editors: Margaret Comaskey, Cecilia Gardner

Production Manager: Barbara Anne Seixas

Layout: Fernando Quiñones and TSI Graphics, Inc.

Picture Editor: PHOTOSEARCH, INC.

Graphics Art Manager: Demetrios Zangos

Line Art: J/B Woolsey Associates

Cover and Part Opener Art: Mick Wiggins

Composition and Separations: TSI Graphics, Inc.

Printing and Binding: Von Hoffmann Press, Inc.

Illustration credits begin on page IC-1, and copyright notices begin on page CN-1; these pages constitute extensions of the copyright page.

Worth Publishers

33 Irving Place

New York, NY 10003

We dedicate this book with love and gratitude to our parents

J. Earle Edwards, Marjorie V. Edwards, Fred H. Lippucci, Marion K. Lippucci

and to our children

John V. Edwards and Elisabeth M. Edwards

About the Authors

DAVID V. EDWARDS is Professor of Government at the University of Texas at Austin, where he has taught American government, international relations, public policy, and social theory since 1965. He was the recipient of a teaching excellence award given by the student body there. Professor Edwards is the author of *The American Political Experience*; *American Government: The Facts Reorganized*; *International Political Analysis*; *Creating a New World Politics*; and *Arms Control in International Politics*, among other works. He has also written for such periodicals as the *Washington Post, The Nation, Intellect, Panorama* (Milan), and *La Quinzaine Litteraire* (Paris). An honors and Phi Beta Kappa graduate of Swarthmore College, he was awarded Woodrow Wilson and Danforth graduate fellowships and received M.A. and Ph.D. degrees in political science from Harvard University. He was twice a Research Associate at the Johns Hopkins University Washington Center of Foreign Policy Research and has also been visiting professor of politics at New York University, and has served as a consultant to the Institute for Defense Analysis, the Danforth Foundation, and the Industrial Management Center. Among the research grants he has received have been a NATO International Research Fellowship and a Rockefeller Foundation Conflict in International Relations Fellowship.

ALESSANDRA LIPPUCCI is a political and social theorist and a lecturer in American government at the University of Texas at Austin. She studied at the Institut d'études politiques in Paris, received a B.A. in international relations from the George Washington University, and a Ph.D. in political theory from the University of Texas at Austin. She has worked on Capitol Hill for former Senator Mark O. Hatfield (R-Ore.) and former Representative Richard L. Ottinger (D-N.Y.), and in the Texas State Legislature for former Representative Hawkins Menefee (D-Houston). In addition to developing and teaching courses in American government, political and social theory, environmental politics, and ethics at the University of Texas at Austin over the past 20 years, she has also published articles on social and legal theory and delivered numerous invited papers and lectures on interdisciplinary topics. She has been a member of the American Political Science Association for 28 years.

Contents in Brief

PART 1
Practicing American Democracy 1

1. **What Is, What's Right, and What Works** 3
2. **Constitutional Practice** 35
3. **Practicing Federalism** 73

PART 2
How Americans Practice Politics 107

4. **Political Culture and Socialization** 109
5. **Public Opinion** 149
6. **Political Participation** 185
7. **Political Parties** 221
8. **Interest Groups** 265
9. **The Media** 305
10. **Campaigns and Elections** 345

PART 3
How American Institutions Work 387

11. **Congress** 389
12. **The Presidency** 437
13. **The Federal Bureaucracy** 481
14. **The Courts and the Legal System** 523

PART 4
Practicing Civil Liberties and Civil Rights 565

15. **Civil Liberties** 567
16. **Civil and Human Rights** 607

Contents

Preface xxiii

PART 1

Practicing American Democracy 1

1 What Is, What's Right, and What Works 3

What Is Politics? 5
What Is Political Authority and How Does It Work? 6
Sources of Political Authority 7
Disputes over Public Policy and the Common Good 9

The Major Actors in American Politics 10
The National and State Governments 10
The People and Their Groups 10

The Rules That Regulate American Politics 14
The U.S. Constitution 14
Constitutional Practice 14
Federalism 15
Representative Democracy 16

The Politics of Knowledge 17
Interpretation 17
The Steps (and Claims) of Political Analysis 20
Context 23

Learning by Doing in American Politics 24
The Adaptive Process 25
Learning by Doing 27

Steering the Nation into the Twenty-first Century 29

Summary 32
Key Terms 33

2 Constitutional Practice 35

The Origins of American Constitutional Practice 37
Magna Carta: The Origin of Colonial Rights 38
Rights in Colonial Founding Documents 38
English Rights and Colonial Rights 41

From Discontent to Nationhood 42
Discontent over Taxes 42
Revolution and Independence 43
State Constitutions 46
The Articles of Confederation 47

Drafting the Constitution 49
Key Disputes 51
The Governmental Machine 54
The Principles and Powers of the Constitution 56
The Powers of Each Branch of Government 59

The Dispute over Ratification 61
The Federalist Argument for Ratification 62
The Anti-Federalist Argument Against Ratification 63
Why the Federalists Won 64

Why the Constitution Still Works 64
Change by Amendment 65
Change by Interpretation 66
Refoundings 69

Summary 70
Key Terms 71
How You Can Learn More About the Founding 71

3 Practicing Federalism 73

What Is American Federalism? 75

The Federal Distribution of Powers 78
Enumerated, Reserved, and Concurrent Powers 78
Implied Powers 79
Inherent Powers 81
The Powers of the Localities 81
Indian Nations 84

The Evolution of American Federalism 86
Dual Federalism, 1836–1933 86
Cooperative Federalism, 1933–1961 88
Creative Federalism, 1961–1969 89
New Federalisms, 1969 to the Present 89

Democracy, Federalism, and the Future 97
Advantages and Disadvantages of Federalism 97
What's Right? Competing Visions of Federalism 101
What Works? Competing Approaches to Reforming Federalism 102
Toward Cyberspace Federalism? 103

Summary 104
Key Terms 105
How You Can Learn More About American Federalism 105

PART 2
How Americans Practice Politics 107

4 Political Culture and Socialization 109

American Political Culture 111
Regulating Order and Change 112
Maintaining Order Through Incremental Change 113
Protecting Diversity 113

Political Socialization 115
Primary and Secondary Political Socialization 115
Political Socialization Is *Political* 116
Political Socialization Promotes Patriotism 119
Does Political Socialization Overpromote Authority? 121
Political Socialization, Political Culture, and Political Institutions Work Together 122

Sources of Conflict in American Political Culture 123
Subcultures 123
Religion 124
Individualism and Communitarianism 126
Political Ideologies 127

Sources of Order in American Political Culture 131
Reduction of Difference 131
Common Laws, Rules, and Procedures 131
Cross-Cutting Allegiances 132

Current Challenges to the American Political Culture 133
Intergenerational Conflict 133
The Decline of Public Trust 136
Heightened Expectations of Government 138
The Downsizing of the American Dream 139
The Growing Gap Between Rich and Poor 141

Revitalizing American Political Culture 142
Upgrading and Equalizing Education 142
Strengthening Community Life 144
Redefining Patriotism and Citizen Allegiance 145

Summary 146
Key Terms 147
How You Can Learn More About Political Culture and Socialization 147

5 Public Opinion 149

What Public Opinion Is and Why It Is Important 151
What Public Opinion Is 151
Why Public Opinion Is Important 152

How Trustworthy Are Polls and Their Interpretations? 159
Survey Methods 160
Constructing the Questions 162
Timing the Poll 164
Interpreting Poll Results 166

How Competent Is American Public Opinion? 168
Political Sophistication 168
Analytical Shortcuts 172
Collective Rationality 173
Public Judgment 174

How to Improve Public Opinion 176
Increase Political Knowledge 176
Practice Collective Deliberation 179
Promote Informed Participation 179

Summary 182
Key Terms 183
How You Can Learn More About Public Opinion 183

6 Political Participation 185

Expanding the Right and Opportunity to Vote 187
Removing State Restrictions on Voting 187
Relaxing Registration and Voting Procedures 191

The Value of Voting 193
Why Voting Seems Right to Americans 193
Reservations About Voting 194
How the Experts Evaluate Voting 195

Explaining the Vote 196
Political Factors 196
Social and Class Factors 199
New Information 203

Other Forms of Political Participation 204
Participating Through Government 204
Participating Outside Government 205
Participating by Resisting 210

Government as a Political Activist 211
Types of Government Activism 211
Types of Government Resistance 212
The Benefits and Costs of Government Response 213
Improved Political Participation Can Strengthen Democracy 214

Summary 216
Key Terms 217
How You Can Learn More About Political Participation 217

7 Political Parties 219

What *Is* the American Party System? 221
How the Two-Party System Affects Government 221

What American Parties Are *Expected* to Do and What They *Actually* Do 223
Party Supporters 223
Party Ideology 226

Parties in the Federal System 231
State and National Organizations 232
Parties Lose Their Nominating Power 234

The Evolution of the Two-Party System 237
The First National Parties 238
The Modern Party System 239

Third Parties in the Two-Party System 245
Third-Party Handicaps 245
Third Parties Still Matter 249

The Two-Party System Today 251
Signs of Failure 251
Signs of Life: Reaching Out 252

Reforming the American Party System 256
Is a Multiparty System Right for America? Experts Disagree 257
How Would a Multiparty System Work in America? 258
The Current Electoral System Promotes Broader Representation and Stability 259

Summary 259
Key Terms 260
How You Can Learn More About Political Parties 261

8 Interest Groups 263

What Are Interest Groups? 265
What Makes an Interest Group "Special" or "Public"? 265
The Problem of Free Riders 266
Indirect Interests 267
Who Belongs to Interest Groups? 268
Why Interest Groups Form 270
What Interest Groups Want 274

How Interest Groups Work 277
Functions 277
Resources 278
Strategies 280

Are Interest Groups Right for America? 285
The Madisonian Dilemma 285
Can a Government Awash in Interest Groups Serve the Common Good? 286
Do Interest Groups Serve Democracy? Experts Disagree 287

Monitoring and Regulating Interest Groups 290
Current Regulations—and Loopholes 291
Proposed Reforms and Obstacles to Them 294
Ethics Regulations 299

Summary 300
Key Terms 301
How You Can Learn More About Interest Groups 301

9 The Media 303

The Media: Mass, Specialized, and People's 305
The Mass Media 306
The Specialized Media: Alternative Voices for Special Interests 309
The People's Media: Individual Access 310

How Do the Media Shape the News? 314
The Journalist's Role 314
The Interests of Owners, Editors, and Producers 321
What Kind of Bias? Media Critics Disagree 325

How the Media Cover Government and Politics 328
The White House Beat 328
The Bureaucracy Beat 330
The Capitol Hill Beat 332
The Judicial Beat 333
Covering the Rest of the World 334

Government's Power to Regulate and to Withhold Funds 334
The Power to Regulate 335
Funding of Public Broadcasting 337

Media Reform and Democracy 337
Do the Media Strengthen Democracy? 337
Media Reforms: What's Right? And What Works? 339

Summary 342
Key Terms 343
How You Can Learn More About the Media 343

10 Campaigns and Elections 345

The Nature of American Elections 347
What Elections Do and Why They Matter 347
Stakes and Resources in Elections 349
Competing Claims to Authority 349
The Political Environment 352

How Elections Have Changed 353
Presidential Elections 353
Congressional Elections 357

The Stages of a Presidential Election 364
The Constitutional Ground Rules 364
The Seven Stages of the Presidential Contest 364

Campaign Reforms and Democracy 375
More Media Responsibility 378
Efforts to Make Elections More Democratic 378

Summary 384
Key Terms 385
How You Can Learn More About Campaigns and Elections 385

PART 3
How American Institutions Work 387

11 Congress 389

What Congress Does 392
The Powers and Responsibilities of Congress 393
The Functions of Parties in Congress 395
The Roles of Members of Congress 401

The Internal Politics of Congress 407
Congress as Two Legislatures: House and Senate Committee Action 407
The Special Roles of Informal Groups and Staffers 414
Congress as Two Legislatures: House and Senate Floor Action 416
The Two Houses as One Legislature: Conference Committees 423

The External Politics of Congress 424
Relations with the President and the White House 424
Relations with the Bureaucracy 427
Relations with Other Actors: The Courts, Special Interests, and Individuals 430
Reforming Congress 432

Summary 434
Key Terms 435
How You Can Learn More About Congress 435

12 The Presidency 437

The Roles and Powers of the President 440
The President's Constitutional Roles 440
The President's Legal Powers 440
The Development of Presidential Roles and Powers 442

Presidential Characteristics 447
Presidential Qualifications, Experience, and Job Requirements 447
Presidential Personality 449
Presidential Health 449

Presidential Skills, Authority, Tools, and Resources 452
Presidential Authority 452
Special Presidential Tools 458
Presidential Resources 460

Running a Presidency 461
The Life Cycle of a Presidency 462
Managing a Presidency 464

Governing and Making Policy 472
Presidential Strategies for Dealing with Congress 472
The Presidency and the Courts 475

Reforming the Presidency 476

Summary 478
Key Terms 479
How You Can Learn More About the Presidency 479

13 The Federal Bureaucracy 481

What Is the Governmental Bureaucracy? 483

Government as a Network of Bureaucracies 483
The Evolution of the Executive Bureaucracy 486
Changes in the Executive Bureaucracy 492

What Makes Bureaucracies Effective—Or Ineffective? 495

The Key Features of a Bureaucracy 495
What Bureaucrats Do 497
The Politics of Bureaucracies 499
Using the Instruments of Bureaucratic Power 501

How the Bureaucracy Interacts with Other Institutions 505

The Presidency, Congress, and the Bureaucracy 505
Bureaucratic Relations with Special Interests, the Media, and the People 509

Reforming Bureaucracy 512

Bureaucracy and Democracy 513
Bureaucratic Ethics 514
Top-Down Bureaucratic Reform 515
Other Reform Proposals 517

Summary 520
Key Terms 521
How You Can Learn More About the Bureaucracy 521

14 The Courts and the Legal System 523

The Sources of Legal Authority 525

Types of Law 525
The Three "Legs" of American Law 526
Judicial Review 529
Judicial Decisions 530

Interpreting the Law 531

Judicial Philosophy 532
Methods of Interpretation 532

The Structure of the American Legal System 537

The State Court System 538
The Federal Court System 539
The U.S. Department of Justice 542

Influences on the Courts 545

Individual Chief Justices 545
Major Events and Developments 546
The Politics of the Appointment Process 547
Television 549
The Effects of Presidential Choices 551

How the Supreme Court Makes Public Policy 551
The Agenda-Setting Process: Deciding to Decide 552
Hearing and Deciding Cases 554
Writing Opinions and Announcing Decisions 555
Compliance 556

Reforming the Legal System 559
Social Inequality Affects Equal Justice 559
Demands for Efficiency Affect Equal Justice 560
Reforms 561

Summary 562
Key Terms 563
How You Can Learn More About the Courts and the Legal System 564

PART 4
Practicing Civil Liberties and Civil Rights 565

15 Civil Liberties 567

What Are Civil Liberties? 568
Communitarians Versus Civil Libertarians 569
The Dispute over the Origin of Civil Liberties 571
Civil Liberties in the Bill of Rights 571
Nationalizing the Bill of Rights 574

Freedom of Religion 578
Interpreting the Establishment Clause 578
Interpreting the Free Exercise Clause 581

Freedom of Expression 583
Freedom of Speech 583
Freedom of the Press 591
Life, Liberty, and Property 592
The Taking of Life 593
The Taking of Liberty 594
The Taking of Property 596

Privacy 598
The Dispute over the Right to Privacy 598
Abortion 600
Sexual Orientation 601
Wiretapping and Electronic Surveillance 601
High-Tech Invasion of Privacy 602
Civil Liberties as Constitutional Practice 603

Summary 604
Key Terms 605
How You Can Learn More About Civil Liberties 605

16 Civil and Human Rights 607

Understanding Civil Rights Disputes 608
Social Factors 609
Legal Factors 610
Political and Economic Factors 612
Systemic Factors 614

Civil Rights Strategies 615
African Americans 616
Women 622
Latinos 625
Native Americans 628
Asian Americans 630
Gays and Lesbians 632
Americans with Disabilities 634
Creating New Rights 634

Civil Rights Remedies 636
Integration: Compulsion and Incentives 637
Affirmative Action for All? 638
Equal Pay and Comparable Worth 643

The Evolving Ethics of Human Rights 645
The U.N. Declaration of Human Rights and Its Instruments 645
Disputes over Civil, Welfare, and Developmental Rights 649

Summary 651
Key Terms 652
How You Can Learn More About Civil and Human Rights 652

Appendix A-1
The Declaration of Independence A-1
Constitution of the United States of America A-4
***The Federalist,* Nos. 10 and 51** A-16
Presidents of the United States A-23
Supreme Court Justices A-24

Glossary G-1

Notes N-1

Illustration Credits IC-1

Copyright Notices CN-1

Author Index AI-1

Subject Index SI-1

Boxes

Why Good Policies Can Languish 9
How a Republican Constitution Works 51
The Origins of the Separation of Powers 61
The Roles and Rules of Constitutional Practice 68
How Living in a Federal System Affects You from Birth to Death 83
The Iroquois and American Federalism in New York State 85
America's Core Values 111
A Crisis of Democracy? 114
George Washington, National Hero 120
The Political, Economic, and Social Dimensions of Ideologies 128
Recent Changes in Values 158
Seven Steps to Public Judgment: The Case of Health Care 177
Deliberative Opinion Polls 180
How Much Can Voters Tell from a Tamale? 197
What Is a Correlation? 203
Multiparty Systems and the American Two-Party System 222
A Libertarian's View of Democrats and Republicans 229
Critical or Realigning Elections 242
Two Models for Reforming the Party System 257
Lobbying, Brussels Style 273
The Keating Debacle: The High Cost of Learning by Doing 275
The Media of Minorities and Women 311
The Framing of Lani Guinier 319
Owner Efforts to Influence Media Content 322
What Works in Presidential Campaigns: Good Running Mates—The Vice President and the Spouse 369
What Works in Presidential Campaigns: Stealing Bases 371
How Democratic Is the Electoral College? 376

Congressional Caucuses 415
What Really Happens: C-SPAN Versus the Congressional Record 419
Congress as a Bureaucracy 426
Congress's GAO Investigates the Pentagon's Smart Weaponry 429
Watergate and the Nixon Presidency 456
The Iran-Contra Affair and the Reagan Administration 470
Governmental Use and Abuse of Information Classification 503
Common Criticisms of Bureaucracy 513
The Rational Basis Test and the Strict Scrutiny Test 535
The Nexus Theory 536
Special Federal Courts 540
Special Enforcement Divisions of the Justice Department 544
The Effects of Presidential Choices on the Supreme Court 552
Explaining Habeas Corpus 595
The Intermediate Scrutiny Test 615
The Montgomery Bus Boycott: *What Worked* 618
The Civil Rights Act of 1964 619
The Nation of Islam 621
The Failure of the Equal Rights Amendment 626
U.N. Conventions Awaiting U.S. Action 650

Political Actors Disagree

Balanced Budget Amendment: Yes or No? 19
How Self-Interested Were the Framers? 53
Defining Marriage 98
Should Elites or Public Opinion Guide the Nation? 170
Presidential Character 450
Supreme Court Justices on Judicial Philosophy 533

Are Children Entitled to Civil Liberties? 570
The Dispute over the Constitutionality of the Religious Freedom Restoration Act 584
Gloria Steinem vs. Milos Forman 588
Are Women and Men Equal? 624
The Dispute over the Sex Gap in Pay 646

Political Action Guides

How to Find Out *What Is*: Accessing Political Information 21
How to Decide *What's Right:* Making Ethical Judgments in Politics 24
How to Write an Effective Letter to the Editor 208
How to Learn to Be a Political Activist 215
Parties Active in the United States Today 246
Getting Information from Groups About Financial Aid 271
How to Read the Morning Paper and Watch the Evening News 326
How You Can Contribute to Political Campaigns 358
How to Find and Interpret Congressional Voting Records 421
How to Communicate Effectively with Your Members of Congress 430

The Politics of Knowledge

Shays' Rebellion: Anarchy or Justice? 50
Censorship in the Schools 118
The Power of Secret Polls 155
Factors That Shape Civil Rights Beliefs and Analysis 610
Defining Equal Opportunity 638

The Politics of Language

Pretested Language in the "Contract with America" 157
The Language of Media Insiders 317
What Should the President Be Called? 453
The Bureaucrat's Ten Commandments 507
Interpreting the Right "to Keep and Bear Arms" 573
The Dispute over the Ninth Amendment 599

Preface

We have taught the American government course required of all undergraduates at the University of Texas at Austin to classes of 200 to 350 for decades. We had used *The American Political Experience*, which David Edwards had written, as it went through four editions in the late 1970s and 1980s. That book emphasized the importance of citizen participation and the situations of women and ethnic and other minorities.

By the 1990s, politics and policy challenges had changed, and so had our approach to teaching the course. We therefore felt it was time to write a completely new book—one that retained the strengths of *The American Political Experience* but was based on the pedagogical principles we had been developing in the classroom.

While we were revising the manuscript, we used several versions of it in our classes. We also used a major daily newspaper as a supplement so that students could see the connections between actual current events and what they were learning from the textbook. Their performance on tests and their comments in class indicated that the analytical tools and principles they were learning from the textbook enhanced their understanding of the political activities and events they were seeing in the daily news. And, because the textbook did the major work of describing and explaining the political dynamics we wanted our students to master, we were free to elaborate upon them in lectures, illustrate them with video clips and newspaper articles, and invite students to discuss and debate them during class. The feedback we got from students personally and in their course evaluations was gratifying. Students expressed greater interest in the course, and their test scores over the semester revealed steady improvement in their ability to analyze political problems and disputes thoughtfully and critically.

Our Approach to the Study of Politics

Throughout the book, we analyze politics in terms of three questions: *What is*? *What's right*? and *What works*? We believe that here we can best convey the purpose and pedagogical features of this book by using the same approach.

What Is Our Pedagogical Approach?

We describe, explain, and evaluate the processes of American politics with the help of a strong, clear pedagogical framework that we introduce in Chapter 1 and use consistently throughout the book. The basis of this framework is our definition of politics:

> Politics consists of disputes over claims to the authority to decide *what is, what's right,* and *what works.*

Through this definition, students are stimulated to address two key questions:

1. Which political actors are making conflicting claims to this authority?
2. How do they try to persuade others that they know *what is, what's right*, and *what works*? In other words, how do they make these claims to authority?

We encourage students to raise these questions with respect to every dispute they encounter—in this text, in current affairs, and in their daily lives.

Because our definition of politics focuses on disputes over claims to authority, we present as much of the subject matter as we can in the form of disputes. Some of these disputes—such as what the Constitution means or how a core American value (liberty, equality, the right to property) should be applied in a particular instance—have persisted throughout the nation's history, while other disputes (over education policy or welfare policy, for example) arose later but have persisted. Still other disputes (such as the dispute over slavery) have been resolved once and for all. As we present these disputes in this text, we point out gaps between political principles (*what's right*) and political practice (*what is* or *what works*). Finally, we show that solutions to some political problems can, over time, become problems themselves, and that much of the problem solving in which political actors engage involves *learning by doing*.

Why We Believe Our Pedagogical Approach Is *What's Right* for a Basic American Government Course

As its title, *Practicing American Politics*, indicates, this book puts the basics of American politics into the normative as well as the descriptive context of political practice. We show that all people, groups, and institutions—including government—affect the political process, either by engaging in politics actively and intentionally or by leaving it to others, and that all are therefore responsible for the quality of American democracy.

The book encourages students to practice politics in ways that accord with their beliefs, values, talents, and expanding body of knowledge. It does so by equipping them with nonideological methods for understanding and evaluating political processes and issues and by giving them tools and information to help them practice politics in a variety of ways throughout their lives.

This practice-oriented approach was inspired by the realization that this text and this course may well be the only sustained encounter students will have with this subject in their lifetimes. The guiding purpose of this book, in two words, is to encourage *good citizenship*—by which we mean an acceptance of the responsibility that each of us bears to strengthen democracy in a changing world, to protect it from "the tragedy of the commons" (situations in which individuals seek their own goals in ways that produce negative consequences for the whole), and to ensure that all of us continue to dedicate our individual gifts and aspirations to the common good, even as we debate what that good is or should be.

How Is Our Pedagogical Approach *What Works*?

When students examine a dispute and discover that its participants see the matter that divides them (*what is*) in terms of their differing needs and goals and their varying perspectives, students confront the fact that politics creates winners and losers among people who feel justified in their views. In asking which party should prevail, or what the outcome of the dispute should be (*what's right*), students confront the ethical dimensions of the dispute and must consult their own consciences. In asking which solution would be the most efficient or affordable (*what works*), students confront the practical side of problems and the necessity of establishing priorities in situations that often involve scarcity, insufficient information, and the need to make painful tradeoffs as, for example, in formulating a policy that promotes cleaner air and public health without crippling auto manufacturers and other industries. In confronting such problems, students discover that political solutions require a willingness to *learn by doing* and to make adjustments in response to that learning.

Although these three questions—*what is*, *what's right*, and *what works*—are often intertwined in any dispute, asking them separately helps students to pinpoint areas of consensus and disagreement. In the case of welfare policy, for example, they will discover that some people agree that a welfare problem exists (*what is*) and may even agree on *what's right* (that certain people should or should not receive a helping hand from the rest of society), but they may not agree on *what works* (what welfare reforms would best address the problem).

Chapter 1 also introduces students to *the politics of knowledge*—strategies of communication that rely on the manipulation of information, logic, and language, often in combination, to bolster a political actor's claims about *what is*, *what's right*, and *what works*. We then equip students with the basic analytical tools (practices of description, explanation, evaluation, and prescription) that allow them to recognize the politics of knowledge when actors employ these strategies and to analyze and evaluate political disputes (and any other kinds of disputes, for that matter). They discover that these analytical tools are often intertwined, and they learn how to use these tools themselves and to recognize when they are being used by others. We were delighted when one of our students exclaimed enthusiastically at the end of a semester: "I have never liked politics because it all seemed such a mess. Now, when I pick up the newspaper, I automatically see an argument in terms of *what is*, *what's right*, and *what works*. And I really understand what's going on!"

Special Features

We've incorporated many special features to reinforce student learning.

Introductory Case Studies in Each Chapter

Each chapter starts with an introductory case study that is designed to perform two important tasks. First, we refer back to the case study throughout the chapter to illustrate the chapter's key points and concepts. Second, as a chapter unfolds we sometimes fill out more areas of the case study. This pedagogical device is used extensively in Chapter 1, for example, where we introduce major political actors, political rules, and features of the political process in terms of the disputes over water scarcity in California. We do the same with other case studies, among them "lemon laws" protecting car buyers (Chapter 3), multicultural college courses (Chapter 4), Ross Perot's presidential campaigns (Chapter 7), the Rodney King affair (Chapter 9), and the implementation of Clean Air Act amendments (Chapter 13).

Critical Thinking Aids

Boxed features called the Politics of Knowledge, the Politics of Language, and Political Actors Disagree appear throughout the text. These boxes stimulate critical thinking and reinforce the pedagogical principles outlined in Chapter 1 by exposing the roots of political disputes so that students learn to analyze political questions critically and think about them constructively.

Participation Aids

Political Action Guides provide students with information on a variety of ways of practicing politics, from how to read the morning paper and watch the evening news to how to get in touch with many political parties.

Internet Aids

Practicing "electronic democracy" via the Internet is encouraged in every chapter. Web site addresses in marginal boxes tell students where they can reach political actors of all types, from government agencies to interest groups to political parties to major media. In addition, the case study in Chapter 6 shows how an ordinary citizen used an electronic bulletin board and e-mail to help solve a homeless problem in her community. And Chapter 9 provides useful information on the people's media.

Integration of Special Features in the Text

We have selected the textual and visual elements of each chapter to complement one another. What students read in the text is directly connected to the visuals they see on the page. Every box, marginal definition, table, figure, photograph, and cartoon has been carefully chosen to illustrate specific points we make in the text. Each chapter thus functions as a coordinate whole.

Coverage

Public Policy

We have integrated our discussions of particular policy issues throughout the book—especially where those issues highlight the politics of federalism and the politics that result from the separation of powers and from the system of checks and balances—to reinforce students' understanding of those central dynamics which they will find in the news every day. For example, *environmental policy* is discussed in Chapter 1, Chapter 8 (Interest Groups), Chapter 11 (Congress), and Chapter 13 (Bureaucracy), among others. *Education policy* is covered in Chapter 1, Chapter 4 (Political Culture and Socialization), Chapter 5 (Public Opinion), Chapter 14 (The Courts and the Legal System), and Chapter 16 (Civil Rights). *Campaign finance* is discussed in Chapter 8 (Interest Groups) and Chapter 10 (Campaigns and Elections). *Economic policy* is treated in Chapter 4 and Chapter 12 (The Presidency).

Cultural Diversity

The changing racial and ethnic composition of our American Government classes, and the growing presence of international students and students with severe disabilities, have encouraged us to focus on the cultural and other differences that both enrich and challenge American democracy. We have integrated coverage of these differences throughout the chapters to foster civility and mutual respect. The pedagogical principles that we use in this book encourage students to view the circumstances of another person or a group from the perspective of that person or group as part of the process of deciding *what is, what's right,* and *what works.*

Comparative Perspectives

Many of our chapters deal with the growing effects of globalization on American politics in such areas as the economy, human rights, scarcity of resources, and the environment. We also have boxed features with comparative coverage of differing political systems (such as federal structures and parliamentary systems) where we believe these differences are especially illuminating, and we integrate these discussions in the text itself wherever possible.

Impacts of Federalism

By encountering different aspects of federalism in virtually every chapter, students discover the many ways in which this form of government structures the behavior of political actors ranging from parties, campaigns, interest groups, and the media to local, state, and national governments. By the time they have finished the book, students will see federalism as a practical reality of political life.

Ethics and Reform

In addition to raising ethical questions (relating to the *what's right* theme) throughout the book, each chapter ends with a section that focuses on the problems and prospects for reform in areas related to that chapter. In these sections students discover that proposals for reform are often contested and thus constitute a central feature of political life.

Supplements to the Text

A talented team of authors has produced a number of supplements to help students master the principles and political dynamics described and explained in our book. Instructors will benefit from a number of supplements designed to enhance lectures, lessons, and the teaching experience.

Student Learning Guide Marilyn Davis, Spelman College. The Student Learning Guide helps students focus on chapter material with features such as chapter summaries, guided study, definitions of key terms, and practice test questions, which include the matching of key terms and multiple choice and essay questions. Correct answers with page references are listed at the end of each chapter.

Instructor's Resources Manual Brian Fife, Indiana University—Purdue University at Fort Wayne. Instructors will find this an invaluable resource. Each chapter contains a chapter of overview and outline, a condensation of chapter themes, definitions of key terms (organized by the chapter's main heads), lecture suggestions, classroom activities, Internet addresses, and additional readings.

Test Bank Jim Henson, Northeast Louisiana University. More than 1,500 multiple choice, fill-in, true-false, and essay questions accompany the textbook. The computerized test system allows instructors to edit questions, import questions, create multiple versions of tests, print in a variety of fonts, and even test students online.

Documents Collection Brian Fife, Indiana University—Purdue University at Fort Wayne. A comprehensive collection of more than 50 primary source documents keyed to chapters in the textbook. Each document is preceded by a short description of its context and background.

Transparencies The transparency set includes approximately 70 four-color acetates of illustrations, charts, figures, graphs, and maps from the text.

The St. Martin's Resource Library in Political Science By special arrangement with St. Martin's Press, we are offering three brief, supplementary books on a range of topics:

Ralph Nader's Practicing Democracy, 1997: A Guide to Student Action, 2nd ed.—Katherine Isaac, Center for the Study of Responsive Law. This valuable resource contains biographical and contact information for over 400 political action groups. It empowers students to become politically active at the local, state, and federal level.

Big Ideas: An Introduction to Ideologies in American Politics—R. Mark Tiller, Houston Community College. This book presents an overview of political, social, and economic ideologies and their connection to politics and policy disputes.

The Real Thing: Contemporary Documents in American Government—Fenyan Shi, Georgetown University. This anthology contains the texts of laws, letters, memos, grants, court opinions, and other documents that can be used for critical analysis.

Acknowledgments

Our greatest debt by far is to each other for the love and familial and intellectual companionship that we have shared for two and a half decades, especially during the seven years of intense partnership in working on this book.

We have dedicated this book to our parents and our children, with profound gratitude for their presence in our lives. We are also grateful for the enormous contributions that our teachers, teaching assistants, students, and friends in Austin, around the nation, and around the world have made to our lives and our work.

For all the wonderful years of friendship and support, we particularly wish to thank Burt and Mary Fagan, Eusebio Pons and Montserrat Porqueras de Pons, Lourdes Mir de Orrange and Rob Orrange, Helena de La Fontaine and Zulfikar Ghose, John and Leslie Cunningham, David Kramer, Carmen Lord, and Joan Balogh and Alan Kubala.

David Edwards also wishes to thank the people in his church, work group, men's group, and dance group, and the others who have made special contributions—especially Tim and Barbara Cook, Kathy Rodgers, and Alexandra Evans.

Alessandra Lippucci also wishes to acknowledge a special debt to Roger and Dagmar Louis, Ed Epperson and Mary Luker, and David Prindle.

We thank all our colleagues and staff members (past and present) in the Department of Government and in other departments at the University of Texas at Austin with whom we have worked and shared years of learning and friendship. We especially wish to thank our teaching assistants in the American government course who participated in the development of the pedagogical base on which this book now stands. For their particular contributions to this book we thank Dean Burnham, John Butler, Suzanne Colwell, Jim Fishkin, Michele Gallman, Michael Hall, Bob Luskin, Susan Marshall, Janice May, Joe TenBarge, Douglas Laycock, H. W. Perry, Luis Plascencia, Robert Moser, Lisa Montoya, and Daron Shaw. We thank the reference librarians at the Tarleton Library, especially David Gunn, and at the Perry-Castañeda Library for their invaluable assistance. We thank Greg Wallace of Wallace Distributors for his contributions of copies of the *New York Times* and the *Wall Street Journal*.

Over the seven years between signing our contract with Worth and completing the final draft of this book, we have worked with dozens of highly competent professionals. Bob Worth and Tom Gay saw the promise of this project and signed it. Our development editors and copy editors—the most demanding we have ever had the challenge and pleasure to work with—began with Jane Tufts and included Susan Seuling, Ann Hofstra Grogg, and Nancy Fleming; their contributions have improved every page. Editorial assistant Howard Unger exceeded his portfolio by being a sympathetic soundingboard and an exceptional resource on the Vietnam period. The versatile Deanna Krickus and Donna MacIver (editorial assistants) facilitated the project's progress in many and varied ways. Margaret Comaskey and Cecilia Gardner (senior project editors) and Suzanne Thibodeau (managing editor), were the ones who energetically tugged, pulled, and finally yanked this project through the production process with unfailing and supportive good spirits. George Touloumes (art director) applied his legendary artistic skills working with Malcolm Grear Designers to create yet another beautiful Worth book. Penny Bice, our supplements editor, and the author team she put together produced the specially designed and carefully edited supplements. Deborah Bull of PhotoSearch good-naturedly sought to fulfill our unusually demanding photo requests.

This book would not be in your hands now if it were not for the leadership of Worth's president, Susan Driscoll, and Catherine Woods (executive editor), who, after joining the company in 1996, finally put this project on a fast track. With their publishing and people skills they made the project the focus of a *team*—the secret to any successful enterprise—and hovered over us until the book was finished. They sat in on key meetings in New York, flew to Austin to hammer out the schedule (over Tex-Mex food), and participated in regular conference calls. They were always there for us, as we knew they were there for everyone else. Those of you who have known the experience of working as a team know that friendship invariably binds those who touch, with common commitment, the same project. We have all worked hard, but working hard together has been one of the most deeply satisfying episodes in our lives, and for this we thank our teammates from the bottom of our hearts.

David V. Edwards
Alessandra Lippucci

Reviewers

The authors want to thank the following reviewers—whom our publisher selected with care, and whose identities we learned only when the book was finished—for their invaluable suggestions and criticisms, which we used to revise and improve the text at every stage. The book is much stronger because of their efforts.

George Agbango
Bloomsburg University of Pennsylvania

Davis Ahern
University of Dayton

Judith A. Baer
Texas A&M University

Paul Benson
West Texas A&M University

Peter Bergerson
Southeast Missouri State University

Jim Calvi
West Texas A&M University

Carol Cassel
University of Alabama

Allan J. Cigler
University of Kansas

Gloria Cox
University of North Texas

Marilyn A. Davis
Spelman College

Arthur English
University of Arkansas, Little Rock

Elizabeth N. Flores
Del Mar College

Patricia S. Florestano
University of Baltimore

Richard R. Johnson
Northwestern Oklahoma State University

Tobe Johnson
Morehouse College

Laurence F. Jones
Angelo State University

Ronald Kahn
Oberlin College

Thomas A. Kazee
Davidson College

Scoot Keeter
Virginia Commonwealth University

Matthew R. Kerbel
Villanova University

Stephen A. Lohse
University of North Texas

Benjamin Marquez
University of Wisconsin

Lee McGriggs
College of the Mainland

Lisa Montoya
University of Texas, Austin

Wayne D. Moore
Virginia Polytechnic Institute

James A. Morrow
Tulsa Community College

Dennis Ogirri
Johnson C. Smith University

David Olson
University of Washington

Timothy O'Neill
Southwestern University

Bruce I. Oppenheimer
University of Houston

Donald L. Robinson
Smith College

David C. Saffell
Ohio Northern University

Jeffrey A. Segal
State University of New York, Stony Brook

Henry Sirgo
McNeese State University

Terry Spurlock
Trinity Valley Community College

Danny G. Sutton
Iowa State University

Mark P. Sutton
Bucks County Community College

Alan Thornton
Howard University

Melvyn Urofsky
Virginia Commonwealth University

Stephen H. Wainscott
Clemson University

James Ward
University of Massachusetts, Boston

Jonathan P. West
University of Miami

Laura Woliver
University of South Carolina

Allan Wyner
University of California, Santa Barbara

Cheryl Young
University of North Florida

Practicing American Democracy

PART 1

What Is, What's Right, and What Works

Dams such as this one in northern California prevent salmon from swimming freely upstream to spawn.

CHAPTER 1

The citizen . . . expects that planes will not crash . . . that elevators will not break their cables, food products will be free of botulism, and pure water will come out when the tap is turned on. If these expectations are *not* met, then some agency of government, or some institution . . . must pay and take the blame. And the legal system will provide—*must* provide—machinery to make sure all this happens by way of prevention, or cure, and certainly by payment of damages.

Lawrence M. Friedman

[Government] covers the surface of society with a network of small complicated rules, minute and uniform. . . . Such a power . . . compresses, enervates, extinguishes, and stupifies a people, till each nation is reduced to nothing better than a flock of timid and industrial animals, of which government is the shepherd.

Alexis de Tocqueville[1]

What Is Politics?

The Major Actors in American Politics

The Rules That Regulate American Politics

The Politics of Knowledge

Learning by Doing in American Politics

Steering the Nation into the Twenty-first Century

What do washing our cars, watering our lawns, and being served a glass of water in a restaurant have to do with politics? Normally, nothing—unless you happen to live in a place where water is scarce, such as southern California. When a valued resource becomes scarce it enters the domain of politics. Right now government asks Californians to conserve water voluntarily, but the time may soon come when it gives them no choice.

A string of droughts in recent years has reduced California's water supply at the same time that urban and suburban areas have continued to mushroom, increasing the demand. Massive farms now compete for this precious resource with the Chinook salmon and the delta smelt that the salmon feed on. Farmers have posted signs warning "NO WATER, NO FARMING, NO FOOD." Farms that once employed hundreds of migrant workers to harvest fruits and vegetables now turn them away, and shops that catered to farmers and workers have shut down. The salmon, which have survived many changes in their habitat, are prevented by large dams from swimming upstream to spawn or are chewed up by the dams' turbines that generate electricity for industry and people. As one politician put it, "The only obstacle the salmon have not been able to overcome was the pouring of concrete across their rivers."[2] Meanwhile, builders and developers want more water to expand the cities and suburbs where most of the state's voters now live. The scarcity of water has become a mainspring of California politics. What brought this crisis about?[3]

In the 1930s, President Franklin Roosevelt relied on federal water policy to lift the Pacific Northwest and California out of the Great Depression. As part of this policy, the national government helped California build a series of dams that created thousands of jobs, provided cheap electricity to homes and businesses, and supplied virtually unlimited water to farms, industries, and cities. As the state's population grew, so did its water projects. Today a massive network of aqueducts, canals, and tunnels transports California water hundreds of miles through the Central Valley Project—the biggest plumbing works on the planet.

Northern California now ships two-thirds of the state's supply of water to southern California, which has two-thirds of the state's population but very little water of its own. Much of this water is used to drench the Central Valley, formerly a desert of 100,000 acres stretching about 500 miles from north to south and 40 to 100 miles from east to west. This long-distance irrigation makes the Central Valley the richest and most productive agricultural area in the country. For years, most Californians, along with Americans nationwide who feasted on the Central Valley's fruits and vegetables, were happy with this arrangement. So were California's farmers, who got all the water they wanted for practically nothing because taxpayers footed much of the bill. So were developers, who built millions of homes, and homeowners, one in every 15 of whom had a private swimming pool.[4] But the era of water abundance has ended.

When a resource becomes scarce, those who value it compete to acquire as much of it as they can, often calling on government to draft laws and regulations that support their interests. In California such pressure has come from agribusiness (large commercial farms) on one side and commercial fisheries (many of which belong to Native Americans), the sport fishing industry, duck hunters, and conservationists on the other. Residents of cities and suburbs who once sided with agribusiness now support conservationists and developers in their efforts to reduce the amount of water going to agribusiness—water that they, as the largest group of taxpayers in the state, are forced to subsidize. Those in the business of pumping water from the north to the south (such as the Metropolitan Water District, founded in 1928), who once pumped 80 percent of the state's water to agribusiness, are now siding with the cities and suburbs.

To balance these interests, the federal government has been trying to reallocate California's water. In 1992 Congress passed a bill that tripled the water allocation for fish and wildlife at the expense of farmers and developers and funded water development projects sought by other water-poor western states. In 1994, in an effort to save the salmon, new federal regulations forced sharp cutbacks in the supply of water to the Central Valley.

The politics of water in California has involved many political actors—federal and state politicians, the Environmental Protection Agency (EPA), Congress, the state of California, the media, special interest groups, and a wide variety of experts. Arguments among such competing actors are the basic stuff of politics. In every political dispute we examine in this book, the key issue is which actors—which individuals, groups, or institutions—have the most credible claim to the authority to answer questions about *what is*, *what's right*, and *what works* with respect to a disputed issue. *What is* the current supply-and-demand situation for water in California? What is the *right* allocation of water among competing interests? *What* public policies *will work* to prevent chronic water shortages and protect the salmon?

This chapter introduces you to the basic concepts and analytical tools that we shall be using to analyze disputes in coming chapters. By the time you finish this book, you should understand what American politics is, how it works, and how to practice it effectively. This chapter examines four basic questions:

What is politics?

What major actors practice American politics?

What rules regulate American politics?

How do knowledge and learning affect political practice?

What Is Politics?

All disputes involve a disagreement over whose authority is the most credible. Disputes among **political actors**—individuals, groups, and organizations competing for authority—are the essence of politics. In a dictatorship, some political actors can get what they want by physical force. In a **democracy**, where political authority rests with the people, political actors must persuade others that what they want is right, is reasonable, or promises to be effective.

How persuasive a political actor is depends on how much authority that actor has—that is, how highly people regard that actor's knowledge, integrity, judgment, or effectiveness. When political actors disagree, each typically asserts its superior authority to decide an issue. That is why this book defines **politics** as disputes over claims to the authority to decide *what is*, *what's right*, or *what works*.

This definition of politics is much broader than social scientist Harold Lasswell's classic definition: "Who gets what, when and how?"[5] In California's water wars the distributive question is obvious: Who will get how much water, when, and by what means? This broader definition of politics exposes the competition among political actors for the authority to decide what the distributive outcome should be. This definition allows us to see that each political actor is claiming to be the highest authority on what the crisis involves (*what is*); what action is the correct one to take (*what's right*); and what action will be the most effective (*what works*).

democracy
The term, from the Greek *demos*, people, and *kratis*, authority or rule, means a system of government in which political authority rests with the people.

politics
The term comes from *polis*, the Greek word for city.

government

The term, from the Latin *gubernare*, to steer (a vessel), refers to the continuous exercise of authority over the members of a political society.

power, force, and authority

Power comes from the Latin *potere*, to be able; force from the Latin *fortis*, strong; authority from *auctor*, Latin for agent or actor.

What Is Political Authority and How Does It Work?

The strongest actor in American politics is the **government**, which consists of (1) public laws, (2) public institutions, and (3) public officials. How does government command respect and obedience when its actions are continually criticized by other political actors—political leaders, interest groups, citizen watchdogs, the media, and the public? The obvious answer is that government has enormous **power** to get other actors to do something that they would not otherwise do. Most people grit their teeth when they pay taxes but recognize the benefits of government protection and services. (Just how much protection and how many services the nation needs are, of course, matters of ongoing dispute.) They also know that tax evaders are punished.

Governments have two types of power at their disposal: force and authority. Authority is the most commonly used form of power in politics, just as force is the most common form of power in war. **Force** physically compels an actor to act against its will—as, for example, when the police chase down and arrest a speeder. **Authority** is recognized or accepted power that obtains obedience without the use of force. In many cases, authority works because people believe it is legal or right (to obey a posted speed limit, for example). In other cases, authority works because people recognize that obedience can be achieved by force. When Indian tribes were told that parts of their reservations would be flooded to build dams in the Pacific Northwest and northern California, they evacuated those areas because they recognized that they would be forcibly removed if they did not evacuate. Most of us stick fairly close to the legal speed limit, because we know the consequences of not complying. This knowledge, and the respect for authority it generates, means that police cars do not have to patrol every mile of highway.

Police in Riverside, California, about to arrest a man in a stolen pickup. He crashed into a tree after leading the police on a short chase.

Sources of Political Authority

Political actors typically draw on four sources of authority—tradition, charisma, expertise, and legitimacy.

Tradition

Many of the legal, religious, and economic practices that influence American politics today have their own sources of authority. However, these sources, such as English common law (Chapter 14), Protestantism (Chapter 4), and capitalism (including **laissez-faire capitalism**), have been reinforced by centuries of **tradition**. American judges today, for example, rely on the same common law principles that guided their colonial and English predecessors. Some traditions, such as Protestantism and capitalism, are also mutually reinforcing. The traditional Protestant values of hard work and self-reliance and **capitalism's** emphasis on private property and economic self-interest are mutually reinforcing in American political culture.[6] Recent efforts to restrict federal social welfare and the government's right to confiscate private property for public use may be traced to these complementary traditions. Traditions also enhance the legal authority of those in high public office. Certainly the image of the Supreme Court justices would suffer if they appeared on the High Bench in suits and dresses—let alone in bathing suits—rather than in their traditional black robes, as would that of a president if no military band played "Hail to the Chief" on formal occasions.

Charisma

A source of authority for some political actors is **charisma**—a personal magnetism that inspires others. Charisma has no necessary connection with character. A charismatic political actor may, depending on one's point of view, seem praiseworthy, like George Washington, or diabolical, like Adolf Hitler. Presidents Franklin Roosevelt (1933–1945) and John F. Kennedy (1961–1963) were also charismatic leaders. President Ronald Reagan (1981–1989) had enough charisma— a combination of friendliness and charm—to sustain his popularity even though it was common knowledge that he sometimes fell asleep or told anecdotes from his Hollywood career in cabinet meetings. Charisma also increased the Reverend Martin Luther King, Jr.'s effectiveness as a civil rights leader and César Chavez's effectiveness as a labor union leader.

Expertise

Political actors who lack charisma must find other ways to bolster their authority. The most common way is to be recognized as a trained or experienced expert in a specialized field. This gives them **expertise**—specialized knowledge that most people

---

capitalism

Capitalism is an economic system in which the means of production (factories, farms, shops) are privately rather than publicly (government) owned. Owners and their assistants operate these enterprises for a profit, employing the rest of the work force as laborers.

laissez-faire capitalism

The theory of laissez-faire (French for "let it alone") capitalism was developed by Scottish economist Adam Smith (1723–1790) in his book *The Wealth of Nations*. This theory's proponents believe government should place no restrictions on economic activity because natural balancing forces in the marketplace will benefit those who are productive and efficient as well as consumers.

tradition

The term describes an inherited, established, or customary pattern of thinking, acting, or behaving that is passed down from generation to generation by word of mouth, writing, or gesture.

accept as accurate and relevant. Political leaders must rely on experts for specialized knowledge because most of what they do and decide involves technical or complex knowledge that goes beyond their personal experience. Presidents, cabinet officials, and members of Congress have access to numerous experts in and out of government who possess specialized information about virtually every subject. The drafters of the Endangered Species Act, for example, relied on the expertise of marine biologists, hydrologists (experts on water flow), and environmental lawyers, among others.

Although expertise may strengthen an official's authority, it may not be enough to guarantee that person's effectiveness or to win public support. President Jimmy Carter (1977–1981), a "policy wonk," mastered impressive amounts of technical policy information, but he lacked broad appeal and the political skills required to advance his policy agenda effectively. He was beaten in his campaign for reelection by Ronald Reagan, who lacked expertise but possessed charisma.

Legitimacy

In American politics, the authority of political actors is also bolstered by **legitimacy**—the appearance of legality or rightness. Whatever its source, legitimacy bestows on individuals, groups, and institutions an aura of correctness that strengthens their authority. Actors acquire legitimacy by adhering to the laws produced by government. Presidents—even the ones we don't like or didn't vote for—have legitimacy in our eyes simply because they have been elected under the law and conform to it. Political actors also acquire legitimacy by adhering to certain religious and moral principles, some of which coincide with secular laws (the prohibitions against theft, perjury, and murder, for instance), and by respecting firmly ingrained traditions of American political culture (such as saluting the American flag).

Sometimes several types of legitimacy converge to strengthen an actor's authority. For example, the president takes the oath of office in the presence of American flags and swears to uphold the Constitution with one hand raised before the Chief Justice of the Supreme Court and the other hand placed on the Bible. Civil rights leaders such as the Reverend Martin Luther King, Jr., and the Reverend Jesse Jackson have used their authority as religious leaders to legitimate the civil rights movement and, in Jackson's case, to run for president and mediate between business and labor. The fact that Jimmy Carter was a devout born-again Christian when he ran for president in 1976 and that conservative televangelist Pat Robertson was a well-known minister when he ran for president in 1988 gave both men strong moral legitimacy with like-minded voters.

Legitimacy is also mutually reinforcing within a political system. California, for example, has abided by the national Endangered Species Act because it recognizes that the U.S. Constitution grants Congress the authority to pass laws legally binding on the states. States and businesses obey the EPA's water protection regulations because they recognize that the EPA is acting legitimately on the basis of authority granted by Congress and the Constitution.

---

policy wonk
This slang term describes someone who understands the nuts and bolts of policy issues.

legitimacy
The term for this type of authority comes from the Latin *leges*, laws.

policy
This term, like the word "police," comes from the French *polire*, to clean, and refers to procedures and programs that governments, businesses, and others adopt to organize their activities and to solve problems.

Why Good Policies Can Languish

In January 1997, floods ravaged Yosemite National Park, damaging cabins, sewers, roads, bridges, and the parking lots of restaurants and shops that cater to 4 million visitors each year—many more than the park can handle ecologically. Each day cars, trucks, and recreational vehicles pollute the mile-long trip through Yosemite Village. These floods focused all too rare attention on the U.S. National Park Service, which must preserve the park's ecosystem and keep the 374 parks in the system accessible to the public at the same time.

In 1980 Park Service staff devised a master plan to restore the balance between the natural environment and visitors by easing traffic, restoring meadows, moving housing outside the park, relocating campsites to higher ground, and giving the riverbanks back to the animals. Why has this plan languished for so long?

As with many good policies, the plan was overwhelmed by more than one unfriendly political environment. First, it coincided with the onset of the Reagan administration, whose Environmental Protection Agency chief had vowed to abolish the agency. Second, it coincided with the administration's initiative to downsize government and cut back on federal services. Third, helping the national parks was not a priority for most lawmakers, who were intent on channeling whatever federal money they could to their own constituencies. In short, this "common good" had no powerful advocates.

So, despite widespread recognition that the national parks were in trouble (*what is*); that this trouble should be remedied (*what's right*); and that the Park Service had developed a remedy that *would work*, nothing was done during two Reagan administrations and one Bush administration. If the Park Service's hopes were raised when Bill Clinton promised to pay greater attention to environmental problems in his 1992 presidential campaign, his first administration's priorities did not include the environment. In American politics, problems *and* solutions often languish until the political climate becomes hospitable to political action.

Source: "Nature's Agenda," *New York Times*, February 15, 1997.

Disputes over Public Policy and the Common Good

Most political disputes involve competing claims to the authority to decide which **public policies**—laws and government regulations or practices—best serve the public, or **the common good**. A key question is, Who gets to define "the public" or "the common good"? In the California water wars, there seem to be many "publics" rather than just one, and there does not seem to be one "good" that is common to all. In such areas as the environment, energy, taxes, and foreign affairs, policymakers must often make painful tradeoffs. Because public policies frequently help some people at the expense of others, it is important that all parties to a policy dispute have fair access to government to present their views on the issue if the authority of government is to survive such tradeoffs. But even when there is a consensus on what the common good is and what policy it requires, the policy may languish, as the box above illustrates.

The Major Actors in American Politics

The major actors in American politics include governmental actors and nongovernmental actors, all competing with one another in the political process.

The National and State Governments

Anyone anywhere in the United States is subject to the authority of two major governmental actors: the government of the nation (the federal government) and the government of the state in which he or she lives. Article VI of the U.S. Constitution makes the federal government the dominant political actor:

> This Constitution, and the Laws of the United States which shall be made in Pursuance thereof; and all Treaties made, or which shall be made, under the Authority of the United States, shall be the Supreme Law of the Land; and the Judges in every State shall be bound thereby, any Thing in the Constitution or Laws of any State to the Contrary notwithstanding.

Although the authority of the federal government is supreme, it is not absolute. The Constitution limits its authority by delegating some specific powers to the federal government, by reserving some general powers to the states, and by allowing the federal and state governments to share powers in certain areas.

The exercise of shared powers has often led to disputes among these governmental actors over which government's authority should predominate in a given domain, such as social welfare, education, or the environment. Such instances of intergovernmental politics, which are clearly visible in the California water wars, are a common occurrence in American politics.

The People and Their Groups

The population living within the nation's boundaries includes not only U.S. citizens but also resident (legal) aliens and illegal aliens. Both citizens and noncitizens are protected by the Constitution.

Political actors include individuals (such as the president), small groups (such as the Sierra Club), and large institutions (such as the Environmental Protection Agency). Most people move in and out of different roles or occupy several roles at the same time. If Jennifer Smith is a customs official, for example, she is a federal bureaucrat and thus is part of the major political actor known as the national (federal) government and of the smaller political actor called the Immigration and Naturalization Service. If she belongs to the Sierra Club, she is at the same time an environmentalist and member of an interest group. When she votes in a California election, she is acting as a citizen of California. When she votes in a national election, she is acting as a citizen of the nation. In this book, the terms "the people" and "the public" refer to citizens and noncitizens acting *outside* any official governmental roles they might have, either alone or in groups.

Political Parties

Many Americans identify with a political party—an organization that helps candidates who stand for its political principles to win elections. Parties do this with the expectation that victorious candidates will promote the policies the parties favor. Because the United States is a federal system with elective offices at all levels of government, the major parties—Democratic and Republican—maintain organizations at the precinct, county, congressional district, state, and national levels and focus on issues that affect voters at each of those levels. While most party decisions are made by party leaders, parties rely on citizen volunteers for a variety of tasks, especially during campaigns. Although many Americans have become disaffected with the major parties and some have turned to "minor," or third, parties, parties are still major actors in the political process because of the role they play in the nomination and election of candidates for the 525,000 elective offices around the country.

Interest Groups

The Constitution permits individuals and groups to assemble and form *interest groups*—organizations that seek to convert the interests (the political, economic, social, or moral goals) of their members or supporters into public policies. The Indians who own most of the salmon fisheries in California have formed interest groups to lobby for more water and, with the help of legal experts, have sued the government in court for access to more water.

Most of the interest groups in the California water wars are private: agribusiness is represented by the Central Valley Family Farm Alliance (a name chosen to camouflage the massive size of these enterprises); the fisheries are represented by the Pacific Coast Federation of Fishermen's Associations; duck hunters, by Ducks Unlimited; migrant workers, by the United Farm Workers; and urban and suburban interests, by the Metropolitan Water District. Organizations such as the Sierra Club, Friends of the Earth, and the Save the San Francisco Bay Association claim to represent the public interest. In this case, urban dwellers and environmentalists, often on opposite sides of disputes, have joined forces to obtain some of the water going to agribusiness. The fact that interest groups often shift coalitions in this way gives their members more chances to compete over a broad range of issues. Some political scientists believe that such competition gives more people a chance to participate in the political process, while others say that the pressure they exert on government prevents public officials from doing what's right for the country, state, or city, or for the people as a whole.

Experts

Many of the issues in politics today are so complex that political actors, including powerful leaders, must rely on experts with specialized knowledge, or expertise, on those issues or on the rules and procedures for handling them. The mass media also hire or invite experts to explain these complex issues to the public and to represent the range of disagreement on them. Experts both inside and outside government help to define policy problems (*what is*); they argue for dif-

> **alien**
> An *alien* is someone who is neither a citizen nor a national of the country in which he or she resides. The term comes from the Latin word for "other."

An organizer for the United Farm Workers union addresses strawberry pickers during their lunch break near Watsonville, California, in the summer of 1996.

ferent goals (*what's right*) and ways of reaching them (policy options); and they often explain why they believe a particular policy will be more effective than others (*what works*). Many questions in the California water wars have remained unresolved because the experts *disagree*. State experts, for example, doubt that the EPA's regulations will actually save the environment, while EPA experts say they will. The EPA maintains that agribusiness can make do with less water, while farmers, who are already making do with less water than before, disagree.

Elites

Elites are powerful individuals who work inside government as elected or appointed officials or outside government as leaders of businesses, religious groups, and other important private organizations. All elites in government are ultimately responsible to the people. Because elected officials can be replaced by voters, they tend to be the most sensitive to public opinion. Appointed officials have a greater range of action because they cannot be voted out of office. Still, those with fixed terms of office may be preoccupied with getting reappointed, and those appointed to indefinite terms by a particular administration may be removed by superiors displeased with their work or responding to public pressure. Officials appointed for life, such as Supreme Court justices and federal judges (who may be removed from office only for extreme misbehavior), are the least subject to the pressures of interest groups and public opinion.

Nongovernmental elites exert considerable influence over the political process outside the public spotlight. Indeed, some political observers maintain that these elites really run the country behind the scenes. Their political power usually comes from their positions as heads of major organizations and businesses that influence campaigns, elections, and policymaking in various ways. Sometimes the same elites succeed in influencing a string of presidents from both major parties.

Dwayne Andreas, chairman and retired CEO of Archer Daniels Midland, a food-processing giant that advertises itself as "Supermarket to the World," has donated huge sums of company money to Democratic as well as Republican presidential campaigns over the last 25 years. During President George Bush's 1992 reelection campaign, Andreas asked the White House to grant his company an exemption from the provisions of the Clean Air Act, which favored methanol over ethanol (a gasoline substitute that includes a product made from corn), so that it could sell more ethanol nationwide. He got the exemption, which one administration official estimated would nearly double the consumption of ethanol. In 1996 Archer Daniels Midland pled guilty to conspiring with competitors to fix the prices of two agricultural products and agreed to pay $100 million in fines. Yet when the 1997 balanced-budget compromise was crafted, ADM's ethanol fuel subsidy, which has cost taxpayers $7 billion, was preserved—with support from both the Democratic White House and Republican congressional leadership. The Cato Institute, a Washington research center, has called the company "the most prominent recipient of corporate welfare in U.S. history."[7]

Dwayne O. Andreas headed Archer Daniel Midland Company for a quarter of a century before he stepped down in 1997 in the wake of a price-fixing scandal. He still chairs the board of the giant food-processing corporation.

Nongovernmental elites often compete with each other in politics, seeking different goals, drawing on different resources, and exercising different amounts of influence. Because their main goal is usually to preserve and expand their own power, they cannot be counted on to serve the common good. However, their organizations do play a major economic role by providing jobs, goods, and services. In the short run, if California agribusiness declines, unemployment will rise, tax revenues will fall, and California produce will cost more. And if the salmon decline, the same things will happen in the fishing industry, and consumers will pay more.

The Media

The American public relies on the media—newspapers, television, and electronic communication systems—for virtually all political information. The media are the main way the public learns about the political activities of other actors, including the activities of the media themselves (see Chapter 9). Participants in the water wars look to the media to track the conflict and pass on new information. Sometimes particular media take sides in a dispute. Not surprisingly, the *Los Angeles Times* has tended to side with the urban and agribusiness interests of southern California.[8] In addition, interest groups and other actors commonly purchase media time to influence public opinion. One group opposed to redistributing water in favor of the salmon budgeted $800,000 for television and radio ads and $100,000 to identify sympathetic news media and, in the words of an internal memorandum, to "feed them information to complement and reinforce the news media effort."[9]

The Rules That Regulate American Politics

All actors—governmental and nongovernmental—practicing American politics are required to abide by formal legal rules that regulate the political system. The most important of these rules are contained in the U.S. Constitution of 1787 and its amendments. Other rules are in laws and regulations.

The U.S. Constitution

The U.S. Constitution is an agreement made by representatives of the people that performs four tasks fundamental to any **political society**. The Constitution

- defines the American people's values and way of life (Chapters 2 and 4)
- distributes ruling political power among the various political actors and institutions (Chapters 2 and 3)
- provides mechanisms that allow political actors and institutions to manage their conflicts (Chapters 2 and 3) and
- helps to regulate the need for public order and the pressures for social change (Chapter 4).

The Constitution outlines the "master" rules that determine what political authority and rule-making powers the national and state governments may exercise. Even if the meaning of these "master" rules is sometimes unclear and their rightful applications are often in dispute, they affect your life on a daily basis, as you will see throughout this book. If you are a student, for example, these constitutional rules are what ultimately protect the privacy of your academic grades and records and prohibit your college or university from keeping any records on your political beliefs and activities. Why is this? The Constitution gives Congress the power to pass laws, and in 1974 Congress passed the Family Education and Privacy Act (FEPA). But because the Constitution gives the states—not the federal government—primary authority over education, FEPA applies only to schools that accept funds from the federal government. However, because virtually every institution of higher learning accepts some sort of federal funds (to help with financial aid, for instance, or to support research), your educational records are probably protected by this national (federal) law.

> **political society**
>
> A political society distributes power to political actors according to some sort of agreement. In tribes this agreement may be only the *division of labor*—delegating tasks such as hunting, gathering, and cooking to particular groups (often men and women). In more complex societies this agreement often takes the form of a *social contract*, such as a constitution.

Constitutional Practice

Constitutional practice (also known as constitutionalism) is an ongoing commitment by the people in a political society to abide by the rules of their constitution and accept the enforcement of its guarantees. Americans take an oath to protect and defend the Constitution when they are sworn into a federal office or enter the military, as do immigrants when they become citizens. But most Americans honor the Constitution because they were raised and taught to accept it as the supreme law of the land, even if they don't know its contents in detail. Thus the Constitution does not get its authority from its actual contents, but rather from the people who attribute authority to it. As a result, the Constitution has been able to serve (with the major exception of the Civil War) as the ultimate authority in the resolution of the nation's political disputes.

While constitutional practice has allowed the political system as a whole to work over time, it has often failed to protect the constitutional rights and liberties of particular groups (see Chapters 15 and 16). What's more, there have always been disputes over what these rights and liberties actually consist of (*what is*) and what protection they deserve in a particular case (*what's right*). Constitutional practice is thus an ongoing, evolving activity in which the rules of the Constitution serve as the nation's primary steering device.

Federalism

Most nations have a **unitary system**, a political system in which a single national government exercises direct authority over the entire nation and its people. If the United States had been settled as one vast territory instead of 13 separate colonies, it might have developed a unitary system, too. But once the 13 colonies became independent states, they insisted on keeping as much of their **sovereignty**, or ruling authority, as they could when they agreed to form a nation. At first they joined together (federated) loosely as a *confederation*, in which the states exercised predominant power over the national government. But when this arrangement did not work the way many in the country wanted it to, political elites representing the states created a *federation*. The rules of this federation divided authority over the people between the national government and the state governments, giving the national government predominant but limited power over the states as well. This form of government, whose blueprint is the U.S. Constitution, is called **federalism** (Chapter 3).

Because the Constitution reserves certain powers to the states, people must obey state laws as well as those of the national government. American citizens thus have a particular kind of dual citizenship: they are citizens of their states and citizens of the nation. Because the Constitution gives more power in certain policy areas to the national government than it does to the states, states—as we've seen in the case of California—must often defer to the authority of the federal government. California must also defer to the treaty that the Klamath Indians signed with Congress in the nineteenth century, granting them the right to stretch gill nets across California rivers to catch salmon, while federal regulations force everyone else to catch salmon one at a time using a single line and hook. However, California, like other states, exercises primary authority in other areas, such as crime and education.

sovereignty
This term, from the French *sov*, above, and *reign*, rule, refers to the power of a ruler.

sovereign
A sovereign has rank or authority over others. A sovereign state is independent of other states and has authority over its own citizens.

popular sovereignty
Originally, the sovereign or ruler was a monarch. In a republic, rulers derive their authority to rule from the consent of the people who are governed—thus the term *popular sovereignty*.

Disputes often arise—and are often settled—under the ground rules of this federal system. The Constitution, for example, stipulates that the U.S. Supreme Court will decide disputes between states. In 1947, when Arizona asked Congress to help finance a major water project like one it had financed for California, Congress refused because Arizona was unable to obtain enough water from California sources to justify the project. Arizona then turned to the Supreme Court in an effort to obtain the required water—enough for 5 million people. California had refused the water because of a 1944 federal treaty requiring it to ship about the same amount of water to Mexico. The stakes were so high in this case that the trial lasted 11 years, making it the longest and costliest case in U.S. Supreme Court history. The Court heard arguments by some 50 lawyers and 340 witnesses. In 1963 the Court reached its decision in *Arizona v. California*: Arizona won, and five years later Congress authorized the money for its water project.[10] California had suffered a bitter defeat that would cost it valuable water. And yet Californians accepted the decision because they knew that, under the rules of the Constitution and of federalism, the Supreme Court had the authority to make it.

Representative Democracy

Ask any American to describe the U.S. form of government and the likely answer will be, *democracy*. Ask what *democracy* stands for and you are likely to get answers such as government by the people (also called **popular sovereignty**), along with a list of "core values" such as individual freedom, freedom of expression, equal rights under the law, majority rule, and constitutional government. (A list of America's core values appears in Chapter 4).

Democracy is typically defined as *rule by the people*, but this definition does not say what powers the people have to rule. In a **direct democracy**, all citizens have a direct say in what government does. In some New England towns, where tradition and size allow it, citizens can still express their views in regular town meetings, where they vote on local policy issues. In a **representative democracy**, the system that has proved more practical for large populations, citizens vote for other citizens to represent them and their interests in government. Thus in a representative democracy the people rule indirectly through their elected representatives.

Most Americans are satisfied with this arrangement because they lack the time, expertise, or inclination to help make the major decisions that running a complex nation requires. They also know that if they disagree with the actions of their elected representatives, they can vote them out of office at the next election. While the drafters of the Constitution accepted the principle of popular sovereignty—the notion that government is legitimated by the people—they had no intention of establishing a direct democracy because they did not believe that ordinary citizens possessed the qualities required to govern wisely. They therefore established a **republic**, that is, a form of government in which supreme power resides in the people and is exercised by representatives responsible to the general electorate (those who are entitled to vote). A republic, they believed, would be governed by wise elites who would serve the common good.

The Politics of Knowledge

Knowledge is the most powerful tool there is in politics. Why? Because politics—disputes over claims to authority made by competing actors—typically relies on persuasion. When political actors try to persuade others that their claims to authority are justified, they practice the **politics of knowledge**—strategies of communication that rely on the manipulation of information, logic, and language (rhetoric), often in combination. This does not mean that their goals are not admirable, just that promoting them in politics requires such strategies. Indeed, since each one of us uses many of the same strategies in everyday life, they should be easy to recognize in the public arena. Familiarizing ourselves with these strategies helps us develop a better understanding of the way the politics of knowledge *works*.

Interpretation

The politics of knowledge always involves acts of **interpretation**. A person who makes an interpretation is claiming to have the authority (1) to explain the meaning of something or (2) to translate a complicated matter into understandable terms. An interpretation is thus a claim about *what is*.

Because people differ in their beliefs and values, they are bound to differ in the interpretations they find persuasive. To maximize their power in the political process, political actors try to persuade as many relevant people as possible (the general public, voters, political leaders, experts) to accept their interpretations. Because effective persuasion depends upon knowing how people are likely to react to knowledge claims, political actors often pay for such information by hiring pollsters to survey public opinion. Once political actors know what particular segments of the population believe and want, they can target and frame their messages to increase their acceptance.

Information Claims

In an effort to serve their cause, political actors convey information in various overt forms, among them:

- *Images*—bumper stickers, yard signs, posters, graphs, flow charts, photographs, and, increasingly, videos and other electronic media
- *Speeches*—lectures, slogans, exhortations, diatribes, songs, chants
- *Gestures*—salutes (of the American flag, showing patriotism), marches (in a national holiday parade, following tradition), raising fists (in a protest, showing defiance), applause (showing appreciation or agreement)
- *Writing*—political arguments, laws, court decisions, regulations, reports, graffiti
- *Statistics*—budget figures, polling data, census data, election results

> **interpretation**
> The term comes from the Latin *interpres*, agent, negotiator. An interpreter claims to have authority to explain the meaning of something or to translate a complicated matter into understandable terms. An interpretation is thus a claim about *what is*.

Political actors also convey information through innuendo that can help their cause or damage their opponents. They even at times *withhold* information when this can help them or damage their opponents.

Logic Claims

Political actors also use logic to persuade others that their cause is based on real circumstances (*what is*), that their cause is *right*, and that their policy proposals *will work*. Many decisions of the Supreme Court, for example, contain a step-by-step presentation of the logic used to legitimate the conclusions the justices reached. Justices who disagree with the decision often file equally logical "dissenting opinions." But the Court's decision does not hinge on which arguments are the most logical, but rather on how many justices those arguments manage to persuade (Chapter 14).

The public is regularly bombarded with competing logical arguments about the state of the nation (*what is*), which of these conditions should be considered strengths and which are weaknesses to be addressed (*what's right*), and which policy proposals *will work*. Before submitting a budget to Congress, for example, the president lays out the logic for the spending decisions in a State of the Union message that is addressed as much to the public as to lawmakers. Immediately following this speech, a spokesperson from the major opposition party uses very different logic to criticize it. The box nearby contrasts the logical arguments of President Bill Clinton and those of Representative J. C. Watts (R.-Okla.), whom the Republican opposition picked to respond, on the need for a constitutional amendment to require balanced budgets.

Language Claims

Language has a special ability to persuade, even inspire, in a way that moves beyond logic. Ringing speeches by presidents—Abraham Lincoln's Gettysburg Address or John F. Kennedy's Inaugural Address, for example—continue to reverberate as they are remembered and quoted by political actors seeking greater authority for their arguments.

Sometimes political actors appropriate the words of popular figures for their own political purposes. This is what Watts did in his rebuttal to Clinton's 1997 State of the Union message: "I'll end my speech with the final words of Kennedy's Inaugural Address: 'Let's go forth to lead the land we love, knowing that here on Earth, God's work must truly be our own.'" When Kennedy delivered this speech in January 1961, it was heard primarily as a call for Americans to take more responsibility for their country and the world, but not as a call to downsize government. Watts certainly was not borrowing Kennedy's rhetoric to support programs that were part of Kennedy's New Frontier, such as the Peace Corps or the Alliance for Progress ($20 billion worth of assistance to Latin American countries). Instead, Watts used the quote to cap his series of arguments calling for Americans to look to themselves and God, not to government, for solutions to the nation's problems. Watts took the Kennedy quote out of context because he wanted to associate himself with a president who still holds a magnetic attraction for many Americans.

Political Actors Disagree

President Bill Clinton

Rep. J. C. Watts (R-Okla.)

Balanced Budget Amendment: Yes or No?

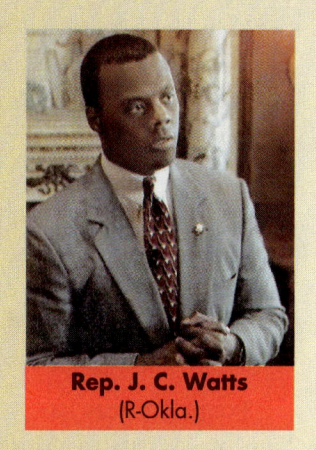

We here tonight have an historic opportunity. Let this Congress be the Congress that finally balances the budget.

In two days, I will propose a detailed plan to balance the budget by 2002.

This plan will balance the budget and invest in our people while protecting Medicare, Medicaid, education, and the environment. It will balance the budget and build on the Vice President's efforts to make our Government work better, even as it costs less. It will balance the budget and provide middle-class tax relief to pay for education and health care, to help raise a child, to buy and sell a home.

Balancing the budget requires only your vote and my signature. It does not require us to rewrite our Constitution. I believe it is unnecessary and unwise to adopt a balanced budget amendment that could cripple our country in time of crisis later on and force unwanted results such as judges' halting Social Security checks or increasing taxes. Let us agree: We should not pass any measure that threatens Social Security. We don't need a constitutional amendment—we need action.

Whatever our differences, we should balance the budget now, and then, for the long-term health of our society, we must agree to a bipartisan process to preserve Social Security and reform Medicare, so that these fundamental programs will be as strong for our children as they are for our parents.

We must get our Government's financial affairs in order. The biggest step in that direction is an amendment to the U.S. Constitution that demands that the Federal budget be balanced.

We are more than $5 trillion in debt. . . . That $5 trillion national debt is more than financially irresponsible, it's immoral. Because someone is going to have to pay the piper, and it's going to be our kids and grandkids.

The American family is already overtaxed. Right now the average family spends about half of every dollar they earn in some kind of government tax or fee. Consider a 5-year-old child. If things continue as they are, by the time they're 25 the tax they could pay will be about 84 cents on the dollar. That's more than a shame, it's a scandal.

The balanced budget amendment will force the Government to change its ways—permanently. No longer will a President or a Congress be able to spend money we don't have, on benefits our children will never see.

In a few weeks we will vote on that amendment. Republicans can't pass it on our own, because it takes a two-thirds majority. So we need Democrat votes, and we need your help. We need you to write or call representatives and senators and tell them to pass the balanced budget amendment now!

A balanced budget amendment will lower your house payment, your car payment, your student loan. Maybe the accumulated savings is only $1,500 a year. Well, $1,500 may not be much to some; however, it's a new washer and dryer or home computer, or money toward a much-needed second car.

Source: President Bill Clinton's State of the Union Address, 1997, and rebuttal by J. C. Watts, quoted in *New York Times*, February 5, 1997, A14.
When the amendment to balance the federal budget was brought up for a vote two months later, it was approved by the House of Representatives but fell one vote short in the Senate.

Political actors also associate new policies they are proposing with past policies that have worked. When President Clinton issued his Call to Action for American Education in his 1997 State of the Union Address, he compared it to America's bipartisan foreign policy during the Cold War era (1946–1989):

> One of the greatest sources of our strength throughout the Cold War was a bipartisan foreign policy; because our future was at stake, politics stopped at the water's edge. Now I ask you [the Congress]—I ask all our nation's governors, and I ask teachers, parents and citizens across America—for a new bipartisan commitment to education, because education is one of the critical national security issues of our future, and politics must stop at the classroom door.[11]

Political actors have also borrowed the techniques of advertisers. The group Northwesterners for More Fish, for example, sounds like a local environmental group concerned with protecting fish. Instead, it's the name of a group of Washington consultants representing big utilities in the Northwest under siege by environmentalists for depleting the fish population. This increasingly common practice of camouflaging one's political agenda with an environmentally friendly name is called "greenscamming."[12]

A related strategy is the use of technical language to confuse, mislead, or conceal. The U.S. military uses technical language to insulate Americans from the brutality of war. When the United States bombed Iraq during the Persian Gulf War in 1991, for example, military officials called the bombings "surgical strikes" to imply remarkable precision in their targeting and delivery—language they reinforced with aerial photos of "smart bombs" zeroing in very precisely on targets. When bombs went astray and hit civilians and nonmilitary buildings, they called this "collateral damage" rather than civilian casualties. Sometimes those wayward bombs were called "incontinent ordnance" to further conceal the extent of their unreliability and their explosive power.

The Steps (and Claims) of Political Analysis

The questions individuals ask about any political issue are shaped by the assumptions they hold about *what is*, *what's right*, and *what works*. This is true of professional political analysts (journalists, pollsters, political scientists, policy analysts) and ordinary people alike. For example, if you believe that salmon are an endangered species and that saving the salmon is the right thing to do, you will want to support public policies likely to achieve your goals effectively. Your assumptions about *what is* and *what's right* will inevitably color your entire analysis of the salmon issue, and you will engage in the politics of knowledge to produce a policy that will achieve the outcome you want.

Many professional analysts remain silent about the assumptions they make about what is, what's right, and what works because the norms of their profession require that an analysis appear to be objective if it is to persuade others. Politicians and ordinary people do the same thing. An analysis is more likely to appear objective if the facts seem to speak for themselves and if the policies prescribed seem to follow logically from the presentation of those facts.

Political analysis typically proceeds in four logically related steps: description, explanation, evaluation, and prescription.

Political Action Guide

How to Find Out *What Is*: Accessing Political Information

The traditional way to find political information was to consult books for background and newspapers for current developments. These essential sources were long ago joined by radio and television, and are now increasingly supplemented by electronic sources accessed via the Internet.

For guidance on books to supplement the information in each chapter, you can consult the "How to Learn More About . . ." feature at the end of each chapter. This feature also lists key reference volumes on the topic of the chapter that you can probably find in your academic library.

Newspaper sources are now most easily and inexpensively accessed via the Internet. You can read most of the text of the day's edition of each of the major national newspapers–among them the *New York Times*, the *Washington Post*, and the *Wall Street Journal*—on the Internet at each paper's World Wide Web home page. For their Web site addresses, see the "Internet box" in Chapter 9. The Web sites of the major television networks are also listed in Chapter 9.

A site for current news and interpretation of particular interest is the AllPolitics page maintained by Cable News Network and Time Inc., with contributions by other providers, including *Congressional Quarterly*. AllPolitics can be reached at *http://www.allpolitics.com*. The National Political Index offers a wide variety of links to some three dozen categories of political information, ranging from elections through government agencies to political games and simulations. It can be reached at *http://pomo.nbn.com/people/hemmerle*. Another site of great value because of the many links it offers is "New Politics," which describes itself as "the non-partisan U.S. political participation resource" and can be reached at *http://www.newpolitics.com*. And the Institute for Global Communications contains five online "communities of activists and organizations": PeaceNet, EcoNet, LaborNet, ConflictNet, and WomensNet, which are gateways to articles, features, and Weblinks on progressive issues. Other Web sites with extensive links are presented in boxes and in the margins throughout this book.

Description

Those who offer a **description** claim to present an accurate picture of the facts about someone or something (*what is*), but facts are always selected with an interest in, or a perspective on, what they are intended to describe. There is no such thing as "pure facts," "plain facts," "self-evident facts," or "objective facts." So when a political actor presents you with a set of facts, you should first attempt to identify the interests that shape the selection and presentation of those facts.

The winners of policy disputes are usually those who convince others that their facts are true. We might assume that there could be no debate over when a war began, but for years veterans' groups argued that the Vietnam War had been underway be-

---

description

The word comes from the Latin *describere*, to copy or transcribe.

fact

The word comes from the Latin *factum*, a thing done or performed. The meaning of any fact depends on its context—the perspective or set of interests that shapes its presentation.

fore 1964, the official date for disability benefits. The 16,000 men and women who had served in Vietnam before 1964 finally won acceptance of their view, and in 1996, Congress moved the war's "starting date" back to February 28, 1961.

People will often agree on a description if it is cast in very broad language. For example, all the political actors involved in the California water wars agree on the broad view of *what is*: the state suffers from a shortage of water. But when the question narrows to where the most serious shortage is—in salmon streams, on farmlands, or in cities—interests diverge, and descriptions of *what is* diverge as well. Conservationists say that agribusiness is getting more water than it really requires, and argue that it should be more efficient. Agribusiness says it has already taken every possible conservation measure. In short, the more a description touches on competing interests, the more likely it is to be contested. The Political Action Guide on the preceding page tells you how to access political information.

Explanation

An **explanation** is an interpretation. In explaining the reasons why a particular state of affairs exists and what the facts it entails mean, the analyst comes very close to assigning praise or blame to political actors and policies. So, for instance, when environmentalists explain that the salmon are dying off because too much water from northern California has been exported to central and southern agribusiness, they imply that agribusiness is to blame for the plight of the salmon. Agribusiness counters that the salmon are dying because a series of droughts have depleted the water supply. There are usually many different explanations for a particular situation. Each explanation, however logical and persuasive, is likely to serve one political actor at the expense of another, thereby fueling political disputes rather than resolving them.

Evaluation

An **evaluation** assigns a value to the evidence produced by the description and explanation. It is a weightier claim about *what is* because it sums up the situation that is in dispute. Because it comes close to deciding how a situation should be dealt with, an evaluation is more likely to be contested than is a description or an explanation. Evaluations, as the box on the balanced budget amendment illustrates, allow decisionmakers to conclude that a particular policy is good or bad, right or wrong, and therefore whether it should be adopted, maintained, altered, or abolished. Evaluations determine the answers to difficult questions, and public officials must constantly weigh the claims of competing values and interests. Do all California homeowners have a *right* to water for their swimming pools? (At the moment they do.) Do all water users have an *equal right* to the state's water? (At the moment they don't.) Do salmon have a right to their habitat? Or are they so valuable in themselves or essential to commercial fisheries that they merit saving regardless of the cost to taxpayers and other consumers of water? The Political Action Guide on the next page describes ways to evaluate political actions and proposals.

explanation
The word comes from the Latin *explanare*, to make plain or to smooth out.

context
This term comes from the Latin *texere*, to weave.

Prescription

A **prescription**—instructions about what should be done to improve a situation—is the most highly charged element of political analysis because it specifies who will be helped and hurt by an action. Thus even if all parties agree on *what is* (the salmon are dying) and *what's right* (the species should be preserved), they may still disagree on how to achieve that goal (hatching more salmon, banning salmon fishing, dismantling dams). Problems like this become especially poignant in situations where people are being raped, tortured, and killed because of their ethnicity or religion, for example. When the former Yugoslavia broke apart in civil war, or when the Hutu and Tutsi tribespeople began killing each other in Rwanda, there was widespread agreement in the United States and the world community that ethnic strife was occurring, that it was wrong, and that it should be stopped. But there was no real agreement about what interventions would *work* to stop the slaughter.

Context

Political actors always evaluate an issue in a **context**—a set of conditions that place the issue in a particular light that suggests how the issue should be dealt with. As we saw in California's water wars, actors often disagree over a policy because they view it in different contexts—that is, with different needs, beliefs, and values in mind. When competing actors place an issue in conflicting contexts, a decision by policymakers to give more weight to one context than another typically determines the outcome of the dispute.

Political observers increasingly point to context as the factor that frames issues differently. An action deplored in one context may be applauded in another. Listen to any policy dispute and you will notice that the arguments often focus on which context is the right one to use in evaluating the issue. In deciding what standards Congress should set for particles of soot and ozone in revising the Clean Air Act, for example, the Environmental Protection Agency in 1997 recommended standards based on health. But businesses and some governors, concerned with the context of dollars, concluded that the costs of complying with the EPA standards were too high. The EPA estimated that compliance would cost from $6.6 billion to $8.5 billion a year, while the benefits would amount to $51 billion to $115 billion a year. In contrast, the President's Council of Economic Advisors, which looked only at the ozone standard, estimated that the benefits from ozone compliance would be a modest $1 billion a year.[13] In such situations, the final policy decision is usually a compromise—as Congress and the president compromised on the Clean Air Act revision.

Political Action Guide

How to Decide *What's Right*: Making Ethical Judgments in Politics

Where do we get our ideas about *what's right*? Most ethicists believe that we learn these values from our family, schools, churches, workplaces, and the mass media. Some believe, however, that we are born with a sense of right and wrong, and that our life experience only serves to heighten—or sometimes to override—this inborn sense.

Whatever their source, personal ethical views tend to emphasize either the integrity or intention of the individual actor or the consequences of actions. The former position, often called intentionalism, holds that intending to do the right thing is the most important criterion for deciding what to do in morally challenging situations and the primary criterion for evaluating actions. The latter position is often called consequentialism. The most common version of consequentialism is utilitarianism, which argues that actions should be designed to maximize the benefits (or utility) to people ("the greatest good for the greatest number") and that actions should be evaluated on what they achieve.

In everyday life, most of us combine elements of intentionalism and consequentialism in deciding how to act or in evaluating someone else's action. We usually try to act in ways that benefit people (ourselves included), but we also recognize certain limits to our actions, such as prohibitions on resorting to murder, theft, or serious lying, even if those actions would, on balance, benefit others.

In practice, we often rely on ethical rules of thumb, such as the Golden Rule (do to others what you would like them to do to you) and the principle of doing no unnecessary harm.

Ethical consensus in a diverse population such as ours is unlikely on all but extreme issues, such as opposition to violent treatment of innocent people by the police. Still, many can agree on some general principles—for example, defending the interests of those who are politically powerless and cannot defend their own interests—for use in politics and other aspects of everyday life.

Traditionally, ethics has focused on justice. In practice, this often means asking whether people get what they deserve. How do we decide what people deserve? We usually start with what they believe they need. Taking a justice perspective on the California water politics dispute, we might start by asking: Do the residents of California get the water they need at a fair price? Do the farmers get the water they need at a fair price? Do the Indians get the fishing opportunities they

Learning by Doing in American Politics

Politics—viewed as disputes over claims to the authority to decide *what is*, *what's right*, and *what works*—is an ongoing *process* that changes as events occur, problems arise, and attitudes evolve. This process regulates conflicting pressures for order and change and allows the political system to adapt to disturbances over time.

need? If the answer to any of these questions is no, we might then ask whether all the claimants deserve what they say they need. The Indians' need for food and livelihood might be judged more significant than the homeowners' need for swimming pools. Today, some would go on to ask other questions, such as: Do the salmon get the treatment they deserve?

Each political actor is likely to answer ethical questions differently because each has different basic interests. In the case of water, which is a scarce—and therefore increasingly expensive—resource, all actors must pay for the eventual outcome or cause someone else (most likely the losing actors or the taxpayers who finance the government's activities) to do so.

The actions of politicians in making water policy can be evaluated either in terms of their success in meeting the needs of involved actors (consequentialism) or in terms of their intentions to do the right thing (intentionalism), or in terms of some combination of these principles.

Another, increasingly popular approach to practical ethics was pioneered by psychologist Carol Gilligan and other feminist theorists. They argue that the traditional ethical emphasis on justice, derived from the views and experiences of males, is misguided, because it ignores the experience of women, which tends to emphasize an ethics of care and relationships. According to Gilligan and her colleagues, the quality of everyday life, for men as well as women, depends profoundly on the overlapping and binding linkages among people that we call care, love, and dependence. According to this view, our society would benefit if decisions about how to treat people were reached, case by case, by considering these relationship aspects instead of simply applying the abstract principle of justice.[1] This perspective would probably emphasize the importance of a water policy that balances the interests of residents, farmers, Indians, and perhaps even the salmon, on the grounds that all these political actors have ongoing relationships and that the health of both society and the political system depends on taking all of them into account.

We cannot say that one approach to determining what's right is always better than the other. But we can say that revealing and deliberating on the ethical principles we are using to decide what's right in each case will facilitate more constructive political action. Ultimately, how you choose to make decisions on the ethical questions you encounter in politics and in your life is up to you.

---

[1] See Carol Gilligan, *In a Different Voice* (Cambridge, Mass.: Harvard University Press, 1983).

The Adaptive Process

Politics never stops, because events, problems, and conflicts ceaselessly disrupt the existing state of things (*what is*). The **status quo**—the current arrangement—has an edge in politics because those who have successfully built it or adapted to it often use the money, information, and power they have acquired to defend it.

Anthropologists say that the more successfully an actor adapts to a particular set of conditions, the harder it is for that actor to adapt to a new set of conditions.[14] But change is the nature of life, and experiences (positive and negative) constantly disturb the status quo. Those forms of life that do not respond to change die.

Adapting to change in the United States is complex because the political system is democratic and federal. American representative democracy permits a great many political actors to participate in politics, increasing the number of disturbances that challenge the system. The federal system furnishes the structure within which these challenges are met. On paper, this structure appears hierarchical, with one system nested inside another: cities reside within counties, counties reside within states, states reside within the nation. In practice, when a particular problem such as water scarcity erupts, the political actors who spring into action in response to it show that the levers of power in the federal system may be accessed in a variety of ways. That Americans are often able to practice politics on many levels and among several branches of government is one reason why the United States has always been a dynamic, creative, and productive society—and one reason some problems take so long to solve.

Learning and Change

When political actors learn from their successes and failures and make appropriate adjustments, the American political system is *working*. California's water wars illustrate this process. As noted earlier in this chapter, the Great Depression disrupted the economic status quo in the 1930s and threatened public order to such a degree that President Franklin Roosevelt launched massive public works projects designed to stimulate economic recovery and restore public order. His decision to build a series of dams in the Pacific Northwest and California proved successful in creating jobs and providing cheap electricity and water, and his policy managed to keep California's land in the hands of small farmers for years. The federal government's response to the economic crisis it faced seemed necessary and fair at the time, and it accomplished its goal in terms of that crisis.

But the dams and irrigation projects had unintended consequences. Family farms gave way to agribusiness. Developers built new cities and suburbs for more and more people. California voters who wanted a booming economy willingly supported the building of more huge water projects. Then nature stopped cooperating. Persistent drought and the contamination of the southern aquifers by salt water and agricultural chemicals caused California's demand for fresh water to far exceed its supply. Today the many interests that depend on water compete for less and less of it. Thus, seventy years after the economic crisis addressed by FDR, California faces a *new* crisis. On one side of the water dispute are the beneficiaries of Roosevelt's original public policy and its consequences: agribusiness, cities, and suburbs. On the other side are the actors suffering from the status quo. Both sides now lay claim to the authority to decide *what is*, *what's right*, and *what will work* in this situation. A satisfactory policy solution has yet to be worked out.

Any policy that government now develops to deal with this new crisis is bound to have its own set of unintended consequences, because the parts of any **system**—in this case the political system—are interrelated: a change in one part affects other parts of the system. Once people understand that all parts of a system affect

status quo

This Latin term derives from *stare*, to stand (the same root as the term state) and *quo*, which. *In statu quo* is Latin for "the state in which," or "what is."

one another, they can attempt to improve the quality of the system by making improvements in any one part, but they must also be prepared to progress by trial and error followed by correction. Unintended consequences inevitably give rise to new problems that require new policy responses. That is the way all human systems work. It is also the way they learn.

> **system**
> A system is a group of elements dynamically related in time, according to some coherent pattern. Every system has a purpose, determined by people with particular goals. Because human observers define a system in terms of its boundaries, its parts, and its purpose, what a system is or should be is often a matter of dispute.
>
> **feedback**
> This term is borrowed from mechanics. In human systems, feedback is information about the operation of the system that allows people to correct the system's errors and improve its performance.

Learning by Doing

Learning by doing is the result of actions that produce positive or negative feedback. Positive effects often stimulate more of the same kind of actions—in this case, building more dams to serve the growth that resulted from the initial dam project (see Figure 1.1). A point may be reached when these additional actions produce negative feedback (water shortages and endangered salmon), indicating that some parts of the system are not working. Negative feedback frequently provokes a reexamination of an issue in a new context, leading to a different evaluation of the issue. The water projects which seemed "right" in the context of agribusiness and urban growth may now seem "wrong" in the context of the water shortage and decline of the salmon.

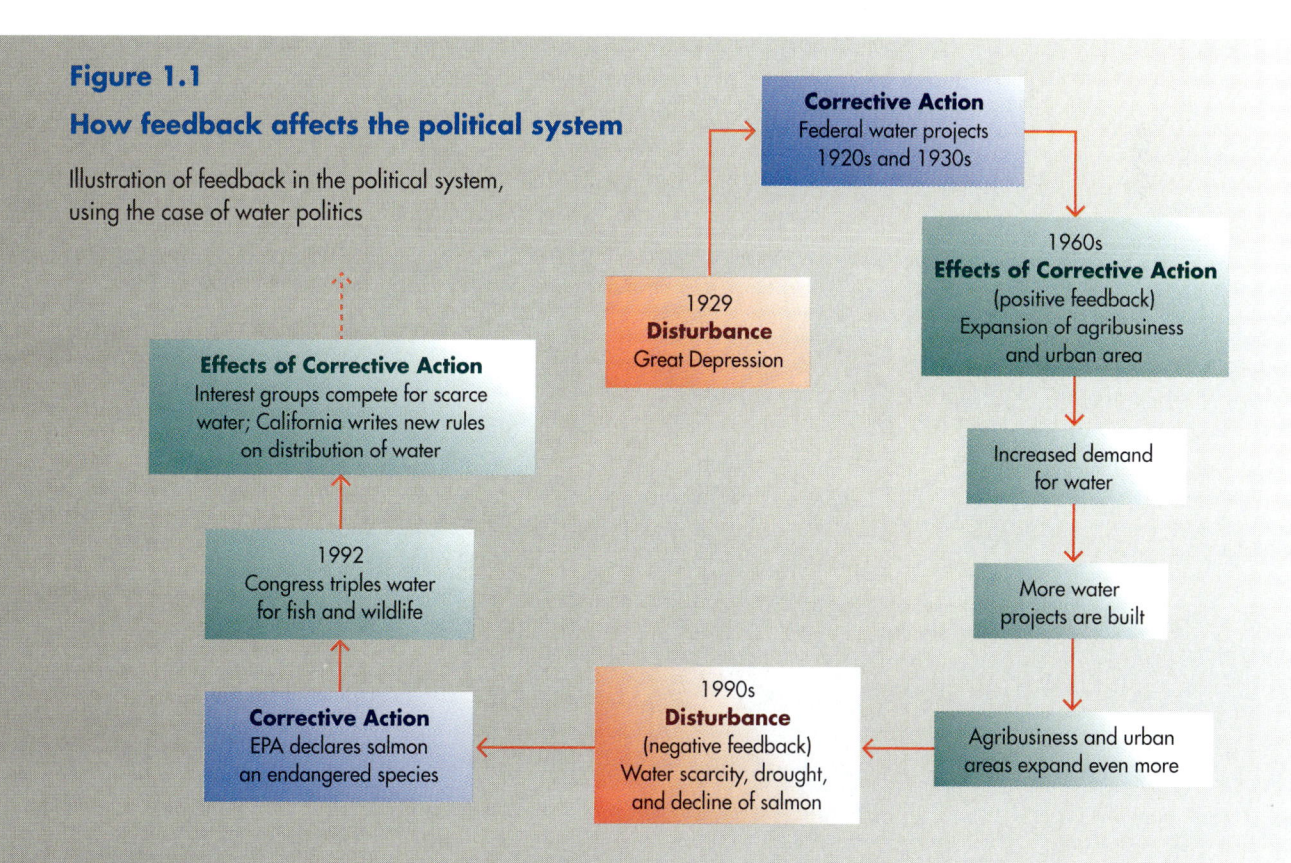

Figure 1.1
How feedback affects the political system

Illustration of feedback in the political system, using the case of water politics

- **1929 Disturbance**: Great Depression
- **Corrective Action**: Federal water projects 1920s and 1930s
- **1960s Effects of Corrective Action** (positive feedback): Expansion of agribusiness and urban area
- Increased demand for water
- More water projects are built
- Agribusiness and urban areas expand even more
- **1990s Disturbance** (negative feedback): Water scarcity, drought, and decline of salmon
- **Corrective Action**: EPA declares salmon an endangered species
- 1992 Congress triples water for fish and wildlife
- **Effects of Corrective Action**: Interest groups compete for scarce water; California writes new rules on distribution of water

Learning by doing is retrospective (backward-looking) until political actors apply the lessons they have learned to other situations. Even then there is no guarantee of success—no two situations are exactly alike, and all actions are subject to unintended consequences. Actors must therefore remain vigilant and ready to take any *corrective action* that seems appropriate. This requires generating new descriptions, explanations, evaluations, and prescriptions (policy options) and then deciding which option is the most appropriate. This ongoing cycle—disturbance → corrective action → negative feedback → new corrective action—is how the political system maintains its stability and develops over time. Figure 1.1 illustrates this cycle in more detail, showing the effects of positive as well as negative feedback and the effects of outside influences such as drought. Once people understand how this process works, they can conduct learning experiments in laboratory-like settings rather than learn passively from failures and mistakes. The photo below, of Marine Corps officers on the floor of the New York Mercantile Exchange, is a striking example of such experimentation.

A political actor whose flexible, adaptive actions suggest an understanding of how this process works may be accused of lacking strong principles and clear policies. Caution and reflection or even inaction by a leader may be interpreted as a sign of cowardice or muddled thinking rather than reflective learning by doing.

Many observers wondered whether Bill Clinton as president was being flexible and pragmatic because he believed that improvisation is the mainspring of the American democratic experiment, or whether he was simply making up his presidency as he went along. The debate raises one of the biggest questions in social science, and indeed, in any person's life: What is the proper relationship between principle (theory) and practice? Experts on theory and practice agree that too much of one or the other does not work. To work, theory and practice must inform each other in the process of trial and error.[15]

Military officers on the floor of the New York Mercantile Exchange try to improve their decision-making skills by observing thousands of screaming traders making instant decisions in chaotic conditions. As one officer explained, "Our problem is that we don't have enough practice making decisions normally to get that kind of confidence." The point of this unconventional exercise was to learn military skills in a laboratory-like setting rather than on the battlefield.

What does such an abstract question have to do with the practice of politics? Everything. Political practice is *always* based on some assumption, principle, or theory, even it is hard to identify and even if the practitioner is not fully aware of it. Ask yourself why you have or have not registered to vote, or why you do or do not approve of the president's policies, and you will come up with some reasons. Explore these reasons and you will find assumptions, principles, and perhaps even a theory that backs them up. Assumptions, principles, and theories allow each of us to steer ourselves through life, just as they enable Americans to steer their democracy through history. It is therefore vital that we know what these guiding ideas are (we must be able to describe and explain them) so we can decide whether we believe they are right (we must evaluate and debate them) and whether they are working (so we can repair or change them when it becomes necessary).

Steering the Nation into the Twenty-first Century

To govern originally meant to steer a vessel. Today the act of governing refers to keeping "the ship of state" on a steady course through troubled waters as well as calm ones. What the destination of the ship of state should be and who decides on the destination are questions that are answered in the political process—that is, while the ship is in motion.

These same questions have preoccupied the members of every political society. Ancient rulers—even pharaohs, kings, and despots who wielded immense power—rarely were able to make dramatic changes in the course of their political societies because the customs and laws of their cultures limited the ways in which those rulers could exercise their power.[16] In today's democracies, the power of leaders is limited both by cultural traditions and customs and by laws. In America, where decisions are made by different branches of government at different levels of government and under pressure from interest groups and public opinion, it sometimes seems that the ship of state has too many navigators and no common vision of where the ship should be going.

In part, the drafters of the Constitution are responsible for this fragmented approach to government because they divided political power among separate entities to prevent its abuse. But they were drafting plans for a minimal ship of state: they expected a class of wise and benevolent rulers to run a limited government on behalf of the common good. Instead, what has grown up is an increasingly democratic political system that permits and even promotes diversity. American democracy allows political parties, interest groups, and a variety of rights activists—African Americans, Latinos, women, the elderly, gays and lesbians, people with disabilities, environmentalists, property owners, animal rights advocates, and others—to organize and make claims to the authority to decide *what is*, *what's right*, and *what works*. Today consumers organize boycotts, unions strike or threaten to strike, and protesters station themselves as close to their adversaries (the White House, nuclear power plants, abortion clinics) as they are allowed to get to garner publicity.

ship of state
The metaphorical use of a vessel to refer to the course of a nation goes back to ancient Greek poetry.

In responding to such claims and challenges, the minimal ship of state has become enormous. Speaking as taxpayers, Americans call for reducing the staggering federal debt and the size and cost of government. Speaking as consumers of government services, they expect government to create and protect jobs; to regulate smoking, alcohol, medicines, and food; and to ensure that everyone has access to affordable health care. Maintaining the equilibrium of such a vessel as well as steering it have become daunting tasks, even for popular political leaders in a time of peace.

Many Americans have the sense that the political system has developed a life of its own, beyond the control of any political actor, even government. They see the country being swept up by powerful currents—such as economic globalization and technological advances—that political leaders can influence only at the margins. America, to be sure, is evolving along with other nations in a world where national boundaries are becoming more difficult, if not impossible, to defend; where issues are often too complex for the public to understand; and where there is no consensus, even among experts, on where America *is* or where it *ought to go*.

As America approaches the twenty-first century, the need for informed opinions and public deliberation has never been greater. Many Americans understand that they do not live in a closed national community, but share common environments with others around the world. And many are trying to sort out the benefits and liabilities of global economic competition—for business, for workers at home and abroad, for prices, for consumer safety, for the environment, and for U.S. sovereignty.

Economic globalization—what it really is, whether it's right, and whether it works for America—will be a major issue in American politics for years to come, not only in its own right but also because it has become a common explanation

American Airlines Pilots picket at Chicago's O'Hare International Airport. President Clinton urged the pilots' union and the nation's second-largest carrier to negotiate a resolution to their dispute.

for many U.S. domestic problems.[17] The public discussion of the issue—the rhetoric of globalization—raises many questions. Are politicians exaggerating the importance of global economic forces? Are businesses using the pressure to compete in these markets as an excuse for cutting wages and not meeting social obligations? When Democrats argue that Americans will be better off once they adjust to global market forces, are they taking this stance to distance themselves from their previous but increasingly unpopular view that government should play a major role in the economy? These and other questions have yet to be answered.

Paul Krugman, an economist who believes that international trade will benefit most Americans and their trading partners abroad, has warned that the rhetoric of globalization poses two risks. One is that Americans may turn to *protectionism*—policies designed to protect the domestic market from foreign influences—thereby reducing the benefits of globalization. The other risk is *fatalism*—the "sense that we cannot come to grips with our problems because they are far bigger than we are." Fatalism, he says, is rampant in Western Europe, where citizens blame world markets rather than their domestic leaders for their nations' failed policies. The United States, he maintains, is in a position to take far better care of its poor than it does: "If our policies have become increasingly mean-spirited, that is a political choice, not something imposed upon us by anonymous forces. We cannot evade responsibility for our actions by claiming that global markets made us do it."[18]

Like this critic, many Americans regard poverty as incompatible with democracy and agree that the poor should be given the tools and the opportunities they need to climb out of poverty. But they strongly disagree among themselves on what these tools and opportunities are (*what is*) and who should provide them (*what's right*). Although politicians would prefer to put this contentious issue (and others like it) at the bottom of the political agenda, they cannot ignore so pervasive and destructive a problem. In 1996 Republican lawmakers convinced the Clinton administration that social welfare programs had grown too costly and did not work. Together they passed new legislation requiring the states to assume social welfare responsibilities that once belonged to the federal government. Today all levels of government are experimenting with new ways of delivering government services. Whether this experiment proves successful or unsuccessful, it is an example of the way Americans maintain the **dynamic equilibrium** of the political system: reevaluating old policies and experimenting with new ones to keep the ship of state in balance while it is moving forward. Indeed, all self-governing systems must remake themselves while they are working. When a consensus develops (as it has on social welfare) that the political system is in disequilibrium—that it no longer works properly in some area—leaders make corrections by rearranging the way that part of the system works (by decentralizing welfare responsibilities, for example) and by setting new goals (deadlines by which some recipients will no longer be eligible for welfare benefits). Using the stream of information (feedback) on how well these corrections are working, leaders then continue to make corrections until there is a consensus that an acceptable equilibrium has been reached.

In American politics, this process goes on in a great many areas at the same time. Those who hold fast to cherished values are always challenged by those who wish to move beyond them. Those who want to protect the national economy are challenged by those who want to globalize it. To be on board the American ship of state is thus to be part of, or at least a witness to, incessant claims that the ship is running into difficulties (*what is*), that it is on the wrong course (*what's right*), and that it is in need of all sorts of repairs (*what works*). If these claims at times seem overwhelming to the political leaders and the people who elect them, Americans should occasionally stand back from the politics of the moment and notice the two hundred years of progress and constitutional practice that have marked the American journey. With one major exception—the Civil War—dynamic equilibrium has been the rule, even when Americans were driven (by war, by economic depression, by struggles for civil rights and liberties) to make major corrections in the political system.

This progress is largely attributable to the fact that Americans have always had magnificent stars to steer by—the right to life, liberty, and the pursuit of happiness—and a self-correcting system of constitutional government that allows them to reevaluate and alter their behavior in light of those stars. In retrospect, America's greatest achievement has been the gradual inclusion (however reluctant) of those who had no legal say in the original political system. But if America has come a long way from the days when Pilgrims and slaves landed in what, for them, was a New World, the nation is about to embark on a new century in which those who came over on different boats are now in the same boat, as the Reverend Jesse Jackson, a descendant of slaves, likes to point out. And the star that is already guiding this New World is the one we now see by satellite—the fragile blue globe known as Spaceship Earth.

Summary

This chapter introduces the main concepts used to analyze politics in this book. *Politics* is defined as disputes over claims to the authority to decide *what is*, *what's right*, and *what works*.

Authority rather than force is the most commonly used and most effective form of power in politics. All political actors, including government, typically draw on four sources of authority—tradition, charisma, expertise, and legitimacy. To preserve its authority in a democracy, government must carry out its tasks in a legal and effective fashion amid criticism and pressure from other political actors. Because democracy permits and even promotes freedom of expression and petition, disputes among political actors are common. The more authority a political actor can muster, the more likely that actor is to achieve its goals. Most actors therefore construct arguments designed to increase their authority and diminish that of their opponents. As a result, the public is often faced with competing assessments of political problems. Most political debates involve competing claims to the authority to decide which public policies best serve the public, or the common good.

All actors that practice American politics—the national (federal) government, the state governments, the people, political parties, interest groups, experts, elites, the media—are required to abide by the rules that regulate the political process. The most important of these rules are laid down in the Constitution of 1787, which provides for federalism and representative democracy. Adherence to these rules over time results in constitutional practice (constitutionalism).

Political actors routinely practice the politics of knowledge—the manipulation of information, logic, and language—to promote their goals. Other actors must decide which political actors are the most credible, as well as which political experts (journalists, pollsters, political scientists) to believe, because they, too, manipulate information, logic, and language in their accounts of politics. The questions people ask about any political issue, as well as the assumptions they make and the goals they seek, tend to shape the answers they get about *what is* (what's really the case about something), *what's right* (what they value), and *what works* (what they believe will effectively achieve a particular goal). Four basic analytical tools are used to answer these questions: description, explanation, evaluation, and prescription. These tools allow their user to place an issue in a particular context that shapes its interpretation and treatment.

Politics is the process by which members of a political society regulate pressures for order and change that allow the political system to adapt to disturbances over time. This adaptive process is extremely intricate and complex in the United States because the political system is required to adhere to the rules of democracy and federalism. In this process, actors learn from their successes and failures and make corrections in their behavior, which is how they improve the political system over time while maintaining its dynamic equilibrium. The greatest challenge facing the political system as it moves into the twenty-first century is the preservation of American values and social order in the face of mounting global economic and environmental pressures.

Key Terms

authority **6**
capitalism **7**
charisma **7**
the common good **9**
context **23**
democracy **5**
description **21**
direct democracy **16**
dynamic equilibrium **31**
elites **12**
evaluation **22**
expertise **7**

explanation **22**
federalism **15**
force **6**
government **6**
interpretation **17**
laissez-faire capitalism **7**
legitimacy **8**
political actors **5**
political society **14**
politics **5**
politics of knowledge **17**
popular sovereignty **16**

power **6**
prescription **23**
public policy **9**
representative democracy **16**
republic **16**
sovereignty **15**
status quo **25**
system **26**
tradition **7**
unitary system **15**

Constitutional Practice

Above: Citizens of Moscow barricade the Russian Federation Parliament building against Soviet tanks, August 21, 1991. *Right:* Soviet coup leaders hold a press conference, August 19, 1991.

CHAPTER 2

We hold these truths to be self-evident, that all men are created equal, that they are endowed by their Creator with certain unalienable Rights, that among these are Life, Liberty and the pursuit of Happiness. That to secure these rights, Governments are instituted among Men, deriving their just powers from the consent of the governed.

Declaration of Independence, 1776

We the People of the United States, in Order to form a more perfect Union, establish Justice, insure domestic Tranquillity, provide for the common defence, promote the general Welfare, and secure the Blessings of Liberty to ourselves and to our Posterity, do ordain and establish this Constitution for the United States of America.

Preamble to the Constitution, 1787

The Origins of American Constitutional Practice

From Discontent to Nationhood

Drafting the Constitution

The Dispute over Ratification

Why the Constitution Still Works

For more than 70 years, since the Revolution of 1917, the Union of Soviet Socialist Republics (USSR) was a Communist dictatorship, with centralized control over virtually every aspect of the republics' affairs and their citizens' lives. In the late 1980s, Soviet Premier Mikhail Gorbachev tried to create a more open society—a movement called *glasnost* (Russian for *opening*)—and halt the arms race that was destroying the economy. In 1990, he allowed the three small Baltic republics of Latvia, Lithuania, and Estonia to declare their independence. In 1991, he and the leaders of the 11 remaining republics agreed to revise the Union Treaty of 1922 in which the Soviet republics had forfeited most of their power to the central government—an agreement that was solidified in the Constitution of 1924. The republics now wanted—and Gorbachev was prepared to give—much of that power back. But on August 19, 1991, before the revised treaty could be signed, eight leading officials who opposed the disintegration of the USSR attempted to topple Gorbachev while he was on vacation in the Crimea.

Then a remarkable thing happened. The citizens of Moscow resisted. In pounding rain, thousands of demonstrators braved columns of tanks to defend their Parliament and the president of the Russian Republic, Boris Yeltsin, from an anticipated attack. They threw up barricades of bathtubs, tree trunks, and buses—anything they could find to stop the Soviet tanks. State television broadcast the astonishing sight of their resistance and the collapse of the coup.

Although Gorbachev was rescued from captivity and restored to his post, the failure of the coup revealed that the collapse of the Soviet Union was irreversible. It dissolved four months later (December 1991) when all the republics declared their independence. Eleven republics agreed to cooperate in a new partnership—the Commonwealth of Independent States (CIS)—in which they retained their status as fully independent states. Many of the republics then drafted new constitutions in an attempt to refound themselves as democracies with capitalist economies. The Russian constitution was approved by national referendum on December 12, 1993. Since then both parliamentary and presidential elections have been held under its rules.

These new republics are learning that simply having a democratic constitution does not guarantee that its principles (*what's right*)—the rule of law, limited government, an open society, and respect for human rights and dignity—will work in practice and over time. Ultimately, the test of these constitutions will be how well they work from day to day and in the face of brute realities. All these republics lack viable constitutional traditions and confront daunting economic and environmental problems. Many are besieged by militant ethnic strife. Demonstrating their capacity to enforce their constitutions' guarantees over time will be a sign of constitutional practice, or constitutionalism. Constitutions matter only when governments and citizens treat them as the supreme authority on how they should practice politics.

The Framers of the U.S. Constitution of 1787 faced similar challenges more than 200 years ago. They had to decide how strong their new Union would be and how much power the national government would have over the states. The Framers viewed the Constitution as a moral, mechanical, and practical document that set forth the nation's core political values (*what's right*); distributed political power among the national government, the states, and the people; and established the rules by which these actors were to practice politics and manage their disputes over time (*what works*). They drafted the document based on the brute realities of their day and their beliefs about how political systems operate (*what is*).

In terms of liberties and rights, the brute reality of their day was that women were not regarded as full citizens, and Indians, indentured servants, and slaves were regarded as noncitizens. In terms of economics, the brute realities were that the southern states depended on slavery, a practice they were not prepared to give up, and that commerce among the states was chaotic. While the document they drafted took account of these realities and acted to change some of them, it also contained rules and procedures that allowed future generations to make their own changes in the Constitution and the political system.

How well has the Constitution worked since then? Experts and ordinary citizens disagree. According to the late Thurgood Marshall, the first African American to sit on the U.S. Supreme Court, the Constitution "was defective from the start, requiring several amendments, a civil war, and momentous social transformation to attain the system of constitutional government, and its respect for the individual freedoms and rights, we hold as fundamental today."[1] And yet Marshall, like many others, used the Constitution to expand individual freedoms (Chapter 15) and rights (Chapter 16).

The Constitution has seen the country through dramatic changes that would severely test any constitution. The country has grown from 13 to 50 states, from a fledgling nation to a world power, from an agrarian to a postindustrial society. The document remains the world's oldest written living constitution providing for a representative form of government and holds the longest record of constitutional practice—achievements that have led constitution writers around the world to study how it was put together and why it has lasted so long.

In this chapter we'll discover how the Framers came to write the Constitution they did and why, after more than two centuries of change, it continues to work—however imperfectly. We'll do this by focusing on the following questions:

What are the origins of American constitutional practice?

What factors shaped the writing of the Constitution?

How does the U.S. Constitution structure American government?

What disputes surrounded the ratification of the Constitution?

Why does the U.S. Constitution still work?

The Origins of American Constitutional Practice

Before a people are prepared to accept a constitution written by their representatives, they must first decide they are "a people" and agree to form a political society. Such a momentous decision is never made overnight. Rather, events and aspirations lead people to a point where they accept their leaders' claims to the authority to act in their name. During the British settlement period, from roughly 1607 to the 1760s, the colonists scattered mainly along the Atlantic coast thought of themselves primarily as English, Dutch, German, Swedish, or some other nationality. Their communities were so isolated that many of them communicated with each other through England by ship.

Why did a majority of these diverse peoples and colonies agree to form a common political society and unite in a war against Britain in 1776? Because the differences that divided them were eventually offset by what they came to share: (1) many adhered to the same principles of natural law and English common law; (2) many were Protestant Christians; (3) most were native English speakers, and others accepted English as the language of commerce; (4) most had suffered the hardships of survival in an undeveloped land; (5) all wanted to expand their economies; and (6) all had grappled with the demands of self-government under the authority of a common government—Britain. By the time the colonies declared their independence, they were actively writing state constitutions that resembled one another in form and content.[2] Ironically, their inspiration for doing so came from their belief in liberties and rights they had inherited from England centuries earlier.

Magna Carta: The Origin of Colonial Rights

The story of how the rights of Englishmen ended up in the U.S. Constitution begins in Runnymede, England, in 1215. For the first time an English monarch, King John, was forced by his rebellious barons to grant **Magna Carta** and submit to "the rule of law." This limitation on royal power established the principle of **limited government** that Americans would one day impose on their national government after independence. Provisions of this Great Charter, which were read aloud to people of all classes in all English villages and towns, guaranteed them such protections as the "judgment of peers" (now called trial by jury) and the "law of the land" (now called due process of law) (see Figure 2.1).

This protection against arbitrary government gained new strength in the seventeenth century when Sir Edward Coke, Speaker of the Parliamentary House of Commons under Queen Elizabeth and Chief Justice under James I, appealed to the Great Charter to justify increasing the power of the Parliament against the king's claim to absolute rule by "divine right." Coke's defense of the peoples' natural rights—the basis for popular sovereignty (Chapter 1)—landed him in prison for 17 months. Before his death he wrote a commentary on Magna Carta, *The Institutes of the Laws of England*, which many colonists then used to justify their rights as Englishmen. An inventory of 47 private libraries throughout the colonies between 1652 and 1791 showed that Coke's *Institutes* was in 27 of them, and that it was by far the most common book on either law or politics. By the time William Penn crossed the ocean to establish the colony of Pennsylvania in 1681, news of his devotion to Magna Carta had preceded him in his published account of his famous trial in London in 1670.

In 1775, the people of Massachusetts chose a state insignia depicting a defender of Magna Carta (1215).

Rights in Colonial Founding Documents

The English men and women who crossed the sea to settle in the New World had been promised by Queen Elizabeth I that they and their descendants would have the same rights as those remaining in England. The colonists insisted on those rights despite living under different founding documents. The chief founding document was the **royal charter** granted to merchant adventurers who wanted to profit from the fish, timber, minerals, and agricultural potential of the New World. These entrepreneurs formed and sold stock in corporations to finance settlements in America and sought royal charters to establish and operate them.

In 1606, King James I granted the Virginia Company of London and the Virginia Company of Plymouth rights to settle land in America. Jamestown, the colony founded by the Virginia Company of London, established a governor, a governor's council, and a people's assembly. These institutions set a precedent for colonial constitution-making and self-government under the authority of the English monarchy. In 1624, the faltering London company lost its charter and the king appointed a royal governor to head

---

Magna Carta

The Magna Carta (Latin for *Great Charter*) is also known as the Charter of English Liberties. Its provisions are derived from universal principles or natural laws (what today we call human rights) that apply to all people, rulers included.

Parliament

Parliament (from the Latin *to speak, to confer*) is a term for national legislatures. In Britain, the Parliament includes an upper House of Lords, composed of the nobility, and a lower House of Commons, which represents ordinary citizens called commoners.

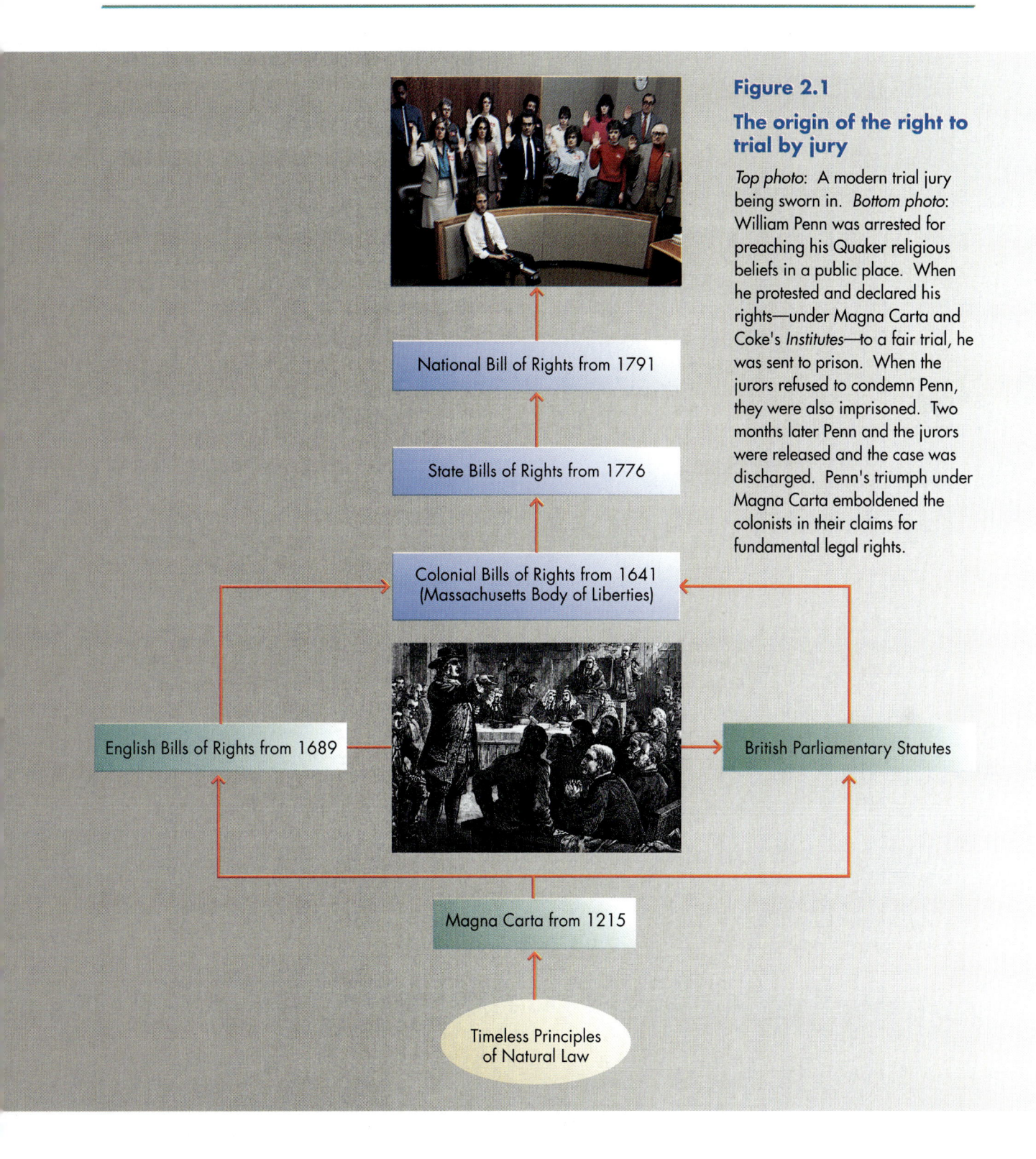

Figure 2.1
The origin of the right to trial by jury

Top photo: A modern trial jury being sworn in. *Bottom photo*: William Penn was arrested for preaching his Quaker religious beliefs in a public place. When he protested and declared his rights—under Magna Carta and Coke's *Institutes*—to a fair trial, he was sent to prison. When the jurors refused to condemn Penn, they were also imprisoned. Two months later Penn and the jurors were released and the case was discharged. Penn's triumph under Magna Carta emboldened the colonists in their claims for fundamental legal rights.

- National Bill of Rights from 1791
- State Bills of Rights from 1776
- Colonial Bills of Rights from 1641 (Massachusetts Body of Liberties)
- English Bills of Rights from 1689
- British Parliamentary Statutes
- Magna Carta from 1215
- Timeless Principles of Natural Law

what then became a royal colony. In 1631, the royal governor and his council, along with the general assembly, agreed to set up courts that would meet regularly in the surrounding settlements and dispense justice according to common law and the principles in Magna Carta.

The signing of William Penn's treaty of peace and friendship with the Delaware tribe inhabiting Pennsylvania.

Other colonies founded themselves on a **compact**. By looking to themselves rather than the king for legitimation, they were already recognizing the principle of popular sovereignty on which the American republic would later be founded. The first and most famous colonial compact was the Mayflower Compact of 1620, signed by the Pilgrims after they crossed the Atlantic on the *Mayflower*. All this compact lacked to be a modern constitution was a description of how political power was to be distributed and institutionalized. This lack was remedied in 1636 with the Pilgrim Code of Law, which contained a detailed list of the political institutions by which the colonists agreed to be governed.[3] Other newly forming colonies adopted similar compacts, such as the Fundamental Orders of Connecticut of 1639. In less than two decades Plymouth, Connecticut, and Rhode Island had created their own governments based on the consent of the governed and on a founding document resembling a modern constitution.

The middle-class English Puritans who founded the Massachusetts Bay Company and who obtained a royal charter to establish a corporate colony were motivated by religion as well as money. They wanted to establish a political community based on Puritan theology —a theology that rested on a **covenant** (a compact that looked to a higher authority, such as God or the king, rather than to the people). In 1635, when colonists demanded written laws "similar to Magna Carta," its assembly responded with the Body of Liberties of 1641. This document was the first colonial **bill of rights**, a document that protects individual liberties, or natural rights. Among its 98 provisions, which bear a striking resemblance to Magna Carta, the Body of Liberties included the right to a trial by jury, a guarantee of due process of law, and a prohibition against cruel and unusual punishment: "No man shall be beaten with above 40 stripes, nor shall any gentleman, nor any man equal to a gentleman be punished by whipping unless his crime be very shameful."[4] While this provision may seem cruel today, it was an important restraint on government's power over the people at the time. The document also protected certain liberties of freemen, women, children, servants, and foreigners and guaranteed citizens and foreigners alike the right to a speedy trial. Nor could government confiscate private property for public use without compensating the owner. After independence, these provisions would become standard features in state and national bills of rights.

The British monarch also granted charters to favored individuals called proprietors. At first colonists in **proprietary colonies**—Maryland, Carolina, New Jersey, New York, and Pennsylvania—had a much smaller say than those in corporately owned colonies over how they would be governed and what rights they deserved. But under pressure from the Crown, all the proprietors eventually agreed to permit assemblies, to follow the laws of England, and to guarantee basic rights.

An exception was William Penn, who formally reaffirmed the rights of Englishmen in 1682 in *The Most Excellent Privilege of Liberty and Property*. In addition to welcoming immigrants of different religions and nationalities, Penn also treated the Indians living in the colony with dignity. Penn's "Holy Experiment," as he called it, was unique among the colonies, but it turned out to be the blueprint for the pluralist, multicultural America of today.

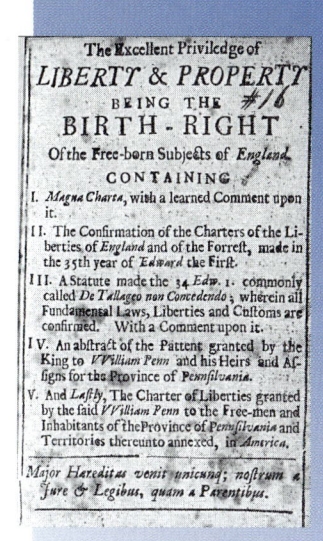

English Rights and Colonial Rights

During the half-century before Penn arrived in Pennsylvania, the English had themselves been engaged in a struggle for rights that ultimately affected rights in the American colonies. Between 1629 and 1640, Charles I ruled without Parliament and imposed taxes by royal decree. His persecution of the Puritans forced many to go to America or into exile. Civil war broke out. The Puritan rebels beheaded Charles in 1649, and their leader, Oliver Cromwell, ruled England from 1649 until his death in 1658. No friend of English liberties, Cromwell is said to have called Magna Carta Magna Farta.[5] His son, who succeeded him, proved a weak leader, and by 1660 Charles II and Parliament, under a restoration agreement, were ruling the country together.

William Penn's guarantee of the rights of Englishmen to the colonists of Pennsylvania, 1682.

The New Mercantilism

The new Restoration government, eager to increase its resources, passed laws strengthening England's traditional policy of mercantilism. The result was a new **mercantilism** aimed at increasing England's favorable balance of trade. The new policy also attempted to standardize and centralize the tasks of colonial administration to further increase the flow of revenues to the Crown. English customs officials now appeared in the colonies. The colonists resented the interference of English bureaucrats in their internal affairs. New Englanders, used to trading freely with the Dutch and the French, complained that their royal charters exempted them from these regulations. Charles rebuffed their complaints, as did his successor, James II. This clash between the new mercantilism and colonial rights began to drive a wedge between England and the colonies.

The Glorious Revolution

If James II was despised in the colonies, he was equally hated at home for revoking domestic charters, ignoring Parliament, and embracing Catholicism. In June 1688, the Dutch prince, William of Orange, husband of James's Protestant daughter Mary, answered a call to rescue England. Five months later, James II fled without a fight and Parliament officially offered the throne to William and Mary, on condition that they accept a Declaration of Rights that increased Parliament's power. A subsequent Bill of Rights (1689) compelled the monarch to call Parliament into session every year and to sign whatever bills it passed. These events, which became known as the **Glorious Revolution**, expanded the rights of Englishmen, and the documents that accompanied the Revolution, along with other features of

> **mercantilism**
> Mercantilism (from the Latin for *merchant*), the economic policy pursued by sixteenth-century European monarchs to regulate domestic industry, agriculture, and trade, encouraged exports and discouraged imports.

> **Whigs and Tories**
>
> These were the two main factions in the British Parliament, emerging around the time of the Glorious Revolution of 1688. While Tories clung to the notion that kings ruled by divine right, Whigs strongly supported the restrictions on royal power contained in the English Bill of Rights.

English law, have served the country as an "unwritten" constitution.

Colonists had difficulty claiming these expanded rights because they conflicted with the policy of mercantilism that made the colonies economically subservient to England. While the colonists considered themselves Englishmen, representatives of the Crown treated them as "colonials" with lesser rights. By the mid-1700s, colonial assemblies were complaining that their royally appointed governors wielded more power over them than the king wielded over the British Parliament. Colonists began to argue, like the Whigs in England, that liberty is threatened by a concentration of power. Newspapers spread the view that tyranny and corruption should be checked by dividing political power up among different government institutions and subjecting them to the watchful eye of elected legislatures.

From Discontent to Nationhood

Meanwhile, Britain had acquired a staggering debt during the French and Indian War (1755–1763) (known in Europe as the Seven Years War), fought against European rivals over claims to empire. Britain expected its prosperous American colonies to help pay the cost of stationing 10,000 British troops in America to safeguard territory won from France, especially because it had reimbursed the colonies for their costs during the French and Indian War and because smuggling and lax enforcement of trade laws by colonists often meant that British tariffs went uncollected.

Discontent over Taxes

Britain therefore imposed customs duties on sugar with the Sugar Act of 1764. Colonial assemblies protested the act in a series of petitions, arguing that it violated their right as Englishmen to consent to any tax laws imposed upon them. But colonists' reaction to this external tax on their imports was mild compared to their fury at the Stamp Act of 1765. This first direct, internal tax ever imposed on the colonies required that all printed matter, including newspapers, pamphlets, legal documents, licenses, diplomas, and even cards and dice, carry an official stamp purchased from the British government. "No taxation without representation!" colonists cried.

When these appeals fell on deaf ears, colonial leaders such as James Otis of Massachusetts pointed out that the rights of Englishmen guaranteed by British law were based on natural (human) rights, which all people share. Otis, who was educated at Harvard and steeped in Coke's commentary on Magna Carta, argued in a treatise that the authority to govern stemmed from "an everlasting foundation in the unchangeable will of God, the author of nature, whose laws never vary." Parliament, according to Otis, thus had a sacred obligation to repeal acts such as the Stamp Act that conflicted with God's natural laws.[6] Parliament ignored Otis's treatise but eventually repealed the Stamp Act to end the American boycott of British imports. But the repeal came too late to reverse the widespread conviction that colonial rights had been trampled on.

Revolution and Independence

American patriots calling themselves "Sons of Liberty" began to spring up in port cities to protest British customs duties. They bridled at the Tea Act of 1773 giving the British East India Company a monopoly on colonial tea, even though the act made tea cheaper than it was in England and cheaper than smuggled tea. After these patriots dumped company tea into Boston Harbor in what became known as the Boston Tea Party, Britain imposed tighter restrictions that the colonists called "the Intolerable Acts."

The First and Second Continental Congresses

These events prompted most of the colonies to send delegates (chosen by their assemblies or by special conventions) to what became known as the First Continental Congress in Philadelphia in September 1774 to address British affronts to their liberties. New England and southern leaders favored military revolt. The Middle Atlantic colonies proposed a compromise that would have given the colonies as a group the power to reject acts of Parliament. They finally agreed on a Declaration of Rights and Resolves that recognized Parliament's right to regulate colonial commerce but rejected its authority to impose taxes and suspend assemblies. They sent their declaration directly to King George III, urging him to revoke the Intolerable Acts. But Parliament was now the dominant political power in Britain, so this effort failed. By the time the delegates disbanded with plans to reconvene, their regional distinctions had softened, prompting Patrick Henry to say, "I am not a Virginian, but an American."

Violence erupted in Lexington, Massachusetts, in April 1775 when British soldiers attempted to seize colonial weapons they feared might be used in an uprising. News of this battle and other bloody skirmishes spread quickly throughout the colonies, and men began to ready their weapons.

The Second Continental Congress began meeting in May 1775. The Revolution was already under way. Many of the delegates, including John Adams of Massachusetts, were attending for the second time. But there were also new faces, among them Thomas Jefferson of Virginia, John Hancock of Massachusetts, and Benjamin Franklin of Pennsylvania. Their first task was to raise an army. Later that year the Congress called upon the colonial assemblies to draft new state constitutions that would provide for "some form of government" independent of the Crown.

Left: American patriots pull down the statue of George III at Bowling Green, New York City. *Right:* Romanians pull down a statue of Lenin in Bucharest before the House of Free Press (previously the headquarters of the Communist party newspaper) on March 3, 1990, six months before the Russian coup.

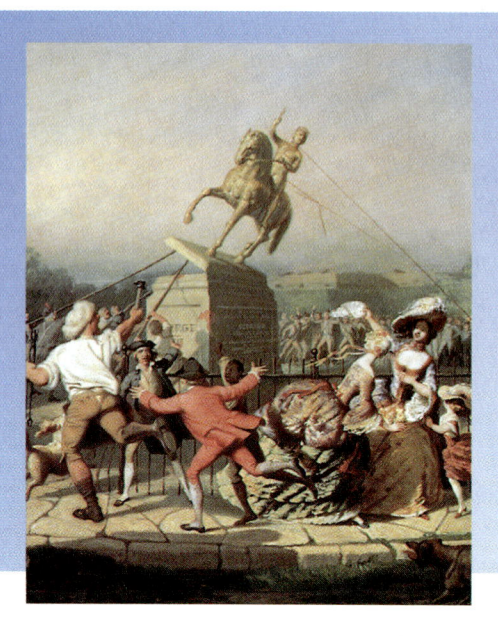

Meanwhile American patriots agitating for total independence increasingly harassed loyalists who preferred reconciliation to revolution. The agitators burned British goods in merchants' shops, threatened ministers who preached loyalist sermons, and whipped up anti-British hostility in towns and in the countryside. Some colonists still undecided were persuaded by Tom Paine's radical pamphlet *Common Sense* (1776), which argued that kingship was incompatible with liberty. Step by step the colonies advanced toward revolution.

The Declaration of Independence

On July 4, 1776, the delegates to the Second Continental Congress approved a formal **Declaration of Independence** from Britain. Thomas Jefferson, its major drafter, knew that the British and colonial loyalists would view the document as an act of treason. His task was to persuade his readers that independence was right and just. Following the familiar format of the compact, he defined Americans as a common people committed to natural law principles and declared their authority to found a government. In addition to relying on the wisdom of the great writers on liberty from Aristotle (384–322 B.C.) to British philosopher John Locke (1632–1704), he also included many of the natural law phrases of colonial legal theorists that were familiar to readers of revolutionary pamphlets, such as the famous assertion that "all men are created equal." In addition, he invoked the popular sovereignty claim in Magna Carta (as popularized by Coke) that governments derive "their just Powers from the Consent of the Governed."

John Locke's view that nature grants people certain rights was incorporated into the Declaration of Independence.

Jefferson wrote the Declaration in the voice of "We," but his use of the term "one people" was ambiguous—a strategy designed to appeal to citizens who identified with their own states as well as to the people of the nation as a whole.[7] This first call for unity on the basis of state citizenship as well as national citizenship would later find a response in the Constitution of 1787. Now the states would only agree to form a loose confederation. As Table 2.1 shows, the commonwealth confederation recently formed by the former Soviet republics is far looser.

TABLE 2.1

Distribution of Powers under the Articles of Confederation, the U.S. Constitution, and the Commonwealth of Independent States

Articles of Confederation 1781	U.S. Constitution 1787	Commonwealth of Independent States 1991
No executive branch	Independent president with extensive powers	Minimal institutional structures include: • Council of the Heads of State (highest coordinating body, convenes twice a year) • Council of the Heads of Government (responsible for economic coordination, convenes twice a year)
No federal judiciary	Supreme Court and inferior federal courts	No judicial structure or formal procedure for settling disputes
Unanimous consent of states required to amend; all states have an equal vote	Simpler amending process requiring consent of three-fourth of states	No special amendment process
Dual Citizenship	Dual Citizenship	No common citizenship
States superior to central government in federal scheme	States have equal votes in Senate; proportional vote according to population in House of Representatives National government superior to states	All 11 republics have an equal vote Every new agreement requires ratification by the republics' legislatures Republics are superior to CIS institutions
Sovereignty located in the states	Sovereignty located in the people	Sovereignty located in the states; each republic must enter international organizations, like the United Nations, or regional organizations, like the EEC, on its own.
Congress *lacks* power to • regulate interstate and foreign commerce • raise taxes • control currency • enforce its laws • enforce treaty provisions	Congress *has* power to • regulate interstate and foreign commerce • raise taxes	No legislative body

Note: The republics gave the CIS virtually no power because they (like the American states under the Articles of Confederation that remembered British tyranny) retain vivid memories of their exploitation under the totalitarian Soviet Union.

Some individuals were so inspired by the Declaration that they embarked on experiments of their own. Virginia planter Robert Carter was one of a number of slave owners, including George Washington, who had come to see slavery as immoral and unjust. He shocked fellow planters with his decision to free his 500 slaves—a substantial number for a planter of that period. However, while Carter had the legal power to emancipate his slaves, he faced the prospect of releasing them into a traditional culture that was not prepared to accept them as free people. Ultimately, Carter released his slaves in groups over time—a process that continued even after his death, according to provisions in his will.

Early reformers such as Carter who sought to abolish the institution of slavery learned the bitter lesson that new ideals—even when written into declarations, constitutions, and laws—are not quickly or easily put into practice. For such change to occur, people's beliefs, social habits, and institutions must also change. Thus while some Americans during this period approached their new state constitutions with the belief that natural justice belonged to all people and would in time bring about a more democratic society, most continued to believe that natural justice applied only to white male property owners.

Today many Americans mistakenly believe that the inspiring promises of the Declaration—especially those of life, liberty, and the pursuit of happiness—are part of the Constitution of 1787. In fact, the missions of the two documents were very different. The Declaration proclaimed—and still proclaims—the visionary political ideals of the American people and millions of others around the world. The mission of the Constitution, as we'll see, was to create a federal system of government that would work.

State Constitutions

Before the Declaration, the Second Continental Congress had called on colonial assemblies, acting as state legislatures, to write their own **state constitutions**. Each state was to choose the form of government that best met its needs. In this heady time, elites and ordinary citizens freely designed and debated new political experiments. To John Adams, a recognized expert on constitutions, it was "a time when the greatest law-givers of humanity would have wished to live. How few of the human race have ever enjoyed an opportunity of [choosing their own form] of government."[8]

All the new state constitutions called for an elected (usually two-house, or bicameral) assembly, a governor (elected by the people or by the assemblies), and a bill of rights. But states gave very different amounts of power to these branches, depending on whether their drafters were conservatives, radicals, or moderates. Conservatives who thought the Revolution was being fought so that local American elites could replace English governing elites wanted strong executive and judicial branches to check popularly elected legislatures. Radicals wanted a popular democracy in which representation was not based on wealth, representatives were kept closely accountable to the people, and the powers of the executive and the courts were severely limited. Moderates chose a middle ground.

Between 1776 and 1798 the states experimented with no fewer than 29 state constitutions (only two of which their legislatures rejected), while thousands of pamphlets and newspapers debated their merits. Those drafted by states controlled by radicals (such as North Carolina) and conservatives (Maryland and New York) worked less well than those drafted by moderates (Virginia).

The Articles of Confederation

Americans had declared themselves unified and independent, but they lacked a way to coordinate their separate states, which claimed **sovereignty**, or independent status. The Second Continental Congress therefore drafted the **Articles of Confederation and Perpetual Union**, which they sent to the states for ratification in November 1777. Meanwhile, the Congress had to beg the states to finance the Revolutionary War with Britain, which had begun in 1776. After five grueling years of war, almost 8,000 British soldiers surrendered to General George Washington at Yorktown on October 19, 1781. The military battle with Britain was finally won, but the political battle among the new states over the new national government was just beginning.

Ratification of the Articles was delayed until March 1781 due to disputes over representation and western lands.[9] The issue was finally resolved when all the "landed" states ceded their western claims to Congress.

A confederation of 13 states seemed to be a natural choice for a nation built out of 13 former colonies. It was also predictable because, having been chosen by their state legislatures, the delegates who drafted the Articles were determined to collaborate as equal states rather than submit to the control of a strong central government.

Defects

The Articles of Confederation were flawed from the start because they failed to grant the national government sufficient authority to govern effectively. Remembering their struggles against Britain, the authors restricted the power of the government, limiting it to a one-house (unicameral) legislature. Congress *was* the government. There was no independent executive or judiciary to enforce its laws.

The rules imposed on the Confederation Congress were equally restrictive. Each state was permitted only one vote in the Congress, and at least nine votes were required to pass a law. Any amendments to alter the Articles required unanimous consent, which meant that each state had the power to **veto** (defeat) any proposed changes. These provisions were designed to give all states, regardless of their size, an equal voice in national decisions and to prevent the national government from swallowing up the states. The states also guaranteed their monopoly over national politics by requiring that only state legislators could serve as delegates to this national Congress. No delegate could serve more than three out of every six years (a move in the direction of term limits). The states also paid the delegates' salaries and could recall them at will.

The Confederation Congress ultimately authorized five executive departments, among them Commerce and Finance, but preferred to set up committees to handle problems as they arose. During his time in the Congress, John Adams sat on more than eighty committees.[10] This reluctance to institutionalize political authority in departments was intended to prevent the new national government from encroaching on state sovereignty. The Congress could only establish post offices, regulate the coinage of money, and oversee Indian affairs. Its

> **confederation**
>
> In a confederation (con, *with* + federate, *to unite*), a compact among sovereign states, the member states retain the predominant power over the common government they establish.

power to appoint military and naval officers and requisition men from the states was worthless because it lacked the power to tax the states to pay for them. The delegates denied it the power to tax because they had learned from experience with the British Parliament that "the power of the purse" was the lifeblood of a state's sovereignty. As a result, the Congress had to ask the states for funds to conduct its business.

The Congress was also denied the power to regulate commerce between the states and between the Confederation and other countries. Instead of uniform national regulations, merchants were forced to deal with 13 different customs schemes. When the Congress in 1784 tried to remedy the problem by passing uniform navigation acts, Rhode Island and North Carolina refused to ratify them.

The Congress was also ineffective in foreign affairs. Britain, for example, had refused to withdraw from a number of western forts, disrupting Indian relations, until America paid off its debts to British creditors and restored the confiscated estates of colonists who had remained loyal to Britain. When the Congress appealed to the states to comply with these requests, they refused. Thus with no executive branch to execute policies of finance, war, trade, and foreign policy, the new national government was powerless to act in critical areas.

Innovations Under the Articles

The Articles nevertheless contained important innovations.[11] First, the Articles made explicit the principle of **dual citizenship** that was implicit in the Declaration—the notion that people are citizens of their states as well as citizens of the nation. For example, the Articles gave "to all the privileges and immunities of free citizens in the several States," thus allowing individuals to move from state to state and to trade and do business with one another on an equal basis. The Articles were thus moving toward the federal form of government the United States has today. Unlike today, under the Articles the national government could act directly only on the states, not on individuals, who came under the authority of the states. Second, the Confederation Congress passed the Northwest Ordinance in 1787 (Chapter 3), providing for admission of new states to the confederation on an equal legal footing, a daring act because their admission would dilute the power of the 13 existing states.

Crisis

No sooner was the war with Britain won than the confederation began to falter. Banks were foreclosing on homes and farms, and prisons were filling with people who could not pay their debts. Nationalists complained that the Confederation Congress was too weak to halt the crisis.

In February 1787, the Congress authorized a committee to convene "for the sole and express purpose of revising the Articles of Confederation." Two circumstances triggered this action. First, New York—the busiest and richest port in the country—had flatly rejected, and thus killed, a proposed amendment that had been circulating among the states for four years to give the Congress an independent source of revenue in the form of import duties. Alexander Hamilton and other nationalists had long been pressing for such an amendment, and all the states were prepared to ratify it except for New York, which refused to share such

Alexander Hamilton (1755–1804) was a framer of the Constitution, coauthor of *The Federalist*, and a proponent of a strong but limited national government.

a rich source of revenue. Second, with no power over the economy, no military force of its own, and no power to command the states to act, the Congress found itself helpless to control popular insurrections flaring up in New Hampshire and other states. The most notorious of these was the farmers' tax revolt in western Massachusetts known as **Shays' Rebellion** described in the box nearby.

Some nationalists viewed the rebellion as evidence that a strong national government was needed to maintain public order. George Washington wrote to fellow Virginian James Madison that "without some alteration in our political creed, the superstructure we have been . . . raising at the expense of so much blood and treasure, must fall. We are fast verging to anarchy and confusion."[12] Physician Benjamin Rush, a Philadelphian who had signed the Declaration, was convinced that "nothing but a vigorous and efficient government can prevent [the people] degenerating into savages, or devouring each other like beasts of prey."[13]

Caricature of Charles Montesquieu (1685–1755), whose theory of the separation of powers advanced in *The Spirit of the Laws* (1748) influenced the American Constitution.

Drafting the Constitution

In May 1787, 55 delegates from all states but Rhode Island (whose legislature was controlled by populists) assembled in Philadelphia to strengthen the confederation by revising the Articles. These delegates were the elites of their day. As lawyers, businessmen, and big farmers familiar with high finance and foreign trade, they understood why the nation could not develop commercially under the Articles. This understanding set them apart from the roughly 90 percent of their countrymen who were subsistence farmers.

Most delegates were also highly educated and, some say, intellectual giants. Thirty-four were college-educated (just to get into King's College—now Columbia University—students were required to be fluent in Greek and Latin), and the others were also remarkably learned. Many had studied the Greek and Roman historians, the Bible, and the influential scientists and philosophers of their day.[14] Having relied heavily on John Locke to justify the break with Britain, the delegates now turned to the French philosopher Montesquieu in designing the national constitution.

The delegates were familiar with the reasons why some governments and empires in history had succeeded while others had failed. Madison, for his part, came armed with statements on the ill-fated history of confederacies and the defects he found in the Articles. With these arguments in hand, the economic crisis brewing, and the fallout from Shays' Rebellion still in the air, the delegates felt justified in exceeding the authority they had been given to amend the Articles. They decided to draft a new document creating a federal system that gave the national government predominant authority over the states.

This decision was a deliberate effort to produce a document that would work—a document based on the realities the nation then faced and on principles the delegates considered right and eternal. However, some scholars argue that critics of the Articles—both then and since then—have exaggerated their weaknesses and that if the Articles had been amended rather than discarded, they would have produced a viable government.[15]

Politics of Knowledge

Shays' Rebellion: Anarchy or Justice?

Shays' Rebellion of 1786 was sparked by a shortage of hard currency (specie) in the new republic. This problem was aggravated by the practice of using promissory notes (IOUs) as a substitute for specie. After the war, exporters in Britain demanded hard currency from American merchants, who then had to demand hard currency from their own customers. Cash-poor farmers, tradespeople, and laborers were suddenly forced to pay in advance for merchandise and pay their loans and outstanding bills in cash rather than in crops and services.

People demanded that their states issue paper money and postpone payments on debts and taxes. Seven states responded by issuing paper money, which they declared valid for the payment of debts, and five states used that money to provide credit to farmers. But creditors fled and merchants closed down to avoid accepting money they considered worthless—behavior the Rhode Island legislature, controlled by populists, tried to stop with fines. But the Massachusetts legislature, which had hiked property taxes to help pay for moving the state capital to Boston, refused to help farmers by stopping the banks from taking back their farms.

Outraged at the foreclosures on their farms, the farmers at first sought peaceful remedies. But when they petitioned for the printing of more money they were accused of wanting to devalue the currency. When they staged peaceful protests, lawmakers remained unmoved. Finally, in desperation, they rebelled. When more than two thousand farmers, organized and led by Revolutionary War veteran Daniel Shays, marched on county courthouses to protest the rise in property taxes, they were quickly crushed by a volunteer army from Boston. (The Massachusetts government had appealed for help to the Confederation Congress, but it was powerless to act.)

Sympathetic historians reject the view that the Shaysites were revolutionary fanatics bent on expanding and devaluing the money supply.[1] They point out that the rebels resorted to insurrection only when their peaceful protests and direct actions failed and that Thomas Jefferson supported their cause. These scholars also point out that the political system was rigged in favor of propertied elites and that the populists were simply trying to obtain some of the justice that they believed they had won in the Revolutionary War. But to Madison, Shays' Rebellion signified the need for a strong central government capable of ensuring public order.

Were the Shaysites anarchists or populist democrats exploited by state and national elites? Although historians still debate this question, the nationalists of the period succeeded in convincing Americans at the time that these men were dangerous anarchists and that the government was too weak to stop them. In such a climate, the call to a convention to strengthen the national government fell on sympathetic ears.

---

[1] This is Herbert J. Storing's view. *What the Anti-Federalists Were For: The Political Thought of the Opponents of the Constitution* (Chicago: University of Chicago Press, 1981). For a pro-Shaysite view, see David P. Szatmary, *Shays' Rebellion: The Making of an Agrarian Insurrection* (Amherst: University of Massachusetts Press, 1980), 57.

The delegates walked into what became the Constitutional Convention of 1787 already agreeing on the general goals contained in the Constitution's short Preamble: commitments to a "more perfect Union," to justice, domestic tranquility, defense, the general welfare, and liberty. They also agreed on the value of rational public debate and they rejected political parties as divisive. Although they accepted the principle of popular sovereignty (that government derives its legitimacy from the people), they insisted that the people be ruled by representatives fit for the task who would be accountable to them. This view—known as **republicanism**, or representative government—was a rejection of direct democracy, where the people themselves vote on all issues (as in New England town meetings).

Most delegates also agreed on how this republican form of government should work (see the box below), viewing the federal and state constitutions as part of a political compact between the nation and the states. In the delegates' eyes the federal form of government (Chapter 1) they were proposing was not drastically different from the confederation they already had. Like the authors of the Articles, they never seriously considered the possibility of abolishing state governments and replacing them with a national government having unchecked direct power over individual citizens.

Key Disputes

The delegates were divided, however, by deep political, cultural, and regional differences. As practical men they knew that compromise was a basic rule of political life as well as the price of a more perfect union. Throughout the stifling four months of summer they met 88 times behind the closed windows and doors of the Pennsylvania State House (now Independence Hall) to work out how much power to give to the national (federal) government and how much to give the states.

How a Republican Constitution Works

A republican, or representative, constitution works in four ways. First, it limits the power of rulers (presidents, governors, and other high officials) by placing them under the authority of its laws. This is the meaning of limited government. Second, it declares which aspects of public life (the public domain) the government may regulate. In other words, it says when government can and cannot intervene in people's affairs. Third, it establishes the institutions of government authorized to act in this public domain. Finally, it defines which people count as full citizens authorized to participate in those institutions. In performing these tasks, the document *constitutes*—brings into existence—the fundamental law that governs a political society, and along with it, the existence of the people of that country. But unless the people actually participate in and defend the political processes which their constitution guarantees, that constitution will not matter. In short, republican principles go hand in hand with constitutional practice.

The 12 state delegations that were the basic voting units of the convention pursued their states' interests by forming coalitions.[16] For example, southern states united against northern states to prevent Congress from exercising unlimited power over commerce because they feared northern merchants would pass trade laws placing southern commodities at a disadvantage. But once they had struck a compromise—in this case Congress was given the power to regulate interstate and foreign commerce but could not levy an export tax—the states formed new coalitions around other issues. The most crucial coalitions aligned large states against small states and northern states against southern states.

Representation: Large States Versus Small States

The key question that confronted these delegates was this: Should a state's number of representatives to Congress be based on its population, as the more populous Middle Atlantic states wanted, or should each state have equal representation, as the smaller states wanted?

The Virginia Plan, a scheme devised by James Madison, would have created a bicameral Congress with representation in each house based on a state's population. The plan appeared to give equal representation to citizens but in practice it would have made the most populous states like Virginia the real power-brokers in Congress. States with smaller populations wanted to keep the same system of representation they enjoyed under the Articles. They therefore backed William Patterson's New Jersey Plan calling for a unicameral Congress in which each state would have an equal vote. This plan appeared to give equal representation to the states, but in practice it gave a voter in a small state like Delaware more say than a voter in New York. The plan would even have allowed a coalition of the seven smallest states, which contained only 25 percent of the population, to dominate Congress. Despite their differences, both plans would have strengthened the national government by giving Congress the power to raise taxes, regulate interstate commerce, and employ military force against the states.

This dispute over representation was settled by the **Connecticut,** or **Great, Compromise** of July 1787, which created a bicameral legislature consisting of two houses of Congress: the Senate and the House of Representatives. (This was not a bold innovation. The Framers were familiar with the two-chambered British Parliament—the House of Lords and the House of Commons—and bicameralism had been a general practice in most of the colonies and states.) Each state would have two seats in the Senate, preserving states' rights, while representation in the House of Representatives would be proportional to a state's population and hence more democratic. By providing the states with so-called equal representation in the Senate, the compromise gave—and still gives—disproportionate representation to sparsely populated states. The compromise also required all bills (proposed legislation) to pass both houses in identical form to become law.

Slavery: Northern States Versus Southern States

Two questions concerning slaves faced the convention. (1) How should slaves count for purposes of political representation and federal taxation? (2) Should the importation of slaves continue to be legal?

Political Actors Disagree

How Self-Interested Were the Framers?

Given that most of the Framers believed that individuals are motivated primarily by self-interest, to what extent did their own self-interest shape their writing of the Constitution? Historian Charles A. Beard, who saw the Constitution as a conservative document which obstructed social progress, argued in *An Economic Interpretation of the Constitution* (1913) that the Framers distributed power in the Constitution to promote the economic stability and prosperity of their own class.

Clearly the Framers were an elite group in terms of education, professional status, and wealth, but their opposition to democracy—as illustrated, for example, by the provision that the Senate be elected by the state legislatures rather than by the people—seems to have reflected the fear among political leaders that most ordinary people lacked information and were easily swayed. When Elbridge Gerry of Massachusetts told his fellow delegates that "the evils we experience flow from an excess of democracy," he quickly added that this did not mean that the people lack virtue; rather, they are easily duped and "daily misled . . . by false reports circulated by designing men."[1]

Historians who have combed through the evidence have found that some of the Framers had economic interests that could have motivated them to draft the Constitution in their self-interest and others did not. However, the evidence, while difficult to assess, shows no strong connection between the amounts and kinds of property the Framers had and the way they behaved at the convention.[2] Thirty-four of the 55 delegates were lawyers. At least 27 were farmers, 19 of whom (northerners as well as southerners) owned slaves. Eight speculated in land to such a degree that they could have been affected by decisions regarding the political representation of western lands and the admission of new states. As many as 30 owned certificates of the public debt and so were creditors of the government. Another complicating factor is the fact that the delegates were representing their states and were voting as state delegations, some of which were strongly divided.[3] Thus most historians now conclude that the economic interests of the Framers did not fundamentally influence the system of government they produced, and even Beard himself softened his argument in his later writings.[4]

It is still true that the lawyers, businessmen, and big farmers among the Framers, who dealt regularly in legal and commercial matters, foreign trade, taxation, and relations among the states, were most likely to understand the limitations of the Articles of Confederation and recognize that the nation could not develop commercially or industrially on such a weak foundation. In contrast, most of the population—roughly 90 percent—were subsistence farmers. With few if any goods to export and little if any money to buy imports, they were not directly concerned with trade and high finance. But the drafters of the Articles were, for the most part, the same people who later drafted the new constitution.[5] It therefore appears that they originally acted, and were continuing to act, from common—largely economic—concerns about *what is*, *what's right*, and *what works*.

---

[1] Quoted in Page Smith, *The Constitution: A Documentary and Narrative History* (New York: Morrow, 1978), 103–104. Gerry was alluding to Henry Knox's exaggerated account of Shays' Rebellion.
[2] The first major critique of Charles Beard's thesis was Robert E. Brown, *Charles Beard and the Constitution* (New York: Norton, 1956). See also Forrest McDonald, *We the People: The Economic Origins of the Constitution* (Chicago: University of Chicago Press, 1958).
[3] Forrest McDonald, *Novus Ordo Seclorum: The Intellectual Origins of the Constitution* (Lawrence: University Press of Kansas, 1985), 219–224.
[4] Michael Kammen, *A Machine That Would Go of Itself: The Constitution in American Culture* (New York: Random House, 1987), 6.
[5] Smith, *Constitution*, 86–87.

Slaves then made up 30 percent of the population in five southern states. The agricultural economies of these states relied on slave labor, and their laws classified slaves as private property rather than as human beings with rights. These states saw an opportunity to maximize the number of representatives they were eligible for in the House of Representatives by counting their slaves—men, women, and children—as people, one for one, in the calculation of congressional seats. At the same time, however, they tried to minimize their tax burden by refusing to have slaves count as people, one for one, in calculating their federal taxes. Northern delegates were outraged. "If you count your slaves for purposes of representation," they shot back, "we'll count our mules."[17] The controversy was settled by the notorious **three-fifths compromise**, which stated that the national census (the basis for calculating both the number of seats a state could hold in the House of Representatives and the rate of federal taxation) would count each slave as "three-fifths" of a person for both purposes. This compromise gave southern states disproportionately greater power in the House of Representatives compared to the northern states until after the Civil War.

The delegates also compromised on the importation of slaves. Abolitionists in the northern states, which were not dependent on slavery, wanted the practice abolished. This demand alarmed South Carolina and Georgia, which insisted on the unrestricted importation of slaves because so many died tending the rice swamps. North Carolina, however, had all the slaves it needed, while Maryland and Virginia had surpluses they would sell to South Carolina and Georgia if the new constitution outlawed the importation of new slaves. The delegates of Georgia and South Carolina stood firm: if the importation of slaves were outlawed, they would not join the Union.

In the end, the delegates decided to exclude the word "slave" from the Constitution while implying the legality of slavery in three passages. First, Article I, section 2, uses the phrase "all other Persons" to refer to slaves in the passage that counts each as three-fifths of a person for purposes of taxation and representation. Second, Article I, section 9, prohibits Congress from preventing "the Migration or Importation of such Persons as any of the States now existing shall think proper to admit" for 20 years, although it allows Congress to levy a $10 head tax on such human imports. Third, Article IV, section 2, requires that a "Person held to Service or Labour in one State, under the laws thereof," who escaped to another state, be "delivered up" to the original owner. (These provisions were nullified by the Thirteenth Amendment, ratified in 1865.)

The Governmental Machine

In designing the new government, the Framers drew on the lessons of the American political experience as well as on the philosophical and scientific thinking of the Enlightenment. These Enlightenment assumptions about the nature of reality strongly determined the Framers' beliefs about what form of government was right for the nation and how well such a government would work.

Age of Enlightenment

Also called the Age of Reason, the Age of Enlightenment began with the Glorious Revolution of 1688 and ended with the French Revolution of 1789. Enlightenment thinkers broke with traditional religious thought by explaining nature and human behavior in rational, scientific terms that could be applied to society for the improvement of humanity. The American Framers were primarily influenced by John Locke in England and by Montesquieu and the authors of the *Encyclopedia* in France.

What Is: The Laws of Nature

Like the Enlightenment thinkers, the framers shared a mechanistic worldview shaped by the principles of the seventeenth-century English physicist Isaac Newton. Newton viewed the universe as an orderly place governed by **laws of nature**. Benjamin Franklin, Alexander Hamilton, and many other Framers also believed human nature to be governed by such laws. And they agreed with Scottish philosopher David Hume (1711–1776) that human beings naturally put self-interest above virtue. These beliefs profoundly affected their views about how government should work. They believed, following John Locke, that a government would work only if it conformed to the laws of nature (*what is*), which could be discerned through observation and reason.

What's Right: Limited Government

These assumptions about "what is" led the Framers to conclude that the right sort of government was a limited government that allowed individuals to pursue their own interests free from government regulation. They accepted Scottish economist Adam Smith's argument in *The Wealth of Nations* (published in 1776, the same year as the Declaration of Independence) calling for laissez-faire capitalism, or free-enterprise capitalism. Such a policy, Smith claimed, would ensure efficiency by allowing the market itself, not government, to regulate the production and distribution of goods and services—as if, in his words, an "invisible hand" were constantly adjusting things for the better. This theory is very much alive today. Its critics argue that government has a responsibility for the general welfare of the people, while its defenders maintain that government manipulation of commerce for political purposes—as the colonists experienced it under mercantilism and as contemporaries experience it in trade policy—will always fail because it violates the law of nature, as do government efforts at "social engineering."

Some nationalists of the day—Madison and Hamilton, for instance—were not laissez-faire purists. They recognized that the pursuit of self-interest often requires individuals to adapt to new circumstances and believed that such change would stimulate nation-building. Because individuals often remain attached to old ways of doing things, Hamilton believed that government should provide incentives for them to change.[18] Hamilton also favored using public money to back up government debt and argued that a national bank would strengthen the nation's economy. (The question of whether the federal government had the constitutional authority to establish a national bank was decided in 1819 in *McCulloch* v. *Maryland*, discussed in the next chapter.)

What Works: A Self-Sustaining System of Government

The Framers intended their governmental machine to run on its own power—to "go of itself" automatically just as the planets circle the sun.[19] They believed such a self-sustaining system of government would be propelled by its different parts and functions and driven by individual self-interest. This tendency to view politics as a kind of mechanics was common in the political writings and debates of the day, which made frequent use of such terms as *revolution, balance, equilibrium, fulcrum, system, reaction, mass,* and *power*. The Constitution, John Dickinson told his fellow delegates, was to be consistent with the laws of gravitation: "Let our Government be like that of the Solar system; let the General [national] Government be the Sun and the States the Planets repelled yet attracted, and on the whole moving regularly and harmoniously in their respective Orbits."[20] Experience has shown, however, that the mechanics of the American system of government (its laws and institutions) do not work by themselves. Instead, the system has worked because political leaders and citizens have used these laws and institutions to manage their differences and to steer the nation in the directions they wanted it to go.

The Principles and Powers of the Constitution

The Constitution is relatively short and scant on details. The Framers couched it in very general language to avoid controversy and to increase its chances of ratification. Following a brief Preamble proclaiming the nation's goals, seven articles distribute political power among various institutions.

The first three articles distribute the tasks of the national government among three separate branches and specify how each is to operate. The fourth article defines the relations among the states. The fifth explains the procedures for amending the document. The remaining articles establish the Constitution as "the supreme Law of the Land" (Article VI) and explain how it is to be ratified (Article VII). The political system created by this Constitution was to operate according to three principles: division of powers, separation of powers, and checks and balances.

The Division of Powers

The principle called the **division of powers** distributes political authority among three political actors: the national government, the state governments, and, once the Bill of Rights was ratified, the people. The Framers called this division of powers federalism. In keeping with the spirit of limited government, the Constitution specifies, or enumerates, the powers it gives to the national government and some of the powers it explicitly gives to the states (Chapter 3). Among these enumerated powers are the power to make treaties, declare war, coin money, establish post offices, establish national courts, and regulate interstate commerce. As we'll see below, the Tenth Amendment to the Constitution (part of the Bill of Rights) "reserves" all other powers "to the States respectively, or to the people."

The Separation of Powers

The republican-minded Framers rejected the European tradition of monarchy—the concentration of legislative, executive, and judicial functions in a single individual—as well as the British practice (adopted in 1787) of permitting the House of Lords to dispense justice. Instead, they chose to split the legislative, executive, and judicial functions among three separate branches of government that were to operate as a system—a solution known as the **separation of powers**.

Article I of the Constitution assigns the task of lawmaking to the **legislative branch**, the Congress. Article II assigns the task of carrying out the laws to the **executive branch**, headed by the president. Article III gives the task of interpreting and applying the law to the **judicial branch**, composed of the courts. Unlike parliamentary systems, officials in each of these branches are independent of one another because they have specific tasks to perform and because they are selected by different procedures and for different terms of office. This arrangement prevents the same individual or group from performing all three functions and thereby dominating the political system. In this respect the separation of powers has been largely successful, but it can also make government cumbersome and fragmented.

> **parliamentary system**
> In this system, the executives (the prime minister and cabinet) are chosen by and from the elected Parliament and depend upon its ongoing legislative support for their continuance in office. This form of government is used in Britain, Canada, and other British Commonwealth nations, among others.

Checks and Balances

In addition to preserving the independence of each branch, the Framers wanted the branches to operate as a system. They therefore made each branch answerable to the others by means of **checks and balances** (see Figure 2.2). If Congress, for example, exerts too much power, the president can retaliate with the presidential veto—which Congress can sometimes override. Checks and balances also help to harmonize other parts of the political system. For example, the bicameral Congress serves the nation as a whole, while each chamber represents a different geographical unit (the Senate, the states; the House, population districts). The main checks and balances included the following:

- The executive branch cannot carry out its functions without a budget passed by Congress.
- Treaties and major presidential appointments, including Supreme Court justices, must be ratified and confirmed by the Senate.
- Both houses of Congress must agree on the form of a bill before it can pass, and the president must then sign it into law—a requirement intended to promote thoughtful and deliberative lawmaking and to avoid hasty action.
- The president can veto a bill passed by Congress, but Congress can override the veto and enact the bill into law with a two-thirds vote in each chamber.
- Congress can formally impeach—that is, charge with misbehavior—and then try any federal civil official, including the president or a Supreme Court justice, and vote to remove the official from office; however, the House impeaches and the Senate tries, so the two houses also check each other.
- The federal courts—based on a power known as judicial review (its origin is described below)—can declare a law passed by Congress or actions of a member of the executive branch unconstitutional and hence invalid.

This system of checks and balances often modifies the behavior of political actors in advance. The very existence of confirmation checks, for example, may deter a president from making controversial nominations. If members of Congress expect the president to veto a bill, they may alter it in ways that will make it acceptable to the president before passing it. Similarly, presidents may sign bills they don't like if they expect Congress to override their veto. The formal record, which hides the real influence of checks and balances, shows that presidential vetoes,

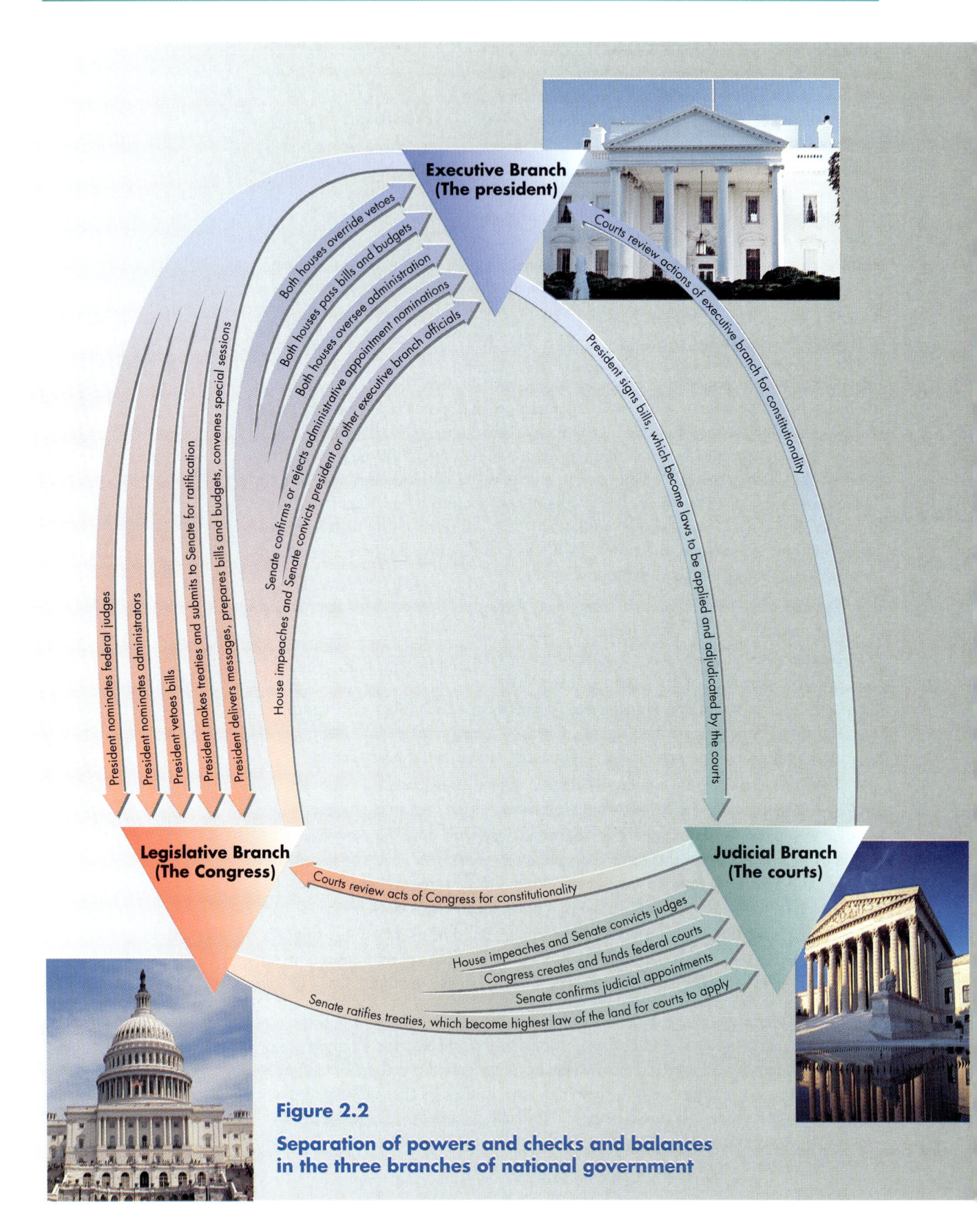

Chapter 2 Constitutional Practice

Executive Branch (The president)

Arrows from Executive Branch to Legislative Branch:
- President nominates federal judges
- President nominates administrators
- President vetoes bills
- President makes treaties and submits to Senate for ratification
- President delivers messages, prepares bills and budgets, convenes special sessions

Arrows from Legislative Branch to Executive Branch:
- House impeaches and Senate convicts president or other executive branch officials
- Senate confirms or rejects administrative appointment nominations
- Both houses oversee administration
- Both houses pass bills and budgets
- Both houses override vetoes

Courts review actions of executive branch for constitutionality

President signs bills, which become laws to be applied and adjudicated by the courts

Legislative Branch (The Congress)

Judicial Branch (The courts)

- Courts review acts of Congress for constitutionality
- House impeaches and Senate convicts judges
- Congress creates and funds federal courts
- Senate confirms judicial appointments
- Senate ratifies treaties, which become highest law of the land for courts to apply

Figure 2.2

Separation of powers and checks and balances in the three branches of national government

congressional overrides, and refusals to confirm presidential appointments are infrequent. Of the 2,400 bills that presidents have vetoed over the last two hundred years, Congress has overridden just over 100. The Senate has rejected fewer than a dozen cabinet appointments and just over two dozen nominations to the Supreme Court.

Checks and balances also tend to increase the number of political deadlocks and delayed responses to crises. Nor do they prevent the legislative or the executive branch from occasionally dominating the political system. Still, by combining the division and separation of powers with the system of checks and balances, the Framers generally succeeded in limiting the government's excesses without undermining its ability to function.

The Powers of Each Branch of Government

When the Framers divided the national government's powers among the three separate branches, they did not always agree on how to specify those powers in the Constitution. As a result, they chose to describe those powers in vague language, causing their meaning (*what is*) to be immediately disputed. But in areas where they agreed, such as on the need to forbid arbitrary taxation and the granting of titles of nobility, they made their meaning perfectly clear.

Congress

Article I provides for a bicameral Congress composed of a House of Representatives and a Senate and establishes minimal rules for the composition and conduct of each chamber. Qualifications of representatives and senators are limited to age, citizenship, and residency. Section 8 consists of 18 clauses restricting Congress to the exercise of 18 enumerated powers—including the power to declare war, levy taxes, and regulate foreign and interstate commerce. The eighteenth clause, however, grants such sweeping authority that it has become known as the **elastic clause**. This clause gives Congress the power "to make all Laws which shall be necessary and proper for carrying into Execution the foregoing Powers, and all other Powers vested by this Constitution in the Government of the United States, or in any Department or Officer thereof." Sometimes called the necessary and proper clause, the elastic clause has been used to stretch Congress's enumerated powers to cope with a vast array of political issues. The courts have also used this clause to derive the principle of implied powers—those powers not specifically mentioned in the Constitution but implied by it because they are necessary for the federal government to carry out its specified, or enumerated, functions (Chapter 3).

The Presidency

Article II sets the president's term of office, establishes election procedures, and limits the qualifications for the presidency to age, citizenship, and residency. Section 2 of the article describes the president's powers and duties as

- commander-in-chief of the military,

- chief administrator of both the executive branch and the judiciary, appointing or nominating key officials and judges enforcing the law,
- chief of state, with power to negotiate with other countries and make treaties (which the Senate must approve by a two-thirds majority),
- chief legislator, with power to propose bills to Congress and sign or veto those that it passes, and
- chief diplomat, appointing ambassadors to and receiving ambassadors from other countries while representing the nation.

The presidency also has its equivalent of the elastic clause in section 3, which gives a president the duty to "take Care that the Laws be faithfully executed." Innovative presidents have interpreted this clause to greatly expand the powers of the presidency (Chapter 12).

The Judiciary

While the Constitution gives Congress what has become known as "the power of the purse" and the executive "the power of the sword," it gives the courts the less visible and tangible "power of the word." The courts have therefore had to develop much of their own authority using the power of legal reasoning.

Article III establishes the court system by saying, "The judicial Power of the United States, shall be vested in one supreme Court, and in such inferior Courts as the Congress may from time to time ordain and establish." As the box nearby explains, this provision went beyond the thinking of Montesquieu, who had inspired the notion of separation of powers but who allowed the judicial functions to remain in the executive branch. However, the Framers said little about what these courts were to do. State and local courts, as the Framers were well aware, were already in place and functioning, so that in creating federal courts they were consciously establishing a dual court system.

The powers of the judicial branch are couched in more general language than those of the other two branches because the delegate who wrote Article III wanted it that way. Gouverneur Morris of New York, a recognized expert on law who drafted the Constitution based on the record of the convention's proceedings, later confessed that he purposely wrote Article III to suit himself. Morris, like Hamilton, had aristocratic and monarchical leanings and put the protection of property above the protection of liberty, although he opposed slavery.[21] However, he wrote Article III in language vague enough to satisfy his more republican colleagues. Morris knew that if he spelled out the powers of the judiciary in exact language he might stir up controversy that could lead the Framers to restrict those powers. So Article III merely established the national Supreme Court as the highest court in the nation and left Congress to set up whatever system of federal courts it saw fit—something it did in the Judiciary Act of 1789. Federal judges serve for life subject to "good Behavior," and Congress may not lower judges' salaries while in office—measures intended to safeguard judicial independence. Judicial power is checked, as we saw earlier, by the presidential power to appoint judges (subject to the advice and consent of the Senate) and by the power of the Congress to increase or decrease the number of federal courts. Morris did not give the judiciary an elastic clause of its own, knowing that judges could achieve the same results through interpretation.

James Madison (1751–1836) was a framer of the Constitution, compiler of the Bill of Rights, coauthor of *The Federalist*, and fourth president of the United States.

The Origins of the Separation of Powers

Most scholars argue that the Framers got the idea for the separation of powers from the *Spirit of the Laws* (1748) by French political philosopher baron de Montesquieu (1689–1755). But as Donald Lutz points out, they also turned to their American political experience. The colonies had followed the English practice of making the judiciary part of the executive, with the monarch the final court of appeal, but with independence most of the new states put the judiciary under their state legislatures. The Framers followed Montesquieu's recommendation of making the federal judiciary a separate branch of government, with its members appointed by the executive for life with the consent of the Senate, but impeachable and removable from office for bad behavior.

The Framers followed Montesquieu's recommendations to exclude the executive from all lawmaking, except for the veto power, and to exclude the legislature from execution of the laws, except for the power to impeach executive branch officials and judges.

He also recommended that the national legislature be bicameral, as in Britain. Britain's upper house, the House of Lords, was made up of nobility, while the lower house, the House of Commons, represented the ordinary citizens called commoners. In the United States there were no lords to serve in the upper house; indeed, the Constitution explicitly prohibits the creation of titles of nobility. In addition, the colonists had developed such a strong distrust of their governors and councils that all but two states created bicameral legislatures so that the upper house, in addition to making the legislative process more deliberative, could keep a close watch on the executive. The Framers thought of the Senate's tasks in similar terms, as a check on the House but, even more important, as a watchdog over the presidency.[1]

Montesquieu's ideas on the separation of powers appealed to the Framers because royally appointed governors often tried to buy off legislators by offering them lucrative positions in the executive branch and colonists had instituted prohibitions on holding more than one office at the same time.

The Framers converted Montesquieu's idea of a separation of powers into separation of roles or functions with shared powers. James Madison, its architect, saw that if the powers of the three branches were completely separated, government as a system would not work. So the framers gave each branch just enough power over the others to incline all three to function effectively as a single, intricate machine.[2]

---

[1] See Donald S. Lutz, *The Origins of American Constitutionalism* (Baton Rouge: Louisiana State University Press, 1988), 158.
[2] Ibid., 157.

The Dispute over Ratification

Moments before the final vote on the Constitution, Benjamin Franklin rose to quell all objections:

> I agree to this Constitution with all its faults, if they are such. . . . For when you assemble a number of men to have the advantage of their joint wisdom, you inevitably assemble . . . all their prejudices, their passions, their errors of opinion, their local interests, and their selfish views. . . . It therefore astonishes me . . . to find this system approaching so near to perfection as it does; and I think it will astonish our enemies. . . . Thus I consent, Sir, to this Constitution because I expect no better, and because I am not sure, that it is not the best.

Franklin then vowed that he would never give the Constitution's opponents any ammunition by disclosing the defects he saw in the document.[22] James Madison echoed this sentiment and sealed his own records of the convention.[23]

Once the Constitution was signed, it was sent to the states, where the battle over ratification had already begun. Those favoring ratification called themselves **Federalists** (they were actually strong nationalists) and labeled their opponents **Anti-Federalists** (who were actually weak nationalists). The Federalists wanted a limited central government strong enough to foster a powerful commercial state. The Anti-Federalists wanted to amend the Articles of Confederation to make the national government more effective without eroding the power of the states. Their debate is a classic example of politics as defined in this book. Each side claimed the authority to decide whether the Constitution should be accepted or rejected based on its views about *what is, what's right,* and *what works.* In fact, the two sides were not solid blocs. Both sides favored a limited national government, and those on each side disagreed among themselves over what those limits should be.

The Federalist delegates won the first battle over ratification procedures. They stipulated that special state conventions composed of popularly elected delegates should approve the document and that the approval of only nine states be required for ratification. This method prevented the Constitution from being treated as amendments to the Articles, which would have required the unanimous consent of the state legislatures, the very bodies that stood to lose powers to the new national government.

When the Anti-Federalists claimed that this device was illegal, the Federalists replied that the nation was not a collection of sovereign states but parts of a single nation (a claim about *what is*), which made it *right* for ratification to be carried out by popularly elected conventions. They also justified their action on grounds that the Articles were, in the words of one delegate, the "*unworkable* machine of a preexisting union."[24]

The Federalist Argument for Ratification

The Federalists' primary argument, as set forth by James Madison, Alexander Hamilton, and John Jay in *The Federalist*, was that the Constitution was right for the nation because it would work. The Constitution would, they claimed, establish an effective national government that would be run by wise and virtuous leaders—men John Adams called the **natural aristocracy**—who were committed to the common good. To Anti-Federalist fears that such a government would be dominated by elites, the Federalists responded that the president and the senators were merely representatives of the people. The Anti-Federalists scoffed at this claim, knowing that power resided in political institutions that could be controlled by elites. Indeed, by establishing large rather than small congressional districts, the Constitution weighted the odds of win-

The Federalist

The major Federalist arguments were published in 85 letters in a New York City newspaper between October 1787 and August 1788. James Madison and Alexander Hamilton, who wrote most of the letters, signed them "Publius" (*the people* in Latin). *The Federalist* had little effect on the ratification debate except in New York. But because it came from the pens of two drafters of the Constitution, it has acquired the status of a quasi-founding document.

natural aristocracy

John Adams, like other elites of his day, believed that nature gives some men greater gifts—education, wealth, a sense of social responsibility—than others, which make these men the best political leaders. When Adams's spirited wife, Abigail, asked her husband to include women in the new constitutional order, he declined.

ning elective office in favor of rich and well-born men who had already acquired experience and reputations in politics and who could afford to run and serve.

Fears that a strong national government would be coercive led Anti-Federalists to call for adding a bill of rights to the Constitution to protect individual liberties. The Federalists argued that this protection was unnecessary, first, because the Constitution limited the national government in ways that denied it the power to grant such specific liberties, and second, because eight of the state constitutions already contained bills of rights. The Anti-Federalists replied that just as bills of rights had traditionally limited governmental power at the state level, a national bill of rights would limit governmental power at the national level. When the Federalists saw that ratification hinged on a national bill of rights, they promised to add one shortly after ratification.

The Anti-Federalist Argument Against Ratification

The arguments the Anti-Federalists used to oppose ratification are still relevant, not only because they resemble arguments put forward by states' rights advocates today, but also because states are currently demanding and receiving unprecedented power from the federal government (see Chapter 3). The Anti-Federalists argued (as many conservative Republicans and Democrats do today) that a strong federal government would be wrong because it would be coercive. They predicted that its great distance from the people would lead to disobedience that would need to be met by military force. They also argued that such a big government would not work effectively because it would be inefficient and pointed out that even among the states themselves "the largest States are the Worst Governed." The Federalists countered that government must have enough public officials and power to function effectively as well as the capacity to coerce obedience when necessary. "Show me a government that can do no harm," said one Federalist, "and I'll show you a government that can do no good."[25]

The Anti-Federalists' greatest fear was that an elite-dominated national government would crush the states, the bastion of the will of the people. This fear led Virginian Patrick Henry, who earlier had galvanized colonists with his cry "Give me liberty or give me death" and then rallied them behind the Articles, to turn against the new Constitution. Anti-Federalists opposed the Constitution's electoral provisions that favored elite interests at the expense of local interests—those of small farmers, traders, and workers. As one delegate to the Massachusetts ratification convention put it: "These lawyers, and men of learning and moneyed men . . . expect to get into Congress themselves . . . and get all the power and all the money into their own hands, and then they will swallow all us little folks . . . just as the whale swallowed up Jonah."[26] The Anti-Federalists denied that a natural aristocracy would represent the people faithfully because they believed that power corrupts all people, including these elites. Strong states, they argued, should act as "watchdogs" to prevent such corruption, and they concluded that the only fair government was one that allowed many classes of people to represent their own interests.

The Anti-Federalists also feared that the national government would impose its own values on the states. They claimed that if the people of a state shared the same basic values, they would strive for relative equality in wealth, influence, and education and would be more successful in schooling virtuous citizens.[27] But Federalists like Madison suspected that such egalitarian sentiments were intended to apply to a relatively like-minded majority that would impose its own values on differently minded individuals and minorities. He doubted that the states could best preserve individual liberties and argued in *The Federalist* No. 10 that a strong national government was needed "to control the effects" of factions—in particular, the power of majorities to interfere with the rights of minorities (see the Appendix). In fact, neither side wanted unchecked majority rule. Rather, they disagreed over where the greatest threat to liberty lay. Both sides feared that majorities might tyrannize others under cover of the law. However, some Federalists believed that adding a national bill of rights to the Constitution as the Anti-Federalists wanted would be enough to control such tyranny.

Why the Federalists Won

The Federalists won the debate over ratification on June 21, 1788, when New Hampshire became the ninth state to ratify the Constitution. They won because they had a concrete proposal in a time of crisis and the Anti-Federalists had none. In addition to sticking their opponents with a negative name, the Federalists were better organized, more famous, and had more newspaper editors on their side. Moreover, the Federalists knew how to sound like good republicans and occasionally even good democrats. Also, the Anti-Federalists were so bent on preventing the tyranny the nation had experienced under the British monarchy that they were unwilling to give the national government enough power to perform its essential tasks. The Federalists succeeded in persuading most citizens that governments were not necessarily tyrannical and that a stronger national government was needed to handle the current problems. Still, they only narrowly defeated the Anti-Federalists, who were popular because most Americans shared their republican, localist values.

Why the Constitution Still Works

The U.S. Constitution has lasted longer than any other written constitution in the world for two related reasons. The document permits political actors to change and reinterpret it to meet new challenges. At the same time, the Constitution promotes stability because it cannot be changed or reinterpreted on a whim. Both these qualities—flexibility and stability—are essential to the life and growth of any nation.

Madison recognized that the Constitution which was being justified in the name of "the people" needed to be responsive to the people. But how responsive? He knew that the revolutionary language of the Declaration proclaiming the people's right "to alter or to abolish" a government to which they did not consent still rang in many ears. Jefferson argued that the Constitution should automatically give each new generation a chance to alter the document as it saw fit and recommended that revisions be made every 19 to 20 years.[28] But Madison feared that such frequent change would be disruptive. Like Hamilton, he held that government should assume the people's consent unless they act collectively and legally to alter the Constitution. Yes, the constitutional machine needed a "safety-valve"[29] to let off popular steam, but that steam should be let off slowly and methodically to prevent the machine from exploding. Madison's concerns have been dealt with in two ways. First, the amendment procedures in Article V have allowed additions to and alterations of the document. Second, the general language of the Constitution has allowed for its reinterpretation and adaptation over time.

Change by Amendment

A comparison of the original Constitution with its 27 amendments (which now constitute almost half the text of the Constitution) reveals that, aside from minor changes and technicalities, the amendments have made few changes in the Framers' governmental design. With three exceptions (the Fourteenth Amendment, which removed the "three-fifths" provision permitting the counting of slaves on that basis for apportioning representatives; the Sixteenth, which allowed Congress to collect an income tax; and the Seventeenth, which required that citizens rather than state legislatures elect senators) the 27 amendments have done little to alter the authority of the three branches. The dramatic growth in the authority of the judiciary and the presidency has been due to other factors, as we'll see in future chapters.

In contrast, most of the remaining amendments were inspired by the Declaration of Independence and made profound changes in civil liberties and civil rights.[30] As we'll see in more detail in Chapters 15 and 16, civil liberties are freedoms from government that the Constitution requires the government to protect, while civil rights are fundamental rights which government acts to protect from the unlawful acts of others, including government itself.

The Bill of Rights

In 1789, two years after the Constitution was written, Madison persuaded his fellow lawmakers to add a bill of rights to the document as the Anti-Federalists had demanded. (Interestingly, Madison barely made it into Congress. Anti-Federalists had succeeded in denying him a seat in the Senate, and he was forced to run for a House seat against James Monroe, which he won.[31]) Many lawmakers were reluctant to amend the Constitution before the government had been stabilized, but Madison argued that further delay would weaken public confidence in the new government. Madison had reduced more than 200 proposals from various state constitutions and state conventions to 12 amendments and managed to obtain the two-thirds majority in each house required for their approval. In 1791, the required three-fourths of the state legislatures ratified the first 10 amendments—what came to be known as the **Bill of Rights** (see the Appendix). Many of its provisions echo Magna Carta.

Amendment Procedures and Their Biases

The Framers made the procedures for amending the Constitution laborious to protect its authority and effectiveness. The procedures were to guard against popular changes that lawmakers considered trivial or inappropriate. In recent years, for example, Congress has refused to propose amendments banning school busing for racial integration, prohibiting burning of the American flag, requiring a balanced federal budget, and (what is hardly surprising) limiting terms for lawmakers.

The procedures involve two separate steps. An amendment must first be *proposed* (it then becomes a formal proposal) and then *ratified*. It can be proposed either by Congress, with a two-thirds majority vote in each house, or by a constitutional convention, which Congress calls if two-thirds of the state legislatures request one (a method that has never been used). Only a fraction of the roughly 10,000 amendments introduced in Congress since 1787 have become formal proposals. Once proposed, the amendment must be ratified by extraordinary majorities—that is, either by three-fourths of the state legislatures or by three-fourths of special state ratifying conventions, whichever Congress directs. Figure 2.3 illustrates this process. In recent years Congress has attached a seven-year time limit for ratification by the states.

Only three amendments have passed through these procedures with relative ease: the Thirteenth, abolishing slavery; the Twenty-first, repealing the Eighteenth, which prohibited the manufacture, sale, and transportation of alcoholic beverages; and the Twenty-sixth, which lowered the voting age from 21 to 18. Typically it takes years to satisfy the requirements, and in some cases ratification fails and the proposed amendment dies. This was the fate of the Equal Rights Amendment (discussed in Chapter 16). A state that votes against ratification can later change its vote but cannot legally rescind (take back) its favorable vote. After ratification the amendment is automatically in force and becomes part of the Constitution.

These procedures have proved to be biased in two ways. First, the requirement for extraordinary majorities in Congress and state legislatures—majorities still composed mainly of white men—makes it difficult for minorities and women to obtain proposal and ratification of amendments that would protect or expand their rights. As we'll see in Chapter 16, the rights of such groups have nonetheless been expanded by elites sympathetic or fearful that their continued restriction might jeopardize law and order. Second, the length of the amendment process prolongs the unfair practices that a proposed amendment seeks to change, such as racial and gender discrimination. These biases have led some groups to look to the courts for speedier remedies.

Change by Interpretation

The Constitution's broad language has facilitated change by interpretation. By the nineteenth century people began to view the Constitution less as a fixed machine and more as a living document that was evolving to accommodate a changing nation. As early as 1835, the astute French observer of the new nation, Alexis de Tocqueville, described the Constitution as "that body of organic laws"[32]—a phrase echoing the nineteenth-century European emphasis on progress and evolu-

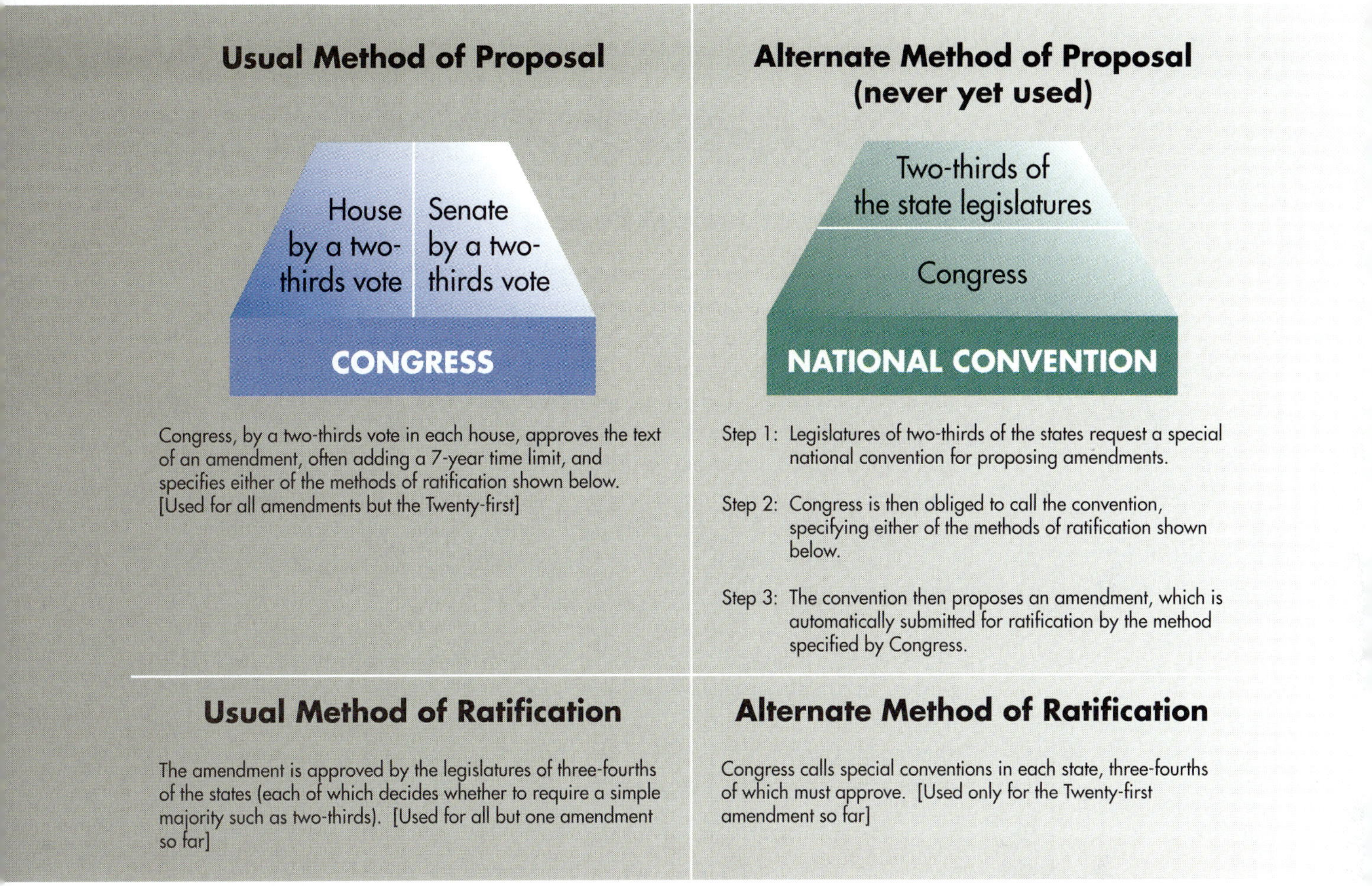

Usual Method of Proposal

CONGRESS
House by a two-thirds vote | Senate by a two-thirds vote

Congress, by a two-thirds vote in each house, approves the text of an amendment, often adding a 7-year time limit, and specifies either of the methods of ratification shown below. [Used for all amendments but the Twenty-first]

Alternate Method of Proposal (never yet used)

NATIONAL CONVENTION
Two-thirds of the state legislatures
Congress

Step 1: Legislatures of two-thirds of the states request a special national convention for proposing amendments.

Step 2: Congress is then obliged to call the convention, specifying either of the methods of ratification shown below.

Step 3: The convention then proposes an amendment, which is automatically submitted for ratification by the method specified by Congress.

Usual Method of Ratification

The amendment is approved by the legislatures of three-fourths of the states (each of which decides whether to require a simple majority such as two-thirds). [Used for all but one amendment so far]

Alternate Method of Ratification

Congress calls special conventions in each state, three-fourths of which must approve. [Used only for the Twenty-first amendment so far]

---

tion. Such "organic laws," however, do not "evolve" without amendments and new interpretations.

The Politics of Constitutional Interpretation

Disputes over what the Constitution means occur because its words do not speak for themselves. Rather, their meaning must be interpreted by people who often have an interest in the outcome, that is, people seeking to prevent or promote change. As one scholar explains, "The Constitution is by its very nature lifeless and inert unless it is put to work in the world by the citizens who live under it."[33] When interests and beliefs coincide, there is wide agreement on what "the correct" interpretation of the Constitution is; when they diverge, as interests and beliefs often do, interpretations of the document conflict. In short, conclusions about "what is" in the Constitution are shaped by what its readers want it to say.

Political actors (government, politicians, parties, interest groups, experts, individuals) often disagree over whether a particular action is constitutional—whether the action is consistent with the Constitution and thus legally enforceable. Because this determination is never impartial, political actors struggle to win such disputes through the politics of knowledge—the manipulation of information, logic, and language (see Chapter 1). In doing so, they are practicing politics as defined in this text—by asserting their superior authority to interpret the Constitution. More specifically, they are practicing the politics of constitutional interpretation.

Figure 2.3

Proposing and ratifying amendments to the Constitution

Although the Constitution lays down certain roles and rules (*what's right*) for this type of political practice, as the box nearby explains, it does not say which political actor has the power to decide constitutional disputes. In 1803, the U.S. Supreme Court successfully claimed this authority in *Marbury v. Madison*, the first case in which the Court declared an act of Congress unconstitutional.[34]

The Power of Judicial Review

The facts of the *Marbury* case require an understanding of their political context. Thomas Jefferson, a Democratic-Republican (successors to the Anti-Federalists), had just won the White House in 1800, defeating Federalist John Adams. The Federalists feared that the new administration would give away national power to the states. So before Jefferson took office, Adams sought to fill 16 new federal judgeships to strengthen the Federalists' hold on the judiciary. On his last day in office Adams appointed one William Marbury to a federal judgeship, but the appointment papers were not delivered before midnight. When President Jefferson prevented their delivery, Marbury petitioned the Supreme Court for a remedy.

Chief Justice John Marshall, an ardent Federalist who had been Adams's secretary of state, used this case to strengthen the power of the courts. He did this in an odd way. Rather than save the job of a single Federalist judge, he held that the Supreme Court lacked the power to see that Marbury got his job because that power, although exercised by colonial judges and included in the Judiciary Act of 1789, was not granted the Court by the Constitution. In taking this action, Marshall made explicit the power of the courts to review and invalidate any laws or actions that violate the Constitution.

The Roles and Rules of Constitutional Practice

The mission of the Constitution was to establish the basic mechanisms of government that would allow people and institutions to manage their political disputes in an orderly fashion from one generation to the next. Because the Constitution is not addressed to an ideal reader or to specific individuals but rather to the *roles* people occupy, it is able to serve all generations who fill those roles.

The Framers created a number of political roles (for example, legislators, presidents, judges, "the people"). They also established rules for exercising the power they attached to those roles. In effect, they created a set of speakers (political actors) and defined the occasions and topics on which they may speak. Those who occupy the role of a member of Congress, for example, will find a list of the occasions and topics suitable for congressional action in Article I. Similarly, the language in Article III tells judges how, in their role as judges, they may think, speak, and act.[1] In addition, the First Amendment creates a platform from which "the people" may speak out, organize, and petition government.

How broadly political actors are able to interpret their roles and rules often determines how powerful they are. Chief Justice John Marshall successfully expanded the role of the courts by laying claim to the power of judicial review, as we saw above. Those occupying the role of "the people" have expanded the powers of the people under the Bill of Rights (see Chapters 15 and 16).

In sum, the Framers created the institutional vehicles people could step into and use, along with a set of instructions on how to use those vehicles in ways that would allow them to maneuver and steer themselves—and the nation. The Framers knew that, once it was launched, they could not control this experiment in government. So they made sure that the political actors they created had the tools they needed to learn by doing: to test their aims and claims in the political process, to adjust them, and to try again.

---

[1] James Boyd White, *When Words Lose Their Meaning: Constitutions and Reconstructions of Language, Character, and Community* (Chicago: University of Chicago Press, 1984), 245.

Judicial review gave the courts, both state and federal, the authority to declare acts of the legislative and executive branches unconstitutional. The final decision is usually made by the highest court in a state, if the matter involves that state's constitution, or by the U.S. Supreme Court, if the matter involves the federal Constitution.

The power of judicial review poses a dilemma to representative democracy, however. On the one hand, the authority of the Constitution is based on the sovereign authority of the people, who elect representatives to government and can vote them out of office at the next election if they choose. Because members of Congress and the president are subject to such electoral control, they are regarded as more accountable to the people than are federal judges and justices of the Supreme Court, who are appointed for life. (Federal judges and justices are, however, confirmed by the Senate, but senators in Marshall's day were chosen by state representatives.) The only popular check on the power of judicial review is the cumbersome process of constitutional amendment. There is, then, a fundamental tension between judicial review and representative democracy.

Refoundings

Many scholars and citizens alike view the events of 1776 through 1789 as the founding of the country—the *only* founding—and look to the Declaration of Independence, the Constitution, and the Framers for legal and moral guidance in assessing *what is, what's right,* and *what works* in political life. However, some scholars now speak of three "foundings":

- the original founding, which produced the Constitution;
- the period of Reconstruction at the end of the 1860s, which produced the Civil War amendments granting citizenship to African Americans; and
- the period of the Great Depression in the 1930s, which produced the New Deal, the country's first system of social welfare.

The justification scholars give for calling these later periods foundings is that they produced legislation by the people's representatives that constituted radical breaks with the past.[35] These radical breaks might well be called "refoundings" because they attempt to reground the nation in a deeper and richer understanding of the promises in the Declaration of Independence and the Constitution. The refoundings in the 1860s and in the 1930s occurred during major national crises. During the turbulent 1960s, the Reverend Martin Luther King, Jr., brought civil rights to the forefront of national politics and compelled the political system to respond. King's refounding inspired the nation—especially minorities and women—with an inclusive vision of democracy that went beyond the republicanism of the Framers.

Arguments legitimating such refoundings can be constructed from the words of the Founders and Refounders themselves. George Washington, for example, did not believe that "we are more inspired, have more vision, or possess more virtue, than those who will come after us." In his retirement he considered himself "a passenger only" on the ship of state, voicing his trust in "the mariners whose duty it is to watch, to steer it to a safe port."[36] And Abraham Lincoln, in the throes of the Civil War, cautioned that "the dogmas of the quiet past are inade-

The Reverend Martin Luther King, Jr., delivers his "I have a dream" speech to 200,000 at the Lincoln Memorial in 1963 during the March on Washington. Many Americans were greatly moved by King's call to blacks to "meet physical force with soul force" and by his plea that the growing black militancy "not lead to a distrust of all white people, for many of our white brothers, evidenced by their presence here today, have come to realize that their destiny is tied up with our destiny and their freedom is inextricably bound to our freedom."

quate to the stormy present. The occasion is piled high with difficulty, and we must rise to the occasion. As our case is new, so we must think anew and act anew."[37] The same argument has been made by refounders worldwide—most recently by reformers in Central and Eastern Europe, the former Soviet Union, and South Africa.

Today some political experts are predicting that the United States is undergoing yet another refounding as conservative Republicans and moderate Democrats attempt to shrink the size of the federal government and shift power to the states. Whether this effort will work as envisaged remains to be seen.

As the nation steps into the twenty-first century, the effectiveness of the Constitution will depend, as it always has, on the quality of the constitutional practice it inspires. The greatest gift its authors have passed on to the people it governs is a set of principles and mechanisms that allow them to manage their conflicts and to overcome obstacles as they pursue their—often very different—visions of what America is and should be.

Summary

The U.S. Constitution has governed the American people for more than two hundred years—a remarkable example of constitutional practice, given their diversity. A constitution based on popular sovereignty will not work unless enough citizens recognize themselves as a national community committed to the values and governing principles that document sets forth.

The American people were not created by the Declaration of Independence. Over time the colonists had acquired experience with self-government under their own founding documents—covenants, compacts, charters, and bills of rights. A national identity developed thanks to, and in opposition to, the authority of their British colonial rulers. British culture—the English language, Protestantism, English common law, and natural law with its notion of the rights of Englishmen—helped to unify the colonies in their struggle for independence. The independent states then drafted their own constitutions and united under the Articles of Confederation to protect themselves from foreign enemies and domestic despots.

When the Articles proved too weak to perform vital domestic and foreign tasks, and Shays' Rebellion provoked calls for a stronger national government, the states sent delegates to a convention with instructions to strengthen the Articles. Concluding that reforming the Articles would not work, they drafted a new federal Constitution in what became known as the Constitutional Convention of 1787.

The delegates easily agreed on the Constitution's guiding principles, but their political and regional divisions led to heated disputes over how to distribute power. Finally, they reached two key compromises: (1) the Great Compromise settled the dispute over representation between the large and small states by creating a bicameral legislature, with the Senate representing states equally and the House of Representatives representing states on the basis of population, and (2) the three-fifths compromise settled the dispute between the northern and southern states over counting slaves for representation and taxation.

The delegates were guided by the wisdom of Enlightenment thinkers (Locke, Hume, and Montesquieu) and lessons learned from the colonial experience. They believed that the new government they were designing would work only if it conformed to the laws of nature and followed a policy of laissez-faire.

The Constitution established a federal form of government that divided power among the national government, the states, and the people. The Constitution further divided national power among three branches: the legislative, the executive, and the judiciary. Each branch can exercise checks and balances over the others to prevent power from accumulating in any one branch. Through an elastic clause or its equivalent, each branch has been able to greatly increase its powers.

Most Federalists, who wanted a strong but limited central government, favored ratification, while most Anti-Federalists, who preferred to amend the Articles, opposed ratification. The Federalists prevailed, and the document was ratified in 1788. In 1791 a national Bill of Rights was added to expand civil liberties. Later amendments extended full rights of citizenship to African Americans and women.

The Constitution has lasted longer than any other written constitution in the world because it permits change while promoting stability and because enough Americans have accepted its authority to govern their political practice. A cumbersome amendment process combined with language general enough to cover new situations gives officials the strength and flexibility they need to govern. In addition, the courts, through the power of judicial review articulated in *Marbury v. Madison* (1803), adapt the Constitution to pressures for change.

Americans have always looked for political guidance to the colonial Founders and Framers and the great leaders who followed them—"refounders" such as Abraham Lincoln, Franklin D. Roosevelt, and the Reverend Martin Luther King, Jr.

Key Terms

Anti-Federalists **62**
Articles of Confederation **47**
Bill of Rights **65**
bill of rights **40**
checks and balances **57**
compact **40**
Connecticut, or Great, Compromise **52**
covenant **40**
Declaration of Independence **44**
division of powers **56**
dual citizenship **48**
elastic clause **59**
executive branch **56**
The Federalist **62**
Federalists **62**
Glorious Revolution **41**
judicial branch **57**
judicial review **69**
laws of nature **55**
legislative branch **56**
limited government **38**
Magna Carta **38**
mercantilism **41**
natural aristocracy **62**
proprietary colonies **40**
republicanism **51**
royal charter **38**
separation of powers **56**
Shays' Rebellion **49**
sovereignty **47**
state constitutions **46**
three-fifths compromise **54**
veto **47**

How You Can Learn More About the Founding

Jillson, Calvin C. *Constitution-Making: Conflict and Consensus in the Federal Convention of 1787.* New York: Agathon Press, 1988. An analysis of how the various factions at the federal convention affected the outcome.

Kammen, Michael. *A Machine That Would Go of Itself: The Constitution in American Culture.* New York: Random House, 1987. An account of how the Constitution has been interpreted in particular eras.

Kyvig, David E. *Explicit and Authentic Acts: Amending the U.S. Constitution, 1776–1995.* Lawrence: University Press of Kansas, 1997. A brilliant analysis of how and why the amendments to the Constitution came to be written.

Lutz, Donald S. *The Origins of American Constitutionalism.* Baton Rouge: Louisiana State University Press, 1988. A compelling study of the colonial founding documents and state constitutions that shaped the Articles of Confederation and the Constitution.

McDonald, Forrest. *Novus Ordo Seclorum: The Intellectual Origins of the Constitution.* Lawrence: University Press of Kansas, 1985. An exploration of the European, and especially English, ideas of law, society, and economics that influenced the Framers of the Constitution.

Madison, James, Alexander Hamilton, and John Jay. *The Federalist.* Edited by Jacob E. Cooke. Middletown, Conn.: Wesleyan University Press, 1961. A collection of newspaper columns written to justify ratification of the Constitution.

Miller, Joshua. *The Rise and Fall of Democracy in Early America, 1630–1789.* University Park: Pennsylvania State University Press, 1991. An argument that the Constitution diminished the democratic tradition developed during the colonial period.

Smith, Page. *The Constitution: A Documentary and Narrative History.* New York: Morrow, 1978. A lively account of debates on the Articles and the Constitution.

Storing, Herbert J. *What the Anti-Federalists Were For: The Political Thought of the Opponents of the Constitution.* Chicago: University of Chicago Press, 1981. A critical analysis of those who opposed the ratification of the Constitution.

Wood, Gordon S. *The Creation of the American Republic.* Chapel Hill: University of North Carolina Press, 1969. An examination of the political ideas that affected the writing of the Constitution.

Practicing Federalism

The above photo shows new cars lined up at a Ford dealership. At right, two demonstrators dressed as lemons stage a protest claiming that the car bought at that dealership was a lemon.

CHAPTER 3

The question of the relation of the States to the federal government is the cardinal question of our constitutional system. . . . It cannot . . . be settled by one generation because it is a question of growth, and every successive stage of our political and economic development gives it a new aspect, makes it a new question.

—**Woodrow Wilson, 1911**

The problem which all federalized nations have to solve is how to secure an efficient central government and preserve national unity, while allowing free scope for the diversities, and free play to the authorities, of the members of the federation . . . so neither the planet States shall fly off into space, nor the sun of the Central government draw them into its consuming fires.

—**James Bryce, 1891**

What is American Federalism?

The Federal Distribution of Powers

The Evolution of American Federalism

Democracy, Federalism, and the Future

Suppose you buy a new car, and then discover something is seriously wrong with it. It came with a warranty, so you take it back to the dealer for repair. But the same problem reappears, so you take it back to the dealer again. And again. And again. You've got a lemon—a new car with a problem your dealer can't fix.

Lemons had become so common by the 1980s that states began passing "lemon laws." Today every state has one. The 1983 New York lemon law says that a new car bought in the state can be returned for a full refund or replacement if the dealer hasn't fixed the same problem in four tries within the first two years or if repairs take 30 days or more.

But what if the dealer refuses to give you a new car or your money back? Either you must sue the manufacturer—something that takes years and costs lots of money—or rely on the New York law's guarantee of "informal dispute resolution" by an impartial arbitrator. When manufacturers picked untrained arbitrators who didn't understand the law and ruled against consumers, New Yorkers complained to their legislators. So in 1986 New York amended its lemon law to require that auto manufacturers offering informal dispute resolution select competent and knowledgeable arbitrators.

The manufacturers, unable anymore to circumvent the law, united to challenge it. The Motor Vehicle Manufacturers Association of the United States (MVMA, a group representing the domestic car makers General Motors, Ford, and Chrysler) and the Automobile Importers of America (AIA, a group of foreign car makers and importers) formed a coalition to challenge the New York state law.

The lawyers could find no basis for overturning the law at the state level because it did not violate the New York state constitution. The only option was to take advantage of the fact that the United States is a federal system and challenge the New York law at the national level. Article VI of the U.S. Constitution provides that federal laws are supreme over state laws. Thus if Congress were to pass a law prohibiting states from having lemon laws, the New York law would be null and void. As it happened, Congress had passed the Magnuson-Moss Warranty Act in 1975, which required that all consumer warranties be clear and that any informal dispute resolution processes be fair and quick. This law made it unlikely that Congress would be sympathetic to the manufacturers.

Nevertheless, the manufacturers and importers came up with a clever strategy to get the New York law overturned. In 1986 they filed suit in the U.S. District Court in New York—one of the 90 lowest-level federal courts located throughout the United States—claiming that the New York law conflicted with the Magnuson-Moss Warranty Act because it gave greater protection to car buyers. Since the supremacy clause of the Constitution makes the federal law supreme, the New York law should be declared null and void. In legal language, they invoked the doctrine of preemption, which provides that the national law automatically overrides any state law on the same subject.

The supremacy clause says that the federal law takes precedence over state law when they conflict. But what counts as a conflict? Sometimes Congress includes explicit language indicating that the new law preempts state laws in that policy area. More often, Congress sets minimum standards that states must meet, a policy called partial preemption because the federal law preempts only those parts of state laws that offer less protection than federal law. Because the Magnuson-Moss Warranty Act said nothing about preemption, the door was opened for anyone to challenge the state law in federal court.

In the New York case, the district court decided in favor of the manufacturers and importers, arguing that "there is no room in this system for states to tinker with the federal criteria." The State of New York then appealed the decision to the Second Circuit Court of Appeals (one of 12 in the United States), also located in New York. This higher court then had to decide just what Congress had intended in passing the Magnuson-Moss Warranty Act.

"The [Magnuson-Moss] Act obviously represents a compromise between warrantors and consumers," the court declared, "and, as is frequently the case in such situations, the process of compromise results in a statute creating problems of interpretation." The court decided to reverse the judgment of the district court on March 26, 1990, and uphold New York's lemon law.

The auto interests then appealed the decision to the Supreme Court, the highest legal authority in the country. In 1991 the Supreme Court announced, in a brief written statement without explanation, that it would not accept the case for consideration, thereby allowing the appeals court's decision to stand. The New York lemon law was not preempted by the Magnuson-Moss Warranty Act, and New Yorkers could invoke it when they believed their new cars were lemons.

Two centuries ago, when the Constitution was newly adopted, a dispute about the purchase of a horse and buggy would never have gotten into federal district court, let alone the Supreme Court. But when you buy a car today, the transaction is governed by a host of national and state laws—whether you or the dealer are aware of them or not. The reason is that you live in a federal political system, in which authority is shared among the national government, the state governments, and the people. In this chapter we'll learn what this means for everyday life and politics as we examine the following questions:

What is American federalism?

How does the Constitution divide powers between the national and state governments?

Why does power shift between the national and state governments?

How does federalism affect American democracy?

How could federalism be renewed to strengthen democracy?

What Is American Federalism?

The U.S. Constitution provides that you are protected by, but must also obey, the laws of two levels of government—those of the nation and those of the state. Thus consumers throughout the United States are protected by the federal Warranty Act, while consumers who buy a new car in a particular state are also protected by that state's lemon law. Both the national level and the state level have direct legal authority over you in certain policy areas, granted to them by the Constitution and so not changeable by Congress. This is why we call the American political system **federalism**. The national or federal government and the state governments together make up the **federal system**.

The Constitution does not mention the third level of government—local government. City, county, and other local governments derive their authority from the state in which they are located and can rule only in areas of policy designated by the state. Altogether, there are 86,743 governments in the United States—one national government, 50 state governments, and the rest local governmental entities (see Table 3.1).

federalism

This term, from the Latin for *being bound together by a treaty*, refers to a system of two levels of government in which each level governs a particular territory and each has direct legal authority over citizens and other residents in certain constitutionally protected policy areas.

federal government/national government

The terms national government, central government, and federal government are synonymous.

TABLE 3.1

How Many Governments Are There in the United States?

National government	1
State governments	50
Local governments:	
County	3,043
Municipal (cities)	19,296
Township (towns)	16,666
School districts	14,556
Special function districts (fire, housing, sewer, highway, airport, etc.)	33,131
Total	86,743

Source: U.S. Bureau of the Census, *Census of Governments, 1992* (Washington, D.C.: Government Printing Office, 1992).

Federalism affects American politics in two ways: First, each citizen has **dual citizenship** (national and state), and many people have split allegiances—to the nation and to their states. Second, Americans have split representation: they are represented politically in governments at each level—the nation, the states, and localities.

As we saw in Chapter 2, this federal structure derived from the transformation of the American colonies, most of which had distinctive local cultures but similar federal structures, into independent states which united under the Articles of Confederation. Citizens jealously guarded the influence they had on their own governance by having their government close by and tailored to their particular circumstances.[1]

When the delegates to the Constitutional Convention of 1787 met to strengthen central control, they assumed that political sovereignty was indivisible. However, they soon concluded that sovereign power could be shared or divided between the states and the central government. In part, this decision was forced on them by desperate circumstances, but Enlightenment ideas also played a role (see Chapter 2). Supporters of a strong central government often cited ancient Greek confederacies as examples of federal systems destroyed by being too decentralized, while opponents cited the Roman Republic as a system ruined by being overly centralized.[2] Contemporary examples were of little help, because neither of the two existing federations, the Swiss and the Dutch, fit the American experience very well.

However, there was another important influence on the drafters: a conscious process of learning from recent experiences in the states. The first new state constitutions drafted at the time of independence had been produced by state legislatures. But the 1780 Massachusetts constitution was drafted by a special convention—not a legislature—and was then ratified at town meetings by those eligible to vote: white male property owners. In other words, the people were clearly the source of sovereignty in Massachusetts. In Philadelphia, the convention delegates gradually came to realize that they did not have to *transfer* some powers from the states to the central government—something many feared would compromise their liberty. Instead, they realized, if the people are sovereign they can decide to *delegate* some powers to their state government and other powers to the national government. This imaginative solution to the problem of sovereign power based on experience in the states was the key to the invention of American federalism by the Framers.[3]

The system the Framers invented, in the words of James Madison in *The Federalist*, No. 39, "is in strictness neither a national nor a federal constitution; but a composition of both"—"a compound republic."[4] Its success has led many other political systems to adapt the federal principle, as shown in Table 3.2, which summarizes the current status of some federal and confederal governmental systems around the world.

It was one thing to create a federal system for 13 existing states. It was quite another to provide for its subsequent expansion. The provision that new states would be admitted to the union on an equal legal footing with the original 13 meant that for the first time in the history of the world large areas colonized by a country would be admitted to a union as equals rather than continually dominated as colonies.

The blueprint for this expansion of the federal union into an "extended republic" was the Northwest Ordinance, passed by the Confederation Congress in 1787 while the Constitutional Convention was under way. The Northwest Ordinance stated that western lands that lay north of the Ohio River and east of the

TABLE 3.2

Selected Federal and Confederal States Around the World

State	Type of Government	Units Constituting the State
Argentina	Federation	23 provinces; 5 regions
Austria	Federation	9 states
Belgium	Federation	3 regions; 3 cultural communities
Brazil	Federation	26 states; 1 federal district
Canada	Federation	10 provinces; 2 territories
China	Dictatorship with formal regional autonomy	5 autonomous regions
Commonwealth of Independent States (formerly the Soviet Union)	Confederation	Russia plus 10 autonomous republics
Federal Republic of Germany	Federation	16 states
India	Federation	25 states
Italy	State with constitutional regions	15 ordinary regions; 5 special status regions
Japan	Constitutionally decentralized state	43 prefectures
Mexico	Federation	31 states; 1 federal district
Nigeria	Federation	21 states
Pakistan	Federation	4 provinces; 1 federal capital; 6 federally administered tribal areas
Spain	Quasi-federation	12 ordinary regions; 3 historically autonomous regions
Switzerland	Federation	20 full cantons; 6 half cantons
United Kingdom	Centralized state with constituent units	England, Scotland, Wales, Northern Ireland, Isle of Man, Channel Islands
United States	Federation	50 states; 1 federal district (Washington, D.C.)

Source: Adapted and updated from Daniel J. Elazar, ed., *Federal Systems of the World* (London: Longman, 1991), app. C.

Mississippi, still controlled by Indians, were to be organized first into territories and then, when a territory's population reached 60,000, into no less than three or more than five states. (This area eventually became Ohio, Indiana, Illinois, Michigan, and Wisconsin.) Territories were to establish their own legislatures. Slavery was forbidden, and education was encouraged.

There was no provision in the Constitution, however, for the expansion of the Union itself beyond the boundaries established in the Treaty of Paris that ended the Revolutionary War. That task would fall to America's third president, Thomas Jefferson, as we'll see shortly.

The Federal Distribution of Powers

The history of the United States can be seen as an ongoing struggle over the allocation or distribution of powers between the states and the central government. The **supremacy clause** means that federal laws override or replace state laws. In practice, however, the situation is much more complicated because five types or categories of powers are allocated between the national government and the states or denied to one or the other. To understand the nature of the federal system and its evolution, we must examine each category of power in turn.

Enumerated, Reserved, and Concurrent Powers

The struggle over the allocation of powers between the states and the national government was resolved—temporarily—in the Constitutional Convention by listing certain powers explicitly granted or *delegated* to the central government and certain other powers explicitly granted to the states. Among these **enumerated powers,** as they are called, the national government was to have supreme power—power over the states and over the people—in certain spheres: in foreign relations, in interstate and foreign commerce, in the coining of money, and in the creation of a postal service. States were to have supreme power—over the citizens and free of central government interference—in other spheres, such as the conduct of elections. There was, however, an important limitation on both these allocations of sovereign powers: neither level of government could overstep the bounds set by the Constitution and any amendments to it because the supremacy clause made the Constitution the highest law of the land.

But what about all the powers not enumerated in the Constitution? To which level of government do they belong? The first session of the new Congress proposed a constitutional amendment stating, "The powers not delegated to the United States by the Constitution, nor prohibited by it to the States, are reserved to the States respectively, or to the people." This proposal, ratified as part of the Bill of Rights, is now the Tenth Amendment to the Constitution.

What are these **reserved powers** referred to in the Tenth Amendment? In *The Federalist*, No. 45, Madison had written, "The powers reserved to the several States will extend to all the objects which, in the ordinary course of affairs, concern the lives, liberties, and properties of the people, and the internal order, improvement, and prosperity of the State."[5] Of course, as part of a newspaper column later collected and published as a book, Madison's assertion lacked the force of law. However, most observers—Framers and citizens alike—understood reserved powers to include the policing of citizen behavior and the regulation of such vital matters as marriage, health, and education.

The central government and the state governments also exercise certain **concurrent powers**—so called because they can be exercised concurrently (at the same time) by both levels. Among these are the power to tax, to pass and enforce laws, and to borrow money. We saw an instance of the exercise of concurrent powers in the lemon law case, in which both the State of New York and the national government exercised their powers to regulate commerce. When concurrent powers are exercised, disputes often arise over whose claim to authority should prevail in a given domain, such as welfare, pollution control, education, or consumer protection. And citizens or special interests may attempt to use the fact of shared authority to contest a particular action or law—as the auto interests did in the lemon law case.

Implied Powers

Many people feared that the general language of the Constitution might let the national government expand its powers too greatly at the expense of the states. Thus when what was to become the Tenth Amendment was being considered in the House of Representatives, one member wanted "expressly" inserted between "Powers" and "delegated to the United States" to safeguard the realm of reserved powers. But Madison objected that it was impossible and imprudent to attempt to "confine a government to the exercise of express powers." It was necessary, he said, to allow for "powers of implication" to avoid having to list each and every national power in minute detail. Madison's logic prevailed, and the government was understood to be one of limited, delegated powers but also one of **implied powers**.[6] The doctrine of implied powers was not formalized by the Supreme Court for another thirty years, but the actual powers of the national government were significantly increased in 1803 with the Louisiana Purchase.

The Louisiana Purchase

Thomas Jefferson took office in 1801 committed to limited government and a literal reading of the Constitution. That same year, Spain ceded the Louisiana Territory to France, and Jefferson feared that the United States would be pinned between British Canada on the north and the French in the west (see Figure 3.1). Unlike Spain, a power then in decline, France under Napoleon was a force to be reckoned with. Moreover, a strong French colony would obstruct westward expansion and the creation of a continental United States with a republican government. In short, Jefferson was faced with two issues fundamental to American nationhood: national security and westward expansion. When Napoleon proved

Figure 3.1

The growth of the United States from its original thirteen states through the Louisiana Purchase and beyond

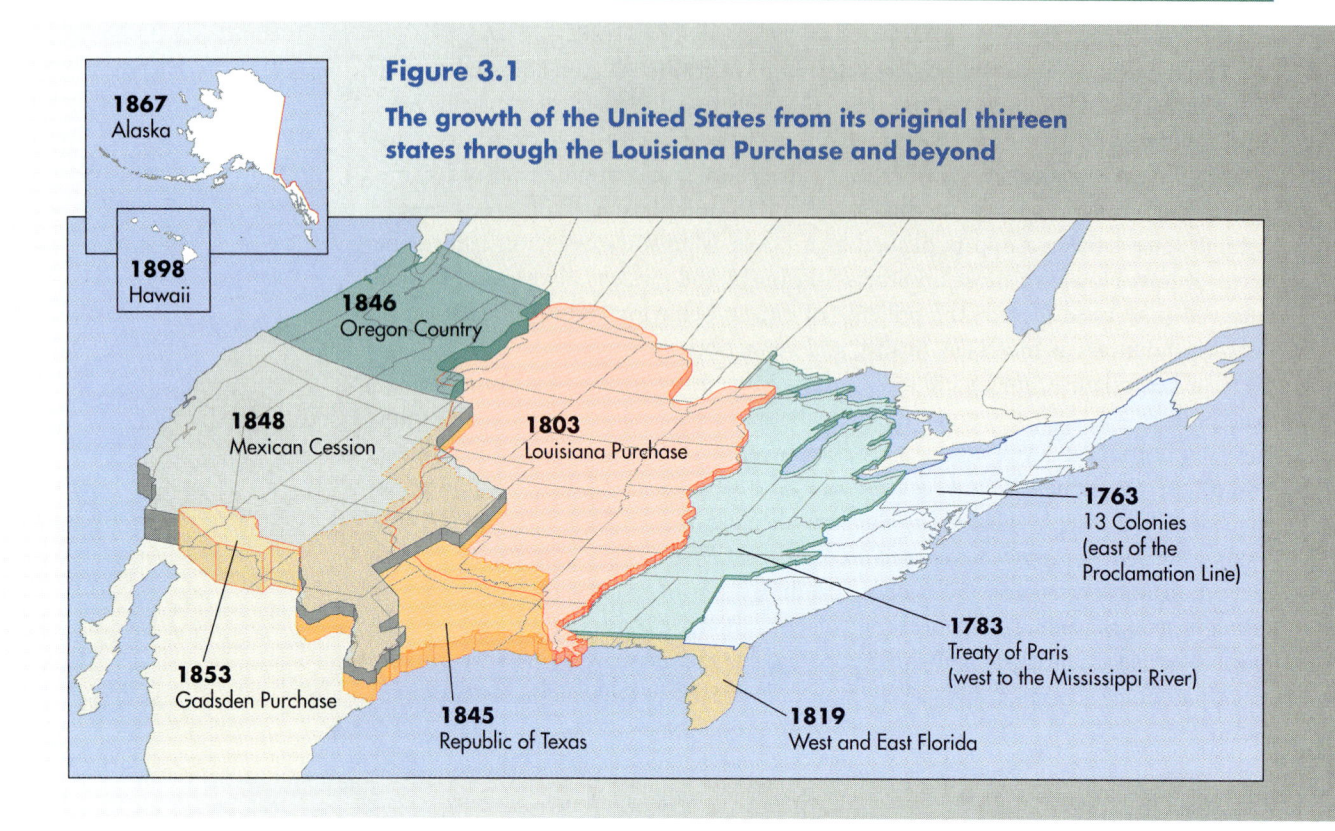

- 1867 Alaska
- 1898 Hawaii
- 1846 Oregon Country
- 1848 Mexican Cession
- 1803 Louisiana Purchase
- 1763 13 Colonies (east of the Proclamation Line)
- 1783 Treaty of Paris (west to the Mississippi River)
- 1853 Gadsden Purchase
- 1845 Republic of Texas
- 1819 West and East Florida

willing to sell the whole Louisiana Territory, Jefferson jumped at the chance to buy it, even though his own literal reading of the Constitution would not have allowed him to do so without a constitutional amendment. With hindsight, we are likely to say he acted wisely, for it is hard to imagine a United States of America without any states west of the Mississippi. But at the time, Jefferson was taking the initiative in asserting an implied power.

McCulloch v. Maryland

Sixteen years after establishing the power of judicial review in *Marbury v. Madison* (1803) (see Chapter 2), Chief Justice John Marshall expanded the power of the federal courts and the federal government in *McCulloch v. Maryland* (1819).[7]

As in *Marbury*, the specific substance of *McCulloch*—the questions of whether the federal government had the power to establish a national bank (the Court held that it did) and whether the State of Maryland had the power to tax it (the Court held that it did not)—was overshadowed by two larger principles. First, Marshall argued that implied powers could legitimately be derived from enumerated powers because a constitution specifies powers only in outline form, so it requires interpretation. Second, Marshall argued that national supremacy forbids the states to interfere in the constitutional operations of the federal government. "The question is, in truth, a question of supremacy," wrote Marshall, "and if the right of the States to tax the means employed by the general government be conceded, the declaration that the constitution . . . shall be the supreme law of the land, is empty." The decision thus both expanded the powers of the central government and contracted the powers of the states—despite the language of the Tenth Amendment.[8]

In the related case of *Osborne v. Bank of the United States* (1824), the Marshall Court allowed a state official who was violating a federal law to be sued.[9] This case established the principle that the national government could enforce federal law against the states. In establishing the supremacy of the Constitution and national law over state law, *McCulloch* and *Osborne* laid the groundwork for the gradual domination of the federal government over the states.

Inherent Powers

To govern more effectively at home and exert more influence abroad, the national government continued to extend its authority to exercise concurrent powers. Then in *United States v. Curtiss-Wright Export Corp.* (1936) the Supreme Court granted legitimacy to another device for the expansion—the doctrine of **inherent powers**.

The question before the Court was whether Congress could constitutionally delegate power to the president in the area of foreign relations—in this case, the power to forbid the sale of arms to Bolivia. The Court said yes, because inherent in the concept of a nation are the powers a national government needs to operate as a nation-state in a world of nation-states. The Court called these inherent powers because any nation must have them in order to function effectively—in other words, they are inherent in the concept of a nation. The Court's actual language was "necessary concomitants of [the nation-state's] nationality." This decision, a century and a half after the Constitution went into effect, legitimated the fifth type of governmental powers in the American federal system. These five types of powers are summarized in Table 3.3.

The Powers of the Localities

The Constitution makes no mention at all of towns, cities, or counties, so their regulation devolves to the states. Madison understood that the diversity of interests found in larger political units might be lacking in smaller units, making tyranny of the majority over the minority a more likely threat on the local level. Still, in the nation's first century, cities and towns generally enjoyed considerable freedom from state or national interference. However, as city populations grew and governments at all levels became more active, states began to limit their localities. The power of states in these matters was expressed in an 1868 decision by Iowa State Supreme Court Justice John F. Dillon. Local governments, he declared, are "mere tenants at the will of the legislature" of the state and therefore must derive their political authority from the states in which they are located. This principle, formalized in commentaries Dillon published four years later, has become known as **Dillon's Rule**.[10]

As cities grew and became harder to manage, states began to grant them **home rule**—local autonomy in municipal affairs. St. Louis was granted home

Dillon's Rule

This principle states that a city's powers are strictly limited to those expressly granted by the state, those necessarily implied by that grant of powers, and "those essential to the accomplishment of the declared objects and purposes" of the city.

TABLE 3.3

Types of Powers in the Federal System

Type of Power	Origin of the Power	Examples
Enumerated (delegated) to the national government	Article I, section 8; Article II, section 2 and other sections; Article III, section 2 of the Constitution	Power to make war, to establish post office, to regulate interstate and foreign commerce, to coin money
Enumerated (delegated) to the state governments	Article I, section 4; Article II, section 1; Article V; and other sections of the Constitution	Power to establish state and local governments, to conduct elections, to ratify constitutional amendments
Reserved to (retained by) the state governments	Tenth Amendment to the Constitution	Powers not delegated to the national government by the Constitution or prohibited to the states by the Constitution (but not specified in the Constitution)
Concurrent in (shared by) the national and state governments	Constitution plus traditional practice	Power to tax, to spend, to build roads, to regulate business
Implied to the national government	Constitution, as interpreted by Supreme Court in *McCulloch v. Maryland*	Any power that is an appropriate, nonprohibited means to a legitimate end
Inherent in the national government	Supreme Court, in *United States v. Curtiss-Wright*	President's power to regulate arms sales
Denied to the national government	Article I, section 9 of the Constitution and Bill of Rights	Ex post facto laws (outlawing something after it is done), bills of attainder (laws declaring someone guilty and prescribing a penalty without a trial), others specified in first eight amendments
Denied to the state governments	Article I, section 10 of the Constitution and Supreme Court when it made the Bill of Rights apply to the states (see Chapter 15)	Make treaties, coin money, regulate interstate commerce, refuse to treat citizens of other states equally with their own

rule by Missouri in 1875, and by 1900, 12 states were granting it. Today 35 states have constitutional or legal home-rule provisions, and two-thirds of the cities of 250,000 or more have home-rule charters.[11] Courts have generally defined "municipal affairs" narrowly to involve such issues as zoning and sewerage, and legislatures have regularly inserted themselves into such local concerns as property law and utility rates. Cities are in a constant struggle to gain more local autonomy—the capacity to take their own policy initiatives without the risk of being overruled by the state government[12]—but because they lack any protection in the Constitution, each city remains at the mercy of its state's government and legal system. However, the division of power between the central government and the states gives cities and counties the opportunity to appeal to the more receptive level of government. Having no place in the Constitution, cities have tended to be marginal players in the great debate over federalism, but like the state and national levels of government, they have considerable influence on the daily lives of citizens and other residents, as the box nearby demonstrates.

How Living in a Federal System Affects You from Birth to Death

At Birth

Local government requires and grants you a birth certificate that records your name (which you cannot change without going to court), date and place of birth, and parentage.

State government regulates the certification of any doctors and nurses who may assist your birth.

National government assigns you a Social Security number (which will identify you for governments and other institutions for life).

If born in the United States, you automatically become a citizen of the *nation* and of the *state* in which you were born.

In Infancy

Local government requires that you get vaccinations against dangerous and communicable childhood diseases and usually offers them free for those who can't afford them.

National government establishes standards for the safety of food, medicine, clothing, and other goods, now and for the rest of your life.

National, *state*, and *local* governments regulate (now and for the rest of your life) the public water supply from which you drink and the air quality, and build and maintain the roads you travel on.

In Childhood

Local government establishes and largely funds the public school you are entitled to attend.

State government requires you to attend a public or private school, or be home schooled, until you meet high school graduation requirements or reach an age in your teens (which varies from state to state). It also sets curricular standards for your schooling and helps fund public education.

National government establishes and funds programs for early childhood education, especially for the disadvantaged.

National government creates, prints, and coins the money you get, use, or save.

National and *state* governments establish and fund various programs of economic assistance for which you may be eligible.

In Early Adulthood

Local government invites you to register to vote if you are a citizen and conducts regular elections for offices at all levels of government in accordance with *national* and *state* election laws.

Local governments (city and county) collect various taxes on property you own.

National, *state*, and *local* governments charge taxes on the telephone you use.

State and *local* governments charge sales taxes on many things you purchase.

State government issues you a driver's license if you pass its test, requires you to register any car you buy, and sells you required license plates for any car you buy.

State and *local* governments run colleges you may attend.

National government establishes and enforces child labor laws and minimum wage laws that regulate any employment you may have.

National government requires all males to register for Selective Service (potential military service) at age 18.

National, most *state*, and some *local* governments tax income from any job you have, and *national* government deducts Social Security contributions from your paycheck, while *state* government deducts unemployment insurance from it, now and for the rest of your life.

National, *state*, and often *local* governments pass and enforce laws to prevent discrimination in school, work, and play because of your race, ethnicity, beliefs, gender, age, or disability.

In Adulthood

State government issues the marriage license and requires blood tests should you decide to marry.

Local government provides fire and police protection and might control your water supply and collect your garbage.

National government issues the passport you need to travel abroad and runs the customs office you must pass through when you return.

National, most *state*, and some *local* governments require you to file annual income tax returns and make and enforce laws affecting your work.

National and *state* governments regulate most aspects of your use of money, including banks and other financial institutions, such as insurance companies and credit card services you use.

In Old Age

National government protects you against certain forms of discrimination based on age.

National, *state*, and sometimes *local* governments pass and enforce laws concerning retirement.

National government pays you Social Security benefits if you qualify.

National and *state* governments regulate the medical care you receive and require payments from you to support it.

Local government issues your death certificate and may investigate the cause of your death.

National and *state* governments supervise the inheritance of your money and goods by those you designate, in accordance with their laws.

Indian Nations

The political status of the Indian nations who occupied much of the territory that became the United States has been quite different from that of the states and localities. During the Revolution, the United States, still without a Constitution, signed a treaty with the Delaware Indians that envisaged the formation of an Indian "state whereof the Delaware Nation shall be the head and have a representative in Congress." The Northwest Ordinance pledged that "the utmost good faith shall always be observed towards the Indians; their lands and property shall never be taken from them without their consent." The Constitution of 1789 gave Congress the power to "regulate commence . . . with the Indian tribes," then viewed as foreign nations. However, the ensuing two centuries have seen violation after violation of pledges and treaties as Indians were removed from choice lands and virtually compelled to live on "reservations" carved out of existing and new states unless they chose to assimilate (see Chapter 16).

The struggle for Native American political power resulted in passage of the Indian Citizenship Act in 1924, granting Indians the right to vote in federal and state elections and requiring them to pay federal taxes and perform military service when drafted. Tribes, however—or nations, as most Indians prefer to call them—have few significant powers and no automatic representation in the federal or state governments, although members may serve in tribal, state, or national offices. Being located within the United States has some interesting effects on the lives and economic opportunities of tribes and their members, as the box nearby illustrates.

The Iroquois and American Federalism in New York State

While the federal system of government has accommodated national, state, and local governments, it has never included Indian nations as a component or governmental level, nor has it generally expanded the liberties of Native Americans. Consider the case of the Iroquois.

In the Revolutionary Era, some Indian nations supported the British, some the Americans. The Iroquois Confederacy of tribes, established long before European settlement began, officially remained neutral. In practice, however, the Oneida and the Tuscarora supported the colonies while the Mohawk, Onondaga, Cayuga, and Seneca aided the British.

The British had promised to protect the interests of the Indians whatever the outcome of the war, but the Treaty of Paris (1783) did not even mention the Indians. Instead it provided that the British would cede all lands south of Canada and east of the Mississippi—which included most of the Iroquois lands—to the United States. The Iroquois protested in vain that, as peoples whose sovereignty had been recognized by treaty in 1768, they alone had the authority to control or cede their land. The State of New York, which claimed more Iroquois land than any other state, had promised each Revolutionary War soldier 600 acres. To fulfill this pledge, New York decided to expel the Iroquois.

The Articles of Confederation gave the Congress the power of "regulating the trade and managing all affairs with the Indians . . . provided that the legislative right of any state within its own limits not be infringed or violated." New York proceeded to make its own treaties with individual Iroquois tribes. Weak, disunited, and without British support, the tribes agreed to accept lands farther west in exchange for the lands they currently claimed.

Even after the U.S. Constitution assigned Indian relations to the national government and a representative from President Washington reached agreement with the Seneca (1791), New York State continued to allow land companies to make separate deals with individual tribes, who often misunderstood the terms of these agreements.[1]

In 1851, Indian nations were assigned territorial "reservations" by the federal government to replace their lands. Today federal law officially regards tribes on reservations as sovereign nations, but this sovereignty is severely limited by the requirement that Indians and tribes obey most federal and state laws. This arrangement affords few advantages to the Indians, but one is that Indian stores on reservations can't be forced to collect state sales taxes. Tribes may charge and collect their own sales taxes, but don't in order to attract non-Indian shoppers.

By the mid 1980s, New York estimated that cigarettes purchased in reservation stores by non-Indian shoppers cost the state $15 million a year in lost sales taxes. So in 1988 the state issued a regulation requiring wholesale distributors of cigarettes to pay taxes on any cigarettes they sold to reservation stores beyond the number that the state calculated Indians would buy for their own use. New York anticipated that these distributors would pass the charges on to the shops, which would pass them on to non-Indian shoppers. The state thus collected the revenue without technically violating the federal prohibition against collecting taxes from reservation store sales.

New York's highest court ruled in 1990 that this novel tax regulation violated tribal sovereignty and was thus illegal. In 1992 the U.S. Supreme Court overturned the state court ruling, as it had a similar one from Oklahoma in 1991, holding the tax regulation to be legal. Iroquois reservation merchants seeking to profit from selling cigarettes to non-Indians suddenly lost in practice the protection that the American federal system and their semisovereign status had granted them in principle.[2]

By 1997, New York estimated the lost tax revenue from reservation cigarette and gasoline sales at $100 million a year. To enforce court rulings, state police began blocking shipments of gas and cigarettes to Indian tribes that refused to be taxed. However, Indian protests were so great that the state backed down and the governor announced that the state would stop trying to collect the taxes. The limited sovereignty of Indian reservations in the federal system had survived another challenge.[3]

Similar issues were also raised when Iroquois nations wanted to open gambling casinos on Indian lands inside New York's boundaries. Congress had passed a law in 1988 requiring tribes to negotiate with their respective states about opening such casinos and granting the tribes the right to sue a state that refused to negotiate in good faith in federal court. New York granted the Iroquois the right to open casinos, although the state constitution made casinos illegal on non-Indian land. Thus the federal system protected this Indian business venture.

Then, in 1996, the Supreme Court ruled that the Seminole tribe, which wanted to open casinos on its reservation in Florida, could not sue the State of Florida in federal court to force it to negotiate, despite the 1988 law.[4] The Court argued that the Eleventh Amendment, which prohibits citizens of another state from suing a state in federal court, prohibits Congress from granting that right to Indians because reservations have a special status in the federal system. So once again what had seemed to be an instance of federalism protecting Indian rights was turned into a limitation by the U.S. Supreme Court, which is the ultimate legal authority for Indian tribes and states alike in the federal system.

---

[1] For the story, see Helen M. Upton, *The Everett Report in Historical Perspective: The Indians of New York* (Albany: New York State American Revolution Bicentennial Commission, 1980), chap. 2; Francis Paul Prucha, *American Indian Treaties* (Ithaca, N.Y.: Cornell University Press, 1994); Francis Jennings et al., eds., *The History and Culture of Iroquois Diplomacy* (Syracuse, N.Y.: Syracuse University Press, 1985).
[2] See Linda Greenhouse, "Court Decision Favors Tax on Reservation Cigarettes," *New York Times*, January 22, 1992; and *Oklahoma Tax Commission v. Potawatomi Tribe*, 498 U.S. 505 (1991).
[3] Raymond Hernandez, "In a Shift, State Won't Try to Tax Sales on Indian Reservations," *New York Times*, May 23, 1997.
4. *Seminole Tribe of Florida v. Florida*, U.S. (1996).

The Evolution of American Federalism

The struggle over the proper distribution of power in the federal system has been replayed time and again. Thomas Jefferson, in keeping with the mechanistic worldview shared by the Framers, used the metaphor of the pendulum to describe how this struggle played out over time. Shortly after the Constitution was drafted, he wrote to a friend, "We are now vibrating between too much [the proposed constitution] and too little government [the Articles], and the pendulum will rest finally in the middle."[13] It never has. Power has tended to flow in one direction or the other from one period to the next, usually driven by concerns that one power center has become too strong and needs to be limited by the other. However, over the course of American history this metaphorical pendulum has defied the laws of physics by swinging ever closer to the central government and ever further from the states, as we shall see in the following survey.

Dual Federalism, 1836–1933

In the Federalist era, under the new Constitution, the central government grew in size and political strength. But after several decades power began to swing back toward the states. President Andrew Jackson (1829–1837) reasserted the old

Anti-Federalist concern for states' rights—a term used by advocates of the view that all rights that the Constitution did not delegate to the national government or deny to the states remain with the states, and that the federal government's claims to implied powers should be resisted and limited.

When Federalist Chief Justice John Marshall died in 1835, Jackson picked Roger B. Taney (served 1836–1864) to succeed him. Taney, a supporter of states' rights, believed that the Court should serve as the arbiter between the equally sovereign national and state powers. The United States was entering the era of what scholars call **dual federalism** in which the national and the state levels of government remain supreme in their own jurisdictions.

In the boom years leading up to the outbreak of the Civil War in 1861, emerging new economic interests often sought assistance from both levels of government. When businesses wanted subsidies or tax breaks, they went to their state governments. When they wanted tariffs to protect them from competition from cheap imports, they had to appeal to the national government. When they wanted transportation improvements such as roads and canals, they appealed to both. The South, however, remained predominantly rural, and efforts to protect its slave society and agricultural economy coalesced in strengthened claims of the states against those of the national government.

The strongest claim of states' rights advocates emerged in the 1830s, when southerners objected to high tariffs passed by Congress. Unable to prevail in Congress, southerners adopted the doctrine of **nullification**, which held that a state convention could declare a national law that it found unacceptable null and void within the state's boundaries and refuse to observe it. A special state convention in South Carolina nullified the national tariffs in 1832 and threatened secession if the national government attempted to enforce the tariffs. Faced with this grave threat, President Jackson got Congress to authorize the use of force to preserve the Union but at the same time to lower the tariff. South Carolina backed down.

However, nullification and secession soon resurfaced as southern responses to efforts to outlaw slavery. Taney's conservative Court, dominated by southern justices, in effect reaffirmed the constitutionality of slavery in *Dred Scott v. Sandford* (1857), a decision (discussed in Chapter 16) that outraged both abolitionists and supporters of the national government.[14]

This shift was reinforced in the Reconstruction era after the war, as Congress passed civil rights enforcement laws and Republican-dominated legislatures, supported by Union troops, passed progressive legislation in southern states. Three constitutional amendments designed to weaken state power were also passed and ratified: the Thirteenth (1865), which outlawed slavery; the Fourteenth (1868), which guaranteed all persons "equal protection of the laws" and protection against any state's efforts to "deprive any person of life, liberty, or property, without due process of law"; and the Fifteenth (1870), which prohibited denying the right to vote "on account of race, color, or previous condition of servitude."

As Reconstruction ended and freewheeling capitalism gained political strength, power began to swing back toward states' rights in what is sometimes called the era of mature dual federalism. The Supreme Court regularly held unconstitutional congressional efforts to regulate business—efforts which ranged from setting a national minimum wage to abolishing child labor. In *Hammer v. Dagenhart* (1918), which declared the Child Labor Act of 1916 unconstitutional,

Chief Justice Roger B. Taney, author of the doctrine of dual federalism.

the Court explicitly endorsed the doctrine of dual federalism, arguing that "the grant of authority over a purely federal matter was not intended to destroy the local power always existing and carefully reserved to the States in the Tenth Amendment."[15]

The First World War led to the national government's taking on new roles, including expanded federal financial **grants-in-aid**—payments to the states to finance such specified state activities as agriculture, vocational education, and highway construction. (The first federal grant-in-aid had been made in 1887.) These programs had the inevitable result: greater federal aid resulted in increased federal control over the states. But the postwar era saw another decline in federal government activism under Republican free-market-oriented administrations.

Cooperative Federalism, 1933–1961

A drastic and unprecedented centralization of power occurred as a result of the economic crisis of the 1930s, and a new era of **cooperative federalism**, in which the national government and the states functioned as complementary parts of a single governmental mechanism, began. In the throes of the Great Depression, Americans looked to Washington for help, and President Franklin D. Roosevelt and the Congress responded with the New Deal, a package of programs to stimulate the economy and create jobs. At first the Supreme Court ruled virtually all of these programs unconstitutional because they involved unprecedented roles for government in the economy. Increasingly, it became clear that the Court was so much at odds with the mood of the country that it could not preserve its authority without accepting this stronger swing of the pendulum toward Washington. And when FDR threatened to "pack the Court" by adding enough liberal members to make a majority for his programs—something he could do with the consent of the Congress because the number of justices is set by law, not by the Constitution—the Court reversed its position and began to declare New Deal programs constitutional. Indeed, in *United States v. Darby Lumber Co.* (1941), which upheld the central government's power to regulate wages in the timber industry, the Court declared that the Tenth Amendment "states but a truism that all is retained which has not been surrendered."[16]

Meanwhile, a new pattern of cooperation between the national government and the states was emerging. From 1932 to 1934, federal grants of funds to states and localities quadrupled, and these grants continued to increase as the depression persisted. Among the new programs were national grants for state and local unemployment and welfare programs and national aid for local publicly financed housing. World War II (1941–1945) cemented the

Workers in the depths of the Great Depression in 1935 widen a street in a federally funded Works Progress Administration program during the era of cooperative federalism, characterized by expanding federal grants to states and localities.

strong role of the federal government in most aspects of life—a role that persisted after the war as the Supreme Court became increasingly active in extending civil rights and civil liberties (as we'll see in Chapters 15 and 16).

Creative Federalism, 1961–1969

In the 1960s cooperation between Washington and the states dramatically increased, and with it the national government became even more dominant in the federal system. The large flow of funds from Washington to the states that had begun with the New Deal swelled under President Lyndon Johnson's Great Society, especially with the wide array of innovative domestic economic policies he called the War on Poverty.

The Great Society programs were launched at the same time that the nation was waging war in Vietnam. President Johnson and the Congress were unwilling to raise taxes to fund these initiatives, given the growing unpopularity of the Vietnam war, preferring to borrow the money, even though that increased the federal deficit. States and cities were, of course, delighted to receive more funds from Washington.

The number of grant programs to states under Johnson's **creative federalism** expanded from about 50 in 1961 to some 420 by the time he left office in 1969. Many of these were **categorical grant programs**—programs that specify the category of activity (such as sewer construction or public housing) on which states and cities are to spend the grant funds and that include detailed regulations, written in Washington, about how the programs are to be carried out. One way Johnson sought to control the programs was to bypass the existing political institutions in states and cities, which were controlled by governors and mayors, and put school districts, nonprofit organizations, and other new and more flexible bodies more sympathetic to the innovative programs in charge. This arrangement has been called "third-party federalism," because programs were executed by third parties rather than the traditional political actors.[17]

President Lyndon Johnson talks with a citizen of Inez, Kentucky, in a 1964 trip promoting his War on Poverty, during the era of creative federalism.

New Federalisms, 1969 to the Present

Presidents since Johnson have consistently sought to return some power to the states, although their approaches have varied with their ideologies and previous experiences. The Republican presidents—Nixon, Ford, Reagan, and Bush—have been conservatives committed to the view that power rightly belongs at the state level, while the two Democrats elected during this period—Carter and Clinton—were former governors who believed that states tended to be more creative, more sensitive to local and regional needs, and more effective than the national government in designing and implementing programs.

Nixon's New Fiscal Federalism, 1969–1977

Many state and local political officials resented being cut out of the process that distributed federal funds to their citizens during the Great Society. They watched helplessly as other leaders—often their political adversaries—dispensed jobs and aid and gained local political power. Most state and local leaders therefore welcomed President Nixon's "new federalism." Its centerpiece was **revenue sharing**, in which the federal government shared money it raised through taxing or borrowing with the states and localities, primarily by providing **block grants**. Block grants consolidated various specific categorical grants into a single sum and gave states and localities more discretion over how to allocate funds within each general area, such as urban development. Liberals and many Democrats in Congress opposed revenue sharing because it decreased the power of the federal government to set priorities; it was in their political interest to continue the almost five hundred existing categorical grants, which made their recipients—especially the poor and disadvantaged, both traditional Democratic constituencies—beholden to them. However, most of the 50 states and many of the 80,000 local governments lobbied hard for the proposed revenue sharing, and it passed Congress in 1972. The program produced $30 billion in block grants over its first four years, and another $26 billion over the next four years after its renewal in 1976. In 1980, in the face of growing economic problems, Congress agreed to cut states from the program but continued to fund localities. However, by 1986, revenue sharing was dead, a victim of fears of growing federal spending deficits. Figure 3.2 portrays the changing scale of federal aid to state and local governments.

Categorical federal grants continued after the demise of revenue sharing. However, as concerns for environmental protection and economic development increased, expanding government programs increasingly overlapped and federal regulation became more complex. The result was growing pressure for more efficiency in what is now usually called **intergovernmental relations**.

The case of fire-fighting, which had long been a local function, illustrates the problem. In 1960, the only federal agency fighting fires was the Forest Service. But over the next 20 years Congress created so many new agencies and new grant programs that when it took office in 1981 the Reagan administration found no fewer than 49 federal agencies involved in state and local fire protection programs. These included parts of every cabinet department except State and Defense, along with 11 other independent federal agencies. Together, they administered 52 grant programs for fire-fighting.[18] The Carter administration sought to foster greater cooperation between states and the national government while limiting new programs, and then the Reagan administration decided it was time to get the spiraling federal bureaucracy under control by making severe cutbacks.

Reagan's New Regulatory Federalism, 1981–1989

Ronald Reagan took office in 1981 pledging to institute a new version of what he, like Nixon before him, called "new federalism."[19] He promised to reduce federal regulation of business and return more responsibilities to the states and localities.[20] Twelve months later, his administration had successfully slashed federal aid to states and cities and enacted nine new block grants to give states and cities a freer hand in spending the federal aid that survived Reagan's budgetary ax. Reagan also cut back federal regulation of industry, allowing states to reclaim that power if they chose to do so.

However, Reagan's attempts to return power to the states met with growing resistance as the country slid into recession. Congress balked at proposed grant cuts in Reagan's second year. At the same time, businesses began complaining that as federal regulation decreased, they found themselves facing different regulations in different states. They began to lobby for renewed standardized federal regulation, especially in areas such as consumer-product safety and trucking.

preemption
This term, from the Latin for *to put aside before considering*, refers to the practice by which a national law automatically *preempts* or supersedes any state law on the same subject if Congress so intends.

Figure 3.2
The pattern of federal aid to states and local governments

This figure depicts the size of federal grants-in-aid to states and cities and also shows them as a percentage of state and local spending.

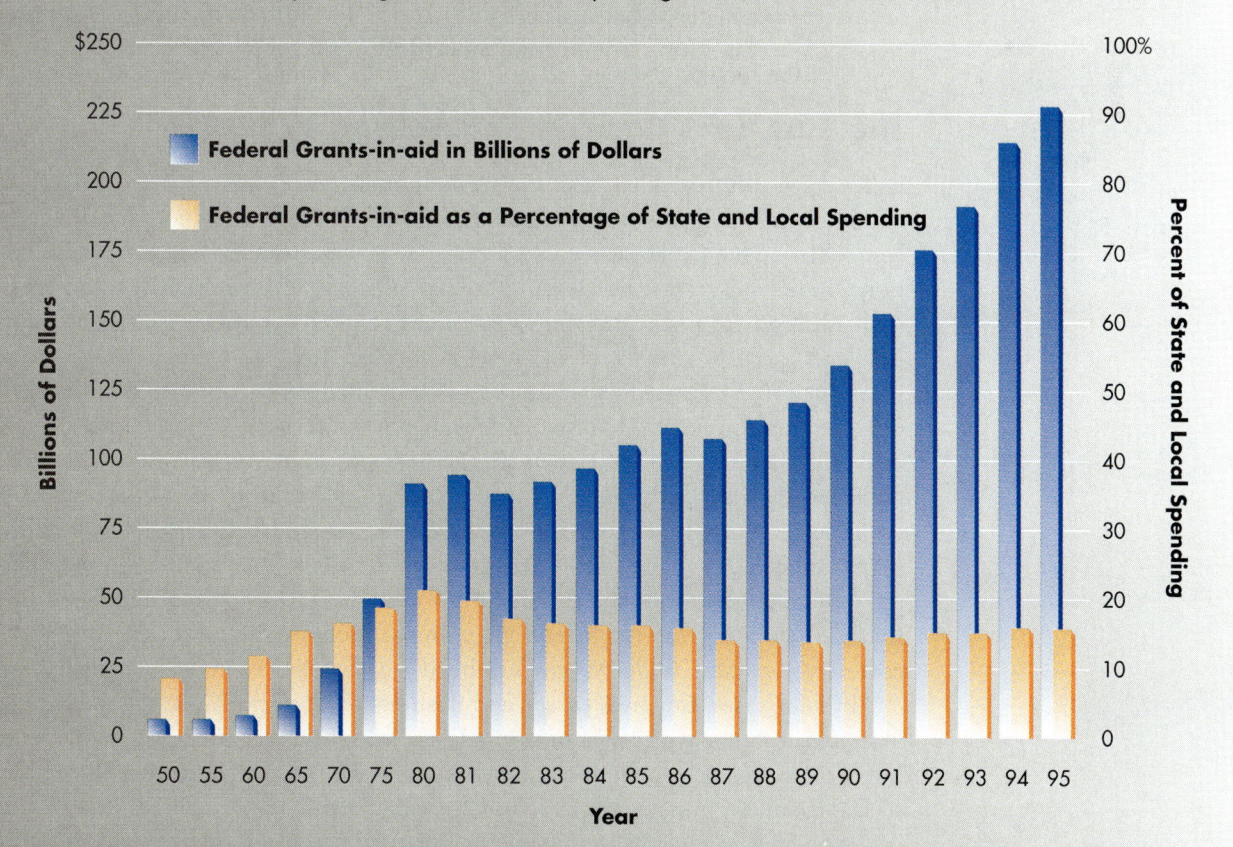

- Federal Grants-in-aid in Billions of Dollars
- Federal Grants-in-aid as a Percentage of State and Local Spending

Source: Advisory Commission on Intergovernmental Relations.

The device for such standardizing federal regulation was **preemption**—the principle whereby national law automatically takes precedence over state laws on the same subject. The auto interests invoked preemption in arguing in the lemon law case that the federal Warranty Act superseded state laws on the issue.[21] During the Reagan years Congress expressly preempted state and local regulation on 91 programs, extending even to raising the legal age for drinking of alcoholic beverages, and enacted 16 new regulatory laws.[22]

The Supreme Court also seemed to disagree with the Reagan attitude toward federalism. In its 1985 decision in *Garcia v. San Antonio Metropolitan Transit Authority*, the Court required the city of San Antonio to abide by federal employment regulations just like a private business.[23] The Court said that states and cities do retain sovereign authority but cannot appeal to the Tenth Amendment to protect it. Instead, their sovereign authority is protected by the structure of the federal government itself—especially the representative structure of Congress. States are represented directly in the Senate and indirectly in the House, it argued, so they must protect their interests through their representatives in Congress. This ruling struck fear into states and cities unsure of how far the Court would go.

Ultimately, the so-called Reagan Revolution had surprisingly little lasting effect on either spending or regulation. By the time the recession ended, tax cuts and large increases in military spending and domestic programs such as Medicare and Social Security had produced skyrocketing federal deficits that made new initiatives in fiscal federalism impossible. The greatest lasting impact of the Reagan years was a change in thinking at the state and local levels. As the federal deficit became a hot political issue, states and cities stopped expecting Washington to solve their problems and instead became major innovators in policy areas ranging from public education through criminal justice to child care.[24]

The Bush Era's Coercive Federalism, 1989–1993

A new recession struck early in the Bush administration while the federal deficit continued to mount, with the result that neither the president nor the Congress controlled by the Democrats could justify departures from the Reagan era limitations on federal grants. However, growing pressures for new regulation in areas such as the environment and workplace safety resulted in more legislative preemption and a sharp increase in the newest popular tool: **mandates**. Traditionally, when the federal government required, or mandated, states or cities to undertake new programs in health, welfare, environmental protection, or other areas, it had provided the funds to pay for them. In the Bush era, however, because of the enormous federal deficits, the federal government required that states or cities come up with the necessary funds to carry out these federal mandates themselves. Because states and cities usually can't borrow and run deficits in their annual budgets like the federal government, they were forced to raise state and local taxes. As **unfunded mandates** from the federal government soon accounted for up to 60 percent of many states' budgets, critics dubbed Bush's policy **coercive federalism**.[25]

In some cases, Congress passed and Bush signed new mandates, including large increases in state payments of medical aid to the poor under Medicaid, along with major increases in air pollution control (in the Clean Air Act Amendments) and in special facilities for the handicapped (in the Americans with Disabilities Act). These new mandates were added to ongoing mandates dating from the Reagan era to re-

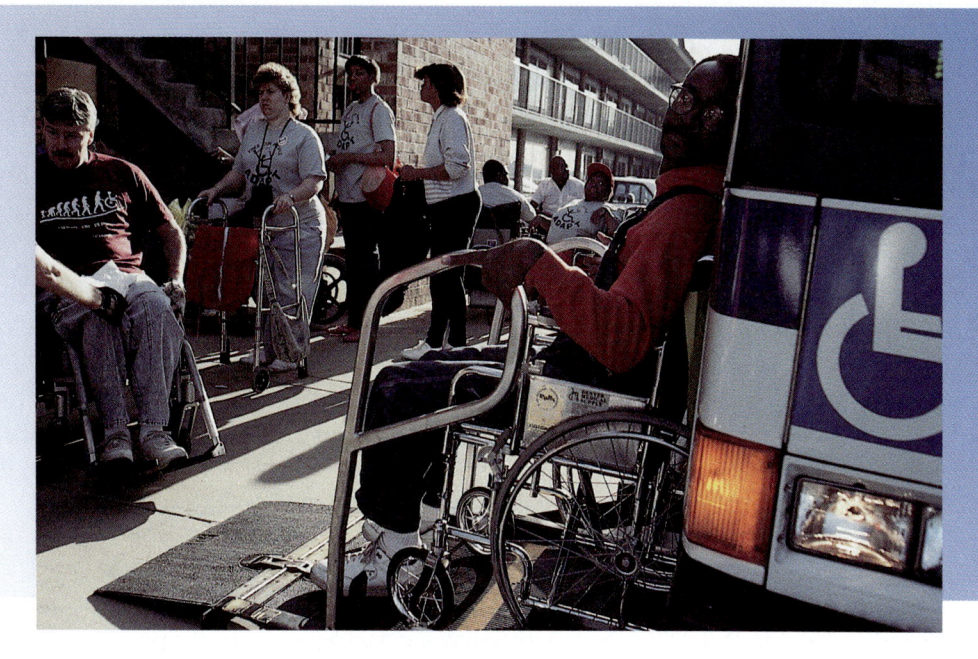

Disabled individuals board a special bus on their way to a 1991 demonstration at national Social Security headquarters to protest their treatment after passage of the Americans with Disabilities Act of 1990.

move asbestos from schools, to clean public drinking water supplies, and to furnish transportation for the disabled. These mandates alone, in coming years, were projected to cost tens of billions of dollars of state and local—not federal—funds.

On top of these legislative mandates, the Bush administration used its own regulatory powers to impose still other mandates on states and cities, such as requiring "drug-free workplaces."[26] In turn, states increasingly adopted Washington's strategy and mandated that their cities undertake certain programs—particularly employee pension, health, and environmental programs—without furnishing the required funds, thereby replicating in cities the same economic difficulties and political distress that had plagued states.[27]

While Washington wielded its mandate "stick," it also increasingly used grants as "carrots" to entice states to adopt particular policies. An example of this "carrot federalism" is the 1992 program passed by Congress to reduce deaths caused by drunk drivers—nearly half of all auto-related deaths. The program offers up to $20 million in grants to a state that adopts tougher drunk-driving laws, such as stricter standards for determining when drivers are legally intoxicated, stricter enforcement of the 21-year-old drinking age, and the taking of licenses of drivers convicted of two drunk-driving offenses within 30 days.[28]

Meanwhile, the Supreme Court had begun to move away from the implications of its decision in *Garcia*, acting to protect some state legislation in the face of claims of federal preemption, as it did in the lemon law case. In 1991 it decided that the federal Age Discrimination in Employment Act did not preempt Missouri's constitutional requirement that state judges retire at the age of 70.[29] The Court justified this limit on the congressional power to preempt by returning to the Tenth Amendment, saying, "As every schoolchild learns, our Constitution establishes a system of dual sovereignty between the states and the federal government," and adding, "In the tension between federal and state power lies the promise of liberty." This language seems to echo the judicial philosophy of dual federalism, in which the Court played the role of a balancer of power in the federal system.

Moreover, the Court also held constitutional certain state and local laws that some argued violated provisions of the Bill of Rights. For example, in 1991 the Court upheld a Michigan law requiring mandatory jail terms for particular crimes, as well as a city ordinance in South Bend, Indiana, forbidding nude dancing.[30] Opponents of these laws had argued that they violated longstanding judicial interpretations of the Eighth Amendment's prohibition of "cruel and unusual punishments" and the First Amendment's protection of freedom of expression.

The Court's recent willingness to limit the federal preemption power has not been lost on environmentalists. They have taken to lobbying governments in states and cities with populations sympathetic to their goals for stricter environmental protection than Congress is willing to pass, hoping that the Court will deny preemption. This strategy proved successful in the Court's 1991 ruling in a case that arose in Casey, Wisconsin, a town of 401 people, which had required a permit for anyone to apply any pesticide to either public or private property in order to protect its shallow well water. When it refused to grant such permits, a local landowner sued on grounds that less strict state and federal laws preempted the local law. The Supreme Court held that the Federal Insecticide, Fungicide and Rodenticide Act of 1972 does not preempt stricter regulation of pesticides and chemical lawn care products by local governments.[31] Environmentalists have also gotten stricter local regulations on disposable bottles and plastic containers passed in cities across the country—regulations that are increasingly holding up in court. For example, it is now illegal to sell certain foods in plastic bottles or plastic cups in St. Paul, Minnesota, and many cities require that toilet paper, paper towels, and newspapers sold within the city limits contain recycled materials.

Meanwhile, states and cities seeking to attract new industry and more jobs are refusing to take stringent steps to protect the environment. Such differences in policy priorities, which the federal system permits, are producing what some are calling **competitive federalism**,[32] in which states and cities with differing policies actively compete with each other for citizens and businesses and the increased tax base they provide. Some believe that this competition, with the diversity it produces, is healthy for the country. Critics argue that the interests of some citizens—usually the least powerful—will suffer when those of other citizens or the interests of business are favored. But supporters of increased diversity respond that federalism has its own correcting mechanism: the mobility of citizens, who can move to another state with more favorable policies if they don't like the policies where they are.[33] However, the poorest citizens in central cities and rural areas are often the least mobile and usually the least able to protect their interests politically.

Many states' rights conservatives have welcomed the trend toward growing diversity and competition among states on the grounds that it strengthens federalism by expanding states' rights. Others argue that this trend will chop up what has been an increasingly national marketplace in which the same goods have been available everywhere. If it does require business and industry to produce and sell different products and services in different parts of the country, the result is likely to be less diversity of products for consumers in any given location and higher costs for all. Some say that this trend violates the Constitution's commerce-clause promise of a nationwide free market, while others counter that it allows states (and their home-rule cities) to exercise their federalism-given rights to regulate business and protect the environment as they see fit.[34]

As the U.S. Supreme Court ceased carving out new rights for citizens, many state courts became more rights-conscious, making increasing use of the bills of rights in the state constitutions. In what some call the new judicial federalism, state courts have declared more than seven hundred state laws in violation of the state bills of rights—a practice that was very rare until the 1970s.[35] Supreme Court Justice William J. Brennan wrote in 1986 that the "rediscovery by state supreme courts of the broader protections afforded their own citizens by their state constitutions . . . is probably the most important development in constitutional jurisprudence in our time."[36] It is a development made possible by the fact that we have a federal system judicially as well as executively and legislatively.

Meanwhile, the Supreme Court has continued to defend state interests. In *New York v. United States* (1992) it held that Congress had crossed the line separating acceptable encouragement and unconstitutional coercion in requiring any state that did not provide a site for disposing of low-level nuclear waste to become the "owner" of any such waste created within its borders and be responsible for any damage caused by the waste.[37] The Tenth Amendment, it held, prohibited Congress from compelling the states to enact or administer what was in fact a federal program. Then, in *United States v. Lopez* (1995) the Supreme Court invalidated a federal law prohibiting the possession of guns in or near schools, arguing that Congress had gone too far in using its powers under the commerce clause (with the claim that guns are sold interstate) for this regulatory purpose.[38]

States increasingly used these decisions, and the anticoercion principle underlying them, to argue against the Brady Handgun Control Act of 1994, which required local law-enforcement officials to perform background checks on purchasers of handguns during a five-day waiting period without providing the necessary funds. The Supreme Court held this provision unconstitutional in 1997 in *Printz v. United States* (Chapter 15).

The Clinton Administration's Reinventing Federalism, 1993–

Bill Clinton assumed the presidency after serving for more than a decade as governor of Arkansas. He sympathized with the objectives of many federal regulatory programs but objected to the inflexibility of federal guidelines and the burden unfunded federal mandates put on states and localities. His campaign had promised to "reinvent government" at the national level—making it more efficient, more creative, more flexible, and more responsive. Once in office, he endorsed a set of principles designed to "reinvent federalism" by reinvigorating the federal-state-local partnership, among them:

- establishing national goals and then allowing states and localities flexibility in choosing the means to achieve them—steering rather than propelling
- waiving national guidelines to enable states and communities to design their own approaches to problem-solving rather than following national guidelines
- coordinating and combining various national programs into broader, more flexible programs
- assuming more fiscal responsibility for problems that fall within the national government's legal or constitutional responsibility
- limiting unfunded federal mandates on state and local governments
- helping states and localities to learn from each others' successes.[39]

The White House Home Page on the World Wide Web, a gateway to the special page devoted to Clinton Administration efforts to reinvent federalism.

devolution
This term, from the Latin for *moving* or *falling away from*, refers to the movement of governing power down from the national government to the lower levels, especially states and localities.

The Clinton administration quickly began granting waivers for experimental deviations from standard federal programs in such areas as health insurance and welfare reform, and it developed more flexible programs in areas such as crime control. Setting national goals, however, proved more difficult because of big and growing differences over *what's right* in most policy areas. And Clinton's failure to get comprehensive health-care reform passed by Congress despite enormous effort only served to emphasize the political difficulty of reinventing federalism. After the Republican sweep of Congress in 1994, a compromise was reached on limiting unfunded mandates. However, that bill did not roll back any existing unfunded mandates, and because it applied only to new legislation, its impact was limited from the start.[40]

Only time will tell whether the latest efforts of politicians and citizens at each level of the federal system will produce significant **devolution** of power from the national level to the states. Table 3.4 summarizes the key features of each stage in the evolution of American federalism.

TABLE 3.4

The Stages of American Federalism

Period	Name	Characteristics
1836–1933	Dual federalism	States and national government sovereign and therefore equal; relations between them characterized by tension rather than collaboration; national government gains strength because of role in promoting economic growth
1933–1961	Cooperative federalism	Federal-state-local sharing of responsibilities for almost all functions; steady growth of national government's powers, especially regulation
1961–1969	Creative federalism	President Johnson's emphasis on partnership of national government, states, cities, counties, school districts, nonprofit organizations; many new programs with many grants made directly to cities
1969–1977	New fiscal federalism	President Nixon's emphasis on decentralization, revenue sharing
1977–1981	Partnership federalism	President Carter's efforts to foster greater cooperation between states and national government while limiting new programs
1981–1989	New regulatory federalism	President Reagan's emphasis on cutting back federal government's role and increasing efficiency; end of revenue sharing
1989–1993	Coercive federalism	President Bush's use of unfunded mandates and preemption to influence state and local conduct
1993–	Reinventing federalism	President Clinton's emphasis on greater efficiency and responsiveness, with national government steering but state and local governments providing the motor; limitations on unfunded mandates and provision of waivers to encourage state experimentation

Democracy, Federalism, and the Future

Federalism was a controversial innovation two centuries ago, and its practice continues to be debated today. Politicians and academics still assess the advantages and disadvantages of a federal system, its effects on American democracy, and possible reforms.

Advantages and Disadvantages of Federalism

For two hundred years, supporters of federalism have argued that one of its great virtues is its tendency to preserve regional diversity. The Framers certainly thought that each state would—and should—construct its own "moral commonwealth," with its own rules regulating voting and marriage, for example, while the national government took on the task of directing foreign relations and facilitating commerce.[41]

Tensions and Inequities

But in practice, the federal system has rarely been harmonious. To the extent that federalism continues to preserve each state's right to maintain its own "moral commonwealth," it may also preserve inequities—in economic opportunities, in freedom of expression, in education, in the availability of health care and abortions. Since the 1960s especially, tensions over federalism have focused on the national government's efforts to engineer social change, as some might put it, or, as others might express it, to protect the civil rights of groups such as ethnic minorities as well as the civil liberties of individuals, including dissenters and even alleged criminals.

Madison's fears that majorities in small local units would deprive minorities of their rights had been realized, for example, in segregation laws in place throughout the South by the end of the nineteenth century. When, starting in the 1950s, action to overturn these laws and their effects came at the national level—in Supreme Court decisions and orders, in congressional legislation, in federal mandates, even in presidential orders to send federal troops—resisters turned again to states' rights as the principle that justified their actions. (For a full discussion of these issues, see Chapters 15 and 16.)

Who has the power to decide *what's right*? Should the national government impose a "moral commonwealth" on states and localities? Should states and localities be able to define and defend local practice even when it conflicts with national policies or interferes with the rights of some individuals? This basic question has rippled through all the hot political issues of past decades—busing, abortion, school prayer, affirmative action, pornography, and, most recently, homosexual marriage. For an account of this very controversial issue, see the box nearby.

Political Actors Disagree

In the Western world, marriage has long been defined as the joining together of a man and a woman by church or state. Governments have often provided special benefits to married couples—especially those with children. Today, however, couples of the same sex are seeking the right to marry and obtain the same legal recognition and benefits heterosexual couples receive. These include family insurance and health benefits, joint tax returns and tax breaks, family visitation privileges in hospitals, and automatic inheritance rights.

Conservatives committed to defending the traditional definition of marriage have been organizing and lobbying lawmakers to prevent the recognition of same-sex marriage rights. In the words of religious broadcaster and former Republican presidential candidate Pat Robertson, "Marriage defined as a man and a woman has been around more than 6,000 years and has served most cultures very well." And a spokesperson for the conservative Family Research Council in Washington, D.C., remarks: "The onus should not be on those defending marriage but on the tiny minority of people who are attempting to radically redefine it. I, for one, won't submit to the tactic of portraying tradition-minded Americans as radicals and close-minded bigots."[1]

In 1993 the Supreme Court of the State of Hawaii ruled that the state's refusal to grant marriage licenses to three gay couples violated the state constitution's explicit prohibition of discrimination on the basis of gender. The court said that unless the state could show compelling reasons for restricting marriage to heterosexuals, this discrimination would have to end. The Hawaii legislature responded by passing a law in 1994 stating that marriage licenses must be restricted to "man-woman units" capable of procreation. However, the state supreme court ruled that this law violated the state constitution.

Critics of this decision feared that gay couples from other states would travel to Hawaii to marry with the expectation—or at least the hope—that their home states would have to recognize their Hawaiian marriages. Why would a marriage license issued in Hawaii under Hawaiian law be legal in another state that does not have a law allowing same-sex marriages? Because Article IV of the U.S. Constitution requires that "full faith and Credit shall be given in each State to the Public Acts, Records and judicial Proceedings of every other State." Just as states must recognize birth certificates and driver's licenses issued by other states, they must also recognize marriage licenses or divorce decrees issued by other states, according to some legal experts. Years ago, Nevada had laws allowing rapid and relatively easy divorce while other states had more demanding divorce requirements. As a result, people seeking a quick divorce went to Nevada, knowing that their home states would have to recognize their Nevada divorces when they returned because of this provision in the federal Constitution.

Defining Marriage

Conservative activists working through organizations such as the Christian Coalition, Concerned Women for America, and Eagle Forum have been pressing state legislators across the country to explicitly outlaw same-sex marriages. They hope that the courts will exempt their states from having to recognize such marriages performed in another state on grounds that they would violate the state's public policies defined by law. By 1997, eight states had laws explicitly outlawing same-sex marriages, and 30 states had laws describing marriage as a civil contract between a man and a woman.

Responding to the same pressures in an election year, the U.S. Congress passed the Defense of Marriage Act in 1996. This law was intended to "inoculate" states against having to recognize same-sex marriages occurring in other states as well as bar federal recognition of same-sex marriages and preclude the granting of federal spousal benefits such as Social Security and veterans' benefits to same-sex marrieds. Opponents of same-sex marriages argued that the act's "inoculation" of other states from the possible requirement that they recognize same-sex marriages performed in any state was constitutional because the second part of the "full-faith-and-credit" article of the Constitution says that "Congress may by general Laws prescribe . . . the Effect" of the article on the states. A U.S. Supreme Court test of this act by supporters of same-sex marriage is likely.

Conservatives are outraged at the possibility that a handful of unelected judges in the state of Hawaii could have the constitutional authority to say what marriage is for the majority of the country. In contrast, gays, lesbians, and their liberal supporters rejoice that these judges are using their state constitution to advance minority civil rights. Recall that the Framers insulated the judiciary from majority rule to protect judges from political pressure—though the Framers certainly never envisioned the prospect of same-sex marriage.

Efforts by political activists to redefine marriage show how deeply entrenched definitions create legally recognized groups or classifications—such as who gets to marry and who doesn't—that exclude some people. When such classifications are recognized and reinforced by public laws, the institution in question becomes a public as well as a private matter. When the classification scheme that reinforces the existing definition of marriage is upheld by public policy, those whom it excludes may petition government to demand their inclusion. Whether government responds to their demand often depends on how socially sensitive the issue is. Legislatures, which have the closest ties to the public of any branch of government, are often reluctant to alter a classification if doing so would strongly offend their constituents. Thus groups seeking expanded civil rights often turn for help to the courts, which are more insulated from public opinion, and the Constitution, which the courts interpret and apply.

The debate over same-sex marriage involves states' rights, congressional power, and ultimately the authority of the Supreme Court in yet another illustration of the ways in which the federal structure of government in the United States affects people's everyday lives.[2]

---

[1] Both quotations from David W. Dunlap, "Fearing a Toehold for Gay Marriages, Conservatives Rush to Bar the Door," *New York Times*, March 6, 1996.
[2] See John P. Feldmeier, "Federalism and Full Faith and Credit: Must States Recognize Out-of-State Same-Sex Marriages?" *Publius* 25, no. 4 (Fall 1995): 107–126.

The national government relies on the supremacy clause and the Fourteenth Amendment for the authority to dictate policies protecting those who are discriminated against regionally or locally. In recent decades, it has also employed mandates to make state and local governments administer—and sometimes design—programs, such as health care (through Medicaid) and compensatory education for the handicapped,[42] that redistribute resources from the rich to the poor. Such programs are usually intended to produce greater equality—a goal often more favored at the national level than at lower levels of government.

Duplication and Competition

The fact that most of the current challenges facing states and cities—economic development, education, environmental protection—do not respect state or local boundaries should generate collaboration among governments at different levels. But problem-solving in a federal context sometimes generates competition instead.

Because a policy adopted at any level of the federal system can affect the others, governments themselves become lobbyists, seeking to influence policy decisions at each level. Policies once adopted are usually implemented in parallel bureaucracies at national and state levels of government and also often in a third bureaucracy at the local level, in what some now call substate federalism.[43] Some argue that this duplication of agencies and efforts is wasteful, while others praise its sensitivity to regional or local conditions.

Participation and Innovation

Even though the Framers of the Constitution did not intend the federal system to be democratic, it gradually evolved in that direction under social, economic, and political pressures. In the process, opportunities for citizens and interest groups to participate multiplied. Points of entry into the system include not only national, state, and city governments but also other local governmental units such as counties and school districts (see Table 3.1.) Supreme Court Justice Louis D. Brandeis (served 1916–1939) pointed out that states and localities, which vary so much among themselves, can serve as "laboratories of democracy." They can experiment with new systems of governance and participation, and their learning by doing can be instructive to others. Many states are now engaged in such experimentation in health-care delivery and welfare reform, among other policy areas.

The differing regional political cultures[44] have also served as fertile ground for the development of political parties, interest groups, and policies that have achieved national influence and brought new participants into American politics. This process has been slow and difficult, of course, first for the propertyless urban white males who lacked the vote at the time of the founding, and then for the women and minorities so long excluded.

Consider the question of how citizens are represented in Congress and in state legislatures. Today we take it for granted that political representation should be based on population, so that a big city elects more representatives to a state legislature or to Congress than a small town. But in the early decades of the new nation, representation in the lower house of most states was based on territory and each city or county was allocated a single representative regardless of its population. At the time the theory was that each territorial unit was a community with its own homogeneous identity and interests, and each unit could therefore be adequately represented by a single individual. The goal was to get a city or town's particular viewpoint expressed in reasoned debate in the legislature, where it would be considered by all present before a decision was reached. Gradually, however, the objective of state politics shifted from making sure that distinctive viewpoints were expressed to weighting each viewpoint's expression by the number of people who held it. So states began shifting the basis for deciding how many representatives to elect from the number of geographical units to the number of white male adults or of taxable inhabitants. No state yet used total population to determine how many representatives would be elected and how big each electoral district would be, however.

The systems by which elections to the U.S. House of Representatives were structured also varied. Some states allowed all eligible (which meant white male and, in some states, property-owning) voters to cast a ballot for all of the state's representatives (called at-large voting). Other states created electoral districts with different-sized populations, each of which elected one representative. Not until 1842 did Congress finally pass a law requiring that elections to the House be by district, with each eligible citizen voting for only one representative.

In effect, the current approach to representation evolved by a process of experimentation and learning by doing in the various states—something that could only occur because the federal structure of the government encouraged each state to decide how to organize itself politically. The system that eventually emerged, in which representation in the House is based primarily on population rather than territory, is grounded in the individual rather than the community. When the electoral system was based on area or territory, it was hard to accommodate the interests of rapidly growing populations and new towns. The shift to a system based on population made political strength rather than community interest the accepted basis of politics.[45] With the expansion of the federal political system that resulted, politics changed and democracy evolved.

What's Right? Competing Visions of Federalism

What's the right way to structure the distribution of power among the national government, the state governments, and the people in a federal system? Three major visions of federalism now compete for the allegiance of the people and the politicians.

The Liberal Vision

From the New Deal through the Great Society, and until the Reagan Revolution, the politically dominant view in national politics and in many states was liberalism. Its primary focus was on manipulating the economy to encourage job opportunity and financial security and, later on, protecting and strengthening individual or group rights to participate in government, the economy, and society. Liberals sought to strengthen the national government so that it could protect the people from severe economic downturns, compel state and local governments to extend rights of voting and access to public accommodations to those who had been deprived of them, and regulate business so that it treated employees and consumers—and the environment—better. In short, the liberal position was to let Washington do what it wished in virtually every area it wished to act in while protecting the individual liberties specified in the Bill of Rights from infringement by the national and the state levels of government.

The States' Rights Vision

The major alternative to liberalism has long been the view that the purpose of federalism should be to protect states' power from encroachment by the national government. This conservative view, which takes its roots to the Antifederalists and the southern Confederacy, is usually described rhetorically as an argument for states' rights, even though on reflection most would agree that only people have rights; states, instead, have powers. Its current manifestation is the view that each state should be allowed to do whatever it wants in any policy area, such as setting speed limits on interstate highways or establishing welfare programs, without interference from the national government—even if some exercises of state power produce outcomes not in harmony with widely supported national goals such as equality.

Montana highway workers remove a speed limit sign in 1995 after the federal speed limit was lifted by a congressional action, allowing each state to set its own regulations. Montana has no daytime limit.

The Libertarian Vision

Those who believe that the primary justification for federalism is to protect individual liberty from governmental interference, whether that be by the national or by the state governments, can be called libertarians (Chapters 4 and 5). Their goal is to prevent Washington and the states from doing most everything they wish to do, leaving or returning power and money as close to the people as possible—even if this means that economic or social equality declines when governments stop fostering it.[46]

What Works? Competing Approaches to Reforming Federalism

"Most debates over federalism are only lightly camouflaged debates over policy," one expert argues. "Citizens as well as political leaders consistently subordinate constitutional questions to immediate policy concerns."[47]

Most proposals for changing American federalism focus on shifting responsibility for particular policy areas such as welfare or medical care from the national to the state level of government or privatizing functions now carried out by government by turning them over to private businesses. Some emphasize the importance of strengthening citizenship by urging and training citizens to be more effective and responsible both in solving problems outside of government and in influencing their governments. The key to constructive changes in the federal system, some say, lies in decentralizing more political authority to the local level: "Unless citizens have the opportunity to solve problems within their own communities—an opportunity that centralized systems have largely destroyed—there is little reason to think that merely sending programs back to state and local governments will have much real impact."[48]

Democratic Reinventers Versus Republican Contractarians

The dominant debate in Washington recently has been between Clintonian Reinventers—those favoring reforming government to make it more efficient and responsive while preserving a major role for the national government in most policy areas—and Republican Contractarians—those favoring major cutbacks in virtually every domestic governmental program in order to shrink government and leave more policy decisions to the states, localities, and citizens.

This is partly a debate about *what's right*, as we've seen, with Republicans tending more toward states' rights than toward libertarianism and Democrats relinquishing some aspects of their liberalism but still favoring national governmental problem-solving rather than state, local, or individual freedom of action. However, because the United States is essentially a pragmatic country, the debate is increasingly focusing on questions of *what works*. The widespread and growing view that governmental approaches developed during the Great Depression no longer work today opened the way for the Republican counterattack on national government activism of the Reagan era and then the effort to execute the "Contract with America," a conservative campaign document endorsed by Republican House candidates before the 1994 elections. Despite strong rhetoric about cutting back government, however, the only major enacted Contract reform with implications for federalism was a limitation on unfunded mandates, as we saw above.

Proposed Constitutional Amendment

Fundamental institutional or structural changes are not as often considered seriously—in part because they generally require constitutional amendments. In 1993, however, the Republican governor of Utah, Michael Leavitt, and the Democratic governor of Nebraska, Benjamin Nelson, proposed that the states call a Conference of the States for the fall of 1995 in Philadelphia to propose constitutional amendments designed to achieve "a long-term leveling of power" between the national government and the states. The call was endorsed by the National Governors Association, the Conference of State Legislatures, and the Council of State Governments.

Foremost among their proposed amendments was one providing that a federal law could be repealed by a vote of two-thirds of the states' legislatures. Like all amendments proposed by Congress, however, this one would require a two-thirds majority in both houses of the U.S. Congress, which would be voting to limit its own legislative power, before it could be submitted to the states for ratification. However, the proposal for a Conference of the States drew opposition from the far right and organized labor, both fearful it might turn into a "runaway convention" like the one that met to amend the Articles of Confederation two hundred years ago but instead produced the Constitution. The diverse opposition eventually forced the organizers to cancel the conference, bringing at least a temporary end to efforts to reform federalism by constitutional amendment.

Toward Cyberspace Federalism?

American federalism was founded on a territorial basis, and it retains that geographical characteristic even today. Rapid developments in technology, however, have fostered such growth in economic, political, and informational interdependence around the globe that some doubt the continued relevance of territorial federalism—at least at the national level. Gradually, more and more political sovereignty may be transferred upward to transnational organizations such as the United Nations and the World Trade Organization—especially in policy areas such as environmental protection, regional peacekeeping, and international trade. This, after all, has already happened on a regional basis in Western Europe, where the member states have created the powerful transnational European Union.

Meantime, the electronic information revolution, ranging from satellite television to the Internet, is already giving citizens inexpensive access in their own homes to information sources located virtually everywhere in the world. Some say that we are now creating—almost without noticing it—a new **electronic frontier** to replace the geographical frontier that was so important in shaping the development of the United States into a continental

---

To access the Constitution, *The Federalist*, historical speeches, and even constitutions from around the world, go to:

http://www.santacruz.k12.ca.us/vft/constitution.html

To access the constitutions of virtually all of the states, go to either of the following sites:

http://www.findlaw.com/11stategove/indexconst.htm

http://www.iwc.com/entropy/marks/stcon.html

For various documents and articles on federalism, including the impact of federal policies on the states, go to the site maintained by the National Conference of State Legislatures:

http://www.ncsl.org/statfed/afipolicy.htm

For more philosophical materials on federalism and other topics, go to:

http://www.voxpop.org:80/jefferson

---

cyberspace

This term, developed from the Greek word for *control* and its English adaptation *cybernetics* (the science of control systems relying on feedback), refers to the nonterritorial space in which information flows without regard to political boundaries or geographical obstacles.

nation. This new frontier is circling the globe and, in the view of some, will increasingly tend to create a virtual global government of a nonterritorial state that some call "cyberspace" or "cyberia." Governments are having difficulty regulating this electronic global network (see Chapter 9). If they do not learn lessons from the American federalist experience about the importance of dividing governing power and responsibilities among appropriate levels of government, they may lose most of that power. The consequence may be a new **cyberspace federalism** in which more functions that have been performed by central governments shift, not to lower-level governments, but to loose electronic transnational networks and to individuals.

Today, the federal distribution of power is heavily influenced, if not shaped, by information—information that informs people everywhere of each other's interests and perspectives as a basis for cooperative, perhaps increasingly nongovernmental, action. In coming chapters, we'll see how profoundly territory and power have already shaped American politics and government, and we'll also find signs that the electronic information revolution is already doing the same.

Summary

When the Framers replaced the Confederation under the Articles with the Constitution's federal system, they divided sovereignty between two levels of government. Each individual then became a citizen of both the nation and a state, and had to obey each level within in its proper sphere of sovereignty.

The Constitution as interpreted by the Supreme Court gives the national government four types of powers: (1) *enumerated*—those specifically listed in the Constitution; (2) *concurrent*—those it shares with the states; (3) *implied*—those necessary for it to exercise its enumerated powers; and (4) *inherent*—those any country must have to function in world affairs. The states have certain powers *enumerated* in the Constitution, the unspecified powers *reserved* to them by the Tenth Amendment, and *concurrent* powers they share with the federal government. Localities depend for their powers on the states in which they are located (Dillon's Rule).

Chief Justice Marshall strengthened the national government in *Marbury v. Madison* (1803), which established judicial review, and *McCulloch v. Maryland* (1819), which asserted national supremacy while developing the doctrine of implied powers. Chief Justice Taney (served 1836–1864) presided over the beginning of the era of dual federalism, in which the Court mediated between two equal sovereignties. After the Civil War established that states could not secede and Reconstruction weakened the southern states, the era of mature dual federalism (1861–1932) featured growing national government involvement in economic growth.

In the era of cooperative federalism, the national government and the states cooperated to generate economic growth. In the 1960s the flow of federal money increased enormously with Johnson's Great Society categorical grant programs. Under Nixon's new fiscal federalism, *revenue sharing* gave states and cities more freedom in spending federal block grants. Reagan's new regulatory federalism reduced the federal role in regulating business and industry, but enormous budget deficits forced cancellation of revenue sharing. The Bush era emphasized *unfunded mandates* while increasing preemption of state laws also strengthened the national government. Meanwhile the Supreme Court began to limit the national government's mandate power while economic difficulties forced states and cities into competitive federalism to attract new business and industry. Clinton then sought to "reinvent" federalism, while new Republican majorities in Congress attempted to reassert states' rights.

Today most problems require cooperation among the levels of government. The levels preserve diversity among states, sometimes promoting innovation and sometimes obstructing progress. The proliferation of governments and bureaucracies gives citizens and interests more opportunities to participate in government and politics. Today the territorial basis of federalism is being eroded by electronic communications and the growth of the global economy and transnational organizations.

Key Terms

block grants **90**
categorical grant programs **89**
coercive federalism **92**
competitive federalism **94**
concurrent powers **79**
cooperative federalism **88**
creative federalism **89**
cyberspace federalism **104**
devolution **96**
Dillon's Rule **81**
dual citizenship **76**
dual federalism **87**
electronic frontier **103**
enumerated powers **78**
federal system **75**
federalism **75**
grants-in-aid **88**
home rule **81**
implied powers **79**
inherent powers **81**
intergovernmental relations **90**
mandates **92**
nullification **87**
preemption **91**
reserved powers **78**
revenue sharing **90**
states' rights **87**
supremacy clause **78**
unfunded mandates **92**

How You Can Learn More About American Federalism

Anton, Thomas. *American Federalism and Public Policy: How the System Works*. Philadelphia: Temple University Press, 1989. A study of the effects of federalism on actions of public officials shaping and implementing public policy.

Beer, Samuel. *To Make a Nation: The Rediscovery of American Federalism*. Cambridge, Mass.: Harvard University Press, 1993. A fascinating account of the history of the competing ideas of nationalism and federalism that influenced the theory and practice of American federalism.

Donahue, John D. *Disunited States*. New York: Basic Books, 1997. An argument by a former Labor Department policymaker that devolution of power to the states will undercut national interests and national values without increasing constructive innovation.

Elazar, Daniel. *American Federalism: A View from the States*, 3rd ed. New York: Harper & Row, 1984. An innovative examination of federalism and political culture, now a classic.

———*The American Mosaic: The Impact of Space, Time, and Culture on American Politics*. Boulder, Colo.: Westview, 1994. A stimulating broad view of the context of American federalism.

Hamilton, Lee C., and Donald T. Wells. *Federalism, Power, and Political Economy*. Englewood Cliffs, N.J.: Prentice Hall, 1990. A study of the economic dimensions of American federalism.

Peterson, Paul, Barry Rabe, and Kenneth K. Wong. *When Federalism Works*. Washington, D.C.: Brookings Institution, 1986. An evaluation of how federalism shapes policy on education, health care, and housing.

Publius: The Journal of Federalism, a quarterly journal of academic federalism studies with one issue each year on "The State of American Federalism."

Rivlin, Alice M. *Reviving the American Dream*. Washington, D.C.: Brookings Institution, 1992. A proposal to restructure both program responsibilities and revenue raising at the national, state, and local levels.

How Americans Practice Politics

PART 2

Political Culture and Socialization

ARE YOU POLITICALLY CORRECT?

Am I Guilty of Racism, Sexism, Classism? Am I Guilty of Ageism, Ableism, Lookism? Am I Logocentric? Do I Say 'Indian' Instead of 'Native American'? 'Pet' Instead of 'Animal Companion'? By John Taylor

ARE YOU POLITICALLY CORRECT?

Am I Misogynistic, Patriarchal, Gynophobic, Phallocentric, Logocentric? Am I Guilty of Racism, Sexism, Classism? Do I Say 'Indian' Instead of 'Native American'? 'Pet' Instead of 'Animal Companion'? By John Taylor

Parodying the notion of political correctness, the lead story in the January 21, 1991, issue of *New York* magazine, the editors circulated half the New York city edition with a man on the cover and the other half with a woman on the cover.

CHAPTER 4

Interior Minister of Lilliput: "But you're a Giant! A monster sent by our enemies to destroy us!"

Gulliver: "I'm not your enemy; I'm just different. . . ."

Minister: "Different! That makes you an enemy!"

Gulliver: "No, I'm different from you and you are different from me. So you see, we're both the same. That makes us equal. . . ."

Jonathan Swift, *Gulliver's Travels*

There is not only contestation about who can legitimately claim to be an American, but also what distinctive features—e.g. language, race, culture—constitute the heart of "American-ness."

Kristen Hill Maher[1]

American Political Culture

Political Socialization

Sources of Conflict in American Political Culture

Sources of Order in American Political Culture

Current Challenges to the American Political Culture

Revitalizing American Political Culture

"Are You Politically Correct?" demanded the cover of *New York* magazine, a popular weekly that often airs current political debates. This time the lead article was about *political correctness*, or *PC*—a derogatory term for language or behavior designed to avoid offending a particular group. The author, an opponent of PC, tells how two Harvard University professors, both well-known civil rights advocates, canceled their course on race relations after students accused them of racial insensitivity in the classroom.[2] One was accused of reading from the diary of a southern planter without giving equal time to the slaves' point of view.

The article explains that the professor, a nationally known expert in his field, had defended his actions by claiming that historians had found no diaries, journals, or letters by slaves. Apparently he was unaware that blacks had been writing, and books by blacks had been published, since the late eighteenth century. Former slaves as well as educated freemen and freewomen had produced a wide array of poetry, prose, memoirs, diaries, sermons, and petitions. Many had been collected in an anthology called *The Slave's Narrative*, published in 1985.[3] That book begins with this statement from historian Richard Hofstadter: "Any history of slavery must be written in large part from the standpoint of the slave"—a statement made in 1944!

The article accuses these students of promoting **multiculturalism**, a movement that gained popularity in the 1980s and early 1990s for its defense of cultural diversity.[4] The article describes multiculturalism as a "new fundamentalism" that threatens the First Amendment right to freedom of expression—in this instance, the right of the two professors to teach their course as they saw fit. But the students had a point. They called for multiple points of view, for telling the story of Columbus's "discovery" of America, for example, from the point of view of the native peoples who experienced it as an invasion. One-sided accounts of history distort facts, devalue the experience of disadvantaged peoples, and deprive all people of the knowledge they need to live in a more civil and democratic society.

This dispute at Harvard is only one among many heated debates in colleges and universities across the country over what new courses should be taught, what traditional courses should be dropped or modified, what ethnic studies programs and majors should be established, and whether teachers of multicultural courses should come only from the cultural groups those courses focus on. As one observer explains, "Academia is hotly contested terrain, and the stakes couldn't be higher. Who will decide what visions of reality young people will be exposed to? Who will become the officially recognized 'experts' advising policymakers in government and influencing public opinion by way of the mass media?"[5]

Conservatives such as William Bennett (secretary of education under Ronald Reagan), Lynne Cheney (head of the National Endowment for the Humanities under George Bush), and Allan Bloom (conservative political theorist, now deceased), have argued that multiculturalism—a perspective valuing and treating all cultures equally—is destroying Americans' faith in their common heritage and citizenship, which a civil society depends on. Liberal historian Arthur Schlesinger and liberals concerned with the breakdown of community have voiced similar concerns.[6] These critics point to religious, ethnic, and racial conflict in the world today—Catholics and Protestants in Northern Ireland; Serbs, Croats, and Muslims in the former Yugoslavia; Muslims and Hindus in India; and intertribal conflict in Africa—to show what weak citizenship bonds can cause.[7] Must multiculturalism's emphasis on ethnic origins and multiple perspectives lead to division?

This dispute over PC and multiculturalism is yet another example of politics understood as disputes over claims to the authority to decide *what is*, *what's right*, and *what works* with respect to American political culture. In this chapter we'll see how American political culture and political socialization influence people's views on these questions and how these views in turn influence disputes over what political culture and socialization *should be*. We'll do this by focusing on four key questions:

> **What are the functions of American political culture and socialization?**
>
> **What are the sources of conflict and order in American political culture?**
>
> **What major challenges does American political culture currently face?**
>
> **How can American political culture and socialization be revitalized?**

American Political Culture

A nation's **political culture** consists of widely shared beliefs and practices about *what is*, *what's right*, and *what works* in society and political life. The core values that hold American political culture together—freedom, democracy, justice, fairness (see the box nearby)—developed gradually out of a common language, laws, political institutions, religious and economic practices, territory, and history.

While there is a strong consensus on these values as abstract political principles, disputes abound over which values should prevail in practice. Government regularly intervenes to settle disputes in concrete situations where the same core value is being contested (freedom of the press often conflicts with a person's freedom to a fair trial, for example) and where core values conflict (as liberty and equality often do). But without the capacity to maintain social order and regulate change, government cannot settle such disputes. Thus the most important value that protects all other American values is the commitment to the rules that govern the political process itself—what we call constitutional practice in Chapter 2.

America's Core Values

Despite their diversity and changing lifestyles, Americans have always shared a small cluster of core values which have held them together as a people and as a nation. These values "are the *unum* in the national motto, *e pluribus unum* [out of many, one]—the unity amid the variety of American life."

- *Freedom*. Valuing political liberty, free speech, freedom of movement, freedom of religious worship, and other freedoms from constraints to the pursuit of private happiness.
- *Equality before the law*. Placing a high value on having the same rules of justice apply to one and all, rich and poor, black and white.
- *Equality of opportunity*. The practical expression of freedom and individualism in the marketplace, which helps to resolve the tensions between the values of freedom and equality.
- *Fairness*. Placing a high value on people getting what they deserve as the consequence of their own individual actions and efforts.
- *Achievement*. A belief in the efficacy of individual effort: the view that education and hard work pay off.
- *Patriotism*. Loyalty to the United States and dedication to the way of life it represents.
- *Democracy*. A belief that the judgment of the majority should form the basis of governance.
- *American exceptionalism*. A belief in the special moral status and mission of America.
- *Caring beyond the self*. Placing a high value on a concern for others such as family or ethnic group; neighborliness; caring for the community.
- *Religion*. A reverence for some transcendental meaning extending beyond the realm of the secular and practical.
- *Luck*. A belief that one's fortunes and circumstances are not permanent and that good fortune can happen to anyone at any time.

Source: Excerpted from Daniel Yankelovich, "How Changes in the Economy Are Reshaping American Values," in *Values and Public Policy*, ed. Henry J. Aron et al. (Washington, D.C.: Brookings Institution, 1994), 23–24.

Regulating Order and Change

A **nation** will thrive only if its people and their institutions successfully regulate pressures for order and change. A political culture strongly affects how much and what kind of order there will be in a society and how much authority government will have to uphold it. The more authority government has, the more influence it exerts over the political culture, and the more effective its regulation of order and change will be.

Why has American political culture been able to preserve the nation's identity while responding to pressures for change—pressures such as immigration, economic depression, war, struggles for social justice, technological advances, and, more recently, multiculturalism? One reason is that the common values, beliefs, and ambitions American political culture supports have withstood disputes over what it means to be "an American."

Americans, like the Framers, have understood that too much order leads to stagnation and too little order leads to chaos. They have come to view their political system as the ongoing process through which they express and reinvent themselves from one generation to the next. In this process, they expect some aspects of the political culture to change, such as the decline of racism and the rise of technology, just as they expect some aspects to stay the same, such as their commitment to the national community and its core values.

Americans also promote the **civility** required to address demands for order and change. Civility—a respect for social order—is crucial in a democracy, which must permit and protect the expression of different viewpoints, and it is especially crucial in a society as diverse as the United States. Equally indispensable are government institutions with enough authority to enforce that civility and manage those differences.

Many governments rely on indoctrination and coercion rather than civility as a means to achieve public order. As the example of Saddam Hussein's Iraq (among many others) has shown, some governments have tried to suppress or eradicate the religious, racial, or ethnic groups that threaten their authority. People who live in a society that is civil as well as democratic sometimes take its benefits for granted. But no political society achieves these benefits once and for all. They must be constantly nourished and tended or the legitimacy of the political system will break down.

Here is an Arab child enjoying Italian pizza in America. Is she an American? People disagree on what "American" means. According to some, an American is someone committed to the nation's core values, regardless of race, ethnicity, religion, gender, or class. In contrast, hate groups such as the Ku Klux Klan contend that only members of certain races, ethnic groups, and religions are "true Americans." Still others reject the notion that Americans share a common cultural or national community, and regard everyone who is a citizen as an American.

nation

A nation (from the Latin for "birth") is a group of people bound together by race, history, or circumstances that lead them to identify themselves as a *people*.

Maintaining Order Through Incremental Change

Order tends to predominate even in a dynamic political culture because most individuals are raised to honor their nation's dominant beliefs—beliefs which legitimate the authority of law and government. American political culture is stable because change tends to be orderly and *incremental*. Disturbances provoke corrective action, which may produce negative feedback and a new corrective action. There are important advantages to this step-by-step approach to change: (1) it does not overly threaten those who support the status quo; (2) it often placates those calling for change even if they dislike its slow pace; (3) it prevents costly mistakes resulting from abrupt and sweeping change; and (4) people generally believe that incremental policies have a realistic chance of working.

Both Democrats and Republicans appear to have lost faith in sweeping change. After the Clinton administration failed to make radical reforms in health care, it switched to a piecemeal approach to public policy. Its Families First program is dedicated to such uncontroversial goals as reducing teen pregnancy and providing tax credits for student loans. "It's incremental by design," explained Senate Minority Leader Tom Daschle (D.-S.D.). "We want it to be something that people can understand and believe can happen."[8] When voters signaled that the reforms in the 1994 Republican "Contract with America" were too drastic and reelected Clinton in 1996, they prompted promises of cooperation and moderation from both parties.

Some political observers worry that the national government has become the slave of incremental change rather than its master.[9] They predict that Washington will continue to change and to face wrenching policy choices but argue that it has lost the capacity to steer the country in new directions: "Having passed through a minimalist stage in its first 150 years and an expansive stage in its next 50, Washington has become what it will be: a large, incoherent, often incomprehensible mass" that is responsive to powerful special interests but incapable of "any broad, coherent program of reform." Others say that this view applies only to the internal workings of government and that dramatic changes can still come from outside shocks such as social movements, depression, and wars.[10] Which view is correct remains to be seen.

Protecting Diversity

If American political culture needs sameness—cultural cohesion—to maintain public order, it also needs difference—cultural diversity—to stimulate new ideas, experimentation, and change. The First Amendment, backed by government, protects people's right to differ in beliefs, values, and behavior within the bounds of civility. Protecting this right is a huge task in a nation where the laws protect both the individual and cultural diversity. The result is that government, no matter what it does or does not do, is constantly criticized by an array of political actors. Ironically, the individual and cultural diversity that American government is obligated to protect guarantees that it cannot please everyone.

Proponents of a strong national culture have long argued that there is too much diversity for government and democracy to handle, as the box nearby indicates. Today they blame the cracks in the political culture on the deterioration of the nuclear family, inadequate discipline in the schools, excessive immigration, economic dislocations, and multiculturalism. Some political scientists agree, saying that the country is undergoing a "culture war" in which some groups seek to assert their values or preferred beliefs and lifestyles over those of others.[11] They attribute this culture war partly to significant social change and partly to severe economic pressures in a complex and culturally diverse society. Multiculturalists warn that perpetuating a political system in which members of the dominant political culture typically decide public policy will ultimately fragment the political culture by alienating less powerful groups, such as minorities and women.

A Crisis of Democracy?

In the mid-1970s some political observers began to speak of a crisis of democracy. Democracy, they argued, was a weak and flawed form of government easily overwhelmed by demands for social change. An elite group of business leaders, politicians (including Jimmy Carter before he became president), and academics from the United States, Western Europe, and Japan formed an organization called the Trilateral Commission to diagnose the problem and prescribe a cure. What was needed, they argued in a report, was not more democracy but more reliance on experts:

> Democracy is only one way of constituting authority, and it is not necessarily a universally applicable one. *In many situations, the claims of expertise, seniority, experience and special talents may override the claims of democracy as a way of constituting authority.* . . . The arenas where democratic procedures are appropriate are, in short, limited.[1]

One reason why democracy has been successful so far, the report concluded, is that not all citizens participate in the democratic process. Some are politically apathetic and passive, while others have been marginalized and denied significant roles in the political process. The report warned that as these marginalized groups—African Americans, Latinos and others—became "full participants in the system" they might "overload" the system with demands it could not meet "and undermine its authority."[2] The report concluded that if these groups are to be allowed to participate fully in the political system, they must limit their demands.

While this elitist and expertise-oriented report was unpopular with advocates of popular democracy, the Reagan and Bush administrations took its warnings seriously. Recognizing that groups competing in the political system for scarce resources are not inclined toward self-restraint, the Bush administration set out to "resocialize" citizens to expect less of government and to rely more on the private sector and volunteer groups. The Clinton administration has attempted to steer a middle course between self-restraint and basic aid to various groups.

If America's leaders and its people are addressing this crisis through the democratic process, is democracy really flawed? So far democracy is proving far more resilient than its critics anticipated.

---

[1] See Michael T. Crozier, Samuel P. Huntington, and Toji Watanuki, *The Crisis of Democracy: Report on the Governability of Democracies to the Trilateral Commission* (New York: New York University Press, 1975), 113.
[2] Ibid., 114.

The dispute between proponents of a strong national culture and cultural diversity is itself an example of the value of diversity—in this case, the fact that the former want families, schools, and government to focus on democracy's ideals (*what's right*—but not fully realized), while the latter want these same institutions to focus on democracy's shortcomings (*what's wrong*—without acknowledging how many ideals have been realized). It is often hard for members of each camp to recognize that the goals of both camps support the political culture as a whole. One camp is the standard-bearer for public order; the other camp calls attention to the nation's unfulfilled promises and the need for change.

But even those who understand that both camps make essential contributions to the political culture will still disagree in each particular instance over which camp's analysis is right and whether their prescriptions will work. In sum, in a democratic political culture people will always disagree over how much and what sort of order there should be and how fast and in what ways that order should be changed. Debates over these issues play a major role in determining what kind of nation America is and will become.

Political Socialization

A political culture maintains itself through institutions that transmit its beliefs, values, and practices from one generation to the next—a process known as **political socialization**. Individuals new to a political society, such as children and immigrants, are taught to accept and live by values that support the political order. They are taught these values by families, churches, synagogues, schools, peer groups, workplaces, government agencies, and the mass media. Political socialization is a far more effective way to achieve public order than coercion, which depends on constant monitoring and enforcement.

Primary and Secondary Political Socialization

Primary socialization occurs principally in the private sphere of the family and in private and public preschools, while secondary socialization occurs largely in public schools and throughout adult life. Primary socialization, during which children are taught basic skills and cultural values—the language, norms (accepted rules of conduct or ways of thinking), beliefs, traditions, and worldview of their parents and caregivers—is largely concerned with instilling civility, order, and a sense of collective identity. Traditionally, children learned more about politics from their fathers, but they now learn about equally from both parents.[12] Because more than half of American families are headed by a single parent or by parents working full-time outside the home, caregivers, teachers, and television now play a greater role in primary socialization.

As children grow, the authority of teachers and TV to explain and describe the world to them begins to rival that of parents, and children enter the stage of

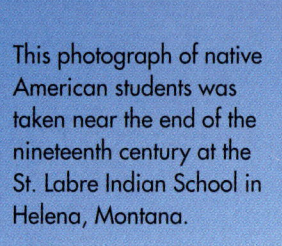

This photograph of native American students was taken near the end of the nineteenth century at the St. Labre Indian School in Helena, Montana.

secondary socialization. Between the fourth and eighth grades they begin to develop critical, even cynical, views of political authority and institutions, often by challenging such authority. Young people typically receive conflicting messages from academic authorities: "Respect and obey us *and* think for yourselves." They also discover that their parents' world is not the only world there is, and some make the painful discovery that their status in society is lower than the status of others. Such knowledge does not usually destroy children's beliefs about what's right, but it can lead them to realize that "right" political values, such as liberty and equality, are sometimes ignored and often conflict in practice. Like adolescents and adults, children are also strongly influenced by the mass media, which they consume at staggering rates. Most nine-year-olds watch more than five hours of TV a day, far more than children in nations that are U.S. trading partners.[13]

The use of certain educational materials, such as multicolored maps in textbooks and classrooms, encourage students to think of themselves as Americans in contrast with other nationalities. Many students first learn to participate in democratic institutions by electing student governments and leaders of youth organizations. In college some join the Young Republicans, the Young Democrats, or other political groups, and some work in political campaigns. Colleges and universities often require courses in American history and politics in an effort to reinforce the ideas of a national history and political community.

Political socialization does not end with school. The mass media, public officials, political candidates, political parties, interest groups, social movements, and religious institutions continue to shape political beliefs and participation throughout life. Serving on a jury or in the military, traveling abroad, watching the Olympics or films that inspire patriotism, or experiencing a national emergency can reinforce a sense of patriotism and national identity. So can personal participation in the political process.

Political Socialization Is *Political*

Because political socialization largely determines what sort of political culture the nation will have in the future, political actors who disagree over what the political culture should be compete in the political process to ensure that the political socialization children receive produces the kind of political culture they want. In the process, each actor makes claims to the authority to decide what sort of political culture is right for the country. Thus political socialization is a major political issue.

Disputes regularly erupt around public school education because public schools are governed by political institutions at the state and local levels, and these institutions are subject to intense pressure from a variety of political actors—parents, teachers, social workers, lawmakers, governors, and the courts. In this political cauldron public schools are supposed to educate children and socialize them to be good public citizens.

How well do public schools perform these tasks? Much depends on the primary socialization teachers have to build on. Much also depends on how effective the educational system is and often on how unequal local social and economic conditions are. It also depends on whether those who evaluate teachers agree with what they are teaching and the way they teach it. Teachers are vulnerable to political criticism because they present themselves as authorities on *what is*, *what's right*, and *what works* in many areas. Because teachers influence the beliefs and behavior of their students, schools at all levels have become major battlegrounds in the culture wars.

Most adults want schools to replicate their own values. Because those values vary from one person or group to the next, educational priorities—the importance of basic skills, social skills, foreign languages, critical thinking, self-esteem—vary. Some want all classes taught in English; others want classes taught in the students' native languages. Some want children to receive sex education and information on sexually transmitted diseases such as AIDS; others want little or no such instruction. Some maintain that teachers who are gay or lesbian should be free to teach; others would bar them from the classroom. Gay, lesbian, and single parents want instruction that increases tolerance for their lifestyles; conservatives often oppose such instruction because they believe it undermines traditional family values. Multiculturalists want the curriculum to include materials from diverse cultural perspectives; proponents of a strong national culture want the curriculum to include materials that preserve and strengthen the national culture. Fundamentalist Christians want the account of creation in the Bible (creationism) taught as fact or at least presented as a theory alongside the theory of evolution; others would ban religious theories from science classes. As the box nearby indicates, disputes rage over which books and teaching materials should be censored.

In 1996 this first grade class in Brooklyn's Public School 114 had 46 children more than there were chairs. In many inner city schools the conditions are so bad that Jonathan Kozol's book *Savage Inequalities* (1991) describes these schools as "death zones" that smother children's enthusiasm for learning and crush their potential to become productive citizens.

The Politics of Knowledge

Censorship in the Schools

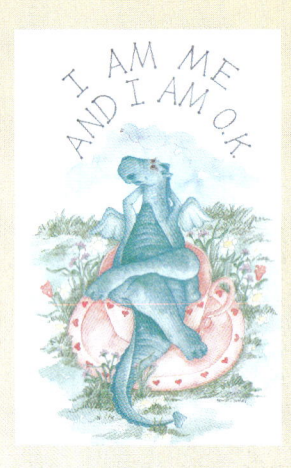

Witchcraft? Some critics of Pumsy, a long-tailed dragon, say that the use of the teacup in this poster reflects the teaching of witchcraft.

Each year school districts nationwide are pressured to ban books and teaching materials that critics claim harm children. The anticensorship group People for the American Way has found that nearly half of the challenges to instructional materials succeed. Seven percent of these challenges are from leftists attempting to ban books they consider racist, such as Mark Twain's *Tom Sawyer*, John Steinbeck's *Of Mice and Men*, and Alice Walker's *The Color Purple*. Thirty-eight percent come from conservative groups, especially the Religious Right.[1]

A chief target of the Religious Right has been material aimed at improving children's self-esteem, such as Quest International, a program sponsored by the Lions Club (a nonpartisan national service organization) that uses skits and other activities to promote honesty, integrity, and service to others in ways that professionals find effective.[2]

Christian conservatives accuse Quest and 15 other self-esteem counseling programs of indoctrinating children in secular humanism (the belief that human beings rather than God determine moral values) and Eastern mysticism. An imaginary blue dolphin named *Duso* (an acronym for *d*eveloping *u*nderstanding of *s*elf and *o*thers) is used by teachers and counselors nationwide to help youngsters' self-esteem and prevent drug abuse. A similar program, Pumsy in Pursuit of Excellence, is now used in 40 percent of public schools. Jill Anderson created Pumsy after discovering that children with high self-esteem outperform those with low self-esteem. By identifying with Pumsy, children learn how to make decisions and solve problems and to access their inner strengths. Pumsy also helps children ward off bullies, drug-pushers, and sex offenders. They practice using these skills in imaginary situations, such as responding to someone pressuring them to do something they know is wrong or unsafe.

Small but vocal conservative Christian groups have run candidates for school boards nationwide to force them to reject Pumsy and similar guidance counseling programs on grounds that they hypnotize children, expose them to schizophrenia, teach them to disobey their parents and hate God, and even to practice witchcraft. The Citizens for Excellence in Education, which spearheads such challenges, warns that Pumsy and Duso are leading children down pathways to the occult under the guise of self-esteem and that the time has come "to revert to Christian control of the public schools."[3] Activist Phyllis Schlafly, head of Eagle Forum (a group that has fought sex education in the public schools), has attacked Pumsy for teaching children "to look at a dragon as a friend instead of their parents."[4] And George Twente, a Christian therapist who has conducted a nationwide anti-Pumsy crusade, asserts that "the problem with Pumsy is that it teaches children to think for themselves."[5]

---

[1] Anne Hazard, "Political Group Releases Censorship Report, Says Public Schools Under Attack," *States News Service*, September 1, 1993.
[2] Dave Miller, a Quest vice president, quoted in Larry Bleiberg, "Questioning Practices," *Dallas Morning News*, June 8, 1993, 2A; Dr. Anne Petersen, vice president of research, University of Minnesota, cited in ibid.
[3] Robert Simons, quoted in Janice Martin, "Religious Right Targets Schools," *Rocky Mountain News*, Denver, Colo., October 24, 1990.
[4] Arthur Salm, "Public Eye," *San Diego Union-Tribune*, April 5, 1993, E2.
[5] George Twente, television program *Attitudes*, Lifetime, New York City, Spring 1992.

Political Socialization Promotes Patriotism

patriotism
The word patriotism comes from *patria*, Latin for "fatherland," a traditional term for the state.

Political socialization strengthens a political culture and loyalty to government when it inspires devotion to **patriotism**, the sense of identification and loyalty one feels for one's country and its governing institutions.

Storytelling and Rituals

A good way to inspire patriotism is to connect the stories of a nation with individuals' own stories.[14] Many adults, for example, associate the stories of Johnny Appleseed, Davy Crockett, and Pocahontas with their childhood. Collective memories also develop from stories about experiences of economic depressions and wars. Epics like "how the West was won" are told and retold in novels, paintings, photographs, and films. Many Americans also feel a sense of kinship through songs, crafts, jokes, and even food (turkey at Thanksgiving, hotdogs at baseball games).

Schools and scout troops promote patriotism through rituals such as saluting and pledging allegiance to the American flag and singing the national anthem or "America the Beautiful." Baseball fans in America stand for the national anthem before a game. American flags fly on national holidays and at half-staff on occasions of national mourning, and they play a central role in events ranging from sports to military and political funerals. This is why so many Americans view the burning of the flag by political demonstrators as an act of desecration.

Reverence for the Ancestors

Reverence for America's ancestors is visible on a daily basis, from statues in parks to coins and bills in people's pockets. (See the box nearby on George Washington.) Leaders turn to the ancestors for guidance in times of trouble, as President Abraham Lincoln did during the Civil War and as congressional leaders did during the

President William Jefferson Clinton marked the birthday of his predecessor and namesake at the Jefferson Memorial in Washington, D.C., on April 14, 1993—250 years after the third President of the United States was born.

Two Lincoln Presenters greet one another at the 1996 annual meeting of Lincoln Presenters in Springfield, Illinois.

George Washington, National Hero

From the time of his death in 1799, American children have been taught to call George Washington "the father of our country," and leaders have invoked his name to inspire patriotism and to legitimate their authority.

When the new Constitution was drafted and the country desperately needed legitimacy at home and abroad, Washington was a famous Revolutionary War general. His house in Mount Vernon, Virginia, was already a national shrine visited by tourists, and his face was stamped on American coins after the Revolution—as it still is. In 1783 the president of Yale University had declared:

> O Washington! how do I love thy name! How have I often adored and blessed thy God, for creating and forming the great ornament of human kind! . . . . Thy fame is of sweeter perfume than Arabian spices in the gardens of Persia. . . . . Listening angels shall catch the odor, waft it to heaven, and perfume the universe![1]

Such extravagant language was commonly used during Washington's presidency, and after his death he was often portrayed in the company of angels. Those who knew that Washington had the usual human failings did nothing to dispel this veneration. John Adams and Alexander Hamilton did not air their disagreements with Washington in public, recognizing even then that the fledgling republic was strengthened by the Washington myth because it helped to give Americans a common hero and a common history. Over time other prominent Founders joined Washington as objects of political worship, among them Thomas Jefferson, James Madison, and Benjamin Franklin.

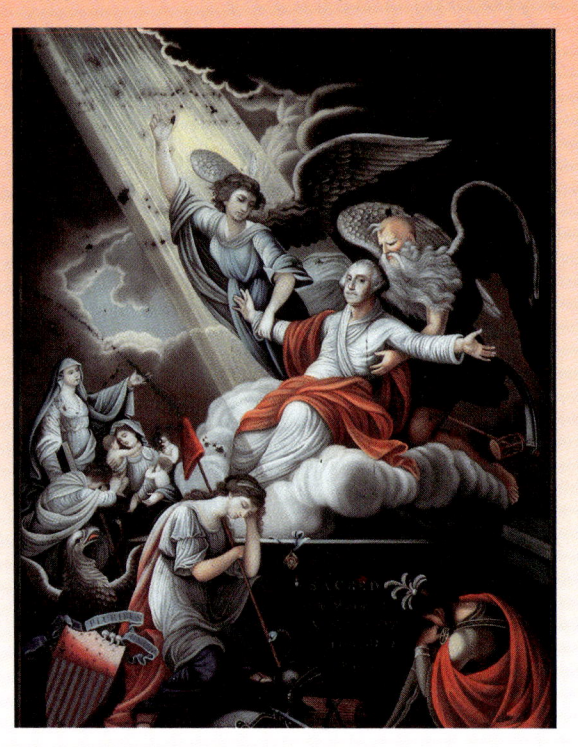

[1] Quoted in Barry Schwartz, *George Washington: The Making of an American Symbol* (Ithaca, N.Y.: Cornell University Press, 1987), 41.

Watergate crisis of 1973. Politicians routinely refer to the greatness of the ancestors to enhance their own authority and to legitimate their own agendas. Listen to any presidential nomination or acceptance speech or State of the Union Address and you will hear the names of ancestors and national martyrs, such as Lincoln and the Reverend Martin Luther King, Jr., invoked to lend authority to the speaker's assertions.

In recent years, multiculturalists have charged that leaders have been misusing the ancestors for political purposes. Right before President Bill Clinton's visit to the Jefferson Memorial, a commentator pointed out that Jefferson did not free his own slaves during his lifetime or attempt to abolish slavery either when he was governor of Virginia or after he became president.[15] But even though Jefferson was in many ways a man of his own times, his Memorial has become a timeless testament to the kinship of all Americans—and perhaps of all humanity.

Respect for Founding Documents and National Celebrations

All cultures safeguard and venerate signs and symbols that commemorate their beginnings and most profound experiences. In the United States, copies of the Declaration of Independence and the Constitution abound (see Appendix), but the original documents are preserved and guarded like sacred texts—sealed in a climate-controlled glass case in the National Archives where they may viewed under guard and where each night an elevator lowers them to a bomb-proof shelter 50 feet below ground.

Americans commemorate their founding with regular celebrations of national holidays and special occasions, such as the bicentennials of the Declaration of Independence and the Constitution. Such celebrations reconsecrate Americans as "We, the People" and recommit them to the nation's core values, but they purposely ignore past mistakes or recast them as positive acts. Fourth of July celebrations do not acknowledge that the winners of the Revolutionary War confiscated the property of those who remained loyal to Britain. Nor do celebrations of America's victory in World War II acknowledge that the U.S. government imprisoned Japanese Americans in "relocation" camps during that war.

Patriotism's resilience in the face of changes in the political culture is visible in many areas. For example, the term *founding fathers* was used to suggest that Americans belong to the same national family until the feminist movement in the 1960s pointed out the paternalism inherent in the term. Some regard such developments as a sign that patriotism is diminishing, while others see patriotism as becoming more sensitive to minorities and women.

This century-old San Francisco statue became the focus of a multicultural controversy in 1996 when American Indians complained about the vanquished Indian at the feet of a Spanish settler and a Franciscan missionary. When the city's Art Commission placed a plaque on the stature decrying the suffering of the Indians, the Spanish consul general and the Roman Catholic Church complained. The Art Commission appointed a new task force to draft new language acceptable to all.

Does Political Socialization Overpromote Authority?

In the 1993 movie *A Few Good Men*, starring Tom Cruise, two Marines are dishonorably discharged for blindly following orders that led to the death of a fellow Marine. Such blind obedience led U.S. soldiers in 1968 to shoot all the men, women, and children in the Vietnamese village of My Lai because they were suspected of aiding the Communist Vietcong. And in 1970, members of the Illinois National Guard shot and killed four students at an antiwar demonstration at Kent State University. These events prompted social critics to fault public and private schools for turning out students who could not think critically and who were ignorant of their rights and of the way the political system works.[16] They urged students to doubt what they read and to demand that teachers, experts, and other authorities provide evidence for their judgments.[17] They also called for educational opportunities in addition to college to teach people how to keep a job, understand their children and their society, and vote responsibly. Liberal and radical scholars began to explore the ways in which authority governs people's lives without their awareness, stunting their critical thinking and individual creativity.[18] They found that trust in authority is so deeply embedded in

founding fathers
The term was only coined in 1918, when Senator Warren G. Harding, elected president two years later, used it in an address to the Sons and Daughters of the American Revolution.

habits of thought and language as to be almost invisible, even to most analysts, and pointed out that people who do not protest against authority may be manipulated by it. They depicted individuals as trapped in a political culture by socialization practices designed to engineer their consent. Individual freedom and democracy, they argued, were merely myths which political socializers manipulate to achieve public order. One critic likened political socialization to "friendly fascism":

> I participate.
> You (singular) participate.
> He, she or it participates.
> We participate.
> You (plural) participate.
> THEY decide.[19]

Conservative critic Robert Nisbet agreed. In *The Twilight of Authority*,[20] he described America as suffering from a "new despotism" and argued that families, schools, communities, science, an intrusive bureaucratic state, and even people's language were stunting individualism and creativity.[21]

Americans seem to have learned from these criticisms, because political analysts, the media, and educators have begun to pay more attention to the ways in which political actors use information, logic, and language to enhance their authority. Today efforts to cultivate critical thinking can be found at all educational levels and in many political science textbooks. This textbook defines politics as disputes over claims to authority in order to increase people's awareness of what those claims to authority are and how they work. People will then be better equipped to decide for themselves whether those claims are right.

Political Socialization, Political Culture, and Political Institutions Work Together

Political culture, political socialization, and political institutions (government) operate as a system in which each component affects the others (see Figure 4.1). Effective political socialization produces a cohesive political culture, which in turn produces political institutions with legitimate authority. Ineffective political socialization produces a fragmented political culture, which in turn produces political institutions lacking legitimate authority. As in any system, no single component precedes and determines the others.[22] Thus a political culture does not come into existence before political socialization or before governing institutions; rather, they develop and work together. Improvement or failure in one area can lead to improvement or failure in the others.

The difficulty in the operation of this model in a representative democracy is twofold. First, a representative democracy depends on the participation of educated citizens who know how to think critically and are not discouraged from or fearful of doing so. Thus a heavy-handed political socialization that promotes respect for authority to the point that individuality and creativity are stifled will undermine the very citizen participation on which its legitimation depends.

Figure 4.1

The American political system

(a) Interactive System

- Political culture
- Political socialization
- Political institutions (government)

(b) Interactive System Over Time

Political socialization · Political institutions · Political culture · Interactions

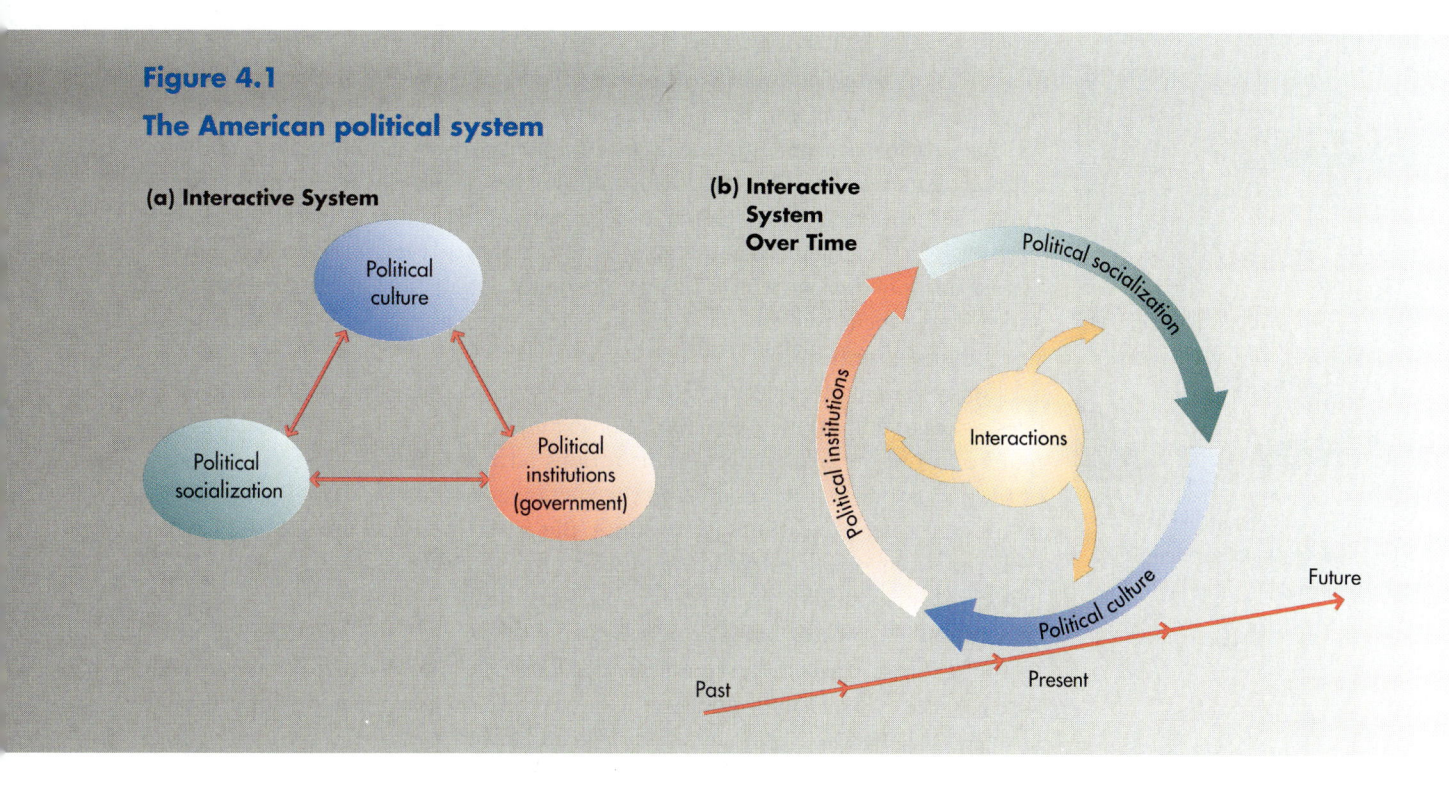

Past — Present — Future

At the same time, too much dispute over claims to authority or too many perspectives vying for legitimacy can also fragment the political culture, impair political socialization, and cause political authority and civility to decline. That is why opposition to multiculturalism is intense. Yet multiculturalists continue to argue that the only way to preserve political institutions is to make them responsive to all citizens, and that means making political socialization and political culture more inclusive. The fact that this expansion has been occurring incrementally suggests a sensitivity in the American political culture to both concerns.

Sources of Conflict in American Political Culture

Today major conflicts persist over subcultures, religion, individualism and communitarianism, and political ideologies.

Subcultures

America's political culture has developed alongside, and often in conflict with, preexisting loyalties to **subcultures**—nondominant cultures nested within the national political culture. The loyalties of those belonging to subcultures often

New citizens brandish their certificates of citizenship.

extend beyond U.S. boundaries. Thus some American Catholics feel a sense of identification with Catholics worldwide, or with Catholics in Ireland, for example, while some American Jews identify with Israel.

As a nation of immigrants planted in a land already home to diverse Indian cultures, America has been multicultural and regionally diverse from the beginning. These differences are tolerated and accommodated in a political culture that supports the American **nation-state**. Although they are exposed to the nation's history and political system in school, members of subcultures also seek to know and preserve their own customs and histories, especially with the current emphasis on multiculturalism.[23]

Many laws and court decisions presently protect certain customs and practices of racial and ethnic minorities. For example, some states and localities now require schools in areas where ethnic groups have reached a specified percentage of the population to offer courses in the languages of those groups. Public schools in Chicago offer classes in 17 languages. But in 1996, when the school board in Oakland, California, declared black English the "primary language" of its 28,000 black students, criticism from blacks and others led the school board to retract its declaration. Advocates of a strong national culture want students to be required to speak and learn standard English, the language they need to succeed in the larger society. Some states and localities have considered formally adopting English as the official governmental language, and there have been recurring efforts to pass a constitutional amendment making English the national language.

Religion

The First Amendment protects (with certain limitations) all recognized religious groups (Chapter 15). Because religious beliefs deeply affect many people's lives and behavior, how they raise their children, and what public policies they prefer, those beliefs often lead to political disputes. Religious disputes become political once religious activists promote their goals in the political process. These disputes—over abortion, the right to die, capital punishment, public aid to religious schools, U.S. support for Israel—also divide believers and nonbelievers, both of whom often oppose the ways in which government responds to such disputes.

The chances that a religious dispute will become political are great in the United States, where more than 1,200 religious groups and 220 recognized religious denominations practice their faiths. Many Native Americans practice their own religions, although some have adopted or were forced to convert to Christianity. Judaism, Catholicism, and Protestantism have common biblical roots, but these do not always provide common ground in politics. A variety of religions have sprung up in the United States as well, among them Mormonism, Jehovah's Witnesses, the Nation of Islam, and New Age spiritual beliefs.[24] In recent years there have been dramatic increases in the followers of Islam, Buddhism, and Hinduism.

nation-state

A state is a set of political institutions (government) which successfully claims the authority to govern a political society within certain territorial boundaries. When the majority of people in this territory accept these claims, the result is a nation-state.

black English

Black English, also known as Ebonics (a combination of "ebony" and "phonics"), American Vernacular English, or jive, is derived from West African culture. Recognition of black English as a distinct language is an effort to destigmatize the language of black students.

Despite such diversity, Protestants have always dominated the American political culture (see Figure 4.2). The vast majority of the early colonists were Protestants, and some settlements were intolerant of other religions, even other forms of Protestantism. Children learned to read and write from books that illustrated the ABC's with biblical statements. By the time of the Revolution, Protestant values had saturated American culture. Protestantism today ranges from conservative (Southern Baptists) to liberal (Episcopalians, Presbyterians, Methodists). The fragmentation of Protestantism, its steady decline in membership,[25] and the increasing influence of non-Protestant religions are diluting Protestant dominance. Many associate this decline with that of institutions that have traditionally promoted civic virtue and a strong national culture—the nuclear family, churches, public schools, community life, and commerce.[26]

Some adherents of the ultraconservative, fundamentalist **Religious Right**— estimated at 1 in 7 Americans, or 14 percent of the population[27]—support what one survey calls "Christian nationalism," the view that America's political problems can be alleviated if government adopts a Christian outlook. Activists of the Religious Right have formed interest groups, such as the Christian Coalition founded by the Reverend Pat Robertson and Ralph Reed (2 million strong with an annual budget of $250 million), to back conservative politicians, to initiate referenda to curtail the rights of gays and others, and to tackle inner-city problems.

Figure 4.2

Profile of religious preference in the United States

How Americans describe their religious preferences when asked. "Other" includes Muslim, Hindu, Buddhist, etc.

- Protestant 60%
- Catholic 24%
- None 8%
- Other 6%
- Jewish 2.5%

Source: Statistical Abstract of the United States: 1996 (116th ed.) (Washington, D.C.: U.S. Bureau of the Census, 1996), p. 70.

Despite the general view that adherents of the Religious Right are concentrated in the rural South and tend to be older and less educated than other Americans, more than a third have attended one year of college, 3 out of 10 are under 35, and a majority live outside the South.[28] Among the liberal groups attempting to stop such initiatives is People for the American Way, which describes itself as "Your Voice Against Intolerance" and launched "Expose the Right!" campaigns in the 1996 elections at state and local levels. Conflict is likely to mount as adherents of the Religious Right feel increasingly threatened by religious diversity, secularism, and what they see as a decline in public morality and as religious moderates and liberals feel threatened by what they perceive as takeovers by extremists.

To maintain their identities as religious minorities, some religious groups such as the Amish in Pennsylvania and Hasidic Jews in Brooklyn attempt to isolate themselves from the political culture at large and socialize their children in their own beliefs and practices. They have their own educational institutions, and those who violate community norms are shunned. Most stay aloof from politics. One scholar calls the members these communities "partial citizens" because their relationship with the political culture at large "rests on something of a bargain: as long as the group stays away from the common life of the country, and doesn't try to eat at the public trough, then society can agree that citizenship has fewer claims on them than on others."[29] Because these "partial citizens" don't vote, don't run for office, and don't get involved in policy debates, they are not perceived as a threat to cultural unity in the way some other subcultures are.

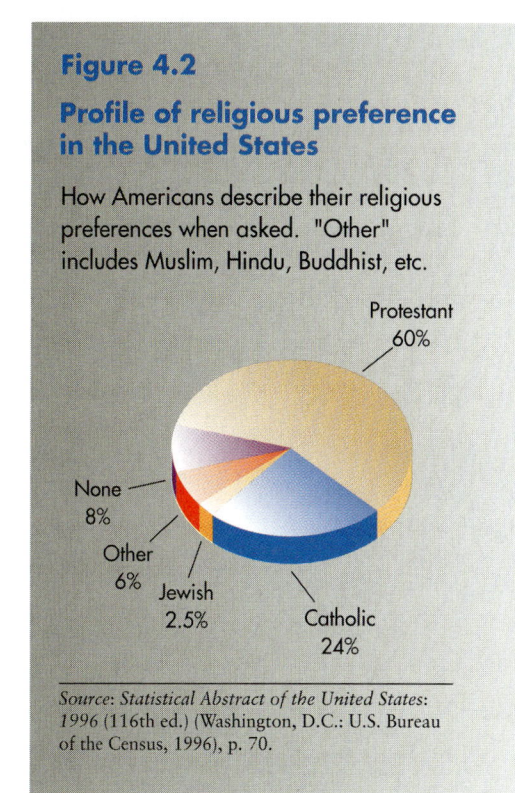

Individualism and Communitarianism

Americans place a high value on **individualism**—the right of each person to think freely and to take initiatives—within the bounds of civility. Many associate individualism with the Protestant ethnic and the accomplishments of courageous pioneers, successful entrepreneurs, inventive scientists, and political heroes like Lincoln, who, we are taught, was born in a log cabin and reached the White House on his own initiative. Individualism ranks high in a political culture that values and protects individual rights to free speech and religion, to petition government, to bear arms, to vote for candidates of one's choice, and to pursue the American Dream.

One scholar, however, maintains that throughout American history individualism has been primarily a privilege of economically successful middle-aged white men, one seldom available to women and young men. Since colonial times, women have been expected to repress their individual aspirations on behalf of family, community, and nation, while young men have been expected to do the same by serving in the military and preparing to assume economic and family responsibilities.[30]

The Framers feared that individualism, which they associated with self-interest, would undermine civic virtue or **communitarianism**, which values the well-being of the community from the local to the national level.[31] They therefore crafted the Constitution so that only elites—"natural" aristocrats who were thought to possess civic and communitarian virtues—would have access to the levers of power. Ordinary citizens who were thought lacking in these virtues were forced to petition government through those elites who were their representatives. But the Framers' precautions did not prevent people of all classes from prizing individualism. Indeed, the generations who grew up on Horatio Alger novels believed that individualism and communitarianism went hand in hand, even though these principles conflict in theory. However, to characterize a diverse nation as individualistic, communitarian, or anything else is simplistic. Individuals move in and out of many circles and live in a world of many *we*'s. As children become adults, they begin to realize that their freedom as individuals and indeed their very lives depend on communities and that individuals and communities survive and thrive together. The individual freedom that fails to respect social rules and conventions will ultimately destroy itself. In short, rights require responsibilities.

In recent years, some liberals have echoed conservative concerns that individual responsibility and civility are eroding and called for strengthening such traditional institutions as families, neighborhoods, and schools.[32] Some in the Clinton administration argue that the country has swung too far in the direction of individualism and the creation of new rights. They criticize the growing "cult of the victim"—

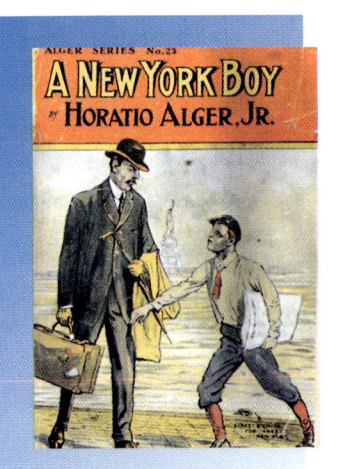

Cover of one of Horatio Alger's (1834–1899) 100 rags-to-riches novels.

appeals for leniency for those who break the law on grounds that their judgment was impaired by psychological factors such as abuse. Proponents of individualism and communitarianism have productive debates over such matters, and both perspectives contribute to an ethical and effective democracy.

Political Ideologies

Conflict in American political culture is also due to differences in **political ideology**—a cluster of concepts (ideology comes from the Greek for "idea" and "logic") that politicians and parties use to gain authority and legitimacy for their stands on *what is*, *what's right*, and *what works*. Some people use a political ideology to screen parties, political candidates, and public policies, but many abandon it when it suits their interests. Most Americans rely on common sense and **pragmatism** (from the Latin for "deed")—a practical approach to problem solving—but these notions are often in turn influenced by political ideologies.

Political ideologies reflect the times. Republicanism, for example, which the Framers preferred to democracy, has evolved toward democracy. Nor do supporters of the same ideology always agree. In the past, ideologues in the former Soviet Union and its Eastern satellites and in the People's Republic of China strongly disagreed over how to define and practice socialism. In Western countries, many disagree over how to define and practice democracy.

In the United States, the most important political ideologies are conservatism and liberalism.

Liberals generally

- support the Democratic party,
- support government intervention in politics and economics to protect and expand civil rights and civil liberties and improve the conditions of the poor, minorities, and women,
- endorse equality as their primary political value, and
- favor a politics of inclusion that seeks representation and participation for all.

Conservatives generally

- support the Republican party,
- oppose massive government intervention in politics and economics and look instead to market mechanisms, states, localities, and volunteerism to resolve the country's problems,
- endorse liberty as their primary political value, and
- support traditional moral, religious, and family values and ask government to enforce them.

Assumptions about human nature greatly influence whether one is inclined to be liberal or conservative and how one evaluates political issues, parties, candidates, and government performance. Liberals tend to believe that human nature is basically good and capable of improvement. Conservatives tend to view human nature as basically selfish and incapable of improvement. In their view, when

The Political, Economic, and Social Dimensions of Ideologies

In the political sphere, the struggle among ideologies consists largely of tradeoffs between three goals: government-imposed order, government-protected individual freedom, and equality of participation legislated and protected by government. The three points of the political triangle shown on the facing page stand for these three goals. Libertarians are located near the extreme of individual freedom, because individual liberty is their foremost goal. Social conservatives, by contrast, are close to the extreme of social order, because they tend to emphasize such policies as strong police forces at home and large military forces abroad, and they favor strictly limited rights of those accused of crimes at home and tend to oppose foreign policies seeking to foster human rights around the world. Democrats tend to favor both civil liberties (government-protected freedoms) and equality, so they are located between those two points, with traditional liberal Democrats closer to the equality point and New Democrats closer to the freedom point.

In the economic sphere, the goals are economic freedom through laissez-faire capitalism; public order through government regulation of the economy; and social equality through government policies that redistribute wealth (such as progressive income taxes and welfare programs). Libertarians remain near the freedom point because they are staunch laissez-faire capitalists. Social conservatives oppose government efforts to achieve social equality through the redistribution of wealth as well as government efforts to achieve public order through economic regulation, but because they make an exception for economic regulation that prevents monopoly and exploitation of consumers, they occupy a middle position on the question of government intervention. Traditional Democrats favor government redistribution of wealth and economic regulation to a far greater extent than New Democrats, who tend to favor reliance on market mechanisms rather than law in many policy areas such as school vouchers and environmental protection.

In the social triangle, the goals are freedom from government interference in everyday life (the main goal of libertarians); government-imposed standards for everyday life (the main goal of social conservatives); and government-engineered equality of status (the main goal of socialists). Because social conservatives strongly favor such government-imposed standards on such issues as prayer in public schools and prohibitions on abortion, they reside at this point, while libertarians reside at the anti-interference point. Democrats, by contrast, tend to favor government protection and expansion of social equality.

Plotting ideological positions as triangles rather than on a linear spectrum helps explain why their adherents often conflict with one another, but also sometimes unite to support a particular policy. For example, the ideologies of third parties could not be more different, but their leaders have united to oppose their exclusion from meaningful participation in the electoral process by the Democratic and Republican parties (Chapter 7).

The political, economic, and social dimensions of ideologies

The triangles at right depict the ideologies of various political groups in the United States. The location of a group in each triangle—political, economic, or social—shows the relative importance it gives to order, freedom, and equality in that policy area.

For example, in the political triangle, **Liberal Democrats** are located near the **equality** point because they tend to favor strong government protection of the right to vote and government financing of campaigns. They are far from the **freedom** point because they tend to oppose people who refuse to pay taxes. They are also far from the **order** point because they tend to oppose government control of political parties. **Traditional Republicans** are farther from the **equality** point because they tend to be less supportive of government financing of campaigns, farther from the **freedom** point because they tend to strongly oppose civil disobedience, and closer to the **order** point because they tend to favor government regulation of labor unions, especially of the right to roganize and to strike.

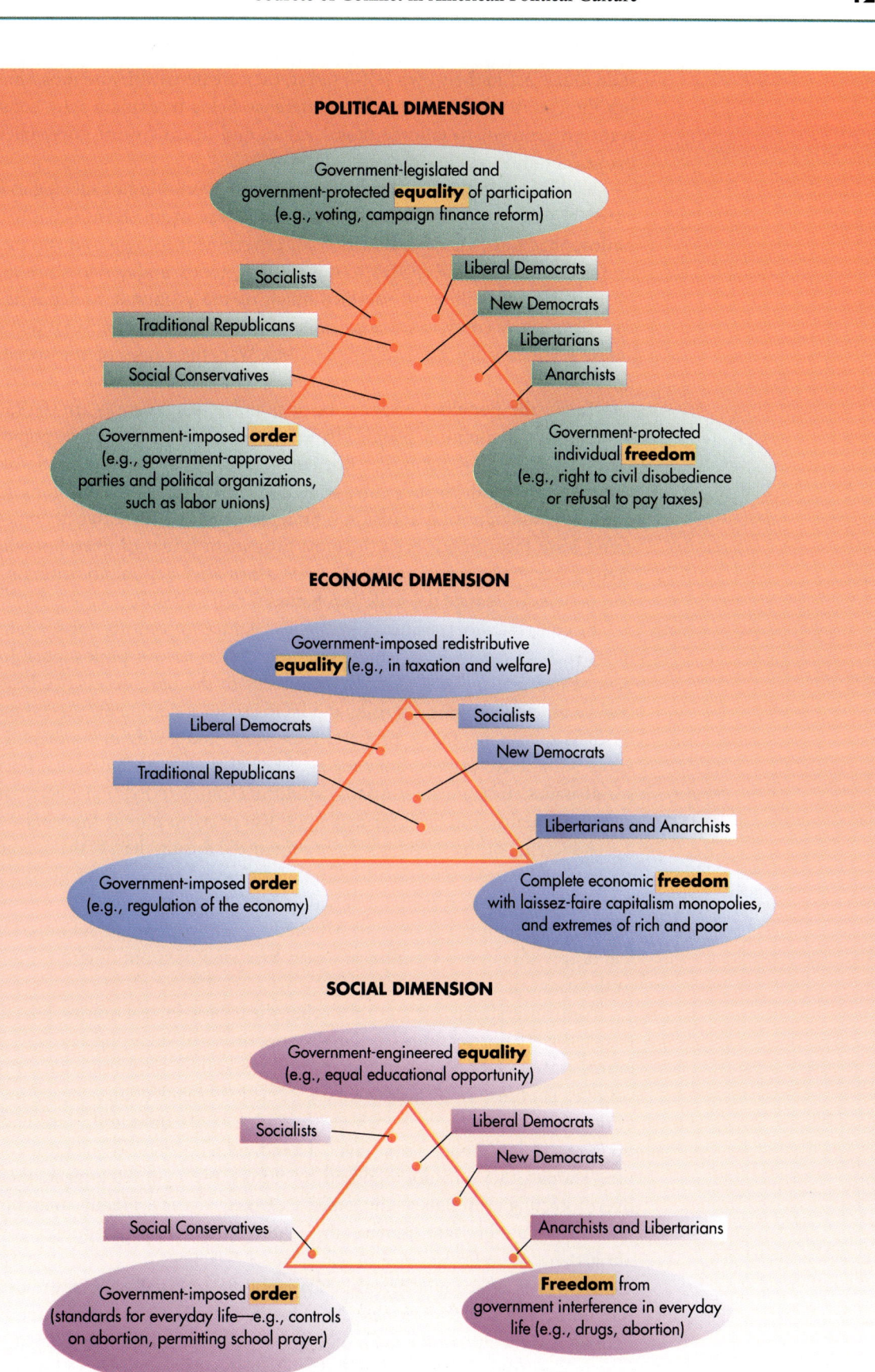

Sources of Conflict in American Political Culture

POLITICAL DIMENSION

- Government-legislated and government-protected **equality** of participation (e.g., voting, campaign finance reform)
- Government-imposed **order** (e.g., government-approved parties and political organizations, such as labor unions)
- Government-protected individual **freedom** (e.g., right to civil disobedience or refusal to pay taxes)

Positions:
- Socialists
- Liberal Democrats
- Traditional Republicans
- New Democrats
- Libertarians
- Social Conservatives
- Anarchists

ECONOMIC DIMENSION

- Government-imposed redistributive **equality** (e.g., in taxation and welfare)
- Government-imposed **order** (e.g., regulation of the economy)
- Complete economic **freedom** with laissez-faire capitalism monopolies, and extremes of rich and poor

Positions:
- Liberal Democrats
- Socialists
- Traditional Republicans
- New Democrats
- Libertarians and Anarchists

SOCIAL DIMENSION

- Government-engineered **equality** (e.g., equal educational opportunity)
- Government-imposed **order** (standards for everyday life—e.g., controls on abortion, permitting school prayer)
- **Freedom** from government interference in everyday life (e.g., drugs, abortion)

Positions:
- Socialists
- Liberal Democrats
- New Democrats
- Social Conservatives
- Anarchists and Libertarians

individuals act in their own self-interest, they create wealth and jobs, thus benefiting the country as a whole. This difference helps to explain why conservatives want government to enforce moral values and liberals want government to improve economic conditions.

In addition to these major ideologies, a number of minor ideologies have persisted in American politics. Inspired by the ideas of nineteenth-century German philosopher Karl Marx, **socialists** want government to own and run most of the nation's economic enterprises to ensure that goods and services are distributed fairly. They are willing to sacrifice much of the economic and political liberty Americans now enjoy for greater equality. But with the collapse of numerous socialist regimes since the end of the Cold War, the ranks of the socialists have declined.

Today the **populists**—advocates of popular democracy—are the loudest defenders of the common people. In recent elections conservative populists have supported Ronald Reagan, Pat Buchanan, Ross Perot, and House Speaker Newt Gingrich. They call for tax cuts, reductions in government, and nonintervention abroad, while opposing abortion, immigration, and affirmative action. The Reverend Jesse Jackson has been the most prominent leader of liberal populists, who favor government assistance to the poor, affirmative action, abortion on demand, and policies to reduce the wide gap between rich and poor.

In contrast, **libertarians**, inspired by eighteenth-century laissez-faire economists such as Adam Smith and contemporary American philosopher John Hospers, want to shrink the size of government to the bare necessities because they believe big government is wrong and ineffective. Government, they argue, has no business taking income or property from some and giving it to others. Here they agree with conservatives, but they agree with liberals on individual liberties and social issues. In sum, libertarians would maximize individual liberty at the expense of equality and have formed a political party to pursue this goal.

Adherents of the Religious Right, organized during the 1970s, operate mainly on the conservative edge of the Republican party. Among their goals are the return of organized prayer in public schools, the banning of abortion and pornography, and the removal of sex and AIDS education from public schools. Often they feel deeply threatened by cultural forces they view as morally wrong and harmful to the traditional political culture.

Neoconservatives sprang up during the 1960s in reaction to liberal policies they felt were not working. Originally supporters of such policies as welfare programs and forced busing, they later argued that only programs that work should survive. They also oppose deep military cuts in the face of an uncertain world and criticize the courts for being too soft on criminals. **Communitarians** have sprung up in reaction to policies that favor the individual to the detriment of community life. Though they are not opposed to cutting the military budget, they oppose overprotecting criminals at the expense of their victims. Finally, **anarchists**, more numerous in the late nineteenth century than today, oppose government altogether.

As this brief account reveals, each ideology is actually a mixture of political, economic, and social positions. As a result, there is some overlap among them, making it difficult to plot them on a linear spectrum from left to right. The box nearby uses triangles instead to depict ideological agreements and disagreements with respect to three political values—individual freedom, public order, and social and economic equality.

⭐ Sources of Order in American Political Culture

For the American political system to work, its many sources of conflict must be moderated by sources of order to achieve a dynamic equilibrium (Chapter 1). Among the major sources of order in American political culture are the ideal of the "*melting pot*"; common laws, rules, and procedures; and cross-cutting allegiances.

Reduction of Difference

America has been described as a "melting pot" in which subcultural differences due to race, ethnicity, religion, and regionalism are homogenized. More recently, it has been described as a "salad bowl," in which those identities are retained but mixed. In both cases, the reduction of subcultural differences strengthens the national political culture, which promotes public order. Many immigrants and their children marry outside their group, Americanize their names, and lose their original languages, religious faiths, racial characteristics, and national identities over generations. A 1990 study showed that 67 percent of American-born Asian Americans and 38 percent of Latino women ages 20–29 married outside their ethnic group, as opposed to only 3 percent of African-American women, a statistic attributed to the latter's radical social and residential isolation.[33] The fastest growing groups, Latinos and Asian Americans, are projected to assimilate at about the same pace as earlier, European immigrants. Thus the influence of militant multiculturalism is being offset by the melting pot, which blurs racial and ethnic boundaries just as it did in the case of earlier immigrants.

In addition, regional differences have been eroded by economic and technological changes. These changes have reduced regional tensions, but at a price, as a political satirist explains:

> People will miss that it once meant something to be Southern or Midwestern. It doesn't mean much now, except for the climate. Out on the Minnesota prairie, the little Swede towns are dying and the vast suburbs are booming, which are identical to the suburbs of Atlanta or Charlotte, where people live on Anonymous Drive in Homogeneous Hills, people who, when you meet them, the question "Where are you from?" doesn't lead to anything interesting. They live somewhere near a Gap store, and what else do you want to know?[34]

The children of this Oakland, California, family illustrate the increasing erosion of traditional racial classifications.

Common Laws, Rules, and Procedures

Adherence to common laws, rules, and procedures ("due process" and "equal protection") promote public order when they are viewed as treating people of different races, ethnic groups, religions, genders, and classes fairly. No political system does this perfectly. Until recently, these constitutional guarantees seemed fair because legal concepts appeared to be neutral. Today, however, there is a growing recognition that these concepts are never neutral because they rest on a decision to support certain specific rules and legal procedures rather than some others.[35] Not even the procedures laid down in the U.S. Constitution are neutral; rather, they "are supported by substantive commitments within the political culture—a certain suspicion of government, a certain kind of individualism, a certain image of the good life, a certain view of how the "'blessings of liberty' ought to be secured."[36] As one political philosopher puts it, "our ancestors' assumption was that the government's only *moral* duty was to insure 'equal protection of the laws'—laws that, in their majestic impartiality, allowed the rich and the poor to receive the same hospital bills."[37] As Americans increasingly discover that their common laws, rules, and procedures are deeply rooted in their political culture—a political culture which favors some at the expense of others—they will come face to face with the question of what their moral duty as members of a national community is.

Cross-Cutting Allegiances

According to one calculation, the identities of most people living in the United States are complicated by some 25 to 30 group differences: biological characteristics, such as gender, race, and age; cultural characteristics, such as ethnicity and religion; and economic and class-related differences resulting from unequal educational opportunities and disparities in occupation and income.[38] These differences may be reduced to two types: (1) those based on characteristics over which people have no control (race, ethnicity, gender), or in many cases very little control, such as class, and (2) those based on beliefs, commitments, allegiances, and tastes over which people have some or a great deal of control, such as religion, political party, interest group, social movement, profession, or an enthusiasm for science fiction, rhythm and blues, or a football team.

Groups based on characteristics are likely to be divisive and destabilizing unless their members also belong to groups sharing common interests. Anyone can belong to the Baptist or Roman Catholic religion and support the same local cause. They may also frequent the same restaurants or opera performances, if they can afford to. These **cross-cutting allegiances** tend to dilute the sense of separation people feel when they are treated solely as blacks, Latinos, poor people, or women, in much the way that the theater assembles "odd lots of humanity, with different backgrounds, different I.Q.'s . . . and emotional responses—and makes them breathe together, laugh together, feel themselves together in the unanimity of their approval or disapproval, belief, or disbelief."[39] Obviously, the stabilizing function of cross-cutting allegiances works best in the absence of discrimination and poverty, and when people are able to come together at will.

The more cross-cutting allegiances there are in the political culture, the more stable the political system is likely to be. Shifts in cross-cutting allegiances have made it increasingly difficult for voting experts to use group differences to predict election outcomes, as we'll see in Chapter 7. Rich blacks, for example, have some common interests with rich whites and other common interests with poor blacks. The positions blacks or whites take on issues are sometimes influenced by race and other times by economics. Gays and lesbians of different races, classes, and

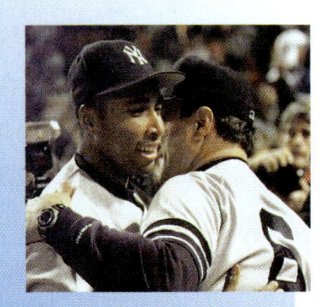

Bernie Williams and Joe Torre embrace after the Yankees win the World Series in 1996, illustrating the ways in which professionalism often cuts across racial and other differences to unite people in a common cause.

religions may share a common political interest in their civil rights, while rich gays and lesbians may have more in common with rich heterosexuals on economic policy.

Other cross-cutting allegiances, such as professionalism and **cosmopolitanism** (from the Greek *cosmos*, universe, and *polis*, city), also reduce cultural tensions. Originally cosmopolitans were people who left their hometowns and regions for the urbanity and sophistication of major cities. Today the universality of cosmopolitanism is being rivaled by suburbanism, a development that has abandoned many poor and minorities to bleak and crime-ridden inner cities. But as suburbs and suburban schools increasingly reflect a broader range of racial and ethnic, if not economic, groups, racial and ethnic tensions will diminish.

American pragmatism is a cross-cutting allegiance. Pragmatists come from a variety of backgrounds and can be found in a cross-section of the public as well as government. Pragmatists, for example, are united by their commitment to practicality and their willingness to examine each problem afresh as it arises. They are also willing to experiment and to learn by doing, and they expect to modify or abandon a policy when it no longer seems right or doesn't work. Pragmatists do, however, disagree over how (or whether) to apply lessons learned from past mistakes to present situations. Those who have opposed U.S. intervention in Haiti, Bosnia, or Africa have often cited Vietnam as a lesson for nonintervention. Supporters of intervention cite the lesson of Munich, where the 1938 failure to resist Hitler's aggression in Europe is thought to have caused or hastened World War II.

Current Challenges to the American Political Culture

Since the 1960s, American political culture has been faced with the following challenges: intergenerational conflict, a sharp decline in public trust, heightened expectations of government, the downsizing of the American Dream, and the growing gap between rich and poor.

Intergenerational Conflict

Experts disagree over the extent to which membership in a generation affects political culture, in part because it is difficult to separate the effects of aging from the influences that mark the beliefs of a particular generation. The "aging" thesis, which can be found as early as Aristotle,[40] holds that for psychological and social reasons people tend toward idealism and extremism in their youth, moderation in their middle years, and conservatism in their later years. The "generation" thesis, popularized by sociologist Karl Mannheim, holds that generations are often marked by major social events that occured when they were between 18 and 25 years old.[41] Members of each generation develop common beliefs about *what is*, *what's right*, and *what works* based on encounters with and memories of intense historical events, such as wars and economic crises.[42] The generation thesis, however, must allow for the fact that each generation is divided by race, gender, class, religion, education, and ideology, and the fact that beliefs often change when individuals move from school into the workplace. In addition, interpersonal contact between generations within the same class tends to moderate intergenerational conflict. Relations between "parent/child, teacher/student, senior/junior colleague, friend/friend, constitute cross-cutting ties between generations."[43] Such factors prevent one generation from making common cause against another. Despite these analytic problems, professional and ordinary political observers routinely refer to the influences of the following three generations on American political culture.

The World War II Generation

The worldview of Americans born between 1920 and 1935 was shaped by the hardships of the Great Depression and World War II. Raised at a time when divorce was rare, most lived in intact families where the father's role as head of the household was clearly defined. Racial segregation—in schools, neighborhoods, public accommodations—was the law in southern states and the custom in many others. In 1940 only 15 percent of 18- to 21-year-olds were in college, and most of their professors were men.[44] Schooled in the virtues of capitalism, this generation was civic-minded, strongly patriotic, and respectful of authority.

After enduring poverty, joblessness, and wartime sacrifice, Americans emerged from World War II with 45 percent of the world's GDP. Corporations bred team players, and the look-alike houses in the suburbs seemed to stamp out look-alike families.[45] This generation was proud of the nation's new superpower status and its stand against communism, and it accepted the first-ever peacetime military draft without protest. As affluence increased, so did conformity. Children of immigrants became assimilated, college students joined sororities and fraternities, and religious congregations expanded. In 1954 Congress added the words "under God" to the pledge of allegiance and a year later it ordered "In God We Trust" inscribed on all American money. Meanwhile, TV beamed a shared vision of the world into an increasing number of living rooms. Those who did not prosper—the rural and urban poor, African Americans, Native Americans, and Latinos—were mostly invisible to those in the suburbs. This postwar affluence continued without serious setbacks until 1973.

This modest tract house was designed after World War II for a Pennsylvania community known as Levittown, named after its developer. These houses were inexpensive because it was cheaper to make them all the same.

The Baby-Boom Generation

The children of the World War II generation were the **baby boomers**—the 60 million people born between 1946 and 1964. Their worldview was shaped by their rejection of the materialism and conformity of their parents, an intense idealism inspired by the youthful President John Kennedy (1961–1963), and their response to the civil rights movement and antiwar protests. While most were ordinary idealists, there were extremist minorities on the right (the youth wing of the John Birch Society and the Young Americans for

baby boomers
This largest generation in American history was called the baby boom because there was a "boom" in the birth rate when soldiers returned from World War II.

Freedom) and on the left (Students for a Democratic Society, or SDS, and the Free Speech Movement). As American casualties in Vietnam mounted, the divisions between the boomers, who regarded the war as immoral, and their parents, who regarded the war as a duty, increased. Protesters organized "teach-ins" on college campuses, and some students occupied buildings, destroyed property, and burned their draft cards.

In 1968 the Vietnamese communists launched a massive surprise military offensive against the United States-backed government of South Vietnam; presidential candidate Robert F. Kennedy (President Kennedy's brother) and the Reverend Martin Luther King, Jr., were assassinated; Chicago police attacked student protesters outside the Democratic National Convention; and U.S. soldiers massacred civilians in the South Vietnamese village of My Lai (something Americans only learned about a year later). These events remain deeply etched in the memories of both generations, though in very different ways.

"Generation X"

At first, the children of the boomer generation were dubbed "Generation X" because their political identity and their ideals seemed unclear.[46] This is changing with the growing awareness of the daunting problems this generation faces. Growing up in the shadow of the boomers, many Xers have gotten the impression that everything meaningful—the political dramas, the social struggles, the excitement of participating—ended with the 1960s. The conspicuous consumption of the Reagan–Bush years and the turn toward profitmaking by those who fought for social justice in the 1960s have led some Xers to become cynics, even though most of them agree with their elders politically in many areas.

The many Xers who hold college degrees do not expect to have the same chances for jobs and prosperity as their parents and grandparents. They also resent the heavy burdens they are projected to bear for Social Security and Medicare benefits to older Americans, most of whom are unprepared for retirement,[47] as well as the massive national debt they will inherit. And they will be outvoted by Americans 65 and older, whose voting rate is the highest in the country—something that gives the older generations an enormous say over how government resources should be distributed.

Xers are also discovering that women who can now have both a career and a family bear exhausting burdens: most women return to work outside the home before a child turns one; women still do 87 percent of the shopping, 81 percent of the cooking, 78 percent of cleaning, and 63 percent of the billpaying.[48] Experts predict that Xers will not return to the nuclear family of the 1950s, and that as women grow more financially self-sufficient, both men and women will have less to gain from marriage. Americans are becoming sexually active earlier but marrying

One of the roughly 2,500 protesters taunting police at the 1968 Democratic National Convention in Chicago.

Figure 4.3
United States population by race or ethnicity

Race or Group	1980	1990	2000 (projected)
White	195,713	208,710	225,532
Black	26,683	30,486	35,454
Hispanic Origin	14,609	22,354	31,366
Asian	3,729	7,458	11,245
Native American	1,420	2,065	2,402

Population (in thousands)

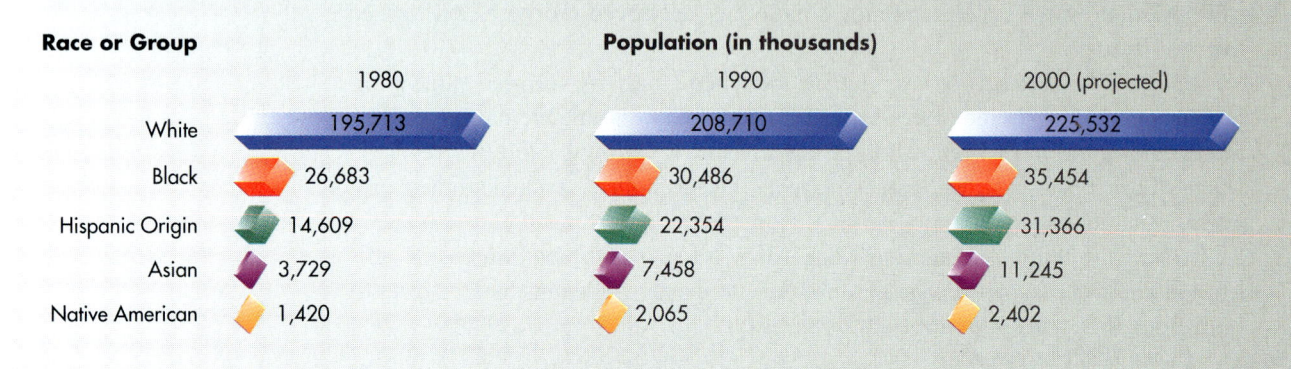

Source: *Statistical Abstract of the United States: 1996* (116th ed.) (Washington, D.C.: U.S. Bureau of the Census, 1996), p. 14.

later, are separating and divorcing more often, and are less likely to remarry. In the twenty-first century, more than 60 percent of children are expected to live with a single parent, usually their mother.[49] Xers are also facing a more racially and ethnically diverse population than their predecessors (see Figure 4.3).

The Decline of Public Trust

The widespread public trust political leaders enjoyed in the 1950s suffered serious blows in the 1960s, even among the World War II generation. In the 1970s, the slogan "Question Authority" appeared on bumper stickers and T-shirts. Figure 4.4 shows that by the mid-1990s public confidence in major social, economic, and political institutions had seriously eroded.

The slogan "Question Authority" is still popular today because a wave of scandals from the 1970s to the present reinforced the skepticism many Americans feel toward their political institutions. In 1974, when the House Judiciary Committee recommended that President Richard Nixon be impeached for his part in the Watergate scandal (see Chapter 12), most blamed the man, not the institution of the presidency. But the discovery of more foreign and domestic scandals in each subsequent administration increased distrust of political institutions in general.

Public distrust intensified when the Iran-Contra hearings exposed the Reagan administration's secret and illegal arms sales to a "terrorist nation" (Iran) to secure the release of American hostages held by pro-Iranian groups in Lebanon. Some of the proceeds were used illegally to fund guerrillas known as Contras who were trying to topple the left-wing government in Nicaragua. At home, televised hearings exposed corruption in the Department of Housing and Urban Development and the savings and loan industry. The "Iraq-Gate" scandal in the Bush administration revealed the government's role in arming President Saddam Hussein's

Iraq, which then invaded Kuwait and provoked the United States and its allies to launch a war in the Persian Gulf. White House staff in the Clinton administration were accused of covering up improper activities by the White House Travel Office and of illegally obtaining information on prominent Republicans from the Federal Bureau of Investigation. Both President Clinton and his wife underwent a lengthy investigation into alleged illegal activities involving a real estate development named Whitewater. Following election to his second term, Clinton faced many questions about party fundraising. At the same time, the House of Representatives reprimanded Speaker Newt Gingrich for his improper use of funds connected with his political action committee. Each of these scandals has driven public trust down.

Americans now question whether their government is reliable and their leaders are trustworthy. Politicians who have tried to deny wrongdoing by blaming errors on the political process have only reinforced public fears that the political system as a whole is flawed.

Figure 4.4
Faith in institutions

According to a survey by the National Opinion Research Center, Americans have less confidence in the leaders of national institutions today than in the 1970s.

Respondents indicated whether they had a great deal, some, or hardly any confidence in the people running the institutions listed.

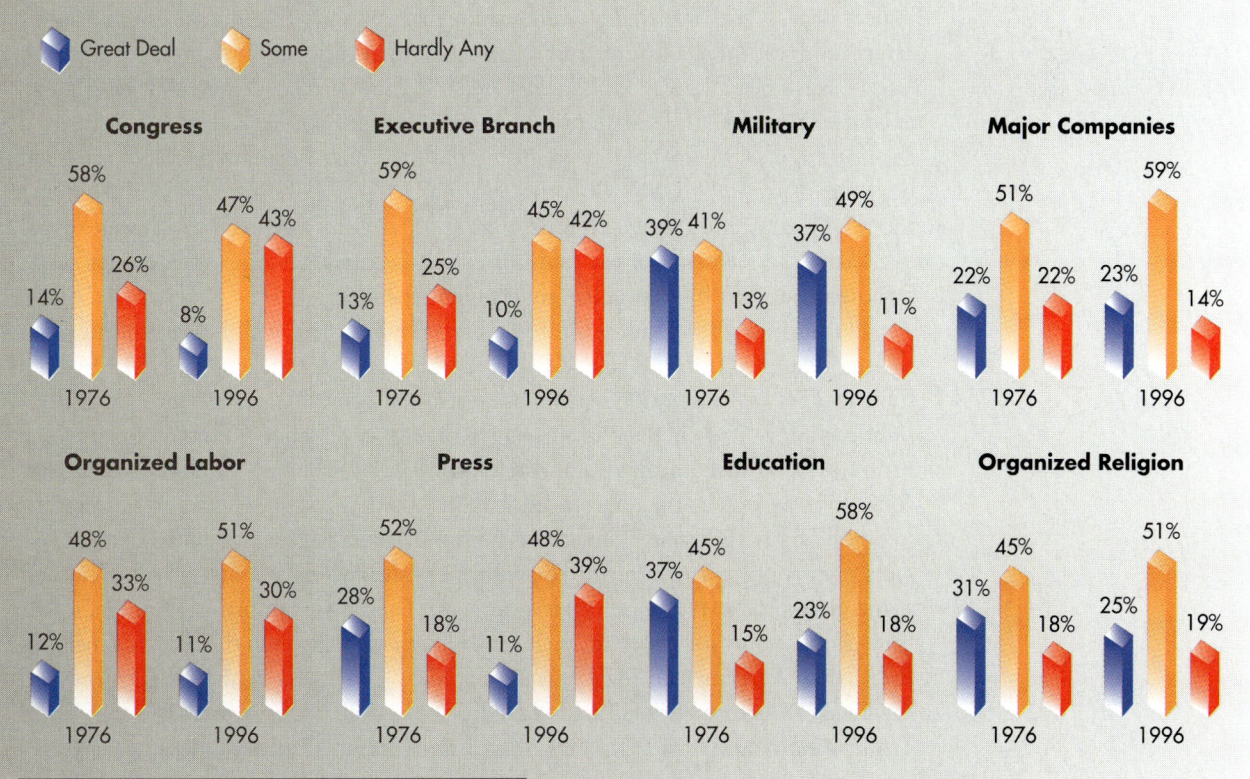

Legend: Great Deal | Some | Hardly Any

Congress
- 1976: 14%, 58%, 26%
- 1996: 8%, 47%, 43%

Executive Branch
- 1976: 13%, 59%, 25%
- 1996: 10%, 45%, 42%

Military
- 1976: 39%, 41%, 13%
- 1996: 37%, 49%, 11%

Major Companies
- 1976: 22%, 51%, 22%
- 1996: 23%, 59%, 14%

Organized Labor
- 1976: 12%, 48%, 33%
- 1996: 11%, 51%, 30%

Press
- 1976: 28%, 52%, 18%
- 1996: 11%, 48%, 39%

Education
- 1976: 37%, 45%, 15%
- 1996: 23%, 58%, 18%

Organized Religion
- 1976: 31%, 45%, 18%
- 1996: 25%, 51%, 19%

Source: Data from *The Public Perspective*, Feb./March 1997, 2–5.

Heightened Expectations of Government

Citizen expectations of government have grown along with the size of the social services "safety net" government has increasingly provided since the 1930s. This aid, which began with unemployment compensation and income security upon retirement, increased dramatically during the 1960s, when the existence of poverty in the midst of plenty led President Lyndon Johnson to declare a War on Poverty and his administration to develop Great Society reform programs, including preschool education, job training, and a domestic peace corps to help the poor at home. Social services expanded to include housing assistance, food stamps, health care for the poor and elderly, and student loans. Paying for these services and a war in Vietnam at the same time weakened the economy.

During the 1970s sociologist Daniel Bell predicted that public demands on government would continue to rise as the nation shifted from an industrial to a **postindustrial society**—a transformation as dramatic as the shift from an agrarian to an industrial society during the nineteenth century.[50] This postindustrial shift, which was also occurring in other industrialized nations, changed American society and political culture in three important ways:

- Institutions grew larger, more hierarchical, and more complex.
- Specialization increased and worker expertise narrowed.
- New technologies displaced labor, causing widespread unemployment.[51]

The social importance of families, schools, and religious organizations declined. These changes shook people's sense of security, self-esteem, values, and political expectations. They were less willing than their parents to embrace a strict work ethic, to invest for the future, and to postpone gratification of their desires. Sociologist Christopher Lasch dubbed the 1970s "The *Me* Decade" to characterize an excessively private and selfish notion of the self that had displaced civic virtue and the notion of service. Character building that had once meant *being* or *doing good* now meant *feeling good*.[52] Government, many felt, was responsible for providing them with a decent, if not a comfortable, standard of living—a view that persisted even after the recession of the mid-1970s and recognition that tax revenues could no longer support high levels of government spending.

During the 1980s the desire for material goods and well-being continued to rise amid perceptions of a declining economy. Americans increasingly blamed their leaders for the nation's problems—a weak economy, persistent crime, poor public schools, and the lack of affordable health care. They preferred to consume rather than to save and invest and relied on deficit spending to finance their personal lives as well as the government.

Polls show that many Americans continue to want government to curb the effects of corporate downsizing.[53] Some see immigrants as a competitive threat and want government to curtail their numbers. They also oppose U.S. policies that they claim export jobs abroad, including U.S. participation in the North American Free Trade Agreement (NAFTA), negotiated by Presidents Bush and Clinton, and the General Agreement on Tariffs and Trade (GATT), transformed into the World Trade Organization (WTO) under the Clinton administration.

The Bush administration set out to "resocialize" citizens to expect less of government and to rely more on the private sector and volunteer groups. The Clinton administration, more sympathetic to citizen demands for government activism but acknowledging budgetary realities, also attempted to reduce public expectations of government. As Clinton and Gore put it, the government "should do less rowing and more steering"—that is, government should develop tax and spending policies that stimulate actors in the private sector to perform many of the tasks that government had been performing[54] (see Chapter 13). However, the Clinton administration remained committed to social programs that prepare Americans—especially children—to become productive citizens.

As the federal debt and public anxiety over economic security mounted during the 1990s, so did public pressure to cut government and taxes. Yet many still expected government to upgrade public education, protect consumers and the environment, provide for universal health care, help find a cure for AIDS, strengthen the economy, stimulate employment, and foster prosperity for a population that had grown larger and was living longer. But government services, like everything else, now cost more—more than many Americans were willing to spend. Evidence of a disjunction between roles as taxpayers and as consumers of government assistance could be seen in 1994 and 1996, when voters put Republicans in favor of strict government downsizing in control of both houses of Congress and Bill Clinton, who favored both downsizing and significant social services, in charge of the White House. As one observer puts it, "Taxpayers will not allow the government to do much more than it does now. But government's client groups will not allow it to do much less."[55]

The Downsizing of the American Dream

One of the strongest common bonds in American political culture has been the **American Dream**—the pursuit of happiness, whether by acquiring and developing property or by achieving artistic, athletic, intellectual, or spiritual goals. Because standards of living for most groups have tended to rise from one generation to the next, the American Dream seemed attainable to many people—that is, until 1973. Since then, real median family income has scarcely grown, average real wages have stayed the same or declined,[56] and living standards have dropped for 80 percent of the nation's workers.[57] The middle class now works longer hours for lower pay, and young workers are discovering that many of the new jobs being created are low-wage, part-time, and without benefits such as health insurance. As a result, many are losing faith in the American Dream (see Figure 4.5).

These changes and the profound disillusionment they have brought have been attributed primarily to global competition, but other factors have played a

The point of this parody is that the evolution of the American Dream brought with it a decline in space and self-sufficiency. Americans who once aspired to their own farm aspired to Levittown tract houses 150 years later. Today they count themselves lucky to share an urban condo with tiny pets and to experience the world around them vicariously on a VCR.

Figure 4.5

American attitudes and the American dream: A survey of parents

(1)	Do you expect your children will have a better life than you have had, a worse life, or a life about as good as yours?	Better life Worse life About as good No children Not sure	46% 20% 27% 6% 1%
(2)	For most Americans, do you think the American dream of equal opportunity, personal freedom, and social mobility has become easier or harder to achieve in the past 10 years?	Easier to achieve Harder to achieve Not sure	31% 67% 2%
(3)	And do you think this American dream will be easier or harder to achieve in the next 10 years?	Easier to achieve Harder to achieve Not sure	22% 74% 4%

Source: Urie Bronfenbrenner et al., *The State of Americans* (New York: Free Press, 1996), 52; Harris Poll data.

role: the energy crisis and inflation of the 1970s, the failure of Reagan-era tax cuts to restore prosperity, the rising costs of government aid to the elderly, the shift to a service economy, technological change, and corporate downsizing. Between 1989 and 1995, parents' expectations that their children would have a better life than they did dropped almost 25 percent. Such deep disillusionment is justified: laid-off workers a generation ago were able to get equivalent jobs, while two-thirds of their counterparts today must work for less. Experts on these trends say that their implications "for all but the wealthiest of Americans would seem to be that the economic aspirations embedded in the American Dream must be significantly scaled back."[58]

Many CEOs argue that the American Dream will become a nightmare if the country does not become more competitive[59] and claim the market itself will make the necessary adjustments. And, indeed, by the presidential election of 1996, the economies of some areas of the country such as Michigan and California seemed on the rebound. According to one report, roughly 60 percent of new service jobs were for professionals and managers.[60] But one commentator also warned: "A culture provides the values of community and caring; if the society does not supply them, the market certainly will not."[61]

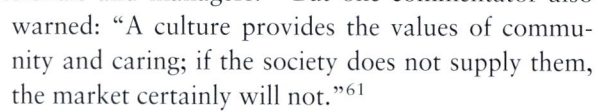

How strongly racism affects the American Dream is a matter of dispute. Most whites believe that blacks enjoy equality of opportunity, while most blacks believe that they do not. Often it is middle-class blacks who are the most disillusioned, for just as the American Dream seems about to come true for them they discover that racism still bars them from promotions, home mortgages, taxis, even courteous service in restaurants. Some observers warn that blacks who give up on the American Dream may turn to black nationalist or separatist movements.[62]

The Growing Gap Between Rich and Poor

Those with the least faith in the American Dream are those who suffer from poverty and prejudice. Studies show that since 1973, as the economic pie has shrunk, ever bigger slices have been going to the rich and ever smaller ones to the poor (see Figure 4.6). People with the fewest skills now earn less. The number of children in families of the working poor has risen 67 percent, to 5.6 million in 1994 from 3.4 million two decades ago,[63] while the chances that such children will get a college education have been falling. The poor and minorities suffer the highest rates of violent crime.[64]

Such trends have created an underclass that may resort to antisocial behavior to meet their needs because they don't need social approval and see no reason to participate in the political process.[65] These people—the poor and uneducated, particularly in urban ghettos and rural areas—elude the main socializing agencies, such as—family, school, church, and clubs, that instruct individuals in the dominant values of the political culture and the promise of the American Dream. Already the United States has a far higher incarceration rate than other industrial democracies.[66] If democracy is to work, experts warn, the nation cannot ignore this alienated underclass.[67]

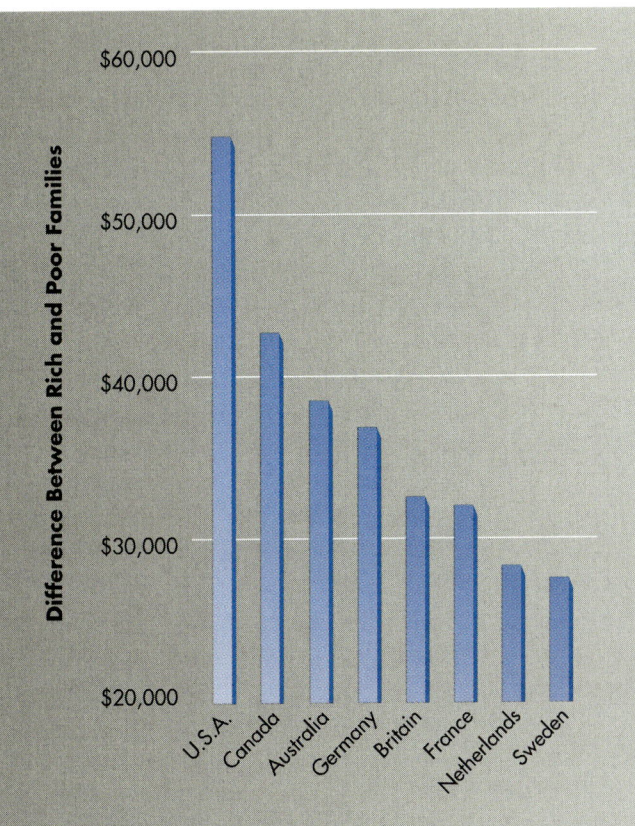

Figure 4.6

Rich and poor families are furthest apart in the United States

This graph shows the difference in after-tax income of a high-income family of four and a low-income family of four. The comparison is between a family at the 90th percentile (that is, having a higher income than 89 percent of the country's families) and a family at the tenth percentile (that is, with a lower income than 90 percent of the country's families).

Source: Urie Bronfenbrenner et al., *The State of Americans* (New York: Free Press, 1996), 149; Luxembourg Income Study data.

★ Revitalizing American Political Culture

These new major challenges to the American political culture suggest the need to upgrade and equalize education, strengthen community life, and redefine patriotism and citizen allegiance.

Upgrading and Equalizing Education

"The answer to all our national problems comes down to a single word: education," said President Lyndon Johnson in promoting his Great Society programs of the 1960s. This was also Bill Clinton's refrain in the 1996 presidential campaign. Today, when the only security workers can count on is the skills and training they can take with them from job to job, getting a good education is more important than ever. Yet more than 40 million adults cannot perform simple tasks involving reading, writing, and math.[68] Census data show that improvements in education reduce poverty, among other benefits (see Figure 4.7).[69] Education is primarily the responsibility of the states, but they have a long way to go in upgrading and

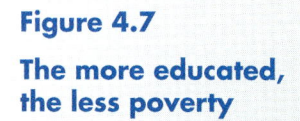

Figure 4.7

The more educated, the less poverty

This figure shows the impact of parental education on the likelihood that a child under 18 will be living below the official poverty line.

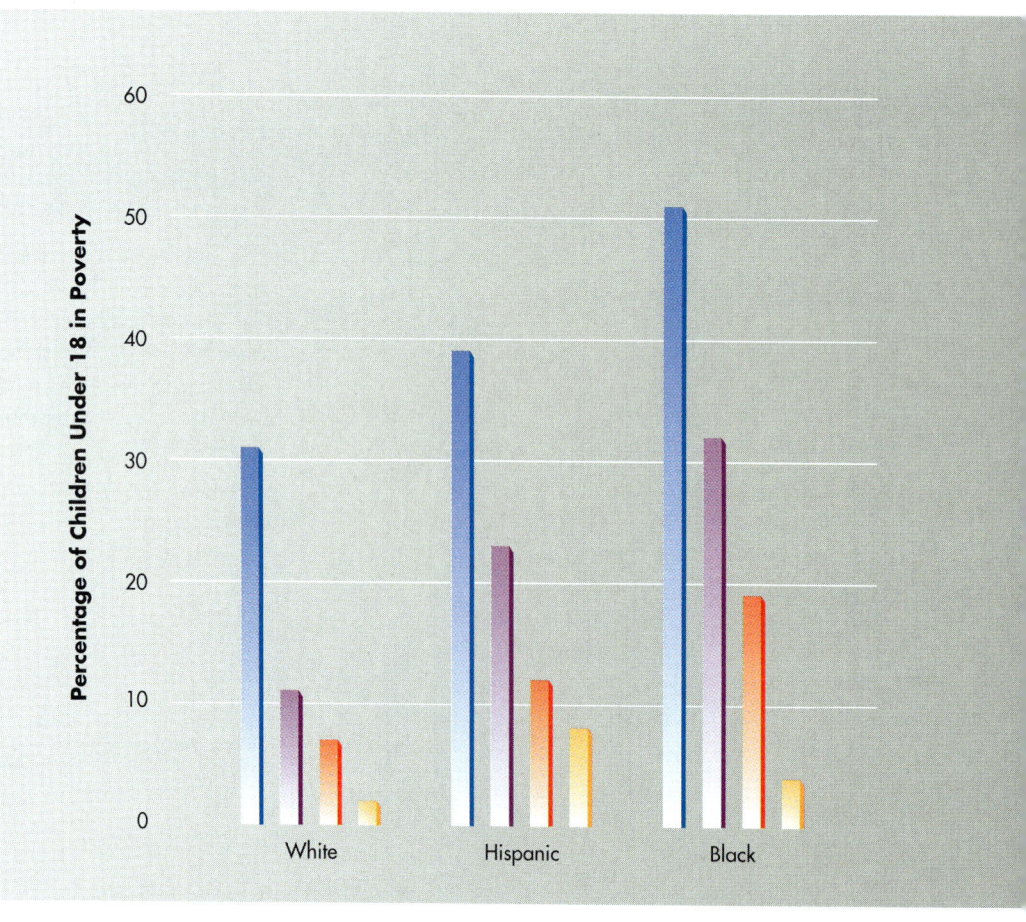

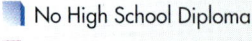

- No High School Diploma
- High School Diploma
- Some College
- College Degree or More

Source: Urie Bronfenbrenner et al., *The State of Americans* (New York: Free Press, 1996), 176; U.S. Bureau of the Census data.

equalizing their educational systems. The Clinton administration supports the right of states to educate their children as they see fit but has proposed that students take national examinations to monitor how well state education works.

Charter Schools and Vouchers

To upgrade educational achievement and reduce violence in the schools, states are experimenting with new ways of teaching and new types of schools.[70] By 1996 more than 25 states had passed laws creating some 260 **charter schools**—experimental schools that operate independently of state authority—and the largest teachers' union in the country, the National Education Association, has begun opening more. Some states now offer **school vouchers**—a payment from government that can be used to pay for a child's education in a public or private school of the parents' choice. Supporters of vouchers argue that people should be able to exercise free choice over where they send their children to school, claim that private schools educate and socialize children more effectively than public schools, and assert that vouchers will do more for minority children than pouring resources into their poor and mediocre public schools. Supporters of public schools maintain that because public schools, in effect, cut across race, ethnicity, gender, and class, they strengthen American political culture and democracy. A popular humorist makes the same point by pretending to look back on the age of public schools from the twenty-first century, an age of school vouchers:

Landel Shakespeare, 7, displays his report card from Our Lady of Peace, a Roman Catholic grade school in Cleveland, Ohio, that he attended on vouchers. Ohio was the first state to issue government vouchers to pay tuition at religious schools. The Shakespeares will receive a total of $1,648, to which they must add the remaining $172 of their son's tuition. Other states, such as Minnesota, issue vouchers only to nonreligious private schools.

> With the introduction of school vouchers, you got to send your kids to schools where they learned the *truth*—your choice—Our Lady of Sorrows, Foursquare Millennial Gospel, Moon Goddess, Malcolm X, the Open School of Whatever, the Academy of Hairy-Legged Individualism, the School of the Green Striped Tie, you name it, and who could argue with the idea of free choice?—until you stop and think that the old idea of the public school was a place where you went to find out who inhabits this society other than people like you.[71]

Equalizing Education

Ninety-percent of America's students attend public schools whose quality often correlates with wealth. But the strongest defenders of public schools live in white suburbs where the quality of tax-supported schools is the highest and diversity is the lowest.[72] If public schools are to perform their academic and socializing functions fairly, then states must remedy these vast inequalities.

Americans who can afford it are increasingly cutting themselves off from the rest of society by living in gated communities. There are more than 25,000 gated communities in the United States today.

But money alone cannot cure education problems that stem from social problems. In 1990, the Kentucky legislature did more than pass a law dramatically narrowing the spending gap between rich and poor school districts. It also called for more creative teaching, improved technology, better counseling, preschools for low-income children, and attention to the many outside influences that affect learning. Between 1990 and 1994 Kentucky raised per-pupil spending 40 percent (it had ranked last in percentage of adult high school graduates, and in 1980 just over half had high school diplomas). Other states may follow Kentucky's example if this major commitment to education pays off. Another encouraging development is the equalization of whites' and blacks' graduation rates between 1985 and 1995.[73]

Strengthening Community Life

For the last 30 years, communitarians and other social critics have been warning about the consequences of the breakdown of American community life. Today communities face increasing unemployment due to downsizing by government and corporations alike and the likelihood that many more jobs will be eliminated permanently due to advances in automation. While manual laborers are displaced, those with intellectual competence and advanced degrees are increasingly able to cut themselves off from the rest of America with "their global linkages, good schools, comfortable lifestyles, excellent health care, and abundance of security guards."[74] If the country is split into the underclass and the isolated rich, who will help out in community service organizations, crisis centers, public shelters, self-help programs, after-school programs, scouting activities, local theater and music groups, conservation programs, and other areas of community life? In the past women have frequently managed such programs as volunteers, but with increasing numbers of women in all classes now in the work force, their ability to sustain such programs has declined precipitously.

Community Service and the Nonprofit Sector

The idea of community service—voluntary outreach not motivated by expectations of material gain—is often inspired by a sense of kinship and connection with others and a desire to return a portion of one's individual knowledge, experience, wealth, and energies to the larger society that has made these achievements possible. Currently the independent sector accounts for 6 percent of the nation's GDP, in contrast to the private (economic) sector, which accounts for 80 percent, and the public (government) sector, which accounts for 14 percent. While this so-called third sector is half the size of government in terms of employees and earnings, in recent years it has been growing twice as fast as the other two sectors. This sector, with its 1.4 million nonprofit organizations—organizations that serve the public welfare instead of earning profits for shareholders—plays a vital role as an advocate for groups whose needs are not being met by the private and public sectors. It has been described as "the bonding force, the social glue that helps unite the diverse interests of the American people into a cohesive social identity. . . . Yet strangely enough, this central aspect of the American character and experience is little examined in . . . textbooks," which focus on the marketplace and government.[75]

Expanding the Third Sector

Innovative policy proposals are now aimed at increasing volunteerism and decreasing unemployment at the community level. For example, the four-day high-tech work week, which gives workers more family and leisure time and increases plant productivity, is already a reality at Hewlett-Packard and Digital Equipment. Other proposals include the shadow wage, which would provide a tax deduction for every hour volunteered to a certified nonprofit organization, and the social wage, which would provide the unemployed with a living wage in return for doing work in their communities.

The adoption of a value added tax—a tax on the value that each stage of production adds to a product, shifting the burden away from income and onto consumption—has also been suggested. A tax of 5–7 percent on discretionary goods and services could raise enough money to finance a social wage and salaries for community service programs. Advocates of a VAT would reduce the regressive impact of the tax by exempting basic necessities and small businesses, as other countries have done.

Redefining Patriotism and Citizen Allegiance

Today communities, towns, and cities worldwide are being transformed by the globalization of finance, multinational corporations, and mass communication across national borders. Airplanes, satellite hookups, global cable TV news, and the Internet are only some of the ways modern technology connects people throughout the world. The nation-state itself is losing power abroad to global corporations and transnational organizations, while at home it is mired in massive debts. In addition, the nation-state is only one of the many settings—from neighborhoods to the world at large—in which Americans practice politics. As one political scientist puts it, the United States "arguably leads this global trend toward a 'national space' that contains many 'international borders'."[76] As people's loyalties and activities expand downward and outward in these ways, patriotism is coming to mean "a personal commitment to make one's country honest and just in all its acts" and to "motivate the whole country to be as good a neighbor in the community of nations as the conscience of individuals motivates them to be in the communities where they live."[77]

Political theorist Michael J. Sandel predicts that before long sovereignty will be dispersed both upward and downward among "a multiplicity of communities and political bodies—some more extensive than nations and some less." No other arrangement, he argues, will inspire the allegiance of citizens. When people enter an airport anywhere in the world, they expect that certain safety and sanitary conditions are being met, and certain international institutions see that they are. But more such institutions will be needed at all levels of social organization. Sandel points out that groups such as the Commission on Global Governance, composed of public officials from around the world, are working to spread a global civic ethic that will move people toward cosmopolitan citizenship—a shared global vision in many areas of life. Other political theorists who recommend expanding this notion downward advocate a rooted cosmopolitanism that reflects a greater sensitivity to racial and ethnic roots.[78] These developments suggest that the revitalization of American political culture is already underway.

Summary

The debate over multiculturalism and political correctness is a reminder that politics and power are intimately tied to education. Knowledge and the language used to convey it express points of view about *what is*, *what's right*, and *what works*. Hence schools at every level find themselves caught in political disputes over *what* should be taught, *how* it should be taught, and by *whom*.

In the United States, political culture—the widely shared beliefs and practices people have about *what is*, *what's right*, and *what works* in political life—is the process by which the American people express and reinvent themselves as a national community from one generation to the next. Among these shared beliefs are the nation's core political values: a commitment to freedom, democracy, liberty, justice, equal opportunity, and capitalism.

American political culture maintains its identity because its people—individuals, groups, organizations, and governing institutions—successfully regulate and balance pressures for order and change. This regulation requires civility—reasonable tolerance for others and respect for the law—learning by doing, and effective political socialization.

Political socialization—the process by which people acquire and develop political beliefs and values and then transmit them to others—gives coherence to a political culture by fostering common beliefs, values, practices, and aspirations. Most people in the United States are also socialized into regional, racial, ethnic, or religious subcultures, and many develop commitments and concerns that extend beyond the nation-state. Primary socialization occurs largely in the home, while secondary socialization occurs in schools, on the job, and in other ways throughout adult life. Political socialization promotes patriotism through storytelling, rituals, reverence for the American ancestors, respect for founding documents, and national celebrations. Political socialization, political culture, and political institutions operate together as a system in ways that continually strengthen or diminish one another.

Major sources of conflict that stem from differences between subcultures, religions, ideals such as individualism and communitarianism, and political ideologies are offset to some degree by sources of order: assimilation; adherence to common laws, rules, and procedures; and allegiances that cut across cultural differences.

Among the challenges facing American political culture today are intergenerational conflicts; the decline of public trust; the erosion of the American Dream; and the growing gap between rich and poor.

Signs of revitalization in American political culture include efforts to upgrade and equalize education; expand volunteerism; and redefine patriotism and citizen allegiance in a world in which domestic and international political actors are altering the traditional role of the nation-state.

Key Terms

American Dream 137
anarchists 128
baby boomers 132
charter schools 141
civility 110
communitarianism 124
communitarians 128
conservatives 125
cosmopolitanism 131
cross-cutting allegiances 130
individualism 124
liberals 125
libertarians 128
multiculturalim 108
nation 110
nation-state 122
neoconservatives 128
patriotism 117
political culture 109
political ideology 125
political socialization 113
populists 128
postindustrial society 136
pragmatism 125
Religious Right 123
school vouchers 141
socialists 128
subcultures 121

How You Can Learn More About Political Culture and Socialization

Bellah, Robert N., et al. *Habits of the Heart: Individualism and Commitment in American Life.* Berkeley: University of California Press, 1985. A captivating account of how these themes are woven in different ways through the lives of a small number of white, middle-class Americans. This slice-of-life approach to public opinion provides a helpful complement to the more common statistical approaches.

Dolbeare, Kenneth M., and Janette Kay Hubbell. *USA 2012: After the Middle-Class Revolution.* Chatham, N.J.: Chatham House, 1996. An argument that the middle-class should pressure government to support policies of economic nationalism to recover the promise of the American Dream.

Graebner, William. *The Engineering of Consent: Democracy and Authority in Twentieth-Century America.* Madison: University of Wisconsin Press, 1978. A compelling account of the ways in which social engineering has disempowered democracy. Especially interesting is the second half of the book, which treats the student protest movements during and after the Vietnam War.

Hochschild, Jennifer L. *Facing Up to the American Dream: Race, Class and the Soul of the Nation.* Princton, N.J.: Princton University Press, 1995. A study of how black Americans relate to the American Dream, based on polls of black respondents from different economic classes.

Ichilov, Orit, ed. *Political Socialization, Citizenship Education, and Democracy.* New York: Teachers College Press, 1990. A rich introduction to the wide spectrum of research in political socialization and its effects on democracy.

Lasch, Christopher. *The Culture of Narcissism: American Life in an Age of Diminishing Expectations.* New York: W. W. Norton, 1978. An influential perspective on American political culture in the 1970s, including a critique of the American educational system that anticipated that of the opponents of political correctness and multiculturalism in the 1990s.

Lea, James F. *Political Consciousness and American Democracy.* Jackson: University Press of Mississippi, 1982. A critical and compelling analysis of how American political culture has been affected by schooling, language, technology, prejudice, and related influences.

Leinberger, Paul, and Bruce Tucker. *The New Individualists: The Generation After the Organization Man.* New York: HarperCollins, 1991. Fascinating case studies of the social, political, and religious values of the children of the conformist generation of the 1950s.

MacLeod, David I. *Building Character in the American Boy: The Boy Scouts, YMCA, and Their Forerunners, 1870–1920.* Madison: University of Wisconsin Press, 1983. An engrossing historical account of how the male child's character was socially engineered to support particular notions of male responsibility and citizenship.

Sinopoli, Richard C. *The Foundation of American Citizenship: Liberalism, the Constitution, and Civic Virtue.* New York: Oxford University Press, 1992. A view of American citizenship from the vantage point of the Framers.

Public Opinion

Above: Newt Gingrich and House Republicans launch their Contract with America in September 1994 in preparation for the midterm elections. *Right:* Republican public opinion expert Frank Luntz observes unseen the focus group behind a one-way mirror.

CHAPTER 5

I argue that representative government [requires] an independent, *expert* organization [to make] facts intelligible to those who have to make the decisions. . . . [We need to abandon the] unworkable fiction that each of us must acquire a competent opinion about all public affairs.

—Walter Lippmann

The democratic way of life rests firmly on . . . the actual experience of the mass of its citizens. . . . Because there are no rigid standards of absolute value, it is all the more vital to measure the standards which the people set for themselves [including] the opinions of the opposition.

—George Gallup[1]

What Public Opinion Is and Why It Is Important

How Trustworthy Are Polls and Their Interpretations?

How Competent Is American Public Opinion?

How to Improve Public Opinion

In September 1994, when Newt Gingrich and House Republicans launched the Republican midterm election platform known as the "Contract with America," its provisions had already been market-tested under the direction of public opinion expert Frank Luntz. To do this Luntz had used *focus groups*—small groups of people representative of a particular sector of the population who are brought together and observed, usually behind a one-way mirror, as they discuss an issue or a candidate. For the focus groups Luntz had chosen those the Republican party most needed to reach—alienated Americans who feared for their futures and distrusted the major parties and big government. Possible "Contract with America" provisions that failed to score a 60 percent popularity rating were dropped, and the remainder were tested in telephone polls to confirm their mass appeal.

Using Luntz's data, Gingrich and his supporters crafted a list of ten items that they promised to bring to a House vote during the first 100 days of the new Congress—term limits, a balanced budget amendment, welfare reform, a stronger national defense, middle-class tax relief, stiffer punishment for criminals, and swifter enforcement of the death penalty. Because the data showed strong disagreement over such social issues as abortion and school prayer, these were dropped from the document. So was the word "Republican," which even Republicans in the focus groups felt would make the contract less appealing to independent voters and disaffected Democrats. Republicans, focus group members had complained, are "mean" and "uncaring" and "don't give a damn about the average person."[2]

After more than 300 Republican House candidates signed the "Contract with America," the Republicans captured both houses of Congress for the first time in almost forty years. Many interpreted this victory as evidence that the "Contract with America" had worked for the Republican party.

Luntz's use of public opinion to field-test the various provisions of the "Contract with America" and then to bolster the Republican agenda as it moved through Congress is a clear example of polls driving public policy and boosting party popularity at the same time. Some observers are concerned that this use of polls will discourage politicians from acting on their own beliefs about *what's right*. "That's always been a problem in American politics," says Sheldon Gawiser, president of the National Council on Public Polls. "Do you talk about what you think or do you talk about what you think [people] want to hear?"[3]

Luntz rejects such criticisms. "I know what people want and I think it's time that the Republican Party starts giving people what they want and stops acting arrogant and saying, 'This is what you need. We know it's good for you.'"[4] The question, of course, is *which* people. Luntz's focus groups consisted largely of white, middle-class people who had paid little attention to politics until Ross Perot and Pat Buchanan made bids for their votes. Moreover, Luntz advises Republicans to disregard African Americans because "they have little common ground with what we stand for."[5] In short, the slogans Luntz pretests come from a fairly homogeneous group of disaffected independents who often determine the outcome of elections but are not typical of the public as a whole.

Luntz also knows that most of the people he polls don't really understand the issues on which they are being queried. He reminds Republicans, for example, that "Americans know almost nothing about the budget, and what they think they know is often wrong."[6] But in his capacity as a partisan pollster, Luntz feels no responsibility to educate the public. His responsibility, as he sees it, is to get his Republican clients elected and reelected.

Political candidates and White House strategists in both parties increasingly rely on focus groups, polls, and other marketing devices to win elections and gain support for their policies. The partisan use, or manipulation, of public opinion might seem to be different from consulting public opinion to formulate party agendas and public policies. In American politics, however, these uses are hard to separate. Are polls and public opinion becoming just another commodity to politicians, interest groups, and the media who can afford to buy data—or even to buy the manufacture of "data" by partisan pollsters—to gain power, attention, or profits?[7] If so, how will this new kind of "public opinion" affect democratic politics?

In this chapter we'll explore the vital role public opinion plays in American democracy by focusing on the following questions:

> **What is public opinion and why is it important in American politics?**
> **How trustworthy are polls and their interpretations?**
> **How competent is American public opinion?**
> **How can public opinion be improved?**

What Public Opinion Is and Why It Is Important

There is no such thing as public opinion in and of itself. Rather, *people*, influenced by their goals, create pictures of what they call public opinion.

What Public Opinion Is

Most specialists on the subject define **public opinion** as the summary of the distribution of expressed attitudes of all or part of the people on some subject at some particular moment. Their definition is very precise because it recognizes that

- people's opinions are never unanimous on anything because individuals are socialized differently, belong to different subcultures, and find themselves in different circumstances;
- public opinion involves only the attitudes people actually express—not those they don't; and
- attitudes expressed at some particular moment can suddenly change: people may feel positive about the social services the federal government provides until they pay the income taxes that finance those services on April 15.

This view of public opinion assumes that we can find out what public opinion is by simply adding up (or aggregating) individual opinions. Some specialists, however, argue that public opinion should be thought of as something different from the mere sum of individual opinions at a given moment because they believe that the American public learns from experience over time, as we'll see.

Public opinion specialists called **pollsters** use **polls** and surveys of individual beliefs and preferences to produce a picture of public opinion. Finding out what public opinion is contributes to understanding politics and affects the practice of politics. When distributions in public opinion remain stable over time, political actors are able to act in a more predictable public environment, whether they agree with its views or not. American public opinion has remained relatively stable in a number of areas: its core values (see Figure 4.1, p. 123); its unwavering support for capital punishment; the general acceptance (with some qualifications and reservations) of sex education in the schools (polls show a steady majority of 80 percent for over 15 years); the rejection of government censorship of the media; the acceptance of the critical role of the press; and the belief that women should receive equal pay for equal work.[8] Figure 5.1 shows what political actors can learn from the way public opinion is distributed.

Particular segments of public opinion are increasingly studied through the use of **focus groups**—small groups of people representative of a particular sector of the population, whose views on particular issues and candidates are studied to help political actors devise strategies to elicit desired reactions from the populations these groups represent. Major political campaigns, like the Republican "Contract with America," make effective use of focus group research.

> **poll**
> A poll is a survey (from the Latin for "oversee") that asks a selection of people questions designed to elicit their opinions on some subject. The word *poll* has the same root as *politics*—the Greek word *polis*, or "city-state."

Figure 5.1

The distribution of public opinion influences political actions

The distribution of public opinion on an issue is typically depicted in three ways that may help a political actor decide how to respond. For example, political actors would tend to respond to a *normal distribution* of public opinion (the bell-shaped curve, a) by pursuing middle-of-the-road policies. When public opinion shows a *skewed distribution* (b) in which the views of most people are similar but skewed toward one end, political actors ignore or depart from those views at great political risk. Public opinion that is fairly evenly divided into two camps on an issue has a *bimodal distribution* (c). Such issues present the greatest challenges to political actors because taking either position risks alienating a great many people, while taking a compromise position between the two risks disappointing everyone.

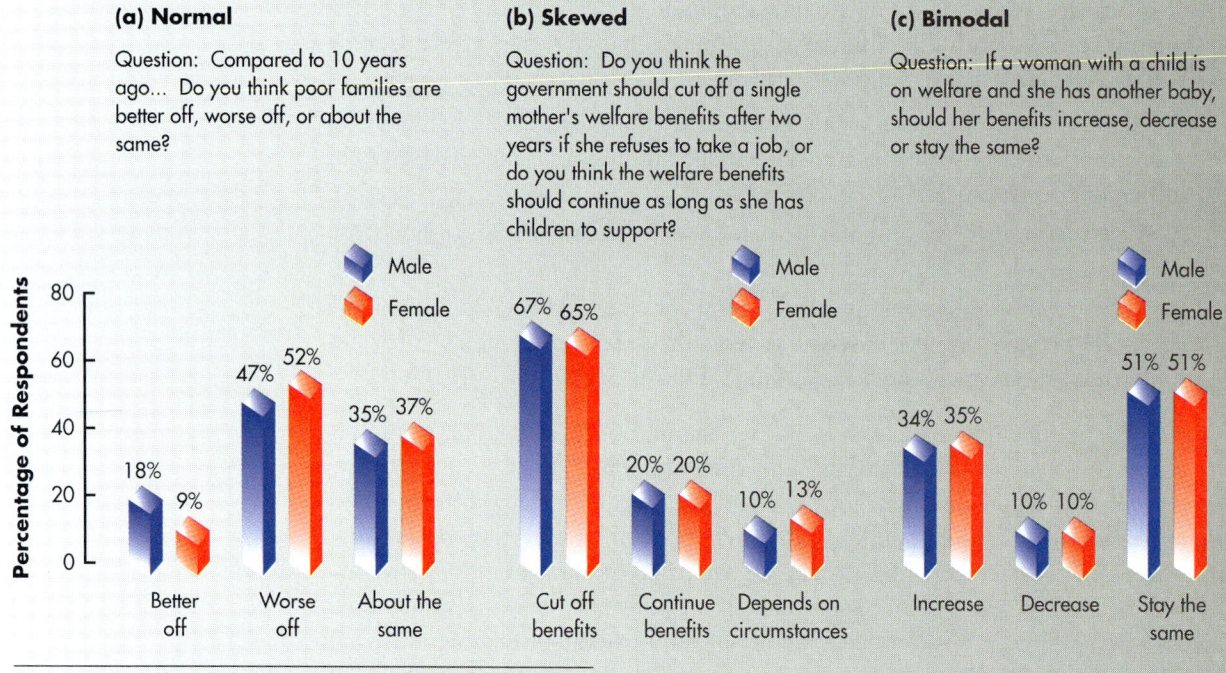

(a) Normal

Question: Compared to 10 years ago... Do you think poor families are better off, worse off, or about the same?

	Male	Female
Better off	18%	9%
Worse off	47%	52%
About the same	35%	37%

(b) Skewed

Question: Do you think the government should cut off a single mother's welfare benefits after two years if she refuses to take a job, or do you think the welfare benefits should continue as long as she has children to support?

	Male	Female
Cut off benefits	67%	65%
Continue benefits	20%	20%
Depends on circumstances	10%	13%

(c) Bimodal

Question: If a woman with a child is on welfare and she has another baby, should her benefits increase, decrease or stay the same?

	Male	Female
Increase	34%	35%
Decrease	10%	10%
Stay the same	51%	51%

Source: (a) Survey by Princeton Survey Research Associates for Knight-Ridder, Jan. 5–15, 1996; (b, c) Survey by Associates Press, June 5–9, 1996; all reported in *The Public Perspective*, August/September 1996, 24.

Why Public Opinion Is Important

Public opinion is important in American politics because it can legitimate political authority, it can make political actors more responsive and effective, it can help political candidates and parties, and it can indicate continuity and change in beliefs and values.

Public Opinion Can Legitimate Political Authority

Public opinion is often used to legitimate political authority. Political actors use public opinion data to show that the public supports their actions and policies. Polls allow them to claim that their actions and policies are *right* or are *what should be* done. Such data may be particularly influential if they are expressed in numbers and graphs that make them look like scientific descriptions of *what is*.

Today the actions and policies of democratic governments tend to be evaluated by their popular appeal. Of course the fact that democracies hold elections already makes them dependent on public opinion. Indeed, studies show that U.S. policies at both the national and state levels tend to reflect public preferences.[9] Recognizing this fact, even some dictators respond—or at least pay lip service—to popular sentiment in order to gain approval both at home and abroad.[10] Some despots—Nazi Germany's Adolf Hitler, Fascist Italy's Benito Mussolini, and more recently, Cuba's Fidel Castro—have managed, as one expert puts it, "to convince even themselves that they truly speak for or, in fact, actually embody, the popular will."[11] Moreover, dictators want to know what their people think even if they choose to disregard it because they can use such information to manipulate popular attitudes and thereby strengthen their grip on power.

When polls show that a majority of the American public favors a particular government proposal and when Congress then turns that proposal into law, democracy appears to be working—that is, the people rather than elites seem to be running the country. And when political authorities appear to be carrying out the will of the people as revealed in polls, their own political authority tends to be legitimated.

Public Opinion Can Make Political Actors More Responsive and Effective

Political actors of every sort, from interest groups to government, consult public opinion for a variety of reasons. One reason government leaders and bureaucrats consult public opinion is to find out what public policies the public wants so they can be more responsive and effective. After the 1992 elections, when *Newsweek* and Gallup polls found enormous discontent with immigration policy,[12] many lawmakers introduced bills to restrict immigration. Just before the presidential election of 1996, Congress passed and President Bill Clinton signed into law a tough immigration control bill in response to public opinion on that issue. There have been similar responses to public pressure for reducing deficit spending and the size of government.

Consulting public opinion lets policymakers know whether people believe existing policies are working as intended, or whether people believe they should be changed or abolished. Public opinion also helps policymakers predict whether a new, experimental, or costly program is likely to have popular support. As competing health care bills wended their way through Congress in 1994, for example, all eyes were on the polls to see which proposals were the most popular, and lawmakers altered their bills accordingly. This was a clear case of lawmakers reacting to positive and negative feedback from polls. Their *learning by doing* followed these steps:

1. Lawmakers launched drafts of their proposed bills.
2. Members of the public reacted to the proposals in polls, whether the respondents were knowledgeable about them or not.
3. Lawmakers then tailored their bills to the views expressed in those polls.

Sometimes government leaders consciously adopt programs that lack public support. In 1994, when polls showed that most Americans opposed sending military troops to Haiti to restore its democratically elected president, who had been deposed by a military coup, President Clinton concluded that Americans did not adequately understand the situation. After attempting to explain and justify the need for U.S. intervention in a nationwide speech, he proceeded with the intervention. The result was another instance of *learning by doing*. The mission's success and the absence of bloodshed turned public opinion around—at least for the time being.

Public Opinion Can Help Political Candidates and Parties

Political candidates who can afford it regularly consult public opinion, not just in focus groups but also with preelection ("horserace") polls designed to give them the information they need to become more effective campaigners and thereby improve their chances of winning. Campaigns routinely spend large sums to learn what the public thinks about the candidates, their opponents, and key election issues. Depending on what they learn, candidates may withdraw, modify, or strengthen their support for those policies. After the 1994 midterm elections, when the public strongly opposed any further tax increases, politicians in both major parties looked for alternative ways of financing government. As we'll see in Chapter 10, candidates also consult public opinion in deciding what issues to focus on. Presidents since Franklin Roosevelt have used preelection polls to develop reelection strategies, but, as the box nearby shows, the Reagan White House was the first to make polling a routine part of the president's reelection strategy.

After using public opinion to help Republicans develop their 1994 midterm election platform—the "Contract with America"—Frank Luntz also armed the Republican candidates with market-tested language they could use in their campaigns. A "Johnny Appleseed" of political rhetoric, Luntz saw himself "planting words and phrases for the Republican candidates all over the country."[13] As a result, he helped to "nationalize" a midterm election that would normally have focused on local issues, thereby providing the Republicans with a unifying, positive agenda they could use against Clinton. Even after the Republican victory, Luntz continued to act as the party's chief pollster, coaching Republicans on political language that could help them create a "post-welfare state" New America that would be "as powerful as the New Deal was 60 years ago." In a lengthy communications strategy memo issued in January 1995, Luntz fed Republicans pretested words and simple slogans (see the box on page 157) designed to elicit favorable responses from the public.[14]

Some politicians use intentionally biased surveys, or **"push" polls,** as a political tool to reinforce their own point of view in the population by making it appear more broadly held than it is in order to create a **bandwagon effect.** When a poll commissioned by Texas billionaire Ross Perot during the 1992 presidential campaign asked whether laws should be passed to prevent special interests from making huge contributions to political candidates, a full 99 percent

"push" poll
This type of poll uses loaded questions to propel the respondent in a particular direction. An example, asking about U.S. participation in the United Nations, might be: "Should American taxpayers be forced to support an organization that infringes on U.S. sovereignty?"

bandwagon effect
The term comes from the tendency people once had to "jump on the bandwagon"—the wagon carrying a band in a parade—as it passed, to share in the merriment.

The Politics of Knowledge

The Power of Secret Polls

Political strategists routinely conduct secret polls to help presidents and presidential candidates boost their public popularity. In *Hidden Power: The Programming of the President*, reporter Roland Perry explains how strategists for Ronald Reagan devised a computerized campaign to engineer his 1980 presidential victory. Unlike "horserace" polls that tell which candidate is ahead at election time, these "attitudinal" surveys are used to "map" the mood of the entire population—its fears, hopes, aspirations, thoughts, and feelings. This map tells the candidate how to frame his campaign messages to win public approval.

Perry explains that this public opinion map was created for Reagan well before he embarked on the 1980 campaign trail. The map, for instance, located fundamentalist Christians in particular states and counties across the country, identifying where Reagan should present a pious image of himself and use religious rhetoric to win votes. To get these data, professional callers claiming to be "independent" sat at computer terminals and typed in responses to more than 20 questions that probed people's religious views. How important was it, for example, that a candidate believe in Christ? What was the respondent's religious faith? Did the respondent believe in Charles Darwin's theory of evolution or the biblical story of creation?

In addition to mapping broad campaign strategies, secret polls are also used to "track," or monitor, the blow-by-blow effects of election battles. For example, if these tracking polls show that a candidate is weakening, strategists can try to shore up his or her image. If polls show that a candidate is perceived as dangerous, strategists can work to make him or her appear peaceful. If polls show that a candidate's opponent is viewed as congenial, strategists can try to tarnish that image.

Tracking polls are also used to map the attitudes of different voting groups such as women, African Americans, Hispanics, Catholics, blue-collar workers, and middle-income suburbanites. Strategists then use computers to separate and file this information into categories and subcategories that can be manipulated and tracked over time. Today computers can be used to program a candidate's campaign from start to finish as well as his or her public image once in the White House.

Richard Wirthlin, Reagan administration pollster, 1980.

Source: Roland Perry, *Hidden Power: The Programming of the President* (New York: Beaufort Books, 1984), vi–vii.

of respondents said yes (see Figure 5.2). But when the question was reworded by other pollsters to ask whether groups have the right to contribute to candidates they support, only 40 percent favored limiting contributions.[15] Increasingly, a politician who claims that a flattering poll is accurate or an unflattering poll is inaccurate is quickly derided by the press.

Candidates and parties can also learn from poll results conducted by independent pollsters. Clinton's mention of the word "education" 43 times and Dole's mention of it 30 times in the first presidential debates of 1996 were efforts to address widespread worries about education revealed in poll after poll. Several weeks before the 1996 presidential election, a poll of roughly 1,000 likely voters conducted by Louis Harris and Associates showed that 63 percent said President Clinton "would do a better job on education" and 32 percent said Senator Dole would. Political observers attributed Clinton's higher rating to his success in communicating that his expanded support for education was basically incremental and mainstream, while Dole's call for downsizing the Department of Education, supporting school choice with vouchers, and curtailing the power of teachers' unions was perceived as too drastic.[16]

Figure 5.2

The question of questions: An experiment in polling

Results of H. Ross Perot's mail-in survey in the 1992 presidential campaign are compared with those for the same question given to a national sample by Yankelovich & Partners, a more neutrally worded version of the question submitted to a national sample, and still another version given to another national sample by the Gordon Black Corporation.

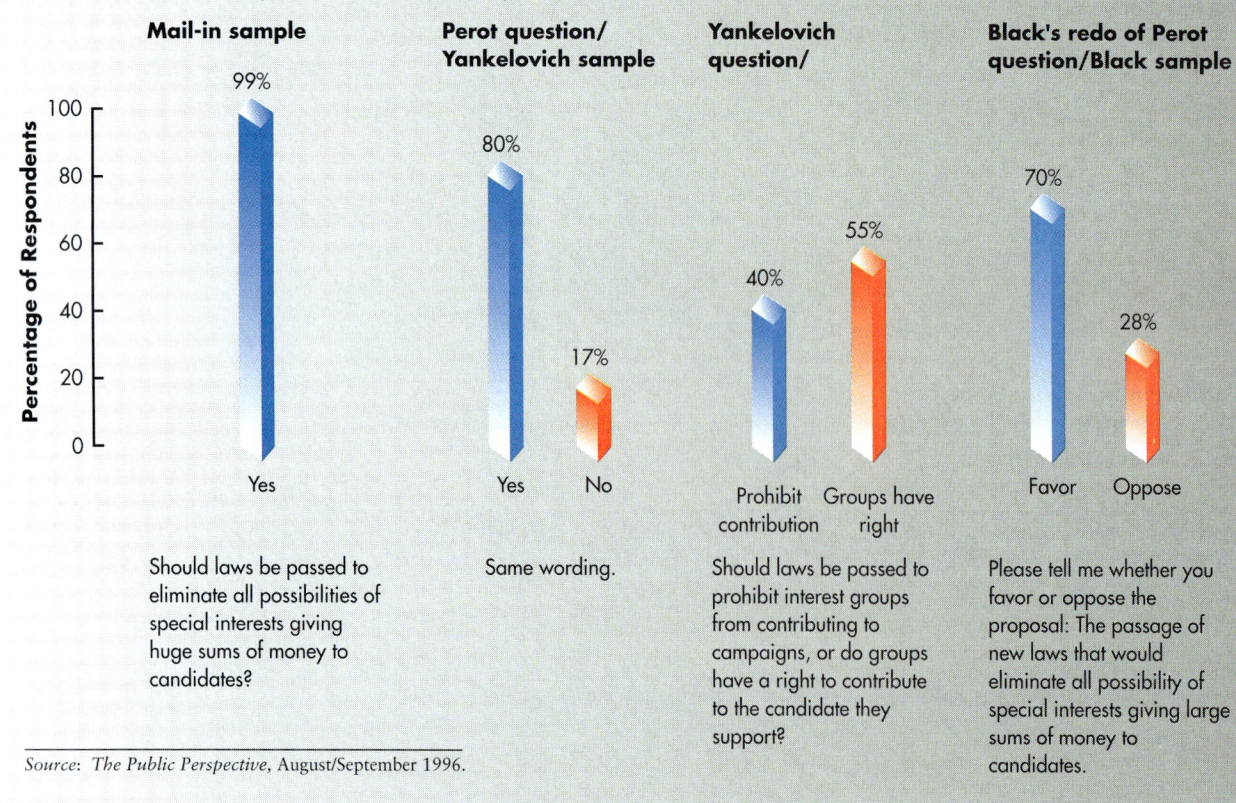

Mail-in sample
- Yes: 99%

Should laws be passed to eliminate all possibilities of special interests giving huge sums of money to candidates?

Perot question/Yankelovich sample
- Yes: 80%
- No: 17%

Same wording.

Yankelovich question/
- Prohibit contribution: 40%
- Groups have right: 55%

Should laws be passed to prohibit interest groups from contributing to campaigns, or do groups have a right to contribute to the candidate they support?

Black's redo of Perot question/Black sample
- Favor: 70%
- Oppose: 28%

Please tell me whether you favor or oppose the proposal: The passage of new laws that would eliminate all possibility of special interests giving large sums of money to candidates.

Source: *The Public Perspective*, August/September 1996.

The Politics of Language

Pretested Language in the "Contract with America"

The following are some linguistic tips from Frank Luntz's January 1995 communications strategy memo to Republican candidates:

- Say you are cutting "bureaucrats," who have no friends, rather than "programs," which have many friends. (When Luntz found that even the educators in his focus groups were willing to abolish the Department of Education so long as student loans were preserved, he advised Republicans to promise that any "truly important" program would be saved even if entire departments were eliminated.)

- Use the refrain, "It's time to put government on a diet." "With the average American family likely to have gained 4 pounds between Thanksgiving and New Year's Day, the diet analogy plays well."

- Instead of threatening to put children whose mothers can't care for them in an "orphanage" (this was Newt Gingrich's language, and its approval rating in focus groups was only 3 to 1), suggest putting abused welfare children in "foster homes" (this term won an approval rating of 5 to 1). "Words matter," Luntz wrote, "and almost any word is better than 'orphanage.'"

- "Talk about denying cash benefits to people who have more kids while on welfare; that strikes a chord with the public."

- "Play up the role of private charities" and stress that they can do more for needy people than government.

- Stress that "the Government is incredibly inefficient. It's like a bad charity that gives more to administration than to the people it's supposed to benefit."

- "The most important reason to eliminate the Federal deficit and balance the budget? For the future of American generations, for the children."

- "Talk about the challenge of irresponsible debt, runaway spending, destructive welfare and an anti-saving tax code in moral—as well as economic—terms. America believes Washington isn't just irresponsible but that it is fostering all the wrong values in our society."

- Repeat the refrain, "If we all ran our personal finances like the Government, we'd all be bankrupt."

- Use the phrase "government-controlled health care."

- Refer to "struggling entrepreneurs" rather than employers and businessmen.

- Respond to Democratic complaints that the Republican agenda is unfair by saying, "Is it 'fair' for Medicare recipients to have an even greater choice of doctors and facilities than the average taxpayers who are funding the system? Is it 'fair' to give student loans for truck driving schools? Is it 'fair' to penalize middle-class families for saving for the future? Is it 'fair' to leave battered children in abusive homes?"

Sources: "House Republicans Get Talking Points: GOP Pollster's Memo Offers Advice on How to Win with Words," *Washington Post,* February 2, 1995; Robin Toner, "Word for Word/Advice for Republicans; Attention! All Sales Reps for the Contract with America!" *New York Times,* February 5, 1995.

Recent Changes in Values

American public opinion reflects recent changes in a variety of areas, as Daniel Yankelovich has recorded. Similar changes appear to have occurred in Western Europe and Japan, generally about five to ten years earlier.

The concept of duty. Less value placed on what one owes to others as a matter of moral obligation.

Social conformity. Less value placed on keeping up with the Joneses.

Respectability. Less value placed on symbols of correct behavior for a person of a particular social class.

Social morality. Less value placed on observing society's rules.

Pluralism. Greater acceptance of differences in ethnicity and life-style.

Sacrifice. Less value placed on sacrifice as a moral good, replaced by more pragmatic criteria of when sacrifice is or is not called for.

Expressiveness. A higher value placed on forms of choice and individualism that express one's unique inner nature.

The environment. Greater value placed on respecting and preserving nature and the natural.

Technology. Greater value placed on technological solutions to a vast array of problems and challenges.

Sexuality. Less moral value placed on "correct" sexual behavior; a loosening of some but not all norms of sexual morality.

Pleasure. Less puritanism about pleasure, especially bodily pleasures; pleasure regarded as a good.

Family. A high value placed on family life, but with a vastly expanded concept of family beyond the traditional nuclear form.

Husband-wife relationships. A far-reaching shift from role-based obligations to shared responsibilities.

Health. Greater value placed on one's own responsibility for maintaining and enhancing health.

Work ethic. A shift from the Protestant ethic valuation of work as having intrinsic moral value to work as a source of personal satisfaction, and therefore less tolerance for work that does not provide personal satisfaction.

Women's rights. A higher value placed on women achieving self-fulfillment by paths of their own choice rather than through roles dictated by society.

Source: Daniel Yankelovich, "How Changes in the Economy Are Reshaping American Values," in *Values and Public Policy*, ed. Henry J. Aaron et al. (Washington, D.C.: Brookings Institution, 1994), 22. Reprinted by permission.

Public Opinion Can Indicate Continuity and Change in Beliefs and Values

Public opinion, when tracked over time, can reveal how the beliefs and values of individuals, particular groups, or the population as a whole have changed, as the nearby box demonstrates. For example, recent surveys show that Americans' core values (Chapter 4) have remained strong and stable despite vast social and economic changes. The greatest shift has been a reduction in *xenophobia* (fear and hatred of what is foreign and strange) toward a greater tolerance for diversity. Polls during the 1930s and 1940s showed that public opinion was openly and actively antiforeigner, antiblack, anti-Catholic, anti-Semitic, and opposed to equality for women. Forty years later only 3 percent of respondents said they would not like to live next door to a Jew, and the percentage willing to accept a Jewish president rose from 47 percent in 1947 to 82 percent in 1987. In 1955, 55 percent of white Americans said they had "a right to keep blacks out of their neighborhood if they wanted to"—a percentage that dropped to 22 percent by 1990. A 1946 poll showed a large majority believed that men were more intelligent and performed better in most jobs (except as secretaries) than women. By 1987, 82 percent said that they would vote for a woman for president.[17]

How Trustworthy Are Polls and Their Interpretations?

Since polls are the best tools available for determining public opinion on a particular subject at a particular time, the obvious question is, How accurate are they? Most people believe that polls are reliable,[18] and the percentage that pays attention to them has risen from 28 percent in 1944 to 55 percent in 1996 (see Figure 5.3). Poll results by reputable polling organizations also tend to be viewed as trustworthy because they attempt to measure public opinion scientifically and to treat all the respondents—and their opinions—equally. However, a number of problems still plague public opinion research.[19] A poll's accuracy, experts say, depends on four main factors:

- the survey and data collection methods used,
- the wording and ordering of the questions,
- the timing of the questions, and
- the interpretation of the data.

Figure 5.3

The accuracy of surveys and the attention paid to polls

Question: Some polling organizations make frequent predictions of election results. What is your general impression of how well they do—do you think they are pretty nearly right most of the time, or do you think their record is not very good?

Question: Do you think poll returns on matters not dealing with elections, but with public opinion toward such things as labor problems or international affairs, are usually pretty nearly right, or not right at all?

Question: Do you follow the results of any public opinion poll regularly in any newspaper or magazine?

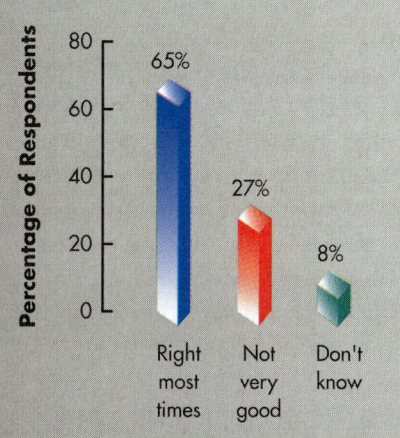

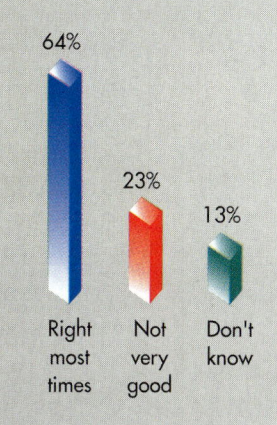

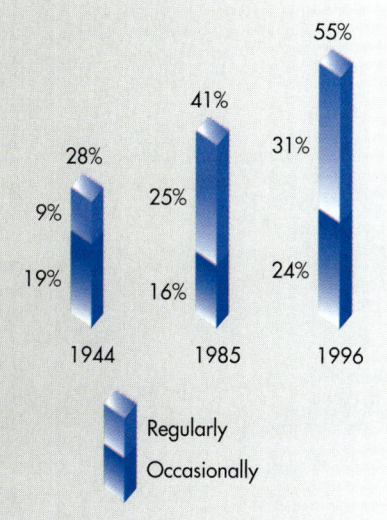

- Right most times: 65%
- Not very good: 27%
- Don't know: 8%

- Right most times: 64%
- Not very good: 23%
- Don't know: 13%

Year	Regularly	Occasionally
1944	9%	19%
1985	16%	25%
1996	24%	31%

(Totals: 1944: 28%; 1985: 41%; 1996: 55%)

Source: Survey by the Gallup Organization, April 25–28, 1996. Reported in *The Public Perspective*, August/September 1996, 55, 51. The 1944 survey was by Hadley Cantril.

Survey Methods

National Opinion Research Center (NORC)

NORC conducts various comprehensive opinion studies, including the well-known "General Social Survey." For information on its current studies as well as discussions of survey research methods, visit

http://www.norc.uchicago.edu

Survey methods have come a long way since the early efforts to sample public opinion; pollsters, like politicians, *learn by doing*. Because they have they profited from their mistakes, pollsters now have a better understanding of the value and limitations of polls. They have also benefited from advances in the social sciences during the last fifty years. The greatest of these advances has been the quantitative revolution—a major shift away from explanations based on description and reasoning to explanations based on numerical, or quantitative, data. Today much research relies on survey data that have been processed or manipulated with the help of computer programs. Social scientists interested in studying public opinion trends often consult such sources as the General Social Surveys (GSS), which specialize in the collection of survey data over time as well as census and other data. These surveys, which have been administered by the National Opinion Research Center (NORC) at the University of Chicago since 1972, offer researchers a bank of 1,500 face-to-face interviews annually (with the exceptions of 1979 and 1981), based largely on the same questions to maintain continuity.

From Straw Polls to Random Sampling

But modern polls and surveys are not the only way of taking the public's pulse. In previous eras there was no way to measure public attitudes unless they were expressed in editorials, publications, and debates or they erupted in strikes, boycotts, protests, or riots. In the early nineteenth century, political observers relied on **straw polls**—nonscientific surveys that tap the opinions of those who happen to be around or who are easy to contact. Abraham Lincoln regularly conducted straw polls during the Civil War when he met with citizens at the White House. "I call these receptions my '*public opinion baths*,'" he once remarked, "for I have but little time to read the papers and gather public opinion that way."[20] Today reporters interview ordinary citizens at work, in bars, and in their homes as part of their campaign coverage. Political observers estimate crowd size at rallies and the number of items—political buttons, T-shirts, and bumper stickers—activists display to support their causes. Politicians tour their districts; count letters, faxes, and phone calls; consult reports from party officials; consider editorials in the media; and estimate the impact of public protests and the results of elections, initiatives (petitions the public signs that can compel a vote by the electorate to produce a law), and referenda (legislative proposals submitted to voters for approval). Population movements may be still another indicator, but they are often hard

The "Million Man March" on the Mall in Washington, D.C., on October 16, 1995, was organized by controversial Nation of Islam leader Louis Farrakhan (see Chapter 16) to inspire African-American men to take greater responsibility for themselves and their communities. New technology that relies on aerial photographs is increasingly able to improve the accuracy of straw polls involving the counting of large crowds. In the case of this march, analysis of the photographs showed that the crowd was well under one million.

to interpret. For example, observers cannot really tell whether the exodus of affluent urbanites to suburbia during recent decades—called "white flight"—is due primarily to racism or to such factors as poor schools, urban congestion, pollution, noise, and crime rates.

When there is a discrepancy between straw polls and public opinion surveys, the latter have more credibility because they are more scientific. What makes these polls more scientific? In the 1930s and 1940s George Gallup and other polling pioneers made use of a scientific advance called **random sampling**—a procedure that permits accurate generalizations and predictions about a group (voters, for example) by questioning some of its members. This procedure assumes that because people of similar backgrounds in similar situations typically hold similar opinions, it is unnecessary to question the entire group. If the survey is well designed, a small number of blue-collar workers in the Midwest, for instance, can be used to represent all blue-collar workers in the Midwest if their unique differences relevant to opinions are screened out. The procedure requires that the sample be randomly chosen, that is, individuals representing a group must be selected in such a way that each member of that group has an equal chance of being chosen. Pollsters achieve random sampling by constructing elaborate pools of numbers from which they draw their sample.[21]

Selecting a sample population that does not represent the entire population will produce lopsided and flawed results, as was dramatically illustrated in 1936. A prominent American magazine, the *Literary Digest*, mailed sample ballots for the presidential election to 10 million voters drawn from its subscribers as well as from auto registration lists and phone directories. When the ballots of the 2.5 million people who sent them back were counted, they showed that Alf Landon would defeat Franklin D. Roosevelt 61 percent to 37 percent. At the same time, a poll conducted by George Gallup, with a much smaller sample, predicted that Roosevelt would win, 56 percent to 44 percent. Gallup's poll was correct. Why? Gallup explained that even a sample as large as the *Literary Digest*'s readership would not be an accurate picture of the entire American electorate because it was skewed in favor of the wealthy—people who, even during the Great Depression, could afford to subscribe to magazines, to have telephones, or to own cars. Requiring respondents to mail back their ballots further skewed the results by producing the views of the most motivated members of the selected population.

The Gallup Organization

To visit the pioneer public opinion survey group's Web site for reports on its latest surveys and to search "The Gallup Newsletter Archives" for accounts of past surveys, contact:

http://www.gallup.com/index.html

Sample Size

For a poll to be accurate, it must survey an adequate chunk of the group being polled. Commercial polling companies such as the Gallup Organization and Louis Harris and Associates use about 1,200 people for national polls. Statisticians calculate that 95 out of 100 samples of this size should produce a **margin of error** of no more than 3 percent either way. Typically, if a poll shows that 45 percent of respondents hold a particular opinion, the actual percentage of

Researchers gather data for a *Los Angeles Times* exit poll following a primary election.

those holding it should be no higher than 48 and no lower than 42. While this level of confidence is not perfect, it is highly predictive.[22] When you find a poll reported on TV or in the paper, look for a statement of its margin of error. Reputable polls typically include their sample size and margin of error along with their results. Polls that don't may not be as trustworthy. The kind of "dial-in" polls often conducted on TV have very high margins of error, again (as in the *Literary Digest* example) because those who (1) are viewing the program, (2) take the trouble to call in, and (3) are willing to pay the phone charge are self-selected and do not represent the entire population.

Coping with Biases in Data Collection

While face-to-face interviews were once the primary method of data collection and are still commonly used by the Gallup and Roper organizations, most polling is now done by phone to save time and money. Because 97 percent of today's households have telephones, the chance of class bias occurring in such a method is far less than it was, say, in 1950, when only 63 percent of households had telephones. However, a different problem is presented by the fact that many of today's telephone numbers are unlisted or connected to answering machines. To cope with unlisted numbers, most pollsters now rely on random digit dialing performed by computers. To cope with answering machines, large professional survey organizations may call back thousands of times, while smaller organizations may call back only about a dozen times. Pollsters also call back if the phone is not answered, but some people never answer their phones. There are also some who don't complete the interview or simply hang up on the interviewer.

To ensure that data collection is not biased, the telephone numbers being dialed must come from all areas of the country. The interviewers, too, must be representative, as race can be a factor. For example, African-American interviewers tend to get more cooperation when talking with African Americans, and whites with whites. Because the data collection process can never be perfect, pollsters must allow for some margin of error.

The Roper Center for Public Opinion Research

This center, located at the University of Connecticut, gathers and archives research results from many of the most important public opinion research organizations. Visit its site at

http://www.lib.uconn.edu/RoperCenter

Constructing the Questions

Pollsters have learned that how they word their questions, the order in which they ask them, and the choices they offer respondents can drastically affect the outcome. They have also learned the importance of coping with "false answers" and inconsistencies.

Wording the Questions

Words—even simple words—mean different things to different people in a particular context. When a 1981 poll asked 51 people whether the questions in a survey about television were clear to them, they said yes. But when questioned further about what the phrase "over a period of years" meant, 7 said it meant no more than 2 years, 19 said it meant 7 years or more, and 19 thought it meant 10 years or more. (The remaining 6 people were not sure or had no opinion.)[23]

Ordering the Questions

The order in which questions are asked can also influence poll results. Pollsters often illustrate this influence with a poll taken at the height of the anticommunist Red Scare in the 1950s. When interviewers first asked respondents whether they thought the United States should allow Communist reporters into *our* country, only 36 percent said yes. But when interviewers preceded this question with one that asked whether the Soviet Union should let American reporters into *their* country, the number of yes answers to the original question jumped to 73 percent.[24]

The order of questions can affect poll results in a broader way as well. Respondents are usually more willing to answer questions of a personal nature (age, income, education level, etc.) toward the end of the interview, once they feel they have gotten to know the interviewer, rather than at the beginning. In addition, respondents usually display more concern about a topic toward the end of the interview, because the interview process itself often tends to increase their interest in it. Also, because people wish to appear logical and consistent, they are often unwilling to contradict their earlier answers. Consider the example of a poll that asks which candidate the respondent supports in the general election and which party he or she identifies with. Pollsters have learned that when they ask respondents their party affiliation *before* asking what candidate they support, respondents are more likely to say they support the candidate of their party. However, when the questions are reversed, more respondents say they support a candidate of another party.[25]

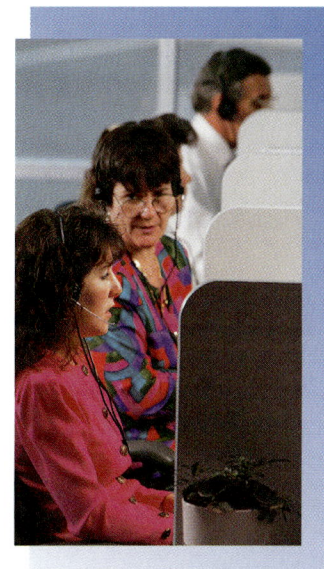

A telephone bank of poll workers in Herndon, Va., in May 1992.

Providing a Reasonable Range of Answers

Failure to provide the respondent with a reasonable range of answers can also affect a poll's outcome. For example, when asked whether "the courts deal too harshly or not harshly enough with criminals," 6 percent said "too harshly" while 78 percent said "not harshly enough." But when given the option "don't have enough information about the courts to say," 29 percent chose this answer while only 60 percent said "not harshly enough."[26] One critic of the wording of certain questions in the 1996 National Issues Convention in Austin, Texas (described at the end of the chapter), found fault with this question:

> If the U.S. does continue to give foreign aid, for what purpose should the aid be given: (1) military support only; (2) economic development only; (3) both military support and economic development?

What is missing, according to this critic, is a fourth choice: giving foreign aid for humanitarian reasons. "Humanitarian assistance easily would have been a more popular response than either economic or military support. Even in the Cold War era when the American public was asked [about humanitarian aid], the responses were overwhelmingly for humanitarian assistance . . . over military aid."[27]

Coping with False Answers

Pollsters have long known that some people make up answers to survey questions about which they know nothing in order to avoid seeming impolite or ignorant.

This effect was clearly demonstrated in a famous study in the 1940s in which college students were asked for, and gave, their opinion on three fictitious national groups—the Danireans, Pireneans, and Wallonians. Pollsters call such answers intended to please the interviewer or make the respondent look good **doorstep opinions.**

Because some surveys want the views only of individuals who are informed about the subject of the poll, pollsters must find ways of screening out those who lack such knowledge. Some do this by questioning individuals about a fictitious person or event and eliminating those who offer "knowledgeable" answers to such questions. Others offer respondents an "escape route." For instance, before asking an individual's opinion of a particular politician, the interviewer first asks whether the respondent has ever heard of that person. If the name is unknown to the respondent, the interviewer will not ask for an opinion.[28] Similar screening techniques are used to detect lying that is motivated by the desire to avoid questions about illegal practices such as drug abuse.[29]

Timing the Poll

Timing can be crucial to a poll's outcome. Gallup discovered this in 1948 when he predicted that Thomas E. Dewey, not Harry Truman, would win the presidential election. The fault, he discovered, lay not in his random sampling but rather in his decision to stop the interviewing ten days before the election, largely because he sensed that voters were apathetic and believed that most undecided voters would not vote. Because Gallup failed to continue polling right up to election day, his results were wrong. The apathetic became more interested and the undecideds made up their minds in the final days of the campaign and then voted after all. Pollsters have now learned to poll right up to election day but remain vexed by potential voters who say they're undecided. The election of 1948 thus taught at least two valuable lessons in how to improve the accuracy of polls as predictors—lessons about sampling and the timing of polls.

Timing problems also afflict **longitudinal studies**—studies that examine changes in the opinions of the same people over time. When pollsters specializing in socialization, for example, want to know how the same people's attitudes and opinions have changed over time, they question the respondents first as adolescents and then as adults. However, it is often difficult to know which changes should be attributed to the influence of aging and which to the effects of intervening historical events. One study attempting to measure changes in public trust of post–World War II baby boomers between the Vietnam (1965) and Watergate (1973) periods was criticized for its failure to distinguish between (1) whether youthful trust tends to decline with age in general or (2) whether youthful trust declined as a result of the disillusionment and skepticism that resulted from the series of dramatic shocks (war, corruption, and political assassinations) to the political system that occurred during that period.[30]

More reliable are longitudinal studies that show the tendency of individuals to describe themselves as liberals or conservatives. Other studies show relatively high levels of stability on basic values such as individualism and egalitarianism, as well as on racial attitudes and on issues such as abortion, marijuana use, and women's rights. Still other studies show relatively low levels of stability on such matters as public trust, political interest, and civic duty.[31]

Longitudinal studies also show that changes in an individual's environment can cause relatively permanent changes of opinion. A famous study of the largely conservative women in the class of 1943 at Bennington College—a small, elite liberal arts school in Vermont—showed that these women were strongly influenced by their largely liberal professors, making a shift to the political left that persisted 20 years later.[32] A follow-up study of the class after 50 years showed the same persistent pattern.[33]

Age-based studies show that opinions are affected by conditions and experiences particular to a given generation as well as by **period effects**—conditions and experiences that affect all age groups. When a more uniform shift in opinion is caused by period effects, experts try to find out whether that shift is the result of new information and learning. A recent study examined three issues that have divided the generations in recent decades: abortion, gay rights, and the role of women in society. To the extent that opinions are based on age or generation, researchers expected differences in attitudes to increase with an increase in knowledge. To the extent that period effects are driving the emergence of these new issues, researchers expected an increase in knowledge to move all three generations in a similar direction. Their analysis showed the influence of both factors. When knowledge level was not considered, the oldest generation—the pre-boomers—was the most conservative on these issues and the post-boomers the most liberal. However, all three groups became more liberal as their knowledge of the issues increased. Because the knowledge levels of the post-boomers were the highest, the gap between them and the other groups was the greatest.[34]

Intergenerational studies also show that some biases persist from generation to generation but in a different form. One 1985 study found that fathers who reflected racist traits in the 1950s (for example, by opposing racial intermarriage) had raised children who as adults in the 1960s reflected what liberal analysts considered to be racist traits (for example, opposition to busing and affirmative action).[35] However, the fact that in recent years some liberals and African Americans have also expressed doubts about busing and affirmative action suggests that the underlying causes of changing opinions require more careful explanations.[36]

Members of the Bennington College class of 1943 at their 1993 class reunion.

Interpreting Poll Results

Interpreting poll results can present difficulties for experts and the public alike. Political scientists, for instance, must explain why the opinions people express sometimes differ from their behavior. One insight grew out of a study that tried to discover why Americans said they supported the principle of racial equality but did not support public policies designed to achieve it. Evidence showed that the biggest gap between principle and practice occurred in the most politically sophisticated rather than in the least politically sophisticated. At first this looked like a case of inconsistency, but deeper examination revealed that educated conservatives consistently disagreed with liberal policies such as school busing and affirmative action. Thus, conservatives and liberals may agree on the *ends* (goals, or *what's right*) of public policy (they may both be committed to racial equality, for example), yet disagree over the *means* (the particular policies, or *what works*) to accomplish those ends.

Experts on public opinion and politics also have difficulty interpreting poll results during an election campaign because publishing the results of a poll can have feedback effects that alter the very opinions it seeks to measure, thereby distorting the democratic process. These effects can be of two sorts: the *bandwagon effect*, described above, in which people decide to shift to the candidate who appears to be winning, and the **underdog effect**, in which people decide to shift to the candidate who appears to be losing. Pollsters have yet to confirm the force of these effects, because both can occur at the same time and their magnitude can vary among different segments of the electorate, and because it is difficult to distinguish these effects from the influence of last-minute campaigning.[37]

Some surveys, however, may be intentionally designed to obtain particular results. Such biases may be built into the research questionnaire—for example, by asking leading questions, as the "push" polls do, or by purposely omitting questions whose answers will detract from the desired result—or worked into an interpretation of the results.

A decision to include or omit the "don't knows" and the "undecideds" can drastically affect the results. It also makes a difference whether the answers are weighted equally and simply added up or weighted on a complex scale and measured accordingly. For example, pollsters who want a yes or no answer on abortion will suppress the distinctions and nuances most people make. A 1989 poll on attitudes toward abortion found that only 9 percent of the population opposed abortion in all instances, and that of the 49 percent who opposed it in general, 39 percent favored exceptions for cases such as rape, poverty, or other circumstances. To be truly accurate, a poll on abortion would have to uncover and report these various qualifications. The poll in question found that 85 percent of the population favor abortion when the woman's life is in danger; 75 to 80 percent if there is a strong chance that the baby will be born

> For discussions about polling theory and practice as well as public opinion polls and raw polling data, visit the Social Science Data Collection at
>
> http://www.ssdc.ucsd.edu/ssdc/pubopin.html

Democratic pollster Celinda Lake and Dole campaign pollster Linda DiVall on CNN in 1997.

with a serious birth defect; 41 percent if the woman is unmarried or does not want to marry the man; and 39 percent when a married woman does not want to have any more children.[38] Thus, asking respondents a number of related questions rather than just a single question can reveal how they feel about various aspects of an issue—aspects that don't show up in an answer to a single question.[39] "Yes" or "no" answers on abortion also hide the fact that support for abortion increases as political knowledge on the issue increases.[40]

As the history of the "Contract with America" indicates, survey results may be manipulated to promote political candidates. Candidates often hire **campaign pollsters**—openly partisan pollsters who arm candidates with favorable or "cooked" data that improve their images and their messages. During the 1970s such pollsters greatly influenced presidential campaigns, and as a result, many achieved national prominence and political influence in their own right. Among these were Louis Harris, who put his talents behind John Kennedy in the 1960 presidential election; Pat Caddell, who first worked for George McGovern, then helped elect Jimmy Carter, and then worked for Democrat Jerry Brown in the 1992 presidential primaries; and Robert Teeter, who helped reelect Nixon in 1972, was President Gerald Ford's chief pollster-strategist in 1976, and worked on the Reagan and Bush campaigns.

According to a close observer of their strategies, these and other influential political pollsters relied heavily on techniques that exaggerated and distorted the positive qualities of their candidates and the negative qualities of their opponents. In the Ford–Carter campaign of 1976, for example, Teeter's polls showed that Americans admired Ford as a person rather than as a leader and that he was a dismal campaigner. In response, Ford's advisors developed the White House "Rose Garden" strategy, which confined the incumbent president to ceremonial functions in the Rose Garden, where he would look presidential—even if he could not act it. Meanwhile, Teeter's polls showed that Americans had not yet developed a firm image of Jimmy Carter, who had been a nationally prominent candidate for only a few months. Ford's campaign strategists later wrote a book in which they

On advice from his pollsters and campaign advisors, President Gerald Ford conducted his 1976 campaign from the safety of the White House Rose Garden.

described their attempts to influence public opinion by making Carter appear as "an Unknown. A man whose thirst for power dominates. Who doesn't know why he wants the presidency or what he will do with it. Inexperienced. Arrogant (deceitful). Devious and highly partisan (a function of uncontrolled ambition). As one who uses religion for political purposes; an evangelic. As liberal, well to the left of center and a part of the old-line Democratic Party." That this image was entirely false did not matter to the top Ford strategists because, as the author of the study puts it, "the art of campaigning is not a search for the Truth, but for *a* truth that the public will buy"—especially at the ballot box.[41]

How Competent Is American Public Opinion?

When it comes to public opinion, competence can be thought of in a number of different ways: as manifesting political sophistication; as the use of analytical shortcuts; as demonstrating rationality; and as exercising public judgment. Political analysts disagree over how short American public opinion falls in each of these areas. As the box on pages 170–171 indicates, some conclude that Americans as a whole are not competent enough to play a substantive role in the policymaking process and that major decisions should be left to experts. Others maintain that American public opinion is competent enough to merit consultation. This dispute has obvious implications for popular democracy.

Political Sophistication

Some polls attempt to measure people's levels of **political sophistication**—that is, the quantity and quality of political information they possess about *what is*, *what's right*, and *what works* in the political process. Political scientists consider the greatest importance of political sophistication to be its effect on the connection between a person's values and the policies and candidates he or she supports—a connection that tends to be "considerably tighter among the more sophisticated."[42] Because such sophistication typically depends on how well educated and wealthy a person is, political sophistication has implications "for the fairness of the contest among interests" in our democracy.[43] Elites and experts, for example, are more likely to heed political opinions that they view as rational and well-informed.

A survey of more than two thousand factual questions about politics asked in national surveys over a fifty-year period found that only 41 percent of those questions were correctly answered by over half the public.[44] In general, surveys show, men are somewhat more knowledgeable than women and whites are somewhat better informed than African Americans, while

while those with higher incomes are more informed than those with lower ones. But most polls have shown that the majority of the public has always had low levels of political sophistication.[45] A 1994 Gallup poll, for example, showed that a third of the population did not know Vice President Al Gore's name.

Political scientist Russell Neuman has found sharp differences in political sophistication in three American "publics" (see Figure 5.4). Political scientists commonly refer to this distribution of political knowledge in the population as **political stratification**. A person's level of political sophistication, according to Neuman, is strongly influenced by the sort of socialization he or she has received.

- *Twenty percent* of the population (the group on the left of Figure 5.4) are unapologetically apolitical and have limited political horizons and vocabularies. These individuals don't vote or keep politically informed and can't be mobilized for political action, even in response to a severe crisis or their own economic self-interest. Economist Anthony Downs suggests several reasons for their lack of involvement: (1) most people are too busy with their own personal lives and interests to make such an investment; (2) the payoff for acquiring vast amounts of political knowledge is generally very small; and (3) because a single voter has very little influence on the system, it does not make sense for most people to bone up on the candidates or the issues.[46] These reasons hold true for the poor and uneducated as well as for the affluent and educated who dislike politics and believe that their participation in the political process would have no impact.

- *Seventy-five percent* of the population (the middle group in Figure 5.4) pay little attention to politics, are mildly cynical about politicians, share common patterns of opinion and behavior, yet vote fairly regularly out of civic duty.

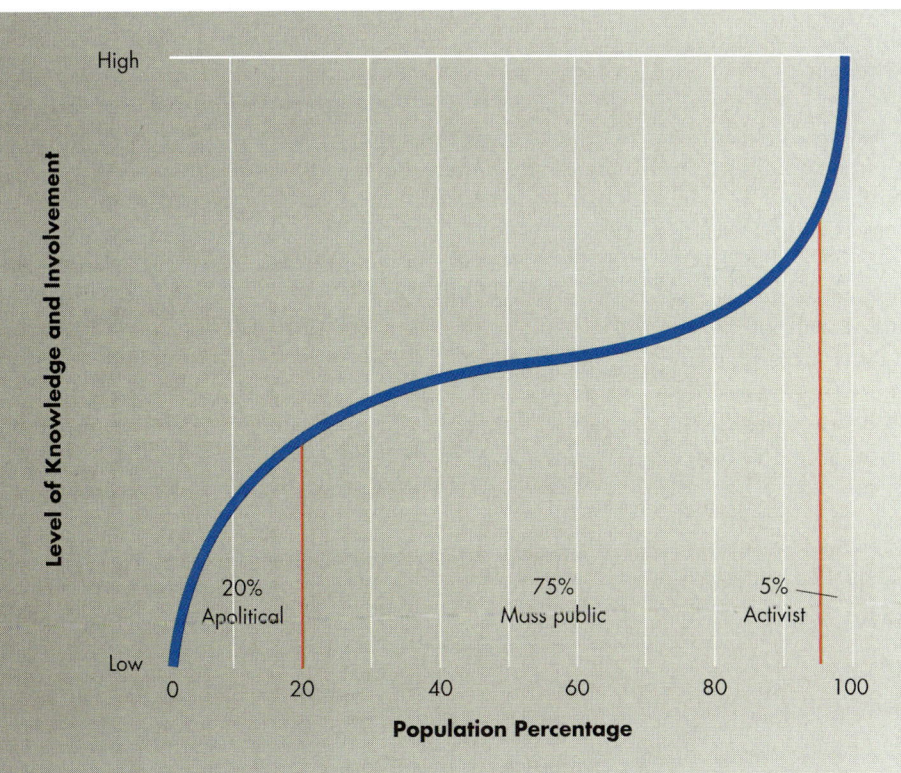

Figure 5.4
The theory of the three publics

- 20% Apolitical
- 75% Mass public
- 5% Activist

Source: Russell Neuman, *The Paradox of Mass Politics: Knowledge and Opinion in the American Electorate* (Cambridge, Mass. Harvard University Press, 1986).

Political Actors Disagree

Walter Lippmann

George Gallup

Should Elites or Public Opinion Guide the Nation?

An Elitist and a Populist Disagree

Experts disagree over how informed Americans should be to merit being consulted on public policies. In a series of books published during the 1920s, journalist Walter Lippmann concluded that public opinion was not competent to guide the country. If experts could not grasp the complex nature of political affairs, he asked, then how could the public, which was far less informed? Members of the public, he argued, form their own pictures of political reality from images shaped by culture and their personality.[1] Given Lippmann's assumption about *what is*—that public policy is merely a collection of individuals biases—his conclusion about *what's right* is hardly surprising: public policy should be decided by experts who are far less biased.

Lippmann's negative views of public opinion were confirmed by the first public opinion surveys conducted in the 1930s, which pictured many Americans as politically apathetic, largely uninformed, and seldom voting on the issues.[2] Surveys in the 1950s and 1960s reached similar conclusions. According to one major study, only a minority of Americans had any meaningful political beliefs, and even fewer had developed their beliefs into a coherent ideological framework.[3] Even more pessimistic is one scholar's recent conclusion that the American public has not become much more sophisticated "by anything approaching elite standards" over the last twenty-five years.[4] Surveys in other Western democracies tell a similar story.[5] In sum, experts from Lippmann to the present suggest that public opinion is not a reliable compass by which to guide a nation.

While Lippmann was arguing for decision making by experts, pioneering pollster George Gallup was warning that opponents of "direct democracy" could lead the country to "antidemocratic government." Gallup did not say that the government could do without experts. "No one denies that we need the best and the wisest in the key positions of our political life," he argued, but he went on to insist that they "be subject to check" by public opinion and urged Americans to "find the right balance" between public opinion and the opinions of elites and experts.[6] In contrast to the nation's Framers, who believed that the years between elections would free elected officials from public demands so they could exercise their own best judgment, Gallup argued that polls might usefully fill in the picture of public concerns between election years and thus make the political system more democratic.

Political Scientists Disagree

Lippmann's and Gallup's dispute over public opinion still divides political scientists today. Michael Robinson, a political scientist at Georgetown University, agrees with Lippmann:

> The central fact of American politics is the behavior of the political elite. Washington is everything. The vagaries of election returns, of course, determine

which of two competing members of the elite will occupy a seat in Congress for a few years. But who gets nominated and, more important, what gets decided as policy in the day-to-day workings of the political process are determined in smoke-filled rooms and on golf-courses. Public opinion is the inarticulate and blurry backdrop for the realities of political life."

Walter Dean Burnham, a political scientist at the University of Texas, sides with Gallup:

Electoral politics is not the backdrop; it is the essence, the keystone of the political process. The big issues, such as military, economic, and welfare policy, are influenced by the electorate's opinions.... Woe to the young elected officials who think they can play politics in Washington without actively courting the opinions, preferences, and whims of the folks back home. It is easy for the power junkies close to the citadel in Washington to forget that the rest of the country is out there. In the final analysis, if a policy is not based on public opinion, it won't survive.[7]

Why do these experts disagree? Political scientist Russell Neuman suggests a number of factors ranging from individual temperament and values, to type of education, to geographical location. He points out, for example, that Robinson begins each day with the *Washington Post*, can't imagine living outside the nation's capital, and specializes in studying the maneuverings of Washington elites. Skeptical of the kind of "number-crunching" central to public opinion research, he believes that only elite opinions really matter. In contrast, Burnham lives hundreds of miles from Washington and, like other experts on public opinion, may well have specialized in this area because he believes that polls help legitimate democracy.[8] Other observers put it this way: "Scratch beneath the veneer of academic sophistication of most American political scientists and you will find middle-class Democrats and Republicans, who have accepted most of the political values to which they were socialized."[9] Those values are usually associated with the belief that elites do not—and should not—run the country,[10] because that would indicate that the American political system is not really democratic.

There is a danger, however, that political scientists who focus exclusively on what the public believes about *what is*, *what's right*, and *what works* may fail to notice the degree to which elites shape and manipulate public opinion. In sum, both Burnham and Robinson shed valuable light on public opinion: Burnham tells us what public opinion is and what it means; Robinson tells us what—at least for the time being—it does not and cannot do. Robinson's approach leads to case studies of political elites, their motives and strategies, while Burnham's approach focuses on election returns and public opinion data.[11] Both approaches are logical, but each gives us a very different "slice" of political reality. When taken together, the slices add up to a more complete picture of how the political process really works.

---

[1] Walter Lippmann, *Public Opinion* (New York: Macmillan, 1941), 29. Lippmann's other books include *The Phantom Public* (New York: Harcourt, Brace, 1925) and *The Public Philosophy* (Boston: Little, Brown, 1955).

[2] For the history of public opinion research, see Philip E. Converse, *Survey Research in the United States: Roots and Emergence, 1890–1960* (Berkeley: University of California Press, 1987).

[3] Philip Converse, "The Nature of Belief Systems in Mass Publics," in *Ideology and Discontent*, ed. David E. Apter (New York: Free Press, 1964), 206–261.

[4] See Robert C. Luskin, "Measuring Political Sophistication," *American Journal of Political Science* (November 1987), 889; "Political Psychology, Political Behavior, and Politics: Questions of Aggregation, Causal Distance, and Taste," in *Political Psychology and Political Behavior*, ed. James H. Kuklinski (New York: Cambridge University Press, 1997).

[5] See, for example, Hans D. Klingemann, "Measuring Ideological Conceptualizations," in *Political Action: Mass Participation in Five Western Democracies*, ed. Samuel H. Barnes and Max Kaase (Beverly Hills: Sage, 1979), 215–254.

[6] George Gallup and Saul Forbes Rae, *The Pulse of Democracy: The Public Opinion Poll and How It Works* (New York: Simon & Schuster, 1940), 261, 262.

[7] Both quoted in Russell Neuman, *The Paradox of Mass Politics: Knowledge and Opinion in the American Electorate* (Cambridge, Mass.: Harvard University Press, 1986), 1, 2.

[8] Ibid., 2.

[9] Michael Margolis and Gary A. Mauser, *Manipulating Public Opinion* (Pacific Grove, Calif.: Brooks/Cole, 1989), 5.

[10] While many political scientists have read books like C. Wright Mills, *The Power Elite* (New York: Oxford University Press, 1956), and Thomas R. Dye, *Who's Running America? The Conservative Years*, 4th ed. (Englewood Cliffs, N.J.: Prentice Hall, 1986), only a very few accept their view that powerful elites dominate American politics.

[11] Neuman, *Paradox of Mass Politics*, 2.

- This middle mass is modestly literate in political matters, keeps track of the big issues, but lacks the background information and political vocabulary necessary to grasp a broad spectrum of issues. This group can be activated by the concerns of fellow citizens, and over the past thirty years has responded to such major issues as the Vietnam War, Watergate, civil rights, women's rights, and environmental protection. Given the high costs of obtaining and processing information, however, many in this group turn to trusted friends, newspaper endorsements, or experts for advice on how to vote, and many even enter the voting booth with "crib sheets" to guide them in voting on the long lists of candidates and propositions. Political analysts call these voters **cue-takers**.

- Only *five percent* of the population (the group on the right in Figure 5.4) are politically active and highly sophisticated—about the same percentage as in other Western democracies.[47] This elite, which includes professional politicians, print and broadcast journalists, academics, and other political experts, is politically articulate and equipped to process large amounts of complex information. Republicans and Democrats within this group are equally sophisticated politically.

Although Neuman confirms the low level of political sophistication among Americans, he takes a middle position between those who say that the average American is not thoughtful or informed enough to make democracy work successfully and those who argue that mass democracy does not require a highly informed electorate to work successfully. Still others argue (as we'll see below) that there are errors in the survey research showing low levels of political knowledge.[48]

According to Neuman, one reason American democracy works and has survived over time while many democracies in Europe and elsewhere have not is that the elite and middle groups in his study do not ignore evidence of political corruption or unresponsiveness. When a crisis arises, they mobilize and take action. It was the tide of negative opinion over the Watergate scandal, for example, that led Richard Nixon to resign the presidency, and, prior to the 1992 elections, when the press revealed that some members of Congress had been regularly overdrawing their accounts at the House of Representatives bank, public anger caused some of them to withdraw from the race and others to be defeated or to barely scrape by. Europeans scoff at Americans for what they take to be such naive, simple-minded demands for virtue in political leaders.

Neuman also believes American democracy works because average citizens are willing to voice meaningful opinions on issues without being experts on them, expressing their views on matters ranging from foreign affairs to the budget and the deficit. Behind this willingness, he claims, is the same faith that sustains the jury system—the basic belief that when people are given the chance to review the facts of a case fairly and openly, their collective judgment will equal, or even surpass, the judgment of the most brilliant legal experts.[49]

Analytical Shortcuts

Some political scientists are now questioning the conventional ("high-information rationality") view of political sophistication. Should political sophistication be determined by how much political information an individual has, by the reasoning the individual uses to organize that information, or by how intelligent the individual is?[50]

Assuming that Neuman is right, how do politically unsophisticated citizens develop meaningful positions on issues? One possibility is that they compensate for their lack of political knowledge with analytical shortcuts: processing what little information they do have in simple and efficient ways, relying on simple "rules of thumb" (what some experts call "low-information rationality"[51]) to sort out political issues.

People who possess such rules of thumb can function effectively even without being politically sophisticated in any of the conventional senses. For example, those who dislike racial minorities do not have to ponder the details of proposed policies that would spend more money on such minorities. Conversely, those who believe that racial minorities deserve all the help they can get may support such policies without examining them extensively or one by one. Individuals use similar types of positive or negative feelings to determine their positions on abortion, gun control, gay rights, and the like. They simply filter complex policies through the broad mesh of their feelings, values, and beliefs—the very images of reality that journalist Walter Lippmann (see the box on p. 170) argued collectively make up public opinion. Those who use such criteria to evaluate a candidate or an issue have little incentive to acquire more knowledge about these matters.

More politically sophisticated citizens filter issues through the use of reason. Studies show that these citizens tend to respond more positively to closely reasoned appeals (logically related explanations for why deficit spending should be curbed, for example), whereas the less sophisticated respond more positively to symbolic appeals (a clock that ticks off the rate of deficit spending per minute, for instance).[52] On the question of whether government should offer or withhold assistance to poor African Americans, one study showed that many people reached their conclusions by reasoning from the causes of poverty. If they attributed poverty to factors blacks were capable of remedying, then they believed that blacks, "following Horatio Alger, . . . should help themselves."[53] But if they attributed poverty to some external force beyond one's control—say, the lingering effects of slavery, or substandard schooling—they concluded that public assistance was reasonable and justified. But to reach this conclusion one must have accurate knowledge of the history of African Americans and the social and legal discrimination they have faced as a group. It has been shown that blacks are more likely than whites to have such knowledge, and are therefore more likely than whites to favor government assistance to blacks.[54]

Collective Rationality

Political scientists Benjamin Page and Robert Shapiro acknowledge that survey data on Americans as individuals show their levels of political sophistication to be low but claim that when their opinions are examined collectively, they appear to be more rational that most experts have assumed.[55] Page and Shapiro prefer to define public opinion as a

rule of thumb
The term, meaning an informal, nonscientific form of measurement, derives from carpenters' occasional use of their thumb rather than a ruler to measure something.

body of opinions that reflects learning over time rather than as the sum of individual opinions that are largely uninformed (as the traditional definition at the beginning of the chapter does). This collective definition allows them to hold a more optimistic view of public opinion—one that legitimates American popular democracy at a time when much of the world is looking to it as a model. In effect, Page and Shapiro are claiming that public opinion is capable of *learning by doing* from generation to generation, even though the individuals who make up those generations are not the same.

Page and Shapiro argue that over time this collective public "holds a number of real, stable, and sensible opinions about public policy and that these opinions develop and change in [response] to changing circumstances and to new information."[56] They reject the notion of the 1970s that there is a crisis of democracy (described in Chapter 4)[57] and the notion of the 1980s that Americans are incapable of grasping complex problems such as the deficit. They also claim that the methods of surveys showing that individual opinions are unstable over time are flawed. They further claim that most studies of political sophistication are little more than "trivia quizzes," which ask respondents to name key political figures, such as members of Congress and Supreme Court justices, and that people have no reason to memorize such information when they can easily look it up. However, they do admit that most Americans know little about how government actually works, how much it spends, what goes on in other countries, or even where those countries are. They accept the findings of studies that show that two out of three Americans would not recognize the text of the Bill of Rights if they saw it, and that nearly 40 percent believe that Israel is an Arab nation.

But Page and Shapiro argue that even if most individual Americans are politically ignorant, they change their policy preferences in light of new information and deliberation. The media, they point out, play a key role in this learning process by publicizing information and stimulating public debate. For instance, news stories revealing who is responsible for a problem may cause individuals to change how they attribute responsibility—whether, for example, they blame the president rather than Congress for an economic recession and high unemployment—and this information may then cause their policy preferences to change. Because studies of public opinion often overlook this learning process, they sometimes conclude mistakenly that individual attitudes fluctuate almost randomly and even appear to be "nonattitudes," or impulsive reactions. This view is also reinforced by the fact that individuals who hold conflicting attitudes about a policy may, under the pressure of the interview, cite one attitude rather than another, depending on their mood or on how the questions are posed. Page and Shapiro argue that this apparent inconsistency often disappears when the opinions expressed by the *same individual* are measured at several different times and averaged together.[58] In sum, these political scientists maintain that the public, like every other political actor, learns by doing over time.

Public Judgment

How should elites and experts respond when the public expresses opinions it is unwilling to support with action? Polls show, for example, that most Americans are concerned about global warming and want government action to reduce it but are unwilling to make even modest sacrifices—such as paying a higher gasoline tax or further controlling auto emissions—to do so.

Pollster Daniel Yankelovich argues that Americans should move beyond mere public opinion, for which they are not held accountable, to **public judgment**—the willingness of respondents to take responsibility for their opinions.[59] So, for example, when the public stops treating global warming as an abstract threat and takes concrete action over time to prevent it, it will have come to public judgment on this issue. Those who have come to public judgment have wrestled with the tough policy issues and have agreed on action to handle them.

Because experts dominate the decision-making process, relatively few Americans, according to Yankelovich, get the chance to develop public judgment and advance the cause of popular democracy. He believes that, unless experts and the public exchange views in a deliberative process characterized by mutual trust,[60] the gap between experts and the public will widen and public participation in politics will decline. Public judgment can grow, Yankelovich claims, if the power gap that divides experts and the public is narrowed. If the gap were narrowed and public judgment contributed effectively to the policymaking process, experts would be less resistant to increased citizen participation.

Public judgment develops gradually over a period of time, according to the steps outlined in the box nearby. On a complex issue such as health care policy, Yankelovich estimates that this sequence of steps will take at least ten years. It took more than a decade of increasingly violent crime before a majority of the public decided in 1994 that it was ready for some form of gun control and Congress finally passed a limited version. It has also taken years for Congress to deal with how little education children get and how much violence they watch on TV. There are many areas in which Congress is not prepared to act until it feels confident that the public will accept its actions.

This distinction between public opinion and public judgment is a prescriptive one, in the sense that Americans are being encouraged to increase their understanding of the issues and to take responsibility for their opinions about them. The motivation for adopting the concept of public judgment is clearly to improve the quality of American democracy. What is less clear is how the concept of public judgment is to be judged. Who decides that the public's judgment on a particular issue is right or wrong?

Yankelovich would rely on the judgment of recognized experts on the issue in question. He reports that when first asked, 63 percent of respondents said they favored a constitutional amendment to balance the federal budget, but when they learned that such an amendment might mean higher taxes, that number shrank to 39 percent. Yankelovich concludes from this finding that the 24 percent who changed their minds had not reached public judgment on the issue because they were not prepared to back up their opinions with higher taxes or spending cuts. Many Americans would object to this conclusion because they believe that government presently wastes enough tax dollars to pay the costs of such an amendment—a view Yankelovich calls "wishful thinking." Instead, he cites the view of economic experts who say that the budget cannot be balanced without raising taxes. However, experts, as we know, often disagree. Nor are spending cuts ever mentioned as a way of balancing the budget. Yankelovich is an expert on public opinion, not economics, yet he expects others to accept the conclusions of the particular economic experts he trusts. In doing so, he resembles the experts he accuses of dominating the decision-making process. There is nothing surprising in Yankelovich's

Pollster Daniel Yankelovich.

attitude, because experts tend to rely on the judgments of other experts—especially those whose views reinforce their own political opinions.

There are other problems with the notion of public judgment. One is the criteria used to define it. Does the fact that Americans are willing to back their opinions up with dollars, or that their opinions hold steady over time, really indicate that they have reached a more mature position on a public policy? Does the fact that a majority of Americans have consistently supported capital punishment mean that their opinions have "matured" and become public judgment? If not, how can we tell when a more mature position has been reached? Must we rely on experts such as Yankelovich to tell us? These questions bring us back to the crux of politics—disputes over claims to the authority to decide *what is*, *what's right*, and *what works*.

Second, how does Yankelovich explain the gap between "a mature body of responsible public judgment"[61] and the failure to put that judgment into practice? One of the issues on which Yankelovich says Americans have reached a firm public judgment is the belief that women should receive equal pay for equal work, but as we'll see in Chapter 16, this goal has yet to be reached.

Third, the concept of public judgment does not address what the Framers of the Constitution called "the tyranny of the majority." In sum, the question of *whose values* should be used to evaluate a public policy as "mature" and "responsible" animates every public opinion dispute.

How to Improve Public Opinion

Political ignorance in America, where access to political information is widely available, is often viewed as the fault of individuals and groups alone. But the fact that political ignorance damages the democratic political system and the public at large makes such ignorance a national problem, one that requires concerted action by a variety of actors, both public and private. In short, the quality of American public opinion is the responsibility of all political actors. Because political knowledge, collective deliberation, and citizen participation operate as a system, failures and improvements in any one of them affect the others.

Increase Political Knowledge

Americans need exposure to more accurate information and debate from schools, public officials, commentators, experts, political parties, and interest groups. The media are essential to such exposure, as Chapter 9 will explain. Schools, especially colleges and universities, promote higher levels of political knowledge, but recent cutbacks in public education funding and increases in tuition are creating substantial differences between the financially advantaged and disadvantaged in obtaining access to political knowledge. Experts say that government financial aid for students "could be the most significant single step toward greater civic literacy—and

Seven Steps to Public Judgment: The Case of Health Care

Stage 1: Dawning Awareness

During the Bush administration a majority of the public was becoming aware that health care costs were skyrocketing, that millions lacked health insurance, and that their own coverage had grown costly and was in danger of erosion. A majority accused the health care industry of being overly greedy and wasteful and blamed lawyers for excessive litigation that has caused the costs of malpractice insurance to skyrocket. At this stage in the public debate, most people were unaware that health care costs are also driven up by the rising costs of new technologies, the rising costs of caring for the elderly and people with AIDS, and the rising costs of administration. While many Americans pointed to the Canadian system of universal coverage as a model to follow, few actually knew much about it.

Stage 2: Greater Urgency

The issue of health care has been raised in various forms in politics for decades, but it was only during the 1992 presidential campaign that it entered this second stage, when people began to feel that action was urgent. This sense of urgency was linked to fears (prompted by rising unemployment) that if people lost their jobs they would also lose their health insurance. Surveys showed that 4 out of 5 then believed that health care had become an emergency.

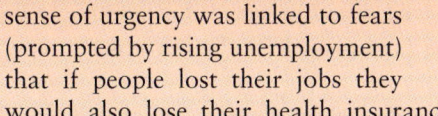

Stage 3: Discovering the Choices

Because President Clinton had made comprehensive health care a centerpiece of his legislative program in 1993, people slowly began to learn about health care problems other than those they had personally encountered and the various policy options Congress was proposing to deal with them. For example, they learned that savings could come from limiting damages in malpractice suits and from preventive medicine—giving people incentives to take responsibility for their own health before they get sick. They also learned (largely under pressure from their employers) about health maintenance organizations (HMOs) and "managed care," which could save money while replacing traditional individual reliance on a personal physician and specialists. Gradually the notion that health care involves a knowledgeable, responsible, cost-conscious consumer and a greater role for government began to dawn on the public.

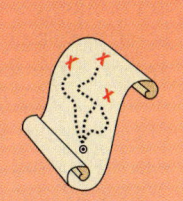

Stage 4: Wishful Thinking

By 1993 the public had reached the stage where people wanted all the options, and while they said they were willing to pay a bit more for them, they had no accurate idea of what these options cost. Polls showed that most Americans had come to view health care as a right rather than as a commodity to be purchased. Ninety-one percent believed that everyone should get the same treatment a millionaire can afford, and 71 percent believed that "health insurance should pay for any treatment that will save lives even if it costs $1 million to save a life." They mistakenly assumed that they paid for 70 percent to 80 percent of those costs when they paid only about 20 percent. At this stage—where opinions are today—Americans have not decided that they are ready to pay for the universal health coverage they say they want. Ultimately, Yankelovich believes, the public will have to accept that health care options will mean higher costs and less choice for individuals, as well as some degree of rationing and limits on technology.

Stage 5: Weighing the Choices

In the stages we've examined so far, the experts and the media do most of the "consciousness raising"

(Continued on next page)

work—formulating policy choices on health care and presenting them to the public. Next people will need to learn what these choices are and what trade-offs they involve in terms of interests and values. According to Yankelovich, the public at this stage will have to accept some federal regulation of costs, the extension of coverage to all, a modest tax hike to pay for that extension, and the decision not to use costly technology to prolong the life of elderly persons during the final months of life. Polls show that the elderly increasingly favor this latter policy.

Stage 6: Taking a Stand Intellectually

At this stage, people who have worked through the options and tradeoffs take an intellectual stand on an issue.

Stage 7: Making an Ethically Responsible Judgment

In this final stage people who put their own interests and beliefs first in previous stages must then reflect on how the policy will affect society at large. They must then come to an ethical public judgment about the policy, meaning that they are willing to support it emotionally, intellectually, and financially. Yankelovich believes "that many years and many crises will have to pass before the American public fully accepts the need to ration, regulate, reform, and even revolutionize health care in America so that it preserves some semblance of a right rather than a consumer good, without bankrupting the nation."

Source: Adapted and updated from Daniel Yankelovich, "How Public Opinion Really Works," *Fortune*, October 5, 1992, 102–104, 108.

---

civil equality."[62] They also point to the lack of public spaces for continuing civic education, which they say schools could help provide both electronically and in classrooms.

Campaigns could also heighten political learning with the cooperation of the media and candidates (see Chapter 10). When Ross Perot used his own money during the 1992 presidential campaign to televise lectures on the economy and the deficit during prime time, a surprising number of viewers tuned in. No political leader had ever dared attempt to explain such complex issues to the public. The Concord Coalition, a pressure group concerned with reducing the deficit, kept up the momentum with nationwide lectures. Because C-SPAN aired many of these lectures, public understanding on the issue grew still further. Members of Congress and even the president began making more use of charts to explain their positions on economic policy, and the 1996 campaign responded to these public demands.

The more political actors treat the public as rational and competent, the more rational and competent it can become. The more they mislead the public with misstatements and lies, the more they undermine that rationality and competence—as well as their own legitimacy.

Practice Collective Deliberation

Improvement in public opinion also depends on rational **collective deliberation**. When collective deliberation is working properly, people receive accurate information and helpful interpretations from political actors, which they then use to develop policy preferences that express their own needs and values.[63] In the process, they usually change their opinions to some degree and increase their levels of political sophistication.

This process has already been demonstrated by a new type of poll known as the **deliberative opinion poll,** which polls individuals twice on particular issues: once in isolation (as conventional polls do) and again after they have been supplied with new information on those issues and have discussed them in a group that represents a cross-section of the public being polled. When individuals are provided with new information and receive feedback from others, they often alter their opinions, or at least increase their tolerance for other points of view. As the nearby box indicates, deliberative polls are an example of *learning by doing*: they provoke opinion change in response to increases in knowledge and debate. Unlike conventional polls, deliberative opinion polls take account of the fact that individuals do not live in isolation from others and that individual beliefs and preferences often change in dialogue with others. In contrast, conventional polls merely record what individuals think before they are challenged to reflect on feedback from other people.

Deliberative opinion polls must be evaluated with caution, however. Unlike the cross-section of people who participate in a deliberative poll, most people in the real world are so divided by race, class, education, and the hustle and bustle of everyday life that they never meet, much less carry on genuine conversations with, a wide range of people different from themselves. If few people have the opportunity for deliberation, are the findings of these polls more wish than reality?

Another error that some specialists claim afflicts deliberative opinion polls is the Hawthorne effect. The concern is that people who participate may become self-conscious in ways that change their behavior as well as their views on the issues being polled. Since the purpose of deliberative opinion polls is precisely that—to raise people's consciousness and equip them with information that allows them to change their views and behavior—those who conduct such polls tend to dismiss this criticism out of hand.

Promote Informed Participation

Political knowledge and participation are intertwined. Political knowledge encourages people to take an interest in politics, to use the media, and to participate politically, while these activities in turn increase political knowledge. Studies show that additional increments of political knowledge measurably improve citizen participation. As two political scientists explain, "All things being equal, the more informed peo-

> **Hawthorne effect**
> In the 1920s researchers at the Hawthorne Works, a Bell System plant, found that any change in structure or operation produced an improvement in productivity. The term now refers to changes in people's opinions that are traceable to the fact that they are part of an experiment rather than to the actual nature of the experiment.

Deliberative Opinion Polls

Unlike opinion polls that record the poorly informed opinions participants already hold, a new kind of opinion poll shows what opinions they would hold if they had more information on the issues and an opportunity to discuss them with experts and with others. Political scientist James Fishkin developed the national deliberative opinion poll to find out whether it increased people's political sophistication.[1]

After some preliminary trials in Europe, a deliberative opinion poll was held in Austin, Texas, in January 1996, when presidential candidates were campaigning for their party's nomination. Known as the National Issues Convention (NIC), the poll randomly selected prospective participants nationwide, and 459 delegates met in 30 groups of 12 people for two and one-half days. Several major foundations and corporations contributed $4 million dollars to pay the delegates' travel, hotel, meals, and expenses, plus stipends of $300 each.

The participants were polled on three major issues—foreign policy, the economy, and the family—first while still at home, and then after the convention, to see whether their opinions had changed. At the NIC they got briefing books and a chance to discuss these issues with experts and among themselves, and to meet with and question for 20 minutes each presidential candidate who participated. Public television agreed to carry five and one-half hours of these events nationwide. How well did the experiment work?

The sample was less random than expected because a winter storm in the Northeast kept some participants from attending, resulting in too many westerners and too few elderly. Second, Senator Bob Dole chose not to attend, and President Clinton sent Vice President Gore. Senator Richard Lugar (R-Ind.) appeared in person, while Senator Phil Gramm (R-Tex.), former Tennessee governor Lamar Alexander (R), and magazine publisher Steve Forbes, Jr. (R), appeared via satellite.

After preparing themselves on the issues and drafting 20 substantive questions for each candidate, many of the delegates were dissatisfied with the responses they received. A Los Angeles delegate complained, "The politicians kind of weaseled out of it. They seemed to do a lot of double talk. And when they tried to explain things they used terms and language no one could understand anyway. They're not really in touch with the general public." The owner of a chocolate factory in Massachusetts agreed: "They launched into their stump speeches. That's their profession." A journalism professor said that the interchange underscored the gap between "the professional political class" and what ordinary citizens wanted to know.[2] But a woman delegate said that what she learned by talking to the candidates was "that these issues that we may have thought were black-and-white or right-or-wrong are more complicated."[3]

Comparison of the predeliberation poll results with the postdeliberation poll results showed marked changes in opinion. Before deliberations, 41 percent strongly agreed with the statement "I have opinions about politics that are worth listening to." After deliberations that percentage rose to 68. On the issue of whether the United States should adopt a single-rate flat tax, the predeliberation poll found 43.5 percent in favor and 43 percent opposed. After deliberations, support for the tax fell to 29.8 percent and opposition climbed to 49.7 percent. On the minimum wage, the preconvention poll showed strong agreement by 26.6 percent of the delegates; some agreement by 32.8 percent; and strong disagreement by 6.7 percent. After deliberation, the strongly agree group climbed to 40.4 percent; the somewhat agree group rose to 34.6 percent; and the strongly disagree group fell to 4.2 percent.[4]

Few first-time experiments are perfect, and conventional pollsters have criticized the NIC's survey design and the methodology.[5] But the real success of the NIC experiment was the deliberation the delegates engaged in. As one delegate explains, "Deliberation is a different kind of talk than debate. The result will almost never be unanimity [full consensus]. If you listen carefully, however, you can often hear a sense of common concerns and areas where people with conflicting values are willing to work cooperatively."[6] David Matthews, president of the Kettering Foundation, one of the conference's sponsors, made much the same point: "The most profound effect of deliberation is to change my opinion of your opinions. . . . This creates a sense of possibility."[7]

This sense of possibility was coupled with feeling of comradeship. In the small groups, people whose paths would normally never cross put party and ideology aside to discuss the three issues before them. One delegate, a minister from California, expressed amazement "at how people from all walks of life could come together for a few days and have a dialogue on a variety of issues. I sat between somebody who couldn't read and a trucker from Pennsylvania and yet we had a common ground."[8] A delegate from Arizona confessed, "The last time I had a discussion on citizenship and democracy was in the seventh grade. I spend more time keeping my driver's license current than my citizenship."[9]

A lawyer from Minneapolis, for example, turned out to be just as concerned about the economic stress on families as this military wife from North Dakota: "Two working people never see their children, and that's not right."[10] As a mother of three quietly told of her day-to-day experiences in a public housing project, an auto mechanic from Buffalo, a businesswoman from New Jersey, and a home health worker from Costa Mesa "all leaned forward in their chairs so they could hear. . . . [This woman] has no credentials as an expert on welfare, but she is an expert in her own life." After intense discussions the group reached a consensus: it was less important to cut back on welfare programs than to make sure that the programs worked. As one delegate put it, "We don't lack for money in this country. We lack accountability."[11]

Hearing experiences firsthand promoted tolerance in group after group. In response to an 84-year-old man's view that a real family must have both a father and a mother who are present in the home, a single working black mother of two firmly contradicted him, saying that hers was just as much a real family. After hearing her out, the man told her he was wrong, and she crossed the room and hugged him.[12] When the conference came to an end, more than a few delegates parted with hugs.

Organizers hoped the conference would increase the political sophistication of those who watched the convention on TV. They also hoped that the candidates would have a better idea of the public's chief concerns, thus improving the quality of public debate during the campaign and the quality of mass democracy.

---

[1] James F. Fishkin, *The Voice of the People*, 2nd ed. (New Haven: Yale University Press, 1997).
[2] Carlos Nieto III, Michael Goldman, and Jay Rosen, School of Journalism, New York University, all quoted in Daniel M. Weintraub, "Conventional Answers Leave Forum Participants Unsatisfied," *Orange Country Register*, January 21, 1996.
[3] Mary Ellen Cox, quoted in Tom Brazaitis and Joe Frolik, "Experiment in Citizenship," *Cleveland Plain Dealer*, January 22, 1996.
[4] Ernest Tollerson, "Opinions Were Changed by Issues Convention Talks," *New York Times*, January 27, 1996,
[5] See *Public Perspective*, April/May 1996.
[6] Quoted in Tom Brazaitis, "Ordinary People Learn That They Are Experts," *Cleveland Plain Dealer*, January 28, 1996.
[7] Quoted in Catherine Flavin and Regina Dougherty, "Conscience and Citizenship at the NIC," *Public Perspective*, April/May 1996, 47.
[8] Mike Schooner, quoted in Robert Bryce, "New Poll Shows Power of a Little Information," *Christian Science Monitor*, January 24, 1996.
[9] Don Worcester, quoted in John E. Yang, "'Real People' Face Issues, Candidates in Experiment on Citizenship," *Washington Post*, January 21, 1996.
[10] Julie Jones, quoted in Thaddeus Herrick, "Issues Delegates' Refrain: Fretting About Keeping Jobs," *Houston Chronicle*, March 10, 1996.
[11] Both quoted in Daniel Weintraub, "America in One Room," *Orange County Register*, January 21, 1996.
[12] Brazaitis, "Ordinary People."

ple are, the better able they are to perform as citizens."[64] Voters must know where candidates stand on abortion and other issues if they are to affect those issues at the polls. Understanding the processes that protect participation is not only essential to one's own participation, but it helps promote tolerance for the participation of others. Studies show that a majority of the public would like to prohibit members of groups they dislike from running for office, speaking in public, teaching in public schools, or even belonging to those groups.[65] However, political tolerance has been found to increase dramatically with an increase in knowledge of civil rights and civil liberties.[66]

The more informed the participation, the more successful it is likely to be. Fortunately, the power of information differs from other sources of political power in two ways: First, information is not finite, so its acquisition by one actor does not mean that there is less of it for others. Second, while more information can help an actor pursue private interests, it also leads to a richer understanding of the public interest and of how the two can be reconciled. Polls showing that "greater knowledge had resulted in more support among older citizens for women's and gay rights, among men for abortion rights, and among whites for race-conscious government programs" support this view.[67] But these polls also suggest that greater knowledge on social issues tends to promote liberal rather than conservative causes. It is important to remember that these polls are making claims about what counts as "greater knowledge," and that assessments of knowledge change over time in response to feedback and changes in the political system. The possibility that race-conscious government programs may have already worked well enough to undermine their continued use is a conclusion many blacks as well as whites are now reaching. Thus it would not be surprising if polls soon treat this conclusion as "greater knowledge," and if members of the public use it to more adequately inform their participation.

Summary

Most specialists define *public opinion* very generally as the summary of the distribution of expressed attitudes of all or part of the people on some subject at some particular moment. Public opinion is important to political actors because (1) it can legitimate their political authority, (2) it can make them more responsive and effective, (3) it can inform political candidates and parties, and (4) it can be an indicator of continuity and change in beliefs and values.

How trustworthy polls are depends on the way surveys are designed, implemented, and interpreted. While survey methods and accuracy have greatly improved since Gallup introduced random sampling in the 1930s, they are not error-free. In addition, polls commissioned by politicians and interest groups are often used to manipulate public opinion rather than to measure it accurately.

Experts disagree over how competent American public opinion is, and therefore what role it should play in American democracy. Disagreement persists over how much power the public should have compared with that of elites and experts, and how politically sophisticated the public must be for elites and experts to heed its political opinions. Elitists have little faith in the public's poorly informed understanding of the world and argue that elites and experts should run the country. Champions of public opinion believe that the public, along with elites and experts, should play a major role in the political process.

Some specialists argue that the public is more

rational and competent to guide policymaking than most studies suggest, while others warn that elites and experts are usurping the power of the public to guide governmental decisionmaking. American public opinion can be improved, specialists argue, through collective deliberation.

Key Terms

bandwagon effect 154
campaign pollsters 167
collective deliberation 179
cue-takers 172
deliberative opinion poll 179
doorstep opinions 164
focus groups 151

longitudinal studies 164
margin of error 161
period effect 165
political sophistication 168
political stratification 169
polls 151
pollsters 151

public judgment 175
public opinion 151
"push" polls 154
random sampling 161
straw polls 160
underdog effect 166

How You Can Learn More About Public Opinion

Delli Carpini, Michael X., and Scott Keeter. *What Americans Know About Politics and Why It Matters.* New Haven: Yale University Press, 1996. An analysis of the role knowledge plays in the political process.

Gallup, George, and Saul Forbes Rac. *The Pulse of Democracy: The Public Opinion Poll and How It Works.* New York: Simon & Schuster, 1940. A highly readable and fascinating account of the rationale for and the workings of public opinion, co-written by the founder of scientific opinion polling.

Herbst, Susan. *Numbered Voices: How Opinion Polling Has Shaped American Politics.* Chicago: University of Chicago Press, 1993. Herbst examines the rise and influence of polls from a politics of knowledge perspective.

Lippmann, Walter. *Public Opinion.* New York: Macmillan, 1941. A valuable and interesting analysis of the phenomena of public and expert opinion in the presurvey period by one of the most influential journalistic thinkers.

Margolis, Michael, and Gary A. Mauser, eds. *Manipulating Public Opinion: Essays on Public Opinion as a Dependent Variable.* Pacific Grove, Calif.: Brooks/Cole, 1989. Short, insightful analyses of how public opinion is manipulated in electoral politics, public policy, and the media.

Moore, David W. *The Superpollsters: How They Measure and Manipulate Public Opinion in America.* New York: Four Walls Eight Windows, 1992. An absorbing account of how pollsters have manipulated public opinion on behalf of presidential candidates since the days of George Gallup.

Page, Benjamin I., and Robert Y. Shapiro. *The Rational Public: Fifty Years of Trends in Americans' Policy Preferences.* Chicago: University of Chicago Press, 1992. The authors argue that American public opinion, when viewed collectively over time, appears more politically sophisticated than it does in studies that focus purely on individuals.

Price, Vincent. *Public Opinion.* London: Sage, 1992. A short, critical history of the problems the concept of public opinion has posed to those who have tried to study it.

Sniderman, Paul M., Richard A. Brody, and Philip E. Tetlock. *Reasoning and Choice: Explorations in Political Psychology.* Cambridge, England: Cambridge University Press, 1991. An argument that ordinary people do reason through their positions on a range of issues.

Yankelovich, Daniel. *Coming to Public Judgment: Making Democracy Work in a Complex World.* Syracuse, N.Y.: Syracuse University Press, 1991. A fresh, positive approach to the topic of public opinion that merits critical attention.

Political Participation

Above: A homeless person in Santa Monica, California.
Right: Santa Monica artist, political activist, and advocate for the homeless Bruria Finkel at her computer.

CHAPTER 6

> Change is happening more quickly than our capacity to absorb it, so often if we wait, problems will seem to have gone away. . . . And those who struggle with the answers often appear misguided, if not inept, making it easy for us to criticize from the sidelines. . . . What I would like to leave you with this afternoon is a different strategy . . . find new ways to be engaged in your community—at any level.
>
> —Deputy Education Secretary Madeleine M. Kunin, May 1996

> You know there are people sleeping in the streets of our cities, you've seen them; you know there is the poison of bigotry infesting our society, you've heard it; you know that we are poisoning our rivers and our skies, you've smelled it, you've choked on it, you've shed tears over the tragedy of it. But what are you going to do about it? Do you have the will?
>
> —David McCullough, biographer, May 1996[1]

Expanding the Right and Opportunity to Vote

The Value of Voting

Explaining the Vote

Other Forms of Political Participation

Government As a Political Activist

Improved Political Participation Can Strengthen Democracy

One summer evening in 1989, artist Bruria Finkel got an idea about how to solve a problem many homeless people faced in her hometown of Santa Monica, California. These people needed a place to take a morning shower, put on clean clothes, and store their belongings so they could go to work or, if unemployed, interview for jobs. How did Finkel know about this problem?

Finkel belonged to the Public Electronic Network (PEN), an "electronic city hall" the city had launched in February 1989 to increase citizen participation in civic life. PEN operates via an electronic bulletin board (e-mail) system—a computer system that allows people to communicate with one another. The city of Santa Monica distributes free user accounts to anyone who registers with the city, and citizens with an account can send e-mail messages from their home terminals or from one of the many public terminals available in public libraries, schools, and city buildings.

Citizens using this electronic system can read information the city posts on the electronic bulletin board about jobs and other matters, communicate their views and questions to other citizens and to city hall, and participate in teleconferences—ongoing interactive conversations—on a variety of issues ranging from homelessness, to crime (the police department runs a teleconference called Crimewatch), to environmental and recycling problems, to a host of social issues such as gun control, AIDS, sexism, and racism.

At first, citizens used the system as an information source, but soon some realized they could use it as a catalyst for political action. In July 1989, a group of users organized the PEN Action Group, which held face-to-face as well as online meetings about specific problems. Bruria Finkel heard about the "morning" problems of the homeless through online conversations with at least two dozen homeless people on the homeless teleconference.

In subsequent meetings with social service agencies, Finkel and others in the PEN Action Group learned that there were no public shower facilities available in the mornings and that the one free laundry service available to the homeless required clients to wear borrowed garments until their clothes could be returned. No lockers were made available because no one wanted to "police" their contents.

Finkel and her group first tried to solve these problems in a conventional, centralized fashion—for example, by leasing a building that would provide these morning services. When these efforts got nowhere, they tried a decentralized approach. They raised $5,000 for a laundry voucher system that would allow the homeless to use vouchers at any participating laundromat. Next the group contacted a locker manufacturer who agreed to donate 30 free lockers to the city for a seven-month trial period. Meanwhile, the city agreed to the group's proposal for a comprehensive study of the problem, and in June 1990, it allotted $150,000 to outfit city restroom facilities with lockers and showers. The city also agreed to open all city showers at 6:00 A.M.

New technology—in this case e-mail—brought citizens together not only in the identification of a problem but in its solution. This kind of political action will become more common as more political actors learn how to use the possibilities for communication computers offer. Right now Santa Monica residents can log onto the teleconference PENhelp.[2]

In this chapter we examine the factors that affect people's willingness and ability to engage in political participation of various sorts. We'll do this by focusing on the following questions:

How have the right and opportunity to vote been expanded in America?

How important is voting?

What are the other ways people can participate in politics?

How can improved participation strengthen democracy?

Expanding the Right and Opportunity to Vote

Political actors—individuals, groups, and even government itself—engage in **political participation** when they attempt to advance their beliefs about *what is*, *what's right*, and *what works* in political life. In the United States these actors try to influence who gets elected, what public policies get adopted, and how government is run. In doing so, they are *practicing American politics*. Most actors practice politics by using existing laws and institutions, some create their own organizations and movements, and a few resort to protest.

Voters, for example, rely on existing laws and institutions to decide who will represent the people in government and to hold elected officials accountable for their actions by reelecting them or voting them out of office. But voting in a country with weak or corrupt political institutions does not assure responsible representation and accountability. Meaningful voting depends on how well other elements in the political system—electoral procedures, campaign finance laws, legislatures, executive branches, courts, parties, interest groups, the media—perform. Because voting affects and is affected by all of these factors, it must be evaluated in tandem with the political system as whole.

Is voting the most important form of political participation in the United States? When President Lyndon Johnson signed the Voting Rights Act of 1965, protecting the right to **vote**, he declared all other rights meaningless without it. Voting, he said, not only gives people "control over their own destinies" but it "is the most powerful instrument ever devised . . . for breaking down injustice and destroying the terrible walls which imprison [people] because they are different from other[s]."[3] But more and more people are discovering, as Bruria Finkel and the PEN Action Group did, that there are many opportunities to practice politics between trips to the polls. Indeed, most politics takes place during these intervals. Voting, then, is just one part—a very important part—of the wider range of activities called political participation.

Today, most people who are U.S. citizens and at least 18 years old are allowed to vote. But it took 182 years to secure these voting rights. First a variety of state requirements and restrictions on voting had to be removed. The states had the power to impose these restrictions because the Constitution of 1787 allows them to regulate voting—even for national elections—so long as these restrictions accord with the Constitution and federal laws. The voting laws in the 50 states thus determine the size of the nation's **electorate**, all those permitted by law to vote.

Removing State Restrictions on Voting

Over the course of the nation's history, the states removed certain voting restrictions on their own initiative. But constitutional amendments and U.S. Supreme Court decisions have struck down state laws that

vote

The word comes from the French *voie*, meaning "voice" or "statement."

made voting dependent upon race, gender, age, payment of a tax, ownership of property, proof of literacy, or lengthy residence in a taxing district. States continue to deny the vote to various groups, such as the mentally ill, prison inmates, convicted felons, violators of elections laws, and the homeless, and they continue to prescribe "The Times, Places and Manner of holding Elections," as the Constitution (Article I, section 4) gives them the power to do. But the Constitution also says that "the Congress may at any time by Law make or alter such Regulations," and the states have been compelled to obey laws passed by Congress prohibiting a variety of restrictions on voting.

Removing Restrictions on Adult White Men

After 1800, growing democratic sentiment, an expanding westward frontier, and the formation of new states began to erode property-owning restrictions on the **franchise**, or right to vote. By 1820 many states had revised their constitutions so that men who paid taxes or served in the militia could vote even though they owned no property. In 1824 this expanded electorate gave populist Andrew Jackson a plurality of votes for president, but the vote in the House of Representatives (no candidate received a majority of the electoral vote) did not go his way; Jackson received a resounding majority of the vote in 1828. By 1840, more than 90 percent of adult white men were eligible to vote.[4]

Removing Restrictions on Adult Black Men

Following the Civil War, a Republican Congress passed the Fourteenth Amendment granting citizenship to "all persons born or naturalized in the United States." The former Confederate states (except Tennessee) could not reenter the Union without ratifying this amendment. When most refused to do so, federal troops enforced the law. During this brief period, known as Reconstruction, federal military rulers registered more than 800,000 black men, thus allowing blacks to win election to state legislatures and Congress. In the 1870s, the Mississippi state legislature elected two blacks to the U.S. Senate and southern states sent 16 blacks to the House of Representatives.

When angry white southerners formed the Ku Klux Klan to terrorize blacks and prevent them from voting, Congress reacted with the Fifteenth Amendment, ratified in 1870, explicity stating that the right to vote could not be "denied or abridged . . . on account of race, color, or previous conditions of servitude." (States outside the South had consistently denied the vote to free black men.[5]) Again Congress imposed this amendment on southern states by force.

After the election of 1876, when the Republican party abandoned Reconstruction and federal troops were withdrawn from the South, Democratic state legislatures quickly found ways to prevent most

Student Nonviolent Coordinating Committee (SNCC) activists register voters in Ruleville, Mississippi, in 1963.

black men from voting. They allowed the Democratic party to set the conditions for voting in primaries by declaring the Democratic party a private club. And because the party completely dominated politics in the South, primaries were the only elections that mattered. In the general election, the Democrats always won. When the Democrats restricted voting in primaries—the so-call **white primary**—they effectively disfranchised black men.

Most southern states also imposed literacy tests on would-be registrants or required voters to display a reasonable understanding of the state constitution if it was read to them. Many states exempted voters from property and literacy requirements if they could prove that they, their father, or grandfather had voted before 1867 (before Reconstruction Republicans came to power). Blacks, of course, were usually told their literacy or "understanding" was deficient, and they never qualified for exemption under the **grandfather clause**. Another strategy for deterring the black vote was the **poll tax**—a fee (usually several dollars) a citizen was required to pay before voting. If all these tests would not keep blacks from the polls, harassment and threats surely did.

The grandfather clause was declared unconstitutional in 1915 and the white primary in 1944.[6] Yet many states still barred blacks from voting, especially in rural areas in the South. Not until the mid-1960s—almost 100 years after the Fourteenth Amendment—did the federal government act to protect the right to vote. In 1965 the Voting Rights Act abolished literacy and other tests and appointed federal examiners to implement the law in states and counties (mainly in the South) where there was evidence of past discrimination. Congress expanded the protections of the Voting Rights Act in 1970, 1975, and 1982 (see Table 6.1). In 1964 the Twenty-fourth Amendment abolished the poll tax for national elections, and in 1966 the Supreme Court outlawed it for all elections.[7]

Removing Restrictions on Women, Native Americans, the Young, and Others

Fifty years after black men got the vote, women won their struggle for **suffrage**, or the right to vote. The Declaration of Independence had promised Americans freedom and equality, but these were not widely thought to apply to women. When the colonies became states, only New Jersey allowed women to vote. This right, which allowed the few women who owned property to vote in state elections, was rescinded in 1807, when women began to vote in greater numbers.

The campaign for woman suffrage later in the century was led by women derisively dubbed *suffragettes*. During the 1890s, by organizing, lobbying, picketing, parading, and even striking, the women's movement persuaded a number of states to grant women the vote. In 1916 both the Republican and Democratic parties endorsed woman suffrage, and in 1920 women's right to vote in all elections was guaranteed by the ratification of the Nineteenth Amendment.

In 1924, an act of Congress declared "all non-citizen Indians born within the territorial limits of the United States" to be citizens of the United States. This left people between the ages of 18 and 21 as the last major group of disenfranchised citizens. During World War II, Georgia

A suffragette marches for the right to vote in New York City, 1910.

suffrage

Suffrage was originally a religious term used for petitioning God to change or improve some situation. But once secularized, the term applied to the voters' power to petition for a political change by means of the vote.

TABLE 6.1

Constitutional Amendments, Federal Laws, Supreme Court Decisions Expanding the Right to Vote

Year	Action	Impact
1870	Fifteenth Amendment	Prohibited voter discrimination because of race, color, previous condition of servitude.
1920	Nineteenth Amendment	Prohibited voter discrimination because of sex.
1924	Indian Citizenship Act	Granted citizenship to Native Americans.
1944	*Smith v. Allwright*	Supreme Court decision prohibited the white primary.
1957	Civil Rights Act of 1957	Authorized Justice Department to go to court to protect voting rights.
1960	Civil Rights Act of 1960	Authorized courts to appoint referees to assist voter registration.
1961	Twenty-third Amendment	Extended right to vote in presidential elections to residents of District of Columbia.
1964	Twenty-fourth Amendment	Prohibited poll tax in national elections.
1965	Voting Rights Act of 1965	Suspended literacy tests and authorized federal voter registrars in seven southern states.
1966	*Harper v. Virginia State Board of Elections*	Supreme Court decision prohibited poll taxes in any election.
1970	Voting Rights Act Amendments of 1970	Lowered minimum voting age for federal elections to 18; abolished state literacy tests; required uniform rules for absentee voting; in effect imposed a maximum 30-day residency requirement for presidential elections.
1971	Twenty-sixth Amendment	Lowered the minimum voting age to 18 for all elections.
1972	*Dunn v. Blumstein*	Supreme Court decision shortened residency requirements for voting in all elections.
1975	Voting Rights Act Amendments of 1975	Authorized federal voter registrars in ten more states; provided for use of ballots printed in more than one language.
1982	Voting Rights Act Amendments of 1982	Extended provisions of 1970 and 1975 amendments; allowed private parties to prove violations.

lowered its voting age from 21 to 18, and at the peak of the Vietnam War, Kentucky and Alaska lowered theirs—attempts to reconcile voting age with draft age and to recognize the contributions of those in the armed services. In the 1970 elections, when more states followed suit, Congress lowered the voting age to 18 for all elections. However, the Supreme Court ruled that Congress could only lower the voting age in *federal* elections—those for president and Congress. Finally, the Twenty-sixth Amendment, ratified in 1971, lowered the voting age to 18 for *all* elections.

Citizens living in Washington, D.C., the nation's capital, were granted the right to vote for president by the Twenty-third Amendment, ratified in 1961. They also vote for their own elected officials, as well as for one nonvoting member of the House of Representatives. So far they have failed to obtain representation in the Senate or the vote for their representative in the House. Citizens in U.S. territories—Puerto Rico, the Virgin Islands, and Guam—vote for their own elected officials but not in federal elections, and have only a nonvoting representative in Congress.

Relaxing Registration and Voting Procedures

The practice of **registration**, which the colonists inherited from England, was often used by elites to protect their own power. Those who intend to vote must register, or sign up, ahead of time with a local bureaucrat in charge of voting—typically a county official who works in a courthouse. In the course of the nineteenth century many states enacted voter registration laws to combat fraud and in effect to discourage certain social groups from voting, but in the twentieth century, as restrictions on voting have declined, so has the proportion of registered voters. Today roughly 190 million Americans are eligible to register to vote, but only 60 percent of them (114 million) are actually registered. About 40 percent, or 76 million Americans, remain unregistered. Continuing a 30-year trend, those registering as Democrats declined by about 1 percent in 1996 (from 50 to 49 percent), while Republican registration held steady at 34 percent.[8]

Today millions of Americans don't know where to register or what the deadlines are. One study showed that about 6 percent of nonvoters in Travis County, Texas, did not know they were actually registered to vote.[9] Registration is also difficult for the third of the country's citizens who change residence between presidential elections, because registration rules vary from state to state, county to county, and city to city. In New York, for example, a person's registration expires if he or she fails to vote in several elections in a row. Other states have made voting easier. Some state registrars now operate out of mobile units and set up booths in schools, supermarkets, shopping malls, and libraries, and more than half allow registration by postcard. In Ohio, McDonald's restaurants give their customers placemats printed with a form they can mail in. In most states, following registration, regular voting keeps registration current.

In 1993, Congress passed the "Motor Voter Act," mandating states and Washington, D.C., to allow citizens to register by mail and at motor vehicle offices. Democrats argued that this national registration system would make it easier for the poor and less educated to register. Republicans argued that the new law would lead to fraud and voting by illegal aliens. In fact, Republicans feared that such a bill would hurt their chances at the polls, just as Democrats expected it would help them. By the 1996 elections 12 million citizens had registered under the law, more than doubling the previous rate. However, some Republican governors have dragged their feet in implementing the law. In 1996, a federal court ordered New York Republican governor George Pataki's Department of Labor to comply with the law, and the U.S. Supreme Court rejected California Republican Governor Pete Wilson's challenge that the law was unconstitutional.

Supporters of registration requirements say that they help to control fraud by preventing people from voting several times in the same contest or by preventing people from voting in the name of people who have moved away or died. Some also believe that registration helps to dissuade ignorant and apathetic citizens from affecting the outcome of elections. Opponents want to abolish registration primarily to increase voter **turnout**—the percentage of eligible (registered or not) voters who actually "turn out" at the polls to vote. But do registration requirements really decrease turnout? Some political scientists like to cite the Dakotas: South Dakota, which requires registration, and North Dakota, which resembles South Dakota in political makeup but doesn't require advance registration, both had a turnout of 61 percent in the 1988 presidential election.[10] But others point

Figure 6.1

The decline in voter turnout

Source: Statistical Abstract of the United States, 1996 (116th ed.) (Washington D.C.: U.S. Bureau of the Census, 1996), p. 287.

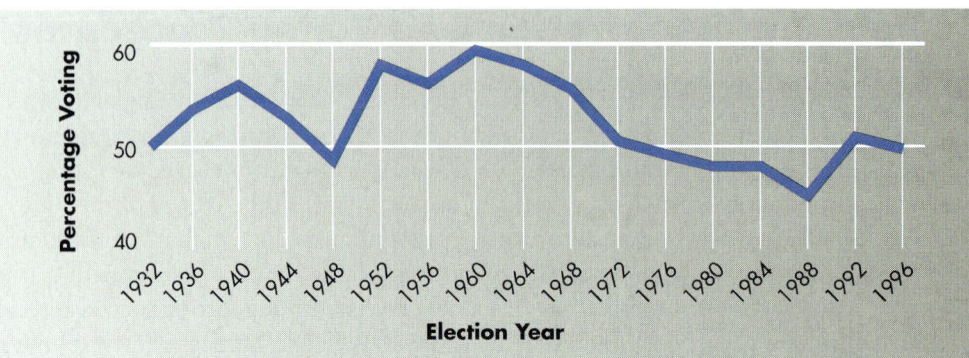

out that the 87 percent of Dakota voters who turn out to vote on election day constitute only one-third of those who are eligible to vote. Abolish registration, they say, and turnout will rise. Still, in every election since 1960 (except for the 1992 election, in which Ross Perot ran for the first time), the percentage of eligible voters voting has declined (see Figure 6.1).

The combination of registration and voting procedures in many states still discourages voting. Citizens who wish to vote must often do two distinct things at two separate times, often in two different places. After registering, they must show up on election day at the assigned polling place in their precinct. This location, which they must find in a newspaper, is rarely where they registered. Moreover, major elections are held on weekdays, and even though the law requires employers to allow employees time off to vote, many employees do not take advantage of this opportunity because they fear reprisals. Although most polling places open at 6:00 or 7:00 in the morning and do not close until 7:00 or 8:00 in the evening, lines are long before and after work. Shortly after the 1996 election, one citizen complained in a letter to the editor: "I cannot understand why, in the age of 'information superhighway,' cell phones, satellite pagers and fax machines, we must trudge to the polling place, wait in line to prove who we are, and punch little perforated cards! This is akin to using oil lamps and washing our clothes in the stream. Why can't we just pick up the phone, call an 800 number and punch in our selections?"[11]

Supporters of popular democracy would like the nation to adopt Wisconsin's practice of permitting persons to register and vote on the same day at the polling place. Many European countries no longer require registration, or make it automatic with the receipt of a driver's license or identification card. They also hold elections on weekends or holidays—sometimes over a two-day period—and make it easy to cast absentee ballots. In the United States, most states limit absentee voting to citizens who have acceptable excuses, such as being sick or planning to be out of town. Texas, however, has pioneered "no excuse" early voting, opening polls to all voters several weeks prior to an election. A drawback of this approach is that those voting this early must base their decisions on political conditions that could change drastically in the final weeks and days of the campaign.

The Value of Voting

Voting has value only in countries with genuine democratic institutions. Voting in the former Soviet Union was a sterile exercise because the results were determined in advance. The fact that the turnout rate in the former Soviet Union was 99 percent shows how essential it is to evaluate voting in connection with the rest of the political system. In Russia and other former Soviet republics today the value of voting is still unclear because their transformation to democracy is incomplete.

The value of voting is somewhat unclear even in established democracies. Higher turnout rates in Western European democracies and Japan suggest that their citizens value voting more highly than U.S. citizens do. But high turnout may be due to their simpler registration and voting requirements and to differences in party and electoral systems. In Australia, Belgium, and Luxembourg, for example, citizens face a fine if they don't vote. In addition, the American two-party winner-take-all system (the party with the most votes wins; see Chapter 7) gives voters less choice and incentive than multiparty systems that allow proportional representation (parties divide the seats according to their proportion of the votes). Such differences among the 27 countries that hold regular elections make it hard to evaluate voter turnout, and hence the value of voting, from democracy to democracy.

Why Voting Seems Right to Americans

Most Americans who do vote always have. They grow up accepting the value of voting and practicing it in a variety of contexts before they ever enter a polling place, routinely voting on what to have for the family dinner, what movies to see with friends, and where to go on class trips.

Most Americans view voting as a legitimate way of making political decisions, for several reasons. First, voting is the legal mechanism (*what is*) their national and state constitutions and their legislatures have prescribed for selecting their political representatives. Second, these constitutions and laws also declare that voting is a fundamental right (that *what is* is also *what's right*). Third, most Americans have been socialized to view voting as their civic responsibility (*what's right*, because one is a citizen). Fourth, Americans tend to believe that the people who are to be affected by decisions should be the ones to make those decisions as often as practicable, or at least have an indirect say in them.

Americans also support voting because it's *what works*, given their vast numbers and responsibilities. Americans have a representative rather than a direct democracy because they cannot handle all political matters themselves. In this respect, voters do much more than decide who resides in the White House, the governors' mansions, and the houses of Con-

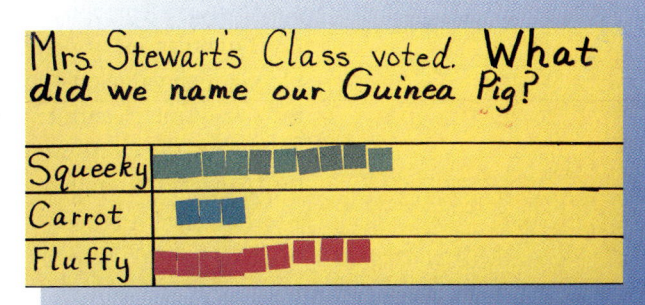

Melba Stewart's 1996 kindergarten students at Casis Elementary School in Austin, Texas, chose the name of their guinea pig (Squeeky) by voting.

gress. They also decide who will serve as their state legislators, who will preside over many of their courts, who will run the schools and assess the taxes, and which bond elections, referenda, and initiatives will succeed.

Reservations About Voting

Despite their confidence in voting, Americans also recognize voting's limitations. Just because a majority vote a certain way does not make that judgment just or right. In the words of a French philosopher, "A vote can render legal that which is unjust."[12] Indeed, we have just seen that in the past majorities have acted to keep minorities and women from voting. In the United States, the principle of majority rule must defer to principles of *what's right* laid down in laws and court decisions.

Americans sometimes discover that when a complex vital issue is at stake, such as what sort of health care policy to adopt, voting may cut short and thus stifle serious deliberation. During the 1992 presidential campaign, for example, when both President George Bush and candidate Bill Clinton promised the country a health care policy, voters were forced to vote for one or the other before knowing what each policy proposal involved. This drawback can arise in voting at all levels of government, from city councils to Congress. Sometimes those who are confident that they can win a particular vote may call for it before lawmakers have had a chance to deliberate, thus preventing them from changing their views or reaching a consensus.

Americans also have reservations about whether voting works in the sense of producing the public policies they want. Only 10 percent say they believe that their vote really affects public policy, while more than half say they vote out of "civic duty." One survey shows that "civic duty" (56 percent) consistently outweighs all other motives combined—candidate preference (14 percent), the need for change (9 percent), party preference (2 percent), and even habit (15 percent).*[13] Some political scientists maintain that voting is primarily a symbolic act allowing citizens to express their loyalty to the political system[14] and to identify with a political party and participate on election day.[15] Others worry that, far from advancing the cause of democracy, such loyalty merely legitimates and reinforces the power of elites to preserve the status quo.[16] The fact that leaders respond to public opinion, which reflects the attitudes of voters and nonvoters alike, may also cause people to devalue the vote.

Low turnout of voters between 18 and 21 suggests that young people do not place a high value on voting. Because lowering the voting age to 18 has expanded the size of the electorate, the poor showing of younger voters has caused turnout figures for the electorate as a whole to decline by several points. This decline, in turn, lowers the value that the electorate appears to place on the vote.

---

*Numbers do not add up to 100 percent because of rounding.

How the Experts Evaluate Voting

Political scientists, pollsters, and political professionals who have dissected voting patterns and election results for more than fifty years have described the following problems with voting:

- Voters don't always get the policies they favor. If voters on the winning side got the policies they voted for, Americans would have a strong incentive to vote. But because candidates support more than one policy, it's hard to know which policy position, if any, accounts for a victory. Also, since neither voters nor parties can force candidates to honor their campaign pledges, there is no way to hold successful candidates accountable, and, indeed, such pledges are routinely broken.[17] Finally, not all voters base their choice primarily on policies; many give greater weight to competence, party affiliation, and a candidate's character.

- All votes—well informed or poorly informed—count the same. In a democracy, each vote is supposed to count the same as every other vote. As Gabriel Almond puts it, elections basically reduce each voter to a bean and then count up the beans.[18] This principle, known as "one person, one vote," is generally accepted as what's right because it conforms to the democratic value of equality. But because elections weigh the choices of informed or uninformed voters equally, they can be a disincentive to politically sophisticated voters.

- Voters have a limited choice of candidates. A voter's choices in a general election are limited to the list of candidates that appears on the ballot. This list is the result of an electoral process shaped by political campaigns, political money, political advertisements, and the fact that the number of candidates is pared down in a primary selection process held by each party. Because voters end up with a small slate of candidates from which they must choose, their accumulated votes only partially reflect the popular will. Hence voting is as much an *effect* as a *cause*.

- Voters can be manipulated by marketing techniques. Voters are supposed to make their choices by weighing the candidates' merits and positions on various issues in terms of their own values and beliefs. In actuality, voter opinions and choices often seem to reflect the effects of successful marketing.[19] But successful marketing is so costly that low-budget campaigns and parties are less likely to mount sophisticated campaigns to win a place for their candidates on the ballot.

- The poor and uneducated are less likely to vote than the affluent and educated. Census figures show that people are less likely to vote if they belong to a racial minority, are uneducated, poor, young, single, or have recently moved.[20] Some specialists believe that the "have-nots," who get few rewards from the political process, register their frustration with the system by not voting.[21] In contrast, census figures show that people are more likely to vote if they are white, well educated, middle aged, married, northerners, government employees, residentially stable, and hold political opinions. However, many educated and affluent people don't vote because they have grown cynical about the democratic process and believe the status quo will prevail no matter who wins.[22] Some experts claim that cynicism is the chief reason why people don't vote;[23] others argue that cynics vote just as often as everyone else.[24]

Explaining the Vote

Most American voters would say that they vote for the best person or that they vote for the candidates of their party. But the research of political scientists, candidates, campaign strategists, media experts, and others reveals that voting decisions are in fact shaped by political factors, which can vary from election to election; social and class factors, which are more enduring; and new information, which either reinforces people's existing views or causes those views to change.

Political Factors

The most important political factors that affect voting decisions are (1) the ideologies and cues voters use to evaluate the major issues and candidates, (2) the attractiveness of the major parties at the time, and (3) and the voters' views of the candidates' characters. How influential these factors are depends on the overall tenor of the times. When times are turbulent, voters typically focus on the issues at hand or on a crisis, if there is one. When times are relatively calm, they often shift their attention to the character of the candidates and may well pay less attention to politics in general.

Ideologies, Shortcuts, and Cues

An ideology, as we saw in Chapter 4, is a political formula for deciding *what is*, *what's right*, and *what works*. It provides its believers with an *information shortcut* for evaluating candidates and issues. People simply measure each candidate, party, and issue against their ideological principles and screen out whatever conflicts with those principles. An even speedier screening device is the *information cue*, an action regarded as politically symbolic, as the tale of the unshucked tamale described in the box nearby reveals. Because political ideologies give citizens more concepts with which to describe, criticize, and evaluate what goes on in the political process than do ordinary information cues, ideologies can help citizens to become informed voters. However, a citizen who relies entirely on an ideology will tend to be highly *partisan*—always voting for the candidates of his or her party without considering the merits of other candidates. Problems can arise when the information shortcuts voters use to save time and energy become combined with the shortcut strategies candidates use to attract votes, such as sloganeering and character attacks. Such a combination can perpetuate a cycle of mass political ignorance that impoverishes public debate and the quality of participation at the ballot box and elsewhere.

Major Issues and Party Identification

Although both major parties still have a core of loyalists, each has lost the broader base of support it once enjoyed. Surveys of presidential elections have shown that, rather than voting automatically for the candidate of the party they identify with, most voters have consistently chosen the person they believed better

How Much Can Voters Tell from a Tamale?

During the 1976 presidential campaign President Gerald Ford attended a rally in San Antonio, Texas, to boost his popularity with Mexican-American voters. As television cameras rolled and reporters looked on, Ford was offered a hot tamale. With a gracious smile the president bit into it without removing the cornhusk wrapper. The next day a photograph of Ford appeared in newspapers and on television stations across the country broadcasting his ignorance of this staple of Mexican-American cuisine.

For most Americans this incident reinforced Ford's reputation as something of a bumbler. Latinos saw it as a clear signal that the president was profoundly ignorant of their culture. How, they wondered, could such a president have their political interests at heart? Most Latinos voted for Jimmy Carter, who won a close election. After Ford lost, he was asked what lesson he had learned from his campaign. "Always shuck your tamales!" he replied.

Today's politicians are learning that they must familiarize themselves with the cultural practices of the ethnic and regional groups whose votes they wish to win. In Maine they had better to know how to eat a lobster. In Jewish communities they should know what *kosher* means and what a *knish* is. Savvy politicians also know how to hobnob with elites and eat caviar. The Reverend Jesse Jackson, an African-American Democratic candidate for president in 1984 and 1988, once complimented former Democratic Senator Lloyd Bentsen of Texas on his ability to "go from biscuits to tacos to caviar real fast, knowing that's just the cultural diversity that makes up America."[1]

Does knowing how to eat ethnic food tell voters how much a politician knows about the issues, and whether he or she is trustworthy? Not really, but it does, some voting specialists believe, convey an important message to the public: "A president who understands and is familiar with an ethnic group is more likely to help ease that group's way into the political mainstream, and will make open disparagement of that group less acceptable. A president with friends from such a group is more likely to understand its sensibilities . . . than one who doesn't even know how to cope with their foods."[2]

---

[1] Quoted in Samuel L. Popkin, *The Reasoning Voter: Communication and Persuasion in Presidential Campaigns* (Chicago: University of Chicago Press, 1991), 3.
[2] Ibid., 3.

---

able to handle the issues they considered to be major. Voters have tended to vote for the Republican candidate when they believed that the major issue was one of foreign policy, and for the Democratic candidate when they believed that issue was the economy. This tendency was reconfirmed in 1992, when Bill Clinton won with his promise to repair what he called a faltering economy, and again in 1996 when he took credit for a robust economy.

The Character Issue

Europeans generally regard public concerns over a candidate's personal morality as unrealistic and even amusing. For Americans, however, a candidate's morality and character matter a great deal. They want to know that a candidate, especially a presidential candidate, is trustworthy, faithful, mature—in short, decent as well as competent. The media, in turn, now feel obligated, or at least entitled, to expose anything in a candidate's private life that seems improper and routinely scrutinize his or her personal history for evidence of illegal or unethical activities, instances of bad judgment, mental instability, and lies. In 1988, for example, Democrat Gary Hart dropped out of the presidential race for the nomination after his marital infidelity was detailed in the press. But when Bill Clinton faced similar allegations during the 1992 primaries, he refused to drop out. Largely because the Clintons addressed the issue together, "head-on," on prime-time television ("60 Minutes") early in the campaign, it died down. Clinton's patriotism was also questioned because he had avoided the draft during the Vietnam War. In 1996, Clinton's campaign was again clouded by questions about his character, among them an accusation of sexual misconduct when he was governor of Arkansas, a special counsel's investigation into his alleged involvement in the Whitewater affair (Chapter 4), and accepting campaign donations from foreign business interests. Exit polls showed that voters put aside these alleged character issues (*what's right*) to vote for the candidate they believed was the more competent (*what works*).

TABLE 6.2

Votes by Groups in Presidential Elections, 1960–1996

	1960 Dem.	1960 Rep.	1964 Dem.	1964 Rep.	1968 Dem.	1968 Rep.	1968 Wallace	1972 Dem.	1972 Rep.	1976 Dem.	1976 Rep.	1976 McCarthy	1980 Dem.	1980 Rep.	1980 Anderson	1980 Other
National	50.1%	49.9%	61.3%	38.7%	43%	43.4%	13.6%	38%	62%	50%	48%	1%	41%	50.8%	6.6%	1.4%
Men	52	48	60	40	41	43	16	37	63	53	45	1	38	53	7	2
Women	49	51	62	38	45	43	12	38	62	48	51	†	44	49	6	1
White	49	51	59	41	38	47	15	32	68	46	52	1	36	56	7	1
Nonwhite	68	32	94	6	85	12	3	87	13	85	15	†	86	10	2	2
Education																
College	39	61	52	48	37	54	9	37	63	42	55	2	35	53	10	2
High school	52	48	62	38	42	43	15	34	66	54	46	†	43	51	5	1
Grade school	55	45	66	34	52	33	15	49	51	58	41	1	54	42	3	1
Employment																
Professional and business	42	58	54	46	34	56	10	31	69	42	56	1	33	55	10	2
White-collar	48	52	57	43	41	47	12	36	64	50	48	2	NA‡	NA‡	NA‡	NA‡
Manual	60	40	71	29	50	35	15	43	57	58	41	1	48	46	5	1
Union members	65	35	73	27	56	29	15	46	54	63	36	1	50	43	5	2
Farmers	48	52	53	47	29	51	20	NA‡	NA‡	NA‡	NA‡	NA‡	31	61	7	1
Under 30	54	46	64	36	47	38	15	48	52	53	45	1	47	41	11	1
30–49 years*	54	46	63	37	44	41	15	33	67	48	49	2	38	52	8	2
Over 49*	46	54	59	41	41	47	12	36	64	52	48	†	41	54	4	1
Protestants	38	62	55	45	35	49	16	30	70	46	53	†	39	54	6	1
Catholics	78	22	76	24	59	33	8	48	52	57	42	1	46	47	6	1
Republicans	5	95	20	80	9	86	14	5	95	9	91	†	8	86	5	1
Democrats	84	16	87	13	74	12	14	67	33	82	18	†	69	26	4	1
Independents	43	57	56	44	31	44	25	31	69	38	57	4	29	55	14	2

Figures for some groups do not add to 100% because of the vote for other minor-party candidates. †less than 1 percent; ‡not available. *1996 data for 30–44 years and over 44.

Social and Class Factors

Political scientists have also found that social and class factors have a deep and long-lasting influence on voting behavior. These factors include psychological attitudes, age, race, gender, education, religion, ethnicity, and socioeconomic status.[25] Table 6.2 indicates how various groups, classified according to some of those factors, voted in presidential elections from 1960 to 1996.

Psychological Attitudes

Psychological attitudes can affect voting behavior in many ways. For example, a person's vote is likely to be affected by whether his or her personality type conflicts with, or agrees with, the personality type of a candidate. A person who dis-

	1984 Dem.	1984 Rep.	1988 Dem.	1988 Rep.	1992 Dem.	1992 Rep.	1992 Perot	1996 Dem.	1996 Rep.	1996 Perot
National	41%	59%	46%	54%	43.2%	37.8%	19.0%	49.2%	40.7%	8.4%
Men	36	64	44	56	41	37	22	43	44	10
Women	45	55	48	52	46	38	16	54	38	7
White	34	66	41	59	39	41	20	43	46	9
Nonwhite	87	13	82	18	77	11	12	77	17	5
Education										
College	39	61	43	57	43	40	17	47	44	7
High school	43	57	46	54	40	38	22	49	38	11
Grade school	51	49	56	44	56	28	16	59	28	11
Employment										
Professional and business	34	66	NA‡	NA‡	NA‡	NA‡	NA‡	NA‡	NA‡	NA‡
White-collar	47	53	NA‡	NA‡	NA‡	NA‡	NA‡	NA‡	NA‡	NA‡
Manual	46	54	NA‡	NA‡	NA‡	NA‡	NA‡	NA‡	NA‡	NA‡
Union members	52	48	NA‡	NA‡	NA‡	NA‡	NA‡	NA‡	NA‡	NA‡
Farmers	NA‡	NA‡	NA‡	NA‡	NA‡	NA‡	NA‡	NA‡	NA‡	NA‡
Under 30	40	60	37	63	40	37	23	53	34	10
30–49 years*	40	60	45	55	42	37	21	48	41	9
Over 49*	41	59	49	51	46	39	15	48	42	8
Protestants	39	61	36	64	41	41	18	41	50	8
Catholics	39	61	51	49	47	35	18	53	37	9
Republicans	4	96	7	93	7	77	16	13	80	6
Democrats	79	21	85	15	82	8	10	84	10	5
Independents	33	67	43	57	39	30	31	43	35	17

Source: Data provided by the Gallup poll; sources for 1996 Federal Election Commission and Voter News Service, data compiled by Joe TenBarge, manager, Government Department Data Archive, University of Texas at Austin.

likes authority may oppose a strong-willed, forceful candidate, while a person who defers to authority may support such a candidate. There are also those whose strong sense of family loyalty leads them to vote for the party their family has traditionally voted for. Evidence suggests that the strongest psychological factor affecting political participation of all types is trust. In contrast to pessimists, who are fearful of the future, "trusters" are upbeat optimists who treat setbacks as temporary and expect that they will be successful on their next try. They are generous with others, get involved in their communities, and take risks for people they have faith in, even in the face of contrary evidence.[26] In 1996, of the 20 percent of voters who based their decision primarily on trust, 8 percent voted for Clinton, 84 for Dole, and 7 percent for Perot.[27]

Generation, Age, and Education

The generation to which a voter belongs as well as age can affect his or her vote. At each presidential election, about 8 percent of the electorate are new voters with different experiences and beliefs about *what is*, *what's right*, and *what works*. While issues are more important to them than to their elders, they tend to vote less frequently than the older generation.

The more formal education a person has, the more likely that person is to vote Republican—with the exception of those with some graduate education, who are more likely to vote Democratic. The less formal education one has, the more likely one is to vote Democratic. Still, a particularly popular candidate may win a majority among voters of all educational levels, as did Lyndon Johnson in 1964, Richard Nixon in 1972, and Ronald Reagan in 1984. In 1992 Bill Clinton won a plurality among all educational levels but was kept from winning a majority by the presence of Perot, who did about equally well among all but postgraduate voters. Clinton maintained this plurality in 1996, as shown in Table 6.2.

Race

Of the 83 percent of whites voting in 1996, 43 percent voted for Clinton, 46 percent for Dole, and 9 percent for Perot. As Table 6.2 shows, the most loyal voters in the Democratic coalition are African Americans. Although the gap in turnout between African Americans and whites has declined, it is considerably wider when age and race are combined and grows even larger when poverty is factored in. Thus poor, young African Americans vote less often than poor, young whites. Even though poor whites outnumber poor ethnic minorities as a whole, the fact that there is a greater *percentage* of minorities at the bottom of the economic scale means that minorities have proportionately less voting clout than whites.

Of the Latinos voting in 1996 (5 percent of the total vote), 72 percent voted for Clinton, 21 percent for Dole, and 6 percent for Perot. Although Latinos are socially conservative and increasingly middle class, their support for Dole was smaller than their support for any other Republican presidential candidate in the last 25 years. In 1984, 40 percent of their vote went to Ronald Reagan. According to one observer, many Latinos believe that anti-immigration Republicans are also anti-Latino. Studies show, however, that Latinos between 18 and 24 are less loyal to the Democrats than their elders and that educated, upwardly mobile Latinos might gravitate to Republicans if they are not pushed away.[28]

Of the Asian Americans voting (1 percent of the total vote), 43 percent voted for Clinton, 48 percent for Dole, and 8 percent for Perot. Of the remaining races combined (1 percent of the total vote), 64 percent voted for Clinton, 21 percent for Dole, and 9 percent for Perot.

Gender

Once there was relatively little difference in the way the men and women voted, and what difference there was sprang mainly from women's greater reluctance to support the use of force in foreign affairs or to subdue urban unrest. This **gender gap**—the tendency for women voters to be less supportive than men of Republican candidates, and for men to be less supportive than women of Democratic candidates—began to grow during the Reagan years due to Republican opposition to abortion, especially after the right wing of the party took control of the national convention and party platform in 1992. That year more women voted than men (54 percent compared with 46 percent) and more women voted for Clinton than did men (46 percent compared with 41 percent), while more men voted for Bush and Perot (38 percent and 21 percent) than women (37 percent and 17 percent). In 1996, the gap widened still further (see Table 6.2). Table 6.3 shows how men and women differed politically right before the 1996 elections.

TABLE 6.3

How All Men and Women Differ Politically

		Men	Women	Gap Size
Party identification	Republican	36%	28%	8
	Independent	31	25	6
	Democrat	30	**43**	13
Political philosophy	Liberal	13%	17%	4
	Moderate	45	**50**	5
	Conservative	38	29	8
Governmental responsibilities	Government should do more to solve problems.	24%	31%	7
	Government is doing too many things better left to businesses and individuals.	**67**	**57**	10
Affirmative action programs should be . . .	Continued	42%	**47%**	5
	Abolished	**52**	36	16

Figures add vertically but may not equal 100 percent. Bold numbers are highest percentages by category.
Source: New York Times/ CBS News Poll; based on telephone interviews with 978 registered voters Sept. 2–4. The question on affirmative action is from a poll conducted Aug. 3–5 with 900 registered voters.
New York Times; October 6, 1996, A14.

Months before the election, political observers speculated on whether "soccer moms" would help vote Clinton back into office. But despite Clinton's effort to "target" soccer moms and exploit the gender gap, exit polls revealed that a far more powerful force for Clinton was the "marriage gap." While married women split their votes between Clinton and Dole (44–44 percent), widows and divorcées gave Clinton his greatest lead—33 points![29] More than half (56 percent) of working women—a group containing many single, divorced, and widowed women—voted for Clinton, while only 35 percent voted for Dole. Although women in 1996 were professionally and financially better off than they had been for years, they were concerned that government was treating the poor as part of the nation's economic problem instead of helping them.[30] Moreover, many women work for the government and nonprofit organizations (14 million out of 24 million jobs).[31] These poll results suggest that the gap between men and women is less significant than the gap between the nuclear family and women who live with economic insecurity, worry about others who live with it, or fear that they may end up living with it themselves. One pollster suggests that some married women did not vote for Dole because, should their marriages fail, they might have to turn to government for support.[32]

Religion and Ethnicity

Roman Catholics typically vote Democratic, while Protestants typically vote Republican. Jews are, after African Americans, the second most loyal group to the Democratic party. Ethnic groups such as the Irish, Italians, and Poles and other Slavs have also tended to vote Democratic, while people of northern European origin have tended to vote Republican. These patterns, which date from the nineteenth century, are hardly surprising because northern Europeans tend to be Protestant, while the other groups tend to be Catholic or Jewish. These patterns were reinforced by the fact that Republican supporters of Prohibition were repelled by the Irish, Italians, and Germans, who drank alcoholic beverages. One change in this pattern is that Republicans have been gaining support from younger Catholics since Ronald Reagan, while older Catholics have remained steadfast Democrats. Analysts believe that Clinton won substantial Catholic support in 1996 due to Republican efforts to cut social welfare programs.[33]

In the presidential election of 1992, white born-again Christian fundamentalists supported Bush over Clinton 59 percent to 25 percent, with 23 percent voting for Perot. Similarly, those who attended religious services at least weekly chose Bush over Clinton 47 percent to 38 percent, with 15 percent voting for Perot.[34] These patterns persisted in 1996. Dole's strength came primarily from the Great Plains and the Southeast, the Protestant heartland, while Clinton's came from the more religiously diverse Northeast, Upper Midwest, West Coast, and parts of the Sunbelt.

What Is a Correlation?

A *correlation* is an apparent relationship between two phenomena (groups of people, periods of time, sets of statistics) that does not seem to be caused by chance alone. For example, people who wear business suits at work tend to vote Republican, whereas people who wear overalls at work tend to vote Democratic. There is, then, an apparent correlation between the type of clothes worn for work and the way one votes. A correlation is not necessarily a *causal relation*, however. It would be misleading to conclude from this correlation, for instance, that party preference is caused by work clothes. (This would be called a *spurious correlation*.) In this example, both party preference and work clothes are traceable to economic status. It is always prudent to treat research conclusions based on correlations as educated guesses, or *hypotheses*. New research may reveal different correlations that may suggest that behavior has different causes. Such ongoing study and revision of explanations is a major way *learning by doing* occurs in the social sciences and explains why political scientists change their understanding of politics over time.

Socioeconomic Status

Studies have shown a correlation between how one votes and one's **socioeconomic status (SES)**—that is, one's occupation, income, and social class. In most of the elections studied, the higher a person's family income, the more likely he or she was to vote Republican, and the lower that income, the more likely he or she was to vote Democratic. In the 1992 elections, among voters making $15,000 or less, Clinton got 59 percent of the votes while Bush got only 11 percent. Bush got 46 percent of those making over $75,000 while Clinton got only 38 percent. In 1996, Clinton again got 59 percent of the vote among those making $15,000 a year or less, Dole 28 percent, and Perot 11 percent. Experts speculate that the decline in turnout among lower-income voters (from 13.8 percent in 1990, to 11.0 percent in 1992, to 7.7 in 1994) is due to their feeling neglected by both parties. The upturn to 11 percent in 1996 may have been a reaction to the Republican-driven cuts in welfare.

New Information

Voters are also influenced by informal sources of information, such as neighborhood yard signs, billboards, bumper stickers, campaign buttons, and the opinions of co-workers and friends.[35] Such opinions can be contagious, causing some people to reassess their own positions. Those who engage in political debate are more likely to waver, while people who have few political conversations often remain neutral or choose not to vote. This new political information voters receive during a campaign must compete with the "stored" information and opinions they already hold. Highly informed voters may be the least receptive to new information because they already possess a significant amount of stored information.[36]

Other Forms of Political Participation

Americans turn out at the polls at lower rates than citizens in other democracies, but they engage in other forms of political participation at higher rates. In these other forms of participation, people are taking direct responsibility for deciding *what is*, acting personally to promote their view of *what's right*, and recommending their ideas about *what works*. As with voting, the value of these other forms of participation depends on how well the other actors and institutions in the political system perform.

Participating Through Government

Americans routinely rely on the nation's traditions, laws, and political institutions to express themselves politically and to reach their goals.

Symbolic Support and Obedience

One way Americans participate politically is to express their solidarity with other Americans and their loyalty to the nation. They salute the flag, sing "The Star-Spangled Banner," and recite the Pledge of Allegiance—small gestures that demonstrate massive public faith in the political system. Similarly, acts of obedience to the law—paying taxes, getting cars inspected, or pulling over in response to a police siren—have the overall effect of legitimating the legal demands of government. And legitimacy, as we've seen repeatedly, is essential to the effective exercise of political authority and the maintenance of public order.

Serving and Working in Government

Americans participate at all levels of government by attending and speaking at city council meetings, testifying at public hearings, contacting their elected representatives about their concerns, and serving on citizen advisory committees. About 1 percent run for and, if they win, serve in one of the half-million elective offices. Finally, more than 15 percent work as bureaucrats in local, state, or national government. Not surprisingly, active participants tend to be educated and to know how the political process works. According to one survey, 42.5 percent of college graduates claimed to have contacted a public official at some time in their lives, as compared with only 10 percent of those who had not graduated from high school.[37] The uneducated, the poor, and the young are the least likely to take such political initiatives.

Legal Action

Both individuals and groups file lawsuits in the courts and press their legislators for laws to achieve justice for themselves or others. In 1996, for example, a mother and daughter won a $16.5 million verdict against a Michigan hospital for refusing to honor the daughter's living will once she had become completely incapacitated.[38] Legal action typically requires strong initiative, money for lawyers' fees, and patience with the slow pace of the legal system.

An important vehicle for achieving wider social goals is class action suits, in which one or more persons sue as representatives of a larger group in a similar situation. For example, members of minority neighborhoods have begun to sue their state and local governments as well as private businesses for practicing **environmental racism**—concentrating waste-processing plants and sites in minority neighborhoods.

In addition, legislatures in 24 states have passed laws granting citizens the power to sign petitions for **initiatives**. When a designated percentage of the electorate files a formal petition for legislative or constitutional changes, the legislature or the total electorate must then vote on the proposals. A *direct initiative* is voted on by the electorate during the next general election. An *indirect initiative* must be approved by the legislature before it is voted on by the electorate. Citizens may also repeal an existing law through a **referendum**, an electoral procedure in which the legislature refers an issue to the people, asking voters to accept or reject a legislative or constitutional proposal. A referendum may be used to gather information about public opinion on an issue, or its results may actually become law. A city government may allow such initiatives while the state in which that city is located may not. Texans who live in Austin, for example, make use of the so-called I&R in city policymaking, even though the state legislature has refused to permit the I&R at the state level. One indignant Texan complained: "Politicians say we Texans aren't qualified to vote on laws, but that is a pathetic argument. We're smart enough to elect them, but we're not smart enough to vote on this?"[39] Some populists are now calling for a national initiative which would allow Americans to bypass Congress and pass laws directly.[40] In some cities and a few states, citizens may also initiate a **recall** election of a public official accused of violating the public trust. Although this device is rarely used, it does allow citizens to remove a public official from office. Typically, it is well-informed citizens who launch and participate in these initiatives, although such initiatives can be a learning experience for others in the community. And, increasingly, business groups and other special interests have organized and funded campaigns for initiatives and referenda in California and elsewhere.

Known as "Brownie Mary," this senior activist long raised and distributed marijuana brownies to San Franciscans with AIDS. In November 1996, California voters approved a referendum allowing doctors to prescribe marijuana for medicinal purposes. The Clinton administration vowed that the Justice Department would take action against such doctors.

Participating Outside Government

Some people engage in political action outside government because they believe that government should play a limited role in public life. As the activities of the PEN Action Group demonstrate, the opportunities for such participation have never been greater thanks to innovations in technology and communications, and individuals and groups are finding creative ways to make a difference from the local to the global level.

Voluntary Action

More than 90 million Americans contribute more than 20 billion hours of voluntary service a year.[41] Citizens of widely varying backgrounds mentor students, staff soup kitchens, lead scout troops, and volunteer in hospitals, churches, and prisons; they also participate in established service organizations such as the Lions and Rotary clubs.

During his administration, President George Bush called on volunteers to multiply and shine like "a thousand points of light." President Clinton echoed this initiative in April 1997 by inviting former presidents Bush, Jimmy Carter, and Gerald Ford to Philadelphia to help lead the Presidents' Summit for America's Future, a national campaign to inspire American voluntarism. Moderate and conservative Democrats and Republicans, and to a greater degree libertarians, support voluntary action because they believe it's *what's right* politically as well as morally. They would like to see voluntary assistance and philanthropic giving reduce or even replace government assistance in many areas, especially welfare. They claim that such assistance works better, reduces the size and cost of government, and strengthens liberty by reducing government's role in people's lives.

Elites and celebrities make news when they mobilize support for their favorite causes. But ordinary people also make a dramatic difference when they "vote" to buy organic foods, recycle, and take public transportation. Ordinary people are also giving more money to charities (see Figure 6.2). Such individual action can have massive cumulative effects and is contagious. You can expand the scope of your participation from the local to the global level with the help of the Political Action Guide on page 215.[42]

Voluntary action can be especially effective when people join forces with others, because groups are more likely to develop an organization, muster public support, and actively pursue their goals over time. Opponents of abortion, for

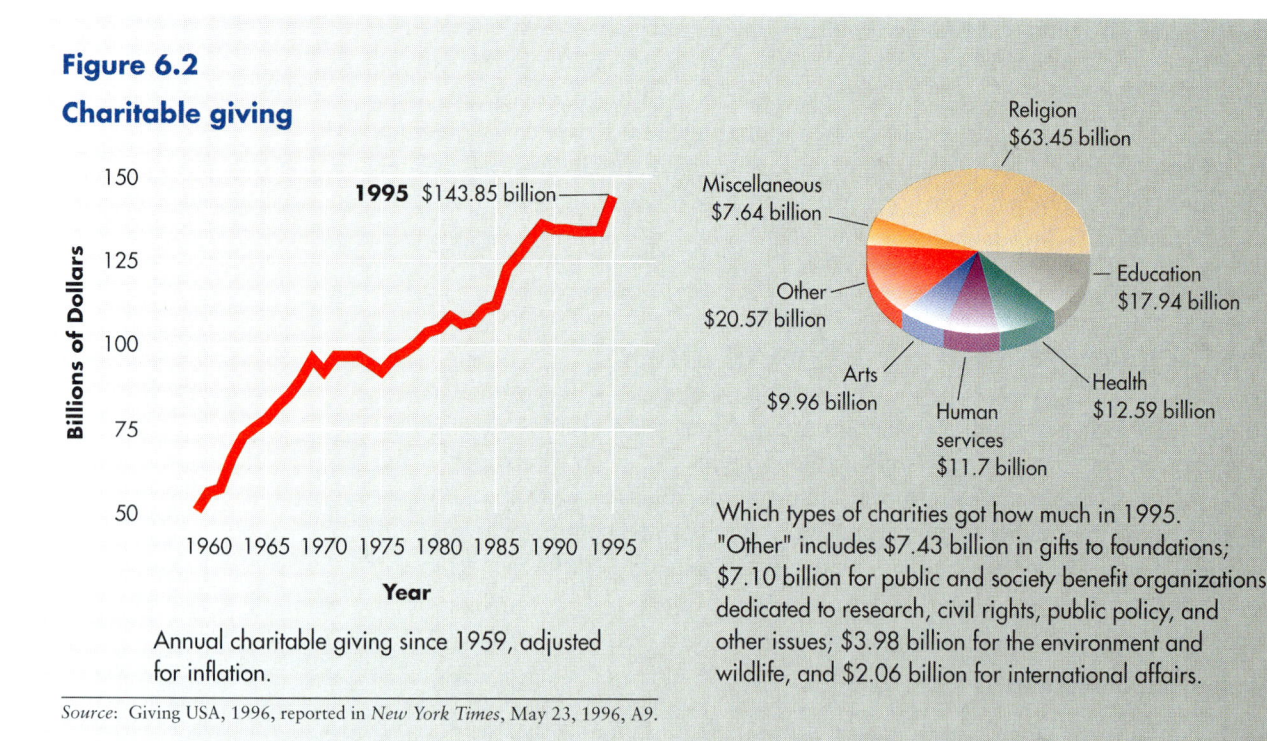

Figure 6.2
Charitable giving

Annual charitable giving since 1959, adjusted for inflation.

Which types of charities got how much in 1995. "Other" includes $7.43 billion in gifts to foundations; $7.10 billion for public and society benefit organizations dedicated to research, civil rights, public policy, and other issues; $3.98 billion for the environment and wildlife, and $2.06 billion for international affairs.

- 1995 $143.85 billion
- Religion $63.45 billion
- Miscellaneous $7.64 billion
- Other $20.57 billion
- Education $17.94 billion
- Arts $9.96 billion
- Human services $11.7 billion
- Health $12.59 billion

Source: Giving USA, 1996, reported in *New York Times*, May 23, 1996, A9.

example, run Human Life Centers to help women find alternatives to abortion. Advocates of children's concerns lobby and hold rallies. The Nature Conservancy buys wilderness land from private owners to keep it wild. And in recent years, a variety of new citizen movements have sprung up to cope with such problems as inadequate public schools, homelessness, child abuse, and battered women. Some citizens have tried to improve public education by acting as mentors or establishing alternative schools. Others concerned about violence and crime have organized groups to patrol their neighborhoods. To expand affordable housing, Millard Fuller of Georgia founded the low-cost housing construction organization known as Habitat for Humanity. Former President Jimmy Carter and his wife Rosalynn help the organization to build houses every year, as do thousands of ordinary Americans in cities throughout the country and the world. Some citizens and businesses try to reduce violence by offering money, concert tickets, or other rewards to those who turn in guns to local police. Some private organizations now make charitable contributions to government, as the H.J. Heinz Corporation did in 1996 when it donated $450,000 to the National Endowment for the Arts to support arts programs for children that Congress had cut back.[43] And in 1997 media owner Ted Turner announced his plan to donate $1 billion over ten years to humanitarian projects of the United Nations.

Dr. Lorraine E. Hale, director of Hale House in New York City, participates in a child-care training program for parents who will take the skills they acquire back to their communities in the Mississippi Delta, Louisiana, and Arkansas. The program was founded by Hale and restaurant owner Sylvia Woods.

Some right-wing critics, such as talk-show host Rush Limbaugh, complain that government appeals for voluntarism are "fleecing corporations" and cajoling them to adopt "a more socialistic attitude." And the *Weekly Standard* has proposed that "the best way for government to encourage voluntarism is to butt out of civil life."[44] On the left, the Reverend Jesse Jackson and others worry that politicians are focusing on voluntarism to avoid blame for dismantling the social welfare system. Some nonprofit groups have expressed the same concern. They point out that the majority of hours volunteered are episodic and do not help build inner-city schools or provide health insurance to the poor. They argue that voluntarism is no substitute for government action in many areas.[45]

Pressure Activities

The First Amendment permits citizens and noncitizens alike to engage in pressure activities to call attention to their causes and to persuade others, including government, to respond to their needs and concerns. They may attempt to influence company officials or TV networks directly by informing them of their views and needs—usually by letter, telegram, telephone, or fax. They may also appeal to fellow citizens and business and community leaders more generally by speaking out in public, distributing information, and writing guest newspaper opinion columns or letters to the editor. They may form or join interest groups, political parties, and social movements.

Political Action Guide

How to Write an Effective Letter to the Editor

Here are some suggestions that can help you write the kind of letter most likely to receive favorable consideration by the editorial desk.

1. Do not write longhand. If possible, *use a typewriter* or *computer* and double-space the lines.
2. *Plan your first sentence carefully*. Try to make it short and interesting. If you begin with a reference to a news item, editorial, or letter in the paper, your letter immediately has added interest for the editor. If you write to criticize, *begin with a word of appreciation, agreement, or praise*. Don't be merely critical; make constructive suggestions.
3. *Deal with only one topic in a letter*. It should be timely and newsworthy. Be sure your meaning is clear. Use simple words and short sentences and paragraphs.
4. *Express your thoughts as concisely as possible*. Check your local paper for the average length of a letter and try not to exceed it.
5. *Avoid violent language or sarcasm*.
6. *Help supply facts* that may be omitted from, or slanted in, news stories or editorials. In many cases, editors will want to pass this information on to the public.
7. *Don't hesitate to use a relevant personal experience* to illustrate a point.
8. *Bring moral judgments to bear* upon issues confronting the nation and the world. Appeal to readers' sense of fair play, justice, and mercy. Challenge them to respond to the issue.
9. *Try to be optimistic and practical*. Out of fear and despair, people may avoid the most pressing issues of the day. But they may take action when they are inspired to do so and are led to believe that there is hope for a solution.
10. *Send your letter (with appropriate adjustments) to editors of newspapers in other cities*. Always send originals, not copies or photocopies. Many papers have a policy against publishing the same letters sent to other papers.
11. *Always sign your name* and give your address, telephone number, fax number, or e-mail address. You can use a pen name or initials for publication, but the editor must know the source of the letter in order to confirm its authenticity.
12. Don't give up looking for your letter too soon. It may not appear for ten days or longer. *Don't be discouraged if your letter is not printed*. You have given the editor the benefit of your thinking. Try again. If one letter in ten is accepted, you have reached an audience large enough to make your effort worthwhile. (But your score will probably be better than that!)

Adapted from "How-to-Write a Letter to the Editor," published by the Friends Committee on National Legislation.

Visionary Action

In his 1992 Inaugural Address Bill Clinton quoted this warning from the Bible: "Without vision, the people perish." The survival of the nation and the world depend on anticipating and addressing future threats, such as safeguarding human health and the environment. But politicians who seek reelection are torn between addressing long-term problems that require vision and accommodating the many groups that are heavily invested in conventional ways of coping with problems—ways that may work in the short run but not in the long run. Unfortunately, the more successful a society is in adapting to current conditions, the harder it is for it to readapt to new conditions.[46] Creative, visionary minds can help the nation make a transition from *what works* today but will not work tomorrow to *what will work* tomorrow. But because visionaries typically threaten the status quo—which the government often supports—they usually work outside government.

The policies visionaries promote sometimes succeed in influencing or even supplanting existing policies if there is a market for doing so and if there is reason to believe that the new policies will work. Developing such a market can take time, however. Visionary ideas usually seep into the public consciousness slowly as they are discovered and publicized by concerned individuals and groups. But once there is a large enough market for these ideas, change begins to happen. Wes Jackson, a proponent of sustainable organic agriculture, has spent decades preparing for a worldwide agricultural crisis caused by large-scale farming based on chemical fertilizers and pesticides—agricultural practices that the U.S. Department of Agriculture supports, even though they are depleting the topsoil, because they work *right now*. Conventional American agribusiness produces more food at cheaper prices than organic farmers can, allowing people to eat for less. But as public awareness of the environmental and health hazards of chemical fertilizers and pesticides has increased, so has the market for organic produce. As a result, organic farming is becoming economically viable, and many consumers can now vote on this issue with their dollars.

When visionary ideas begin to penetrate debates over public policy or gain a toehold in government, they are typically attacked by entrenched interests. In some cases, such as the opposition of conventional medicine to alternative or complementary medicine, this resistance is not just financial; it also involves the defense of an entrenched system of scientific beliefs about *what is*, *what's right*, and *what works* in human health. Once again, market forces are having an impact on this debate. Currently, more than 30 percent of the public use some form of alternative medicine to treat autoimmune, degenerative, and terminal diseases such as AIDS, arthritis, and cancer.[47] This trend led Congress in 1992 to establish a new Office of Alternative Medicine in the National Institutes of Health to study the effectiveness of acupuncture, herbal medicine, homeopathy, mind-body control techniques like visualization and guided imagery, and electromagnetism. Some insurance companies now cover some of these types of treatments. Despite strong opposition from the medical establishment—one Stanford doctor suggested calling the new Office of Alternative Medicine "The Office of Astrology"[48]—citizen efforts proved crucial. Democratic Senator Tom Harkin of Iowa, chair of the appropriations subcommittee that funds health research, was persuaded to push for the new office by AIDS activists and the testimony of friends and other members of Congress who had benefited from alternative medicine.

Electronic Action

As Bruria Finkel's efforts to help the homeless show, new technologies such as e-mail may be used by all types of political actors to network with fellow citizens and people worldwide to pursue common political and social goals. For example, such forms of electronic communication can be used to pack city council meetings for important votes, to connect schools and hospitals in rural areas with needed information, and to debate policy issues such as public health. A housewife in Los

Organic agricultural visionary Wes Jackson has received a "genius" grant from the MacArthur Foundation. At his Land Institute in Salinas, Kansas, he and his students study the ancient, hardy prairie ecosystem to develop alternative farming methods that do not destroy the valuable topsoil lost daily through conventional agriculture.

To learn more about electronic action, contact the Center for Civic Networking, PO Box 65272, Washington, D.C. 20035; 202/362-3831:

civicnet.org

complementary medicine
This term conveys a willingness to coexist with conventional medicine, while *alternative medicine* conveys an intent to replace it.

Angeles who was upset at all the anti-Clinton criticism she saw on the Internet set up her own Web site—"Clinton, Yes!"—to publicize Clinton's achievements. Such civic networking allows people to bypass the mass media as well as government.

Lawmakers and government officials are also using e-mail. Republican Senator John Ashcroft of Missouri, for example, has used the Internet to mobilize popular support for term limits. According to one specialist in civic networking, the government could save tax dollars spent on treating people in emergency wards if it used the Internet to educate the public about health problems.[49]

Doing Nothing

A less obvious form of political activism is to be politically inactive. Some people feel that they can remain separate and aloof from politics either because they dislike or feel alienated from it, or because they don't believe their participation will make a difference. This is a misconception. Doing nothing is *doing something* because it has political consequences for democracy by leaving decisions and influence to others. For every instance in which Americans do nothing politically, American democracy becomes less democratic and therefore less legitimate.

Participating by Resisting

Resistance—yet another form of political action—may be used against fellow citizens, businesses, or government itself. In some instances, such resistance is protected by the Constitution; in others, it is illegal and subject to punishment.

Obstructionism

Some political activists attempt to influence others, including government, by legally obstructing their functions. Public employees, schoolteachers, and citizen groups occasionally organize strikes, work slowdowns, or boycotts. Sometimes they create physical obstructions, as American farmers did in the 1970s when they drove their tractors into Washington, D.C., demanding government assistance. Occasionally legislatures have limited obstructionism, as Congress did in 1994 when it passed the Freedom of Access to Clinic Entrances Act prohibiting protesters from physically obstructing the entrances to abortion clinics. A pioneer of this sort of **direct action** was the late Saul Alinsky, who trained people to be effective protesters during the 1960s. Alinsky taught that protesters need not always carry out direct action for it to be effective. Sometimes it is enough merely to leak the plans.

Right-to-life activists engage in civil disobedience in front of St. Patrick's Cathedral in New York City.

Civil Disobedience

When individuals and groups commit acts of **civil disobedience**—that is, when they intentionally break the law to call public attention to a law or policy they believe to be unjust—they expect to be caught and punished. Indeed, being carried off to jail is a way to attract media attention and public support. In the 1960s TV news commonly showed the police bodily dragging civil rights and antiwar activists into custody. Today, arrests are more likely to be provoked by anti-abortion protesters and environmentalists.

Dr. Jack Kevorkian, a pathologist who favors legalizing physician-assisted suicide for the terminally ill, has participated in a number of such suicides despite criticism from the medical profession, religious leaders, and the public and despite repeated arrests and trials. Kevorkian's home state of Michigan responded to his activism by passing a law prohibiting physician-assisted suicide. The issue has been in the courts ever since.

Uncivil Disobedience

Acts of **uncivil disobedience**—rioting, arson, assassination, bombing, and other forms of terrorism—are aimed at subverting the political order. Those who send bombs through the mail or kill doctors who perform abortions, for example, often end up hurting their cause as well as incurring state punishment. Other forms of uncivil disobedience may go undetected or unpunished: bribery of public officials, shoplifting or other theft by those who claim they are "striking a blow against capitalism," the "liberation" of animals from experimental laboratories by animal rights activists, and vandalism on the Internet. Unlike those engaged in civil disobedience, those who commit subversive illegal acts attempt to escape punishment. Because most people view such acts as dangerous and unjustified, uncivil disobedience is generally less effective politically than civil disobedience.

The bombing of a government building in Oklahoma City on April 9, 1995, was an act of terrorism that killed 167 people. Timothy MacVeigh was convicted of this crime in 1997.

Government As a Political Activist

Government actors—leaders, lawmakers, judges, bureaucrats, and the agencies they serve—are major participants in the political process. Government actors continually respond to external and internal pressures at all levels in the federal system, even as they actively promote their interests and policies. Government is primarily concerned with bolstering its authority to govern by persuading citizens that its policies are both legitimate (*what's right*) and effective (*what works*). To do this, public officials often try to involve citizens in the policy process—but usually on government's terms.

Types of Government Activism

Government actors engage in many of the same types of activism as citizens. Public officials, for example, frequently display their loyalty to the American people and the nation through such symbolic acts as addressing the public on national holidays and honoring veterans and service men and women who have died in action.

Often the personal presence of a top official is intended to convey support or disapproval in the name of the American people. Government actors also seek to influence public opinion by making speeches and releasing news to the mass media.

When government actors come to the aid of states and communities suffering from natural disasters such as hurricanes, floods, and earthquakes, they are doing so in the name of all Americans. The federal government also supplies roughly 10 percent of the budgets of many private charities, uses federal funds to help equalize the disparities between rich and poor school districts, and spends about 1 percent of the budget on foreign aid.

Federal as well as state governments also rely on legal action. At the federal level, the U.S. solicitor general in the Justice Department files suits that the administration would like to contest in court. In recent years, a number of states have filed suit against tobacco companies in an effort to recover health care costs due to smoking-related illnesses.

Government actors sometimes innovate, especially under pressure. When Congress rejects mandatory action, as it has in the case of standards for energy efficiency, bureaucrats sometimes try to get citizens to take such action voluntarily. The Department of Energy and the Environmental Protection Agency now look for "smarter ways" to alert consumers to energy-efficient products. For example, both agencies now offer manufacturers of appliances, building materials, and computers an "Energy Star" seal of approval if they meet government energy-efficiency standards. The purpose of this logo is to identify energy-efficient products for consumers who may wish to vote for them with their dollars.

The EPA is also experimenting with incentives that grant companies greater flexibility to meet marketplace demands in return for carrying out more environmental cleanup than the law requires. Companies participating in the EPA's pilot program had to agree to reduce overall pollution, collaborate with local residents, and meet all legal pollution limits before being allowed to circumvent the complex regulations that control the discharge of pollutants. For example, Intel, which makes computer chips, can now switch manufacturing processes more quickly because it no longer has to get new EPA permits, thus increasing its competitive advantage. Corporations, regulatory specialists, and lawmakers who want to strengthen the economy and clean up the environment welcome such experiments. But environmentalists and labor groups worry that these changes will increase toxic chemical hazards in the workplace and in communities.[50] Such innovations create a need for strong watchdogs as well as a willingness to *learn by doing*.

Representing the American people at the ceremonies observing the 50th anniversary of the Allied invasion of Normandy, France, during World War II, President Clinton honors the American soldiers who died in action.

Types of Government Resistance

Government can also resist citizen demands with a number of tactics that may be used separately or in combination:

- Delaying action: a tactic used, for example, to avoid treating Vietnam and Gulf War veterans contaminated by chemical agents
- Tokenism, or doing a little of what is asked in order to appear more responsive than it really is: foot-dragging by the Central Intelligence Agency and the Pentagon, for example, in declassifying military and other documents after Congress passed a law in 1991 requiring them to do so

- Discrediting requests as too costly, unworkable, or unrepresentative of the popular will: the response of most lawmakers to term limits, for example
- Ignoring, suppressing, or covering up the request by punishing the requesters, jailing them, or keeping them from public attention: falsely declaring dead the 200 U.S.-trained Vietnamese secret agents who sought back pay, for example.[51]

Decisions by government actors *not to act* in particular circumstances—denying requests for lower taxes, higher import quotas, or subsidies, or requests by other countries to send U.S. troops to quell a crisis abroad—are a form of both resistance and activism because these decisions not to act have important, even grave, consequences.

Less overtly, government can use its authority and its claims to represent the people to promote the views it wants the people to have. Political scientist Murray Edelman argues that the legitimacy Americans ascribe to their government is really fraudulent because it is manufactured by government and used largely to justify the status quo.[52] This fraudulence is made worse, Edelman says, by government's frequent co-optation of dissenters: giving them a stake in the political process through recognition, jobs administering social programs, and other incentives so they will moderate their dissent. Some observers say that the social programs of President Lyndon Johnson's Great Society were actually efforts to co-opt and quiet segments of the population that were protesting and rioting in the 1960s. Such criticism puts government in a double bind: if it does not respond to dissenters by attempting to include them in the political process, it is accused of fostering dissension and protest; if it includes such groups, it is accused of cooptation.

When government acts to provide services such as disaster relief, it does so on behalf of the entire American public. Here a National Guardsman distributes clothing to victims of Hurricane Andrew in Florida.

The Benefits and Costs of Government Response

Various federal officials conduct public hearings around the country to get citizen input, criticism, and advice on policy issues. Hearings can have three important benefits. First, local input can lead to better policies, because centralized bureaucracies often lack the detailed knowledge of local problems necessary to identify and formulate effective policies. Second, public hearings can result in greater acceptance of policies, because citizens are usually more willing to accept and help implement policies that take account of their own input. Many school districts, for example, involve parents and teachers in the selection of school principals. Third, local involvement can make government more responsible, because informed and involved citizens are better equipped to evaluate whether a policy is working properly and to hold public officials accountable for their performance.

Government's responsiveness to citizen input is not without its costs and problems, however. For example, government often hires more people and spends more tax dollars on public opinion surveys and public hearings to gather citizen input and keep the public informed. And when citizens request further study of a policy, the delay in implementation can raise costs due to inflation. Major delays can occur when ordinary citizens lack the technical expertise to understand how a policy is supposed to work, so more time must be spent on educating members of the public who want to be involved. In addition, citizens are sometimes more concerned about how a policy will affect their neighborhoods than with the benefits the policy will provide to a larger geographical area. For this reason, citizens often oppose the location of halfway houses for the mentally ill or for prisoners on probation, or waste incinerators, in their own neighborhoods. Such opposition is now known as **NIMBY**—an acronym for "not in my back yard." Citizens may also hold values different from those of public officials and policy experts proposing a policy. Disagreements arise, for example, over what sort of sex education should be taught in public schools and whether information on sexually transmitted diseases and condoms should be made available to sexually active high school students. Finally, because those who respond to government initiatives are usually of higher SES (white suburban and city dwellers, mostly Protestants), such support is not representative. Although some activists attempt to represent the interests of the poor, people in rural areas, and others who don't participate actively in the political process, government tends to be more responsive to the most politically active. Those who believe that citizen participation is vital to democracy say that any uneven response is a small price to pay for the benefits of a healthy political system,[53] but those adversely affected by citizen input may well think otherwise.

Improved Political Participation Can Strengthen Democracy

As we have seen throughout this text, improvement in any one part of the political system can cause improvement in the system as a whole. As political participants improve and increase their stock of political knowledge and expand the scope of their participation, they *learn by doing* and the quality of democracy spirals upward.

Voting is a good place to start. "Smart" voting can start the upward spiral in the following way:

- The more politically competent voters are, the more likely they are to elect competent officials as their representatives.
- The more competent the elected officials, the more competent the experts they are likely to hire.
- The more competent the experts, the better the advice they are likely to give policymakers and the more effective government is likely to be.
- The more these leaders and experts pursue policies that increase the number of well-informed voters, the more participation and democracy will spiral upward.

In a democracy the need to improve participation never ends because the responsibilities of public life never end and political problems never run out. Unfortunately, such problems seldom receive the attention they deserve until a crisis

Political Action Guide

How to Learn to Be a Political Activist

If you are interested in becoming an effective political activist, you may wish to consult these general guides:

- Ed Schwartz, *Net Activism: How Citizens Use the Internet* (Sebastopol, Calif.: O'Reilly and Associates, 1996): 1-800-889-8969 or http://www.ora.com
- "Liszt" is a national directory of e-mail discussion groups in every area from art to science to health: http://www.liszt.com
- Katherine Isaac, *Ralph Nader Presents: Practicing Democracy, a Guide to Student Action* (New York: St. Martin's Press, 1995), offers tools and contacts for individual and group activism in public education, research, direct action, citizen lobbying, initiative and referendum, community law, shareholding, the media, fundraising, women's organizations, children's advocacy, human rights, poverty and hunger, world peace, and government agencies: 1-800-321-9299
- Neighborhood Online Web page is devoted to neighborhood activism in Philadelphia and throughout the nation: http://libertynet.org/community/phila/natl.html
- Richard Zimmerman, *What I Can Do to Make a Difference* (New York: Penguin Books, 1992), offers information on activism in areas such as protecting the rain forests, saving endangered species, and helping youth and the homeless: 1-800-253-6476 or http://www.penguin.com/usa/usa-home.html
- Earth Works Group, *Fifty Simple Things You Can Do to Save the Environment* (Berkeley, Calif.: Earth Works Press, 1989), urges individuals to donate money and time to the causes they support and to buy products that protect the environment from producers who practice occupational safety and refrain from animal testing; recommends investing in socially responsible money funds such as the Pax World Fund, Working Assets Money Fund, and Fidelity Environmental Services; recommends using socially responsible credit cards, such as the Working Assets Visa Card, whose companies donate a percentage of their profits to enviromental and other change-oriented causes: (408) 724-3212 or http://www.earthworks.com
- *Whole Earth Review*, a journal that examines such topics as "Electronic Democracy" (no. 71, summer 1991): (415) 256-2800 or http://www.well.net/mwec/wer.html
- Mark Satin, *New Options for America* (Fresno, Calif.: Press at California State University, 1991), proposes alternatives to the harmful long-term consequences of economic growth and strategies for downsizing the welfare state and promoting individual responsibility: (209) 278-4240 or http://www.csufresno.edu

occurs or an existing policy—the availability and affordability of health care, for example—breaks down. And no matter how carefully crafted the new policies may be, some will turn out to be flawed when they are implemented because the ultimate test of any new idea is whether it *works*. All who practice politics must inevitably *learn by doing* through trial and error.

Because American democracy—indeed, all of human life—works in this way, expectations of accountability should be flexible. The fact that elected officials frequently find themselves faced with new circumstances that demand a departure from, or even a reversal of, their campaign promises is a good reason for evaluating candidates and leaders on their integrity and judgment rather than their particular stands on the issues.

People usually find it harder to take effective political action than they anticipated. Unexpected complications and lack of cooperation often produce frustration and disappointment. Well-intended actions have unintended consequences. One activist advises not to try to move a mountain in a day, but instead to "chip away at it."[54]

In "chipping away" at the problems that face the nation and the world, activists also reinforce their constitutional right to political participation. A promise in print, even in so lofty a document as the Constitution, remains only a promise until it is put into practice. Political participation should not be left entirely to elites, experts, and professional activists. "We each have a public life. Every day—at school, where we work, where we worship, within civic and social groups, as well as the polls—our behavior shapes the public world. Public life draws on the strengths of all of us."[55]

The challenges of living in—let alone governing effectively—an experimental democracy are daunting. Political actors must diagnose and address problems that change month to month and year to year as the country grows larger and more complex. In such a democracy, the tasks and responsibilities of citizenship can only grow. There is no "hidden hand" to do the work of democracy for us. We must practice it ourselves for it to flourish.

Summary

Political actors—individuals, groups, or even government itself—engage in political participation when they attempt to advance their beliefs about *what is*, *what's right*, and *what works* in political life. Voting is the legal procedure that permits the electorate to choose its representatives for public office and hold them accountable. In setting voting requirements, state legislatures define the American electorate. However, states may not set voting requirements that violate the U.S. Constitution or laws of Congress protecting citizens' fundamental right to vote.

Over the past century, state voting restrictions based on registration, property, race, gender, and youth have been relaxed or abolished by the U.S. Supreme Court and Congress. Those who want voter turnout to increase favor easing or eliminating remaining registration requirements.

Citizens as well as voting experts are ambivalent about the value of voting. Most Americans have been socialized to view voting as a legitimate form of decision making (*what's right*), even if they have reservations about it and don't believe it always delivers the policies they want (*what works*). Some experts regard voting primarily as a symbolic gesture of loyalty that legitimates the political process and reinforces the status quo.

Turnout is affected by psychological attitudes, age, race, gender, education, religion, and ethnicity. White, well-educated, middle-aged, and married individuals are more likely to vote than uneducated, poor, young, and single individuals. Advocates of equal representation worry that the current low voter turnout is abandoning democracy to elites.

In addition to voting, citizens participate in politics in other ways. Some participate *through* government, expressing their loyalty through symbolic actions, serving and working in government, and engaging in legal actions, including filing lawsuits and making use of the initiative, referendum, and recall. People also participate *outside* government through voluntary action, pressure activities, visionary actions, and using new electronic communication technologies. Participation also takes the form of resistance—sometimes legal, such as obstructionism, and sometimes illegal, such as civil disobedience. Government actors also engage in political action—sometimes by initiating citizen involvement in the political process and other times by delaying policies, discrediting and co-opting activists, or suppressing dissenters.

Political participation is an interactive process in which improvement by any political actor can provoke improvement in other actors, causing the quality of democracy to spiral upward. The participation of well-informed citizens who *learn by doing* is crucial to democracy.

Key Terms

civil disobedience **210**
direct action **210**
electorate **187**
environmental racism **205**
franchise **188**
gender gap **201**
grandfather clause **189**
initiative **205**
NIMBY **214**
political participation **187**
poll tax **189**
recall **205**
referendum **205**
registration **191**
socioeconomic status (SES) **203**
suffrage **189**
turnout **191**
uncivil disobedience **211**
vote **187**
white primary **189**

How You Can Learn More About Political Participation

Edelman, Murray. *Symbolic Uses of Politics.* Urbana: University of Illinois Press, 1964. An argument that citizens are not as free as they think they are because elites manipulate their political opinions through images and symbols.

Ginsberg, Benjamin. *The Captive Public: How Mass Opinion Promotes State Power.* New York: Basic Books, 1986. A compelling argument that citizen participation expands state power in ways that circumscribe people's freedom.

Gomes, Ralph C., and Linda Faye Williams, eds. *From Exclusion to Inclusion: The Long Struggle for African American Political Power.* New York: Greenwood Press, 1992. Chapters document the historic struggles of blacks and others that led to the Voting Rights Act of 1965 and the extent of their influence on elections since that bill was passed.

Key, V. O., Jr. *The Responsible Electorate: Rationality in Presidential Voting.* Cambridge, Mass.: Harvard University Press, 1966. Key shows voters to be rational decision makers who are concerned with major policy issues, the character of public officials, and the performance of government.

Ladd, Everett Carll. *Where Have All the Voters Gone? The Fracturing of America's Political Parties,* 2d ed. New York: W.W. Norton, 1982. An analysis of the effects that the decline of parties has had on elections.

Natchez, Peter B. *Images of Voting/Visions of Democracy.* New York: Basic Books, 1985. A critique of the forty years' worth of voting studies that portray American voters as incompetent.

Popkin, Samuel L. *The Reasoning Voter: Communication and Persuasion in Presidential Campaigns.* Chicago: University of Chicago Press, 1991. A provocative argument that voters make rational decisions about issues, candidates, and parties with the help of information shortcuts.

Sharp, Gene. *The Politics of Nonviolent Action.* Boston: Porter Sargent, 1973. The most comprehensive study of the theory and practice of nonviolent action.

Shienbaum, Kim Ezra. *The Electoral Connection: A Reassessment of the Role of Voting in Contemporary American Politics.* Philadelphia: University of Pennsylvania Press, 1984. An argument that those who vote are the beneficiaries of the political system, yet they vote largely for symbolic rather than self-serving reasons.

Verba, Sidney, and Norman Nie. *Participation in America: Democracy and Social Equality.* New York: Harper & Row, 1972. A seminal study of the social and economic factors that affect citizen participation.

Zimmerman, Joseph F. *Participatory Democracy: Populism Revived.* New York: Praeger, 1986. A clear account of the costs and benefits of citizen participation by a scholar who believes that the benefits of democracy outweigh the costs.

Political Parties

Above: H. Ross Perot, presidential candidate of the Reform party, appears on "Larry King Live," July 10, 1996. *Right*: A member of the Reform party collects signatures in New Braunfels, Texas, on a petition that would allow Ross Perot or another member of his party to get on the state ballot for the 1996 presidential elections.

CHAPTER 7

No free country has ever been without parties, which are a natural offspring of freedom.

James Madison, 1821

The spirit of party serves always to distract the public councils, and enfeeble the public administrations. It agitates the community with ill-founded jealousies and false alarms; kindles the animosity of one part against another; foments occasional riot and insurrection.

George Washington, 1796[1]

What *Is* the American Party System

Parties in the Federal System

The Evolution of the Two-Party System

Third Parties in the Two-Party System

The Two-Party System Today

Reforming the American Party System

In January 1992, after Texas billionaire Ross Perot suggested on the "Larry King Live" cable TV show that he might be willing to run for the presidency as an independent if volunteers put him on the ballot in all 50 states, thousands of Americans organized and did just that. Many hoped that someone so successful in business might be able to fix the economy and end the stalemate between the Democratic-controlled Congress and the Republican-controlled presidency. Democrats and Republicans blamed each other for the stalemate. But as Perot said sarcastically throughout his campaign, "It's not the Republicans' fault, of course, and it's not the Democrats' fault.... Somewhere out there there's an extraterrestrial that's doing this to us, I guess."[2]

Perot had an advantage that most independent and third party presidential candidates lack. As a billionaire, he could buy blocks of TV time to get the media visibility and public support a candidate needs to win. In addition, Perot's supporters believed that his wealth would insulate him from special interests. They also liked his political rhetoric: "Let's just get under the hood and fix the engine." "Let's just do it." "It's just that simple." By midsummer, volunteers had gotten Perot's name on the ballot in all 50 states, and he and President George Bush led Arkansas Governor Bill Clinton in most polls.

Suddenly, on the day Clinton was to accept the Democratic party's presidential nomination, Perot suspended his campaign. The reason he gave was that his candidacy could throw the election into the House of Representatives, where lawmakers rather than the people would pick their president—a consequence that, he claimed, would severely damage American democracy. Perot also said he sensed that the Democratic party under Clinton was being reborn, and with it a meaningful two-party system. Skeptics suggested that Perot's real reason for ending his campaign was its disarray. Loyal volunteers, some of whom had quit their jobs to work full time in Perot's campaign organization, United We Stand, America, felt betrayed when they were pushed aside by the few campaign professionals Perot had hired. And these pros, who disagreed among themselves, got angry at Perot when he would not let them run things their way.[3]

Then, just as suddenly, Perot decided to reenter the race in October, a month before the general election. He managed to regain much of his popular support, especially after his performance in the presidential debates and a blitz of *infomercials* (30- and 60-minute TV commercials) outlining his program to fix the economy through common sacrifice. Perot got 19 percent of the vote, the biggest showing for an independent or third party candidate since Theodore Roosevelt's run in 1912. Perot lost the election but succeeded in mobilizing many Americans disaffected with the two major parties.

At first, Clinton and the Democratic majorities in both houses of Congress seemed to cooperate, but gradually that cooperation broke down and popular discontent with the status quo grew. The result was the stunning Republican victory in the 1994 congressional elections that gave the party control of both houses. Once again the two branches of government were divided by stalemate, and complaints about the two-party system increased. Once again Perot stepped forth to organize the discontented.

In September 1995, Perot announced that he would build a new party on the base of the million or so dues-paying members he claimed still made up United We Stand, America. This new Reform party was to run a "world-class" presidential candidate in 1996 on a platform of a balanced budget constitutional amendment, congressional term limits, a simpler tax code, and campaign finance reform. The party would not run its own candidates for Congress and other offices but would endorse individual Democrats and Republicans who supported the party's goals.

In an unusual national primary in which votes were cast by mail, telephone, and the Internet, Perot defeated Richard Lamm, former Democratic governor of Colorado, for the Reform party's nomination. Again, Perot chose a political unknown as his running mate: his advisor on trade issues, Washington economist Pat Choate. Again, Perot got on the presidential ballots of all 50 states. This time he accepted $29 million in federal funds from the Federal Election Commission and used a large portion of it to buy TV time the night before the election. Perot won 8 percent of the popular vote—about half the percentage he had won in 1992.

Does Perot's success as a political outsider reflect the bankruptcy or imminent demise of the current two-party system? Would the country be better served by a broad array of very different parties? Or has Perot's candidacy prompted the Democrats and Republicans to revitalize themselves? This chapter will explore the American party system by focusing on the following questions:

What is the American party system and how does it work?

How have the two major parties evolved?

Why are third parties excluded from full participation in the political process?

What is the status of the two-party system and how might it be reformed?

What *Is* the American Party System?

A **political party** is a group that organizes to elect candidates to public office under the name, or "label," of that group. Unlike most other countries with representative governments, Americans have usually had only two **major parties** from which to choose. Major parties are those that are strong enough—that have enough political and organizational power—to win major elections. A number of minor parties, often called **third parties**, occasionally contest elections, but they almost always lose because, as we'll see, the major parties control the rules of the electoral process that protect their "duopoly." This is why the American **party system**—the system in which the major political parties compete in the electoral process and persuade certain segments of the population to identify with them over a given a period of time—is often called a **two-party system**.

How the Two-Party System Affects Government

In the United States, two parties dominate the party competition for the authority to determine *what is*, *what's right*, and *what works*. In multiparty parliamentary systems, that competition is more democratic. The box on page 222 outlines the main differences between these kinds of party systems and their effects on their respective political systems.

In the American presidential system, the presidency may be controlled by one party and one or both houses of Congress may be controlled by the other party—a situation known as **divided government**. In the 38 years from 1954 to 1992, the Democrats controlled the House of Representatives—and the Senate in all but six of those years—while Republicans held the White House for all but 12 years. Clinton's election in 1992 marked the first time since the Carter administration (1980–1984) that government was not divided. But the Republican sweep of Congress in 1994 returned divided government—a situation that was perpetuated by the 1996 elections.

party

This word comes from the Latin *partire*, "to partition" or "to divide." Thus a party represents only a *part* of the people. Among other words with the same root are *partisan* (one giving allegiance to a particular party) and *participation* (taking a part or a role in something).

Multiparty Systems and the American Two-Party System

Multiparty systems allow candidates from more than two parties to compete in local elections and win seats in the national legislature. These systems typically rely on proportional representation (PR), a type of representation in which each party receives seats in the national legislature in proportion to the votes it receives nationally. The use of PR is not the only important difference between multiparty systems and the American two-party system. The United States relies on a presidential system of government—one in which the person who wins the nationwide, or general, election becomes the head of government. This arrangement differs from a parliamentary system of government, such as that of Canada or Great Britain, in which the head of government (usually called the prime minister) is selected by a majority vote of the members of parliament. Thus in a parliamentary system the head of government and the majority in the national legislature belong to the same party or governing coalition. (Many parliamentary systems do have two legislative bodies, and it is possible for the opposition to control the "upper house," but because it plays no role in selection of the head of government, this split does not result in divided government of the sort so common in the United States.) In such systems, members of the ruling parties almost always vote with the government because the government must resign and call new parliamentary elections if it loses a major vote in parliament. Such party discipline is absent in the United States, where the president rules for a fixed four-year term regardless of how Congress votes.

The result of divided government is often **gridlock**, or political stalemate. By resisting compromise both branches can block legislation because a bill must be passed by both houses and signed by the president to become law. Gridlock typically intensifies as elections approach because each party wants to deny the other any policy victories and blame it for blocking needed legislation. In the 1992 presidential campaign, President George Bush pleaded for voters to reelect him and give him a Republican Congress he could work with, while Bill Clinton promised that if elected he and the Democratic Congress would cooperate to revive the nation's economy. Ross Perot was able to exploit the gridlock issue by stressing his independence from both major parties and from the special interests attached to them. He promised that if elected he would "take a chainsaw to the aisles of Congress" (the two parties sit on opposite sides of the aisles in each house) and force the two parties to cooperate on his legislative program. Many political experts dismissed this claim because Perot would have lacked the traditional levers of power, such as rewards and punishments, that a president can use on members of his own party to bring them into line.

gridlock
This term was first developed by journalists to describe big-city traffic congestion in which vehicles approaching a crossroads from all four directions stop and block each other from advancing: the traffic "grid" is "locked." Applied to politics, the term suggests a traffic jam in which competing interests block each other so completely that progress is impossible.

What American Parties Are *Expected* to Do and What They *Actually* Do

What American parties are expected to do is not necessarily what they actually do. Political parties are expected to

- link people with government by aggregating (bringing together) the political interests of various groups and turning them into public policy proposals,
- recruit qualified candidates and organize campaigns to elect them,
- encourage their candidates, once elected, to represent the party's policy proposals and interests in government and unite under party leaders to convert them into laws, and
- help to get those laws implemented by bridging the separation of powers and coordinating policymaking.

Critics say parties do a poor job of linking people with government by aggregating interests because they water down their positions to attract votes. The British ambassador made this same criticism almost a century ago: "The two parties in the United States resemble two bottles, each bearing a label describing its contents, and each being quite empty."[4]

Do parties recruit qualified candidates and help get them elected? Parties, we'll see in a moment, no longer control who runs for office under their labels or how campaigns are conducted, although they still organize and preside over the nominating process, raise money for their candidates, and help get out the vote. And the major parties still write the rules—at least indirectly, in Congress and in state legislatures—that determine who gets to be on the ballot at election time.

Do elected officials promote their party's goals once in office? Because the major parties no longer choose the candidates, they no longer have much control over their behavior in office. Elected officials often deviate from party platforms and ideology, disagree among themselves on matters of policy, and form coalitions across party lines to support the policies they back. Although presidents try to get the support of members of their own party, they often fail. Meanwhile, the party out of power often encourages partisan division on policy questions, thus contributing to gridlock when government is divided. Still, imagine what politics would be like if there were no strong parties to aggregate interests in a multicultural country as complex as the United States. Elites, wealthy and famous candidates, political consultants, special interests, and political action committees (PACs)—committees set up by interest groups or candidates to raise and distribute money to influence elections—would have a far greater say in the political process. And with no major party labels to identify other candidates, incumbents would have an even greater advantage than they do now. Moreover, the media would be unable to "filter" their coverage of the candidates through the familiar "screens" of party affiliation.[5]

Party Supporters

Americans don't formally belong to a party in the same way that people do in many countries, where they carry membership cards, pay dues, and attend regular meetings. Rather, Americans simply decide whether or not to identify with the party of their choice. Those who identify with a party may be candidates, officeholders, convention delegates, activists, or voters.

Political Candidates and Officeholders

Candidates who seek public office usually do so under a party label, are formally nominated by the party organization to represent it in an election, and are then listed as affiliated with that party on the ballot. Both houses of Congress and most state legislatures are organized around party membership. Members of the **majority party**—the party holding the most legislative seats—serve as chairs of committees and usually dominate the proceedings. The majority leader in each chamber comes from the majority party. Both parties have whips in each chamber to rally party members behind important legislation the party supports or the president's agenda if the president happens to belong to their party. These party leaders belong to the party elite. The president, who stands at the top of his party, typically appoints party members to staff the major positions in the executive branch. The fact that parties and government are intertwined in these ways affects how public policies are designed and implemented. It also explains why gridlock can occur and why officeholders must often form coalitions across party lines to advance their policymaking interests.

Party Activists and Convention Delegates

Party activists are **loyalists** or **professionals**. Loyalists are committed volunteers who help at party headquarters at election time, donate money and services, distribute political literature and campaign signs, and serve as delegates to their party conventions at the county, state, and national levels. Professionals are political experts paid to run party organizations at the national, state, and local levels from one election to another. They also hire pollsters, fund-raisers, and advertising experts to work on important campaigns. Some 5 to 10 percent of Americans volunteer to work for a party from time to time.

In general, loyalists have cared more about the candidates and issues in an election than the professionals, who have focused on the survival of the party as an institution. Loyalists have also been more inclined to fight for principles (*what's right*), while the pros have been pragmatists who often compromise and negotiate with adversaries within the party (*what works*). Because parties choose both loyalists and professionals as convention delegates, these conflicts have often been played out on the convention floor. In recent elections, however, Republican party pros under Ronald Reagan, George Bush, and Pat Buchanan have taken much the same stands as party loyalists. So have supporters of Ross Perot and other third party candidates. This trend was especially strong in 1992 and continued in 1996 despite Robert Dole's efforts to moderate party rhetoric. In 1996, Dole was faced with the problem of how to sustain the enthusiasm of his party's hard-core loyalists who help to get out the vote and still appeal to the moderate Republicans and independent voters he needed to win the election.

In their 1968 convention, Democrats under the leadership of liberal Senator George McGovern of South Dakota pushed through new party rules that democratized the selection of national convention delegates and affected party organizations from the national to the local level. The most controversial of these **McGovern Reforms** was a proportional representation quota system. Delegations had to reflect race, age, and presidential preference "in reasonable relationship to their presence in the state's population." These reforms shrank the power of party elites and professionals and expanded the power of the loyalists. They also increased the number of state primaries because adopting the primary was an easy way state party organizations could meet the reform requirements.[6] The reforms helped McGovern win the presidential nomination in 1972, but when he managed to carry only Massachusetts and the District of Columbia, party elites began watering down the reforms. When the Democrats lost the White House to Ronald Reagan in 1980, party pros curbed the power of the loyalists still further by creating appointed **superdelegates** (party officers and elected officials), most of whom could go to the convention "uncommitted"—free to vote for any candidate and to make deals to nominate a candidate who could win the general election.

For decades Republican party elites have resisted similar reforms by pointing to the Democrats' fragmentation and frequent failures to win the presidency. Fewer women and minorities hold key Republican party positions compared with the Democrats, but party elites have made some voluntary concessions to these groups to retain their loyalty and to attract new members and more voters. In 1996, when Republicans lost significant support from women voters, some party elites acknowledged that women should be given greater policymaking power in the party.

Party Voters

To be a Republican or a Democrat in the United States, you just declare that you are one. Or, as political scientists say, you *identify* with a party, an affiliation called **party identification**. Figure 7.1 shows party identification in presidential election years since 1952. Because "joining" a party is so easy, neither party can demand **party loyalty**—your promise to vote for its candidates. And because there are no membership requirements, voters may shift from one party to another as they choose—something Americans do more and more often. When voting patterns shift dramatically and change the balance of power between the two parties for a generation or more, political scientists say that a **realignment** has occurred. A **dealignment** has occurred when a significant number of voters no longer wish to identify with a party and become independents. Although the number of Democrats has declined in recent years, they still outnumber Republicans. Democrats and Republicans together outnumber independents, but each party must attract independent votes to win. In 1996, half the independents who had supported Perot in 1992 voted for Dole, while the remainder split equally between Perot and Clinton.[7]

A Republican party storefront office in Vincennes, Indiana.

FIGURE 7.1
Party identification, 1952–1996

Year	Strong Democrat	Weak Democrat	Independent-leaning Democrat	Pure Independent	Independent-leaning Republican	Weak Republican	Strong Republican	Apolitical
1952	22%	25%	10%	6%	7%	14%	14%	3%
1956	21	23	6	9	8	14	15	4
1958	27	22	7	7	5	17	11	4
1960	20	25	6	10	7	14	16	3
1962	23	23	7	8	6	16	12	4
1964	27	25	9	8	6	14	11	1
1966	18	28	9	12	7	15	10	1
1968	20	25	10	11	9	15	10	1
1970	20	24	10	13	8	15	9	1
1972	15	26	11	13	11	13	10	1
1974	18	21	13	15	9	14	8	3
1976	15	25	12	15	10	14	9	1
1978	15	24	14	14	10	14	8	2
1980	18	23	11	13	10	14	9	3
1982	20	24	11	11	8	14	10	2
1984	17	20	11	11	12	15	12	2
1986	18	22	10	12	11	15	11	2
1988	18	18	12	11	13	14	14	2
1990	17	19	12	11	13	17	11	2
1992	18	18	14	11	12	14	11	1
1994	15	19	13	10	11	14	16	1
1996	19	20	14	9	11	15	13	0

Source: American National Election Studies, Center for Political Studies, University of Michigan.

Party Ideology

Both major parties have been successful in attracting voters with a wide range of interests and political ideas and in building coalitions that enable them to win elections. However, because voters are free to shift parties, and because one party may build a broader-based coalition in a particular election, it is difficult to pinpoint permanent ideological differences between the two parties over time.

Ideological differences between the parties are usually reflected in the national party platforms adopted by the nominating conventions. Both major party platforms tend to include similar "planks"—or statements—on general issues such as education but reveal major differences on controversial issues such as abortion and government regulation. Both parties often word some planks ambiguously to avoid alienating factions within the party. Because platforms do not bind a party's candidates if they are elected, the platforms are usually viewed as a campaign ritual that unites the party or as a way of resolving disputes within the party rather than as serious policy commitments. But when one faction of the party dominates the platform, as ultraconservative Republicans did in 1992 and to some extent in 1996, the platform can be internally divisive.

As we saw in Chapter 4, most Americans tend to be more pragmatic than ideological. Still, such diverse groups as organized labor, ethnic and racial minorities, environmentalists, feminists, and pro-choice advocates generally find greater support under the Democratic label, while business groups, Christian fundamentalists, and advocates of a strong military generally prefer the Republican party. Republicans favor downsizing government and allowing states, localities, and the private sector to solve many social and economic problems. New Democrats who favor such efficiency measures agree that government should downsize but want it to take an active role in addressing social and economic problems. Republicans believe that reducing regulations on business will allow it to prosper and benefit society at large by creating more jobs and thus taxable income. Democrats doubt that this approach really works and want government to help reduce the gap between rich and poor. Today the Democratic party's core supporters are working-class and lower-middle-class voters. In 1996 about a quarter of all voters came from union households, and 6 out of 10 of them voted for Democrats.[8] But the party has also attracted more middle-class voters as the size of the working class has declined. Indeed, it is not easy to tell the political behavior of these two classes apart.[9]

Democrats are divided between traditional liberals who favor strong government intervention, particularly on behalf of the poor, and New Democrats who resemble liberal-to-moderate Republicans. Evidence of this split could be seen in the decision of four southern Democratic senators not to seek reelection in 1996: Howell Heflin of Alabama, David Pryor of Arkansas, Sam Nunn of Georgia, and J. Bennett Johnston of Louisiana. Meanwhile, Clinton's New Democrats were clearly trying to move the party toward the center. At the Democratic National Convention in 1996, the speeches of liberals Jesse Jackson and former New York Governor Mario Cuomo were scheduled outside of prime time. And immediately following Clinton's reelection a number of administration liberals resigned.

Left: Republican presidential candidate Bob Dole campaigns at CellTech in New Hampshire in February 1996. *Right*: President Bill Clinton addresses a meeting of Emily's List, a liberal organization, composed mainly of Democrats, that supports women's bids for public office. Behind Clinton is Ann Richards, former governor of Texas.

FIGURE 7.2

Republican party factions

Two Republican surveys taken after the 1996 election indicate that the Republican party is divided into five groups. Deficit hawks (about 30 percent of those interviewed) who favor eliminating the deficit are likely to be men over 45; supply-siders (about 20 percent) who favor tax cuts rather than deficit reduction tend to be younger men; moralists (about one-fifth) who emphasize issues such as abortion prohibition are likely to be older and female; cultural populists (about a quarter of the party) who oppose elitism are generally younger women; and progressives (less than 10 percent) who support programs such as government action to help the disadvantaged.

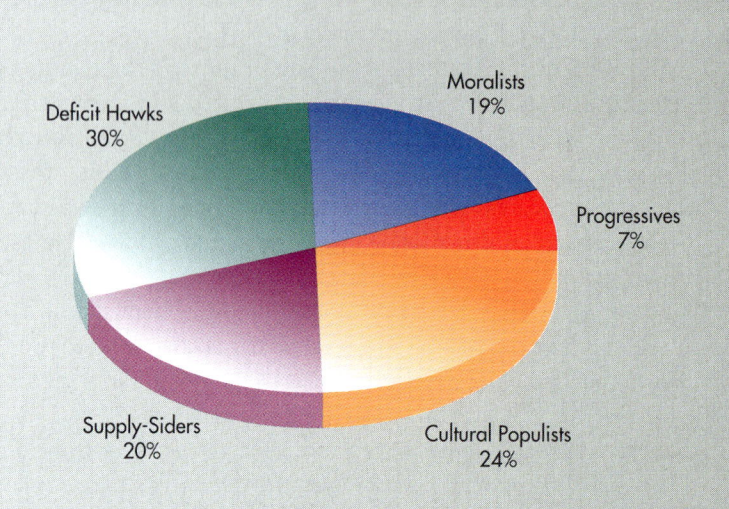

- Deficit Hawks 30%
- Moralists 19%
- Progressives 7%
- Cultural Populists 24%
- Supply-Siders 20%

Source: Washington Post National Weekly Edition, March 3, 1997, 35.

But today the deepest ideological divisions are in the Republican party (see Figure 7.2). Once divided along regional lines (liberals in the Northeast versus conservatives in the West and Midwest), the party is now split into ideological factions.[10] Many of the more senior Republicans tend to be moderate on social issues, conservative on defense and fiscal issues, committed to keeping federal spending in their constituencies, and willing to make deals with Democrats to pass legislation. The confrontational newcomers—many of whom now come from the South (House Speaker Newt Gingrich is from Georgia and Senate Majority Leader Trent Lott is from Mississippi)—oppose abortion, favor school prayer, and want government reduced to a minimal, even libertarian, level.[11]

The Political Spectrum

While both parties have been shifting toward conservatism, any attempt to assess the ideological differences between the major parties is necessarily shaped by *who* is doing the assessing and from *what point of view*. Political scientists commonly locate or "plot" party loyalists, or **partisans**, on a line called a **political spectrum** to indicate how strongly they are attached to liberal and conservative principles. The typical political spectrum places extreme liberal principles on the left end of the line, extreme conservative principles on the right end of the line, and moderate principles in the middle. The spectrum explains why ultraliberal groups are often called "left-wingers" and ultraconservative groups, "right-wingers."

While this simple device is a useful way of illustrating ideological differences on many issues, it does

left and right

The use of *left* and *right* to designate political ideology dates from the French Revolution, when the conservatives sat on the right side of the National Assembly and radicals on the left.

A Libertarian's View of Democrats and Republicans

The following excerpts are the thoughts of A. Lawrence Chickering:

Both political parties—Democrats and Republicans, including the conservatives and liberals within each—are conspirators in an effort to foil [local self-government]. Both parties want to control governance, but not to have to work too hard to change society. Both would rather bask in applause for their self-proclaimed wisdom or compassion.

Democrats think everything happens in Washington: the only way to fix society's problems is to spend more money, to grease the big federal machine so that it works properly. They believe the poor and minority groups cannot really run their own lives. Although many of them would [say they oppose] bureaucratic management of the poor, that is where their prescriptions and political alliances tend to lead. They have shown little interest in working to stimulate low-income people to achieve real self-governance, because they are convinced that self-governance only benefits the well-to-do. For the disadvantaged, only the national government machine can provide.

Republicans are no better. While they talk a lot about getting government "off people's backs," most of them are content to see social policy administered from afar. They may believe in the ability of people to run their own lives—or at least say they do—but very few of them have shown any interest in actively working to empower low-income and minority groups at the local level, helping them to acquire the skills and financial help they need to make themselves genuinely independent. Most Republicans' interest in the machine of government is strictly negative: they want to stop it. . . .

It is easy to see why the public has withdrawn from participation in most arenas of "public life": because it has been left no room to do anything except passively receive things from what many state and local officials refer to as "the national delivery system." People know that government has made a mockery of the original notion of "public" policy, and they want no part of it.

It does not have to be this way. Governments can provide services without also delivering them. They can pay and leave delivery to others, as they did after World War II with the GI Bill. At that time, the U.S. government wanted to provide access to higher education for returning war veterans but did not want to create and run a lot of colleges for them. Instead, it provided vouchers (the equivalent of money), which were redeemable at accredited colleges. Choice of institution remained with the veterans.

This bill, which allowed millions of young people a chance to go to college, is the model for a very different way of organizing public services [public housing, legal, and social services] from any we have at present. Structuring our political system to encourage real participation and self-governance by citizens would end the crisis in our politics by restoring to people control over their own lives.

Source: A. Lawrence Chickering, *Beyond Left and Right: Breaking the Political Stalemate* (San Francisco: ICS Press, 1993), 181, 184–185.

not work for all issues. In Chapter 4, these differences were plotted on a series of triangles (see page 129). For example, many conservative Republicans believe that burning the American flag is a treasonous act that should be punished, while many liberal Democrats believe that flag-burning is an example of freedom of expression and is therefore protected by the First Amendment. Libertarians, whom political scientists would normally place to the right of Republicans on the political spectrum on issues such as downsizing government, agree with the liberal Democrats on flag-burning. Their argument is an instance of a cross-cutting allegiance, a concept also discussed in Chapter 4.

To supporters of third parties, which have stronger ideological goals, the differences between the ideologically broad major parties, which compete for many of the same voters, seem very small. Thus supporters of third parties often conclude that the major parties give voters very little choice at the ballot box. But to Republicans on their party's right wing and to Democrats on their party's left wing, the differences between the major parties seem very great. To Republicans and Democrats who stand at the ideological center of their parties, the differences between the two parties seem small.

Not surprisingly, party activists tend to be more extreme in their ideological positions than those who vote only in general elections; that is why they appear near the ends of the political spectrum. Republican convention delegates as a whole tend to be more ideologically extreme than Democratic delegates as a whole; that is why the former appear to be closer to the conservative end on the political spectrum and the latter closer to the liberal end.

Those calling themselves independents fall virtually in the middle of the spectrum. Their numbers doubled between 1964 and 1974, and they have since remained about one-third of the electorate. While many switch back and forth between the major parties in presidential elections, as a group they lean toward Republicans more often than toward Democrats, having favored Republicans in every postwar election except Lyndon Johnson's in 1964 and Clinton's in 1992 and 1996. Their vote helps explain how the Republicans have been able to win the presidency so often in recent decades.

The Strategy of Convergence

Differences between the major parties tend to decline when campaigns heat up because neither party can win the general election with party supporters only. Both parties know they will pick up a greater number of votes if they move closer to the center of the ideological spectrum, where most voters lie. Political scientists call this "competing for the middle." Thus when Democrats move from the left toward the center and Republicans move from the right toward the center in their campaign rhetoric, they are pursuing a **strategy of convergence**, as illustrated in Figure 7.3.

In 1996, Dole tried to make moderates feel welcome under the Republican party's "big tent." But the "big tent" metaphor had not worked for the Bush campaign in 1992, and in 1995 a Bush aide warned that "the sucking sound you hear is the shrinking of the inclusive big tent of Republicanism."[12] A journalist who tracked Clinton's middle-of-the-road campaign describes how he "cast himself as Ronald Reagan, peddling the politics of good humor [and] asked, like President Reagan, whether voters considered themselves better off than four years ago. And on the final weekend of the campaign, he brazenly borrowed the Reagan slogan, 'It's morning in America.'"[13]

The strategy of convergence tends to work well in general elections when the nominees of the two parties compete with one another for the ideological middle but not when the candidates are competing for their party's nomination and must appeal to their party's activists. These activists, or loyalists, we've just seen, are motivated more by ideology than is the general electorate and tend to support candidates like themselves. Today, however, media coverage of the nomination races makes it harder for candidates who win in the more ideological primaries to

FIGURE 7.3

The strategy of convergence

1 = Typical original position of candidates for Democratic nomination
2 = Typical original position of candidates for Republican nomination
3 = Typical general election position of Democratic candidate
4 = Typical general election position of Republican candidate

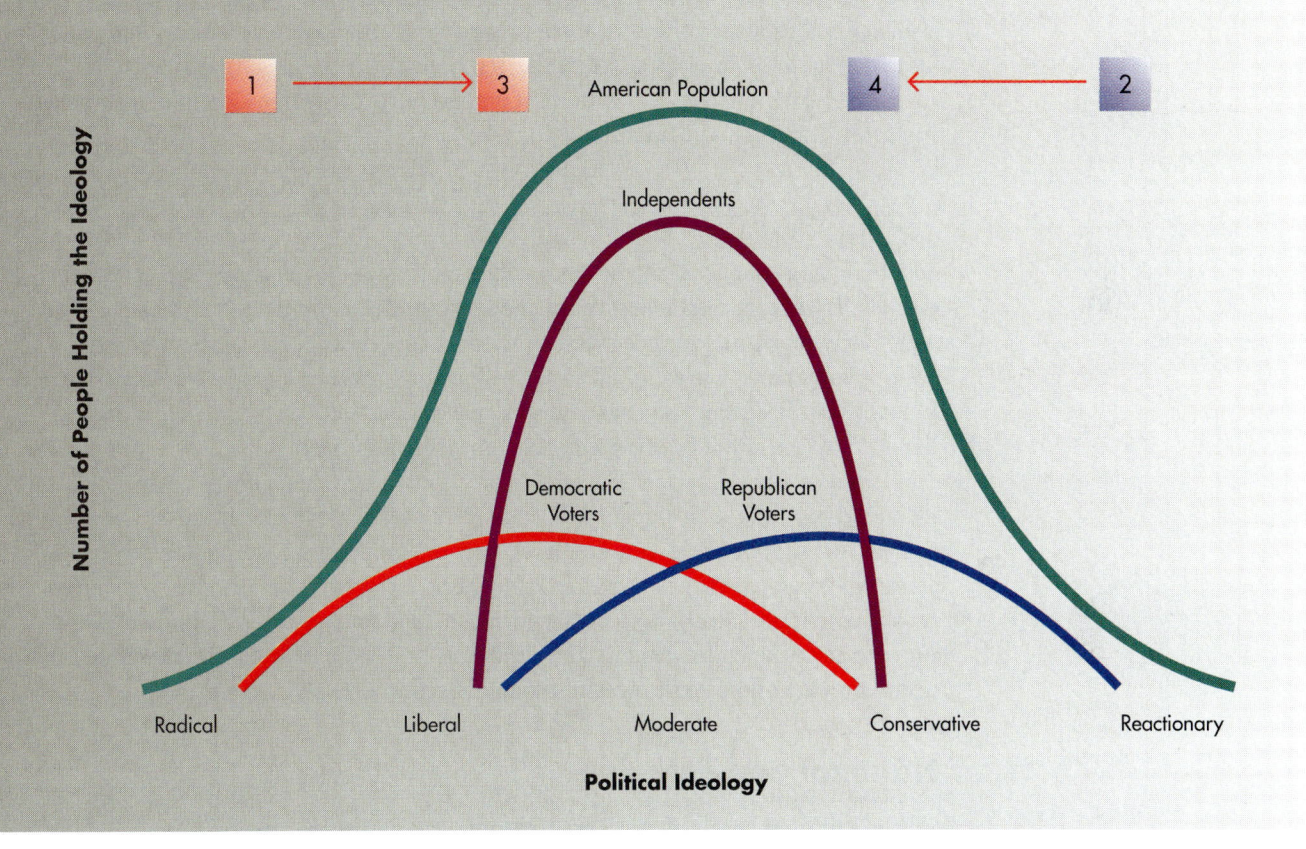

pursue a strategy of convergence in the general election because attentive voters already identify them with the more extreme positions they took to win nomination. Figure 7.3 illustrates the pressures on the major party candidates to diverge in the primaries and to converge in the general elections.

Parties in the Federal System

The work parties do is structured by a major political reality: they must operate in the federal system. Parties design presidential campaigns in a winner-take-all system that focuses on the states. In this system, the candidate who wins the most popular votes in a state is then entitled to all that state's *electoral* votes (Chapter 10). The fact that parties must work within the federal system helps explain why party organizations are similar and why their goals often differ. To work effectively, each party must have local, state, and national organizations because elections are conducted at each of these levels.

State and National Organizations

At the state and local levels, each party maintains a statewide committee with connections to local offices and usually writes its own state platforms and holds state conventions in election years. At the national level, each major party maintains four organizations: a national committee, a campaign committee in each house of Congress, and a national convention.

State and Local Organizations

The main goal of parties at the state and local levels is to get their own candidates elected. To do this they solicit campaign contributions and usually draft their own state party platforms to reflect state and local concerns. But while parties' organizations sometimes wield significant power at the state and local levels, they are no longer the iron-fisted party machines that monopolized many local elections earlier in this century. These big-city machines such as New York City's Tammany Hall Democratic organization began to erode as the practices party bosses used to deliver votes—handing out jobs, social services, Thanksgiving turkeys, and even money to supporters—were replaced by unemployment compensation, food stamps, and government-supported medical care. Party bosses also lost power due to anticorruption legislation and growing media scrutiny. Still, candidates continue to seek the endorsements and organizational help of both big-city and suburban mayors and other powerful political figures.

National Committees

At the national level, each party's national committee oversees party activities such as fundraising and candidate recruitment during the years between national elections. The national committee is composed of party officials from each state, along with state party chairs and any others party leaders appoint. The Republican National Committee (RNC) has 150 members, while the Democratic National Committee (DNC) has 350—a reflection of its effort to represent a more diverse clientele.

Although the RNC and the DNC head the organizations of their parties, they exert little control over the party committees and candidates at the state and local levels. Nor do they have significant influence over presidential campaigns. The most national committees can do is offer support by raising money, running campaign schools for candidates, and producing and buying media time for "generic" campaign ads aimed at increasing support for all the candidates on their ticket rather than for particular candidates—a strategy begun by the Republicans in 1980.

Normally the chairs of these committees remain neutral during the primaries to avoid alienating a candidate who might wind up as the party's nominee, but occasionally they intervene against a candidate they believe might damage the party's long-term strength. In practice, each party's presidential nominee selects the chair of the national committee for the election period. During the campaign, the national committee supports its party's candidate, but its role has decreased since the candidates of parties receiving 5 percent of the popular vote in the previous election are eligible for tax dollars through a checkoff on income tax forms—money they use to hire their own campaign staffs, professional handlers, media experts, pollsters, and other specialists. However, when a candidate runs out of funds before the general election because of a challenging primary struggle, the national committee can step in and spend its own funds in general support of the party and its candidates, as the RNC did for Bob Dole in 1996. After the election, the presidential victor selects a new party pro or prominent politician to run the national committee, while the losing party often faces a fight over possible choices among party pros representing those planning to seek the nomination in four years' time.

Congressional Campaign Committees

Each party organizes one campaign committee in the Senate and another in the House to raise campaign money, recruit promising candidates to run for office, help reelect incumbents, and support the party's challengers around the country for seats they don't hold. The committees supporting House campaigns are the Democratic Congressional Campaign Committee and the National Republican Congressional Committee. Those supporting Senate campaigns are the Democratic Senatorial Campaign Committee and the National Republican Senatorial Committee. The elected members of each party in each house also organize into party caucuses or conferences to plan legislative strategies, as we'll see in Chapter 11.

Congressional committees must compete with individual candidates for campaign contributions. This is a difficult task because loyalists usually prefer to give to individual candidates in hopes of gaining access to those elected officials later on. But monetary limits on contributions to individual candidates have led big donors to give to party committees as well. One way the campaign committees solicit contributions is by inviting voters to special events where they get to meet prominent party leaders. Often these committees merely add to the campaign war chests of individual representatives and senators, allocating most funds for close races in hopes of increasing the party's strength in the House and Senate.

National Conventions

National conventions, which date from the 1830s, top the governing structure of each party. Their purpose was—and still is—to bring together party activists from the states (and the District of Columbia, Puerto Rico, and territories such as Guam) every four years in the summer prior to the November presidential election to nominate candidates for the presidency and vice presidency and to write rules governing party activities. These delegates also adopt the party platform, which reflects their ideology and electoral strategy.

Most convention delegates are selected at the local and state levels in party primaries and caucuses, although both parties also make party leaders special

> **caucus**
> This word is believed to have been borrowed from an Algonquian word referring to a gathering.

delegates. Because Republicans tend to prefer orderly conventions, they select about 2,000 delegates and alternates from a fairly homogeneous pool of supporters. A poll of their 1996 delegates showed that these delegates were overwhelmingly white, male, and middle-aged and that 1 in 5 was a millionaire. They were also "more conservative" than delegates eight years before, more conservative than Republicans generally, and more conservative than their presidential candidate, Bob Dole (see Figure 7.4).[14] Republican convention rules also limit debates over controversial issues such as abortion, and ultra-conservative populist candidate Pat Buchanan was not permitted to address the convention in 1996, even though he won more than 3 million votes in the primaries.

The Democratic party selects delegates representative of the party's diverse supporters. Its roughly 4,000 delegates and 4,000 alternates long made conventions raucous, divisive, and unpredictable. But in 1992 the party, tired of its 12-year losing streak, ran an orderly and unified convention, while the Republicans were deeply divided over the legacy of Ronald Reagan. Still, as the most interesting aspects of convention politics take place behind the scenes, even divisive conventions don't generate the huge TV audiences they once did, and the major television networks have repeatedly cut back on their gavel-to-gavel coverage, leaving a gap filled by Cable News Network and C-SPAN. In 1996, even as both parties tried to overcome public indifference to the predictable outcome of their conventions by downplaying ideology and staging crowd-pleasing speakers and events, even fewer tuned in to a ritual stripped of all genuine drama and dissent. One conservative Republican observer predicted that "scripting, squelching, and screening its way to party loyalty may leave the party talking to itself."[15]

Parties Lose Their Nominating Power

In recent decades, parties have lost the strong control they once had over the nomination process. At the turn of the twentieth century, state and local party machines controlled nominations using the **secret party caucus**. Party bosses met in "smoke-filled rooms" to pick the candidates they wanted to run for president and for state and local offices. This system changed with the rise of primary elections.

The Rise of Primaries

Party reformers eventually succeeded in replacing the secret party caucus with the **direct primary**—an election in which the voters, rather than party bosses, decide which candidates the parties will nominate.

primary
This is the first, or *prime*, election in a series followed by the general election, which includes all candidates who win their primaries.

FIGURE 7.4

Comparing Republican delegates with the voters

Comparisons of 1996 delegates to the Republican National Convention with Republican voters and all voters.

	Delegates	Republican voters	All voters
Government			
Government is doing too many things better left to businesses and individuals	91%	78%	59%
Trade			
Free trade must be allowed, even if domestic industries are hurt by foreign competition	53%	34%	31%
Values			
Government should do more to promote traditional values	56%	44%	42%
Government should have a favorable opinion of the Religious Right	55%	39%	31%
Abortion			
Abortion should be permitted in all cases	11%	22%	27%
Abortion should be permitted but subject to greater restrictions than it is now	12%	17%	14%
Abortion should be permitted in cases such as rape or incest, or to save the woman's life	38%	39%	39%
Abortion should be permitted only to save the woman's life	27%	16%	14%
Discrimination			
Necessary to have laws to protect racial minorities from discrimination	30%	39%	51%
Not necessary	60%	56%	44%

	Delegates	Republican voters	All voters
Affirmative action			
Most of these government programs should be continued	9%	28%	45%
Most of these government programs should be abolished	78%	61%	43%
Immigrant children			
Children of illegal immigrants should be allowed to attend public schools	26%	46%	54%
Should not be allowed	58%	48%	41%
Assault weapons			
Oppose the nationwide assault weapons ban	51%	33%	24%
Demographics			
Men	64%	53%	46%
Women	36%	47%	54%
White	91%	95%	84%
Black	3%	2%	11%
No college	7%	43%	51%
Some college	92%	56%	48%
Family income under $50,000	23%	60%	71%
Family income $50,000 to $75,000	18%	19%	14%
Family income over $75,000	47%	17%	11%
Conservative	70%	50%	11%

Source: New York Times/CBS News poll of the delegates, cited in James Bennet, "The Delegates: When Image Meets Reality," *New York Times*, August 12, 1996, A1.

Primaries are run according to rules adopted by state legislatures—bodies controlled by Republicans and Democrats. Some forty states now use a **closed primary** in which voters must declare their party affiliation and choose from among the candidates on that party's ballot. Other states use an **open primary**, which allows voters to choose candidates from any party they wish. Only a few states have a **blanket primary**, which lists qualified candidates of all parties on a single ballot and allows voters to choose among them. Since the 1960s, as the parties have become more democratic, states have come under increasing pressure to adopt the primary or to widen participation in their conventions and in **nonsecret caucuses**—open meetings in which voters or party members gather to choose their nominees.[16] This method, which is used mainly in western and New England states, is praised as an example of grassroots democracy but criticized because it produces narrowly partisan candidates who don't appeal to a broad enough chunk of the electorate to win in the general election.

Under the primary system, candidates may run for office at any level without the backing of their party. For example, when former Georgia Governor Jimmy Carter sought the Democratic presidential nomination in 1976, he had few ties to and virtually no backing from party leaders but still managed to win by getting public support during the primary process. In most states, there are few requirements to run in a primary. Either a candidate must sign up (and often pay a modest "filing fee") or submit a nominating petition bearing a required number of signatures. Supporters of such requirements argue that they restrict the race to serious candidates, while others complain that they impose hardships on candidates who lack name recognition and the money to get it. The party nominees for each office are selected in the primary election. The nominees of all the parties who have met their state's legal requirements then compete in the **general election**. In a general election, held in early November in even-numbered years, candidates from all parties compete for thousands of federal and state offices. Every fourth year, when presidential candidates run, the election is called a *presidential election*. Two years later, midway in the president's term of office, the election is called a *mid-term, off-year*, or *congressional election*.

Winner-Take-All Versus Proportional Representation

Most Republican state presidential primaries now operate according to the winner-take-all principle: whoever wins the most votes wins all the convention delegates of that state. This practice attracted attention during the 1992 primaries when Pat Buchanan won 25 to 30 percent of the votes in most states, but President Bush, thanks to his party's rules, won virtually all the delegates. In 1996 Buchanan again won significant percentages of the votes in many states but gained very few delegates and therefore lost the nomination early in the primary season to Bob Dole.

The Democratic primaries use the principle of proportional representation by which each state's delegates are allocated in proportion to each candidate's percentage of the state primary vote. This rule seems fair (*what's right*), but it works against the party in the general elections. In 1992, for example, it kept the candidacies of former Governor Jerry Brown of California, former Senator Paul Tsongas of Massachusetts, and Governor Bill Clinton of Arkansas alive through the spring primary season. These candidates were still attacking one another when

Republican presidential candidate Pat Buchanan campaigns in New Hampshire in the winter of 1996.

the Republicans knew that President Bush would be their nominee and were uniting behind him. One prominent Democrat complained, "We Democrats have forgotten that the point of the nominating process is not to choose a candidate but to elect a President. We have created a nominating system that lets marginal candidates serve as spoilers."[17] In 1996 this was not a problem because Clinton was an incumbent and his renomination was never really in doubt.

Criticism of Primaries

While some oppose the present primary system, claiming that it weakens the party and often tends to promote losing candidates, others criticize it for strengthening the power of the upper and middle classes to the disadvantage of the poor and less educated. They argue that while direct primaries are touted as a democratic reform because they increase opportunities for citizen participation, in practice these primaries give only the "illusion of popular rule."[18] In fact, primaries may actually undermine lower-class interests because the relatively few voters who turn out for them tend to be party loyalists who come from more advantaged groups.[19] Moreover, many primaries exclude independents—the largest number of voters in America today—because the Republicans and Democrats in the state legislatures who write the rules that determine ballot access increase their chances of renomination if primary voters are party loyalists.

A National Primary?

The rise of the direct primary has led to suggestions that a national primary be held in the late spring prior to the general election. One political scientist sees the national primary as a natural outgrowth of two hundred years of American nominating practices: presidential candidates were first chosen by caucuses in Congress, then by national party conventions, then by a mixture of state primaries and caucuses, and finally, he anticipates, by a national presidential primary, thereby "eliminating official parties and exalting the individual voter."[20] Others worry that individual voters are not well enough informed to shoulder this responsibility and that a national primary would merely reflect the ignorance of American mass democracy.

The Evolution of the Two-Party System

Why did political parties appear at all in American politics? They are not mentioned in the Constitution, and the Framers dismissed them as divisive factions (see James Madison's *The Federalist*, No. 10, in the Appendix). Jefferson distanced himself from both the Federalist and the Anti-Federalist "parties," proclaiming in 1792 that belonging to a party "is the last degradation of a free and moral agent. If I could not go to heaven but with a party, I would not go there at all."[21] Yet shortly thereafter Jefferson himself founded a party, and in just four years parties became respectable. Why this sudden shift?

The First National Parties

Parties developed (they became *what is*) by doing useful work. Even before they were formally established, political coalitions resembling parties were performing valuable functions. In Chapter 2 we saw how the political coalitions at the Constitutional Convention forged the compromises that persuaded the delegates to sign the Constitution and how the Federalists and the Anti-Federalists then organized and publicized the debate over ratification. In the first session of Congress, caucuses and regional voting blocks aggregated interests to bring order to an institution that represented diverse regions, classes, and cultures. In later sessions supporters of aggregated interests began to help elect each other.[22] Parties soon began to organize campaigns to compete for the presidency and other top offices. Ironically, the factionalism that Madison originally associated with parties was being tamed and managed by the parties themselves in ways that made the political system work more effectively.

Federalists and Jeffersonian Republicans

Soon after the Constitution was ratified, Madison and Jefferson joined forces against Alexander Hamilton, thus splitting the Federalists into two groups that became the first national political parties. Madison and Jefferson called themselves Republicans and jestingly labeled Hamilton's group "anti-Republican." John Quincy Adams later remarked that much confusion could have been avoided if these parties had been rightly named. The Federalists, he said, should have been called the Nationalist party, in keeping with their nationalist goals, while the Republicans should have been called the Federalist party because they believed in a federalist system that gave political weight to the states.[23]

Hamilton's Federalists were the ancestors of today's Republican party. They supported the old Federalist policy of creating a strong national government capable of protecting the country from foreign enemies and fostering economic development. (The modern Republican party has also made defense and economic growth top priorities.) The Federalist party drew most of its strength from New England and the coastal regions of the Middle Atlantic states and South Carolina—regions with strong commercial interests. The Federalists believed that stimulating the development of industry would ultimately benefit everyone.

The ancestor of today's Democratic party, the Madison–Jefferson Republicans, pointed to the virtuous farmer as the model of economic and political independence. Republican support came largely from the interior and the South, which favored a weaker, more frugal central government and agrarian interests (small landholders, farmers, and frontier dwellers)—interests defended by the Anti-Federalists and still cultivated by the Democratic party today. In 1800, when Jefferson ran against Federalist John Adams for the presidency, the Jeffersonians called themselves Democratic-Republicans to highlight their devotion to democracy. The Democratic-Republicans proved to be better coalition-builders than the Federalists because they were open to a broader range of economic groups and ideologies. The social elitism and the commercial economic policies pursued by the Federalists led to a gradual defection from the party by those members of the business community who saw greater opportunities opening up under the Jeffersonian Democratic-Republicans.[24]

Jacksonian Democracy

In 1828 Democratic-Republican Andrew Jackson defeated John Quincy Adams' bid for reelection by portraying himself as a democrat running against an aristocrat. Jackson's state-centered politics was popular, and the recent abolition of the property requirement for voting in most states won him the support of rural and urban workers. The more nationalist right wing of the Democratic-Republicans reacted by splitting off to form the National Republican party under the leadership of Henry Clay, Daniel Webster, and Jackson's first vice president, John C. Calhoun. This group favored a stronger national legislature rather than a dominant popular president. In 1832 it joined with the fragments of the old Federalist party, which favored commerce, industry, and finance, to form the Whig party. The faction of Democratic-Republicans that stayed loyal to Jackson eventually became known as the Democratic party. Over the next 25 years the struggle between the Democrats and Whigs was leading toward today's two-party system when it collapsed in the conflict over slavery.

Slavery split the Whigs, bringing to an end what scholars call "the second party system." Whigs from the South joined the pro-slavery Democrats, while Whigs opposed to slavery formed a new Republican party in 1854, which opposed extending slavery to the new western territories seeking admission to the Union. The Republican party was the first—and so far the only—third party ever to become a major party in U.S. history. The evolution of the American party system is shown in Table 7.1.

This caricature of Andrew Jackson, from the year he was elected president (1828), was drawn by David Claypool Johnston in the style of sixteenth-century Italian artist Arcimboldo. Johnston used images of dead Native Americans to construct the head of the former Indian fighter.

The Modern Party System

When Republican Abraham Lincoln was elected president in 1860 without any help from the South, the rift between the two parties over slavery and economic issues proved too deep to resolve at the ballot box, and southern states seceded from the Union to form the Confederacy. Peaceful competition between the two parties would pick up only after the Civil War came to an end, but it would continue to reflect regional loyalties.

Reconstruction and the "Solid South"

For decades after the Civil War, white southerners remained embittered against the Republican party and northern Reconstruction policies, which had stripped them of their slave labor supply and forced them to sit next to former slaves in state legislatures and on trains. A violent white backlash prompted Congress to require the former Confederate states to ratify the Fourteenth Amendment (which enlarged the concept of citizenship to include blacks) and the Fifteenth Amendment (which gave freedmen—but not women—the right to vote). But soon intimidation and violence prevented the freedmen from exercising that right, and the Democrats regained control of the southern state legislatures. By the time Reconstruction came to an end in 1877, a Democratic "solid South" counterbalanced the almost equally solid Republican north.

> **Whig party**
>
> The American Whig party took its name from a comparable British party of an earlier period, whose name derived from the Gaelic word *whiggamor*, meaning "cattle driver" or "cattle thief." It came to be used to describe Scottish Presbyterians, and in politics referred to progressive reformers identified with commerce and manufacturing interests.

TABLE 7.1

The Evolution of the American Party System

Era	Year			
The Preparty Period	1789			Federalist-Washington
	1792			Washington
	1796	Democratic-Republican		J. Adams
The First Party System	1800	Jefferson		—
	1804	Jefferson		—
	1808	Madison		—
	1812	Madison		—
	1816	Monroe		—
	1820	Monroe		—
	1824	J. Q. Adams		—
	1828	Democratic-Jackson		National Republican,
	1832	Jackson		Whig
	1836	Van Buren		—
The Second Party System	1840	—		W. H. Harrison
	1844	Polk		—
	1848	—		Taylor
	1852	Pierce		—
	1856	Buchanan	Constitutional	Republican
	1860	Southern —	Union	Lincoln
	1864	Democrat —		Lincoln
	1868	—		Grant
	1872	—		Grant
The Third, or Modern, Party System	1876	—		Hayes
	1880	Rough —		Garfield
	1884	balance Cleveland		—
	1888	—		B. Harrison
	1892	Cleveland		—
	1896	—	Populist	McKinley
	1900	—		McKinley
	1904	—		T. Roosevelt
	1908	—		Taft
	1912	Republican Wilson	Progressive	—
	1916	dominance Wilson		—
	1920	—		Harding
	1924	—		Coolidge
	1928	—		Hoover
	1932	F. D. Roosevelt		—
	1936	Democratic F. D. Roosevelt		—
	1940	dominance F. D. Roosevelt		—
	1944	F. D. Roosevelt		—
	1948	Progressive Truman	States' Rights	—
	1952	—		Eisenhower
	1956	—		Eisenhower
	1960	Kennedy		—
	1964	Johnson		—
	1968	—	American	Nixon
	1972	Republican —	Independent	Nixon
	1976	dominance Carter		—
	1980	—	Independent	Reagan
	1984	—		Reagan
	1988	—		Bush
	1992	Clinton	Independent	—
	1996	Clinton	Reform	—

The Republican Ascendancy and the Rise of Populism, 1877–1932

In the industrial Northeast, growing numbers of European (often Roman Catholic) immigrants were pressured to vote Republican by factory owners. Workers would often find this warning in their last pay envelope before a presidential election: "Don't come back to work if the Democrat wins the election." Republicans, who had captured the loyalty of Protestants there, continued to dominate this region and the Midwest well into the twentieth century. From 1877 to 1932, only two Democrats won the White House: Grover Cleveland (1885–1889 and 1893–1897) and Woodrow Wilson (1913–1921).

Meanwhile, in the 40 years following the Civil War, a new political movement called **populism**, which emphasized the concerns of ordinary people, sprang up in the South and West. Farmers united against rate-gouging railroads, which monopolized the transportation of their goods to city markets, and banks, which charged high interest rates and seized farms for nonpayment of mortgages. Populist parties such as the Greenback party, the People's party, and the Farmers' Alliance of the 1880s and 1890s, which sought to take power away from the elites and give it to the people, were too small to win the presidency, but they siphoned off support from the Democratic party, which stood closest to them politically.

Populism collapsed after the election of 1896, when the Democrats nominated the People's party candidate, William Jennings Bryan, and lost, but in both major parties, **progressivism** flourished between the end of the nineteenth century and the First World War. This reform movement sought to remedy the problems of industrialization, urbanization, and agrarian poverty through limits on monopolies, the passage of labor laws, and improvements in the way government worked. When Theodore Roosevelt and fellow progressives broke with the Republican party in 1912 to run as the Progressive, or "Bull Moose," party, they won 27 percent of the vote. Even as late as 1924 the Progressive candidate, Robert La Follette, won 16 percent of the vote.

The Democrats' New Deal Coalition, 1932–1945

From the election of Lincoln in 1860, the Republicans controlled the presidency with only three interruptions until the election of Democrat Franklin D. Roosevelt in 1932. Roosevelt managed to hold on to the White House for the next 13 years, and his party held on to it for another 7 years after his death in office. What stopped the Republicans' winning streak?

This dramatic realignment, or shift in party loyalties (see the box nearby), was triggered by the stock market crash of 1929 and the Great Depression that followed. Almost one-third of the work force was unemployed. Roosevelt defeated Republican Herbert Hoover and then embarked on a "New Deal" consisting of programs that used government resources to create jobs and stimulate the economy. Beneficiaries of these programs formed a New Deal coalition that kept the Democrats in power for four straight elections. While Roosevelt continued to help small farmers—a traditional Democratic voting block until

> **populism**
> This term, from the Latin *populus*, meaning "the people," refers to the concerns of ordinary folk such as workers and small farmers, as opposed to the rich and powerful.
>
> **GOP**
> Republicans began using the initials for *grand old party* to refer to their party in the 1870s. Democrat Harry Truman liked to say they stood for "grand old platitudes."

Critical or Realigning Elections

A critical or realigning election is one in which voters shift party allegiance in ways that affect the political balance between the parties for a long period of time, bringing about major changes in what the parties stand for. An election that produces a critical realignment differs from maintaining elections, which do not disrupt power relations between the parties, and from deviating elections, which produce only temporary shifts in voter allegiance.

A critical, realigning election is a sign of upheaval and a major watershed in the nation's political history. So far, political scientists have identified five presidential elections in the country's history as critical, realigning elections. These elections are outlined below.

Party Realignment in Critical Elections

Election	President	Party	Party Realignment
1800	Jefferson	Democratic-Republican	Jefferson's victory ended Federalist control of the presidency and ushered in a quarter-century of Democratic-Republican party dominance.
1828	Jackson	Democrat	Jackson's victory shattered the National Republicans, established the Democrats as a major party, and prompted the creation of the Whig party.
1860	Lincoln	Republican	The Republicans replaced the Whigs as the second major party. For the next quarter-century the nation was divided between the pro-Republican North and pro-Democratic South.
1896	McKinley	Republican	The Republicans, now the party of business, hard money, and cities, defeated a coalition of Democrats and Populists, who represented farmers, the South, and the West.
1932	F. D. Roosevelt	Democrat	Roosevelt ended Republican party dominance by committing the federal government to an active role in promoting economic recovery from the Great Depression.

recent decades—his decision to strengthen labor unions with the National Labor Relations Act of 1935 (which legalized collective bargaining by unions with management) further polarized politics along class lines. Critics complained that inefficient government administrators had replaced the captains of industry as the nation's economic managers.

As divisions among the classes increased, regional party loyalties began to break down. The Great Depression led less well off Americans to flock to the Democrats, while the rich and middle-class professionals gravitated to the Republicans. Republicans were increasingly seen as the party of the rich, Democrats as the party of the poor. In later decades this image would haunt the Democrats, who still saw the poor as their natural constituency but who no longer wanted to be perceived as incapable of fostering prosperity for all.

The Postwar Era

Following World War II, the Democrats were still able to elect Harry Truman over Thomas Dewey in 1948—an election most people expected Dewey to win because the economic prosperity of the postwar period made poverty less of a campaign issue. But the issue of civil rights was tearing the New Deal Democratic coalition apart, turning blacks and liberals against white southerners and white labor. The segregationist States' Rights party—the "Dixiecrats"—won in southern states, and the progressive independent candidate Henry Wallace, who ran on a platform for world peace, attracted wide support from liberals, blacks, farmers, and labor. Despite these erosions of traditional Democratic supporters, Truman won by waging a tough campaign as an underdog.

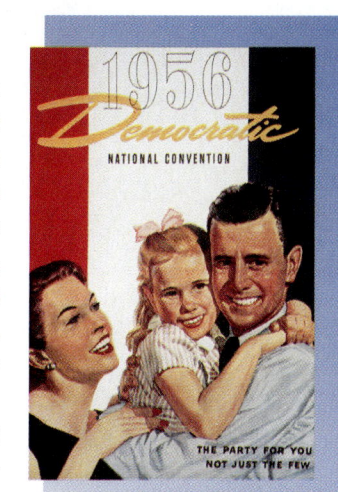

However, widespread corruption in the Truman administration and popular discontent with the Korean War, which had begun in 1950, led Republican General Dwight D. Eisenhower to an easy victory in 1952 that cut across class lines and further damaged the New Deal Democratic coalition. "Ike," as he was affectionately called, was reelected by a landslide in 1956 on a platform promising continued "peace, prosperity, and progress"—again, party goals that cut across class lines. Although Eisenhower's popularity won him eight years in office, the Republican party failed to elect his less popular vice president, Richard M. Nixon, to the presidency in 1960. Nixon's defeat in one of the closest presidential races in American history was partly due to an economic slowdown that revived the issue of class, but it was also due to the youthful charisma of Democrat John F. Kennedy, who pledged "to get this country moving again."

Vice president Lyndon Johnson became president when Kennedy was assassinated on November 22, 1963. Johnson, a protégé of Franklin D. Roosevelt, was then elected in 1964 on a populist platform that promised to revive the economy, help the poor, and keep the peace. Johnson quickly sent Congress dozens of proposals to solve domestic problems, but he also escalated the war in Vietnam. The military was then drafting all who lacked legitimate excuses or powerful connections—a policy that cut across class lines and scarred American families everywhere. With opposition to the war mounting and the nation bitterly divided, Johnson decided not to seek reelection in 1968.

The cover of the 1956 Democratic National Convention Program associates the party with the values of stability and conformity that predominated in the 1950s—values shared by Democrats and Republicans alike.

The Era of Divided Government

Republican Richard Nixon barely defeated Johnson's vice president Hubert Humphrey, but the Democrats retained control of both houses of Congress. Nixon won reelection in 1972 by appealing to issues that cut across class. In addition to his promise to "wind down" the war in Vietnam, he appealed to what he called the "silent majority" of Americans to support his "law-and-order" campaign against student radicals and school busing for racial integration—issues that splintered the old and aging New Deal coalition. But the Watergate scandal forced Nixon to resign in 1974 and hand over the presidency to Vice President Gerald Ford.

In 1976, during the worst recession since the 1930s, former Democratic governor of Georgia Jimmy Carter won the presidency by reviving the tra-

silent majority

In a speech, President Richard Nixon appealed to "the great silent majority of my fellow Americans" for support against the "vocal minority" of anti–Vietnam War dissidents. His claim that this majority existed (*what is*), that its views on Vietnam were *right*, and that he had the authority to speak for it, worked temporarily to bolster his Vietnam policy.

ditional Democratic coalition of white and black support in the South. But in 1980, with the economy again faltering and Carter's failure to free American diplomats taken hostage in Iran, many Democrats defected and helped to elect Republican Ronald Reagan, a former movie actor and governor of California.

Reagan had attracted a broad spectrum of voters and won a Republican majority in the Senate for the first time since 1954—an outcome he claimed gave him a popular mandate to change the direction of the country. He had promised to lower taxes, curb inflation, reduce unemployment, and strengthen defense with an economic reform program that became known as Reaganomics, which ultimately tripled the national debt. Democrats—especially those in the House of Representatives, which they still controlled—were in a quandary. If they obstructed Reagan's popular reforms, they stood to lose popularity. If they supported them, they stood to lose their traditional base of support. They tried to cover both flanks by refusing to fund new federal programs and by seeking tax relief for the poor and middle class as well as the wealthy. In 1984, with the economy booming again, Reagan easily won reelection. However, in the mid-term elections of 1986, the Democrats took advantage of government scandals to regain control of the Senate and increase their hold on the House. Ordinarily they would have been in a position to launch new spending programs that would have broadened their base of support, but the massive deficit and public resistance to raising taxes kept this impulse in check.

In 1988 George Bush, Reagan's vice president and a convert to conservatism, handily defeated Democratic Governor of Massachusetts Michael Dukakis. Bush's inaugural promise to make America a "kinder, gentler nation" took a back seat to foreign policy pursuits: the winding down of the Cold War, the invasion of Panama to unseat alleged drug kingpin and military dictator Manuel Noriega, and the Gulf War to oust Iraq from Kuwait following its invasion of that oil-rich sheikdom. By the campaign season of 1992, however, voters—many jobless and without health insurance—blamed Bush for what they saw as a faltering economy and turned to Democrat Bill Clinton, who promised change.

As we saw earlier, the failure of the Clinton administration and the Democratic-controlled Congress to work together effectively led to a Republican sweep in the 1994 congressional elections, perpetuated in 1996, and the return of divided government. In an effort to make his second term productive, Clinton called on party leaders to put partisanship aside and cooperate around "the vital center."

As major party leaders moved toward this "vital center," populists became more assertive. Candidates on the right (Pat Buchanan and David Duke), on the left (Jesse Jackson and Ralph Nader), and in the middle (Ross Perot) campaigned on populist themes, and some sought to form alliances. A key organizer expressed their anticorporate views this way: "We are ruled by big business and the government as its paid hireling, and we know it. The big corporations . . . have taken control of our work, our pay, our housing, our health, our pension funds, our bank and savings deposits, our public lands, our air waves, our elections, our very government. It's as if American democracy had been bombed." But how well these alliances will work is unclear. As another populist organizer put it, "Getting progressives together is kind of like loading frogs into a wheelbarrow."[25]

This campaign button for Republican presidential candidate George Bush associates him with four of the nation's most popular Republican presidents.

Third Parties in the Two-Party System

Presidential power has shifted between two major parties throughout American history, with third parties playing only a minor role in governance. (The Political Action Guide on page 246 describes these third parties and tells how to contact those that are still active.) Americans have become so used to the two-party system that until recently few have questioned its legitimacy. While they have a choice to vote for or against each party's candidates, they can't vote for or against the two-party system itself. This system operates like a vise, forcing voters to choose between two slates of candidates and squeezing out competition from third parties. As discontent with government leadership mounted in the 1990s, polls found large percentages of Americans favoring third party activity.[26] However, the prospect of a third party becoming a real alternative to the two dominant parties is unlikely due to the handicaps such a party faces.

Third-Party Handicaps

Three things have kept all third parties, with the exception of the Republicans, from becoming major players in the American party system over the last 200 years. First, although they can select candidates and run campaigns, third parties lack the power to reform the electoral process (which the major parties dominate) in order to level the playing field for all parties. Second, they lack money and media exposure. Finally, they lack legitimacy.

Electoral Handicaps

Because the American system of electing presidents requires successful presidential candidates to win separate primary elections in a large number of states around the country, a purely regional candidate or one who fails to build a strong national base cannot win. This difficulty drives most candidates to associate themselves with one of the two major parties, which have long-standing organizations in all 50 states.

In addition, the two major parties benefit from the fact that Americans elect most public officials in **single-member districts** by **plurality voting**. This system means that a district elects only one candidate to a public office and that the candidate who gets the most votes wins, even if his or her vote total is only a *plurality* (one vote more than the person in second place receives) rather than a *majority* (one vote more than 50 percent). In this winner-take-all system, only candidates belonging to the strongest parties can win. So, for example, a Libertarian running for the House of Representatives who receives 15 percent of the vote will lose the election as well as the right to any representation whatsoever in the House. Moreover, even if Libertarian candidates win 15 percent of the vote in *all* 435 congressional races, the party will still receive no representation in Congress. As a result, they can't promote their goals in office and thus gain more support. This feature of the current system has led some reformers to advocate proportional representation.

Political Action Guide

Parties Active in the United States Today

The Major Parties

Democratic Party (Democratic National Committee, 430 S. Capitol St. SE, Washington, D.C. 20003. http://www.democrats.org) Founded in its present form in 1848.

Republican Party (310 First St. SE, Washington, D.C. 20003. http://www.rnc.org) Founded in 1854.

Third Parties

Not all third parties have the same bases of support. Some are primarily ideological, some are single-issue, and some are factional.

Ideological parties are committed to political beliefs that differ sharply from those of the major parties. The most active of these parties today are:

Communist Party of the U.S.A. (239 West 23d St., New York, N.Y. 10011. http://www.hartfordhwp.com/cp.usa) Founded in 1919, this party seeks to abolish capitalism and redistribute wealth.

Libertarian Party (1528 Pennsylvania Ave. SE, Washington, D.C. 20003. http://www.lp.org) Founded in 1971, this party is committed to maximizing individual liberty, slashing big government, and privatizing the economy. Libertarian candidates on ballots at state and local levels sometimes cut into Republican strength to tip some elections toward the Democrats.

Natural Law Party (51 West Washington Ave., Fairfield, Iowa 52556) Founded in 1992 by supporters of the Maharishi Mahesh Yogi, this party seeks to employ knowledge and technologies such as Transcendental Meditation to harmonize human institutions with the laws of nature. It ran candidates for president and vice president in 35 states in 1992 and in all states in 1996.

New Alliance Party (200 West 72d St., Suite 30, New York, N.Y. 10023) Founded in 1988, this party managed to acquire enough signatures to get its presidential candidate, Lenora Fulani, on the ballot in every state and the District of Columbia and to acquire a significant amount of federal matching funds for its campaign. Although it did the same in 1992, Fulani did not run in 1996.

Socialist Labor Party (PO Box 50218, Palo Alto, Calif. 94303) Founded in 1891, this party seeks "the peaceful abolition of capitalism via the ballot, backed up by an industrial organization." It runs national and local candidates and publishes the newspaper *Weekly People*.

Socialist Party, USA (275 Seventh Ave., New York, N.Y. 10001. http://www.socialist.org) Formerly the Socialist party, this moderate socialist party founded in 1901 by Eugene V. Debs became the most successful socialist party in American history, attracting over a million votes in elections during the Great Depression.

Socialist Workers Party (14 Charles Lane, New York, N.Y. 10014) Founded in 1938, this party currently calls for economic revolution, feminist goals, and an end to racism. In 1980 it managed to get its presidential candidate on 29 state ballots but its influence has declined with the collapse of socialist states in Eastern Europe and the former Soviet Union.

Single-issue parties condense their politics into a single, often emotional, vision that attracts voters who agree with it. Today's most active single-issue parties are:

Green Parties of North America (1710 Connecticut Ave. NW, Washington, D.C. 20036) Founded in 1972, this party is affiliated with Green parties in European and other countries that are committed to environmental protection.

National Socialist White People's Party, formerly called the American Nazi party (2507 North Franklin Rd., Arlington, Va. 22201) Founded in 1959, this extreme right-wing party is composed of people who describe themselves as "White Americans of Aryan descent who accept the National Socialist teachings of Adolf Hitler without reservation and are willing to submit themselves to Party discipline." Its program, among other goals, calls for "A White America."

Prohibition Party (P.O. Box 2635, Denver, Colo. 80201) Founded in 1869 to oppose the consumption of alcohol, this party still runs presidential candidates.

Right-to-Life Party Founded in 1980, this party runs candidates who oppose abortion.

U.S. Taxpayers Party (450 Maple Ave. East, Vienna, Va. 22180. http://www.ustaxpayer.org) This party, which opposes taxes and abortion, was founded in 1992, and ran Howard Phillips as its candidate in 21 staes in 1992 and in 39 states in 1996.

Factional parties are those that have split off from an existing major party, usually to protest its presidential candidate. Today the main factional party that continues to field presidential candidates is a conservative party:

American Independent Party (8158 Palm St., Lemon Grove, Calif. 92045) In 1964, conservative Alabama governor George Wallace broke with the Democratic party to campaign for "law-and-order" and against school busing. Although the Republican party adopted much of this program, the party has continued to run presidential candidates.

Reform Party (http://www.reform-party.org) Founded in 1995 by Ross Perot, this party attracted voters from both major parties in 1996.

247

Lack of Money and Media Exposure

The media tend to neglect third-party candidates in favor of potential winners. Because third-party candidates get little free media coverage, it is harder for them to attract enough contributions to pay for ads that promote their positions. Moreover, the 1974 Federal Election Campaign Act (FECA), written by Republican and Democratic lawmakers, gives federal matching funds to major party presidential candidates *prior* to an election and to third parties candidates *after* the election, when it is too late to use them to improve their name recognition. To get any government funding at all, a party must have received at least 5 percent of the votes cast in the last election—a percentage that is extremely hard for a third party to meet. By winning 8 percent of the votes in the 1996, Perot's Reform party became eligible for federal financing in the year 2000. But he would have had to have won 25 percent to be eligible for funding equal to that of the two major parties.

Third-party candidates are also routinely excluded from the televised presidential and vice presidential debates—again, because those who decide who can participate are often major party leaders. The decision by the Commission on Presidential Debates to include Ross Perot and his running mate Admiral James Stockdale in the 1992 debates hinged on permission from the Bush and Clinton campaigns. The commission excluded the Libertarian candidates even though they were on the ballot in all 50 states. In 1996, when Perot asked to be included in the two presidential debates, the commission rejected him on grounds that his election was unrealistic—a conclusion it based on his showing of roughly 7 percent in the polls. Perot (who had refused to debate his underdog opponent Richard Lamm in the Reform party's national primary) fumed that "two registered puppies" were shutting "this cur dog" out of the debates.[27] He sued the commission in court, arguing that his receipt of federal funds entitled him to debate, but lost.

With the exception of billionaires like Perot, few independent and third party candidates can afford to fly around the country campaigning in private planes like the major candidates. In the 1988 primaries, a number of third-party candidates—

Four third-party presidential candidates take advantage of the free nationwide TV exposure provided by CNN's "Larry King Live" in July 1996: (*from left to right*) King, Harry Brown (Libertarian party), Ralph Nader (Green party), John Hagelin (Natural Law party), and Howard Phillips (U.S. Taxpayers party).

whose ideologies clashed but whose pockets were equally empty—got together and chartered a plane. This cooperation enabled them to visit college campuses as a group, where they delivered ideologically different campaign messages from the same podium. In 1996, several of the most prominent third-party candidates, who had also been excluded from the presidential debates, aired their views on Larry King's TV show following each of the two debates and following King's solo interview with Perot.

Lack of Legitimacy

Third parties also lack legitimacy. Most Americans still view particular third parties—especially those out of the ideological mainstream—as disruptive. Although they increasingly endorse the *idea* of a third party, few Americans believe in changing the system to equalize competition among the major and minor parties. A 1980 study showed that only 1 in 100 identified with a third party.[28] Even the Supreme Court has done little to help third parties gain a more equal electoral footing. Third parties won 64 percent of their cases during the Court's more liberal era—the 1950s and 1960s—compared with 27 percent in the Court's more conservative succeeding decades.[29] In 1997 the Court dealt third parties a further setback by upholding a Minnesota ban on fusion tickets—the practice of permitting candidates to appear on more than one party's ballot. Such cross-endorsements were common in many states before the major parties succeeded in banning them. In handing down the decision, Chief Justice Rehnquist declared: "the Constitution permits the Minnesota legislature to decide that political stability is best served through a healthy two-party system."[30]

Third Parties Still Matter

Despite sizable handicaps, third parties and independent candidates often affect election outcomes, even though they cannot win in the present system (see Table 7.2). Of the last 38 presidential contests, 16 victors (40 percent) failed to win with popular majorities—most recently Bill Clinton in 1992 and 1996.[31] Third parties also take stands or back policy innovations that eventually find their way into the programs of one or both of the major parties. The major parties often adopt proposals first made by third parties in order to attract more voters and thereby limit the appeal of the party that originally sponsored the proposal. The 1996 Democratic and Republican platforms incorporated the goal of deficit reduction that Perot's campaign organization had called for in 1992 and his Reform party was calling for in 1996. Some say that third parties may actually strengthen democracy and the performance of the two-party system by pressuring the major parties to listen to the disaffected: third parties "are a weapon citizens can use to force the major parties to be more accountable. . . . They represent the needs and demands of Americans whom the major parties have ignored." If this is so, then those who vote for third parties may not necessarily be "throwing away" their votes, as they are often criticized for doing. One specialist even asserts that those who have cast their votes for third parties throughout American history have probably cast the most powerful votes of all.[32]

TABLE 7.2

Third Party Issues Adopted by Major Parties

Third-Party Platform(s) and Issues	Adaption in Major Party Platform(s)	Subsequent Enactment: Constitutional Amendment or Congressional Statute
Prohibition party (late nineteenth century)		
Prohibition	—	Eighteenth Amendment (1919) (repealed by Twenty-first Amendment, 1933)
Woman suffrage	Democratic (1916); Republican (1916)	Nineteenth Amendment (1920)
Direct election of senators	Democratic (1908)	Seventeenth Amendment (1913)
Populist (People's) party (1892)		
Direct election of senators	Democratic (1908)	Seventeenth Amendment (1913)
Free coinage of silver	Democratic (1896)	Defeat of issue with passage of Gold Standard Act (1900)
Immigration restrictions	Democratic (1896)	Many statutes, particularly in early 1920s
(Graduated) income tax	Democratic (1908)	Sixteenth Amendment (1913) and subsequent legislation
Shorter working hours	Democratic (1908)	Wages and Hours Act (1935);
Socialist party (1904–1912)		
Woman suffrage	Democratic (1916); Republican (1916)	Nineteenth Amendment (1920)
(Graduated) income tax	Democratic (1908)	Sixteenth Amendment (1913) and subsequent legislation
Shorter working hours	Democratic (1908)	Wages and Hours Act (1938)
Socialist party (1928)		
Public works and unemployment insurance for the unemployed	Democratic (1932, 1936)	Statutes passed in 1933
American Independent party (1968)		
Toughness on crime	Republican (1968)	Omnibus Crime Control and Safe Streets Act (1968) and subsequent legislation
Perot's United We Stand, America (1992)		
Deficit reduction	Democratic (1996); Republican (1996)	FY 1998 budget agreement (between President Clinton and Republican-controlled Congress)

Source: Adapted from J. David Gillespie, *Politics at the Periphery: Third Parties in Two-Party America* (Columbia: University of South Carolina Press, 1993), 26–27.

The Two-Party System Today

During the 1970s and 1980s scholars, journalists, and party pros joined in what one observer called "an almost universal chorus to sing of the . . . weakening, decline, and decomposition" of the two-party system.[33] When the Republicans ran ultraconservative Barry Goldwater for president in 1964 and were trounced, some said the Republican party was finished because it had been captured by the right. Four years later its moderate standard-bearer Richard Nixon won. In the next election, when Nixon trounced ultraliberal George McGovern, some said the Democrats were finished because they had been captured by the left. But moderate Jimmy Carter regained the White House for them four years later. Also, following Republican post-Watergate defeats in 1974, pundits wrongly predicted that the Republicans would become a permanent minority party.

Some asserted that Reagan's and Bush's 12-year dominance of the presidency signaled the death of the Democratic party, only to see Clinton beat Bush in 1992. Others cited the continuing weakness of Republicans in Congress and in many states as evidence that the Republicans were no longer a truly national party, only to see them gain control of both houses of Congress and a majority of state governments in 1994 and 1996. Still others pointed to the steady decrease in voter turnout since the Kennedy–Nixon election of 1960 as a sign that both parties were in decline, until turnout actually increased in 1992. Two commentators observed, "we do not know if major parties are failing because they are ideologically out of touch with their electorates, poorly organized, underfinanced, badly led, nonaccountable, corrupt, overwhelmed by unethical or fanatical competition, unable to rule effectively, or some combination of these factors."[34] Whether—beneath all these vacillations—the two-party system is indeed declining or whether it is merely undergoing major changes remains the subject of lively debate.

Research now suggests that predictions of decline may have been premature. By the mid-1980s, some specialists asserted that parties were never really strong in the past and that truly national parties were only then beginning to emerge.[35] Optimists claim that the major parties are in the process of recapturing voter loyalty by reaching out to traditional party voters (as the Republicans did with their "Contract with America") as well as to new or previously underrepresented constituencies—particularly women, African Americans, and Latinos. The major parties also appear to be revitalizing their organizational capabilities at the national level by making better use of technological innovations such as databases and electronic mail.[36] Or the parties may merely be realigning—changing in ways that will eventually stabilize the party system. But even if the party system stabilizes, many fear that the lack of party discipline characteristic of weak parties will result in ongoing divided government and gridlock.[37]

Signs of Failure

Voter dissatisfaction with major parties is worldwide. In the United States experts blame party troubles on a variety of factors. Parties, as we saw above, have lost control of the nominating process and have lost respect due to divided government and gridlock. In addition, political action committees and special interest groups lure candidates away from the political center, where the parties want them to be, with promises of financial, organizational, and voter support. Disaffected voters are dealigning (detaching) themselves from parties in ever greater numbers, and many are practicing politics through social movements such as direct action groups, economic co-ops, food banks, clinics, and counseling centers.

Dealignment—what one political scientist calls the "onward march of party decomposition"[38]—seems to occur during political upheavals that cut across party lines and affect vast segments of society. For example, voters' disenchantment with parties rose markedly in the wake of the Vietnam War, the Watergate scandal, and the racial turmoil of the 1960s, as was clear from the 10 percent drop in voter turnout between 1960 and 1988, the doubling of voters calling themselves independents between 1964 and 1974, and the continuing decline in registration over the same period. In 1988 only half of those eligible to vote actually did so. These developments even led some observers to speak of a "nonvoter party."[39] Other political scientists view dealignment as evidence that parties are growing stronger.[40] They argue that dealignment forces parties to improve their organization and to get better at mobilizing and persuading voters.[41] They also fault voting-behavior studies for assuming that voters are as important for party viability as party organization.

There may also be a connection between declining partisanship and the arrival of a new, more educated generation that doesn't like being told how to vote by party elites. These voters are more inclined to vote a **split ticket** (that is, select candidates from both parties for different offices in a single election) instead of the automatic **straight ticket** (voting for the entire "party slate" of candidates). Today ticket-splitters—even the strongly partisan—are common in national elections and growing in state and local elections. Below the presidential level, where voters often know little more than the candidate's party affiliation, most partisans stick to their party's ticket, whereas independents split tickets regularly.

Signs of Life: Reaching Out

Because both major parties have been losing support among their traditional constituencies, they are reaching out to women and ethnic minorities.

Women

After women received the right to vote in 1920, neither party did much to welcome them.[42] The one exception was the Democrats' decision that year and the Republicans' decision in 1924 to represent men and women equally on their national committees. This policy has continued and been extended to many party committees at the state and local levels. Before World War II, women had only a small voice in national conventions, serving mainly as alternates who only participate when delegates leave the convention floor. Not until the McGovern Reforms of 1972 did women's status in the Democratic party really improve. This improvement grew out of the feminist movement of the 1960s and 1970s and major changes in American society: a large increase in numbers of working women, a

Representative Susan Molinari delivers the keynote address at the 1996 Republican National Convention in San Diego. In June 1997 Molinari resigned from Congress to become a TV news commentator.

delay in marriage age, and lower birth rates—all changes that fostered an increase in women's political activism. These changes pressured the Republicans to allow more women to participate, but rather than mandating quotas, Republicans have formally recommended that state organizations try to represent women and minorities in proportion to their numbers in the population. In 1988, however, the 50-year-old National Federation of Republican Women, a group subsidized by the Republican National Committee to organize the women's vote, was granted a seat on the 28-member RNC Executive Council. It is the only women's group in the party to have its own Washington office and a permanent president.

But formal equality does not necessarily ensure equal political power. True, more women now run for and are appointed to public office, almost half of local school boards are composed of women, and in the 1990s more women than ever made it into Congress. Still, the number of women in leadership positions dramatically declines as the power of the office increases. In 1984 the National Organization for Women (NOW) and other women's groups helped to get Democrat Geraldine Ferraro on the presidential ticket as Walter Mondale's running mate, but no woman has yet been elected president or vice president, and no woman has run on either major party ticket since Ferraro.

In the presidential elections of 1992 and 1996, a growing **gender gap**—the tendency for women voters to be less supportive than men of Republican candidates and for men to be less supportive than women of Democratic candidates—was evident as moderate Republican women, who constitute a large part of the party mainstream, deserted Bush and Dole because the party opposed abortion and favored cutting federal programs affecting families (Table 6.4). Dole tried but failed to get their support with symbolic gestures, such as inviting a young abortion-rights moderate, Representative Susan Molinari of New York, to give the keynote address at the national convention. The gender gap was especially pronounced in the South, where a large majority of white men supported Republicans while moderate women chose Democrats.

African Americans

African-American voters identified with the Republican party of Lincoln up until the 1930s but then shifted to the Democrats. Figure 7.5 depicts the history of this race gap. Democrats took an interest in African Americans only after they took jobs in the industrial North. In the southern states, blacks were excluded from voting by poll taxes and literacy tests and thus had no power in party organizations, which were controlled by segregationist white Democrats (Chapter 6). It was not until 1936 that a black delegate was seated at the Democratic National Convention and not until 1948 that the party took a lukewarm stand in favor of civil rights for blacks. With the passage of the Civil Rights Act in 1964, the party's black membership shot up. But no president since Lyndon Johnson has won a majority of both white and black votes in a general election—not even southerner Jimmy Carter, who lost the majority of white votes but still won the presidency in 1976 thanks to a large majority of black votes. Yet even in northern urban areas African Americans were excluded from the party hierarchy.

Since then, some African Americans have attempted to amplify their voices by switching party allegiance. Frustrated by their failure to advance economically under the Democrats during the 1970s, some shifted to the Republican party as "Freedom Americans." As a spokeswoman for the group explained, "Democrats don't need to bait the hook if they already got the fish. . . . They love to have us in

FIGURE 7.5

Republicans and the race gap

Beginning with the Civil War, black voters allied themselves with the Republican party up until the 1930s. Here is a look at how they have voted since then, and which party they have identified with.

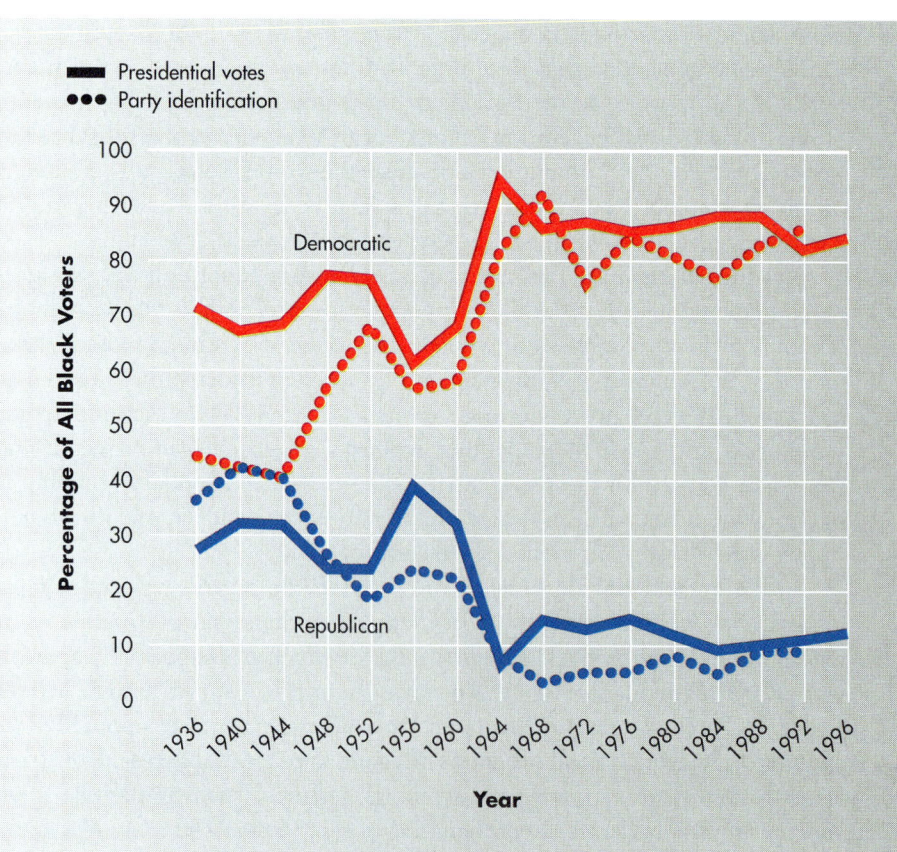

Source: Joint Center for Political and Economic Studies, reported in *New York Times*, September 19, 1996, A16. Voter data for 1996 from Voters News Service.

their party, but they're not going to vote for any of us."[43] In 1980 Ralph Abernathy, leader of the Southern Christian Leadership Conference (SCLC) founded by the Reverend Martin Luther King, Jr., abandoned the "Democrats only" strategy and supported Reagan. However, in 1984 African Americans joined the Democrats in droves to support the presidential campaign of the African-American Jesse Jackson, who conducted effective registration drives everywhere he went. Today, a host of African-American mayors and state and national legislators hold public office nationwide, some in part because they attract a significant percentage of white voters.

In 1992 blacks backed Clinton, and Jesse Jackson stumped for him, despite the fact that his policies were aimed at pleasing the middle class. Blacks still supported Clinton in 1996, despite his signing of a welfare law that they and other liberals strongly opposed, because they felt they had no promising alternative. But angry attacks on Clinton and the Democrats as "the lesser of two evils" were broadcast on black radio and TV stations across the country.

Latinos

Thirty years ago Latinos were not a major force in American politics.[44] This situation is rapidly changing. Today Latinos are the fastest-growing ethnic group in the country and are widely predicted to become the largest ethnic group early in the twenty-first century. Until recently, Latinos have had less clout at the ballot box than the population as a whole for two reasons: youth and noncitizenship. The Latino population is younger than other ethnic groups. In 1992, 34 percent of this population was under 18 and so could not vote. Twenty percent are between 18 and 24, the age group with the lowest voter turnout. (This age group is only 14 percent of the population as a whole.) In addition, only 19 percent of Latinos are in the 55 and older age group—the group with the highest voter turnout nationally—compared to 30 percent of the national as a whole. Finally, Latino voter turnout has tended to be low, especially in primaries, compared with that of the overall population.[45]

In 1992 more than 4 out of 10 adult Latinos (roughly 6 million) were resident aliens or illegal aliens and were thus ineligible to vote. In contrast, only 11 percent of whites and 8 percent of blacks could not vote in 1992 because they lacked citizenship. Specialists say that noncitizenship will remain the largest obstacle to Latino voting strength throughout the 1990s. Yet the potential strength of Latinos, especially as noncitizens become citizens who register and vote, is great. The passage of a stringent immigration law in 1996 at the urging of Republicans has given noncitizens a strong incentive to seek citizenship.

Most Latinos register as Democrats or vote for Democrats, and they are more widely represented in that party's organizations than in Republican organizations.[46] (An exception is the Cuban population in Miami, whose large percentage of upper-middle-class professionals usually vote Republican, although Clinton has wooed some of them away with his harsh policy against Castro's Cuba.) Latinos routinely show high levels of support for presidential candidates. In 1988, 70 percent turned out for Michael Dukakis, who could speak Spanish, as well as for congressional candidates.

In 1992, 92 percent of elected Latino officials who identified with a party called themselves Democrats in comparison with 8 percent who called themselves Republicans, although many were elected to local, nonpartisan offices. Figure 7.6

Loretta Sanchez defeated ultraconservative Republican Robert J. Dornan in their 1996 California race for a House seat by such a narrow margin that he contested the election, accusing her campaign of obtaining illegal votes. She is the only Latino in the House.

FIGURE 7.6

Distribution of Latino elected officials, January 1997

The charts show the characteristics of these 4825 officials by (a) party affiliation, (b) state, (c) gender, and (d) level of office.

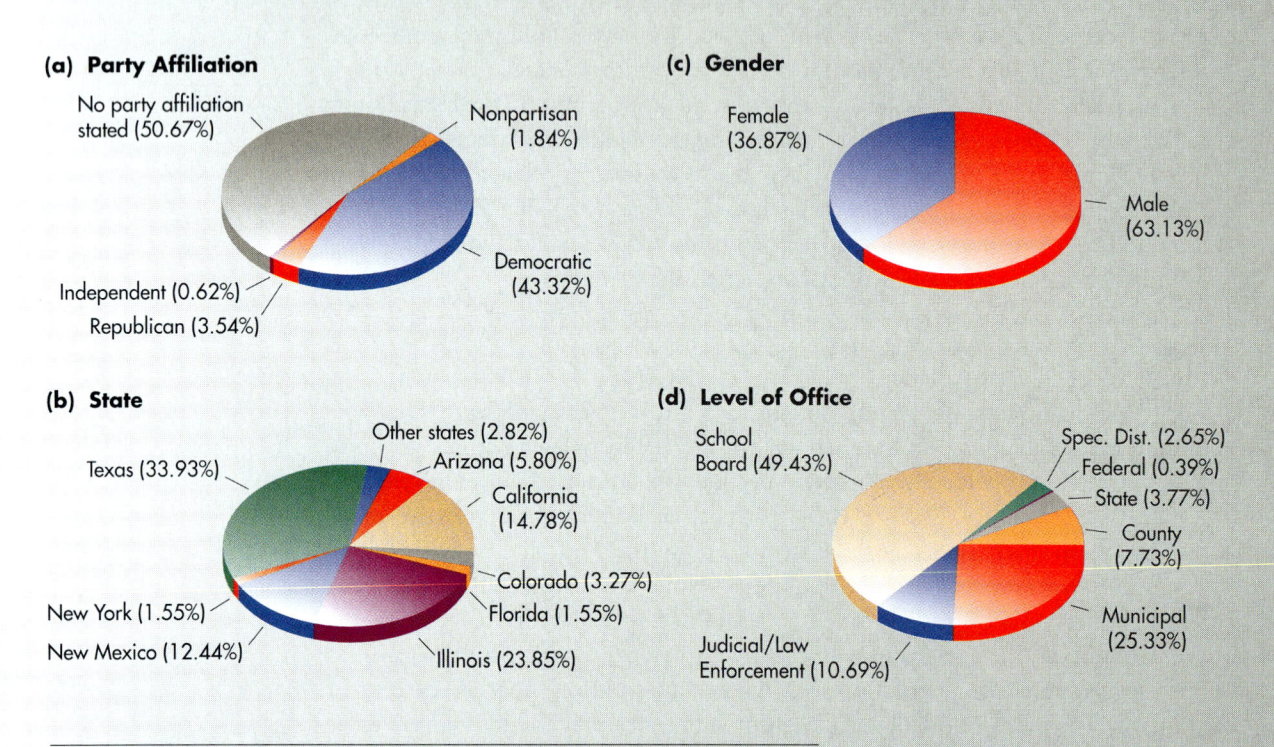

(a) Party Affiliation
- No party affiliation stated (50.67%)
- Nonpartisan (1.84%)
- Democratic (43.32%)
- Independent (0.62%)
- Republican (3.54%)

(b) State
- Texas (33.93%)
- Other states (2.82%)
- Arizona (5.80%)
- California (14.78%)
- Colorado (3.27%)
- Florida (1.55%)
- Illinois (23.85%)
- New Mexico (12.44%)
- New York (1.55%)

(c) Gender
- Female (36.87%)
- Male (63.13%)

(d) Level of Office
- School Board (49.43%)
- Spec. Dist. (2.65%)
- Federal (0.39%)
- State (3.77%)
- County (7.73%)
- Municipal (25.33%)
- Judicial/Law Enforcement (10.69%)

Source: National Association of Latino Elected Officials, *National Roster of Hispanic Elected Officials.*

shows party identification for Latino elected officials in 1997 as well as percentages of Latino officials by state, gender, and level of office. Between 1984 and 1993, the number of Latino elected officials at all levels of government increased by about 41 percent. Twenty percent of these officials at the national level are women, while in Latino communities women hold 30 percent of these posts. In the 1980s, 9 of the 10 Latinos in Congress were Democrats, and 9 more won election to the House in 1992 (8 of them Democrats). In 1996, 18 Latinos won election to the House.

Reforming the American Party System

The two proposals described in the box nearby for reforming the American party system—the responsible party government model used by parliamentary systems and the party realignment model based on strong ideological or other interests—are unlikely prospects because they are out of step with American political culture. Only the multiparty alternative receives serious debate.

Two Models for Reforming the Party System

Responsible Party Government

Advocates of responsible party government want two strong parties that are accountable to American voters. The parties would pledge themselves to a particular program and compel their members to vote for and implement it. This way voters would know in advance what they were getting, and if their party disappointed them, they could oust it at the next election. Politics would become more issue-oriented and predictable, and special interests would cease to be major players in the system. But critics say such a system would be unstable, confrontational, and lead to an inflexible Congress. They also fear that lawmakers, who are now relatively independent and deliberative, would lose the freedom to legislate as their reason and conscience dictate, as well as the power to serve as a check on the president or the executive branch when they believe this is necessary.

Party Realignment

If the party realignment reform were adopted within the two-party system, voters would attach themselves to the parties on the basis of some widespread distinction such as economic class or political ideology. If they chose class, this might produce an upper- and middle-class party of wealthy businesspeople and professionals and a working-class party of labor and intellectuals.[1] If they chose ideology, the outcome would group conservatives in one party and moderates and liberals in the other. Such a reform could deepen class and ideological divisions and make it harder to achieve consensus on policy and other matters.

[1] For an examination of this proposal, see David Broder, *The Party's Over* (New York: Harper & Row, 1972).

Is a Multiparty System Right for America? Experts Disagree

Does a strong two-party system make for "a healthier, stronger government?"[47] Some experts believe that the unifying and stabilizing character of the two-party system counterbalances the fragmentation of government resulting from the separation of powers and checks and balances that the Framers designed to frustrate would-be despots. While the Framers may have protected the country from despots, supporters of the two-party system say they also made it hard for leaders to govern effectively and therefore created the need for the coalition-forming powers of the major parties. Parties thus work to counter the fragmentation that the Framers built into the political system.[48] A nineteenth-century political theorist summed this view up nicely when he said that checks and balances "balance the government only," while parties "balance society itself." Conflict between the major parties, he argued, has the positive effect of sifting opinions through a great many minds so that when they become public policy they do not take society by surprise.[49]

In contrast, proponents of third parties view the major parties as the sort of despots the Framers sought to avoid, arguing that in a healthy democracy all parties should compete on an equal basis. Their argument resembles Madison's view in *The Federalist*, No. 10, that an interplay of competing interests would prevent a few large interests from dominating politics. However, political scientists who support the two-party system have interpreted Madison's assertion as expressing the need for precisely the kind of broad coalition-building that major parties must undertake to win. They even use the term "Madisonian" to describe the way major parties often get competing groups to make concessions that reduce conflict between rich and poor and other sectors of society.[50] Madison, they say, would have criticized third-party politicians who refuse to compromise and accommodate other interests. Because defenders of third parties prefer parties that take clear stands and stick by them, they view coalition-building politicians as opportunists who cloud the differences among groups just to get elected.

How Would a Multiparty System Work in America?

At first glance, a **multiparty system** seems much fairer than the present system because it would allow parties to be represented in government based on their strength among voters. Voters would be able to choose from a greater number of smaller parties, which would furnish clearer choices and coherent policy agendas, and seats in Congress would probably be allocated by proportional representation (PR). So why don't Americans shift to this system? Because the issue of fair representation is actually more complicated.

Proportional Representation Would Limit Regional and Local Representation

Critics of PR point out that it would limit the regional and local representation of the current electoral system, because candidates selected to represent minority parties would come from national lists rather than local districts. As the Anti-Federalists pointed out long ago, the political interests of regions vary. The major parties try to address these differences by recruiting candidates and backing issues that voters in those regions support, and they often try to nominate presidential candidates with particular regional strengths. In the South, Republicans have increasingly dominated presidential elections and have been acquiring a greater number of congressional seats by opposing abortion and supporting prayer in public schools—which would be unpopular with many Republicans, let alone Democrats, in the Northeast. And in the Northeast and the Midwest, Democrats have maintained their strength by supporting the concerns of labor and urban ethnic groups. Republican strength in the South has also been helped by choosing southern white male candidates, while Democratic strength in the Northeast has been helped by recruiting union members and African-American candidates.

Proportional Representation Tends to Foster Shaky Governments

Proportional representation has also been considered to produce shaky governments by fostering too many parties and too much competition among them. Parties must usually form coalitions to rule, and governments run by coalitions tend to be unstable because any of the parties in a ruling coalition may become disaffected over a particular issue and pull out of these temporary alliances or, worse, defect to the opposing side. The examples of numerous Western European governments have not been lost on American political experts or on many of these governments themselves, which have modified their systems of proportional representation in the direction of winner-take-all systems. In these modified systems, European parties are forced to form coalitions *before* rather than after elections—something that limits representation but promotes stability.

The Current Electoral System Promotes Broader Representation and Stability

The American electoral system promotes stability by favoring the strongest parties. To be strong, a party must attract as many voters as possible. Thus the parties are compelled to win the confidence of a variety of groups, such as liberals, conservatives, men, women, ethnic minorities, labor, business, environmentalists, pro-life, pro-choice, young, and old. Many in these groups will decide to support a major party that does not fully represent their interests but can win rather than a minor party that strongly represents their interests but is destined to lose.

By contrast, the smaller, more ideologically coherent parties fostered in PR systems are likely to be dominated by a particular special interest and run by a committed elite and its own experts. This situation can increase the power gap between elites and experts on the one hand and elites and ordinary citizens on the other, thereby decreasing the opportunities for popular participation in government. Furthermore, the bargaining among many small parties required to form a coalition government tends to give vetoes over many policy options to small ideologically committed groups whose votes are vital to the coalition. Thus ordinary citizens might lose even more power and representation under PR than under a two-party system. For the time being, then, it is likely that the American party system with its two dominant parties and array of third parties is likely to continue very much as it is.

Bill Clinton, a delegate to the American Legion's Boys' Nation in July 1963, shakes hands with President John F. Kennedy at the White House.

Summary

The American party system is dominated by two major parties: the Republicans and the Democrats. This two-party system is associated with the presidential system of government, while multiparty systems are associated with parliamentary systems of government. In the two-party system, the presidency may be controlled by one party and one or both houses of Congress may be controlled by the other party—a situation that produces divided government and often gridlock.

Defenders of the two-party system say these parties perform the indispensable functions of (1) aggregating political interests, (2) recruiting qualified candidates and organizing the electoral process, and (3) formulating and implementing public policy. Critics say the system is unrepresentative, domineering, and fails to give voters authentic choices of candidates and policies. Third party and independent candidates complain that they cannot win in this system because they lack the power to reform the electoral process, money and media exposure, and legitimacy. Above all, they lose because the winner-take-all rules of the electoral system—single-member districts and plurality voting—benefit the major parties.

While both parties have been moving toward the right, they attract quite different constituencies. The Republican party tends to appeal to conservatives, businesspeople, and those who want to downsize government, while the Democratic party tends to appeal to liberals, labor, minorities, and those who want government to play an active role in problem-solving. Yet both parties are strikingly similar in (1) their inability to control membership and foster party loyalty, (2) their common dependence upon party activists–loyalists as well as professionals, (3) the common *federal* structure of their organizations at the national, state and local levels, and (4) their tendency to resort to a strategy of convergence on ideological issues in general elections. Both parties are also divided by internal ideological divisions.

Another similarity is that elites in both parties lost significant power when the parties replaced the practice of nominating candidates by secret party caucuses with the direct primary system. However, the Republicans adopted winner-take-all primaries while the Democrats adopted primaries based on proportional representation and state nominating caucuses. Democrats also reformed the rules governing the selection of delegates to their national convention. The McGovern Reforms that took effect in 1972 opened the process to women, minorities, and other underrepresented groups. Party elites later watered down these reforms when they produced candidates too far to the left to win in the general election. Still, these reforms and the party's support and passage of civil rights legislation have attracted more women and minorities to the Democratic than to the Republican party.

Both major parties also share a common history. Emerging in a climate hostile to parties, they built coalitions in Congress and in the electorate and formed party organizations at all levels of government. National parties underwent a number of changes until Lincoln's Republican victory in 1860, which divided the country into the anti-slavery Republican north and the pro-slavery Democratic south. Regional competition between the two parties was interrupted in 1932 by 20 years of the New Deal coalition under Democrats Franklin D. Roosevelt and Harry Truman, and until the Democrats generally dominated Congress, while the Republicans have tended to dominate the presidency.

Increasing dealignment and the rise of independents have weakened both parties, but political experts disagree over whether the major parties are in permanent decline or simply undergoing a slow realignment. The signs of decline in recent decades include (1) loss of control over the nomination process, (2) divided government and gridlock, and (3) competition from PACs, special interests, and social movements. The signs of life include reaching out to new constituencies. While proponents of third parties would like to replace the two-party system with a multiparty system and proportional representation, the more stable and regionally representative American two-party system is likely to endure.

Key Terms

blanket primary **236**
closed primary **236**
dealignment **225**
direct primary **234**
divided government **221**
gender gap **253**
general election **236**
gridlock **222**
major party **221**
majority party **224**
McGovern Reforms **225**
multiparty system **258**

national conventions **231**
nonsecret caucus **236**
open primary **236**
partisans **228**
party identification **225**
party loyalists **224**
party loyalty **225**
party professionals **224**
party system **221**
plurality voting **245**
political party **221**
political spectrum **228**

populism **241**
progressivism **241**
realignment **225**
secret party caucus **234**
single-member districts **245**
split ticket **252**
straight ticket **252**
strategy of convergence **230**
superdelegates **225**
third party **221**
two-party system **221**

How You Can Learn More About Political Parties

Baer, Denise L., and David A. Bositis. *Elite Cadres and Party Coalitions: Representing the Public in Party Politics.* Westport, Conn.: Greenwood Press, 1988. A critical look at why various party theorists conflict in their assessments of parties and an analysis of how new coalitions of elites may be affecting the party system.

Black, Gordon S., and Benjamin D. Black. *The Politics of American Discontent: How a New Party Can Make Democracy Work Again.* New York: John Wiley, 1994. An analysis of recent political trends making the argument that a new party could be effective.

Cox, Gary W., and Samuel Kernell, eds. *The Politics of Divided Government.* Boulder, Colo.: Westview Press, 1991. Essays on the causes and consequences of divided government and the role the major parties play in it.

Epstein, Leon D. *Political Parties in the American Mold* Madison: University of Wisconsin Press, 1986. A look at how scholarship has affected our understanding of parties and an argument that parties are inherently imperfect but necessary institutions.

Gillespie, J. David. *Politics at the Periphery: Third Parties in Two-Party America.* Columbia: University of South Carolina Press, 1993. A comprehensive examination of the history and nature of significant third parties in the United States.

Hoadley, John F. *Origins of American Political Parties, 1789–1803.* Lexington: University Press of Kentucky, 1986. A compelling picture of how parties emerged from the preparty coalitions dating from the Federalists and the Anti-Federalists and how they solidified during the First Congress.

Huckfeldt, Robert, and Carol Weitzel Kohfeld. *Race and the Decline of Class in American Politics.* Urbana: University of Illinois Press, 1989. A study of the effects of race and class on political parties.

Lunch, William M. *The Nationalization of American Politics.* Berkeley: University of California Press, 1987. A condensed account of party history and power shifts in the party system and an analysis of how the nationalized parties are faring in today's government.

McSweeney, Dean, and John Zvesper. *American Political Parties: The Formation, Decline and Reform of the American Party System.* New York: Routledge, 1991. One of the clearest and most concise critical accounts of the history and dynamics of the American party system.

Maisel, Sandy L., ed. *The Parties Respond: Changes in the American Party System.* Boulder, Colo.: Westview Press, 1990. Essays by various experts on parties, on topics ranging from party history and changes in party organization to the function of parties in government and the electoral arena.

Pomper, Gerald M. *Voters, Elections and Parties: The Practice of Democratic Theory.* New Brunswick, N.J.: Transaction Books, 1988. An argument, in Part 3, that currently weak parties must be strengthened in the interests of a healthy democracy.

Rosenstone, Steven J., Roy L. Behr, and Edward H. Lazarus. *Third Parties in America: Citizen Response to Major Party Failure.* Princeton, N.J.: Princeton University Press, 1984. A lucid account of why third parties fail at the ballot box but succeed in influencing the major parties and thus strengthening the party system.

Shafer, Byron E. *Bifurcated Politics: Evolution and Reform in the National Party Convention.* Cambridge, Mass.: Harvard University Press, 1988. A look at how the nomination process has progressed from secret caucuses to open primaries, reducing the national party convention to the nominator of last resort.

Shafer, Byron E., ed. *The End of Realignment: Interpreting American Electoral Eras.* Madison: University of Wisconsin Press, 1991. Essays by leading scholars debating the concept of realignment.

Sundquist, James L. *Dynamics of the Party System.* 2d ed. Washington, D.C.: Brookings Institution, 1983. An analysis of the historical development of the American party system.

Interest Groups

Above: Actress Meryl Streep testifies in March 1989 on behalf of the Natural Resources Defense Council at a congressional hearing on the dangers to children of apples treated with the pesticide Alar. *Right*: Scientist Bruce Ames defends the safety of apples treated with Alar, October 1988.

CHAPTER 8

> Within minutes of the time I conclude my address to Congress Wednesday night, the special interests will be out in force. Those who profited from the status quo will oppose the changes we seek. . . . Many have already lined the corridors of power with high-priced lobbyists.
>
> **President Bill Clinton, 1993**

> Congress shall make no law . . . abridging [limiting] . . . the right of the people peaceably to assemble, and to petition the Government for a redress of grievances.
>
> **First Amendment to the U.S. Constitution**[1]

What Are Interest Groups?

How Interest Groups Work

Are Interest Groups Right for America?

Monitoring and Regulating Interest Groups

The old adage "An apple a day keeps the doctor away" was called into question on February 26, 1989, on the CBS news program "60 Minutes." The controversy sparked that Sunday night grew into a classic demonstration of how interest groups operate in tandem with other actors—government agencies, the media, and the courts—to achieve their objectives.

"60 Minutes" reported a finding by the Natural Resources Defense Council (NRDC)—an environmentalist group—that the pesticide Alar, then used on red apples, posed "an intolerable risk" of cancer in children. Uniroyal, Alar's manufacturer, instantly denied the charge, as did the apple-growing industry and the U.S. Environmental Protection Agency (EPA). As the conflict accelerated, consumers were caught in the crossfire, and the apple industry faced a financial disaster.

- **The environmentalists' claims** The NRDC had paid a public relations firm $40,000 to get its version of the facts about Alar on "60 Minutes" and then on the "Donahue" talk show. It also delivered its message in TV ads, including one in which Meryl Streep—chair of the NRDC's Mothers and Others for Pesticide Limits—scrubbed vegetables at a kitchen sink while explaining to a little boy why such care was necessary. The NRDC also publicized evidence that the EPA planned to ask the apple-growing industry for a two-year phase-out of the use of Alar, indicating that the federal agency was worried about its long-term effects.

- **The industries' response** Before the "60 Minutes" segment had ended, a representative of the apple growers was phoning a leading Washington, D.C., public relations firm to plan a response. Soon a million-dollar media blitz carried the message "An apple a day is still good advice." To ward off future threats, the growers also launched a multimillion-dollar public relations campaign, "Food Watch—Safe, Abundant Food for All." The campaign's TV spot aired on Thanksgiving Day 1990, featuring what one of its producers described as "families and feasting, Grandma and apple pie, and Judy Collins [singing] . . . 'Amazing Grace' with the Mormon Tabernacle Choir . . . in the background."[2] The twenty-year-old Agriculture Council, a private group representing agribusiness companies, joined in. William F. Kirk, chair of the council and head of international sales of agricultural chemicals at du Pont, launched a campaign to bolster consumer confidence in food producers across the board—a campaign one employee described as developing "relationships with key media people and feeding them a steady diet of pro-industry information."[3] Council-supplied reading informed lawmakers that food technology could both solve world hunger and protect the environment.
- **The EPA's position** The EPA's policy was intended to accommodate its two conflicting official duties: guarding the public's interest by establishing and monitoring safe tolerance levels for pesticides in and on food, and balancing that interest against the needs of the industries and others it must regulate. The agency recognized that pesticides might be a health hazard: As the NRDC had predicted, the EPA, in May 1989, classified Alar as a probable cause of cancer in humans. But the EPA also understood that bankruptcy and unemployment take a heavy toll on the health of the economy and on people's lives, which is why it gave the growers two years to phase out Alar use. The message was mixed: Yes, Alar causes cancer; no, it does not constitute a "health emergency."

Unsure of what and whom to believe, Americans turned to the media. Public fear mounted as experts voiced their disagreement in the spotlight of media publicity. Many consumers voted with their feet in supermarket aisles, avoiding apples and apple products. Schools yanked apples off lunch counters, and grocers pulled them from shelves. Uniroyal voluntarily halted sales of Alar and recalled stocks still on shelves. The industry worried that consumers' fears would put apple growers out of business and hurt the profits of processors and supermarkets.

When the dust settled, the apple growers had suffered economic damage, and they held the NRDC and the media to blame. In November 1990, they filed a lawsuit alleging losses of millions of dollars due to false statements by "60 Minutes." In 1993, a U.S. district court upheld the program's right to free speech, concluding the growers had failed to produce sufficient evidence of false statements. Two years later, a U.S. appeals court agreed, and that decision was left standing when the U.S. Supreme Court refused to review the case on April 29, 1996. Though Alar was off the market, the real question of whether it was a threat to human health had not been resolved. As one apple grower explained, "You can use all the facts in the world. If a mother thinks it's going to poison her kid, what can you do?"[4] One grocer summed it up nicely: "We're dealing with perception here . . . not . . . reality."[5]

The Alar controversy offers a brief glimpse of how interest groups attempt to convince others that their perception of *what is* is the right perception. In this chapter, we explore how interest groups practice politics in the United States by asking these questions:

What are interest groups, and what do they want?

How do interest groups work?

Do interest groups serve the common good and democracy?

Why are interest groups so hard to monitor and regulate, and what can be done about this?

What Are Interest Groups?

An **interest group** or lobby is an organization that seeks to convert the interests (the political, economic, social, or moral goals) of its members or supporters into public policies. Thousands of interest groups pursue these goals, often by **lobbying**—attempting to influence public officials to win their support.

What Makes an Interest Group "Special" or "Public"?

Interest groups are often classified as "special" or "public," depending on whose interests they claim to serve. A **special interest group** seeks to promote public policies that serve the interests of its own members and supporters. The Agriculture Council, which supported the growers in the Alar dispute, represents its members, the agribusiness companies. A **public interest group** claims to promote public policies that serve the interests of vast segments of the public. Although children who eat apples are not members of the NRDC, that organization claimed to serve their interests.

Whether a group represents a "special" or "public" interest invariably depends on one's interpretation of *what's right*. To avoid legitimating a group's claim to authority it may not deserve, commentators increasingly refer to "self-described public interest groups." In short, how a group is classified depends on who is doing the classifying and whether that person shares the group's goals. People primarily concerned with public health would, for example, accept the NRDC as a public interest group because it seeks to protect the public from hazardous chemicals. Those primarily concerned with economic health might instead argue that the NRDC is not a public interest group because it tries to limit the use of pesticides, thereby preventing farmers from producing more food at lower costs.

lobby
The term originated in mid-seventeenth-century England where the practice was conducted in a public waiting room, or lobby, near the House of Commons. In the United States lobbying is often conducted in areas adjacent to the Senate and House floors.

Conflicting claims like these are a reminder that politics consists of disputes over claims to authority to decide *what is, what's right,* and *what works.*

The Problem of Free Riders

The goals so-called public interest groups seek seldom serve the entire population or serve everyone equally. In the Alar case, for instance, the NRDC served all consumers of red apples, a group far smaller than all consumers of, say, clean air. Also, Alar-free apples mean more to a child, who has a lower tolerance for pesticides, than to an adult, just as clean air means more to an asthmatic or a jogger than to most others.[6]

Alar-free apples and clean air are **collective goods** (also called *public goods*)—goods that, once provided to some members of an actual or a potential group, cannot be denied to others in that group.[7] Thus all consumers of red apples—not only members of the NRDC—get the "collective good" of Alar-free apples if that chemical is banned. Similarly, all people—not only members of environmental groups that lobbied for clean air legislation—get the benefits of cleaner air.

People who do not join a group because they know they can enjoy its benefits for free are **free riders,** and public interest groups that promote collective goods are vulnerable to them. In *The Logic of Collective Action*, Mancur Olson argues that it is rational for individuals not to join or pay dues to an interest group that benefits everyone and gives them a "free ride."[8] Most people in the public radio and public television audiences, for example, know they can enjoy the programs without contributing to them. Olson argues that rational individuals join organizations only when they have an incentive to do so, and he identifies three possible incentives:

- **Material benefits** The Sierra Club, for instance, offers its members *Sierra* magazine, with beautifully illustrated articles on nature and analyses of environmental issues; discounts on books and calendars; an opportunity to participate in more than 250 nature treks around the world; and local chapter activities. Professional associations, for example, sponsor conferences and trips; labor unions provide benefits from collective bargaining; the National Rifle Association (NRA) offers a magazine, insurance policies, and hunting and shooting competitions. But the main reason people join a self-described public interest group is to promote its goals. This motive allows the NRA's much smaller adversary, Handgun Control, Inc., to attract members who receive nothing but the satisfaction of supporting its gun-control efforts.

- **Job requirements** Some unions have contracts with employers specifying that all employees must join the union. Many professionals join organizations that enhance their contacts and reputations; about half of U.S. doctors, for example, belong to the American Medical Association.

- **Psychological rewards** Some people join groups to experience solidarity with others in support of a common cause, such as crime prevention or animal rights. These psychological feelings are often reinforced by magazines, newsletters, and award ceremonies.

Adam Werback, 23, the youngest head of the Sierra Club, and his predecessor, David Brower.

The National Rifle Association's convention in Dallas, Texas, in April 1996.

How do groups cope with the free-rider problem? Some try to get others to pay for the free riders by seeking financial support from wealthy individuals and charitable foundations. Others target material, selective, and psychological benefits to actual members.

Indirect Interests

Groups prohibited from lobbying U.S. public officials directly, such as think tanks and foreign interests, do so indirectly.

Think Tanks

Policymakers and members of Congress often seek information from policy research institutions called **think tanks**, which specialize in various kinds of policy expertise. Because think tanks are classified by the Internal Revenue Service as educational institutions that benefit the public interest, they are tax-exempt. (The rules for tax exemption are discussed below.) To maintain this status, think tanks must refrain from lobbying. Nevertheless, these knowledge brokers are often strongly partisan. Indeed, many shape their activities to the declared policy goals of the current administration or its political opposition in order to maintain access and influence. In the 1960s, liberal economists in the Brookings Institution and military consultants of the RAND Corporation advised President Kennedy on economic policy and Vietnam. Experts from both think tanks, among many others, were also eager to supply President Johnson with proposals for his Great Society programs. In the 1970s, the Nixon administration sought advice from the conservative American Enterprise Institute (AEI). The Reagan administration also consulted the conservative Heritage Foundation, with a staff of 135 and an annual budget of $135 million. Both think tanks then hired many departing Reagan administration officials. Liberal Democrats turn to the Institute for Policy Studies, founded in 1963, and the Center for National Policy, founded in 1981, among others.[9] The Clinton administration has consulted and hired staffers from the Progressive Policy Institute, which generates ideas for moderate Democrats. And the Cato Institute, founded in 1977, puts out books, reports, and media-outreach programs to win converts and influence policy toward libertarian goals.

Not all think tanks are partisan. Many receive funding from nonpartisan as well as from partisan sources. Still, decisions on whom to hire, what to study, and how to publicize research results make think tanks more activist than the name suggests.

Foreign Interests

Because foreign interests have no constitutional right to petition the U.S. government directly, they do so indirectly by hiring American lobbyists—usually Washington lawyers—to represent them. Many Washington law firms specialize in lobbying for foreign governments, foreign businesses, royal families in the Middle East, and other powerful foreign interests such as foreign political parties, as well as U.S. citizens and corporations based abroad. When Ross Perot made foreign lobbyists a chief target during his 1992 and 1996 presidential campaigns, many foreign lobbyists lowered their public profile. Many have been turning to American firms with an interest in allying themselves with a foreign firm to carry their mutual concerns to federal and state lawmakers. Boeing Company, for instance, pressures lawmakers to keep China's most favored nation trade status because China routinely buys hundreds of millions of dollars worth of Boeing aircraft.[10]

Who Belongs to Interest Groups?

Interest groups may represent individuals or groups. Some, such as the National Committee for Adoption, allow both interested individuals and groups to join.

Individuals

Most Americans belong to at least one formal organization (see Table 8.1). The formal organizations most individuals join include places of worship and sports or recreational groups, not groups actively involved in politics, such as the NRDC or the NRA.[11] Individuals who pay dues or fulfill certain obligations can join some special interest groups, such as the conservative Christian Moral Government Fund or the liberal Americans for Democratic Action (ADA), or some public interest groups, such as the Concerned Women for America or the League of Women Voters. But membership in other groups is restricted to individuals with specific qualifications. Professional groups such as the American Bar Association (ABA) and the National Education Association (NEA)—which represents 1.9 million school teachers and administrators—are restricted to members of their professions. Similarly, only lobbyists can join the American League of Lobbyists. Groups that provide material benefits—such as group travel rates, group insurance rates, and information bulletins—expect members to pay dues. Seven out of ten Americans belong to one association and one out of four belongs to four or more.[12]

TABLE 8.1

Many Americans Belong to Various Types of Groups

Organization	Percentage of Population Who Belong			
	1980	1984	1988	1991
Religious-affiliation groups	30.0	33.3	34.3	33.2
Sports groups	17.0	21.1	19.5	17.5
Labor unions	18.0	14.1	12.8	9.6
Professional or academic societies	12.8	15.3	13.5	16.3
Fraternal groups	10.4	9.1	8.4	9.0
School service groups	9.9	12.2	12.4	14.3
Service clubs	8.9	10.4	11.0	8.9
Hobby or garden clubs	8.4	8.8	10.3	10.8
Literary, art, discussion, or study groups	8.4	8.7	8.5	9.2
Youth groups	8.0	9.4	10.7	8.6
Veterans groups	7.4	6.9	8.4	7.0
School fraternities or sororities	4.2	5.8	4.3	4.7
Farm organizations	4.0	4.2	3.4	3.2
Political clubs	3.1	3.9	4.4	3.7
Nationality organizations	2.5	3.3	2.2	4.5

Source: Roger H. Davidson and Walter J. Oleszek, *Congress and Its Members*, 4th ed. (Washington, D.C.: Congressional Quarterly Press, 1994), 297.

Groups

Just as individuals group together to pool their resources and gain greater policy-making clout, interest groups form associations to pool resources and promote their common interests.

- *Special interest associations* differ in size, membership, and the work they do. **Peak associations** are large umbrella groups that represent a vast array of organizations at a very general level. Examples include the National Association of Manufacturers (NAM) with 12,000 corporate members, the U.S. Chamber of Commerce, and the Business Roundtable. The American Federation of Labor and Congress of Industrial Organizations (AFL-CIO), which represents more than 100 labor unions, which in turn represent 15 million workers, is also a peak association. **Trade associations** represent business groups in a particular industry—shipping, farming, defense contractors—and offer their members assistance tailored to their needs.

- *Public interest associations* bring together local chapters of national groups. Examples include the National Audubon Society (environmentalists), Rotary International (public service), the United Way of America (charity funding), the Urban League (urban African Americans and other minorities), and the Child Welfare League of America (children's concerns).

- *Media associations* are composed of media groups, such as the Newspaper Publishers Association, the National Press Club, and the National Cable Television Association.

- *Government associations* enable governors and mayors to join forces to lobby the federal government for help in solving state and local problems such as crime, inner-city decay, and pollution and to pursue common goals, such as economic development, social welfare, and public works programs. (You can watch the meetings of the National League of Cities, the U.S. Conference of Mayors, and the National Governors Association each year on C-SPAN.)

Why Interest Groups Form

According to political scientist David Truman's "disturbance theory," interest groups form when a particular class or category of people experiences a threatening disruption or disturbance.[13] The Reagan administration's threat to slash student loans during the 1980s, for example, strengthened the U.S. National Student Association and led to the foundation of the National Student Lobby, which defends such loans. As the nearby Political Action Guide shows, other organizations, including the National Association of Financial Aid Administrators, sponsor World Wide Web sites to support this interest.

But not all interest groups form in response to threats. Factory workers, for example, have had an incentive to form trade unions since the Industrial Revolution but did not do so for decades. Many groups form slowly and often falter before they succeed. Moreover, people frequently delay joining an interest group until they have proof that the group works and can deliver on its promises. Sometimes a dynamic, charismatic leader—such as consumer activist Ralph Nader or the late organizer of farm workers Cesar Chavez or televangelist Pat Robertson—is the key to a group's successful formation. The ability to attract educated and politically sophisticated members also helps. As we saw in Chapter 6, people with a higher socioeconomic status are more likely to participate in politics than are the poor and uneducated, who are underrepresented in the political process and outmatched by competitors for favorable public policies. But the process of group formation does not fully explain *why* interest groups form, either. A better view comes from a quick look at the growth of interest groups over the past seventy years.

Top: Cesar Chavez addresses the first United Farm Workers convention in Fresno, California, in 1973. *Bottom:* Televangelist Pat Robertson.

Where Do Interest Groups Come from, and Why Do They Multiply?

From James Madison's day until just after the Civil War, Americans depended primarily on political parties to voice their concerns to government. Gradually, groups representing different political ideologies and economic interests formed to influence government. Roughly 50 lobbyists were operating in Washington by the end of the Civil War.[14] By 1929 that number had reached 500, and at the height of the New Deal, 6,000. By the 1990s the number had jumped to over 40,000.[15] What led to this interest group explosion?

vested interest
The term comes from the French word for a protective cloak or garment. Vested interests seek to preserve the benefits they already receive.

Political Action Guide

Getting Information from Groups About Financial Aid

Here are a few of the many sources of information that public and private groups provide for obtaining scholarships and other financial aid:

Online

- The Financial Aid Information Page, which is on the World Wide Web (http://www.finaid.org) is sponsored by the National Association of Student Financial Aid Administrators. It contains information on scholarships and grants, as well as warnings about fraudulent search firms. The association has another site (http://www.nasfaa.org) that offers consumer scholarship tips.
- The College Board Web site (http://www.collegeboard.org) contains a database of scholarship sources called Expan Scholarship Search. A similar database is available in many libraries and guidance counselors' offices through a software program called Fund Finder, also from the College Board.
- The Student Loan Marketing Association home page (http://www.salliemae.com) offers information on scholarships, grants, and student loans.
- SRN Express (http://www.rams.com/srn/search.htm) is a free Web version of the database of the Scholarship Resource Network, a search firm. It focuses on private-sector aid, like academic scholarships.

Books

- *College Costs and Financial Aid Handbook,* 14th ed. (New York: College Board, 1994). This how-to book includes an outline of major aid programs, a discussion of how financial need is determined, and a look at college costs.
- *The Scholarship Book*, 5th ed., by Daniel J. Cassidy (Englewood Cliffs, N. J.: Prentice Hall, 1996). This is a guide to private-sector scholarships, grants, and loans.
- *Financial Aids for Higher Education*, edited by Oreon Keesler (Dubuque, Iowa: Brown & Benchmark, annual). It lists more than 3,000 sources of financial aid, with details on eligibility criteria.

- **Government-sponsored reforms** Between 1929 and the end of the twentieth century, expanding government programs created new **vested interests**—interest groups receiving benefits from government. New Deal programs gave farmers vested interests, and farmers then organized to defend and retain them. In the 1960s, Great Society programs like Head Start, Medicare, Medicaid, and food stamps spawned interest groups to defend and expand them.
- **Opposition to vested interests** From the late 1960s to the late 1970s consumer, labor, and environmental groups mobilized to challenge vested business interests that had dominated the economy for decades. The government responded by creating ten federal agencies, among them the Consumer Product Safety Commission (CPSC) and the Occupational Safety and Health Administration (OSHA). Environmental groups such as the NRDC gained influence.[16] During the 1980s business interests, with help from the Reagan and Bush administrations, were able to limit the political success of these movements.

- **Social movements** An increasingly diverse population gave rise to groups that have challenged dominant beliefs and cultural practices such as segregation, the traditional role of women, and discrimination against gays and lesbians. Gay rights groups, for example, became politically active after the "sexual revolution" of the 1960s allowed sexuality issues to be openly discussed. A 1994 directory listed 400 gay groups, up from 300 in 1990.[17] When the conservative backlash of the Reagan era threatened these new social movements, citizens' and public interest groups grew to the tens of thousands; today, they receive more than $4 billion each year from 40 million members who want their interests defended.[18]

- **Defenders of the traditional social order** Traditionalists such as the Christian Coalition (discussed in Chapter 4) have organized to support traditional family values and to oppose abortion, gay rights, and the ban on school prayer. Similar groups have formed to lobby for the adoption of English as a national language and to oppose affirmative action and illegal immigration.

- **Increased intergovernmental lobbying** In recent decades, governmental groups such as the National League of Cities, the U.S. Conference of Mayors, and the National Governors' Association, along with city and state agencies, have organized to lobby the federal government. Many of these groups maintain offices in Washington, D.C.

- **Technological innovation** New technologies trigger new interest groups. The Air Line Pilots Association (ALPA) was formed in 1931, as airplanes began to be used for both commercial travel and military and cargo purposes. Similarly, interest groups grew up as the use of telephones, radio, television, and computers became common. Today the Internet is spawning Web sites of all types—from underfinanced groups such as the AIDS group Mothers Against Jesse [Helms] in Congress to do-it-yourself stock investors. In this newest round of innovation, proponents of Internet regulations have provoked defenders of these and other Web sites to organize against them.[19]

Lobbyists traditionally gather in the corridors of power, where they hope to obtain access to public officials.

Lobbying, Brussels Style

Life as a lobbyist in Brussels, at the headquarters of the European Union, is much brighter than life as a Washington lobbyist. In 1994 more than 3,000 non-Belgian companies and governments hired more than 20,000 lobbyists—twice the number they employed in 1990—to influence Union commissioners to draft regulations favorable to their interests. There is roughly one lobbyist for every 1.3 commissioners. If Washington lobbyists labor under a negative image and must work hard to gain access to public officials, "Eurolobbyists" in Brussels have no image or access problem. Lobbying activities are mostly out in the open, and Brussels officials work hard to give lobbyists the information and technical advice they need to support the interests of the groups they represent. In return, lobbyists such as those representing the American Chamber of Commerce often provide the Union's commissioners with policy studies that go well beyond their organization's relatively narrow interests.

Like Washington lobbying, effective Eurolobbying requires that lobbyists contact insiders—politicians and business leaders. To facilitate these contacts, former members of the European Parliament and other officials have organized lobbying firms that specialize in particular areas, such as industry, agriculture, and telecommunications; the firms also may tailor their services to people from specific countries. Foreigners can take a crash course in French and English on how to lobby Brussels style from an independent organization called the European Institute for Public Affairs.

Americans and other foreigners in Brussels can also learn how to use the many technologies that give them access to business information. Over 180 Infocenters throughout the member nations of the European Union supply instant data on available services, as well as on market conditions, for companies large or small. The Union-run Business Corporation Network helps those interested in forming joint ventures to make contact with one another.

Rounding out these amenities is the Brussels cuisine, which elevates even the lowly french fry to a peak gastronomic experience. How well would such services work in the United States? That is food for thought.

Source: Adapted from Ronald Facchinetti, "Why Brussels Has 10,000 Lobbyists," *New York Times*, August 21, 1994.

- **Loss of power by political parties** As the power of political parties has dwindled, people have turned to interest groups such as the liberal ADA and the conservative Christian Coalition, and to groups within political movements, such as the National Organization for Women (NOW), the National Association for the Advancement of Colored People (NAACP), and the National Gay and Lesbian Task Force.
- **Decentralization of government programs** Interest groups have multiplied at the state and local levels in the wake of the transfer of programs from federal to local jurisdiction during and since the Reagan era.[20]
- **The globalization of the economy** Lobbyists representing foreign interests are on the rise in Washington, D.C., as is their spending. These lobbyists—one-third of whom are former federal officials[21]— operate at all levels of government. The Japanese government and companies alone hired more than 125 American law firms, economic consultants, and public relations experts between 1988 and 1992.[22] To see how U.S. and other foreign lobbyists fare in Brussels, Belgium, the headquarters of the 15-nation European Union, read the box above.

But even with so many diverse reasons for forming, interest groups are remarkably similar in what they want from government, the topic we turn to next.

What Interest Groups Want

Most interest groups pursue multiple goals. Women's groups, for example, seek equal pay for equal work, legal support for family leave for pregnancy and child care, research funding for women's health problems, and, in many cases, abortion rights. Other groups are **single-issue groups** ardently pursuing one goal and resisting compromise on its attainment. The National Abortion Rights Action League and the National Right to Life Committee, for example, lobby on abortion policy. The Citizen Flag Alliance supports a constitutional amendment to ban flag-burning. Single-issue groups have increased in number since the 1970s, in part because broadly focused interest groups, like the broadly focused major political parties, rarely give their full support to a particular cause.

All groups, whether special or public, single-issue or multi-issue, want one or more of the following: (1) government money; (2) federal regulation, deregulation, or reregulation; and (3) social or moral reforms.

Monetary Benefits

The largest number of interest groups are *economic groups* seeking monetary benefits from government. Defense contractors pressure the Department of Defense for government contracts to build plants and manufacture planes, submarines, and other military hardware. The American Farm Bureau Federation and the National Farmers' Association try to ensure that farm subsidies and other benefits are protected and increased. Labor groups such as the AFL-CIO and the Teamsters seek a higher minimum wage and increased protection for unions' rights to bargain collectively with management. And many businesses hire lawyers to lobby for tax loopholes that would allow them to keep more of their income.

John Sweeney, head of the AFL-CIO, addresses a labor group outside the 1996 Democratic National Convention in Chicago.

Not all interest groups seeking monetary benefits are for-profit organizations. Private charities as well as state and city agencies lobby Congress to continue funding or to expand social welfare programs. Social Security recipients pressure Congress through the American Association of Retired Persons (now, with over 30 million members, the second largest organization in America after the Catholic Church) to protect Social Security payments—even those of the wealthy. And on the other side of the fence is the National Taxpayers Union (NTU), which wants to cut government spending and reduce taxes—a monetary benefit if it allows wage earners to keep more of what they make.

The Keating Debacle: The High Cost of Learning by Doing

During the 1980s, Charles Keating, head of the financially troubled Lincoln Savings and Loan in Arizona, asked five senators to pressure the Federal Home Loan Bank Board, the federal agency that regulated S&Ls, to delay closing his bank. Ethical questions were raised because all five senators had accepted large contributions from Keating—something that was not illegal—and each had met with the bank regulators twice on Keating's behalf. As a result, his bank was allowed to function for two more years until the Federal Deposit Insurance Corporation (FDIC)[1] finally shut it down in 1989 with a massive deficit. Although the senators argued that they were only doing for Keating what they would do for any citizen, the Senate Ethics Committee found that they had exercised poor judgment. Keating was tried and sentenced to twelve and a half years in jail for financial wrong-doing that cost taxpayers $132 billion, and three of the senators decided not to seek reelection.

In December 1996, after Keating had served four and a half years, a federal judge tossed out his conviction on grounds that the jury had improperly discussed an earlier conviction. By then few people seemed to care because they had come to view the real culprit as misguided government policies. Congress had allowed thrifts—savings and loan associations and savings banks—to expand into a variety of new businesses about which they knew little, and lax oversight made thrifts an easy target for crooks. One federal commission later attributed the crisis to "a systematic breakdown in the political system."[2]

Breakdown or not, the real estate industry bounced back in just a few years. The resort hotel Keating had built in Phoenix is now owned by the Sheraton Corporation and is thriving. (Guests pay $450 a snifter for Hardy's Perfection Cognac.) Government bureaucrats responsible for seizing and selling roughly $500,000 billion in real estate—home mortgages, luxury hotels, and even race horses—managed to put a major portion of these assets into private hands in just a few years, although at a substantial loss to taxpayers. And the thrift industry, which experts say is obsolete, is shrinking. In 1985, when the thrift crisis was gathering momentum, 3,262 federally chartered thrifts held $1.1 trillion in assets. By the middle of 1996, 1,436 thrifts held $771 billion in assets. "So what have we learned?" asked one journalist. "Mr. Keating is free and bitter, and government regulators say they are wiser."[3] The Keating case illustrates the ways in which widespread illegal behavior can thrive on misguided regulatory policies and a lack of government oversight.

---

[1] Founded in 1933, the FDIC shares regulatory powers with the states over state-chartered banks not in the Federal Reserve System and over mutual savings banks.
[2] Quoted in James Sterngold, "For Some, It's Still a Wonderful Life," *New York Times*, December 8, 1996, Section 4, 3.
[3] James Sterngold, in ibid.

Regulation, Deregulation, or Reregulation

High on many interest groups' wish lists are new federal regulations and the protection of old regulations. In 1970, in response to labor groups, Congress passed the Occupational Safety and Health Act (OSHA). But business lobbies during the Reagan and Bush years and during the first Clinton administration forced OSHA to rely on consensus-building rather than regulations to achieve its goals. Only when Clinton began his second term in 1997 did he announce plans to set mandatory rules to prevent repetitive motion injuries, which affect hundreds of thousands of workers from computer programmers to meatpackers—injuries that produce roughly $20 billion in compensation costs each year.[23] Thus, whether regulations that groups seek become laws *(what is)* and whether those laws are enforced *(what works)* often depend on the political context in which they exist.

President Bill Clinton addresses the 1993–1994 U.S. Chamber of Commerce convention.

Deregulation—the removal of regulations—has worked in a number of areas: the airlines, trucking, and overnight delivery services. Occasionally, usually after *learning by doing*, groups will ask the federal government for *reregulation* (the reimposition of regulations). During the Reagan years, the savings and loan (S&L) lobby persuaded Congress to deregulate the industry so that S&Ls could compete more effectively with banks and other financial institutions by investing in commercial real estate, which is more profitable than home mortgage investment. However, as the box on page 275 explains, the federal agency that regulated S&Ls failed to monitor the new high-risk ventures. Within two years they began to fail and S&Ls began to fold. When taxpayers discovered to their dismay that they were legally bound to bail out large portions of the industry, outcries for *reregulation* led the Bank Board to impose sharp restrictions on S&L real estate investments.

Social, Moral, and Political Reforms

Interest groups motivated by their religious or humanitarian beliefs about *what's right* regularly pressure government for favorable policies and laws that will bring about social, moral, and political reforms. They may request that existing laws be abolished, preserved, or enforced more rigorously, that new laws be enacted, that constitutional amendments be adopted, or that more conservative or liberal judges be appointed to the bench. The Roman Catholic Council of Bishops, for example, lobbies government on issues from abortion to school prayer to human rights—as do other religious groups. The Friends Committee on National Legislation, a Quaker group, and Amnesty International, among others, lobby for civil rights, human rights, and prison reform, both at home and abroad.

The nation's eight Roman Catholic cardinals lead a prayer vigil at the U.S. Capitol in September 1996 aimed at persuading members of the House to override President Clinton's veto of an early version of a bill banning some late-term abortions.

How Interest Groups Work

Interest groups practice politics by performing a variety of functions that benefit the public, government, and their own members and supporters. These functions require adequate resources as well as effective strategies.

Functions

Interest groups practice politics through the following activities.

- **Representing citizens to government** Interest groups use lobbyists to present the views of their members to all branches and levels of government. They lobby the courts through *amicus curiae* briefs and by pressuring the Senate to reject judicial nominees who would be likely to rule against their interests.

- **Educating the government** Interest groups often hire experts to explain to government officials the potential impact of a proposed policy. Many lawmakers and bureaucrats appreciate this information. As one former member of Congress put it: "If you have an 800-page health-care bill and three paragraphs deal with the dentists, it is very helpful to have a dental lobby in Washington and in the district [to explain] the impact of those three paragraphs. . . ."[24] Groups that can afford it often hire "lawyer-lobbyists" to persuade lawmakers to word laws in their favor and to open or close particular loopholes. Some interest groups even draft legislation for lawmakers.

- **Educating the public** Groups educate the public by making statements to and through the media, publishing reports, and maintaining Web sites. At the NRDC's Web site (http://www.nrdc.org), the public can consult reports on the monitoring of beach pollution in coastal states and many other topics.

- **Setting the policy agenda** By alerting the public to new issues and pressuring government to address them, as the NRDC did in the Alar case, interest groups also serve as agenda setters. Without such actions, certain issues might never make it onto the policy agenda. In response to the NRDC's concern about coastal water pollution, for example, North Carolina and Key West, Florida, started monitoring programs in the summer of 1997. Government can't anticipate all problems, and sometimes it prefers to avoid controversy, as the EPA did when it granted the pesticide industry a two-year phaseout for Alar.

- **Ensuring that policies are carried out** By acting as watchdogs, interest groups try to ensure that the bureaucracy implements policies that have been enacted. If implementation lags, the interest group alerts government officials and may even take the government agency to court to achieve compliance.

- **Socializing members into the political process** Interest groups teach their members basic political skills, such as how to lobby effectively for their goals. Groups often ask members to contact their representatives in Congress, for example. Having learned these skills, members may then use them in other political arenas or teach them to colleagues or family members.

- **Keeping members informed** Interest groups mail out "alerts" to warn members of new problems or important upcoming votes in Congress so they can urge their representatives to defend their interests. Increasingly, interest groups also provide the computer-based facilities for members to send electronic messages to public officials expressing their views on policy questions. Because the vast number and complexity of government regulations can be overwhelming, some groups hire "watchdog" lobbyists—often Washington lawyers—to study any regulations that affect their interests. These watchdog lobbyists alert interest groups to benefits they might otherwise overlook and warn them when they might unknowingly be violating the law.[25]

Resources

Effective interest groups usually have active, efficient, and highly visible organizations. This requires physical resources, such as money and office space; human resources, such as leaders, experts, and members; and organizational resources, such as technologies that link leaders and members.

Physical Resources

Groups raise money through membership dues, direct-mail solicitations, and fund-raisers. Money attracts money, so the more a group spends on advertising and benefits for its members, the more contributions and members it is likely to attract. The richer and bigger the group, the more doors it opens to lawmakers seeking campaign contributions and votes. Groups that can afford toll-free numbers make it easy for people to join and contribute over the phone. Some even tailor their phone number to carry their political messages, like the antitax group 1-800 BE ANGRY.[26] With enough money, an interest group can house a paid professional staff in a Washington office (ideally on K Street, known as Lobbyists' Row) within easy reach of lawmakers, bureaucrats, legal experts, and direct-mail specialists. Over 40,000 registered lobbyists now have Washington offices.

Less wealthy groups may have to operate from small local offices, and they may be unable to contribute to political campaigns. Such groups depend on support from volunteers and helpful bureaucrats. Their public exposure comes from press releases, testimony before lawmakers and other government bodies, and Web sites on the Internet.

Human Resources

We noted earlier in the chapter that an interest group's success depends in part on charismatic and resourceful leaders. It also needs a staff of competent experts and responsive members. But the most visible and indispensable human resource is the lobbyists who provide political expertise in three domains: financing the right campaigns, developing the right contacts, and establishing the right kind of reputation. Effective lobbyists know which campaigns to back because they know which political actors, bureaucrats, and experts can help to get their interests enacted into law. Lobbyists use their contacts to maintain these relationships by supplying these public officials with accurate information about technical questions and the views of powerful people outside government.²⁷ Such lobbyists establish reputations of being trustworthy brokers in the political process, as one lawmaker explains: "It doesn't take very long to figure out which lobbyists are straightforward, and which ones are trying to snow you. The good ones will give you the weak points as well as the strong points of their case. If anyone ever gives me false or misleading information, that's it—I'll never see him again."²⁸

Lobbying efforts work best when an active and vocal group of members can be counted on to send faxes, write letters, make phone calls, or participate in demonstrations. Narrowly focused groups such as the American Israel Public Affairs Committee (AIPAC) and the NRA, or morally motivated groups such as right-to-life or antiwar groups, tend to be tightly organized, and their members have high levels of commitment. Lawmakers take notice when these "true believers" band together as a bloc of single-issue voters—especially if the members are dispersed across the country and of mixed gender or ethnicity.

K Street in Washington, D.C., commonly known as "Lobbyists' Row."

The longtime practice whereby political interest groups use celebrities to endorse causes—as the NRDC used Meryl Streep—has recently become organized. A public affairs consulting firm and a theatrical press agency jointly formed a company called Cause Celêbre in 1997 to match celebrities and causes in ways that benefit both. A celebrity seeking an appealing cause can pay the company a fee to find one, as can a group looking for a suitable celebrity.²⁹

Organizational Resources

No interest group can be effective if its leaders, lobbyists, and members are unable to communicate quickly, make decisions efficiently, and take targeted direct lobbying action. Organizational resources that enable quick and efficient action can compensate for a lack of money or a relatively small membership. AIPAC, the lobby for Israel, has formidable organizational powers. As one House Democrat put it, "If I cast a vote against Israel, every Jew in my district will know about it, and be on my back."³⁰

Another powerful, because well-organized, group is the Association of Trial Lawyers of America (ATLA), which has 60,000 members and a budget of more than $19 million. After a long and unsuccessful struggle to curb the strength of trial lawyers, Senator Mitch McConnell (R.-Ky.) remarked: "The perception is that AIPAC is the strongest lobby in town. Wrong. The strongest lobby in Washington by far is ATLA."³¹ Why is ATLA so powerful? According to one lobbyist, "Some groups have brawn, like the National Rifle Association, and some have brains, like the environmentalists. The trial lawyers have both."³² ATLA, for example, gives major sums of money to a political action committee (PAC) which gives it to political parties to support their candidates. Lawyers also relate easily to lawmakers because many lawmakers are also lawyers.

Strategies

Successful interest groups draw on five key strategies: contributing to political candidates; adapting to changing circumstances; cooperating with other political actors to build coalitions; using "inside strategies" to manipulate the levers of Washington politics; and using "outside strategies" to bring grassroots pressure to bear on lawmakers.

Contributing to Political Candidates

Interest groups spend their money with the intent of ensuring that whoever wins does so with their support. Many contribute to candidates of both major parties running for the same office, and they often support candidates who are running unopposed. Wealthy groups, such as the National Association of Manufacturers or the AFL-CIO, use a *blanket strategy*—backing a large number of candidates. Those with less money favor a *target strategy*—channeling their resources to influential members on committees that directly affect their agendas. One lobbyist using this strategy explained, "[Lawmakers] are always having $50 or $100 a plate fund-raising dinners or receptions, and I'll contribute to some of these, if they're given by people on the committees I work with. It's not much, certainly not compared to big business or big labor, but you would be surprised at how closely members pay attention to even the smallest contributions. I see them as basically insurance—insuring that I'll get beyond the receptionist when I need to see these guys."[33] Groups also donate "in-kind" campaign contributions. Some provide free public opinion surveys or telephone banks to get out the vote. A company may loan an executive, a lawyer, or some other expert to a campaign.

Adapting to Changing Circumstances and Learning by Doing

An interest group's strategies and tactics must adapt to changing political conditions. Sometimes lobbying lawmakers is the most profitable strategy; other times filing a lawsuit may be best. The NRDC learned this in some of the battles it fought before it took on the Alar case. The Yale law students who founded the NRDC originally patterned their organization on the NAACP Legal Defense Fund, which primarily pushed for civil rights in the courts. At first, this strategy worked well because the NRDC's lawyers, poring over new federal environmental regulations, found technicalities on which to base lawsuits that they eventually won. When the states devised strategies to avoid complying with these regulations, the NRDC pressed the EPA to force the states to comply. The EPA did nothing until the NRDC filed suit against it and won. The NRDC court victory required the states to impose a surcharge on commuter parking to cut down on driving and, therefore, on auto pollution. The NRDC soon learned, however, that legal action alone would not change the system. Congress undercut the NRDC victory by passing a law prohibiting the EPA from enforcing the surcharge. This setback forced the NRDC to adapt—to learn how to lobby Congress to achieve its goals. In 1973 it formed the National Clean Air Coalition to coordinate lobbying by civic, religious, public health, and labor organizations. And, when the NRDC turned to Madison Avenue hard-sell tactics (like the Meryl Streep commercial it used in its Alar battle), it usually won.

Interest groups must also be flexible enough to change as the political process changes. Since World War II the executive branch has seized the initiative in a number of policy areas, especially regulation. Lobbyists interested in regulatory issues then had to shift their attention from Congress to the bureaucracy. Changes in Congress have also placed new demands on lobbyists. The increasing turnover in membership in recent years has given lobbyists a host of new lawmakers to "educate." In addition, reforms that began in 1968 have changed the pecking order in Congress. The old seniority system, which gave the greatest power to the most senior lawmakers, has given way to a system that spreads power more evenly among the members. Because the same small elite no longer dominates committees year after year, lobbyists must spend more time and resources informing a broader range of lawmakers of their concerns.

Lobbyists also have more meetings to prepare for and attend since the Legislative Reorganization Act of 1970. These **sunshine rules** exposed much of the legislative process in the House to public light, requiring the recording of votes on amendments. Lobbyists and the public now can see what positions lawmakers take on controversial issues. The law also shed light on committee activities that had previously cloaked lawmakers' concessions and compromises in secrecy. According to one observer, the rules are "great for lobbyists, but the members of Congress hate [them]. There in the back of the hearing room are all these lobbyists . . . giving a thumbs-up or a thumbs-down to specific wordings or provisions [of a proposed law]. It's a fishbowl for them."[34]

Cooperation and Coalition Building

Effective interest groups cooperate and build coalitions because, while groups' goals often clash, they sometimes coincide. Business and labor, for instance, rarely agree on wages and job security, but they cooperate in their support for tariffs on imports because they both benefit from them. Tariffs raise the cost of foreign goods, which gives consumers an incentive to buy American goods. In the auto industry, for example, management and the unions cooperate in pushing for tariffs and quotas on foreign-made cars to obtain higher profits for the auto industry and higher wages for auto workers. Groups sharing a category—large and small oil companies, for example—sometimes join forces to push for tax breaks, in this case, for drilling new oil wells. They do so even though they are simultaneously competing fiercely on other issues, such as oil import policies, which affect only the big companies that can afford foreign operations.

Interest groups also form coalitions to support common goals. Some coalitions, such as trade associations, are ongoing institutions; others may form to deal with a particular issue and then disband. One such temporary coalition formed to oppose environmentalists' efforts to strengthen the Clean Air Act of 1990. Environmentalists backed strong tailpipe-emission controls and an increase in the average fuel-efficiency rate from 27.5 to 40 miles per gallon by the year 2000. American carmakers, claiming these requirements would force them to shrink big cars to the size of a small Honda, hired an influential Washington lobbyist to identify users of large, American cars and to pull together a coalition that would lobby to defeat the proposals. Lawmakers were soon deluged with letters, calls, and telegrams from people who depend on the safety and carrying capacity of large cars—the elderly, people with disabilities, the police, and volunteer organizations such as Big Brothers, Big Sisters, and Scout groups that shuttle groups of people around. The coalition even flew an Alabama sheriff, a Nebraska farm bureau president, and a senior citizen from Florida to the capital for a press conference. The coalition prevailed.[35]

Inside Strategies

Part of effective lobbying is knowing how to press the levers of power inside the Washington policy community, or "Beltway." **Inside strategies** include contacting lawmakers and their aides and government bureaucrats directly and getting publicity in the Washington media, where government officials are likely to see it.

Information is essential to inside strategies. Lobbyists, lawmakers, and bureaucrats who specialize in a particular policy area typically meet regularly to share information, to discuss the potential impact of proposed laws, and even to agree on legislative strategies. Government officials may also seek advice from lobbyists who were once government officials themselves. The lobbyist who helped U.S. carmakers form the coalition, for example, was a former congressional aide. When lobbyists, lawmakers or their staffs, and involved bureaucrats work together on policy issues, the arrangement is known as an **iron triangle**, representing the three "angles" of the policymaking process. Iron triangles can also be viewed as informal **issue networks** because the participants constantly move in and out of these relationships as issues change. (See Chapter 13.)

Most insider lobbying still centers on Congress. Lobbyists' tactics for the House and Senate differ because the institutions differ. A lobbyist has greater access to House members than to senators, for example, because House members have fewer committee assignments and fewer constituents than do senators. House members usually are also less pressed for time than busy senators, who often palm lobbyists off on their staffs. Some lobbyists prefer working in the House, where the legislative process, governed by numerous rules and formalities, is more predictable. Others feel more at home in the Senate, which is less hampered by rules, less predictable, and sometimes more open to personal influence.

Lobbyists must be seen if they are to be heard. Knowing how to maneuver in this world of elites means forming influential friendships and getting invited to the right parties. Social access is often political access, so lobbyists routinely invite lawmakers and staff members to lunch or for a quick cup of coffee during a lull in legislative action.

Outside Strategies

Outside strategies stimulate grassroots support for an issue, and they offer a powerful one-two punch in combination with inside strategies. Public interest groups were the first to develop and refine grassroots strategies, but other groups, especially conservative religious lobbies, have also adopted them. Outside strategies may be direct, indirect, or both.

- *The direct approach* establishes direct contact with carefully targeted citizens and attempts to rally them to the group's cause. Some groups hire experts to locate and profile pockets of likely supporters by Zip Code. The group then mails out messages tailored to their concerns.

  Many groups—televangelists, businesses, public interest groups—supplement direct-mail tactics with technologies that provide easy access to large numbers of people. The U.S. Chamber of Commerce, for example, uses a sophisticated phone bank to alert its 215,000 corporate members when their support is needed on some issue. Contacted members can automatically send messages to legislators by pressing 1 to send a personal mailgram or letter, pressing 2 to send a voice-mail message, or pressing 3 to have the Chamber's computer place a direct personal phone call to their representative's office.[36]

The American Bankers Association uses a databank to personalize this process. "Every member of Congress went to school with somebody, or played on a football team with somebody, or dated somebody's sister," explains one lobby official. "We do nothing more than focus and organize those people at an important point in time."[37] His association's databank holds 10,000 members' names and ranks their connections to lawmakers from "slight" to "very close." When he spots a lawmaker willing to raise corporate taxes, he consults the databank, finds names of the lawmaker's friends, and has them fire off a letter opposing the idea.

Technology's contribution to lobbying continues through the World Wide Web on the Internet. One Washington lobby firm, Marlowe & Co., created the Web site Netlobby to enable the firms it represents to e-mail targeted members of Congress. Netlobby furnishes sample letters, talking points, and relevant statistics to Web site visitors. With a click of the mouse, visitors can then fire off letters to key lawmakers and public officials.[38]

Some groups simply send members preprinted letters and postcards with the precise message they want lawmakers to receive so that members can just sign them and drop them in the mail. Many lawmakers view such letters as phoney "Astroturf" rather than as authentic grassroots lobbying. Some even have their aides phone signers to see if they really know or care about the issue. (Mail campaigns have on occasion turned out to be fakes, the letters forged or "signed" by dead people.) Staffers don't read or count postcards, but they sometimes weigh them. Some lawmakers see these cloned messages as an opportunity to build political support and answer them for this reason.

- The *indirect approach* generates grassroots support by launching mass-media campaigns to publicize a group's cause. The interest group may purchase full-page newspaper ads, buy radio or television spots, or hold press conferences in hopes of gaining media attention. Following the infomercial model, a public relations firm may present the client's message in an electronic press release, narrated by actors playing reporters and designed to look like a TV news story. The hope, of course, is that the media will run the release as a news story. Glossy publicity folders called media kits are routinely sent to newspapers to generate stories favorable to clients.

Observers disagree about how influential grassroots campaigns are, but many people have built successful lobbying-for-hire businesses on the widespread belief that they matter. National Strategies and Marketing Group, formed by some inside-the-Beltway Democrats, specializes in mobilizing grassroots support for its clients. It successfully did so when one client, a toxic-waste disposal firm that used land-based incinerators, wanted to keep the EPA from approving a competitor's application to burn wastes at sea. National Strategies lobbied the EPA by forming a grassroots organization, which it called Alliance to Save the Ocean. The strategy buried the client's economic interests beneath the facade of a public interest—the environment.[39]

Marlowe & Co., the firm that created Netlobby, can be reached at http://www.cais.com/marlowe

A display of the shoes of gun victims on the Mall in Washington, D.C., in October 1996, organized by gun control advocates.

TABLE 8.2

What Washington Lobbyists Do

Technique	Percentage of Groups That Use Techniques
Testify at hearings	99
Contact government officials directly to present your point of view	98
Engage in informal contacts with officials—at conventions, over lunch, etc.	95
Present research results or technical information	92
Send letters to members of your organization to inform them about your activities	92
Enter into coalitions with other organizations	90
Attempt to shape the implementation of policies	89
Talk with people from the press and the media	86
Consult with government officials to plan legislative strategy	85
Help to draft legislation	85
Inspire letter-writing or telegram campaigns	84
Shape the government's agenda by raising new issues and calling attention to previously ignored problems	84
Mount grassroots lobbying efforts	80
Have influential constituents contact their legislator's office	80
Help to draft regulations, rules, or guidelines	78
Serve on advisory commissions and boards	76
Alert legislators to the effects of a bill on their districts	75
File suit or otherwise engage in litigation	72
Make financial contributions to electoral campaigns	58
Do favors for officials who need assistance	56
Attempt to influence appointments to public office	53
Publicize candidates' voting records	44
Engage in direct-mail fund raising for your organization	44
Run advertisements in the media about your position on issues	31
Contribute work or personnel to electoral campaigns	24
Make public endorsements of candidates for office	22
Engage in protests or demonstrations	20

Source: Key Lehman Schlozman and John T. Tierney, *Organized Interests and American Democracy* (New York: Harper & Row, 1986), 150.

Lobbying-for-hire groups sometimes coordinate outside and inside strategies to squeeze public officials from both directions. For example, when Morgan Stanley, a large Wall Street investment company, wanted to buy a federally owned freight company, it hired a three-company team of lobbyists-for-hire to win broad support for its purchase. They used insider lobbying to pressure lawmakers in Washington and outside strategies to gather support from shippers, mayors, and others at the grassroots level.[40] (Despite the strategy, the campaign failed.) For a list of lobbying techniques used by Washington lobbyists, see Table 8.2.

Are Interest Groups Right for America?

Do interest groups serve the United States and the common good when they pressure government for public policies that support their goals? The Framers did not think they would. Do interest groups serve democracy? Some political scientists say they do, others say they don't.

The Madisonian Dilemma

The Framers believed that the common good is best served when individuals separately pursue their own private interests. But the First Amendment to the Constitution permits individuals to organize themselves into interest groups to petition government for assistance. This conflict between the Framers' beliefs and the law they wrote has been called the **Madisonian dilemma**.

James Madison was keenly aware that the people's constitutional right to petition government was bound to generate political conflict. As he explained in *The Federalist*, No. 10, interest groups permit people to pursue their own self-interest in ways that can *promote the common good*, but interest groups can also pressure government to adopt policies that benefit their own special interests *at the expense of the common good*.

Madison believed that rival groups with different interests would inevitably spring up and compete with one another for government support, and he feared that large "majority factions" would overpower and suppress minorities. How could "the mischiefs of faction" be cured? Madison ruled out any governmental restrictions on people's freedom to pursue their own self-interest for two reasons: he thought such restrictions would be "worse than the disease," and he supported the people's right to petition government. He argued that factions should be tolerated, but he predicted that their effects would be limited in three ways:

- *The separation of powers and checks and balances would make it hard for any single group to dominate the entire government.* Madison was only partly right about this. True, the three branches of government are limited by checks and balances at the federal and state levels. But the fact that government is divided into branches and levels provides interest groups with many points of access. Not only can some interest groups lobby all three branches, but they often use one branch of government against another to do this. The tobacco companies, for example, lobby the Food and Drug Administration, contribute to presidential and gubernatorial campaigns and to federal and state legislative candidates, and pressure state attorneys-general to protect their interests from lawsuits.

- *The "natural aristocracy" of intelligent and enlightened people, whom Framers believed would gravitate toward public service, would protect the common good from the selfishness of interest groups.* In *The Federalist*, No. 10, Madison admitted, however, that government could not always be counted on to ensure that the common good prevails: "It is in vain to say, that enlightened statesmen will be able to adjust these clashing interests, and render them all subservient to the public good. Enlightened statesmen will not always be at the helm; nor, in many cases, can such an adjustment be made at all."

- *Competition in the growing national economy would give rise to so many competing interest groups that no one group would be able to monopolize the marketplace of interests.* As we'll see shortly, political scientists still disagree over the truth of this argument, but they agree that the number of interest groups has mushroomed well beyond Madison's wildest imagination.

Can a Government Awash in Interest Groups Serve the Common Good?

Does the explosion of interest groups mean that certain segments of the population are getting their way at the expense of the population as a whole? Not necessarily. As we saw in the Alar case, one of government's jobs is to mediate between conflicting interests. Although interest groups can deliver the political support that government and politicians want, government controls information that interest groups want. Government can therefore influence the policies of interest groups, just as interest groups can influence the policies of government.[41]

In addition, as interest groups have multiplied and specialized, government has sometimes been able to exploit their differences to keep one from benefiting at the expense of other groups or the public. This is a big change since the 1950s, when entire policy areas were dominated by one or two large organizations. In the 1950s, for instance, the American Medical Association (AMA) spoke for the entire medical community and the American Farm Bureau Federation (AFBF) spoke

Members of the National Black Farmers Association protest outside the White House in December 1996 against discrimination in the federal lending program to farmers.

for the entire farming community. Today these groups face competition on many policy matters from newer medical and farming groups, as well as from groups representing different interests.

This splintering of power reduces the relative power of any one community of interests, which makes all of them easier for government to control. Lawmakers passed the Tax Reform Act of 1986, for example, because interest groups were so divided over the issues that they effectively canceled one another out. Similar divisions among interest groups have allowed Congress to deregulate the airlines, telecommunications, and trucking industries.

Do Interest Groups Serve Democracy? Experts Disagree

Most Americans appreciate the representation interest groups provide but are deeply suspicious of their influence on public officials and public policies. For decades, scholars and political observers have been similarly split on the issue, with pluralists arguing that interest group competition fosters democracy, and elite theorists arguing that such groups are irrelevant because privileged insiders dominate all policymaking.

The Pluralists' Argument

Pluralist theorists argue, as Madison did, that competing interest groups balance one another in the political arena, thereby contributing to social stability and the common good. Public policy, these political scientists claim, reflects an equilibrium of interest group demands that changes only when one or more groups mobilize and succeed in getting a new policy adopted. In their view, *policy is the outcome of the contest between competing interest groups*. Public officials merely act as umpires in the disputes among interest groups, rather than choosing the policies they believe will best serve the nation's needs. The classic, founding pluralist text was David Truman's *The Governmental Process*.[42]

Robert Dahl's *Who Governs?*—a classic study of local politics—offered the first concrete evidence to support these claims.[43] Dahl found that competing groups in New Haven, Connecticut, reached political decisions by bargaining and compromise, with no single group always getting its way. The book, published in 1961, had an enormous impact on scholars who interpreted its descriptions (*what is*) as evaluations (*what's right*) and prescriptions (*what works*). In their minds, Dahl was saying not only "This is the way things are" but also "This is the way things should be." Many concluded that competition among interest groups helps rather than hinders democracy.[44]

But Dahl also had critics. In their view, the local issues he had studied threatened neither the status quo nor the elites in New Haven, and therefore his research had not proved that controversial issues could be effectively addressed or resolved by interest groups politics or that pluralism actually fosters democracy. Some scholars pointed out that groups such as minorities, women, antiwar protesters, and the poor lacked access to government because they lacked access to the interest groups that had long shaped the policies on civil rights, war, and poverty. In a truly pluralistic society, these critics argued, such groups would not have needed to resort to urban riots, civil disobedience, and violence because government would have heeded their petitions, as it had those of other groups.

Still others criticized Dahl for not recognizing that interest group politics is inherently conservative—that once a group gets what it wants from government it becomes a vested interest, which then tries to exclude competing groups from gaining similar privileges. In *The End of Liberalism*, Theodore Lowi attacked this positive view of interest groups—a view political scientists call **interest group liberalism**. As interest groups have ballooned, Lowi argued, government has grown oppressively big, ineffective, and corrupt. Interest groups, he said, undermine democratic government by pressuring government officials to bargain informally with lobbyists, largely behind closed doors, thus distorting public policies.[45]

The Elite Theorists' Argument

The pluralists were also attacked by the **elite theorists**, who drew their arguments from sociologist C. Wright Mills' *The Power Elite* [46] and similar books. Elite theorists argue that a small group of privileged insiders—wealthy families, powerful politicians, corporate executives, and military leaders—dominate policymaking at the federal, state, and local levels. They claim that it is this highly centralized and authoritarian grip on political power, not the democratic process, that determines policymaking decisions.

A 1992 PBS "Frontline" documentary illustrated just how cozy this elite world can be. Occupying vacation apartments in the same building in Bal Harbor, Florida, at that time were former Speaker of the House Tip O'Neill (now deceased); former Senator Howard Baker; Senator Robert Dole; former cabinet member Elizabeth Dole; Jack Stephens, a major contributor to both major parties; TV commentator David Brinkley; Democratic party leader and former ambassador to Russia Bob Strauss; and Dwayne Andreas, chairman of the board of Archer Daniels Midland—whom we saw lobbying for ethanol in Chapter 1. As the TV program pointed out, these people were more than friends: "Bob Dole went to bat for ethanol and got big contributions from Dwayne Andreas. Andreas contributed to Howard Baker's big fund-raiser and to Tip O'Neill's big retirement dinner. Andreas's firm, ADM, sponsers David Brinkley's show. And ADM appointed Bob Strauss to its board of directors." No matter who won the 1992 presidential election, "Frontline" concluded, these people would have access to the White House.[47]

Elite theorists maintain that all groups, including the most democratically inclined, are governed by the **iron law of oligarchy**, or rule by elites. These scholars therefore pay little attention to interest groups as political actors because they are convinced that elites conduct political affairs directly with government, bypassing both the public *and* the special interest groups.[48]

Hyperpluralism and Demosclerosis

Today some political observers warn that **hyperpluralism**—the excessive proliferation of interest groups—will clog the political process and cause it to break down. Critic Jonathan Rauch compares hyperpluralism to "the tragedy of the commons," an ecological phenomenon in which public lands are stripped by animal grazing because common ownership gives everyone an incentive to use the lands and no one an incentive to maintain them. Rauch argues that hyperpluralism will cause American democracy to develop **demosclerosis:**

> Demosclerosis is a version of . . . the tragedy of the commons. . . . In a common-resource situation, if everybody tries to win, everybody loses. . . . The universe of public policies is a kind of commons. If you see others rushing to get favorable laws and regulations passed, you rush to do the same so as not to be left at a disadvantage. But government can only do so much. Its resource base and management ability are limited, and its adaptability erodes with each additional benefit that interest groups lock in. So if everybody descends on Washington hunting some favorable policy, government becomes rigid, overburdened, incoherent. Soon it's despoiled. Everybody loses.[49]

Rauch argues that politicians tend to react to hyperpluralism by pandering "to interest groups frantically while denouncing them furiously."[50] In the days when only a few powerful people and political machines dispensed political favors in smoke-filled rooms, they did a good job of "keeping the lid on interest group frenzy—they just didn't do it particularly fairly," says Rauch. When Congress made the process fair by abolishing the seniority system, "we abolished the venal gatekeepers. But that was only the good news. The bad news was that we also abolished the gate."[51]

How Democratic Are Interest Groups?

Interest groups have been criticized for being undemocratic both in failing to represent all Americans and in limiting the participation of their members. Few would disagree that most interests are represented to some extent by interest groups. However, critics claim that economic interests—businesses and high-income groups in particular—tend to dominate because they have more money, trained talent, technology, time, and other resources to run efficient organizations on a sustained basis. Compared with weaker groups like the unemployed and the working poor, powerful economic interests such as corporations also have more interest groups to represent them.

Critics also argue that even self-described public interest groups don't represent all Americans. Although some groups, such as labor unions and the NRA, recruit members from lower-income groups with less education,[52] members of most interest groups tend to be professionals and managers with college educations and high incomes. Among the members of Common Cause, the liberal reform "citizens lobby," 43 percent have completed graduate or a professional school and the average member's family income is twice the national average.[53] Of the NRDC's 130,000 members, 85 percent have at least a bachelor's degree and the average member's income is $68,000. NRDC board members meet at the Harvard Club in New York City, and Kennedy and Rockefeller family members work on the group's staff—something that has led to charges of "limousine environmentalism."

Elite theorists argue that these socioeconomic differences often divide leaders and group activists from the membership they are supposed to serve. Some accuse the middle-class leaders of civil rights organizations, for example, of failing to represent the views of the average African American. Studies show that civil rights leaders tend to be liberal on social issues and conservative on economic issues, whereas their followers are just the reverse, favoring the death penalty and criticizing free-market capitalism.[54]

Do interest groups practice democracy internally? Few interest group leaders, including those who run "public interest" groups, allow members much say in their organizations. Only about half the groups allow any member participation at all. Most are dominated by elites and experts—evidence that the iron law of oligarchy applies inside interest groups. Exceptions are some women's organizations that have been shifting to collective leadership and that keep close links with their grass roots. Wider Opportunities for Women (WOW), for example, has recently switched to a work-team model of organization based on consensus management.[55] In general, however, leaders of most groups claim that democracy hampers their effectiveness, which depends on being able to act independently of members, often on short notice and on the advice of legal or other experts.[56] Interest groups thus end up concentrating power in elites who manage the experts they hire. In short, the political effectiveness of most groups is gained at the expense of participation *within* the groups themselves. This may be fine with many members who lead busy professional and family lives and are content to "vote" for a cause either by paying their annual dues or by refusing to renew their membership.

Whatever their members' views, many public interest groups can afford to ignore them because their financing comes largely from foundations and from federal grants and contracts. In the 1960s and 1970s, federal contributions even went to community development organizations such as the Reverend Jesse Jackson's Operation PUSH, but in the Reagan years the funds were sharply cut in an effort to weaken liberal activists. The funding role of foundations is significant: One-third of the mainly liberal self-described public interest groups have traditionally received half or more of their funds from the Ford Foundation or similar sources; one-tenth have received more than 90 percent.[57] Some of these liberal groups are "public interest" law firms that don't bother to recruit members and, while they may follow progressive policies, organizationally they resemble the commercial corporations they oppose in court.[58] The Nader Public Citizen network of organizations actually prohibits formal member participation in the specialized research and action groups for which Public Citizen raises money.[59] Is this lack of internal democracy a bad thing? It may not affect the functioning of the groups themselves, but it could cause citizens to become less informed, less vigilant, and less politically active.

Monitoring and Regulating Interest Groups

Efforts to monitor and regulate interest group activities must confront the seemingly unresolvable problem stated in the Madisonian dilemma: Interest groups have a constitutional right to organize and petition government, and this right allows them to affect public policies in ways that help themselves at the expense of others. Would-be reformers must also resolve several other problems. The laws on the books are largely the result of incremental responses to particular scandals, abuses, and growing concerns about public ethics rather than a carefully crafted body of legislation.[60] Even these existing laws are not properly enforced. And, finally, reform efforts are stymied by strong disagreements not only over how to define and evaluate the problem (*what is*) but also over how to correct it (*what's right* and *what works*).

Current Regulations—and Loopholes

Until the 1970s, both the federal government and the 50 states focused their attention on monitoring lobbyists rather than regulating them.

Laws About Monitoring Lobbying Activities

Domestic lobbyists must obey laws designed to move lobbying activities into the open where they can be monitored and to restrict those activities within ethically acceptable boundaries. The 1946 Federal Regulation of Lobbying Act requires domestic lobbyists, and often the groups they represent, to register with the Clerk of the House and the Secretary of the Senate. They must file quarterly financial statements detailing many of their activities (to make it harder to hide ill-gotten gains) and refrain from certain activities (such as accepting a percentage of the financial benefits they obtain for the interest group they represent).

The registration requirement is ineffective for a number of reasons:

- There is no agreement on the definition of *interest group* or *lobbyist* (*what is*). Should government agencies and federal bureaucratic organizations such as the American Public Welfare Association[61] be required to register, for example? Although federal law usually excludes these actors, some states and localities do not.

- Because the law applies only to those whose "principal purpose" is to influence Congress and raise money for that purpose, lobbyists often avoid registering. Many trade associations, for example, claim that their *primary function* is updating their members on industry developments and that lobbying is only a *secondary function*. At present, less than half of the lobbying community is registered.[62]

- Lobbyists who do register typically file only sketchy reports. The 1977 Foreign Agent Registration Act (FARA) requires lobbyists for foreign governments and businesses to file reports with the Justice Department every six months, detailing their political contacts on behalf of those governments. However, the law does not prohibit resident aliens and the domestic subsidiaries of foreign corporations from making political contributions. (Interestingly, while FARA explicitly prohibits foreign nationals from contributing directly or indirectly to American political campaigns, the Reagan administration persuaded Congress to set up a foundation to give money to political parties fostering democracy in other countries. This formalized a long-standing covert U.S. government policy of supporting foreign political movements friendly to the United States.)

Although some observers believe the lobby laws are too limited, others say they are too invasive. Labor unions, business groups, Nader's Public Citizen network, the American Civil Liberties Union, and a number of religious and environmental organizations have fought laws requiring increased disclosure. These groups claim they invade the privacy of organizations and their supporters and violate their constitutional right to petition government.

Groups differ not only on whether lobbying laws are constitutional but also on who should enforce these laws and who should be monitored by them. Predictably, interest groups push for lobbying laws that favor themselves and restrict their opponents. Business lobbies, for example, want unpaid lobbyists such as Ralph Nader to register. Common Cause and other self-proclaimed public interest groups want restrictions on indirect grass-roots lobbying, a specialty of business groups. Corporations bidding for military and other contracts vigorously oppose the extension of lobbying laws to cover contacts with the executive branch. Small interest groups with limited staffs and budgets oppose the requirement of filing regular financial statements as too demanding.

Laws Prohibiting Bribery and Valuable Gifts

The old-fashioned bribery from the industrial era days when corporate "robber barons" paid off lawmakers to get special advantages over their competitors has largely disappeared. Occasional scandals still erupt, such as "Koreagate" in the late 1970s, in which a Korean businessman was accused of bribing several dozen lawmakers and politicians to promote policies favorable to his government. In general, however, gift-giving replaced bribes as professional lobbyists replaced amateurs. In 1996, in an attempt to reduce conflict of interest "gifts"—junkets to swank resorts, meals in fancy restaurants, tickets to Washington Redskin football games—Congress passed reforms that limit the value of items or services a lawmaker can accept. The House limits gifts to T-shirts and other items of nominal value; the Senate limits gifts to items worth less than $50. Money still seeps through the many loopholes in the campaign finance laws, however.

Campaign Finance Laws and Political Action Committees (PACs)

How much money should interest groups be able to donate to political candidates? Richard Nixon won the presidency in 1968 with the help of huge sums of private money—much of it anonymous and some of it illegal—including a gift of a record $2,800,000 from an insurance magnate. As a result, the Democratic-controlled Congress passed the Federal Election Campaign Act (FECA) of 1971. FECA and its 1974 amendments required interest groups and candidates to disclose contributions greater than $100, including the donor's name, address, and profession. Individual contributions were limited to $1,000 and group contributions to $5,000 per election. (Primaries, runoffs, and general elections count as separate elections.) But while the law capped an individual's gifts to all political candidates at $25,000 per year, it placed *no such total limit on*

President George Bush addresses a group at a White House banquet.

what a group could give. This loophole gives members of interest groups a motive for giving indirectly through their **political action committees (PACs)**—organizations that pool individual members' contributions and dole them out as they see fit. (We'll say more about FECA in Chapter 10 on Campaigns and Elections.) **Bundling**, as this practice is called, produces large sums of money that can get a candidate's attention, as the head of the machinists union's PAC explains:

> If you walk up to a candidate and give them $10—which is about all some of our members can afford—it doesn't mean a goddamn thing. But if we as an organization walk up to a candidate and give him or her $10,000, it means a whole lot more. Also, our union is big and strong in some places and we have hardly any members in others. By pooling the money, we can put New York members' money into Wyoming or New Hampshire, where a senator's vote is just as important to us.[63]

Although **hard money**—contributions made directly to candidates—is limited, a loophole allows both individuals and groups to make unlimited contributions directly to political *parties*. These contributions are known as **soft money**, and parties may use them only to publicize their stands on the issues, for voter registration drives, and for generic (not candidate-specific) political advertising. The Supreme Court upheld the soft-money distinction in *Buckley v. Valeo* (1976), declaring that such donations are a form of free speech protected by the First Amendment. But as a former senator pointed out, those who can afford to donate the most money usually get the loudest speech.[64] As Figure 8.1 shows, soft-money donations skyrocketed during the 1996 campaign to triple the amount spent in 1992. Table 8.3 lists the top overall contributors to both parties in 1996.

FIGURE 8.1

Hard and soft money donations in 1992 and 1996

The political parties are collecting record amounts of both "hard money," which must be reported to the Federal Election Commission and comply with contribution limits, and "soft money," which is raised outside FEC limits and is prohibited from being used to promote individual candidates. In practice, the spirit of that restriction is often circumvented.

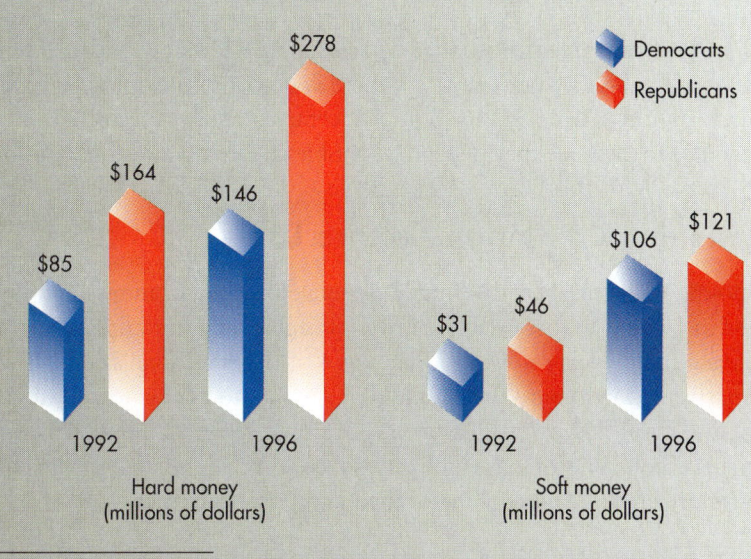

Democrats
Republicans

Hard money (millions of dollars):
- 1992: $85 (Democrats), $164 (Republicans)
- 1996: $146 (Democrats), $278 (Republicans)

Soft money (millions of dollars):
- 1992: $31 (Democrats), $46 (Republicans)
- 1996: $106 (Democrats), $121 (Republicans)

Source: Time, November 11, 1996.

TABLE 8.3

Top Overall Campaign Contributors in 1996

Rank	Contributor	Total	Democrat	Republican
1.	Philip Morris	$2,741,659	$ 608,704	$2,131,955
2.	A.T.&T.	2,130,045	858,462	1,270,583
3.	Assoc. of Trial Lawyers of America	2,106,325	1,747,725	353,600
4.	Teamsters Union	2,097,410	2,005,250	87,160
5.	Laborers Union	1,938,250	1,778,750	153,500
6.	Int'l Brotherhood of Electrical Workers	1,821,710	1,785,260	31,950
7.	RJR Nabisco	1,765,306	341,406	1,423,900
8.	National Education Assoc.	1,661,960	1,618,110	38,850
9.	American Medical Assoc.	1,633,530	321,114	1,309,166
10.	American Federation of State/County/Municipal Employees	1,616,125	1,578,700	32,425
11.	United Auto Workers	1,592,298	1,583,323	3,475
12.	Ernst & Young	1,590,215	791,290	798,675
13.	National Auto Dealers' Assoc.	1,563,175	268,000	1,293,175
14.	Food and Commercial Workers Union	1,510,395	1,480,645	20,750
15.	United Parcel Service	1,479,581	510,569	966,512
16.	National Assoc. of Realtors	1,406,233	471,628	934,105
17.	Machinists/Aerospace Workers Union	1,396,375	1,383,625	7,750
18.	National Assoc. of Homebuilders	1,338,049	243,000	1,095,049
19.	Marine Engineers Union	1,317,165	582,165	735,000
20.	Atlantic Richfield	1,278,678	416,553	860,125

Source: Center for Responsive Politics; *New York Times*, October 18, 1996. *Note:* Includes soft money to the national parties, PAC money to candidates, PAC and individual contributions to the Clinton and Dole campaigns, and individual campaign contributions to all federal candidates.

Proposed Reforms and Obstacles to Them

Despite general agreement that campaign finance laws regulating interest groups and lobbyists don't work (*what is*), there is no consensus on what to do about it (*what's right*). Lawmakers have little incentive to adopt reforms with real teeth (*what works*) because they depend on lobbies for campaign contributions.

Tightening Campaign Finance Laws

Proposals to strengthen the fragile Federal Election Commission (FEC), established in 1974 to enforce election laws, by replacing party-appointed commissioners (each major party now appoints three of the six commissioners) with strong nonpartisan watchdogs, by persuading Congress to adequately fund the commission, and by providing instantaneous electronic rather than monthly disclosure of campaign contributions are unlikely to be enacted because lawmakers do not want more effective monitoring of their campaign activities.

Bill Clinton failed to act on his 1992 campaign promise to tighten campaign finance laws while the Democrats still controlled Congress. And the Republican reformers who swept into Congress in 1994 did not act. When a citizen in a New Hampshire town meeting suggested that Clinton and Gingrich set up an independent commission to recommend reforms, the two made headlines by shaking hands on the idea, but then dropped it. The same morning in 1995 that Clinton signed an agreement to abide by the legal limit of $37 million during the 1996 primary campaign, entitling his campaign to $13 million from U.S. taxpayers, he hosted one of the many coffee klatches he held for major campaign donors to the Democratic National Committee (DNC). The DNC, acting as an extension of the Clinton-Gore campaign, spent the $44 million raised from these events, which included overnight stays in the Lincoln bedroom, for pro-Clinton advertising—a scheme that nullified the spending cap. Later Clinton blamed Democratic party fundraisers—"the other campaign, not mine"—for these evasions of the law.[65]

Clinton's promise of reforms during his 1996 campaign coincided with accusations that his campaign had accepted illegal contributions from an Indonesian company through its American lobbyist John Huang, a former Commerce Department official, and that the campaign might have accepted money from Chinese agents through Asian Americans with political connections to the Democratic party.[66] Under intense media scrutiny, the DNC announced that it was returning money from "unverifiable or improper sources."[67] When the DNC announced that it would no longer accept legal donations from subsidiaries of foreign companies and would limit soft-money donations to $100,000 from any source, it loudly challenged the Republicans to do the same. But companies quickly complained, causing the DNC to have second thoughts.[68] Democrats and the liberal press then accused some Republicans, such as Senator Alfonse D'Amato, of campaign finance abuses.[69]

Estimates are that both major parties collected three times as much soft money as they had in 1992 and spent $120 million on advertising. The total for the two campaigns—roughly $2.7 billion—was the largest in U.S. history.[70] And the newly elected Congress did nothing to stop this flood of soft money—to no one's surprise.

Some political analysts point out that capping or banning soft-money contributions would further weaken political parties and thereby strengthen the power of interest groups, which are often viewed as alternatives to parties. And defenders of PACs argue that underdog candidates (such as presidential hopefuls Senator Eugene McCarthy in 1968 and former Senator Paul Tsongas in 1992, and many House and Senate challengers) cannot launch campaigns without help from either PACs or large donors. So this reform would leave the political field to incumbents, millionaires, and those they support. Incumbents oppose this reform because PACs help them raise money for reelection. Senators must raise an average of $10,000 every week of their six-year terms to finance their reelection campaigns. More than half that money usually comes from PACs.[71] Lobbyists don't want to do away with PACs either, because, as one of them put it, "No public official would do anything for you. How would you ever get anything done?"[72] What does this reliance on PACs say about the representativeness of American democracy? The Constitution may call PAC-dependent members of Congress "representatives," says one critic, but when they are "obligated to outsiders for 60 percent or 80 percent of their campaign funds, whom do they *really* represent?"[73] A former lawmaker answers this question quite candidly: "You've got 14 phone messages on your desk. Thirteen of them are from constituents you've never heard of, and one of them is from a guy who just came to your fund-raiser two weeks earlier and gave you $2000. Which phone call are you going to return first?"[74]

Polls show that two out of three contributors and an even larger percentage of the public oppose using tax dollars to finance congressional and even presidential campaigns. (Since 1974 the FEC has distributed voluntary tax contributions to presidential primaries, nominating conventions, and general election candidates but not to congressional campaigns.) However, 52 percent of donors indicated that they would support **public campaign financing** if it were accompanied by strict limits on how much candidates could spend.[75] Such a solution could help to restore confidence in the electoral process because it would reduce the need for campaign fundraising and thus the need for politicians to court donors with tax breaks, subsidies, tariffs, and federal contracts—which taxpayers and consumers must pay for.[76] (The Cato Institute estimates that such "corporate welfare" costs taxpayers $60 billion each year.[77]) It would also eliminate the distraction of fund raising from the official duties of elected officials. But many citizens don't want government that involved in elections, or would rather see their tax dollars spent for other purposes. They also balk at financing campaigns that they regard as too negative and empty.

Closing the "Revolving Door"

Is Congress playing the role of the fox guarding the chicken coop? So many lawmakers and executive branch officials go on to become lobbyists that the phenomenon is now known as the **"revolving door"** syndrome. These new lobbyists use their governmental contacts and expertise to make money in the private sector.[78] Ex-lawmakers know many current lawmakers as well as the rules and strategies of the legislative process, and, unlike other lobbyists, are allowed onto the House and Senate floors during debates. President Clinton promised in 1992 to slam the revolving door, but he didn't manage to do so before his deputy chief of staff, Roy Neel, slipped through. Before his first year was out, Neel had accepted an offer of $500,000 a year to run the U.S. Telephone Association, the high-powered lobby for regional and local telephone companies. Other administration officials and many members of Congress defeated in the elections of 1992, 1994, and 1996 also became Washington lobbyists.

While reform advocates campaign for measures that would bar retiring or defeated government officials from taking lobbying jobs in the private sector for several years after leaving the government payroll, the revolving door has begun turning in the opposite direction. Lobbyists are now taking jobs inside Congress. A top strategist for the Health Insurance Association of America who helped to kill Clinton's health plan landed the directorship of the House Ways and Means Committee when the Republicans won control of Congress. The vice president of the American Forest and Paper Association and a strong backer of the timber industry became a staffer for the Senate Energy and Natural Resource Committee, which oversees the management of federal forests. Because the revolving door has so seldom ushered outsiders inside government, there are no regulations on this practice.

Closing Loopholes in the Tax Laws

> By calling some campaigning a "charity," candidates let their wealthiest backers take big tax deductions and force the rest of us to compensate the Treasury. That sounds starkly fraudulent, and it is. But it is nonetheless becoming common practice. When alert journalists catch them at it, the politicians merely twist their way around the arcane rules of the I.R.S. with a wink and a smirk, as if to say, Doesn't everybody do it?[79]

No, not everyone does it, but understanding the "arcane rules" and knowing who is breaking them is something citizens need to do if they want the culprits caught and punished.

Tax laws exempt not-for-profit organizations from federal taxation. The Internal Revenue Service (IRS) recognizes two kinds of not-for-profits: nonlobbying do-good "charitables" such as the Urban League and think tanks, and lobbying advocacy "noncharitables" such as the NRA and the Tobacco Institute.[80] The IRS does not tax either group, but when you file your income tax form, you can deduct only your contributions to the charitables from your taxable income. This is a form of subsidy because, when you send a check for $100 to United Way, your church, a foundation, a public interest group, or a think tank, you do not have to pay an additional $25 to $39 in taxes on that money, depending on your tax bracket. If your contribution were taxed, you might send a smaller amount—perhaps $75 or $60. By giving you that deduction, the government gets less money from you in taxes and must make up that shortfall by increasing taxes on everyone. In other words, taxpayers will pay $25 to $39 to enable you to contribute $100 to the interest group of your choice. The rationale for these public subsidies (taxpayers' support) of not-for-profits is that they contribute to "the common good."

Thus charitable, educational, and religious groups benefit the most from tax exemptions, but there is a tradeoff: They also are the most severely restricted in terms of political activity. Groups that violate this prohibition lose their tax-exempt status. For example, a federal court ruled that a medical society had broken the law against electioneering by printing in its newsletter the names of political candidates who were members of the society. This alone would not have violated the law, but the fact that the newsletter stated the society's opposition to socialized medicine did.

Some argue that these IRS rules prevent charities from accomplishing their goals through public policies and violate their First Amendment rights to free speech and to petition government. Others argue that the law protects taxpayers from having to subsidize each group's political goals. The U.S. Supreme Court has concluded that while Congress may not penalize

tax loophole or tax expenditure

Tax loopholes, or exemptions, get this slang name because they are holes in the tax laws or regulations that benefit particular groups. The government officially calls such loopholes "tax expenditures" because they decrease revenue—which makes them the equivalent of actual government spending.

groups that lobby, it is not required by the First Amendment to give tax breaks to those that choose to lobby.[81] Thus any charity that chooses to lobby loses its tax-exempt status.

Many not-for-profits make wise and honest use of the subsidies they receive, but others abuse them, often for partisan causes. Nonlobbying partisan think tanks, which count as charitables because they are conducting policy research, educating the public, and monitoring government, often operate at the same levels of indulgence as well-to-do corporations. Employees of the American Enterprise Institute (AEI), for example, enjoy large salaries, expense accounts, and a dining room with fine silver and china engraved with the AEI logo. The libertarian Cato Institute, which advertises itself as a watchdog on government waste and has even published a book outlining the abuse of nonprofit tax subsidies,[82] held a tax-deductible "Benefactor Summit" in the Virgin Islands! The liberal group People for the American Way has been equally adept at manipulating not-for-profit exemptions. American taxpayers indirectly foot the bill for all of these write-offs because the taxes these organizations do not pay are made up for by ordinary taxpayers.

Outlawing "Split Groups"

In the 1970s, groups on the left and the right muddied the write-off waters still further by setting up "**split groups**"—what one critic has called mating "the noncharitable studhorse with the charitable mare" and breeding a "hybrid worth millions in government subsidies."[83] The idea was the brainchild of Senator Jesse Helms (R-N.C.), who hired archconservative lobbyist Richard Viguerie to form a series of noncharitables—the Congressional Club, Conservative Caucus, Committee for the Survival of a Free Congress, and a PAC called the National Conservative Political Action Committee. Viguerie then coupled these noncharitables with a parallel set of charitables—the Coalition for Freedom, Institute of American Relations, Institute on Money and Inflation, and American Family Institute—run by the same people and sharing the same offices, equipment, staff, management, contributors, and ideology. By this device, Helms was able to divert money that would have gone to tax payments and use it to pay for "educational" materials, salaries, plane trips, banquets, projects, and consultants to further his ultraconservative agenda. Tax returns for 1989 showed that the foundation attached to Helm's Conservative Caucus paid nearly 30 percent of the Caucus's wages, although it earned only about 17 percent of the Caucus's income. In addition, one fund raiser, which grossed slightly more than $1 million, cost slightly less than $1 million. It netted the Caucus only $205,651, 40 percent of which went to pay Viguerie for his assistance.[84]

In a roundabout way, the Supreme Court has upheld the legality of split groups. In a 1983 decision, the Court denied "charitable" status to an organization favoring statehood for the District of Columbia, but it stated that the group could set up a complementary group that *was* a charitable.[85] Today hundreds of split groups abound on both left and right: the NAACP, the ACLU, Friends of the Earth, Gun Owners of America, and many more. At present, however, the IRS has no system for tracking the transfer of funds between the organizations of split groups, so taxpayers have no idea how much they are being bilked by them.

Why have Congress and the IRS been so lax in preventing abuses of not-for-profit exemptions? The reason is simple: The very groups and think tanks that serve as watchdogs on government waste are themselves beneficiaries of the regulations, and many members of Congress, who influence IRS regulations, in turn benefit from partisan activities by these groups.

Ethics Regulations

As scandals involving Congress and the executive branch have escalated in recent decades, bipartisan ethics committees in both the House and Senate have been busy. Ethical issues involving the executive branch and federal agencies come before regular House and Senate committees and subcommittees and sometimes before independent prosecutors.

Congress has consumed tremendous resources investigating allegations of unethical activities by members of all three branches of government, some focusing on campaign contributions. Until the scandals surrounding the 1996 presidential campaign broke out, the most famous such case to come before the Senate Ethics Committee during the 1980s was the Keating debacle described on page 275. In 1997, after a prolonged investigation by the House Ethics Committee, Speaker Newt Gingrich was fined $300,000 for using tax-exempt educational organizations—the Abraham Lincoln Opportunity Foundation and the Freedom Foundation—to sponsor partisan activities. The fine—set to reimburse the Ethics Committee for the costs of its investigation—was imposed not only because the Speaker's activities were thought likely to have bilked taxpayers of hundreds of thousands of dollars, but also because he had impeded the investigation.

Ultimately, ethics committees and regulations cannot substitute for individual integrity and a commitment to the spirit of the law. Laws, as one sociologist put it, represent the "*ethical minimum*" of a society.[86] When people divorce their individual interests from those of society, their actions are likely to backfire somewhere down the line. Practicing an ethics that attempts to mesh public and private interests is not only *what's right*, it is also likely to be *what works*—especially in the long run.

GOPAC, formed by House Speaker Newt Gingrich to promote Republican candidates to public office, distributed to its members tapes of lectures Gingrich (shown here) had delivered at Reinhardt College. The House Ethics Committee later found that Gingrich had violated campaign laws in mixing educational with partisan activities.

Summary

Interest groups organize primarily to compete for favorable government policies. They hire experts, including lobbyists and public relations firms, to influence lawmakers, bureaucrats, the media, and the public. Groups may be either special or public. Special interest groups provide material benefits to members; public interest groups provide collective goods that serve some segments of the population more than others. Free riders often enjoy these goods for free.

Interest groups represent individuals, groups, or both. Peak associations are composed of vast numbers of groups, such as big business and big labor; trade associations represent businesses in the same industry. Local chapters of public interest organizations also form associations, as do media and government groups. Foreign interests attempt to influence the U.S. government by hiring American lobbyists. Think tanks influence government through their expertise, which is often partisan.

Interest groups form and multiply for a variety of reasons, among them to respond to problems or threats, to preserve or oppose vested interests in government programs, and to defend the status quo. They seek three kinds of benefits: government spending; regulation, deregulation, or reregulation; and social, moral, and political reforms by: (1) representing citizens to government; (2) educating lawmakers and bureaucrats; (3) setting policy agendas; (4) acting as watchdogs; (5) socializing citizens; and (6) educating members and the public.

Interest groups need physical, human, and organizational resources and rely on five key strategies: forming PACs, tailoring their activities to government operations, building coalitions, developing "inside" strategies (within Washington), and developing "outside" (grass-roots) strategies.

The growth of interest groups since World War II and the development of high-tech lobbying raise anew the Madisonian dilemma: ensuring that interest groups retain their First Amendment freedom to petition government in their own behalf, without undermining policies aimed at the common good. Both the public and political theorists are ambivalent about whether interest groups serve the common good. Pluralist theorists argue that the greater the variety of interest groups, the more likely they are to balance one another and produce equitable policy outcomes. Elite theorists argue that interest groups fail to provide equal or effective representation and that big business, big labor, and professional groups have the resources and expertise to win most policy battles. Some observers warn that hyperpluralism, an excess of interest group activity, distorts the policymaking process. Very few groups practice internal democracy.

There is little agreement on what laws would best monitor and regulate lobbyists. Domestic lobbyists must register and report their activities to Congress; foreign lobbyists must register with the Justice Department. And while some not-for-profits—charitables and noncharitables—make good and fair use of federal tax exemptions, others develop practices such as split groups to avoid paying taxes. Interests groups have found similar loopholes in the campaign finance laws. Politicians have yet to respond to growing calls for significant campaign finance reform.

As the scandals involving Congress and the executive branch have multiplied in recent years, ethics committees have been active in both houses. When special interests consistently put their own interests above the public interest, they may impair the political system that protects those very interests.

Key Terms

bundling **293**	iron law of oligarchy **288**	public interest group **265**
collective goods **266**	iron triangle **282**	revolving door **296**
demosclerosis **288**	issue network **282**	single-issue group **274**
elite theorists **288**	lobbying **265**	soft money **293**
free rider **266**	Madisonian dilemma **285**	special interest group **265**
hard money **293**	outside strategies **282**	split group **298**
hyperpluralism **288**	peak association **269**	sunshine rules **281**
inside strategies **282**	pluralist theorist **287**	think tank **267**
interest group **265**	political action committee (PAC) **293**	trade association **269**
interest group liberalism **288**	public campaign financing **296**	vested interest **271**

How You Can Learn More About Interest Groups

Berry, Jeffrey M. *The Interest Group Society.* Boston: Little, Brown, 1984. A lively survey of how interest groups affect their membership, parties, and policymaking.

Birnbaum, Jeffrey H. *The Lobbyists: How Influence Peddlers Get Their Way in Washington.* New York: Random House, 1992. A former reporter's interesting behind-the-scenes look at lobbying in the Reagan era.

Browne, William P. *Politics, Programs, and Bureaucrats.* Port Washington, N.Y.: Kennikat Press, 1980. A study of the interaction of interest groups and bureaucrats in the policymaking process.

Cigler, Allan J., and Burdett A. Loomis, eds. *Interest Group Politics*, 4th ed. Washington, D.C.: Congressional Quarterly Press, 1995. A reader with chapters on many different interest groups, including the National Organization for Women, the Christian Right, and agriculture.

Garson, David G. *Group Theories of Politics.* Beverly Hills, Calif.: Sage, 1978. A critical history of the development of pluralist theory.

Knoke, David, and James R. Wood. *Organized for Action: Commitment in Voluntary Associations.* New Brunswick, N.J.: Rutgers University Press, 1981. An analysis of how interest groups galvanize public support to achieve collective public policies.

Mack, Charles S. *Lobbying and Government Relations: A Guide for Executives.* New York: Quorum, 1989. A lobbying guide for executives, describing the rationales for lobbying, inside and outside strategies, forming coalitions, financing, and ethics.

Rauch, Jonathan. *Demosclerosis: The Silent Killer of American Democracy.* New York: Times Books, 1994. A caustic critique of the deadly effects of interest group politics on American democracy.

Schattschneider, E. E. *The Semi-Sovereign People.* New York: Holt, Rinehart & Winston, 1960. A classic study on the general functioning of interest groups.

Scholzman, Kay Lehman, and John T. Tierney. *Organized Interests and American Democracy.* New York: Harper & Row, 1986. A general analysis of interest groups, based on original survey data.

Smith, James Allen. *The Idea Brokers: Think Tanks and the Rise of the New Policy Elite.* New York: Free Press, 1991. A history and survey of the role of think tanks in the policymaking process.

Truman, David. *The Governmental Process*, 2nd ed. New York: Alfred A. Knopf, 1971. The study of group interests that inspired pluralist theory.

Vogel, David. *Fluctuating Fortunes.* New York: Basic Books, 1989. A study of the ups and downs of corporate interests.

The Media

This videotape of Rodney King being beaten by Los Angeles police officers was taken by a bystander and broadcast around the world. The exoneration of four officers charged with the assault touched off three days of rioting, which also received intensive media coverage.

CHAPTER 9

By shaping our picture of the world on an almost minute-to-minute basis, the media now largely determine what we think, how we feel and what we do about our social and political environment.

—Robert Stein

The most serious threat to a free press is the progressive corruption of news and information by entertainment, fiction and moral indifference. The whole purpose of a free press is to inform a free society. News may not be truth, but it is supposed to be linked to reality and to the facts which a nation needs for its own governance.

—Michael J. O'Neill, former editor of the *New York Daily News*[1]

The Media: Mass, Specialized, and People's

How Do The Media Shape the News?

How the Media Cover Government and Politics

Government's Power to Regulate and to Withhold Funds

Media Reform and Democracy

Rodney King, an African American, was overtaken by Los Angeles (L.A.) police on March 3, 1991, after a high-speed chase. King refused to be searched or handcuffed, and in the late-night conflict that ensued, four officers clubbed him with nightsticks and kicked him 56 times in 81 seconds. Although the officers' final report indicated an ordinary arrest, a witness with a video minicamera thought otherwise. He sold a videotape of the incident to a local TV station, and that broadcast was picked up by the Cable News Network (CNN) and other networks. Seeing the tape, many viewers were outraged at what seemed a clear case of police brutality or at least excessive force.

Spurred by the exposure, the Los Angeles district attorney investigated and later charged four officers with assault with a deadly weapon and excessive use of force, and two with also filing a false police report. At trial, defense lawyers argued that King had led the police on an 8-mile chase at speeds over 100 miles an hour before being apprehended and claimed that the video's first two seconds—usually edited out on television—depicted King rising from the ground to attack the officers before the beating.[2] On April 29, 1992, after seven days of deliberation, the jury found the defendants not guilty on all counts but one. They deadlocked on the count of unnecessary force against Laurence Powell, the officer most active in the beating on the videotape.

Newspaper, TV, and radio coverage was extensive; the Court TV cable channel broadcast the entire trial live. Within an hour of the live announcement of the verdict on television and radio, violence had erupted in south-central Los Angeles, a largely African-American area. Once again, a bystander recorded events with a video camera, including the brief resistance and then withdrawal of police. Unchecked, the angry mob began torching and looting. Helicopter news crews broadcast the riot live to local audiences and fed the footage to the national networks. They also transmitted the dramatic assault on Reginald Denny, a white truck driver dragged from an 18-wheeler and severely beaten by several African Americans.

These televised reports produced responses of their own. Some viewers, hearing of the police withdrawal, joined in the destruction and looting. Other area residents—also African Americans—saw Denny's beating on television and ran to the scene, rescued him, and helped get him to a nearby hospital, apparently saving his life. Another viewer, President Bush, asked for prime airtime to condemn the violence. "What you saw and I saw on the TV video was revolting," he said that night, and he promised federal troops would help restore law and order.

Despite a dusk-to-dawn curfew, the rioting, torching, and looting continued for three days and nights. When it ended, 58 were dead, 2,300 were wounded, 1,200 local businesses had been destroyed, and property damage was estimated at $1 billion.

As the fires died down, counterreactions set in. The federal government charged the four officers with depriving King of his civil rights; two were eventually convicted and given prison sentences. Having viewed videotapes supplied by the local media, the L.A. police, led by Police Chief Daryl Gates and with pre-arranged live TV coverage, arrested four men for the assault on Denny. Two of the four received light prison sentences, roughly comparable to those handed down against the two officers.

Ethnic groups charged that the media's selective reporting had distorted the picture of what had really happened.[3] Korean immigrant merchants claimed they had been shown firing at looters but attacks on them had not been shown. And although the media had covered the riots in African-American neighborhoods, those in nearby Mexican-American and Salvadoran neighborhoods were not reported because the media did not know those areas well. (Later studies supported this observation: 51 percent of the 5,000 rioters arrested by L.A. police were Latinos, while only 38 percent were African Americans.) And others noted that when similar but more limited disturbances had occurred in San Francisco, Seattle, and Atlanta, they did not receive the same comprehensive live and national coverage given the L.A. riots.

Some observers also criticized the media's short attention span. When President Bush visited the scene a week after the King verdict and endorsed an urban development program, media coverage was sparse. Journalists' initial interest in the L.A. riots had moved the problems of inner cities much higher on the national political agenda. But their interest in those problems was quickly displaced by the upcoming presidential election—another event increasingly tailored to and shaped by the media.

The Rodney King affair illustrates the extraordinary power of the mass media to influence U.S. politics, and it raises troublesome questions about the role the media play in the United States. In many countries, the government owns and operates the major media, decides what citizens should know, and then provides it. In the United States, the media are privately owned but are protected by the First Amendment, which guarantees freedom of the press. Broadcasters are also given free use of the public airwaves. Should these provisions, which make the media the only private businesses with constitutional protections, carry with them special obligations beyond entertaining audiences and making a profit for shareholders? If so, what are those obligations? Educating citizens about the political process? Raising issues of public concern and exploring possible solutions? Being the watchdog of democracy?

In this chapter we explore these issues by focusing on five questions:

What types of media report the news, and what do they report?

How do the media shape our images of political reality, and how can we defend ourselves against this?

How do the media report on politics and government, and how do politicians and government react to and influence this coverage?

How much power does government have over the media, and what forms does that power take?

How do the media strengthen American democracy, and how could they be reformed to be more responsible guardians of it?

The Media: Mass, Specialized, and People's

Almost everything we know about politics (and many other popular topics) comes to us via the **media**—the means of communication or transmission of information. Two centuries ago, that communication was by means of paper and print (the *print media*); more recently, much of it has been via airwaves (the *broadcast media*). Today, many messages are electronically transmitted by facsimile machines, telephone lines, and online computer information providers (*electronic media*). Regardless of the format, the transmissions have had a common element: political actors—journalists, experts, various groups and individuals, and, of course, politicians—have used the media to transmit their assertions about *what is, what's right,* and *what works.* This tradition has a long history in the United States.

The media wield tremendous power in the United States today. In this chapter, we examine that power and what it means for a democracy. We begin by considering the three main types of media: the mass media, which are the most influential media covering U.S. politics today; the specialized media, which target limited audiences; and the people's media, which bypass traditional channels and enable person-to-person transmission, usually electronically.

media

Media is a plural term; the singular is *medium,* derived from the Latin *medius,* for "middle." In communications, a medium is the means by which the sender of a message communicates with the receiver.

The Mass Media

The **mass media** are *mass* in three senses: they reach large masses of people; they themselves are massive organizations; and they transmit a mass, or standardized, message to their audiences.

Mass Audiences

The audience to whom the mass media deliver their messages is enormous. There are now more than 260 million Americans, and more then 98 percent of U.S. homes have at least one television set—more than have telephones or toilets. The average adult viewer watches TV almost three hours each day. (The average child aged 6 to 17 watches four hours daily.) Americans also buy some 61 million newspapers each day, and many of them are read by several people. Asked to name their favorite source or sources for news, most Americans—69 percent—said they rely on television, while 43 percent said newspapers, and only 16 percent said radio (see Table 9.1). Asked which news source (one source only) they considered most reliable, 56 percent said TV, 22 percent said newspapers, and 7 percent said radio.[4] Four decades ago, newspapers took top place (Table 9.1).

Concentrated Ownership

With few exceptions, the mass media are business corporations that must make a profit to survive, and this has contributed to an increasing trend toward greater concentration of ownership. There are three stages in the ongoing process of media concentration:

1. *Local newspapers are bought by national newspaper chains, and local radio and television stations are bought by national broadcasting chains.* Newspapers form chains such as that owned by Gannett (*USA Today* and 90 other dailies), Thomson (70 dailies), and Knight-Ridder (35 dailies). Today only 350 dailies—most of them in small towns—are independently owned.[5] Most commercial television stations are now affiliated with one of four large networks: ABC, CBS, NBC, and Fox. The commercial radio stations also tend to be linked into four large national networks: CBS, NBC, ABC, and Mutual.

The press center at the 1992 Barcelona Olympics, which accommodated 4,000 accredited members of the media.

TABLE 9.1

Which Media Do Americans Rely on for Their News?

Source of most news (in percentages)

Question: "First, I'd like to ask you where you usually get most of your news about what's going on in the world today—from the newspapers or radio or television or magazines or talking to people or where?" (More than one answer is permitted.)

	1959	1963	1967	1972	1976	1982	1986	1992	
Television	51%	55%	64%	64%	64%	64%	66%	69%	(1)
Newspapers	57	53	55	50	49	44	36	43	(2)
Radio	34	29	28	21	19	18	14	16	(3)
Magazines	8	6	7	6	7	6	4	4	(5)
People	4	4	4	4	5	4	4	6	(4)

Most believable news source (in percentages)

Question: "If you got conflicting or different reports of the same news story from radio, television, the magazines, and the newspapers, which of the versions would you be most inclined to believe—the one on the radio or television or magazines or newspapers?" (Only one answer is permitted.)

	1959	1963	1967	1972	1976	1982	1986	1992	
Television	29%	36%	41%	48%	51%	53%	55%	56%	(1)
Newspapers	32	24	24	21	22	22	21	22	(2)
Radio	12	12	7	8	7	6	6	7	(3)
Magazines	10	10	8	10	9	8	7	4	(4)
Don't know/ no answer	17	18	20	13	11	11	12	12	(5)

Source: Adapted from Harold W. Stanley and Richard G. Niemi, *Vital Statistics on American Politics,* 4th ed. (Washington, D.C.: Congressional Quarterly Press, 1994), Table 2-12, p. 74.

2. *National chains are combined into media conglomerates.* Many of the news media companies are now owned by large conglomerates—corporations involved in diverse activities ranging from home appliances to cinema. For example, RCA, the electronics corporation that owns NBC, is itself owned by the giant conglomerate General Electric, and CBS is owned by the electronics giant Westinghouse. There is also a growing trend toward media-only conglomerates—companies that own newspapers, TV stations, radio stations, magazines, and even book publishers. ABC is part of Capital Cities/ABC Inc., which in turn is owned by the Walt Disney Company. Disney also owns 8 local television stations, 21 radio stations, 9 daily newspapers, and various book publishers, magazines, and cable companies. *Newsweek* is owned by the *Washington Post*, which also owns TV and radio stations. *Time* is part of the enormous media conglomerate Time Warner, Inc., which also owns Turner Broadcasting, which is the parent of CNN (Cable News Network), among others. Time Warner also is the largest magazine publisher and the second-largest cable company in the United States.

3. *National conglomerates are being bought by global conglomerates.* As one observer puts it, "Five media corporations dominate the fight for the hundreds of millions of minds in the global village."[6] One of these corporations is Time Warner, which, in addition to its U.S. interests, is also the largest record company and one of the largest book publishers in the world. Headquartered in New York City, Time Warner has subsidiaries in Australia, Asia, Europe, and Latin America. Another global giant is the Walt Disney Company, with its extensive holdings. The other three leading global media companies are headquartered abroad: Bertelsmann in Germany, Hachette in France, and News Corporation in Australia. Each of the three has major holdings in the U.S. market, including many products that compete with those of the other global giants. Few of these products are particularly distinctive.

Concentrated ownership translates into less competition, both within a specific medium and between different media. Being owned by a chain or conglomerate may give a newspaper or broadcaster more information sources and increased operating funds, but as that outlet grows stronger it tends to overwhelm its local competitors. In 1920, for example, 700 cities had competing newspapers with different owners; today, fewer than 50 cities can make this claim. And the answer cannot be found in population figures: In 1910, 100 million Americans were reading 2,400 daily papers. By the mid-1990s, 260 million Americans were reading only 1,570 dailies.[7]

Standardized Messages

As noted earlier, the large media corporations are commercial operations, and they must keep investors happy by showing a profit. To do so, they sometimes share costs and always attempt to reach the largest possible audience.

The United States has more than 1,100 commercial TV stations, some 1,600 daily newspapers, and nearly 10,000 commercial AM and FM radio stations. Seems a lot, doesn't it? But that doesn't translate into 13,000 different viewpoints on the world. Most of these media organizations get at least some of their news from the Associated Press (AP), a news service that is staffed by reporters, photographers, and editors located around the world and that is owned jointly by the media outlets using it. The media also share other sources. Print and electronic news media use reports from such national and international news services as Reuters (based in Great Britain) and the New York Times News Service. Local radio and TV stations pick up programs fed to them by the national networks.

Media corporations find it cost-effective to standardize production processes and materials. That means paper communications are turned out in large print runs, and audiotapes, videotapes, and films are mass produced.

And so are the messages. To appeal to a large audience, a message must be easily understood, regardless of the educational level of the viewer or reader. The giant corporations that control the media therefore tend to aim for the lower middle in their editing and programming, sometimes simplifying content to the point that critics accuse them of "dumbing it down."

Intensifying this trend toward homogenization is the media's dependence on advertising for most of their revenue. The media acted as they did in the Rodney King case primarily because the video and the riots were dramatic news, and dra-

---

Major Newspapers on the Web

About a thousand dailies have a Web presence. Among the leaders are:

Chicago Tribune
http://www.trib.com

Christian Science Monitor
http://csmonitor.com

New York Times
http://www.nyt.com

(This site, called *Cyber-Times*, includes a helpful set of references to and links to other media that would normally be considered competitors.)

San Jose Mercury News
http://www.sjmercury.com/main.htm

(This site, called *Mercury Center* and created by the chain owner Knight-Ridder, was the pioneer in newspapers on the Web.)

Wall Street Journal
http://www.wsj.com

(Unlike most newspapers, this site charges for access.)

Washington Post
http://www.washingtonpost.com

matic news increases *ratings* (the percentage of the television viewing audience watching the station) and *circulation* (the number of newspapers sold). Higher ratings and circulation draw more advertising, and that results in greater profits.

Americans pay no direct cost to receive network TV or radio, and they pay little to get cable TV. The price of most magazines doesn't even cover the cost of printing and mailing, let along staff salaries. Advertising makes up the difference and accounts for any profits the business shows—and for the 10 largest media companies, that's a lot of money. Disney, Time Warner, Viacom Inc., News Corp., Sony, TCI (TeleCommunications Inc., the largest cable system owner), Seagram (owner of MCA), Westinghouse/CBS, Gannett, and General Electric together made more than $80 billion in media business revenues in one recent year.[8] With advertisers picking up such a big tab, perhaps it's not surprising that the media companies carefully avoid content that might alienate or offend advertisers or potential buyers of advertisers' products.

The effect of all this concentration and standardization is that consumers are getting less and less news from the mass media. As large conglomerates have taken control of the major news media, spending on television documentaries and investigative newspaper reporting has declined, as has daily news coverage.[9]

With many different news sources providing the same information, Americans now get choice without diversity. Your choice between the NBC and CBS evening news or between *Newsweek* and *Time* magazines or even between NBC's news and *Time* magazine may not make much difference in terms of the content you get. And, unlike residents of most other countries, Americans cannot look to the public media for better coverage. The United States has only a small public-media sector, primarily the television stations of the Public Broadcasting System (PBS) and its radio affiliates of National Public Radio (NPR) and American Public Radio (APR). Even these public media rely heavily on financial contributions from businesses. Neither are they immune from the concentration trend: 391 local non-commercial radio stations make up the NPR network, and PBS links 349 non-commercial TV stations.

The Specialized Media: Alternative Voices for Special Interests

Perhaps you, like many other Americans, prefer getting at least some of the news from specialized national and local political media that more directly address the issues you consider important. If so, you can choose among thousands of books, hundreds of thousands of magazine articles, millions of newspaper articles, dozens of cable TV channels, and at least a handful of radio stations. Small-circulation magazines include *The Nation* (liberal), *The New Republic* (moderate), and *The National Review* (conservative). Specialized electronic political information carriers, such as those cited throughout this book, target computer-literate news seekers. The C-SPAN cable TV channels carry the proceedings of both houses of Congress and other public affairs programs. Now that 60 percent of American households receive cable television, the average household has access to four dozen cable channels in addition to the affiliates of the four major networks.

Major Broadcast Media Web Sites

ABC
http://www.abc.com

Eye on the *Net@CBS*
http://www.cbs.com

NBC
http://www.nbc.com

CNN Interactive
http://www.cnn.com

This site, like the cable station, covers breaking news, replete with video clips and a fast search engine that will locate stories on requested topics.

C-SPAN
http://www.c-span.org

A Web version of the two cable channels that cover American politics with a special focus on both houses of Congress.

Corporation for Public Broadcasting
http://www.cpb.org

National Public Radio
http://www.npr.org

PBS Online
http://www.pbs.org

This site has "The News-Hour with Jim Lehrer" in hypertext with graphics.

An especially visible area of growth among media covering the interests of specialized audiences is that directed to ethnic minorities and women, as the box nearby shows.

Alternative news weeklies are also a source of diversity. These local papers, distributed free, now serve almost 6 million people and earn some $250 million in advertising annually.[10] Their editorial slants vary, but most cover topics such as environmental pollution more critically, and controversial issues such as gay rights more sympathetically, than the major media. However, the very success of the alternative press has made even it subject to the trend toward absentee ownership by chains that bring more resources to the papers. This trend may also foster the same negative tendencies afflicting mainstream chain newspapers: less distinctively local flavor, less critical local news coverage, and more sensitivity to advertisers.[11]

> **Media Links on the Web**
>
> NewsLink
>
> http://www.newslink.org/menu.html
>
> This site includes links to some 700 newspapers, 450 broadcast, and 650 magazine links. It's been described as a newsjunkie's heaven.
>
> Progressive Networks Inc.
>
> http://www.prognet.com/prognet
>
> This organization seeks "to bring the networking power of the Internet to bear on social and political issues," sponsoring What's New in Activism Online.

The People's Media: Individual Access

A third and growing U.S. media sector—one that politicians have been slow to notice but that ordinary citizens take very seriously—is the **people's media**, which enables ordinary citizens to communicate among themselves and, sometimes, with their leaders. These popular media range from talk shows to online computer networks, and they share two characteristics the others generally lack. First, receivers can control the kinds of messages they receive and can tailor them to their own interests. Second, receivers increasingly fill a second role as well: that of senders.

From Ham Radio to Talk Shows

In previous eras, private individuals could spread news, opinions, or entertainment to people beyond the reach of their voice or the mails only if they had access to a printing press or, later, the radio or television airwaves. This changed when technological breakthroughs in miniaturization enabled such individuals to become ham radio operators, sending and receiving short-wave messages to anyone who would tune in—even abroad. With the advent of citizens' bands—a range of radio-wave frequencies allocated for the use of private citizens—some motorists became local broadcasters, using radios in their cars and trucks. With a mere trip to a local copy shop, individuals soon became publishers of a sort, taking advantage of photocopying when it fell within the range of most people's wallets. Then, in the 1980s, affordable fax (facsimile transmission) machines made the trip to the store unnecessary.

> **C-SPAN**
>
> C-SPAN (Cable-Satellite Public Affairs Network) was established to carry the gavel-to-gavel proceedings of the House of Representatives and other public affairs programming, such as congressional hearings, public affairs conferences, and political speeches. When the Senate decided to allow telecasting as well, a second C-SPAN channel was created. Both are funded by the cable television industry, not the federal government.

During the 1980s an older form of radio and television—the listener/viewer-call-in program or talk show—gained new prominence. Such shows have traditionally been local, but the most prominent and influential are now national. Their pioneers were Larry King, on whose CNN show Ross Perot first declared his availability for the 1992 presidential campaign (Chapter 7), and the outspoken conservative Rush Limbaugh.

The Media of Minorities and Women

Ethnic minorities and women have participated actively in the media since the colonial era, but to do so they have usually had to found their own publications or buy their own radio or television stations. The 273 radio stations and 27 television stations owned by members of various minority groups are less than 3 percent of all stations, and many have smaller audiences than other stations in their markets. Although their impact on national politics and economic life is limited, they often meet important needs of their own audiences.

African Americans

The first black-owned and black-operated newspaper, *Freedom's Journal*, was founded in New York City in 1827. Since the late nineteenth century, African-American newspapers have developed in most large cities, and today there are 227, most published weekly. The *Amsterdam News*, established in 1909 and published weekly in New York City, takes the record for longest continuing period of publication. The Brooklyn (New York City) *Daily Challenge* has the largest circulation: 79,000. There are also 88 African-American periodicals of various types and a nationally distributed cable channel, Black Entertainment Television, which reaches 34 million subscribers. More than 20 TV stations and 450 radio stations nationwide have some programming aimed at a black audience. Many of them are serviced in part by the National Black Network or the Sheridan Broadcasting Network. African Americans own 19 television stations and 181 radio stations.

Latinos

There are now five dailies among the 329 Spanish-language newspapers in the country, with a combined national circulation of about 10 million. The most prominent of these is New York City's *El Diario*, with a daily circulation of 51,000. Some papers are bilingual, and their success has led some originally English-language papers in the South and Southwest to publish sections in Spanish. The English-language *Miami Herald* began publishing a section called *El Nuevo Herald* in 1987. The *Herald* became the nation's first quadrilingual newspaper in 1994, when it added many features in Creole for Haitian readers and began publishing a page of Brazilian news in Portuguese. There are also 82 Spanish-language magazines published in the United States.

Spanish-language programs are developed by Telemundo, Galavision, and Univision, the latter a cable channel carried on nearly 600 systems serving almost 10 million viewers. The Spanish Information Service network furnishes Spanish-language news to radio stations. Latinos currently own 7 television stations and 85 radio stations.

Native Americans

The first Native American newspaper, the bilingual *Cherokee Phoenix and Indian's Advocate*, was founded in 1826 in a town northwest of Atlanta. Since then, more than 1,100 Indian newspapers and magazines have appeared. The largest independently owned newspaper currently published is the weekly *Indian Country Today*, published by Oglala Sioux in South Dakota since 1981. Many other Indian nations have their own newspapers, such as the *Mohawk Akwesasne Notes* and the *Navajo Times*, or magazines. There are no Native American television stations, but there are 5 radio stations.

Women

Most of the 20 women's newspapers and 214 women's magazines published in the United States focus on lifestyle (fashion, food, and housing, but also increasingly careers) rather than political and economic affairs. The leading exception is *Ms.* magazine, founded in 1969 and now published bimonthly. There are no women-owned TV or radio stations, and women-oriented cable TV programming focuses on lifestyle topics. Annual studies by the professional group Women, Men, and Media show that news about women is on the increase in U.S. media, but men still receive more attention. The majority of journalists are men.

Sources: *Gale Directory of Publications & Broadcast Media* (Detroit: Gale, 1994); *Black Americans Information Directory*, 3d ed. 1994–1995 (Detroit: Gale, 1994); *1994 Working Press of the Nation* (Burlington, Iowa: National Research Bureau, 1994); "Boast of Success: Hispanic Newspapers Say They're Generally Profitable, Growing," *Editor & Publisher*, February 12, 1994, p. 13; "Miami Herald Now Quadrilingual," *Editor & Publisher*, April 9, 1994, p. 18; *Media Report to Women* (Washington, D.C.: Women's Institute for Freedom of the Press, 1993); "Slow Gains by Minority Broadcasters," *New York Times*, May 31, 1994.

Susan Swain and her guests, Senator Ernest Hollings (D-S.C.) and Senator John McCain (R-Ariz.), respond to viewer call-ins on a C-SPAN program.

The popularity of Limbaugh's radio and TV talk shows and the fact that most talk-show hosts around the country are conservatives led observers to assume that talk audiences are also overwhelmingly conservative. Thus many were surprised by a 1994 study that showed those audiences relatively evenly divided among conservatives (35 percent), moderates (29 percent), and liberals (24 percent).[12] The first nationally prominent liberal talk-show host, Texas populist Jim Hightower, did not begin broadcasting until 1994, and his show was canceled when Disney bought ABC a year later. The conservative dominance has led some to call for regulations requiring broadcasters to give equal time to various sides of controversial questions. (Some are asking for reinstatement of the fairness doctrine, discussed later in this chapter.)

But not all talk shows are partisan. C-SPAN, which reaches 22 million viewers a week, carries regular daily call-in programs that allow viewers to talk with journalists. When Congress is not in session, lawmakers occasionally appear and respond to callers' uncensored views.

The effect talk shows have on citizen behavior is unclear. Talk shows democratize the expression of opinions somewhat by offering outlets and audiences to ordinary people—at least those with the time to participate. Some critics worry, however, that many talk-show hosts foster a combative style of expression that may further corrupt political discourse; others fear that citizens may believe participation in talk shows is a sufficient substitute for political action.[13]

The Computer Revolution: Online Political Communication

Nothing has so transformed communication as the development of the relatively inexpensive and powerful personal computer attached to a phone line by a modem. With systems like these, anyone who pays a subscription fee to a service provider can access the **Internet**, a global network connecting more than 20,000 registered computer networks in 63 countries. With this access come multiple communication opportunities:

modem
A modem (short for modulator-demodulator) is a device attached to a computer that enables it to "talk" to another computer by converting its digital signal into an analog sound wave that can be transmitted over telephone lines. The receiving modem then converts the wave back to a digital signal for the receiving computer.

- The ability to write and send **e-mail** (electronic mail) instantly and cheaply to anyone in the world who can receive e-mail—even the president (at president@whitehouse.gov).
- An opportunity to leave messages or requests for information on more than 150,000 **computer bulletin boards** and to carry on spirited debates with the other 12 million Americans who use these boards. To make government news and information databases more readily available, the federal government in 1993 established FedWorld Gateway, an umbrella service that links more than one hundred government agency bulletin boards and can be reached via the FedWorld Web site as well.
- Use of the **World Wide Web** (**WWW**, or the Web), the multimedia network made up of hundreds of thousands of Web sites set up by institutions or individuals to offer information to anyone who wants it (or, in the case of some businesses, anyone who wants to pay for it). Access to each site is via a home page maintained by the owner.

According to one recent count, more than 37 million people now access the 2 million host computers of the Internet, mostly through the World Wide Web. Another study found that 23 percent of Americans and Canadians use the Internet, and 9 million of them use it daily. Even people without computers now can have e-mail and access to the Web if they own a television set, buy a Web-TV box for several hundred dollars, connect it to a phone line, and pay the service provider's fee.[14]

Political parties, candidates, and interest groups routinely use these media and technologies (Chapter 10). The ready availability of so much information and the nationwide spread of connections among telephones, televisions, and computers have led politicians and businesses alike to commit themselves to construction of a national **information superhighway**. Most of the data paths—telephone wires, television cables, and satellites—already exist, although they are being continually upgraded technologically as the traffic grows and technology improves.

All this innovation could produce an information utopia that promotes democracy—but only if access for getting and posting information is easy, free or inexpensive, and virtually universal. Although nobody owns the Internet, access to it still depends on businesses, educational institutions, or private firms that charge for their services, so difficulty and cost may prevent most citizens from using the superhighway. Even if free access is given to those who can't afford to pay, their equipment and their neighborhood wiring are likely to be inferior.[15] The 20 million Americans who are blind or have other physical disabilities that impair their use of telecommunications equipment will also require special devices to convert text into sound. That will be an expensive proposition for individuals, unless government regulations make it a required feature of every machine on the highway. A precedent was set by federal regulations governing the provision of visual captions for television programs. Once networks began broadcasting captions on a separate band, deaf viewers who wanted to read them had to buy a set-top decoder that cost hundreds of dollars. When federal regulations required all new TV sets to be equipped with

President George Bush addresses the nation during the 1991 Los Angeles riots. The "closed caption," developed to aid the hearing-impaired, is transmitted with the TV picture and is accessed via a special computer chip in the television set.

information superhighway

This national information infrastructure, similar in a sense to the interstate highway system for vehicles, is being constructed as a web of electronic paths that connect public institutions, workplaces, and homes. It is being expanded to accommodate not only words but also voice and video.

> **public-access cable**
>
> This is a programming arrangement in which a local cable company offers airtime and usually a production studio and equipment free to local government bodies, citizen groups, and even interested individuals, without controlling program content, and carries such programming on dedicated channels. Most local companies—more than 2,000 at last count—offer public-access programming, many of them under requirements of the franchise they receive from the local government.

decoders, producers developed a small computer chip that displayed captions; their cost was less than 25 cents each.

Alternative Television

Alternative television is an outgrowth of two video trends. The first is the development of lightweight, relatively inexpensive camcorders—the type used in the Rodney King case. Using such equipment, virtually anyone can produce an advanced videocassette and then use a VCR to edit it. An interesting innovation is "MTV News Unfiltered" (see page 324). The second trend creating new media opportunities is local **public-access cable**, which allows people to use a cable company's equipment and assistance to make programs and televise their messages on local-access cable stations.

Not surprisingly, these two inexpensive video technologies have fostered new citizen action groups that create their own programs locally. The commercial cable industry currently feeds alternative programming to local-access groups around the country via its National Community Network. The future of such alternative television is unclear.[16] In an era of growing consolidation and standardization among the major media, however, it could contribute to the strengthening of democracy by diversifying media messages.

How Do the Media Shape the News?

When we read the paper or watch the evening news, we tend to consider the media authorities on politics and government. Why? Because their stories have compelling content—statements by participants, quotations from official documents, dramatic photos and video images—and because they claim or imply that their reports come from authorities inside government or behind the scenes. We have no way of challenging these accounts, so we grant the media authority to describe, explain, and interpret political reality to us. But should we? The media have the power to influence our views of *what is, what's right,* and *what works.* To be critical consumers of news, we must understand the obstacles to accuracy and completeness built into the news process—especially journalists' own attitudes and biases, the sources they rely on, and the interests of the owners, editors, and producers who determine what makes it into the paper or onto the TV news.

The Journalist's Role

Most older journalists attended journalism schools that taught them to be neutral or objective observers and reporters, but journalism education today usually recognizes that this is not possible. Leaving aside for the moment the dictates of editors and company policies (those are covered later in this chapter), no reporter can give us all the news, even about politics—there simply is too much going on.

Furthermore, a journalist attempting to be an impartial observer for the absent public runs the risk of becoming a dupe of public officials. From the viewpoint of objective neutrality, when an official says something, it's news, whether it's true or not and whether it's the whole truth or only a piece of the truth.

A journalist preparing a report must therefore select from the enormous detail of real life and present those aspects he or she considers important. And, as many people commented about the coverage of the Rodney King incident, when selection occurs, so does distortion—because something has been left out. That means that journalists—even those who believe they are representatives of the people or defenders of the public interest—are giving a skewed picture of political reality. The picture can be skewed by one or more of several factors, including the reporter's values, his or her sources, the context in which the story is presented, and the reporter's view of the role of the journalist.

Journalists' Values, Beliefs, and Culture

Journalists, like the rest of us, construct their own images of reality based on their experiences and situations. Their basic values, which they may not even be aware of, much less question, will influence the way they report, especially when they are covering violations of their own basic beliefs. According to one study, most journalists believe that

- America's government and values are superior to those of other cultures;
- government of the people, by the people, and for the people is superior to the self-interested government found in the behavior of many politicians;
- the capitalist free-enterprise system is the best system in the world; and
- small-town values are preferable to the values held by residents of big cities, with all the chaos and problems that accompany big-city life.[17]

A reporter who believes in moderation and order, for example, may rely primarily on official sources and may not give readers or viewers detailed information on official misconduct or on demonstrations or campaigns by nongovernmental change activists.

Some skewing of reports is a consequence of personal characteristics and social connections. The typical journalist in America today is 36 years old, white (92 percent), with a bachelor's degree (82 percent), and makes just over $30,000 a year.[18] These are hardly the characteristics of a powerful elite, but they are not typical of the American people either. Washington journalists—particularly television journalists—are even less typical because they often enjoy the same income and social standing as those they cover. The most prominent have even become celebrities in their own right, serving as panelists on TV news shows and earning $30,000 or more for a single speech to a business or lobbying group.[19]

Washington reporters and politicians increasingly share a common language that only news junkies are likely to understand fully, as the box nearby reveals. "Washington news gathering," writes one observer, "is an interaction among elites. One elite reports on another elite."[20] They also often socialize with each other. For example, *New York Times* State Department correspondent Thomas Friedman played tennis with President Bush's secretary of state and campaign manager James Baker while reporting on him. NBC's Andrea Mitchell covered the

Left: ABC television star journalist Sam Donaldson (at right) socializes with James Carville, a political advisor to President Bill Clinton. *Right:* Newlyweds Alan Greenspan, chairman of the Federal Reserve, and NBC television correspondent Andrea Mitchell.

Clinton campaign while living with Alan Greenspan, a Republican whom Bush had appointed to chair the Federal Reserve.[21] Clinton later reappointed Greenspan and won reelection, and in 1997 Mitchell and Greenspan married in what was the Washington social event of the year. Such relationships—as we saw in Chapter 8—are not uncommon. Do they compromise the reporters? The Washington press corps has yet to address this question of professional ethics, which we'll examine later in this chapter.

Nor is there agreement on the appropriateness of politicians becoming journalists and vice versa—a growing trend recently. There have been occasional successful transitions: Pat Buchanan went from journalist to Nixon White House aide to journalist to Reagan aide to journalist to occasional presidential candidate. Tim Russert, an aide to Senator Daniel Patrick Moynihan (D-N.Y.), became NBC's Washington bureau chief. David Gergen worked in the Nixon, Ford, and Reagan White Houses, then became a *US News & World Report* editor, returned to work in the Clinton White House, and then returned to the magazine. But even successful transitions through this "revolving door" may raise questions about the independence of the press.

The Influence of Sources and Beats

A journalist's report may also be influenced by the interests of *sources* (the people who supplied the information for the report) and by his or her **beat** (the particular office, figure, or policy area to which the reporter has been assigned).

Sources generally are people trying to advance their own interests by getting their views into the media. To get information out, a government official need only contact a wire service or a major paper. The national wire services and the major daily newspapers get most of their material from government officials, and the TV and radio networks get most of their material from the wire services and major papers. One ten-year study of the news operation of news magazines and networks found that 70 to 85 percent of news sources are political, economic, social, or cultural celebrities rather than "unknowns." Fully 20 percent of all domestic news comes from the president, and another 20 percent from the cabinet.[22]

Most stories on the front pages of the nation's two leading newspapers, the *New York Times* and the *Washington Post*, come either from U.S. government officials or from foreign or international officials, according to another study. Simi-

Politics of Language

The Language of Media Insiders

A prominent journalist, himself a media insider, offers this account of how media insiders describe the passage of a day reporting on the administration:

> The day is composed, not of hours or minutes, but of *news cycles*. In each cycle, *senior White House officials* speaking *on background* define *the line of the day*. The line is echoed and amplified *outside the Beltway* to *real people*, who live *out there*, by the President's *surrogates*, whose appearances create *actualities* (on radio) and *talking heads* (on television). During the *roll-out* of a new policy, the President, coached by his *handlers* and working from *talking points* and *briefing books* churned out by *war room* aides, may permit his own head to talk. There are various ways in which he might do this, ranging from the simplest *photo op* to a *one on one* with a media *big-foot*, to the more elaborately orchestrated *media hit* (perhaps an *impromptu* with real people) to the full-fledged spectacle of a *town hall*.
>
> The line, a subunit of the Administration's thematic *message*, is reinforced by *leaks* and *plants* and *massaged* through *the care and feeding* of the press. It is adjusted by *spin patrol* and corrected through *damage control* when *mistakes are made* or *gaffes are committed* that take attention *off-message* and can create a dreaded *feeding frenzy*. Reaction to the line is an important part of the cycle, and it comes primarily from Congressional leaders of both parties, the strange-sounding *biparts*, whose staff-written utterances are often delivered directly to *media outlets* via *fax attacks*. The result of all this activity passes through the *media filter*, where it is cut into tiny, easily digestible *sound bites* and fed to already overstuffed *pundits*, who deliver the ultimate product of the entire process, a new piece of *conventional wisdom*.

Source: Excerpted from Michael Kelly, "The Game," *New York Times Magazine*, October 31, 1993, pp. 64–65.

---

larly, most are accounts of public and official events or are derived from briefings and **leaks**—confidential information about what's happening or what's being considered, passed on secretly by bureaucrats, usually middle-level officials. Only one-quarter come from what the trade calls "enterprise"—interviews, spontaneous events, and reporters' own analyses.[23]

The sources that compete to tell their stories want you and others to accept them as authorities about *what is, what's right*, and *what works*. As one observer has noted, "The primary source of reality for news is not what is displayed or what happens in the real world. The reality of news is embedded in the . . . relations that develop between journalists and their sources, and in the politics of knowledge that emerges on each specific newsbeat."[24] The media's beat system strengthens such relations by immersing journalists in specific areas of government, politics, and policy. Journalists are usually assigned to a particular beat for a year or more. By focusing on one office, figure, or policy rather than on other actors or issues, they build expertise. But the beat system also tends to encourage specialization that distorts accounts by leaving out marginal actors and the broader context.

The myopia created by the beat system is intensified by television's quest for images. Ron Nessen, a longtime TV newsman and then press secretary to President Ford, observed that

> TV focuses almost entirely on the "visible" Government in Washington—The President, Congress, the Cabinet departments and the Supreme Court. Television virtually ignores the "hidden" Government that is responsible for much of what happens here—the 3200 lawyers, the 2500 trade associations, the innumerable lobbyists, foundations, Washington representatives and consultants. . . . In fact, just about the only time the "hidden" Government ever attracts the attention of the cameras is when someone breaks the rules and gets caught, for bribery, conspiracy or peddling influence. Otherwise, for TV, it's not a story.[25]

Framing: Placing Events in a Context

We often depend on journalists and editors—and the experts they choose to interview—to analyze and interpret the news. One need only read about Medicare reform or genetic cloning to know that much of the news today involves complex and technical subjects. One NBC News pamphlet asserted that a reporter has an obligation "to put news into perspective, to interpret and to analyze," because "the bare statement of a development may confuse and mislead when it is divorced from essential background and context."[26] Interpretation is one instance of the more general phenomenon of **framing**—putting a news item in a particular context that influences readers or viewers to draw particular conclusions about it. Journalists are usually unaware that they have framed a story in a way that generates a particular interpretation because framing is unavoidable. Putting a report on a program called "the news" or in the news columns of the paper is an act of framing. So is choosing a particular photo or film to illustrate a story, and so is the wording of the headline above the story. As one analyst concluded, "News frames are almost entirely implicit and taken for granted." But, in fact, news frames "determine what is selected, what is excluded, what is emphasized. In short, news presents a packaged world."[27]

But invisibility does not prevent—and indeed it may even strengthen—the tendency of such frames to influence the way we interpret what appears to be a simple news account of someone's statement or action. Consider the Rodney King videotape. It began with a scene of King charging the police who were trying to arrest him. That framed King as a dangerous man. But then the police began repeatedly beating him while he was down on the ground. This footage was more dramatic, and it framed King's experience as an instance of police brutality. Television stations broadcast that second excerpt over and over again. This instance of media editing and framing contributed to the fury so many felt at the not-guilty

framing

If you encounter some splashes of paint on a wall, you might conclude that the person who painted the room was sloppy. But if those splashes of paint have a picture frame around them, giving the names of the painting and the artist, you'll see them as a piece of modern art. We use this information about *what is* to interpret the content or meaning of the painting and even to evaluate its success in representing its subject. We interpret statements about political reality in the same way. The term for this is "framing."

The Framing of Lani Guinier

Lani Guinier, an African-American law professor at the University of Pennsylvania, was President Clinton's choice to be assistant attorney general for civil rights during his first term. Her candidacy ended in a barrage of hostile framing by the media.

As a professor, Guinier had advocated innovative electoral systems for city councils and other collective bodies. Her goal was to achieve limited representation in the political process for minority interests that otherwise could never garner enough votes to elect a representative in single-member–district elections. In her nomination press conference, she explained in detail (too much detail, it later seemed) how such a system of weighted voting might work. The next day, a *Wall Street Journal* editorial called her "Clinton's Quota Queen" for advocating such electoral changes—even though she had never used the word *quota* or advocated quotas, which had become politically very controversial in that time of racial division. Other journalists and media seized on the epithet: a computer search soon thereafter found 337 articles referring to Guinier as a "quota queen." As the attack continued, Clinton decided that Guinier's nomination had become just too controversial, and he insisted that she withdraw her candidacy, even though she was a longtime friend. "In the rush to prejudgment," Guinier later remarked, "I was dismissed without the usual journalistic intervention of primary reporting or the political courtesy of a formal hearing. The attacks on my reputation were promulgated and then repeated by too many journalists who seemed ignorant of their subject."

This framing of Guinier by the media succeeded in creating an image of *what is* that was far removed from the facts but so politically powerful that it overrode both the facts and a longtime friendship in destroying a nominee's candidacy.

Source: Debra Gersh Hernandez, "'Gotcha Journalism' Takes No Prisoners," *Editor & Publisher*, April 23, 1994, p. 101.

---

verdict, and therefore also contributed to the rioting and looting that followed. Another instance of framing killed President Clinton's nomination of Lani Guinier as assistant attorney general for civil rights, as the box above recounts.

In an attempt to minimize framing, journalists often try to avoid the influence both of their own political views and of politicians' claims. Many take refuge in a technical focus—for example, by concentrating on political strategy rather than policy substance when reporting on campaigns and legislative struggles. "Political reporters tend to be politics-wonks rather than policy-wonks, absorbed in 'inside baseball' analysis rather than fascinated by the question of how government should run the country," says one scholar.[28] Adopting a technical focus may help avoid certain kinds of framing, but it is another type of framing and may prevent their giving a fuller picture of politics that takes the issues and the actors' attitudes seriously.

The Journalist's Goal—What Should It Be?

If the whole truth is unattainable and real objectivity is impossible, what should be the goal of the journalist attempting to report the news? Journalists themselves disagree, but the most frequently named goals are accuracy, balance or fairness, and partisanship.

- *Accuracy.* Some say the goal should be providing an accurate account of what someone said or did, of an event the journalist observed, or of the information the journalist uncovered. This sounds appropriate, but what happens if the news source is lying or covering up important aspects of the situation? Accurate reporting will then spread the lies or abet the cover up. And if the reporter or a witness interviewed by the reporter saw only a small and atypical portion of the whole event, accurate reporting may even mislead.
- *Balance or fairness.* Those who argue for balance or fairness believe the journalist's goal should be to report both sides of a story or be equally critical in examining the words or deeds of both parties to an event or a controversy. But stories usually have more than two sides because others are affected by what is said or done. Who decides how many sides should be covered, and on what basis? Furthermore, "fair" reporting of criminal or irresponsible activities may encourage support for crime or irresponsibility. Many thought that the extensive live coverage of the rioting in Los Angeles after the Rodney King verdict only encouraged more violence.
- Partisanship. Some journalists believe that they and the media should abandon any pretense of neutrality and instead serve as avowed political partisans, as newspapers and journalists did when political parties financed most newspapers. They assert that the media should always be watchdogs—critics of the established order—because an adversarial media is one of the few possible checks on government's abuse of power today. Critics of this viewpoint argue that an adversarial media can so discredit government that it may damage democracy over time. Moreover, they say, journalists who become regular critics of the government may lose access to many of the authoritative sources they need to validate their reports.

If objective reporting is impossible, accuracy is insufficient, balance and fairness may prove irresponsible, and partisanship may damage democracy, what should journalists and the media do? Perhaps their only answer is to attempt to make any inescapable biases of their reporting more explicit or obvious. Then the public can be defensive consumers of the news by taking framing and other biases into account. (We return to the topic of bias and defensive consuming of the media later in this chapter.) But journalists aren't the only people media audiences have to defend themselves against.

Ted Koppel became a media star and his late-night ABC news program, "Nightline," became a ratings winner for its coverage of the Iran hostage crisis in 1980, which dragged on for more than a year.

The Interests of Owners, Editors, and Producers

"Journalists no longer hold the commanding position they once did in the ever-expanding universe of news and information," notes a former editor of a big-city paper. "They simply do not have the power and control they [once] exercised."[29]

Why? In part, because there is so little time and space in which to present the news. Reality today consists not only of what several hundred thousand political actors in Washington, D.C., are saying and doing but also of what 6 billion other people around the world are experiencing and doing. Of that whole sphere, we get what producers or editors choose to fit into less than 20 minutes of reporting on the evening television news, into the three-minute hourly news on commercial radio, or into the *news hole* in the paper. No matter which channel they watch or which paper they read, Americans usually get the same "big stories." The other less glamorous or less striking—but perhaps more consequential—developments are rarely covered in the commercial media. As one journalist observed, "It often seems to me that at any given moment, 99 percent of the journalists are covering 1 percent of what's happening in the world."[30] However, time and space are not the only factors limiting media coverage. The media have their own agendas, which include attracting advertisers, increasing their audience, and focusing on personalities and human drama. And these agendas and the "bottom line" are more important to the conglomerates that have replaced the previous owners.

> **news hole**
> This is a term newspaper people use for the space that is not occupied by advertising and that is available for news, which must be written to fit into the space.

Attracting Advertisers

Making money—not reporting the news—is at the top of the agenda for the major mass media. The larger the audience a program or paper attracts, the higher the advertising rates it can charge. News programs and newspapers are under pressure to attract large audiences. An audience increase of 1 percent for a network's evening news telecast can be worth more than $10 million a year in increased advertising revenues.[31] Television news programs have had great success in attracting viewers by replacing hard news with soft news that entertains readers or offers advice on handling their personal problems. As newspapers lost their audiences to TV, they learned to follow television's example.

In choosing what news to report, producers and editors cannot help but feel the pressure of holding on to the advertisers who put up the money that supports their organization. If the organization is owned by a conglomerate, they are also likely to feel pressure to shape or even suppress bad news that might threaten the owner's other investments. A former president of NBC News relates one such story in the box on page 322.

Increasing the Audience—That's Entertainment

The news content of the mass media is now prepared under tight time deadlines by writers, performers, and editors encouraged to entertain by furnishing stunning content with an obvious immediate significance. One form of political entertainment popular with media and consumers alike is the **media event**. These largely ceremonial events include political anniversary celebrations, funerals of political leaders, presidential inaugurations, and even the Olympics. Media events may celebrate political leadership or "portray an idealized version of society, reminding society of what it aspires to be rather than what it is."[32]

Owner Efforts to Influence Media Content

Lawrence Grossman, who was president of NBC News when General Electric bought NBC, tells this story of pressure to influence media content from on high:

> Early in the morning of Tuesday, October 20, 1987, I received an angry phone call from Jack Welch, the hard-nosed chairman of GE. . . . Welch was calling to complain about the way we were reporting the previous day's sudden stock market plunge. He thought our pieces were undercutting the public's confidence in the market, which would certainly not help the stock of NBC's new parent company. He felt no qualms about letting his news division know that he thought NBC's reporters should refrain from using depressing terms like "Black Monday" to describe what had happened.

Although Grossman did not pass the instructions on to NBC's reporters, other media officials might have done so. Indeed, Grossmann points out, GE's potential influence is extensive. Through NBC it owns the major financial cable news service, and it funds various programs on public TV and radio, as well as investing in various cable companies. As the trend toward concentrated ownership continues, editors, producers, and journalists will likely experience more frequent instances of pressure to shape or suppress stories that could prove harmful to the parent company's financial health.

Source: The quotation is from Lawrence K. Grossman, "Regulate the Medium," *Columbia Journalism Review* (November-December 1991): 72.

Serious reformers have difficulty getting promising solutions considered because the media prefer quick fixes and cosmetic solutions that make better sound bites. Some stage events for the sole purpose of getting media coverage. The Center for Science in the Public Interest did this when it wanted to publicize the danger of heart attacks caused by the daily consumption of too much saturated fat. Knowing that another press release criticizing the typical American diet would attract no media attention, the Center held a news conference replete with striking visuals, bowls of popcorn, and tantalizing sound bites, highlighting its discovery that most movie theaters were using coconut oil—a saturated fat—to make their popcorn. It showed that a typical movie serving contained more than 900 calories and 60 grams of fat, 43 of them saturated—more than twice the government's recommended daily limit—even without any added "butter" topping! This entertainment orientation produced publicity so great and so negative that one theater chain after another announced it was changing to unsaturated canola oil.[33] One 1960s radical activist, now a sociology professor, points out that political movements

> become "newsworthy" only by submitting to the implicit rules of newsmaking, by conforming to journalistic notions . . . of what a "story" is, what an "event" is, what a "protest" is. . . . Mass media define the public significance of movement events or, by blanking them out, actively deprive them of larger significance. . . . For what defines a movement as "good copy" is often flamboyance, often the presence of a media-certified celebrity-leader . . . but these qualities of the image are not what movements intend to be their projects, their identities, their goals.[34]

Politicians who want extraordinary coverage have also learned to take the entertainment route. Six members of Congress protested Japanese trade policy by taking sledge hammers to a Toshiba radio and got extensive TV coverage even though they were only 6 of 435 House members. Publicity-seeking extremists (terrorists, for example) also fare well on television—more so than their political strength merits. Even demonstrators who aren't violent often get more coverage than moderates on the left and right, because presenting views that clearly conflict makes better television and has the trappings, if not the substance, of objectivity.

The Use of News Routines and Narratives

Three editorial practices—news routines, narratives, and episodic news reporting—further limit the news we receive. All focus attention on high-profile or dramatic people and their stories, rather than on political processes, public policies, or general conditions.

News routines are principles editors use to select events and people to cover. They tend to give the most attention to two groups: people at the top of society, who have higher income, status, and power and who serve as leaders, official sources, and experts; and those at the other extreme, who tend to be pictured as deviants and troublemakers.[35] The vast range of individuals in between, who do most of the work in politics and who have most of the day-to-day influence in most government agencies, usually get little attention.

Republican members of Congress gather on Capitol Hill in 1987 to smash an imported Toshiba radio. This dramatic "media event" was staged to protest the Japanese manufacturer's sale of technology to the Soviet Union.

A second editorial practice is the presentation of news accounts as *narratives* to enhance their dramatic impact. Television news emphasizes the visual, the dramatic, and the personal—qualities best captured in stories. "For a story to work, there must be something in it that touches your heart, that gets across some kind of emotion—anger, joy, fear," wrote a CBS News managing editor. "Don't just give me the facts; tell me a story. Unless there's human drama, the facts get lost."[36]

Relying on narratives is good entertainment, but does it encourage serious analysis? If it is compelling, the human drama will probably distract attention from important facts about underlying conditions and policies, such as background information that can show why the drama happened in the first place. For example, the human drama surrounding the Los Angeles riots after the Rodney King verdict showed people looting and setting fires, victims fleeing violence, innocent people being beaten, and merchants and residents using arms to defend themselves. These emotional snapshots led many to define these events in terms of law and order and obscured the underlying social and economic conditions that many believed made the city a powderkeg ready to explode.

In a similar fashion, an emphasis on drama in campaign reporting often results in highlighting poll results rather than issues and personal scandal rather than underlying institutional problems. Moreover, by reporting "stories" with beginnings and endings, the media convey the impression that they are telling the whole story, or at least all that is important about the story, when the underlying issues may be far from resolved.

The third and more subtle distortion is the tendency to cover the news *episodically*—as individual instances of such happenings as unemployment, homelessness, or drug abuse. Episodic news reporting makes for good visuals on television and compelling human interest stories in newspapers, but it misleads people into thinking that the problems portrayed are individual and momentary. From such a close viewpoint, the influence of broad social, economic, and political factors is hard to see, and people tend to conclude that individuals—victims and perpetrators—are solely responsible for developments. Episodic coverage may do little to generate interest in public policy concerns. In contrast, *thematic* news coverage explores the pervasiveness of problems and explanations of their deeper causes—aspects vital to effective public policy. Such coverage is not compelling to today's audiences because "talking heads" on television and quotes from experts in the newspaper are not entertainment. The danger, as one scholar notes, is that over time, episodic reporting can result in "the trivialization of public discourse and the erosion of electoral accountability."[37] Given this distorted picture of political reality, people may not see the connections among events or develop conclusions about causes and solutions. As a result, neither politicians nor the government are held responsible, and problems tend to be neglected.

The "New News" and "Gotcha Journalism"

The search for personal stories went into high gear in 1992 when MTV, the pop music cable network, expanded its own nascent news department and covered the presidential primaries in a way that emphasized personalities—to the background beat of rock music. *Rolling Stone* media critic Jon Katz used the term the **"New News"** to characterize this "heady concoction, part Hollywood film and TV movie, part pop music and pop art, mixed with popular culture and celebrity magazines, tabloid telecasts, cable and home video." As other examples of New News he cited Court TV, the Larry King and Rush Limbaugh talk shows, and network evening news magazines such as "Inside Edition." Among the topics favored by New News media are sexual harassment and race relations. What Katz called the "Old News"—balanced, moderate, objective, detached, fact-oriented—is, he wrote, "pooped, confused and broke," watched only by aging citizens, not by youth.[38]

The New News took another leap forward when MTV developed its weekly program "MTV News Unfiltered," which turns viewers into reporters. Viewers are invited to phone in their own news stories, and MTV editors pick the most promising and ship camcorders to the proposers so they can produce their own news segments. The network then airs the best—unedited—during the Sunday morning program and intersperses others throughout its schedule. Topics vary from issues of interest to all ages, such as Gulf War Syndrome, to youth issues, such as dress codes and public service projects run by teens. In each case, the voice is unique and nonprofessional, and the implication is that individual citizens, young as well as old, can make a difference.[39]

The New News has faced severe criticism from some. Given an obsession with profits and the necessity to make a report stand out in the sea of information, the New News approach can be very attractive to media owners. "No need for bureaus in far-flung lands. No need to focus on the serious stuff of running a nation. Too expensive and too boring," writes one political reporter turned journalism professor. The result, he says, is that American journalism "is increasingly seen as a business of hucksters and character assassins" and a business unworthy of public trust.[40]

Going a step beyond the New News is **"gotcha journalism"**—investigative journalism intended to catch public officials in seemingly compromising positions or to unearth claims that they engaged in inappropriate acts at some earlier time. Investigative journalism came to prominence when journalists published criticisms of the Vietnam War in the 1960s, and it flourished with the support of liberal politicians emphasizing environmental and consumer concerns in the 1970s and 1980s. Many journalists with liberal views sought out negative stories on the Nixon, Carter, and Reagan administrations. The tables turned with the growth of conservative political newspapers (such as the *Washington Times*), magazines (the *American Spectator* and the *Washington Standard*), and book publishers (Regnery and Free Press). Conservative attention focused particularly on candidate Clinton, his administration, and the first lady. Ethical questions dogged Clinton into his second term, as reporters searched for details of Hillary Rodham Clinton's business dealings (Whitewater) and Bill Clinton's personal conduct while Arkansas governor (the Paula Jones sexual harassment charges). Nominees for important positions in his administration faced unusual probes, as had some Bush nominees.

Where New News places a premium on entertainment, gotcha journalism often seems to value apparent scandal more than information—even when covering the major institutions of American government. Its impact on the lives of many political actors has been immense, and many fear that it also seriously undermines popular confidence in government.

What Kind of Bias? Media Critics Disagree

It is easy for one person to see bias in someone else's account, but most of us have difficulty recognizing our own biases. This helps explain why most people—conservatives, liberals, and moderates—agree that the mass media are biased but disagree on what these biases are. Consider the way this tendency shows up in the stands taken by these professional media critics:

- The right-wing group Accuracy in Media (AIM) describes its function as combating "media distortion and abuse"—which it does by attacking what it considers left-wing bias in most media.
- The left-wing group Fairness and Accuracy in Reporting (FAIR) describes its function as correcting bias and imbalance by focusing on "the narrow corporate ownership of the press, the media's allegiance to official agendas and their insensitivity to women, labor, minorities and other public interest constituencies."
- The Media Research Center was founded by the finance director of Pat Buchanan's 1992 campaign.
- The Center for Media and Public Affairs, founded by two social scientists, is an outgrowth

bias
The word *bias* originally meant a "slanting line." It has become a metaphor for the different "slants" or "takes" people have on reality—including, of course, journalists.

Political Action Guide

How to Read the Morning Paper and Watch the Evening News

The Washington news that gets to us via the evening news on TV or in the morning paper has already been "processed" by the source in government, by the reporter, and by the editors in New York who prepare it for television, for the *New York Times*, for the Associated Press, or for another news service. So you probably shouldn't take this news to be an accurate account of *what is*, for it usually means something more than, or different from, what it seems to say. Here are some general guidelines on how to interpret it.

1. Don't mistake a "trial balloon" for a fully developed, agreed-upon, official policy or course of action. Often an official will "leak" a proposal to find out what popular reaction would be were it to become policy.
2. Don't mistake a "hostile leak" for a "trial balloon." Often an opponent of a particular policy proposal will leak it to stimulate hostile reactions that would encourage its advocates to withdraw it.
3. Remember that there is always a time lag between an erroneous accusation and a correction, and that denials and corrections usually get less "play" than accusations. So don't assume that what you hear at first is true. (This is less of a problem in political campaigns now because of new technology; see Chapter 10.)
4. Pay careful attention to the type of denial that is made. A quick "blanket denial" of a fast-breaking story is usually made by a low-level official who wouldn't be in a position to know whether it was true or not—such as a press secretary—in hopes that the whole thing will blow over. As soon as the involved officials "get their act together," they are likely to issue a "cover story" designed to be a plausible explanation of what happened. Such stories may in fact cover up the truth, as was the case with the Nixon White House's handling of the Watergate break-in. So it's best to suspend judgment until more facts are in.
5. A "no comment" response usually means that the accusation or account is true. The involved officials think it so likely that a particular story will be confirmed by events or study that they don't dare risk denying it.

of their study of the national press corps, which concluded that the press consists predominantly of secular, white, male, eastern-educated liberals out of touch with mainstream America.

- The Institute for Media Analysis focuses primarily on the *New York Times* and criticizes the media from an antigovernment perspective.[41]

Although each group advocates what might be called "defensive news consumption," each would make different recommendations as a result of its political orientation.

Many organizations emphasize that citizens should diversify their information resources. Although reporters may seem to be doing this for us when they quote "experts" who have different opinions on a topic, some studies show the diversity is more apparent than real. A study conducted at the University of Minnesota examined every network TV newscast for 29 months, and it found that the interviewed experts—whom it called **news shapers**—were "remarkably homogeneous. . . . They

6. What day it is may make a big difference in how believable or how important an account is. Sunday is a slow news day, so officials are likely to make statements—either privately or on interview shows like "Meet the Press" or "Face the Nation"—that aren't really that important but will be inflated by reporters and editors seeking news to report in Monday's paper. Such a story is often called a Monday-morning plant because it is designed to appear in the Monday news.
7. Very little really important news is released on Friday because people tend to be away from their TV screens Friday night, and hardly anybody reads the paper on Saturday.
8. The Sunday papers have the largest newspaper audiences, so outsiders such as government critics and activists often release their major news on Saturday, as a Sunday-morning plant.
9. Most news is not as bad as reporters make it out to be. Usually it's less serious than it seems, as was the case with accusations in the Whitewater affair that plagued the Clinton administration. Reporters have a tendency to make a story seem more important than it is so that it—and they—will get more attention.
10. However, the really bad stories are almost always worse than reports suggest. Hardened reporters have difficulty believing that issues like Vietnam, Watergate, or the 1996 Asian campaign finance scandal can be as bad as they are, and because they're often afraid they'll lose their access to important public official sources if they overstate such matters, they're cautious.

In sum, when you encounter an important story, it usually helps to ask first who would benefit from, and who would be hurt by, people's believing the report. Then, in the days that follow, watch for reports of the activities and statements of both parties. Keep your own scorecard.

Source: See Austin Kiplinger, *Washington NOW* (New York: Harper & Row, 1975), pp. 270–72, where points 1, 3, 4, 5, 6, and 9 are presented and developed. For a behind-the-scenes account by a network news director, see Av Westin, *Newswatch: How TV Decides the News* (New York: Simon & Schuster, 1983). For other guidance, see Robert K. Manoff and Michael Schudson, eds., *Reading the News* (New York: Pantheon, 1986); Martin A. Lee and Norman Solomon, *Unreliable Sources: A Guide to Detecting Bias in News Media* (New York: Carol, 1990), esp. Chapter 3, "Media Con Games: How to See Through Them"; Neil Postman and Steve Powers, *How to Watch TV News* (New York: Penguin, 1992).

---

tend to be men rather than women, East Coasters rather than West, and Republicans (along with a few conservative Democrats) rather than critics of the political establishment . . . ex-government officials (mostly from Republican administrations), and 'scholars' from conservative Washington, D.C., think tanks"[42] (Chapter 8). Another study found that the media now rely overwhelmingly on a few think-tanks for expert analysis—foremost among them the Heritage Foundation (which is conservative), the Brookings Institution (centrist), the American Enterprise Institute (conservative), and the Cato Institute (libertarian).[43]

When prestigious newspapers and news programs interview certain people, they grant them authority by certifying them as experts. ABC news anchor Peter Jennings warns that "television seems to give people an instant set of credentials. Just appearing on the box, whether you're a guest or being quoted, has its own set of electronic credentials, and sometimes they don't match reality."[44] Similarly, the inclusion of particular *views* grants them greater legitimacy in the minds of the audience—at the expense of views that have been excluded. What this all means is that because most Americans depend on the national print and electronic media, they are relying on preselected sources whose credentials are not always clear and whose opinions tend to converge.

So, whatever your political orientation, you need to protect yourself against the ways in which both politicians and the media are able to shape the public's images of reality. Some effective strategies are seeking out foreign newspapers and magazines, trying to see things from the adversary's point of view, studying the historical origins and evolution of current situations, and viewing matters in a broader social and economic, as well as political, context. The late Erwin Knoll, editor of the left-wing monthly *The Progressive*, advised that

> you say to yourself every time: "Who's telling me this and why? What have they got to gain by saying it? How does it connect to what I was told yesterday? How does it connect with what I saw or heard or read somewhere else?" Once you start applying that process to the news, you'll be amazed at how much more insight you have.[45]

The Political Action Guide on pages 326–327 offers specific suggestions on how to be a defensive consumer of political news.

How the Media Cover Government and Politics

Many journalists cover Congress, and some are assigned to the bureaucracy, but the White House and Supreme Court beats are considered more prestigious.[46] Network reporters assigned to the White House get so much exposure on television that they become celebrities and are allowed to keep their assignments indefinitely. The Supreme Court beat is usually assigned to journalists with law degrees. Journalists on most other Washington beats are rotated every several years to give them varied experiences and prevent them from becoming too sympathetic to the people and institutions they cover.

The White House Beat

The president gets more coverage than anyone else in government—but even the president's TV coverage is less than it used to be. The average length of a direct quote from a president on TV news was 45 seconds in 1968; today it is less than 10 seconds.[47] Because television increasingly emphasizes entertainment rather than information, presidents now try to speak in brief sound bites that are more likely to make it onto the news.

About 60 reporters for TV and radio networks, newspapers, and magazines are members of the White House press corps. Most of them are white (95 percent) and male (69 percent); their average age

beat
Journalists call assignments "beats" because originally someone covering a particular news source had to "beat the pavement" doing this on foot.

is 42.[48] The president's press secretary coordinates communications between the Oval Office and this small army of journalists. Most press secretaries, like most White House reporters, have been white men; Dee Dee Myers, Clinton's first press secretary, was the first woman to hold this post.

The White House Correspondent

Covering the president may seem glamorous, but it's usually drudgery. Reporters spend most of the day in cramped press quarters trying to get phone calls returned by bureaucrats or waiting on so-called stakeouts—in the words of one, "*waiting* on the curvy driveway outside the West Wing for key players to emerge from a meeting with the president [or] *waiting* outside a house in the bitter cold while the president enjoys a leisurely meal inside" in case something happens to the president.[49] White House journalists call it the "body watch."

Both the White House and the media editors generally prefer coverage of trivial activities and anecdotes about the presidency or the presidential family rather than of serious policy issues, because it is noncontroversial and entertaining.[50]

When the president takes a trip, 50 to 100 correspondents go along on the press plane, but because they won't all be able to squeeze into the helicopters, press facilities, and meeting rooms with the president, they designate a small pool of three or four to be their collective eyes and ears. These few correspondents report back to the rest, who then file their own stories as if they had been there. "It's actually possible to travel overseas with a president and never see him," says one veteran White House correspondent—something correspondents never tell the public.[51]

The Press Secretary and the Office of Communications

As the press corps' major source of information about the president, the White House press secretary has great power to help shape the accounts of a presidency. But this power is only as good as the press secretary's credibility. The press corps must believe that he or she knows what's going on and will never knowingly lie to them. President Carter's press secretary, Jody Powell, once estimated that he could control the content of about 85 percent of the stories by White House correspondents just by emphasizing or avoiding particular issues in his briefing and by being accessible to the journalists informally throughout the day.[52] To prepare daily media briefings, the press secretary reads the major daily papers, calls officials in agencies about which the journalists might ask questions, and often talks with the president.

Aiding the press secretary is the White House Office of Communications, which manages all White House relations with all the media, local as well as national, and tries to coordinate the public relations activities of the executive branch agencies in order to control the public agenda.[53] Its primary concern is image making.

Dee Dee Myers (at right), President Clinton's first press secretary, meets the press.

Presidential Strategies for Controlling the Media

Richard Nixon, who created the Office of Communications, explained that presidents "must try to master the art of manipulating the media not only to win in politics but in order to further the programs and causes they believe in; at the same time they must avoid at all costs the charge of trying to manipulate the media. In the modern presidency, concern for image must rank with concern for substance."[54]

President Reagan's top three aides met every morning to pick the day's theme—the "story line"—and to pass the word to the communications director and press secretary and send it by computer to senior officials throughout the government and their press spokespersons.[55] Meanwhile, the president's "handlers" would try to keep him from speaking off the cuff to journalists he ran into during the day. This highly coordinated strategy gave the White House tight control over what appeared on the television news most nights. But just to make sure, White House aides would telephone correspondents just minutes before they filmed their stories to put the White House spin on the story.[56]

The Bush administration used the media more sparingly. To maintain warm personal relations with White House correspondents, President Bush met regularly with individual reporters in such informal settings as dinner at the White House or a game of horseshoes, a tennis match, or jogging. Such meetings were supposed to make it harder for them to file hostile reports.

President Clinton's experience with the press was quite different. During large parts of his two terms, he faced largely hostile media coverage, often focused on charges of alleged extramarital affairs and questionable financial dealings during his tenure as governor of Arkansas. His comments and speeches also were hard to condense into brief media sound bites. During a time when Washington media coverage focused increasingly on political power struggles, Clinton tended to speak at length on the substance of policy debates. When the Republicans captured Congress in 1995, media coverage targeted the contest between Clinton, House Speaker Newt Gingrich, and Republican presidential candidate and Senate Majority Leader Bob Dole, emphasizing "the game of politics" to an extent that increased public hostility toward the media.[57] However, as Clinton focused his re-election message, his media coverage grew more positive—so much so that most observers thought he was treated better than Dole was during the 1996 presidential campaign (Chapter 10).[58] Even so, much of the coverage once he began his second term proved unusually adversarial.

The Bureaucracy Beat

Some reporters' beats are buildings, such as the Defense Department's Pentagon or the State Department. On occasion, reporters need special backgrounds for such assignments. During the Cold War era, for example, the Pentagon was usually covered by people with military expertise. Reporters who cover issues must deal with a number of bureaucracies. Covering the environment, for example, means covering not only the Environmental Protection Agency but also such departments as Energy and State. Whatever their specific beat, most reporters assigned to the bureaucracy get their information from three sources:

want more than canned segments, legislators can now give them "radio beepers" (interviews with beeps in the background indicating they're recorded), two-way press conferences, "video town meetings," and call-in shows with toll-free 800 numbers. This massive exploitation of electronic media may help explain why most citizens, who have low opinions of Congress as an institution, have high opinions of their own representatives and usually reelect them regularly.

Members of both the House and Senate also use cable television to impress the folks back home. Thanks to C-SPAN's gavel-to-gavel coverage of all floor proceedings, their speeches are delivered to their constituents at home and to viewers around the nation—more often than not with only a handful of their fellow legislators on the floor.

The Judicial Beat

The media's relationship with the federal courts is very different from the ones they have with the executive and legislative branches. Most federal courts get little media coverage outside the city in which they are located or in which a case originated. The U.S. Supreme Court does get major media coverage of its decisions on controversial topics, such as abortion or the death penalty, but legal experts find this coverage weak. As noted earlier, the law is a technical field, and unless reporters have legal training—and fewer than a dozen do—they are unlikely to understand the reasoning and the significance of a decision. Furthermore, the cases most likely to get media coverage are those in which the Court's vote is close rather than those with the greatest legal significance.

Coverage is further limited by the severe restrictions the federal courts put on the media. Journalists are allowed to attend and report on courtroom proceedings, but they may not use audio and video equipment, or even still cameras. More important, journalists are barred from the conferences in which judges decide how to rule on a case—the court equivalents of congressional committee and floor debates. Thus reporters rarely learn how a court reached a particular decision.

Although conferences are closed, decisions and any opinions issued with them become available almost immediately on the Internet. The Court nevertheless depends on the media to convey its decisions not only to the citizenry but even to the many lower courts, which are expected to follow its guidelines, and to public officials whose behavior might be affected by the decision. Why then do the courts make it difficult for the media to cover them comprehensively? Some observers believe the answer lies in the ideological struggles and the interpersonal arguments that occur quite regularly among judges (Chapter 14). If the media reported these conflicts, the authority and legitimacy of the courts might decline, and their effectiveness—and with it the legitimacy of the law—would be curtailed.

Court coverage is nonetheless growing. Journalists increasingly speculate on ideological divisions among the justices and attempt to discern patterns and trends in the Supreme Court's decisions. Some justices have recently started granting interviews to select journalists and giving occasional public speeches on court decision making—an unprecedented development. When William Rehnquist became the new chief justice, he even wrote a book on how the Court operates.[65]

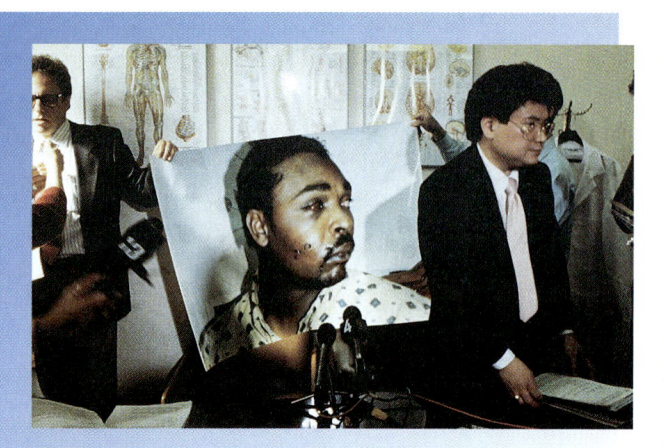

Attorney Steven Berman (at right) stands before a photograph of Rodney King at the televised state trial of the police officers accused of beating him.

Although the Supreme Court still refuses to allow cameras into its chamber, it did rule in *Chandler v. Florida* in 1981 that televised coverage of a court trial does not violate a suspect's constitutional rights.[66] Shortly thereafter, most states began experimenting with allowing some trials to be televised. In 1992, the new nationwide Court TV cable channel started telecasting whole state and local court trials that were of public interest—such as the trial of the Los Angeles police accused of mistreating Rodney King and the murder trial of football legend O. J. Simpson. Since 1991, federal courts have been experimenting with allowing cameras in some federal civil trials, and a similar experiment in criminal trials seems likely. So the trend toward greater openness will probably continue—but only at the pace decided by the courts.

Covering the Rest of the World

If we rely on the media for coverage of U.S. events, we are even more dependent on them as sources of information about what's happening in the rest of the world—the setting for U.S. foreign policy as well as a growing percentage of the country's economic activities. But the media's global coverage is not very comprehensive. Foreign coverage is very expensive, and only 20 American newspapers, 6 wire services, and 8 TV and radio networks have foreign bureaus.[67] One study found that only 0.3 percent of the 150,000 U.S. journalists working for U.S. media organizations are assigned to overseas news bureaus, and most of them are stationed in industrialized countries rather than in the developing world. In fact, the study found, "More U.S. reporters cover the New York Yankees than the entire continent of Africa."[68] This means that most reporting of foreign news must come from a few U.S. reporters or from foreign news services such as the British Broadcasting Corporation and Reuters. And most of the sources that overseas journalists rely on are government officials. The result is that the view of the rest of the world that Americans get through this very small journalistic window is severely limited and often distorted.

Government's Power to Regulate and to Withhold Funds

The media can influence political actors by the way they cover them, but governmental actors hold two cards of their own: the power to regulate and, in the case of public broadcasting, the power to withhold federal funds.

The Power to Regulate

Regulation is the key determinant of which media Americans have and what content those media will—or will not—carry. The First Amendment guarantees freedom of the press, but it says nothing about radio and television. During the evolution of radio and television broadcasting, the U.S. government has taken two somewhat contradictory positions:

- The federal government controls the issuing of radio and television broadcast licenses on the grounds that the airwaves over which most transmission occurs are a public good.
- The courts classify broadcasting as part of the press for constitutional purposes, thereby limiting the extent to which government can legitimately influence content.

The Federal Communications Commission (FCC)

Soon after radio began operating in 1920, the secretary of commerce laid down regulations to ensure that broadcast signals could be clearly heard and would not overlap. In 1926, after a court ruled this practice unconstitutional, competitors began using signals that interfered with each other. Urged by the broadcasting industry, Congress in 1927 created the Federal Radio Commission and gave it the power to regulate the airwaves. That commission was reconstituted in 1934 as the **Federal Communications Commission (FCC)** and given broader regulatory powers to achieve "a fair, efficient, and equitable" broadcasting system responsive to the "public interest, convenience, or necessity." The FCC still regulates the broadcast media.

The FCC is an independent regulatory agency supposedly removed from politics because its seven members are appointed for seven-year terms, but it still gets drawn into the political arena in three main ways:

- The president, with the approval of the Senate, appoints a new member whenever someone's term expires.
- Congress and the president must agree on the FCC's annual budget.
- FCC decisions often are appealed to the courts.

These practices give both citizen groups and business interests opportunities to influence the FCC indirectly.

Who Can Have a License?

The FCC has contended that radio and television should be basically local institutions. The FCC is empowered to issue licenses to stations to use the public airwaves, although few frequencies are still available. It can revoke or refuse to renew licenses when they come due every three years, but it does so only rarely, when a station drastically violates its guidelines. It also regulates how stations should serve the public interest—but in a way that avoids censorship.

Believing that stations should reflect community interests, the FCC traditionally limited the number of radio and TV stations a network or a chain could own, both locally and nationally. This policy changed when the Telecommunications Act of 1996 allowed single ownership of any number of television stations as long as the total did not exceed more than 35 percent of those available in the nation.

What Content Is Regulated?

The FCC expects broadcasters, as local institutions, to reflect local needs and desires, serving the basic purpose of developing an informed public opinion through the public dissemination of news and ideas concerning the vital public issues of the day. Further, the news and ideas should come from "diverse and antagonistic sources." To ensure that broadcasters provided news and information to the public, the FCC initially required stations to do some nonentertainment broadcasting. Then, under President Reagan, the FCC began to deregulate broadcasting and abolished that requirement on grounds that citizen needs were being met.

In 1929 the Federal Radio Commission had developed a policy to foster the airing of a wide range of opinions that came to be called the **fairness doctrine**. It allowed broadcasters to editorialize but also required them to present "different attitudes and viewpoints concerning those vital and often controversial [community] issues." However, broadcasters challenged the fairness doctrine in court on the grounds that it infringed their right to free speech. They also argued that it was no longer necessary because the growth of other electronic media such as cable television provided sufficient diversity of opinion. In 1987, the FCC abandoned the fairness doctrine on the grounds that it "chills speech" and "contravenes the First Amendment and thereby disserves the public interest."[69]

Despite abandoning the fairness doctrine, the FCC maintains several guidelines to foster fairness:

- The **personal attack rule**, also called the **right of rebuttal rule**, provides that when a station broadcasts an attack on the honesty, integrity, or character of a person or group other than in its news or election coverage, the station must give the subject of the attack the right to rebut the charge.
- The **equal time rule** requires a broadcaster to offer equal access to its airwaves to all candidates for a given office if it sells or grants such access to one candidate anywhere but in its news programs.
- The **reasonable access provision** guarantees that candidates for federal office will have reasonable access to buy unedited airtime during campaigns.
- The **political editorializing rule** requires that if a station endorses a candidate for public office in an editorial, it must give other candidates for that office a chance to reply on the air.

Other Laws and Regulations Affecting the Media

The U.S. Supreme Court occasionally deals with questions of First Amendment rights to news gathering (Chapter 15). The courts have also protected ordinary citizens against libel in the media—something against which public figures get only very limited legal protection. The Telecommunications Act of 1996 that deregulated ownership of cable systems and television and radio stations also required television manufacturers to insert the **V-chip**—a computer chip that allows parents to block material rated as offensively violent or sexual, and it banned pornography on computer networks.

When Congress tried to prohibit sending or displaying "indecent" material on the Internet, the Supreme Court unanimously ruled the Communications Decency Act of 1996 an unconstitutional infringement of the First Amendment.[70]

Most obscenity protections and most legal protection of journalists and the media now occur at the state level. All 50 states today have open meeting laws and open records laws giving the media the right to demand access to state and local government activities. In addition, journalists in most states may refuse to reveal confidential information to courts as a result of protections granted by laws in 28 states and court decisions in most others.[71] Thus here, as in so many spheres of activity, the federal system of government affects the practice of politics in the United States.

Funding of Public Broadcasting

When government funds the media, it can make demands concerning content—something that borders on censorship. Congress in 1997 appropriated about 14 percent of the funding for public radio and television through the Corporation for Public Broadcasting (CPB), but that appropriation declines every year. The rest of public broadcasting's funds comes mostly from businesses, foundations, and people who subscribe to or become members of their local stations.

Public broadcasting was created in 1967 to produce and distribute programs that were too controversial or too specialized for the commercial networks. Since then it has been criticized by conservative groups for carrying too many liberal programs and commentators, by both conservative and religious groups for occasionally carrying programs that they consider indecent, and by liberal groups for being too dependent on white males as its experts. Public broadcasting has accommodated these concerns to such an extent that many media analysts now find its programming, both on television through the Public Broadcasting System (PBS) and on radio through National Public Radio (NPR), American Public Radio (APR), and Public Radio International (PRI), bland and increasingly similar to that of various cable channels and even sometimes the networks.

The "V-chip" that TV manufacturers must install in every set to enable adults to prevent children from tuning in to overly violent or sexual programs.

Media Reform and Democracy

Few would deny that the media now play a dominant role in American politics. As we have seen, however, even media officials and journalists disagree over the role the media *should* play. Academic experts and other observers raise other questions, such as whether the net effect of the media is to strengthen or weaken democracy. Practitioners and observers alike also argue over what constitutes ethical media conduct and whether reforms are needed to achieve it.

Do the Media Strengthen Democracy?

The power of the media is limited, according to most research, by the fact that people can choose whether to expose themselves to particular media.[72] Still, most specialists on the media agree that the media can play a positive roll in helping set the policy agenda, legitimating political actors, fostering deliberation, and making the system more representative.

Helping Set the Policy Agenda

By publicizing problems, identifying key issues, and suggesting causes and solutions, the media play a major role in setting the policy agenda for Congress and the president. Television network news, for example, put the elimination of racism on the political agenda in the 1950s and 1960s, with its graphic portrayals of the rough treatment of peaceful black Americans and civil rights demonstrators at the hands of police in southern cities. In the late 1960s and 1970s, the networks put ending the Vietnam War on the agenda by telecasting graphic film of the war—particularly of U.S. casualties—into American homes, making this the first "livingroom war."[73] During the 1980s and 1990s, eliminating sexism and protecting the environment have been media targets.

Fostering Legitimation, Deliberation, and Representation

The media also lend legitimacy to the campaigns of political candidates and the efforts of interest groups. Some individuals running for election find themselves anointed, first as serious candidates and later as frontrunners. Anointment virtually guarantees a flow of campaign funds and continued media attention (Chapter 10). Others who are dismissed by the media as nonserious or without hope of victory are more or less guaranteed to fail, no matter how qualified.

Activist groups, like individual politicians, receive both free publicity and a legitimate status in the minds of politicians and the public when the media take them seriously. Those ignored or dismissed are unlikely to gain further popular support, let alone access to decision makers.

Some media activities do foster deliberation—the thoughtful discussion of problems and possible solutions like that which once occurred in town meetings. The late social historian Christopher Lasch stressed the importance of deliberation:

> What democracy requires is public debate, not information. The kind of information it needs can be generated only by vigorous popular debate. We do not know what we need to know until we ask the right questions, and we can identify the right questions only by subjecting our own ideas about the world to the test of public controversy. . . . When we get into arguments that focus and fully engage our attention, we become avid seekers of relevant information. Otherwise we take in information passively—if we take it in at all.[74]

Perhaps the media should emphasize public debate more, rather than trying to convey information. Too great a focus on information, as Lasch feared, could foster a view of the public as a passive audience, virtually helpless before the onslaught of information overload and manipulative media bombardment.

When the media accurately convey to politicians the views of the people on public issues, they strengthen the system's representativeness. They also do this when they inform the citizenry about candidates and issues at election time. But representative democracy also assumes that the best decisions on political questions will result from deliberation by elected leaders and those they appoint rather than from direct citizen participation.

Media Reforms: What's Right? And What Works?

At a time when government regulation of the media is diminishing, those who call for media reforms often propose responsible media self-regulation and increased citizen access.

Media Self-Regulation

Can the media regulate themselves? Opinions are mixed. In principle, an ethical journalist is "a humane truth teller who seeks justice and protects freedom as a faithful steward of his or her craft," according to one expert, who goes on to concede that no journalist can live up to this standard.[75] A former reporter and editor who runs an academic program for journalists makes a more telling criticism of journalists:

> Few have first-hand knowledge of the impact of the American power structure on the daily lives of those who are most vulnerable to and dependent upon the exercise of power. Almost none live in truly integrated neighborhoods. Increasingly, their children are in private, not public schools. Most of them socialize with government officials and civic and social leaders they cover. Their values and their perspectives tend to merge.[76]

President Clinton conducts an electronic town meeting in Detroit.

Furthermore, while all major national political officials are now required to reveal their personal financial investments as well as their income sources, neither journalists nor editors nor media executives face any such requirements. There are growing calls for legally requiring such disclosure because media figures now have such important roles in shaping public political discourse. Such calls may fly in the face of current trends toward deregulation, but many critics argue that the media have fallen behind in their social obligation to observe high standards of accuracy or balance and that they fail to reflect the diversity of society by giving access to various points of view and rights of reply to those they criticize.

Media insiders disagree, saying that if a problem exists, it can be solved by self-regulation. Early in the twentieth century, journalists and then editors began adopting codes calling for decency, fair play, sincerity, truthfulness, accuracy, and impartiality. However, such codes have always lacked enforcement provisions because of fears that the codes themselves might become instruments of censorship as powerful as any governmental interference. And lacking any means of enforcement, they have had little impact on journalistic practice in the face of pressures to reach larger audiences.[77]

Doubting that the media will ever effectively police themselves and fearing that politicians either will refuse to regulate or will reflect the views of powerful interests in any further regulation efforts, some say the burden inevitably rests with citizens themselves. These observers recommend, first, that citizens exercise "consumer sovereignty" and patronize only those media that behave responsibly. Second, they would like to see increased citizen access to the media.

Increased Citizen Access

"Freedom of the press belongs to the man who owns one" quipped the first media critic, A. J. Liebling.[78] Many activists agree, calling for democratization of ownership and access instead of the current trend toward ownership by a few large corporations sharing preferences for profitable entertainment rather than news. Some base their recommendations on a claim that individual citizens and minority groups have *rights* of access to the media and *rights* to be served by the media as they wish. Consumer advocate Ralph Nader took this position when offering the following principles for protecting citizen access at the onset of the computer revolution:

- Every electronic communications technology must be operated in the interest of all citizens.
- The literacy that is the people's birthright must also include media literacy—the teaching of the use of video equipment and computers.
- Every citizen has the right to an opportunity to reach an audience.
- Every citizen has the right to all the information necessary to make rational choices as a voter and as a consumer.[79]

Implementing such citizen access rights would likely require greater proliferation of small-scale, locally based, interactive, and participative people's media rather than centralized and professionalized mass or specialized media. Trends in communication technology appear to be leading the United States in this direction.

Can the New Technologies Help?

Three important trends seem likely to shape the interplay of communications and politics in years to come:[80]

- *The proliferation of technologies.* The public can already use televisions as well as computers and modems, via either telephone lines or cable, to receive an enormous array of information.
- *The decentralization of access to information and transmission lines.* Decentralized access now exists, but only for those who can afford the equipment, pay the fees for expanded access, and master the required technical knowledge. If decentralization of technology and access proceeds at a rapid pace, there could be much more diversity in the messages we receive.
- *Increasing interactivity of senders and receivers.* Experiments in interactivity in which political actors and citizens interact through the media are now going on in various U.S. cities. Although we do not yet know what the most effective use of interactivity is, we can be sure that for democratic deliberation to flourish, technology must become both universally available and interactive.

Is Teledemocracy the Answer?

Teledemocracy—interactive electronic networks connecting all citizens to a central databank by telephone or television—could easily provide more comprehensive accounts of public concerns. Ross Perot advocated a national "electronic town meeting" as the ideal way to make important decisions: "We go to the American people on television, explain it in great detail, and say, 'Here are the alternatives that we face. Which of these alternatives, as owners of the country, do you feel is best for the country?' The American people react, by congressional district, and we know what the people want."[81]

Would such a system work? Many fear that the effect of such a process might be manipulation of ill-informed public opinion—especially because people's answers depend on the way a question is put (Chapter 5) and because only small percentages of the people ever participate in any type of direct political activity (Chapter 6). Electronic town meetings might actually diminish the true deliberation that effective democracy requires.[82]

Implications for Democracy

We cannot foresee whether the unprecedented access that government, business, and citizens now have to information and to the means of communication will strengthen or undermine the status quo. Modern government as it exists today has used the mass media to help centralize its authority and control. But political opposition has also used the media—mainly the alternative press but increasingly video and computer technology—to mobilize forces of opposition and advocate change.[83]

For all their great potential, however, technological advances may actually hinder democracy to the extent that they "magnify the problems of equality and access, of amplified leaders and voiceless audiences, that have plagued mass media politics."[84] Many people still fear the new electronic technology, and many still have neither the knowledge nor the money to use it. And all of us face the challenge of information overload and anxiety. After all, a typical weekday edition of the *New York Times* contains more information than the average person was likely to encounter in a lifetime at the time America was founded.[85] Citizens who lack the money, basic knowledge, and time required to make good, effective use of these remarkable information resources are likely to view the new technology as elitist and oppressive rather than useful, liberating, and empowering. If this happens, some citizens will be increasingly information-rich and some—probably most—will be information-poor. Furthermore, new technologies diversify *sources* of information and *means* of communication, but no one yet knows how much they will diversify the *content* of communication. Greater access to transmission lines could mean greater opportunity for control. And, finally, the technology could be exploited by any government that engages in electronic eavesdropping, uses shared databases to intimidate citizens, or disperses insidious propaganda.[86]

Whether the new mass and alternative media will enhance U.S. democracy will ultimately depend on the extent to which those seeking to strengthen democracy are able to use them to achieve greater access, more participation, and better democratic deliberation. It will also depend on each person's willingness to patronize the media that behave responsibly and to withhold support from those that don't.

Summary

The media are the print-based, broadcast-based, and computer-based channels through which information is sent and received. They have become the major authorities about what is happening in politics and what political actors, experts, citizens, and others believe should happen. The major print and broadcast media are called mass media because they reach mass audiences, their messages are standardized, and their ownership and control are increasingly concentrated in the hands of large corporations that own newspapers, television stations, radio stations, and other media. Various specialized media reach narrower audiences with information and opinion. And the people's media—the alternative press; talk shows; e-mail; the Internet and its computer bulletin boards and World Wide Web; and inexpensive video equipment and public-access cable—use technology to offer individuals and groups greater access.

The reports the media provide are not necessarily accurate, nor are they always what citizens need. They are shaped and limited by journalists' basic values, the interests of their sources, the organization of reporting into beats, the impact of framing, and journalists' differing views of their proper goals: accuracy, balance or fairness, and partisanship. The reports are also influenced by the interests of owners, editors, producers, and advertisers, including making profits by entertaining. The editorial practices of using news routines, narratives, and episodic reporting reach their peak in the current trend toward the "New News" and "gotcha journalism."

Media coverage of the president, the bureaucracy, Congress, and the courts is limited by struggles between reporters seeking information from officials and officials seeking to conceal information and manipulate the media. Most coverage relies primarily on official sources rather than on investigative reporting, and staged media events are common. Reporting of foreign news is limited and often distorted.

The government regulates the media through the Federal Communications Commission, which has the power to issue broadcast licenses; through partial funding of public broadcasting; and through various laws and guidelines. The recent trend toward deregulation has resulted in elimination of the fairness doctrine and increased the trend toward media chains and conglomerates.

The media play important roles in American politics by anointing candidates and setting the policy agenda. They may strengthen American democracy by informing the public and fostering public debate on issues. Media professionals tend to favor self-regulation, while others may prefer more government regulation. Calls for reform often focus on broadening ownership or at least access. Technologies are proliferating, and sometimes competing, with the result that access to information and transmission lines is decentralizing. New technology—manifest in the people's media—could produce an information utopia but might instead create a well-informed elite and information-poor average citizens. It's too early to know whether the result will be stronger or weaker democracy.

Americans would be wise to develop strategies of self-defense, understanding how media technology and practices tend to distort media reports and seeking out competing accounts from various experts and participants.

Key Terms

beat **316**
computer bulletin boards **313**
disinformation **331**
e-mail **313**
equal time rule **336**
fairness doctrine **336**
Federal Communications Commission (FCC) **335**
feeds **332**
framing **318**

gotcha journalism **325**
information superhighway **313**
Internet **312**
leaks **317**
mass media **306**
media **305**
media event **321**
New News **324**
news routines **323**
news shapers **326**

people's media **310**
personal attack rule (or right of rebuttal rule) **336**
political editorializing rule **336**
public-access cable **314**
reasonable access provision **336**
teledemocracy **340**
V-chip **336**
World Wide Web (WWW) **313**

How You Can Learn More About the Media

The best way to follow the media in American politics on a regular basis is to read these specialized magazines: the *Columbia Journalism Review*, the *American Journalism Review* (formerly the *Washington Journalism Review*), the *Media Studies Journal*, the *IRE Journal* (a bimonthly published by the Investigative Reporters and Editors), and the *Media Culture Review*. For particular attention to civic networking and other forward-looking aspects of the communications revolution, see the quarterly *Whole Earth Review*. The impact of the media is regularly examined in *The New Citizen*, published quarterly by Citizens for Media Literacy, 34 Wall Street, Suite 407, Asheville, NC 28801; its e-mail address is: cml@unca.edu. An organization especially interested in the future implications of the media is Computer Professionals for Social Responsibility, Box 717, Palo Alto, CA 94301; its e-mail address is cpsr@cpsr.org. Among the most helpful books are the following:

Bagdikian, Ben. *The Media Monopoly*, 5th ed. Boston: Beacon Press, 1997. The leading study of the trend toward concentration of ownership and control of the major mass media.

Fallows, James. *Breaking the News*. New York: Random House, 1996. A critique explaining "how the media undermine American democracy."

Hertsgaard, Mark. *On Bended Knee: The Press and the Reagan Presidency*. New York: Farrar, Straus & Giroux, 1988. A revealing investigation of news management by the Reagan White House.

Hess, Stephen. *The Washington Reporters*. Washington: Brookings Institution, 1981. *Live from Capitol Hill! Studies of Congress and the Media*. Washington: Brookings Institution, 1991. Two books by the leading expert on the Washington press corps.

Iyengar, Shanto. *Is Anyone Responsible? How Television Frames Political Issues*. Chicago: University of Chicago Press, 1991. A study of framing and episodic versus thematic reporting.

Iyengar, Shanto, and Donald R. Kinder. *News That Matters: Television and American Opinion*. Chicago: University of Chicago Press, 1987. A study of media influence based on experimental research.

Lappé, Frances Moore, and Paul Martin Du Bois. *The Quickening of America: Rebuilding Our Nation, Remaking Our Lives*. San Francisco: Jossey-Bass, 1994. An action guide, Chapter 6 of which is devoted to "Making the Media Our Voice."

Maltese, John Anthony. *Spin Control: The White House Office of Communications and the Management of Presidential News*. Chapel Hill: University of North Carolina Press, 1992. A study of the development of White House efforts to influence news reporting since the Nixon administration.

Schudson, Michael. *The Power of News*. Cambridge, Mass.: Harvard University Press, 1995. An interesting study of the history of newspapers and the contributions the media make to democracy.

Soley, Lawrence C. *The News Shapers: The Sources Who Explain the News*. New York: Praeger Press, 1992. An examination of the homogeneity of experts consulted by the mass media.

Willis, Jim. *The Shadow World: Life between the News Media and Reality*. New York: Praeger Press, 1991. A reflective account by a practitioner.

Campaigns and Elections

Above: The hunt country around Middleburg, Virginia, where Democratic leaders met to plan the party's strategy for the 1992 presidential election. *Right:* Democratic National Committee chair Ron Brown (at microphone) and fundraiser Pamela Harriman join Richard Gephardt (between Brown and Harriman), Bill Clinton (behind Harriman), and other potential candidates outside Harriman's home to meet the press after the strategy meeting. (The photograph was taken from a videotape of the PBS *Frontline* episode called "The Best Campaign Money Can Buy.")

CHAPTER 10

> It's hard for the other guy to say dirty things about you if your fist is in his mouth.
>
> —James Carville, Democratic party campaign strategist

> Campaigns are about definition. Either you define yourself and your opponent, or they do. What you want to do is define yourself on your terms and define them on your terms. Victory goes to the aggressor.
>
> —Mark McKinnon, Democratic party campaign strategist[1]

The Nature of American Elections

How Elections Have Changed

The Stages of a Presidential Election

Campaign Reforms and Democracy

On June 13, 1991, 21 people—part of the group of 150 wealthy Democratic party supporters called the Managing Trustees—met in secret at Pamela Harriman's horse farm in Middleburg, Virginia. Harriman was a longtime fundraiser, member of the Democratic National Committee, and heir to the $75 million estate of her husband Averell Harriman, former governor of New York. Her guests that day included business leaders, investors, and other wealthy individuals who, as Managing Trustees, gave at least $200,000 a year to the Democratic party. (The party has another group of 300 who give only $100,000 a year and are called merely "Trustees.") In 1991, the group hoped to select the next nominee and develop a message and strategy that would win the 1992 election.

With that election still 16 months away, President Bush's popularity remained high following the Gulf War. But polls showed that popularity was due primarily to successes in foreign affairs and was counterbalanced by a perception that he had neglected domestic affairs and an economy mired in recession. The Managing Trustees believed that the millions of Democrats who had voted for Ronald Reagan and George Bush in the past three elections would back a candidate whose main message was the need to ease the economic distress and insecurity of the middle class. They were searching for a "New Democrat" who would focus on domestic concerns not as a traditional liberal relying on big government, but as a moderate working in partnership with business. They had therefore invited would-be candidates to meet with them at Harriman's farm.

A handful of hopefuls accepted, among them Senator Lloyd Bentsen of Texas, Senator Bill Bradley of New Jersey, Governor Bill Clinton of Arkansas, House Majority Leader Dick Gephardt of Missouri, Senator Tom Harkin of Iowa, Senator Jay Rockefeller of West Virginia, and former senator Paul Tsongas of Massachusetts. Each was asked whether he would run on the agreed message and strategy if the Managing Trustees pledged to raise money for his campaign. The Managing Trustees were particularly impressed by Clinton's youthful vigor, quick mind, knowledge of the issues, and self-identification as a New Democrat. Speaking with the press after the meeting, Clinton declared, "Working people are making less money and working longer hours . . . than they were 10 years ago. They're worried sick . . . that their kids are going to get sick and they won't be able to pay the bills. . . . And they're worried that the schools aren't very good, and . . . they won't be able to send them to college."[2]

It was the message the Managing Trustees wanted to hear, and they went on to raise millions of dollars to back his successful primary campaign against five other Democrats. After Clinton's nomination in July 1992, they raised even more money than they had for the 1988 general election campaign.

The same evening the Managing Trustees convened in Middleburg, the Republican Senatorial and Congressional Committees were holding their annual President's Dinner fundraiser at the Washington Convention Center. The event, attended by 4,100 Republicans in formal dress, raised more than $7 million. Republicans had pioneered the practice of organizing an elite corps of large-scale contributors; their counterpart to the Managing Trustees is Team 100, some 200 chief executives of large corporations. Team 100 had raised $25 million for candidate Bush in 1988 in only 90 days and was already hard at work filling his coffers for the next campaign. In 1992, each team member gave $100,000 or more to the party and received special invitations to White House briefings and private meetings with President Bush. In August 1992, the Republicans renominated Bush.

After running an efficient campaign that stuck to the strategy worked out at the secret Middleburg meeting, Clinton outspent and soundly defeated both Bush and billionaire H. Ross Perot, who spent more than $60 million of his own money. At the inauguration, the Managing Trustees had their own gala in the Washington building housing the Organization of American States—the same elegant building in which Team 100 had celebrated Bush's victory four years earlier.

More than half of the 20 million Democrats who had voted in the primaries had voted for Clinton, assuring him of the nomination. Some 13 million Republicans voted in their primaries, 10 million for Bush. Thus 20 million Americans got their favorites nominated. Nearly 105 million people voted for someone in the November election. But of the 260 million Americans who would be governed by the new president, only 44 million had voted for him. And the only access most of these voters had to their new president's victory celebration was watching the parade along Pennsylvania Avenue or on TV. (The morning after the inauguration, however, Clinton did hold an open house at the White House for any person who wished to come—something no president since Andrew Jackson had done, and something Clinton did not repeat after his 1996 reelection.)

The story of the Managing Trustees and Team 100 illustrates the critical role money plays in American elections. But money isn't everything. The quality of the candidate matters, as does the credibility of the candidate's claim to authority. And the candidate's stand on the issues voters care about also matters. To understand the many factors that shape how elections are fought and won, we focus on four basic questions in this chapter:

The Nature of American Elections

What roles do elections play in American politics?

How has the increasing importance of money and media changed presidential and congressional campaigns?

What strategies do candidates use to get support in the key stages of the campaign?

What changes might make elections more ethical, more issue-oriented, less influenced by big money, and more responsive to the general population?

The Nature of American Elections

As we've seen in the preceding chapters, opinion polls, political activism, parties, interest groups, and the media all influence elections and help shape what happens in government. None of them, however, can substitute for **elections**—the process in which citizens cast votes to choose a person to hold public office and govern at the local, state, or national level. Elections do more than just select government officials, however, and election campaigns have changed considerably in recent decades.

What Elections Do and Why They Matter

For the first time in history, most of the world's population lives under some relatively democratic system of government. In these systems, elections are becoming the most popular way of choosing leaders, although they aren't the only possible way. In ancient Greece, for example, all eligible Athenian citizens drew lots to decide who would occupy leadership positions, which rotated periodically.

When the United States was founded, elections—which are now a hallmark of the American political system—were relatively rare. Elections persist because they not only perform several basic and practical functions but also affect citizens and the political system at a deeper and more encompassing level.

For a remarkable index to virtually all the political information on the Web, go to the National Political Index:
http://pomo.nbn.com/people/hemmerle

Basic Functions

Every two, four, or six years, Americans must decide who among them will fill some portion of the approximately 525,000 elective offices. Whether the office in question is that of president or of recorder of deeds, elections serve five important functions:

- *Elections select public officials as specified by law.* Local, state, and national laws require that many governmental posts be filled by election, and they specify how and when most of these elections take place.

election

The word *election* comes from the Latin word *eligere*, "to choose," and refers either to the choice voters make among candidates for an office or to voters' decision to approve or disapprove a policy position in a referendum or other vote.

These are portions of the bilingual ballot used in the 1994 Democratic primary election in Texas. Registered Democratic voters selected their party's candidates for public offices ranging from United States senator to state judges and county and local officials.

- *Elections reveal public opinion about what government is or should be doing.* Victory and defeat are often attributed to voter reactions to the positions candidates take on issues, and in some states and cities, elections also include referenda and initiatives that enable citizens to express directly their views on policy questions (see Chapter 6).
- *Elections influence government policy.* A president or party that wins by a large margin can claim a **mandate**—the voters' approval—to implement campaign proposals.
- *Elections evaluate officials' performances.* When voters reelect—or fail to reelect—office holders, they are making a public performance evaluation, or engaging in **retrospective voting**.[3]
- *Elections evaluate campaign promises.* With their votes, citizens engage in **prospective voting**—they announce their appraisals of candidates' claims to authority, sincerity, and plausibility and of their ability to represent voters' interests. According to one survey, voters' expectations of parties' future performance strongly influenced their votes in nine recent elections.[4]

Deeper Effects

Elections also affect voters and the political system at a deeper and more comprehensive level. Since the first U.S. election, citizenship rights have been expanded, giving more groups the right to vote (see Chapter 6). Among the functions elections perform for this increasingly diverse group of voters are the following:

- *Elections make people feel involved.* Elections are public rituals; as citizens are socialized to participate in them, the legitimacy of the political system is strengthened.
- *Elections encourage peaceful political action and therefore strengthen the existing political system.* They suggest that people unhappy with the status quo should resort to ballots, not bullets. They also condition citizens to believe that political action should be occasional rather than frequent, occurring at a regularly scheduled time—election day.
- *Elections preserve a (limited) role for mass political action.* They foster involvement in selecting officials rather than in influencing policy.[5] In doing so, they both preserve and limit the sphere of citizen action.
- *Elections focus citizen frustration.* When conventional politics fails to produce the results citizens want, or when their actions don't seem to matter, voters become frustrated, which in the short run is likely to produce apathy. In

the longer run, frustrated citizens may turn to less conventional political action, such as civil disobedience and even rioting (see Chapter 8). Such reactions can undermine the dominant role elections usually play and may threaten the system's legitimacy.

Stakes and Resources in Elections

The stakes in elections vary—from one election to another, and from one political actor to another. Candidates run for office to fulfill their ambitions, to advance their policy interests, or both. Parties back candidates hoping their election will advance party policy interests and enable party supporters to be appointed to government jobs. Special interest groups deliver money, votes, or useful information to candidates in the expectation that winners will listen to and act on their views on policies.

Most individual citizens also have policy interests. Few give anything more than their votes to their preferred candidates, but some committed volunteers who care about the candidates or the issues donate their money, time, and services (see Chapter 7). Others donate these things hoping the winner will support their causes and perhaps even appoint them to some government job.

Campaign resources include both money and information. Candidates use the money they receive from special interests, individuals, and (in the presidential contest) the federal government to stage events that attract free media coverage and to buy advertising, both of which are costly but both of which win votes.

Candidates also need persuasive ideas about *what is, what's right,* and *what works* to use in campaigns and policymaking. They once got their ideas from their own experience or from local or national political figures who claimed to know the preferences of voters and interest groups. Today they often pay large fees for the surveys or professional expertise of pollsters, campaign consultants, and policy specialists.

Competing Claims to Authority

Competing claims to authority are what elections are ultimately about, because authority wins votes and decides elections. As we saw in Chapter 7, voters have grown more independent and more skeptical. As a result, candidates now have a difficult time determining what will persuade voters that their images of reality are superior to those of other candidates. They make credible *claims to authority* by referring to such traits as experience, character or life history, expertise, age, religious views, ethnicity, or gender.

Incumbency Versus Outsider Status

Incumbents campaign to maintain their authority in the minds of voters, while challengers campaign to undermine that authority and substitute their own claims. Traditionally, a strong claim to authority was **incumbency**—running for reelection while holding office. Most people still recognize a president in office as an authority—often *the* authority—on the world situation, with privileged access to secret information. Many also recognize the president as an authority on domestic affairs, although here they are not so quick to deny their own expertise gained from daily experience with the economy, health care, crime, education, and so on. Incumbents do everything in their power to appear "presidential," appearing in the White House rose garden for media photo opportunities and using the presidential seal as a backdrop everywhere they appear.

Incumbency does not always guarantee reelection. Most Senate and House incumbents seeking reelection have tended to win, in what was formerly known as the **incumbency advantage**. However, as skepticism has grown among voters, as the media have scrutinized candidates' private lives, and as the financial attractions of lobbyist jobs have beckoned, many congressional incumbents have lost primaries or chosen not to run again. (The section on congressional elections below discusses these developments in more detail.)

Challengers often campaign as outsiders when there is widespread anti-incumbency or anti-Washington sentiment. In 1992, Bill Clinton staked his claim quite carefully when he pointed to his 12 years as governor. In part, it was a claim that he was an authority on how to govern, to counter fears that he was too young or too inexperienced to be president. But he also wanted to remind voters that he was not a "Washington insider." In 1996, Robert Dole of Kansas, a Washington insider and congressional leader for three decades, quit the Senate not just to be freer to run his presidential campaign but also to appear more of an outsider. But Ross Perot outdid all other candidates in 1992 and 1996, claiming that as an outsider who had never held elective office he was uniquely qualified to "clean up the mess in Washington."

Character and Life History

Skeptical of campaign promises, citizens have increasingly looked to the candidate's character and life experience. Making an effective claim to authority on the basis of character is risky because character is difficult to convey. Some candidates make this claim indirectly, by referring to their military service or family life. In the 1992 campaign, for example, Bush's advertising frequently featured "warm fuzzies"—colorful, reassuring film of President Bush and his family.

More often, candidates claim character by challenging their opponents' claims to it. They may cite a lack of military service, a failure to pay appropriate taxes for household help, or an allegation of marital infidelity. In 1996, when Republican challenger Dole could not excite voters with his policy proposals, he raised Clinton's character as an issue.

Claims to authority based on relevant experience are often more successful than claims to character, but they, too, can backfire, especially if voters hear the wrong message. In 1988, Michael Dukakis claimed authority by citing his experience as governor of Massachusetts, but that claim backfired when the Bush campaign responded by citing Dukakis's veto of a bill requiring the recitation of the Pledge of Allegiance in Massachusetts schools. This, they implied, was evidence of his lack of patriotism. To highlight his commitment to national defense, Dukakis then arranged for the media to see him riding in a tank, but his authority crumbled further when his apparent insecurity in the vehicle brought widespread ridicule. Bush, who had taken two previous tank rides—and a fire engine ride—without criticism, looked even better by contrast.[6]

Bob Dole resigned from the Senate seat that he had held for 27 years in order to appear more like an "outsider" during the 1996 presidential campaign—a stance that is believed to appeal to disaffected voters. To appear more informal, he removed his necktie—but continued to wear French cuffs. Here he gives a thumbs-up to supporters the day after announcing his resignation.

Expertise

Outsiders face a special challenge in demonstrating that they are knowledgeable about the issues the officeholder must deal with. A govenor seeking the presidency is likely to know many domestic issues well, but is unlikely to have foreign policy expertise; a senator, in contrast, will have voted on some foreign affairs issues. As a longtime "policy wonk," Clinton had no trouble demonstrating expertise as a challenger, and that helped him defuse Bush's advantage as an incumbent in 1992. With policy problems becoming increasingly complex, expertise has tended to be a more effective claim to authority at all levels.

Maturity Versus Youth and Vigor

Some candidates try to capitalize on their age as a claim to authority. Younger candidates may claim that youth brings fresh ideas and energy. Older ones may claim that age brings valued experience. Bush was 22 years older than Clinton in 1992, and each candidate tried to exploit that difference. Because Bush's policies were unpopular at that time, he tried to emphasize his own experience and maturity. He cited his "lifetime of public service" and charged that Clinton couldn't be trusted with the job of president because he would have to learn on the job—particularly in foreign affairs. Voters fed up with "politics (and politicians) as usual" felt Bush's experience was at least in part grounds for disqualifying him.

When Ronald Reagan ran for reelection in 1984, his lackluster performance in the first debate with Walter Mondale made his age—he was 73—an issue. So when the topic came up in the second debate, Reagan declared, "I will not use my opponent's youth and inexperience against him." Thus with humor Reagan defused a potential liability, although Mondale was himself 56 years old and had been in politics most of his adult life.

Gender, Ethnicity, and Religion

Women and ethnic minority candidates may exploit their gender or ethnicity as a source of authority—especially to entice new voters to the polls. Mondale tried to use gender to his advantage by picking Representative Geraldine Ferraro of New York as his running mate in 1984—the first woman ever to be nominated for a presidential ticket by a major party. But it was not enough to overcome Reagan's popularity and Mondale's own unpopular pledge to raise taxes if elected.

Jesse Jackson used his status as the first African American to wage a serious campaign for a major party's presidential nomination in 1988 to register many first-time voters, white as well as black. Carol Mosely Braun (D-Ill.) did the same in becoming the first black woman senator in 1992.

It was long thought essential for a presidential candidate to be a Protestent, because no Jew or professed atheist had ever won the office and no Catholic had triumphed until John Kennedy in 1960. In recent elections at all levels, the Religious Right has become so active (see Chapters 4 and 6) that many candidates—from Democrat Jimmy Carter in 1976 through Republican congressional candidates since 1988—have advertised their "born-again" Protestant faiths as claims to authority. But such claims increasingly alienate voters concerned to preserve the separation of church and state (see Chapter 15). So using religion as a claim to authority can be a problematic tactic, just like most other such claims.

Jesse Jackson's bid for the 1988 Democratic presidential nomination drew the support of many whites as well as blacks and other minority members—many of whom registered to vote for the first time.

Walter Mondale and his running mate, Geraldine Ferraro—the first woman to appear on a major party's presidential ticket—appear together at a rally in Austin during the 1984 campaign.

The Political Environment

No matter what resources or authority a candidate can claim, the campaign and election take place in a context or environment governed not only by laws and regulations but also by the day-to-day developments in the political world. Once the campaign is under way, challengers and incumbents have little choice but to make the most of these circumstances, but both will try to paint the picture of *what is* in colors that favor their candidacy. An incumbent, describing the accomplishments of the past term, will paint a rosy picture of the present. The challenger, listing failures and persistent problems, will create a dark and gloomy image of the same present. The one who misjudges the public mood can lose the election.

If voters believe the times are good economically, campaigns may be able to rely on "atmospherics" such as the 1984 Reagan theme that it was "morning in America." But if voters believe times are bad, an incumbent who tells them otherwise courts trouble, as Bush did in the 1992 campaign when he denied that the country was in a recession, despite polls showing that most Americans thought it was. When late in the campaign he admitted that there were economic problems and pledged to fix them in a second term, skeptical voters interpreted his statement as an admission of inaction and wondered why they should trust him to change if re-elected.

Clinton, the challenger, had only to adhere to the formula agreed to in the Middleburg meeting with the Managing Trustees—focus on the economy and related issues such as affordable health care and call on Americans to have "the courage to change." By holding that line he overcame scandals and primary setbacks while crystallizing his New Democrat image. (Lest he and his supporters forget this, Clinton's chief campaign advisor, James Carville, posted a sign at campaign headquarters saying simply, "The economy, stupid!")

This cartoon from the 1976 campaign mocks the tendency of the incumbent (in this case Gerald Ford) to depict the situation as better than it is and of the challenger (Jimmy Carter) to depict things as worse than they are.

While maintaining its own focus, each side in an election challenges the other's claims to authority. In the 1996 campaign, Dole tried unsuccessfully to convince people that the economy was weak, while Clinton took credit for the improvement that most Americans were feeling and statistics were showing, and raised fears that Republicans would worsen things by threatening Social Security and Medicare. With a strong economy and low unemployment, people voted their pocketbooks. The election seemed to ratify the political status quo, reelecting the president and granting the Republicans continued control of Congress. It also reflected trends that have transformed elections at all levels.

How Elections Have Changed

In previous chapters, we've noted many developments that continue to change the American political process. The electorate has grown and become more diverse. Breakthroughs in communications technology have altered the roles played by the media. The McGovern Reforms and new election regulations have reduced the power political parties can exercise and increased the importance of money in every election. In this section we examine how some of these trends are shaping the way Americans elect their presidents and their members of Congress.

Presidential Elections

Few observers would say that American voters get to choose the best possible candidate—especially at the presidential level. At all levels, party dominance has given way to candidate dominance, but candidates are in turn dominated by their dependence on the media they need to reach voters. And that means they are also dominated by the search for money to pay for media coverage and ads.

From Party Dominance to Candidate Dominance

Until the 1960s, political parties controlled the presidential nomination process (see Chapter 7). Local party leaders wielded enormous power because they selected—or were themselves—delegates to state and national nominating conventions. People who wanted to run for office had to gain the support of these local figures, and they also had to rely on donations from wealthy members of their party. Battles over who received the party's blessing were fought among party leaders behind closed doors in smoke-filled rooms. The media gave little coverage to the actual nominating process for offices, and the drama at the national convention was confined largely to roll-call voting by state delegations controlled by state party leaders. Once nominated, candidates for national and state offices depended primarily on party fund raising.

In 1968, much of this changed, as the McGovern Reforms (see Chapter 7) reformed the nomination process in the Democratic party, opening the process to challengers who built support among voters rather than leaders. These reforms also increased the number of convention delegates selected in the binding primaries and party caucuses.

Candidates need less help from a party's national organization than they did before the McGovern Reforms of 1968 took effect. Steve Forbes used his huge personal fortune to finance his 1996 Republican presidential primary campaign. He is shown here campaigning in Iowa.

Four years later, Richard Nixon further fragmented party control when he constructed his own campaign reelection organization—the Committee to Re-Elect the President (CREEP)—independent of the Republican party. CREEP raised millions of dollars from businesses and executives in secret campaign contributions, some obtained through coercion. CREEP's employees also broke into Democratic party headquarters in the Watergate building in Washington, D.C., and searched for secret documents on campaign strategy. The coerced business contributions were eventually revealed, and the Watergate burglars were captured in the act. This combination of financial corruption and "dirty tricks," which became known as Watergate, resulted in a new law to regulate campaign finance. Nevertheless, since CREEP, all major party candidates have followed Nixon's lead and run their own election campaigns independently, relying on party organizations only for assistance.

The campaign finance reforms launched after Watergate have helped shape the presidential nominating process that exists today. The reforms, as we'll see shortly, have forced candidates to start campaigning much earlier in order to establish an identity in multiple states, raise money for campaign organizations, and get media exposure.[7] As one analyst describes it, "What was once a relatively straightforward task conducted largely out of public view has been transformed into a long and tortuous media circus."[8]

Together, the McGovern Reforms, the Nixon campaign innovations, and the campaign finance reforms have produced a nominating process that is decidedly focused on the candidate.

From Activist Dominance to Media Dominance

Campaigns centered on the candidate rather than on the party are inevitably dominated by the media. When political parties ran the campaigns, they organized paid workers (often workers on the payrolls of cities and states the party controlled) and volunteers to turn out the vote for their candidates. Individuals running their own campaigns needed a less labor-intensive mode of campaigning to break their dependence on the parties, and they found it in the media.

The first political commercials on television appeared in 1952—the year television began broadcasting convention proceedings (see Chapter 9). At that time, only about 15 million American homes had TV sets—a total that climbed to about 54 million by 1960 and now exceeds 100 million. The media are now indispensable because they bestow credibility by anointing some individuals as front-runners and separating them from the rest of the pack of contenders as plausible national candidates. Studies show that in most elections, roughly one-third of the voters choose their presidential favorite before the parties hold their conventions, another third decide during the conventions, and the final third make up their minds during the fall campaign.

Party nominees seek two types of media exposure:

- **free media**—news coverage that can boost their standing with voters; and
- **paid media**—advertising, mainly on television.

Candidates spend about half of their money on TV ads. During the 1996 campaign, that amounted to a record $400 million—or 30 percent more than in 1992—with the three major presidential candidates spending some $29 million each.[9] They bought almost 1,400 hours—that's 58 days of TV ads—in 1996.[10]

Imagery has become a central—perhaps the central—element in campaigning. Bush's successful 1988 campaign was largely devoid of substantive policy commitments—except for his ill-fated pledge of "no new taxes." Because Clinton seemed most comfortable in direct interaction with people, his 1992 campaign bought television time for unrehearsed "town meeting" question-and-answer sessions with ordinary voters, had him play the saxophone wearing sunglasses and discuss urban problems on a youth-oriented talk show, and then sent him on bus tours after the convention. Each of these activities personalized "Bill" to a certain group of voters to overcome attacks on his character, show his mastery of policy questions, and generate images designed to capture TV screens and attract voters.

As the influence of the media has mounted over the last three decades, so has criticism of them. Studying the 1972 presidential contest, the first in which parties had lost their dominant role to candidate organizations, two political scientists concluded that "the only noticeable effect of network campaign news is an increased tendency for voters to view elections as a lot of nonsense rather than a choice between fundamental issues."[11] The major influence on voters, the study found, was political advertising. By 1980, the media were being criticized for increasingly focusing on the horse-race aspects of the campaign instead of the issues, the candidates' policy positions, and their characters, abilities, public records, and personal backgrounds.[12] Now, at the end of the twentieth century, television has become the major information source for voters throughout the campaign, whatever the nature of the coverage.[13]

By 1988, the media—responding to criticism from candidates, analysts, officials, and voters—had begun paying more attention to candidates' policy positions. Democratic challenger Jerry Brown, dissatisfied with media coverage, helped strengthen that trend when in 1992 he pioneered the **infomercial**—a 30-minute commercial prepared by a candidate and broadcast as paid media, usually on cable stations, where advertising is less expensive. Ross Perot relied almost entirely on 60-minute infomercials on networks in 1992 and 1996, and his televised lectures, replete with graphs and charts, were unexpectedly popular.

In 1992 and 1996, the media started scheduling longer interviews, especially in talk-show format, and they increased network analyses of candidates' positions on issues. In 1994 and 1996, some local media experimented with "civic journalism" programs, polling citizens about problems and solutions and virtually compelling candidates to respond to citizen concerns in their campaigns.

Nevertheless, as we saw in Chapter 9, the mass media are in the entertainment business, not the citizen information business, and their news departments are in the news business, not the citizenship business. The media cover candidates' qualifications, records, and issues only as long as large audiences tune in to hear about them. For that reason, media dominance often seems to weaken democracy rather than performing a public service for voters. And media dominance, as noted earlier, has a direct connection to money dominance.

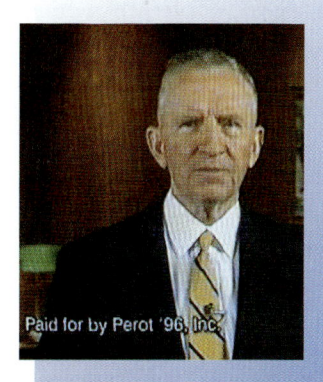

The infomercial—a paid television program—has been heavily used by Ross Perot and other candidates to communicate their policy positions to the public.

TABLE 10.1
Presidential Election Campaign Spending, 1996

Clinton prenomination	$ 38 million
Clinton general election	62 million
Democratic party ("soft money")	122 million
	$222 million
Dole prenomination	$ 42 million
Dole general election	62 million
Republican party ("soft money")	$141 million
	$245 million
Perot prenomination	$ 8 million
Perot general election	29 million
	$37 million
Other third-party candidates	
Browne (Libertarian) prenomination	$ 1 million
Hagelin (Natural Law) prenomination	$ 1 million

Sources: Federal Election Commission data; Anthony Corrado, "Financing the 1996 Elections," Chapter 4 in Gerald M. Pomper et al., *The Elections of 1996* (Chatham, NJ: Chatham House, 1997); Candice J. Nelson, "Money in the 1996 Elections," in *America's Choice: The Election of 1996,* ed. William Crotty and Jerome M. Mileur (New York: Dushkin/McGraw-Hill, 1997), Chapter 12.

For official information from the Federal Election Commission on campaign regulations, contributions, etc., along with the text of *FEC Reports*, go to its site:

http://www.fec.gov

From Organization Dominance to Money Dominance—and Efforts to Control It

The reliance on media coverage has caused campaign costs to skyrocket. In 1960, when television was new and national party organizations ran campaigns, a presidential election cost a total of $20 million. By 1992, Clinton and Bush had each spent about four times that amount (see Table 10.1).[14] Even allowing for inflation, that's an enormous increase. In response both to this astronomical increase in spending and to growing public disquiet, Congress has occasionally sought to limit the role of money in campaigns in a way consistent with protecting the rights of citizens and interest groups to influence politics—and, critics say, consistent with protecting the advantages of incumbency.

The earliest efforts to regulate campaign finance were limited to restrictions on federal employees. The Pendleton Civil Service Act (1883) was intended to protect federal employees from coercion by their superiors, and it therefore banned soliciting or receiving federal campaign donations in federal buildings. The Hatch Act of 1939 (modified in 1994) restricted political activity by federal employees, barring all but elected officials from soliciting political donations in most cases. The first serious and broad-ranging attempt at reform was the **Federal Election Campaign Act (FECA)** of 1971, which set limits on an individual's contributions to candidates but not to political parties. FECA also barred foreign nation-als from contributing to U.S. state and federal elections.

When FECA proved too weak to prevent the financial corruption in the Nixon reelection campaign in 1972, Congress established the bipartisan independent Federal Election Commission (FEC). The FEC was charged with gathering and publicizing information on campaign contributions and spending and with administering public funding of presidential campaigns.

In spite of these measures, campaign costs—especially in the primaries—continue to soar, and fundraising groups such as the Managing Trustees and Team 100 play ever-increasing roles. Money is now more important than ever to candidates, and, ironically, that's partly because of the FEC rules. To become eligible for federal matching funds, presidential candidates must first raise $5,000 in private contributions of $250 or less in each of 20 states. To do this, they must start raising funds long before primary season. Those who meet the requirement receive up to half the primary campaign spending limit, which the FEC set at $39 million for 1996. (To find out how you can contribute to a campaign, see the nearby Political Action Guide.) Each of the two major parties also receives more than $11 million in federal funds for its national nominating convention—a subsidy that helps protect the two major parties against challenges from third parties.

Since 1976, each major-party presidential candidate has chosen to accept matching federal funds for the general election campaign instead of raising private contributions beyond the required qualifying amounts. However, each party and all independent groups interested in the campaign are still free to raise unlimited amounts of **soft money**—other funds they can spend in support of their preferred candidate, as long as they do not give it directly to the candidate. The Supreme Court seemed to put its blessing on soft money in June 1996, when it ruled that political parties have the right to spend unlimited amounts of money on campaigns so long as they act independently of the candidates.

> **soft money**
> This term distinguishes the money raised by parties and special interests from that raised by candidates' campaigns. There are strict limits on who can contribute money to candidates and how much one individual can contribute, which makes that hard money to raise. There are few limits on who can contribute to parties and no limits on how much, which makes that money easier to raise—or soft money.

FECA originally limited the amounts individuals could contribute to their own campaigns and the total amount each candidate for a particular office could spend. It also limited the amounts political action committees (PACs) could spend to support political candidates or policy agendas. These limits were struck down in 1976 when the Court in *Buckley v. Valeo* declared such spending limits unconstitutional constraints on free speech.[15] (Buckley was a wealthy New York senator who wanted to spend his own money on his campaign and argued that the congressionally imposed limits violated his right to freedom of expression.) The Court also struck down spending limits on individual campaigns at the same time, with the sole exception of publicly funded (thus far, only presidential) campaigns. The Court has followed four main guidelines for evaluating the constitutionality of campaign finance regulations:

1. Regulations requiring disclosure of the sources and amounts of contributions, and regulations accompanying voluntarily accepted public funding of campaigns, are permissible as long as they do not seriously hurt minor parties or independent candidates.
2. Limitations on the size of contributions to candidates are acceptable if intended to prevent undue influence of special interests.
3. Restrictions on spending in behalf of candidates by business corporations operated for profit are constitutional.
4. No other limits on spending in elections are constitutional.

Since the Court's 1976 decision, PACs have become major players in federal elections. Some 5,000 PACs are now involved at federal, state, and local levels (see Chapter 8). They must report their contributions, but few voters see the resulting FEC reports, just as few voters notice the credit lines in small type on electronic and print commercials prepared and paid for by PACs. But presidential candidates and members of Congress notice.

PACs tend to give more heavily to incumbents than to challengers, who need inordinately large sums to dislodge officeholders. This may help to explain why incumbents, whether Democrats or Republicans, favor either the status quo or public financing that would effectively limit the amount challengers could spend.

Congressional Elections

Congressional elections have been altered by many of the same trends that have influenced presidential elections, especially by the decrease in party dominance,

Political Action Guide

How You Can Contribute to Political Campaigns

Contributions to state and local campaigns are governed by state and local laws, while contributions to presidential campaigns are governed by federal law. As the law stands, here's how you can contribute to your favorite presidential candidate or party.

- You can contribute up to $1,000 per year to each candidate, $20,000 per year to a national party, and $5,000 per year to a political action committee (PAC), up to a total of $25,000 per year. Cash contributions are limited to a total of no more than $100. For amounts beyond that, you must make your contributions by check, wire transfer, or other traceable method.

- If you are a labor union member, your union can contribute a portion of your dues to a candidate through a PAC, either directly to candidates (hard money) or indirectly to parties (soft money). However, unions, like corporations, must work within legal limits: $5,000 per candidate per election, $25,000 per party per year, $5,000 to another PAC per year, and no limit on the total amount they give in any one year.

- Like corporations and labor unions, you as an individual can give unlimited soft money to national parties to pay administrative costs and for "party-building" activities such as get-out-the-vote drives and ads supporting or opposing an issue. These donations cannot be given directly to candidates running for federal offices.

- You may make unlimited independent expenditures for or against a candidate, if you report them to the Federal Election Commission. You could, for example, pay for an ad describing why the candidate's election would benefit some group of people or the country in general, so long as your expenditure was not coordinated with, or under the direction of, the campaign run by the candidate or party.

- Your employer cannot legally solicit you to contribute to a campaign or party.

- If you are neither a U.S. citizen nor a permanent resident, you cannot make any contribution, either in your own name or in the name of others.

the increased dependence on media and money, and the incumbency effect. Those running for House seats also face the possibility that their district may be altered or abolished during reapportionment or redistricting.

From Party Dominance to Candidate Dominance

Individuals running for the House or Senate now get some funds from individuals and from the party's congressional campaign committee, but most also get large sums directly from PACs. Consequently, candidates need not defer to their party, or even to a president who is the leader of that party. With the decline in party-based voting, the **coattail effect**—the ability of a popular presidential candidate to carry everyone else on the party's ticket into office "on his coattails"—has decreased. Many voters now routinely vote a **split ticket**, choosing a president from one party and a senator, representative, or other candidate from the other. Split-ticket voting helps explain the split outcome of the 1996 elections, which produced a Democratic president and a Republican House and Senate.

Veteran Washington journalist David Broder summarized the growing tendency of members of Congress to vote independently of both president and party: "In our era of debilitated political parties, Washington is run by 536 individual political entrepreneurs—one president, 100 senators, and 435 members of the House." Pointing out that each got to Washington on his or her own and each chooses an office to seek, raises money, hires pollsters and ad-makers, and recruits volunteers on his or her own, Broder concluded that "each of them is scrambling to remain in office, no matter what."[16]

Media Dominance, Money Dominance, and the Incumbency Effect

In all but the least populous states, and in most congressional districts, candidates can meet only a fraction of the potential voters. With the party no longer able to deliver the vote, candidates for House and Senate seats depend on expensive mass media to reach the voters, and campaign finance has therefore become a critical issue.

The average Senate incumbent spent $2.8 million in 1992. The average challenger wasn't far behind, at $1.5 million. Average contestants for open seats—where no incumbent was running—spent $2 million. These sums were about 25 percent more than the comparable figures in 1990, just two years earlier.[17]

For the 1996 election, Senate and House candidates raised $659 million. Seventy-six of those candidates spent at least $1 million, but 17 of them lost anyway—in most cases to incumbents who spent even more.[18] Total spending by Senate incumbents was $80 million, versus $57 million for challengers; House candidates spent $407 million, two-thirds of it by incumbents.[19]

Parties still work hard and spend big to reelect incumbents. Once Clinton's reelection seemed assured, thanks in large part to massive spending by the Democratic party, the Republican party spent $30 million in the last four weeks of the campaign in a successful effort to hold its majorities in Congress. Partly as a result of that great outpouring of dollars, 12 of the 13 Republican senators running for reelection won and only 18 of their representatives lost.

Traditionally, most Senate and House incumbents who have sought reelection have won (see Figure 10.1). House incumbents typically win with more than 60 percent of the vote. Why? Incumbents have five advantages when they seek reelection:

1. Constituents recognize their names more readily than those of most challengers.
2. The media give them extensive exposure during their terms in office.
3. Special interests want to preserve their access to incumbents, and they contribute heavily to their campaign chests, making the current campaign finance regulations an incumbency protection system.
4. Voters tend to credit and reward their own members of Congress for casework—services they provide to constituents (see Chapter 11).
5. Voters tend to credit their members for pork-barrel legislation—government actions that benefit the district, such as contracts for highway construction and defense production—whether the representative did or did not actually play a role in "bringing home the bacon" (see Chapter 11).

Figure 10.1
Incumbent Reelection Rates

The curves in this graph show the percentage of victorious incumbents running in both primary and general elections. The occasional dramatic lows in Senate contests reflect major political developments such as the controversy over the Vietnam War (1968), the impact of the Watergate scandal (1976), and the Reagan sweep (1980).

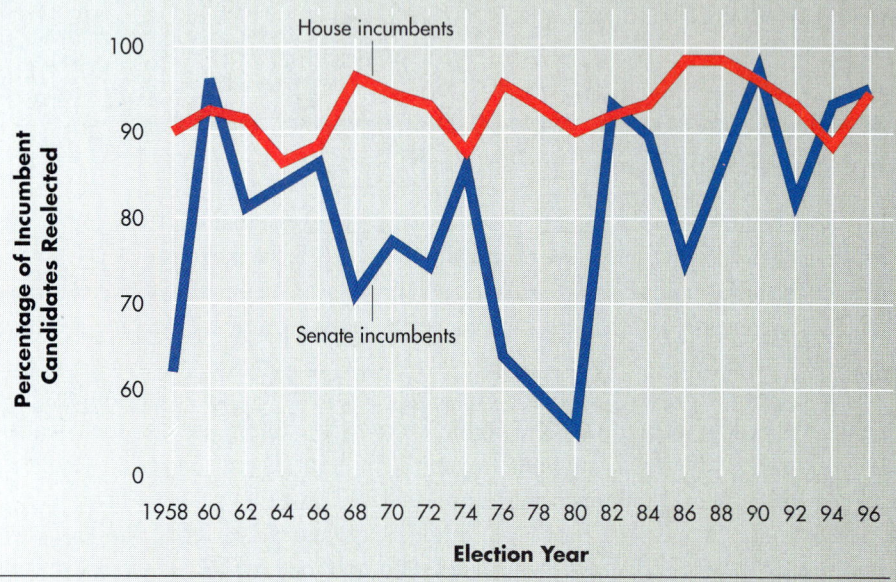

Source: Norman J. Ornstein, Thomas E. Mann, and Michael J. Malbin, *Vital Statistics on Congress, 1995–1996* (Washington, D.C.: Congressional Quarterly Press, 1996).

Despite these built-in advantages, incumbency is no longer the plum it once was. Growing numbers of incumbents in recent elections have failed to be reelected and others have chosen not to run. Among the reasons are scandals (discussed in Chapters 9 and 11), the strenuousness of continuous campaigning, and lucrative offers from lobbying firms. In 1992 alone, 74 incumbents chose not to run, 20 lost primaries, and 27 lost in the general election. The same pattern recurred in 1994, with the result that more than half of all representatives had been elected for the first time in the 1990s—an astonishing turnaround. And when 15 new senators were elected in 1996, that brought the number of senators serving their first or second terms up from half in 1995 to two-thirds in 1997. Consequently, many now use the term **incumbency effect** rather than *incumbency advantage* to describe the advantages and disadvantages of running for reelection.

The Threat of Reapportionment

The greatest threat to congressional incumbency occurs every ten years when **reapportionment** reassigns House seats among the states in accordance with the latest U.S. census data on population growth or decline. After the 1990 census, for example, California gained seven seats and New York lost three.

House members are elected every two years from geographical districts within their states. Until 1929, the total number of House seats was based on population, beginning with an original 59 members. In 1929, when the number of representatives reached 435, Congress decided that further growth would make House processes unwieldy and it set a permanent total of 435. To ensure that districts could be approximately the same size across the nation despite population shifts, as the Constitution dictates, the seats are reapportioned among the states after each ten-year census. Reapportionment does not affect the Senate because the Constitution guarantees two senators to every state, regardless of size or population.

Each of the smallest states has only one representative (see Figure 10.2) along with its two senators, all elected at large. Every other state is divided into House districts. Thus almost all House elections occur in small and somewhat distinctive districts that now average about 575,000 residents.

The Impact of Redistricting

When a state gains or loses one or more seats through reapportionment, the state's legislature must **redistrict**—redraw the lines that divide populations into approximately equal, geographically based units. Many state legislatures initially refused to redraw their congressional districts, thereby protecting incumbent—usually rural—members against urbanization. They also refused to redraw state legislative districts, with the same effect. Finally, in *Baker v. Carr* (1962), the Supreme Court declared that the state legislature's refusal to redistrict state legislative districts as population shifted, as had occurred in Tennessee, was unconstitutional because it deprived citizens of equal protection under the law. Two years later, in *Wesberry v. Sanders* (1964), the Court extended this protection to

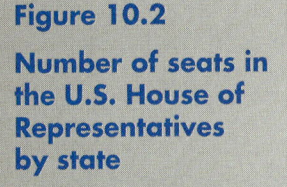

Figure 10.2

Number of seats in the U.S. House of Representatives by state

Each state is represented by two senators in the U.S. Senate, but representation in the House is constitutionally determined by a state's population

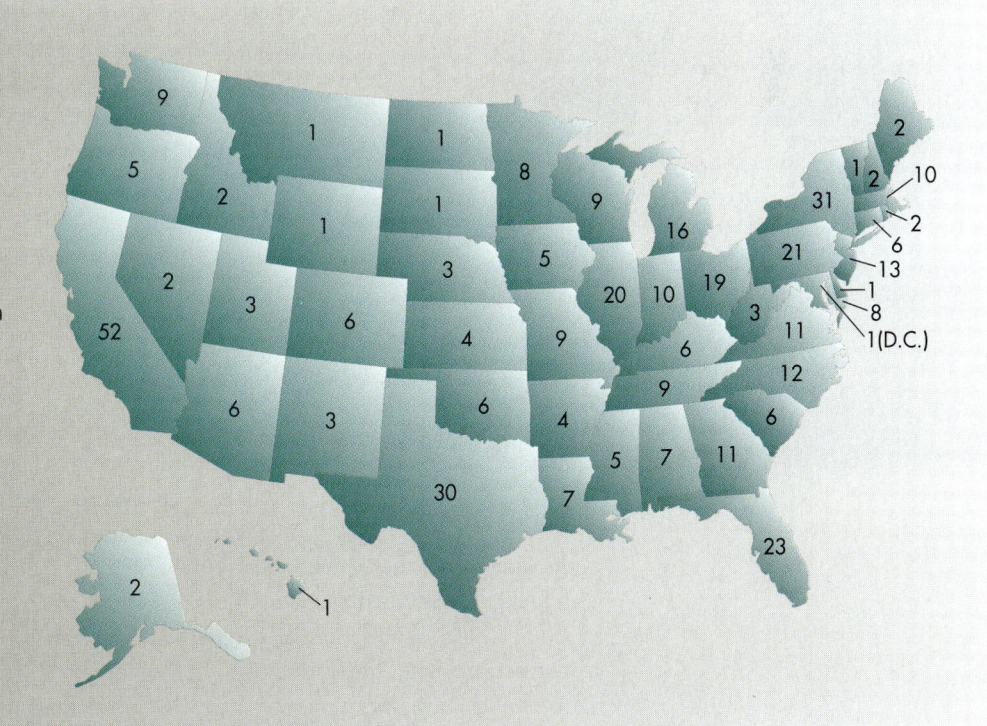

gerrymandering

This practice of designing unusually shaped districts to increase the election chances of a particular party is named for Elbridge Gerry, governor of Massachusetts. In 1812, the state legislature carved up that state's Essex County to create a district that looked like a salamander.

congressional districts. Then in *Reynolds v. Sims* (1964), a case involving Alabama state legislative districts, the Court asserted that the principle underlying redistricting should be one person, one vote.[20]

Redistricting is always highly political, with no consensus on the right or fair way of drawing district lines. The process is usually dominated by the party controlling the state legislature, which creates districts that maximize the electoral chances of its candidates. If no one party controls both houses of the legislature, or if the governor is of a different party, bargaining helps determine district lines.

Gerrymandering is redistricting to benefit some particular group or interest, and it can create strikingly bizarre shapes. Gerrymandering has been used both to prevent ethnic groups from influencing elections and to better their chances of being represented. For example, when black Americans began to vote following the Voting Rights Act of 1965 (see Chapter 6), white-dominated legislatures used two techniques to minimize the effect of their votes:

- *packing*, concentrating ethnic minority voters in a few districts so that they could elect only a few persons; and
- *stacking*, spreading them so thinly across many districts that they could not elect anyone.

Amendments to the Voting Rights Act in 1982 required that redistricting be done in a way that increased the likelihood that Latinos and African Americans would be able to elect Latino and African-American representatives to Congress. To create districts dominated by ethnic minorities (or ethnic majorities), legislatures had to draw very unusual district boundaries that combined geographically dispersed pockets of voters. Justice Department approval was required before the new politically drawn districts could go into effect, and they then could be contested in the courts. After redistricting, the number of African Americans in the House increased in 1992 from 25 to 38, and Latinos from 11 to 17.

Critics condemned such districts as **racial gerrymandering**, and in the years after the 1990 census, when the issue of representation for ethnic minorities reached prominence, lawsuits were filed in five states. The first and probably most dramatic case of so-called racial gerrymandering to reach the U.S. Supreme Court was the redesign of the 12th congressional district in North Carolina. Following federal guidelines, the North Carolina legislature had created that district to enable the election of a black representative—something that had not occurred in the state since Reconstruction. The serpentine district combined African-American sections of Charlotte and Durham, two large cities 160 miles apart, and numerous small black communities scattered along Interstate Highway 85, which connects the two cities (see Figure 10.3). Charging that the Justice-approved district discriminated against

Rep. Cynthia McKinney (D-Ga.) celebrates her reelection to the House of Representatives in 1996. McKinney had first been elected in a "racially gerrymandered" district, but was reelected despite the redrawing of her district's boundaries to put blacks in the minority after the Supreme Court's adverse rulings in *Shaw v. Reno* and other cases.

white voters in the region, who could not elect anybody but an African-American representative, citizens sued the U.S. Justice Department. In 1993, the U.S. Supreme Court ruled 5 to 4 in *Shaw v. Reno* that the district was so "extremely irregular" that it seemed designed to "segregate the races for the purposes of voting." The Court ordered the lower court to consider the protest while holding open the possibility that a state might be able to offer "sufficiently compelling justification" for a racial gerrymander. It then sent similar cases from other states back to lower courts with orders to reverse racial gerrymandering.[21]

In the 1996 elections, five of the African Americans who had been elected in the racially designed districts won reelection despite court-ordered redistricting. Nevertheless, voting patterns in their districts remained highly polarized racially, and many thought the candidates were reelected because they were incumbents and despite their race. In 1997, there were 37 African Americans and 18 Latinos in the House.

Figure 10.3

The 12th congressional district.

The district follows Interstate 85, winding through urban centers to pick up a high concentration of black voters.

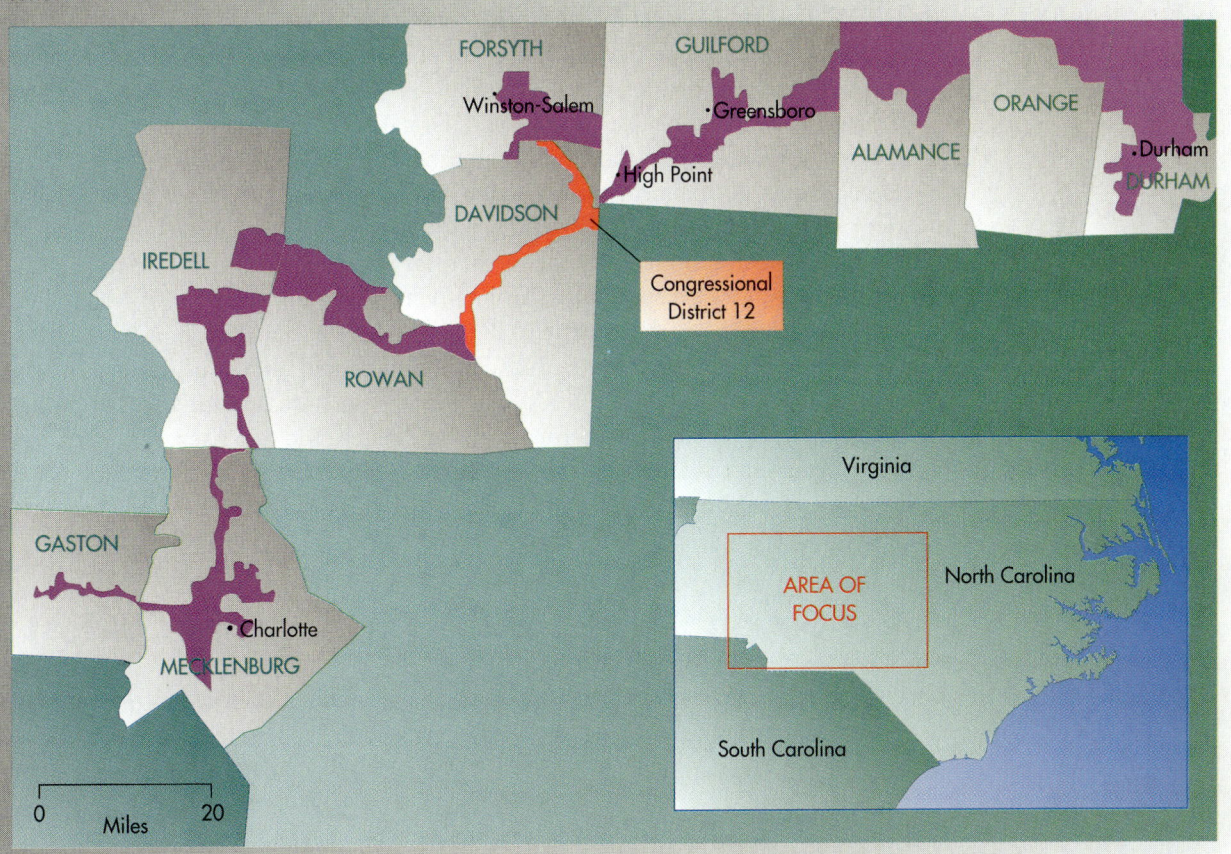

The Stages of a Presidential Election

When the Founders wrote the basic rules for presidential elections into the Constitution, they could not foresee the key role parties would soon play, let alone the dominant roles that special interests, money, and the media now have. Since those rules were written, the process of electing a president has grown into a seven-stage, winner-take-all contest. (Chapter 12 covers the qualifications and responsibilities of the presidency.)

The Constitutional Ground Rules

George Washington became America's first president when each state legislature chose presidential electors who then gathered as members of the Electoral College in the state capital to cast their votes for president and vice president. Washington had no opposition, and electors chose John Adams, the second-best available person, as vice president. When Washington left office after two terms, political parties were transforming presidential politics. John Adams, a Federalist, was elected president, but the Constitution's provision that the second-highest vote getter would become the vice president produced a Republican vice president (Thomas Jefferson), dividing executive authority between the parties.

With greater party discipline, the Republican party's candidates for president and vice president tied for president in the next election. That put the election into the House, where Federalists perpetuated the stalemate for months before finally acceding to the election of the Republican candidates. In 1804 the Republican-sponsored Twelfth Amendment was passed, requiring separate ballots for president and vice president and enabling the winning party to elect its own slate to both offices.[22]

The Constitution had left the method for selecting electors to the states, and by 1824 all states except South Carolina (which held out until 1860) had shifted this responsibility to those citizens eligible to vote. From this point on, citizens voted state by state in a general election, and shortly afterward electors voted state by state in the Electoral College. Each new state admitted to the Union added another possible battleground for candidates. Today, 51 separate elections, one in each of the 50 states and the District of Columbia, are conducted every four years on the first Tuesday after the first Monday in November.

The Seven Stages of the Presidential Contest

Over the last two centuries, the election of a president has evolved into a national contest consisting of seven stages:

1. A secret preprimary
2. A silent primary
3. State primaries and caucuses
4. The political parties' national conventions
5. The general election campaign

6. A popular election
7. An official Electoral College election

At each stage, candidates can win or lose, and their organization will attempt to exploit the process to its own benefit. And after the sixth stage, victor and potential challengers alike begin thinking about the next election four years hence and how they will organize their campaigns to gain authority in the minds of big financial contributors, media commentators, party officials, and voters.

The Secret Preprimary: Filling the War Chest

The first stage in the campaign is the **secret preprimary**, a fundraising process that occurs out of public view. Only an independently wealthy candidate like Ross Perot could run a plausible presidential campaign without raising large sums of money before the official season begins, and nothing dissuades rivals—or at least guarantees their eventual defeat—so effectively as a large campaign war chest in place long before the primaries. In the 1992 presidential campaign, the secret preprimary opened a full 16 months before the general election and 8 months before the first primary, when the Managing Trustees met at the Harriman farm.

Potential donors such as the Managing Trustees have various motives for giving to the party and its candidates. Some believe the party's victory is in the country's best interest. Some anticipate access to the candidate or other officials after the election. Others are seeking an ambassadorship. (Of Clinton's 98 ambassadorial appointments in his first year, 38 were political appointments rather than career diplomats;[23] Pamela Harriman became the U.S. ambassador to France.) Still others enjoy the satisfaction of being behind-the-scenes kingmakers. But whatever their motives, donors are unlikely to give unless they find the potential candidate authoritative in presenting a promising campaign message and strategy.

For an incumbent, the preprimary stage means raising enormous sums to scare off potential challengers and to pay for early advertising that will frame the election as a choice between a strong incumbent and a dangerous or divisive rival candidate or party. Eighteen months before the 1996 general election, the Democratic party began a national TV campaign focusing on crime and the budget, attacking the Republican Congress, and featuring President Clinton. The ads, along with other election activities, were financed by $250 million in soft money that the party had raised, mostly from large donors. Many of the donors were invited to small dinners with Clinton or Vice President Al Gore, and some stayed overnight in the White House's Lincoln bedroom. These funds supplemented Clinton's reelection campaign spending, which was limited by law. Although the total frightened off any potential challengers within the Democratic party, the amount was dwarfed by the $400 million the Republican party raised in comparable efforts.[24] When these enormous sums, and the tactics the two parties had used to raise them, were revealed after the election, pressures for campaign finance reform increased dramatically.

The Silent Primary: Campaigning for Media Attention

The second stage in the campaign is the **silent primary** (sometimes called the *hidden primary*); it derives its name from the fact that voters have yet to cast a single vote in an actual primary. Candidates who have secured early financial backing can use it during this stage to boost perceptions of their authority, credibility, and

Information on many aspects of the 1996 electoral campaign can still be found at:

http://campaign96.com

A guide to sites dealing with the 1996 campaign can be found at:

http://www.aboy.com/general.html

Information on many aspects of the 2000 electoral campaign, and a guide with links to other sites, can be found at:

http://www.newpolitics.com

which describes itself as "the non-partisan U.S. political participation resource."

promise in the minds of media people. Those who do not already have one will hire a competent (and therefore costly) campaign staff and attempt to gain early public recognition—often through effective speech making—in the critical period leading up to the first primaries.[25]

During this period, journalists begin anointing potential candidates who seem to have a real chance of winning and weeding out lackluster candidates. Those taken seriously by the media will probably also be taken seriously by the groups of large donors who fund the later stages of the primary campaigns. Media anointing also helps candidates engage the interest of party leaders at all levels, who want a winner at the top of the ticket in November. No wonder, then, that this period is devoted to **impression management**—efforts to manage or manipulate the media's images of candidates so that the media will pass those favorable images on to the primary voters.

The Democratic party's unprecedentedly early and extensive TV advertising campaign was designed with a dual purpose, both related to impression management. First, it was intended to improve Clinton's image after the party defeat in the 1994 congressional elections. Second, it was meant to create a negative image of the conservatively assertive Republican Congress long before most potential voters were thinking about the election—an image the eventual Republican nominee would have to overcome before defining himself (or herself) in the voters' minds. The effort cost $85 million, but as Clinton strategist Dick Morris noted, "We created the first fully advertised Presidency in U.S. history."[26]

State Primaries and Caucuses: Locking Up the Nomination

In the third stage, the voice of the people—or, more accurately, the voice of the party faithful and the issue-motivated citizens who vote in primaries and caucuses—will be heard. Before the McGovern reforms, New Hampshire kicked off the primary elections, but now Iowa's **primary caucus**—a gathering of party supporters who vote their presidential preferences face-to-face in precinct meetings—

plays that role. The Iowa caucuses serve as an early, if sometimes unreliable, barometer of candidate strength among party enthusiasts.

Primaries and caucuses attract the more ideologically extreme party supporters, and candidates who take extreme policy positions to win their votes can alienate the more centrist voters and independents who are crucial to victory in the general election. Clinton avoided this trap in 1992, winning the nomination as a moderate. Incumbent George Bush, facing a primary challenge by conservative commentator Pat Buchanan, was caught in the trap when he felt he had to move to the right to get renominated. In 1996, Bob Dole, the Republican leadership's favorite, faced a similar challenge by Buchanan and another from wealthy publisher Steve Forbes. Forbes spent some $25 million of his own money attacking Dole and advocating a *flat tax*, a uniform tax rate on all incomes that he attempted to sell as fairer and simpler than the current system but that would have enabled the rich to pay less than they now do in taxes. Both Bush and Dole lost the support of some moderate Republicans and independents when they shifted to the right.

The National Convention: The Candidate's Coming-Out Party

Both parties' nominations are usually locked up well before the fourth stage, the national conventions. With primaries the determining factor in nominations, both political parties have converted their conventions into opportunities to showcase their candidates to the American people. Democratic strategists demonstrated their skill at this in 1992, building on the results from two sets of polls, one showing Clinton trailing both Bush and Perot and the other showing that Americans knew little about Clinton as a person. They produced a glitzy biographical film focusing on Clinton's humble beginnings (his father's death in an auto accident before Clinton was born; his being raised by his mother, who was abused by his alcoholic stepfather). The film also showed highlights of his political career, from his participation in the Boys' State mock national legislature, where he was greeted by (and photographed with) President John F. Kennedy, to his years as

The major parties' national nominating conventions have become media spectacles, with the Republicans (*left*) and Democrats (*opposite*) trying to "out-glitz" each other to hold viewers' interest.

governor of Arkansas. Knowing that convention highlights would be telecast nationally, the strategists scheduled the film to precede the acceptance speech, counting on it not only to create sympathy for Clinton but also to create a stark contrast with Bush's widely known patrician family background. They also structured the convention proceedings to limit disruption and dissension—problems that had beset every Democratic convention since 1964 and made many Americans question the party's ability to govern. Hollywood producers put on a nightly convention show that combined stars and multimedia reminiscent of the extravaganzas developed by the Reagan forces for the 1980 and 1984 Republican conventions. The convention also spotlighted Clinton's choice as running mate, Senator Al Gore (D-Tenn.), and Clinton's wife, Hillary Rodham Clinton, to maximize the appeal of the New Democrat, new-generation ticket (see the box on page 369).

This strategy worked. Clinton got a large postconvention bounce into a lead he never relinquished. When the Republican convention featured rightwing attacks on both Bill Clinton and Hillary Rodham Clinton, moderate and independent viewers were alienated instead of energized, and Bush never recovered his footing. In 1996, Dole also needed a boost from convention redefinition, but he failed to get it despite staging what most observers considered the glitziest convention ever and selecting a younger and more charismatic running mate, Jack Kemp (see the box on page 369). The convention did perform another typical function—converting the nominee from the choice of a faction to the leader of a party coalition—but it was too little, too late, to turn candidate Dole into President Dole.

The General Election Campaign: Holding Your Base, Building Coalitions

A 1996 Democratic party TV ad attacks Bob Dole's record on "family leave" legislation intended to allow workers to take unpaid leaves of absence to care for a newborn or a sick family member.

A primary goal of the fifth stage—the general election campaign—is to create an even broader electoral coalition. Campaign strategists work hard to etch in the minds of potential voters favorable images of their candidate and unfavorable images of the adversaries. If they are successful, the candidate is awarded the authority to govern.

General election campaigns are organized on two levels:

• *The national campaign* is organized around themes and issues that strategists believe are relevant to and will interest large numbers of people around the country. This portion of the campaign is more important for its influence on opinion polls than for its direct impact on voters. The media use national opinion polls to create images of momentum and collapse and to update viewers on the current status of the horse race. These reports focus attention on one candidate at the expense of others, and that attention often brings with it more votes.

What Works in Presidential Campaigns: Good Running Mates—The Vice President and the Spouse

Experts believe that elections are won and lost at "the top of the ticket" by the presidential nominees, but candidates always seek to enhance their claims to authority by choosing a running mate who brings special strengths to the ticket. Most candidates also try to make effective use of their spouses.

The Vice President's Contribution

Conventional wisdom says that even a strong vice-presidential candidate won't help the campaign much, but a bad choice could cost the ticket several percentage points. Nevertheless, vice-presidential candidates are chosen carefully, and they were traditionally intended to balance the ticket by providing a contrast with the presidential candidate's region, generation, or ideology.

In 1988, George Bush chose staunchly conservative junior senator Dan Quayle of Indiana to strengthen his grip on his Reaganite base. After four years of observing the vice president's dutiful service, many Americans still weren't sure Quayle was qualified to become president should that become necessary, and some Republicans advocated replacing him. Bush retained him to avert further erosion of his conservative support, but Quayle's continued presence on the ticket did not add to its appeal to moderates and independents.

Clinton's choice of Al Gore—senator from Tennessee and fellow southerner, fellow Baptist, and fellow baby boomer—didn't balance the ticket in the traditional sense, but it did add Gore's experience in foreign policy and arms control—issues Clinton had never dealt with as a state governor. Gore also was an experienced campaigner, having run for the Democratic nomination in 1988. Finally, he had an impeccable moral image and strong environmentalist credentials, as the author of the best-selling book *Earth in the Balance* (Boston: Houghton Mifflin, 1992). Republicans tried unsuccessfully to portray Gore as an environmental extremist, with Bush himself calling him "Ozone Man."

In 1996, Republicans chose veteran politician Robert Dole to face the Clinton–Gore ticket. An uninspiring candidate himself, Dole first sought retired general Colin Powell, an African American with strong bipartisan national support, as his running mate, but Powell declined the offer. Dole then turned to former representative Jack Kemp, who had also been Bush's secretary of housing and urban development. Kemp, once a professional football quarterback and an old adversary of Dole's, brought to the ticket political experience, empathy for the poor and for African Americans, and energy and youthfulness. But his economic policy preferences clashed with Dole's, just as his personality did, and the ticket never seemed coherent; nor did it galvanize the needed support among independents. Once again, the election outcome was shaped by the top of the ticket.

The Spouse's Role

So far, all American presidents have been men, and their wives traditionally functioned as helpmates during the presidential campaigns and the president's term in office. Edith Wilson and Eleanor Roosevelt were exceptions, but the real departure from this pattern began with Rosalyn Carter, who campaigned actively and then advised her husband Jimmy once he took office. Nancy Reagan was less active on the campaign trail but was regularly—often controversially—involved behind the scenes in the White House. She was particularly criticized for consulting an astrologer, who, some said, indirectly influenced her husband's decisions.[1] Barbara Bush was a warm campaigner who devoted her energies to literacy campaigns rather than policy involvement once her husband won the presidency.

The storm that swirled around Hillary Rodham Clinton as candidate's wife and first lady was unprecedented. A prominent lawyer and children's activist, she was Bill Clinton's virtual partner when he was governor, heading a special state taskforce on education reform. During the campaign she won the support of voters who expected her to be a liberal influence on her husband, and she excited many working women, feminists, and others who believe marriages should be partnerships. But she also outraged many traditionalists and conservatives during the campaign, and she became even more controversial during her service as first lady—especially when she headed the unsuccessful effort to reform health care during President Clinton's first term.

Elizabeth Dole was an active campaigner for her husband, Bob, during his 1996 bid for the presidency. She had served as secretary of transportation in Ronald Reagan's cabinet (1983 to 1987) and as secretary of labor in George Bush's cabinet (1989 to 1991). Her role as candidate's spouse was nearly a role reversal, for the Dole camp had at one point considered her for the vice-presidential spot eventually awarded to Kemp.[2] Head of the American Red Cross, she proved an active campaigner, mixing comfortably with crowds in ways Dole couldn't. During the campaign, Dole joked about accompanying her on the campaign trail, and after he lost he recommended that she be the party's presidential candidate in 2000, so he might finally get into the White House—as first man!

[1] Nancy Reagan, *My Turn: The Memoirs of Nancy Reagan* (New York: Random House, 1989).
[2] Evan Thomas, "Victory March," *Newsweek*, November 18, 1996.

- *The local campaign* is waged in each state, and it is the key to winning the presidency. Once constructed primarily of crisscrossing trips from city to city, this campaign is today waged primarily in the major media markets—areas, often overlapping state boundaries, that center on a major city surrounded by densely populated suburbs and that are served by major TV stations and newspapers which can carry the candidate's message to a large number of people. In the heat of the campaign, most candidate appearances are scheduled in the major media markets in states with large numbers of Electoral College votes that the candidate has a good chance of winning.[27]

Successful image making is increasingly difficult in this era of media-dominated elections. The media are less and less likely to pass along favorable propaganda handouts from the campaigns, preferring instead to analyze strategies and even issue statements, watching for strategic posturing, mistakes, and cover-ups. They also pay close attention to attacks by adversary camps.

Election campaigns, local or national, are designed to influence particular groups of voters. Strategists divide these groups into candidates' **bases**—voters who will remain loyal unless alienated by something the candidate does. Each candidate then embarks on a three-part strategy:

1. Solidify his or her own base.
2. Woo first-time and independent voters.
3. Split off pieces of the opponent's base, ideally winning them over as a new part of his or her electoral coalition, but at least denying their votes to the other candidate, either by encouraging them to vote for a third-party candidate or by so disgusting or disappointing them that they stay home on election day.

The Reagan campaigns polished the art of base-splitting and added an innovation. They used **wedge issues**, particularly social issues such as abortion, school prayer, and school busing, to slice off lower-middle-class voters who otherwise would have voted Democratic because of that party's stand on economic issues. In subsequent elections, such **base politics** have been central to campaign strategies, as the box nearby explains.

What Works in Presidential Campaigns: Stealing Bases

Each political party now courts an unstable base: The Republican base constantly threatens to disintegrate, and, as we saw in Chapter 6, the Democratic base is shrinking. Candidates thus face the dilemma of trying to make all the diverse subgroups happy without alienating any of their own members or the large number of independent voters essential to a presidential victory.

The Republican Base

The loose consortium of the Republican base consists of three groups:

- business interests and upper-class citizens;
- libertarians;
- social conservatives, including the Religious Right.

This coalition is particularly hard to hold together in bad economic times. Business interests, which benefit from the established order and usually oppose government intervention, support government subsidies and protection during bad times. Libertarians, who on principle oppose government intervention in virtually everything but police power and military self-defense, also favor greater civil liberties—for everyone, including gays and lesbians and women who want abortions. Social conservatives, mainly middle-class voters, oppose government intervention in business, except possibly in bad economic times. They generally favor government intervention to protect social and religious values, including laws to prevent abortion, and oppose civil rights for gays and lesbians.

The Democratic Base

Major subgroups of the Democratic base—labor, liberals, and minorities—are shrinking:

- Labor is losing political strength; only 20 percent of all workers now belong to unions.
- Liberals have been in retreat since Reagan and Bush succeeded in associating the term *liberalism* with big government, high taxes, and permissiveness toward criminals and deviants.
- Minorities—ethnic, gender (working women), and lifestyle (especially gays and lesbians)—have traditionally been staunch Democrats. But a growing percentage of white ethnic minorities, including Polish, Irish, and Italian Americans, have advanced economically and, like most of the middle class, increasingly vote Republican.

Capturing the Swing Votes

Swing voters—independents—are vital to presidential election, for neither party's base could elect a winner without them. Although one in every three people is a self-labeled independent, few are *pure independents*, who admit to no party leaning, are very diverse in their views, and vote much less frequently than either party loyalists or "leaners." *Leaners*, who also call themselves independents, tend to be economically comfortable and politically moderate and to behave more like party loyalists—closet Democrats and Republicans.[1]

Leaners are the swing voters courted by campaign strategists. They were the "Reagan Democrats" who, during the prosperous 1980s, were more interested in social issues than in economic policies. They were the closet Republicans driven toward Clinton in 1992 and 1996, as Buchanan's primary challenges forced both Bush and Dole to take more conservative stands. Many were baby boomers—the 60 million Americans born between 1946 and 1964—who not only were more comfortable with the Democrats' more moderate stands on social issues but also were attracted by the "double-boomer" ticket that promised "responsible change" at a time when the economic slump was threatening their well-paying jobs.

Both parties also look for votes among young, first-time voters. In the Reagan era, young voters tended to identify with Republicans. In 1992 and 1996, Clinton won the youth vote by presenting himself as the "new generation" candidate, even appearing on MTV.[2]

Stealing the Opponent's Base

Gaining an independent's vote gives you an advantage of one, but getting the vote of an opponent's supporter gives a net advantage of two. In the 1980s, Reagan campaign strategists successfully peeled away lower–middle-class Democrats, but the Republicans found that wedge issues could not hold these voters during the poor economic times of 1992. A similar effort in 1996 actually alienated moderate Republican voters.

To win in 1992, Clinton had to pick up about 10 percent of Bush's 1988 voters—or a significant majority of new voters—to supplement the 46 percent that Dukakis got in 1988. In addition to campaigning on fiscal responsibility and welfare reform, Clinton used wedge issues to shave off more liberal Republicans. He focused on women's rights—particularly abortion rights—and also courted gays and lesbians. He said little about helping African Americans or the poor. Clinton again used wedge issues to attract the women's vote in 1996. Clinton's strategy would not have worked if Perot had drawn away a substantial part of the Democrats' base. Perot failed to cut into the Clinton base substantially enough to affect the outcome in either election.

Another way to peel away blocs of voters is to attack the opponent's character or patriotism. In 1992, the attacks on Bush pointed to a major character liability for conservatives—abandoning his 1988 "No new taxes!" pledge. Some 17 percent of self-described conservatives voted for Perot in 1992, and 18 percent for Clinton. Republicans counterattacked with veiled references to Clinton's alleged marital infidelity and by contrasting his avoiding the draft with Bush's service as a fighter pilot (the 1992 campaign) and with Dole's war wounds (the 1996 campaign). Clinton's "positives" fell, but Americans nevertheless voted their pocketbooks in both elections.

[1] Bruce E. Keith et al., eds., *The Myth of the Independent Voter* (Berkeley: University of California Press, 1992).
[2] Christopher Georges, "Mock the Vote: What's Wrong with MTV's Hot New Political Coverage," *Washington Monthly*, May 1993, pp. 30–35.

Effective campaigns require flexible tactics and up-to-date information about voters' views and adversaries' records and daily activities. Equally essential are quick and definitive decision making and rapid communication of decisions and orders. The Reagan campaigns excelled at these strategies, using advanced electronic communications systems and simplified and focused messages that were standardized and controlled across the country. Campaign activities were coordinated with journalists' schedules to maximize exposure on nightly television news. This careful timing kept the Democrats on the defensive, delaying their responses to Republican attacks until the next day; by that time, of course, Reagan's messages had received full and unanswered play on the evening news and in the morning papers.

Both the Reagan and Bush campaigns perfected **opposition research**—studies of the actions and statements of the opposition, which were then computerized for instant retrieval whenever the campaign needed them. The Democrats duplicated this capability in 1992 with funds pledged by the Managing Trustees at the Middleburg meeting. They also adopted the Republican practices of using focus groups (see Chapter 5) and **tracking polls**—nightly telephone calls to carefully selected people who answer questions about their current presidential preference and their reactions to the day's developments, including each campaign's issue message. The campaign then uses that up-to-the-minute information to craft the next day's messages.

The Clinton forces ensured that their candidate's responses would not be held over until the next day, as had happened to the Democrats during the Reagan campaigns. Through computer networks and fax machines, the Democratic candidates and their campaign offices around the country were able to retrieve and fax relevant materials to key media instantly so their responses made it into the very stories presenting Republican charges—within the same "news cycle," as media professionals call it. In the midst of the 1992 campaign, one journalist remarked that "both on the attack and the defense, Mr. Clinton's campaign often seems more military than political, and has shown itself adept at the sort of warlike politics that are generally thought of as the specialty of Republican operations."[28] The campaign even called its central office "the War Room."

By contrast, the Bush campaign never developed a clear uniform message, lacked a single commander, and never seemed able to learn from its mistakes.[29] Nor did the Republican party, for many of the same criticisms were made of the Dole operation four years later, when it faced an even slicker Clinton reelection operation.

The Popular Election: Getting Out the Vote

Over 96 million Americans—49 percent of those eligible to vote—went to the polls on November 5, 1996, to record their choice for president, for representative in Congress, and, in one-third of the states, for senator. They also voted for various state and local offices. That turnout, the lowest percentage since 1924, contrasted with 1992's turnout of 55 percent. At the presidential level, the voters chose Dole, Clinton, Perot, or one of the 18 lesser-known candidates, such as consumer advocate Ralph Nader, running on the Green party ticket, or Harry Browne, running as a Libertarian (see Table 10.2).

TABLE 10.2

The 1996 Presidential Vote

A total of 21 presidential candidates were listed on the 1996 ballot in at least one state. Following is each candidate's vote total and percentage of the nationwide popular vote, and the state in which each did best.

Candidate (Party)	Popular Vote	Percentage	Best Showing
Bill Clinton (Democrat)	47,401,054	49.24	D.C., 85.19%
Bob Dole (Republican)	39,197,350	40.71	Utah, 54.37%
Ross Perot (Reform)	8,085,285	8.40	Maine, 14.19%
Ralph Nader (Green)	684,871	0.71	Oregon, 3.59%
Harry Browne (Libertarian)	485,120	0.50	Arizona, 1.02%
Howard Phillips (U.S. Taxpayers)	184,359	0.19	Virginia, 0.57%
John Hagelin (Natural Law)	113,659	0.12	Montana, 0.43%
Monica Moorehead (Workers World)	29,082	0.03	Ohio, 0.24%
Marsha Feinland (Peace & Freedom)	25,332	0.03	California, 0.25%
Charles E. Collins (Independent)	8,899	0.01	Colorado, 0.19%
James Harris (Socialist Workers)	8,463	0.01	D.C., 0.14%
Dennis Peron (Grassroots)	5,378	0.01	Minnesota, 0.22%
Mary Cal Hollis (Socialist)	4,764	0.00	Oregon, 0.14%
Jerome White (Socialist Equality)	2,438	0.00	Michigan, 0.04%
Diane Beall Templin (American)	1,847	0.00	Utah, 0.19%
Earl F. Dodge (Prohibition)	1,298	0.00	Arkansas, 0.05%
A. Peter Crane (Independent)	1,101	0.00	Utah, 0.17%
Ralph Forbes (America First)	932	0.00	Arkansas, 0.11%
John Birrenbach (Ind. Grassroots)	787	0.00	Minnesota, 0.04%
Isabell Masters (Looking Back)	752	0.00	Arkansas, 0.08%
Steve Michael (Independent)	408	0.00	Tennessee, 0.02%
"None of these candidates"	5,608	0.01	Nevada, 1.21%
Scattered write-ins	24,475	0.03	New Hampshire, 0.49%

Source: Adapted from *CQ Weekly Report,* January 18, 1997, p. 187.

Ralph Nader campaigns in California as the Green party's 1996 presidential candidate.

Voters continued to show up at polling places until they closed, but the major campaigns were able to predict the outcome long before that, based on exit polls and their expert knowledge of key bellwether—trend-setting or typical—states and key precincts. When the election results were broadcast that evening, the public learned what the campaigns had known from about noon onwards—Clinton had been reelected. He received 49.2 percent of the presidential votes (up from 43 percent in 1992) to Dole's 40.7 percent (compared with Bush's 38 percent in 1992) and Perot's 8.4 percent (down from 19 percent in 1992). Clinton's margin was over 8 million votes (up from 1992's 6 million). For a breakdown of which groups voted for which candidates, see Table 6.2 on pages 196–197.

The Electoral College: The Official Election

Most Americans believed that they had voted for Dole, Clinton, or Perot on November 5, and most believed that Clinton had won the presidency by 8 million votes. But they were wrong on both counts. The *real* presidential election occurred not on November 5 but on December 16. The votes cast on November 5 were not cast for Bush or Clinton or Perot but rather for slates of **presidential electors** whose names were not even listed on the ballots of most states. The electors chosen by the voters in each of the 50 states and the District of Columbia are collectively referred to as the **Electoral College**—a body that never actually meets but whose members cast the ballots state by state in their own state capitals on December 16, 1996. Their votes were sent to Washington, D.C., where they were opened and counted in a special session of Congress on January 9, 1997. *That* was the moment Bill Clinton was officially elected president—by a vote of 379 electoral votes to 159 for Dole and none for any of the other candidates, including Perot.

In keeping with the Framers' federalist design, states get as many **electoral votes** as they have senators and representatives in Congress. In every state, each presidential candidate's campaign selects the slate of electors, who are pledged to vote for that candidate if he or she gets a plurality (one vote more than anyone else) in the state in November. As long as electors honor their pledge, the Electoral College vote is no surprise.

Under certain conditions, however, the Electoral College can produce a victor other than the leading popular vote getter. This happened only once, in 1888, when the Electoral College elected Benjamin Harrison even though Grover Cleveland had won more popular votes. A third candidate could produce a similar result by taking a substantial number of votes in a few big states at the expense of the candidate winning the national popular vote. The election would then go to neither the third candidate nor the winning candidate but to the person who had placed second in the popular vote. Some feared this outcome when Perot ran in 1992 and 1996; subsequent exit polls showed, however, that he drew similarly from both candidates' support. Perot's presence may have drawn enough votes in several states to shift them from one candidate to the other, but Clinton's margins of 202 electoral votes in 1992 and 211 in 1996 did reflect the popular vote outcomes.

bellwether state

This term comes from *wether*, literally a male sheep that leads the flock by wearing a bell. It originally referred to someone who set a trend followed by others in politics. It has come to mean a state that tends to vote like the nation and so can be used to predict the outcome of an election before results in other states are known.

A final way the Electoral College could overturn the popular vote is by means of **faithless electors**—those who break their pledge to a candidate. Bolting is illegal in only half the states and carries a penalty (a small fine) in only five of those states. Only 8 of the almost 17,000 electors chosen since the first election have bolted, but because bolting cannot be effectively prevented anywhere, it remains a potential problem.[30] For example, in 1976, Jimmy Carter won a popular vote plurality of almost 2 million votes and had an electoral vote margin of 297 to 241. That election was very close—a shift of only about 5,000 votes in Ohio and Hawaii would have changed the Electoral College votes to give Ford a majority, despite Carter's popular plurality. Or, if only 29 of Carter's pledged electors had bolted and voted instead for Ford, Ford would have been returned to office.

A president elected by popular vote could lose under one other condition—no candidate winning the required majority of Electoral College votes. The Constitution provides that in case of an Electoral College tie, the House of Representatives would pick the new president, with each state's delegation casting one vote regardless of its size, and that the Senate would pick the new vice president. This happened in the 1824 election, when the House elected John Quincy Adams president, even though Andrew Jackson had won more popular votes. (The controversy this caused was lessened by Jackson's landslide victory in the next election.) In March 1877, the House again elected a president—Rutherford B. Hayes—who was not the popular vote winner—Samuel Tilden. That election was thrown into the House when Congress set up an electoral commission to rule on disputed electoral votes. No election since has overturned the preference of the people expressed in the November popular vote, but several have come close. So candidates, citizens, and journalists continue to criticize the Electoral College as antidemocratic, while some political scientists challenge this conclusion, as the box nearby explains.

Presidential electors pledged to vote for Bob Dole, who took Texas in the 1996 presidential election, gather in Austin to cast their ballots in the Electoral College election that actually determined the outcome.

Campaign Reforms and Democracy

As presidential campaigns have grown longer and more negative in the past few decades, an increasing number of people have called for such reforms as more responsible media coverage, more ethical campaign practices, and more informative campaigns.

How Democratic Is the Electoral College?

Many experts fear that if a candidate who wins the national popular vote does not win the presidency in the Electoral College, the public will question the legitimacy of the winner's election; beyond that, the public may begin to distrust the election system itself, and may perhaps even conclude that the United States is not really a democracy at all. Given these fears, why don't we replace the Electoral College system with the national popular election that most citizens think we have?

Efforts to replace the Electoral College with direct popular election have failed because of an informal coalition of two types of states that believe they benefit from the Electoral College. States with small populations, such as Alaska and Nevada, believe the Electoral College gives them more representation than their population size would merit, since each state gets two electors for its two senators in addition to the number its population entitles it to in the House. But the small states, too politically weak to preserve the Electoral College by themselves, depend on support from big urban states. These states have the most electoral votes, and so get the most attention from candidates—and promises to their big population blocs, such as ethnic and suburban voters. Thus the conventional explanation for the persistence of the Electoral College is that the small rural states and the large urban states unite against everyone else to preserve it.

But do these states, and the groups of voters within them, really benefit from the Electoral College? Experts are not so sure. A study of what experts call "the biases of the Electoral College" after the 1990 reapportionment found a net overall advantage to large states that in practice makes the votes of certain groups more important—especially those of urban voters, Jewish voters, those who live in the Far West, Hispanics, and foreign-born citizens. Electoral College biases disadvantage rural citizens, inhabitants of the mountain, midwest, southern, and eastern states, and African American voters.[1]

Whether the conventional wisdom or this expert analysis is more accurate, it is clear that powerful political interests appreciate the existing system for the benefits they believe it gives them. But how democratic is a system that gives special benefits to some states and their voters at the expense of everyone else?

Clearly the Electoral College system violates the basic democratic principle of "one person, one vote"—a principle has been the basis of voting law reforms in Congress, state legislatures, and the courts (Chapter 6). The Electoral College actually functions instead on the principle "One Californian, 2.6 votes, and one resident of a small state, less than one vote."

However, a look at the actual impact of the Electoral College on the way candidates campaign challenges the assumption that it would be more democratic to have direct election of the president, in which everyone's vote would indeed count the same because all votes for each candidate would simply be added up, with the largest national total winning. To maximize the number of voters they reached, candidates in a direct election would spend virtually all of their time and advertising money in the "major media markets." Thus the actual impact of direct elections on candidates' behavior might well penalize voters in smaller states or rural areas even more than the Electoral College system does. So if our concern is protecting the interests and rights of various electoral minorities scattered around the country, the Electoral College may actually make presidential elections more democratic by getting candidates to pay attention to citizens in less populous areas.

Still, many who fear outcomes that might challenge the legitimacy of the whole electoral system favor direct election of the president. Direct election might produce a minority victor, for such a "winner-take-all" provision tends to attract many candidates. Fearing that this too could threaten the legitimacy of the electoral outcome, some argue for requiring some minimum winning percentage of popular votes—say 40 percent. However, this would require a runoff election and could further weaken the two-party system by encouraging independent candidacies. Because any change in the Electoral College requires a constitutional amendment, it seems unlikely that anything will be done unless and until someone wins the presidency in the Electoral College while losing the popular election.

---

[1] Lawrence D. Longley and James D. Dana, Jr., "The Biases of the Electoral College in the 1990s," *Polity* 25, no.1 (Fall 1992): 123–145.

American campaigns have often—perhaps usually—been dirty. When Thomas Jefferson ran for president, the president of Yale University warned that if the author of the Declaration of Independence were elected, the Bible would be burned and "our wives and daughters [might become] the victims of legal prostitution." When Andrew Jackson ran as the first "man of the people" in 1828, his opponents spread false allegations that his mother, then dead for 50 years, had herself been a prostitute. Abraham Lincoln's opponents called him a despot, a liar, a thief, a buffoon, a robber, a tyrant, a butcher, and an old scoundrel, along with such names as "Ignoramus Abe."[31]

Recent presidential campaigns have been characterized by increasingly negative attacks on opponents' records, statements, and character. Charges have been made both by candidates and by their surrogates—running mates or other individuals campaigning in place of the candidate. In the 1988 campaign, for example, supporters of President Bush waged an ugly ad campaign against Dukakis by focusing on convicted murderer Willie Horton, who committed rape and robbery while on a weekend furlough from a Massachusetts prison while Dukakis was governor. What the ads failed to mention was that the Massachusetts program was very similar to a federal furlough program supported by the Reagan-Bush administration. In the 1996 campaign, ads sponsored by organized labor attacked Republicans for allegedly favoring cuts in Social Security and Medicare, when in fact they had only supported limiting increases in funding for those programs.

Even Abraham Lincoln, now regarded as one of the greatest presidents, was subjected to negative attacks, especially in connection with the Civil War. In this 1864 cartoon by a northern critic, Columbia, a symbol of the United States, demands the return of the 500,000 additional soldiers that Lincoln has just ordered to be drafted.

Attacks like these are part of the price of running for office, because, as we'll see in Chapter 15, the law does not protect politicians from libel or slander—written or spoken remarks that injure one's reputation. Nevertheless, there are unofficial boundaries that candidates are expected not to cross. President Bush crossed one of them toward the end of the 1992 campaign, when—his claim to authority based on maturity having failed, and threatened with defeat—he declared, "My dog Millie knows more about foreign policy than these two bozos." Partisan crowds loved the "red meat" rhetoric, but others thought it language unfit for a president.

Candidates may be able to have it both ways at once, by declaring noble principles of behavior while also reminding everyone of the suspicions or allegations others raise about the adversary. Bush tried this in 1992 when he was asked whether the allegations of Clinton's marital infidelity were appropriate material for the campaign; he responded that he and his campaign would "stay out of the sleaze business." Terms such as *sleaze* may imply that there could be something to such allegations.

Does negative campaigning win elections? There is no doubt that it drives up a candidate's "negatives" in opinion polls, and it does tend to alienate voters, perhaps keeping some from going to the polls. But as the 1992 and 1996 elections remind us, voters generally pay more attention to other considerations.

More Media Responsibility

The media were roundly criticized for being manipulated by the negative 1988 Republican campaign that won Bush the White House. When the 1992 campaign rolled around, they were taking pains to report on negative campaigning and were developing new ways to assess campaign ads. Cable News Network (CNN) pioneered the "ad police," who, led by correspondent Brooks Jackson, ran news stories about national political ads and gave them bright red labels reading *Unfair, False,* or *Misleading.* Other networks, local stations, and newspapers followed CNN's lead. Citizens also actively participated in call-in shows and citizen forums, criticizing candidates' negative campaigning and inattention to policy issues.

Polls consistently find that most citizens believe the media have no right to pry into candidates' private lives. This issue came into the national spotlight in 1988, after several journalists staked out Democratic candidate Gary Hart's Washington apartment and then reported that they had seen a woman who was not Hart's wife leave the apartment. While journalists, politicians, and citizens alike debated the propriety of journalists' staking out candidates' private lives, Hart felt compelled to withdraw from the race. By 1992, after much soul searching, the mainstream media had grown more hesitant to publicize such activities. But they again joined in, citing a newsworthy public controversy, when nightclub performer Gennifer Flowers was interviewed in the supermarket tabloid the *Star* about her allegations of an extramarital affair with Bill Clinton. Clinton eventually denied the allegations on a special edition of the TV news magazine *Sixty Minutes.*

The media may have helped deter personal attacks on Clinton in 1996, however. In that election, the Dole campaign focused on Clinton's character as revealed by the Whitewater investment and alleged cover-up, rather than on his private life. Some analysts believed the restraint was in part attributable to fears in the Dole camp that a more personal attack on Clinton would cause the media to run a story about a woman they had located who swore she and Dole had been sexually involved before his divorce from his first wife.[32]

Media coverage of negative campaigning, like the campaigning itself, could end in one of two ways. The media could voluntarily refuse to provide coverage for negative campaigning, even at the cost of losing audience to less responsible sensationalist organizations. Alternatively, American citizens could show their disapproval by withholding votes from practitioners of negative campaigning to show that such tactics are counterproductive.

Efforts to Make Elections More Democratic

Elites, special interest groups, and various experts play significant roles in choosing candidates for elected offices. Elites such as the Democrats' Managing Trustees and the Republicans' Team 100 wield a great deal of influence in money-dominated campaigns. Special interest groups contribute enormous sums of money to candidates and become key players to the extent that officeholders feel obliged to represent their interests rather than the public interest.

Even high-placed campaign workers are now political professionals, with their own journals and newsletters, foremost among them the bimonthly *Campaigns and Elections*, published in Washington since 1979.[33] One can now get a graduate degree in political campaign management from various schools, including the Graduate School of Political Management in New York City.[34] Campaign strategists and managers gain their knowledge of practical politics by working in one campaign after another. Those who run a victorious campaign often join the staff of the victor because the reelection campaign begins the day the victor takes office and experienced campaign professionals are a valuable asset.

We have also seen that victors are chosen by only a small fraction of the eligible voters, and that the process by which political parties choose their major candidates may produce leaders who are unlikely to represent the broad spectrum of views held by the American public.

If all of this concerns you, you are not alone. Many now argue that campaigns and elections are in need of reform. Some proposals would modify the existing system. Others assert that the system needs improvements in campaign content, legal regulation of campaign advertising, substantial reforms in the nominating process, further enforced regulation of campaign finance practices, and better methods of increasing voter turnout. Let's examine some of the most prominent proposed reforms.

Improving the Content of Campaigns

The most comprehensive recent set of campaign reform proposals was developed by a commission of former politicians, journalists, and academics convened by the Markle Foundation in response to the negative content of the 1988 campaign. This commission found that voters act as if elections belong to the candidates rather than to them, and that they fail to "grasp the fact that democracy grants them the power to demand candidate and media performance that is much more to their liking, and more responsive to their needs."[35] To correct this situation, the commission recommended the following steps:[36]

- Establish a permanent, nonpartisan foundation to educate citizens about democracy and their role in it.
- Ask candidates to pledge to conduct clean campaigns.
- Require presidential candidates to participate in four debates if they wish public campaign funding.
- Encourage broadcasters and publishers to evaluate the truth of the claims that candidates make in their advertising and to avoid being manipulated by the candidates.
- Establish a 20-hour election day so that polling hours through the 50 states would be concurrent, and prevent media from making public projections of winners while the polls are still open because such projections may dissuade citizens from voting.
- Simplify voter registration.

The most striking thing about these proposals—and similar proposals that have been made in one election after another—is that they lack foolproof enforcement mechanisms and depend primarily on good-faith efforts by candidates and journalists.

Regulating Campaign Advertising

Those who believe good-faith efforts will fail have concluded that the only hope for real reform is legal regulation of campaign advertising. One proposed law would avoid the inflammatory and misleading impact of short commercials by requiring any advertisement of 10 minutes or less to consist only of a "talking head" in front of a camera, accompanied by a line identifying the candidate and party the ad is supporting. Proponents of this idea believe it would encourage more informative speech in place of the currently popular but misleading voice-over rhetoric and dramatic visuals.[37] Another proposal would require that a station carrying a negative ad about a candidate grant that candidate free time to respond. This provision would cost the media advertising dollars and so encourage them to reject negative ads. It might also be challenged in court as an infringement of candidates' right to free speech.

Changing the Nominating Process

The current lengthy, costly, exhausting campaigns tend to be self-selecting processes that favor individuals with the qualities that make good campaigners—sheer endurance, charisma to attract the media, and an ability to appeal to various local and regional interests while avoiding stands that might upset significant blocs of voters. Unfortunately, these qualities differ greatly from those that make a good president—especially the ability to lead public opinion while managing an enormous bureaucracy and negotiating with members of Congress. This is the basic premise underlying proposals for revising the process by which presidential candidates are chosen. Although many people favor simplifying the nominating process, they disagree on how it could best be accomplished.

The most drastic proposal is for a **national primary,** a national qualifying election, held in May or September, in which every voter could vote for a preferred candidate in his or her party. The winner of each party's primary would then be the party's candidate in the general election. Critics of this proposal agree that a national primary would simplify the nominating process but say that the plan would make it impossible for citizens to watch how the candidates handle themselves when dealing with changing issues, campaigning in different regions of the country, and coping with the inevitable campaign disasters, and to change their minds about whom to support as a result.

Another proposal calls for strengthening the role of parties through **preprimary national conventions**, where party professionals would scrutinize candidates and then select the party's official nominee. That individual would then have to compete in a national primary against any preprimary losers who received a substantial percentage of the vote and wanted to challenge him or her. The preprimary would enable party leaders to eliminate candidates who, in their opinion, lacked substantial party support, were unlikely to be good candidates, or would probably not make a good president. The ability to challenge the official nominee would preserve a role for party supporters around the country should the leaders' selection be unpopular. Supporters say this proposal would eliminate the advantage a candidate can now gain by doing well in early state primaries and caucuses that are unrepresentative of the electorate as a whole. Furthermore, a convention followed by a primary would get more media attention, and therefore more voter attention, than the current extended primary and caucus system.[38]

A less drastic and more popular proposal calls for scheduling a series of **regional primaries,** perhaps spaced three or four weeks apart. Candidates could then focus their attention better, spend their energies and resources more effectively, and gain more focused media attention. Voters could evaluate candidates over a longer and more diverse competition, and candidates would be required to develop appeal in various regions of the country to win their party's nomination. Since 1988, some southern states have coordinated their primaries to occur on the same day, now called Super Tuesday. The large bloc of delegates elected on that day focuses candidates' attention and can maximize the South's impact on the nomination process if it occurs at the right moment. In the 1996 campaign, however, Super Tuesday had little impact, and key states decided to move their primaries to earlier dates in the year 2000 campaign season. The regional primary proposal would institutionalize the Super Tuesday approach for the entire country. Inevitable disputes over when each region would hold its primaries would have to be resolved through the political process, or perhaps by drawing lots.

Critics of the regional primary proposal point out that this option has at least one disadvantage: With so many state primaries on the same day, candidates would depend on media exposure—and therefore on large sums of money—even more than they do now.

Coordinating any major change would be difficult because the nomination process is determined by a combination of state laws and party rules. Because incumbents generally fare well under any system, the most fervent change advocates are usually the disappointed leaders of the party that lost the last election, who believe that a different process would produce a more nationally viable candidate for their party. Until the 1992 election, Democrats favored reform because the process had produced a string of victorious Republican candidates. Any impetus for reform before the year 2000 will probably come from Republicans concerned about their intraparty ideological battles. But any major changes will require the consent of state legislatures, which the 1996 elections left quite evenly split between the parties, with Democrats controlling 20, Republicans 18, and the rest divided between the two.

Reforming Campaign Finance

The favorite target of most election reformers today continues to be campaign finance, despite recent efforts to impose new controls. The stakes are enormous. Every vote finally cast in the presidential election costs its recipient somewhere between $2 and $5. Through the income tax checkoff option, taxpayers pay an additional $13 per vote by underwriting much of the general election presidential campaign spending and a portion of the primary election expenditures, to the tune of some $130 million in 1996.[39] But much of the money spent by presidential candidates and all of the money spent by congressional candidates comes from contributions, and many of those contributions come from special interests seeking particular favors from the candidates they support. A system with these underpinnings amounts to "honest graft,"[40] in the words of a critical journalist, and those who would reform it have proposed the following:

> **"honest graft"**
>
> The term *graft* refers to money or property gained through political corruption. The term *honest graft* is traceable to a turn-of-the-century New York City political boss, George Washington Plunkitt, who distinguished between blackmailing someone you have political power over (dishonest graft) and getting rich by using inside information to make investment decisions (honest graft). Today, such activity is no longer considered permissible.

- Ban soft money, limit contributions from PACs, and limit congressional campaign spending. (These terms were specified in a bill sponsored by Senators Russell Feingold [D-Wis.] and John McCain [R-Ariz.], which failed to pass Congress in 1997.)
- Amend the Constitution to limit the First Amendment right to free speech as interpreted by the Supreme Court, so that spending caps become constitutional. (This proposal was defeated in Congress in 1997.)
- Provide federal funding for congressional candidates who agree to spending caps on their campaign. (This measure is similar to the current provisions for presidential campaigns.)
- Give candidates free or cheaper media (TV, radio, newspaper) advertising, perhaps in exchange for their agreeing to spending caps.
- Require all candidates and parties to disclose all contributions more fully, more frequently, and more publicly, perhaps on the Internet.

Efforts to further limit contributions and spending continue to meet resistance from incumbents and challengers alike, as well as from the parties, many special interests, the advertising media, and even the Supreme Court. Some nonpartisan advocates of strong grassroots politics also oppose such reform because it would tend to inhibit competition by challengers and limit influence by underrepresented interest groups. These critics instead favor greater disclosure of just who gives how much to whom, and public financing of congressional campaigns.[41]

Three of the four major networks plus PBS and CNN launched an interesting experiment in the 1996 presidential election. They gave the major candidates free minutes for statements, and a study found greater accuracy and fewer attacks in these free statements than in candidate advertising. Even though a poll found only 23 percent of the voters knew of the experiment, most participants thought it worth expanding in the next presidential election, despite criticism that it undemocratically denies free time to minor-party candidates.[42] One prominent proposal calls for stations to make "deposits" to a "national time bank" that would give vouchers to all qualifying congressional candidates, who could use them to buy media advertising according to their own campaign strategy. However, broadcasters, which are extremely powerful in Washington, oppose such proposals with claims that they would cost them a fortune and violate their First Amendment rights.[43] For a look at how some other democracies regulate campaign finance, see Table 10.3.

Increasing Voter Turnout

A final and primary concern of those interested in the American electoral process is that, whatever the election and whatever the process, very few citizens actually vote. Some propose that citizens be required to vote or pay a fine, as in some European countries with much higher turnouts. Opponents of this controversial proposal point out that it could merely require ill-informed citizens to cast meaningless—but perhaps consequential—votes.

Others argue that low turnout results when citizens are too busy to inform themselves, and so never become interested enough to vote. "The challenge to the future of American campaigns and hence to American democracy," wrote one an-

TABLE 10.3

How Other Democracies Handle Campaign Finance

Britain

Candidates for Parliament
- Official campaign period lasts only a few weeks.
- Any group or individual, including foreigners, can donate to parties or candidates.
- Spending is limited for candidates, but not for parties.
- Parties are allocated free TV time.
- Contributions do not have to be disclosed.

Germany

Candidates for parliament (Bundestag)
- All financing of candidates is done through political parties. Corporate contributions are legal.
- Contributions are tax deductible, up to $3,750 per year.
- Parties are allocated free TV time.
- The federal treasury gives parties more than 60 percent of their campaign funds. Private or corporate contributions are matched up to a total of $144 million per year.
- Contributions under $12,000 do not have to be disclosed.

Japan

Candidates for parliament (Diet)
- Corporations can contribute directly to candidates.
- Annual contribution limits are considerably higher than in the United States. Individuals may give candidates up to $83,000, but no more than $12,000 to a single candidate, and up to $166,000 to parties. Corporate limits range from $62,500 to $833,000, depending on company size.
- Contributions under $416 to do have to be disclosed, and loopholes abound to avoid reporting higher donations.

Canada

Candidates for Parliament
- Unions and corporations can contribute directly to candidates and parties.
- Contributions are not limited, but spending is. Each candidate's limit depends on the size of the district and ranges from $37,500 to $48,750. In 1993 the two largest parties could spend $7.5 million each.

Russia

Candidates for president
- Candidate spending is restricted. In the 1996 presidential election, the spending limit was $3.5 million.
- Enforcement of disclosure requirements is generally lax. President Boris Yeltsin's 1996 reelection campaign reportedly attracted tens of millions of dollars that were never reported.

Source: Washington Post National Weekly Edition, March 3, 1997, p. 10.
Note: All dollar amounts based on exchange rates as of March 1997.

---

alyst, "is how to bring back the excitement and the music in an age of electronic campaigning. Today's campaigns have more to do because an educated, media-centered society is a broadened and segmented electorate which is harder to rally."[44] But any effort to involve more citizens in campaign events such as rallies and town meetings would make campaigns even more expensive and longer—two changes few favor.

Some suggest that low turnout is caused by the infrequency of elections. If the United States had more elections, held more often, voting would become habitual, according to this viewpoint. Electing more officials at the local, state, and perhaps even national levels—perhaps on the same national election day—might produce a higher turnout.

Ultimately, reforms can do little to protect the electoral system unless citizens inform themselves about the candidates and the issues and then choose to vote. Citizens are more likely to accept this responsibility if the media encourage them to do so and furnish the information they need to make informed choices—and if special interests lose their financial stranglehold on campaigns. But changing the behavior of the media and the special interests requires major reforms, and reforms themselves require an informed and responsible citizenry to press for them, given the extent to which politicians are compromised by the current system. Thus in the end it is up to you and all other Americans to become and remain responsible voters. Citizens who do not inform, defend, and assert themselves ultimately have only themselves to blame for the quality of the political candidates and the actions of the political leadership at all levels of elected government.

Summary

Elections perform five basic functions: selecting public officials, revealing public opinion, influencing government policy, evaluating officials' performances (retrospective voting), and evaluating campaign promises (prospective voting). Elections also have other deeper effects, such as making citizens feel involved, encouraging peaceful citizen action, preserving a limited role for mass political action, and focusing citizen frustration when elections don't turn out as desired.

Candidates, parties, interest groups, and individuals each have their own stakes in elections. All usually have policy interests, and all use different resources—money, votes, information, and ideas.

Candidates compete by making claims to authority to characterize reality—*what is*, *what's right*, and *what works*—for voters. These claims may appeal to incumbency, character and life history, expertise, age, religion, ethnicity, gender, or other characteristics. Election outcomes depend on the political environment—laws, regulations, and daily developments.

Both presidential and congressional elections have changed since the 1960s, from party dominance to candidate dominance, from activist dominance to media dominance, and from organization dominance to money dominance. Efforts to control the role of money through laws and regulations supervised by the Federal Election Commission have been limited by the Supreme Court and have not been very successful.

Congressional elections have also been affected by the incumbency effect—better name recognition, special media exposure, special interest contributions, and voter credit and reward for casework and pork-barrel legislation. House seats can disappear through reapportionment, and redistricting—which is called gerrymandering when it creates unusually shaped districts to determine election outcomes—can create or eliminate districts.

Presidential elections now have seven stages: a "secret preprimary," in which wealthy individuals and vested interests select and contribute to their preferred candidates; a "silent primary" in which candidates use impression management to convince the media of their seriousness and viability; the party primaries and caucuses, in which candidates try to win a majority of convention delegates; the party conventions, which showcase the candidates; the general election campaign, 51 different campaigns conducted simultaneously; the popular election; and the official Electoral College election, in which electors selected by voters on election day vote state by state to select the president.

The negative campaigning that has characterized elections, particularly in 1988, has caused voters and the media to pressure candidates to make campaigns and their coverage more issue oriented. Reformers have proposed rules to improve campaign content by limiting negative messages and character attacks and instead focusing on issues; to regulate campaign advertising; to make changes in the nomination process, such as holding a national primary, a preprimary national convention, or regional primaries; to further regulate campaign finance; and to increase voting turnout. Ultimately, the quality of American elections depends primarily on the quality of citizenship exercised by Americans.

Key Terms

base **370**
base politics **370**
coattail effect **358**
election **347**
Electoral College **374**
electoral votes **374**
faithless electors **375**
Federal Election Campaign Act (FECA) **356**
free media **355**
gerrymandering **362**
impression management **366**

incumbency **349**
incumbency advantage **350**
incumbency effect **360**
infomercial **355**
mandate **348**
national primary **380**
opposition research **372**
paid media **355**
preprimary national convention **380**
presidential electors **374**
primary caucus **366**
prospective voting **348**

racial gerrymandering **362**
reapportionment **360**
redistricting **361**
regional primaries **381**
retrospective voting **348**
secret preprimary **365**
silent primary **365**
soft money **357**
split ticket **358**
tracking polls **372**
wedge issues **370**

How You Can Learn More About Campaigns and Elections

For inside information by and about campaign organizers, strategy, and tactics, see the periodical *Campaigns and Elections*, published at 1835 K Street N.W., Suite 403, Washington, D.C. 20077. You can get a wide variety of official reports on campaign regulations and spending by contacting the Federal Election Commission, 999 E Street N.W., Washington, D.C. 20463 (800-424-9530). You may also write for a free subscription to *The Record*, a monthly periodical the FEC publishes, which summarizes recent election news developments and publications. The most detailed reference on the history of American elections is Congressional Quarterly's *Guide to United States Elections*, 3rd ed. (Washington, D.C.: Congressional Quarterly Press, 1994), which includes information on elections from 1789 through 1992. For further information, consult the following books.

Buchanan, Bruce. *Electing a President: The Markle Commission Research on Campaign '88.* Austin: University of Texas Press, 1991. A critique of the 1988 elections with recommendations for reforming the process and its coverage by the media.

Crotty, William, and Jerome M. Mileur, eds., *America's Choice: The Election of 1996.* New York: Dushkin/McGraw-Hill, 1997. A collection of analyses of various aspects of the 1996 elections.

Ehrenhalt, Alan. *The United States of Ambition: Politicians, Power, and the Pursuit of Office.* New York: Times Books, 1991. An analysis of the motivation of politicians in the United States.

Jackson, Brooks. *Honest Graft: Big Money and the American Political Process.* New York: Alfred A. Knopf, 1988. A reporter's study of the extent of big money's penetration of American politics.

Jacobson, Gary C. *Politics of Congressional Elections*, 3rd ed. New York: HarperCollins, 1992. A study of how people win elections to Congress.

Morris, Dick. *Behind the Oval Office: Winning the Presidency in the Nineties.* New York: Random House, 1997. A memoir by a Clinton strategist in the 1996 election.

Pomper, Gerald M., et al. *The Election of 1996: Reports and Interpretations.* Chatham, N.J.: Chatham House, 1997. A collection of analyses of major stages of the 1996 campaign and election.

Sabato, Larry, ed. *Millennium: The Elections of 1996.* Boston: Allyn & Bacon, 1997. Another collection of analyses of major stages of the 1996 campaign and election.

Sorauf, Frank. *Inside Campaign Finance: Myths and Realities.* New Haven, Conn.: Yale University Press, 1992. An analysis of the politics of campaign finance by an expert on the role of money in politics.

How American Institutions Work

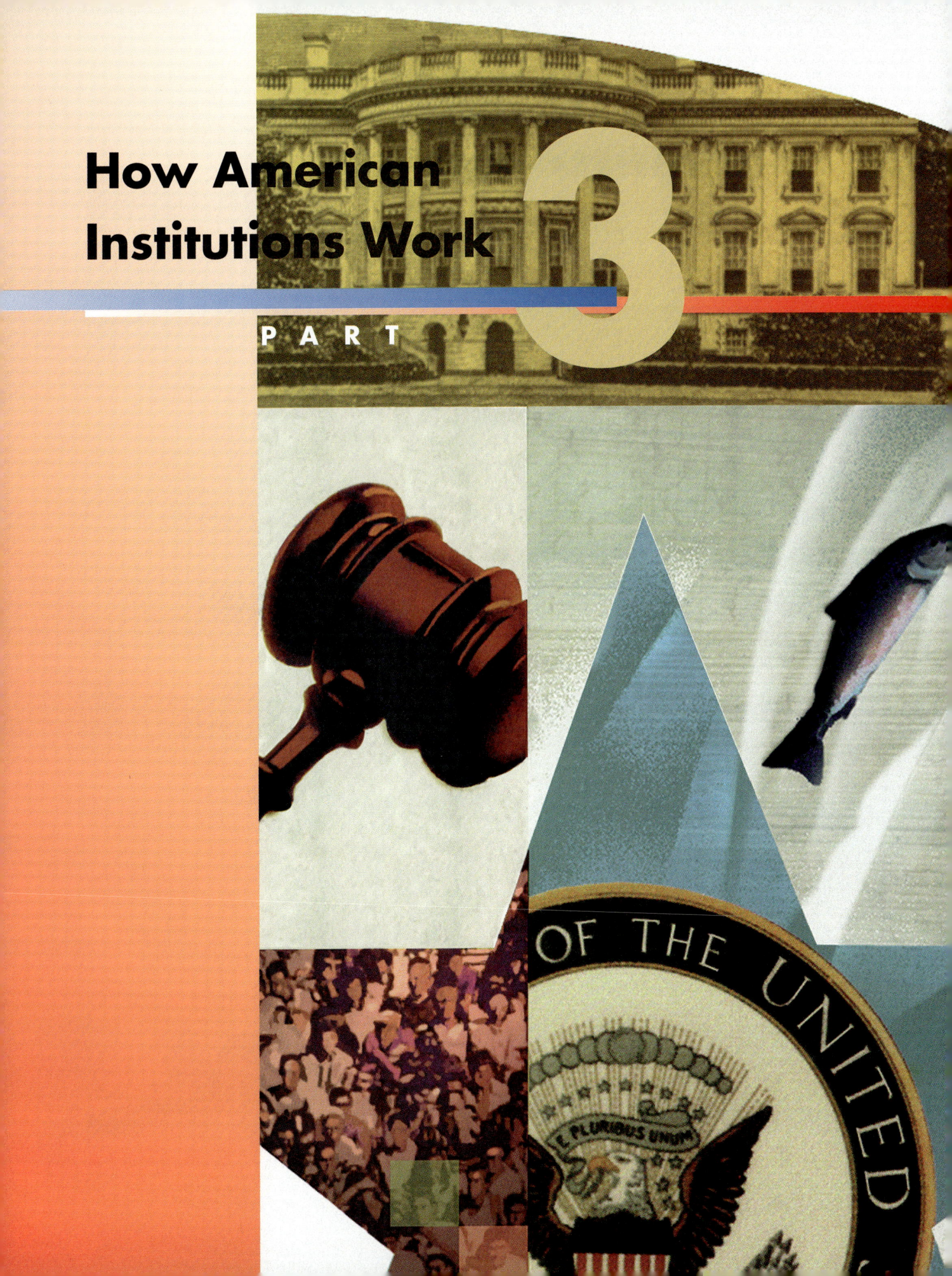

PART 3

Congress

Above: Industrial air pollution in Baton Rouge, Louisiana.
Right: Representative Henry Waxman (D-Calif.) (*center*) confers with aides on the Clean Air Act Amendments of 1990.

CHAPTER 11

I have seen in the Halls of Congress more idealism, more humaneness, more compassion, more profiles of courage than in any other institution that I have ever known.

—Hubert H. Humphrey, former Democratic senator from Minnesota and former vice president

It's every man for himself. Every senator is a baron. He has his own principality. Once you adopt that as a means of doing business, it's hard to establish any cohesion.

—James B. Pearson, former Republican senator from Kansas[1]

What Congress Does

The Internal Politics of Congress

The External Politics of Congress

Reforming Congress

Take a deep breath. The air you just breathed was polluted, no matter where you are—indoors or out, in a large industrial city, in a suburb, or on a farm. Air pollution is an inevitable consequence of modern life. Some of the chemicals that industries and farms depend on end up in the air, as do the by-products of the burning of gasoline and other fuels.

When researchers in the 1960s found that pollution can endanger people's health, Americans began turning to government for protection. A series of ecological disasters—coastal oil tanker spills, an oil well blowout off California beaches, and chemical waste discharges from factories that killed large numbers of fish—coupled with books proclaiming an ecological crisis prompted Congress to pass the National Environmental Policy Act of 1969 and President Richard Nixon to create the Environmental Protection Agency in 1970. Congress, which had passed a weak Clean Air Act in 1967, strengthened it in 1970 and again in 1977 by limiting auto pollution and requiring reductions in emissions from coal-burning power plants thought to cause the "acid rain" that was killing fish and poisoning lakes in northeastern states and Canada.

Despite these steps, air quality in many cities continued to deteriorate, and lung diseases increased. Environmentalists and health professionals joined forces with Democrats in Congress to seek stricter regulations, but their efforts were stymied by the Reagan administration's campaign to reduce government regulations on industry. When George Bush won the 1988 election, he decided to make good on his pledge to be "the environmental president" by strengthening the Clean Air Act to further limit power plant pollution and auto tailpipe emissions and to encourage the development of cleaner alternative auto fuels made from natural gas or corn. For the first time in a decade, the president and congressional leaders were agreed in principle on the need to legislate improved air quality.[2]

The president's proposals, cast as amendments to the existing Clean Air Act, were combined into what is called a *bill*—a piece of draft legislation—in July 1989. They were submitted to both houses of Congress, because both houses must approve a bill before the president can sign it into law. Lobbyists for automobile producers, electric utilities, and other polluters, along with members of Congress from districts and states with big polluters, wanted to kill the bill if possible, or otherwise weaken it by attaching crippling amendments. Environmental advocates, on the other hand, finding the Bush proposals too weak, wanted to strengthen the proposals by amending the bill.

Any draft legislation—whether proposed by the president or by a member of the House or Senate—is "referred," or sent, to a committee of members concerned with the topic. This referral is made in the Senate by the majority leader— the leader of the party which has a voting majority. In the House, the Speaker, who has been selected by the party that dominates the House, makes the referral. Each committee's job is to study the bill and decide whether to recommend its passage to the whole Senate or House. If the bill seems important, the head of the committee—called the chair—often refers it to one of its subcommittees, which can get testimony from interested parties such as administration officials, lobbyists, and academic or business experts, and may then vote to amend the bill before recommending it to the whole committee for its decision on whether to recommend its passage to the whole Senate or House.

In the Senate, Majority Leader George Mitchell (D-Maine), long an environmentalist, made the Clean Air Act Amendments his top priority. He referred the bill to the Environment and Public Works Committee, whose 16 members included 5 environmentalists from New England, the area most affected by acid rain, and only one senator from the Appalachian and Midwestern states that burn polluting coal. Chairing the Environmental Protection Subcommittee to which the bill was referred was Max Baucus (D-Mont.).

Because both the subcommittee and the whole committee were dominated by New England environmentalists, after relatively quick deliberation, the committee reported out a bill that was stronger—and much more costly to polluting industries—than the original Bush bill. Mitchell called the clean air bill up as the Senate's first business in 1990 but found immediately that it did not have enough support to pass. Many Republicans were hesitant to support it because the White House thought it too strong, and many Democrats from other regions wanted it modified to take account of their objections—something the committee had not done because it was so homogeneous. But to complicate matters, senators could not agree on what changes they wanted. Some opposed the acid rain provisions, others rejected the auto emissions provisions, and still others disliked the proposals supporting alternative fuels less polluting than gasoline.

In the Senate, a small minority can prevent a vote by "talking a bill to death," because Senate rules require the votes of 60 of the 100 senators to cut off debate. Thus Mitchell decided to arrange secret negotiations among the bill's Senate supporters, its Senate opponents, and Bush administration aides. It took months to work out a compromise acceptable to Senate supporters and the Bush administration. Neither environmental nor business lobbyists were happy with the compromise, but the Senate leadership and the Bush aides agreed to oppose all amendments proposed from the floor during debate in order to preserve the compromise, which then passed the Senate by a vote of 89 to 11 on April 3, 1990.

The situation in the House was equally difficult but quite different. There the Bush bill had been referred to the Energy and Commerce Committee, whose 43 members were representative of the country at large and of the House as a whole. Its chair, John Dingell (D-Mich.), represented a part of the Detroit area that is home to the "big three" automakers, General Motors, Ford, and Chrysler, and was married to a lobbyist for GM. Dingell, a staunch opponent of auto emissions regulations, agreed to sponsor Bush's bill in the House because he knew he couldn't prevent passage of a bill and wanted as much control over its contents as possible. He referred the bill to the Health and Environment Subcommittee, chaired by his arch-enemy, Henry Waxman (D-Calif.), who represented part of the Los Angeles area that included Hollywood and had a terrible smog problem. A longtime champion of auto emissions cutbacks, Waxman was bound to try to strengthen the Bush bill. But over the years Dingell had appointed many moderates to Waxman's subcommittee—something a powerful committee chair can do—and he was confident they would resist Waxman's efforts.

Both Waxman and Dingell agreed that a new clean air bill was inevitable, and both wanted a significant bill passed to prove that they were effective leaders in the House, but they disagreed strongly on what the bill should contain. Rather than risk defeat, they took the unusual step of agreeing to compromise their differences early in the process and develop a bill they would then both pledge to support on the House floor—a difficult decision because each knew that such a compromise would be attacked by both environmentalists and industry interests.

Waxman's subcommittee approved a draft of the compromise clean air bill in early October 1989. Despite their agreement, Dingell delayed scheduling debate by the full committee until the following March, when it became clear in the Senate that Mitchell and the White House had made a deal that would stick. Neither Dingell nor Waxman wanted administration people involved in their own deal making because each feared the Bush people would side with the other. The White House disliked being excluded but could do nothing in the face of agreement by the two committee titans. The House committee deliberations took a month of strenuous, late-night, secret meetings of key players. Finally, on April 5, the drafting was finished. When the bill reached the House floor, it passed by a 415 to 15 vote on May 23, after only two days of debate and several minor amendments.

When the House and Senate pass different versions of the same bill, one house may simply approve the draft passed by the other. However, on a major issue such as this the significant differences are compromised in a *conference committee*. The House Speaker and the Senate majority leader each appoint members to this committee—usually those recommended by the chairs of the committees that have debated the bill—to represent the interests of their body in the compromise negotiations.

Dingell and representatives more sympathetic to environmental protection struggled for a month over who would be the House conferees. Finally, the

Speaker forced a compromise, selecting an astonishing 130 members from 9 committees, while the Senate sent 9 from 2 committees. White House aides were once again barred from participating in the negotiations and had to sit in a nearby room and communicate with their supporters by hand signals. Negotiations lasted from July 13 until October 22, when a compromise bill that combined many of the stronger provisions of each chamber's original draft was agreed to. Both chambers then passed the compromise by overwhelming votes, and on November 15, 1990, President Bush signed the Clean Air Act Amendments of 1990.

The legislative process had worked, and all Americans' lives would be affected for decades to come by the terms of the agreement negotiated over 15 months. This case illustrates the actual day-to-day workings of Congress that we'll explore more fully in this chapter by focusing on five key questions:

> **What does Congress—the government's lawmaking institution—actually do?**
>
> **How do conflicting goals make being a member of Congress difficult?**
>
> **Why is it hard for Congress to legislate successfully?**
>
> **Why is it hard for Congress to prevail in struggles with other political actors?**
>
> **What reforms might improve the performance of Congress and its members?**

What Congress Does

The Framers considered Congress the key actor in the new American government and expected it to engage in thoughtful deliberation. Today, however, it is often locked in struggles with the executive branch when not stalemated internally, and the public holds it in low esteem. Polls find that more than half of the people approve of the job their own representative is doing but only 20 to 30 percent approve of the job Congress as a whole is doing. However, most Americans know little about Congress. A poll taken as the 1994 midterm elections approached found that only a third of respondents could name a single bill passed by the current session, even though Congress had recently approved a deficit reduction package, approved the North American Free Trade Agreement (NAFTA), established a new youth national-service program, and passed a reorganization of the bureaucracy that cut 70,000 jobs, among many other important laws. Most could not even name their own representative, let alone identify the party leaders in either house. Indeed, 40 percent believed that the Republicans controlled Congress—something that hadn't been true for 40 years but that resulted soon thereafter because of voters' negative assessment of Congress.[3] Such public ignorance makes it hard for Congress to operate effectively. To understand why, we must examine the functions Congress performs. In the following section we will examine the roles members adopt in fulfilling their responsibilities.

The Powers and Responsibilities of Congress

Today, most consider the president the key to the national government, but the Framers established Congress as the first branch in Article I. Even though they were establishing a representative system of government, the Framers made "the people" the legitimating force in the new republic. The Senate, whose members were elected by state legislatures until 1912, was to represent the states and take a longer view because senators were given six-year terms. The House of Representatives, with members directly elected by the people every two years, would represent the people, paying special attention to their local concerns. As the collective voice of "the people" in a representative republic, Congress had the primary responsibility to ensure that the people's voices were heard, their interests considered, and the common good preserved, through laws that would shape policy.

At the founding, the country contained 13 states with fewer than 3 million people (excluding Indians and slaves), and the government employed a mere 50 bureaucrats. Over the next 200 years the number of states quadrupled, the population multiplied almost a hundred times, and the federal bureaucracy increased by a factor of 600,000. Not surprisingly, Congress changed drastically, too.

Congress first met in New York in 1789, and then in Philadelphia, moving to its current location, the Capitol building in Washington, in 1800. Early Congresses ordinarily met from the harvest season until spring planting, passing fewer than a hundred bills every two-year session. Today, Congress meets virtually year-round, with occasional "recesses" at holiday times. The Senate gained two new members whenever a new state joined the Union, reaching its current 100 when Alaska and Hawaii were admitted in 1959. The size of the House grew with population until 1913, when a new law limited it permanently to 435 to prevent it from becoming unwieldy. Eventually, nonvoting members from the District of Columbia, American Samoa, Guam, Puerto Rico, and the Virgin Islands brought the total to 440.

"The Old House of Representatives," an 1822 painting by Samuel F. B. Morse.

The Powers Granted to Congress

Article I, section 8, grants Congress the power "To lay and collect Taxes [and] Duties [on imported goods], . . . to borrow Money, . . . to regulate Commerce with foreign nations, and among the several States," as well as to establish rules by which foreigners may become American citizens. It also grants Congress the power to write bankruptcy laws, coin money and regulate its value, provide for punishment of counterfeiting, establish post offices, enact patent and copyright laws to protect the property rights of inventors and authors, and create lower federal courts under the Supreme Court. In foreign affairs, Congress is granted the power to declare war and to provide for armed forces. Finally, Congress is granted the power to govern the federal city, which we call the District of Columbia, or Washington, D.C.

Two centuries of experience have shown that among the most important of these enumerated powers are the powers to tax, to regulate commerce, and to ratify treaties—the latter granted to the Senate alone in Article II. Article II also gives the House the power to impeach (that is, accuse or indict) and the Senate the power to try and, if convicted, remove from office officials guilty of "Treason, Bribery, or other high Crimes and Misdemeanors." Article IV gives both houses the power to admit new states to the Union. And Article V grants the power to propose constitutional amendments to the states by a two-thirds vote of both houses—a power Congress has used to increase its other powers, especially furnishing a new president between elections if necessary (the Twentieth Amendment) and levying an income tax (the Sixteenth).

The most important power granted to Congress is the power "to make all Laws which shall be necessary and proper for carrying into Execution the foregoing Powers, and all other Powers vested by the Constitution in the Government of the United States, or in any Department or Officer thereof." This last clause of Article I, section 8, is called the **necessary and proper clause**, but it is also known as the **elastic clause** because Congress has used and stretched it so much.

The Six Key Functions of Congress

Congress makes policy with the president when passing new laws, such as the Clean Air Act Amendments, and when passing the national government budget each year, because the budget determines what government can and cannot do. All bills for raising revenue are supposed to originate in the House. Occasionally, Congress attempts to make policy on its own by passing a resolution declaring its views on a particular subject—but because such views are not cast as formal legislation, they are not binding on the rest of the government or the people. The Senate has two exclusive functions: giving its "Advice and Consent" to treaties (by a two-thirds vote) and to key appointments to the executive and judicial branches. Impeachment is another function enumerated in the Constitution. Finally, oversight of the other two branches by means of investigations and hearings is not specified but has been added, in practice, as a function.

Congress thus has six key functions:

- legislating
- budgeting
- ratifying treaties
- confirming appointments
- impeaching and removing officials from office
- overseeing the conduct of the executive and judicial branches.

The Senate Select Watergate Committee, chaired by Sam Ervin (D-S.C.) (*center*), meets in 1974 to perform the least frequent of Congress's six functions—considering whether to impeach the president, Richard M. Nixon.

To accomplish this work, Congress must first achieve agreement among enough of its 535 elected members and the thousands of assistants, each with his or her own views of *what is, what's right,* and *what works,* and then prevail in power struggles with the other branches of government. It can be done, as we saw in the case of the Clean Air Act Amendments. But it is rarely easy. So to understand the role of Congress in American governance we must examine Congress not only as a legislature consisting of two houses but also as a body organized by two major parties, each with its leaders, and as an assemblage of hundreds of individuals, each with his—and increasingly her—own career objectives and agendas.

The Functions of Parties in Congress

Although not mentioned in the Constitution, parties arose soon after the new government was instituted (Chapter 7) and immediately became influential in Congress, where they have three important functions: creating rules that help shape the way each house operates, furnishing legislative leaders, and organizing elections, a function described in Chapter 10.

Creating the Rules

Each chamber sets its own operating rules. Relying largely on precedent, Thomas Jefferson compiled the Senate's first parliamentary manual to provide "order, decency, and regularity" in its operation, and the House did the same. Each rule book was shaped by the distinctive qualities of the body, as we'll soon see, as well as by the common requirement that majority and minority rights be protected and that power be distributed among members, committees, and the leadership. Each body readopts its rules by a vote at the beginning of each session and can change its rules whenever it sees fit, but because predictability is very appealing, important changes are infrequent. Normally, each member votes with his or her party colleagues on rule changes, but occasionally an issue is so controversial that some members cross party lines. For example, an effort in 1995 to modify the Senate **cloture** rule, which currently requires agreement by 60 percent of those senators present and voting to limit debate and move toward a vote, failed because a majority of Democrats joined all Republicans to defeat a proposal to lower the requirement.

Each party in each chamber also develops its own party rules to specify how it selects its leaders, assigns members to committees, and conducts its other business. These rules, too, tend to persist from one session to the next, but when new leadership wants greater power, for example, it may seek changes. The many liberal Democrats elected to the Senate in the 1970s wrested some power from southern conservatives who chaired most committees by modifying the principle of **seniority**, by which the majority party member who had served longest on a committee was automatically elected chair of that committee by all party members.

Providing Legislative Leadership

While members of both chambers are elected as Democrats or Republicans (independents and third party members are rare), party affiliation determines voting only at the start of each two-year session when the leaders of each chamber are formally elected by the chamber's entire membership. In practice, each party first selects its candidates in a **party**

cloture
This term, French for the action of closing, was originally applied to the closing of debate in the French Assembly by the will of the majority.

seniority
This term comes from the Latin *senex*, meaning "old" or "elder"; it is also the root of the word *Senate*.

caucus—a private meeting of all its members. In the formal election in the whole House or Senate, all members of the party almost always vote for the winners of the caucus contests and the majority party candidates thus become House Speaker, Senate majority leader, as well as all committee chairs. The 1997 election was unusual in that a handful of Republican House members withheld their votes from Speaker Newt Gingrich (R-Ga.) because of ethics charges pending against him. Gingrich had been elected Speaker two years earlier after being chosen minority whip in 1989 over a senior colleague because he was an unusually partisan and effective leader.

Once leaders are chosen, party loyalty is usually weak in both chambers, but party leaders still play important roles off the floor. They represent the body as well as its majority or minority to the president, to the media, and through the media to the public. This role becomes especially important when the president belongs to the other party, because these leaders automatically become the leading national voices for their party.

Leadership in the House

The **Speaker of the House** decides which committee to refer a bill to, thereby often determining its fate. As presiding officer, the Speaker—or a chosen substitute—decides who will be allowed to speak during debate. The Speaker also appoints members of the powerful Rules Committee, which schedules important legislation for floor consideration and decides how much debate and amendment will be allowed. And as party leader in the House, the Speaker has considerable informal power to determine committee chair and membership decisions—a power that Gingrich has wielded more than any other Speaker in nearly a century.

Representative Dick Armey (R-Texas), House majority leader (*center*), confers with Speaker of the House Newt Gingrich (R-Ga.) (*right*) in a Republican leadership meeting.

"You know, you ask me what are my powers and my authority around here," ruminated Thomas P. "Tip" O'Neill, who served as Speaker from 1976 to 1986:

> The power to recognize on the floor; little odds and ends . . . like those trips to China, trips to Russia . . . ; or other ad hoc committees or special committees, which I have assignments to; plus the fact that there is a certain aura and respect that goes with the Speaker's office. He does have the power to be able to pick up the telephone and call people. And Members oftentimes like to bring their loyal political leaders or a couple of mayors. And oftentimes they have problems from their area and they need aid and assistance, either legislative-wise or administrative-wise. We're happy to try to open the door for them, having been in the town for so many years and knowing so many people. We do know where a lot of bodies are and we do know how to advise people. And I have an open-door policy.[4]

As important as these "little odds and ends" are, a Speaker's effectiveness depends even more on skill in political infighting. A senior Democratic representative described it this way after watching Sam Rayburn (D-Tex.), Speaker whenever the Democrats controlled the House from 1940 to 1961, considered by many the most effective Speaker in modern history: "To maintain personal influence the Speaker is forced to engage in a savage political scramble involving sectional interests, local claims and personal advancements. . . . All too often, wise and just legislation becomes a subordinate issue and frequently a total casualty."[5] The situation is little different today.

> **whip**
> The term originated in English fox hunting, where the *whipper-in* kept the hounds from straying as they pursued the fox, and from there it came to be used in the British Parliament for efforts to compel party loyalty on key votes.

The Speaker's chief lieutenant is the **majority leader**—the majority party's floor leader, elected by the party caucus, who helps plan the legislative agenda and serves as a go-between for the Speaker and party members. Party **whips** aid the majority leader, constantly assessing the prospects for pending bills by keeping tabs on voting inclinations and "whipping" members into line to vote "with the party" on important bills. Whips are appointed by the leadership.

The Speaker is a partisan leader in the House, but the Presidential Succession Act of 1947 also makes the Speaker second in line behind the vice president in the presidential succession, followed by the president pro tempore of the Senate (see below). Thus far, however, no Speaker has succeeded to the presidency. The closest that one has come was in the Nixon era, when Vice President Spiro Agnew was forced to resign in the face of corruption charges. But, following procedures outlined in the Twenty-fifth Amendment, Nixon replaced Agnew with Representative Gerald Ford well before Nixon himself resigned in the face of certain impeachment over the Watergate affair. Ford then became the only unelected vice president to succeed to the presidency.

Leadership in the Senate

The vice president of the United States officially presides as president of the Senate, but in fact only appears on ceremonial occasions and when his presence could make an important difference. If he is presiding—but only then—he can vote to break a tie as well as recognize speakers and refer bills to committee. In practice, the vice president rarely presides. Nor does the longest-serving member, who is officially **president pro tempore** (that is, president for the time). Normally, junior majority members take turns at the thankless job of presiding.

The majority leader is the real power in the Senate. Normally, he (no woman has yet been majority—or minority—leader) consults with the **minority leader**—the minority party's floor leader—about scheduling. However, rules allow the majority leader to speak ahead of anyone else and therefore to shape the course of debate by "yielding" (deferring) to a senator who has a key amendment. This debate-controlling role is especially important when partisanship increases and consultation with the minority party decreases, as happened when the Republicans took control of the Senate in 1995.

Behind the scenes, the leadership practices may be less than statesmanly. Lyndon Johnson (D-Tex.) moved to the Senate after learning leadership skills from Speaker Rayburn in the House and developed his own brand of leadership, often called "The Treatment." Historian and former LBJ aide Arthur Schlesinger summarized Johnson's own description of his technique as Senate majority leader:

> The Treatment began immediately: a brilliant, capsule characterization of every Democratic Senator, his strengths and failings, where he fit into the political spectrum; how far he could be pushed, how far pulled; his hates, his loves. And who must oversee all these prima donnas, put them to work, knit them together, know when to tickle this one's vanity, inquire of that one's health, remember this one's five o'clock nip of Scotch, that one's nagging wife? Who [but the majority leader] must find the hidden legislative path between the South and the North, the public power men and the private power men, the farmers' men and the unions' men, the bomber-boys and the peace-lovers, the eggheads and the fatheads?[6]

By contrast, Robert Byrd (D-W.V.) described his majority leadership role this way: "I don't have power but I have knowledge of the rules. I have knowledge of the precedents. I have knowledge of the schedule. So I'm in a position to do things for others."[7] Byrd emphasized the importance of cultivating those in the other party—referred to as those on "the other side of the aisle" because a large aisle separates the Democratic desks from the Republican desks. As Senate majority leader prior to resigning to conduct his presidential campaign, Bob Dole (R-Kans.) maintained cordial relations with Democrats. His successor, Trent Lott (R-Miss.), at first played a more assertive role, instead cooperating more closely with his former House colleague Gingrich in opposing Clinton initiatives and pressing a Republican agenda. However, in time his attention returned to Senate concerns.

As in the House, party leaders in the Senate are assisted by deputies and whips. Legislative priorities are set by each party's Policy Committee. Committee assignments are officially made by the Democratic party's Steering Committee and the Republican party's Committee on Committees. Each party also has campaign committees—as in the House—to raise funds and distribute them to members seeking reelection (see Chapter 7).

The Question of Party Unity

After the votes that organize the House and Senate at the beginning of each session, strong party unity is usually limited to highly partisan moments, such as the end of a congressional or presidential term, when parties maneuver for electoral advantage. The Senate tends to perform its special functions—ratifying treaties and confirming appointments—in a bipartisan manner, and the much rarer function of impeachment and trial is so important that it tends to be conducted quite nonpartisanly in both chambers.

Partisan voting is most prominent in times of divided government, when it tends to produce **gridlock**—a government "traffic jam" in which competing interests block all movement (see Chapter 7). Divided government occurred in only 8 of the 58 years from 1897 to 1954, but then in 26 of the next 38—always taking the form of Democratic control of one or both houses of Congress with a Republican in the White House. A trend toward more consistent party voting on legislation and the budget, shown in Figure 11.1, began to increase significantly when conservative Republican president Ronald Reagan set the agenda against opposition from liberal congressional Democrats. The trend

Figure 11.1
Rising partisanship

This graph shows the percentages of representatives and senators who voted with their party on party unity votes—those in which a majority of one party votes one way and a majority of the other party votes the opposite way. The rising percentage of party unity votes indicates that congressional parties are more frequently at odds with each other.

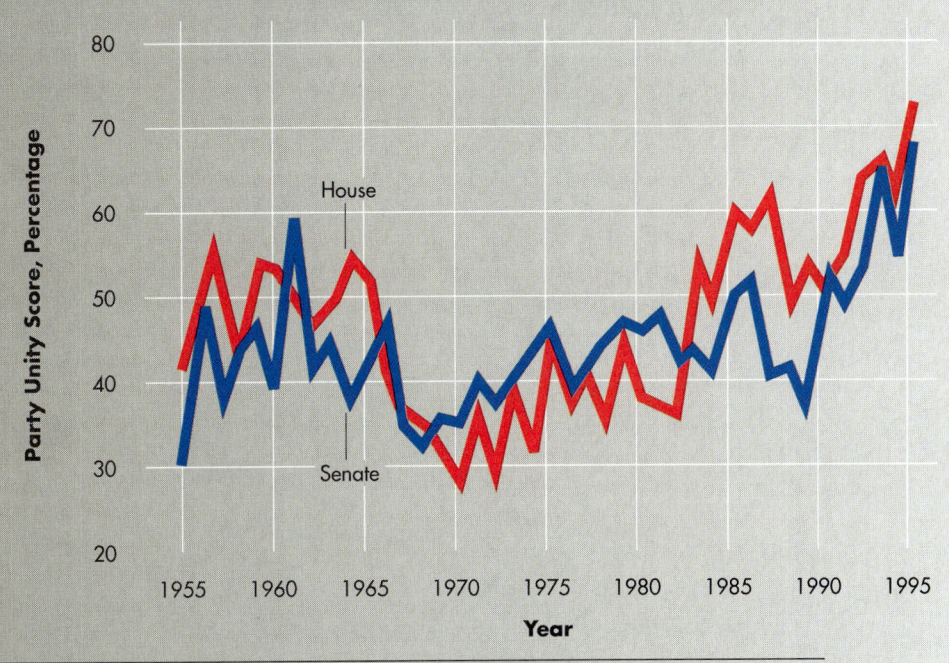

Sources: Norman J. Ornstein, Thomas E. Mann, and Michael J. Malbin (eds.), *Vital Statistics on Congress, 1993–1994* (Washington D.C.: Congressional Quarterly Press, 1994) 208; Dan Carney, "As Hostilities Rage on the Hill, Partisan-Vote Rate Soars," *Congressional Quarterly Weekly Report*, 27 January 1996, 199.

toward more partisan voting—and partisan exercise of oversight investigations of the executive branch—increased as the 1994 midterm elections approached, when House Republicans voted with conservative Democrats to oppose President Bill Clinton's initiatives, and Senate Republicans, aided by conservative Democrats, suddenly unified to oppose virtually every Clinton program in hopes of gaining more seats. (This cross-party alliance of conservatives is nothing new; from Franklin Roosevelt's day on, the so-called conservative coalition of Republicans and southern Democrats tried to block progressive legislation.) The tactics worked extraordinarily well—so well, in fact, that Democrats, newly the minority party, used them effectively against the Republican Senate leadership as the 1996 elections approached, forcing Republicans to give way on key Clinton issues such as immigration and welfare reform to avoid appearing ineffective.[8] Figure 11.2 depicts the strength of each party in each chamber and control of the presidency for every two-year congressional session since 1933.

Figure 11.2

Party strength in Congress and control of the White House

In the years shown in blue, both houses of Congress were controlled by the party in opposition to the president. Independents are not shown. Figures are for the start of each session.

President	Congress	Senate (Dem / Rep)	House of Representatives (Dem / Rep)
Roosevelt	1933, 73d	60 / 35	310 / 117
Roosevelt	1935, 74th	69 / 25	319 / 103
Roosevelt	1937, 75th	78 / 16	331 / 89
Roosevelt	1939, 76th	69 / 23	261 / 164
Roosevelt	1941, 77th	66 / 28	268 / 162
Roosevelt	1943, 78th	58 / 37	218 / 208
Truman	1945, 79th	56 / 38	242 / 190
Truman	*1947, 80th*	45 / 51	188 / 246
Truman	1949, 81st	54 / 42	262 / 171
Truman	1951, 82d	49 / 47	234 / 199
Eisenhower	1953, 83d	47 / 48	213 / 221
Eisenhower	*1955, 84th*	49 / 47	232 / 203
Eisenhower	*1957, 85th*	49 / 47	233 / 200
Eisenhower	*1959, 86th*	64 / 34	283 / 153
Kennedy-Johnson	1961, 87th	65 / 35	262 / 175
Kennedy-Johnson	1963, 88th	66 / 34	258 / 176
Johnson	1965, 89th	68 / 32	295 / 140
Johnson	1967, 90th	64 / 38	248 / 187
Nixon	*1969, 91st*	58 / 42	243 / 192
Nixon	*1971, 92d*	54 / 44	255 / 180
Nixon-Ford	*1973, 93d*	57 / 43	243 / 192
Ford	*1975, 94th*	61 / 38	290 / 145
Carter	1977, 95th	61 / 38	293 / 142
Carter	1979, 96th	58 / 41	276 / 159
Reagan	1981, 97th	53 / 46	242 / 191
Reagan	1983, 98th	55 / 45	269 / 166
Reagan	1985, 99th	53 / 47	253 / 182
Reagan	1987, 100th	55 / 45	259 / 176
Bush	1989, 101st	55 / 45	260 / 175
Bush	1991, 102d	56 / 44	267 / 167
Clinton	1993, 103d	56 / 44	256 / 178
Clinton	*1995, 104th*	54 / 46	231 / 203
Clinton	*1997, 105th*	55 / 45	227 / 207

Democrats / Republicans

The Roles of Members of Congress

> **representation**
> This term comes from *re-* ("again") and *present* ("offer"), so a representative is someone who offers or presents again the views of someone to another.

Congress can carry out its six functions well only if most members adopt them as goals. Whether they do or not depends on which of the various possible roles they adopt or emphasize—representative advocate, responsible deliberator, ambitious politician, effective colleague, loyal party member, policy advocate, service provider, or profiteer.

The Representative Advocate Versus the Responsible Deliberator

Should members of Congress accept their constituents' views of *what is, what's right,* and *what works,* or should they rely on their own judgment? Most people want their member of Congress to represent them by presenting their views in debates. This, after all, is the root meaning of the term *representation.* But a House member who wants to be representative must decide whom or what to represent. Should it be the views of all of the roughly 600,000 people in a typical district, whether or not they voted for him or her—or voted at all? Only about half vote in presidential election years and less than a third in off-year elections, after all, and about half of those who do, vote for the loser. Should the member represent the views of the apathetic and the adversary? Should one somehow represent constituents' extensive ignorance on most congressional issues?

No member can be typical of the district population in gender, since the population is equally male and female. Furthermore, the overall composition of Congress is not very similar to the American population in any other way. Both houses are still composed largely of older white male lawyers and businesspeople, as Table 11.1 portrays quite clearly, although this is less true today than it used to be. How important are gender, ethnicity, education, and profession, in which members are so different from their constituents? As we saw in Chapter 5, it's hard to correlate such personal attributes with political views on most issues. So perhaps this dissimilarity of members and their constituents is not so important for representativeness. Some districts are remarkably homogeneous in terms of income or ethnicity—and therefore quite different from other districts. For example, residents of Maryland's Washington suburban district have about ten times the average family

Senator Nancy Kassebaum (R-Kan.) (*left*) and Representative Patricia Schroeder (D-Colo.) discuss their impending retirement in 1996 in the Women's Caucus Reading Room in the Capitol. On the wall behind them are photographs of all the women then serving in the House of Representatives.

TABLE 11.1

The Composition of Each House of Congress, 1997

	House	Senate
Total membership	435	100
Party affiliation		
Republican	227	55
Democrat	207	45
Independent	1	0
Women	51	9
Ethnicity		
African American	37	1
Latino	18	0
Asian American	3	2
Native American	0	1
Religious affiliation (largest ones)		
Roman Catholic	127	24
Baptist	58	9
Methodist	46	13
Presbyterian	43	10
Episcopalian	31	11
Jewish	25	10
With law degree	172	53
Average age	52	58

Source: Congressional Quarterly Weekly Report, January 4, 1997.

income of residents of the Bronx district in New York City. But most House districts are diverse in themselves. The typical senator has an even greater problem representing some 5 million people.

A member who advocates constituents' views rather than his or her own views is acting as a **delegate** or agent of the voters. House members—but not senators—commonly hold this view of their role, often voting as they believe their constituents would wish. However, studies find that these beliefs about constituents' views, which representatives get from opinion polls, faxes, phone calls, and letters, as well as face-to-face meetings with constituents, are often inaccurate and vague.[9]

In any case, most members are also expected to represent the views of businesses and other interest groups in the district or state—views that sometimes conflict with those of most individuals. In the case of the Clean Air Act Amendments, for example, John Dingell was the representative for the auto manufacturers with factories in his district and the auto workers who lived and worked there, as well as for those residents forced to breathe noxious auto emissions, and he had to choose which views to emphasize. Henry Waxman, by contrast, represented a district with no auto factories, in which everyone suffered from daily smog, so his choice was easy.

One representative expressed the rationale for the delegate role concept quite clearly: "I'm here to represent my district. . . . This is part of my actual belief as to the function of a congressman. . . . What is good for the majority of districts is good for the country. What snarls up the system is these so-called statesmen-congressmen who vote for what they think is the country's interest. . . . Let the senators do that. . . . They're paid to be statesmen; we aren't."[10]

Some reject the delegate role because it is virtually impossible to carry out accurately. Others reject it because they believe it the duty of a representative to vote for what's best for the district, the state, or the nation, regardless of public opinion or special interests. Such a role, commonly called **trustee**, was endorsed by the British politician Edmund Burke, who argued in 1774 that a lawmaker should listen to and respect the opinions of his constituents but owes it to them to rely on his own judgment. "His unbiased opinion, his mature judgment, his enlightened conscience, he ought not to sacrifice to you, to any man, or to any set of men living," Burke told his constituents. "Your representative owes you, not his industry only, but his judgment, and he betrays, instead of serving you, if he sacrifices it to your opinion."[11] Studies have found that in most legislative bodies a majority of representatives view their role as being a responsible deliberator, or trustee.[12]

Edmund Burke (1729–1797) addresses Britain's Parliament.

The Ambitious Politician

Whatever they may say to constituents or interviewers, scholars generally find that many representatives actually behave instead as politicos.[13] The **politico** is concerned primarily with his or her own career, focusing on reelection or other personal advancement and varying his or her views and votes depending on the electoral circumstances and likely financial benefits such as campaign contributions. Today, most campaign contributions come not from constituents but from special interests located outside the member's district. The politico must be sensitive to the wishes of such large contributors while avoiding taking positions unpopular among constituents that could jeopardize his or her prospects for being a career politician.

Until the twentieth century, few members made Congress a career. Indeed, at the turn of the century, 44 percent of House members were serving their first term and the average senator was in his second. By the 1980s, turnover was rather rare in both chambers, but in the 1990s, turnover again increased, and after the 1994 elections, only 65 percent of Democrats and 45 percent of Republicans had served more than four years in the House. One-fourth of the Senate, moreover, had served less than three years (Chapter 10).

In earlier decades, new members advanced through an **apprenticeship system** by attaching themselves to more senior members who guided their slow progress into subcommittee chair and then committee chair positions, where they would serve for decades if their party retained control of the House or Senate. In the 1970s discontented younger Democrats forced reforms that made committee chairs face election by their party colleagues and so enabled less senior members to advance more rapidly. In recent years, many senior members of both chambers have chosen to leave, disenchanted with what the job has become. As he retired early, Senator Tim Wirth (D-Colo.), who had first served in the House, made a typical complaint: "All the time it took to raise funds was time not spent talking with constituents, not tending to legislative business and not actually campaigning. . . . Unhappily, the first loyalty of any candidate is too often to self and re-election, rather than to any broad political organization or community of like-minded activists."[14] Those who retire or lose an election often become Washington lobbyists—earning much more money because they know many of the players, understand the legislative process, and as ex-members have the right to lobby their former colleagues on the floor of the body they previously served in.

The Effective Colleague Versus the Loyal Party Member

Traditionally, the best way to be effective, unless one was chair of a powerful committee, was to be a loyal party member. Informal "rules of the legislative game" called on members—especially new members—to defer to their party's leadership when it asked for their votes unless the interests of their constituents were seriously at stake. Newer members were also expected to be quiet, and all were expected to be civil to each other, even across party lines. "Should the new legislator wish to be heard," George Washington wrote in 1787, "the way to command the attention of the House is to speak seldom, but to important subjects."[15] Almost 200 years later, newly elected Senator Joseph Clark (D-Pa.) asked Senator Hubert Humphrey (D-Minn.) how to behave. "In essence he said, 'Keep your mouth shut and your eyes open. It's a friendly, courteous place. You will have no trouble getting along. . . . Don't let your ideology embitter your personal relationships. It won't if you behave with maturity. . . . And above all keep your mouth shut for awhile.'"[16] These traditional rules are perhaps best summarized in the axiom of the legendary Sam Rayburn: "If you want to get along, go along." However, as we shall see, such restraint and civility have recently declined considerably.

Party leaders today can still sometimes make successful claims to authority—the essence of politics—with members. Members of the president's party may sometimes be persuaded to support an imperiled presidential initiative, and opposition members may be prevailed upon to oppose presidential proposals regardless of their merits.

Another traditional way to be effective was to specialize in one particular policy area, thereby earning deference from other members on those issues. But liberals elected in the 1970s and conservatives elected in the 1980s and 1990s have generally refused to be limited by specialization, just as they refused to defer automatically to party leadership.

The Policy Advocate

Some members come to Congress primarily to advance their particular policy interests, while others with stronger personal ambitions seek to be effective policy advocates to establish a legislative record to use as a claim to authority in seeking higher office. Whatever the motivation, effective policy advocacy requires first getting one's policy proposal on the public agenda—usually through adroit exploitation of the media, which is increasingly difficult because so many assertive members are competing for media attention. But once on the agenda, a proposal must be passed by both houses of Congress, and passage usually requires building a temporary coalition across party and regional lines through good collegial relations, as John Dingell did with the Clean Air Act Amendments.

The Service Provider: Pork, Casework, and Assistance to Special Interests

All members of Congress provide services to their state or district, to constituents, and to local and distant special interests. Even those who constantly call for cutting government spending claim credit for "bringing home the bacon" by getting public works projects such as highways, federal government office buildings, federal grants to local governments, schools, and research organizations, and government contracts to businesses for goods or services. Collectively, these projects are known as **pork-barrel** items, or "**pork**" for short.

Constituents who ask a member for help in dealing with the federal bureaucracy—or even just for a free pamphlet on baby care—get special attention from the member's staff because a response can earn a vote next election. The staff worker sends requests to the relevant government bureaucrats, who respond because bureaucrats want to please those who

"pork"

This term, short for *pork barrel*, comes from the practice, common before the days of refrigeration and chemical preservatives, of preserving meat or fish in a barrel of pork fat. When times were bad, or in winter, one went "to the pork barrel" for food. That's approximately what members of Congress do, too—going to the federal treasury for funds for local projects.

casework

This term is applicable because the activities involve working on the "case" of an individual by contacting bureaucrats or others who can help the constituent.

Steamtown, a museum of steam railroading equipment established in abandoned railyards in Scranton, Pa., is widely considered an example of "pork" because it was created and maintained with federal funds, during a time of very tight budgets, in the home district of Joseph McDade of Pennsylvania, who is the most senior Republican in the House and sits on the Appropriations Committee.

control their budgets. Studies find that about a quarter of a member's time and half to two-thirds of his or her staff's time is spent on such **casework**—as it is called—primarily involving Social Security and veterans' benefits.[17]

Members also serve the needs of special interests, usually businesses or groups, but occasionally wealthy or powerful individuals, in or out of the district, by intervening with the bureaucracy or "carrying" (sponsoring) a particular piece of legislation—often one the interest group has drafted—in hopes of campaign contributions.

The Profiteer

Many people believe that members are motivated less by the welfare of their constituents and the country than by a hunger for personal gain. In fact, however, few legislators feel their lives are privileged financially or materially, and fewer get rich while serving in Congress. Members do receive a number of special privileges—called perquisites of office, or "**perks**"—and salaries ($133,600 a year) that are much greater than a typical American worker's income but smaller than those of many corporate executives. To avoid calling attention to salaries and having to vote for raises, Congress passed a law in 1990 providing for automatic annual cost-of-living salary increases unless it votes to reject them. However, the widespread unpopularity of Congress has forced members to vote to reject raises every year since 1992. With their income most must maintain two homes—one in their district and one in the very expensive Washington area. What makes senators' and representatives' lives more comfortable are the various personal perks they receive, among them use of the Senate and House gyms for only $400 a year and medical insurance and treatment for only $520 a year, subsidized meals in the Senate and House dining rooms, free parking in Washington and at its airports, and free car washes, plants, and flowers. They also receive very generous pensions. When the value of these perks is added to the member's salary, the average

conflict of interest

This term refers to a situation in which someone acts in his or her role as a public official in a way that benefits that person as a private individual. In other words, one's own personal interest is in conflict with the public interest.

TABLE 11.2

The Typical Representative's Average Day

Activity	Average Amount of Time Spent on Activity
In the House chamber (2 hours, 53 minutes)	
In committee/subcommittee work (1 hour, 24 minutes)	
Hearings	26 minutes
Business	9 minutes
Markups	42 minutes
Other	7 minutes
In his/her office (3 hours, 19 minutes)	
With constituents	17 minutes
With organized groups	9 minutes
With others	20 minutes
With staff aides	53 minutes
With other representatives	5 minutes
Answering mail	46 minutes
Preparing legislation, speeches	12 minutes
Reading	11 minutes
On telephone	26 minutes
In other Washington locations (2 hours, 2 minutes)	
With constituents at Capitol	9 minutes
At events	33 minutes
With leadership	3 minutes
With other representatives	11 minutes
With informal groups	8 minutes
In party meetings	5 minutes
Personal time	28 minutes
Other	25 minutes
Other (1 hour, 40 minutes)	
Total (11 hours, 18 minutes)	

Source: U.S. House of Representatives, Commission on Administrative Review, *Administrative Reorganization and Legislative Management*, 95th Cong., 1st sess., 1977. H. Doc. 95–232, 18–19.

total comes to $175,746, bringing the total cost of maintaining each member, including expenses for staff and office costs, to $903,694 per representative and $1,125,066 to $2,685,000 per senator.[18] Many of these perks benefit reelection campaigns, such as free long-distance telephone lines in their homes, free postage (called the *franking privilege*) for mailings to constituents, plus calendars and photos to give to constituents.

Hearing of the pay and perks members receive and the large pensions most receive, many conclude that members are mere profiteers—a belief reinforced by scandals such as the Keating Five case (Chapter 8) and the House Bank scandal (Chapter 9). The Bush administration sought to make political capital against the Democratic-controlled Congress with an attack on congressional perks at the time of the House Bank uproar—until members of Congress retaliated by describing the even bigger perks of the president and his assistants (Chapter 12). Such attacks help explain the low repute in which many now hold Congress.

A more serious charge leveled against some members is **conflict of interest**. While judges and executive branch officials usually remove themselves from decisions involving, say, a company they own stock in if their decision could benefit themselves, members of Congress rarely refrain from voting on legislation in which they have a personal financial interest. Nor have they been known to sell or relinquish control over their stocks and other such investments before taking office in order to prevent such situations from arising and to eliminate even the appearance of possible conflicts of interest. On most issues that come before them, however, most members of Congress have no personal material interest.[19]

The Persistent Questions for Members: *What's Right?* and *What Works?*

Members of Congress often find it difficult to balance the requirements of these varied and often conflicting roles: representing their constituents (as a delegate, trustee, or politico), managing their careers, acting as a loyal party member and as a colleague, serving their constituents, and in some cases advancing their own personal fortunes. The more time and energy spent on one role, the less remains for the others. As Table 11.2 indicates, in a typical day the average House member spends almost three hours in the House chamber, an hour and a half in committees, just over three hours in the office, and two hours at various other Washington locations. Thus members must decide what the right thing to do is on issue after issue, bearing in mind the questions of *what will work*, not only for the country but also for their political future—but with little time and energy for the kind of deliberative thinking that the Framers expected of members. To get a better sense of the constraints and possibilities they face, we must examine how Congress actually works, both internally and externally in its relations with the rest of government and other actors.

The Internal Politics of Congress

Congress is really two legislatures—the House and the Senate—each acting somewhat independently through its own unique system of committees and rules on issues that concern its members. But because a bill must be passed by both chambers to become law, the two chambers must also act as one legislature to create and approve compromises. Figure 11.3 offers a concise map of the stages a bill must go through to become a law—stages we saw occurring in the case of the Clean Air Act Amendments and will now analyze by examining the politics of this legislative process.

Congress as Two Legislatures: House and Senate Committee Action

Most of each chamber's work is done in its committees and subcommittees, which are sometimes called "little legislatures" or "the workshops of Congress." Table 11.3 summarizes the workload of each chamber of Congress in a recent two-year session. Committees and subcommittees conduct hearings on public questions and on proposed legislation, at which bureaucrats, experts, and citizens testify. They also "**mark up**"—that is, examine section by section and amend—proposed legislation and then vote on whether to recommend its passage.

Every bill introduced by a member of Congress is referred to a committee for consideration, or screening, but only 10 to 30 percent ever get "reported out" of committee for possible consideration on the floor.

The Evolution of the Committee Systems

In the early years of the republic, when the demands on government were limited and membership was small, each house debated subjects on the floor and then set up special, or ad hoc, committees to draft

ad hoc and standing committees
Special, or *ad hoc* (Latin for "to this" or "for this" particular function), committees, which are temporary and have designated goals, are distinguished from standing committees, which are ongoing, or *stand*, from one session to the next.

Chapter 11 Congress

Figure 11.3
How a bill becomes law

These are the basic steps of the most typical route.

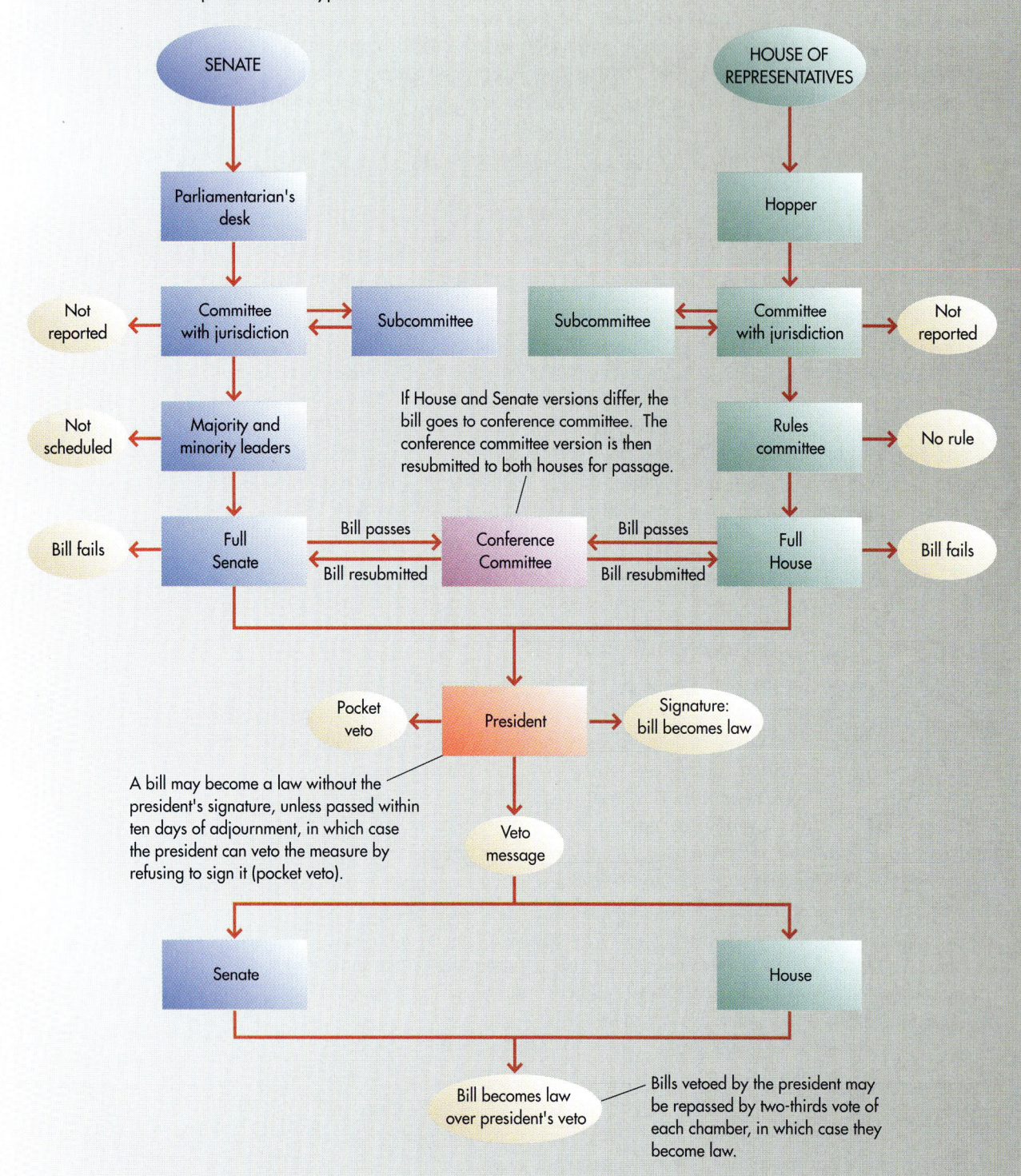

SENATE → Parliamentarian's desk → Committee with jurisdiction ↔ Subcommittee
- Not reported
- Committee with jurisdiction → Majority and minority leaders
  - Not scheduled
- Majority and minority leaders → Full Senate
  - Bill fails
- Full Senate → Conference Committee (Bill passes / Bill resubmitted)

HOUSE OF REPRESENTATIVES → Hopper → Committee with jurisdiction ↔ Subcommittee
- Not reported
- Committee with jurisdiction → Rules committee
  - No rule
- Rules committee → Full House
  - Bill fails
- Full House → Conference Committee (Bill passes / Bill resubmitted)

If House and Senate versions differ, the bill goes to conference committee. The conference committee version is then resubmitted to both houses for passage.

Full Senate / Full House → **President**
- Pocket veto
- Signature: bill becomes law
- Veto message

A bill may become a law without the president's signature, unless passed within ten days of adjournment, in which case the president can veto the measure by refusing to sign it (pocket veto).

Veto message → Senate and House → Bill becomes law over president's veto

Bills vetoed by the president may be repassed by two-thirds vote of each chamber, in which case they become law.

Source: Richard Pious, *American Politics and Government* (New York: McGraw-Hill. 1986), 390.

TABLE 11.3

Congressional Workload, 104th Congress, January 1995 to October 1996

	Senate	House
Days in session	343	122
Time in session	2,875	2,524
Measures introduced and referred to committee	2,661	5,329
Measures reported out of committee for action	509	771
Measures passed*	822	1,022
Bills vetoed**	1	15
Vetoes overridden	0	1

*For the most part, the same measures are included in House and Senate totals.
**Indicates in which chamber the vetoed bill originated.
Source: *Congressional Record, Daily Digest,* January 7, 1996; updated electronically.

legislation for consideration by the full body. But within 25 years, both houses had established regular standing committees, each to deal with issues in a particular policy area. Members of standing committees developed subject expertise so other members could depend on committee judgment.

Gradually, committee chairmen (no women then served) became very powerful because seniority, rather than competence or loyalty to party leadership or the president, determined who headed committees. The seniority system, whereby the majority party member who had served the longest on a committee was automatically elected chair, benefited members with *safe seats*—in the modern era, conservative southern Democrats and conservative midwestern Republicans who never faced serious electoral opposition. In the 1960s and 1970s, scores of younger and more liberal newcomers from northern and western cities and suburbs forced through reforms in party rules that required the election, by all party members, of committee and subcommittee heads and *ranking* minority party members (those who would become chair if their party controlled the chamber). Newer members representing closely contested districts or states and worried about their reelection prospects sought positions on committees and subcommittees dealing with subjects relevant to their constituents, so the number of committees and subcommittees grew and members got appointments to four to six committees and subcommittees instead of one or two. The result was narrower specialization and the kind of bargaining among factions on and between committees that we saw with the Clean Air Act Amendments.

In the 1980s, two developments decreased committee workload: severe budget pressures, brought on by high deficits, that limited how much legislation was given serious consideration; and divided government's tendency toward stalemate and less legislating. Still, member committee and subcommittee assignments continued to increase, with House members averaging 6 and senators 11 appointments.[20] When the Republicans gained control of both chambers in 1995, they had little success at cutting the number of committees, managing only to convert three minor House committees into subcommittees of other standing committees and to reduce the number of subcommittees from 118 to 86.

Committee Structures and Assignments

Committee assignments are made by the Democratic party's Steering and Policy Committee and the Republican Committee on Committees, with strong input from the party leader. Members seek assignments to the committees with the most power or prestige, especially the money committees. Each chamber has a Budget Committee, which adopts general budgetary guidelines early in the year. Each chamber's Appropriations Committee then recommends final spending levels for all federal programs, making them even more important. The Framers provided that all revenue-raising bills originate in the House because only it was directly elected by the people who would be paying the taxes, so the House Ways and Means Committee is even more important than the Senate Finance Committee. The House Rules Committee, which decides which bills reported out of other committees will be debated on the floor and what kind of debate will be allowed, has no counterpart in the Senate, where the leadership schedules floor deliberations and debate is effectively unlimited. (The Senate Rules and Administration Committee has no role as floor debate gatekeeper, instead controlling internal operations and handling legislation on campaign finance and election laws.)

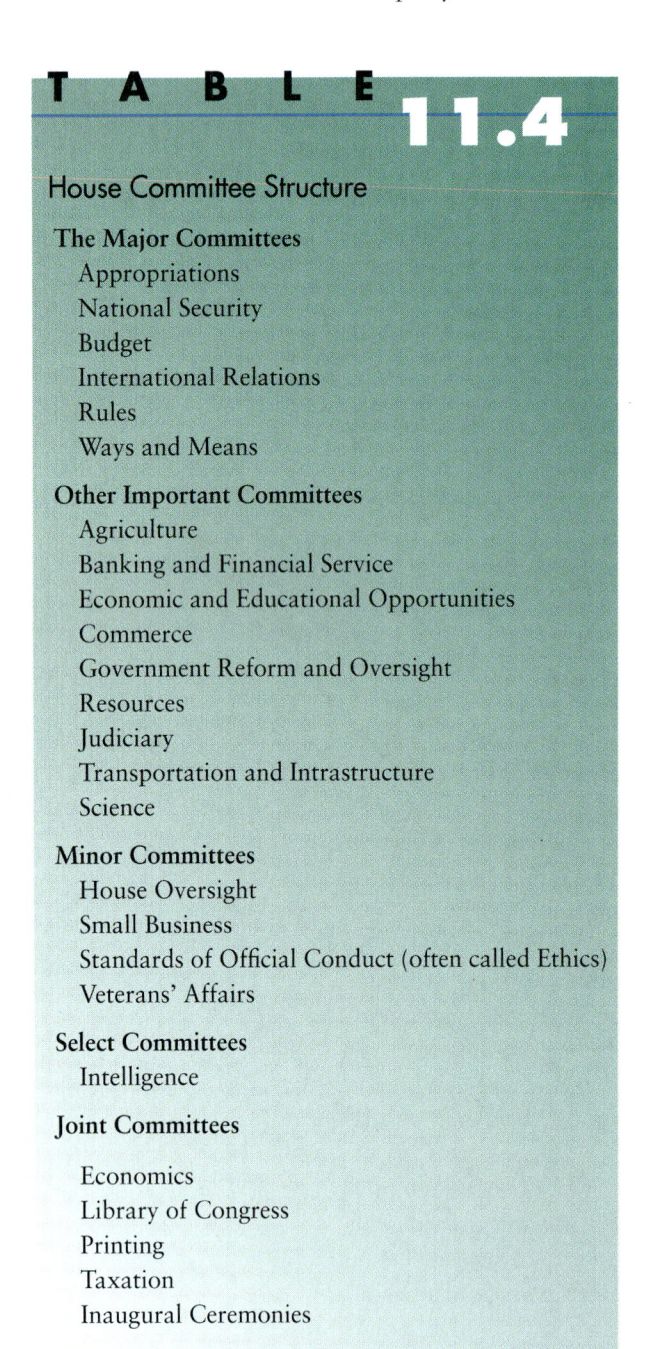

Each chamber has many *substantive* or *policy* committees that make policy and spending recommendations in areas such as banking and agriculture. The Senate Armed Services Committee and the House National Security Committee (until 1995 called the Armed Services Committee) have long been attractive because national defense is important and military spending is geographically dispersed. The Senate Foreign Relations Committee is more important than its House counterpart, International Relations (formerly Foreign Affairs), because the Senate approves treaties and ambassadorial appointments. The House Commerce Committee (formerly Energy and Commerce) and the Senate Environment and Public Works Committee, both of which dealt with the Clean Air Act Amendments, are among the more important but less prestigious committees.[21]

Each chamber also has some *select* committees—usually temporary committees created to undertake a major investigation such as Watergate or the Iran-

TABLE 11.4

House Committee Structure

The Major Committees
- Appropriations
- National Security
- Budget
- International Relations
- Rules
- Ways and Means

Other Important Committees
- Agriculture
- Banking and Financial Service
- Economic and Educational Opportunities
- Commerce
- Government Reform and Oversight
- Resources
- Judiciary
- Transportation and Infrastructure
- Science

Minor Committees
- House Oversight
- Small Business
- Standards of Official Conduct (often called Ethics)
- Veterans' Affairs

Select Committees
- Intelligence

Joint Committees
- Economics
- Library of Congress
- Printing
- Taxation
- Inaugural Ceremonies

Contra affair or to deal with a current issue outside existing committees' jurisdictions. There are also several *joint* committees with an equal number of members from each chamber, established to avoid unnecessary duplication of effort on less controversial matters such as printing government documents and the Library of Congress. The current committee structures of the House and Senate are depicted in Tables 11.4 and 11.5.

House members rarely get the committee assignments that enable them to get benefits for their district, such as Commerce for an oil-producing district representative or Agriculture for someone from a farm state, because the competition is so great. Because there are fewer senators, most serve on one of the top five committees: Appropriations, Budget, Finance, Armed Services, and Foreign Relations. However, a senator with national ambitions may want a committee with high visibility but little relevance to the senator's state, such as Foreign Relations.

The Committee-Subcommittee Process

When the content of bills was simpler, the leadership (the Speaker in the House and the majority leader in the Senate) referred a bill to the committee having jurisdiction over the subject unless it feared that that committee would "pigeonhole" or "bottle up" a bill it badly wanted passed, as southern committee chairs routinely did with civil rights legislation into the 1960s. The trend today is toward more comprehensive bills—called **omnibus bills**, or **megabills**—which deal with many facets of general problems such as trade, crime, health care, energy, and environmental protection. Omnibus bills have become popular as the workload has increased. Their special appeal was once explained by Leon Panetta (D-Calif.), then chair of the House Budget Committee:

> You can use large bills as a way to hide legislation that otherwise might be more controversial, as a way to be able to slam-dunk issues that otherwise might be torn apart, as a way to avoid hard votes that Members would have to account for at election time, as a way to avoid angering special-interest groups that use votes to decide contributions to campaigns and as a way to guarantee that the President will have to accept it.[22]

Instead of the standard **single referral**, omnibus bills often get **multiple referral**, being sent to two or more committees with relevant interests and expertise—up to 15 in a few cases—for consideration at the same time. Less common, but used occasionally, are

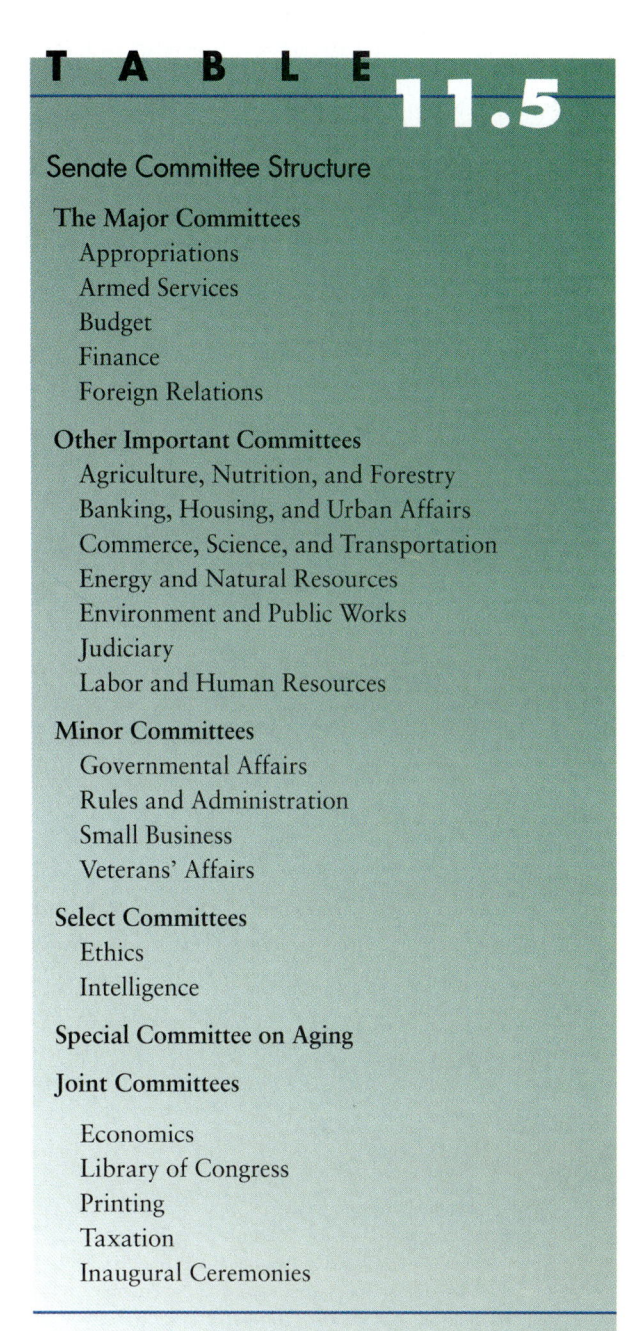

TABLE 11.5

Senate Committee Structure

The Major Committees
  Appropriations
  Armed Services
  Budget
  Finance
  Foreign Relations

Other Important Committees
  Agriculture, Nutrition, and Forestry
  Banking, Housing, and Urban Affairs
  Commerce, Science, and Transportation
  Energy and Natural Resources
  Environment and Public Works
  Judiciary
  Labor and Human Resources

Minor Committees
  Governmental Affairs
  Rules and Administration
  Small Business
  Veterans' Affairs

Select Committees
  Ethics
  Intelligence

Special Committee on Aging

Joint Committees
  Economics
  Library of Congress
  Printing
  Taxation
  Inaugural Ceremonies

A House committee holds hearings on the 1993 siege by federal law-enforcement agencies against the Branch Davidian cult's compound in Waco, Texas.

sequential referral, in which first one committee and then another considers a particular bill, and *split referral*, in which different parts of a bill are sent to different committees at the same time. In the House, if the committees do not act by a Speaker-set deadline, the bill is considered automatically discharged and eligible for floor consideration. This power of time-limited referral rarely needs to be used because its threat is always present.[23] The Senate relies on multiple referral for about 10 percent of its workload, the House for about one-quarter.[24] Multiple referral appeals to members wishing an early say on many bills but severely complicates the legislative process.

Until recent decades, committees were the scene of the real legislative action in both chambers, and most members deferred to committee judgment on most bills that made it to the floor. In the Senate, committees remain the major vehicles for legislative decision making in most instances. Some Senate committees—Budget, Rules and Administration, and Veterans' Affairs—still have no subcommittees. Most others use subcommittees for holding hearings but do the markup in full committee. The Clean Air Act Amendments case was unusual in that the leadership engineered special negotiations off the floor to overturn the committee's action because the committee's bill was too strong for both the Senate and the White House. But even in such cases, all members usually have a chance to affect the final outcome on the floor.

The situation in the House is quite different. Because the large size of the parent committees makes real debate and negotiation on the details of most bills impossible, most important legislating now occurs in subcommittees, which hold hearings, mark up bills, and write reports—as happened in the case of the Clean Air Act Amendments. Committee chairs have also lost some power, because the Speaker works with the Rules Committee to schedule each bill and decide what sort of floor debate and amendment (called a *rule*, explained later) to grant it.

omnibus bill

The noun *omnibus* (from the Latin *omni*, "all," and *bus*, "vehicle") is a public vehicle that transports many people. We usually shorten it to *bus* when referring to such a vehicle. The adjective *omnibus* means to provide many things at once, or to contain, convey, or include many items, as an *omnibus* bill does.

Committee Deliberation

In both chambers, two-thirds of the bills referred to committees die there. But if a bill is reported out of committee, it is likely to be passed by the House or the Senate as a whole, as Table 11.3 shows. Although these statistics make Congress appear inefficient and perhaps unresponsive to citizen interests, many bills are introduced by members for show, having been drafted by special interests and carried to please interest groups and impress constituents at reelection time with the number of bills they have introduced on important subjects.

The bills most likely to get serious consideration are those with many sponsors, those on major issues of the day, and those sent to Capitol Hill by the administration. If the committee leadership is uncertain what it wants to do with a bill, it may invite the relevant executive agencies to comment on it. It then decides whether to drop the bill, consider it in the whole committee, or refer it to one of its subcommittees.

If a bill is being seriously considered, the whole committee or subcommittee usually holds hearings on it and marks it up before voting on whether or not to report it out. A bill reported out by a subcommittee goes to the whole committee, which may hold further hearings and further mark it up before voting on whether to report it out to the whole chamber. But even if the committee reports the bill out, it is only scheduled for floor debate if the leadership so wishes.

This complex committee process thus has four key stages intended to guarantee that significant legislation receives careful consideration before decisions are taken: (1) opportunities for interested groups in and out of government as well as some individuals to express their views; (2) deliberation by involved members; (3) negotiation of differences to produce a bill that is both substantive and politically appealing enough to pass; (4) development of a record of testimony and conclusions by the committee about the bill's merits and the intentions underlying it—called **legislative intent**—summarized finally in a committee report. Legislative intent has two important uses. Bureaucrats can refer to it in deciding how to implement the law, and the courts often use it as a basis for resolving challenges to the law. With so many policy questions facing Congress and so many interested parties, it is rare that a bill successfully navigates these four stages of the committee process: expression, deliberation, negotiation, and reporting.

Committee Leadership

Each committee has two leaders: the chair from the majority party and the ranking minority party member. The chair's procedural powers include calling and chairing meetings for hearings and markups, establishing meeting agendas, hiring and firing most committee staff, and allocating such committee resources as office space and funds. The chair also consults with the party leadership over changes in committee membership at the start of each two-year session. When a committee bill reaches the floor, the chair usually acts as floor manager and recommends majority party conferees for the conference committee if it passes. The ranking minority member supervises minority staff, oversees appointment of minority members to subcommittees, recommends minority conferees, and may assist in managing bills on the floor.

Until the reforms of the 1970s, committee chairs ran their committees as personal fiefdoms. Now that chairs are elected, their power is more dependent on personal skills, expertise, and knowledge of the rules—and support of the leadership. Some committee chairs are legendary for the way they exercise their power. John Dingell, whom we met in the Clean Air Act struggle, chaired the House Energy and Commerce Committee until Democrats lost control in 1995. He was virtually born into the House, winning his father's congressional seat on his death in 1955. A big man physically, he commanded the attention of his colleagues by his use of his prerogatives. In the words of a Republican committee colleague: "Sometimes I think he is an arbitrary and capricious son of a bitch, and other times I think he is a great parliamentarian. . . . Dingell is formidable not because he has more friends than anyone else, nor because he is more skilled, [but] because he takes the skill he has and combines it with good staff work, a thorough knowledge of the issues and a bulldog determination not to let go. He is the most tenacious member of Congress."[25] In the words of a legislative aide, "He is a skillful legislator. He is as devious as hell. And he demands loyalty."[26]

The Special Roles of Informal Groups and Staffers

The 535 voting members of Congress face an enormous workload and are beset by hundreds of executive branch agencies and thousands of interest groups as well as citizens on the outside trying to influence them. To cope, they rely heavily on informal interest groups and staffers for help.

The Coordinating Influence of Informal Groups

Members have organized themselves into some 120 informal interest groups,[27] which scholars and journalists call *caucuses* but Congress calls *legislative service organizations* to make them seem less interest-oriented. The major types are described in the nearby box.

Most of these caucuses analyze issues and legislation for members, and many attempt to get issues on the congressional agenda and mobilize support inside and outside of Congress. Occasionally, one has a major influence on public policy. The Senate Children's Caucus brought publicity to the issue of sexual abuse of children by conducting nationally reported hearings, for example; the Congressional Caucus for Women's Issues fostered laws reforming military pensions for women and strengthening child support payment enforcement; and the Congressional Black Caucus, which has 39 members, has negotiated key changes in pending legislation in exchange for its members' support on controversial bills.[28]

These informal groups never got direct support from Congress, but until Republicans stopped the practice in 1995, some managed to get their own paid staff and office space by collecting dues from members or by inviting interest groups and other outsiders to fundraisers. Some have coordinated activities with outside lobby groups funded by businesses, labor groups, or other special interests.

Congressional Caucuses

Some of the informal congressional groups known as caucuses are *partisan*—limited to members of one party. Among them are the Democratic Study Group, organized in 1959 when newly elected liberals were seeking to reform House procedures, which soon grew to include most House Democrats; the Conservative Democratic Forum, founded by southern House Democrats (called Boll Weevils) who supported Reagan economic policies; the Northeast-Midwest Republican Coalition, made up of liberal House Republicans (who came to be called Gypsy Moths); and the Conservative Opportunity Society, made up of House Republicans.

The *bipartisan* caucuses organize around regional interests or policy interests. Among those most prominent in the House have been the Congressional Agricultural Forum, with 75 members; the Congressional Human Rights Caucus, with 150; and the Pro-Life Caucus. The Senate has had fewer caucuses, most of them bipartisan—among them the Senate Western Coalition; Concerned Senators for the Arts; the Pro-Life Action Task Force for Women, Children, and the Unborn; and the Senate Human Rights Caucus.

Among the *bicameral* groups—those which include members from both chambers—have been the California Democratic Congressional Delegation; the Congressional Corn Caucus; the Congressional Friends of Human Rights; the Congressional Caucus for Women's Issues; the Congressional Black Caucus (founded in 1971); and the Congressional Hispanic Caucus (founded in 1976).

Congressional Staffs

Each senator and representative has personal staff assistants, and each committee and subcommittee has majority and minority party staffs. When Congress reorganized itself in 1946 it decreased the number of committees and increased the number of staff, then a mere 200. Today, close to 10,000 staff assist the 540 members and some 4,000 work for the 300 committees and subcommittees. Some staffers with decades of experience have inside knowledge on which new arrivals on Capitol Hill depend and so become the chief administrative and legislative aides or senior committee staffers. Many, however, are recent college graduates looking for exciting jobs and willing to work the long and irregular hours.

Congressional staffers are sometimes called "unelected representatives" because in both chambers they do most of the bill writing, committee research, speech writing, and constituent service. They also organize each member's daily activities and provide briefings on committee and floor activities. They are the main conduits lobbyists use to get messages—and campaign contributions—to members. In fact, staffers often serve as intermediaries among legislators, lobbyists, officials from the White House, and executive agency specialists as bills are being drafted and compromises constructed, and even during floor action.[29]

President Bill Clinton and potential presidential candidates General Colin Powell (*left*) and Newt Gingrich attend the Congressional Black Caucus's annual formal fundraising gala in 1995.

Congress as Two Legislatures: House and Senate Floor Action

The biggest differences between the House and Senate, summarized in Table 11.6, derive from the different lengths of their terms of office and from their different rules—especially those governing floor action. Floor consideration is far from automatic for bills with committee approval. Senate rules protect the minority party, and even the individual member, wishing to obstruct passage. By contrast, the House is governed by majority rule, and once a House measure makes it to the floor, a determined majority can generally work its will quickly.

Debate

While it appears that the essence of floor action is voting, the decisions that determine the ultimate fate of most bills are usually reached long before.

In the House, as major bills are approved by committee they are listed in order of their approval on a calendar. Bills that raise or spend money go on the Union Calendar, while all other major bills go on the House Calendar. Bills involving private matters such as immigration requests or personal claims against the government go on the Private Calendar, and noncontroversial bills go on the Consent Calendar. The Speaker and majority leader then determine which of these bills will reach the floor on the special days set aside for these types of bills. The leadership can bring money bills to the floor at any time, but House Calendar bills must first obtain a **rule**—a certification setting a time limit for debate and specifying what amendments, if any, will be allowed—from the Rules Committee. Until the 1970s, the Rules Committee, dominated by southern conservatives, acted independently in scheduling legislation, killing most liberal bills by simply refusing to grant them a rule. Reforms have given the majority leadership greater authority over the Rules Committee, but it can still grant special priority to a bill and specify whether and how it can be amended on the floor and how much debate will be allowed, or it can grant an *open rule* allowing unlimited amendment.

When a bill is called up on the floor, the House as a whole first passes (or on rare occasions amends) the rule drafted by the Rules Committee. The House then converts itself instantly into a **Committee of the Whole**—a parliamentary device to enable it to operate with different rules such as a smaller **quorum** (the number of members required to be present for business to go on).

Debate on the bill lasts for the time specified in the rule—usually several hours but occasionally, on highly visible and controversial bills, up to ten—divided equally between the bill's majority and minority floor managers, who are usually the chair and ranking minority member of the committee that approved the bill. Following general debate, votes are taken on whatever amendments the rule allows. The House then reconvenes as the House for the final vote. If the bill passes, it is sent to the Senate—or, if the Senate has already passed a similar measure, the two versions may go to a conference committee.

In the Senate, where fewer rules restrict the legislative process, partisan politics can easily delay or thwart passage of a controversial bill. The Senate has only two calendars: the Calendar of General Orders

quorum
This term is Latin for "of whom," a phrase commissions used to designate that members of a body be a particular number of people. Today the term refers to a fixed number of members of any body who must be present for its transactions to be legitimate.

TABLE 11.6

Important Differences Between the House and the Senate

	House	Senate
Special constitutional powers	Initiates all revenue bills (Article I, sec. 7)	Must give "Advice and Consent" to treaties (Article II, sec. 2)
		Must approve many major presidential appointments (Article II, sec. 2)
	Passes all articles of impeachment (Article I, sec. 2)	Tries impeached officials (Article I, sec. 3)
Structure	Larger (435 voting, 5 observers)	Smaller (100)
	More hierarchically organized	Less hierarchically organized
	Power less evenly distributed	Power more evenly distributed
	Shorter term (two years,), all elected at once	Longer term (six years), one-third elected every two years (Article I, sec. 3)
Leadership	Centralized in practice under the Speaker	Less centralized in practice
Legislative procedures	Bills introduced into "the hopper" and referred to committee by the Speaker	Bills normally referred by majority leader but may be introduced from the floor
Committee procedures	Committees almost always consider bills first	Committee consideration may be bypassed
	Speaker may create ad hoc committees	No ad hoc committees may be created
	Committee action more influential than floor action for final decision	Floor action as important as committee action for final decision
	Subcommittees do markup before committee action	Subcommittees mainly used for holding hearings
	More committees and subcommittees	Fewer committees and subcommittees
Scheduling	Generally controlled by majority party leadership and Rules Committee	Generally mutually agreed by majority and minority leaders
	System of "calendars" and special days for calling up different types of bills	Informal consultation with major efforts to accommodate senators' scheduling requests
Floor debate rules	Rigid rules favor majority	Flexible rules protect minority
	Debate limits set by Rules Committee	Debate limits rare, set by full Senate via unanimous consent or cloture
	Amendment rules determined by Rules Committee, with "nongermane" (irrelevant) amendments prohibited on floor	Amendments controlled by full Senate, with "nongermane" (irrelevant) amendments allowed
Other key characteristics	Acts more quickly	Acts more slowly
	Tends to be impersonal	Tends to be more personal
	Less prestige for institution and members	More prestige for institution and members
	Less media coverage of members	More media coverage of members
	More member specialization with fewer committee assignments	Less member specialization with more committee assignments

and the Executive Calendar (used for treaties and presidential nominations). There is no committee that schedules bills, and Senate rules allow unlimited debate and amendment. The majority leader must therefore consult with the

filibuster

This term derives from the Dutch word for "freebooter," which in the sixteenth century referred to marauders or pirates and adventurers.

minority leader to decide which bills to bring to the floor, because a bill is only likely to get consideration and a vote if the Senate votes to suspend its rules by a **unanimous consent agreement** that limits debate and specifies what amending will be allowed on the floor.

If such unanimous consent agreement cannot be reached, the leadership may still bring a bill up for consideration, but in that case opponents can **filibuster**—talk a bill to death, usually by reading irrelevant materials for many hours on end—unless and until 60 percent of the Senate votes for *cloture*, limiting debate to 30 more hours, at which time a vote must be taken.

The cloture rule, which originally required the assent of two-thirds of all senators, was liberalized in the 1960s to require the assent of only 60 percent of those present and voting. In the next two decades there were about a hundred filibusters, most of which succeeded in getting the contested legislation withdrawn. In recent years, however, the annual average has shot up to 15, and in the month preceding the 1994 midterm elections Republicans made unprecedented use of the threat to filibuster. Anticipating that they might be able to regain control of the Senate in the coming elections, they decided to deny the Democrats and President Clinton any legislative victories. Democrats had enough votes to win any partisan vote but lacked the 60 votes required for cloture. So all Republicans had to do to stop consideration of any bill was begin—or even threaten to begin—a filibuster. They did so successfully on health care, campaign finance reform, lobbyist registration, and other major Democratic bills. The result was a record 28 Republican filibusters in two years, and the Democratic leadership had to file motions to vote on ending filibusters an unprecedented 72 times.[30] Republicans paid a price, however, as Democrats used the same strategy against them to prevent the 104th Congress from passing Republican legislation before the 1996 campaign.

These filibusters and objections were matters of party strategy, but a single senator could have achieved the same result, either by threatening to filibuster or by objecting to suspending the rules. In the words of former representative and senator John Culver (D-Iowa), "If you just want to be unpleasant and have a temper tantrum and if you just want to be excessively self-obsessed, you can have a field day in the Senate. . . . You really can't do that the same way in the House. The rules of the Senate are congenial to permitting the least consequential member to shut the place down if he's smart enough or willful enough to do it."[31]

The House and Senate are both governed by sets of formal rules that "protect majority and minority rights, divide the workload, help contain conflict, ensure fair play, and distribute power among members."[32] If the will and the votes are there, either chamber can act. If not, obstructionists can prevail, constrained only by fear that the tactics they use today may be used against them next time.

Style and Civility

Each chamber has its own distinctive floor style. The differences in size of the body and in length of term between elections, plus differences in constituencies, make the Senate a kind of "club" and the House a kind of "fraternity." In the Senate, floor conduct still tends to be leisurely and genteel—rather like a men's club. However, time pressures have increasingly taken their toll. In the view of Ernest

What Really Happens: C-SPAN Versus the Congressional Record

If we wish to know what Congress actually does, we might think that a sensible place to look would be the *Congressional Record*. This official daily publication, which describes itself as containing "proceedings and debates of the Congress," has been published every day Congress has been in session since 1872. A glance at it suggests that it prints every word every member says on the floor of either house, for it averages some 250 pages of small print a day.

On October 18, 1972, the *Congressional Record* reports, Representative Hale Boggs (D-La.), who was majority whip, addressed the House. "In the next few minutes," he is quoted as saying, "I would like to note for members the great amount of significant legislation enacted during the session." After doing so, according to the report, he wished every representative a Merry Christmas and a Happy New Year. Observers might disagree about the impressiveness of the record of that session of Congress. But no one could fault the sentiments, coming as they did just as the Congress was about to adjourn for the year. However, any follower of Congress, or any reader of the daily paper, would question the report that Hale Boggs had addressed the House that day—for Hale Boggs had been killed in an airplane crash in Alaska two days earlier.

Such bizarre reports can occur because Congress has developed a way of allowing members to record not what they actually said but what they would have said had they been present and had there been time. Members are so busy with other important tasks that they are rarely on the floor. Indeed, unless an important vote is actually being taken, no more than a handful of members are likely to be on the floor. But to "make a record" that they can use with the voters, Congress makes three concessions to the truth in the *Congressional Record*. First, during a session a member can ask permission to "revise and extend my remarks" at a later time. That permission is always granted "without objection." The member then submits the text of what he or she would have said, and it is printed as if it had actually been said in that day's *Congressional Record*. So the fact that a speech appears in the *Congressional Record* is no guarantee that it was ever delivered.

No one could know whether a particular speech had actually been given without sitting endlessly in the gallery above the floor—until the House began allowing live television of its proceedings in 1979, followed by the Senate in 1986, over special cable channels (C-SPAN 1 and 2) created by the cable industry and furnished to cable companies. At that point, viewers around the nation (and even around the world, once the State Department began transmitting the signal via satellite) could follow every speech in Congress. Ironically, however, this step, which did constitute a move toward "truth in representation," also fostered yet another deceptive practice. This second concession to the truth is the practice of "special orders"—a provision by which, when the day's business is through, individual members may address the House for up to an hour each on subjects of their choice. These speeches are carried live on C-SPAN and then printed in the *Congressional Record* as if they were part of the regular session. Because the business day is over, no one else attends other than another member awaiting his or her turn to speak. But the House runs the cameras that transmit the signal to C-SPAN, and members insist that the camera not show the empty chamber except for an occasional shot. So a viewer tuning in would know that this was not a real session of the House only if he or she read and understood the caption saying that the House is considering special orders.

The third concession to the truth is the longstanding practice of allowing any member to revise the stenographic record of what he or she actually said on the floor of either house before it is printed in the *Congressional Record*. Members do this regularly, especially when they get carried away on the floor and want to conceal what they said from posterity—or from whoever reads the *Record*.

The lesson here is that citizens may need to consult more than just the apparently authoritative sources if they wish to know the whole truth about what really happens in Congress.

Hollings (D-S.C.): "There is no longer any senatorial club. . . . You do not get to see the other Senators. . . . You have five breakfasts and eight dinners and seven other things, and by the time I finish my speech here I have to get back to the staff because they have four appointments waiting in the office. So the collegial relationships are a thing of the past."[33]

In the House, floor behavior is more informal. In the words of one observer, "The House has the feel of a fraternity: members punch arms, slap thighs, joke, and those whose families stay in their districts often share houses, like graduate students."[34] Behavior on the floor has deteriorated somewhat in recent years. In 1985, Robert Dornan (R-Calif.) grabbed Thomas Downey (D-N.Y.) by the tie and accused him and other Democrats of being weak on national defense. In 1990, when Henry Hyde (R-Ill.) made hostile remarks to Barney Frank (D-Mass.), Craig Washington (D-Tex.) took offense, and Robert Walker (R-Pa.) responded in a way that forced colleagues to restrain the two from fighting.[35] Furthermore, as the box nearby reveals, reports of what occurs on the floor that appear to be official may actually be quite inaccurate.

Deterioration has reached the Senate, too. In 1995, freshman senator Rick Santorum (R-Pa.) outraged many older members in both parties by constantly referring to President Clinton as "Bill" on the floor—a violation of a longstanding custom of respect. His defense was that "the Senate is a stuffy place" and his language merely reflected today's public discourse.[36] Partisan scraps and angry reactions by women or ethnic minority members to their treatment by white male members have also become more frequent as party tensions have risen and the composition of Congress has diversified.[37]

At an informal level, the gulf between party leaders has become even more pronounced as partisanship has increased. As Speaker, Tip O'Neill would play cards after work and golf on weekends with his Republican counterparts, but once Gingrich became Speaker, he and House Minority Leader Richard Gephardt (D-Mo.) did not even speak to each other,[38] so coordination had to be done by aides. The situation got so bad that in 1997 junior House members of both parties organized a special informal weekend retreat to improve civility, but its effects were short lived.

Voting

Most final voting is conducted electronically in the House or by "roll call" in the Senate and recorded so that constituents (and potential opponents) can discover how their representatives voted. However, a recorded vote on final passage may be misleading, because the critical votes often come on earlier amendments or even on procedural questions such as which amendments to allow or on technical features such as when the bill will take effect. The many votes—procedural as well as substantive—on most important measures allow a lawmaker to appear to come out on both sides of an issue. For example, a member may vote to authorize a program but then vote against funding it, or vote for a substitute version of a bill but then vote against the final passage of the actual bill. Such behavior can make the bill's supporters believe that the lawmaker favors the concept while also pleasing those who oppose the bill. The Political Action Guide nearby tells how you can learn how members vote—and what their votes really mean.

roll-call vote

Before electronic voting was introduced, a vote was recorded by roll call: Each member announced his or her vote when the clerk called the representative's name. The Senate still uses roll-call voting.

Political Action Guide

How to Find and Interpret Congressional Voting Records

All "record" or "roll-call" votes on the floor of either chamber on bills and amendments are printed in the *Congressional Record,* which you can find in most large libraries. The *Congressional Quarterly Weekly Report* (see the bibliography at the end of this chapter), available in many libraries, prints records of all important votes. Some newspapers, such as the *New York Times* and the *Washington Post,* print the breakdown of votes on major topics. And many local papers print weekly summaries of how local representatives and senators voted on key bills.

The Library of Congress offers *Thomas,* a link to congressional information named for Thomas Jefferson, on the Internet at http://thomas.loc.gov. *Thomas* provides the full text of bills, a directory of committees, the weekly schedule, and the text of every issue of the *Congressional Record,* including a record of all votes, along with other relevant materials. Information on House proceedings can be found at www.house.gov and on Senate proceedings at www.senate.gov.

However, unless you've been following a certain issue and know just what was being voted on, published recorded votes are not likely to tell you very much. Members of Congress may vote with public opinion in their constituency on final passage of a bill but may have voted against public opinion in committee or during the amending process. Members may also change their vote once floor voting is completed. For example, members who voted with the party leadership or with a special interest and against the interests of their district, and then discover when they see the final tally that their vote was not crucial, may have their vote changed for the record. Such members may thus get credit in public for voting with their constituency, when in fact they voted against it the first time around.

To examine key votes—which usually come on amendments before the final vote on passage of a bill—you really need studies prepared by interest groups. More than 60 organizations prepare such lists after each session of Congress, rating all members by whether they vote as the groups believe they should. Among the major rating groups—to which you can write for their latest set of ratings—are:

- AFL-CIO Committee on Political Education (COPE), 815 16th St. NW, Washington, D.C. 20004
- American Conservative Union, 422 First St. SE, Washington, D.C. 20003
- American Farm Bureau Federation, 425 13th St. NW, Washington, D.C. 20004
- Americans for Democratic Action, 1424 16th St. NW, Washington, D.C. 20036
- Consumer Federation of America, 1012 14th St. NW, Washington, D.C. 20005
- Environmental Action, 1346 Connecticut Ave. NW, Washington, D.C. 20036
- League of Women Voters, 1730 M St. NW, Washington, D.C. 20036
- National Associated Businessmen, Inc., 1000 Connecticut Ave. NW, Washington, D.C. 20036
- Women's Lobby, Inc., 1345 G St. SE, Washington, D.C. 20003

There are many possible influences on each voting decision of each member—constituency interests, party line, ideological commitment, and leadership wishes—and we have no sure way of knowing why particular members vote as they do, even if they give reasons publicly.[39] While, as we have already noted, members most often "vote their constituencies," many votes also follow party lines—Democrats voting one way, Republicans the other—because the parties in Congress are becoming increasingly ideologically coherent. The liberal wing of the Republican party has virtually disappeared, and conservatives in the Democratic party, almost exclusively from the South, have been replaced by Republicans or themselves switched parties. Recently elected members of both chambers tend to be more conservative or less willing to compromise than their party leaders.

"The Senate has become a band of 100 individual operators," concludes one observer. "There's very little a leader can do to impose his will on the members any more."[40] This **legislative free-lancing**, as Washington insiders call it, reached new heights in Clinton's first two years, when many Democratic senators refused to support such major leadership bills as a budget reduction package (Chapter 12) and health care reform. After the Republican sweep of 1994, Republicans, too, exhibited more free-lancing.

Are these votes, whether party-line or free-lance, well-informed? Members haven't the time or the staff assistance to study carefully most of the bills they vote on. "There are just too many votes, too many issues, too many meetings, too many attention-demanding situations," complained one representative. "We're going to committee meetings, subcommittee meetings, caucuses—a caucus of the class with which you were elected here, the rural caucus, the steel caucus, you name it—and we're seeing constituents and returning phone calls and trying to rush back and forth to the district, and then we're supposed to understand what we're voting on when we get to the House floor."[41] Table 11.3 reveals that members studying only bills coming to the floor for votes would have to study some 5,300 bills a year, many of them consisting of hundreds of pages of legal language. Floor debates are rarely enlightening. If each representative spoke for only one minute on each bill, each House debate would take more than seven hours. And in the 1995–1996 session, since the House passed 1,022 bills, there would have been barely enough time for each member to speak for one minute on each bill if the House had remained in session 24 hours a day year-round. Senators could speak longer on each bill, but since debate is often unlimited, it would be impossible to have full debate on most bills.

Given these constraints, members may resort to the traditional practice of vote trading commonly known as **log-rolling** and often euphemistically called "mutual accommodation." The late Sam Ervin (D-N.C.), a folksy senator who rose to fame chairing the committee investigating the Watergate scandal, expressed this approach well in his description of his relations with Senator Milton Young (R-S.D.). "I got to know Milt Young very well. And I told Milt, 'Milt, I would just like you to tell me how to vote about wheat and sugarbeets and things like that, if you will just help me out on tobacco and things like that.'"[42]

To vote on a bill's merits, members often resort to **cue-taking**—looking to trusted colleagues of either party who share one's political orientation on the issue at hand for guidance on how to vote. If you watch voting on amendments closely, you can sometimes see a key member giving a thumbs-up or thumbs-down signal to others watching for guidance. In the words of the late senator Edmund Muskie (D-Maine):

> People have all sorts of conspiratorial theories on what constitutes power in the Senate. It has little to do with the size of the state you come from. Or the source of your money. Or committee chairmanships, although that certainly gives you a kind of power. But real power up there comes from doing your work and knowing what you're talking about. Power is the ability to change someone's mind. . . . The most important thing in the Senate is credibility. *Credibility! That* is power.[43]

The Two Houses as One Legislature: Conference Committees

The constitutional requirement that legislation be passed in identical form by both chambers requires that the two chambers function frequently as a single legislature. There are three ways the two chambers can reach agreement on common language. Sometimes—especially on minor bills, and at the end of a session when time is very short—one chamber simply adopts and passes the language approved by the other. Often, however, the two chambers send measures back and forth between them, voting on each other's proposed amendments, until the drafts come to be identical. The most controversial measures (about one in every four or five bills that become law)—such as the Clean Air Act Amendments—go to a **conference committee**.[44]

Conference committees are ad hoc committees—that is, each is appointed for the sole purpose of negotiating a compromise on a particular piece of legislation. Because they usually have the final say on what a bill contains, they are sometimes called "the third house of Congress." Before the congressional reforms of the 1970s, they generally consisted of the 5 to 12 most senior members of the committees that had first considered the bill in each chamber, and they deliberated in secret. Today, formal conference committee deliberations are open, although informal behind-the-scenes discussions are crucial to the negotiating process. Two recent developments have increased the size and composition of conference delegations: multiple referral, which involves more committees, and omnibus bills, which give more members an interest in conference outcomes.

Conferees are chosen by the House Speaker and the Senate's presiding officer after consultation with leaders of the involved or interested committees and then approved by unanimous consent. The conferees, known as "managers," include members of both parties and may include specialist members not on the involved committees—a practice that tends to favor the House, which with its larger membership is more likely to have a specialist on any given subject and to produce very large delegations, such as the House's 130 members from nine committees versus the Senate's 9 members from two committees on the Clean Air Act Amendments.

Each chamber's delegation has a single collective vote in the conference committee, and both sides are expected to compromise in order to create a new bill that each chamber can approve in identical form. Normally, the negotiation produces a true compromise, with each side giving way on some provisions and getting its way on others. Often, a chamber will insert a provision during markup primarily to have something to trade in conference later on.

Occasionally, on complex legislation such as appropriations bills, when conferees reach agreement on all but a handful of provisions, they may make a partial conference report on the situation. In such a case, each chamber votes to approve the partial report and then each takes up the remaining issues, voting on the floor for proposed compromises, which are sent back and forth between the chambers (as in the second route to agreement, discussed above), until total agreement is finally reached.

The conference process can be difficult when one chamber has "instructed" its delegates not to give way on certain provisions of its bill. Occasionally, a "runaway conference" produces a "compromise" that incorporates provisions that were not in either chamber's bill.[45] President Reagan once remarked, "You know, if an orange and an apple went into conference consultations, it might come out a pear"—to which majority leader Jim Wright (D-Tex.) responded that the conferees should instead "make fruit salad."[46]

When the compromise is reported back for a final vote, either chamber may vote to *recommit* (send back) the bill to the conference committee, where it dies if Congress adjourns without approving a new compromise.

Of course, any bill passed in identical form by both houses can only become law if the president signs it, or if both houses pass it again after a presidential veto, this time by at least a two-thirds majority, or if the president neither signs nor vetoes it, thus allowing it to become law without his approval.

The External Politics of Congress

The Constitution's separation of powers requires that Congress have close and continuing relations with the executive branch, the courts, special interests, and constituents. Many of these relations are conducted by Congress's own bureaucratic agencies, which are described in the box on page 426.

Relations with the President and the White House

Congress has occasionally deferred to a strong presidency, especially at the beginning of an administration elected on an activist platform or when Congress has close partisan ties with the president, as was the case with Thomas Jefferson, Franklin Roosevelt, and at first with Lyndon Johnson. More typically, the two branches operate to check and balance each other,[47] and in periods of divided government congressional influence is often strongest.

The Framers provided that the president "recommend to [Congress's] Consideration such Measures as he shall judge necessary and expedient"—the constitutional basis for the annual State of the Union Address, which the president uses to attempt to shape the public policy agenda. In a time of severely limited governmental resources, however, the primary device for agenda control, and the policymaking that it permits, is spending and the annual budget that controls this spending. And because it has to approve that budget each year, Congress has a major role in public policy. Neither Congress nor the president can develop a program or solve a major national problem without the other's participation. But each is chosen by different constituencies, often in different elections, so each is likely to respond to different situations and cues from the public. The resulting divergence and frequent discord make governance difficult and encourage each branch to attempt to strengthen its position against the other.

Either the president or Congress can use two possible strategies for increasing its power over the other. The *intragovernmental strategy* involves making alliances with the bureaucracy or the courts to increase support for its efforts in the struggle with the other. Confronting a Democratic-controlled Congress and a liberal Supreme Court, President Richard Nixon nominated conservative judges to gain influence in the court system. The strategy's success was limited because the Senate rejected two of his Supreme Court nominees and several who were confirmed turned out to be much more liberal than expected (Chapter 14). Nixon also tried to gain greater control over the bureaucracy by carefully selecting loyal appointees, but this effort also came to naught when the Watergate scandal broke and some of his appointees deserted him when he was charged with illegal acts and "abuse of power" (Chapter 13).

Congress countered Nixon's efforts with an *extragovernmental strategy* of gaining support from various interest groups outside of government. As growing segments of Congress became disillusioned with the Vietnam War, they aligned themselves with antiwar interest groups and conducted televised hearings on the war and on the Watergate scandal to galvanize public support. Nixon was forced to end the war and ultimately to resign, and Congress consolidated and expanded its power at the expense of the weakened presidency. First, it passed the War Powers Act in 1973, over Nixon's veto, which requires the president to consult with Congress before undertaking sustained military operations abroad. And when the Nixon administration *impounded* (refused to spend) money Congress had appropriated for its favorite projects, Congress sued to force the spending, thereby strengthening popular support for Congress at the expense of the presidency. Congress also passed the Budget and Impoundment Control Act of 1974 to prevent future impoundments.

The struggle between Congress and the presidency has continued in subsequent administrations—

Newt Gingrich, newly elected as Speaker of the House, and President Clinton shake hands at a joint appearance in New Hampshire after spontaneously agreeing to create a nonpartisan committee to recommend changes in campaign finance laws. The commission was never actually established.

Congress as a Bureaucracy

Congress must oversee not only the executive branch bureaucracy but also its own, which includes each member's personal staff, each committee's staff, and four major support agencies, along with smaller bodies ranging from the Capitol Police Force through a television studio to a computer service.

Support Agencies

The major research support agencies of the Congress are the Congressional Budget Office, the General Accounting Office, the Congressional Research Service, and the Library of Congress.

- The Congressional Budget Office (CBO) gives Congress its own estimates of the cost of proposed programs and forecasts the likely development of the economy, so Congress can make decisions without simply relying on those developed for the executive branch by its Office of Management and Budget. When major health-care reform reached the public agenda after the 1992 elections, CBO analyzed the likely cost and evaluated the workability of each of the reform proposals offered by the White House and congressional groups. It concluded that the comprehensive plans would be too costly and complicated, while the less ambitious plans would fail to make much difference in how many Americans had health insurance and how affordable such coverage would be. These CBO studies—along with massive lobbying by many varied special interests—helped doom comprehensive health-care reform in 1994.[1]

- The General Accounting Office (GAO) is a semi-independent oversight agency. Its professional analysts evaluate the performance of government agencies and the spending of federal funds and make recommendations to Congress. Most of these recommendations are also made available to the media and the public.[2] Its director, called the comptroller general, is appointed for a 15-year term so that he or she will be relatively free from political pressures.

- The Congressional Research Service employs some 800 researchers to answer questions on anything from any member—even including requests forwarded from constituents for help on high school term papers. Its research projects and monographs give Congress a valuable source of information independent from the information provided by the executive branch agencies—a resource that no other legislative branch anywhere else in the world has.

- The Library of Congress, the nation's official library as well as Congress's own, serves as the official depository of every book published in the United States as well as all government documents. It is now developing a National Digital Library to make much of its collection of over 100 million items available online.

The growth of these specialized support agencies has given members of Congress more, but not necessarily better, information about policy problems and alternatives, but at the cost of introducing an even wider array of differing assumptions about *what is*, *what's right*, and *what works*, each of which members of Congress must either accept or challenge—or ignore.

---

most recently as the Republican-controlled Congress has sought to compel changes in Clinton administration policy on the budget, environmental protection, taxes, and welfare. Battles in this struggle are won by one side or the other, but the war never ends—thanks to the constitutional provisions invented by the Framers. In general, Congress fares better in domestic policy contests than in foreign policy battles, where Congress remains, in the words of a recent study, "a subsidiary, though still important, actor in a decision-making process that continues to be led by the president. And in that decision-making process Congress and its members play the valuable role of critic and legitimizer."[48] (We'll examine these struggles from the president's perspective in the next chapter.)

The Congressional Budget

Congress is the overseer and evaluator of the budgets of the executive and judicial branches, but Congress develops and approves its own budget. As a result, spending has skyrocketed as both houses have sought to develop—singly as well as in the joint agencies just described—the capabilities to answer the executive branch in disputes over policy and to evaluate policy proposals. The annual congressional budget exceeded $1 billion for the first time in 1993 and has continued to climb since, passing 1.7 billion in 1998.

Legal Regulations on Congressional Conduct

Just as Congress's budget is unregulated by outside powers, so is Congress's own conduct in the realms of employment practices and ethics—both causes of increasing controversy. Congress passes the laws that require safe workplaces and prohibit job discrimination in the nation's businesses and in the rest of the federal government but has traditionally exempted itself from the provisions of these laws. Why? The official reason is that if the laws covered Congress, the executive branch would be the enforcement mechanism and that would violate the separation of powers and give the executive branch powerful leverage over Congress.

Critics of Congress argued, however, that the real reason for these exemptions was to allow Congress to continue its discriminatory practices. Certainly, the internal record of Congress in terms of racial and gender discrimination has been very poor until quite recently.[3] Until the Kennedy-Johnson administration, the only jobs African Americans could get on Capitol Hill were as waiters, janitors, and brass polishers. Women—even white women—fared little better. As better jobs gradually opened up for women and minorities, their pay always lagged behind that of white males. But unlike the rest of the country, Congress could not be sued for such discriminatory treatment because it had exempted itself from the legislation that required everyone else to behave better. When Republicans gained control in 1995, by an almost unanimous vote, Congress passed the Congressional Accountability Act requiring Congress to abide by many of the same workplace rules it has imposed on the rest of society. After President Clinton issued an executive order banning smoking in all federal buildings in 1997, however, Congress became the only remaining federal refuge for smokers.

---

[1] Richard Wolf, "The Office That Roared in Health Debate," *USA Today*, September 1, 1994.
[2] You can subscribe to a free monthly publication that summarizes the findings of the most recent studies and offers you a chance to request free copies of the reports that interest you from the GAO through *Thomas*, the Library of Congress's Internet link (http://thomas.loc.gov).
[3] The best firsthand account—a fascinating one—is a memoir by the pioneer in the campaign to get better treatment for African Americans behind the scenes as head of the Senate Dining Room: Robert Parker, *Capitol Hill in Black and White* (New York: Dodd, Mead, 1986).

Relations with the Bureaucracy

All Congress—or the president—can do is make policy decisions and proclaim them through laws or presidential executive orders (Chapter 12). It is then up to the bureaucracy to implement these decisions—usually by converting broad general statements into specific programs and regulations and carrying out the resulting instructions.

Relations between Congress and the president may change when the presidency changes hands, but those between Congress and the bureaucracy are usually much more stable. Legislators and bureaucrats consult regularly over budgets, appointment of high-level officials, decisions about where to locate projects, and proposals to establish, reorganize, or abolish programs or agencies. Some of these relationships are very stable (see discussion of so-called iron triangles in Chapters 8 and 13). Congressional staffers doing casework to cope with the needs of constituents or the desires of special interests contact bureaucrats regularly. Congress also plays longer-term roles in policy and implementation by inserting a legislative veto in certain laws and conducting oversight of many important agencies and programs.

The Legislative Veto

In 1932 Congress began to insert in some bills a provision that once an agency develops a program, it must submit the program to Congress, which decides whether to accept or veto the program. This **legislative veto** was designed to allow Congress to keep control over a law's implementation while delegating to bureaucrats the power to convert the law into specific regulations. There are three versions of this legislative veto: the two-house veto, in which both houses consider the program; the committee veto, in which a congressional committee considers it; and the one-house veto, in which either house may veto it. The War Powers Act, for example, has a two-house veto provision, while the Trade Act of 1974, which lowered tariffs, has a one-house veto. Congress had built one or another type of legislative veto into almost 300 major laws but had used it less than a hundred times by 1983,[49] when the Supreme Court ruled the device unconstitutional in *Immigration and Naturalization Service v. Chadha*. The Court held that Congress "must abide by its delegation of authority until that delegation is legislatively altered or revoked" and argued that both houses must agree on such action.[50]

The primary effect of the legislative veto had been to encourage regular informal consultation and even compromise between the executive and legislative branches. Congress has continued to insert legislative vetoes in some key legislation, hoping that the Court will eventually approve at least limited use of such provisions. Meanwhile, however, Congress has been forced to rely more heavily on laws prohibiting certain behaviors by the executive, thereby heightening conflict between the branches.

The Oversight Function

Congressional **oversight**—review of executive branch agencies and the programs and policies they administer—is the only regular way Congress, and thus the people, can get information on how well the bureaucracy is doing its job. When Congress reorganized itself in 1946, it directed each committee to continually monitor the execution of laws by the administrative agencies under its jurisdiction by holding hearings in which bureaucrats testify about their past activities and future plans.

Congress has passed laws requiring that executive branch agencies themselves regularly prepare some 5,000 reports to Congress on such bureaucratic activities as enforcing the laws, spending, and policy evaluation. However, such required reports are hard to find and still harder to read. Investigations get more media attention and sometimes unearth more information, but they are difficult to organize and costly in money and members' time. Most observers do not believe Congress handles its oversight efforts particularly well—with occasional dramatic exceptions, mainly investigations such as Watergate and Iran-Contra. The General Accounting Office, which audits expenditures and evaluates agencies, does perform some oversight by investigation, such as the instance summarized in the box nearby.

Effective oversight is more likely during divided government and when Congress wants to protect certain agencies against presidential interference—as when the Reagan administration tried to abolish or curtail many agencies that were longtime favorites of Congress. Competition among programs brought on by the ballooning federal deficit in the 1980s and 1990s also fostered more oversight intended to determine which programs most deserve scarce resources. In the conclusion of a recent study, "The knowledgeable pushing, hauling, poking, and advocacy of Congress as it keeps a watchful eye on policy and administration . . . is far from perfect, not even pretty or neat, but we could do far worse."[51]

Congress's GAO Investigates the Pentagon's Smart Weaponry

During and after the Gulf War, the Defense Department and military contractors claimed that the new "smart weaponry"—"stealth" fighter jets designed to avoid detection by enemy defenses, computer-guided attack missiles, and "smart bombs" intended to find their targets by themselves—were extremely effective in finding and destroying targets in Iraq. After the war, Senator David Pryor (D-Ark.) and Representative John Dingell (D-Mich.) asked Congress's General Accounting Office to report on the actual performance of these extremely expensive weapons so they would know whether Congress should appropriate funds to buy large quantities of the weapons, as the Pentagon had requested. The GAO spent four years studying more than a million Pentagon and contractor documents and interviewing pilots, planners, and battlefield commanders to prepare a 250-page secret document.

A brief summary of that report released publicly in July 1996 found that the Pentagon's claims "were overstated, misleading, inconsistent with the best available data, or unverifiable." Instead, it concluded, these new weapons performed about the same as the older, cheaper weapons. The study found, for example, that pilots could not tell whether a target was a tank or a truck nor whether it had already been destroyed. New high-tech sensors could not see through clouds, rain, fog, smoke, or high humidity. Smart bombs only hit their targets 40 percent of the time, not the 80 percent the Pentagon had claimed.

When the report was released, the Defense Department did not dispute its findings. It said instead that it would deal with the problems by improving its smart weapons. Meanwhile, however, the cost of smart bombs being built and planned had already reached more than $58 billion—a sum the GAO pointed out is more than the government spends each year on the Federal Bureau of Investigation, the war on drugs, immigration control, the federal court systems, and prison construction.

Source: Tim Weiner, "'Smart' Weapons Were Overrated, Study Concludes," *New York Times,* July 9, 1996.

Political Action Guide

How to Communicate Effectively with Your Members of Congress

Most members of Congress are so busy, as we've seen in this chapter, that they can't possibly read all their mail—incoming or outgoing. However, you can take certain steps to make it more likely that the member of Congress to whom you write will see your letter. If your letter asks a question that cannot be answered by a form letter, someone will have to answer your letter personally. If you are an expert on the matter your letter discusses or have otherwise written a particularly analytical letter with well-thought-out arguments, it is likely that the staff member who opens the letter will set it aside for the member of Congress to read personally. But the best way to assure that the member will read your letter is to refer to any personal contact you might have had with him or her or with his or her family, friends, or staff.

The following are some helpful hints prepared by Representative Morris K. Udall (D-Ariz.) for the League of Women Voters:

1. Be sure your letter is addressed properly: to Senator _____ or Representative _____, at the U.S. Senate or the U.S. House of Representatives, Washington, D.C. 20515 (House) or 20510 (Senate).
2. If the subject of your letter is a bill or issue, mention it in the first paragraph.
3. Write as soon as possible; don't wait until a bill has been passed.
4. Keep your letter as brief as possible.
5. Give your reasons for taking a stand. Be specific and constructive.
6. Don't make threats or berate your representatives.
7. Say "well done" when it's deserved.

You can also contact your member of Congress by e-mail, phone, telegram, or personal visit.

Phone calls can be made simply by dialing (202) 224-3121, the number for both the House and Senate, and then asking for the member's office. When the receptionist answers, give your name and ask for the legislator by

Relations with Other Actors: The Courts, Special Interests, and Individuals

As part of the separation of powers, the Constitution directs Congress to set up "a supreme Court" and the Senate to pass upon, or *confirm*, the president's appointments to it. It also gives Congress the power to create whatever lower courts it deems necessary, and Congress has successfully claimed the power to confirm appointments to these federal judgeships as well. Congress also approves the budget of the judicial branch, as it does that of the executive branch.

The Supreme Court, in turn, has the constitutional power—developed in 1803 by Chief Justice John Marshall in *Marbury v. Madison* (Chapter 2)[52]—to assess the constitutionality of acts of Congress and regularly interprets congressional legislation. It rarely declares laws unconstitutional, generally deferring to the Congress on the grounds that it is elected by the people (see Chapter 14). However, cases occasionally come before the Court that have profound implications for Congress, such as the state laws establishing term limits for members of Congress, which the Court ruled unconstitutional in 1995.

name. If he or she is not in or is busy, ask to speak with the legislative assistant who handles the subject you're concerned about. He or she talks almost every day with the legislator and helps develop his or her positions on issues, and so your views are quite likely to be noted.

To make an electronic connection, you can visit the House's Website, www.house.gov, or the Senate's, www.senate.gov, and follow the instructions given there.

If you can get to Washington, you may be able to visit your legislator personally. Write or phone for an appointment before you go. A better bet, however, is to visit your legislator when he or she is in the district—most weekends, most holidays, and during congressional recesses. You'll find a listing in the phone book under "U.S. Government" for your legislator's local or district office. This office is always staffed by one or more assistants who will be happy to hear your views as well as to arrange appointments in the home district.

The most likely way to get to see your legislator, however, is to invite him or her to speak to a group, even one you set up just for the occasion. Most legislators are especially interested in speaking to student groups. At such a meeting, you will usually get to express your views, too. After the visit write a letter of thanks and restate your views. If the legislator does what you urged, write again to say "well done."

Positive contacts with your legislator—whether by mail, phone, or personal visit—will make it easier for you to have access the next time an issue that concerns you arises. And if you find yourself in general agreement with your legislator, volunteering to help in the local office or in the next campaign can be an excellent way to strengthen your access and even your influence. It is also a fascinating way to learn more about politics from the inside.

Many observers consider Congress a virtual captive of special interests. Most members' campaign funds come from political action committees (PACs) and wealthy individual contributors (see Chapters 8 and 10), and members do spend much of their time introducing bills for powerful business interests, public interest groups, and individuals and intervening with government bodies to aid groups and individuals. The public interest may indeed often be a casualty of such close relations to special interests.

However, the Framers designed the government so that any special interest wanting government to do something must convince either the executive branch or the Congress—or often both—to agree, or the action cannot be undertaken. And the First Amendment also protects the right of every citizen to attempt to influence Congress. The Political Action Guide nearby suggests ways of making sure your messages and your visits have maximal impact upon your legislators. Only if you and your friends and neighbors and co-workers—and many others like and unlike you—do so are your representatives likely to become *your representatives*. And only if they do will it be possible for the Congress to become, as the Framers intended, the representative branch—the *first* branch—of our government.

Reforming Congress

Some observers attribute the frequent failure of Congress to deal effectively with matters of public policy, a major source of its current low esteem, to its rules and procedures, despite recent reforms. The greater democratization that has been achieved has actually made it harder for the body as a whole and for the party leadership to act effectively—especially when dealing with a resolute president. Both the ease of delay in the Senate, where debate is virtually unlimited, and the difficulty of amendment in the House, where the majority party can usually have its way if it is united, can be obstacles to effective policymaking because both chambers must agree on any law. The fragmented committee jurisdictions in both chambers and use of omnibus bills, which require that many different committees process any proposals for major change in most policy areas, also make innovation difficult, as we've seen. So democracy seems to come at the expense of efficiency and effectiveness, and vice versa.[53]

Others believe that the basic problem is the people in Congress, many of whom do not wish to do more than Congress currently does. Many of the new, highly spirited members, whose presence might seem to bode well for policy innovation over time, are conservatives who believe that Congress (and government as a whole) should do less. Furthermore, the partisan wrangling that developed in the Reagan era and has turned into gridlock since suggests that even activist members may have trouble fostering the unity required for effective policy initiatives or for severe cutbacks in government. In short, "the system is biased either toward compromise and incremental change, or toward confrontation and inaction."[54]

A Joint Committee on the Organization of Congress in 1992 favored realigning committee jurisdictions to fit current policy issues such as health care and the environment and imposing term limits on committee chairs, but powerful committee chairs in both chambers blocked these reforms. After gaining control in 1995, House Republicans reduced individual members' committee assignments and limited the terms of chairs, but rejected a proposal to switch from annual budgets to a two-year budget so that agencies could plan better and Congress could consider programs more carefully.

Today there is considerable popular support for term limits, a constitutional amendment requiring a balanced budget, and cutting congressional salaries, perks, and staff to remove personal incentives for members to become careerists. But experts doubt that such popular reforms would improve the operation or the output of Congress. Both experts and public opinion support curtailing the influence of special interests, but they disagree on how to do this. Most experts favor campaign finance reform to limit PAC spending in exchange for at least partial public financing of congressional campaigns, but most people oppose public financing.

Thus Congress must come up with reforms substantial enough to regain legitimacy in the public's mind. Many believe that the place to start is ethics. People grant legitimacy to those they perceive as acting correctly. In professions from law and business to journalism and politics, correct action is defined as ethical action. The array of recent congressional scandals—among them the House Bank (Chapter 9), the Keating Five (Chapter 8), and Speaker Gingrich's misuse of tax-exempt funds and giving misinformation to the Ethics Committee investigating him, along with public allegations of sexual misconduct by some members—have fostered greater public concern about members' ethics. Most close observers believe that ethical conduct in Congress is much higher now than it has ever been, but public perceptions are what matters. In the recent words of one member, "The truth is, the quality of the Congress is better than it was years ago, and yet people think we're a bunch of dumb scoundrels."[55]

There is no unanimity on what appropriate ethical conduct by members of Congress actually is, but three principles of legislative ethics are widely endorsed:

- *Autonomy.* Legislators have an obligation to deliberate and decide free from improper influence by special interests or their own personal interests.
- *Accountability.* Legislators should give constituents sufficient information about their personal finances, campaign contributions, and deliberations on particular issues, so that voters can decide whether to reelect them.
- *Responsibility.* Legislators should behave (and appear to behave) in ways that facilitate the effective functioning of Congress and that strengthen democracy.[56]

But such general principles do not give members sufficient guidance on how to act in particular situations, and as we saw with media ethics (Chapter 9), it is hard to develop a code of ethical conduct that effectively instructs someone who is unsure of what to do.[57]

Underlying this practical difficulty is the fact that we, the people, are not clear about what we wish legislative ethics to achieve. Is it independent ethical judgment by legislators? or more ethical policy decisions? or decisions more in harmony with the ethical views of constituents? or less appearance of ethically compromised behavior by legislators? Unless we are clear about what we want, we can't expect legislators to behave in ways that will impress us with their integrity.[58]

Currently, each chamber has an Ethics Committee (the House's is called Standards of Official Conduct) composed of current members that offers ethical advice to any member who requests it and sits in judgment of the conduct of any fellow member charged by another member with an ethics infraction. Occasionally, the committee reaches a negative finding that leads a member to resign, as did Senator Bob Packwood (R-Ore.), who had been accused of sexual harassment by former staffers, in 1995. In 1997, the House Standards of Official Conduct Committee levied an unprecedented $300,000 fine on Speaker Gingrich—the estimated cost of the investigation resulting from his providing it incorrect information. Some believe this process would work better if the committee consisted of outsiders—perhaps ethical specialists from other professions or perhaps esteemed former members of Congress—who would bring prestige and a public image of impartiality to the investigations and rulings.

Instead of agreeing on ethics reform, let alone passing a procedural reform package, however, many members continue to engage in "Congress-bashing" whenever they campaign for reelection—"running for Congress by running against Congress." Such posturing increases popular misunderstanding of the challenges facing Congress internally while distracting popular attention from the policy problems facing the nation. It also creates greater public disillusionment with politics and politicians that may eventually bring about a real crisis of legitimacy for Congress and even the federal government as a whole.

"More so than at any other time in the nation's history, Congress is elected and organized to serve the disparate elements of a self-interested public rather than to identify and foster the shared concerns of a public-spirited citizenry," writes one

Jim Wright (D-Texas) was forced to resign as Speaker of the House after being accused (by Newt Gingrich) of ethics violations in 1988. Besides being charged with a conflict of interest between his business dealings and some of his legislative efforts, Wright was criticized for taking "royalties" of $55,000 on a book that an aide had written in his name and a friend of his had published.

specialist. "Congress increasingly lacks the ability to recognize the mutual concerns and shared interests of the public and the ability to discover new governing principles that could resolve our policy dilemmas and renew public faith in government."[59]

Unless Congress finds the will, the capacity, and the ideas necessary to meet this challenge, its legitimacy will decline further and policy responsibility will inevitably shift increasingly and perhaps even irreversibly to the presidency. Admirers of the system of separation of powers and checks and balances fear that such a shift could threaten the long-term survival of democracy. The hope is that newly elected reformers concerned about the image and the effectiveness of Congress can reach bipartisan agreement with committed veterans to create reforms that improve the conduct of members and once again make Congress a vibrant first branch of the federal government.

Summary

Congress was granted certain specific powers in the Constitution and has six key functions: legislating, budgeting, ratifying treaties, confirming appointments, impeaching officials, and overseeing the other branches.

Parties have three important functions in Congress: creating rules that help shape the way each house operates, furnishing legislative leaders (House Speaker, majority and minority leaders, and whips; Senate majority and minority leaders and whips), and organizing elections. In recent sessions, party unity has increased as partisan division has intensified.

Each member must decide which of the possible roles to adopt: representative advocate (delegate), responsible deliberator (trustee), ambitious politician (politico), effective colleague, loyal party member, policy advocate, service provider (furnishing "pork" and doing casework), or profiteer (enjoying "perks" and perhaps having a conflict of interest).

Congress is really two legislatures, the House and the Senate. Each operates as a committee system in which members are assigned to committees and subcommittees by the party leadership. Bills are referred to committees, where they may be marked up and sent to the floor for debate if the leadership agrees. Both chambers are supposed to deliberate before voting on legislation on the floor, but the large workload and limited time make deliberation difficult. The size of the House (435 voting members) and its rules make deliberation virtually impossible there. The smaller Senate (100 members) has rules protecting minority rights, which encourage filibusters unless cloture can be agreed to by 60 percent of those voting. Because knowing all legislation well is impossible, members tend to rely on cue-taking, advice from their staffs, and guidance from caucuses of members with shared interests in deciding how to vote. Rather than depending on party leadership, they are likely to do legislative free-lancing. Once legislation is passed in different forms by both chambers, it must be compromised, either by one chamber accepting the other's language or by negotiation in a conference committee.

Congress has its own support agencies such as the Congressional Budget Office and the General Accounting Office. It develops its own budget and regulates its own conduct. It also often engages in power struggles with the president and the executive branch, not only when there is divided government but also when both branches are controlled by the same party. Its role in policymaking is significant, but Congress rarely initiates new policies, usually instead influencing the shape of policies proposed by the executive, especially through its role in approving the budget.

Popular discontent with Congress has led to renewed interest in reform, but experts disagree about which rules and procedures should be changed, and Congress has been slow to act on ethics reform. Public confidence in Congress is unlikely to increase significantly until these issues are successfully dealt with.

Key Terms

apprenticeship system **403**
casework **405**
cloture **395**
Committee of the Whole **416**
conference committee **423**
conflict of interest **406**
cue-taking **422**
delegate **402**
elastic clause **394**
filibuster **418**
gridlock **398**
legislative free-lancing **422**
legislative intent **413**

legislative veto **428**
log-rolling **422**
majority leader **397**
"mark up" **407**
megabills **411**
minority leader **397**
multiple referral **411**
necessary and proper clause **394**
omnibus bills **411**
oversight **428**
party caucus **395**
"perks" **405**
politico **403**

"pork" **404**
pork barrel **404**
president pro tempore **397**
quorum **416**
rule **416**
seniority **395**
single referral **411**
Speaker of the House **396**
trustee **402**
unanimous consent agreement **418**
whip **397**

How You Can Learn More About Congress

Aberbach, Joel. *Keeping a Watchful Eye.* Washington, D.C.: Brookings Institution, 1990. A study of the politics of congressional oversight.

Bacon, Donald C., Roger H. Davidson, and Morton Keller, eds. *The Encyclopedia of the United States Congress* (New York: Simon & Schuster, 1995). A four-volume history of Congress containing more than a thousand articles and almost as many illustrations, tables, and charts, written by more than 550 authorities.

Baker, Ross K. *House and Senate,* 2nd ed. New York: W.W. Norton, 1995. A detailed comparison of the two chambers.

Congressional Quarterly. *Guide to Congress,* 4th ed. Washington, D.C.: Congressional Quarterly Press, 1991. A very comprehensive account, in more than 1,000 pages, of the history and operation of Congress.

Congressional Quarterly Weekly Report. The most authoritative and comprehensive weekly account of current happenings in Congress and background on them, available in academic libraries.

Davidson, Roger H., ed. *The Postreform Congress.* New York: St. Martin's Press, 1992. A collection of scholarly studies of various aspects of how Congress now functions.

Davidson, Roger H., and Walter J. Oleszek, *Congress and Its Members,* 4th ed. Washington, D.C.: Congressional Quarterly Press, 1994. A classic, comprehensive scholarly study updated.

Dodd, Lawrence C., and Bruce I. Oppenheimer, eds. *Congress Reconsidered,* 5th ed. Washington, D.C.: Congressional Quarterly Press, 1993. A wide-ranging collection of recent analyses by specialist scholars.

Gold, Martin, et al. *The Book on Congress: Process, Procedure, and Structure,* rev. ed. Washington, D.C.: Big Eagle Publishing, 1992. A comprehensive survey of the operation of each chamber, including thorough coverage of rules and procedures.

Hinckley, Barbara. *Less Than Meets the Eye.* Chicago: University of Chicago Press, 1994. A study of "the myth of the assertive Congress" in foreign policymaking.

Lindsay, James M. *Congress and the Politics of U.S. Foreign Policy.* Baltimore: Johns Hopkins University Press, 1994. Another study of the limited role of Congress in foreign policy making.

Mezey, Michael L. *Congress, the President, and Public Policy.* Boulder, Colo.: Westview Press, 1989. A study of the changing role of Congress in various aspects of public policy.

Price, David E. *The Congressional Experience.* Boulder, Colo.: Westview Press, 1992. An interesting account of what it's like to be a representative by someone who was first a political science professor.

Schneier, Edward V., and Bertram Gross. *Congress Today.* New York: St. Martin's Press, 1993. An updating and expansion of Gross's classic 1953 book *The Legislative Struggle,* focusing on legislative strategy.

To find out what your own congressional district is like, check the volume for your state issued after the 1990 census by the U.S. Census Bureau. Or, for a capsule description, look up your congressional district in the *Almanac of American Politics,* published every two years by *National Journal,* or in *Politics in America: Members of Congress in Washington and At Home,* published every two years by *Congressional Quarterly.*

The Presidency

Above: President Bill Clinton meets with congressional leaders Thomas Foley (D-Wash.), the speaker of the House (*at left*), and Senate Majority Leader George Mitchell (D-Maine) (*right*) in the Cabinet Room of the White House to plan legislative strategy for the Clinton administration's first budget. *Right*: Vice President Al Gore stands by as the Senate votes on the budget, ready to cast the tiebreaking vote as presiding officer.

CHAPTER 12

Executive [presidential] leadership, to produce intended real change, must be solidly founded in power and principle.

—**James MacGregor Burns**

Everybody believes in democracy until he gets to the White House and then you begin to believe in dictatorship, because it's so hard to get things done. Every time you turn around, people resist you and even resist their own job.

—**An aide to President John F. Kennedy**[1]

The Roles and Powers of the President

Presidential Characteristics

Presidential Skills, Authority, Tools, and Resources

Running a Presidency

Governing and Making Policy

Reforming the Presidency

Bill Clinton assumed the presidency on January 20, 1993, committed to cutting the annual federal deficit—the amount that government spending each year exceeds revenue. The deficit, then averaging a quarter of a trillion dollars a year, had quadrupled the national debt to over 4 trillion dollars in the 12 years of Reagan-Bush Republican presidencies. Clinton's fiscal conservatism derived from his view that uncontrolled deficits prevent investments in the new technologies, worker training, and education needed to make the United States more competitive in the global economy and improve the deteriorating economic situation of the middle class. He had pledged to cut the deficit in half during his term. However, changing budgetary priorities is hard for a new president, who inherits a budget based on the goals of the outgoing administration.

The current budget process has three stages, once the president has submitted a proposed budget to Congress. First Congress passes a budget resolution setting general targets for spending and taxes for the fiscal year beginning the following October 1. The second stage, called "reconciliation," involves passing legislation and revising existing laws to implement whatever changes in tax laws and spending for particular programs have been required by the terms of the budget resolution. This is the stage in which Clinton could seek specific changes in

Reagan-Bush practices and policies. The final stage is passage—by October 1—of the 13 separate annual appropriations bills that provide money for the ongoing operations of the government. Clinton added a fourth stage—an "economic stimulus" package for the current fiscal year to be passed immediately to quickly improve the economy's performance.

A week after the election, Clinton began meeting with Democratic congressional leaders—Speaker Thomas Foley (D-Wash.), House Majority Leader Dick Gephardt (D-Mo.), and Senate Majority Leader George Mitchell (D-Me.) to get ideas and support for his deficit-control plans. He then met with committee chairs having jurisdiction over his economic proposals. Then at a bipartisan news conference he pledged to work for consensus on his forthcoming economic program.

Meanwhile, Democratic congressional leaders tried to enlist the support of newly elected members, arguing that they would sink or swim politically depending on whether their party leader, the president, successfully broke the Washington gridlock that had so troubled voters in 1992.

In mid-December 1992, Clinton began to generate public support for his proposals by hosting a two-day economic summit in Little Rock with 300 business leaders, economists, and interest group representatives. These nationally televised roundtable discussions gave Clinton a chance to demonstrate his policy and budgetary expertise as well as his concern for fiscal responsibility.

A month after his inauguration, Clinton presented his economic package in a nationally telecast address to Congress. Clinton's options in shaping the package had been limited by several key factors. First, interest payments on the national debt, over which no one had any control, were $210 billion a year. Second, two-thirds of the entire budget—Social Security and Medicare (which together totaled a third of all spending) and most defense spending—were considered politically untouchable. So the only possible sources of major cuts were "discretionary" spending (which included such items as the Federal Bureau of Investigation and air-traffic control) and aid to the poor, a traditional Democratic program that had taken serious hits throughout the previous 12 years. So the task for Clinton and the congressional Democrats was particularly difficult—and painful. The only way to achieve substantial deficit reduction acceptable to most Democrats was through tax increases, so Clinton proposed a $337 billion increase over five years, including a broad tax on energy use. He also proposed a $25 billion economic stimulus package, partly to strengthen weak spots in the economy and partly to appeal to Democratic liberals.

Most congressional Democrats were pleased, but the many interest groups that would suffer from the proposed cutbacks were upset. To limit opposition while the budget resolution was drafted, the administration and its congressional allies remained vague on likely spending changes. House leaders prohibited amendments to the budget document, and it passed easily in less than a month. The House also easily passed the economic stimulus bill the same day, again under a "no amendments" rule. Because Clinton had decided to depend entirely on Democratic votes rather than seeking bipartisan agreement in advance, all Republicans opposed the budget bill, and only three supported the stimulus package.

Major parts of the reconciliation bill then went to the Ways and Means Committee, where Chairman Dan Rostenkowski (D-Ill.) continued the partisan approach by convening committee Democrats alone for three days of meetings to draft and approve the bill's various provisions. When he finally convened the actual committee, the Democrats suppressed their differences and passed the bill on a party-line vote.

When the reconciliation bill came to the floor, the Democrats were short of the required majority because conservative Democrats insisted on provisions controlling Social Security and Medicare spending, so Majority Leader Gephardt, with the president's agreement, negotiated a compromise. The bill then passed by just 6 votes.

In the Senate, Republican opposition forced the leadership to withdraw the stimulus package. On the reconciliation bill, Democrats from energy-producing and energy-consuming states forced large cutbacks in the energy tax, but then had to cut Medicare spending to keep the required deficit-reduction effects. As in the House, the leadership negotiated compromises off the floor. The final vote was 49–49, with all Republicans and 6 Democrats opposed, so Vice President Al Gore cast the tie-breaking vote.

The conference committee took several months to reach a compromise. But lacking votes in both houses, the president had to take an active role. In an August 3 telecast, he asked the American people for support. But Minority Leader Robert Dole's (R-Kans.) telecast response urged citizens to express their opposition and supplied the phone number of Congress. Three million Americans called their representatives, most opposing the bill.

The next morning, Clinton met with the House Democratic Caucus, promising to make further spending cuts if conservatives supported the bill. He invited key members of Congress to the White House to watch him sign pledges to control entitlement spending and reduce the deficit-reduction targets. He lobbied undecided members by telephone.

Finally, on August 5 the House voted. The White House kept an open phone line to the cloakroom just off the floor so the president could lobby members up to the last moment. As the voting neared an end, the count stood at 217–216. Only one member had yet to vote: Marjorie Margolies-Mezvinski (D-Pa.), newly elected from a suburban Philadelphia district. She had announced her opposition earlier that afternoon, but just before the voting told Clinton she would support him if he needed her vote. He did. The final dramatic vote, 218–216, was carried live on CNN and C-SPAN.

The next evening, the Senate voted. Once again, Gore broke the tie.[2] The new president had won a victory, by the narrowest of margins, after using most of the tools at his disposal to convince members of his own party in Congress. In this chapter, we'll learn how the president wins—or loses—such battles, in Congress and elsewhere in the government, by answering the following questions:

What are the roles and powers of the president?

How do presidents differ in terms of personality and skills, and how do these qualities affect their success?

How do presidents develop and use presidential authority?

How do presidents manage the presidency?

How do presidents govern and make policy?

How might the presidency be reformed?

The Roles and Powers of the President

The president of the United States is frequently called the most powerful official of the most powerful nation on earth. He sits atop an executive branch of almost 3 million federal government bureaucrats and almost 2 million members of the armed forces—all of whom he is supposed to direct. He also governs a nation of 265 million people. How does he do all this? The Framers specified five roles for the office of president in the Constitution, and every president fulfills these. However, to be effective in today's much more complex world, a president must also play additional roles developed by innovative presidents over the country's two-hundred-year history.

The President's Constitutional Roles

Article II of the Constitution specifies the major roles of the presidency:

- *commander in chief* of the armed forces
- *chief administrator* of the executive branch departments ("he shall take Care that the Laws be faithfully executed") and the courts, nominating judges
- *chief diplomat*, making treaties while conducting the country's foreign relations
- *chief legislator,* proposing new laws to Congress and signing or vetoing laws passed by Congress
- *chief of state*, appointing ambassadors to and receiving ambassadors from other countries while representing the nation in ceremonial occasions.

The Framers rejected both an "elective kingship," in which an individual would be elected but then would rule as a king, and a plural executive or committee that would rule collectively, perhaps by majority vote, before settling on a president. This "vigorous executive," as Alexander Hamilton described the role in *The Federalist*, No. 70, was a controversial compromise between those wanting an executive with "competent," or effective, powers, and those seeking to limit presidential powers. The separation of powers between the legislative and executive branches departed from the British parliamentary system—the system used by most democracies around the world today (see Chapter 7).

The President's Legal Powers

The Constitution specifically grants the president certain powers to execute the five presidential roles. Among these **enumerated powers** are appointment, treaty making, the veto, and the right to pardon offenders. The appointment power enables the president to fulfill the role of chief administrator, while the treaty-making power is vital to the role of chief diplomat, for example.

TABLE 12.1

The Roles of the President

Informal Title	Responsibility	Source and/or Prime Originator	Occasion for the Innovation or Experience Encouraging It
1. Commander in chief	Leading nation's military forces	Constitution, Article II, sec. 2; Washington	Revolutionary War
2. Chief administrator	Managing executive branch and enforcing law	Constitution, Article II, sec. 2; Washington	Appoints and fires executive branch officials; meets with cabinet for the first time on November 20, 1791
3. Chief diplomat	Making and implementing foreign policy	Consitution, Article II, sec. 3; Washington	Issues neutrality proclamation
4. Chief legislator	Proposing bills to Congress and signing or vetoing bills passed	Consitution, Article I, sec. 7; Article II, sec. 3; Washington	Submits proposed legislation to Congress
5. Chief of state	Appointing and receiving ambassadors	Consitution, Article II, secs. 2, 3; Washington	Experience under Articles of Confederation
6. Party leader	Organizing party support for the presidential program	Jefferson	Assumes leadership of Democratic-Republicans
7. Representative of the people	Voicing the concerns of the people in government	Jackson	Proclaims himself the "people's president" and develops "spoils system"
8. Mobilizer of the government	Organizing and exercising the routine and emergency governmental wartime powers	Lincoln; Wilson	Lincoln during Civil War; Wilson in World War I
9. Moral leader	Offering moral guidance on issues to people	Lincoln; Wilson	Gives moral dimension to war aims, Lincoln in the Civil War and Wilson in World War I
10. Mobilizer of the people	Organizing the power of public opinion to influence government	Theodore Roosevelt	Uses presidency as "bully pulpit"; initiates press conferences
11. World leader	Exercising U.S. power in world affairs	McKinley; Theodore Roosevelt; Wilson	McKinley initiates Spanish-American War; Roosevelt intervenes in Latin America; Wilson leads World War I peace process
12. Social reformer	Developing and implementing programs to solve social problems	Theodore Roosevelt	Trust-busting and campaigning to regulate monopolies
13. Manager of the economy	Influencing economic developments through governmental action	Wilson; Franklin Roosevelt	Wilson initiates income tax, leads industrial war production; Franklin Roosevelt initiates anti-Depression government programs

Congress has passed laws (more formally known as statutes) granting the president further powers vital to fulfilling the role of chief administrator. These **statutory powers** include developing the budget for congressional approval (as we saw in the opening case study), governing by special powers in times of emergency such as war or economic crisis, and reorganizing the executive branch for greater efficiency.

The greatest growth in presidential powers, however, has probably been through what are called **inherent powers**—powers an executive branch of government requires to carry out its duties of implementation. The Constitution says that "the executive Power shall be vested in a President," and presidents have been engaged in defining through practice (*what works*) just what those words imply ever since. For example, the Constitution envisaged the president as *a* legislator, not *the chief* legislator; subsequent practice strengthened the president's role.

The Development of Presidential Roles and Powers

The legal words that describe the roles and powers of the president are only words until they are interpreted and put into practice by particular presidents. In the republic's early decades, the president was less important than Congress. A century ago, presidents often answered the front door of the White House themselves. But the power, prestige, and duties of the office have expanded as strong presidents have successfully claimed authority.

George Washington: Founding the Presidency

Called the father of his country for his service as chief military leader during the Revolution and as the first president, George Washington was also the father of the presidency. He set vital precedents for his successors in developing the powers necessary to carry out the five constitutionally specified roles. For example, the Constitution gives the president the right to appoint officials with senatorial approval, but says nothing about removing officials. Knowing that being *chief administrator* would mean little if he could not fire people whose work he disapproved of, Washington claimed that authority, too. He also established the practice of meeting regularly with the heads of the three departments created by the first Congress (State, War, and Treasury) plus the attorney general (the government's chief lawyer). These heads (called secretaries) of departments formed what we now call the **cabinet**—a Washington legacy not mentioned in the Constitution.

Washington also initiated the practice of submitting proposed legislation to Congress and seeking support for it there, and the president, rather than Congress, has been *chief legislator*, taking the lead in developing policy via legislation, ever since. In vetoing legislation he disliked or believed unconstitutional, Washington made the veto power, granted by the Constitution, an effective presidential tool. He also withheld from Congress his own papers and documents on a diplomatic matter on grounds that Congress was not constitutionally entitled to them. Some 150 years later, this precedent, which still protects presidential actions from the prying eyes of political opponents, was labeled *executive privilege*. As *commander in chief*, Washington used troops to put down a rebellion in Pennsylvania. And as *chief diplomat*, he made foreign policy without consulting Congress, surprising Congress and laying the groundwork for active foreign policymaking by subsequent presidents. In related action, he asserted his authority as *chief of state* to appoint and receive ambassadors and to host ceremonial occasions.

> **lame duck**
> A president, once reelected, cannot run again—he has had his wings clipped and can no longer fly. The term, first applied in the 1830s to politicians considered politically bankrupt, gradually came to be applied to officeholders whose power has been curtailed because they must soon leave office as a result of statutory limitation or defeat.

Washington's voluntary resignation after serving two terms, which made certain that the office would not become a lifetime possession of any one person, set a precedent observed by all his successors until Franklin Roosevelt, who was elected to four straight terms during the Great Depression and World War II. Roosevelt's controversial shattering of the precedent resulted in the Twenty-second Amendment, ratified in 1951, limiting a president to two terms.

This two-term limitation has a dual effect on a president's power. Once reelected, a president becomes a **lame duck**, losing clout with party members, who know they won't have to deal with him much longer. However, not having to worry about reelection, lame-duck presidents are freer to innovate and make controversial decisions for which they may be remembered.

The Presidency in the Nineteenth Century

Thomas Jefferson (1801–1809), the third president, added a sixth role to those specified in the Constitution: *party leader*. Jefferson retained close ties with his Democratic-Republican party supporters in Congress, and presidents have since been expected to lead their party in Congress, whether it has a majority or not.

Proclaiming himself the "people's president," Andrew Jackson (1829–1837) added a seventh role: *representative of the people*. In the people's name, he abolished the practice of allowing bureaucrats to hand their posts over to their sons and, on the principle that "to the victor belong the spoils," replaced many with people loyal to him to make the bureaucracy more responsive (Chapter 13). Another Jackson innovation was relying for advice less on the department heads (the official cabinet) than on his own informal advisors (called his **kitchen cabinet**). These two innovations increased the loyalty and support he received, making it easier to democratize the presidency. He also strengthened the presidency by using the veto with great effect and strengthened the Union in the Nullification Crisis of 1832–1833 by successfully resisting South Carolina's effort to *nullify* (render without legal effect within its boundaries) a national law—in this case, a tariff.

Abraham Lincoln expanded the president's roles and powers in time of war. Confronting the prospect

Members of the public flock to Andrew Jackson's inaugural celebration at the White House in 1829. Jackson pioneered a new presidential role: representative of the people.

of a civil war while Congress was not in session, Lincoln suspended certain constitutional liberties, spent funds that had not yet been appropriated, blockaded southern ports, and banned "treasonable correspondence" from the U.S. mails. These acts, of doubtful constitutionality, were performed in the name of his powers as commander-in-chief and chief executive and to "preserve, protect and defend the Constitution." He was, in sum, the originator of the emergency powers that underlie the eighth role of the president—*mobilizer of the government for war.*

Moreover, throughout the conflict—particularly in interpreting its meaning for the survival of democracy and an end to slavery—Lincoln pioneered a ninth role of the presidency: *moral leader*. His gift for speech, for moving rhetoric and for envisioning the present in the framework of history, elevated the authority of the president even as it inspired ordinary citizens. Lincoln's Gettysburg Address and Second Inaugural Address are well known. Here is what he had to say to Congress in December 1862 regarding his plan for compensated emancipation:

> In *giving* freedom to the *slave* we *assure* freedom to the *free*—honorable alike in what we give and what we preserve. We shall nobly save or meanly lose the last, best hope of earth. Other means may succeed; this could not fail. The way is plain, peaceful, generous, just—a way which if followed the world will forever applaud and God must forever bless.[3]

Lincoln's role as moral leader, acknowledged even in his own day, has endured to this day, changing forever what citizens look for in their president.

Abraham Lincoln delivers the Gettysburg Address, initiating the presidential role of moral leader.

Refounding the Presidency: Theodore Roosevelt and Woodrow Wilson

The modern presidency traces to the contributions of Theodore Roosevelt (1901–1909) and Woodrow Wilson (1913–1921). "Teddy" Roosevelt added a tenth role: *mobilizer of the people* to increase the influence of public opinion on government. To that end, he took advantage of the emerging mass-audience newspapers and magazines by inventing the presidential press conference, which he used as a "bully pulpit" to generate popular support for his programs.

Roosevelt also developed an eleventh presidential role, pioneered by his predecessor, William McKinley (assassinated in 1901), in the Spanish-American War of 1898: that of *world leader* exercising American power in world affairs. Capitalizing on the nation's newfound enthusiasm for empire and its traditional endorsement of "rugged individualism," Roosevelt developed the policy of "gunboat diplomacy," using armed forces to police the internal politics of Latin American countries to protect American lives and business interests and seize new colonies. He also used the new role of world leader to mediate a peace treaty between Russia and Japan in 1905.

Theodore Roosevelt was the first to play the presidential role of mobilizer of the people.

As a progressive, Roosevelt intervened in an unprecedented way in American business in the name of conservation and fairness. He protected natural resources against commercial plunder, striking miners against mineowners, and consumers against unsafe food and drugs. He also used government power to weaken monopolies ("trust-busting") and regulate the railroads. These policies, which he called the "Square Deal"—an astute use of the politics of language—developed a twelfth presidential role: *social reformer.*

> **conscription**
> This term comes from the Latin *conscribere* (*con*, meaning "together," plus *scribere*, "to write or enter in a list"). It was first used in a law passed by the French Republic in 1798 to require compulsory enlistment of citizens in the military and has been used by other governments since. Its more common name is "the draft."

Woodrow Wilson, formerly a political science professor, combined skill at party leadership with an activist conception of the presidency to forge a highly successful legislative record, including a lowered tariff for freer international trade, a new antitrust (antimonopoly) law, and new federal regulation of banking and business. He also introduced an income tax on wealthy individuals after the Sixteenth Amendment was ratified in 1913—which enabled the federal budget to expand from $800 million a year to over $18 billion in 1919. The Overman Act of 1918, passed during World War I, gave the president virtually dictatorial power over the economy for the duration of the war.

Wilson thus created a thirteenth role for the president: *manager of the economy.* In this role he transformed the United States into a modern nation-state and made World War I the first total war, compelling the country's military forces, augmented by conscription, and its industrial productive forces, financed through the new income tax revenue, to serve the war effort.

Taken as a whole, these Wilsonian measures marked the end of the limited government favored by the Framers. Although some of this authority expired with the end of the war, the innovations set the stage for the bureaucratization of government.[4] Wilson thus laid the groundwork for the large and powerful executive branch we have today, but at the price of the efficiency and personal mastery of previous activist presidents. Troubled by Congress's tendency to dominate the president, he argued that only the president, with a national constituency, could get both Congress and the people to deliberate on policy questions. He believed that a president derived his authority from the people and should therefore remain alert to their moods and interests to maintain that authority and foster policy cooperation.[5] Wilson used the devices pioneered by Roosevelt to bring the president closer to the people, creating what some call the "plebiscitary presidency."

Wilson also attempted to revive the role of moral leader by calling the World War "the war to end all wars" and "to make the world safe for democracy," and engineering a peace plan that created a new League of Nations to police the peace. However, the Senate refused to ratify the treaty, and Wilson's effort to take his case to the people failed. A backlash to his energetic efforts to expand the authority of the presidency led temporarily to a weaker presidency.

The Modern Presidency: Franklin Roosevelt and His Successors

The office languished under passive presidents until the Great Depression enabled Franklin Delano Roosevelt to launch the "New Deal"—an activist

Franklin Delano Roosevelt delivers a radio broadcast during the Great Depression; he pioneered the presidential role of manager of the economy.

domestic agenda greatly expanding the authority and size of the executive branch. Roosevelt was a charismatic orator, an effective campaigner who exploited the new national radio networks in marshaling public support, and an innovative organizer. He developed two special groups of assistants. A team of experts from universities, called his "brains trust," developed new policies and legislation, while a set of informal political advisors and assistants formed FDR's version of the "kitchen cabinet." The broad range of new programs led to irreversible governmental domination of the economy under presidential guidance. Roosevelt's mastery of the presidency during the twin crisis of the Depression and World War II won him four terms—twice as many as any other president—in which he drew together all of the previous elements of presidential roles and powers.

On his sudden death, Roosevelt was succeeded by his little-known vice president, Harry Truman (1945–1953), who proved to be an activist but not an innovator. Dwight Eisenhower (1953–1961) temperamentally and philosophically believed that strict limits should be placed on the exercise of presidential authority. He was particularly hesitant to use federal power to enforce racial integration in the public schools after the 1954 Supreme Court decision declaring segregation unconstitutional (Chapter 16). Nor was he willing to exert moral authority to encourage integration by asserting that racial segregation was morally wrong.

John Kennedy (1961–1963) defeated Eisenhower's vice president, Richard Nixon, on the slogan "Let's get America moving again," and proposed various legislative initiatives, including the first major civil rights bill in almost a century, but his legislation was languishing in Congress when he was assassinated. His successor, Lyndon Johnson (1963–1969), capitalized on the public distress at Kennedy's assassination and his own southern origins to further develop the role of moral leader, getting strong civil rights and voting rights bills through Congress and then engineering a massive expansion of the government's role in social reform (the War on Poverty) and a package of social and economic reform measures (the Great Society) including urban renewal and aid to education. However, Johnson's activism in getting the country into an unwinnable war in Vietnam—morally questioned by many others publicly and by Johnson privately[6]—led to his decision not to run for election to a second full term.

Richard Nixon (1969–1974), his successor, claimed to be a conservative but still extended the social reformer role with the first major efforts at environmental protection and new worker safety and health programs and once again asserted the president's role as world leader by developing closer relations with communist adversaries China and the Soviet Union. Still, as we'll see shortly, he was forced to resign in the face of likely impeachment for abuse of presidential powers at home and abroad. Ronald Reagan (1981–1989), while professing opposition to governmental social reform, took an activist approach in attempting with mixed success to curtail that government involvement, exploiting the powers of the presidency to force change through large-scale (often secret) use of his presidential prerogatives such as executive orders. George Bush (1989–1993) attempted to claim Reagan's conservative mantle but without Reagan's activism, setting the stage for Clinton's more activist but politically moderate presidency.

Presidential Characteristics

In the two centuries of presidential governance, the trend has been toward an expansion of the roles, especially by strong activist presidents. While most have entered the office with similar qualifications, their personal strengths and weaknesses have shaped the institution of the presidency and influenced their administrations' successes and failures as well.

Presidential Qualifications, Experience, and Job Requirements

Most presidents have been remarkably similar in background, even though the Constitution sets only three minimal requirements: being a native-born citizen of the United States, being at least 35 years old, and having lived in the United States for at least 14 years. All presidents have been white males; most have had Anglo-Saxon ancestry; all but one have been Protestants. John Kennedy, a Roman Catholic, overcame resistance to Catholic nominees by winning in 1960. Jews, atheists, and African Americans still face such resistance, although widespread interest in the prospect of General Colin Powell's presence on the 1996 Republican ticket may indicate a new openness to African-American candidates. Women still face resistance, and Walter Mondale's crushing 1984 defeat by Ronald Reagan after selecting Representative Geraldine Ferraro (D-N.Y.) as his running mate did not improve women's prospects, even though polling showed that she was not a significant factor in the outcome.

Any differences in upbringing and education tend to be balanced by rather similar work experience. Many presidential candidates are trained as lawyers, but few actually practice law for long, instead working their way up through elective politics—most often through a governorship or Congress. Eisenhower, a retired military general serving as a college president, was the only exception in generations. Military experience was expected of candidates, but as war has become less frequent and less popular, finding attractive candidates with military service records has become harder. By 1996, most candidates for either major party's nomination lacked any military experience, and Bob Dole's effort to make Clinton's avoidance of military service an issue failed. "Outsider" status—never having served in the federal government—can be an advantage when antigovernment sentiment is strong, but outsiders may have trouble working with Congress, as did former governors Carter and Clinton. Figure 12.1 portrays the governmental routes taken by all major-party presidential nominees since 1932.

448 Chapter 12 The Presidency

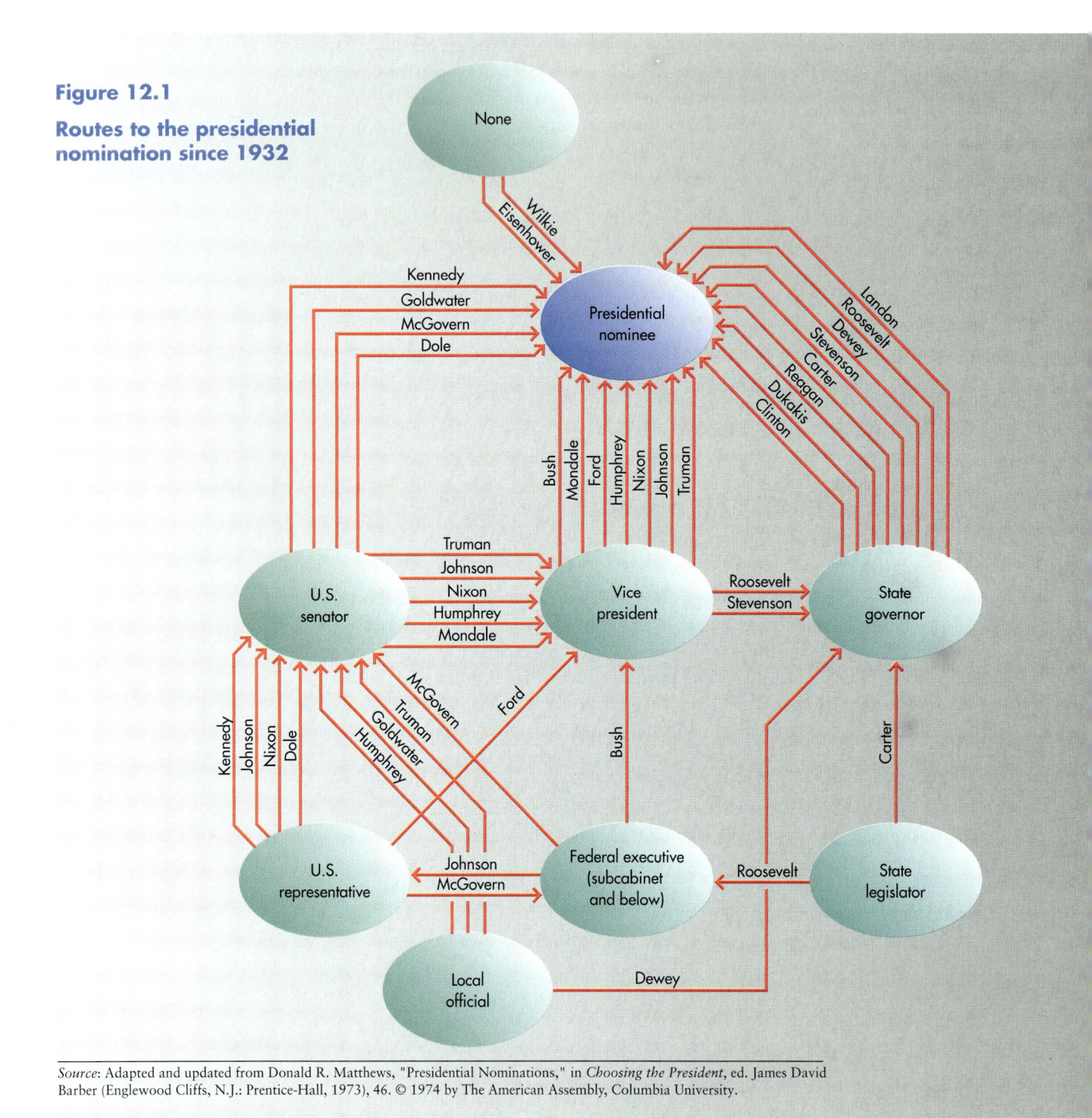

Figure 12.1
Routes to the presidential nomination since 1932

Source: Adapted and updated from Donald R. Matthews, "Presidential Nominations," in *Choosing the President*, ed. James David Barber (Englewood Cliffs, N.J.: Prentice-Hall, 1973), 46. © 1974 by The American Assembly, Columbia University.

Johnson and Nixon, with long national elective political careers, were probably the best prepared recent presidents, yet each overstepped political bounds in ways that terminated his career prematurely. So previous political experience may not prevent disastrous presidential mistakes such as Vietnam and Watergate. As Lyndon Johnson lamented to his aide Bill Moyers on taking office, "You know, Bill, I've been in both the House and Senate and in all that time no one told me how to be

President."[7] Despite an impressive government-service record, Bush had difficulty reading the political pulse accurately—perhaps because most of his service was appointive rather than elective. What accounts for these disappointments and failures? It may be that the job requirements have simply become too great for *any* individual.

Presidential Personality

The office of president makes great psychological demands on a person. The president must establish and maintain a successful relationship with the American people at the same time that he must coordinate policy goals with members of Congress and executive branch bureaucrats, all under severe resource limitations and time constraints.[8]

Growing recognition of these psychological demands has led experts who study presidents to agree that certain personality traits are always desirable in a president, among them charisma, intelligence, integrity, and decisiveness. Among other traits commonly thought important are honesty, determination, tenacity, and aggressiveness.[9] Political scientist James David Barber's study of what he calls "presidential character"—style, character, and worldview, as well as childhood experiences—assesses and predicts presidential performance, as the box nearby reports. Barber's focus on presidential character implies that if voters select the right person for the job, things will go well. Experience suggests differently, however. President Gerald Ford's first press secretary observed that success in the White House is largely determined by "the possession of personal attributes that are in public demand at an hour of public need"[10]—something no president can control.

Whatever attributes a president brings to the presidency, the job will affect the occupant. Bruce Buchanan's study of recent presidents finds four effects that may have serious implications for presidential performance:

- Stress from the overwhelming demands of the job may bring on a physical and/or emotional breakdown (Wilson).
- Deference by colleagues may cause and accentuate distortions in perception (Johnson).
- Frustration over obstacles may erode personal scruples (Nixon).
- Dissonance—a conflict of views within one's own mind—may encourage equivocation and lying (Nixon).

Such experiences, Buchanan fears, may lead presidents to base decisions on faulty grounds, distorted information, or wishful thinking and may lead to battling with other legitimate powers, such as Congress or the courts, or even risking war to save face.[11]

Presidential Health

Until recently, neither the media nor the public paid any attention to the health of the president unless one fell seriously ill, nor did they inquire about the health of candidates. Woodrow Wilson, who had a stroke

personality
This term is used by analysts as shorthand for psychological predispositions or character and temperament—such qualities as an inclination toward activism or passivity, a need for privacy, a sense of self-esteem, and a drive or motivation for power or for achievement.

Political Actors Disagree

The leading student of presidential character is political scientist James David Barber, who published the first edition of his book *The Presidential Character* in 1972. Barber divides all presidents along two dimensions in two ways, as the diagram depicts. First, he separates those he calls the *actives*, who devote a lot of energy to the job, from the *passives*, who seldom take initiatives. Second, he divides both groups into the *positives*, who seem generally happy and optimistic, and the *negatives*, who seem sad or irritable.[1] Combining these two distinctions yields four categories of presidents, each with a unique character and approach to the office.

Presidential Character

Experts disagree over how accurately Barber's categories capture the key qualities of presidential personality. Some point out that if the picture of a president's personality is faulty, then conclusions about how he goes about his work will also be faulty. For example, Barber warns that the *active-*

Emotional Attitude Toward the Presidency

	Positive	Negative
Active	Tends to show confidence, flexibility, a focus on producing results through rational mastery	Tends to emphasize ambitious striving, aggressiveness, a focus on the struggle for power against a hostile environment
	Examples: Jefferson, Franklin Roosevelt, Truman, Kennedy, Ford, Carter, Bush, Clinton	Examples: John Adams, Wilson, Hoover, Lyndon Johnson, Nixon
Passive	Tends to show receptiveness, compliance, other-directedness, plus a superficial hopefulness masking inner doubt	Tends to withdraw from conflict and uncertainty and to think in terms of vague principles of duty and regular procedure
	Examples: Madison, Taft, Harding, Reagan	Examples: Washington, Coolidge, Eisenhower

(Energy Level in Doing the Job)

Source: Adapted from James David Barber, *The Presidential Character*, 3rd ed. (Englewood Cliffs, N.J.: Prentice-Hall, 1985).

that destroyed his health, remarked that "men of ordinary physique and discretion cannot be Presidents and live, if the strain be not somehow relieved," suggesting that otherwise the country would have to pick its presidents "from among wise and prudent athletes—a small class."[12] Franklin Roosevelt suffered partial paralysis from polio, but the press refrained from photographing him in his wheelchair in order not to alarm the public and did not report his final serious illness until he died in office in 1945. Thereafter, illnesses were usually reported, but not always their severity.[13] Dwight Eisenhower suffered three serious illnesses in office: a heart attack, an intestinal problem, and a minor stroke. John Kennedy suffered from a chronic back ailment that required special braces, exercises, and chairs, and his Addison's disease also required regular doses of very strong medicine—a fact officially denied until well

homeopathy

Homeopathy is a medical practice using remedies that are made primarily of natural substances specially diluted and agitated. Widely practiced in Europe and elsewhere, it is increasingly popular in the United States.

negatives may have difficulty controlling their aggressiveness because they are motivated by anxieties and guilt. They also try to resolve their own psychological problems in the public sphere by winning struggles on their own rather than compromising with other political actors. The result may be fixation on a politically disastrous policy, such as Woodrow Wilson's refusal to compromise with the Senate on the League of Nations, Lyndon Johnson's rigidity on Vietnam, and Richard Nixon's covering up of Watergate.

Other experts contest such conclusions. For example, Alexander George, author of a psycho-biography of Wilson, attributes Wilson's uncompromising behavior to his strong moral principles, in contrast to Nixon, who, he claims, was driven by personal ambition. Barber grants that Nixon may deserve a special subcategory of *active-negative*—those threatened not by defeat of their moral principles but rather by attacks on their independence. But George argues that if Nixon deserves this special subcategory, then so do Herbert Hoover and Lyndon Johnson, for other reasons.[2]

It is also unclear whether Barber was correct to classify George Bush as an *active-positive*.[3] Although active in foreign affairs, Bush often seemed uninterested in actually governing—in controlling the bureaucracy and implementing his own policy agenda. Instead, he seemed to prefer behind-the-scenes personal contacts and public ceremonial events. But as we'll see, this approach allowed him to expand presidential power by governing without Congress.

By contrast, Clinton, another *active-positive*, had an intense interest in politics, policy, and governance. When confronted with political opposition, Clinton's inclination was usually to attempt to construct a compromise, as he did on welfare reform in 1996 and tax reform in 1997.

Disputes over Barber's work, not so much among academics as among journalists,[4] have led some to suggest that we need new categories for assessing our presidents' characters and predicting presidential performance.

---

[1] James David Barber, *The Presidential Character,* 4th ed. (Englewood Cliffs, N.J.: Prentice-Hall, 1992).
[2] See Alexander George, "Assessing Presidential Character," *World Politics* 26 (January 1974): 234–282.
[3] James David Barber, "The Silver Spoon in Bush's Mouth, and Policies," *New York Times,* January 27, 1990.
[4] For a thoughtful examination of Barber's theory and some of the scholarly debate over it, see Michael Nelson, "The Psychological Presidency," in *The Presidency and the Political System,* ed. Michael Nelson, 3rd ed. (Washington, D.C.: Congressional Quarterly Press, 1990), Chapter 8.

---

after his assassination. Lyndon Johnson had gallbladder and hernia surgery as president, and he once suffered from pneumonia. The public was told when Reagan had cancerous growths removed from his colon and face, but how close he came to death from a would-be assassin's bullet was not revealed until he was safely convalescing. Bush was treated for an overactive thyroid (Graves' disease) and for a while took a drug some considered mind-altering while he was making decisions that led to the Gulf War. Clinton took regular shots for his allergies until he switched to homeopathic remedies.

Most people now agree that voters should know the medical history of candidates as well as the state of health of a sitting president because these conditions are likely to affect the president's ability to serve effectively. But there is still no way to guarantee public access to such information if a candidate or president seeks to conceal it.

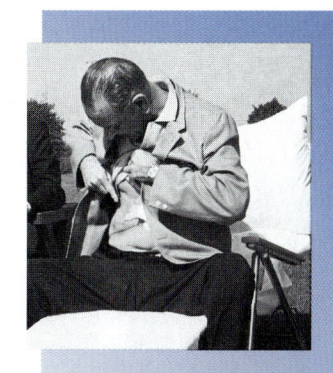

President Lyndon Johnson shows reporters the scar from a gallbladder operation he underwent while he was in office.

Presidential Skills, Authority, Tools, and Resources

While scholars do not agree on the most desirable personal characteristics of presidents,[14] they recognize that the key to an effective presidency is getting other people to comply. The ability to perform the following tasks seems essential to presidential effectiveness today:

- *Managing information.* Because a president cannot know enough about most matters to decide without assistance, he must manage the flow of information to him so that he gets what is most vital.
- *Managing people.* A president should be appropriately accessible, even to in-house critics who disagree with him, and should take others' recommendations seriously even when they conflict with his inclinations.
- *Managing the policy process.* A president must be able to delegate responsibilities to competent subordinates rather than trying to micromanage.
- *Deciding.* A president should make good decisions in a timely manner rather than deciding prematurely or procrastinating.
- *Selling policy "inside the Beltway."* A president should be able to convince Washington insiders using his political acumen or insight about individual motives and his ability to bargain and build coalitions.
- *Selling policy "outside the Beltway."* A president should be able to convince the American people to accept his decisions as appropriate by effectively using political rhetoric and by employing whatever authority he has.

No president will be equally competent at each of these key tasks, but presidents who show talent in most of them will likely be effective in getting and exercising the authority that makes the presidency work.

Presidential Authority

Political actors have authority—the assumed or recognized capacity to exercise power—when others recognize that they can use the necessary resources (force, money, information) to get their way if they choose to. When people recognize this authority as legal or otherwise appropriate, it is said to be *legitimate*—and is therefore likely to be even more effective.

Powers specified in the Constitution or the laws, or developed by custom or convention, tend to become attached to the office of the presidency in the minds of citizens and those of the president's subordinates as well. In other words, the president's orders and requests have a legitimacy that induces compliance. But a president perceived as unethical can lose this legitimacy, as happened to Nixon in the waning days of his presidency, when subordinates disregarded his orders. A president perceived as ineffective can lose this authority, as happened to Clinton when his massive ef-

---

"inside the Beltway" and "outside the Beltway"

These terms refer to people and concerns centered within the federal government as opposed to those residing outside the capital and so lacking the "insider" perspective or emphasis. They derive from the Washington Beltway, the local name for the interstate highway that rings Washington, D.C., and nearby suburbs.

The Politics of Language

What Should the President Be Called?

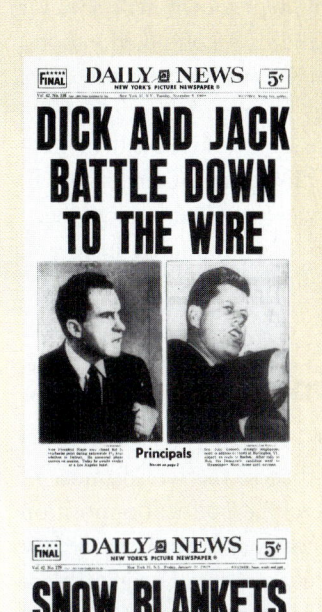

The American presidency was the first such office in the world, so when George Washington was inaugurated, there was no precedent to guide what he should be called. Almost immediately the issue of his title was debated in Congress. The Senate, as the more elitist chamber, seemed to favor "His Elective Majesty" or "His Elective Highness" or maybe even "His Mightiness." John Adams, Washington's vice president, suggested "His Most Benign Highness" and "His Highness, President of the United States and Protector of Their Liberties," a proposal that was roundly booed (and prompted some senators to chide Adams as "His Rotundity" and "His Superfluous Excellency," in return). Ultimately the more democratic House of Representatives prevailed. The new chief executive would be called, simply, "President of the United States." While this title was used in public, in private Washington's longtime friends continued to call him "the General."

When John Kennedy took office at age 43 he was the youngest president ever elected, and some newspapers referred to him in headlines as "Jack"—the name his friends had used. "The White House"—as presidential aides are usually referred to (because it gives *them* more authority)—quickly let it be known that "the President" (as aides call him because it gives *him* more authority) thought this nickname demeaned the dignity (by which they meant the authority) of the president and asked that it be stopped. Newspapers, believing "Kennedy" too long, compromised on "JFK," thereby preserving presidential authority. The Kennedy administration was particularly sensitive to the issue of presidential authority because Kennedy was succeeding a military hero, General Dwight Eisenhower, who had brought with him so much personal authority that he had no problem with newspapers calling him "Ike."

When James Earl Carter took office, he let it be known that he preferred to be called "Jimmy Carter" in the press, and William Jefferson Clinton, another southerner, has insisted on being called "Bill Clinton." But even longtime friends are expected to use "Mr. President," the title that has become a tradition over the past two hundred years.

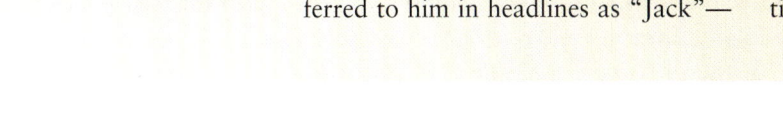

fort at comprehensive health-care reform collapsed. Furthermore, an innovative, activist president may need to expand the authority inherited with the office.

Sustaining Presidential Authority

Efforts to solidify and even increase presidential authority often build on the symbolic and ceremonial aspects of the office, beginning with the inauguration ceremony, with its oaths sworn on Bibles, parade, and bands playing "Hail to the Chief." Presidential authority is also sustained by the president's living in an official residence, the White House, and his conducting such official business as welcoming other heads of state and presiding over special dinners and other ceremonial events. Presidents speak from a rostrum graced with the presidential seal and an American flag. They are called—even by their close friends—"Mr. President," as the box above explains.

This classic photograph shows Harry Truman at a desk in the Truman Library in Independence, Missouri, with the famous sign "The Buck Stops Here."

Are symbols gaining over substance? The vision that presidents offer seldom goes beyond general values.[15] One scholar concludes, "The setting of a speech now dictates what a president will say. Or presidential staffs do. Or audience composition does. Or political traditions do. Or media coverage does. The thoughts and feelings of presidents themselves rarely do."[16] Late in his second term, President Reagan, who got his start in movies and then moved to television, told an interviewer: "There have been times in this office when I've wondered how you could do the job if you hadn't been an actor."[17]

Exercising Presidential Authority

Although the American presidency is considered the most powerful political office in the world, most of its occupants complain that they are powerless to overcome political opposition and achieve their objectives. The presidency is not a command office. As Harry Truman contemplated turning the office over to former general Dwight Eisenhower, he mused: "He'll sit here and he'll say, 'Do this! Do that!' *And nothing will happen.* Poor Ike—it won't be a bit like the army."[18] "People talk about the powers of a President, all the powers that a Chief Executive has, and what he can do. Let me tell you something—from experience!" Truman remarked after three years on the job. "The President may have a great many powers given to him in the Constitution, and may have certain powers under certain laws which are given to him by the Congress of the United States; but the principal power that the President has is to bring people in and try to persuade them to do what they ought to do without persuasion. That's what the powers of the President amount to."[19] While presidents certainly try to persuade other political actors to do their bidding, effective presidents also build coalitions to get support for their policies and lead the public at large in the direction they want to go.

Most of the important things a president wants to do require cooperation from other parts of government. Congress must pass legislation and appropriate money to establish and fund programs. Bureaucrats must follow orders to develop and carry out programs. The courts, if asked, may rule on whether programs and the laws establishing them are constitutional. And the people decide whether or not to accept the programs and the president who proposes them. In other words, most presidential powers are shared powers. Presidents must persuade others to accept their position—their beliefs about *what is, what's right,* and *what works.* In the words of a classic study of presidential power by Richard Neustadt,

> The essence of a President's persuasive task with congressmen and everybody else is to induce them to believe that what he wants of them is what their own appraisal of their own responsibilities requires them to do in their interest, not his. Because men may differ in their views on public policy, because differences in outlook stem from differences in duty—duty to one's office, one's constituents, oneself—that task is bound to be more like collective bargaining than like a reasoned argument.[20]

While many Americans feel that bargaining and compromising with the many competing political actors and interest groups are an unfortunate requirement of the system of shared powers, others call it a virtue. "There is merit to a system," writes Barbara Kellerman, "that tends to stall unless the governor consents to negotiate with representatives of the governed . . . in keeping with the democratic ideal that power be shared."[21] Negotiation in a system of several parties, regional differences, many interest groups, and cross-cutting issues usually involves building coalitions. By the time presidents take office, they have already developed two different coalitions of voters: one to win their party's nomination and a broader one to win the general election, as we saw in Chapter 10. Once in office, presidents must then develop a third: a **governing coalition**—a collection of groups or special interests in the public at large that generally support the president's program.[22]

If the president's governing coalition is strong and cohesive enough, it will arise in Congress as well, making the president more successful. At the outset, the coalition's strength depends on how broad the president's electoral support was and on whether members of Congress support the chief executive, perhaps fearing electoral disapproval if they do not. Bill Clinton, who took office with an unusually small electoral coalition as the victor in a three-way race, soon found his early governing coalition shrinking. Congressional Democrats decided that Clinton had become so unpopular in their districts that voters might punish them next election for supporting him. Many lost anyway, and Republicans gained control of Congress, only to see Clinton's popular support rebound at their expense. Clinton's limited legislative success in his fourth year depended on building momentary coalitions that included Republicans—an arrangement that brought him criticism, as effective coalition-building often does, for what ordinary citizens tend to consider unprincipled "politics as usual." When he won reelection and Republicans retained control of Congress, Clinton made even greater efforts to govern across party lines.

Clinton, like his predecessors, found that persuasion and bargaining are not enough. A president must also provide leadership by projecting a vision of *what's right*—of where the country should go—that the people as a whole and other political actors find compelling. "The Presidency is . . . preeminently a place of moral leadership," remarked Franklin Roosevelt, a master at it. "All our great Presidents were leaders of thought at times when certain historic ideas in the life of the nation had to be clarified."[23]

Articulating a vision that clarifies the hopes, dreams, and responsibilities of the American people can energize them to express their support for the president's preferred policies and even sometimes to volunteer their help. To some presidents, such visionary leadership seems to come naturally. Inspired by President Kennedy's inaugural challenge to "Ask not what your country can do for you—ask what you can do for your country,"[24] thousands of Americans joined the Peace Corps, established by executive order six weeks later. When he declared in May 1961 that the United States should commit itself to putting a man on the moon by the end of the decade, the country's politicians and scientists united in support of the expensive Apollo program that eventually did just that. George Bush, on the other hand, complained that he didn't know how to handle what he called "the vision thing," and voters in 1992 agreed. Dole, facing the same difficulty, was no match for Clinton's future-oriented campaign rhetoric in 1996.

Whether visionary leaders or not, all presidents eventually resort to the leadership strategy that political scientists often call "going public,"[25] promoting policies

Watergate and the Nixon Presidency

On June 17, 1972, five men were arrested in the Democratic party offices in the Watergate office building in Washington. The following January the seven men eventually indicted for the break-in were tried. Five confessed, and the other two were found guilty by the jury. Federal Judge John Sirica gave long sentences to the group. In response, one of the men, James McCord, wrote Sirica a letter saying that the men were under political pressure to plead guilty, that some had lied during the trial, and that the break-in had been approved by higher-ups. Sirica read the letter aloud in court, in effect reopening the case.

One result was hearings on the affair by a Senate select committee, which began May 17, 1973, and ended several months later. Another result was Nixon's appointment of Archibald Cox as special Watergate prosecutor. Cox took over the Justice Department's investigation on May 18, 1973, and served until Nixon ordered him fired in what was called the "Saturday Night Massacre" of October 20. Yet another result was greater investigation by the media. That investigation was hampered by what came to be called a White House cover-up. Dan Rather, then CBS's White House correspondent, termed it "the deadly daily diet of deceit sent us from the White House.... They lied, schemed, threatened, and cajoled to prevent network correspondents from getting a handle on the story. And they succeeded."[1]

As the scandal unfolded—despite the cover-up—Nixon aides increasingly claimed that the president was being "hounded from office" by the press. However, the conventional account of Watergate as primarily a media achievement is at best only partially true. Indeed, Bob Woodward and Carl Bernstein's memoir, *All the President's Men,* and the subsequent movie highlight not only Judge Sirica's role but also—especially—the contribution of "Deep Throat."[2] "Deep Throat" was the source of major leaks to "Woodstein," as the pair came to be known. His or her identity is still not publicly known. The common supposition is that he or she was a government bureaucrat close enough to the parties involved to be very well informed but far enough away to escape suspicion.

Other members of the executive branch were also important. Clearly, Special Prosecutor Cox and his successor, Leon Jaworski, played vital roles in pursuing the case in the face of White House resistance and obstruction. John Dean, once the president's counsel and then a leading witness against his White House colleagues before the Senate Watergate Committee, was also important. Another important figure was Alexander Butterfield, previously a Nixon aide, who revealed in his Senate testimony that Nixon had installed a system to tape all his conversations. Many still believe that without this knowledge and the texts of tapes that were eventually obtained, Nixon would have been able to serve his full term as president.

But those tapes would never have reached the special prosecutor or the Congress and the public were it not for the federal courts, which ruled that

in Washington by appealing directly to the American people for support. When an effective president "goes public" by getting constituents to put pressure on their representatives, as every president since Teddy Roosevelt has, he generally puts the argument in terms of the public interest—an interest he alleges is opposed by well-organized special interests. A classic formulation was Reagan's presentation of his tax reform proposal in a national television address in 1985: "The proposal I am putting forth tonight for America's future will free us from the grip of special interests and create a binding commitment to the only special interest that counts, you, the people who pay America's bills. It will create millions of new jobs for working people and it will replace the politics of envy with a spirit of partnership."[26] To be effective in exercising presidential authority, a president must not only have a wide range of political skills but must also "appear presidential"—that is, well-suited to the office—and must offer a vision of *what's right*.[27]

Nixon had to turn the tapes over once they were subpoenaed. (In recent years, the National Archives has been making the tapes available to the public.)

Even after the court rulings, the media revelations, and the bureaucratic leaks, Nixon was still president—with two and a half years left to serve. Why did he then resign? While all this was going on, Nixon's popularity was taking a severe beating. By the time he resigned, only one in four Americans approved of his conduct in the presidency.

The articles of impeachment that the House Judiciary Committee voted on through those final days were an appalling indictment. Article I cited the cover-up, an illegal obstruction of justice on a grand scale. It was passed by a vote of 27 to 11 on July 27, 1974. Article II covered abuse of power, with emphasis on a wide range of violations of citizens' constitutional rights. It passed by a vote of 28 to 10 on July 29. Article III cited Nixon's defiance of congressional subpoenas commanding him to turn over tapes and documents. It passed the next day.

These articles were a stunning bill of particulars, of "high Crimes and Misdemeanors" (as the Constitution defines impeachable offenses). But offenses rather similar to these had been committed at one time or another by other presidents.

Still, Nixon's presidency had been one in which people in and around the White House had been guilty of breaking and entering, illegal wiretapping, theft of private documents, lying to a grand jury, falsifying records presented to a grand jury, and various violations of campaign finance laws. Thus, the "tone" of the Nixon administration was not one to foster concern for legality among its own employees. And Nixon himself escaped trial and punishment for his own role in Watergate and its cover-up; he was pardoned by Gerald Ford, the very man whom he had chosen to be vice president when Spiro Agnew was forced to resign because of corruption.

Some would say that Nixon's fall was the result of his administration's perpetration of so many misdeeds at the same time, and at such high levels, and of discovery of his own involvement in these affairs. Still others would point to his having ignored Congress, alienated the bureaucracy, downgraded the cabinet, ceased to attend adequately to the special interest groups, and lost the support of the Republican party by running for reelection on his own.[3] As a result, this analysis goes, he had lost the political base that is essential to effective governance. The best explanation of his fall may be this unique combination of transgression and erosion in an era when politics had become very visible and public expectations of leaders had increased.

---

[1] Dan Rather, "Watergate on TV," *Newsday,* December 16, 1973.
[2] Bob Woodward and Carl Bernstein, *All the President's Men* (New York: Simon & Schuster, 1974).
[3] Nicholas Hoffman, "The Breaking of a President," *Penthouse,* March 1977.

Abusing—and Even Losing—Presidential Authority

The exercise of presidential authority or cruder forms of power can also be overdone, of course. Richard Nixon was accused of such abuses of presidential power as meddling with the Internal Revenue Service by trying to get confidential information on citizens' tax returns and then ordering the IRS to investigate them, ordering illegal wiretapping of certain citizens, maintaining a secret spy unit in the office of the president, and covering up illegal actions by subordinates. These abuses and their aftermath, which collectively came to be called *Watergate,* are summarized in the box nearby.

Much of Nixon's abuse of power was attributed to the growth of "an imperial presidency"[28]—presidents acting more like all-powerful emperors than like elected officials in a system of separation of powers. His elected successor Jimmy Carter

Jimmy Carter delivers a telecast wearing a sweater both to emphasize the importance of conserving fuel oil by keeping the thermostat low and to demonstrate his "deimperializing" of the presidency.

therefore sought to "deimperialize" the office by actions such as carrying his own luggage while campaigning, walking up Pennsylvania Avenue during his inauguration rather than riding in the presidential limousine, and selling the presidential yacht. However, some thought he went too far, and his successors have sought to strike a balance between commanding authority and "common man" qualities. Reagan, for example, combined a "folksy" image with a "tough on communism" stance. Yet Reagan's very emphasis on image seems to have encouraged subordinates to take initiatives on their own, perhaps believing they were doing what the president would have wished them to do if only he had told them. The Iran-Contra affair (see the box on page 470) is a case in point, evidence that detachment from presidential authority can undermine it just as quickly as direct orders that push the limits of legitimacy.

Special Presidential Tools

To achieve their objectives presidents can, of course, use existing laws (which can also be amended or reinterpreted) to develop and implement programs. However, they have been ingenious in developing additional tools, foremost among them the executive order, the executive agreement and its recent complement, the congressional-executive agreement, executive privilege (see above), the veto, and various prerogative powers.

The Executive Order

The president's responsibility to "take Care that the Laws be faithfully executed" has been used by every president since George Washington to justify the **executive order**, which requires agencies or individuals to take specified actions, thus bypassing Congress. Most of the more than 13,000 executive orders presidents have issued are routine efforts to achieve uncontroversial goals such as implementing laws passed by Congress, but some have been issued when presidents have had to act alone or quickly, as in national emergencies, and some have been kept secret because they would be controversial.

Occasionally, an executive order is challenged in court on the grounds that it oversteps the president's authority, but the courts have upheld the president's power to issue such orders even when they have declared a specific order unconstitutional. Presidents Johnson, Nixon, and Reagan significantly extended the use of executive orders: Johnson to fight a war in Vietnam without having Congress first declare it, Nixon to abolish programs and agencies established by Congress without its approval, and Reagan to conduct illicit military operations in Central America against the explicit orders of Congress. All three also used their powers less openly to involve the Federal Bureau of Investigation (FBI) and the Central Intelligence Agency (CIA) in domestic spying and violation of the civil liberties of citizens.[29]

Executive Agreements

The Constitution requires that treaties with foreign nations be ratified by a two-thirds vote of the Senate. Since the founding, presidents have bypassed this onerous requirement by making **executive agreements** with other countries. An executive agreement is, practically speaking, a treaty that will not be submitted to the Senate.

The practice was upheld by the Supreme Court in 1920 in *Missouri v. Holland*.[30] In recent years, presidents have made increasing use of **congressional-executive agreements** when an agreement with other countries would require congressional implementation. In these cases, the president has sought advance agreement from Congress to make the agreement on condition that Congress approve it by a simple majority of both houses rather than by a two-thirds majority of the Senate—a provision known as "fast track." Both the North America Free Trade Agreement (NAFTA) and the expansion of the General Agreement on Tariffs and Trade into the World Trade Organization were congressional-executive agreements approved by both houses in 1994.

The Veto

The constitutional provision that the president can veto a bill passed by Congress gives him a powerful weapon. To **veto** a bill, the president returns it unsigned with his objections to the chamber that originated it. Few bills are vetoed, but the threat of a veto often prompts modifications that will make a presidential veto less likely because overriding a veto requires a two-thirds majority of both chambers. Of the 1,437 bills vetoed from 1789 through 1996, only 105 were overridden. If Congress is in session and the president does not sign a bill within 10 weekdays, the bill becomes law anyway. However, when Congress adjourns, a bill unsigned in 10 days dies—a practice called the **pocket veto**. In 1996, Congress added a new weapon to the president's arsenal to take effect in 1997: a limited **line-item veto**. This tool allows the president to veto certain specific items within an appropriations bill without killing the whole bill. Long sought by presidents, this innovation could expand presidential power considerably, but it has been challenged by those who consider it an unconstitutional abdication of power by Congress. And in any case the authority expires in 2005 unless extended by Congress.

Prerogative Powers

Sometimes emergencies require the president to act without congressional cooperation. Such **emergency powers** were first recognized by the Supreme Court in 1936, in *United States v. Curtiss-Wright Export Corporation*, where they were termed *inherent powers* (Chapter 3).[31] Prominent instances include Lincoln's Civil War era suspension of civil liberties and exercise of powers normally belonging to Congress while it was in recess, and Roosevelt's incarceration of Japanese-American citizens in detention camps during World War II—both actions eventually upheld by the Supreme Court.[32] However, when Truman used emergency powers to seize private steel mills when a strike was threatened so the federal government could operate them to furnish supplies for the Korean War, the Court declared the seizure unconstitutional.[33]

These are instances of a broader category of powers called **prerogative powers**—extraordinary powers outside the bounds of the written Constitution that the president can exercise in times of emergency—especially foreign emergency. Congress has also claimed prerogative powers, such as conduct-

prerogative

This term, derived from the Latin *praerogare*, meaning "to ask first" or "to ask before," refers to a prior right or privilege that originally belonged to a king. The *royal prerogative* meant that the sovereign was subject to no restriction or interference.

ing independent investigations, subpoenaing witnesses, and the legislative veto. Prerogative powers are not absolute, depending on acquiescence of the other branches, which is usually given in emergencies. They can always be challenged in the Supreme Court, as the legislative veto was (Chapter 11). Furthermore, Congress can respond to presidential claims to prerogative powers by cutting appropriations, overriding vetoes, investigating executive behavior, or passing laws such as the War Powers Act of 1973 (Chapter 11), which requires consultation with Congress before an extended deployment of American troops abroad.[34]

Presidential Resources

In addition to the authority of the office and these special tools, the president can use five key resources to convince others to do what he wishes: jobs, money, access, support, and information.

Jobs: Presidential Appointments

The president's constitutional power to appoint people to run executive branch departments and agencies has been limited by the professionalization of the bureaucracy (Chapter 13), so today an incoming president can appoint only about 3,000 of the almost 3 million federal employees who serve in his administration. About a thousand of these are what are called policy or political positions for people who run various agencies and serve as presidential assistants in and around the White House, with the rest "supporting" positions, such as clerical staff, chauffeurs, cooks, and gardeners. These thousand policy jobs are a source of great power to new presidents, for they can appoint not only their own political friends and supporters but also the friends of people, such as members of Congress, whose support they want. The Senate must approve major nominations but almost always does so even when controlled by the opposition party.

Money: Budgetary Allocations

Congress is a major budget actor, but the president can use decisions on money as political resources because he proposes the allocation of funds to each agency and program, may use the line-item veto in some instances, and ultimately oversees executive branch spending of final budget allocations.

Access: The Opportunity to Get Word to the President

No individual gets anything from the president without being granted access—the opportunity to see the president or to contact him by phone, fax, or letter—by the president or his chief of staff (see below). Access is valuable because the president's time is scarce and so many seek it: 100 senators, 435 representatives, 50 governors, hundreds of mayors; many of the thousand policymaking appointees; representatives of special interests, many of whom gave money to the president's campaign in hopes of obtaining such access later; and the president's own staff—

more than 500 in the White House Office alone. And this list doesn't even include the representatives of almost 200 other countries, let alone the rest of the American people—more than a million of whom write the president every year.

Support: The Opportunity to Get Something from the President

The greatest "gift" a president can give to another politician is a program the politician wants for his or her constituents. But any instance of support for a member's legislation is a valuable presidential resource. "A President can't whip members of Congress into line. All he can do is work out a relationship with the members that is comfortable for them and that keeps the lines of communication open," remarked Larry O'Brien, who lobbied Congress for Presidents Kennedy and Johnson. "It's a very fragile thing, and it can break apart so easily if you lose touch with each other. The little things are so important—returning their phone calls and setting aside time on the President's schedule for informal, off-the-record meetings with members; getting their constituents on the White House VIP tours; helping them get publicity and speakers in their districts; . . . answering their questions; getting them information that lets them justify their support for something the President wants to do."[35]

Information: The Knowledge for Effective Action

Presidents have access to more information than any other individuals on earth, ranging from staff summaries of media coverage, reports by thousands of executive branch policymakers, and regular reports from the government's special intelligence organizations, including the FBI on domestic matters and the CIA and other agencies on foreign affairs, to advice from individuals. Presidents can use this information in making decisions, withhold it from those they wish to deceive or punish, or give it to those they wish to reward. They can also "leak" it to the media to mobilize support for something they are planning or mobilize opposition to something someone else is planning. And they regularly use information from their own pollsters to shape, or manipulate, public opinion.

Running a Presidency

Regardless of their particular agendas, presidents face the same basic challenges: encouraging economic growth to enlarge the tax base and improve people's lives on the domestic front and preserving the country's place in the world. In the Cold War era that began with the end of World War II in 1945, this latter responsibility entailed maintaining a strong military and using it to protect U.S. interests abroad. Today it has come to mean protecting U.S. opportunities to trade freely with other nations and to borrow money to finance the ever-growing national debt. These domestic and foreign policy spheres are no longer really separate. The strength of the domestic economy, including jobs and profits, depends on such factors as the price of oil on the world market and global purchases of American goods and services. The strength of the global economy depends heavily on the economic health of the world's largest trader, the United States. And the strength of the nation abroad depends on the health of the economy at home. Furthermore, problems such as the quality of the environment, which affect everyday life and economic policy at home, are now global problems that ultimately must be addressed globally as well as nationally.

To meet these challenges, a president-elect must construct a new administration that suits his own style. He must then navigate the stages all administrations go through as they move toward the next election, all the while attempting to put his stamp on the way the bureaucracy conducts the nation's business.

The Life Cycle of a Presidency

Every presidency goes through stages, starting with the transition and the claim of a mandate. At the outset a presidency has a **honeymoon**, when people have high hopes for a new beginning and opponents fresh from defeat tend to hold their critical tongues, allowing the new president to dominate the news as he staffs his new administration and develops his early policy agenda. The honeymoon inevitably gives way to a period of increased struggles with Congress as the midterm elections approach. Those elections typically cost the incumbent's party some seats in Congress, thereby setting the stage for the runup to the next presidential election, during which conflicts with Congress intensify. Let's look at each stage in more detail.

The Transition, the Mandate, and the Honeymoon

Since the 1960s, presidents-elect—or at least their staffs—have engaged in careful planning for the transition to office. The outgoing administration cooperates in briefing newcomers about administrative processes and ongoing domestic and foreign issues. Indeed, issue briefings now begin during the presidential campaign. The official transition occurs when the president is sworn in, usually by the Chief Justice of the Supreme Court, and control over the satchel containing the codes and communication equipment the president needs to launch a nuclear strike—called "the football" by the officers who carry it—is passed to the incoming president.

Every president claims to have a **mandate** from the electorate to undertake his key policy preferences on taking office, even though the most any victor can claim is that about a quarter of the people gave a general endorsement to his program. Claiming a mandate can help generate public support and acquiescence from Congress, but since the astonishing precedent set by Franklin Roosevelt's administration, the first 100 days of a presidency are generally regarded as critical to the successful exploitation of whatever mandate an incoming president claims. "You've got to give it all you can, that first year," Lyndon Johnson once told an aide. "Doesn't matter what kind of majority you come in with. You've got just one year when they treat you right, and before they start worrying about themselves."[36] But that was in the 1960s. Today, the policy process is so complex, the political context so full of special interests and competing players, and the public so impatient with government that the honeymoon rapidly gives way to political struggle—even if there are no unanticipated political surprises such as foreign crises.[37]

Ronald Reagan is followed closely by a uniformed officer carrying "the football" containing nuclear launch codes that goes everywhere with the president.

The honeymoon that lasted a year in Johnson's time lasted only weeks for Clinton, who in his first term had unusual trouble finding acceptable candidates for key jobs and satisfying key constituencies with his early policy priorities. His personnel problems were unprecedented because he had pledged to select a cabinet that "looked like America" in its ethnic and gender makeup. He therefore had to find prominent people for his cabinet who could pass not only the traditional tests of political suitability and competence but also the new test of diversity.

Clinton's honeymoon was also cut short by a policy problem that grew out of his attempt to keep a campaign pledge. His promise to gays and lesbians that he would change the regulation banning them from military service ran into strong opposition not only from the political right but also from the military and even critics in his own party in Congress. And when he had to back down, his administration looked ineffective at the outset, his approval ratings plummeted, and the struggles over personnel and campaign promises distracted him from other priorities—especially economic and health-care reform. He eventually got most of his economic package approved, as we saw, but then failed at health-care reform. The result: Clinton's honeymoon dreams turned into the political nightmare of the Republican sweep of the midterm congressional elections of 1994.

After the Honeymoon: A Rocky Marriage or a Virtual Divorce?

The second major stage of any presidency is increasing interbranch struggle as conflicting political agendas take hold—the "worrying about themselves" that Johnson described. A third of the senators and all House members face reelection after two years of the new administration, and even members of the president's own party increasingly emphasize priorities that reflect their regional and ideological concerns rather than those of the White House. Their concerns inevitably make it difficult for the president to get his own legislative agenda adopted, so he must compromise more than at the outset.

The marriage becomes increasingly rocky because, in the terms favored by many political scientists, the president is in a cycle of decreasing influence over Congress, and probably over public opinion as well. Carter's vice president, Walter Mondale, already a longtime political veteran, summarized it this way on their inauguration day, "You know, a president . . . starts out with a bank full of good will and slowly checks are drawn on that, and it's very rare that it's replenished. It's a one-time deposit."[38]

Midterm elections provide another opportunity for politicians and the media to assess the public temperament. The president's own party always loses seats in both houses of Congress—sometimes losing control of one house, as happened to Reagan in 1986, or both houses, as happened to Clinton in 1994. These elections bring on the next stage—interbranch struggle that increases as the next presidential election approaches. If major presidential hopefuls are members of Congress who oppose the president to establish their own credentials as independent and more attractive choices, the result is likely to be stalemate, and it may even be a virtual divorce if members of the president's own party conclude that supporting him is a political liability.

By the second half of the term, the president and the staff have learned how to be effective in domestic policymaking, but this "cycle of increasing effectiveness" coincides with a "cycle of decreasing influence" in Congress and so the policy agenda must be restricted.

The Special Case of the Second-Term President

A reelected president begins the second term with valuable experience and at least some carryover staff, but he is also weaker because he is a lame duck. Knowing the ropes usually makes the president appear more competent, and he may generate higher approval ratings, as Reagan and Clinton did (see Figure 12.2). But presidential effectiveness also depends on the ability to sustain support in Congress, and that decreases once a president becomes a lame duck on reelection. The jockeying for political position in Congress that beset the second two years of the first term intensifies immediately, because both parties will have primary contests for the next presidential election. The president may even face nascent opposition from an ambitious vice president or cabinet members.

Managing a Presidency

Putting competent people in jobs that allow them to use their talents effectively, finding appropriate roles for the vice president and the presidential spouse, and then developing effective administrative procedures are keys to any administration's success.[39]

Presidents generally begin with close personal friends in whose capabilities and loyalty they have confidence. Andrew Jackson had his "kitchen cabinet," FDR his "brains trust," Carter his "Georgia Mafia," Reagan his "California Mafia," and Clinton his "Friends of Bill." Often these close advisors serve informally, from the sidelines. Some campaign staffers who specialized in policy areas (policy wonks) are placed in positions where they can advocate those policies, while others (brokers) are given the task of producing coherent policy out of competing ideas endorsed by disagreeing experts and competing interest groups. Still others (politicos) have the task of analyzing the implications of policies for the president's political power and reelection prospects. But because most longtime friends are strangers to Washington, too much reliance on them can jeopardize an administration's political effectiveness. To help newcomers avoid serious mistakes, the president needs "old Washington hands"—people who have served in earlier administrations and already know the ropes so they can handle dealings with Congress and the bureaucracy. A study of presidential appointments since 1961 found that 62 percent of all White House staff appointments were close presidential associates. In the larger Executive Office of the President, it was only 38 percent. In the key cabinet posts (State, Defense, Treasury, and attorney general), the percentage was 33, while in the rest of the cabinet it was only 20.[40] Each president makes his own mix of these differing types, so some administrations are stronger in the campaign realm while others are stronger in policy.

President Reagan with First Lady Nancy Reagan at his side.

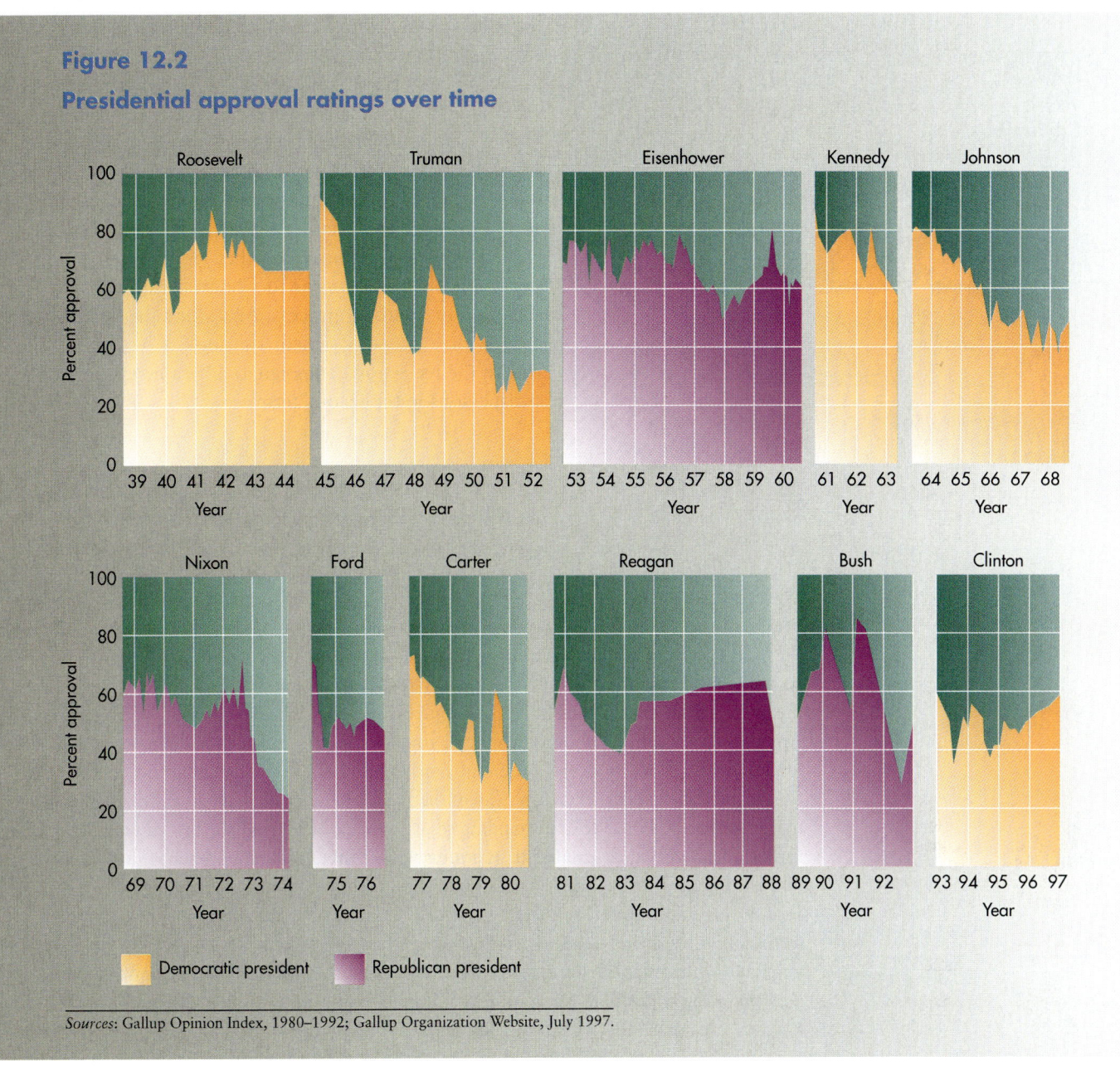

Figure 12.2
Presidential approval ratings over time

Sources: Gallup Opinion Index, 1980–1992; Gallup Organization Website, July 1997.

The Evolving Role of the Presidential Spouse

Presidents have often relied on their wives for counsel, and first ladies have always served as White House hostesses and as symbols of both their husbands and the nation's women. In some recent administrations they have also played vital roles, but none has had the active policy role that Hillary Rodham Clinton assumed when her husband took office.[41] She was given responsibility for developing the Clinton proposals for the administration's policy centerpiece—health-care reform—along with

First Lady Hillary Rodham Clinton speaks at a rally in Portland, Oregon, in support of the health-care reform package whose development she directed.

an office in the White House and a much larger staff of professionals than any predecessor.

Many Americans welcomed the new prominent role of the first lady—herself an accomplished lawyer—as a step forward for women and as needed assistance to an overworked president. But some complained that it is inappropriate for a presidential spouse to have important policy responsibilities because she is not accountable either to the American people through election or to Congress through the nomination approval process. And when the health-care reform proposal failed, she took a less active role in the reelection campaign and became even less conspicuous in the second term.

The Vital Twin Roles of the Vice President: Standby Equipment and Special Assistant

The status of the vice president is unique in two ways. Having been elected, the vice president can't be fired, even by the president. And serving in the executive branch, the vice president also has the role of presiding officer in the Senate, thereby transcending the separation of powers. The first vice presidents were the runners-up in the presidential contest and therefore sometimes political adversaries. The Twelfth Amendment, ratified in 1804, changed that by making each president run on a "ticket" with his own vice presidential candidate. However, the job had little political significance except when a president died in office until the Twenty-fifth Amendment was ratified in 1967. Responding to growing concern that a disabled president might be unwilling or unable to relinquish the office, this amendment allows the vice president to temporarily assume the powers and duties of a president who decides he is unable to perform the duties of office, or, in cooperation with the cabinet, to declare a president disabled and become "acting president."

The same amendment also for the first time provided for replacement of the vice president should he or she die, leave office (as Nixon's Spiro Agnew did), or become president (as Gerald Ford did). In each case, the vice president is to be replaced by someone nominated by the president and confirmed by a majority vote of both houses of Congress. The Presidential Succession Act of 1947, drafted when some feared that a nuclear attack might wipe out most of Washington, already provided that if both the president and the vice president should die at the same time, the Speaker of the House would become president. Next in line is the president pro tempore of the Senate, followed by various cabinet officers.

Until recently, the vice president has been, in the words of Ford's choice, Nelson Rockefeller, "standby equipment," used mainly for such ceremonial duties as attending the funerals of foreign dignitaries. Eisenhower did invite Nixon to attend cabinet meetings and represent the nation in some foreign travels, and Kennedy assigned Johnson the tasks of coordinating space exploration and racial desegregation programs, as well as lobbying Congress on key issues. However, it was not until Gerald Ford sought major domestic policy advice from Rockefeller, who had long served as governor of New York, that the office took on day-to-day political importance. Jimmy Carter gave Walter Mondale, a former senator, special lobbying duties on key bills and the role of special counselor on virtually all important presidential decisions. Mondale was also given an office close to Carter's, in contrast to his predecessors, who were relegated to the neighboring Executive Office Building.[42] As Reagan's vice president, George Bush was less visible, in part because Reagan's conservative followers were distrustful of him as a conservative-come-lately. When he became president, Bush gave Dan Quayle, his conservative vice president, the task of cultivating conservative support by public speaking and chairing a special Council on Competitiveness (see below).

Never before had a president and vice president resembled each other so closely as Bill Clinton and Al Gore, both in their forties, southerners, and moderate Democrats. Clinton made Gore a major advisor on policy and politics and gave him extensive policy responsibilities, including directing the National Performance Review commission charged with "reinventing government" (see Chapter 13). Still Gore, like his activist predecessors, was frustrated by the office's lack of formal power as well as by the challenge of being the loyal subordinate while preparing to run for the presidency on his own.

The Cabinet

The president's cabinet, a fixture since Washington, is formally a creature of Congress, for both chambers have the constitutional authority to create or abolish departments and the Senate approves the president's key nominations. Figure 12.3 depicts the expansion and changes in cabinet departments. The cabinet includes the heads of the various executive departments plus the president and vice president, but the president may assign other key officials "cabinet rank" and may invite other interested parties to attend cabinet meetings.

In theory, cabinet meetings have two major functions: to allow presidents to express their policy goals to the heads of the 14 executive branch departments and other offices granted cabinet-level status, and to allow department heads and other high presidential aides to discuss policy questions that cross normal departmental lines. In practice, however, cabinet meetings have become more of a formality than a fruitful exchange of views, primarily because, although appointed by the president, most department heads come to think in terms of the interests and needs of their departments instead of those of the president. Nixon recognized the problem: "When an individual has been in a Cabinet position . . . for . . . a certain length of time he becomes an advocate of the status quo; rather than running the bureaucracy, the bureaucracy runs him."[43] The policy burden then shifts to the White House staff, which has to supervise the activities of the cabinet departments for the president and serve as an alternative cabinet at the same time.

President Clinton introduces the members of his first-term cabinet, selected to "look like America," following their swearing-in in 1993.

Figure 12.3
The development of the president's cabinet and other major offices

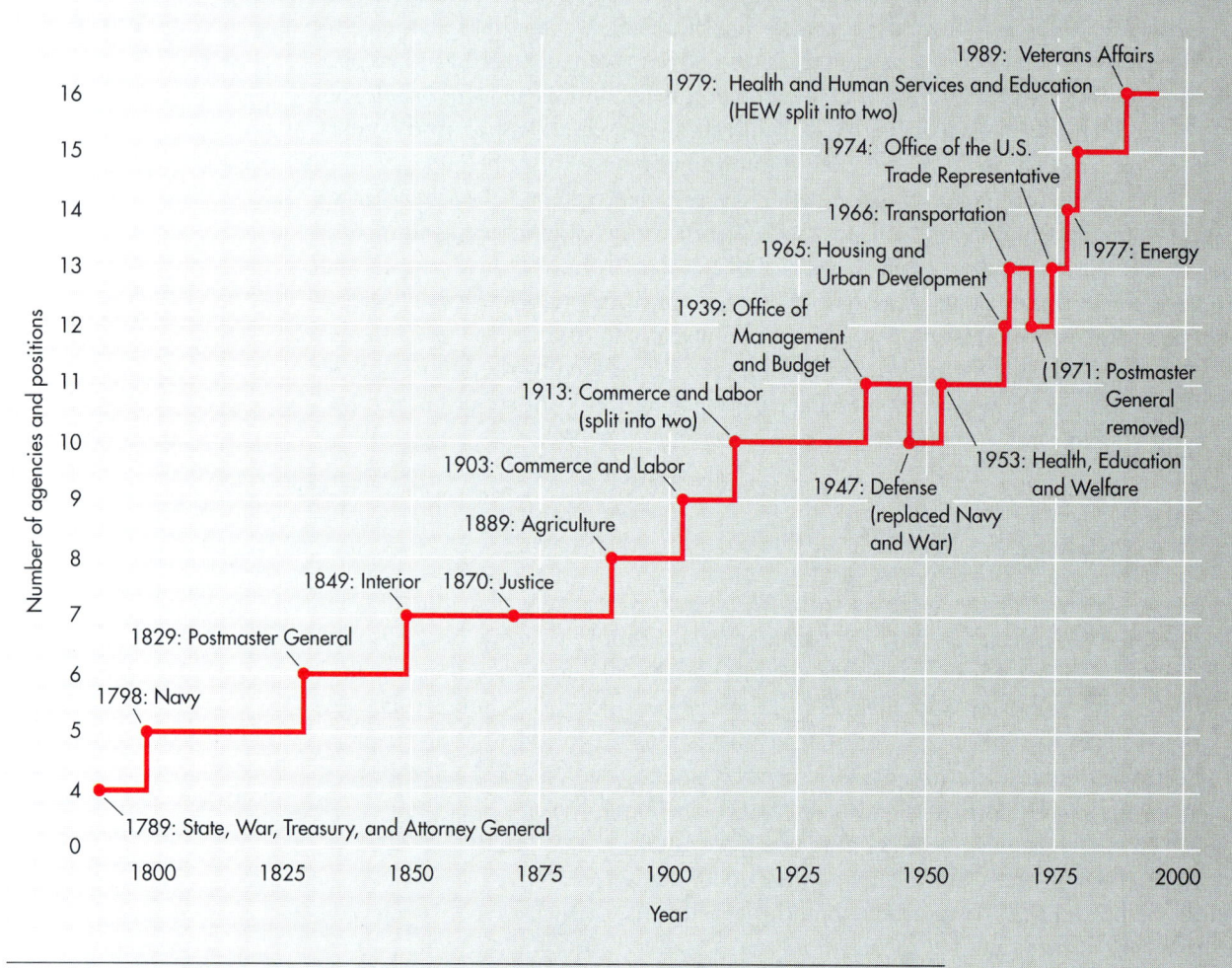

Number of agencies and positions vs *Year*

- 1789: State, War, Treasury, and Attorney General
- 1798: Navy
- 1829: Postmaster General
- 1849: Interior
- 1870: Justice
- 1889: Agriculture
- 1903: Commerce and Labor
- 1913: Commerce and Labor (split into two)
- 1939: Office of Management and Budget
- 1947: Defense (replaced Navy and War)
- 1953: Health, Education and Welfare
- 1965: Housing and Urban Development
- 1966: Transportation
- (1971: Postmaster General removed)
- 1974: Office of the U.S. Trade Representative
- 1977: Energy
- 1979: Health and Human Services and Education (HEW split into two)
- 1989: Veterans Affairs

Source: Adapted from *Washington Post*, February 9, 1993, A15. © 1993 The Washington Post. Reprinted with permission.

The White House Staff and the Executive Office of the President

There was no White House staff at all until a clerk was appointed in 1857. Around 1900 the White House office consisted of a few presidential assistants, bookkeepers, messengers, secretaries, cooks, and household staff. By 1932 it included only 37 people.

Under Franklin Roosevelt, however, the White House staff began to grow rapidly, developing and overseeing the many new New Deal programs, until it was overwhelmed. The resulting reorganization revolutionized the presidency. It created the **Executive Office of the President** (EOP) and moved the Bureau of the Budget out of the Treasury Department into the EOP to help Roosevelt oversee and coordinate the bureaucracy while developing better control by managing the purse strings.

When the White House operation grew so large that much of it was moved across the street into the Executive Office Building, a new White House staff grew up in its place. This new staff, eventually called the **White House Office**, was formally a part of the EOP, intended to coordinate relations between the president and the rest of the government. The executive branch ballooned again during World War II, and in 1946 a Council of Economic Advisers (CEA) was created in the EOP to advise the president and ease the transition to a peacetime economy. In 1947, a National Security Council (NSC) was added to advise on foreign and defense policy.

Truman, like Roosevelt, had a staff organized like a circle with himself at the hub. Eisenhower, a retired general, replaced that "hub and spokes" system with a pyramid. He sat at its tip, aided by a powerful chief of staff supervising the still-growing bureaucracy beneath him. Kennedy and Johnson, both activist presidents, returned to a version of the Roosevelt model, adding more special agencies to perform tasks under presidential guidance that were not being done satisfactorily in the cabinet departments. Nixon extended this approach by further centralizing and personalizing the presidency. One expert on executive organization, who helped Carter organize his staff, described the operation and limitations of this model:

> The personalized presidency largely depends on the leader's ability to mobilize public opinion to put pressure on the government to perform as he desires and to support what he believes is right. If the President lacks this skill, he cannot compensate in the long run by relying on the inherent strength of the office. The centralized presidency largely depends on the leader's ability to keep lines open to those outside his immediate circle and to resist minutiae. If the President is suspicious of cabinet members and relies too heavily on overworked assistants, he is apt to lose perspective and even his sense of reality.[44]

Many observers attribute the Vietnam debacle under Johnson and the Watergate catastrophe under Nixon to the failure of their centralized, personalized presidencies—products of the long-term trend toward larger White House staffs and the consequent weakening of the cabinet. Some justify this centralization on the grounds that most important policy questions transcend the narrow responsibilities of departments, believing that the less specialized EOP can better coordinate policy. During the Nixon and Johnson years, virtually all major policy was developed by the White House staff. However, it then had to be "sold"—as the common expression goes—first to the president, then to Congress and to organized interests who might otherwise oppose it, and then to the executive branch bureaucrats who previously developed policy and were still charged with implementing it. One scholar refers to this development as "the emergence of a presidential branch of government separate and apart from the executive branch."[45] This process has actually created a "little government" (some 600 or so in the White House Office and more than 1,000 more in the rest of the Executive Office of the President) within a government (the 3 million employees in the executive branch bureaucracy). As a result, the president must not only move the nation but also move Congress and his own bureaucracy!

The Iran-Contra Affair and the Reagan Administration

Riding the crest of his landslide reelection and continuing high popularity, President Ronald Reagan in 1985 sought a major foreign policy success to guarantee his place in history.

People working on the president's National Security Council (NSC) staff proposed selling arms to Iran. The United States sells weapons to many countries. But Iran had been denied such weapons for years because it sponsored terrorist attacks on Americans and its allies in the Middle East were holding a handful of American citizens as hostages. The arms sales were apparently intended to secure the release of these hostages.

At the same time, the president wanted to continue giving military aid to rebels (called "Contras") fighting to overthrow the Marxist-leaning government of Nicaragua. Congress had lost patience with this policy and in 1984 passed the Boland Amendment to a budget bill prohibiting sending military aid to the Contras.

NSC staffers thus developed a new policy proposal: selling arms to Iran and using profits from these sales to help finance the Contras. But because both actions were contrary to announced U.S. policy, and also violated certain U.S. laws, they were to be done covertly—under cover. The arms were to be shipped to Iran via other countries, and the profits were to be passed to the Contras via secret bank accounts in various countries.

Somebody approved the plan. (President Reagan later denied that it was he. Secretary of State George Shultz and Secretary of Defense Caspar Weinberger both opposed it when they heard it proposed, and so were excluded from further planning sessions.) Lieutenant Colonel Oliver North, a marine assigned to the NSC, supervised its execution. He had the assistance of some employees of the Central Intelligence Agency (CIA) as well as various private citizens. The program continued for a year until a newspaper in Lebanon "blew its cover," revealing that the United States was engaged in trading arms to Iran for hostages.

That revelation caused an outcry. The Reagan administration first claimed it was only selling the arms to strengthen the position of moderates in the Iranian government, so that they would be more friendly toward the United States in the future.

A quick investigation in November 1986 by Attorney General Edwin Meese 3d revealed, however, that arms sale profits were diverted to the Contras. This revelation caused greater outcry because Congress had expressly prohibited such mil-

Warned of the problems this approach had created, Carter attempted to run a cabinet-centered administration but never managed to achieve sufficient control over his own government. The Reagan forces then hired very slowly, only after checking the political and ideological loyalty of job candidates. They picked cabinet secretaries unsympathetic to many of their departments' programs and forced them to make drastic budget cuts as they took office, thereby alienating them from the employees they would be supervising. Furthermore, they centralized decision making in the White House staff at the expense of the cabinet departments. But Reagan's detached management style limited his administration's effectiveness in reshaping policy and practice over the long haul and led to policy conflicts[46] and, some argue, to the Iran-Contra scandal summarized in the box above.

Bush, with a lifetime of public service experience, wanted to avoid such mistakes. He delegated authority to negotiate with other actors to trusted aides under his general guidelines and maintained loyalty with telephone calls and personal notes. Having no overarching agenda for his administration, he did not insist on day-to-day control. This pragmatic approach suited his temperament but not that of many of the Reagan holdovers in his administration, several of whom later wrote scathing accounts of his presidency.[47]

itary aid. So the administration set up a special commission headed by former Senator John Tower (R-Tex.) to investigate the operation of the NSC. It also appointed a special prosecutor to determine whether anyone involved should be charged with illegal conduct in what soon came to be called "Irangate" or "Contragate."

But Congress was not satisfied by these measures, so each house set up its own special investigating committee. The Tower Commission reported its conclusion that "the president did not seem to be aware of the way in which the operation was implemented and the full consequences of U.S. participation." However, to discover how the policy had been developed and who was responsible for it, the congressional committees held combined hearings in the summer of 1987.

In all, there were 40 days of public hearings (many of them nationally telecast) and 4 days of closed or secret sessions. The 28 witnesses testified for 250 hours. The committees also examined 1,059 documents supplied by the participants in the affair.

What was concluded?

1. The president had denied that he knew about the Contra fund diversion, and no witness contradicted that. Former NSC head Rear Admiral John Poindexter, who was forced to resign when the scandal broke, said that he approved the program but didn't raise the matter with the president because he assumed Reagan would have approved it.

2. The Reagan administration's policy process worked very badly in this affair. Small groups of people, in and out of government, acting in secrecy against the will of Congress and violating the law, created and implemented policies that hurt the U.S. standing in the Middle East and around the world when they were revealed. Nor did those policies actually achieve their objectives of freeing the hostages and strengthening the Contras.

3. Foreign policy should be made with the participation of the Department of State (which was excluded from the debate over the Iran-Contra affair) and executed by it and other official representatives with operational experience, rather than by staff members of the NSC and the CIA plus interested private citizens.

4. Reagan's management style of giving blanket authority to subordinates and not checking up on what they did made these developments possible. His detachment was an important failure in presidential leadership.

The Clinton administration struck most observers and many participants as adrift from day one. Clinton, a "policy wonk" rather than an administrator, failed to establish priorities,[48] and neither periodic reorganizations nor personnel changes brought discipline. Only after Clinton's job approval rating plummeted and his party lost control of Congress did the administration refocus its energies, resisting the conservative programs pushed by the Republican Congress and emphasizing such popular positions as protecting Medicare and fighting crime, all the while negotiating trade agreements and peace accords abroad. The strategy won Clinton reelection and brought his approval ratings to all-time highs, even though it brought few new legislative programs.

The Chief of Staff

No president is especially concerned with administration except when popular perceptions of incompetence affect his image as a leader. To oversee the running of the White House staff every president designates a **chief of staff**, a chief gatekeeper who decides who gets on the president's daily schedule, sees that the president gets a wide range of views and options, and tries to prevent his being blindsided by crises. But some chiefs of staff act so forcefully as gatekeepers or policy advocates that they ultimately undermine the president they serve. When Reagan's chief of staff, Donald Regan, acted more as a chief executive than as a staff person, he was forced to resign.[49] Bush's chief of staff, conservative former New Hampshire governor John Sununu, controlled access so tightly that the president was forced to open a post office box at his summer home in Kennebunkport, Maine, as a "back channel" for his top advisors and cabinet heads to use in reaching him.[50] Sununu's gruffness proved an asset, serving as a "lightning rod" for criticism that would have been directed at the president when something went wrong in the White House. But Sununu, like most of his predecessors, was replaced when too many bad things had happened to the administration, as was Clinton's first chief of staff, a close boyhood friend who proved insufficiently strong in setting priorities. His replacement, Leon Panetta, a veteran of Congress and of Clinton's Office of Management and Budget, brought needed "insider" political sensitivity to the administration and helped engineer its new coherence after the Democrats lost control of Congress. In his second term, Clinton turned to an experienced White House administrator, Erskine Bowles.[51]

Former California congressman Leon Panetta (wearing glasses, flanked by Budget Director Alice Rivlin and Treasury Secretary Robert Rubin) was President Clinton's second chief of staff.

Governing and Making Policy

The system of shared powers requires the president to share policymaking with Congress, whatever its political composition, and to keep an eye on the courts, which can thwart policy by declaring executive actions or legislation unconstitutional. Thus each president selects aides to lobby members of Congress and adopts an approach to dealing with Congress as part of his governance strategy, and each develops a way of relating to the courts.

Presidential Strategies for Dealing with Congress

Relations between the president and Congress are far more complicated than party composition would suggest, because legislators tend to be members of Congress first and members or adversaries of the president's political party second. Former president Gerald Ford once remarked: "When I was in the House for 25 years I almost always looked down Pennsylvania Avenue at the White House, regardless of whether Democrats or Republicans were there, and wondered why they were so arrogant. Then, when I was in the White House myself, I looked up at the Congress and wondered how there could be 535 irresponsible members of Congress."[52]

Presidents with legislative experience know how to lobby legislators, whatever their party, while those lacking such a background tend to fare better when they leave legislative politicking to their **congressional liaison**. Until this century, open lobbying by the president was considered unseemly. Franklin Roosevelt was the first president to send his own representatives to talk with legislators—something he had to do because he was disabled. Truman continued the practice, but as a former senator he didn't want to infringe on congressional powers, so his liaisons confined their work to doing favors for members and discussing patronage jobs. Eisenhower then created a formal Office of Congressional Relations (OCR), and from then on congressional liaison took on more importance as the number and complexity of issues before Congress increased. Starting with Reagan, administrations have assigned some OCR staff to deal with policy questions and others to specialize in serving members from particular geographical regions.[53]

Presidents must develop strategies for dealing with Congress as an institution on the budget and other legislation, as well as ways of relating to particular members who have special powers over such matters as confirmation of presidential appointments. Each president selects among four basic strategies.

Governing *over* Congress: Domination

No president since Lyndon Johnson, who won a landslide election in 1964 after succeeding to the presidency when Kennedy was assassinated, has been able to dominate Congress, and even Johnson eventually ran into difficulty. Having been a representative and then a powerful Senate majority leader, Johnson knew how Congress worked better than any president before or since. He also knew the personal interests and foibles of virtually every important member, and he used this knowledge to garner votes, as we saw last chapter.[54] He readily gained passage of his Great Society legislation and only lost effectiveness by continuing the Vietnam War long after congressional—and popular—support had eroded.

Richard Nixon, despite his service in Congress, had no taste and little talent for congressional relations. Unable to dominate the domestic agenda with Democrats controlling Congress, he decided to *"take over* the bureaucracy and *take on* the Congress,"* in the words of one participant-observer.[55] (We'll see how he tried to take over the bureaucracy in the next chapter.) He took on the Congress by refusing to spend funds appropriated by Congress for various programs. This tactic—called **impoundment**—led to court battles, all of which the administration lost, and passage of the Budget and Impoundment Control Act of 1974, which requires congressional approval of any presidential impoundments. Nixon's efforts, the last gasp of "the imperial presidency," brought about a series of laws transforming presidential-congressional relations (see Chapter 11).

Governing *with* Congress: Collaboration

Collaboration seems the preferable strategy under divided government, yet few presidents have seriously tried it, and fewer have succeeded at it. Ronald Reagan made an effort to do this when he took office with the first Republican Senate majority since 1954 and enough conservative House Democratic support to get his economic reform package passed. Thereafter, however, as the economy slumped and Democrats gained seats in the 1982 midterm elections, his working majorities disappeared and he was forced to cooperate on a more equal basis. The result was passage of important legislation such as the 1986 tax reform, which had bipartisan support—and bipartisan opposition.

Clinton took office with Democrats controlling both houses and the leadership guaranteeing he could get his legislative program passed without bipartisan collaboration. They were wrong, and a unified Republican opposition in both houses successfully blocked Clinton's desperate efforts to get legislation through before the midterm elections. Clinton then declared his willingness to collaborate with the new Republican majorities, but the Republican leadership asserted that it would cooperate, but not compromise, knowing full well that a strategy of collaboration depends on compromise. This stand forced Clinton into resorting to the third strategy: opposition.

Governing *Against* Congress: Opposition

A president facing a Congress controlled by an opposition party unwilling to collaborate may be tempted to adopt a strategy of opposition, hoping to gain voter support for his party by convincing voters that Congress stood in the way of his program's adoption but risking being blamed for governmental inaction. Harry Truman used this strategy effectively in 1948, proposing major laws that the Republican Congress refused to pass and then winning a stunning upset by running against "the do-nothing Congress." George Bush tried the same strategy, but voters remembered his collaboration with Democratic congressional leaders on the 1990 "budget deal" that produced a large tax increase intended to cut the federal deficit, and Bush's strategy failed. Clinton's situation was different. The new Republican majority in the House had come to power pledged to implement the conservative "Contract with America," and the growing unpopularity of that package allowed Clinton to play the role of resister of unpopular change so effectively that popular opinion blamed the Republicans for shutting down the government in the 1995–1996 budget stalemate. Clinton's reelection proved that while governing against Congress is a risky strategy, it can sometimes prove successful. Nonetheless, he frequently returned to a strategy of collaboration in his second term.

Governing *Without* Congress: Circumvention

Every president occasionally circumvents Congress, especially on issues of alleged national security where secrecy is deemed important. However, George Bush, although described by journalists as a "minimalist" who believed that "that the best course was to do as little as possible,"[56] adopted a pioneering strategy to protect the presidency by circumventing Congress.

Bush's strategy had three parts. First, hundreds of times, when signing a bill passed by Congress, he issued a "signing statement" declaring that certain provisions of the bill violated the Constitution and therefore had no binding legal force and would not be implemented. Predecessors had vetoed such bills, with the subsequent congressional override making the bill law anyway and placing Congress clearly on record as believing the bill constitutional—a statement of *legislative intent* that could influence a later Supreme Court decision on the matter. Bush's strategy allowed the administration to delay implementing a bill it opposed while avoiding further expression of congressional intent, daring opponents to challenge the administration in court.

Bush's second tactic was to invoke secrecy when "necessary" in the conduct of foreign policy, usually by using secret directives to the National Security Council. This tactic—used by his predecessors as well—shielded his decisions and actions not only from public debate but also from congressional knowledge. He employed the tactic in secretly supporting Iraq's dictator Saddam Hussein until Iraq invaded Kuwait[57] and then in attempting to justify going to war against Iraq without getting congressional approval. The third tactic was creating a Council on Competitiveness authorized to reverse regulations proposed by Bush administration agencies to implement laws passed by Congress on the environment, health, and safety regulation that it concluded unduly limited the global competitiveness of the United States.

President George Bush signs the Civil Rights Act of 1991 in a public ceremony. Following the signing, Bush issued a "signing statement" contesting the constitutionality of some of its provisions—an instance of "governing against Congress."

These three tactics significantly increased presidential power without accountability to Congress or to the electorate and blurred the constitutional principles of separated and shared powers, establishing what a congressional insider called a "semi-sovereign presidency."[58] Reflecting on his experience as the 1996 elections approached, Clinton remarked: "One of the things I have learned in the last two years is that the President can do an awful lot of things by executive action."[59] And, like his predecessors, he sought to prevent Congress from getting easy access to information about wrongdoing in the executive branch, as we'll see in the next chapter.

The Presidency and the Courts

The Supreme Court in 1803 established the principle that it could declare laws of Congress unconstitutional in *Marbury v. Madison* (Chapter 2),[60] but it did not declare a presidential action unconstitutional until after the Civil War. In that instance, it barred execution of a civilian sentenced by a military commission for releasing and arming rebel prisoners during the war despite President Lincoln's argument that his execution, while contrary to existing laws and judicial procedures, was the lesser evil during a civil war.[61] By the time this decision was handed down, the war was over and Lincoln had been assassinated. The precedent of striking down a president's action had been established, but only after the issue was moot.

This power was not invoked again until the Court prohibited Franklin Roosevelt from removing a federal trade commissioner for a policy disagreement without going through legal channels.[62] It then invalidated Truman's seizure of the steel mills (see above) because it usurped congressional authority.

Five more instances of the Court overruling presidential actions involved Nixon. One was his effort to prevent publication of the *Pentagon Papers,* a secret

Defense Department analysis of U.S. involvement in the Vietnam War that had been illegally leaked to newspapers. Another was his electronic surveillance (wiretapping) without a prior court order of a person accused of bombing an office of the Central Intelligence Agency. The third, and most damaging, was ordering Nixon to turn over secret tapes of White House conversations to the special prosecutor investigating the Watergate scandal despite White House claims of executive privilege—a decision that precipitated Nixon's resignation. After he left office, Nixon lost a case contesting his impoundment of money appropriated by Congress as well as a case contesting the government's putting his presidential papers in federal custody to prevent their destruction so that historians would eventually have access to them.[63] Then in 1988 the Court overruled a presidential action in an ethics case.[64]

Most of these decisions were handed down so long after the actions in question that they did not seriously hamper the conduct of the office. The fact that so few presidential actions have been declared unconstitutional indicates that the courts are slow to reach such decisions even when the questioned action seems a flagrant abuse of power. Instead, the Court tends to declare such matters *political questions*—that is, questions of politics or policy involving relations between the Congress and the president that the Court asserts should be settled in the political process by the parties involved instead of by the judicial branch.

The courts rarely pose grave threats to the presidency, but their legal interpretations regularly influence policy and action, and the president may think twice before undertaking a constitutionally questionable action for fear of a legal entanglement. So presidents seek to appoint sympathetic judges to the bench to protect their power and increase the chances that the courts will sanction their actions—a strategy that has produced mixed results, as we'll see in Chapter 14.

Reforming the Presidency

What reforms might produce better presidents? Some believe the nature of the primary and general election campaigns must be changed so that better people win election, others focus on improving the presidency as an institution, and still others favor fundamental changes in the structure of government.

The electoral process, as we saw in Chapter 10, favors people with talents quite different from those needed for effective governance. The rigors of campaigning may filter out those lacking knowledge and stamina (both qualities valuable to a president) but some believe that better candidates would run—and better potential presidents might survive the process—if campaigns were shorter. This result could be achieved by replacing the current structure of contests spread across the country between January and June with a single national primary or several staggered regional primaries (see Chapter 10).

Sometimes we discover too late, however, that a winner is ill-suited to the job, and the Constitution provides no way (except impeachment and conviction for "high crimes and misdemeanors") of disposing of a mistake until the next election. Some critics therefore support a recall procedure similar to that provided in some states and many cities, whereby a certain percentage of voters signing a petition can compel a popular vote on whether to remove an official from office. However, there is no agreement on how many signatures should be required to start recall proceedings, and some fear that a president threatened with recall might try to placate the public in ways that could damage the country.

Given these difficulties, some recommend institutional reforms to make it easier for less gifted individuals to be effective presidents. But because these institutional reformers disagree over whether the presidency should be strengthened or weakened, there is little agreement on which reforms to support. Some favoring strengthening the presidency see virtue in a multiple advocacy system in which a neutral aide would take steps to see that whenever an issue comes up, those arguing for different positions get equal chances and resources to present their views.[65] Others, believing that there is little necessary connection between the foreign policy tasks of the president and the domestic tasks and that each is large enough to be a full-time job, suggest electing one president for each set of responsibilities.[66] Others, including former Senator Mark Hatfield (R-Ore.), have proposed splitting the domestic responsibilities into several elected offices—in effect, election of a cabinet. But such a plural executive would increase specialization, make it harder to take account of the growing interconnections among policy areas, and inevitably increase the political struggles among the various specialized subpresidents. Furthermore, campaigns for nomination and election would become more costly and complex, and the fragmentation of presidential power might dissuade good people from seeking each office.

Some arguing for more fundamental structural changes in government favor adopting the parliamentary system used in most Western democracies, in which the head of government is elected by the legislature. Others would settle for adopting its provision for the "confidence vote," by which Congress could take a "vote of confidence" on the president, with a negative vote—perhaps by a two-thirds majority—removing the chief executive and either replacing him with the vice president or producing a new election for president and perhaps for the Congress that voted "no confidence."[67] But some prefer to experiment with the parliamentary practice of "question time," which requires cabinet members and the president to appear regularly before one or both chambers to answer questions from members. Others favor allowing—or perhaps requiring—the president to select some or all cabinet members from sitting members of Congress to create closer relations between the branches.

But while supporters of parliamentary government want the president and Congress to be more sensitive to voters and mandates, other reformers argue that presidents are already too sensitive to public opinion and overly obsessed with reelection. They propose that the president be elected to a single six-year term to ease the physical and psychological burdens of the office and to allow time for developing and implementing a comprehensive program. But many doubt that the change would reduce the role of politics in the White House, and some believe that the isolation from politics this reform would achieve would not be positive: "A president who remains aloof from politics, campaigns, and partisan alliances does so at the risk of becoming the prisoner of events, special interests, or his own whims."[68] Woodrow Wilson, in fact, argued: "A four-year term is too long for a President who is not a true spokesman of the people, who is imposed upon and does not lead. It is too short a term for a President who is doing, or attempting, a great work of reform, and who has not had the time to finish it. To change the term to six years would be to increase the likelihood of its being too long, without any assurance that it would, in happy cases, be long enough."[69]

Some who celebrate the political nature of presidential-congressional relations support repealing the Twenty-second Amendment so a second-term president would not be a lame duck. Others favor abolishing the midterm election to allow more time for a president to get organized, develop programs, and attempt to get them through Congress before Congress becomes too obsessed with the next election. If House terms were lengthened to four years and Senate terms to eight years, with one senator from each state elected every four years, each election could be a referendum on both the president and Congress, thereby making it more likely that the president could effectively pursue programs for longer than the honeymoon. Or, to keep everyone closer to public opinion, House terms could be three years and the president given a single six-year term.

At present, however, no reforms have broad enough support to be instituted.[70] The presidency might better serve the country if, instead, the public reduced its enormous expectations of an office that was purposely limited in its capacity to govern by the system of separated powers and checks and balances.

Summary

The Constitution outlines five major roles of the president: commander in chief of the armed forces, chief administrator of the government, chief diplomat, chief legislator, and chief of state. George Washington established the office in practice, creating important precedents such as the cabinet and executive privilege. Strong successors added eight more roles: party leader (Jefferson), representative of the people (Jackson), mobilizer of the government for war (Lincoln), moral leader (Lincoln), mobilizer of the people (Teddy Roosevelt), world leader (McKinley, TR, and Wilson), social reformer (TR and Wilson), and manager of the economy (Wilson and FDR).

The presidency has enumerated powers (listed in the Constitution), statutory powers (granted by laws), and inherent powers (those belonging to it because it is an executive). These powers create authority, which presidents often attempt to increase, sometimes abuse, and frequently find difficult to exercise.

The Constitution requires that presidents be native-born citizens of the United States, at least 35 years of age, and U.S. residents for at least 14 years. No special experience is required, but most have had similar experience as elected state and/or national officials. Because the office places great demands on its occupant, scholars study presidential personality to discover the most promising qualities but so far have not reached consensus on this. Presidential health has become of greater concern in recent decades as many presidents have suffered serious illnesses or temporary disabilities. Presidents differ in their skills, among them managing information, managing people, managing the policy process, making decisions, and selling policy both inside and outside the Washington Beltway.

To be effective, presidents must sustain the authority they inherit with the office; exercise their authority, primarily by building coalitions, projecting their vision of *what's right*, and mustering public support; and avoid the abuses of power that have haunted the office in recent times. The tools available to presidents include laws, executive orders, executive agreements, congressional-executive agreements, vetoes, executive privilege, and various prerogative powers. The leading presidential resources are jobs, money, access, support, and information.

Each presidency evolves from an opening "honeymoon" phase when an electoral mandate is claimed through an increasingly difficult relationship with

Congress as midterm elections approach. Second-term presidents are essentially lame ducks who find it increasingly difficult to command the support of Congress.

Presidents staff their administrations with close personal advisors, politicos, policy specialists, and career officials. They increasingly depend as well on their spouses and vice presidents (who often serve as special assistants as well as "standby equipment"). Surrounding the president are the cabinet (heads of the executive departments) and their assistants on the White House staff and those in the Executive Office of the President. Each president organizes his staff in his own way, attempting to avoid the problems of predecessors, but experience suggests that there is no ideal way.

Presidents must share policymaking with Congress and depend on a special liaison office to lobby Congress. Presidents choose among four different strategies for relating to Congress: domination, collaboration, opposition, and circumvention. They often try to supplement their power by selecting judges who will likely support their programs. Still, the courts only very occasionally check presidential power by ruling particular actions unconstitutional.

Experts disagree on whether the presidency should be made more powerful or less powerful, and few proposed reforms have widespread support.

Key Terms

cabinet **442**
chief of staff **471**
congressional-executive agreement **459**
congressional liaison **473**
emergency powers **459**
enumerated powers **440**
executive agreement **458**
Executive Office of the President **469**

executive order **458**
executive privilege **443**
governing coalition **455**
honeymoon **462**
impoundment **473**
inherent powers **442**
kitchen cabinet **443**
lame duck **443**

line-item veto **459**
mandate **462**
pocket veto **459**
prerogative powers **459**
statutory powers **442**
veto **459**
White House Office **469**

How You Can Learn More About the Presidency

Barber, James David. *The Presidential Character*, 4th ed. Englewood Cliffs, N.J.: Prentice Hall, 1992. The classic study of presidential attributes.

Campbell, Colin, and Bert A. Rockman, eds. *The Clinton Presidency.* Chatham, N.J.: Chatham House, 1995. Assessments of the Clinton White House by various experts.

Edwards, George C., III, John H. Kessel, and Bert A. Rockman, eds. *Researching the Presidency: Vital Questions, New Approaches.* Pittsburgh: University of Pittsburgh Press, 1993. An interesting collection of papers by scholars.

Hess, Stephen. *Organizing the Presidency*, 2nd ed. Washington, D.C.: Brookings Institution 1988. A classic study assessing the effectiveness of various ways of organizing the White House.

Jones, Charles O. *The Presidency in a Separated System.* Washington, D.C.: Brookings Institution 1994. A study emphasizing the role of Congress and its own agenda, as well as presidential styles, in influencing policy outcomes.

Lowi, Theodore J. *The Personal President: Power Invested, Promises Unfulfilled.* Ithaca, N.Y.: Cornell University Press, 1985. A critique of the contemporary presidency and presidents.

McDonald, Forrest. *The American Presidency: An Intellectual History.* Lawrence: University Press of Kansas, 1994. An examination of the origins of the presidency and its evolution into a complex and powerful institution by a leading historian of the founding.

Nelson, Michael, ed. *The Presidency and the Political System*, 4th ed. Washington, D.C.: Congressional Quarterly Press, 1994. A valuable collection of articles on various aspects of the presidency.

Neustadt, Richard E. *Presidential Power and the Modern Presidents: The Politics of Leadership from Roosevelt to Reagan.* New York: Free Press, 1990. A revision of the classic study of presidential leadership as persuasion.

The Federal Bureaucracy

Above: Air pollution in Los Angeles. *Right*: Environmental Protection Agency head Carol Browner announces new regulations on urban pollution to implement the Clean Air Act Amendments of 1990.

CHAPTER 13

I thought I was the President, but when it comes to these bureaucracies, I can't make them do a damn thing.

—**Harry S Truman**

Bureaucracy is often thought of as some kind of alien force, . . . as a "they" that opposes us and hence is apart from us. Actually, bureaucracy is . . . public institutions operating within our communities. It is public employees living in our neighborhoods. . . . It is collective action in our behalf.

—**Charles T. Goodsell,
former federal bureaucrat[1]**

What Is the Governmental Bureaucracy?

What Makes Bureaucracies Effective—Or Ineffective?

How the Bureaucracy Interacts with Other Institutions

Reforming Bureaucracy

Passage of the Clean Air Act Amendments in October 1990, after years of struggle and months of intense bargaining (see Chapter 11), was widely hailed as a bipartisan victory for the environment. But the amendments had serious implications for virtually every major industry in the country, and experts put the cost of compliance at a staggering $25 billion. Soon after President George Bush signed the bill, some of the 19,200 bureaucrats in the Environmental Protection Agency (EPA) began writing the regulations that would put the principles stated in the legislation into practice.

Among the many complex provisions were several designed to curtail smog in urban areas by requiring automakers to sell cleaner-running cars, oil companies to produce reformulated gasoline for sale in cities with the worst air, and states to establish centralized facilities for testing auto emissions in those cities. While the EPA allowed the 28 states involved to choose their own programs for achieving the required pollution cutbacks, it recommended that states with cities having the most serious problems institute auto emission inspections by centralized testing stations. Such stations scattered around each city would be required to use equipment that tests a car while it is running on a treadmill—something more like actual driving than the standard idling test that local gas stations administered. Centralized test stations were required because the treadmill equipment cost $150,000, much more than local gas stations could afford. Cars in violation of the strict standards would have to be repaired by local stations and then retested centrally. The EPA argued that this program would produce major cutbacks in urban pollution. But drivers faced increased cost and hassle, and local gas stations faced lost inspection business. As the January 1, 1995, deadline for states to pass legislation complying with these antismog mandates approached, rebellion spread among the auto industry, the oil industry, states, and consumers.

The law provided that the EPA could cut off billions of dollars in federal highway funds to states that failed to establish the required programs on time—a powerful incentive to states to obey such a federal mandate. But following the November 1994 elections, when Republicans calling for cutbacks in government regulation won control of Congress and key state governorships and legislatures, Pennsylvania, New Jersey, Virginia, Texas, and other states indicated a willingness to forgo these federal highway funds to satisfy unhappy citizens and special interests—a development that astonished EPA regulators. Fearing that the new antiregulation Congress might even attempt to repeal major sections of the Clean Air Act, EPA administrator Carol Browner, a Clinton appointee, met with the governors of five states in early December and promised that the EPA would allow states greater flexibility in designing alternatives, as long as clean air targets were eventually met. For example, states would be allowed to use less expensive and less accurate testing equipment so long as they supplemented it with random roadside inspections and other measures.

Experts working for environmental groups feared that Browner's compromise was the beginning of a capitulation that could reverse nationwide progress toward cleaner air. Other experts disagreed. Some pointed out that the cities targeted for cleanup were selected on the basis of air testing that included data from the scorchingly hot summer of 1988; based on these data, 89 urban areas outside California had been classified as violating federal smog standards, 18 of them having "serious" or "severe" problems. Hot summers always cause increased smog, these critics pointed out, but no summer since 1988 had been nearly so hot. Had more typical years been used, they claimed, no cities outside California would have needed the stringent measures. Indeed, the EPA's own figures for 1989–1991 found only 37 areas outside California in violation, only 4 of them seriously so.[2] However, public health advocates claimed that 140 million Americans breathing unhealthy air would benefit from the new EPA regulations, and if another hot summer occurred, everyone would benefit from the more stringent standards.

Early in 1995, governors or legislatures in state after state suspended their tailpipe emission inspection programs, awaiting final EPA rules specifying how much credit toward the required goals they would get for adopting various emission-control options. But businesses with state contracts to provide the emissions testing sued for breach of contract. Two years later, a state district judge in Texas ordered the state to pay $160 million in damages to the bankrupt Tejas Testing Technology Company. Meanwhile, the EPA continued to try to find a balance between *what's right* and *what works,* but every effort to do so proved highly controversial.

The EPA and other governmental bureaucracies are important political actors. Bureaucrats determine not just how public policies work in practice but what the policies actually are. To understand why, we must ask:

What are the U.S. government bureaucracies, and how have they evolved?

What makes bureaucracies effective—and ineffective?

What do bureaucrats do?

What roles do bureaucracies play in the national government today?

How should bureaucracies be reformed?

What Is the Governmental Bureaucracy?

Have you ever worked for a government or a public college or university? If so, you were a government bureaucrat. And if you served in the military, you were also a government bureaucrat. One of every six Americans working today is a government bureaucrat. There are more than 18 million bureaucrats at the national, state, and local levels, from the president to your local garbage collector. Of these, 2.8 million people work for the agencies charged with running the national government and putting policies into practice.[3] Most of what we do every day is affected by what federal bureaucrats do. They regulate businesses, collect taxes, influence what we see on television, and even decide how much rat feces will be allowed in the peanut butter we buy. To perform these many and varied tasks effectively, they are organized into bureaucracies.

Government as a Network of Bureaucracies

"The governmental bureaucracy" is really a complex network of many bureaucracies. Each of the three levels of government (national, state, and local) has three branches (executive, legislative, and judicial). The executive branch at each level is composed of many different bureaus, each made up of executives, managers, and staff, and the other two branches include various bureaus as well.

Most of the 2.8 million bureaucrats (they'd rather be called "civil servants") at the national level are organized into 14 departments (see Figure 12.3 on page 468), the Postal Service (a public corporation employing some 850 million), and close to 2,000 agencies within the executive branch, as we saw in the last chapter. The major departments and agencies of the executive branch bureaucracy are shown in Figure 13.1. In the legislative branch, some 31,500 people staff the hundreds of Senate and House offices that serve members and committees as well as such support agencies as the Library of Congress, the General Accounting Office, and the Congressional Budget Office. Even the judicial branch has a small bureaucracy of some 29,500 to administer the court system.[4] This same pattern is repeated in each of the 50 states and at the local levels (counties and cities). Although our main focus in this chapter is on the executive

bureaucracy

The term comes from the French word *bureau* ("desk" or "office") and *-cracy* (form of government), so a *bureaucracy* is literally a government of desks or offices.

Figure 13.1
The U.S. government

The Constitution

Legislative Branch
The Congress
Senate   House
Architect of the Capitol
United States Botanic Garden
General Accounting Office
Government Printing Office
Library of Congress
Congressional Budget Office

Executive Branch
The President
The Vice President
Executive Office of the President:
White House Office
Office of the Vice President
Council of Economic Advisors
Council on Environmental Quality
National Security Council
Office of Administration
Office of Management and Budget
Office of National Drug Control Policy
Office of Policy Development
Office of Science and Technology Policy
Office of the U.S. Trade Representative

Judicial Branch
The Supreme Court of the United States
United States Courts of Appeals
United States District Courts
Territorial Courts
United States Court of International Trade
United States Court of Federal Claims
United States Court of Appeals for the Armed Forces
United States Tax Court
United States Court of Veterans Appeals
Administrative Office of the United States Courts
Federal Judicial Center
United States Sentencing Commission

Department of Agriculture | Department of Commerce | Department of Defense | Department of Education | Department of Energy | Department of Health and Human Services | Department of Housing and Urban Development

Department of the Interior | Department of Justice | Department of Labor | Department of State | Department of Transportation | Department of the Treasury | Department of Veterans Affairs

Independent Establishments and Government Corporations

African Development Foundation
Central Intelligence Agency
Commodity Futures Trading Commission
Consumer Product Safety Commission
Corporation for National and Community Service
Defense Nuclear Facilities Safety Board
Environmental Protection Agency
Equal Employment Opportunity Commission
Export-Import Bank of the U.S.
Farm Credit Administration
Federal Communications Commission
Federal Deposit Insurance Corporation
Federal Election Commission
Federal Emergency Management Agency
Federal Housing Finance Board
Federal Labor Relations Authority
Federal Maritime Commission
Federal Mediation and Conciliation Service
Federal Mine Safety and Health Review Commission
Federal Reserve System

Federal Retirement Thrift Investment Board
Federal Trade Commission
General Services Administration
Inter-American Foundation
Merit Systems Protection Board
National Aeronautics and Space Administration
National Archives and Records Administration
National Capital Planning Commission
National Credit Union Administration
National Foundation on the Arts and the Humanities
National Labor Relations Board
National Mediation Board
National Railroad Passenger Corporation (Amtrak)
National Science Foundation
National Transportation Safety Board
Nuclear Regulatory Commission
Occupational Safety and Health Review Commission
Office of Government Ethics

Office of Personnel Management
Office of Special Counsel
Panama Canal Commission
Peace Corps
Pension Benefit Guaranty Corporation
Postal Rate Commission
Railroad Retirement Board
Securities and Exchange Commission
Selective Service System
Small Business Administration
Social Security Administration
Tennessee Valley Authority
Thrift Depositor Protection Oversight Board
Trade and Development Agency
U.S. Arms Control and Disarmament Agency
U.S. Commission on Civil Rights
U.S. Information Agency
U.S. International Development Cooperation Agency
U.S. International Trade Commission
U.S. Postal Service

Source: U.S. *Government Manual*, 1996–97. (Washington D.C.: U.S. Government Printing Office, 1996).

TABLE 13.1

Types of Federal Bureaucrats and Their Tasks

Level	How They Are Appointed	How They Are Recruited	Their Typical Orientations	Their Major Tasks
Top management	By high-level elected or appointed official	From political and occasionally civil service ranks; loyalty to administration usually important	Short-term service; relatively unrestricted by red tape; much and varied experience, but not always in similar jobs	Developing and implementing president's program; long-range planning; protection of the agency
Middle management	By competition	By examinations testing administrative competence	Career ambitions; devotion to procedural rules; sometimes hostile to both politically appointed agency head and Congress	Overseeing daily operations of the agency
Professional and technical staff	By competition	By examination or by selection from lists of licensed professionals	Devoted to professional work; often hostile to and ignorant of politics; oriented more toward professional peers than toward agency	Performing technical and professional tasks, such as those of the lawyer, engineer, and accountant
Clerical, manual, and routine worker staff	By competition	By examinations testing relevant skills or straight hiring	Low skill levels, low aspirations; see government work as a "a job"	Performing routine tasks essential to getting agency's work done

Source: Adapted, expanded, and updated from Charles Adrian and Charles Press, *The American Political Process* (New York: McGraw-Hill, 1965), 528.

branch bureaucracy at the national level, most of what we say applies to state and local bureaucracies as well.

Each department, agency, or bureau in this network of bureaucracies is composed of two types of officials: those appointed by the chief executive or other political figures, and those belonging to the permanent bureaucracy. Most of the political appointees are top management executives who concentrate on policymaking.

The permanent bureaucrats, or career officials, are divided into managers and staff. The managers—often called middle management—are career civil servants who have some policy responsibility and run the agencies from day to day. The staff consists of professional and technical experts in law, engineering, accounting, and whatever other specialized areas the agency needs plus clerical, manual, and other staffers who do routine tasks. Table 13.1 summarizes how each type of bureaucrat gets into government and what the typical orientations and tasks of each are.

The Evolution of the Executive Bureaucracy

There were bureaucracies in this country long before there was a United States. The British government set up bureaucratic agencies to administer its colonies, as had the Dutch and Spanish. But the real growth and distinctive development of the American governmental bureaucracy began after independence, and it continues to this day.

Bureaucracy and the Constitution

Even though neither "bureaucracy" nor "administration" appears anywhere in the Constitution, it is clear that the Framers expected a bureaucracy to be established to help carry out government's responsibilities. They required that the president "take Care that the Laws be faithfully executed" and gave the executive the power to "require the Opinion, in writing, of the principal Officer in each of the executive Departments, upon any Subject relating to the Duties of their respective Offices." Clearly a president could not execute the laws without considerable help from governmental employees. However, the Constitution also gave Congress the power to appoint officials of departments, which suggests that the Framers expected Congress to take the lead in creating the federal bureaucracy. And as part of the legislative check on the presidency the Constitution gave Congress the power of advice and consent on certain key presidential appointments.

The Constitution said nothing about which particular departments, bureaus, or agencies should be created, so George Washington and his administration had to invent, design, and justify each department to Congress, which then had to pass laws establishing them. Alexander Hamilton took the lead in designing the Departments of State, War, and Treasury, which he adapted from their predecessors under the Articles of Confederation. Hamilton had written, in *The Federalist,* No. 72, that "administration should consist of the simple execution of executive details"[5]—a nonpolitical view of administration that did not last long. Congress agreed with Washington that only the president could remove department heads. (The sole exception to this is, of course, the power of impeachment and conviction for "Treason, Bribery, or other high Crimes and Misdemeanors," which the Constitution assigns to the House and Senate, and which they have exercised only rarely.) This first major delegation of power by Congress to the executive has since become a vital tool in the president's power to expand the scope of his authority by both increasing and controlling the functions of the bureaucracy.

Once the necessary agencies were established and staffed, stability was achieved through consistency. In the early years, many prominent citizens willingly became professional public servants and often served in the same offices from one president to the next. Indeed, some even passed their offices on to their sons. The Framers believed that such a "natural aristocracy" had the education and civic virtue to serve the common good and therefore needed few curbs on its behavior.

inferior officers

The Framers stated in Article II, section 2, that Congress could delegate the power to appoint assistants to the courts or to the heads of departments rather than the president. In doing so, they opened the way for grave conflicts between Congress and the president, for bureaucrats appointed by assistants without presidential approval could owe their ultimate loyalty to those officials or to Congress and therefore jeopardize presidential authority and policy. Congress has, however, generally refrained from exercising this power.

From "Spoils" to Merit in Staffing

As ordinary citizens became more politically active, they demanded not just the vote but also their share of government jobs. Andrew Jackson, elected in 1828 as a "man of the people," feared that the bureaucratic elite which had served the previous presidents might not implement his program. He therefore fired 252 of the 610 holdovers—more bureaucrats than his six predecessors combined had removed in 40 years—and replaced them with loyal supporters.[6] When a political ally asserted, "To the victor belong the spoils," the **spoils system**, in which the winner of an election rewards political supporters with government jobs, got its name. (Some who think this term too crass prefer to call the practice **patronage** because jobs are provided by the boss, or patron.) The spoils system was not, strictly speaking, a Jacksonian invention, for Jefferson had done the same thing on a much more limited scale.

When Jackson discovered that putting his own people in top slots did not produce the pliable government he wanted, he reorganized the government into permanent offices to be occupied by rotating employees. His strategy for making the bureaucracy more responsive to his will had two parts.[7] First, he separated the functions or roles of government offices from the personal qualities of the individuals who performed them, so that trained workers could be interchangeable. Second, he arranged these functions in a hierarchy with specified functional responsibilities, rules and regulations, and clear lines of command, so each employee would know what his responsibilities were and whom to obey. These reforms to foster competence in the nonaristocratic new recruits became the first step toward the creation of a modern bureaucracy.[8]

This Jacksonian bureaucracy was not yet fully modern, because the selection of bureaucrats was not yet based on merit. It took 50 more years of discontent with government performance and the assassination of the newly elected president James Garfield in 1881 by a disappointed office seeker for Congress to pass the **Pendleton Act**—known officially as the Civil Service Act of 1883—which began to replace the spoils system with a merit-based permanent career civil service. The act established a bipartisan Civil Service Commission to supervise competitive exams for about 10 percent of the jobs in the national bureaucracy. Since then, new laws have extended this requirement to about 85 percent of federal government jobs. Many of the other 450,000 jobs are awarded by other merit systems, such as those operated by the Foreign Service (for diplomats) and the Federal Bureau of Investigation (for FBI agents).

Despite the civil service system, career bureaucrats often found themselves subject to pressures to support the party in office during campaigns, and so in 1939 Congress strengthened the system by passing the **Hatch Act**. This act made it illegal for federal civil servants to participate in political campaigns except for voting and contributing money to candidates. The terms of the act have recently been modified somewhat, but the act continues to protect civil servants from partisan political pressures.

The Hatch Act was not intended to prevent political superiors from firing non-civil-service employees. But over recent decades the Supreme Court has limited that practice as well. A 1976 decision, *Elrod v. Burns*, declared it unconstitutional for a new sheriff to fire all non-civil-service employees in his office who did not belong to his political party, arguing that "political beliefs and association

This cartoon depicts a statue "honoring" President Andrew Jackson for introducing the "spoils system" by kicking out carryover bureaucrats and replacing them with people loyal to him.

constitute the core of those activities protected by the First Amendment."[9] Fears that this principle might be extended to presidential appointments have proved unfounded, and incoming presidents continue to replace the approximately 2,000 political appointees of the previous administration.

How the Bureaucracy Ballooned

In Andrew Jackson's time, the executive branch occupied four drab buildings located at the corners of the grounds on which the White House stood. Today the executive branch is located in 441,000 buildings scattered throughout Washington, around the nation, and around the world. Indeed, the government now owns 2.7 billion square feet of office space (which cost more than $165 billion to build) and rents another 242 million square feet (for rental fees of over $2 billion a year).[10]

These staggering figures are hard to grasp. But compare them to the world's largest office building, the Sears Tower in Chicago, which is 1,454 feet tall (about the length of five football fields), has 110 stories, and contains 4.5 million square feet of office space. The U.S. government owns the equivalent of 600 Sears Towers in office space and rents the equivalent of 54 more.

The number of employees ballooned as well. In Jackson's time, the government employed about 5,000 people. Today the figure is about 2.8 million (see Figure 13.2). The total has decreased slightly during President Bill Clinton's tenure, and has been declining steadily in per capita terms (that is, as a percentage of the population) since the early 1970s.

Why the enormous growth in the federal bureaucracy throughout American history? Four factors have been instrumental:

- *Population growth.* Coping with more people has required more government offices in more places, with more employees.
- *Emergencies and crises, such as wars and depressions.* Wars require both mobilization of soldiers and governmental direction of war-making industrial

The bureaucracy has grown enormously in the past century and a half. The map at left shows the executive branch buildings that surrounded the President's House in Washington, D.C., in 1828. They include the Departments of State, War (now Defense), Navy, and Treasury. (The other highlighted buildings are hospitals, churches, and the like.) The map at right shows the same area today, with government buildings highlighted in gold. (The buildings shown in pink are museums and other cultural institutions.)

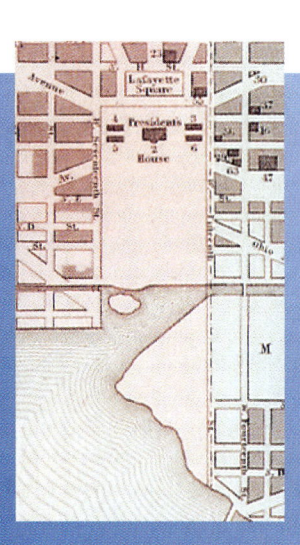

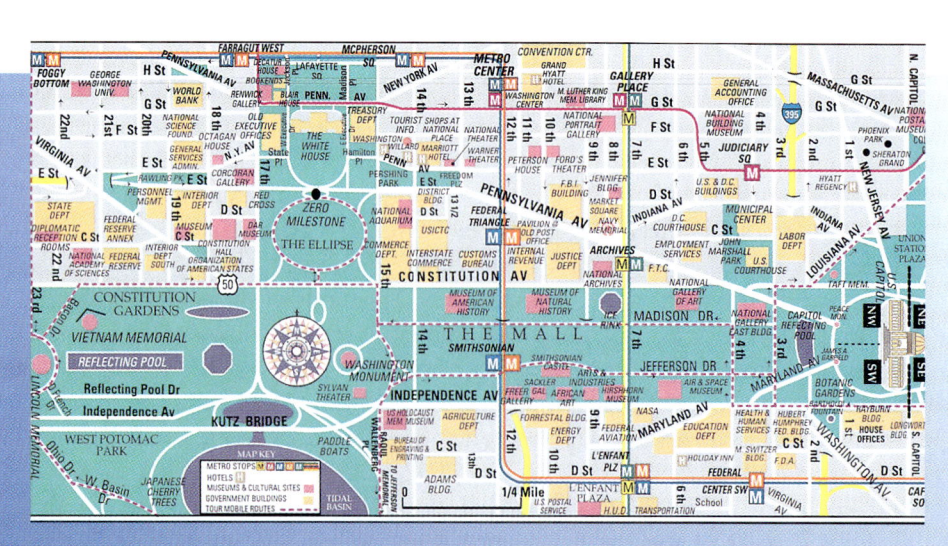

Figure 13.2

The growth in number of civilian federal government employees

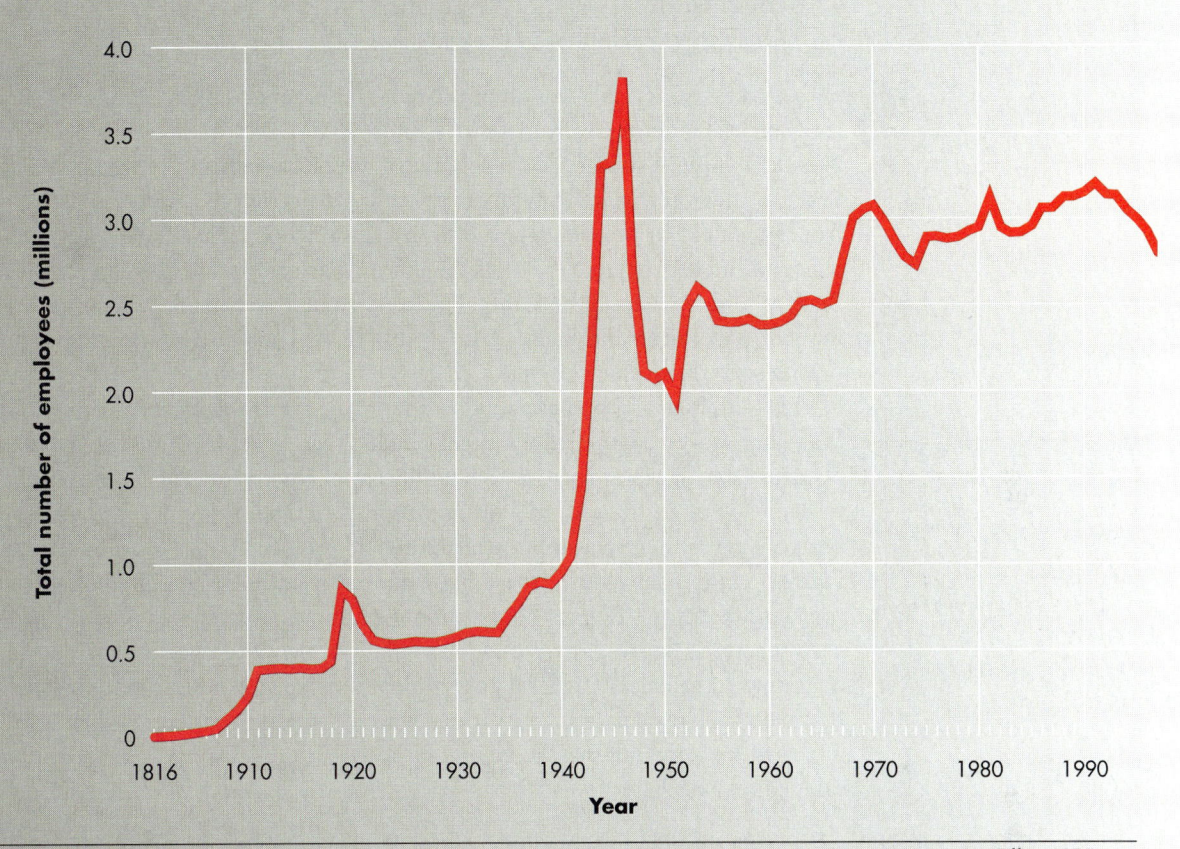

Source: 1816–1970: U.S. Bureau of the Census, *Historical Statistics of the United States* (Washington, D.C.: U.S. Government Printing Office, 1975), 1102–1103; 1971–1995: U.S. Office of Personnel Management, *Federal Civilian Workforce Statistics, Employment and Trends*, bimonthly release, updated from *Statistical Abstract of the United States 1997* (Washington, D. C.: U.S. Government Printing Office, 1997).

capacity, so they inevitably increase the size of the national bureaucracy. Postwar conversion of industrial capacity to peacetime uses and economic growth both require regulation, which means more bureaucrats to make rules, ensure compliance, and administer penalties. Government intervenes in times of depression to bolster the economy and put the jobless back to work through programs that require an army of new bureaucrats. Other major events have similar effects.

- *Science and technology*. New industrial technologies—from the cotton gin to the nuclear power plant, from railroads to airplanes, and from the telegraph to television and the Internet—raise issues such as patent and copyright protection for developers, subsidies for producers, and safety for consumers, and governmental responses to each of these concerns require more bureaucrats.

• *New governmental responsibilities.* Pressures to alleviate or resolve long-standing social problems such as child labor, killer diseases, poverty, and environmental degradation have given rise to new governmental agencies with specific responsibilities in these areas.

In recent years, the growth of the federal bureaucracy has stabilized. In a typical year, the federal government hires more than half a million new people. Until President Clinton took office, a slightly smaller number quit, retired, or died each year, so that the federal bureaucracy tended to grow at a slow but steady rate from president to president—even under those who attacked the bureaucracy as wasteful, inefficient, and bloated, as Jimmy Carter, Ronald Reagan, and George Bush all did. As part of his campaign to reinvent government, which we'll examine below, Clinton did succeed in shrinking the bureaucracy slightly—the first president to do so since Carter.

As buildings and bodies grow, so do budgets. In the first three years of George Washington's presidency, the federal budget averaged $1.42 million a year. Four decades later, Jackson spent $15.2 million in his first year. Today, the administration spends more than $2 million *a minute, 24 hours a day*. So the entire annual budget of Washington's administration would finance about 30 seconds of today's administration. Of course, these figures are not adjusted for inflation. Washington's and Jackson's dollars bought about ten times as much as ours do now. But even when the figures are adjusted for inflation, the difference is enormous, and it continues to grow. The federal government now spends a billion dollars every six hours or so. How much is that? If you started to count a billion dollars in $1 bills at the rate of one bill per second, eight hours a day, seven days a week, it would take you 95 years!

How the Bureaucracy Has Thickened and Widened

In recent decades, as the size of the bureaucracy has stabilized, a new concern has surfaced: the changing shape of the bureaucracy. The distance between the top and the bottom levels of the various cabinet departments has increased drastically just since 1960. Until that time, departments were headed by a political appointee, called a secretary, supported by up to five levels of assistants established by statute: deputy secretary, under secretary, assistant secretary, deputy assistant secretary, and deputy administrator. Since 1960, when the first associate deputy secretary position was created by presidential order, more and more levels have been added in a phenomenon that political scientist Paul Light calls **bureaucratic thickening**.[11] Today there are 52 levels of administrative positions in the federal government (listed in Table 13.2). Not all of these layers exist in each of the 14 cabinet departments, and only 17 are common to most departments. However, virtually every department has dozens of levels.

This increase in the number of officials between the president and the front-line bureaucrat—those who actually deal regularly with the public, issuing checks or conducting inspections, for example—makes it almost impossible for policymakers to know what's going on in the field. It also makes getting presidential orders carried out very difficult. In 1983, there was 1 employee in the middle level

TABLE 13.2

The 52 Levels of Bureaucracy in Washington Today

Secretary	Assistant Deputy Administrator
Chief of Staff to the Secretary	Associate Administrator
Deputy Chief of Staff	Deputy Associate Administrator
Deputy Secretary	Assistant Administrator
Chief of Staff to the Deputy Secretary	Deputy Assistant Administrator
Associate Deputy Secretary	Associate Assistant Administrator
Under Secretary	Principal Office Director
Principal Deputy Under Secretary	Office Director
Deputy Under Secretary	Principal Deputy Office Director
Principal Associate Deputy Under Secretary	Deputy Office Director
Associate Deputy Under Secretary	Assistant Deputy Office Director
Assisstant Deputy Under Secretary	Associate Office Director
Associate Under Secretary	Deputy Associate Office Director
Assistant Secretary/Inspector General/General Counsel	Assistant Office Director
Chief of Staff to the Assistant Secretary	Deputy Assistant Director
Principal Deputy Assistant Secretary	Principal Division Director
Deputy Assistant Secretary	Division Director
Associate Deputy Assistant Secretary	Deputy Division Director
Deputy Associate Deputy Assistant Secretary	Associate Division Director
Assistant General Counsel/Inspector General	Assistant Division Director
Deputy Assistant General Counsel/Inspector General	Deputy Assistant Division Director
Administrator	Subdivision Director
Chief of Staff to the Administrator	Deputy Subdivision Director
Principal Deputy Administrator	Associate Subdivision Director
Deputy Administrator	Assistant Subdivision Director
Associate Deputy Administrator	Branch Chief

Source: Paul Light: "How Thick Is Government?" *American Enterprise,* November–December 1994, 60.

for every 1.6 employees on the frontline in the federal bureaucracy. Today the ratio is about 1 to 1.

Why does such thickening occur? The short answer is, because citizens want more services out of government and special interests want more officials to whom they can have direct access. Among the more specific reasons are to have posts with more prestigious titles with which to recruit top appointees, to rebuild agency morale, to conduct the frequent "wars on waste," to increase the expertise available to decisionmakers, and to strengthen the department's position in negotiating with other agencies or other countries.

At the same time as the number of levels have increased, the size of each level has also increased, a phenomenon that Light calls **bureaucratic widening**. In 1960, there were 451 occupants of the administrative hierarchy of the cabinet departments. By 1980, that number had more than tripled, to 1,579, and when

Clinton took office it had grown to 2,393.[12] The same process has occurred in the presidential agencies (the White House Office, the Office of Management and Budget, and the Office of the Vice President) and in the two key congressional bureaucracies—those of the leadership and those of the committees.

Changes in the Executive Bureaucracy

Bureaucracy is always subject to criticism, but critics disagree over what's wrong as well as over what should be done. People unhappy with the extent to which government agencies respond to political pressures and special interests have sought to "depoliticize" bureaucracy by establishing independent agencies. Politicians wanting the bureaucracy to be more efficient and responsive have tried two sorts of reform: reorganizing personnel and restructuring agencies.

"Depoliticizing" Bureaucracy: The Independent Agencies

Virtually every aspect of your daily life—from the food you eat for breakfast to the clothing you wear to bed, from the fees and practices of the hospital you were born in to the disease you may die of, and even the casket you may be buried or cremated in—is affected by what independent agencies do.

The independent agencies are listed as "Independent Establishments and Government Corporations" at the bottom of Figure 13.1. Some, such as the National Capital Planning Commission and the Railroad Retirement Board, have little relevance to most Americans. Some foster important activities, as do the National Science Foundation and the National Foundation on the Arts and Humanities. Many furnish valuable services, as do the Equal Employment Opportunity Commission, the Farm Credit Administration, the Peace Corps, the U.S. Postal Service, and the Federal Emergency Management Agency.

The most important of these independent agencies are the **independent regulatory commissions** (IRCs). The oldest surviving IRC, the Federal Trade Commission, is concerned with regulating certain aspects of the economy. The Federal Communications Commission regulates television and radio, as we saw in Chapter 9. Each IRC regulates a type of commercial activity or a sector of the economy. Usually the objective is to protect "free enterprise" from its own abuses, but some are concerned with protecting the consumer from business abuses such as unsafe food and drugs or the citizen from industrial abuses such as pollution and dangers in the workplace. These IRCs have grown in number and expanded in responsibilities as businesses, industries, and citizens have demanded more protection from the consequences of large-scale business and industry.

The early IRCs were designed to be as free of politics as possible. Most are run by boards or commissioners appointed by the president and confirmed by the Senate. The commissioners generally serve for five to seven years, and most boards must contain members of both major parties. Terms are staggered, so that the commission usually includes appointees of various presidents. Regulatory agencies created since the 1960s, such as the EPA and the Occupational Safety and Health Administration (OSHA), are less autonomous. Headed by a single administrator whom the president appoints and can remove, they are more politically responsive to the president.

Just as Congress makes laws, these agencies make rules for the organizations and activities they regulate. They propose regulations, publicize them, hold public hearings that give interested parties an opportunity to comment, and then pass them by vote. These regulations are called **administrative law** because they are made administratively by bureaucrats rather than by Congress. Congress has given these rules the force of law, which makes these IRCs quasi-legislative bodies. And Congress has also given the IRCs a quasi-judicial function, empowering them to hear and resolve disputes among parties that fall under their regulatory power and investing their resolutions with the same judicial status as court decisions. As a result, IRCs are sometimes called "the fourth branch of government."

While the combining of legislative and judicial responsibilities in these agencies was intended to insulate them from politics, it has turned out to have the opposite effect. IRCs are continually plagued by interest group politics. Thousands of interest groups, as we saw in Chapter 8, pressure these independent agencies to adopt the policies they favor. Concerned citizens, too, increasingly try to influence agency decisions. This politicking is due primarily to the congressional requirement that the agencies be open to citizen and interest group input.

Because IRCs are torn in different directions by competing interests, the regulations they issue are often controversial. Businesses demand certain types of regulations, and citizens demand other types. While few would want to return to the days of unsafe food and unregulated pollution, critics—especially on the political right—often complain that there is too much regulation and that many rules are unnecessary or ineffective. Regulation, they point out, also has negative consequences—raising the prices of goods to American consumers and making American products less competitive on the world market, where competitors do not face such regulations.

Reorganizing Personnel

The Civil Service Reform Act of 1978 reorganized personnel in three ways to make it easier to assemble teams of highly competent officials to implement new programs. It created a **Senior Executive Service** (SES) of some 8,500 top civil servants who would be eligible for large cash bonuses for good work but would also be liable to transfer or demotion for bad work. It also streamlined the appeals process for bureaucrats who are fired, so that firing for incompetence can be more quickly sustained if justified, and created a Merit Systems Protection Board to hear appeals of employees charging mistreatment. It also prohibited reprisals against **whistleblowers**—employees who disclose evidence of gross mismanagement by the government.[13]

The impacts of these reforms have not been as great as hoped. Firings continue to be rare: Somewhere between 12,000 and 30,000 of the 2.8 million executive branch bureaucrats are dismissed for all causes each year, fewer than 250 of them for incompetence. To be fired for incompetence or misconduct, an employee must be given written notice with reasons and specific examples 30 days in advance. The employee then has the right to have an attorney and to reply orally or in writing and to appeal, if the firing is carried out, to the Merit Systems Protection Board and then to the U.S. Court of Appeals.

For information about whistleblowing, consult the site maintained by the Government Accountability Project:

http://www.whistleblower.org/gap

whistleblower

This term refers to someone who "blows the whistle on," or makes public, illegal or inappropriate conduct by some person or agency.

Mary Schiavo, inspector general of the Department of Transportation, testifies before the House Subcommittee on Aviation in 1996. Schiavo "blew the whistle" on federal handling of aviation safety regulations and inspections when she resigned and wrote a book.

Superiors still find that these processes severely limit their ability to make employees responsive. They therefore tend to resort to other ways of coping with an inept subordinate, such as promoting the person to a job where he or she can do less harm, transferring him or her to a different job or to a location away from the center of power, or creating a "special assignment" that requires the employee to travel away from the office frequently. Other approaches involve threatening changes that will make the job unattractive in order to entice a resignation, such as transferring the employee to a place he or she doesn't want to live, or offering a good recommendation if he or she quits, with the threat of a bad reference should he or she refuse to quit and later wish to change jobs. These strategies also perpetuate the incentive to hire a second employee to do the job being done inadequately by the first one, and thereby to increase the size of the bureaucracy.

Restructuring the Bureaucracy

Responsiveness and efficiency have been the twin goals of continuing efforts to restructure the bureaucracy—often with the effect of widening it, as noted earlier. Twelve of the 17 presidents in this century have attempted such restructuring.[14] Harry Truman achieved important reforms by centralizing authority in the hands of the people responsible for managing programs. He also presided over reorganization of the defense establishment and the economic policy agencies. But he lost his enthusiasm for reorganization because he concluded that, in the words of one historian, "reorganization proposals faced such strong opposition that expenditures of time, energy, and political resources ordinarily make them too costly to be undertaken on a large scale. The combined opposition from executive agencies, congressional committees, and pressure groups [was] almost impossible to overcome, especially in the case of plans that were most desirable to the executive."[15]

Most structural changes that pass Congress involve creating new departments by combining programs from various existing departments. Jimmy Carter created two new departments, Energy and Education. Ronald Reagan pledged to abolish these two new departments on grounds that they were unnecessary and meddled in areas the government should stay out of, but he was stymied because special interests liked having separate departments, and Congress agreed. When Reagan then proposed creating a new department for international trade and industry to make administration more rational in this increasingly important area, he found that the special interests preferred the existing structure, which they knew how to influence, and he lost that struggle, too. Reagan then had to settle for a reform he didn't really favor but couldn't oppose because of its political popularity: converting the Veterans Administration into a cabinet department. The effort by the Republican-controlled 104th Congress to abolish the Commerce Department was similarly unsuccessful.

What Makes Bureaucracies Effective—Or Ineffective?

We have thus far been examining government bureaucracies, but we should remember that bureaucracy is also a fact of modern life in business and in every large organization, public or private, from General Motors to the Girl Scouts. All bureaucracies share certain key features, and bureaucrats in business use similar strategies to those used in government to get their way.

The Key Features of a Bureaucracy

A **bureaucracy** in its pure form is a type of organization that integrates a group of specialized human activities into a hierarchy with legal or rule-based authority to achieve continuous conduct of business.[16] Bureaucracies have existed in the Western world from ancient Rome to the present, all marked by five key characteristics. Each feature can make a government bureaucracy more effective or open it to criticism, depending on how sensitive bureaucrats are to the political context in which they work—a context of many bosses and many constituencies.

Continuous Conduct of Business

Presidents come and go, but the bureaucracy enables government to continue its work without serious interruption. Its continuity explains why the bureaucracy is sometimes called "the permanent government." For example, the Clean Air Act Amendments enacted under George Bush's presidency were implemented under Bill Clinton's presidency and his appointed EPA head—thanks to the thousands of EPA employees who had stayed on the job. Such bureaucratic continuity gives incoming administrations the carryover expertise essential to effective governance in times of rapid and continuous change. However, this same continuity also tends to create a vested interest in ongoing policies and practices that can make change more difficult.

Hierarchical Organization

Any bureaucracy is organized in a hierarchy, with superiors (or supervisors) giving orders to subordinates. Hierarchical organization makes it more likely that administration policies will be carried out. But hierarchy may also prevent important information from moving upward to decisionmakers, inhibiting the "feedback" needed for effective *learning by doing* that can improve policies and practices.

Task Specialization

Bureaucrats specialize in particular tasks so that any bureaucrat can be readily replaced by another expert with the same skills and training. This "division of labor" is supposed to increase efficiency, but in practice, because most policy questions are complex and their implications cut across these specializations, it can sometimes lead to fragmentation of effort, conflicts among policies, and inaction.

Law-Based and Rule-Based Authority

Bureaucrats get their authority from the laws that set up their agencies and the rules that organize them. In other words, the basis of bureaucratic authority is legal rather than personal, and a bureaucrat can claim authority and win political struggles by appealing to such laws and rules. These rules also protect bureaucrats from political pressures by ensuring that they are appointed and promoted on the basis of merit. Bureaucratic rules also specify the **standard operating procedures** (SOPs) bureaucrats are expected to follow in their day-to-day activities in order to increase efficiency and maintain the chain of command. Because bureaucrats do not personally own or control their own offices or those of their subordinates, they cannot pass their position on to someone else, nor can they hire or fire employees at will.

Because career bureaucrats get their authority from formal rules rather than from personal loyalty to superiors or to the public, their primary loyalty is usually to the bureaucratic body they are charged with administering rather than to the president or members of Congress. In contrast, other organizations, such as small businesses, may get their authority from the personal qualities or dictates of their chief administrators, who can hire and fire subordinates more freely.

Business via Written Documents

Organizations based on personal loyalty tend to operate by word of mouth and personal interaction. By contrast, a bureaucracy conducts its business largely through written documents, which allow bureaucrats to pass information upward to decisionmakers and to pass orders downward to those who carry them out. A bureaucracy is an "assembly line of information" in both directions,[17] and orders and information are purposefully intended to be clear and easily understood by those who receive them. The **paper trail** this practice leaves behind can make bureaucrats more accountable to other political actors, the media, and the people. It can also offer bureaucrats protection against charges of misbehavior as well as provide material evidence when there is bureaucratic or executive wrongdoing.

The Differences Between Public and Private Bureaucracies

The five formal features of governmental bureaucracy are also characteristic of nongovernmental organizations (NGOs, or the private sector). However, a governmental—or public—bureaucracy differs from a typical private bureaucracy in three important ways.

- *Goals.* The goals public bureaucrats must serve are imposed upon them by the political process. By contrast, business bureaucrats, at least those at the top, typically select their own goals.
- *Spending requirements.* Unlike their private sector counterparts, public sector bureaucrats are required to spend the resources they get as the president or Congress dictates.

Internet Addresses for Major Federal Agencies

You can get access to some of the information the federal government collects and manages or search for a particular agency via the Federal Web Locator:

http://www.law.vill.edu/Fed-Agency/fedwebloc.html

Among agencies of interest are the following:
Department of Commerce
Bureau of the Census
http://www.census.gov

Bureau of Economic Analysis
http://www.bea.doc.gov

FEDWorld
http://www.fedworld.gov

Department of Defense
http://www.dtic.dia.mi/defenselink/

Department of Education
http://www.ed.gov

Department of Health and Human Services
http://www.os.dhhs.gov

Centers for Disease Control
http://www.cdc.gov

National Institutes of Health
http://www.nih.gov

- *Funding.* Public sector bureaucrats can't keep any resources (what the private sector calls "profits") they save or make on their activities, such as collecting taxes or charging user fees at national parks. Instead, they must turn these funds over to the Treasury for reallocation through the budgetary process. As a result, public officials are not motivated by profits and often pay less attention to costs than they should—hence the periodic scandals about $600 toilet seats and $200 hammers bought by the Pentagon.

As a result of these differences, public sector bureaucrats tend to focus more on their institutional constraints and the interests of their particular bureau than on national policy goals.

What Bureaucrats Do

As we saw in the operations of the EPA in the opening case study, bureaucrats perform four functions vital to effective ongoing operation of any government: gathering and managing information, developing policies, converting policies into programs, and implementing programs. These functions are summarized in Figure 13.3.

1. *Gather and manage information.* Policymakers need information to act, and bureaucrats help them get it by monitoring the political, military, social, and economic environments for potential challenges and opportunities. They also help identify and define problems for their bosses.
2. *Develop policies.* Before top officials decide what to do, they usually review a range of options, including arguments for and against each choice, prepared by specialists in their agencies. These specialist bureaucrats usually act on orders of the political leadership. Sometimes, however, they develop policies on their own, even if the policies conflict with the views of their political superiors, because they are so committed to their area of expertise and responsibility or to a particular policy approach.
3. *Convert policies into programs.* Bureaucrats convert policy guidance—in the form of an executive order, a memo, or a law—into a program, a set of specific government actions designed to implement a policy decision. If a policy's objective is complicated, bureaucrats may have considerable discretion about how to convert the policy into programs.
4. *Implement programs.* Once programs have been developed, they are converted by bureaucrats into specific orders to other bureaucrats who will actually carry them out. Most of the time bureaucrats can use five ways of implementing programs:
    - *Deliver goods or services.* The Agriculture Department delivers food stamps to welfare agencies, which distribute them to people with low incomes, for example, while the Forest Service runs national forests.
    - *Regulate goods or behavior.* The Food and Drug Administration restricts the distribution of drugs and regulates the labeling of foods, while the EPA issues regulations implementing the Clean Air Act and penalizes firms for violating them.

Department of Justice
http://www.usdoj.gov

Department of Labor Bureau of Labor Statistics
http://stats.bls.gov

Department of State
http://dosfan.lib.uic.edu

Department of the Treasury
http://www.ustreas.gov

Bureau of Public Debt
http://192.239.92.204/treasury/bureaus/pubdebt

Central Intelligence Agency
http://www.is.gov

Environmental Protection Agency
http://www.epa.gov

Federal Communications Commission
http://www.fcc.gov

National Aeronautics and Space Administration
http://www.hq.nasa.gov/HQ_homepage.html

National Archives and Records Administration
http://www.nara.gov/1

National Science Foundation
http://www.nsf.gov

- *Furnish legal protection or guarantees.* To get people or firms to do certain activities, an agency may offer them special protection. For example, the federal government gives financial guarantees to banks that make student loans.
- *Handle money payments.* The government makes payments to retirees entitled to Social Security benefits and to college students who qualify for Pell grants, for example, and collects our Social Security "contributions" and our income tax payments.[18]
- *Adjudicate disputes.* With so many bureaucratic regulations on the books, and so many bureaucrats enforcing them, conflicts of interpretation (over who must do what) and conflicts of jurisdiction (over who should be allowed to do what) are bound to arise among agencies, between an agency and a nongovernmental organization, or between an agency and a citizen. Such disputes sometimes end up in the courts but are more often handled within the bureaucracy through political negotiation or administrative legal procedures.

Figure 13.3

The levels of bureauracracy and the stages of bureaucratic activity

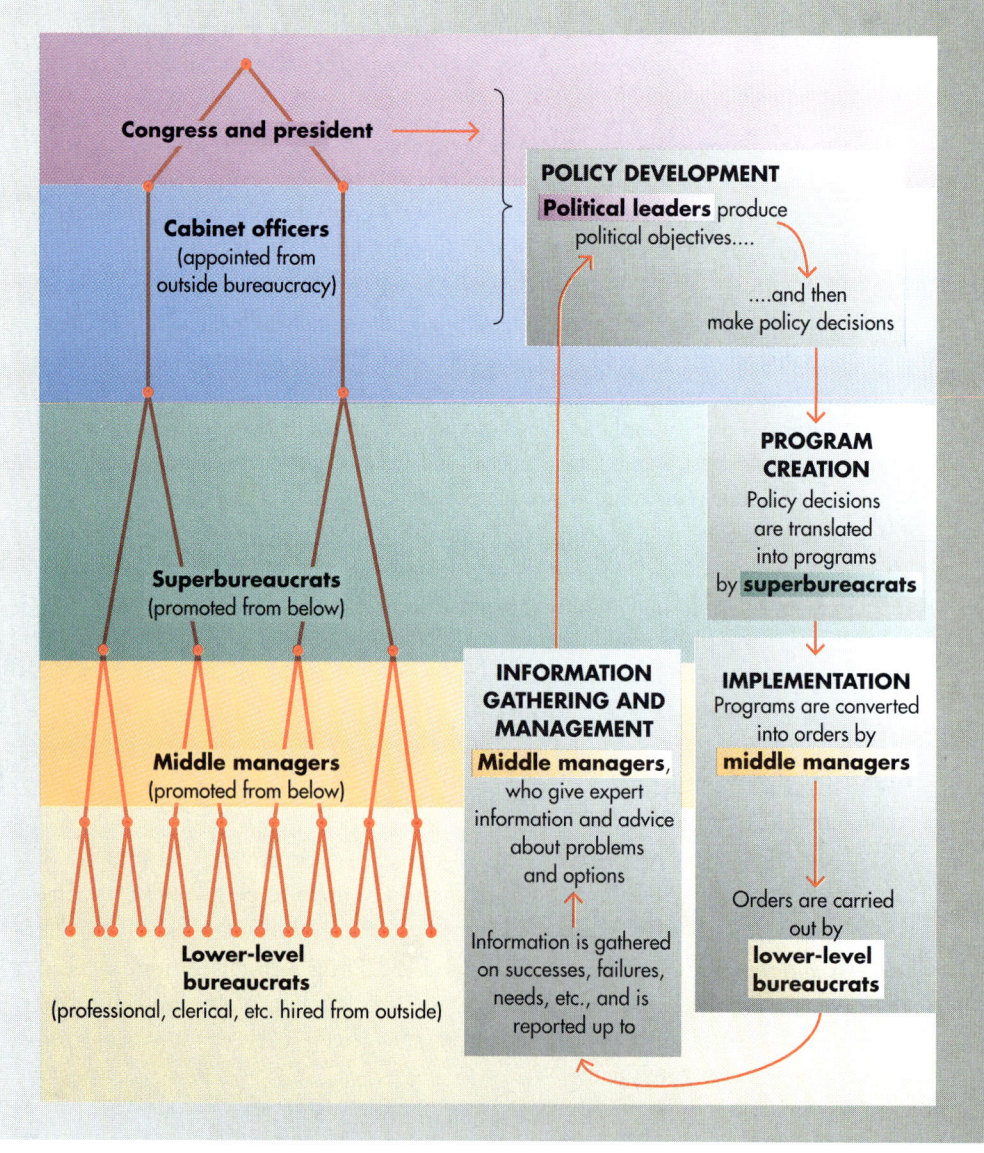

Congress and president

Cabinet officers (appointed from outside bureaucracy)

Superbureaucrats (promoted from below)

Middle managers (promoted from below)

Lower-level bureaucrats (professional, clerical, etc. hired from outside)

POLICY DEVELOPMENT
Political leaders produce political objectives....
....and then make policy decisions

PROGRAM CREATION
Policy decisions are translated into programs by **superbureacrats**

IMPLEMENTATION
Programs are converted into orders by **middle managers**

Orders are carried out by **lower-level bureaucrats**

INFORMATION GATHERING AND MANAGEMENT
Middle managers, who give expert information and advice about problems and options

Information is gathered on successes, failures, needs, etc., and is reported up to

The Politics of Bureaucracies

As political bodies, bureaucracies are constantly engaged in struggles to get their way. In a government that is actually a network of bureaucracies, interagency conflict over money and authority is inevitable. Because the budgetary pie is always limited, agencies find themselves competing for resources with other agencies with similar interests. They also struggle over jurisdiction whenever a major new governmental project cuts across the established responsibilities of existing agencies. The result is **bureaucratic politicking**—the perpetual struggle among different agencies for scarce resources and greater responsibilities.[19]

Scholars studying policymaking in various substantive areas find that bureaucratic politicking has the following tendencies:

- Bureaucrats and their decisions tend to be driven more by agency interests, such as survival, expansion of their spheres of responsibility, and a greater share of the budgetary pie, than by policy-relevant considerations such as efficiency, effectiveness, or the national interest.
- Bureaucrats are competing for power, position, and prestige within their agencies.
- Policy tends to be characterized by bargaining, accommodation, and compromise.[20]

How successful an agency is depends on many factors, among them the concept of effectiveness used to evaluate it, the role adopted by the leadership, the organizational culture, and the use of such power sources as information, expertise, secrecy, and discretion by its bureaucrats.

Conflicts over Goals and Interests

Political actors disagree over how to evaluate a bureaucratic agency's effectiveness because they disagree over what the agency should do. A political leader such as a president or an appointed agency head will want bureaucrats to adopt his or her political program and to work to achieve it by offering good ideas and being loyal and skillful in following orders. The leader may also want the agency to use resources efficiently—that is, at costs reasonable given the benefits and the alternatives. However, career managers who are the day-to-day leaders of an agency, coordinating the activities of hundreds or even thousands of specialists, may have quite different leadership goals, foremost among them:

- protecting the interests—whether budget or missions—of their agency
- advancing a particular program or policy—most often one that benefits the agency's clientele, such as the Agriculture Department's concern to help farmers rather than consumers

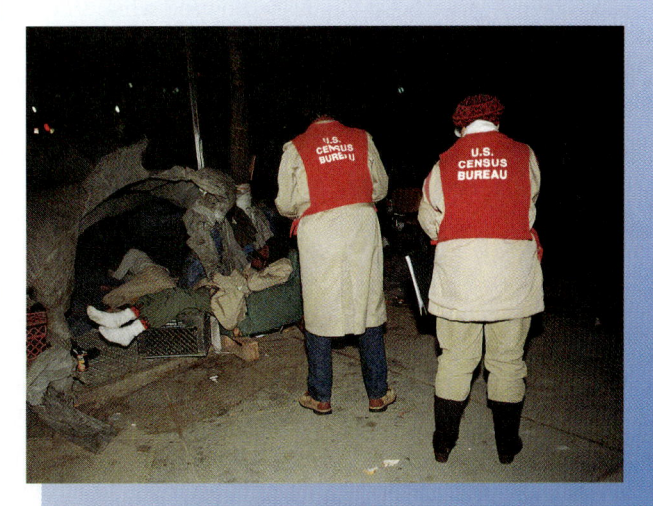

Census Bureau employees approach homeless people in Washington, D.C., to interview them for inclusion in the 1990 census.

- responding to the popular will, usually as their political superiors define it
- defending the national interest, even when that means sacrificing these first three interests
- advancing their own careers.[21]

Some observers of bureaucracy think the personal political attitudes or ideologies of officials are important in how well bureaucracy functions, but most experts believe ideology rarely plays a major role, except in cases such as civil rights enforcement.[22] These diverging interests—typically leaders seeking responsiveness and bureaucrats seeking resources—can make leaders and bureaucrats adversaries. However, bureaucrats need leaders to get them resources, and leaders need bureaucrats to carry out their policies. So, despite diverging ideas about bureaucratic effectiveness, they must cooperate. Any in any case, how effective particular motivations may be will depend on such other factors as the agency's culture and the administration's intent.

Organizational Culture

The motivation of superiors may have less impact on an agency's effectiveness if the organizational culture of the agency—its shared sense of mission—elicits a strong and unified commitment by most employees. Many observers point to the Social Security Administration as an example. Its employees share the longstanding commitment of the American people to furnishing retired people with pensions after they have contributed to the program during their working lives.[23]

In the Central Intelligence Agency, on the other hand, the motives of superiors can be crucial because the agency has two very different missions—intelligence gathering and "operations," or covert activities such as destabilizing or even overthrowing other governments. The people who work in the analytical, or "white," side of the agency have a different organizational culture from those working in the clandestine, or "black," side. The agency itself suffers because each branch devalues the other, so some have suggested splitting the agency into two by function. However, the covert side couldn't function effectively without the intelligence furnished by the white side. Furthermore, both branches need secrecy to function at all, and providing such security to both separately would be less efficient and more costly. Thus they remain joined—a discordant union of conflicting agency cultures.

Administration Intent

We normally assume that a bureaucracy's effectiveness should be measured by the success of the policy it is carrying out, but there are often conflicts between the goals of the political leadership of an administration and the long-term policy responsibilities of an agency established by law and tradition. In such cases, the administration may seek to impose its goals on a reluctant bureaucracy.

During the Reagan and Bush administrations, the federal government was often caught failing to implement major parts of health, environmental, and housing laws passed by Congress and signed by the president. For example, two decades after the Environmental Protection Agency was ordered to identify and regulate hazardous air pollutants, it had issued emission standards for only seven chemicals. Seven years after Congress in 1984 ordered the cleanup of toxic waste dumps that pollute land and water supplies, the EPA had issued no final regulations to accomplish that task. As a result, cleanup was delayed, the affected industries still did not know what they would be required to do, and people went right on breathing bad air and drinking dangerous water, often without knowing it.

Why the delays? Recent efforts have been hampered by a combination of highly complex and sometimes contradictory directives from Congress plus foot-dragging by the bureaucracy under orders from political officials ideologically opposed to enforcing the laws. But delays often occur even when bureaucrats know what to do and want to do it. Under a policy adopted by the Reagan administration and continued by the Bush administration, every agency first had to clear proposed regulations with the Office of Management and Budget, which often demanded changes designed to lessen the paperwork or financial cost to business.[24] While the Clinton administration ended this requirement, it was severely limited by the enormous federal debt and deficit and by the requirement imposed by the 1991 budget agreement that any spending increases be offset by spending cuts. So the administration's intent is, in turn, affected by the larger political environment.

Using the Instruments of Bureaucratic Power

Whatever the political context and whatever the administration's goals, bureaucrats can enhance the chances of a policy's success—or sabotage it—by making judicious use of six important resources: information, expertise, secrecy, discretionary authority, administrative law, and support from clientele groups.

Access to Information

Information is the key to power and effective action in virtually every area of a complex society—especially politics. Even money, if it is to be used effectively, must be properly channeled, and allocation requires information. Votes, too, are usually won by information about preferences and projected policy outcomes.

While Americans consume some 7 trillion words a day through the electronic and print media, and close to 2 million Americans work in information-related professions,[25] no private group—whether it be a business, a mass medium, or a university—has as much access to information as the federal government. The federal government is the world's largest collector, producer, publisher, and disseminator of information,[26] each year spending an estimated $100 billion collecting nearly 300 billion bits of data. Citizens and private organizations spend an estimated $140 billion gathering and reporting much of this information to government. The rest the government gathers by itself—often in secret.[27] This enormous collection of information can be a source of great power, but it is also often a source of severe problems of information management because of the hierarchy, specialization, and centralization of the government.[28]

Bureaucrats decide who gets access to the information they gather. The information management policies they develop serve various purposes beyond effective policymaking, such as increasing support for programs the bureaucracy favors, limiting public awareness of alternatives, or preventing opponents in or out of government from learning about the failures of programs. Indeed, as one expert puts it, "Agencies tend to utilize information as a private political resource rather than as a program-oriented social good."[29] The requirements of democracy and those of bureaucracy often conflict, however. An effective democracy depends upon a well-informed citizenry, while a powerful bureaucracy usually requires strict information management. We'll see how "bureaucratic propaganda"[30] and secrecy practices work as we examine policy battles in government throughout this book.

Use of Expertise

Experts analyze information for accuracy and recommend how to use it to develop, implement, or kill particular policies and programs. Experts may believe themselves to be scrupulously fair, offering their best judgment on questions put to them, but the questions are usually selected and posed by elected officials or political appointees with their own political agendas. Thus, even when expert professionals in government try to serve the public interest as they see it, they may be overruled by superiors with different objectives—sometimes by the president himself. EPA administrator Carol Browner's sudden willingness to cooperate with the governors of major states in making auto emissions regulations more flexible was likely influenced by the importance of those large states to Clinton's prospects for reelection in 1996.

When political actors disagree with an agency's experts, they often seek out other experts—elsewhere in the government, in academia, or in think tanks—whose views they prefer. So the public and politicians alike find themselves confronted with alleged experts who disagree among themselves on the facts (*what is*), and sometimes on the values (*what's right*), of the issue in question. In such a situation, it is often hard for citizens to know which experts to believe. Politicians and bureaucrats with access to the government's vast information resources and to stables of experts eager to be advisors usually have an advantage over citizens, private organizations, and even other bureaucrats without such access. Ultimately, access to expertise can be even more important than access to information, because it is experts who decide what counts as information and what that information really means.

Secrecy

Often the most effective way to control information is to keep it secret. Secrecy allows it to be used for whatever purposes, in whatever ways, and at whatever times its controller wishes. Bureaucrats specialize in secrecy, classifying information into such categories as "top secret," "secret," and "confidential"—and even "eyes only" and "burn after reading." The official purpose of **classification** is to protect national security by removing sensitive government information from open access. There are 47 different—and often conflicting—security programs operated by government agencies, ranging from the military to the Department of Transportation, and 7,000 bureaucrats with the authority to classify documents. The box nearby describes the government's use and abuse of classification.

Discretionary Authority

Bureaucrats usually enjoy large discretionary authority in devising programs. Laws and executive orders rarely specify what is to be done down to the last detail because most matters are too complex for anyone but specialists to design. Furthermore, both Congress and the president often use ambiguous language to avoid alienating one side or another in policy debates.

Governmental Use and Abuse of Information Classification

No one knows how many government documents are classified today. Most agencies maintain files of the classified documents that they might need to refer to, and no outside source keeps track of them. When the military is finished using its classified documents, it turns them over to the National Archives for secure storage—but insists that most of them remain classified. The National Archives measures the classified military documents it holds in cubic feet: 80,000, which works out to an estimated 200 million pages. But that doesn't include diplomatic papers, nor documents still held by government agencies. In 1992, a historian working in the Archives found a 1917 report on American troop movements in Europe during World War I among the classified documents. When it had been reviewed in 1976, Army officials had decided it still needed to be classified! When efforts were made to limit the extent of classification in 1992, the Defense Department created a new category, "Unclassified Controlled Nuclear Information," which allowed it to treat unclassified information as if it were classified.[1]

No one denies that some documents really should be classified to protect national security. However, the classification system is prone to abuses. The most serious abuse is the use of classification to cover up illegal or controversial government activities, to protect incompetence, or to avoid embarrassment. Because political officials and bureaucrats decide what the national interest is and what information should be classified, they can readily use secrecy to increase their power and advance their own objectives.

In addition to concealing information, bureaucrats can also give—or "leak"—classified information to the media in order to discredit particular persons or programs, or to gain support for programs they favor.

Bureaucratic language itself also contributes to secrecy by distorting the conventional meaning of words or by inventing new words which to outsiders seem to be *jargon*—a specialized vocabulary used by an occupation. (The word comes from an old French term for the chattering of birds, which the word is thought to echo.) When bureaucrats use jargon that the public cannot understand, or when they use words euphemistically to reduce or heighten their impact on public opinion, then jargon becomes a *particular type of secrecy*. Sometimes jargon is more irritating than consequential. For example, bureaucrats may say they are "prioritizing" when they mean that they are "ranking in order of importance," or they may say that something is "highly scenario-dependent" when they mean that "the outcome depends on what happens." In other cases, however, as we saw in Chapter 1, bureaucrats use jargon to conceal what the public would find objectionable if it were expressed in ordinary language.[2]

One of the peculiarities of the government's system of classification is that some official documents are considered more "secret" than others.

---

[1] Stephen Budiansky, "Secrets: Cone of Silence," *U.S. News & World Report*, March 2, 1992, 13.
[2] For interesting accounts, see William Lutz, *Doublespeak: How Government, Business, Advertisers, and Others Use Language to Deceive You* (New York: HarperCollins, 1989), and Murray Edelman, *Political Language* (New York: Academic Press, 1977).

Some agencies tend to exercise more discretion than others because such "statutory ambiguity"[31] is especially common in regulatory areas such as environment, health, and occupational safety, where no one can anticipate the situations and circumstances agencies will confront, or the technical questions agency experts will have to decide, in implementing a particular policy.

Discretion is indispensable to policy implementation, but it can damage democracy by interfering with the accountability of elected officials to their constituents. Once elected, these officials make decisions on which they are supposed to be judged in the next election. But this accountability virtually disappears when nonelected experts and bureaucrats exercise so much implementation discretion that the programs no longer resemble what the elected officials voted on.[32]

Discretion tends to be curtailed only when Congress or the president decides that an agency has acted inappropriately. In such a case, a presidential order or congressional legislation—usually in the form of an appropriations rider or a new oversight committee—puts limits on the agency's freedom to act. For example, during the Nixon administration, when Congress discovered the CIA's illegal involvement in various covert operations—including attempts to overthrow foreign governments—it created a special congressional oversight committee charged with keeping an eye on CIA activities. This policy area is so sensitive that the committee deliberates in secret, making secret reports to Congress when it sees fit. At first the CIA cooperated with the committee, but cooperation was suspended when the Reagan administration's CIA director, William Casey, wanted the agency to undertake new activities that he doubted the committee would approve. One was assassinating Middle Eastern terrorists who threatened Americans in the region. Casey got Saudi Arabia to secretly finance the plan so he wouldn't have to request funds from Congress. Casey also arranged the sale of arms to Iran through Israel in exchange for the release of American hostages held in the Middle East. These illegal sales were made at inflated prices, so the proceeds could be funneled, against the expressed wishes of Congress, to the Contra rebels who were trying to overthrow the leftist Nicaraguan government. Despite the program, few hostages were freed, and when the arms delivery to the Contras failed, the operation became public. It became known as the Iran-Contra affair (see the box on page 470) and, not surprisingly, led to further efforts by Congress to restrict the CIA's discretionary authority.[33]

Administrative Law

Bureaucrats exercise a more formal kind of discretionary authority in their power to develop and apply administrative law. Statutes establishing agencies and programs usually contain an "elastic clause" instructing the administrator to make any rules "necessary" or "appropriate" to accomplish the purposes of the statute. The agency then draws up and publishes the rules and regulations it deems necessary. When an agency believes its regulations have been violated, or when a party contests its regulations, the agency often holds an administrative hearing. The order or decision issued by the hearing judge is just as binding as that of any court. This dual administrative and judicial role—implementing policy and adjudicating conflicts—significantly increases the power of the bureaucracy, even though such administrative rulings can often be appealed to the regular courts by discontented parties.[34]

Clientele Group Support

Agencies can also increase their effectiveness in policy battles by encouraging clientele groups to support them. Many bureaucratic agencies are, in fact, termed "clientele agencies" because their primary mission is to serve the interests of a particular clientele. The Agriculture Department, whose mission is to look out for the interests of farmers, fights efforts to cut government subsidies for farmers. In return for such protection, farm groups lobby lawmakers and other agencies for policies the Agriculture Department wants. Similarly, the Departments of the Interior, Labor, Commerce, Housing and Urban Development, Energy, Education, and Health and Human Services, as well as many regulatory agencies, defend the interests of their clienteles and in return receive the same kind of support. Bureaucrats who work in clientele agencies tend to have unusual power because the clienteles they serve are eager to lobby Congress and the president for increases in agency budgets and against limitations on agency powers.

How the Bureaucracy Interacts with Other Institutions

Even in the most harmonious of times, a three-way struggle goes on at the heart of government. The president and his staff attempt to get Congress to agree with his policy wishes and to get the executive branch bureaucracy to carry out those wishes. Congress and its own, smaller bureaucracy try to shape policy by legislating and by influencing both the president's policy decisions and the executive branch bureaucracy's implementation of laws and executive orders. Caught in the middle, the executive branch bureaucracy tries to follow these often conflicting orders while maintaining its own integrity and discretionary authority—and managing conflicts between various bureaus and agencies. And all the while, everyone has to be aware of the wishes of special interests and the people, and of the occasional attention of the courts and the continual attention of the media.

The Presidency, Congress, and the Bureaucracy

The president, as we saw in Chapter 12, appoints the top officials in each office of his own bureaucracy—the White House Office and the Executive Office of the President. He organizes the White House Office to suit his political style and to advance his own goals.[35] The Executive Office of the President oversees the enormous "permanent government" bureaucracy in the cabinet departments and the independent agencies and conducts most relations with Congress, the courts, and relevant state and local bureaucracies.

The effectiveness of presidential bureaucrats is often limited, however, because most are new to government service and must learn the political ropes. Moreover, many—including some cabinet secretaries—don't stick around very long. By the second half of a president's first term, many of these "in-and-outers" are on their way out, usually because they prefer to make more money in the private sector using the contacts and knowledge they've gained in government service or because they've had difficult relations with the career bureaucracy or with Congress.

Presidential-Bureaucratic Relations

The president appoints key bureaucratic leaders in virtually all agencies (the top management level in Table 13.1), issues orders to each agency, proposes each agency's budgetary appropriations and signs each appropriation into law, occasionally alters an agency's procedures, and sometimes even reorganizes an agency without congressional approval. It is little wonder he believes that the bureaucracy should be accountable to him.

The president and his own bureaucracy face two difficult problems in achieving and maintaining this accountability: keeping track of what these many large bureaucratic organizations are doing, and controlling their behavior when it matters to him. Fear that the presidency will not get vital information about what the various agencies are doing has been a major reason for the expansion of the president's own personal bureaucracy. By now, each important bureaucratic agency is being monitored by someone close to the president.

This strategy was developed to new heights in the Reagan administration, which practiced "counterstaffing" in an effort to maximize its ability to bring about drastic change. The strategy had three key components:

- selecting appointees to head key agencies who were strongly committed to the administration's desire to cut back old programs and undertake new policies and would anticipate that career bureaucrats would attempt to sabotage their efforts
- selecting appointees with little experience in the particular policy area so they would lack strong ties to those clientele groups seeking to continue current policies
- shifting officials from one bureau to another to prevent their "going native"—becoming advocates for their agencies or programs rather than for the administration's new policies.

This practice created friction, not just between the president's own bureaucrats and the permanent bureaucracy but also between the administration and interest groups, especially in controversial areas such as environmental policy.

But the Reagan approach was not typical. The president commonly relies more on influence than confrontation in his efforts to control the bureaucracy, for "in order to be successful, presidents must realize that the bureaucracy is their ally and that the bureaucracy will be a better ally to one who leads by persuasion than to one who leads by command."[36] And the president is in any case more likely to be effective when trying to slow an agency than when prodding an agency.[37]

Bureaucratic Resistance and Initiative

Bureaucrats can resist the president. One effective weapon of resistance a bureaucrat has is time, because while presidents come and go, the bureaucracy persists.

The Politics of Language

THE BUREAUCRAT'S TEN COMMANDMENTS

According to Leslie Gelb and Morton Halperin, two former national security bureaucrats, most bureaucrats usually follow their own version of the Bureaucrat's Ten Commandments:

1. Don't discuss domestic politics on issues involving war and peace—even if they influence your view.
2. Say what will convince, not what you believe.
3. Support the consensus.
4. Veto other options so that only yours remains.
5. Predict dire consequences if other options are adopted.
6. Argue timing, not substance.
7. Leak what you don't like.
8. Ignore orders you don't like.
9. Don't tell likely opponents about a good thing.
10. Don't fight the consensus and don't resign over policy.

Source: Adapted from Leslie H. Gelb and Morton H. Halperin, "Diplomatic Notes: The Ten Commandments of the Foreign-Affairs Bureaucracy," *Harper's*, June 1972, 28–37.

So bureaucrats unhappy with their treatment by a president, or discontented with policies he is attempting to impose, can often simply outlast him, even engaging in passive resistance. An aide to President Dwight Eisenhower once remarked that after six years in office, "The President still feels that when he's decided something that ought to be the end of it . . . and when it bounces back undone or done wrong, he tends to react with shocked surprise."[38]

Such resistance can even extend upward to presidential appointees, who may have a clearer sense than the president of what can reasonably be obtained from the permanent bureaucracy. "Half of a President's suggestions, which theoretically carry the weight of orders, can be safely forgotten by a Cabinet member," remarked an aide to President Franklin Roosevelt. "And if the President asks about a suggestion a second time, he can be told that it is being investigated. If he asks a third time a wise Cabinet officer will give him at least part of what he suggests. But only occasionally, except about the most important matters, do Presidents ever get around to asking three times."[39]

A more active measure of resistance is the **leak**—the anonymous communication to a trusted reporter of information the president wishes kept confidential. Items commonly leaked are proposed policies or actions. Indeed, one of "The Bureaucrat's Ten Commandments" developed by two former bureaucrats is "Leak what you don't like" to alert possible opponents so they can attack and resist a proposal before it is enacted.[40] The other principles for winning bureaucratic struggles are summarized in the box above.

Another mode of bureaucratic resistance is **backchanneling**, which allows one to circumvent the normal bureaucratic chain of communication by resorting to a hidden route—often someone on the outside who can convey information or exert pressure on key decisionmakers. In the Reagan administration, it was widely believed that Reagan's wife Nancy was the most reliable backchannel to her husband but that she would only act as such if she strongly agreed with what she was asked to communicate.[41] Hillary Rodham Clinton has played the same role. Shortly after resigning, Labor Secretary Robert Reich described her response to his complaint that he couldn't get memos to his longtime friend, the president: "Send them to me. I'll see that they get to him. Use blank sheets of paper without any letterhead or other identifying characteristics. Just the date and your initials."[42]

On the other hand, bureaucrats can sometimes use the president to achieve their own policy goals. For example, they can begin to implement a policy without informing their high-level political superiors, knowing that once the policy is in place the president will be unlikely to reverse it and reveal thereby that he is not in charge. Bureaucrats can also use the president to strike back at a hostile or unsupportive Congress by supplying the president with information that can be used to frustrate lawmakers' agendas, for bureaucrats are the custodians of virtually everything the government knows about policies and practices—and much that is known about politicians.

During a bill-signing ceremony at the White House, Secretary of Labor Robert Reich listens to First Lady Hillary Rodham Clinton, who served as his "backchannel" to the president.

Congressional-Bureaucratic Relations

Congress expects the bureaucracies to be accountable to it because Congress created most of the agencies, authorizes their programs, appropriates their budgets every year, and holds regular oversight hearings to determine whether key agencies are behaving properly. The Senate also confirms top presidential appointments. To exercise its influence, Congress has its own set of bureaucracies, which we examined in Chapter 11—office staffs, committee staffs, and support agencies including the General Accounting Office (which investigates executive branch conduct) and the Congressional Budget Office.

If any agency behaves in a way that upsets powerful members of Congress or follows presidential directives at odds with the wishes of Congress, or if it faces a Congress in which hostile interest groups have significant power, the result may be congressional involvement that creates paralysis. An expert study of the operations of the Consumer Product Safety Commission, the Occupational Safety and Health Administration, and the EPA concluded that "opposing groups are dedicated to crippling the bureaucracy and gaining control over its decisions" in these areas, and they pressure Congress to pass legislation creating "fragmented authority, labyrinthine procedures, mechanisms of political intervention, and other structures that subvert the bureaucracy's performance and open it up to attack."[43]

But bureaucrats can also use Congress to get what they want—especially in contests with the president. If a president shrinks an agency's budget, operating autonomy, or missions, its officials may ask Congress to restore these through legislation. President Nixon sought to prevent the Legal Services Division of the Office of Economic Opportunity, created in the Johnson years, from continuing to furnish free legal assistance to the poor. So the agency went to Congress and got itself converted into the Legal Services Corporation (LSC), headed by a governing board whose members, while nominated by the president, were subject to confirmation by the Senate. When Reagan became president, he proposed shutting the agency down. When Congress refused to go along, he then tried to stack its governing board with people who would change its policies, but the Senate refused to confirm most of his nominees. So the LSC continued to furnish free legal aid to the poor against the wishes of its titular head, the president. Only when Republicans gained control of both houses of Congress in 1994 were they able to eviscerate the LSC (Chapter 14).

Patterns of Cooperation

Instances of struggle remain atypical. "What is surprising is not that bureaucrats sometimes can defy the president," writes James Q. Wilson, "but rather that they support his programs as much as they do. The reason is rather simple....[B]ureaucrats want to do the right thing. The more skillful of Reagan's conservative appointees proved that: Though most bureaucrats were much more liberal than their political superiors and though there were pockets of resistance, in many agencies . . . the careerists served the policies of their ideologically distant chiefs."[44]

What prevents the ongoing struggle between the presidency and the Congress over control of the bureaucracy from producing stalemate and paralysis? Some agencies have long been typically more responsive to the president, among them the Departments of State, Treasury, and Justice and the Central Intelligence Agency. Others are generally more responsive to Congress, among them the Departments of Agriculture, Interior, Housing and Urban Development, and Veterans Affairs. Furthermore, both the president and Congress have an interest in the bureaucracy's functioning effectively because neither can conduct the affairs of government itself.

Nor can the courts, which depend on government agencies to carry out their orders because they have only minuscule bureaucracies for housekeeping, they depend on government agencies to carry out their orders on matters ranging from a major public policy issue such as school desegregation to small matters like disposing of a *habeas corpus* petition from an individual prisoner. Courts hand down decisions ordering agencies to change the way they act and expect the agencies to enforce these orders on themselves.[45] As we'll see in Chapter 14, the courts often defer to recommendations by the executive branch on how to handle particular cases. And in some cases, a bureaucratic agency may be able to use the courts to its own ends. For example, an agency may informally encourage special interests to sue it in order to get a court order to force the agency to do something it wants to do that is against the president's wishes.

Bureaucratic Relations with Special Interests, the Media, and the People

The bureaucracy has relations of mutual dependence with special interests, the media, and the people, as it does with Congress and the presidency.

Special Interests

Interest groups try to coordinate their policy efforts with bureaucrats and congressional members or staffers through informal arrangements that political scientists call "iron triangles," "subgovernments," and "issue networks." As we saw in Chapter 8, lobbyists for special interest groups, career bureau chiefs, and lawmakers heading the committees or subcommittees involved in some policy areas meet regularly to decide important questions about programs and budgets, often without consulting presidential assistants. These **iron triangles** or **subgovernments** allow bureaucrats who are unable to win through infighting with other agencies in the executive branch to achieve their objectives in another way.

Iron triangles first sprang up in such policy areas as agriculture, water, and public works, where the major political actors tended to outlast presidents and specific issues alike. However, they are less common now for several reasons. Both government and special interests are becoming increasingly specialized as interests grow more complex and change more rapidly. Take the case of agriculture. In the past, "agriculture" meant "the farm problem," and its solution involved guaranteeing stable incomes to farmers facing uncertain weather and fluctuating interest rates on loans carrying them from planting to harvest. The iron triangle composed of farm lobbyists, key bureaucrats from the Agriculture Department, and staffers from the congressional agriculture committees and subcommittees developed the government's agricultural policies and administrative rules through ongoing consultation and negotiation. Today, however, the world of agriculture is so big and complex that most problems involve whole clusters of interests, not just three sides. While agricultural policies still involve farmers, they also involve giant grain companies that seek to export surplus grain to other countries. Because food may be used as a lever against hostile foreign countries or a support for friendly ones, the State Department now takes an active interest in agricultural policy. And because petroleum fuels farm machinery and is used to make fertilizer, pesticides, and herbicides, agricultural policies must deal with oil and natural gas interests. Furthermore, oil is sometimes used by foreign countries as a weapon against the United States, and grain can be used to make substitute fuel, so the Defense Department now has a strong interest in agricultural policy. In addition, agricultural policymaking must take account of the multibillion-dollar food stamp welfare program, which indirectly supports farm prices. Thus agricultural policy has broadened to include clusters of policies—farm, defense, energy, trade, welfare, and health, among others—and results from "webs of influence" exercised by many different political actors and their experts in competing policy areas.

These new policy systems are now generally called **issue networks**—"shared knowledge groups" that bring together large numbers of interested parties with overlapping technical expertise.[46] Unlike iron triangles, issue networks continually form and disband according to the policy issues under consideration. Policy actors constantly move in and out of these networks, so no individual or clique is able to dominate the policy process over time. This lack of control makes long-range planning virtually impossible, so policy often lacks coherence and consistency, and direction is more and more a matter of incremental change.[47]

The Media

The media get valuable information on policy successes and failures, plans, and attitudes from ambitious or discontented bureaucrats. Bureaucrats in turn use the media to leak confidential information, accusations, and other things they can't say publicly. Sometimes they take these actions on orders from higher-ups, other times to sabotage policies of their superiors that they oppose. They also sometimes use media to leak **disinformation**—false information intentionally presented as true. For example, in 1986 the president's national security advisor John Poindexter secretly arranged for the State Department to leak information to several leading newspapers about phony administration plans to attack Libya, which he hoped would scare Libya's leader, Colonel Muammar Qaddafi, who opposed American policy in the Middle East. Only later did the press discover that it had been duped.

Despite such incidents, television and other media have become valuable—and sometimes indispensable—sources of domestic and even international information. In the early days of the Gulf War, for example, Defense Secretary Richard Cheney told the press that he was getting most of his information on the effects of U.S. bombing raids on Iraq by watching television's Cable News Network, which had a correspondent stationed in downtown Baghdad. The scandalous corruption in the Department of Housing and Urban Development in the Reagan years was uncovered in congressional hearings because Representative Tom Lantos (D-Calif.) read an article in the *Washington Post* about misbehavior in HUD and investigated, after the congressional committees responsible for HUD oversight had missed the story.

The People

We all depend on federal bureaucracies for protection against various threats—ranging from foreign enemies abroad to faulty products—and for performance of the essential tasks of government as well as for information we need to be responsible citizens.

Take the meat and poultry inspectors who protect us from food poisoning and fraud. Despite these bureaucratic activities, some 5 million Americans get food poisoning every year, and more than 4,000 die of it. Still, managers of meatpacking companies often complain that inspectors make their work harder and more costly. After several deadly outbreaks, the government in 1996 tightened inspection practices, but the new standards still allow 25 percent of all chicken and 18 percent of all hogs to be contaminated with fecal matter when they leave the slaughterhouse for the grocery store. Why? Because the Clinton administration bureaucrats had to compromise with the meatpacking industry and a Congress responsive to its pressures.

However much we may complain about bureaucracy in general, or criticize it in cases where it defers to special interests we disapprove of, when faced with problems we cannot handle we often turn to a government bureaucrat for assistance. "The public really does exercise a great deal of influence over the federal bureaucracy, or at least some people do," concludes one scholar. "Most agencies listen to a comfortable circle of friends and supporters," especially their clients and outside professional expert advisors, along with their critics in government, the media, and the public.[48]

The public also serves as the primary source of new bureaucrats. As we've noted, the federal bureaucracy hires over half a million people each year for jobs located everywhere in the country and in many places around the world. Governmental bureaucracies also depend on the people for the tax money that finances their salaries and activities and for feedback about policies and proposed regulations that people offer by testifying at hearings, complaining to public officials, or filing lawsuits.

Bureaucracies also construct very detailed databases on each one of us out of census data and various surveys conducted by government agencies. As a result, they know what we do, where we live, how much money we earn, how we spend money, and what we think about various questions. Many believe that this information threatens our civil liberties, as we'll see in Chapter 15. Bureaucrats use most of the information they gather to improve policy and regulation. However, they also sell some of it to private businesses, which repackage it for resale at high prices—a practice many believe is contrary to the rights of citizens whose taxes pay for the gathering of the information.[49]

Reforming Bureaucracy

The original argument for bureaucracy was that it could increase both equity (getting fair and equal treatment) and efficiency—both long valued in American politics. According to most citizens today, however, bureaucracy's biggest problems are limits on *efficiency* from waste and "red tape" and insufficient *equity*. Bureaucracy does serve equity in the sense that it tends to operate impersonally—that is, by treating apparently similar people similarly. But critics say the result in particular cases is often insensitivity and even inhumanity. Bureaucracy serves efficiency by operating in standardized ways, using the same procedures and rules over and over in similar cases rather than necessitating a new way of coping with each individual case. But critics say the consequences may be unresponsiveness to particular needs, arbitrary rule by bureaucrats acting in a standardized way without actual legal authority, and slowness in responding to emergencies.

Some say that these two values—equity and efficiency—are tradeoffs, and one has to decide which value to emphasize. Others say that a bureaucracy with appropriate authority and adequately trained and paid personnel can advance both equity and efficiency.

Most outside experts and political actors agree that the biggest problem with bureaucracy today is *accountability*—the capacity of the president, and sometimes Congress, to control what bureaucrats do. Activist citizens, however, often advocate increased citizen access to and control of the bureaucracy. And some reformers argue that the bureaucracy should become more representative of the population as a whole in terms of gender and ethnicity, so that it will offer more job opportunities to and be more sensitive to the concerns of those groups who so far benefit least. Finally, some of the targets of bureaucratic regulation—particularly business and industry—argue that the *scope of government action* undertaken by bureaucracy is too broad and should be drastically limited by privatizing or decentralizing certain functions long the province of government.

Bureaucracies are easy targets for criticism because every agency, every policy, and every action tends to benefit some people and hurt others. The box nearby summarizes common criticisms. To cope with such criticisms, specialists have proposed various reforms.

red tape

The term *red tape* derives from the red ribbon used in previous centuries to tie up legal documents in England.

Bureaucracy and Democracy

Bureaucracies were never intended to be democratic, as we have seen. Bureaucrats are not chosen by the people, nor are they supposed simply to do the will of the people.[50] The Administrative Procedure Act of 1946 does require minimal public participation in federal agency programs by mandating public notice and comment during rule making and opportunities for groups to be heard during adjudications. Furthermore, in recent decades many government agencies have provided for increased citizen input through such practices as conducting opinion surveys, creating toll-free "800" telephone numbers, setting up Web pages on the Internet, and staging hearings on proposed new regulations at various locations around the country. But only citizens with time and money are usually able to take advantage of these opportunities.[51] Indeed, to find out that rules are being considered, you usually have to read the *Federal Register*. Have you ever even seen, let alone read, a copy of this turgid and enormous daily book? Few citizens—even attentive citizens—have.

> For interesting advice on "How to Get What You Want and Need from the Bureaucracy," visit this Web site maintained by Bob Alman of San Francisco:
>
> http://www.ontheweb.com/usca/bureaucra.html

Common Criticisms of Bureaucracy

Almost everyone has something to say about what's wrong with bureaucracy. But there are some common themes in the critiques offered by scholars and political actors. These are:

- *Clientelism*. Bureaucratic agencies tend to serve and even protect and promote the interests of those they are supposed to oversee, often at the expense of the public interest or of citizens in general.
- *Incrementalism*. Bureaucracies tend to operate slowly and cautiously rather than efficiently and imaginatively, resisting change wherever possible.
- *Arbitrariness*. Bureaucracies tend to apply abstract rules to concrete individual cases in ways that ignore the special merits or concerns of those being affected.
- *Imperialism*. Agencies seek to expand their own powers and responsibilities at the expense of other agencies and programs, regardless of broader considerations of how best to meet needs.
- *Parochialism*. Agencies focus narrowly on their own goals and thereby miss the big picture of government policy and the public interest.
- *Waste*. Bureaucracies, because of their size and procedures, use resources less efficiently than the private sector.

When agencies try to respond to such problems, they sometimes come up with solutions as bad as the difficulty that led to the original "bureau-bashing." For example, to respond to criticisms of clientelism, a bureau may engage in *particularism*—responding to particular people, organizations, or legislative districts. This changes the beneficiaries but does not address the real underlying concern that the public interest is not being served. Similarly, responding to charges that incrementalism prevents progress, an agency may shift its focus to outputs (such as funds given to the poor) rather than outcome (such as numbers of people raised from poverty by the program) in order to create an illusion of progress through quantitative "bean counting," as it's sometimes called.[1]

---

[1] See William T. Gormley, *Taming the Bureaucracy: Muscles, Prayers, and Other Strategies* (Princeton, N.J.: Princeton University Press, 1989), Chapter 1.

Bureaucratic Ethics

Public officials are expected to be public servants—"custodians of the public trust." They take an oath to uphold the Constitution and the law. But bureaucrats cannot be voted out of office, and dismissal, as we've seen, is very difficult. Therefore we usually depend on the personal integrity of such officials to keep them from wrongdoing.

Sometimes the question is not so much wrongdoing as a "judgment call"—at least to the participants trying to decide *what's right*—and we often disagree among ourselves when it comes to specifying *what's right* for a bureaucrat.[52] When Admiral John Poindexter and Colonel Oliver North deceived Congress during the Iran-Contra affair, their conduct was illegal, but their motive was not greed. Rather, these bureaucrats thought their conduct was right because they believed that they were serving "the national interest," or at least President Reagan's wishes. Most Americans disagreed once the facts about their actions were brought to light in a congressional investigation.

Three ethical dilemmas tend to be particularly difficult for bureaucrats. Should they lie for a cause or a policy that seems good? Should they obey orders from a superior when the orders seem immoral? Should they leak secret information to reveal an illegal or unethical plan or action? In each case, the bureaucrat has to decide for himself or herself what's right.

Many ethical questions are not dilemmas, however, and in some cases appropriate behavior has been written into federal laws. The law provides some guidance in avoiding **conflicts of interest**—cases in which an individual benefits personally from something he or she does in an official capacity. Bureaucrats who decide what firms get government contracts must relinquish control of their own financial investments, for example, to avoid the potential for personal gain. The Ethics in Government Act, passed in 1978 after the Watergate scandal, requires that members of Congress and 3,000 of their bureaucrats, along with federal judges and 12,000 high-ranking executive branch officials, publicly disclose their assets each year so that observers can be alerted to possible conflicts of interest. The law also prohibits former bureaucrats from engaging in "influence peddling"—selling to special interests their ability to get access to former colleagues—for a time after they leave office.

Bureaucrats may face less stunning but perhaps more consequential challenges in fulfilling their roles in the policy process. For example, should a bureaucrat, who is unelected, help to create public perception of a problem, mobilize constituencies for a program to solve a problem, or draft legislation for Congress in the absence of orders from above? The laws do not address this question, so the bureaucrat must decide what's right for himself or herself. The same holds for opportunities bureaucrats may have to weaken or kill a program by hiring incompetent people to administer it or by obstructing or subverting its implementation.

Concern with this broad range of ethical questions has led to various approaches to guiding bureaucratic behavior. One approach involves laws and rules, such as those concerning financial disclosure and conflict of interest. General principles place the emphasis on individual responsibility of the bureaucrat.[53] Over recent decades, most federal agencies developed their own ethical standards. However, the standards tended to vary considerably from one agency to the next,

Oliver North explains in a congressional hearing why he decided to break the law in acting as he believed his boss, President Ronald Reagan, wished him to during the Iran-contra affair, when he was a member of the national security staff.

making it almost impossible for the public to know what was required. Finally, the Office of Government Ethics, at President Bush's direction, developed a single, comprehensive, and understandable ethics code to apply uniformly to all employees in the executive branch. That code took effect in 1992, replacing more than 100 different and often conflicting agency regulations dealing with such questions as receiving gifts from outside sources and avoiding financial conflicts of interest. But ethical codes cannot possibly cover all cases where ethical considerations arise, and the more general they are made to cover the wide range of possibly relevant cases, the less helpful they are likely to be in actually deciding what to do in particular cases.[54]

Top-Down Bureaucratic Reform

Every president takes office promising to "fix" the bureaucracy—usually by "trimming fat," "ending waste," and increasing "effectiveness." Presidents Reagan and Clinton brought quite different views about *what's right* and *what works* in bureaucracy to the presidency, and their actions in office reflected these differences.

Reagan's Accountability Initiative

President Reagan achieved unprecedented accountability by adding new layers of political loyalists on top of the career bureaucracy and instituting tighter budgetary and policy controls over the activities of career bureaucrats through the Office of Management and Budget. Whenever a president achieves greater accountability, however, two things inevitably happen. First, the most qualified and experienced career bureaucrats tend to leave government service because they have lost the responsibility that gave them job satisfaction. Second, the political loyalists depart from accepted practices and sometimes even violate the law. Halfway through the Reagan administration, almost half of the newly designated Senior Executive Service veterans had left the government. Their departure was followed by a series of scandals culminating in the Iran-Contra affair. Many observers attributed the extent and magnitude of these scandals to the weakening of the career bureaucracy brought about by Reagan's instituting greater accountability.

Clinton's "Reinventing Government" for Efficiency and Economy

Bill Clinton entered office with a different orientation toward bureaucratic reform—one shaped by his 12-year experience as governor of Arkansas and his enthusiasm for the arguments of two experts on government reform who wrote a 1992 national best-seller called *Reinventing Government*.[55]

Shortly after taking office, Clinton charged Vice President Al Gore with leading a National Performance Review to recommend ways of "reinventing," or restructuring, the federal government. After studying the operation of the major bureaucratic agencies and evaluating a wide range of proposals for reform, the NPR—which insiders quickly dubbed REGO (short for *reinventing*

> National Performance Review (the home of the Clinton "reinventing government" program):
> http://www.npr.gov

government)—came up with seven goals for executive agencies: developing a clear vision, creating a team environment, empowering employees, putting customers first, communicating with employees, cutting red tape, and creating clear accountability.[56] The NPR also made three novel reform recommendations:

- Instead of calling for greater business efficiency, the NPR recommended stimulating experimental initiatives that would empower bureaucrats, pushing decisions down to the level where they meet citizens face to face, converting "large, top-down, centralized bureaucracies" into organizations that constantly learn, innovate, and improve.

- Instead of the traditional call for greater democratic accountability, the NPR recommended that agencies be made more "entrepreneurial"—more responsive to citizens—through "market-style incentives," based on competition, rewards, and sanctions. This approach is sometimes called the "antibureaucracy" model because it emphasizes delegation and flexibility rather than hierarchy and rules.[57] The approach originated in the private sector, and its effectiveness in the public sector remains to be seen.

- Instead of restructuring government to expand the power of the president to lead, as the ten previous presidential commissions on improved governmental functioning had recommended, the NPR recommended a focus on restoring the reputation of the government, which had lost the trust of the people, by emphasizing service to citizens, who should be considered as customers.[58]

Vice President Al Gore, appointed by President Bill Clinton to head his National Performance Review, charged with "reinventing government," releases an NPR report while standing amid stacks of the kind of government paperwork that the report recommended be eliminated.

To implement these transformations, the NPR recommended simplifying rules and procedures so agencies could easily survey citizen satisfaction with public services, develop their own job application forms tailored to their own special needs (to replace the single complex form used by all agencies), and simplify the "procurement process" by which government buys goods and services so as to prevent waste and scandalous overcharging. In addition, it encouraged agency heads to create "innovation labs" charged with developing new ideas on how government workers can do their jobs better.

At first cynics doubted that anything would change, but Gore began supervising efforts to put these recommendations into practice. Innovation labs were created in a hundred agencies, and procurement was reformed. Some agency programs were cut while others were transferred to the states, where they might be handled with more flexibility and efficiency. Finally, bureaucratic rolls were cut by 100,000, with plans for cutting another 200,000 put in place.

When Republicans won control of both houses of Congress in 1994, the new House leadership brought with it yet another reform agenda, the "Contract with America." Its focus was on curtailing the scope of governmental activity, especially regulation of industry. However, as we saw in Chapter 11, skepticism in the Senate, resistance by Clinton, and growing public opposition combined to prevent most of these proposals from becoming law.

Other Reform Proposals

Most proposed reforms that receive support today have remained popular for decades without being put into practice. Political actors want to increase the bureaucracy's accountability to them. Advocates of democracy and citizen participation want to foster greater representativeness in bureaucratic ranks, and lobbyists for business and industry tend to want to curtail government's scope.

Making Bureaucracy More Accountable

Advocates of increased accountability tend to favor "sunset laws" and "sunshine laws." A **sunset law** requires that an existing program or agency be regularly reviewed for its effectiveness. If it passes that review, its life is extended; if not, the program is terminated or the agency abolished or reorganized. The sun, in other words, automatically sets on any program or agency that is not purposely extended after a fixed period of time. Such laws have been pioneered with considerable success in state government to make agencies more responsive to political leadership and overcome the inertia we discussed above. However, the same vested interests that oppose bureaucratic restructuring tend to oppose sunset laws.

A **sunshine law** requires that an agency conduct its meetings and make its decisions in public, so that the media and interested citizens can observe what happens. This provision could both alert those interested in a policy area to what an agency is planning and encourage the agency to refrain from doing things that would be unpopular if known publicly. But neither Congress nor the executive branch is likely to favor any more "sunshine" than now prevails because it would complicate the policy process.

There is in place now "an awesome armada of policies, mechanisms, and processes to oversee bureaucracies and cause those that do not act in the public interest to change course," concludes one expert, but the will to use these means is lacking—and probably for good reason.

> If all existing accountability mechanisms worked as they could, they would probably hobble the bureaucracies in their essential work; administrators and their staffs would be so busy responding to queries and procedures aimed at accountability that there would be insufficient time to plan, organize, and supervise the work for which they were being held accountable. Overcontrol encourages timidity, breeds inaction, and stimulates unnecessary conflict.[59]

Making Bureaucracy More Representative

Today, when growing numbers of civil servants are experts, the bureaucracy remains largely middle-class.[60] According to the government itself, 56 percent of bureaucrats are men and 36.5 percent have at least a B.A. degree. Their average age is now 43.2, average length of service is 14.2 years, and average salary is $37,700.[61] Few of the poor serve in any but menial jobs, but their exclusion is a result more of the special skills demanded by the increasingly complex tasks and procedures of the bureaucracies than of overt discrimination. But as two specialists have pointed out, "Representativeness is not by itself sufficient to provide a responsive, controlled bureaucracy. A bureaucracy drawn from all walks of life, but all-powerful and unaccountable, would be, practically speaking, as dangerous as any other uncontrolled group."[62]

It is increasingly difficult to recruit competent and well-trained bureaucrats from the traditional applicant "pool," and some say this difficulty argues for expanding the pool by emphasizing representativeness. A recent blue-ribbon panel of experts concluded that current trends would leave the country with "a government of the mediocre, locked into careers of last resort or waiting for a chance to move on to other jobs." It called for more flexible leadership and a broader talent base as well as better pay and working conditions for bureaucrats and advocated "careful attention to the recruitment of minority students."[63] The Clinton administration deliberately sought to make the government "look more like the American people," with particular emphasis on recruiting ethnic minorities and women. However, Table 13.3 shows how far there still is to go.

If hiring people who collectively look like the American people is difficult, bureaucrats can at least be urged to consult more extensively with the people affected by programs. Current citizen participation provisions have tended to be more for show than for real, especially as views expressed at bureaucracy-sponsored hearings can easily be ignored when policy is finalized and implemented. Studies have shown that the most effective citizen participation takes the form of boards elected by community constituencies and granted specified legal authority to play a policy role.[64] Writing this provision into policy legislation, and even into the laws that create key agencies, could increase the representation of people's views.

TABLE 13.3

Women and Minorities in the Federal Bureaucracy

Level of Salary and Responsibility	Women's Share (51 percent of population) 1976	1992	African Americans' Share (12 percent of population) 1976	1992	Hispanics' Share (9 percent of population) 1976	1992
Lowest (grades 1–4) $10,000–19,000	78%	74%	23%	29%	5%	7%
Middle (grades 5–8) $16,000–$29,000	60	57	19	23	4	6
Higher (grades 9–12) $24,000–47,000	20	21	10	12	4	5
Highest (grades 12–15) $42,000–$77,000	5	21	5	7	2	3

Source: Office of Personnel Management, *Annual Report to Congress on the Federal Opportunity Recruitment Program, Fiscal Year 93*, series CE-104 (Washington, D.C.: U.S. Government Printing Office, 1993).

Limiting Scope by Privatizing and Downshifting Functions

In the 1980s, many corporations underwent **downsizing**—shrinking by eliminating workers who were unneeded or too expensive and shucking off divisions or product lines that were no longer competitive and profitable. The first major downsizing of the bureaucracy since the 1950s occurred when the Reagan administration tried to weaken agencies whose responsibilities it disapproved of. Downsizing increased under Clinton's REGO, primarily to save money being paid to bureaucrats who had job security, high incomes, and fringe benefits such as health insurance. Some downsizing can be accomplished by **privatizing**, also called **outsourcing**—turning functions over to private companies that become outside sources of work and often can furnish the services more cheaply than government because they use temporary workers who earn low wages and have no benefits. The federal government has privatized such programs as student loans, and many state and local governments outsource work ranging from garbage collection to computer programming. The federal government has long been privatizing functions by such activities as making grants to private bodies, guaranteeing loans made by private banks, and subsidizing particular activities through direct payments (as to farmers) or tax breaks.[65] "From libraries to police, prisons to social services, fire protection to sophisticated planning, private and nonprofit agents have eagerly stepped in as governments have tried to shrink," concluded one recent study. "Although the results of the American version of privatization have varied widely, the overriding lesson is that there is no function left that only the public sector can deliver."[66] Most Americans still expect the federal government to play the major role in such areas as national defense and environmental protection. But increasingly advocates of downsizing call for **downshifting**—shifting functions from the national level to the states and in some cases to localities.

Although the lessons of downsizing by privatizing and downshifting are still being learned, it is already clear that downsizing for its own sake is unlikely to bring either greater cost effectiveness or greater service-delivery efficiency. The appropriate goal, as critics increasingly remark, is *rightsizing*. But what is the right size for bureaucracy? Neither experts nor citizens nor even bureaucrats themselves can agree, so it seems likely that only experimentation and *learning by doing* will answer the question.

Because bureaucratic agencies, like other political actors, are political organizations, they cannot be insulated from politics, as the early merit system reformers hoped. Nor can they be made both highly efficient and accountable to the public, as advocates of organizational restructuring and citizen participation have hoped. Efficiency today requires dependence on technical experts, which makes organizations

"THEY REVISED IT. NOW IT'S THE 'PRETTY-CLEAN AIR ACT'."

less subject to control by other political actors—but no less political. Thus the problems bureaucracies present us with seem as likely to persist as the problems the agencies are charged with handling. One specialist concludes that public management "is a world of settled institutions designed to allow imperfect people to use flawed procedures to cope with insoluble problems."[67] The quality of bureaucracy's performance ultimately depends most on the caliber of people who decide to become bureaucrats. If current efforts to reinvent government inspire bright and concerned people to work for government, bureaucracy may become more effective and more responsible. But the question of to whom it should be responsive—the president, Congress, the people, or some concept of the public interest—will always be decided each time a bureaucrat acts.

Summary

One in every six Americans works for a government bureaucracy—federal, state, or local—and some 2.8 million are federal bureaucrats. Bureaucracy is not mentioned in the Constitution, but the Framers expected the president and Congress to create one. The American bureaucracy has evolved from an aristocratic system through the spoils system originated by Andrew Jackson in 1829 to the merit system established by the Pendleton Act in 1883 and eventually extended to cover 85 percent of all government employees. Major subsequent reforms include the Hatch Act of 1939, designed to protect bureaucrats from political pressure, and the reforms that in 1978 created a Senior Executive Service of top civil servants and protected whistleblowers. The bureaucracy has continued to balloon, thickening and widening in recent decades as well. The independent agencies, including the independent regulatory commissions, are a special case of bureaucracy, established to remain somewhat independent of both the president and Congress but nonetheless highly political. Major factors in the growth of the bureaucracy have included population growth, wars and depression, science and technology, new programs, and new social responsibilities. As bureaucracy's networks have expanded, political conflicts have proliferated.

The five key features of a bureaucracy are continuous conduct of business, hierarchical organization, task specialization, law-based and rule-based authority, and business conducted via written documents. The four necessary functions bureaucrats perform in government are gathering and managing information, developing policies, converting policies into programs, and implementing programs. Public bureaucracies share these features and functions with private sector bureaucracies but are different in three ways: Their goals are imposed on them by the political process, they must spend their resources in ways specified by the president or Congress, and they cannot keep any resources they don't spend.

Political actors have differing goals for bureaucracy, so there are debates over its political effectiveness. Bureaucratic effectiveness depends on leadership orientations, organizational culture, and administration intent as well as the skillful use of the instruments of bureaucratic power: access to information, use of expertise, secrecy, discretionary authority, administrative law, and clientele group support. Effectiveness can be limited by interagency conflict, bureaucratic politicking, and budgetary constraints.

The bureaucracy is accountable to the president and to Congress. Presidents use their own bureaucracy to try to control the other bureaucracies in competition with Congress, but bureaucracies can resist and even use the president. Congress also uses its own bureaucracies to try to control or influence the executive branch bureaucracies, but bureaucracies can also use Congress. Special interests, the media, the courts, and the people also use the bureaucracies and are in turn used by them.

Current reform programs include Clinton's reinventing government initiatives, which are designed to make bureaucracy more effective and less costly. Among other reform goals are increasing accountability, making bureaucracy more representative, and limiting the scope of government by privatizing and downshifting functions. Reform, like every other aspect of bureaucracy, is very political.

Key Terms

administrative law 493
backchanneling 507
bureaucracy 495
bureaucratic politicking 499
bureaucratic thickening 490
bureaucratic widening 491
classification 502
conflict of interest 514
disinformation 511
downshifting 519

downsizing 519
Hatch Act 487
independent regulatory commissions 492
iron triangle 510
issue networks 510
leak 507
outsourcing 519
paper trail 496
patronage 487

Pendleton Act 487
privatizing 519
Senior Executive Service 493
spoils system 487
standard operating procedures 496
subgovernment 510
sunset laws 517
sunshine laws 517
whistleblower 493

How You Can Learn More About the Bureaucracy

Burke, John P. *Bureaucratic Responsibility.* Baltimore: Johns Hopkins University Press, 1986. An examination of individual responsibility for ethical conduct of bureaucrats.

Cook, Brian J. *Bureaucracy and Self-Government: Reconsidering the Role of Public Administration in American Politics.* Baltimore: Johns Hopkins University Press, 1996. An argument that American bureaucracy has been kept under control but that bureaucracy-bashing has served to limit public influence on bureaucracy.

Fesler, James W., and Donald F. Kettl. *The Politics of the Administrative Process.* Chatham, N.J.: Chatham House, 1990. A helpful overview of American public administration emphasizing the politics of bureaucratic decisionmaking.

Goodsell, Charles T. *The Case for Bureaucracy,* 2nd ed. Chatham, N.J.: Chatham House, 1985. A polemical but well-informed defense of bureaucracy by a former federal bureaucrat.

Gormley, William T. *Taming the Bureaucracy: Muscles, Prayers, and Other Strategies.* Princeton, N.J.: Princeton University Press, 1989. An interesting analysis of how political actors wrestle with and within the bureaucracy.

Hummel, Ralph P. *The Bureaucratic Experience,* 2nd ed. New York: St. Martin's Press, 1982. A comprehensive psychologically based attack on the bureaucratization of contemporary life.

Kettl, Donald F. *Reinventing Government? Appraising the National Performance Review.* Washington, D.C.: Brookings Institution, 1994. An early evaluation of the Clinton administration's efforts to reform bureaucracy.

Ryan, Susan M. *Downloading Democracy: Government Information in an Electronic Age.* Creskill, N.J.: Hampton Press, 1996. A useful guide that includes chapters on electronic sources of federal information.

Reich, Robert. *Locked in the Cabinet.* New York: Alfred A. Knopf, 1997. A remarkably candid journal kept by Clinton's longtime friend and first-term secretary of labor.

Seidman, Harold, and Robert Gilmour. *Politics, Position, and Power,* 4th ed. New York: Oxford University Press, 1986. A classic study of the ways political influence operates within the federal bureaucracy.

Wilson, James Q. *Bureaucracy: What Government Agencies Do and Why They Do It.* New York: Basic Books, 1989. A comprehensive contemporary classic analyzing the politics of American bureaucracy.

The Courts and the Legal System

In 1968, when Demetrio R. Rodriguez sued the state of Texas for allowing great gaps between rich and poor school districts, his son was in third grade in a crowded, ill-equipped San Antonio classroom like the one shown here. Rodriguez lost his case. He is shown at right in 1993 in front of a trailer classroom in the Edgewood school district in San Antonio. Conditions had not changed. "My grandchildren deserve better," he said.

CHAPTER 14

Orthodox thinking about the Supreme Court still maintains that the Court is a "legal" rather than a "political" institution. But that pretense has long been under attack. There is a growing realization, to the point of . . . unanimous acknowledgment, that the Justices do in fact make policy—legislate—however much some instances of judicial legislation may be deplored.

—**Arthur S. Miller**

A theory of judging that allows the courts to choose the political results is wrong, no matter in which direction the results tend.

—**Robert H. Bork**[1]

The Sources of Legal Authority

Interpreting the Law

The Structure of the Legal System

Influences on the Courts

How the Supreme Court Makes Public Policy

Reforming the Legal System

Do courts have the authority to order state governments to equalize the quality of education in public schools? Demetrio Rodriguez thought so.

Rodriguez's children attended school in a poor section of San Antonio, Texas. In 1968 he filed suit in federal district court against the San Antonio Independent School District, claiming that children have a constitutional right—either directly guaranteed by, or implicit in, the Fourteenth Amendment—to equality of education.

Like districts in most states, Texas school districts are authorized by the state government and financed largely by taxing property—homes and businesses—within each district. Because rich school districts raised far more money per child through property taxes than poor districts, students in rich districts had well-equipped science and computer labs, sports complexes, and other facilities, while students in poor school districts often had to share textbooks. Rodriguez's lawsuit claimed that these disparities in the financing of public education were unconstitutional.

In 1973 the Supreme Court issued its 5–4 decision in *San Antonio Independent School District v. Rodriguez*.[2] The majority concluded that the Constitution does not *explicitly* (in its text) or *implicitly* (by "reading between the lines") guarantee equality of education. Texas (and by inference all other states) was therefore free to finance its schools however it wished. Rodriguez—and children in poor school districts throughout the country—had lost.

In his dissenting opinion, Justice Thurgood Marshall, joined by William O. Douglas, strongly disagreed with "the majority's labored efforts to demonstrate that fundamental interests . . . encompass *only established* rights which we are somehow bound to recognize from the text of the Constitution itself. . . . I would like to know where the Constitution guarantees the right to procreate or the right to vote in state elections or the right to an appeal from a criminal conviction." They accused the Court of retreating from its historic commitment to "equality of educational opportunity" and denounced an education system "which deprives children in their earliest years of the chance to reach their full potential as citizens."[3]

Twenty years later, 68 school districts joined by numerous individual schoolchildren and their parents, represented by the Mexican American Legal Defense and Education Fund and supported by Texas Rural Legal Aid and other groups, filed a suit in Texas state court against the state of Texas in the person of the state education commissioner, William Kirby, claiming that education is a fundamental right according to the Texas constitution (not the U.S. Constitution). In *Edgewood Independent School District v. Kirby* (1989), the Texas Supreme Court agreed, stating that the existing system was not "efficient" because it did not provide for a "general diffusion of knowledge." In fact, the spending ratio between the richest and poorest school district was 700 to 1. The court immediately directed the state legislature to devise an equitable system of public school finance. Since then, three more Edgewood cases (1989–1995) have led to legislation, upheld by the court, reducing disparities between rich and poor districts to 28 to 1.[4]

More than half the states in the country are currently entangled in similar lawsuits over the funding of public education. At issue in these lawsuits is whether the state courts should require legislatures to equalize educational opportunity by equalizing educational resources. This is not a new question, for states have been playing an ever larger role in the redistribution of wealth through taxing and spending policies.[5] Federal courts are also involved in the redistribution of wealth because they must rule on the legality of federal policies, such as setting a minimum wage, providing Social Security retirement benefits, and supplying social services for the needy. Today virtually all American courts have a say in "who gets what, when, and how."

In this chapter we examine the American legal system in terms of the following questions:

What are the sources of legal authority in the United States?

How is the American legal system organized?

How do the courts make public policy?

What is being done to reform the judicial process?

The Sources of Legal Authority

The **American legal system** consists of (1) several types of law, which are (2) interpreted and applied by federal, state, and local courts and (3) enforced by federal, state, and local law officers. Together this system provides the basis for public order as well as opportunities for social change.

Types of Law

Laws are basic rules of conduct designed to promote public order. Whether we are aware of it or not, we all depend on laws to get us through traffic in relative safety, to provide us with safe drinking water, to ensure that we are not unfairly evicted from our apartments, and to protect our freedom to vote for any candidate we choose. What kind of laws perform these tasks, and where do they come from?

There are two types of law in the United States: private and public. In **private law,** also known as **civil law,** government acts *indirectly* as a referee, or adjudicator, of disputes involving private citizens. Private law consists of (1) tort law, which involves injuries to someone's person or property (examples include assault, auto collision, slander, invasion of privacy, negligence, product liability); (2) property law, which deals with ownership and possession of tangible items and intangible rights; (3) contract and business law, which is based on the right to acquire or use private property; (4) corporate law; (5) inheritance law; and (6) family law. Unlike criminal law, which is concerned with punishment, private law seeks to compensate the injured party.

Public law deals primarily with the powers and institutions of government, the rights and duties people have with respect to government and one another, and the relations they have with people in other nations. Public law consists of (1) constitutional law; (2) statutes (laws enacted by federal and state legislatures); and (3) administrative law (drafted by government bureaucracies to implement legislative statutes). Most criminal laws are statutes designed to punish those found guilty of violating them. Public cases always involve government or one of its institutions as at least one party to the lawsuit. Public law, then, involves government *directly*, which is why political scientists study it and why it is the main focus of this chapter.

Public law encompasses all **criminal law,** or statutes that punish parties for **crimes**—violations of a law or government regulation involving the general public. Crimes are divided into **felonies** (major offenses) and **misdemeanors** (minor offenses). Convictions for a felony usually result in imprisonment for more than a year, with or without a fine, or in execution. Felonies include murder, rape, aggravated assault, manslaughter, kidnapping, arson, burglary, robbery, bribery, price fixing, and tax evasion. Convictions for a misdemeanor usually result in a fine with or without a prison sentence of less than a year. Misdemeanors include littering, traffic violations, trespassing, public disturbance, prostitution,

> **felony**
> This word, derived from Old French *felon*, meaning "villain" or "rogue," was once used for "cholera" and is related to "gall" or "bitterness."
>
> **misdemeanor**
> This word is derived from the Latin *minus*, in the sense of "wrong," and the Old French *démener*, meaning "to behave."

and simple assault. Government (federal, state, or local) is always the prosecutor in criminal cases. In the first O. J. Simpson trial in 1996, for example, the state of California prosecuted Simpson for the crime of murder and he was found not guilty. In the second Simpson trial in 1997, the parents of the murder victims filed a private civil suit against Simpson for "wrongful death" to recover damages. The *Rodriguez* and *Edgewood* cases were matters of public law because they involved a relationship between private individuals (parents of public school students), public institutions (state school districts), and public officials.

Both public and private law distinguish between **substantive law,** which concerns the actual content or substance of a law, and **procedural law,** which concerns the legal methods used to adjudicate matters of substantive law. Substantive law addresses the facts and circumstances of a particular case. Procedural law is intended to ensure that the case is dealt with fairly, according to procedures specified by the law. The most powerful guarantee of procedural fairness is the due process clause of the Fourteenth Amendment: "nor shall any State deprive any person of life, liberty, or property, without due process of law." Rules of law classify people into groups to facilitate the resolution of disputes. Certain classifications, however, have been challenged as unconstitutional under the equal-protection clause of the Fourteenth Amendment (see Chapter 16). Plaintiffs in the *Rodriguez* case, for example, argued that the Texas scheme for public school financing unconstitutionally classified school districts on the basis of wealth.

Questions of law are decided in courts by judges and sometimes by juries. In criminal and personal injury cases, for example, the judge presides over the court but a jury decides the case. **Juries** are groups of 6, 12, or 23 citizens who are authorized to listen to both sides of a case and to give a **verdict**, or ruling on it. Because juries are composed of ordinary citizens, both sides of a case must be explained in ordinary language rather than in the legal jargon of experts. Juries are thus a reminder that "the people" are an important source of legal authority.

The Three "Legs" of American Law

In contrast to many Continental European countries, which rely on a single civil code, legal authority in the United States stands on three main "legs": common law, constitutional law, and legislation. In addition to inheriting most of their legal principles from England, Americans have developed their own legal tradition. As a result, American judges have more opportunities to interpret and "make" law once a case comes before them.

civil codes

Civil codes, used mainly in Continental Europe, are collections (codifications) of all the laws of a given country. Such comprehensive codes generally restrict the authority of judges because they are required to apply the code to particular cases. Louisiana, once ruled by France, is the only state in the Union that relies significantly on this type of law. American legislatures use codes only to codify specific areas of the law. Examples include codes of criminal conduct, legal procedure, elections, commercial law, and the like.

Common Law

The oldest "leg" of American law and that of most other English-speaking countries is **common law**—case law generated by judges and government bureaucrats. For this reason, common law is often called judge-made law. Common law originated in twelfth-century England when judges began to travel around the country (what was once called "riding circuit") dispensing justice according to custom. The right to a trial by a jury of one's peers is a legacy of English common law that Americans enshrined as constitutional law in their national and state bills of rights. So is the **adversary system** of justice that Americans have used since colonial times.

In contrast to the **inquisitorial system** practiced in many western European countries, the adversary system assumes that justice will result from a vigorous but controlled debate between a **plaintiff** (who brings the complaint) and a **defendant** (who is accused of having caused harm)—both usually represented by lawyers. This system assumes that there are two sides to a case which deserve an equal hearing—that is, two contested versions of the facts (*what is*) and views about what the outcome should be (*what's right*).

> **inquisitorial system**
> In this major alternative to the adversary system, judges take the lead role in asking questions of the parties and in reaching a decision—a process resembling an official inquiry. This system is used in Continental European countries and elsewhere.
>
> **stare decisis**
> This Latin term for the principle of precedent means "to stand by that which is decided."

Judges turn to common law (and sometimes to natural law) when constitutional provisions and legislation cannot help them decide a case or when the existing law seems ambiguous. Common law is based on the doctrine of *stare decisis*, which means that judges must defer to the authority of previous decisions unless they find "good cause" for overturning them. If no relevant case law is available in one state, a judge will first look for one in another state or in federal case law or **customary law**, which is a body of regulations deriving from custom (the practices of social, professional, business, and other communities) that is usually recognized as enforceable by government. If several relevant precedents exist, the judge decides which one best fits the current case. In announcing the verdict, the judge cites the rule of law derived from the previous (or "controlling") case and explains how it determined the verdict.[6]

Common law can be a force for change as well as a servant of the status quo. Judges get to decide how far old laws apply to new situations and whether an existing precedent should be honored or ignored. Do privacy rules that apply to written mail also apply to electronic mail? When do biological parents lose their parental rights? The sort of reasoning involved in common law is one in which the "rules change as the rules are applied."[7]

Constitutional Law

Constitutional law consists of the actual text of the Constitution (including amendments) as well as all the decisions that the Supreme Court has handed down over more than 200 years. These decisions recount the struggles over constitutional interpretation since ratification and trace the gradual growth of democracy to the present day. (Each state constitution generates its own body of case law.) Federal and state judges, potential litigants, lawyers, and other political actors turn to constitutional law, the supreme law of the land, for guidance on matters dealing with the powers of government and the rights of individuals.

Legislation

The third "leg" of American law is **legislation,** the deliberate creation of new law by federal, state, and local lawmakers. In earlier centuries, laws were widely viewed as

> A searchable version of the U.S. legal code:
> http://www.law.cornell.edu/uscode

ordained by God, nature, or custom and were thus not to be tampered with. As societies have grown more secular, scientific, and democratic, they have crafted new laws to meet their needs. This development has set traditionalists against reformers and led to heated debates over what laws should or should not be enacted (*what's right*).

All legislation must conform to the U.S. Constitution. State legislation must also conform to the constitution of the state that enacts it. Local legislation by counties and cities must conform to the constitutions of the United States and of the particular state. The possibilities for lawmaking at the various levels of the American legal system are so numerous that laws often conflict. When they do, judges decide, in particular court cases, which law applies according to the principles in Figure 14.1, and the court with the highest authority on the matter makes the final decision.

There are five types of U.S. legislation:

- *Treaties* are agreements with other countries that are signed by the president and ratified by a two-thirds majority of the Senate. According to the supremacy clause in Article VI of the U.S. Constitution, ratified treaties are, like federal statutes, the supreme law of the land.
- *Congressional executive agreements* are international agreements (such as the North American Free Trade Agreement) signed by the president and voted into law by the House and Senate according to procedures negotiated with the president.

Figure 14.1

The Hierarchy of Authority in the Dual Legal System

In the American dual legal system, the law that is higher in the hierarchy takes precedence when there is a conflict. The U.S. Constitution, at the top, takes precedence over all other types of law. State constitutions take precedence over other state and local laws.

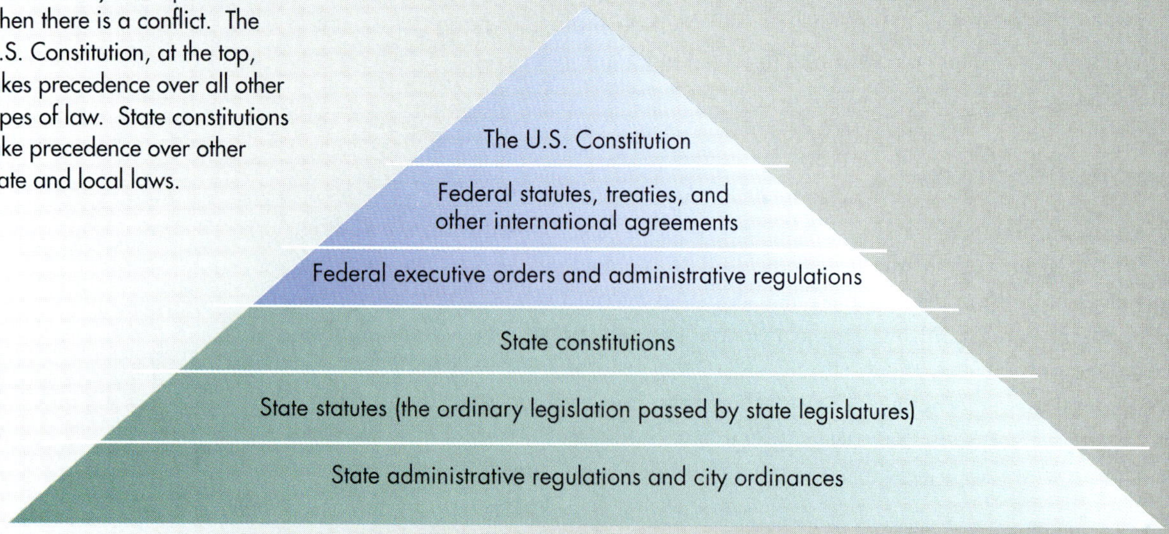

The U.S. Constitution

Federal statutes, treaties, and other international agreements

Federal executive orders and administrative regulations

State constitutions

State statutes (the ordinary legislation passed by state legislatures)

State administrative regulations and city ordinances

Source: Adapted from Edwin W. Patterson, *Jurisprudence: Men and Ideas of the Law* (Brooklyn: Foundation Press, 1953), 198, 259.

- *Executive orders* are issued by the president or state governor and have the status of law unless their constitutionality is successfully challenged. Presidents from George Washington to the present have issued some 13,000 presidential executive orders (see Chapter 12).[8]
- *Statutes* (also called bills or acts) are laws enacted by elected legislative bodies (such as Congress and the state legislatures) and signed into law by the chief executive (the president or a governor).
- Administrative law consists of regulations made by bureaucratic agencies at the federal, state, and local levels to implement legislation.

Of these five types of legislation, citizens have the greatest say over statutes because they elect their legislators and legislators have the authority to abolish or rewrite statutes in accordance with citizen demands. In contrast, citizens have the least control over administrative law because it is written by unelected bureaucrats in the administrative agencies who are insulated from the voters. These agencies have enormous authority to write the regulations implementing legislation as they see fit because lawmakers need to write statutes in very broad language to facilitate passage and they often lack the foresight and expertise to anticipate the details of implementation. Thus laws often include a catchall phrase authorizing bureaucrats to make whatever rules are "necessary" or "appropriate."

Administrative law is growing faster than any other type of law; indeed, it is beginning to outstrip statutory law in its impact on people's economic and social lives. Because this authority gives unelected bureaucrats sweeping discretionary powers to implement policy, it is increasingly viewed as undemocratic. To counter this concern, Congress and state legislatures, as we saw in Chapter 13, allow or instruct administrative agencies to establish their own internal court systems to review compliance with their regulations and to hear complaints about them. Individuals or businesses unhappy with the ruling of an administrative court may appeal the case to the regular courts, which generally compare the ruling with the original statute establishing the agency. The court then considers whether the appropriate methods were followed and whether the agency adjudicator was unduly influenced by politicians or interest groups.[9]

Judicial Review

As we saw in the discussion of *Marbury v. Madison* (1803) in Chapter 2, **judicial review**—the power of the courts to declare acts of the state and federal legislative and executive branches unconstitutional—does not appear in the Constitution. Critics who equate democracy with majority rule argue that judicial review is antidemocratic because it permits unelected judges to overturn policies enacted by popularly elected lawmakers. Those concerned with civil liberties and minority rights point out that the Framers of the Constitution distrusted majority rule and that bills of rights explicitly protect individuals and minorities from coercion by majorities and government. It is a fundamental mistake, they argue, to equate democracy with majority rule. As they see it, the courts actually strengthen democracy when they protect individual freedom and minority rights.[10]

While it is difficult to do, majorities acting through their representatives can overturn a federal or state court decision with a constitutional amendment. For example, the Eleventh Amendment, ratified in 1798, overruled a Supreme Court decision, *Chisholm v. Georgia* (1793), for the first time. The Supreme Court had ruled that Article III of the Constitution granted it jurisdiction in cases involving suits brought by citizens of one state (in this case South Carolina) or foreign country against another state (in this case Georgia). Denying that the Court had such jurisdiction, the Georgia legislature passed a resolution stating that any federal marshal who tried to enforce the Court's decision would be declared a felon and hanged. The amendment resolved the issue by taking the disputed jurisdiction away from the federal judiciary. The Thirteenth Amendment abolishing slavery and the Fourteenth Amendment granting "all persons born or naturalized in the United States" citizenship overrode *Dred Scott v. Sandford* (1857), which declared that blacks, free or enslaved, were not citizens of the United States. The Sixteenth Amendment, ratified in 1913, reversed the Supreme Court's decision in *Pollock v. Farmers' Loan and Trust Co.* (1895) declaring unconstitutional the income tax Congress imposed in 1894. And the Twenty-sixth Amendment ratified in 1971 overrode *Oregon v. Mitchell* (1970), declaring unconstitutional an act of Congress granting 18- to 20-year olds the right to vote in state elections.[11]

The Court itself may overrule or ignore decisions that the justices or the public come to see as mistakes or as outdated. By one measure, it has done this more than 150 times since 1789.[12] Thus, although the Supreme Court is the court of last resort, its decisions are not always final.

Judicial Decisions

Because beliefs about *what's right* and *what is needed* in American society change over time, so do laws and their interpretations. Changes in the law are usually incremental because laws that change too fast (before new beliefs have become widespread) or too slowly (after beliefs have lost their credibility) lose their legitimacy. Such a loss can seriously erode the effectiveness of government, which depends on the authority of law to achieve voluntary compliance. While legislatures bear the main responsibility for ensuring that laws are fair and effective, courts bear some of this responsibility as well. However, they are only permitted to exercise it when a case comes before them.

Judges are adjudicators when they decide cases but become legislators and policymakers when they provide remedies that extend beyond the parties to a case. When this happens, judges "do in fact 'make law.'"[13] Their decisions become legal **precedents**—models for deciding future cases. While these decisions receive the most attention in this chapter, they are far outnumbered by routine decisions that reinforce established law.

Making Public Policy Case by Case

Unlike the president, who can issue an executive order, or a legislator, who can sponsor a law, judges must wait for socially significant cases to come before them before they can make public policy. Thus when groups turn to judges for policy solutions—for example, women and minorities who have trouble persuading lawmakers to enact policies they consider just, or lawmakers who wish to avoid politically troublesome policy decisions—they look for a suitable case to put before the courts, just as Rodriguez did. Few of the 10 million cases that come before U.S. courts each year are suitable for judicial policymaking, but those that are raise issues still unsettled by the law, such as abortion, affirmative action, the right to die, and government's right to confiscate private property. In constitutional cases involving perceived social harms, a judge is responsible for providing a **remedy**. A remedy is any relief a court can provide for a litigant who has been wronged or who is about to be wronged. The two most common remedies are judgments entitling plaintiffs to collect money from defendants and orders (called *injunctions*) requiring defendants to refrain from injurious behavior or to undo its consequences.[14]

Cases used as vehicles for policymaking typically involve a plaintiff representing a large interest group against a public institution such as a school, hospital, prison, or independent government agency. The plaintiff's primary goal is usually to alter the behavior of the defendant or to reform an institution.[15] The suit filed by Rodriguez, for example, was a **class action suit** intended to force the state of Texas to provide parity (equality) in education. In a class action suit—also called a representative action—one or more persons sue or are sued as representatives of a larger group in similar circumstances. The outcome of such a lawsuit applies to members of the larger group as well.

This practice of using individual cases as vehicles for judicial policymaking sometimes forces judges to become administrators who must supervise the reforms they "legislate."[16] Some experts—and occasionally the courts themselves—question whether judges and jurists are qualified to act as administrators. Experts also question whether it is right for a plaintiff and a defendant to remain parties to a suit when judges are using them to make public policy.[17]

Interpreting the Law

Because a law cannot speak for itself, people must interpret it. Political actors—judges, lawmakers, interest groups, legal experts, ordinary citizens—interpret a law in terms of their beliefs about *what is, what's right,* and *what works.* As a result, their interpretations often clash. Such differences may also lead to disputes over a case, as the criminal trial of O. J. Simpson in 1996 illustrated:

> From its very beginning, the Simpson case has served as a screen onto which people would project their own meanings: whether as a feminist morality play about wife-beating or as a story of white society's revenge on a black man who made good or as proof that money and clever lawyers can outfox justice every time.... Disagreement arose [not only] about interpretation but [also] about simple fact.[18]

The First Amendment allows anyone to express an opinion about a case, and the adversary system invites lawyers to develop and recommend partisan interpretations, but only judges have the authority to decide how a law is to be officially interpreted in that case, and their decisions stand until a higher court reaches a different conclusion or a legislature changes the law.

Judicial Philosophy

A judicial opinion is shaped by a **judicial philosophy**—the set of beliefs about *what is*, *what's right*, and *what works* that guides legal judgments. Felix Frankfurter (named to the Court in 1939) helped establish the principle that the Senate should be able to reject a nominee on the basis of judicial philosophy but that it is improper for a nominee to answer questions directly related to controversial issues affecting the Court.[19]

What determines a judge's judicial philosophy? One factor is professionalism. Law schools and the legal profession socialize men and women to hold similar views about what laws mean and how they should be applied. Yet judicial philosophies still differ because individuals differ in their views about *what is*, *what's right*, and *what works* in many areas of life, including their attitudes toward the law. Proponents of **judicial restraint** want judges to operate strictly within the constitutional limits they claim constrain the role of the courts. Proponents of **judicial activism** want judges to play a more active policymaking role. Examples of each judicial philosophy appear in the box nearby.

It is a mistake to connect judicial restraint with conservative policies and judicial activism with liberal policies. In the 1920s and early 1930s, for example, conservative-minded activist justices overturned pro-labor laws. Recently, conservative activist justices have overturned laws banning handguns near schools and requiring local law-enforcement officials to do background checks on people who want to purchase guns (Chapter 15). The term *judicial activism* suggests that this approach to the law has a greater impact on the nation than does judicial restraint, but, in fact, both approaches can profoundly affect politics, as restraint did in *Rodriguez* and activism did in *Edgewood*.

judicial philosophy
This high-minded term has an aura of authority that comes from joining "judicial" (derived from Latin for "judgment") with the term "philosophy" (the pursuit of wisdom).

Methods of Interpretation

Like judicial philosophy, the method used to interpret the law in a particular case drastically affects its outcome. A survey of Supreme Court decisions

Political Actors Disagree

Supreme Court Justices on Judicial Philosophy

William Brennan   **Warren Burger**

In *Plyler v. Doe* (1982) the Supreme Court declared unconstitutional a Texas law allowing local school districts to deny free education to children of illegal aliens. The following excerpts from opinions in that case set forth conflicting judicial philosophies.

Judicial Activism: Associate Justice William Brennan

Education has a fundamental role in maintaining the fabric of our society. We cannot ignore the significant social costs borne by our Nation when select groups are denied the means to absorb the values and skills upon which our social order rests.

In addition to the pivotal role of education in sustaining our political and cultural heritage, denial of education to some isolated group of children poses an affront to one of the goals of the Equal Protection Clause: the abolition of governmental barriers presenting unreasonable obstacles to advancement on the basis of individual merit. [Illiteracy] is an enduring disability. The inability to read and write will handicap the individual deprived of basic education each and every day of his life . . . . We may appropriately take into account the costs [of the Texas law] to the Nation and to the innocent children who are its victims.

Judicial Restraint: Chief Justice Warren Burger

Were it our business to set the Nation's social policy, I would agree without hesitation that it is senseless for an enlightened society to deprive any children—including illegal aliens—of an elementary education. I fully agree that it would be folly—and wrong—to tolerate creation of a segment of society made up of illiterate persons. . . . However, the Constitution does not . . . vest in this Court the authority to strike down laws because they do not meet our standards of desirable social policy, "wisdom," or "common sense."

Source: Plyler v. Doe, 457 U.S. 202 (1982).

---

shows that justices make use of a number of different interpretive methods and are also influenced by a variety of legal and nonlegal factors.[20] Recourse to different methods of interpretation gives justices more options with which to balance pressures for social order with pressures for change as well as to safeguard their authority, which too many unpopular decisions can erode. However, justices often disagree over which method should be applied in a particular case.

Interpreting the Law in Terms of *What Is*

Strict proponents of judicial restraint, such as Justices Antonin Scalia and Clarence Thomas, consistently turn to **originalism** as the only right method of legal interpretation. Originalists try to identify the original meaning set forth by the drafters and ratifiers of a law and then apply that meaning to the case before them. Originalists fall into two camps: textualists, who look for the meaning of a law in the written text itself; and intentionalists, who seek the meaning of a law in the intentions of its drafters by studying the original committee reports, hearings, and debates that led up to the drafting of the law.[21] (Regardless of the method used to interpret a statute, once that interpretation is made it is then treated as a part of that statute and becomes a judicial precedent as well, if the Court majority agrees.) Textualists, however, disagree among themselves on what particular words and phrases meant more than 200 years ago (particularly as historians continually revise their understanding of the founding period) and what they mean today. Intentionalists disagree among themselves over whose intentions count: those who drafted the Constitution or those who signed or ratified it. Their task is further complicated by the fact that the drafters, signers, and ratifiers did not approve of all its provisions and were agreeing to a package of compromises.

Originalists oppose judicial activism for two main reasons. First, they accuse judicial activists of imposing their own political views on the judicial process. While Chief Justice Charles Evans Hughes (served 1930–1941) once claimed that "the Constitution is what the judges say it is,"[22] in practice judges are constrained by legal rules and procedures and by fellow judges. As we'll see below, a justice must get support for his or her policy preferences from a majority of fellow justices (who have their own policy preferences and judicial philosophies) to prevail. Second, originalists argue that judicial activism violates the basic premise of democracy: majority rule. If society needs new policies, originalists argue, then let democratically elected lawmakers—not unelected justices—enact them. But this view, as we've just seen, downplays the constitutional responsibility of the federal bench to protect the rights of minorities from infringement by majorities.

Prominent Supreme Court justices have rejected originalism as unworkable because, as Chief Justice John Marshall pointed out, words cannot be limited to particular meanings: "Such is the character of human language that no word conveys to the mind, in all situations, one single definite idea; and nothing is more common that to use words in a figurative [metaphorical] sense."[23] Judge Learned Hand, a leading twentieth-century jurist, likened the process of judging to being an artist. Yes, the justice must be familiar with the lawbooks but "should never trust them for . . . guidance"; instead, the justice should rely on an "almost instinctive sense of where the line lies between the word and the purpose behind it" and "must somehow manage to be true to both."[24] Before Felix Frankfurter (served 1939–1962) took his seat on the Court, he, too, declared that words in the Constitution can mean so many different things "that they leave the individual Justice free, if indeed they do not compel him, to gather meaning, not from the Constitution, but from reading life."[25]

Interpreting the Law in Terms of *What's Right*

Some judges and justices apply methods of interpretation that support their views of *what's right*. For example, the constitutional provision invoked by a case (advocates for *Rodriguez* invoked the equal protection clause of the Fourteenth Amendment)

The Rational Basis Test and the Strict Scrutiny Test

The Supreme Court has developed two standards of review—the rational basis test and the "close" or strict scrutiny test—to evaluate equal protection challenges to state law.

The rational basis test, the Court's traditional standard of review, defers to the states in two ways. It presumes that the state's purposes in drafting the law whose constitutionality is being questioned are valid. The Court is satisfied if it sees a rational relationship between the state's purpose in passing the law and its prescriptions for carrying out the law. This test also defers to the state's judgment on classification (the grouping of certain people together for legal purposes; see Chapter 16). In the *Rodriguez* case, the majority's decision to apply this test determined its outcome.

The strict scrutiny test imposes much stricter standards of justification on the states. Instead of deferring to a state's judgment on a classification, that classification is regarded as "suspect" and the state must show "a compelling state interest" that justifies its use. In addition to determining whether the purpose of the law is valid, the justices also look to see whether it violates some fundamental right in the Constitution, because a fundamental right always takes precedence over a government power.

The importance of which test the Court applied in *Rodriguez* was made clear at the very beginning of the decision. Justice Lewis F. Powell explained:

> [We] must decide, first, whether the Texas system of financing public education operates to the disadvantage of some suspect class [the poor children in the state] or impinges upon a fundamental right [equality of education explicitly or implicitly protected by the Constitution], thereby requiring strict judicial scrutiny. If so, the judgment of the District Court [which held for Rodriguez] should be affirmed. If not, the Texas scheme must still be examined to determine whether it rationally furthers some articulated state purpose and therefore does not constitute an invidious discrimination in violation of the Equal Protection Clause of the Fourteenth Amendment.

Justice Powell then rejected the claim that Texas should be subject to the strict scrutiny test because it discriminated against poor children and mustered an array of precedents and arguments to justify his reliance on the rational basis test. He concluded: "We cannot say that such disparities [in school financing] are the product of a system that is so irrational as to be invidiously discriminatory. [The] constitutional standard under the Equal Protection Clause is whether the challenged state action rationally furthers a legitimate state purpose or interest. We hold that the Texas plan abundantly satisfies this standard."

Like Justice Powell, Justice Thurgood Marshall, joined by William O. Douglas, began his dissent with the question of which test was appropriate to this case:

> [The] Court apparently seeks to establish today that equal protection cases fall into one of two neat categories which dictate the appropriate standard of review—strict scrutiny or mere rationality.
>
> I . . . cannot accept the majority's labored efforts to demonstrate that fundamental interests, which call for strict scrutiny of the challenged classification, encompass only established rights which we are somehow bound to recognize from the text of the Constitution itself.
>
> I would like to know where the Constitution guarantees the right to procreate, or the right to vote in state elections, or the right to appeal from a criminal conviction. These are instances in which, due to the importance of the interests at stake, the Court has displayed a strong concern with the existence of discriminatory state treatment.

Source: San Antonio Independent School District v. Rodriguez, 411 U.S. 1 (1973).

---

may present judges and justices with different "tests" or standards of review. Choosing one standard of review rather than another can determine the outcome of the case, as the box on the rational-basis and strict-scrutiny tests, above, explains. Judges and justices also come up with theories to justify *right* results, as the box on the nexus theory (page 536) illustrates.

The Nexus Theory

When judges or justices seek to confer constitutional status on a right that does not appear explicitly in the Constitution, they sometimes connect it with an explicit constitutional right. In the *Rodriguez* case, Justices Thurgood Marshall and William O. Douglas used this nexus theory (*nexus,* meaning "to connect or link") to claim that equality of education is a fundamental, or constitutional, right. First they described how the theory itself should work. They then provided examples of how the theory has worked in the past and concluded with how it should work in the present case:

How the Theory Should Work

[The] determination of which interests are fundamental should be firmly rooted in the Constitution. The task in every case should be to determine the extent to which constitutionally guaranteed rights are dependent on interests not mentioned in the Constitution. As the nexus between the specific constitutional guarantee and the nonconstitutional interest draws closer, the nonconstitutional interest becomes more fundamental and the degree of judicial scrutiny applied when the interest is infringed on a discriminatory basis must be adjusted accordingly.

How the Theory Has Worked in the Past

It cannot be denied that interests such as procreation, the exercise of the state franchise, and access to criminal appellate process are not fully guaranteed to the citizen by our Constitution. But these interests have nonetheless been afforded special judicial consideration in the face of discrimination because they are, to some extent, interrelated with constitutional guarantees. Procreation is now understood to be important because of its interaction with the established constitutional right of privacy. The exercise of the state franchise is closely tied to civil and political rights inherent in the First Amendment. And access to criminal appellate processes . . . [is] implicit in the [guarantee] of due process of law. Only if we closely protect the related interests from state discrimination do we ultimately ensure the integrity of the constitutional guarantee itself. This is the real lesson taken from our previous decisions.

How the Theory Should Apply in *Rodriguez*

Education directly affects the ability of a child to exercise his First Amendment rights, both as a source and as a receiver of information and ideas. [Of] particular importance is the relationship between education and the political process [especially voting].

Source: San Antonio Independent School District v. Rodriguez, 411 U.S. 1 (1973).

Critics denounce these result-oriented practices as "legislating from the bench." Defenders argue that such flexibility is appropriate to a living, evolving Constitution. In the *Edgewood* case, the Texas Supreme Court relied on intentionalism ("we consider 'the intent of the people who adopted'" the Texas State Constitution) as well as on textualism ("we rely heavily on the literal text") to declare the state's system of school finance unconstitutional—a goal the court's liberal majority believed was right. But the court did so "with the understanding that the Constitution was ratified to function as an organic document to govern society and institutions as they evolve through time."[26]

Interpreting the Law in Terms of *What Works*

In choosing an interpretive method, some judges and justices consider whether the court can provide a workable remedy once it has defined a wrong. Judges seeking effective remedies must keep one eye on the law and the other on conditions that affect its application.[27] The justices in the *Rodriguez* case may have felt that any remedy for the Texas school finance problem would have demanded excessive resources and oversight of other branches of government—a prospect that "could have chilled the enthusiasm even of a Court quite appalled by unequal educational financing."[28] The Court does not mention a concern for effectiveness in the decision, although it acknowledged that the case involved "the most persistent and difficult questions of educational policy, another area in which this Court's lack of specialized knowledge and experience counsels against premature interference with the informed judgments made at the state and local levels."[29]

Similar concerns for effectiveness may have affected the *Edgewood* decision, all the more so because judges on the Texas Supreme Court are elected, and these judges were operating in a very different economic context. In ordering the state to design a more equitable system of public school finance, these judges understood that times had changed since the 1970s, when Rodriguez lost his case. In those days, the Texas oil-based economy was still booming. But by the 1980s, the oil industry had collapsed. Business leaders wanting to diversify and strengthen the sluggish economy called for educating minority children to become productive workers in a wider variety of jobs. Projections showed that Texas schools would be teaching 75 percent minorities by the year 2000 and that these minorities would soon dominate the work force. It is entirely likely—but nowhere stated in the decision—that the judges felt freer to do what they believed was morally *right* because it was also *right* for the state economy.

The Structure of the American Legal System

The Constitution created only one court—the federal Supreme Court—but gave Congress the authority to create whatever federal courts it wished. Congress could have allowed the already existing state courts to handle matters of federal law, giving the Supreme Court the final word on decisions.[30] Instead, Congress set up a separate federal court system under the Judiciary Act of 1789, giving the United States a **dual legal system**. These two distinct legal systems—one at the federal level and 50 at the state level—coexist and interact in what is often a slow and creaky process. In addition, Washington, D.C., has its own legal system, as do many Native American tribes. Under the Constitution's system of checks and balances, federal and state courts rely on law-enforcement offices in federal and state executive branches.

This dual system means that people with grievances are not restricted to a single legal system, as in unitary states. Those with **legal standing**—the right to file suit—can sometimes take their case to the federal courts or to the courts of one or another state, depending on its subject matter and type of law involved. We've already seen that Texans seeking equality in education took their cause to their state supreme court and won after a similar case had lost in the U.S. Supreme Court some twenty years earlier. Some divorcing parents move to another state if its laws are more hospitable to their child custody claims. If the dual court system sometimes promotes legal confusion and excessive litigation, it also allows federal, state, and local judges

> **Native American courts**
>
> The U.S. government recognizes American Indian nations as dependent rather than independent sovereigns, meaning that they are forbidden to enact laws that violate the U.S. Constitution and federal statutes. However, under the Indian Self-Determination Law (1961), each Indian nation exercises jurisdiction over its own people through Native American courts. In general, cases that come before Native American courts involve disputes among people living on a reservation or involve at least one person who does.
>
> **legal standing in federal courts**
>
> For a federal court to decide a case, the litigant must have legal standing—that is, the litigant: (1) must allege a palpable (not abstract or hypothetical) personal injury that is likely to be redressed by the relief being sought; (2) must not raise general grievances that are more appropriate for legislatures to address; and (3) must make a complaint that falls within the zone of interests protected by the law that is being invoked.
>
> **jurisdiction**
>
> This term is also used with respect to a particular legal system. For example, to say that the law varies "from jurisdiction to jurisdiction" means that it varies from one legal system to another.

to develop and exchange new ideas and to *learn by doing* in different "judicial laboratories."

Federal courts have **jurisdiction**—the authority to hear and decide a case—over most cases involving the Constitution and federal law, although Congress has granted state courts concurrent jurisdiction—the right to be heard in either federal or state courts—in some federal cases. Two types of jurisdiction operate in both the federal and state court systems: original jurisdiction and appellate jurisdiction. Courts with **original jurisdiction** are generally at the bottom of the court systems and tend to be trial courts. In a trial court, the facts of a case are determined, the relevant law is applied, and the decision is often final because higher courts—courts with **appellate jurisdiction**—only hear cases on appeal from lower courts that involve legal errors (violations of due process). Thus parties that have lost a lawsuit in a lower court may yet win if an appellate court finds that the lower court has committed some error of law. Among the common violations of due process are the improper selection of a jury or admission of illegally obtained evidence. The higher court will either *uphold* the lower court's decision (affirm it) or *reverse* it (strike it down). In some instances, however, the appellate court sends the case back to the lower court with instructions on how to reconsider it. And some lower-court decisions are final—as, for example, when a defendant accused of a criminal act is found not guilty. The finality of such a not guilty verdict is protected by the Fifth Amendment's prohibition against *double jeopardy*—being tried twice for the same crime.

The State Court System

In the American legal system the states do most of the work. Each of the 50 states has its own court system, established by the state constitution and legislature. All state legislatures have allowed cities and counties to set up their own courts. States also set up special courts to handle particular tasks, such as juvenile crime.

All states have three broad categories of courts:

1. courts of original jurisdiction, which are trial courts that hear a case for the first time
2. courts with appellate jurisdiction, which hear cases on appeal from courts of original jurisdiction
3. supreme courts (or their equivalent), which hear cases on appeal from the state appeals court.

State and local courts have jurisdiction over roughly 98 percent of the cases in the country—from private adoption proceedings to public murder trials. These courts—county courts in particular—handle most of the criminal cases, mainly because there are far fewer federal than state crimes. State supreme courts issue more than 10,000 rulings every year, most of which are final because few people appeal successfully to the U.S. Supreme Court. State supreme courts also exercise judicial review over executive orders and legislative statutes in their states.

Judges are elected in 39 states. The fact that they can be voted on and off the bench makes them vulnerable to public opinion. Rules governing juries are also decided by state law and vary from state to state.

The Federal Court System

The federal courts hear disputes involving the Constitution and federal legislation. They derive their authority from two sources. Article III of the Constitution allows Congress to create whatever federal courts it chooses. These are called constitutional courts. Congress has also passed statutes creating special courts to handle cases in areas of federal law such as taxation, patents, and claims against the government, which would otherwise overburden the constitutional courts. These legislative, or special, courts are described in the box nearby.

All federal judges are appointed by the president with the approval of the Senate. Constitutional court judges and some legislative court judges are appointed for life; most legislative court judges are appointed for terms of between 12 and 16 years. In principle, their long-term appointments make them less vulnerable than elected state judges to public opinion and the politics of the moment.

Federal District Courts

District courts, the lowest courts in the federal court system, are where cases dealing with federal law first enter the federal court system. These courts handle about 1 percent of the cases in the entire legal system and hear both criminal and civil cases. Most, but not all, of these cases involve federal crimes—areas of the law that are largely settled and therefore make poor vehicles for policy making. These are also the only federal courts that hold trials, use juries, and call witnesses.

Counting the District of Columbia, Puerto Rico, and the territories (Guam, the Mariana Islands, and the Virgin Islands), there are 94 federal district courts. More than half coincide with state boundaries, but larger states including California, New York, and Texas contain as many as four districts each. In 1978, Congress increased the number of district judges from 400 to 517 to cope with rising caseloads. A busy district court may have as many as 27

The current U.S. Supreme Court (*left to right*): Clarence Thomas, Antonin Scalia, Sandra Day O'Connor, Anthony Kennedy, David Souter, Stephen Breyer, John Paul Stevens, Chief Justice William Rehnquist, and Ruth Bader Ginsburg.

Special Federal Courts

The following courts have original jurisdiction over special types of cases:

Claims Court

This successor to the U.S. Court of Claims (1955–1982) was set up by Congress in 1982 to relieve itself of the burden of considering each claim citizens make against the government, which can only be sued with its consent. Claims Court judges hear claims against the government for confiscating property for public use, injuries resulting from negligence by government employees, back pay, and claims referred to it by Congress and the executive departments. The president appoints, and the Senate approves, 16 judges who serve 16-year terms. Individual judges hear cases in Washington, D.C., or wherever they are needed around the country. Disputed decisions are appealed to a special appellate court (the Court of Appeals for the Federal Circuit), which handles special subject matter.

U.S. Tax Court

This court was set up by Congress under the Tax Reform Act of 1969 primarily to hear disputes between taxpayers and the Internal Revenue Service. The president appoints, and the Senate approves, 19 judges who serve 12-year terms. Taxpayers don't need to hire a lawyer and pay only a small fee to appeal tax decisions to this court. Cases involving small sums are settled without a trial, don't set legal precedents, and can't be appealed. Cases involving large sums may be appealed all the way up to the Supreme Court.

Court of International Trade

This court, formerly the Customs Court, was established by Congress in 1982 to handle disputes over tariff laws and duties the government levies on imported goods. Plaintiffs may be claiming that they are eligible for government assistance under the Trade Laws of 1974 and 1979, or they may be seeking relief for economic injuries they have suffered as a result of imports. The president appoints, and the Senate approves, 9 judges for life terms. Appropriately, the court sits at the country's main port of entry, New York City. Again, because these cases deal with special subject matter, they are appealed to the Court of Appeals for the Federal Circuit, and finally to the Supreme Court.

U.S. Court of Military Appeals

Known as the "G.I. Supreme Court," this court was set up by Congress in 1950 as part of a reform effort to uphold military discipline while providing justice to Americans in the armed forces. This court reviews court-martial cases, decisions regarding top military officials (including those involving the death penalty), discharges for bad conduct, and long prison terms. The president appoints, and the Senate approves, 3 civilian judges for 15-year terms. Although the judges are civilians, they do not apply regular criminal law but rather a special body of military law written by Congress.

U.S. Patent and Trademark Office

This administrative agency has jurisdiction over patent law disputes. Like the Federal Trade Commission, the Security and Exchange Commission, and the National Labor Relations Board, these cases are appealed directly to the appeals courts.

---

judges assigned to it. Normally only one judge hears each case, but in special cases the law requires three judges. In criminal cases, however, district courts must provide judge-and-jury trials as required by the Sixth Amendment.

Disputed decisions in cases dealing with constitutional issues, such as *Rodriguez*, are appealed directly from federal district courts to the Supreme Court (see Figure 14.2). Most cases, however, are appealed to an intermediary appellate court.

Figure 14.2
How cases come before the U.S. Supreme Court

THE FEDERAL COURT SYSTEM — U.S. SUPREME COURT — **THE STATE COURT SYSTEM**

- Original jurisdiction → U.S. Supreme Court
- Requests for review ← State supreme court ← State courts of appeal ← State trial courts (e.g., Kirby case)
- U.S. Court of Appeals for the Federal Circuit ← U.S. Court of Federal Claims, U.S. Court of International Trade, U.S. Court of Veterans Appeals
- 12 courts of appeals ← 94 district courts (e.g., Rodriguez case); Independent Regulatory Agencies (e.g., Securities and Exchange Commission, National Labor Relations Board, Federal Trade Commission)
- U.S. Tax Court
- U.S. Court of Military Appeals ← Courts of military review for all the services

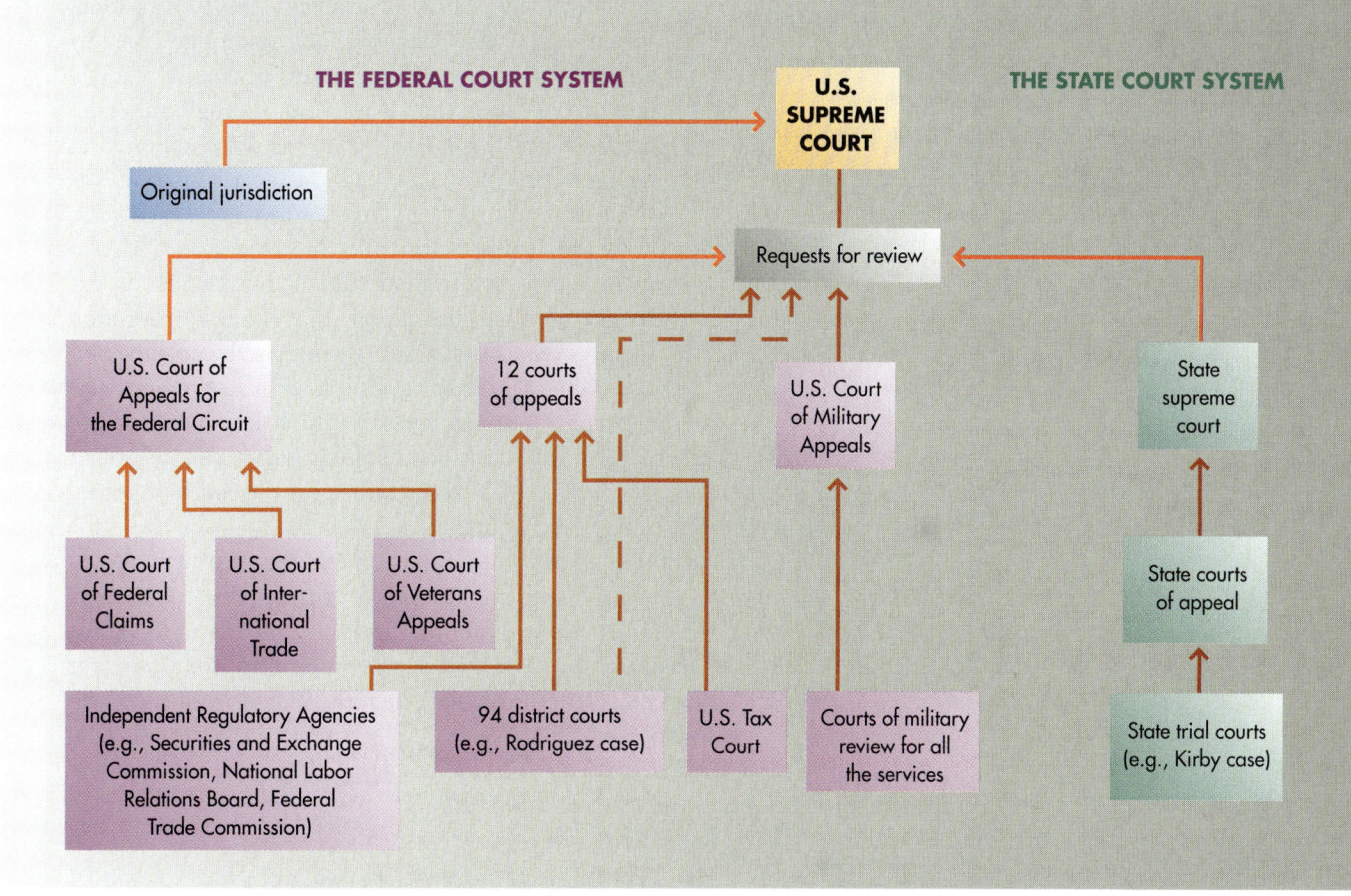

Federal Appellate Courts

Above the district and special legislative courts are intermediary appellate courts—the U.S. Courts of Appeals—also known as **circuit courts**. Like state appellate courts, federal appellate courts do not revisit the facts of a case but determine whether the procedures that led to the decision were fair and followed "due process." They also hear appeals from administrative agency courts, described in Chapter 13. The United States and its territories are divided into 12 circuits, each having one court of appeals. In 1982 Congress established a special thirteenth circuit court to hear cases nationwide in particular areas of the law, such as those appealed from the Court of International Trade and other special courts. From 4 to as many as 23 judges sit on these circuit courts, but each case is usually heard by only 3 judges.

The U.S. Supreme Court

At the apex of the dual legal system stands the U.S. Supreme Court, which hears cases involving violations of federal law (such as a treaty, the Constitution, statutes passed by Congress, and regulations issued by administrative agencies). Congress decides how many justices will sit on the Court. Prior to 1869, the number varied from six to ten but has since stabilized at nine—a chief justice and eight associate justices. The Court is in session from October to June of each year.

Cases come before the Supreme Court in two main ways: by original jurisdiction, which is extremely rare but mandatory (that is, the Constitution requires the Court to hear them), and by appellate jurisdiction and direct appeal (as with *Rodriguez*). The Supreme Court is therefore primarily a court of appeals, the court of last resort, reviewing decisions made by state supreme courts and by the lower federal courts. Figure 14.2 traces the various avenues of appeal by which a case may reach the Supreme Court.

Generally, the Court chooses to hear only those appeals that deal with a *substantial federal question*—a question with implications for public policy. The Court signals its willingness to hear an appeal by granting a **writ of *certiorari*** ordering the lower court to deliver its record of the case. By the unwritten **rule of four**, any four justices can agree to "grant cert." If cert is denied, then the judgment of the lower court stands (*stare decisis*). Ninety-five percent of all cert petitions suffer this fate. Roughly half of these rejected cases are filed by indigents, 80 percent of whom are prison inmates seeking review of their sentences.

> **original jurisdiction of the Supreme Court**
>
> The Constitution specifies three types of cases that fall under the original jurisdiction of the Supreme Court: (1) disputes between states (typically involving disputes over claims to water, minerals, and oil); (2) disputes between a state and the federal government; (3) cases involving diplomats.
>
> **writ of *certiorari***
>
> This writ, or order in writing (*certiorari* means "to be informed of" in Latin), is granted by the Supreme Court to cases it agrees to hear. In legal slang, to *grant cert* means that a higher court orders a lower court to certify and send up the record of a case for review.
>
> **indigent**
>
> This is a legal term (from the Latin *indigere*, to "need") for a person who is poor.

The U.S. Department of Justice

Most law-enforcement efforts in the American legal system occur at the state and local levels. The crimes people worry about most—murder, assault, rape, arson, theft, child abuse—are investigated and prosecuted by state and local governments. The states may establish their own law-enforcement mechanisms, so long as they do not violate the U.S. Constitution, federal law, or their own constitutions. At the federal level the responsibility for law enforcement lies mainly with the Department of Justice, that part of the executive branch which investigates and prosecutes crimes Congress has written into federal law. Federal crimes include discrimination, welfare abuse, drug dealing, kidnapping, racketeering, airplane highjacking, carjacking, illegal immigration, possession of "controlled substances," and tax, stock, and certain other forms of fraud.

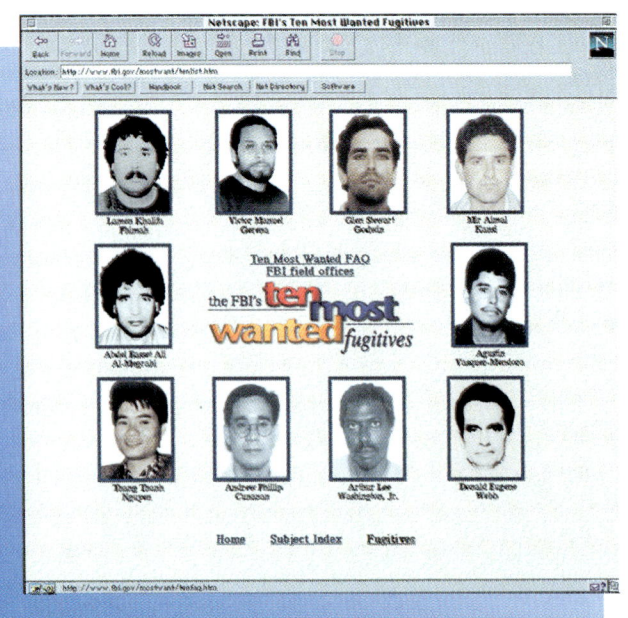

The public once could view photographs of the FBI's most wanted fugitives on post office walls. Today, they can be seen on the bureau's Web site.

The Department of Justice is headed by the attorney general, who oversees the deputy and associate attorneys general, the solicitor general, the Federal Bureau of Investigation, and special enforcement divisions in areas such as business regulation, civil rights, and natural resources. The president nominates these top officials, and the Senate confirms them.

The Attorney General

Appointed by the president to run the Department of Justice, the **attorney general** is torn between the responsibility to impartially enforce the law and loyalty to the president who nominated him or her. The attorney general oversees an enormous bureaucracy that monitors the enforcement of an ever-increasing number of policies stemming from Congress, the executive branch, and federal court decisions. The attorney general's primary responsibilities involve the investigation and prosecution of the federal crimes described above, the enforcement of a massive number of administrative laws, and the handling of interest group litigation.[31]

Attorney General Janet Reno appears before the Senate Judiciary Committee in April 1997 to defend her decision not to appoint an independent counsel to investigate fundraising practices of the Clinton reelection campaign. The attorney general is legally empowered to appoint an independent prosecutor to investigate cases of high-level wrongdoing in the executive branch.

The Solicitor General

The **solicitor general** is the key legal player on the president's team. Working with a staff of about 20 lawyers under the attorney general, the solicitor general decides which cases in the appellate courts the administration should ask the Supreme Court to hear. More than half the Court's caseload consists of such recommendations. The solicitor general also represents the interests of the federal government by submitting *amicus curiae* briefs—arguments intended to influence the Court in the direction of administration policies. If the federal government is a party in a case, the government is represented by the solicitor general.

Solicitors general differ in the degree of partisanship they bring to their job. President Ronald Reagan's second solicitor general, Charles Fried (1985–1989), was candid about his desire to help dismantle "large parts of the welfare-bureaucratic state"; to undercut "the exaggerated faith in bureaucracy and government expertise" inherited from the New Deal; to restore faith in "capitalism and free enterprise"; and to discipline "the wanderings of the federal judiciary almost half of whose members had been appointed during the brief incumbency of President Carter."[32]

The Federal Bureau of Investigation

The Federal Bureau of Investigation (FBI) is the main investigative arm of the Justice Department, with almost a quarter of its employees. The FBI investigates all violations of federal laws except those that

amicus curiae briefs
A *brief* is a short written summary of the relevant arguments that will be presented in a case. *Amicus curiae* (Latin for "friend of the court") briefs are often submitted by the solicitor general and by other individuals and interest groups—such as civil rights groups—when a case speaks directly to their concerns.

Special Enforcement Divisions of the Justice Department

Antitrust Division

This division enforces federal antitrust laws that protect the free enterprise system from monopolistic practices that reduce competition in the marketplace. Among its other duties are advising government bodies such as the Nuclear Regulatory Commission (which licenses nuclear reactors), agencies that regulate bank mergers, and agencies that lease mining rights on federal lands. Its Consumer Affairs Section files civil and criminal suits against those who have violated the regulations of agencies responsible for consumer protection (the Food and Drug Administration, the Federal Trade Commission, and the Consumer Product Safety Commission).

Civil Division

This division handles litigation from all the departments and agencies of the federal government, including members of Congress, cabinet officials, and other federal employees. Because the federal government is engaged in a wide variety of activities—construction, buying, selling, shipping, energy production, insurance, banking—the lawsuits this division handles vary widely and it typically confronts constitutional and policy issues.

Civil Rights Division

This division, founded in 1957, now enforces civil rights laws prohibiting discrimination due to race, ethnicity, religion, age, gender, or disability in connection with voting, education, employment, housing, credit, the use of public facilities and accommodations, and in the administration of federally assisted programs.

Criminal Division

This division enforces criminal statutes that do not fall under the authority of other divisions. Enforcement is carried out by particular sections of the division, such as Organized Crime and Racketeering; Narcotics and Dangerous Drugs; Fraud; Public Integrity (which ensures the honesty of public officials and the electoral process); Internal Security (which oversees statutes related to national security, such as the Foreign Agents Registration Act); International Affairs (which deals with international crime and extradition); and Enforcement Operations (which handles matters such as electronic surveillance and witness relocation).

Land and Natural Resources

This division handles lawsuits in federal and state courts involving natural resources sought or owned by the federal government and the protection of the nation's environment. It enforces laws controlling endangered species, water, mineral rights, air and noise pollution, hazardous wastes, wetlands, and the exploitation of Indian lands.

Tax Division

This division is responsible for representing the U.S. government and its officials in civil and criminal cases related to internal revenue laws that do not come before the U.S. Tax Court.

Congress has assigned to special enforcement divisions in the Justice Department, described in the box above. (There are also specialized law-enforcement agencies in virtually every executive department. The Bureau of Alcohol, Tobacco and Firearms, for example, is a branch of the Treasury Department.) The FBI investigates espionage, sabotage, terrorism, kidnapping, bank robbery, interstate gambling violations, and the assault or killing of the president or a federal officer. It has 56 offices across the country and 20 more overseas, which cooperate with their counterparts in foreign countries.

The heroic reputation that the FBI developed under J. Edgar Hoover (1924–1972) for capturing a number of notorious gangsters was tarnished when

Court said, the Sierra Club would have to show that *particular* individuals would suffer if federal parkland was not preserved.[82] While this policy clearly increases the Court's efficiency by lightening its caseload, it also deprives groups of a powerful tool to advance their causes through the courts. Because the makeup of the Court has changed very little since then, this situation has not changed.

Reforms

These issues have prompted a variety of reforms in both the federal and state judicial systems: the creation of new judgeships, the reorganization of judicial districts, and the use of new technologies that facilitate data collection and record keeping. Other reforms include turning to cheaper and faster alternatives to jury trials and judge-made decisions, as well as to cheaper sentencing procedures. In the past courts have dealt with disputes either by sending them to trial or, if a trial was not called for, by dismissing them. Today less than 10 percent of criminal cases go to trial in federal courts.[83] By cutting down on jury trials, courts also cut down on the high costs of the adversary system and due process. As efficiency measures, these reforms work, but in some cases at the expense of *what's right*.

Alternatives to Trials

Among the alternatives to trials are alternative dispute resolution and plea bargaining. **Alternative dispute resolution**, which includes mediation and arbitration procedures, allows litigants and the courts to negotiate and settle a dispute short of trial.[84] Courts call the lawyers together without their clients to work out alternative solutions to the controversy, and judges act as managers to facilitate a final settlement.[85] If this procedure fails, civil or criminal cases may be given a full trial, with or without a jury.

Plea bargaining involves bargaining in which the accused person agrees to plead guilty to a reduced charge in return for a lesser sentence than he or she is likely to receive if convicted in a trial. This procedure prevents the majority of criminal cases from coming to trial, thereby avoiding the costs of a trial and the public humiliation that might involve. Opponents of plea bargaining say it gives too much discretionary power to prosecuting attorneys, while advocates say that without plea bargaining criminal cases would overwhelm the courts.

These alternatives reflect an administrative approach to justice that in some cases produces fairer results for poor people who can't match their adversaries in lawyer power in the adversary system. In Germany, for example, the inquisitorial system allows judges to take "an active role in questioning witnesses and seeking the facts rather than passively supervising the battle between the prosecutor and the defense attorney."[86] As a result, the German judge can often compensate for a weak attorney who faces a strong government prosecutor. But in the United States, where many state judges are elected and are former prosecutors, judges may tend to favor prosecutors.

Alternative and Mandatory Sentencing

Overcrowded prisons have led many judges to devise innovative types of **alternative sentencing** for people who pose little risk to the community, a strategy that frees up

Joe B. Brown, a local Tennessee judge, has attracted publicity for his alternative sentencing practices, such as allowing a burglary victim to visit the burglar's home and take something of equal value as the burglar watches. Legal experts disagree over how effective these sentences are.

This sign at the end of a farmer's driveway is a condition of his probation. He was given this shaming penalty for attacking another farmer. Judges nationwide are requiring convicted drunk drivers to put special license plates on their cars, shoplifters to advertise their crimes in the local paper, and batterers to apologize publicly to their victims.

prison space for truly dangerous criminals. Judges may require individuals to perform community service as a way of understanding the damage they have done while providing needed assistance to communities. They sometimes require first-time offenders to complete a job training course, get a school diploma, or go through a drug rehabilitation program.[87] New technologies such as monitoring devices people can wear on their legs allow them to live at home and report to parole officers. Some judges are also experimenting with the controversial practice of "shaming."

Both the federal government and the states increasingly rely on **mandatory sentencing**—specifying particular punishments for particular categories of crimes (for example, requiring the death penalty for the murder of a police officer or a prison guard). For drug-related offenses, federal mandatory guidelines prescribe long prison terms regardless of the circumstances. Mandatory sentencing is intended not merely to expedite criminal cases but also to cut down on the discrimination that researchers show taints sentencing procedures.[88] The crime bill passed in 1994—popularly known as "three strikes and you're out"—provides that conviction for three violent federal offenses carry a mandatory sentence of life in prison without parole. The drawback of mandatory sentences is that they deprive the judge of the flexibility to grant leniency in cases that warrant it.

The problems facing the American legal system today will not be resolved overnight by reforms such as these. The local news confirms on a daily basis that laws, courts, police, and prisons do not deter crime or even inflict punishment to everyone's satisfaction. There is no substitute for civility and mutual respect that are formed in childhood and reinforced throughout one's life by strong families, communities, and schools. A healthy economy and a smaller gap between rich and poor can also contribute to a lawful and just society.

Summary

The American legal system consists of (1) several types of law (public and private), which are applied by (2) federal, state, and local courts and enforced by (3) federal, state, and local law-enforcement officers. From the federal Supreme Court down to the local sheriff's office, these laws and institutions promote public order and manage social change by resolving disputes among citizens and between citizens and government.

Legal authority at both the federal and state levels is based on (1) common law, (2) constitutional law, (3) legislation, (4) judicial review, and (5) judicial decisions. Although judges primarily resolve disputes in relatively settled areas of the law, they make policy when the law is ambiguous or when they interpret the law to meet social needs. Judges sometimes act as administrators when they devise and oversee remedies. Unlike elected officials, however, judges can only make policy case by case. Judges rely on their power of judicial review to determine whether a law is unconstitutional and issue decisions that become precedents for future cases—decisions that lawmakers and courts sometimes alter or reverse.

Political actors often disagree over what a law says and how it should be applied, but only judges have the authority to decide how a law is to be interpreted in a particular case. Judges' decisions are strongly influenced by their judicial philosophy (restraint or activism) and the methods they use to interpret the law.

The structure of the American legal system, as determined by the Constitution and the Judiciary Act of 1789, is a dual legal system composed of state and federal courts of original jurisdiction, appellate courts, courts for special areas of the law, and the U.S. Supreme Court, which tops both court systems. While complex and cumbersome, this dual system provides options and "laboratories" for experimentation. Both court systems rely on law-enforcement mechanisms in executive branches. The states bear the heaviest caseloads and the greatest responsibility for law-enforcement primarily because there are many more state crimes than federal crimes. The U.S. Department of Justice, headed by the attorney general, is responsible for investigating and prosecuting federal crimes.

American courts are responsive to federal and state constitutions, legal precedents, rules of procedure, and legal traditions. They are also influenced by powerful personalities, major events (wars, economic depressions), the politics of the appointment process, media publicity, and the judicial choices presidents make.

The Supreme Court makes public policy by choosing to hear cases with policy implications for the nation. It tends to hear cases that preserve the authority and legitimacy it needs to obtain compliance. State courts have found ways to avoid compliance, and such challenges test and refine the decisions of both court systems.

Disparities in wealth affect the quality of justice in the American legal system. Justice is also affected by how well courts work. Hampered by swollen dockets and scarce resources, courts have instituted measures that serve efficiency but not necessarily justice. Clearly American laws, courts, and police do not completely deter crime or even impose punishment to everyone's satisfaction. But factors such as mutual respect, strong families and communities, good schools, a healthy economy, and a smaller gap between rich and poor can also contribute to a lawful and just society.

Key Terms

adversary system **527**
alternative dispute resolution **561**
alternative sentencing **561**
American legal system **525**
amicus curiae briefs **543**
appellate jurisdiction **538**
attorney general **543**
brief **554**
circuit court **541**
civil law **525**
class action suits **531**
common law **526**
concurring opinion **555**
constitutional law **527**
crime **525**
criminal law **525**
customary law **527**
defendant **527**

dissenting opinion **556**
docket **553**
dual legal system **537**
felony **525**
inquisitorial system **527**
judicial activism **532**
judicial philosophy **532**
judicial restraint **532**
judicial review **529**
juries **526**
jurisdiction **538**
laws **525**
legal standing **537**
legislation **527**
majority decision **555**
mandatory sentencing **562**
misdemeanor **525**
oral argument **554**

original jurisdiction **538**
originalism **534**
plaintiff **527**
plea bargaining **561**
political questions **554**
precedents **531**
private law **525**
procedural law **526**
public law **525**
remedy **531**
rule of four **542**
senatorial courtesy **547**
solicitor general **543**
stare decisis **527**
substantive law **526**
summary disposition **555**
verdict **526**
writ of *certiorari* **542**

How You Can Learn More About the Courts and the Legal System

Bodenheimer, Edgar, John B. Oakley, and Jean C. Love. *An Introduction to the Anglo-American Legal System*, 2nd ed. St. Paul, Minn.: West Publishing, 1988. A clear discussion of how the legal system classifies itself and its subject matter, with case illustrations.

Bork, Robert H. *The Tempting of America: The Political Seduction of the Law.* New York: Touchstone, 1990. A survey of the Supreme Court from an originalist standpoint, along with an account of Bork's Senate confirmation hearings.

Carter, Lief H. *Contemporary Constitutional Lawmaking: The Supreme Court and the Art of Politics* New York: Pergamon Press, 1985. A provocative argument comparing the interpretive work of judges to the creative work of artists, with a theory of how to act normatively now that the artifices of interpretation have been exposed.

Chemerinsky, Erwin. *Interpreting the Constitution.* New York: Praeger, 1987. A highly readable discussion of the debate surrounding the proper method of interpreting the Constitution.

Cooper, Phillip J. *Battles on the Bench: Conflict Inside the Supreme Court.* Lawrence: University of Kansas Press, 1995. The most comprehensive account of behind-the-scenes disagreements.

Dimond, Paul R. *The Supreme Court and Judicial Choice: The Role of Provisional Review in a Democracy.* Ann Arbor: University of Michigan Press, 1989. A detailed discussion of the debates surrounding judicial review and its effect on democracy.

Edley, Christopher F., Jr. *Administrative Law: Rethinking Judicial Control of Bureaucracy.* New Haven: Yale University Press, 1990. A detailed analysis of the functions and problems affecting this fastest-growing area of the law.

Galloway, Russell W. *Justice for All? The Rich and Poor in Supreme Court History, 1790–1990.* Durham, N.C.: Carolina Academic Press, 1991. A short, readable history of the liberal and conservative eras of the Supreme Court and their effect on the poor.

Heydebrand, Wolf, and Carroll Seron. *Rationalizing Justice: The Political Economy of Federal District Courts.* Albany: State University of New York Press, 1990. An analysis of the judiciary's efforts to increase its efficiency in the face of diminishing resources and mounting responsibilities.

Murphy, Walter. *Elements of Judicial Strategy.* Chicago: University of Chicago Press, 1964. A fascinating look at the inner workings of the Supreme Court, in terms of both the opportunities for and constraints on the Court's capacity to make public policy.

Perry, H. W., Jr. *Deciding to Decide: Agenda Setting in the United States Supreme Court.* Cambridge, Mass.: Harvard University Press, 1991. Absorbing interviews and analysis exposing the politics and legal technicalities involved in setting the Court's agenda.

Post, Gordon C. *Our Legal System and How It Works.* Ann Arbor: University of Michigan Law School, 1931. A classic work on the functions of the legal system, with particular attention to the use of language and the relevance of context.

Tarr, G. Alan, and Mary Cornelia Aldis Porter. *State Supreme Courts in State and Nation.* New Haven: Yale University Press, 1988. A valuable view of the American legal system through the eyes of state supreme courts.

Practicing Civil Liberties and Civil Rights

PART 4

Civil Liberties

In 1989 Melody DeShaney (*right*), the mother of Joshua DeShaney, filed suit in the Winnebago County courthouse (*above*) against the Wisconsin Department of Social Services for failing to protect her son from beatings by his father, to whom the state had given custody.

CHAPTER 15

[The Federal Elections Campaign Act of 1971] affirmatively enhances First Amendment values. By reducing in good measure the disparity due to wealth, the Act tends to equalize both the ability of all voters to affect electoral outcomes, and the opportunity of all interested citizens to become candidates for elective federal office. This broadens the choice of candidates and the opportunity to hear a variety of views.

—*Buckley v. Valeo, U.S. District of Columbia Circuit, 1975*

A restriction on the amount of money a person or group can spend on political communication during a campaign necessarily reduces the quantity of expression by restricting the number of issues discussed, the depth of their exploration, and the size of the audience reached. This is because virtually every means of communicating ideas in today's mass society requires the expenditure of money.

—*Buckley v. Valeo, U.S. Supreme Court, 1976*[1]

What Are Civil Liberties?

Freedom of Religion

Freedom of Expression

Life, Liberty, and Property

Privacy

Civil Liberties as Constitutional Practice

When the parents of one-year-old Joshua DeShaney divorced, the boy was placed in the custody of his father, who, according to his new wife and visiting social workers, severely beat him. Only once did the Winnebago County, Wisconsin, Department of Social Services intervene, hospitalizing the boy until he was fit to be returned to his father. After a particularly savage beating at age four, Joshua collapsed into a coma, suffered permanent brain damage, and was institutionalized.

Joshua's mother then sued his social worker and the Department of Social Services for damages, claiming that they should have intervened to protect the boy. Because Wisconsin had a law limiting any damages that could be recovered for official misconduct to $50,000, Joshua's mother filed suit in federal court. She charged the Department of Social Services with depriving Joshua of protections under the due process clause of the Fourteenth Amendment and the Fourth Amendment, which affirms "the right of the people to be secure in their persons."

Does the Constitution protect a child from being beaten until comatose by an abusive parent? Although many Americans might think so, the Supreme Court declared 6–3 in *DeShaney v. Winnebago County Department of Social Services* (1989) that the Fourteenth Amendment offers no such protection. Chief Justice William H. Rehnquist cited a long list of precedents holding that the due process clause of the Fourteenth Amendment says only what the federal government may *not* do and nothing about what it *should* do. He explained that the amendment was designed to protect people from government, not to protect private individuals from each other. Only the states have the authority to regulate such behavior by passing criminal laws. Thus the amendment imposed no obligation on Wisconsin to guarantee Joshua "certain minimal levels of safety and security." But it might have, Rehnquist admitted, if the state had had a "special relationship" with the boy—for example, if Joshua had been abused in a foster home approved by the state.[2]

In his dissent, Justice William Brennan argued that the fact that Wisconsin had set up a child protection program and had told people in the community to report instances of child abuse to it constituted the sort of special relationship that a state has with prisoners and inmates in mental institutions—a relationship that entitles them to bodily protection. By depriving the child of help from other sources, Brennan said, the state program "effectively confined Joshua DeShaney within the walls of [his father's] violent home."[3] (The state ultimately tried and convicted the father, Randy DeShaney, of child abuse.)

Many people thought the Court's decision was callous. Uppermost in their minds was the issue of *what's right*, and the suffering of a defenseless child was clearly wrong. But uppermost in the minds of the justices was a question of law. Because these justices favored judicial restraint and a strict reading of the Constitution, they found nothing in the Fourteenth Amendment that gave government the power to right such a wrong. To grant government such powers was, in their view, to violate the Constitution's limits on government. Thus the Court did what it believed was *right* with respect to the Constitution, which, as the majority of the justices saw it, was their job. But this majority also had a mission: to give back to the states some of the power they had lost as a result of activist interpretations of the Fourteenth Amendment (such as Brennan's) by their liberal predecessors on the Supreme Court. Could a different Court have decided the case as Brennan wanted? Yes, if a majority of the justices had agreed with Brennan.

In this chapter we'll examine the disputes that have always surrounded civil liberties in American politics by asking the following questions:

> **What are civil liberties and where do they come from?**
>
> **Under what circumstances are people entitled to civil liberties under the U.S. Constitution?**
>
> **How have the courts defined and upheld civil liberties in a changing society?**
>
> **Why are civil liberties vital to constitutional practice?**

What Are Civil Liberties?

To live in the United States is to be entitled to certain liberties and rights, such as freedom of religion, speech, and the press; freedom from cruel and unusual punishments; freedom to own property; and the right to be tried by a jury of one's peers. A **liberty** or **right** is a power or privilege an individual claims to possess by nature, tradition, or law. The terms *liberties* and *rights* are often used interchangeably, but strictly speaking:

> **liberties and rights**
> One reason *civil liberties* are often called *rights* is because the Founders, following British tradition, listed their liberties in documents called *bills of rights* rather than *bills of civil liberties*.

- **Civil liberties** are *freedoms from government*, freedoms that the constitutions of the nation and the states require those governments to protect.
- **Civil rights** are *claims against government* to take positive steps to protect people from the unlawful actions of others, including government.

Because the United States is a federal system composed of a national government and state governments, civil liberties claims must be made to the appropriate government, as the *DeShaney* case illustrates. But the fact that a majority of the Supreme Court has the authority to decide what level of government is appropriate (*what's right*) makes this decision a *political* one in the sense we are using the term *political* in this book.

Civil liberties in the Constitution are supposed to belong equally to all, citizens and noncitizens alike, no matter how distasteful their beliefs are, so long as they behave civilly. (Whether civil liberties should be extended to children is a matter of dispute, as the box nearby explains.) The principle requires government to remain neutral toward those who exercise their civil liberties. When groups as different as fundamentalist Christians, gays and lesbians, veterans, and Ku Klux Klanners parade down the main streets, police officers are supposed to stand by only to keep the peace.

Communitarians Versus Civil Libertarians

In Chapter 4 we saw that the freedoms of individuals and groups are inseparable from communities that respect those freedoms and inseparable from government's responsibility to maintain law and order. Communitarians argue that the drafters of the Bill of Rights never intended for individuals "to be completely free, to possess things totally, to be treated justly without being asked to act justly."[4] But harsher critics blame an excess of individual liberties for what they see as a decline in American culture. They view the breakdown of the nuclear family, the fall of educational standards, the increase of obscenity in the arts and entertainment, and the rise of illegitimacy, teenage violence, and racial tensions as evidence of this decline.[5]

In contrast, **civil libertarians**—those who rank civil liberties as the highest political value, as activists of the American Civil Liberties Union (ACLU) do—regard these same "facts" as the price for upholding basic freedoms. The primary obligation of government, in their view, is not to overreach the limits that the Constitution places upon it. But communitarians respond that the Framers never anticipated that community life would be shaken by such cultural diversity and rapid technological change, or that civil liberties would collide incessantly in the public arena and in the courts. Imagine their reaction to today's disputes over rap lyrics, the legalization of marijuana, same-sex marriage, and cloning research.

> **Leading Civil Liberties Organization**
> American Civil Liberties Union
> http://www.aclu.org

Political Actors Disagree

Are Children Entitled to Civil Liberties?

Are children—minors who have not yet reached the majority age of 18 and are therefore not yet full citizens—entitled to any civil liberties?[1] The answer to this *what is* question has changed over time as the society has changed its views about *what's right*.

During the colonial period children, from infants to older teenagers, were treated as servants and the *property* of their parents, who made all their decisions and demanded strict obedience.[2] The terms *no person* and *the accused* in the Bill of Rights—language that could have been interpreted to apply to everyone—were applied only to adults. In 1967, however, the Supreme Court held that young people brought before a juvenile court were entitled to due process.[3] In doing so, the Court was extending an existing right to a new group of people, thus widening the coverage of the Bill of Rights.

In 1969, however, the Court recognized children as "persons" under the Constitution who possess "fundamental rights which the state must respect." These rights, the Court said, "do not mature and come into being magically" the day one becomes of voting age.[4] But the Court has not been clear about what these rights are. Children still lack the right to bail and trial by jury,[5] and in 1979 the Court upheld state laws allowing parents to commit their minor children to state mental institutions without granting the child a hearing, on the assumption that most parents act in the best interests of their children.

In 1975 the Court upheld the rights of Amish parents to remove their children from public schools after the eighth grade in order to preserve their community's religious way of life—a decision that continued to view children as parental property.[6] Courts are taking a similar approach in custody and adoption suits, upholding laws that generally award children to biological parents rather than adoptive parents, unless there is proof of neglect, abuse, or abandonment. Advocates of children's liberties argue that adult property rights should not supersede what's best for the child.

Questions of children's civil liberties are increasingly being raised by various state laws and court cases. Some states have passed laws denying unmarried minor girls the right to seek an abortion without parental consent. In *Bellotti v. Baird* (1979) the Supreme Court struck down a Massachusetts law requiring such minors to petition a judge for an abortion if one or both parents refused.[7] The case made it clear that children's rights may differ from those of adults in situations that might cause them undue harm. But undue injury received no such consideration in the *DeShaney* case (1989), in which the Court denied that Wisconsin had "an affirmative 'duty'" to protect Joshua DeShaney from abuse at his father's hands.[8]

---

[1] See Denise M. Trauth and John L. Huffman, "Heightened Scrutiny: A Test for the First Amendment Rights of Children," in *Censorship, Secrecy, Access, and Obscenity,* ed. Theodore R. Kupherman (Westport, Conn.: Meckler, 1990), 71–90.
[2] See "Parental Consent Requirement and Privacy Rights of Minors: The Contraceptive Controversy," *Harvard Law Review* 88 (1975): 1001–1020 (student note).
[3] *In re Gault,* 387 U.S. 1 (1967).
[4] *Tinker v. DeMoines,* 393 U.S. 503 (1969). See also *In re Gault.*
[5] See Hillary Rodham, "Children's Rights: A Legal Perspective," in *Children's Rights: Contemporary Perspectives,* ed. Patricia A. Vardin and Ilene N. Brody (New York: Teachers College Press, 1979), 21–36. Hillary Rodham later changed her name to Hillary Rodham Clinton.
[6] *Wisconsin v. Yoder,* 406 U.S. 205 (1975).
[7] *Bellotti v. Baird,* 61 L. Ed. 2d 797 (1979).
[8] *DeShaney v. Winnebago County Department of Social Services,* 109 S. Ct. 998 (1989).

Communitarians want to preserve the morality of communities so that they will do *what's right* and function in a civil manner. Civil libertarians are more concerned with preserving civil liberties (*what's right*) even if that disrupts the community. But only civil communities can effectively teach respect for civil liberties. In sum, both groups contribute in different but essential ways to the practice of democracy.

The Dispute over the Origin of Civil Liberties

Are you born with civil liberties, or does government give them to you? How people answer these questions affects their views of what civil liberties are and who is entitled to them.

When the Founders and Framers wrote what they believed to be *natural* liberties into law and thus made government responsible for protecting them, these natural liberties became known as *civil* (legal) liberties. However, those who believe that civil liberties originate in natural law rather than in the legal documents that spell them out feel justified in (1) returning to natural law to justify particular liberties that do not appear in those documents and in (2) citing the authority of natural law to claim that civil liberties apply to all people everywhere, regardless of what any document says.

While natural law principles are enormously inspiring as they appear in the Declaration of Independence and as they are used to legitimate human rights today, they have also been used to deny liberties to minorities and women (see Chapter 16). Critics of natural law therefore insist that civil liberties come into existence only in a civil society whose members have agreed to write them into the laws of government. Authority over civil liberties is thereby removed from those who claim to speak for nature, religion, or science and entrusted to human lawmakers. Thus in a democracy, the people, acting through their representatives, have the ultimate say over what civil liberties are (*what is*) and whether their exercise in concrete situations is legitimate (*what's right*). This does not mean that the people and their representatives are not influenced by their beliefs about God, religion, nature, and science in deciding what civil liberties are and when they apply. Many disputes explored in this chapter show that they are. The difference is that peoples' claims to authority in these areas are subject to the democratic processes of criticism, deliberation, majority vote, and the judgment of the courts.

When vandals destroyed outdoor Chanukah menorahs in the winter of 1996, residents throughout Newtown Township, Pennsylvania, displayed menorahs in their windows to show support for their Jewish neighbors.

Civil Liberties in the Bill of Rights

According to a Supreme Court ruling issued a half-century ago, the purpose of the Bill of Rights, ratified in 1791,

> was to withdraw certain subjects from . . . political controversy, to place them beyond the reach of majorities and officials and to establish them as legal principles to be applied by the courts. One's right to life, liberty, and property, to free speech, a free press, freedom of worship and assembly, and other fundamental rights may not be submitted to a vote; they depend on the outcome of no elections.[6]

The Bill of Rights was written in an era when royal officials invaded households at will, smashed printing presses, held people in prison for years without a trial, and often tortured them to get confessions to crimes. Civil liberties that are asserted in the first eight amendments to the Constitution (see Table 15.1) include specific actions the federal government is forbidden to take, such as compelling you to testify against yourself, as well as legal procedures it must

inalienable right

An *inalienable* right or liberty is one that cannot be alienated (taken or given away) without due process of law.

guarantee you if it legitimately curtails your rights. The Fifth Amendment, for example, does not say that the federal government may not deprive you of life, liberty, or property—only that when it does so it must abide by "due process of law." Because these prohibitions are worded as "thou shalt not" actions, they are sometimes called *negative rights*. In contrast, the Ninth and Tenth Amendments protect *positive rights*, although what these rights consist of is debatable because their wording is so vague. The Ninth Amendment declares that rights not spelled out in the Constitution are retained by the people. The Tenth Amendment states that those powers not given by the Constitution to the federal government nor prohibited to the states "are reserved to the States respectively, or to the people."

Civil liberties, while *inalienable,* are not *absolute.* Individuals are required by law to sacrifice some of their private rights for the privilege of living in a civil society protected by government. The Founders followed English philosopher John Locke (1632–1704) and English jurist William Blackstone (1723–1780) in maintaining that government protects what remains of a person's natural liberty after the public welfare has been served.[7] Because people have always disagreed over just how much individual sacrifice the public welfare requires, they have always disagreed over how extensive civil liberties are

TABLE 15.1

The Eight "Thou Shalt Not" Provisions in the Bill of Rights

The Federal Government Shall Not:

1. violate the freedom of religion, speech, the press, and petition (First Amendment)
2. violate the "right of the people to keep and bear Arms" (Second Amendment)
3. quarter any soldier "in any house, without the consent of the owner" (Third Amendment
4. violate the "right of the people to be secure in their persons, houses, papers, and effects, against unreasonable searches and seizures" (Fourth Amendment)
5. hold any person "to answer for a capital, or otherwise infamous crime, unless [indicted by] a Grand Jury," try any person twice for the same offense (double jeopardy), deprive any person "of life, liberty, or property, without due process of law," or take private property for public use "without just compensation" (Fifth Amendment)
6. deprive "the accused" of "the right to a speedy and public trial" in criminal cases (Sixth Amendment)
7. deprive anyone of the "right of trial by jury" in common law cases (Seventh Amendment)
8. require excessive bail or inflict "cruel and unusual punishments" (Eighth Amendment)

The Politics of Language

Interpreting the Right "to Keep and Bear Arms"

Both supporters and opponents of gun control claim that the Second Amendment is on their side. Their constitutional dispute is over the proper context in which to interpret "the right of the people to keep and bear Arms." The declaration of this right is preceded by the statement that a "well-regulated Militia" is "necessary to the security of a free State."

But what is a *militia*? In 1791, a militia consisted of free male citizens armed with muskets, rifles, and bayonets, whereas in the 1990s it consists of the National Guard units of the 50 states armed with sophisticated modern weapons. Gun-control advocates say that the amendment is obsolete (it is no longer *what is*) because it only authorizes "the people" as a body (a *militia*) to bear arms for the specific purpose of protecting society. The amendment does not, they claim, authorize individuals to carry weapons for any reason. Opponents of gun control, backed by the National Rifle Association, claim that the "right of the people" in this amendment is meant to protect individuals, just as the rights in the First, Fourth, and Ninth Amendments are.

The Supreme Court has addressed this issue twice in this century. In 1939 it upheld the National Firearms Act of 1934, which required the registration of sawed-off shotguns on the grounds that this weapon bore no "reasonable relationship" to a well-regulated militia.[1] The Court refused to review an Illinois case in which a town banned handguns in the home. The federal appeals court had upheld the law on grounds that the Second Amendment was a limitation on the federal government, not the states.

In 1997 the Court ruled 5–4 that Congress may not require states to help administer background checks on people seeking to purchase guns.[2] The decision was a major victory for states' rights advocates and for opponents of gun control.

---

[1] *United States v. Miller* (1939), 425 U.S. 435 (1975).
[2] *Printz v. United States*, 65 U.S.L.W. 4731 (June 27, 1997), No. 95-1478.

---

or should be. Today the liveliest disputes involve the rights to have sexual and other types of privacy, to have abortions, to choose physician-assisted suicide, to exercise control over one's private property, and, as the box nearby discusses, to own, carry, and use guns.

Recent Supreme Courts have given less protection to civil liberties under the Bill of Rights than have their immediate predecessors. As a result, people have been turning to their states for such protection, as advocates of same-sex marriage did in Hawaii (see Chapter 3). Originally, though, state bills of rights offered fewer protections than the Bill of Rights, and when individuals sought protection under the Bill of Rights from state laws they claimed violated its provisions, the Supreme Court denied their appeals. It did so for the same reason it gave in *DeShaney*: that the provisions of the Bill of Rights limit only the power of the federal government, not the power of the states. Natural law theorists have argued in vain that people have a preexisting entitlement to these natural liberties and that states, no less than the federal government, have an obligation to protect them.

Nationalizing the Bill of Rights

The ratification of the Fourteenth Amendment in 1868 gave the Supreme Court a legal mechanism for *nationalizing* the Bill of Rights, that is, imposing its fundamental liberties on the states. By 1972, the Court had nationalized most of these liberties with the help of the amendment's due process clause: "All persons born or naturalized in the United States . . . are citizens of the United States and of the State wherein they reside. No State shall make or enforce any law which shall abridge the privileges or immunities of citizens of the United States; nor shall any State deprive any person of life, liberty, or property, without due process of law."

Some justices argued that the amendment "incorporated" all provisions of the Bill of Rights, not just the selected rights that the Court recognized as fundamental. Advocates of **total incorporation** maintained that all the provisions in the Bill of Rights were fundamental and that it was wrong for the Court to pick and choose among them. But the Court chose the path of **selective incorporation**—a case-by-case process—to allow the states more freedom in the federal system. Table 15.2 shows which liberties the states are now obligated to protect and which liberties have not been incorporated.

The Doctrine of Dual Citizenship

According to the doctrine of dual citizenship (see Chapter 2), Americans are citizens of their states and of the nation. The Supreme Court issued its first decision on the question of whether the citizen of a state is protected by the Bill of Rights in *Barron v. Baltimore* (1833).[8] Barron, the owner of a commercial wharf, sued the city of Baltimore for ruining his wharf by dumping sand and gravel into it. In taking his property without providing just compensation, Barron argued, the city had violated the Fifth Amendment. The Court under Chief Justice John Marshall held that the Fifth Amendment applied exclusively to the federal government, not to the states. Because the state of Maryland lacked a law similar to the Fifth Amendment, Barron had no way of obtaining just compensation. The *Barron* decision,

Clarence Gideon, an indigent drifter, wrote this petition for a writ of *certiorari* from a Florida prison, where he was serving time for breaking into a poolroom. He had not had a lawyer and was not entitled to one under that state's constitution. In 1963 the U.S. Supreme Court, in *Gideon v. Wainright*, extended the right to free legal counsel to defendants in state felony trials.

TABLE 15.2

Incorporated and Unincorporated Liberties

Incorporated Liberties

Issue	Amendment Involved	Supreme Court Case	Year
Freedom of speech	First	*Gitlow v. New York*	1925
Freedom of the press	First	*Near v. Minnesota*	1931
Right to a lawyer in death-penalty cases	Sixth	*Powell v. Alabama*	1932
Freedom of assembly and right to petition	First	*DeJonge v. Oregon*	1937
Free exercise of religion		*Cantwell v. Connecticut*	1940
Separation of church and state	First	*Everson v. Board of Education of Ewing Township, NJ*	1947
Right to a public trial	Sixth	*In re Oliver*	1948
No unreasonable searches and seizures—the "exclusionary rule" for evidence	Fourth	*Mapp v. Ohio*	1961
No cruel and unusual punishment	Eighth	*Robinson v. California*	1962
Right to a lawyer in all criminal cases	Sixth	*Gideon v. Wainwright*	1963
No compulsory self-incrimination	Fifth	*Malloy v. Hogan*	1964
Right of privacy	First and others	*Griswold v. Connecticut*	1965
Right to an impartial jury	Sixth	*Parker v. Gladden*	1966
Right to a speedy trial	Sixth	*Klopfer v. North Carolina*	1967
Right to jury trial for all serious crimes*	Sixth	*Duncan v. Louisiana*	1968
No double jeopardy	Fifth	*Benton v. Maryland*	1969
Right to counsel for all crimes involving a jail term	Sixth	*Argersinger v. Hamlin*	1972

Unincorporated Liberties

Right to keep and bear arms (Second Amendment)
Ban on quartering troops (Third Amendment)
Right to a grand jury indictment (Fifth Amendment)
Guarantee of trial by jury in civil cases (Seventh Amendment)
Prohibition on excessive bail and fines (Eighth Amendment)

*Although the right to a trial by jury in criminal cases has been incorporated, only federal courts are required to have 12-person juries and unanimous verdicts in noncapital cases.

which protected states from suits filed against them by their citizens under the Bill of Rights, reinforced the doctrine of dual citizenship—a doctrine the Court used to protect the states from interference by the federal government for almost a century.

Although the Fourteenth Amendment appeared to call for a single, national definition of citizenship, the Supreme Court said it did not. In the *Slaughter-House Cases* (1873), the Court reviewed the complaints of New Orleans butchers threatened with bankruptcy by the Louisiana legislature's decision to give a single corporation a monopoly over the slaughterhouse business.[9] The butchers argued (as Barron had) that their property was being taken without just compensation in violation of the Fifth Amendment, which the Fourteenth Amendment imposed on the states. But the Court held that the intent of the Fourteenth Amendment was a narrow one—to protect "Negroes as a class"—not to provide general federal protection for citizens. This decision made it clear that the Court wanted the Fourteenth Amendment to be read expansively when a case involved racial discrimination but wanted remedies in other cases to be sought under state law.

The first crack in the doctrine of dual citizenship came when the Court declared in *Gitlow v. New York* (1925) that the First Amendment's freedom of speech was a *fundamental right* that belonged to people in the states under the due process clause of the Fourteenth Amendment.[10] During the 1930s and 1940s other First Amendment provisions (freedom of the press and assembly) were also recognized as fundamental rights (*what is*).

In *Palko v. Connecticut* (1937), however, the Court balked at adding **double jeopardy**—the right not to be tried twice for the same crime—to this list.[11] Connecticut was seeking the death penalty for Frank Palko, who was already serving a life sentence for murder, on grounds that legal (due process) errors had been made during his trial. Palko claimed that this action violated his Fifth Amendment protection against double jeopardy. The Court ruled that this provision did not apply to the states, and Palko was executed because Connecticut did not have a law or a constitutional provision protecting its citizens from double jeopardy. In *Palko*, Justice Benjamin Cardozo made the case for selective incorporation by explicitly stating that only the *fundamental rights* of the First Amendment—freedoms of speech, press, and religion—applied to the states. The decision meant that states could follow their own laws on liberty whether they conflicted with the Bill of Rights or not. This practice lasted until the 1960s, when the Court, under the activist Chief Justice Earl Warren, widened the scope of the Fourteenth Amendment by applying most of the provisions in the Bill of Rights protecting persons accused of crimes to the states (see Table 15.2).

Nationalizing the Fourth Amendment

The Fourth Amendment protects people "in their persons, houses, papers, and effects, against unreasonable searches and seizures," unless they are presented with a valid **search warrant**—a judicial writ specifying the cause of the search, the area to be searched, or the items to be seized. Until the 1960s, about half the states allowed criminal evidence that had been seized with a search warrant that had been issued by a judge on the basis of **probable cause**—a reasonable belief that a crime has been committed and that a search will turn up evidence of it. But once the Warren Court nationalized the Fourth Amendment ban on unreasonable searches and seizures in *Mapp v. Ohio* (1961),[12] all states had to abide by the **exclusionary rule**—the exclusion of evidence obtained from illegal searches. This decision was controversial because it allowed individuals to go free who might otherwise have been found guilty.

In *Miranda v. Arizona* (1966) the Warren Court upheld a person's right under the Fifth Amendment not to provide self-incriminating evidence.[13] *Miranda* overturned the conviction of a man who, after two hours of police questioning without a lawyer present, had signed a written confession to the crimes of rape and kidnapping. Today the failure of the police to read the so-called *Miranda* warning to an individual at the time of arrest can lead to acquittal.

Although the Warren Court was widely criticized for overly protecting the rights of alleged criminals at the expense of victims and public safety, the less activist Burger and Rehnquist Courts let these decisions stand, with certain modifications. The Court ruled, for example, that "technical violations" of search and seizure could not be used to free known criminals and held that illegally obtained evidence was allowed if it would have come to light anyway.[14] The Court also made a *good-faith exception* for evidence gathered by police officers who had been issued a faulty warrant and allowed the *Miranda* rule to be dispensed with in instances where there was an "overriding" danger to public safety.[15] In 1996, President Bill Clinton issued an executive order authorizing physical searches without a court order to obtain suspected foreign intelligence information.

STATEMENT OF RIGHTS

Before we ask you any questions, it is my duty to advise you of your rights.

You have the right to remain silent.

Anything you say can be used against you in court or other proceeding.

You have the right to consult an attorney before making any statement or answering any question, and you may have an attorney present with you during questioning.

You may have an attorney appointed by the U.S. Magistrate or the Court to represent you if you cannot afford or otherwise obtain one.

If you decide to answer questions now, with or without a lawyer, you still have the right to stop the questioning at any time, or to stop the questioning for the purpose of consulting a lawyer if you so desire.

HOWEVER

You may waive the right to advice of counsel and your right to remain silent and answer questions or make a statement without consulting a lawyer if you so desire.

WAIVER

I have read the above statement of my rights or have had them read to me. I understand my rights and waive my rights freely and voluntarily, without threat or intimidation and without any promises of immunity.

_____
Signature

Date: _____ Time: _____

Witnesses: _____
_____

Shown here is an example of the printed "*Miranda* warning" that police must read to criminal suspects upon arrest. The Supreme Court's decision in *Miranda v. Arizona* (1966) required that "Prior to any questioning, the person must be warned that he has a right to remain silent, that any statement he does make may be used against him, and that he has the right to the presence of an attorney, either retained or appointed."

Procedural Due Process Versus Substantive Due Process

Advocates of judicial restraint argue that the due process clause guarantees only **procedural due process**—the fair application of the law (*what's right*) in accordance with the rules and customs of the legal system (*what is*). In this view, the due process clause may not be used to evaluate the substance of any particular law, no matter how much a judge or a justice may dislike it. (This was Chief Justice Rehnquist's argument in *DeShaney*.) These advocates therefore criticize judicial activists for supporting **substantive due process**—the view that courts have a responsibility to decide whether the substance of a law is reasonable and to use the due process clause to exercise that responsibility. But who decides what is reasonable? Liberal judicial activists condemn the Taney Court for using substantive due process in *Dred Scott* (1857)[16] but applaud its use to expand civil liberties and civil rights. Conservative judicial activists have applauded its use by the Taft and other Courts to protect private property.[17] Many of the arguments over the nationalization of the Bill of Rights spring from this deeper debate over judicial philosophy (see Chapter 14).

Freedom of Religion

The First Amendment was intended to protect religious freedom by maintaining government's neutrality in the face of different religions and by allowing people to worship freely. It states that "Congress shall make no law respecting an establishment of religion" and has often been tested. In fact, government has never been completely neutral toward religion, and the courts have vacillated when forced to choose between upholding religious freedom and other values government is called upon to protect.

Interpreting the Establishment Clause

The **establishment clause**, which prohibits government from sponsoring or supporting any particular religion, was inspired by the American colonists' distaste for state-supported and state-endorsed religion. Looking to James Madison and Thomas Jefferson, who had drafted the First Amendment, the Supreme Court concluded in *Everson v. Board of Education of Ewing Township* (1947) that "neither a state nor the Federal Government can set up a church. Neither can it pass laws which aid one religion, aid all religions, or prefer one religion over another." Nor is government permitted to force people to believe or disbelieve in any religion, or be taxed "in any amount . . . to support any religious activities or institutions, whatever they may be called, or whatever form they may adopt to teach or practice religion." The Court then cited Jefferson's own view that the establishment clause was intended to erect "a wall of separation between Church and State."[18]

Most have understood the *Everson* decision to mean that government must remain *neutral* with respect to religion—that is, it must do nothing to advance or retard it. The courts have interpreted neutrality to mean that no tax dollars are to be spent on religion and that no Bible reading or prayer are to be allowed in public schools. In 1962 the Court disallowed even the nondenominational prayer, "Almighty God, we acknowledge our dependence upon Thee, and beg Thy blessings upon us, our parents, our teachers, and our Country."[19] Yet the House of Representatives starts each day with a prayer by the House chaplain, who is on the House payroll, and the military employs chaplains to minister to the troops. Critics complain that government employment of chaplains violates the First Amendment, while others say that chaplains are merely enabling public servants to practice their religion freely. So far the courts have permitted government hiring of chaplains and the imprint "*In God We Trust*" on money.

The courts must know what a religion is if they are to uphold the principle of government neutrality toward religion. However, defining a religion—particularly one not based on a notion of God—is difficult in a country of diverse religious beliefs. In 1979, a federal court determined that a school board was establishing a religion when it required the teaching of Transcendental Meditation—a system of meditation with no theological content—in the public schools.[20] In 1985, however, another federal court said that a public school could require students to read a book on secular humanism—a nonreligious philosophical approach to life that many Christians consider a threat to Christianity.[21]

Aid to Parochial Schools

Despite *Everson*, many states give aid, either directly or indirectly, to parochial (church-run) schools, because they lessen the burden on public schools and provide a benefit to children. The Court has devised certain guidelines that allow it to approve some forms of state aid and not others. In *Everson*, for example, a taxpayer had complained that a state transportation program that helped parochial as well as public schools violated the state as well as the federal Constitution. The Court ruled against the taxpayer on grounds that the transportation program helped children more than it did religion.[22]

The Court has also upheld federal and state construction grants to religious colleges because college students "are less impressionable and less susceptible to religious indoctrination" than precollege students.[23] The Court struck down programs to maintain and repair nonpublic (including parochial) schools, tuition assistance for low-income families, and tuition tax deductions for other families, saying that they furthered religious over secular interests and excessively "entangled" church and state.[24] In doing so, the Court was following the three tests it had outlined in *Lemon v. Kurtzman* (1971) when it struck down a state program that paid the salaries of teachers who taught secular subjects in parochial schools.[25] Its rationale: The states would become excessively entangled in religious affairs because they would have to monitor the teachers to be sure that no religion crept into their secular subject matter. For a law concerning religion to be constitutional, it must, the Court said:

- have a primary secular legislative purpose (as the state transportation program in the *Everson* case did);
- not advance or inhibit religion; and
- not excessively entangle government with religion.

These requirements became known as the **Lemon** test.

The main question underlying these establishment clause disputes is not *whether* government should give aid to religious institutions but *how much*. For example, religious institutions already benefit indirectly from many public services such as police and fire protection, water and sewage treatment, public highways, and sidewalks. Children in private (and hence parochial) schools are eligible for the federal school lunch program, just as children in public schools are. People can also deduct contributions to religious institutions from their federally taxable income. The courts have found that none of these incidental aids to religion violates the First Amendment.[26] There is still disagreement over whether a particular form of aid is "incidental" or not and what sort of federal or state aid parochial schools should get.

In 1994 the Supreme Court held that New York's creation of a separate school district to benefit a group of disabled Orthodox Jewish children violated the establishment clause.[27] The state had created the district, which consisted of a single schoolhouse, to protect the children from public ridicule and trauma. But in 1997 the Court overruled a 1985 precedent prohibiting public school teachers from teaching federally financed remedial classes inside parochial schools (teachers had been holding classes in cramped and costly mobile units parked on the street outside).[28] The decision further clouded the question of when federal taxes may be used to support parochial schools.

Religious Displays on Public Property

Traditionally, the Supreme Court has prevented Congress from outlawing certain religions, but a more conservative Court has been moving toward support of certain religions[29]—a position consistent with the Reagan administration's request in *Lynch v. Donnelly* (1984) that the Court "make sure that the hand of government does not suppress this vital freedom" of religion.[30] Writing for the majority, Chief Justice Warren E. Burger ruled that Pawtucket, Rhode Island, was not violating the establishment clause by including a nativity scene in its Christmas display, saying that it was also important to "accommodate" religious expression. In his dissent, Justice William J. Brennan argued that the crèche might offend non-Christians and nonbelievers by conveying "the message that their views are not similarly worthy of public recognition nor entitled to public support. It was precisely this sort of religious chauvinism that the Establishment Clause was intended forever to prohibit." Justice Sandra Day O'Connor, who sided with the majority, disagreed, arguing that the key issue was whether government aid to a religion could be seen as "endorsing" that religion: "Endorsement sends a message to nonadherents that they are outsiders, not full members of the political community, and an accompanying message to adherents that they are insiders, favored members of the political community. Disapproval sends the opposite message." She concluded that the crèche did not signify such an endorsement.

Five years later the Court came to a different conclusion. This time the issue was whether a county courthouse could display a crèche with the sign "Glory to God in the Highest" on its staircase and an 18-foot menorah, or Jewish Chanukah candelabrum, outside the building.[31] The Court held 5–4 that the crèche violated the First Amendment, while the menorah did not. The majority decided, following O'Connor's rationale in the *Lynch* case, that the crèche constituted the "endorsement" of a religion because of its sign, whereas the menorah, because it stood next to a Christmas tree, was merely a holiday symbol. The menorah thus escaped suppression because the majority viewed it in a secular context: "In the shadow of the tree, the menorah is readily understood as simply a recognition that Christmas is not the only traditional way of observing the winter-holiday season." In his minority opinion, Justice Anthony Kennedy argued that the O'Connor standard of "endorsement" did not work and resulted in government hostility toward religion.

Interpreting the Free Exercise Clause

The **free exercise clause** prohibits government from interfering with a person's right to worship or not to worship. (Because expressions of religious beliefs are considered forms of speech, they are also protected by the free speech clause of the First Amendment.)[32] The First Amendment is silent, however, about what government should do when religious freedom conflicts with other protected values. In such cases the Court has ruled that freedom of belief is absolute, but not freedom of religious practice. Government may therefore regulate religious actions in the public interest, although how much weight it should give the public interest has always been a matter of dispute.

This colonial-style house in Queens, New York, is the Masid Abu Bakr Sediq mosque, serving Afghan immigrants.

Conflicts Between Religion and Business

In 1961, Orthodox Jews used the free exercise clause to challenge a Pennsylvania law requiring businesses to close on Sundays to provide "a family day of rest." They argued that because their religion required them to close their stores on Saturdays, the law would injure their businesses. In upholding the law, the Court distinguished between the freedom to believe and government's authority to regulate the practice of religious belief.[33] Dissenters argued that it was "fanciful" for the state to insist that everyone rest on the same day and that Jews should not be made to choose between their religious faith and their economic survival.

In 1963, the Court held that a member of the Seventh-Day Adventist Church, who was fired by her employer for refusing to work on Saturday (the Sabbath day of her religion) but had made a good-faith effort to find non-Saturday employment, was entitled to state unemployment compensation.[34] The Court explained that its decision was not intended to foster the "establishment" of the Seventh-Day Adventist religion but rather to ensure the state's "obligation of neutrality in the face of religious differences."

Conflicts Between Religion and Public Health

Native Americans and immigrants whose religious practices are unfamiliar to most Americans have had to turn to the courts for protection against majority-minded state legislatures, particularly when those practices have affected the public health and safety. In 1992 Florida attempted to ban the traditional African Caribbean religion of Santería practiced mainly by Cuban immigrants, claiming that its ritual sacrifice of animals caused a public health hazard. In oral argument before the Supreme Court, the attorney for the state of Florida argued that no church should have a right to engage in animal sacrifice, suggesting that the public distaste for this religious practice outweighed the issue of public health.[35] One defender of the Santería Church pointed out that the state of Florida allows the boiling of live lobsters, the poisoning of rodents, the killing of aged pets, and the hunting of animals. "Anyone can kill an animal for sport, food, conscience or profit, but not for an exercise of religious worship." Justice O'Connor suggested that instead of banning animal sacrifice the state of Florida might instead have banned inhumane killings and regulated the disposal of the carcasses—an ordinance that Chief Justice Rehnquist said would have been "easier to defend." Mainstream religious organizations sided with the Santería Church for fear that such a ban might erode their own religious rights. In 1993 the Court decided that a city may ban Santería practices so long as the ban accords with neutral rules, such as the state's anticruelty statute, but not if the ban is aimed at religious practices alone.

Conflicts Between Religion and the Law

In the past, government could limit religious liberties only if it had a compelling interest in doing so. Thus, while government banned alcohol during Prohibition, it exempted churches that used sacramental wine. But in 1990 the Supreme Court held that there was no exemption from laws that applied equally to all, as long as the law did not target a specific religion for discrimination.[36] Angered that government no longer had to meet the compelling-interest standard, Congress overwhelmingly passed the Religious Freedom Restoration Act of 1993, requiring government to meet that standard. In 1997 the Court ruled in *City of Boerne v. Flores* that Congress had exceeded its authority because the act did not attempt to remedy a specific act of religious discrimination.[37] The opposing claims in this dispute, outlined in the box on pages 584–585, attracted national attention because of its anticipated impact on this law and federalism.

Conflicts Between Conscience and Military Service

In 1917 Congress exempted from compulsory military service anyone "who, by reason of religious training and belief, is conscientiously opposed to participation in war in any form," defining religious belief in terms of "a Supreme Being involving duties superior to those arising from any human relation" as distinct from "political, sociological, or philosophical views or a merely personal moral code."[38] The courts therefore denied exemptions to **conscientious objectors** (COs)—those who object to military service for reasons of conscience—who did not believe in a traditional God. In 1965, however, the Supreme Court found a CO qualified for an exemption on the basis of his "belief in and devotion to goodness and virtue for their own sakes, and a religious faith in a purely ethical creed [without] belief in God, except in the remotest sense."[39] Calling attention to "the richness and variety of spiritual life in our country," the Court broadened the definition of religious belief to include definitions of God that differed from traditional theism. In 1967 Congress deleted the term "Supreme Being" from the law. In 1971, however, the Court rejected the request for exemption of a CO who refused to serve in a particular conflict—the Vietnam War—because he believed it, rather than all war, to be immoral.[40] The Court held that objections could not be selective but must apply to all wars.

Freedom of Expression

Censorship—official restrictions on freedom of expression—has existed wherever there is government. William Penn, like many others, left Europe to escape from it (see Chapter 2). The First Amendment protects freedom of expression in various forms: "Congress shall make no law . . . abridging the freedom of speech, or of the press; or the right of the people peaceably to assemble, and to petition the government for a redress of grievances." Freedom of expression is essential to democracy, which depends on debate and deliberation. One of these debates focuses on freedom of expression itself: Does it apply only to politics, or does it include the arts, the sciences, and business?

Freedom of Speech

Without freedom of speech, the freedoms of the press, assembly, and petition—indeed, democracy itself—are meaningless. But for government to protect freedom of speech, it must be clear about what speech *is*. Is speech merely words, or does it include lyrics in rap songs, soft money campaign contributions, and flag-burning? The Court has held that it does include all three of these things. Freedom of speech is not absolute, however. Congress and the courts have limited or banned several types of speech on a number of grounds: national security, public safety, obscenity, defamation, hate speech, sexual harassment, and commercial advertising.

National Security Exceptions

Crisis is the context in which governments most often mute or silence their critics. The U.S. Congress's first crackdown on government critics was the Alien and Sedition Acts of 1798, which were inspired by an undeclared war against France in which the United States sided with Britain. The acts were clearly unconstitutional, but they expired after three years and thus were never tested before the Supreme Court. Figure 15.1 describes two more recent crises in which the U.S. government has restricted freedom of speech in the name of national security. The key test is the **clear and present danger** doctrine, articulated in 1919 by Justice Oliver Wendell Holmes in *Schenck v. United States*, summarized in Figure 15.1 (page 586).[41]

Mario Savio, a 21-year-old philosophy student, rallied thousands of students at the University of California at Berkeley in 1964 to assert their First Amendment right to assemble and protest on college campuses, spearheading what came to be known as the Free Speech Movement.

Political Actors Disagree

St. Peter the Apostle Church

Model showing proposed new wing

The Facts of the Dispute

In 1991, when St. Peter the Apostle Catholic Church in Boerne, Texas, could no longer accommodate its growing congregation, it applied for a building permit to expand. The city government denied the permit because the church was in a historic district. The church sued the city under the 1993 Religious Freedom Restoration Act, which states that "government shall not substantially burden a person's exercise of religion" without a compelling interest. Did the city's need to preserve the historic district constitute a compelling interest? When the case reached the Supreme Court, observers around the nation were less interested in how the decision would affect Boerne than with how it would affect the constitutionality of the act.[1]

The Dispute over the Constitutionality of the Religious Freedom Restoration Act

The Dispute over the Facts

Those seeking to expand the church argued that the church was "old" but not "historic." Those who wanted to preserve it disagreed. These claims about *what is* clearly determined people's views about *what's right*. The city government and many residents saw the facts as they did because they wanted to preserve the picturesque flavor of their city, which also attracted tourist dollars. Church members wanted to accommodate the people of the city. Architects attempted to placate the

Public Safety Exceptions

To help it set legitimate limits on speech, the Supreme Court has distinguished between three types of speech:

- **Pure speech.** The peaceful expression of ideas to a voluntary audience is routinely protected.
- **Speech plus.** Verbal expression combined with an action, such as marching or picketing, is protected if it does not obstruct traffic or endanger public safety—as it might, for example, by falsely shouting "Fire!" in a crowded theater or by uttering words that "are likely to cause a fight."[42]
- **Symbolic speech.** Using symbols such as wearing armbands in protest or burning the American flag to express an opinion is sometimes protected and sometimes not.

584

two sides by designing a new wing that would be built behind the church's original façade. But the constitutional issues at stake at the national level made their conciliatory solution irrelevant.

Interested Parties

The states had been the most vocal critics of the Religious Freedom Restoration Act, arguing that it "overprotects" religious freedom. Boerne's attorneys pointed out that prisoners were using the act to sue for the right to practice their "religions," some of which advocated white supremacy, the possession of firearms, and violations of prison rules. But other attorneys praised the act's protections for Jewish convicts and members of other religions viewed as legitimate.

The solicitor general defended the act on behalf of the Clinton administration, which was sensitive to the act's popularity with religious institutions. Defenders of property rights wanted the act upheld because they regarded the city's refusal to grant the church a building permit as a taking of its property without just compensation.

The Dispute Between Congress and the Supreme Court

The politics—that is, the disputes over claims to the authority to decide *what is, what's right,* and *what works*—driving this case at the national level was plainly visible.[2] Congress and the Supreme Court had already disagreed over the correct interpretation (*what's right*) of the Constitution's protection of religious freedom (*what is*). In passing the Religious Freedom Restoration Act, Congress was declaring its authority to defend religious freedom from the Court's 1990 decision denying religious exemptions from laws that apply equally to everyone. In the *Boerne* case, however, the Court was declaring its authority to decide this controversy. Thus when it declared the act unconstitutional, the Court was limiting congressional authority and reasserting its own authority of judicial review. Justice Anthony Kennedy underscored this point in his majority opinion: "The power to interpret the Constitution in a case or a controversy remains in the judiciary." Kennedy wrote that Congress had exceeded its authority in expanding the First Amendment's guarantee of freedom of religion: "Congress does not enforce a constitutional right by changing what it is." In this case, the Court used its power of judicial review to declare its own view of what the First Amendment is and what its proper application involves.

---

[1] *City of Boerne v. Flores*, 65 U.S.L.W. 4612 (June 25, 1997), No. 95-2074.
[2] See Dan Carney, "Religious Freedom Act Overturned, Curbing Congress' Power," *Congressional Quarterly Weekly Report*, June 28, 1997, 1526–1527.

When young men burned their draft registration cards to symbolize their opposition to the Vietnam War, the Court called this an illegal act rather than the expression of a political idea. But when Iowa students were suspended for wearing black armbands to school to protest the same war, the Court overturned the suspensions, declaring that students do not "shed their constitutional rights to freedom of speech or expression" when they enter a school.[43]

Since then, the Court has tended to defend freedom of expression that does not breach the peace. In 1977, for example, it held that members of the National Socialist party (the American Nazis) were permitted to stage a peaceful march in a largely Jewish neighborhood.[44] When in 1989 the Court struck down a Texas law forbidding the desecration of the American flag,[45] Congress reacted with the Flag Protection Act of 1989. But this act was quickly declared unconstitutional in *United States v. Eichman* (1990), with conservative justices Antonin Scalia and

Figure 15.1
Context Determines National Security Exceptions for Free Speech

Context
War against Germany, declared on April 6, 1917.

Executive Action
President Woodrow Wilson used the precedent of the expired Alien and Sedition Acts to justify restrictions on German aliens and acts of censorship. The government used the Espionage Act to crack down on the Industrial Workers of the World, a militant antiwar labor union, arresting more than 300 "Wobblies."

Congressional Action
Congress passed the Espionage Act (1917) to restrict speech that might inspire acts of disloyalty. It also authorized the postmaster general to ban any mail he judged to be a "willful obstruction" of the war effort, including left-wing journals and books containing criticism of the Allies. In 1918 Congress passed the Sedition Act, banning "disloyal, profane, scurrilous, or abusive language" about the U.S. government.

Judicial Action
In *Schenck v. United States* (1919) the Court tested the constitutionality of the Espionage Act. Schenck, a pacifist and socialist, had sent prospective draftees leaflets urging them to resist the draft on grounds that it violated their constitutional rights. Citing wartime emergency, the Court ruled unanimously against Schenck, who was sentenced to 20 years in prison. Justice Oliver Wendell Holmes articulated the rationale: "The question in every case is whether the words used are ... of such a nature as to create a clear and present danger ... that Congress has a right to prevent. ...[When] a nation is at war, many things that might be said in time of peace are such a hindrance to its effort that their utterance will not be endured so long as men fight and that no Court could regard them as protected by any constitutional right."

Context
The Cold War (began 1945) and the Korean War (1950–1953). In 1950 Senator Joseph McCarthy (R-Wis.) was accusing political critics of being Communists or Communist sympathizers and therefore guilty of treason.

Congressional Action
In 1950 Congress passed the Internal Security Act (also known as the McCarran Act) which attempted to force the Communist Party to register as a subversive organization. Congress claimed that an international Communist conspiracy created a clear and present danger to the nation. President Truman vetoed the bill as "the greatest danger to freedom of speech since the Sedition Act of 1798," but Congress overrode the veto by huge majorities.

Supreme Court Action
In *Dennis v. United States* (1951) the Court upheld the convictions of 11 Communist party leaders for violating the Smith Act of 1940 by conspiring to teach and advocate the violent overthrow of the government, even though the men had no actual plans to overthrow the government. Once the fear of Communism abated, the Court softened its position, holding that the government could only act against such threats if there were a likelihood they might be carried out.[1]

---
1. *Yates v. United States*, 354 U.S. 298 (1957).

Anthony Kennedy joining forces with the liberal justices.[46] Applauding this decision, Ira Glasser, the head of the ACLU, said that "what the flag stands for is the freedom to defile it."[47] A subsequent attempt to pass a constitutional amendment outlawing flag-burning quickly fizzled out.

Obscenity Exceptions

In the past, states have used their obscenity laws to suppress sex manuals, information on contraception, abortion, population control, and art and entertainment involving sexual expression. Times have changed, but the tension between those who seek to restrict and those who seek to allow such material persists. Some people want the freedom to buy pornography on the bookstands and to watch sexually explicit material on stage, on television, and at the movies. Others want government to outlaw or at least regulate such materials. The broadcast industry has responded with a controversial ratings system and a V-chip designed to help viewers and parents block programming they consider objectionable.[48] As the box nearby explains, some feminists want to outlaw pornography that exploits and degrades women. But some fear that if state censorship is allowed to gain a foothold in the area of obscenity, it will creep into other areas of expression. Still others say it is possible to distinguish between morally offensive sexual material and sexual material with some artistic or socially redeeming value. How have the courts dealt with these competing claims?

Until 1957, courts tended to uphold government censorship of some sexually explicit material as morally corrupting to young people, while rejecting its complete suppression. But that year a Supreme Court ruling that obscenity would no longer enjoy constitutional protection because it was of no positive value to society left the states free to regulate obscenity.[49] But it also left the Court with the problem of how to protect material that was not obscene, a problem that required the ability to distinguish between obscene and unobscene material (*what is*). In 1973 the Court decided that material would be considered obscene if:

- "the average person, applying contemporary community standards, would find that the work, taken as a whole, appeals to the prurient interest";
- "the work depicts or describes, in a patently offensive way, sexual conduct specifically prohibited by law"; or
- "the work, taken as a whole, lacks serious literary, artistic, political or scientific value."[50]

How well these tests have worked is debatable. Today local communities are largely permitted to regulate obscenity as they see fit, so long as they abide by some basic principles established by the Court. For example, cities may restrict the sale of pornographic materials to particular areas or pass

In 1990, city police declared obscene 7 of the 175 photographs by Robert Mapplethorpe exhibited in a Cincinnati museum. This cartoon ridicules this attempt at censorship by placing Mapplethorpe's photographs in the context of U.S. policies the cartoonist characterizes as "truly obscene art." The scandal led conservatives in Congress to slash the budget of the National Endowment for the Humanities (NEH), through which Mapplethorpe had indirectly received federal grant money.

Political Actors Disagree

Gloria Steinem v. Milos Forman

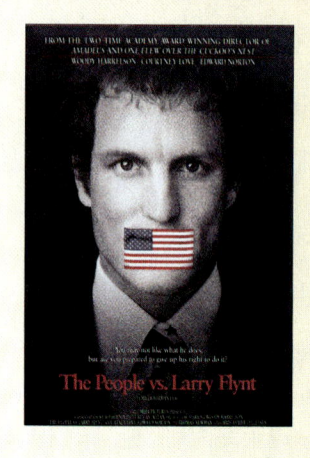

This dispute over what the film *The People vs. Larry Flynt* is about shows how conflicts over *what is* are shaped by conflicting views of *what's right*. The views of Gloria Steinem, a founding editor of *Ms.* magazine, are clearly influenced by her feminist ideology. The views of Milos Forman, the film's director, are influenced by the loss of his family in Nazi concentration camps and by his experience of censorship under the former Czech communist dictatorship.

Gloria Steinem

Larry Flynt the Movie is even more cynical than Larry Flynt the Man. *The People vs. Larry Flynt* claims that the creator of *Hustler* magazine is a champion of the First Amendment, deserving our respect. That isn't true.

Let's be clear: A pornographer is not a hero, no more than a publisher of Ku Klux Klan books or a Nazi on the Internet, no matter what constitutional protection he secures. And Mr. Flynt didn't secure much . . .

In this film, produced by Oliver Stone and directed by Milos Forman, *Hustler* is depicted as tacky at worst, and maybe even honest for showing full nudity. What's left out are the magazine's images of women being beaten, tortured and raped, women subject to degradations from bestiality to sexual slavery.

---

zoning laws that require "adult" movie theaters to be located some distance from churches, schools, parks, or homes. The Court has been more concerned with upholding restrictions on child pornography, while protecting the right of individuals to possess obscene materials in their own homes.[51] In 1996 the Court upheld a 1984 law permitting cable operators to control sexually indecent material aired on commercial—but not public access—channels they lease. In 1997, in a major victory for the broadcast television industry, the Court unanimously struck down the Communications Decency Act of 1996, which had made it a crime to display "indecent" material online that would be accessible to minors.[52]

Defamation Exceptions

Those who make false statements that defame, or injure, a person's personal or professional reputation may be sued for monetary compensation for the damage—whether these statements are written defamation (**libel**) or oral defamation

Filmgoers don't see such *Hustler* features as "Dirty Pool," which in January 1983 depicted a woman being gang-raped on a pool table. A few months after those pictures were published, a woman was gang-raped on a pool table in New Bedford, Mass. Mr. Flynt's response to the crime was to publish a postcard of another nude woman on a pool table, this time with the inscription "Greetings from New Bedford, Mass. The Portuguese Gang-Rape Capital of America."

Nor do you see such typical *Hustler* photo stories as a naked woman in handcuffs who is shaved, raped and apparently killed by guards in a concentration-camp-like setting. You won't meet "Chester the Molester," the famous *Hustler* cartoon character who sexually stalks girls. (The cartoonist, Dwaine Tinsley, was convicted in 1990 of sexually molesting his daughter.) . . .

On the contrary, the Hollywood version of Larry Flynt, played by the charming Woody Harrelson, is opposed to violence. At an anti-censorship rally, he stands against a backdrop of beautiful images of nude women that are intercut with scenes of Hiroshima, marching Nazis and the My Lai massacre. "Which is more obscene," the Flynt character asks, "sex or war?" Viewers who know *Hustler*'s real content might ask, "Why can't Larry Flynt tell the difference?" . . .

So, no, I am not grateful to Mr. Flynt for protecting my freedom, as the film and its enthusiasts suggest I should be. No more than I would be to a racist or fascist publisher whose speech is protected by the Constitution. . . .

The truth is, if Larry Flynt had published the same cruel images even of animals, this movie would never have been made.

Fortunately, each of us has the First Amendment right to protest.

Milos Forman

One can't really argue with Gloria Steinem because she's accusing the film of something it is not. It does not glorify pornography. [This] is like saying *Romeo and Juliet* glorifies teenage suicide. The film is about free speech and the price we pay for it. When the Nazis and Communists first came in [to Czechoslovakia], they declared war on pornographers and perverts. Everyone applauded: who wants perverts running through the streets? But then, suddenly, Jesus Christ was a pervert, Shakespeare was a pervert, Hemingway was a pervert. It always starts with pornographers to open the door a little, but then the door is opened for all kinds of persecution.

Sources: Gloria Steinem, "Hollywood Cleans Up *Hustler*," *New York Times*, January 7, 1997, A13; Milos Forman, quoted in Bernard Weintraub, "'Flynt' Receives Thumbs Up by New Reviewers: A.C.L.U.," *New York Times*, February 21, 1997, B3.

(**slander**). Both libel and slander are limitations on the freedoms of speech and press. Libel is generally considered more serious because the written word is more lasting than a spoken remark.

In some cases, however, people have a legal right, or *privilege*, to make statements that would otherwise be considered libelous or slanderous. In the case of lawmakers, high executive officials, and judges, this privilege is *absolute*, or unlimited, when they are conducting official business. A lesser, or *qualified privilege*, is available to those who comment on public officials, entertainers, and a number of other public figures, so long as the comments are not made with *malice* (knowledge that the statements are false or show a "reckless disregard" for the truth).[53]

Hate Speech and Sexual Harassment Exceptions

Much of the debate over **hate speech**—speech that insults and degrades others on the basis of race, religion, gender, or some other characteristic—has been waged on college campuses. In 1992 the Supreme Court struck down a Minnesota hatecrimes law forbidding the burning of crosses and display of Nazi swastikas that "arouse anger, alarm, or resentment in others on the basis of race, color, creed, religion or gender" because the law was "content-based"—that is, it banned particular categories of fighting words rather than all types of fighting words.[54] This decision effectively destroyed the rationale for speech codes.

Many states have adopted antibias laws that require additional punishment for those who target their victim on the basis of race, religion, disability, or sexual orientation. Some civil libertarians argue that such laws erode freedom of expression by punishing thought, thus creating an unconstitutional category called "thought crimes." When the state of Wisconsin expanded the sentence of a 19-year-old black youth for assaulting a 14-year-old white youth after seeing the movie *Mississippi Burning*, about the murder of three civil rights activists, civil libertarians objected. In 1993, the Supreme Court upheld Wisconsin's action on grounds that the criminal act deprived an individual of his or her personal safety.[55] In its decision the Court stressed the distinction between thought and action, as it had previously done in "gay-bashing" and abortion clinic demonstration cases: a person is free to assault gays and doctors who perform abortions with words, but not with deeds.

Does the First Amendment protect sexist speech? Because the law on sexual harassment (Title VII of the Civil Rights Act of 1964) fails to define "harassment" and "offensive" behavior, it does not punish offensive language unless it targets a particular individual. The ACLU initially defined sexual harassment as a pattern of behavior that hinders or prevents an employee from carrying out his or her job, but it now supports suits such as the one brought by a woman against her employer who told dirty jokes and made vulgar remarks even though she was not touched, propositioned, or denied promotion. In 1993 the Supreme Court decided that sexual harassment cases could be based on a wide range of evidence suggesting that the individual has been subjected to "a hostile environment" as a result of gender.[56]

Commercial Speech Exceptions

Commercial speech—especially advertising—was not granted any First Amendment protection prior to the 1970s because the Supreme Court classified it as commerce rather than as speech. As a result, the Court left such issues to the states to regulate. But starting in 1975 it struck down state regulations barring advertising by abortion clinics, prescription drug companies, and lawyers.[57] While agreeing with state regulations on false and deceptive advertising, the Court has ruled that consumers are entitled to know the cost of goods and services so they can weigh their purchasing decisions. But civil libertarians argue that the Framers never intended for the First Amendment to cover speech that lacked political content and that in protecting commercial speech the Court has overreached its authority and created a new property right. Justice Lewis F. Powell, who drafted many of these decisions, explained that commercial speech does not deserve or receive the same protection as political speech. His four-part test holds that commercial speech merits protection if it is not false and misleading, and can be regulated only if the state has a "substantial" interest in regulating it, the regulation is proportional to the interest, and the regulation is as minimal as possible.

Because all four parts of this test raise questions over *what is*, they are subject to dispute. This problem has led civil libertarians to predict that the Court is miring itself in the same sort of descriptive dilemmas as those that bedevil its obscenity tests.

Freedom of the Press

Freedom of the press is vital to democracy because it provides citizens with much of the information they need to practice politics effectively. But this freedom is not absolute, and its exercise is complicated by new forms of media. Traditionally, freedom of the press applied to the products of printing presses—pamphlets, magazines, newspapers, and books. Today these and other forms of communication, such as radio, TV, film, video, and Internet communications, are known as *media*. While all forms of media that convey political views are protected, printed publications receive the greatest protection. The Privacy Protection Act of 1980 protects the media as well as publishers from unreasonable search and seizure (such as the taking of a reporter's notes). However, the Supreme Court has ruled that because government grants broadcast media the *privilege* (not the *right*) of using the public airwaves, they are subject to licensing and regulation by the Federal Communications Commission (see Chapter 9).

No Prior Restraint and Confidentiality

Except in rare instances, such as national security, government may not censor (exercise prior restraint over) materials before they are published, although punishment may be inflicted later if their publication is illegal. This doctrine of **no prior restraint** is intended both to protect a free press and to foster a responsible press. Occasionally, however, the government has violated this doctrine. In 1971, a federal district court agreed to the Nixon administration's request to stop the press from publishing *The Pentagon Papers*—an exposé of secret Defense Department documents admitting to policy misjudgments during the Vietnam War. But the Supreme Court quickly overruled the district court, saying that the press was free to "bare the secrets of government and inform the public."[58]

To protect reporters who refuse to divulge their sources, even to grand juries investigating crimes, some 28 states have passed *shield laws*. While the Supreme Court has refused to grant reporters complete confidentiality, it has also ruled that the press can be sued for breaking its promise of confidentiality.[59] Many newspapers have paid fines and legal costs, and their reporters gone to jail, to protect their sources and the principles of confidentiality.

What rights do individuals have against the news media? Although public personalities, as we have seen, are not immune from media publicity, ordinary individuals and even businesses have sometimes persuaded the courts that their privacy has been invaded by the media—at least in cases where their names are already in the public record.[60]

Pretrial Publicity Versus the Right to a Fair Trial

The most vexing cases are those in which freedom of the press conflicts with a person's Sixth Amendment right to an impartial jury. The Supreme Court has tended to rule, even in sensational cases where pretrial publicity might bias potential jurors, that the press should not be "gagged" because judges may exercise a variety of options—such as postponing the trial until public attention subsides, moving the trial to another location, sequestering the jury, or enjoining the jurors to focus solely on the evidence—to protect the rights of the accused.[61]

National Security Restraints

Can official government agencies withhold information from the media? Do the press and the public have "a right to know"? The government has the right to withhold information by *executive privilege* (see Chapter 12) and, since 1917, has restricted sensitive national security information to those with a "need to know." The federal government's security classification system breaks most classified information into *confidential*, *secret*, and *top secret* categories. Critics have complained that the government sometimes relies on these devices to prevent politically damaging leaks to the press, thus hindering the public's ability to assess the government's competence (see Chapter 13).

In response to these criticisms, Congress passed the Freedom of Information Act in 1966, giving the press and the public greater access to information in the executive branch and even allowing them to sue the government if necessary. However, in exempting nine different categories of information (including national security issues, policymaking documents, personnel files, and "internal" agency documents), the act failed to provide the comprehensive access critics had called for. Subsequent amendments to the act loosened these restrictions somewhat. However, the Privacy Act of 1974 requires an individual's written consent before personal documents can be released, thus tightening many restrictions still further.

Life, Liberty, and Property

The Fifth Amendment declares, "No person . . . shall be deprived of life, liberty, or property, without due process of law; nor shall private property be taken for public use, without just compensation"—words reinforced by the Fourteenth Amendment.

Because the Supreme Court has never formulated a rule to help it identify unlawful *takings* of property, courts and regulators have made those judgments case by case. They first identify the property in question (*what is*) and then decide what process is due its owner (*what's right*). Government may not take away property (a life, a house, a piece of land, a government job, Social Security payments, welfare benefits, a prisoner's parole, or school attendance via suspension) without warning (passing a statute or issuing a notice) and granting a hearing (either before or after the taking) so the person or group affected can respond.

The Taking of Life

Because there is no appeal once the death penalty has been imposed, fairness in carrying out the penalty is vital. In its 5–4 *Furman v. Georgia* (1972) decision, the Court banned the death penalty throughout the country, saying that it was violating the Eighth Amendment prohibition against "cruel and unusual punishments."[62] The Court did not say that the death penalty was unconstitutional (that the *substance* of the law was wrong) but rather that it was unfairly applied (a failure of *due process*). The penalty is imposed more often on blacks, men, and the poor. The *Furman* decision led the 37 states with the death penalty to stop all executions. But four years later the Court reversed itself in *Gregg v. Georgia*, declaring the death penalty constitutional if the states used fair guidelines in imposing it.[63] Thus at a time when more and more nations were abolishing capital punishment, federal and state legislatures were revising and salvaging their death penalty statutes.

Opponents of capital punishment also make the due process argument that disqualification of potential jurors who oppose the death penalty makes juries unrepresentative of a defendant's peers. In 1995 Congress terminated its financing of resource centers charged with helping indigent death-row inmates find a lawyer.[64] Distressed by such due process problems, in 1997 the American Bar Association called for a moratorium on executions.[65]

As hundreds await execution across the country and executions are carried out with increasing frequency, debates about capital punishment continue: Is it morally and legally right? Does it work to deter criminal behavior—especially murder? Religious leaders and legal theorists are split on these questions. Originalists, for example, point out that the drafters of the Constitution did not intend for the phrase "cruel and unusual punishments" to apply to the death penalty because the death penalty was routinely carried out at the time the document was written. Others, such as Justice Brennan, have argued that because the death penalty is no longer routine it has become "unusual" and therefore "cruel" and unconstitutional. Brennan declared that electrocution, for example, was "the technological equivalent of burning people at the stake."[66]

Capital punishment may work as retribution ("an eye for an eye"), but studies suggest that it does not deter the crimes it is intended to punish. Nor is it efficient. Because lawyers and interest groups can use legal technicalities to delay execution for years—at great cost to the taxpayers—a life sentence is now cheaper than execution. The Rehnquist Court has attempted to speed the process by further restricting the procedures by which state death penalty cases can come before the Supreme Court (see the box on page 595). The 1994 omnibus crime bill, which made 60 additional federal crimes subject to the death penalty, sharply restricted death-row appeals: Death-row inmates are now allowed only one appeal in a federal court within six months of sentencing, although the Court ruled in 1997 that the crime bill does not apply to inmates with pending petitions.[67] Since some inmates have been found innocent years after sentencing (60 during the past ten years[68]), more innocent people will inevitably be executed unless the Supreme Court intervenes—a power it retains in "exceptional circumstances." But as one scholar concludes, this penalty will always involve subjective judgments: "If the jury thinks a particular murder is heinous, it will be able to justify the death penalty; if the jury is sympathetic toward a particular defendant, it will find [ways] to avoid imposing death."[69]

The Taking of Liberty

Some of the ways in which government (legislatures, courts, regulators) deprives people of liberty are widely accepted, such as statutes that confine and punish people convicted of crimes and those that permit or require confinement of the mentally ill. Still others, such as prohibitions of physician-assisted suicide, are more controversial within and outside the legal community.

Prisoners

Once behind bars, do prisoners retain any civil liberties? Very few. Jail, by its very nature, severely restricts freedom of speech, assembly, and protest, although inmates are allowed to receive strictly limited visits from family members. Only in rare cases may prisons refuse an inmate's request to marry. Speech and beliefs that might endanger discipline are curtailed, although courts remain divided over whether prisoners may circulate petitions to express their grievances. Religious practices that might be disruptive are also restricted, although most prisons actively encourage religious activities in the belief that they promote order. Initial hostility toward Muslims—for example, refusal to serve meals without pork or to serve meals after sunset during their holy month of Ramadan—has declined, with some prompting from the courts. Inmates may wear religious medals, and Native Americans have the right to refuse haircuts for religious reasons. Political rights are limited, and each state decides whether felons may vote or not.[70]

In the past, most prisons denied women access to vocational training that would give them marketable skills once they left prison, forcing them to do most of the cooking and cleaning. Today, prisons are required to treat women and men equally in the areas of jobs, vocational training, education, and recreational facilities.

Do prisoners have a right to be rehabilitated? Few prisons offer any meaningful opportunities for rehabilitation. Most lack psychological counseling, and the vocational programs do not prepare inmates for promising jobs. Most prisons are officially termed "corrections" facilities, but according to the ACLU, "The gap between the rhetoric of

Dennis Williams is released from prison on July 3, 1996, after spending 18 years on death row for a double murder that he did not commit. This case highlighted the dispute between those who favor speeding up the appeals process in death penalty cases (which now takes an average of about 8 years) and those who say that doing so will result in the execution of innocent people.

recidivism
This term (from the French for "relapse") is the return of a released prisoner to his or her former criminal behavior.

> ### Explaining *Habeas Corpus*
>
> When supporters of the death penalty complain that death-row inmates are using writs (court orders) of *habeas corpus* to delay their executions, what do they mean? Such writs are used to test the constitutionality of federal and state criminal convictions—in other words, to determine whether a person's right to due process of law has been violated?
>
> Americans inherited the right of *habeas corpus* (Latin for "You have the body") from English common law. When presented with a writ of *habeas corpus,* the government official who has confined an individual must produce that individual at a particular time and place so that the court can decide whether the individual is being illegally detained and, if so, can order his or her release.
>
> The Framers placed this protection against unlawful imprisonment in Article I, section 9, clause 2 of the Constitution: "The Privilege of the Writ of Habeas Corpus shall not be suspended, unless when in Cases of Rebellion or Invasion the public Safety may require it." In addition, federal courts were granted the authority to issue such writs by the Judiciary Act of 1789. This authority was extended to state prisoners in 1867, when the integrity of southern judges was in doubt in the aftermath of the Civil War.
>
> For decades death-row inmates have used this right, often repeatedly, to obtain reviews of their cases or as a tactic to delay their executions. In recent years supporters of the death penalty have tried to limit these appeals. The 1994 omnibus crime bill now restricts inmates to a single appeal, which must be made within six months of conviction.

'corrections'—rehabilitation, education, training, treatment—and the reality of prison life—idleness, despair, solitude, dehumanization—grows greater each year."[71] In recent years the courts have begun to suggest that this failure amounts to "cruel and unusual punishment" and that prisons have a constitutional duty to rehabilitate inmates, or at a minimum to ensure that they don't deteriorate in mind and body. Yet despite evidence that the recidivism rate is closely tied to education,[72] the 1994 federal omnibus crime bill cut all tax subsidies for college educations for prisoners across the nation.

The Mentally Ill and the Terminally Ill

The Supreme Court ruled in 1975 that the Constitution protects the liberty of the mentally ill and that governments can only detain them against their will if they might endanger themselves or others or if they can't survive on their own. As a result of this ruling and financial pressures on the states, people with mental disorders have been increasingly "deinstitutionalized"—forced onto the streets with no supervision. Many are homeless. City social workers and police may no longer pick such people up and take them to hospitals or shelters without court approval. This tension between the liberties and needs of the mentally ill and those of the community is likely to continue as policymakers and concerned citizens search for fair and viable mental health policies.

In a 1996 decision affecting 12 states, a federal judge overturned a Washington state law banning physician-assisted suicide, saying that a terminally ill adult "has a strong liberty interest in choosing a dignified and humane death."[73] Critics, including the American Medical Association, say that in an age of managed health care and cost-cutting the decision could sway doctors and relatives, especially unscrupulous ones, to encourage the terminally ill to choose assisted suicide. In 1997 the Court held unanimously that states may prohibit doctor-assisted suicide.[74] But the Court then refused to hear a challenge to Oregon's "Death with Dignity Act," letting stand the nation's only law permitting physician-assisted suicide.

Members of the Hemlock Society, a group that advocates the right of the terminally ill to choose to end their suffering by taking their own lives, demonstrate outside the U.S. Supreme Court building.

The Taking of Property

Americans inherited their belief that property is a natural liberty which limits government from the English philosopher John Locke and the Scottish economist Adam Smith (1723–1790). The Framers wrote these limits into the Constitution in two places: (1) the **contracts clause** (Article I, section 10), which states, "No State shall . . . pass any Law impairing the Obligation of Contracts," and (2) the **takings clause** in the Fifth Amendment, which states, "Nor shall private property be taken for public use, without just compensation."

Since the New Deal era, courts have made reluctant use of constitutional protections of property and contract in cases that would have seriously interfered with social and economic regulations.[75] But in recent years the Rehnquist Court has been showing fresh concern for these rights.

The Contracts Clause

From colonial times, economic liberty was understood to mean one's freedom to contract, or make contractual arrangements.[76] The Supreme Court has interpreted the obligation of a contract to mean "the law which binds the parties to perform their agreement."[77] Between the 1880s and the 1930s, the Court strongly defended the freedom of contract between employers and employees, even though employers clearly dominated this relationship, on the grounds that it was the only honest way most people could acquire property.[78] On this basis, the Court struck down a state law limiting the hours bakery employees could work, held that contracts forbidding workers to join a union were legal, and declared a minimum wage law for women unconstitutional.[79]

During the New Deal, however, the Court began to address the inequities in contracts between employers and employees. Concluding that the emergency of the Depression overrode the contracts obligation, the Court upheld a Minnesota law granting temporary relief to homeowners threatened by foreclosure.[80] The Court argued that in some circumstances the economic interests of some individuals (the bankers who held mortgage notes, for example) must be sacrificed to assist the community at large.

The Takings Clause

Many of the nation's highways, public parks, and military bases owe their existence to the takings clause of the Fifth Amendment, which is based on the power of **eminent domain**: the right of government to take (confiscate) private property for public use so long as it provides just compensation to the owner.

Originally, the fact that taxpayers were footing the bill for *takings* was supposed to ensure that takings were for public rather than private use. Over time, however, the Court decided that a wider range of uses could benefit the public even if the public did not actually possess the property. Thus in 1981, when Detroit confiscated land belonging to the ethnic neighborhood of Poletown for a new Cadillac assembly plant expected to employ 6,000 people, the action was justified on the grounds that the city was attempting to improve its faltering economy. And in 1984, when the Court upheld Hawaii's Land Reform Act of 1967 redistributing the property of one group of private citizens to another, the Court pointed out that it had "long ago rejected any literal requirement" that confiscated land must "be put into use for the general public."[81]

Despite the pleas of the community, in 1981 the city of Detroit confiscated and razed the neighborhood of Poletown—1,400 homes, 16 churches, 144 local businesses and schools, and this hospital—to make way for a General Motors plant that would provide thousands of jobs. The Supreme Court upheld the constitutionality of this taking of private property.

Recent takings cases have become intertwined with speech cases. San Diego banned all noncommercial billboards and placed restrictions on commercial billboards to improve public safety and the city's image. These improvements, city officials hoped, would attract businesses that would expand the city's tax base and allow the city to upgrade schools and public services. Thus by taking property (posted signs) away from some members of the community, the city was acting to enhance the property of the community as a whole. But instead of treating this case as a conflict between two property rights (one view of *what is*), the Supreme Court treated it as a conflict between property and speech (a different view of *what is*). The Court decided that because noncommercial billboards communicate information, they fall under the protection of the First Amendment.[82]

Another contentious issue is whether government must also compensate property owners when it restricts the *use* of their property without actually taking it. In 1993 the Supreme Court ruled that a South Carolina law protecting its beaches from erosion by blocking construction of private beachfront homes stripped the land of its economic value and required compensation for the loss.[83] This decision marked a shift in regulatory takings policy in favor of property rights and gave people new leverage against environmental regulations that injure them economically.

> **just compensation**
> The Supreme Court has defined *just compensation* as the amount of cash a willing buyer would have paid a willing seller for the property at the time of the taking.

Government can no longer halt development without compensation by claiming that the development conflicts with the public interest unless it can show that the development would cause a definite nuisance. It is not yet clear how this ruling will affect the environment. Nor is it clear whether the government will now be required to provide federal disaster relief to beachfront owners whose property suffers erosion. The courts must decide when the protection of private property becomes too high a price for the public to bear.

Privacy

Under what circumstances may government invade a person's privacy? The English philosopher John Stuart Mill argued in *On Liberty* (1859) that government may restrict individual privacy only to prevent harm to others and to society. But deciding what constitutes such harm (*what is*) often involves people's views about morality and religion (*what's right*), which is why privacy issues provoke such heated disputes. Mill's principle would surely have allowed government to restrict the liberty of Joshua DeShaney's father, but under the rules of American federalism this responsibility (according to the Supreme Court) fell to the state of Wisconsin, not the federal government.

Americans have always acted as if they were entitled to personal liberties not listed in the Constitution in such uncontested areas as marriage, procreation, travel, and the education of their children. But what about same-sex marriage, the adoption of children by same-sex couples, and sexual practices that do not lead to procreation?

In 1928, in a famous dissenting opinion, Justice Louis Brandeis claimed that the Framers sought to protect Americans in their beliefs, their thoughts, their emotions, and their sensations through "the right to be let alone—the most comprehensive of rights, and the right most valued by civilized man."[84] But this was a dissenting opinion, not the law.

The Dispute over the Right to Privacy

It was not until 1965 in *Griswold v. Connecticut* that the Warren Court formally named and used the **right to privacy** to strike down a Connecticut law forbidding the use of contraceptives by married couples and banning the circulation of birth control information for that purpose.[85] This decision was subsequently used to uphold the privacy of sexual relations in cases dealing with married and unmarried persons.

Opponents of judicial activism accused the Court of overreaching its authority in *Griswold* by creating (prescribing) a new constitutionally protected civil liberty. But Justice William O. Douglas wrote the opinion as if the Court had *found* (discovered, not created) this right. By indicating that the Court had merely uncovered a liberty that was in the Bill of Rights all along (a *what is* that had gone unnoticed), Douglas defended the Court's claim to the authority to say *what is* and *what's right* about privacy. The Third, Fourth, and Fifth Amendments, he argued, protected specific "zones of privacy." In declaring that some of these liberties (such as the intimacy of marriage) were ancient liberties that preceded the Bill of Rights, Douglas appealed

The Politics of Language

The Dispute over the Ninth Amendment

The Ninth Amendment states, "The enumeration in the Constitution, of certain rights, shall not be construed to deny or disparage others retained by the people." Until recent decades, this amendment has languished in obscurity in part because its meaning was unclear. It has now become highly controversial because its vague wording allows advocates of judicial restraint to argue that it was intended only to restrict the powers of the federal government and advocates of judicial activism to argue that it protects liberties not listed in the Bill of Rights.

Advocates of judicial activism, and of privacy rights in particular, say the Framers inserted this language in the Bill of Rights to let it be known that the people had other natural liberties besides the civil liberties listed in the document. What were these unenumerated natural liberties? Some have claimed that they include a variety of rights ranging from marriage, procreation, travel, and clean air, to those in the United Nations Declaration of Rights, which includes the right to a vacation.[1] Because these other rights have never been precisely defined, they remain a source of ongoing controversy and a source of leverage for judicial activists.

---

[1] Edward J. Erler, "The Ninth Amendment and Contemporary Jurisprudence," in *The Bill of Rights: Original Meaning and Current Understanding,* ed. Eugene W. Hickock, Jr. (Charlottesville: University Press of Virginia, 1991), 435.

---

to the centuries-old authority of common law and natural law. He expanded the authority of the Bill of Rights still further by arguing that these "specific guarantees in the Bill of Rights have penumbras, formed by emanations from those guarantees that help give them life and substance." In other words, these enumerated liberties imply additional liberties that include the right to privacy.

But some justices believed instead that marital privacy is protected by the due process clause of the Fourteenth Amendment. Justice John Marshall Harlan, for example, defended the use of substantive due process in this case. Other justices believed that marital privacy is protected by the Ninth Amendment. Justice Arthur Goldberg wrote a concurring opinion (joined by Justice Douglas and Chief Justice Earl Warren) stating that the Ninth Amendment, which he argued applied to the states through the Fourteenth Amendment, protected marital privacy as an unenumerated right. But Justice Hugo Black, an advocate of total incorporation of the Bill of Rights, nevertheless dissented because he could find no such right in any of the first eight amendments to incorporate and because he believed that the Ninth Amendment was intended to limit the federal government, not to protect the unenumerated rights of the people. For a discussion of the disputes over the Ninth Amendment, see the box above.

penumbra

This astronomical term, from the Latin *pen,* "partial," + *umbra,* "shadow," is used in painting as a metaphor for places where light and dark are blended together. Justice Douglas made use of the metaphor to make the specific guarantees in the Bill of Rights nebulous enough to accommodate the right to privacy.

Abortion

In *Roe v. Wade* (1973) and its companion case, *Doe v. Bolton* (1973), the Berger Court used the right to privacy to strike down state restrictions on abortion.[86] Because many people regard abortion as an act of murder and therefore a violation of religious, moral, and legal codes, and many others regard it as a woman's privacy right, this decision remains highly controversial today. Justice Harry A. Blackmun began the majority opinion by bowing to both sides of this controversy and then declared that the right to abortion was not absolute. The decision recognizes:

- a woman's *fundamental*, or absolute, right to privacy and thus to abortion, during the first trimester of her pregnancy;
- a state's right to protect the woman's health by requiring that abortions be performed by a doctor and, during the second trimester of pregnancy, under proper medical conditions; and
- a state's right to intervene, if it chooses, to safeguard the life of the fetus, during the third trimester of pregnancy.

Opponents of abortion complained that the right to abortion was absolute in practice because *Doe v. Bolton* allows a woman to abort at any point in the pregnancy if her health is jeopardized and, because "health" includes "mental health," a woman can always find a psychologist who will justify her request for an abortion. Opponents of judicial activism again complained that the Court had overreached its authority, while judicial activists argued that the Court was merely updating the unenumerated liberties in the Ninth Amendment.

In 1976, the Burger Court struck down a Missouri law barring women from obtaining an abortion without their spouses' consent,[87] but in 1980 it narrowly upheld a law limiting the use of federal funds for abortion that critics argued unfairly limited abortion as an option for poor women.[88] The Rehnquist Court, which favored judicial restraint, agreed to accept certain state restrictions on abortion in *Webster v. Reproductive Health Services* (1989), which upheld a Missouri law (1) refusing to allow abortions in publicly funded state hospitals; (2) prohibiting doctors paid by state funds from performing abortions except to save the pregnant woman's life; and (3) requiring women seeking abortions to submit to a test for "fetal viability" to ensure that an abortion would not be performed on a fetus that was capable of living outside the womb.[89] While this decision did not overturn *Roe*, it restricted abortions to private clinics, which critics said were less accessible and more expensive, placing poor women at a disadvantage. Justice O'Connor, who sided with the majority, disagreed, finding that no *undue burden* was placed on women seeking abortions in that state.

In 1992, without overruling *Roe*, the Rehnquist Court upheld Pennsylvania restrictions on the access to abortion.[90] In that state women are now required to be informed by doctors about fetal development, to give their formal consent to the abortion or, if they are minors, obtain parental consent and wait 24 hours between their consent and the abortion. The

---

Justice Harry Blackmun began the majority opinion in *Roe v. Wade* by acknowledging the Supreme Court's "awareness of the sensitive and emotional nature of the abortion controversy, of the vigorous opposing views, and the deep and seemingly absolute convictions that the subject inspires."

fetal viability

In *Roe v. Wade* the Supreme Court defined *viability* as the point at which the fetus is "potentially able to live outside the mother's womb albeit with artificial aid." In 1973 that point was roughly 28 weeks, the end of the second trimester. But technological advances have moved that point back in some instances to 24 weeks. These developments, both sides of the abortion debate agree, make viability a shaky foundation for constitutional rights.

Court struck down as an *undue burden* the requirement that women notify spouses of abortion plans on grounds that it exposed them to spousal abuse and possible violence.

In 1996, Congress passed but President Clinton vetoed the Partial Birth Abortion Act criminalizing a particular procedure used in some late-term abortions. This was the first time that Congress had passed a law outlawing a specific abortion procedure.[91]

Sexual Orientation

In 1982, Michael Hardwick was arrested in his bedroom with another man by Atlanta police armed with an expired warrant (Hardwick had failed to pay a fine for public drunkenness) and charged with sodomy. The charge was later dropped, but Hardwick took the state to court anyway to test the constitutionality of Georgia's sodomy law. Hardwick argued that his right to privacy in his bedroom and his home was equivalent to that which the Supreme Court had already recognized in *Griswold* and *Roe*. By a 5–4 majority the Court held in *Bowers v. Hardwick* (1986) that the right to privacy did not extend to homosexual acts between consenting adults, even in the privacy of their own homes.[92] The majority claimed that the Court lacked the judicial authority to further expand the types of behavior classified as a *fundamental* and hence *constitutional* right. The Court did not say whether heterosexuals could practice sodomy under the Georgia law.

Gay rights advocates argue that those states that still criminalize oral and anal sex not only deprive homosexuals of their right to privacy but also discriminate against heterosexuals and some disabled people. They also fault the Court for failing to learn from the way other democracies have dealt with homosexuality, pointing out that in a case similar to *Bowers* the highest court in the European Community extended the right to privacy to homosexuals. (The civil rights of gays and lesbians are discussed in Chapter 16.)

Wiretapping and Electronic Surveillance

Does the Constitution protect individual privacy from government wiretapping and electronic bugging? Law-enforcement and security agencies claim they need these devices to apprehend spies, kidnappers, and organized criminals. When the telephone was still a new technology, the Supreme Court exempted it from protection against unreasonable search and seizure under the Fourth Amendment.[93] In 1934, the Federal Communications Act outlawed wiretapping, and in 1937 the Court ruled that wiretap evidence obtained without a court order was inadmissible in federal court.[94] Only in 1967, when the Court ruled that wiretapping violated the Fourth Amendment, did wiretapping evidence become inadmissible in state courts.[95] That same year the Court held that telephone booths could not be tapped without a warrant, although it did not extend this protection to cordless phones—an omission that was later corrected.[96]

When fears for the public safety increase, so does the likelihood that the courts will give public safety priority over individual privacy. In the wake of antiwar protests and riots following the murder of Dr. Martin Luther King, Jr., the Omnibus Crime Control and Safe Streets Act of 1968 permitted government officials at all levels to use wiretapping and bugging in certain situations if legal warrants were obtained and to use that evidence in court. A year later Richard Nixon's attorney general used this technology without first getting a warrant to eavesdrop on domestic groups he considered a threat to the national security. The Supreme Court ruled that such wiretapping violated the Fourth Amendment,[97] although it refused to say that its ruling applied to the wiretapping of foreign agents.

High-Tech Invasion of Privacy

Pretty Good Privacy

A free product that can safeguard your e-mail against hackers.

http://www.pgp.com

Internet Privacy Coalition

A coalition that provides information on encryption policy.

http://www.privacy.org/ipc

Cyberspace Law Institute

http://www/cli.org

Today high technologies threaten individual privacy on every side, from credit bureau and medical information databases to computerized mailing lists, caller ID, and files on Web site visitors (cookies). There are calls for a national identity card to help employers screen out illegal aliens. Advanced forms of electronic information—such as closed circuit TV systems that can digitally scan, record, reconfigure, and identify a person's face—when combined with geographic tracking may eventually allow an individual's location to be pinpointed worldwide. Industry is also vulnerable to electronic theft of its ideas and money. Research and development (R&D) ideas and contracts worth millions of dollars have been filched electronically by rival companies. Criminal gangs and expert "hackers" in search of corporate profits have forced companies to spend billions on information security. Government agencies are especially vulnerable to such attacks because 95 percent of their communications travel by commercial networks.[98] (For ways to protect your privacy, consult the Internet Web sites nearby.)

Congress has been slower than the Supreme Court to recognize privacy rights. In 1970 it passed the Fair Credit and Reporting Act, which places limits on records that private and public institutions can develop and distribute; in 1974 it passed the Family Education Rights and Privacy Act of 1974 (see Chapter 1), which guarantees individuals the right to inspect, correct, and amend information about themselves in government files and to prohibit any government agency from making such files available to other agencies without the individual's permission; and in 1980 it passed the Privacy Protection Act, which attempted to defend privacy from new invasive technologies. Legislative efforts are under way to force companies to disclose what sort of information they collect on visitors to their Web sites and allow them an opportunity to get off the marketers' lists.[99] The Internet box nearby tells you how to contact the Cyberspace Law Institute, an online think tank that explores legal issues dealing with the Internet.

Privacy in the workplace preoccupies employers and employees alike. Despite opposition from employers' groups, which argued that polygraphs (lie detectors) were needed to expose billions annually in

cookies

This new computer term refers to a recent technology that allows Web sites to track individual users. A Web site attaches a tiny file on a visitor's computer that acts as a tracking beacon. Although cookies don't divulge your name, they do tell what kind of company you work for, what articles you read, what products you've bought, and whether you might be a frequent flier. Marketing experts can then use this information to attract more customers.

employee theft, Congress passed federal restrictions on polygraphs. Employers also lobbied for random drug testing in order to protect themselves from lawsuits resulting from injuries caused by employees on drugs. But federal courts have held that random drug testing, with the exception of screening airline pilots and train conductors to ensure public safety, violates the Fourth Amendment's prohibition against unreasonable searches and seizures.[100] The privacy of employees with HIV and AIDS is protected by laws covering people with disabilities (see Chapter 16). Whether the results of genetic screening of a person's chromosomes, or DNA, should also be protected is still being debated. Opponents argue that because genetic screening can be used to predict genetic dispositions to depression, schizophrenia, sickle cell anemia, and alcoholism, among other health problems, and can even be used to characterize ethnic and genetic traits including IQ, such information can be used to prejudice a person's employment, eligibility for health insurance, and educational opportunities. In early 1993 the military initiated a program to provide "genetic dog tags" for civilian and military personnel in order to facilitate the identification of corpses in cases where metal dog tags, fingerprinting, and dental records cannot be used. The Pentagon has also welcomed the prospect of genetic screening.[101] But civil libertarians argue that such initiatives will further erode individual liberties.

The courts have begun to rule on high-tech privacy issues. In 1993 a federal court ruled that the Privacy Protection Act of 1980 applied to electronically stored information. The decision pleased newspaper reporters who rely on computers, but not federal law-enforcement officials who feared it might restrict their monitoring of computer bulletin boards and electronic mail.[102] The 1994 omnibus crime bill was an effort to preserve privacy in electronic communications while ensuring that government can still eavesdrop for purposes of law enforcement and national security.

Civil Liberties as Constitutional Practice

When political actors disagree over what civil liberties are and who is entitled to them, they try to win the dispute by claiming that the Constitution—the highest legal authority in the land—supports their views of *what's right*. If the liberty they are claiming is not explicitly mentioned in the document and its amendments, they often devise arguments (as in *Griswold*) to show that it is implicit in the liberties that *are* mentioned in the document.

This strategy is, of course, the proper way to present civil liberties claims to fellow actors and to the courts, and civil liberties lawyers are trained to do just this. The justices of the Supreme Court, the court of last resort for such disputes, also evaluate these claims in terms of the Constitution and judicial precedent. But as human beings with different personal beliefs and judicial philosophies, their evaluations often differ, as we saw in the *DeShaney* and other cases. Thus the civil liberties decisions of the Court, like all its decisions, are not based on *true* interpretations of the Constitution but rather on the agreements of at least five of its nine justices.

When political actors comply with these decisions, they allow American democracy to work. How well it works and how rightly its liberties are recognized and applied are judgments that the people, because of those very liberties, are free to express and to act upon.

Summary

Civil liberties are individual freedoms *from government* that are spelled out in constitutions and bills of rights—freedoms that government is obliged to protect. These liberties, which Americans have inherited from English common law and natural law, apply to citizens and noncitizens alike.

Civil liberties conflicts have arisen over whether residents in the states may appeal to the Bill of Rights for protection against state laws that violate its provisions. Originally, the Supreme Court said no, arguing that Americans were citizens of their own state and the national government and were therefore subject to two different sets of laws under the doctrine of dual citizenship. Gradually, however, most provisions in the Bill of Rights were selectively *incorporated* (applied to the states). In the 1960s the Warren Court widened the meaning of the Fourteenth Amendment to protect the rights of persons accused of crimes. The exclusionary rule now excludes evidence from criminal trials that has been gathered in violation of a person's civil liberties, and the *Miranda* rules warn individuals of their right not to incriminate themselves at the time of their arrest.

Often the Court is asked to decide whether the freedoms of an individual or a group take priority over the freedoms of other individuals or groups, or over considerations for society at large. To mediate such disputes fairly, the Court is supposed to maintain a position of neutrality toward the parties involved, especially in the area of religion, where it is guided by the establishment clause and the free exercise clause. Some have criticized the Court for failing to maintain a strict "wall of separation" between church and state by allowing some aid to parochial schools. The Court has also been criticized for endorsing religion in some instances and for exhibiting hostility toward it in others. Obviously neutrality looks different to people with different interests.

Similarly, the courts must also balance freedom of speech and the press with a variety of other interests—national security, public safety, the suppression of obscenity, and commercial interests. Clashes among the states, the federal government, and the people in these areas have led the Supreme Court to develop guidelines such as the doctrines of *clear and present danger* and *no prior restraint* and tests to evaluate obscenity and commercial speech issues.

Property rights, which once enjoyed strong protection from the courts, have eroded as the provisions of the contracts clause and the takings clause have been relaxed, although the current Court seems interested in reinforcing these rights. Finding the proper balance between private economic rights and the interests of society continues to be part of the general task of balancing individual and social interests.

All three branches of government, and increasingly the courts, now deal with issues of personal privacy ranging from reproductive and sexual practices to high-tech invasions of medical, financial, credit, insurance, and other personal records. Although Congress has passed a number of laws protecting such information, defending personal privacy in an era of high-tech information gathering, storage, and retrieval is becoming increasingly complex.

When Americans recognize the importance of returning to the Constitution decade after decade to mediate their disputes over civil liberties, they demonstrate their commitment to constitutional practice and show that American democracy works.

Key Terms

civil libertarians **569**
civil liberties **569**
civil rights **569**
clear and present danger **583**
conscientious objector **582**
contracts clause **596**
double jeopardy **576**
eminent domain **597**
establishment clause **578**
exclusionary rule **577**
free exercise clause **581**
hate speech **589**
Lemon test **579**
libel **588**
liberty **569**
no prior restraint **591**
probable cause **576**
procedural due process **577**
pure speech **584**
right **569**
right to privacy **598**
search warrant **576**
selective incorporation **574**
slander **589**
speech plus **584**
substantive due process **577**
symbolic speech **584**
takings clause **596**
total incorporation **574**

How You Can Learn More About Civil Liberties

Dorn, James A., and Henry G. Manne, eds. *Economic Liberties and the Judiciary.* Fairfax, Va.: George Mason University Press, 1987. Examines the importance of economic rights in general and in a variety of specific situations, both as a basic individual liberty and as an important check on governmental power.

Epstein, Richard A. *Takings: Private Property and the Power of Eminent Domain.* Cambridge, Mass.: Harvard University Press, 1985. Asserts the importance of property rights in a variety of court cases with the help of a theory based on libertarian ideas.

Faux, Marian. *Roe v. Wade: The Untold Story of the Landmark Supreme Court Decision That Made Abortion Legal.* New York: Macmillian, 1988. A highly readable narrative of the legal actions of the actors and events that led up to the *Roe v. Wade* decision, and its reception by the press and the public.

Finkelman, Paul, and Stephen E. Gottlieb, eds. *Toward a Usable Past: Liberty Under State Constitutions.* Athens: University of Georgia Press, 1991. An unusual view of civil liberties and the debate over federalism from the perspective of the states from the eighteenth century to the present.

Glendon, Mary Ann. *Rights Talk: The Impoverishment of Political Discourse.* New York: Free Press, 1991. A compelling argument that the discourse about civil liberties has overemphasized the absolute and private nature of individual rights and neglected the importance of the communities that teach respect for rights.

Kupherman, Theodore R., ed., *Censorship, Secrecy, Access, and Obscenity.* Westport, Conn.: Meckler, 1990. Twenty-two essays that draw on excerpts from Supreme Court decisions to summarize the basic issues of these four related subjects.

Leahy, James E. *The First Amendment, 1791–1991.* Jefferson, N.C.: McFarland, 1991. A brief history and useful overview of American civil liberties.

Locke, John. *A Letter Concerning Toleration; A Second Letter Concerning Toleration; A Third Letter Concerning Toleration; A Fourth Letter Concerning Toleration.* Locke's argument that toleration is essential for civil society; available in many editions of the works of John Locke.

Mill, John Stuart. *On Liberty.* An argument that justifies liberty primarily on behalf of imaginative individuals, originally published in 1859 and available in many editions.

Price, Janet, Alan H. Levine, and Eve Cary. *The Rights of Students: The Basic ACLU Guide to a Student's Rights,* 3rd ed. Carbondale: Southern Illinois University Press, 1988. A useful handbook on student rights in the areas of the First Amendment, personal appearance, discipline and due process, corporal punishment, tracking and competency tests, handicaps, sex, marriage, pregnancy, school records, grades, and private schooling.

Richard, David A. J. *Toleration and the Constitution.* New York: Oxford University Press, 1986. Analyzes civil liberties from the standpoints of toleration, respect for the self-determining moral powers of conscience, and the requirement of government neutrality.

Rudovsky, David, et al. *The Rights of Prisoners: The Basic ACLU Guide to Prisoner's Rights,* 4th ed. Carbondale: Southern Illinois University Press, 1988. A handbook describing the sometimes clear and the sometimes dubious state of civil liberties inside American prisons.

Wagman, Robert J. *The First Amendment Book.* New York: Scripps Howard, 1991. A short, clear history of the First Amendment from the point of view of the American Civil Liberties Union, illustrated with cartoons.

Civil and Human Rights

The question of whether the children of illegal immigrants are constitutionally entitled to a free public education is the most recent of many disputes over civil rights that have arisen during the country's history.

CHAPTER 16

The important question has always been: Who belongs? Over the generations, as America's answers to that question have become more inclusive, the law has served sometimes to widen the embrace of the national community and sometimes as a barrier to further inclusion.

—**Kenneth L. Karst,
Belonging to America**

To take advantage of contradictions, to open up silences, to turn the rules against the rulers, to work for change within existing cultural traditions—these generally are the most effective strategies available to traditionally oppressed and marginalized groups.

—**Michael W. McCann,
Rights at Work**[1]

Understanding Civil Rights Disputes

Civil Rights Strategies

Civil Rights Remedies

The Evolving Ethics of Human Rights

Do the children of illegal aliens have a right to attend public school?

Many Americans in states with large immigrant populations—New York, Florida, Illinois, New Jersey, Colorado, and those bordering Mexico—say no, arguing that this increases their tax burden, which is already too high.

In 1975, Texas passed a law allowing school districts to bar these children or charge them tuition. Two years later, the Tyler school district decided to charge illegal aliens $1,000 per child per year in tuition. At the time there were about 40 illegal alien children from Mexico among its 16,000 students. Since their families were poor, they were forced to drop out of school. The Mexican American Legal Defense and Education Fund (MALDEF) filed a class action suit—*Plyler v. Doe* (1982)—in federal court on behalf of those children, claiming that the Texas law violated the Fourteenth Amendment, which guarantees equal protection under the law.[2]

Lawyers for the children argued that Texas has welcomed illegal aliens because they are a source of cheap labor. Many of them pay federal income taxes (Texas has no income tax) and all pay high state and city sales taxes. Like most states, Texas finances its public schools largely by taxing property owners (see the account of the *Rodriguez* case in Chapter 14). So anyone who pays rent pays property taxes indirectly, because landlords include taxes in the rent. Thus most illegal aliens support the cost of schools just like any resident.

The State of Texas argued that any person who is in the state illegally is technically not within the state's jurisdiction and thus not protected by the Fourteenth Amendment. Texas also argued that the federal Immigration and Naturalization Service (INS), which guards the nation's borders, had failed to keep these children out of the state, so that if they were to be educated at all, the federal government should pay the cost. When the district court ruled for the plaintiffs, the state appealed the case to the U.S. Supreme Court. In 1982 the Court (5–4) struck down the Texas law, saying that it unfairly penalized the children for legal circumstances beyond their control.

At issue was not, as in the *Rodriguez* case, whether these children were deprived of equality of education but the fact that they were getting no education at all. The Court majority argued that this deprivation hurt society as well as the children, because "education provides the basic tools by which individuals might lead productive lives to the benefit of us all. . . . We cannot ignore the significant social costs borne by our Nation when select groups are denied the means to absorb the values and skills upon which our social order rests." The dissenting justices argued that it would be "senseless for an enlightened society to deprive any children"—including illegal aliens—of an elementary education, but asserted that the Constitution does not give the Court the authority "to strike down laws because they do not meet our standards of desirable social policy, 'wisdom,' or 'common sense.'"[3]

Plyler remains controversial because it's on the cutting edge of civil rights. Because the Court decision imposed yet another unfunded federal mandate on the states, efforts to overturn it by constitutional amendment or state action continue to this day.

Our examination of the development of civil rights and human rights in the United States will be guided by the following questions:

What factors shape civil rights disputes and their analysis?

What strategies have groups used to win and expand their civil rights?

What civil rights remedies have been tried, and how well have they worked?

How has the United States responded to human rights initiatives?

Understanding Civil Rights Disputes

Civil rights are fundamental rights that government acts to protect from the unlawful actions of others, including government itself. But analysis of civil rights depends, as the box on pages 610–611 illustrates, on the context within which they are analyzed and the perspective of the analysts. Disputes arise because political actors disagree over:

> **de facto and de jure**
> The term *de facto*, which is Latin for "in fact," refers to the actual state of affairs, while *de jure*, which is Latin for "in law," refers to the legal state of affairs.

- what counts as an unlawful action (*what is*),
- what positive steps, if any, government should take to remedy the injustice (*what's right*), and
- how effective these remedies are (*what works*).

All civil rights claims are shaped by social, legal, political, and economic factors that give rise to discrimination. In the context of civil rights, **discrimination** is the making of distinctions that harm a person for belonging to a particular class or group. Throughout U.S. history some distinctions have enforced **segregation**—methods of discrimination that erect arbitrary (unreasonable or capricious) barriers between individuals or groups. Segregation imposed by social, economic, and political practices is **de facto segregation**. Examples include housing patterns, traditions in the arts, marginalization of the aged and people with disabilities, gender-based occupations, and the tradition of a white male presidency. Segregation imposed by law is **de jure segregation**. Examples include laws that classify people based on race, national origin, citizenship, gender, or legitimacy of birth.

The key ethical question in civil rights claims is: Can such distinctions be justified? The key political question is: Who has the authority to make such distinctions, whether they are justified or not? In other words, who is certified to define individuals as members of particular groups and to define particular groups as entitled to certain rights? The answers to these questions have varied over time and in response to the social, legal, political, economic, and systemic factors discussed below.

Tatum Harmon is a dancer with the Alvin Ailey Company in New York City. For many years, de facto segregation meant that numerous arts groups were exclusively white.

Social Factors

Civil rights disputes arise over difference. If everyone in the United States belonged to the same culture, race, gender, generation, religion, and economic class, such disputes would be rare. However, members of many groups maintain their collective identity by regarding their beliefs, practices, and accomplishments as superior to those of members of other groups. They then use these views of *what is* to justify treating these "others" as inferior, perhaps as free or low-wage labor. Today discriminatory views based on race (racism), gender (sexism), class (classism), age (ageism), and homosexuality (homophobia) are increasingly held to be morally wrong and incompatible with democracy. The development of a more tolerant and inclusive culture in which groups are regarded as different rather than as superior or inferior has been provoked by wars, civil rights struggles, new technologies, and progress in science and social science. Civil rights activists complain, with reason, that such progress has been painfully slow and is still incomplete.

The Politics of Knowledge

Factors That Shape Civil Rights Beliefs and Analysis

In attempting to understand your own views and those of others on a civil rights event, dispute, or policy, notice the ways in which context (frameworks of reality) and perspective (points of view) are interrelated and influential. As the following example of slavery illustrates, it is helpful to distinguish among the political actors who are direct participants, observers who comment from a distance, and professional analysts who claim to present a neutral, balanced, or accurate picture.

Political *Participants in* Slavery

In the context of slavery, the perspectives of slaves, slaveholders, and abolitionists were shaped by the different roles each played—roles that led them to perceive, explain, and evaluate that institution differently. For many slaveholders, slavery was right; the Constitution gave them a right to property, and slaves were their property. Their prescription: Preserve the institution. For slaves and abolitionists, slavery was a violation of a person's natural liberty. Their prescription: Abolish it. Public officials could be found on both sides of the issue. In 1857, the justices of the Supreme Court upheld slavery in *Dred Scott v. Sandford*, while in 1865, members of Congress and state legislatures abolished slavery with the Thirteenth Amendment.

Political *Observers of* Slavery

Slavery was legally abolished, but its effects did not immediately disappear. Some contemporary observers explain the social, economic, and political status of African Americans today in terms of the "lingering effects" of slavery—an explanation (*what is*) that supports the prescription that the nation ought to take action to erase these effects (*what's right*). These observers often support affirmative action and quotas as remedies for racial discrimination. Others who see no connection between slavery and the current status of African Americans (*what is*) maintain that all people in the United States should be treated solely on the basis of merit (*what's right*).

Professional *Analysts of* Slavery

The perspectives of professionals who analyze slavery are influenced by the context in which they conduct their

Legal Factors

As the epigraph to this chapter indicates, law has sometimes been used "to widen the embrace of the national community and sometimes as a barrier to further inclusion." These different outcomes are due to the fact that American law is actually a network of laws that regulate order and change and do not guarantee particular results.

Civil Liberties

Progress in civil rights depends on civil liberties: the constitutional freedom to speak out, assemble, petition, march, and protest. Before black men and women were allowed to vote, some used their freedoms of speech and petition to lobby analysis as well as by their personal views. Context, in this case, includes historical distance, area of expertise (scholarship, journalism, television documentary), and the audience (other scholars, students, the general public) the analyst is attempting to reach.

But professional analysts are also human beings with feelings, ethics, and beliefs, so their pictures of slavery cannot be neutral. Thus if you are seeking a complete picture of slavery, you must compare analyses based on a variety of perspectives and speculate on the reasons for their differences. Why, for example, might the Harvard professors who specialized in civil rights (Chapter 4) have omitted documents written by slaves from their history course? Why have women historians—in particular black women historians—shown a greater interest than men historians of either race in exploring the hardships of women slaves? And why did the genealogist who traced the descendants of Thomas Jefferson's slaves choose this subject to investigate?

You will not find much scholarship examining the reasons why professional analysts choose to focus on a particular subject, such as slavery, in the first place, or why they treat it one way rather than another. You must therefore learn to raise these questions yourself, to locate contrasting analyses, and to reach your own conclusions on the subject.

Genealogists at Monticello, Thomas Jefferson's home in Virginia, are tracing the descendants of 200 of Jefferson's slaves. The members of the family shown here are descendants of Wormley Hughes, a plantation gardener. Lucia Stanton, one of the researchers, explained, "We wanted to shed light back into the shadows of slavery and give voice to those whose lives and achievements went unrecorded."

legislators for that very right, just as gays and lesbians use those freedoms to promote their civil rights claims today.

Governments rarely expand civil rights voluntarily or because it is morally right. Expansion is generally a response to pressure from activists representing sizable groups of actual or potential voters. Black activist Frederick Douglass put this quite plainly in 1857:

> Power concedes nothing without demand. . . . Find out what any people will quietly submit to and you have found out the exact measure of injustice and wrong which will be imposed upon them, and these will continue till they are resisted with either words or blows, or with both. The limits of tyrants are prescribed by the endurance of those whom they oppress.[4]

black codes or Jim Crow laws
These were laws purposely crafted, especially in the South, to discriminate against African Americans. The term originated in an eighteenth-century plantation song about a black crow. When a performer in "black-face" popularized the song as a jig, the term came to be used for *Negro*.

The Reverend Martin Luther King, Jr., expressed the same view a century later in a letter he wrote while in jail for civil disobedience: "We know through painful experience that justice is never voluntarily given by the oppressor." Civil liberties make it possible to advance (or restrict) civil rights within the context of law.

Federalism and the Separation of Powers

Civil rights disputes are affected by federalism because parties to a dispute seek its resolution in the context—federal or state law—most favorable to them. Thus the plaintiffs in *Rodriguez* and *Plyler* claimed that the State of Texas was violating their rights under the U.S. Constitution, while Texas claimed their concerns fell under state authority.

Federalism has played a major role in civil rights since the country's founding. The Framers justified giving slavery a limited legal life in the Constitution in order to give federalism as a form of government a permanent life. Federalism allowed the imposition of civil rights laws on southern states during Reconstruction (see Table 16.1) as well as the enactment of "black codes" and Jim Crow laws that bypassed those civil rights laws. Thus the rules of federalism (*what is*) do not, by themselves, result in justice (*what's right*).

Civil rights claims based on the Constitution must look to one of the federal government's three branches for legal remedies. Actors may pressure Congress for legislation; the executive branch for legislative initiatives, executive orders, bureaucratic regulations, and law enforcement; and the courts for favorable judgments. Because lawmakers and presidents, as elected officials, are more sensitive to majorities than unelected judges and justices, political actors with unpopular complaints often turn to the courts for remedies.

Justice Thurgood Marshall regarded the Constitution as "defective from the start." He noted that "several amendments, a civil war, and momentous social transformation" helped to bring about the constitutional liberties and human rights that "we hold as fundamental today." Black Americans "were enslaved by law, emancipated by law, disenfranchised and segregated by law; and finally, they have begun to win equality by law."

Political and Economic Factors

Many of the political and economic concerns that divide liberals and conservatives ideologically—in particular, what role government should play in society and what should be done about economic inequality—also divide them on civil rights issues. Libertarians, conservative Republicans and Democrats, and many moderates favor civil rights remedies that are consistent with a smaller, more limited government. They argue, as the Anti-Federalists did, that the Constitution may not be used to remedy problems that are not addressed in the document. The Constitution, as they interpret it, limits the powers of government to the maintenance of order and the protection of fundamental liberties. That is why Chief Justice William H. Rehnquist rejected the expansion of civil liberties in *DeShaney* (Chapter 15) and the expansion of civil rights in his dissent in *Plyler*. In contrast, those who view the Constitution as an instrument for defending and expanding civil rights, as Justice Thurgood Marshall did, are more likely to favor government policies that enforce and expand civil rights protection.

Because there is no neutral observer to decide which side is right, partisans in the political process must defend their opinions on an ongoing basis. The

TABLE 16.1

The Civil War Amendments and Early Civil Rights Acts

Thirteenth Amendment, 1865

"*Section 1.* Neither slavery nor involuntary servitude, except as a punishment for crime whereof the party shall have been duly convicted, shall exist within the United States, or any place subject to their jurisdiction.

Section 2. Congress shall have power to enforce this article by appropriate legislation."

Fourteenth Amendment, 1868

"*Section 1.* All persons born or naturalized in the United States, and subject to the jurisdiction thereof, are citizens of the United States and of the State where-in they reside. No State shall make or enforce any law which shall abridge the privileges or immunities of citizens of the United States; nor shall any State deprive any person of life, liberty, or property, without due process of law; nor deny to any person within its jurisdiction the equal protection of the laws."

Fifteenth Amendment, 1870

"*Section 1.* The right of citizens of the United States to vote shall not be denied or abridged by the United States or by any State on account of race, color, or previous condition of servitude.

Section 2. The Congress shall have power to enforce this article by appropriate legislation."

Civil Rights Act, 1866

This act defined certain citizenship rights of freedmen, such as the right to own and rent property, to make contracts, and to have access to the courts (but not the right to vote).

Reconstruction Act, 1867

This act organized the defeated South (except for Tennessee) into five military districts, each governed by a Union general charged with registering all adult black men and former Confederates and supervising the election of a convention to draft a constitution guaranteeing black suffrage.

Ku Klux Klan Acts, 1870, 1871

These acts authorized the president to use federal prosecutors and military force to stop secret organizations from using coercion to deprive citizens of the right to vote and of equal protection of the laws.

Civil Rights Act, 1875

This act granted blacks equal rights in public accommodations, such as hotels and theaters.

The Voiding of the Civil Rights of African Americans

In 1878, the Supreme Court declared unconstitutional a Louisiana law prohibiting discrimination in transportation.
In 1882, the Court voided the Ku Klux Klan Act of 1871.
In 1883, the Court declared unconstitutional the Civil Rights Act of 1875.
In 1896, the Court upheld state laws segregating public facilities in *Plessy v. Ferguson*.

---

debates these disputes stimulate, however, expand the possibilities for steering the ship of state. From such a perspective, the two sides are complementary, even at the extremes: libertarians supply the ballast of "ordered liberty," while egalitarians rock the boat with demands for a more just, inclusive society and a far smaller gap between rich and poor. Eliminate one of these groups from the political system (or those in the middle), and the ship of state is likely to capsize.

Systemic Factors

Four major systems—social, economic, political, and legal—allow American society to function. Their overlapping rules routinely classify people into groups. For example, current gender classifications require a person to marry a member of the opposite sex (a social rule) if the marriage is to be recognized by law (a legal rule). Economic classifications designate a person as a buyer or seller, an employer or employee, a landlord or tenant. Political classifications categorize you as a youth or senior citizen, a voter or nonvoter, an elected or an unelected official, or eligible or not eligible for welfare. Legal classifications determine what rights and duties you have and what penalties you must pay in particular circumstances.

The equal protection clause of the Fourteenth Amendment requires states to apply their laws to all people *equally*. States may put people in different groups in order to treat them differently so long as those classifications are "rational" (nonarbitrary). However, the equal protection clause requires that persons whom a law places in the same group must be treated in the same way.[5] Federal courts may declare a legal classification "arbitrary" and unconstitutional if they find no rational basis for it. In 1938 Justice Harlan Fiske Stone suggested that a standard of review more stringent than rationality should apply to statutes "directed at particular religions or nationalities or racial minorities."[6]

Suspect Classification

In equal protection cases, federal courts must decide whether the challenged state law unfairly treats the group claiming discrimination. As we saw in Chapter 14 (p. 535), the Supreme Court has developed two main standards of review—the **rational basis** and **strict scrutiny tests**—to help it decide whether the classification made by the challenged law is *rational* (in which case the Court defers to the judgment of the state on the matter) or *suspect* (in which case the classification does not fit the purpose of the law or the purpose itself is not legitimate).

In *Loving v. Virginia* (1967), for example, the Supreme Court held that even though a Virginia law prohibiting racial intermarriage applied equally to all races, its purpose—to maintain segregation—was not legitimate. Thus at issue in cases involving **suspect classification** is the legitimacy of the classification itself. In *Loving*, the Court declared that classifications based on race are inherently suspect and carry "a very heavy burden of justification"—meaning that the state must show that it has a "compelling state interest" in making such a classification.[7] These phrases signal the Court's decision to apply the *strict* ("heightened" or "close") *scrutiny* test rather than the rational basis test.

Once the doctrine of suspect classification had become firmly established in race and alien cases (in 1971 the Court held that state statutes seeking to exclude aliens from welfare benefits are subject to strict scrutiny[8]), efforts were made to apply it to other forms of discrimination: illegitimacy (in 1968 the Court upheld the right of illegitimate—"nonmarital"—children to sue for the wrongful death of a parent but refused to elevate the group to a *suspect* status[9]); gender (in 1971 the Court struck down an Idaho statute providing that when two or more persons were entitled to inherit same property, the male would have priority over the female[10]); the poor (*Rodriguez*); and illegal immigrants (*Plyler*).

The Intermediate Scrutiny Test

In several footnotes to *Plyler v. Doe* (1982) Justice William J. Brennan, Jr., identified the following classifications that the Supreme Court will subject to strong, if not strict, scrutiny:

- [Classifications that] reflect deep-seated prejudice rather than legislative rationality in pursuit of some legitimate legislative objective. Legislation predicated on such prejudice is easily recognized as incompatible with the constitutional understanding that each person is to be judged individually and is entitled to equal justice under the law.
- Classifications treated as suspect tend to be irrelevant to any proper legislative goal.
- Certain groups, indeed largely the same groups, have historically been "relegated to such a position of political powerlessness as to command extraordinary protection from the majoritarian political process."
- [Legislation] imposing special disabilities on groups disfavored by virtue of circumstances beyond their control suggests the kind of "class or caste" treatment that the Fourteenth Amendment was designed to abolish.

Source: Plyler v. Doe, 457 U.S. 202 (1982), quoting *U.S. v. Carolene Products Company*, 304 U.S. 144 (1938).

Intermediate Scrutiny

Since the 1970s, the Supreme Court has developed and made increasing use of a third standard of review known as the **intermediate scrutiny test**. Because this test falls between the rational basis and strict scrutiny tests, it gives the Court greater flexibility in reviewing equal protection cases. Intermediate scrutiny does not automatically defer to the judgment of state legislatures but does allow them to employ classifications based on gender, illegitimacy, and alienage if the classifications are not arbitrary and serve some substantial state purpose. The Court used this standard of review in *Plyler*. Because the Court does not always indicate when it is using this standard, it is useful to survey Justice William J. Brennan's list of the classifications that are subject to intermediate scrutiny (see the box above).

Civil Rights Strategies

Civil rights expand in two ways:

- through the creation of *new civil rights* by new laws or constitutional amendments, new interpretations of existing laws and statutes, or new regulations drafted by federal bureaucracies; and
- by increasing the *number of groups* (African Americans, women, Latinos, Native Americans, people with disabilities) entitled to existing rights.

Once any group gets a new civil right, other groups want it, too. But their members often pursue varied strategies to get it based on their views of *what is*, *what's right*, and *what works*. Some have sought equal treatment and assimilation by using the rules of the legal, political, and economic systems. Others, convinced that these rules are stacked against them, have resorted to individual resistance, mass protest, civil disobedience, separatism, and militancy. Pragmatists have switched strategies or used them in combination. If differences over strategy have made it hard for some groups to forge united fronts, their diversity has allowed them to attract a wide range of supporters.

African Americans

African Americans have fought for civil rights through the **civil rights movement**, which relied on legal and political activism and civil disobedience, militancy, and self-help initiatives.

Legal Activism

NAACP:
http://www.naacp.org

The legal vanguard of the civil rights movement was—and still is—the National Association for the Advancement of Colored People (NAACP). Founded in 1909 by a group of blacks and whites including W.E.B. Du Bois, the NAACP attempted to use the white majority's professed ideals and legal institutions to end lynchings and all forms of racial discrimination. The NAACP was buttressed by other organizations such as the American Civil Liberties Union and sympathetic white churches and synagogues. But progress was slow and hampered by a white backlash and Ku Klux Klan terrorism, even outside the South. Race riots erupted in the 1920s.

The Congress of Racial Equality (CORE), formed during World War II, relied on a "nonviolent direct action" strategy inspired by the Gospels and the pacifist tactics of India's Mahatma Gandhi. Following their service in segregated units in that war, African Americans demanded and began to receive more equal treatment. Nazi Germany's atrocities had awakened many Americans to the dangers of racism, and African Americans expected the principles of freedom and equality they had fought for abroad to be applied to them at home.

Even though by the mid-1950s the NAACP had won most of its suits against southern laws that kept blacks from voting, black voting did not increase. Literacy tests and polls taxes were still legal, uneducated blacks did not understand the importance of voting, and registration efforts were hampered by intimidation and violence. In 1950, for example, the head of the Florida NAACP and his wife organized a large and successful voter registration drive. On Christmas Eve 1951 they were killed by a house bomb.[11]

NAACP lawyer Thurgood Marshall (who would be appointed the first black Supreme Court justice in 1967) had also won suits against white southern universities that put an end to the doctrine of **separate but equal**—the principle that laws providing separate public facilities for blacks were constitutional so long as the facilities were equal—in higher education. This doctrine, which the Supreme Court had upheld in *Plessy v. Ferguson* (1896), was finally abolished in public schools in *Brown v. Board of Education of Topeka* (1954).[12] School officials had ordered Linda Carol Brown, a seven-year-old black girl living in Topeka, Kansas, to travel 21 blocks to an all-black school rather than attend the all-white school just four blocks from her house.

African American and black

Polls show that seven out of ten African Americans prefer the term *black*, in part because it is more inclusive (some blacks' ancestors do not come from Africa) and in part because it suggests political cohesion in the face of discrimination based on skin color. In this book the terms are used interchangeably.

If the case had been decided in the 1952–1953 session, when it first came before the Court, the decision would not have been unanimous and might even have upheld segregation.[13] But the decision was delayed, and Chief Justice Fred Vinson, who had been ambivalent on the issue and had exerted no leadership among the justices, died. In 1953 President Dwight Eisenhower appointed Earl Warren, an opponent of segregation, to take his place. Warren supplied that missing leadership.

Writing for a unanimous Court in 1954, Warren set aside the dispute over the original intent of the Fourteenth Amendment as "inconclusive." He focused instead on the "present place" of public education—what he called "the very foundation of good citizenship"—in American life. His conclusion: "In the field of public education the doctrine of 'separate but equal' has no place. Separate educational facilities are inherently unequal" and therefore violate the "equal protection of the laws guaranteed by the Fourteenth Amendment." Citing sociological evidence provided by experts, Warren added that segregated schools have "a detrimental effect upon the colored children" that "generates a feeling of inferiority as to their status in the community that may affect their hearts and minds in a way unlikely ever to be undone."[14]

The next year, in a follow-up case to implement *Brown*,[15] the Court gave federal trial courts the task of determining how its guideline "with all deliberate speed" should be applied to school districts required to achieve **desegregation**—the removal of racial barriers. The Court also required local school systems to develop their own desegregation plans. After ten years of delay by states and local school districts, the Court abandoned its "all deliberate speed" doctrine because it clearly had not worked.[16]

Political Activism

The *Brown* decision inspired fresh political strategies: boycotts, voter registration campaigns, and civil disobedience. Following his success in the Montgomery bus boycott, described in the box nearby, the Reverend Martin Luther King, Jr., organized the Southern Christian Leadership Conference (SCLC) among black activist churches in the South to broaden his strategy of passive resistance and civil disobedience. Marshall and other NAACP lawyers feared that this strategy would undermine their success in the courts, and segregationists fought back with new laws and violence. In 1957, when Arkansas Governor Orval Faubus ordered that nine black children not be admitted to an all-white high school in Little Rock, it took federal troops sent by President Eisenhower to achieve integration. At the same time, Congress passed the Civil Rights Act of 1957, the first civil rights legislation since 1875. Although the new law established the U.S. Civil Rights Commission and expanded the Justice Department's role in civil rights, it did not abolish discrimination.

In February 1960 black college students in Greensboro, North Carolina, staged a "sit-in" at a drugstore lunch counter, refusing to leave until they were served.

Federal troops escort black students into Little Rock Central High School in 1957. The students had run a gauntlet of angry, taunting whites protesting the integration of the formerly all-white school.

The Montgomery Bus Boycott: *What Worked*

On December 1, 1955, just six months after the second *Brown* decision, a quiet 42-year-old Montgomery, Alabama, seamstress named Rosa Parks boarded a rush-hour bus. When Parks and three other blacks were asked to move to the back of the bus, Parks refused and was arrested. The then-unknown 26-year-old charismatic minister, Martin Luther King, Jr., and his 29-year-old minister friend Ralph Abernathy persuaded Parks to allow her arrest to be used as a test case of bus segregation laws. When NAACP lawyers saw that Parks's case might be delayed indefinitely in the state court system, they filed a similar federal suit—*Browder v. Gayle*[1]—on behalf of five black women. As a result, both city and state bus segregation were declared unconstitutional.[2]

Black activists (mainly women) organized a bus boycott for December 5, the day of Parks's trial.[3]

Virtually every black in the city found another way to get to work the day that Parks was found guilty and fined $10. The bus boycott lasted for 382 days thanks to a giant car pool staffed by more than 200 volunteers with 22 station wagons paid for by local black churches. The boycott cemented political solidarity among blacks for the first time in the city's history and attracted national attention.

The lesson of Rosa Parks and the Montgomery bus boycott is clear: The political effects of individual and community action can be greatly magnified when they are backed by effective institutional support and legal expertise. Black community organizers, the expertise of NAACP lawyers, the *Brown* and *Browder* decisions, and nationwide media attention all helped to make the boycott work.

---

[1] *Browder v. Gayle* 142 F. Supp. 707 (M.D. Ala. 1956), affirmed in *Gayle v. Browder* 352 U.S. 903 (1956).
[2] For a full account of these events, see Catherine A. Barnes, *Journey from Jim Crow: The Desegregation of Southern Transit* (New York: Columbia University Press, 1983), Chapter 7.
[3] Jo Ann Gibson, *The Montgomery Bus Boycott and the Women Who Started It* (Knoxville: University of Tennessee Press, 1987).

Before long, black students, joined by sympathetic white students, were staging such sit-ins throughout the South. Soon scores of southern eating places started serving blacks. The sit-in strategy worked because it gave an army of students a role in the civil rights movement and it gave the media an easy way to cover and contrast the issues under dispute. That same spring, students from throughout the South met in Raleigh, North Carolina, to form the Student Non-Violent Coordinating Committee (SNCC).

In 1961 CORE organized black and white "Freedom Riders" to conduct sit-ins against segregated interstate buses and bus terminals in Montgomery—segregation that the Supreme Court had already declared unconstitutional.[17] The activists were brutally attacked by whites, but with protection from 600 federal marshals, support from the SCLC and SNCC, and a ruling by the Interstate Commerce Commission that interstate buses would be desegregated, they succeeded.

Increasingly, moderate blacks, including King, reacted to these events by asserting the right of blacks to

Black demonstrators "sit in" at a segregated Woolworth's lunch counter in Charlotte, North Carolina, in the early 1960s. They have been refused service; note that the waitresses have left the counter.

The Civil Rights Act of 1964

The major provisions of the act
- prohibited discrimination in voter registration and facilitated lawsuits filed to fight such discrimination;
- prohibited discrimination in public accommodations involved in interstate commerce;
- permitted the Justice Department to file lawsuits to end segregation in public schools and facilities;
- allowed for federal funds to be withheld from state and local programs that practice discrimination;
- prohibited employers from discriminating on the basis of race, color, religion, national origin, or gender; and
- established the Equal Employment Opportunity Commission (EEOC) to investigate and enforce prohibitions against discrimination in the workplace.

self-defense. On Good Friday, 1963, King led a "jail-in," a mass march into Birmingham against the orders of the chief of police. On television Americans saw protesters singing "We Shall Overcome" while being attacked by police dogs, beaten with cattle prods, and sprayed with firehoses. From his jail cell King composed his celebrated "Letter from Birmingham Jail," quoted on page 612.

In June 1963, the assassination of Mississippi NAACP leader Medgar Evers touched off nationwide demonstrations, and in August, a massive March on Washington for Jobs and Freedom culminated in King's celebrated "I Have a Dream" speech (Chapter 1). President John Kennedy had already sent Congress what would become the Civil Rights Act of 1964, which President Lyndon Johnson signed into law once Congress passed it after Kennedy's assassination. The new law, which prohibited discrimination in voter registration, public accommodations, and employment (see the box above), provoked a violent white backlash. Even before it was passed, one black and two white SNCC activists engaged in a voter registration campaign known as Freedom Summer were murdered near Philadelphia, Mississippi. Their deaths, now immortalized in the movie *Mississippi Burning*, were a brutal reminder that civil rights workers still lacked legal protections. By the end of the summer 80 workers had been beaten, 1,000 arrested, and 37 churches bombed.[18] SNCC reacted to the backlash by abandoning nonviolence and forming its own all-black vigilante group.

In 1965, after King's widely publicized march from Selma to Montgomery, Congress passed the Voting Rights Act of 1965 (Chapter 6). In 1968, Congress passed the Fair Housing Act, which outlawed de facto discrimination by private individuals seeking to rent or sell their homes directly or through real estate agents. A few days later King was gunned down in Memphis while organizing black sanitation workers. His murder sparked urban rioting in the nation's

Fifty years ago, James (*left*) and Robert Paschal helped to feed and house the civil rights movement. Now they have decided to sell their Atlanta hotel and restaurant to Clark Atlanta University, a predominantly black college.

capital and in 125 other cities. When order was restored, moderate blacks vowed to carry on King's agenda through such organizations as the National Urban League, led by Whitney Young and later Vernon Jordan, and the Reverend Jesse Jackson's People United to Save Humanity (PUSH) and Rainbow Coalition.

The Black Power Movement

Growing evidence that peaceful civil rights strategies were not working led some blacks to turn to the **black power movement**. Its predecessor, black nationalism, had been introduced by Marcus Garvey, a native of Jamaica, in 1916. Garvey promoted black self-esteem and a back-to-Africa movement among small black farmers in the South and blacks who had migrated to northern ghettos. Rejected by middle-class blacks and plagued by other difficulties, Garveyism collapsed in 1925.

The black nationalists who emerged in the 1960s accused middle-class civil rights leaders of neglecting poor and working-class blacks, their main recruits.[19] By 1964 more than two dozen black nationalist organizations were operating in Harlem alone.[20] Their inspiration came from activists and writers such as third world advocate Frantz Fanon (author of *Wretched of the Earth*, 1961), novelist James Baldwin, poet and playwright LeRoi Jones (later known as Imamu Amiri Baraka), Louis Lomax, and Stokely Carmichael (later known as Kwame Touré), for a time president of SNCC. These activists wore African clothes, jewelry, and hair styles to project a positive black identity and endorsed the slogan "Black is beautiful." Literary figures, artists, and filmmakers made social protest the centerpiece of a black arts movement. In the late 1960s, black college students demanded—and often got—courses and degrees in black studies.

In 1966 in Oakland, California, Bobby Seale and Huey Newton formed the Black Panthers to train armed patrols to protect black neighborhoods against police brutality. Newton and other leaders were jailed or shot by police, but the party grew to more than 5,000 members and 30 chapters nationwide in just three years before specializing in community activism: increasing voter registration, political participation, and creating free breakfast programs.

While black nationalists were less likely to vote and organize politically than other blacks, they nevertheless played key roles in political campaigns, helping to elect black mayors and supporting Jesse Jackson's 1984 and 1988 presidential bids. At the height of the movement, only 7 percent of black nationalists favored a separate black state,[21] and blacks as a group have generally opposed an automatic "vote black" strategy.[22] Today the most controversial black nationalist group is the Nation of Islam, discussed in the box nearby.

Nation of Islam:
http://www.noi.org

Economic Activism

Some African-American leaders, such as Booker T. Washington (1856–1915), had long advocated obtaining economic power by following the rules of the white majority. Once blacks owned land, ran businesses, and bought products, he argued, they would naturally be accepted as full citizens.

Since the 1980s, this strategy has been revived by black conservatives, such as talk-show host Tony Brown, who argue that welfare programs perpetuate dependency and poverty. They prescribe a nationwide **self-help movement** aimed at achieving education and economic self-sufficiency. Blacks, these activists point out,

The Nation of Islam

The Nation of Islam (NOI) was founded by Wallace Fard in the 1930s in Detroit's black ghetto. Fard argued that blacks had been brought to America against their will but were really descendants of the Islamic religion, whose God was Allah. Fard preached that if blacks would organize as Black Muslims, they would one day regain the power that whites had stolen from them. Although the NOI shares a belief in Allah with other Muslims around the world, it has developed its own antiwhite doctrine.

By the time Fard retired, there were 8,000 Black Muslims and a number of mosques. His successor, Elijah Poole, later known as Elijah Muhammad, the son of a southern Baptist minister, took his place and was regarded as a prophet by his followers. Membership grew rapidly. Mosques and schools sprang up across the country, along with a legion of young militant men known as the Fruit of Islam. Their political goal—to achieve economic independence for blacks by fostering black-owned businesses and services—first took root in Chicago. Leaders claim that obedience to a strict traditional morality protects Black Muslim families from the ravages of teen pregnancy; abuse of drugs, alcohol, and tobacco; and even unemployment.[1]

The most famous Black Muslim was Malcolm Little, later known as Malcolm X, who was assassinated in 1966. His father—a Garveyite—had been murdered by a racist group. Today the Nation of Islam's most passionate spokesman is Louis Farrakhan, responsible for organizing the Million Man March in 1995. Critics have attacked Farrakhan for his anti-Semitic statements, for his connections with Libyan president Muammar Qaddafi, and for seeming to turn a blind eye to reports of modern-day slavery in Africa and the Middle East.[2]

Louis Farrakhan preaches, with Fruit of Islam guards behind him.

---

[1] Minister Robert Muhammad, quoted in Robbie Morganfield, "Nation of Islam Spreads Self-Help Message," *Houston Chronicle*, September 11, 1994.
[2] Arthur J. Magida, *Prophet of Rage: A Life of Louis Farrakhan and His Nation* (New York: Basic Books, 1996).

---

earn more than $300 billion a year, so that if blacks bought from black rather than white entrepreneurs, they would have the capital required to lift themselves out of poverty. In Brown's words, "The Chinese help the Chinese, the Koreans help the Koreans, the Cubans help the Cubans, but blacks help everyone else. We have conducted the most successful business boycott in history against ourselves."[23]

Some scholars point out, however, that blacks have been supporting themselves as entrepreneurs and buying from one another ever since the colonial period.[24] Although many states restricted black economic activities and black inventors had trouble securing patents until after the Civil War, many black entrepreneurs, especially in the North, built successful businesses that enabled their children to get good educations and professional jobs. Proponents of self-help and black organizations such as the Urban League are now appealing to middle-class blacks to help finance economic consortiums, African-American banks, and community development projects to assist black professionals, contractors, vendors, and workers.

Women

The legal status of American women at the time of the country's founding was the same as their status under English law: unmarried women were legally dependent on their fathers and married women, on their husbands. Only widows could sign a contract or sue. Despite the rhetoric of freedom and equality in the Declaration of Independence (the first edition of which was printed by a woman[25]), state constitutions, with the exception of New Jersey's (see Chapter 6), denied women the vote. As early as 1819, state legislators restricted abortion and divorce, permitting divorce only in cases of extreme cruelty, adultery, or desertion. Divorced women had no right to the custody of their children, however.

Unequal status was widely legitimated by the belief, held by many white men and women alike, that women belonged to a sphere separate from men and that their natural moral superiority would be compromised if they engaged in the rough-and-tumble activities of business and politics. This view of *what is* restricted middle-class white women to teaching, mission work, abolitionist societies, and the temperance movement and condemned them to de facto segregation. However, as women became leaders in these areas, they pressed for their right to participate in the political process, where they *learned by doing*.

Early Reformers

Women's efforts to participate through education were hampered by the widespread belief that female brains were inferior to male brains—a "fact" that justified training girls only for housework or, if they were wealthy, for sewing, painting, and singing. Education for the daughters of slaves was illegal, and it was rare for free black females in the South. Northern public schools excluded all blacks, male and female.[26]

Still, education was women's main way up in the world. In the nineteenth century, female academies began to train teachers, but women were paid half the rate of men teachers and were expected to resign when they married. State laws barred women from jobs in the legal profession, and colleges and professional schools refused to admit women. But starting in the 1830s women were admitted to Oberlin College, and Mount Holyoke was established specifically for women. After the Civil War state universities in the West and Midwest, short on students, also became coeducational. Only with the development of separate colleges for men and women did many women, however, have access to higher education.

The medical profession was the first to lower its barriers to women, in part because many women disliked being treated by male doctors. Still, women interns and doctors were often segregated in women's hospitals.

When women reformers tried to study law to get the tools to wage a legal fight for suffrage and equal rights, they had to learn law from their fathers, brothers, and husbands, because most law schools rejected them. In the early 1870s, Belva Lockwood was turned away because her admission would "be likely to distract the attention of the young men,"[27] and, as the nearby box discusses, the Supreme Court denied Myra Bradwell's petition to be admitted to the Illinois bar.

The Equal Rights Movement

Women's struggle for equal rights gained momentum with their participation in the abolitionist cause. In 1840, American women delegates at the World Antislavery Convention in London were refused admittance. When their American male colleagues came to their defense by refusing to participate, a compromise was reached: the women were allowed to sit in the balcony on condition that they sat behind a curtain so they would not distract the men.[28] Outraged, the women convened the Women's Rights Convention at Seneca Falls, New York, in 1848 and adopted the Women's Declaration of Sentiments. When the drafters of the Fourteenth Amendment restricted protection of political representation to adult male citizens, women leaders focused on reforming their state constitutions.

Women turned to their states for institutional protection because the states had the power to police business and private property in the interest of health, welfare, and safety. The chief women's organization in the late nineteenth century, the Woman's Christian Temperance Union, not only opposed alcoholic beverages but also fought for child labor laws, improved working conditions for women, city sanitation, the abolition of prostitution, and other progressive causes.

Progressives at the turn of the century supported women's suffrage, but by 1910 only a handful of western states had granted women full voting rights. Women activists meeting in New York in 1914 began to call themselves *feminists*, asserting their right to break out of the "separate sphere" stereotype, to pursue a career, and to free themselves from double standards in social life and sexual morality. The country's rationale for fighting in World War I—to make the world safe for democracy—undercut the rationale for denying women the vote, and the Nineteenth Amendment was ratified in 1920. But many state laws drafted to protect women in the workplace—by fixing maximum daily or weekly working hours and by excluding them from occupations like mining, bartending, and jobs requiring heavy lifting—remained obstacles to greater equality.

Pioneer feminist Betty Friedan addresses a rally in New York City's Times Square in 1992.

Political Actors Disagree

Natural law (a claim about *what is* and *what's right*) has been used to legitimate the liberties in the Declaration of Independence as well as the human rights declarations of the United Nations. Sometimes, however, natural law has been used to legitimate claims that contradict one another, as the following examples illustrate. Elizabeth Cady Stanton used natural law to claim that men and women are equal, while Justice Joseph Bradley and Sears Roebuck used it to argue that women are different from men and are therefore not entitled to equal treatment.

Elizabeth Cady Stanton

Taking the Declaration of Independence of 1776 as her model, Stanton cast American men in the role of tyrannical King George III in the Seneca Falls Declaration of Sentiments and Resolutions of 1848—a year of revolutionary upheaval in Europe:

> We hold these truths to be self-evident: that all men and women were created equal....
>
> The history of mankind is a history of repeated injuries and usurpations on the part of man toward woman, having in direct object the establishment of absolute tyranny over her....
>
> He has never permitted her to exercise her inalienable right to the elective franchise.

Are Women and Men Equal?

> He has compelled her to submit to laws, in the formation of which she had no voice.
>
> He has withheld from her rights which are given to the most ignorant and degraded men—both natives and foreigners....
>
> He has made her, if married, in the eye of the law, civilly dead.
>
> He has taken from her all right in property, even to the wages she earns....
>
> He closes against her all avenues to wealth and distinction which he considers most honorable to himself. As a teacher of theology, medicine, or law, she is not known.
>
> He has denied her the facilities for obtaining a thorough education—all colleges being closed against her....
>
> He has endeavored, in every way that he could, to destroy her confidence in her own powers, to lessen her self-respect and to make her willing to live a dependent and abject life....
>
> Resolved, that woman is man's equal—was intended to be so by the Creator, and the highest good of the race demands that she should be recognized as such.[1]

NOW (National Organization for Women):
http://www.now.org

The Revival of Feminism

During the 1950s, middle-class white women raised their families and supported their husbands as they climbed the corporate ladder, while women in the labor force worked for less than equal pay and unprotected from sexual harassment. At least 10,000 women died yearly from back-alley abortions, and there were no shelters to protect abused or raped women. Women's studies programs in universities were unheard of. It was not until the 1960s that feminism was rediscovered and pushed to new heights over the next 15 years by a number of determined women activists. These women foresaw that the piecemeal legislation they had been seeking from state governments would not produce equality and began to lobby for a comprehensive law that would.

Two organizations—the National Organization for Women (NOW), founded in 1966 primarily by white, middle-class women, and the National Women's Po-

Justice Joseph Bradley

Denied admission to the Illinois bar, Myra Bradwell appealed to the Supreme Court but was again turned down in 1873. In his concurring opinion, Justice Joseph Bradley argued:

> Civil law, as well as nature herself, has always recognized a wide difference in the respective spheres and destinies of man and woman. Man is, or should be, woman's protector and defender. The natural and proper timidity and delicacy which belongs to the female sex evidently unsuits it for many of the occupations of civil life. . . . One of [the special rules of law in most states] is, that a married woman is incapable, without her husband's consent, of making contracts which shall be binding on her or him. This very incapacity [was one reason why the Supreme Court of Illinois found] a married woman incompetent to fully perform the duties and trusts that belong to the office of attorney and counselor.
>
> It is true that many women are unmarried and not affected by any of the duties, complications, and incapacities arising out of the married state, but these are exceptions to the general rule. The paramount destiny and mission of woman are to fulfill the noble and benign offices of wife and mother. This is the law of the Creator. And the rules of civil society must be adapted to the general constitution of things, and cannot be based on exceptional cases.[2]

If this case seems like ancient history, consider that occupations were as segregated in 1970 as they were in 1900.[3] And consider the 1988 case of the *EEOC v. Sears Roebuck*, in which a federal appellate court said that Sears did not discriminate against women in giving them lower-paying jobs than men because women freely choose the "ethic of care" (a concern for family values) over high pay: "Women's 'ethic of care' enables them to rise above the fray, so they are not truly hurt when they are excluded from high-powered, competitive jobs in commission sales."[4]

---

[1] Quoted in Diane Ravitch, ed., *The American Reader: Words That Moved a Nation* (New York: HarperCollins, 1990), 83–85.
[2] *Bradwell v. Illinois*, 83 U.S. 130 (1873).
[3] Claudia Goldin, *Understanding the Gender Gap: An Economic History of American Women* (New York: Oxford University Press, 1990), 4.
[4] *EEOC v. Sears Roebuck & Co.*, 839F 2d 302 (1988).

---

litical Caucus (NWPC), founded in 1971 to serve as the umbrella organization for 300 state and local caucuses—began a national campaign to add an **Equal Rights Amendment** (ERA) to the Constitution that would guarantee equal treatment for women and men. The box on the next page recounts its failure.

National Women's Political Caucus:

http://www.incacorp.com/nwpc

Latinos

The conditions that Mexican Americans, people of Hispanic origin, and other groups increasingly classified as Latinos sought to escape in their struggle for civil rights are directly connected to their exploitation as laborers. Following the Mexican Revolution of 1910, many Mexicans migrated to the American

The Failure of the Equal Rights Amendment

> Equality of rights under the law shall not be denied or abridged by the United States or by any State on account of sex.

Had this simple amendment been ratified, the Equal Rights Amendment (ERA) would have shifted the burden of proof in discrimination cases from men and women claiming to have suffered discrimination onto those accused of discrimination.

But the amendment process was designed to allow only the ratification of proposals with strong national support. From 1923 to 1972, the ERAs proposed in each session of Congress and backed by every president lacked such support. But by the end of the 1960s, the women's movement and feminist organizations seemed to have changed the political climate. Public opinion, both major parties, and most political leaders were now for the ERA.

Within a year after Congress submitted the ERA for ratification in 1972, 30 states had ratified it. But then, with only eight more states needed, anti-ERA campaigns by Phyllis Schlafly's Eagle Forum and others spread fears that the amendment would subvert traditional family values, force women into the labor force and into combat, and require coed toilets. State legislators recoiled from such political heat. As a result, only five more states ratified the ERA before the deadline was reached, and some states even tried to rescind (take back) their ratification. Congress then extended the deadline until June 30, 1982. The National Organization for Women (NOW) called for an economic boycott of the states that had not yet ratified the amendment. But resistance grew, and in the 1980 presidential campaign the Republican party struck support for the ERA from its platform. The new deadline passed with the ERA still three states short of the number required for ratification. The ERA has since been reintroduced into Congress but has failed to get the necessary two-thirds vote.[1]

Because the ERA was never ratified, the status quo continues: Those with discrimination claims must file suit in local, state, or federal court and rely on existing laws against discrimination. More than 800 sections of the U.S. Code make gender-based distinctions, and there are thousands more such laws at lower levels. So even without the ERA these laws may be challenged in federal court under the equal protection clause of the Fourteenth Amendment or in the 17 states that have put ERAs in their own constitutions. But such legal processes are exceedingly slow and costly. A national ERA would have made it easier to win such challenges and to halt the placement of gender distinctions in new laws and regulations.

---

[1] For detailed accounts of this process, see Jane J. Mansbridge, *Why We Lost the ERA* (Chicago: University of Chicago Press, 1986); Mary Frances Berry, *Why the ERA Failed* (Bloomington: Indiana University Press, 1986).

Southwest to work in agriculture, mining, factories, and on railroads. During the Great Depression more than 300,000 were deported to shrink the welfare rolls. In the 1940s, violence against those who remained became widespread, with vigilante groups in south Texas and even law-enforcement officials (mainly the Texas Rangers) badgering, beating, and murdering Mexicans to scare them off their land. The few Mexican-American children who went to school endured substandard, segregated conditions with inexperienced teachers. Few learned English, and most dropped out to work in the fields.

By the 1960s, with one-third of their 4 million living below the poverty line, Latinos were the "most neglected, least sponsored, most orphaned major minority group in the United States,"[29] suffering widespread discrimination in education, voting rights, employment, salaries, housing, and the legal system. Children were typically sent to vocational rather than academic schools and classified as mentally retarded more often than other students because of teachers' prejudices and the Anglo-oriented tests used to evaluate them.

Accommodation and Assimilation

Like black activism, Latino activism developed in two stages. The first, initiated by middle-class community leaders concerned with accommodation and assimilation, sought acceptance and fair treatment from the dominant Anglo culture by following its rules. But when more than half a million Mexicans immigrated to the United States following World War I, Anglos feared they would be inundated by the "flood" of immigrants, and Mexican-American citizens feared that newcomers would undercut their salaries and take their jobs. In 1929 middle-class Mexican Americans met in Corpus Christi, Texas, to form the League of United Latin American Citizens (LULAC). Its priority—to fight segregation in education—was based on the belief that public schools would socialize their children and equip them for equal opportunity. LULAC also opposed attempts to classify Mexican Americans as anything but white (Census Bureau regulations were requiring employers to report Latinos as "colored") to avoid the legal hardships imposed on blacks.[30] LULAC successfully challenged California's policy of segregated schools in state court and went on to defeat the same policy in Texas and in other southwestern states. In 1954, LULAC lawyers won a Supreme Court victory against the State of Texas prohibiting the exclusion of Mexican Americans from jury duty.[31]

When Mexican-American veterans returned home after World War II expecting fair and equal treatment, they were met with discrimination. In response, Texas civil rights activists created the American G.I. Forum to provide proper burials for Mexican-American soldiers rejected by private mortuaries and cemeteries and to help veterans obtain their government benefits. The group then worked for increased political participation, school desegregation, and assistance to illegal aliens.

By far the most visible Latino actor in American politics has been the Mexican American Legal Defense and Education Fund (MALDEF), a public interest law firm. Launched in 1968 with help from the Ford Foundation and modeled on the NAACP Legal Defense and Education Fund, MALDEF fought the *Rodriguez* and *Plyler* cases, even though the *Plyler* case angered some Latinos because it raised property taxes to pay for educating illegal aliens.

Hispanic
This term (literally, "lover of Spain") originally referred to immigrants predominantly from Spain. It was first used by the federal government during the Nixon administration, which created the Office of Hispanic Affairs out of the Offices of Mexican American and Puerto Rican Affairs. In 1980 the Census Bureau adopted the term. Today many reject it as Eurocentric.

Latino
Spanish-speaking U.S. residents disagree over what to call themselves, and the connotations associated with the various terms change over time. The 1992 Latino National Political Survey shows that intellectuals prefer the pan-ethnic term *Latino*, while others prefer *Hispanic*, *Mexican*, *Mexican American*, *Puerto Rican*, or *Cuban*.

Anglo
This term is widely used in the Southwest to differentiate the dominant white population and culture from the black or African-American and the Latino or Mexican-American. It derives from the English origin of the culture but is extended to all people who are not obviously black or Latino so long as English is their native language.

illegal aliens
Those who dislike the negative connotations of *illegal aliens* prefer the term *undocumented workers*. Those who dislike the euphemism of that term may decide that *illegal aliens* is a more accurate choice. It is impossible to avoid the politics of language in either case.

LULAC:
http://www.mundo.com/lulac.html

MALDEF:
http://www.maldef.org

Polls show that Mexican Americans are split along class lines on the issue of illegal immigration. Until the mid-1960s, leaders favored restricting it, but during the 1970s and 1980s they ignored the issue, turning their attention to economic, educational, and discrimination issues. While many expressed alarm that the government was losing control of U.S. borders, Mexican-American elites (mainly employers) did not object to the influx of illegal aliens who provided a cheap source of labor. In 1986 Congress passed legislation prohibiting the hiring of illegal aliens.

Protest Politics and Community Activism

During the 1960s, militant Latino advocates for the poor and working class rejected LULAC's strategy of accommodation. In 1962 labor leader Cesar Chavez began organizing farm workers in Delano, California. Meanwhile, the sight of aid flowing to blacks following the big-city riots of the mid-1960s led some Latinos to conclude that militancy worked. Reies López Tijerina in New Mexico organized efforts to regain lands lost in the Anglo conquest, even appealing to the Mexican government for support and occupying certain forests until expelled by U.S. troops. In Denver Rodolfo "Corky" Gonzalez founded La Crusada para la Justicia (Crusade for Justice) to protest policy brutality, the Vietnam War, and the failure of the Great Society programs to eliminate poverty. Under the leadership of José Angel Gutierrez, these new militants, who called themselves Chicanos, formed La Raza Unida in Crystal City, Texas, in 1969. The party flourished for several years in various parts of the Southwest and then faded.

Since the 1970s, community organizers have utilized the protest tactics of Saul Alinsky (Chapter 6) to improve local services. They have also trained community leaders and helped Latinos craft political organizations out of their churches, unions, service organizations, and neighborhood groups. Focusing on local police protection, housing, paved streets, job training, and economic development, they have avoided hard-to-win goals such as bilingual education and a more sympathetic policy toward Central America. Many would now like to mobilize Latinos as a "national minority" to increase their political power.

Chicanos

Originally this term came from *Mejicano*, meaning "little Mexican kid" in Spanish. During the 1960s Mexican-American activists used it to assert their ethnic and racial (*mestizo*) identity. Mexican Americans are the descendants of Spanish Europeans and Native American peoples. Every October 12, El Dia de la Raza (The Day of the Race), Spanish-speaking Americans throughout the hemisphere celebrate the birth of Chicano peoples.

Native Americans and Indians

Though these terms are used interchangeably in this book, it is important to note that Indian peoples prefer to call themselves by the names of their respective nations. Native Americans are citizens of the nation, the state in which they reside, and the Indian nation to which they belong.

Native Americans

Native Americans have endured a long history of injustice that began with the taking of their lands by European colonists. The injustice continued with the Indian Removal Act of 1830, which called for the relocation of southern Indians to territories across the Mississippi River that were, in the next half century, again taken for white settlement. The last violent confrontation was the Wounded Knee Massacre in 1890,[32] but efforts were already under way to Christianize and assimilate the Indians. In 1887, Congress passed an act that permitted reservation land to be allotted to individuals legally "severed" from their tribes, with the result that tribal sovereignty was undermined and more than half of reservation lands were lost to native peoples.[33]

Assimilation

As with black and Latino activism, Native American activism developed in two stages—one traditional, the other militant. The goals of the Society of American Indians (SAI), formed in 1911, were "pan-Indianism" (uniting all Indians) and assimilation into the dominant culture. After thousands of Indians volunteered in World War I, Congress granted Indians citizenship and the right to vote in 1924. The law did not take full effect until 1948, however, when the Supreme Court struck down clauses in Arizona's and New Mexico's constitutions forbidding Indians from voting. In 1934, as part of the New Deal, Congress passed the Indian Reorganization Act, which allowed tribes to write their own constitutions, run their own judicial systems (subject to limitations by Congress), and determine tribal membership. That same year Congress granted tribes federal aid for education, medical, and other services, which were administered by states and later by private organizations.

Pan-Indianism intensified with the return of World War II veterans, who, no longer willing to tolerate discrimination, founded the National Congress of American Indians (NCAI) in 1944. Like the NAACP, the NCAI lobbied government and litigated in the courts to end inequalities. When Congress terminated the legal standing of tribes in 1953, forcing Native Americans off their reservations and into major urban centers where there was greater access to training and jobs, the NCAI led the opposition. Although the program was halted in 1958, by 1960 some 60,000 Native Americans resided in urban ghettos.

> Native American resources on the Net:
> http://www/nypl.org/research/chass/grd/intguides/native/html
>
> NCAI:
> http://www.ncai.org

Militant and Legal Activism

With the formation of the militant National Indian Youth Council (NIYC) in the early 1960s, these strategies of assimilation began to meet resistance. Militants objected, for example, that the American Civil Rights Act of 1968, which extended provisions in the Bill of Rights to protect members of tribes from tribal punishments, violated tribal justice and self-determination. They launched "direct action" protests, such as the 1969 occupation of Alcatraz island (an abandoned federal prison) and the 1973 American Indian Movement (AIM) occupation of Wounded Knee, South Dakota, site of the 1890 massacre.

After President Richard Nixon called for reforms in 1970, Congress restored some ancestral lands to their owners and made the Bureau of Indian Affairs (BIA) more responsive. But when Congress and the BIA resisted most of Nixon's proposals, national Native American organizations marched on Washington in 1972 to publicize their cause. They occupied the BIA for six days and found records revealing that the agency had mishandled Indian money, neglected Indian safety, and failed to protect Indian property rights.[34]

By the late 1970s, tribes in a number of states filed (and sometimes won) suits to obtain lands illegally taken from them more than 100 years ago. President Jimmy Carter tried to increase the role of Native Americans in government, choosing a

Blackfoot as his assistant secretary of the interior for Indian affairs and a Chippewa to head the BIA. Meanwhile, more and more tribes sought to regain ancestral water and fishing rights through lawsuits supported by a nonprofit law firm, the Native American Rights Fund.

The Reagan administration reduced the federal government's role in Native American affairs, cutting spending, giving tribes control of about one-third of the BIA's programs, and encouraging partnerships with private corporations. Some tribal leaders feared that this policy would shift dependency to the private sector, which would withdraw support once the tribes' natural resources were exhausted.

In 1996, a federal court upheld a claim by an Alaskan tribal government to the authority to tax nonnatives who use their land. The fact that native tribes own more than one-tenth of the state's territory has alarmed state officials, who have apportioned $1 million for an appeal to the Supreme Court.[35]

Bill Clinton was the first president to invite leaders of all the Native American tribes to meet with him and top administration officials at the White House. Indian leaders were pleased that Clinton treated the talks as government-to-government consultations. He is shown at left with Gaiashkibos (*center*) of the Chippewa people in Wisconsin and Wilbur Between Lodges (*right*) of the Oglala Sioux of South Dakota.

Environmental Activism and Casino Gambling

When Native American activists struggle to protect their environments, they are also struggling to protect their religions. Today they conduct direct-mail campaigns in an effort to preserve dozens of sacred sites on 720 million acres of federal lands.

In recent years, more than 200 tribes have turned to casino gambling and bingo halls as a way of rebuilding their nations.[36] Disputes over the practice abound, even among Indians themselves. Federal and state officials wanting reservation casinos to pay taxes just like those outside reservations were overruled by Congress, which in 1988 recognized Indian sovereignty over gaming. The law, however, imposed regulations on Indian gambling not imposed on state gambling: only tribal governments may own and benefit from gambling, and they must first negotiate compacts with their states to determine what types of gambling will be permitted.[37] Opponents of the law argue that the casino owners are not legitimate Indians, while advocates say that casinos will help lift tribes out of poverty. Some Indians fear that gambling will erode their sense of community and tradition.

Asian Americans

Asian Americans
This term includes the following ethnic groups: Japanese, Koreans, Chinese, Filipinos, Southeast Asians, Pacific Islanders, and East Indians.

Today Asian Americans are better educated and more prosperous than most minorities. According to the 1990 census, they constitute 3 percent of the population (7.3 million people) and are also the fastest-growing minority. Still, like other minorities, they have an appalling history of discrimination.

Immigration Quotas and Internment

In the mid-1800s, the U.S. government admitted Chinese immigrants to work in factories and build railroads. When their numbers alarmed white Californians, Congress passed the Chinese Exclusion Act (1882), which kept Chinese laborers out of the country for ten years. Renewed periodically, this act was the start of immigration restrictions that culminated in the Immigration Act of 1924, which severely limited immigration and set quotas for nationalities based on numbers of foreign-born in the 1890 census. Chinese and Japanese continued to be excluded.

> **concentration camp**
>
> One cannot avoid the politics of language in naming these camps. Those who rely on the euphemisms of *internment camps* or *detention camps* seek to distance them from connotations of *concentration camp*, a term associated with Nazi Germany's extermination camps for Jews. But Justice Hugo Black used the harsher term *concentration camp* in his *Korematsu* dissent. Scholars who use it today are attempting to underscore the extreme injustice done under cover of law.

When, in the 1890s, Japanese immigrants began to come to the United States in larger numbers, they encountered the same hostility the Chinese had faced. Eventually California law prohibited the Japanese from buying or leasing land, and in 1907 President Theodore Roosevelt prevented the segregation of Asian children by San Francisco schools by negotiating an agreement whereby the Japanese government would prevent Japanese laborers from immigrating to the United States. After Japan attacked Pearl Harbor in 1941, President Franklin Roosevelt signed an executive order authorizing the exclusion of suspect persons from designated "military areas." More than 110,000 persons of Japanese descent—two-thirds of them native-born Americans—were removed from West Coast states and placed in concentration camps, forcing them to sell their businesses and property at below market value.[38] In *Korematsu v. United States* (1944) the Supreme Court upheld the action by asserting the "pressing public necessity" of winning the war.[39] That same year, when it was clear that Japan would be defeated and the camps were already being dismantled, the Court ruled that the federal government had no legal authority to imprison Japanese Americans who were loyal, law-abiding citizens.[40]

Political Activism

Inspired by the black power movement of the 1960s, students of Asian descent at the University of California formed the Asian American Political Alliance (AAPA) in 1968 to protest racial oppression and the Vietnam War. The pan-Asian movement soon spread to other campuses. Major universities introduced courses in Asian-American studies, and Asian-American scholars, artists, and filmmakers worked to retrieve the Asian-American past. Some activists followed the Black Panther strategy of community activism and urged traditional civil rights organizations such as the Japanese American Citizens League to revive the issue of internment. In 1988, Congress responded with a public apology and $20,000 to each of 60,000 victims still alive.

Ultimately this movement was unable to incorporate the new refugees from Vietnam, Laos, and Cambodia. Since 1965, when Congress ended immigration

Japanese American Citizens' League:
http://jacl/org

quotas, more poor and unskilled Chinese have come to the "Chinatown" ghettos of major cities, increasing the levels of poverty, crime, and social conflict. Many Chinese who have been illegally smuggled into the country have had to work as virtual indentured servants—often in the underworld economy as prostitutes and drug sellers—to pay for their trip. Thirteen percent of Asian Americans now live in poverty due to a lack of English and job skills. Asian-American women have waged their own struggle against the "triple oppression" of gender, poverty, and the paternalism of their native cultures.[41]

Gays and Lesbians

Before the sexual revolution of the 1960s, gays, lesbians, and bisexuals often hid (closeted) their sexual preferences to escape discrimination. While some still do, more are "coming out of the closet" as public opinion becomes more supportive (see Figure 16.1).

Political Activism

Until recently, sodomy was illegal in every state, though few people were prosecuted for it. Although the *Bowers v. Hardwick* ruling in 1986 (Chapter 15) did not protect the sexual privacy of gay men,[42] it prompted an outpouring of contributions to the major gay and lesbian lobbying group, the National Gay and Lesbian Taskforce.

Gays and lesbians are split over strategy because sexual preference cuts across a wide range of beliefs and experiences. Some activists, such as Torie Osborne, favor linking gay rights with progressive causes. Others, such as the Log Cabin Republicans, seek assimilation as political and economic conservatives. So far no single leader has emerged to unite these different groups. Some activists have tried to network with the National Organization for Women and in 1994 persuaded the NAACP to endorse a gay march for the first time. At the international level, Amnesty International, a human rights group with branches around the world, launched a campaign in 1991 to protect the basic human rights of gay men and lesbians, including those imprisoned solely because of their homosexuality. It also released a study on human rights abuses against homosexuals that details torture, imprisonment, "disappearance," rape, and murder. The organization calls for abolishing antihomosexual laws that persist in many countries and a number of American states.

National Gay and Lesbian Task Force:
http://www.ngltf.org

Legal Activism

Until recently, the armed forces did not accept acknowledged homosexuals, and homosexuality was cause for dishonorable discharge. Gays and lesbians turned to the courts for protection. Commanders argued that gays and lesbians undermine "unit cohesion." Critics of exclusion argue that military units can learn to assimilate gays and lesbians just as they have learned to assimilate African Americans and are learning to assimilate women.

In 1992 a federal judge ordered the Navy to reinstate flier Keith Meinhold after he was dismissed for admitting his homosexuality. During the 1992 presidential campaign Bill Clinton declared it was time for gays and lesbians to be able to serve their country without having to lie. But once in office, where he

Figure 16.1
Public opinion on gay and lesbian rights

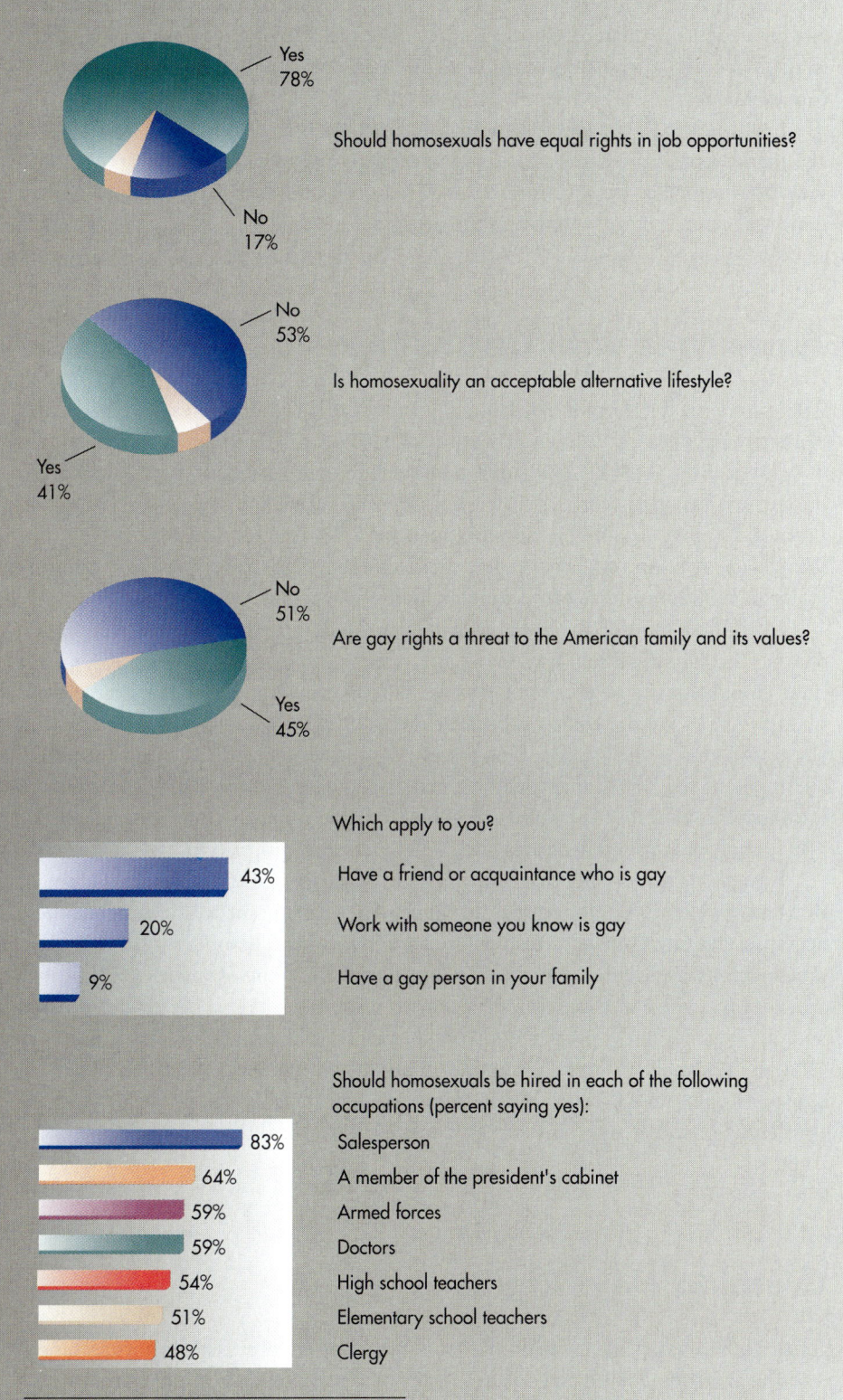

Should homosexuals have equal rights in job opportunities?
- Yes 78%
- No 17%

Is homosexuality an acceptable alternative lifestyle?
- No 53%
- Yes 41%

Are gay rights a threat to the American family and its values?
- No 51%
- Yes 45%

Which apply to you?
- 43% Have a friend or acquaintance who is gay
- 20% Work with someone you know is gay
- 9% Have a gay person in your family

Should homosexuals be hired in each of the following occupations (percent saying yes):
- 83% Salesperson
- 64% A member of the president's cabinet
- 59% Armed forces
- 59% Doctors
- 54% High school teachers
- 51% Elementary school teachers
- 48% Clergy

Source: *Newsweek* poll published September 14, 1992.

faced a resistant military and a rising tide of public opposition, he settled instead for a "don't ask, don't tell, don't pursue" policy that allows gays and lesbians to remain in the military if they keep their sexual preference to themselves. In 1994 the Clinton administration decided not to appeal the Meinhold case to the Supreme Court, saying it would cloud the issue because it had preceded the current Clinton policy. In April 1996, Congress repealed legislation forcing the dismissal of military personnel with HIV, the virus that causes AIDS.

In *Romer v. Evans* (1996), the Supreme Court by a 6–3 margin struck down an amendment to the Colorado constitution denying gays and lesbians the right to seek legal remedies for discrimination based on homosexuality.[43] Editorial pages variously criticized and supported the decision.[44]

Americans with Disabilities

Civil rights for the 43 million disabled people in the United States have been won primarily by federal laws and regulations. In 1990 Congress passed the Americans with Disabilities Act (ADA), prohibiting the federal government from discriminating against disabled workers and requiring affirmative action in their hiring and promotion plus "reasonable accommodations" for disabled workers. By the time the law took effect in 1992, it had been expanded to cover private employers (some 500,000 businesses) and to include the right to sue.

In its first month, more than 26,000 disabled workers filed discrimination charges through the Equal Employment Opportunity Commission (EEOC) against their employers. These were not just workers in wheelchairs. Half of these complaints were for back problems, because the ADA classifies as disabled people with back problems, arthritis, high blood pressure, and heart problems. Upon receiving a complaint, the EEOC investigates it and refers workers with valid complaints to lawyers who take the complaints to court or arrange out-of-court settlements. By 1994, about 2 million businesses had come under the authority of the ADA.

Business leaders argue that many lawsuits lack merit and that the requirement of "reasonable accommodations" is vague. They also point to the expense these accommodations involve as well as the hike in workers' compensation they must pay. Proponents counter that the so-called expenses are investments that improve worker productivity. Moreover, people with disabilities have a strong incentive to succeed because the workplace also ends their social isolation. And those with jobs pay taxes. The public is often sympathetic to the needs of the disabled because, as columnist George Will reminds us, few of us are likely to change our skin color or our gender, but we all could become disabled "on the drive home tonight."[45]

Equal Employment Opportunity Commission:
http://www.mcaa.org/labor/eeco/aeupdat.htm

Creating New Rights

In the United States the creation of new rights—for children, the unborn, animals, and the environment—has tended to occur over an extended period during which advocates and critics debate their merits. Some of their concerns have made it into the law, while others are being heeded by politicians, the media, the law, businesses, and international organizations.

Children

Recognition of children's civil rights, like that of children's civil liberties (Chapter 15), has been slow because children have long been regarded as parental property. Interest groups such as the conservative Child Welfare League of America, founded in 1920 as a league of voluntary organizations, and the liberal Children's Defense Fund, a nonprofit organization of lawyers, researchers, and lobbyists, actively lobby for children's concerns, which keep growing.

Federal concern for children's welfare dates from the first White House conference on children in 1909 and the establishment three years later of a Children's Bureau to study and report on the condition of children. In 1918, despite widespread support for a new federal law restricting child labor by banning the interstate transportation of factory goods produced by child labor, the Supreme Court struck down the law as exceeding the scope of the commerce clause. In his dissent, Justice Oliver Wendell Holmes noted ironically that the Court upheld laws banning interstate commerce in alcoholic beverages but not "the product of ruined lives."[46] In 1941 the Court finally broadened its interpretation of the commerce clause.[47] In the 1960s, Head Start addressed the educational needs of poor children. Widely recognized as a success, its budget is always in danger of being cut back—a danger increased by welfare reform in 1996. And the needs of children increase as the poor become poorer—a trend that has intensified since the 1980s, so that one-fourth of all American children now live in poverty.[48]

> Children's Defense Fund:
> http://www.ohio.life.org/people/cdf.htm

The Unborn

The belief, held by Catholics and many non-Catholics, that human life begins at conception runs counter to the English common law principle that life begins at birth. Experts from scientists to ethicists have produced no evidence or arguments to resolve this dispute over *what is* and, therefore, *what's right*. In such situations, the matter is often turned over to the courts. Efforts by the Supreme Court in *Roe v. Wade* (1973) to reach a compromise on a woman's right to privacy (abortion), the interest of the state, and the interest of the fetus did not settle the dispute (Chapter 15). Although some right-to-life advocates accept abortion in cases involving rape, incest, or the threat pregnancy poses to a woman's life, purists insist that all human life—including that of frozen embryos[49]—is sacred and requires protection. So far the Supreme Court has refused to take a position on when a human life begins. If it did it would find itself faced with two conflicting fundamental rights. Those who see no solution to this impasse have emphasized the importance of policies and programs that prevent unwanted pregnancies.

> **fetus**
> Those who use the scientific term *fetus* (Latin for "offspring," "to grow," "to come into being") distance themselves from the difficulty that surrounds naming and defining the unborn human being. Those who use the term *baby* are making a claim for the humanity of the unborn person. Here again, the politics of language is impossible to avoid.

Animals

Do animals have the same sort of rights as humans? Or do humans have certain *duties* toward animals even though animals lack rights? In 1973 Congress passed the Humane Care for Animals Act, which listed these duties: the provision of wholesome food and water, adequate shelter, veterinary care to prevent suffering, and basic humane care and treatment. It also outlawed the cruel beating of domestic animals and animal fights as sport. But such duties do not entail rights.

So far the language of rights has been tailored to human beings who understand what those rights are and how they apply to them. Animal rights advocates point out, however, that we attribute rights to children and the mentally retarded even though they lack an understanding of the meaning and application of rights. Children's rights, for example, are protected by "proxy," by advocates acting on their behalf. Opponents of animal rights point out that "children will grow up, mentally retarded ones might possibly be treated or even cured," and that even healthy people can be incapacitated and need protection.[50] These distinctions have not dissuaded animal rights advocates from trying to obtain money, supporters, and laws that protect domestic animals from conditions of cruelty, painful experiments, and starvation, and wild animals and their habitats from destruction.

The Environment

Unlike human beings, the natural environment is incapable of filing legal suits to protect rights, seeking restitution for damages, and obtaining compensation as the injured party.[51] Indeed, many Westerners assume that the natural environment has no voice or consciousness. But if the environment were treated as a child or a mental incompetent and assigned a guardian (such as an environmental interest group or a government agency) with the power to file suits on its behalf, environmental rights might become law. At present, however, government typically intervenes in environmental matters only when human interests are at stake. And even when private landowners file suit against polluters for poisoning crops, for example, they base their claims not on the rights of the crops but on their right to the money those crops could have brought.

Civil Rights Remedies

Government efforts to remedy social, political, economic, and legal discrimination through court decisions, laws, public policies, and implementing regulations have led to sharp disputes over the legitimacy of these remedies (*what's right*) and their effectiveness (*what works*). One reason is that people disagree over the meaning of **equal opportunity**, as demonstrated in the box on pages 638–639. Another reason is that opinion often substitutes for hard evidence. In the case of the Americans with Disabilities Act of 1990, for example, federal and state agencies bound by its mandates have failed to gather the data needed to track the act's effectiveness.[52] Without knowing *what is*, it is impossible to know how well a policy is *working*. Thus many remedies have been proposed, tried, revised, or abandoned in an inefficient and highly political process of *learning by doing*.

Integration: Compulsion and Incentives

When none of the federal government's civil rights initiatives—the Supreme Court's decisions striking down state segregation laws, the president's use of federal troops and voting registrars, Congress's civil rights laws—put an end to discrimination, the government shifted to a policy of **integration**, bringing the races together. The assumption was that if whites and blacks with the same educational and professional backgrounds and interests got together, racial conflict would subside. This approach has worked best for those with the highest socioeconomic status (SES). In the military services, people of different races, ethnic groups, and religions have been forced to live and work together since President Harry Truman desegregated the military by executive order in 1948. After racial conflict broke out among U.S. troops in Vietnam, the military developed workshops to reduce such conflict.

Bringing private citizens together has proved far more difficult.[53] Compulsion was tried most extensively in public education, where, once segregated schools were outlawed, separation was due to segregated neighborhoods. The courts resorted to two types of mandates to achieve racial balance: the **pairing of schools** (requiring black, white, and brown schools within a school district to combine) and the **busing of students** (requiring school districts to transport students of one race to a school whose students were primarily of another race). Court-ordered, or "forced," busing was tried in various northern and southern cities but quickly lost political support. Many concluded that the only other way to end school segregation was to end residential segregation. But in 1964 the Supreme Court declined to review a decision by lower federal courts which held that the *Brown* decision did not require ending residential segregation.[54] Although the Fair Housing Act of 1968 prohibited discrimination in sales and rentals, the practice of **redlining**, whereby lending institutions denied mortgages in areas they designated as slums, diminished its effect. Moreover, few blacks could afford housing in white neighborhoods, and the Courts required desegregation only *within* school districts, not *across* school district lines. As a result of 40 years of **white flight**—the exodus of whites from the inner cities to the suburbs—more children are attending all-black or all-white schools now than at the time of Martin Luther King's death. Two-thirds of all black children know few, if any, whites.[55]

The incentive approach—allowing students to transfer to a different school—has generally worked better than compulsion. Blacks are more likely to transfer to white schools than whites to black schools because white schools usually have better resources. In recent decades school districts have experimented with the incentive of **magnet schools**—schools specializing in subject areas such as math, science, and the performing arts, which attract students of all races and ethnic groups. However, magnet schools have been criticized for their expense and for robbing regular schools of their top talents, and many school boards are trying to do away with them.

The Politics of Knowledge

Defining Equal Opportunity

Americans take pride in being "the land of opportunity," and liberals and conservatives alike tend to agree that equal opportunity means getting an equal place at the starting line. But where, exactly, is this starting line located? As early as prenatal care and parental education and day care, or in public school and higher education and the job market?

Wherever the starting line is, individuals do not start out with the same chances of winning. As economist Alan Blinder points out, some of us are born into wealthy families, or with minds capable of pursuing well-paid and satisfying professions, or with the talent and drive for success in business. Some of us benefit from "good upbringings" that provide the education and instill the values that promote "success." Others of us are born into poverty, or with a lesser capacity for education and economic success, or into circumstances in which these goals are not expected or supported. In short, people approach the "equal opportunity" starting line with vastly *unequal* chances of winning.[1]

Blinder then moves beyond describing equal opportunity (*what is*) to the moral question of fairness or equity (*what's right*). What should be done to equalize the competition for equal opportunity, and who should do it? Americans are still debating whether civil rights should include "economic" or "welfare" rights. That all children in America are entitled to a free public education in nonsegregated schools is widely accepted, but the Supreme Court rejected their entitlement to equality of education in *Rodriguez*.[2]

Deciding where to draw the equal opportunity starting line, especially in education, is a politically sensitive issue. Conservatives strongly oppose policies aimed at achieving equal outcomes, or *equality of results*. Liberals argue that the "the bare right" to attend school is not enough. Children, they say, must be "furnished with enough parental guidance and support, enough nurturing day care, enough nutrition and health care, enough exposure to books, music, and art, enough inspirational teachers and other motivational influences, enough psychological counseling if needed, to want schooling, to stick with it, [and] to make the most of it."[3] These critics argue that "real opportunity" should replace the misleading slogan of "equal opportunity."

Many conservatives regard these liberal concerns as fine ideals but don't

Affirmative Action for All?

Minorities and women face a dilemma: they need good educations to get good jobs, but they need good jobs to afford neighborhoods with good schools. The federal government has tried to integrate the workplace through **equal employment opportunity** (EEO)—a personnel policy that guarantees the same opportunities to all individuals—and by prohibiting employers from discriminating on the basis of "race, color, religion, sex, or national origin" (Title VII of the Civil Rights Act of 1964). Ironically, opponents of the act supported including the category "sex" in the bill in the hopes that extending coverage to women would defeat the bill; instead, it helped the bill pass.

believe that Americans should be forced to pay for them. They also doubt that money alone can buy intangibles such as "inspiration" and "motivation" (*what works*). One study found that the investment of $40 million in four cities (Dayton, Little Rock, Pittsburgh, and Savannah) with a high proportion of disadvantaged youth did not raise test scores significantly, although it did lower the dropout rate slightly. A Heritage Foundation study has also found that many of the states which spend the most per pupil have the lowest test scores.[4] However, critics of these studies say that the money has been spent foolishly and often failed to affect the students.

Such disputes are even more contentious in the area of affirmative action, where the use of quotas is aimed at producing specified results. In the *Adarand* case, Justice Clarence Thomas argued that it was "irrelevant whether a government's racial classifications are drawn by those who wish to oppress a race or by those who have a sincere desire to help those thought to be disadvantaged. In each instance it is racial discrimination, plain and simple." Justice John Paul Stevens disagreed: "There is no moral or Constitutional equivalence between a policy that is designed to perpetuate a caste system and one that seeks to eradicate racial subordination."[5]

Pragmatists say that those who search for neutral principles (which they argue do not exist) by asking whether a policy is "fair" or results in "reverse racism" avoid responsibility for solving real-world problems. Their prescription: Start asking "What's wrong and how can we fix it?"[6]

---

[1] Alan Blinder, *Hard Heads, Soft Hearts: Tough-Minded Economics for a Just Society* (Reading, Mass.: Addison-Wesley, 1987), 23–24.
[2] *San Antonio Independent School District v. Rodriguez*, 411 U.S. 1 (1973).
[3] James MacGregor Burns and Stewart Burns, *A People's Charter: The Pursuit of Rights in America* (New York: Knopf, 1991), 450.
[4] The five-year study was conducted by the Annie E. Casey Foundation and completed in June 1993. For a discussion of this debate, see "True or False: More Money Buys Better Schools," *Business Week*, August 2, 1993, 62.
[5] *Adarand Constructors, Inc. v. Peña*, 115 S. Ct 2097 (1995).
[6] Stanley Fish, "When Principles Get in the Way," *New York Times*, December 26, 1996, A27.

In 1965 President Lyndon Johnson issued an executive order calling for the implementation of EEO laws by **affirmative action** (AA)—more aggressive policies aimed at overcoming the effects of past discrimination. If business, labor, and educational institutions wanted to receive federal contracts or tax dollars, they would have to follow federal nondiscrimination guidelines to ensure that they recruited, trained, and promoted a sufficient percentage of workers from previously excluded groups, even if those workers had not themselves been victims of discrimination. Companies with large federal contracts and labor unions with persistent patterns of discrimination were required to develop AA plans that would open more opportunities to "underutilized" minorities and women in any job category. Similarly, colleges and universities receiving federal funds were required to admit women and minority students in proportion to their percentage or availability in the population.

These numerical **quotas** angered those (mainly white men) who were rejected by an employer or a university while minorities with the same or lesser merit were accepted. Critics have attacked quotas as **reverse discrimination** and reverse racism because they give minorities preferential treatment at the expense of whites and men who are themselves innocent of discrimination. Critics also point out that the language in Title VII prohibits racial discrimination against all races, including whites. Defenders of quotas claim they are necessary to cope with the lingering effects of segregation and to break the cycle of economic and educational poverty that makes a mockery of equal opportunity.[56]

Advocates also claimed that the best quota is one based on **proportionality**—the proportional percentage of minorities in the population as a whole rather than in some lesser group, such as a student body. Key issues have been whether courts should rely on local or national populations to determine proportionality and whether, in employment cases, they should use the *labor* pool or the *job applicant* pool as the base population. Some judges have argued that firms should use the applicant pool because minorities apply for blue-collar jobs in greater proportion than their percentage in the population. However, such a policy of proportionality would perpetuate the patterns of racism that result in whites having white-collar jobs and minorities having blue-collar jobs.[57]

Affirmative Action in Universities

Allan Bakke, age 32 and a Vietnam veteran and engineer, had been rejected in 1973 and 1974 by 11 different medical schools, even though his record was superior to the records of minorities who were accepted by the University of California at Davis Medical School under its AA program. Bakke claimed that the university's use of race as a criterion of admission violated the equal protection clause of the Fourteenth Amendment and the Civil Rights Act of 1964. The university argued that the people of California would benefit if more minority students became doctors because many would practice in ghettos and improve the health care of minorities and the poor. In 1978 the Supreme Court held, in *Regents of the University of California v. Bakke*, that university AA programs were constitutional.[58] But it also held that Bakke should be admitted to the U.C. Davis Medical School because its admissions policy improperly used race as the sole criterion for the 16 positions it held open for minority students. (This was a less-than-proportional quota because 16 positions represented a smaller percentage than the minority population in California.) The Court held that race could be one but not the only criterion. The Court also rejected proportionality as a standard for deciding such cases.

Eighteen years later, in *Hopwood v. Texas*, a federal appeals court surprised the academic world by striking down the University of Texas Law School's AA admissions program, stating that race could not be used at all as a factor in admission, "even for the wholesome purpose of correcting perceived racial imbalance in the student body."[59] (The law school was not adhering to rigid quotas: the Texas population is 11.6 percent black and 25.6 percent Latino, while the 1992 entering class was 8 percent black and 10.7 percent Latino.) The Supreme Court let the decision stand even though it was at odds with the *Bakke* decision.

Affirmative Action in the Workplace

In 1971 the Supreme Court ruled, in *Griggs v. Duke Power Company*, that it was a violation of Title VII to require applicants to have a high school diploma and pass an intelligence test to be eligible for jobs (which until then had been filled only by whites) that did not require such qualifications.[60] And in 1979 the Supreme Court, in *United Steelworkers Union v. Weber*, concluded that Title VII did permit policies based on racial preferences.[61] Brian F. Weber, a white employee in Kaiser Aluminum's plant in Gramercy, Louisiana, argued that because of the company's voluntary AA program he was passed over for promotion in favor of blacks with less seniority. The Court found voluntary racial quotas to be consistent with the Civil Rights Act of 1964.

In *Fullilove v. Klutznick* (1980), New York contractors challenged the constitutionality of a congressional statute requiring that 10 percent of federal grants for local public works projects be set aside for minority-owned businesses, even if they are not the lowest bidders, so long as they are controlled by "Negroes, Spanish-speaking, Orientals, Indians, Eskimos, or Aleuts." The Court upheld the law on grounds that the constitutional power to provide for the "general welfare" gives Congress "latitude" to allocate special rights to racial and ethnic minorities "to achieve the goal of equality of opportunity."[62]

But in 1984 the Court backtracked, holding that AA programs did not prevent minorities who were the last to be hired from being the first to be fired unless the employee could prove that the layoff was discriminatory.[63] In 1987, the Court upheld a decision requiring the all-white Alabama police force to hire one black trooper for every white trooper until blacks made up one-quarter of the police force—their proportion in the state population—and also ruled that women and minorities may be employed and promoted ahead of white men even when companies have no previous record of discriminating against those groups.[64]

But the Reagan administration, which opposed AA, argued that the courts should apply the strict scrutiny test to all race-based laws and policies, and the Supreme Court also began to treat quotas and race as a suspect classification. In 1989 the Court held that the city of Richmond's set-aside program for minority businesses violated the equal protection clause.[65] Richmond had required contractors who received city construction contracts to set aside 30 percent of their contract allowance for subcontractors whose businesses were at least 51 percent owned by minorities—a policy that was based on the proportionality principle but that conservatives complained discriminated against whites.

The Court continued this conservative course in *Wards Cove Packing Co. v. Antonio*,[66] a 1989 decision that modified its *Griggs* ruling, which had called for

Jean Marie Burr coaches Brown University's women's basketball team. In 1997 the Supreme Court refused to hear an appeal from Brown, and thus let stand a federal district court decision that found Brown in violation of Title IX, the federal law prohibiting sex discrimination at universities. The decision found that Brown had failed to offer women and men opportunities to participate in sports that were in close enough proportion to their respective undergraduate enrollments.

proportional representation of minorities in each occupation. In *Wards Cove* the issue was whether Alaskan salmon canneries that employed mainly whites in skilled jobs and mainly minorities in unskilled jobs were practicing discrimination. While a federal appeals court said that the canneries would have to show that they could not do business without this imbalance, the Supreme Court held that such a requirement was too costly and time consuming and predicted that businesses faced with such a requirement would turn to racial quotas to protect themselves from lawsuits. The Court thus shifted the burden of proof in such cases from the employers to the plaintiffs. This shift coincided with evidence that blacks and whites had very different perceptions of how blacks were treated in their communities (see Figure 16.2).

As the Court made it harder for workers to sue for discrimination, civil rights activists turned to Congress and state legislatures for support. In 1991 Congress attempted to shift the burden of proof in employment discrimination cases back to employers with the Civil Rights Restoration Act, which undercut the Court's decision in *Ward's Cove*. But in 1993, the Court shifted the burden of proof back to employees. In *St. Mary's Honor Center v. Hicks*, plaintiffs claimed that their dismissal as a result of their company's restructuring created a **disparate impact**

Figure 16.2
Public opinion on the treatment of blacks, 1990

Question: In your opinion, how well do you think blacks are treated in your community—the same as whites are, not very well, or badly?

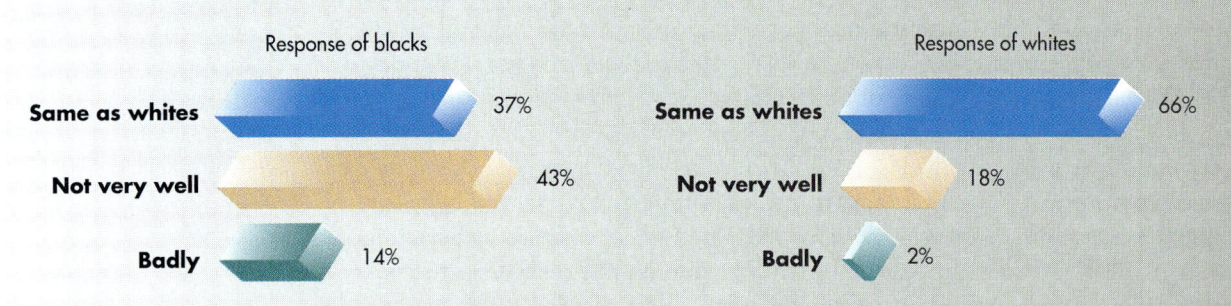

Response of blacks
- Same as whites: 37%
- Not very well: 43%
- Badly: 14%

Response of whites
- Same as whites: 66%
- Not very well: 18%
- Badly: 2%

Question: Looking back over the last ten years, do you think the quality of life of blacks has gotten better, stayed the same, or gotten worse?

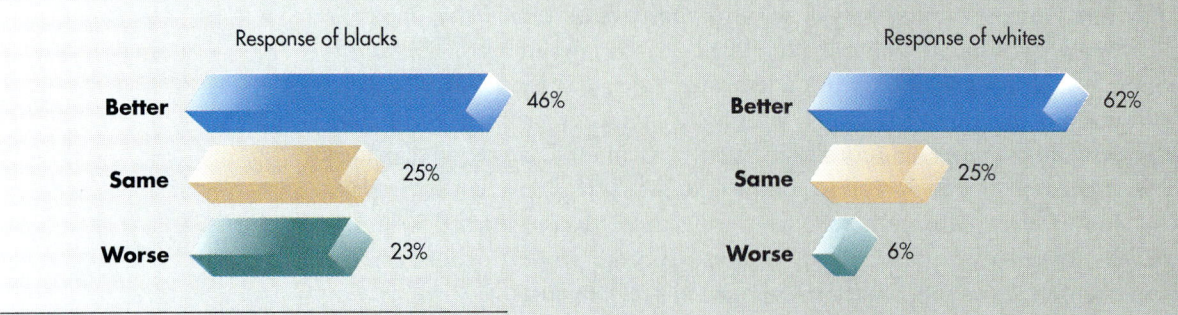

Response of blacks
- Better: 46%
- Same: 25%
- Worse: 23%

Response of whites
- Better: 62%
- Same: 25%
- Worse: 6%

Source: "Social Issues," *Public Perspective*, April/May 1997, p.55.

on older workers, hitting them harder than others.[67] Their company said its motive for firing older, more experienced workers with higher salaries was to become more competitive in the marketplace. But the older workers argued that even if the discrimination was unintended, it was illegal under Title VII. Justice Antonin Scalia, writing for the Court, held that intent is necessary to show discrimination. Some experts predict that disparate impact will soon be applied to minorities and women and will dominate the civil rights agenda in the future.

In 1995 the Court ruled in *Adarand Constructors, Inc. v. Peña* that AA programs must be narrowly targeted to the past discrimination they seek to remedy.[68] The decision prompted the Clinton administration to review all federal AA programs. Deciding to "mend" rather than "end" them, the administration directed federal agencies to reform or abolish any AA program that was (1) quota-based; (2) created preferences for unqualified individuals; (3) resulted in reverse discrimination; or (4) persisted after the remedy was no longer needed.

Equal Pay and Comparable Worth

In the context of a democracy, lower wages for women seem unjust. In the context of capitalism, lower wages for women are simply *what is*. The marketplace does not treat men and women equally in terms of skills, effort, and responsibility for two reasons. First, the rules of the economic system place a higher value on the handling of money than on the handling of people. Because women do most of the teaching, nursing, and child care, they end up with lower salaries than mostly male bankers, lawyers, and accountants. Second, the rules of the social system have herded women into these low-paying jobs and occupations. The result is that their low wages strongly affect the ability of single and divorced women to support themselves and their children, and of married women to have egalitarian marriages.

Equal Pay

Today men earn roughly 20 to 30 percent more than women (depending on wage level) despite policies aimed at closing this wage gap. In 1963 Congress extended wage protection to some—but far from all—women workers through the Equal Pay Act. In 1972 Congress amended the Equal Pay Act to cover professions, and presidents have issued executive orders banning job discrimination against women and minorities by the federal government and federal contractors. Yet patterns of unequal salaries persist. After narrowing for 20 years, the wage gap began widening again in 1997.

In 1973, the Supreme Court held that "statutory distinctions between the sexes often have the effect of invidiously relegating the entire class of females to inferior legal status without regard to the actual capabilities of its individual members." Sex discrimination, the Court said, "was rationalized by an attitude of 'romantic paternalism' which . . . put women, not on a pedestal, but in a cage."[69] Yet in 1976 the Court ruled that bias in health insurance programs against pregnant workers was not sex discrimination, and a year later it ruled against laws granting sick leave for pregnancy.

In 1978 Congress passed a new pregnancy disability law, effectively overturning the Court's 1976 decision on pregnancy insurance and making it illegal for an employer to refuse to hire or promote a woman because she is pregnant, to fire a worker who becomes pregnant, or to force a woman to take maternity leave. In recent years Congress has guaranteed women the right to obtain credit, participate equally in school sports, receive pensions, obtain tax deductions for child care expenses, and attend private military academies.

Comparable Worth

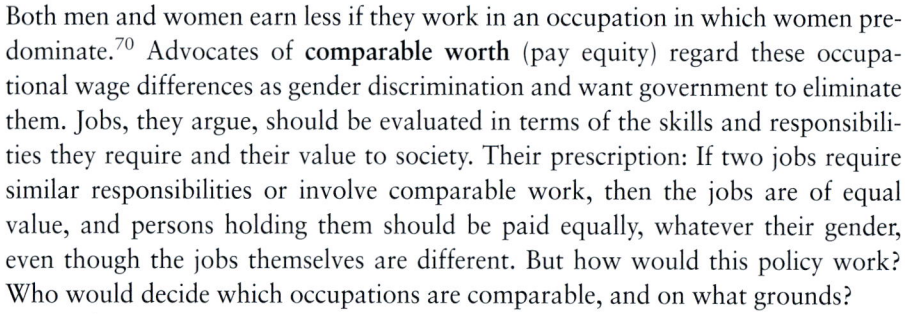

Both men and women earn less if they work in an occupation in which women predominate.[70] Advocates of **comparable worth** (pay equity) regard these occupational wage differences as gender discrimination and want government to eliminate them. Jobs, they argue, should be evaluated in terms of the skills and responsibilities they require and their value to society. Their prescription: If two jobs require similar responsibilities or involve comparable work, then the jobs are of equal value, and persons holding them should be paid equally, whatever their gender, even though the jobs themselves are different. But how would this policy work? Who would decide which occupations are comparable, and on what grounds?

So far these thorny questions have been addressed piecemeal in the courts. In one case, Washington County, Oregon, classified women prison guards as "matrons" and men prison guards as "deputy sheriffs"—a classification used to justify paying the women guards 30 percent less than the men. The women sued and in 1981 the Supreme Court supported their claim.[76] More than a hundred states and cities have since revised their pay structures, and many have raised the pay of jobs held primarily by women. But Congress has passed no laws to remedy the problem in the private sector.

The Reagan administration opposed comparable worth on grounds that, in the words of its head of the Civil Rights Commission, it "is preferential treatment, just like [racial] quotas."[71] A fellow commissioner cast the argument in terms of equality of opportunity and **equality of results**, a distinction conservatives have used to frame the issue to favor their position:

> The attempt to write comparable worth into Federal laws marks a reversal of the civil rights revolution. Comparable worth moves from the assertion of civil and political equality, which we all support, to economic and social equality, which many of us do not support. Guaranteed economic and social equality have never been a part of the heritage of a free country because they ultimately impinge on freedom, by making government the arbiter of the rewards of human effort.[72]

As the box on pages 646–647 shows, political actors disagree on the reasons for the wage gap. One expert sympathetic to this concern suggests that

> acknowledging the connection between skill and gender may open the wage relationship to greater scrutiny, revealing that what society deems valuable is in fact part of a field of social conflict, determined not by intrinsic value, 'natural' merit, or abstract market forces but by power relations. This discovery places comparable worth substantially beyond the meritocratic view of the labor market."[73]

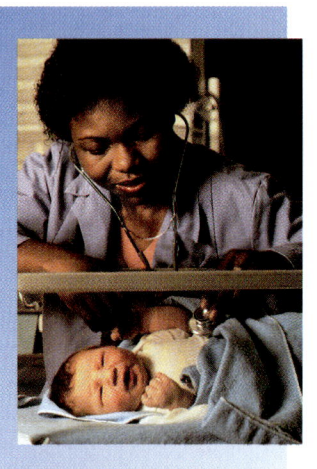

On average, women earn less than men even in jobs of comparable responsibility and difficulty.

The Evolving Ethics of Human Rights

Men are born and remain free and equal in respect of their rights.
—Article I, French Declaration of the Rights of Man, 1789

All human beings are born free and equal in dignity and rights.
—Article I, United Nations Universal
Declaration of Human Rights, 1948

Human rights are the natural rights people hold simply because they are human. Human rights descend from the Old Testament, Magna Carta (1215), the Declaration of Independence (1776), the French Declaration of the Rights of Man (1789), and the Covenant of the League of Nations (1919). Commitment to human rights was renewed in the 1940s with the establishment of the United Nations following the Nazi extermination of millions of Jews, Gypsies, homosexuals, and people with disabilities.

The concept of human rights, like the concept of civil rights, has been expanding at a rapid rate with the passage of more than 70 U.N. resolutions, as Table 16.2 suggests. Like civil rights in the United States, human rights at the international level have been expanded by the creation of *new* rights and the extension of existing rights to new groups. This expansion has occurred in three major waves:

1. the extension since the 1950s of the civil and political rights generated by Western democracies (the sort that appear in the American bills of rights) to other countries
2. the creation since the 1960s of new social, economic, and cultural rights (known as welfare rights)
3. the creation since the 1970s of developmental rights in so-called third world countries.

The U.N. Declaration of Human Rights and Its Instruments

In 1947, shortly after it was created, the United Nations established the Commission on Human Rights. Led by Eleanor Roosevelt, the widow of President Franklin D. Roosevelt, this group of international representatives drafted the Universal Declaration of Human Rights, the first attempt in human history to define human rights for all peoples and to set standards for determining violations. The U.N. General Assembly passed this nonbinding declaration unanimously in 1948.

The goals of the declaration were then translated in 1966 into two covenants intended to bind the countries that sign them even though the United Nations lacks an enforcement mechanism. The first was the International Covenant on Economic, Social and Cultural Rights (ICESCR), which covers basic economic and cultural rights, such as health, education, social security, the right to work

Political Actors Disagree

The Dispute over the Sex Gap in Pay

Feminist advocate: We need comparable worth when studies evaluating equally demanding jobs show that women's jobs pay roughly 20 percent less than men's jobs.

Business critic: Of course there is a sex gap in pay. But much of it is caused by nondiscriminatory factors. After all the relevant adjustments are made, the gap is much smaller. Some of it results from women's roles as wives and mothers, which are determined either by biology or by socialization, as can be seen from the fact that the sex gap in pay between never-married men and never-married women is much smaller than the overall sex gap in pay. Some of the 20 percent sex gap in pay is undoubtedly due to past discrimination against women by educational institutions, in not admitting women to certain programs or counseling them in different directions than men. Even if there was sex discrimination in the labor market in the past, very little remains. Women have made tremendous progress, as evidenced by the fact that there is very little difference in the pay of the youngest cohort of men and women workers.

Sociologist advocate: Yes, there has been improvement, but the gap is still large. Women still earn 76 percent of what men do, up from about 67 percent in 1969. Also, let's not exaggerate how much progress is indicated by the fact that younger cohorts show a smaller sex gap in pay than older cohorts. To some extent, this represents the fact that within each cohort, women's earnings fall farther and farther behind men's over the life cycle, in part because women are concentrated in dead-end jobs that offer fewer promotions and less generous pay increases with seniority. And the most obvious way that women's home responsibilities affect their pay is by reducing their years of employment experience. Finally, the comparison of never-married women with never-married men is unfair because single women have much less human capital (earning power) than single men. And even within this group the sex gap in pay is substantial.

Laissez-faire critic: Perhaps the pay gap is explained by some unmeasured but nondiscriminatory factors, such as ambition or assertiveness. I don't believe that discrimination can persist for long in competitive markets because it is costly to employers.

Socialist-feminist critic: What? Surely capitalists make money by sex discrimination. When they pay women less, they make more money than if they paid women fairly. This is one reason that capitalism and patriarchy go hand in hand.

Laissez-faire critic: No, the real problem is that you socialists often forget that capitalists compete with each other! True, a firm that employs men in high-paying jobs and women in lower-paying jobs makes more money than it would if it employed the same people in the same jobs but paid women more. But if some employers discriminate against women, any other employer can save money by hiring women in men's jobs for less than they currently pay men in such jobs, but more than the women could make elsewhere in women's jobs. Then both the firm and the women would benefit. Surely some

---

and to form and join trade unions, and the right to participate in science and culture. So far 118 countries have signed the ICESCR.

The second and stronger covenant was the International Covenant on Civil and Political Rights (ICCPR), which is "immediately enforceable" in all 115 countries, including the United States, that have signed it since 1976. Sixty-seven countries (though not the United States) have signed the Optional Protocol, which permits those individuals who have had their covenant rights ignored to contact the U.N. Human Rights Commission directly.

A United Nation declaration of rights does not work (it lacks the force of law) until it is turned into a

convention

Convention, covenant, and *treaty* are interchangeable concepts when used to refer to international agreements.

profit-maximizing firms will do this, and when enough of them do it, the nondiscriminatory portion of the wage gap will gradually erode to nothing. In this sense, capitalism is woman's best friend! So what do we need all this government intervention for?

Religious Right critic: I agree completely. The market works!

Business critic: Hear, hear.

Author of this dialogue (sociologist Paula England): This argument that competitive markets counteract discrimination follows from laissez-faire capitalist assumptions. But when members of conservative religious and business groups clothe themselves in the same argument, I suspect an argument of convenience rather than principle. After all, fundamentalist religious groups do not take the laissez-faire position on pornography. Nor do businesses seeking to defend government subsidies, such as tariffs. But is the laissez-faire argument that unaided market forces will destroy discrimination correct?

Sociologist advocate: All this talk about competitive markets might make sense, if it weren't for the fact that many firms have internal markets, especially in the jobs men hold. Internal labor markets mean that there are structured sequences of promotions into higher-level jobs. Workers not already employed in the firm can't compete for these higher-level jobs. Thus, there is no marketwide competition to tempt employers to look for more economical (female) labor in higher-level jobs, as they would if people were hired into these jobs from the external market. So free-market competition just doesn't apply to jobs above the bottom rung of these job ladders.

Laissez-faire economist: Yes, many firms have internal markets. Their job ladders trade off low starting wages for steep wage increases, promotions, job security, and other benefits because the costs of search and on-the-job training make turnover especially expensive. But, roughly speaking, workers looking for jobs know what sort of contracts various jobs offer. So there is enough competition at entry level to provide the erosion of discrimination, even if there isn't market competition higher up the job ladder.

Sociologist Paula England: Yes, market pressures can erode discrimination, but there is no guarantee that it won't take hundreds of years, since the process only works through new cohorts entering firms' internal markets. Women should not have to wait that long for justice.

Notice that sociologist Paula England agrees in part with the laissez-faire claim that market forces erode competition (*what is* and *what works*) but undermines that claim with one of her own: Market forces work far too slowly (*what is*) to be compatible with justice (*what's right*). Thus, speaking from the perspective of an expert, the remedy England prescribes is the same as that of the feminist critic above: comparable worth.

Source: Adapted from Paula England, *Comparable Worth: Theories and Evidence* (New York: Aldine de Gruyter, 1992), 281–283.

---

legal instrument such as a convention and ratified by a specified number of states. For a U.N. convention to have the force of U.S. federal law, for example, it must be:

- adopted by the United Nations
- signed by the U.S. president
- ratified by two-thirds of the Senate
- implemented by enabling legislation passed by both the House and Senate.

Thus when the United States recently ratified the ICCPR, it agreed to enforce its provisions in U.S. courts of law. If U.S. domestic law should conflict with the covenant, the covenant has the greater authority. Thus, a woman whose state does not protect her from marital rape could, for example, appeal directly to the ICCPR.

TABLE 16.2

U.N. Declarations of Human Rights: A Selected Chronology

Year	Declaration	Description
1948	Convention on the Prevention and Punishment of the Crime of Genocide	Recognizes genocide as a crime under international law and states that those accused of it, in wartime or peace, can be tried either by the country in which the crime was committed or by such international tribunals as have jurisdiction.
1959	Declaration of the Rights of the Child	Maintains that children shall enjoy special protection and be given opportunities and facilities, by law and other means, to enable them to develop physically, mentally, morally, spiritually, and socially in a healthy and normal manner in conditions of freedom and dignity.
1960	Convention Against Discrimination in Education (UNESCO)	Parties agree to ensure, by legislation where necessary, that there is no discrimination in the admission of pupils to educational institutions; to make primary education free and compulsory; to make secondary education generally available and accessible to all, and higher education equally accessible to all on the basis of individual capacity; and to make certain that the factors relating to the quality of education provided are equivalent in all public education.
1965	International Convention on the Elimination of All Forms of Racial Discrimination	States condemn racial discrimination and undertake to pursue by all appropriate means and without delay a policy of eliminating racial discrimination in all its forms, to promote understanding among the races, and to discourage anything that tends to strengthen racial division.
1966	International Covenant on Economic, Social, and Cultural Rights	States recognize rights to which all people are entitled, including the right to work, to just and favorable conditions of work, to social security, to an adequate standard of living, to the highest attainable standard of physical and mental health, to education, to take part in cultural life, and to enjoy the benefits of scientific progress.
1967	Declaration on the Elimination of Discrimination Against Women	All appropriate measures shall be taken to abolish existing laws, customs, regulations, and practices that discriminate against women and to establish adequate legal protection for equal rights of men and women.
	Declaration on Territorial Asylum	Asylum granted by a state to persons seeking asylum from political persecution shall be respected by all other states. No such person shall be subjected to such measures as rejection at the border, expulsion, or compulsory return to any state where he or she may be subjected to persecution except for overriding reasons of national security or to safeguard the population.
1979	Convention on the Elimination of all Forms of Discrimination Against Women	All appropriate measures shall be taken to abolish existing laws, customs, regulations, and practices that discriminate against women and to establish adequate legal protection for equal rights of men and women.

TABLE 16.2

U.N. Declarations of Human Rights: A Selected Chronology (*Continued*)

1981	Declaration on the Elimination of All Forms of Intolerance and of Discrimination Based on Religion or Belief	All persons shall have the right to have a religion or belief of their choice, and shall have the freedom, either individually or in community with others and in public or private, to manifest their religion or belief in worship, observance, practice, and teaching.
1984	Convention Against Torture and Other Cruel, Inhuman, or Degrading Treatment or Punishment	Defines torture as any act by which severe physical or mental pain or suffering is intentionally inflicted by, at the instigation of, or with the acquiescence of someone acting in an official capacity, whether to obtain information or confession; to punish, intimidate, or coerce; or for reasons based on discrimination. State parties must prevent torture in their jurisdictions and ensure that it is legally punishable.
1989	International Convention on the Rights of the Child	Children shall enjoy special protection and shall be given opportunities and facilities, by law and other means, to enable them to develop physically, mentally, morally, spiritually, and socially in a healthy and normal manner in conditions of freedom and dignity.

Source: Lucille Whalen, *Contemporary World Issues: Human Rights* (Santa Barbara, Calif.: ABC-CLIO, 1989), 12–18.

The U.S. Senate has not ratified certain conventions, which are listed in the box nearby, for fear that they might: (1) be used against the United States for its treatment of minorities and others; (2) erode the nation's sovereignty; or (3) injure the nation's political and economic interests in the world. Because few Americans are aware that these conventions exist, there is little pressure on the president and Congress to support them. The Senate did, however, finally ratify the Genocide Convention in 1988, almost 40 years after the United Nations had approved it, amending the U.S. Criminal Code to make genocide a federal offense.

Disputes over Civil, Welfare, and Developmental Rights

Civil rights and welfare rights were entangled in the Cold War confrontation that divided East and West from the end of World War II to 1990, and developmental rights still divide the Northern (the so-called first world) and Southern (the so-called third world) Hemispheres.

U.N. Conventions Awaiting U.S. Action

- In 1965 the United Nations adopted the Convention on the Elimination of All Forms of Racial Discrimination (the Race Convention), which President Jimmy Carter sent to the Senate in 1978 for ratification. It has still not been ratified even though U.S. domestic laws now meet the requirements.
- In 1990 the Senate ratified the 1984 U.N. Convention Against Torture and Other Cruel, Inhuman, or Degrading Treatment or Punishment, but the implementing legislation is still pending in both the House and Senate.
- Also pending are ratification of the 1979 Convention on the Elimination of All Forms of Discrimination Against Women and the 1989 International Convention on the Rights of the Child.

Civil and Welfare Rights

Americans have been slow to accept egalitarian social, economic, and cultural rights because these **welfare rights** clash with their core values of individual liberty and the right to property. Their opposition to these collective rights softened with the development of U.S. welfare programs during the Great Depression and Franklin Roosevelt's call in 1944 for an "economic bill of rights." Once the country could afford to pay for them, more and more Americans began to favor rights they believe government should provide in addition to the rights they believe government should protect, such as the right to equality of education. But the rise of conservatism in the 1980s and the collapse of the Soviet Union and Central and Eastern European "welfare states" in 1990–1991 renewed opposition to these welfare rights.

Developmental Rights

In 1977 the U.N. General Assembly declared that the "unjust economic international order" obstructed human rights in developing countries, which were entitled to **developmental rights**—the rights a nation has to develop in terms of its own cultural values. In adopting the 1986 Declaration on the Right to Development, the United Nations was recognizing that violations of human rights in developing countries are caused not only by repressive governments but also by the Western social, economic, political, and legal systems that discriminate against them. With the passage of this declaration, the United Nations linked its universal human rights goals to global issues of development. It rejected as authoritarian the notion that there is one universal (Western) model of development (*what is*) that all countries should follow (*what's right*) and affirmed the right of countries to adopt the model that best suits their own values, needs, and goals (*what's right* and *what works*).

This important shift in U.N. policy, previously grounded in Western values that assume that all people share the same "human nature," came in response to third world critics, who reject this assumption.[74] Some observers fear that this shift will undermine U.N. legal protections for universal human rights and warn that repressive regimes could defend repression in the name of their cultural traditions, values, and economic systems and thus use the U.N. declaration to legitimate brutal behavior.[75]

This dispute pits two seemingly irreconcilable views of *what's right* against each other: the fundamental human rights of individuals throughout the world (universality) versus the rights of individual countries to determine precisely how they will develop (contextuality). Some have tried to create common ground by establishing a universal core of rights that countries may not violate while recognizing their right to cultural diversity in all other areas.[76] This solution does not work, however, because it so closely resembles the dispute it attempts to resolve. Some observers say that without some common ground, human rights, as an international enterprise, will fail.[77]

Yet logic and theory rarely solve such problems and often make them appear hopeless. Practice, ongoing deliberation, and *learning by doing* are more likely to build consensus on human rights issues because such incremental activities alter peoples' attitudes as they engage in them. That is why it is vital to support the domestic and international institutions and organizations such as Amnesty International that keep people engaged with human rights issues.

Amnesty International
http://www.amnesty.org

Summary

Civil rights are fundamental rights that government protects from the unlawful actions of others, including government itself. How civil rights are regarded and addressed depends on the context in which they are placed and the perspective from which they are analyzed. All civil rights claims about *what is*, *what's right*, and *what works* are shaped by social, legal, political, and economic factors.

The equal protection clause of the Fourteenth Amendment requires that legal classifications be rational and that persons classified in the same group be treated equally. The U.S. Supreme Court is the highest authority on whether a law unfairly treats a group claiming discrimination. Using the rational basis, strict scrutiny, and intermediate scrutiny tests, the Court determines whether the classification made by the challenged law is constitutional.

Civil rights expand through the creation of new rights and by increasing the number of groups entitled to existing rights. Some activists have followed strategies that adhere to the rules of the social, economic, political, and legal systems, while others have adopted more militant strategies. African Americans pioneered the struggle for civil rights with the civil rights, black nationalist, and self-help movements. Women, Latinos, Native Americans, Asian Americans, gays and lesbians, and Americans with disabilities have adopted strategies of assimilation, legal activism, and militancy to end discrimination. Advocates for the rights of children, the unborn, animals, and the environment are attempting to expand civil rights to include these groups.

Government has sought to end discrimination by abolishing legal segregation and adopting policies of equal employment opportunity and affirmative action. Companies, labor unions, and educational institutions seeking federal contracts and funds have been forced to follow federal guidelines to ensure that they recruit, train, and promote a sufficient percentage of workers from previously excluded groups, even if the individual workers themselves had not been discriminated against. These quotas have been called reverse discrimination by those who complain that others are given preferential treatment. Liberals have tended to favor government intervention to remedy past discrimination, while conservatives have claimed that such *equality of results* is unconstitutional. The Supreme Court, whose rulings have varied with its ideological makeup, has attempted to steer a middle course between these two positions. Women seeking equal pay and comparable worth have been helped to some degree by Congress and the courts, but men still earn roughly 20 to 30 percent more than women.

Universal human rights have been developing since the United Nations was founded in the 1940s. During the 1950s, the focus was on expanding the civil and political rights generated in Western democracies to other countries. In the 1960s, the focus shifted to the creation of new social, economic, and cultural rights (welfare rights). In the 1970s, the United Nations recognized the developmental rights of so-called third world countries. Disputes have arisen between the industrialized democracies and third world advocates over the legitimacy of these new rights. For this and other reasons, the United States has yet to ratify a number of U.N. human rights conventions.

Key Terms

affirmative action **639**
black power movement **620**
busing of students **637**
civil rights **608**
civil rights movement **616**
comparable worth **644**
de facto segregation **609**
de jure segregation **609**
desegregation **617**
developmental rights **650**
discrimination **609**

disparate impact **642**
equal employment opportunity **638**
equal opportunity **636**
Equal Rights Amendment **625**
equality of results **644**
human rights **645**
integration **637**
intermediate scrutiny test **615**
magnet schools **637**
pairing of schools **637**
proportionality **640**

quotas **640**
rational basis test **614**
redlining **637**
reverse discrimination **640**
segregation **609**
self-help movement **620**
separate but equal **616**
strict scrutiny test **614**
suspect classification **614**
welfare rights **650**
white flight **637**

How You Can Learn More About Civil and Human Rights

Burns, James MacGregor, and Stewart Burns. *A People's Charter: The Pursuit of Rights in America.* New York: Alfred A. Knopf, 1991. An overview of the development of rights in the United States that emphasizes major court cases and historical events. The authors favor the expansion of rights, especially for the poor and children.

Carmichael, Stokely, and Charles V. Hamilton. *Black Power: The Politics of Liberation in America.* New York: Vintage, 1967. An argument very influential in its day, calling for strategies of protest and militancy to achieve civil rights.

Deloria, Vine, Jr., ed. *American Indian Policy in the Twentieth Century.* Norman: University of Oklahoma Press, 1985. Essays on the federal government's policies regarding American Indians during this century in the areas of human rights, voting, resource rights, and economic development.

Edelman, Murray. *Politics as Symbolic Action: Mass Arousal and Quiescence.* Chicago: Markham, 1971. An explanation of why large groups of oppressed people tolerate and sometimes acquiesce in their own oppression.

Espiritu, Yen Le. *Asian American Panethnicity: Bridging Institutions and Identities.* Philadelphia: Temple University Press, 1992. An analysis of the multicultural and multilingual factors that complicate the Asian-American struggle for civil rights.

Fiscus, Ronald J. *The Constitutional Logic of Affirmative Action.* Durham, N.C.: Duke University Press, 1992. A defense of proportionate quotas as a response to distributive justice.

Goldin, Claudia. *Understanding the Gender Gap: An Economic History of American Women.* New York: Oxford University Press, 1990. An exploration of the history and continued existence of gender discrimination in the workplace.

Juviler, Peter, and Bertram Gross et al. *Human Rights for the 21st Century: Foundations for Responsible Hope.*

London: M. E. Sharpe, 1993. Essays on the prospects of human rights following the demise of the Soviet Union.

Karst, Kenneth L. *Belonging to America: Equal Citizenship and the Constitution.* New Haven, Conn.: Yale University Press, 1989. The author shows how U.S. and especially constitutional law have contributed to the ideal of equal citizenship.

Oliver, Michael. *The Politics of Disablement.* New York: St. Martin's Press, 1990. A study of the ways in which the politics of language, capitalism, social welfare, and the ideology of individualism create dependency in people with disabilities.

Salomone, Rosemary C. *Equal Education Under Law: Legal Rights and Federal Policy in the Post-*Brown *Era.* New York: St. Martin's Press, 1986. A study of the federal government's role in promoting and limiting equality of education since *Brown v. Board of Education of Topeka* (1954).

Skerry, Peter. *Mexican Americans: The Ambivalent Minority.* New York: Free Press, 1993. Skerry's account of Mexican Americans focuses on their political goals as well as their divisions over assimilation, protest politics, and political strategies.

Smedley, Audrey. *Race in North America: Origin and Evolution of a Worldview.* Boulder, Colo.: Westview Press, 1993. An absorbing and nuanced account of the development of the concepts of race and racism in U.S. and European history.

Stone, Christopher. *Should Trees Have Standing?* Los Altos, Calif.: William Kaufmann, 1974. A study of why Western law does not recognize environmental rights.

Tushnet, Mark V. *Making Civil Rights Law: Thurgood Marshall and the Supreme Court, 1936–1961.* New York: Oxford University Press, 1994. A detailed and highly readable account of Marshall's 25 years of legal activism with the NAACP.

APPENDIX

The Declaration of Independence

The Unanimous Declaration of the Thirteen United States of America

When in the Course of human events, it becomes necessary for one people to dissolve the political bands which have connected them with another, and to assume among the Powers of the earth, the separate and equal station to which the Laws of Nature and of Nature's God entitle them, a decent respect to the opinions of mankind requires that they should declare the causes which impel them to the separation.

We hold these truths to be self-evident, that all men are created equal, that they are endowed by their Creator with certain unalienable rights, that among these are Life, Liberty, and the pursuit of Happiness. That to secure these rights, Governments are instituted among Men, deriving their just powers from the consent of the governed. That whenever any Form of Government becomes destructive of these ends, it is the Right of the People to alter or to abolish it, and to institute new Government, laying its foundation on such principles and organizing its powers in such form, as to them shall seem most likely to effect their Safety and Happiness. Prudence, indeed, will dictate that Governments long established should not be changed for light and transient causes; and accordingly all experience hath shown, that mankind are more disposed to suffer, while evils are sufferable, than to right themselves by abolishing the forms to which they are accustomed. But when a long train of abuses and usurpations, pursuing invariably the same Object evinces a design to reduce them under absolute Despotism, it is their right, it is their duty, to throw off such Government, and to provide new Guards for their future security.—Such has been the patient sufferance of these Colonies; and such is now the necessity which constrains them to alter their former Systems of Government. The history of the present King of Great Britain is a history of repeated injuries and usurpations, all having in direct object the establishment of an absolute Tyranny over these States. To prove this, let Facts be submitted to a candid world.

He has refused his Assent to Laws, the most wholesome and necessary for the public good.

He has forbidden his Governors to pass Laws of immediate and pressing importance, unless suspended in their operation till his Assent should be obtained; and, when so suspended, he has utterly neglected to attend to them.

He has refused to pass other Laws for the accommodation of large districts of people, unless those people would relinquish the right of Representation in the Legislature, a right inestimable to them and formidable to tyrants only.

He has called together legislative bodies at places unusual, uncomfortable, and distant from the depository of their public Records, for the sole purpose of fatiguing them into compliance with his measures.

He has dissolved Representative Houses repeatedly, for opposing with manly firmness his invasions on the rights of the people.

He has refused for a long time, after such dissolutions, to cause others to be elected; whereby the Legislative powers, incapable of Annihilation, have returned to the People at large for their exercise; the

State remaining in the mean time exposed to all the dangers of invasion from without and convulsions within.

He has endeavoured to prevent the population of these States; for that purpose obstructing the Laws of Naturalization of Foreigners; refusing to pass others to encourage their migrations hither, and raising the conditions of new Appropriations of Lands.

He has obstructed the Administration of Justice, by refusing his Assent to Laws for establishing Judiciary powers.

He has made Judges dependent on his Will alone, for the tenure of their offices, and the amount and payment of their salaries.

He has erected a multitude of New Offices, and sent hither swarms of Officers to harass our People, and eat out their substance.

He has kept among us, in times of peace, Standing Armies without the Consent of our legislature.

He has combined with others to subject us to a jurisdiction foreign to our constitution, and unacknowledged by our laws; giving his Assent to their Acts of pretended Legislation:

For quartering large bodies of armed troops among us:

For protecting them, by a mock Trial, from Punishment for any Murders which they should commit on the Inhabitants of these States:

For cutting off our Trade with all parts of the world:

For imposing taxes on us without our Consent:

For depriving us of many cases, of the benefits of Trial by jury:

For transporting us beyond Seas to be tried for pretended offences:

For abolishing the free System of English Laws in a neighbouring Province, establishing therein an Arbitrary government, and enlarging its Boundaries so as to render it at once an example and fit instrument for introducing the same absolute rule into these Colonies;

For taking away our Charters, abolishing our most valuable Laws, and altering fundamentally the Forms of our Governments:

For suspending our own Legislatures, and declaring themselves invested with Power to legislate for us in all cases whatsoever.

He has abdicated Government here, by declaring us out of his Protection and waging War against us.

He has plundered our seas, ravaged our Coasts, burnt our towns, and destroyed the lives of our people.

He is at this time transporting large armies of foreign mercenaries to compleat the works of death, desolation, and tyranny, already begun with circumstances of Cruelty & perfidy scarcely paralleled in the most barbarous ages, and totally unworthy the Head of a civilized nation.

He has constrained our fellow Citizens taken Captive on the high Seas to bear Arms against their Country, to become the executioners of their friends and Brethren, or to fall themselves by their Hands.

He has excited domestic insurrections amongst us, and has endeavoured to bring on the inhabitants of our frontiers, the merciless Indian Savages, whose known rule of warfare, is an undistinguished destruction of all ages, sexes, and conditions.

In every stage of these Oppressions We have Petitioned for Redress in the most humble terms: Our repeated Petitions have been answered only by repeated injury. A Prince, whose character is thus marked by every act which may define a Tyrant, is unfit to be the ruler of a free people.

Nor have We been wanting in attention to our British brethren. We have warned them from time to time of attempts by their legislature to extend an unwarrantable jurisdiction over us. We have reminded them of the circumstances of our emigration and settlement here. We have appealed to their native justice and magnanimity, and we have conjured them by the ties of our common kindred to disavow these usurpations, which, would inevitably interrupt our connections and correspondence. They too have been deaf to the voice of justice and consanguinity. We must, therefore, acquiesce in the necessity, which denounces our Separation, and hold them, as we hold the rest of mankind, Enemies in War, in Peace Friends.

We, therefore, the Representatives of the United States of America, in General Congress, Assembled, appealing to the Supreme Judge of the world for the rectitude of our intentions, do, in the Name, and by Authority of the good People of these Colonies, solemnly publish and declare, That these United Colonies are, and of Right ought to be FREE AND INDEPENDENT STATES; that they are Absolved from all Allegiance to the British Crown, and that all political connection between them and the State of Great Britain, is and ought to be totally dissolved; and that as Free and Independent States, they have full Power to levy War, conclude Peace, contract Alliances, establish Commerce, and to do all other Acts and Things which Independent States may of right do. And for the support of this Declaration, with a firm reliance on the Protection of Divine Providence, we mutually pledge to each other our Lives, our Fortunes, and our sacred Honor.

John Hancock

Button Gwinnett	George Wythe	James Wilson	Josiah Bartlett
Lyman Hall	Richard Henry Lee	Geo. Ross	Wm. Whipple
Geo. Walton	Th. Jefferson	Caesar Rodney	Saml. Adams
Wm. Hooper	Benja. Harrison	Geo. Read	John Adams
Joseph Hewes	Thos. Nelson, Jr.	Thos. M'Kean	Robt. Treat Paine
John Penn	Francis Lightfoot Lee	Wm. Floyd	Elbridge Gerry
Edward Rutledge	Carter Braxton	Phil. Livingston	Step. Hopkins
Thos. Heyward, Junr.	Robt. Morris	Frans. Lewis	William Ellery
Thomas Lynch, Junr.	Benjamin Rush	Lewis Morris	Roger Sherman
Arthur Middleton	Benja. Franklin	Richd. Stockton	Sam'el Hunington
Samuel Chase	John Morton	Jno. Witherspoon	Wm. Williams
Wm. Paca	Geo. Clymer	Fras. Hopkinson	Oliver Wolcott
Thos. Stone	Jas. Smith	John Hart	Matthew Thornton
Charles Carroll of Carrollton	Geo. Taylor	Abra. Clark	

Constitution of the United States of America

Adopted by Congress: 17 September 1787
Put into effect: 4 March 1789

(Preamble)

WE THE PEOPLE of the United States, in Order to form a more perfect Union, establish Justice, insure domestic Tranquility, provide for the common defence, promote the general Welfare, and secure the Blessings of Liberty to ourselves and our Posterity, do ordain and establish this Constitution for the United State of America.

ARTICLE I

(Legislative powers)

Section 1. All legislative Powers herein granted shall be vested in a Congress of the United States, which shall consist of a Senate and a House of Representatives.

(The House of Representatives, how constituted, apportionment, impeachment power)

Section 2. The House of Representatives shall be composed of Members chosen every second Year by the People of the several States, and the Electors in each State shall have the Qualifications requisite for Electors of the most numerous Branch of the State Legislature.

No Person shall be a Representative who shall not have attained to the Age of twenty-five Years, and been seven Years a Citizen of the United States, and who shall not, when elected, be an Inhabitant of that State in which he shall be chosen.

[Representatives and direct Taxes shall be apportioned among the several States which may be included within this Union, according to their respective Numbers, which shall be determined by adding to the whole number of free Persons, including those bound to Service for a Term of Years, and excluding Indians not taxed, three fifths of all other Persons.][1] The actual Enumeration shall be made within three Years after the first Meeting of the Congress of the United States, and within every subsequent Term of ten Years, in such Manner as they shall by Law direct. The Number of Representatives shall not exceed one for every thirty Thousand, but each State shall have at Least one Representative; and until such enumeration shall be made, the State of New Hampshire shall be entitled to chuse three, Massachusetts eight, Rhode-Island and Providence Plantations one, Connecticut five, New-York six, New Jersey four, Pennsylvania eight, Delaware one, Maryland six, Virginia ten, North Carolina five, South Caroline five, and Georgia three.

When vacancies happen in the Representation from any State, the Executive Authority thereof shall issue Writs of Election to fill such Vacancies.

The House of Representatives shall chuse their Speaker and other Officers; and shall have the sole Power of Impeachment.

(The Senate, how constituted, impeachment trials)

Section 3. The Senate of the United States shall be composed of two Senators from each State, [chosen by the Legislature hereof,][2] for six Years; and each Senator shall have one Vote.

---

[1]Changed by Section 2 of Amendment XIV (1863).
[2]Changed by Section 1 of Amendment XVII (1913).

Immediately after they shall be assembled in Consequence of the first Election, they shall be divided as equally as may be into three Classes. The Seats of the Senators of the first Class shall be vacated at the Expiration of the second Year, of the second Class at the Expiration of the fourth year, and of the third Class at the Expiration of the sixth Year, so that one-third may be chosen every second Year [; and if Vacancies happen by Resignation, or otherwise, during the Recess of the Legislature of any State, the Executive thereof may make temporary Appointments until the next Meeting of the Legislature, which shall then fill such Vacancies].[3]

No Person shall be a Senator who shall not have attained to the Age of thirty Years, and been nine Years a Citizen of the United States, who shall not, when elected, be an Inhabitant of that State for which he shall be chosen.

The Vice President of the United States shall be President of the Senate, but shall have no Vote, unless they be equally divided.

The Senate shall chuse their other Officers, and also a President pro tempore, in the absence of the Vice President, or when he shall exercise the Office of the President of the United States.

The Senate shall have the sole Power to try all impeachments. When sitting for that Purpose, they shall be on Oath or Affirmation. When the President of the United States is tried, the Chief Justice shall preside: And no Person shall be convicted without the Concurrence of two thirds of the Members present.

Judgement in Cases of Impeachment shall not extend further than to removal from Office, and disqualification to hold and enjoy any Office of honor, Trust or Profit under the United States: but the Party convicted shall nevertheless be liable and subject to Indictment, Trial, Judgment and Punishment, according to Law.

Section 4. The Times, Places and Manner of holding Elections for Senators and Representatives, shall be prescribed in each State by the Legislature thereof: but the Congress may at any time by Law make or alter such Regulations, except as to the Place of Chusing Senators. The Congress shall assemble at least once in every Year, and such Meeting shall [be on the first Monday in December,][4] unless they shall by Law appoint a different Day.

(Election of senators and representatives)

Section 5. Each House shall be the Judge of the Elections, Returns and Qualifications of its own Members, and a Majority of each shall constitute a Quorum to do Business; but a smaller number may adjourn from day to day, and may be authorized to compel the Attendance of absent Members, in such Manner, and under such Penalties as each House may provide.

(Powers and duties of the houses of Congress: quorum, rules of proceedings, journals, adjournment)

Each House may determine the Rules of its Proceedings, punish its Members for disorderly Behaviour, and, with the Concurrence of two thirds, expel a Member.

Each House shall keep a Journal of its Proceedings, and from time to time publish the same, excepting such Parts as may in their Judgement require Secrecy; and the Yeas and Nays of the Members of either House on any question shall, at the Desire of one fifth of those Present, be entered on the Journal.

Neither House, during the Session of Congress, shall, without the Consent of the other, adjourn for more than three days, nor to any other Place than that in which the two Houses shall be sitting.

Section 6. The Senators and Representatives shall receive a Compensation for their Services, to be ascertained by Law, and paid out of the Treasury of the United States. They shall in all Cases, except Treason, Felony and Breach of the Peace, be privileged from Arrest during their Attendance at the Session of their respective Houses, and in going to and returning from the same; and for any speech or debate in either House, they shall not be questioned in any other Place.

(Compensation and privileges of senators and representatives)

No Senator or Representative shall, during the Time for which he was elected, be appointed to any civil Office under the Authority of the United States, which shall have been created, or the Emoluments whereof shall have been encreased during such time; and no Person holding any Office under the United States, shall be a Member of either House during his Continuance in Office.

Section 7. All Bills for raising Revenue shall originate in the House of Representatives; but the Senate may propose or concur with Amendments as on other Bills.

(Legislative procedures: bills and resolutions)

---

[3]Changed by Clause 2 of Amendment XVII (1913).
[4]Changed by Section 2 of Amendment XX (1933).

Every Bill which shall have passed the House of Representatives and the Senate, shall, before it become a Law, be presented to the President of the United States; If he approve he shall sign it, but if not he shall return it, with his Objections to that House in which it shall have Originated, who shall enter the Objections at large on their Journal, and proceed to reconsider it. If after such Reconsideration two thirds of that House shall agree to pass the Bill, it shall be sent, together with the Objections, to the other House, by which it shall likewise be reconsidered, and if approved by two thirds of that House, it shall become a Law. But in all such Cases the Votes of both Houses shall be determined by Yeas and Nays, and the Names of the Persons voting for and against the Bill shall be entered on the Journal of each House respectively. If any Bill shall not be returned by the President within ten Days (Sundays excepted) after it shall have been presented to him, the Same shall be a Law, in like Manner as if he had signed it, unless the Congress by their Adjournment prevent its Return, in which Case it shall not be a Law.

Every Order, Resolution, or Vote to which the Concurrence of the Senate and House of Representatives may be necessary (except on a question of Adjournment) shall be presented to the President of the United States; and before the Same shall take Effect, shall be approved by him, or being disapproved by him, shall be repassed by two thirds of the Senate and House of Representatives, according to the Rules and Limitations prescribed in the Case of a Bill.

(Powers of Congress) **Section 8.** The Congress shall have Power To lay and collect Taxes, Duties, Imposts and Excises, to pay the Debts and provide for the common Defense and general Welfare of the United States; but all Duties, imposts and Excises shall be uniform throughout the United States;

To borrow money on the credit of the United States;

To regulate Commerce with foreign Nations, and among the several States, and with the Indian Tribes;

To establish an uniform Rule of Naturalization, and uniform Laws on the subject of Bankruptcies throughout the United States;

To coin Money, regulate the Value thereof, and of foreign Coin, and fix the Standard of Weights and Measures;

To provide for the Punishment of counterfeiting the Securities and current Coin of the United States;

To establish post Offices and post Roads;

To promote the Progress of Science and useful Arts, by securing for limited Times to Authors and Inventors the exclusive Right to their respective Writings and Discoveries;

To constitute Tribunals inferior to the Supreme Court;

To define and punish Piracies and Felonies committed on the high Seas, and Offences against the Law of Nations;

To declare War, grant Letters of Marque and Reprisal, and make Rules concerning Captures on Land and Water;

To raise and support Armies, but no Appropriation of Money to that Use shall be for a longer Term than two Years;

To provide and maintain a Navy;

To make Rules for the Government and Regulation of the land and naval Forces;

To provide for calling forth the Militia to execute the Laws of the Union, suppress Insurrections and repel Invasions;

To provide for organizing, arming, and disciplining the Militia, and for governing such Part of them as may be employed in the Service of the United States, reserving to the States respectively, the Appointment of the Officers, and the Authority of training the Militia according to the discipline prescribed by Congress;

To exercise exclusive Legislation in all Cases whatsoever, over such District (not exceeding ten Miles square) as may, by Cession of particular States, and the acceptance of Congress, become the Seat of the Government of the United States, and to exercise like Authority over all Places purchased by the Consent of the Legislature of the State in which the Same shall be, for the Erection of Forts, Magazines, Arsenals, dock-Yards, and other needful Buildings;—And

To make all Laws which shall be necessary and proper for carrying into Execution the foregoing Powers, and all other Powers vested by the Constitution in the Government of the United States, or in any Department or Officer thereof.

Section 9. The Migration or Importation of such Persons as any of the States now existing shall think proper to admit, shall not be prohibited by the Congress prior to the Year one thousand eight hundred and eight, but a tax or duty may be imposed on such Importation, not exceeding ten dollars for each Person.

(Restrictions on powers of Congress)

The privilege of the Writ of Habeas Corpus shall not be suspended, unless when in Cases of Rebellion or Invasion the public Safety may require it.

No Bill of Attainder or ex post facto Law shall be passed.

No capitation, or other direct Tax shall be laid, unless in Proportion to the Census or Enumeration herein before directed to be taken.[5]

No Tax or Duty shall be laid on Articles exported from any State.

No Preference shall be given by any Regulation of Commerce or Revenue to the Ports of one State over those of another: nor shall Vessels bound to, or from, one State, be obliged to enter, clear, or pay Duties in another.

No Money shall be drawn from the Treasury, but in Consequence of Appropriations made by Law; and a regular Statement and Account of the Receipts and Expenditures of all public Money shall be published from time to time.

No Title of Nobility shall be granted by the United States: And no Person holding any Office of Profit or Trust under them, shall, without the Consent of the Congress, accept of any present, Emolument, Office, or Title, of any kind whatever, from any King, Prince, or foreign State.

Section 10. No State shall enter into any Treaty, Alliance, or Confederation; grant Letters of Marque and Reprisal; coin Money; emit Bills of Credit; make any Thing but gold and silver Coin a Tender in Payment of Debts; pass any Bill of Attainder, ex post facto Law, or Law impairing the Obligation of Contracts, or grant any Title of Nobility.

(Restrictions on powers of states)

No State shall, without the Consent of Congress, lay any Imposts or Duties on Imports or Exports, except what may be absolutely necessary for executing its inspection Laws; and the net Produce of all Duties and Imposts, laid by any State on Imports or Exports, shall be for the Use of the Treasury of the United States; and all such Laws shall be subject to the Revision and Controul of the Congress.

No State shall, without the Consent of Congress, lay any duty of Tonnage, keep Troops, or Ships of War in time of Peace, enter into any Agreement or Compact with another State, or with a foreign Power, or engage in War, unless actually invaded, or in such imminent Danger as will not admit of delay.

ARTICLE II

Section 1. The executive Power shall be vested in a President of the United State of America. He shall hold his Office during the Term of four Years, and, together with the Vice-President, chosen for the same Term, be elected as follows.

(Executive power, election and qualifications of the president)

Each State shall appoint, in such Manner as the Legislature thereof may direct, a Number of Electors, equal to the whole Number of Senators and Representatives to which the State may be entitled in the Congress: but no Senator or Representative, or Person holding an Office of Trust or Profit under the United States, shall be appointed an Elector.

[The Electors shall meet in their respective States, and vote by Ballot for two persons, of whom one at least shall not be an Inhabitant of the same State with themselves. And they shall make a List of all the Persons voted for, and of the Number of Votes for each; which List they shall sign and certify, and transmit sealed to the Seat of the Government of the United States, directed to the President of the Senate. The President of the Senate shall, in the Presence of the Senate and House of Representatives, open all the Certificates, and the Votes shall then be counted. The Person having the greatest Number of

---

[5]See Amendment XII (1804).

Votes shall be the President, if such Number be a Majority of the whole Number of Electors appointed; and if there be more than one who have such Majority, and have an equal Number of Votes, then the House of Representatives shall immediately chuse by Ballot one of them for President; and if no Person have a Majority, then from the five highest on the List the said House shall in like Manner chuse the President. But in chusing the President, the Votes shall be taken by States, the Representation from each State having one Vote; a quorum for this Purpose shall consist of a Member or Members from two thirds of the States, and a Majority of all the States shall be necessary to a Choice. In every Case, after the Choice of the President, the Person having the greatest Number of Votes of the Electors shall be the Vice-President. But if there should remain two or more who have equal Votes, the Senate shall chuse from them by Ballot the Vice-President.][6]

The Congress may determine the Time of chusing the Electors, and the Day on which they shall give their Votes; which Day shall be the same throughout the United States.

No Person except a natural born Citizen, or a Citizen of the United States, at the time of the Adoption of this Constitution, shall be eligible to the Office of President; neither shall any Person be eligible to that Office who shall not have attained to the Age of thirty-five Years, and been fourteen Years a Resident within the United States.

[In Case of the Removal of the President from Office, or of his Death, Resignation, or Inability to discharge the Powers and Duties of the said Office, the same shall devolve on the Vice-President, and the Congress may by law provide for the Case of Removal, Death, Resignation, or Inability, both of the President and Vice-President, declaring what Officer shall then act as President, and such Officer shall act accordingly, until the Disability be removed, or a President shall be elected.][7]

The President shall, at stated Times, receive for his Services, a Compensation, which shall neither be encreased nor diminished during the Period for which he shall have been elected, and he shall not receive within that Period any other Emolument from the United States, or any of them. Before he enter on the Execution of his Office, he shall take the following Oath or Affirmation:—"I do solemnly swear (or affirm) that I will faithfully execute the Office of President of the United States, and will to the best of my Ability, preserve, protect and defend the Constitution of the United States."

(Powers of the president)

Section 2. The President shall be Commander in Chief of the Army and Navy of the United States, and of the Militia of the several States, when called into the actual Service of the United States; he may require the Opinion in writing, of the principal Officer in each of the executive Departments, upon any subject relating to the Duties of their respective Offices, and he shall have Power to Grant Reprieves and Pardons for Offences against the United States, except in Cases of Impeachment.

He shall have Power, by and with the Advice and Consent of the Senate, to make Treaties, provided two-thirds of the Senators present concur; and he shall nominate, and by and with the Advice and Consent of the Senate, shall appoint Ambassadors, other public Ministers and Consuls, Judges of the supreme Court, and all other Officers of the United States, whose Appointments are not herein otherwise provided for, and which shall be established by Law: but the Congress may by Law vest the Appointment of such inferior Officers, as they think proper, in the President alone, in the Courts of Law, or in the Heads of Departments.

The President shall have Power to fill up all Vacancies that may happen during the Recess of the Senate, by granting Commissions which shall expire at the End of their next Session.

(Powers and duties of the president)

Section 3. He shall from time to time give to the Congress Information of the State of the Union, and recommend to their Consideration such Measures as he shall judge necessary and expedient; he may, on extraordinary Occasions, convene both Houses, or either of them, and in Case of Disagreement between them, with Respect to the Time of Adjournment, he may adjourn them to such Time as he shall think proper; he shall receive Ambassadors and other public Ministers; he shall take Care that the Laws be faithfully executed, and shall Commission all the Officers of the United States.

(Impeachment)

Section 4. The President, Vice President and all civil Officers of the United States, shall be removed from Office on Impeachment for, and Conviction of, Treason, Bribery, or other high Crimes and Misdemeanors.

---

[6]Superseded by Amendment XII (1804).
[7]Affected by Amendment XXV (1967).

ARTICLE III

Section 1. The judicial Power of the United States, shall be vested in one supreme Court, and in such inferior Courts as the Congress may from time to time ordain and establish. The Judges, both of the supreme and inferior Courts, shall hold their Offices during good Behaviour, and shall, at stated Times, receive for their Services, a Compensation, which shall not be diminished during their Continuance in Office.

(Judicial power, courts, and judges)

Section 2. The judicial Power shall extend to all Cases, in Law and Equity, arising under this Constitution, the Laws of the United States, and Treaties made, or which shall be made, under their Authority;—to all Cases affecting Ambassadors, other public Ministers and Consuls;—to all Cases of admiralty and maritime Jurisdiction;—to Controversies to which the United States shall be a Party;—to Controversies between two or more States;—between a State and Citizens of another State;—between Citizens of different States;—between Citizens of the same State claiming Lands under Grants of different States, and between a State, or the Citizens thereof, and foreign States, Citizens, or Subjects.

(Jurisdiction)

In all Cases affecting Ambassadors, other public Ministers and Consuls, and those in which a State shall be a Party, the supreme Court shall have original Jurisdiction. In all the other cases before mentioned, the supreme Court shall have appellate Jurisdiction, both as to Law and Fact, with such Exceptions, and under such Regulations as the Congress shall make.

The trial of all Crimes, except in Cases of Impeachment, shall be by Jury; and such Trial shall be held in the State where the said Crimes shall have been committed; but when not committed within any State, the Trial shall be at such Place or Places as the Congress may by Law have directed.

Section 3. Treason against the United States, shall consist only in levying War against them, or in adhering to their Enemies, giving them Aid and Comfort. No Person shall be convicted of Treason unless on the Testimony of two Witnesses to the same overt Act, or on Confession in open Court.

(Treason)

The Congress shall have Power to declare the Punishment of Treason, but no Attainder of Treason shall work Corruption of Blood, or Forfeiture except during the Life of the person Attainted.

ARTICLE IV

Section 1. Full Faith and Credit shall be given in each State to the public Acts, Records, and judicial Proceedings of every other State. And the Congress may by general Laws prescribe the Manner in which such Acts, Records and Proceedings shall be proved, and the Effect thereof.

(Full faith and credit clause)

Section 2. The Citizens of each State shall be entitled to all Privileges and Immunities of Citizens in the several States.

(Privileges and immunities of citizens, fugitives)

A Person charged in any State with Treason, Felony, or other Crime, who shall flee from Justice, and be found in another State, shall on demand of the executive Authority of the State from which he fled, be delivered up, to be removed to the State having Jurisdiction of the Crime.

[No Person held to Service or Labour in one State, under the laws thereof, escaping into another, shall, in Consequence of any Law or Regulation therein, be discharged from such Service or Labour, but shall be delivered up on Claim of the Party to whom such Service or Labour may be due.][8]

Section 3. New States may be admitted by the Congress into this Union; but no new State shall be formed or erected within the Jurisdiction of any other State, nor any State be formed by the Junction of two or more States, or parts of States, without the Consent of the Legislatures of the States concerned as well as of the Congress.

(Admission of new states)

The Congress shall have Power to dispose of and make all needful Rules and Regulations respecting the Territory or other Property belonging to the United States; and nothing in this Constitution shall be so construed as to Prejudice any Claims of the United States, or of any particular State.

Section 4. The United States shall guarantee to every State in this Union a Republican Form of Government, and shall protect each of them against Invasion; and on Application of the Legislature, or of the Executive (when the Legislature cannot be convened) against domestic Violence.

(Guarantee of republican form of government)

---

[8]Superseded by Amendment XIII (1865).

(Amending the Constitution)

ARTICLE V

The Congress, whenever two-thirds of both Houses shall deem it necessary, shall propose Amendments to this Constitution, or, on the Application of the Legislatures of two-thirds of the several States, shall call a Convention for proposing Amendments, which, in either Case, shall be valid, to all Intents and Purposes, as part of this Constitution, when ratified by the Legislatures of three-fourths of the several States, or by Conventions in three-fourths thereof, as the one or the other Mode of Ratification may be proposed by the Congress: Provided that no Amendment which may be made prior to the Year One thousand eight hundred and eight shall in any Manner affect the first and fourth Clauses in the Ninth Section of the first Article; and that no State, without its Consent, shall be deprived of its equal Suffrage in the Senate.

(Debts, supremacy, oaths)

ARTICLE VI

All Debts contracted and Engagements entered into, before the Adoption of this Constitution, shall be as valid against the Untied States under this Constitution as under the Confederation.

This Constitution, and the Laws of the United States which shall be made in Pursuance thereof, and all Treaties made, or which shall be made, under the Authority of the United States, shall be the supreme Law of the Land; and the Judges in every State shall be bound thereby, any Thing in the Constitution or Laws of any State to the contrary notwithstanding.

The Senators and Representatives before mentioned, and the members of the several State Legislatures, and all executive and judicial Officers, both of the United States and of the several States, shall be bound by Oath or Affirmation, to support this Constitution; but no religious Test shall ever be required as a Qualification to any Office or public Trust under the United States.

(Ratification)
(The first ten amendments—known as the Bill of Rights—were passed by Congress on September 25, 1789. They were ratified by three-fourths of the states by December 15, 1791.)

ARTICLE VII

The Ratification of the Conventions of nine States shall be sufficient for the Establishment of this Constitution between the States so ratifying the Same.

DONE in Convention by the Unanimous Consent of the States present the Seventeenth Day of September in the Year of our Lord one thousand seven hundred and Eighty seven and of the Independence of the United States of America the Twelfth.

IN Witness whereof We have hereunto subscribed our Names.

(Freedom of religion, the press, and assembly, and right of petition)

AMENDMENT I

Congress shall make no law respecting an establishment of religion, or prohibiting the free exercise thereof; or abridging the freedom of speech, or of the press; or the right of the people peaceably to assemble, and to petition the Government for a redress of grievances.

(Militia and the right to keep and bear arms)

AMENDMENT II

A well regulated Militia, being necessary to the security of a free State, the right of the people to keep and bear Arms, shall not be infringed.

(Quartering of soldiers)

AMENDMENT III

No Soldier shall, in time of peace be quartered in any house, without the consent of the Owner, nor in time of war, but in a manner to be prescribed by law.

(Protection against unreasonable search and seizure)

AMENDMENT IV

The right of the people to be secure in their persons, houses, papers, and effects, against unreasonable searches and seizures, shall not be violated; and no Warrants shall issue, but upon probable cause, supported by Oath or affirmation, and particularly describing the place to be searched, and the persons or things to be seized.

(Grand juries, double jeopardy, self-incrimination, due process, and eminent domain)

AMENDMENT V

No person shall be held to answer for a capital, or otherwise infamous crime, unless on a presentment or indictment of a Grand Jury, except in cases arising in the land or naval forces, or in the Militia, when in actual service in time of War or public danger; nor shall any person be subject for the same offence to be twice put in jeopardy of life or limb; nor shall be compelled in any criminal case to be a witness against himself, nor be deprived of life, liberty, or property, without due process of law; nor shall private property be taken for public use, without just compensation.

AMENDMENT VI

(Criminal court procedures)

In all criminal prosecutions, the accused shall enjoy the right to a speedy and public trial, by an impartial jury of the State and district wherein the crime shall have been committed, which district shall have been previously ascertained by law, and to be informed of the nature and cause of the accusation; to be confronted with the witnesses against him; to have compulsory process for obtaining witnesses in his favor, and to have the Assistance of Counsel for his defence.

AMENDMENT VII

(Trial by jury in common-law cases)

In suits at common law, where the value in controversy shall exceed twenty dollars, the right of trial by jury shall be preserved, and no fact tried by a jury, shall be otherwise reexamined in any Court of the United States, than according to the rules of the common law.

AMENDMENT VIII

(Bail, fines, and cruel and unusual punishments)

Excessive bail shall not be required, nor excessive fines imposed, nor cruel and unusual punishments inflicted.

AMENDMENT IX

(Retention of rights by the people)

The enumeration in the Constitution, of certain rights, shall not be construed to deny or disparage others retained by the people.

AMENDMENT X

(Reserved powers of the states)

The powers not delegated to the United States by the Constitution, nor prohibited to it by the States, are reserved to the States respectively, or to the people.

AMENDMENT XI

(Suits against the states)

(Proposed March 4, 1794, ratified February 7, 1795)
The Judicial power of the United States shall not be construed to extend to any suit in law or equity, commenced or prosecuted against one of the United States by Citizens of another State or by Citizens or Subjects of any Foreign State.

AMENDMENT XII

(Election of the president and vice-president)

(Proposed December 9, 1803; ratified June 15, 1804)
The Electors shall meet in their respective states and vote by ballot for President and Vice-President, one of whom, at least, shall not be an inhabitant of the same state with themselves; they shall name in their ballots the person voted for as President, and in distinct ballots the person voted for as Vice-President, and they shall make distinct lists of all persons voted for as President, and of all persons voted for as Vice-President, and of the number of votes for each, which lists they shall sign and certify, and transmit sealed to the seat of the government of the United States, directed to the President of the Senate;—the President of the Senate shall, in the presence of the Senate and the House of Representatives, open all the certificates and the votes shall then be counted;—The person having the greatest number of votes for President, shall be the President, if such number be a majority of the whole number of Electors appointed; and if no person have such a majority, then from the persons having the highest numbers not exceeding three on the list of those voted for as President, the House of Representative shall choose immediately, by ballot, the President. But in choosing the President, the votes shall be taken by States, the representation from each state having one vote; a quorum for this purpose shall consist of a member or members from two-thirds of the States, and a majority of all the States shall be necessary to a choice. [And if the House of Representatives shall not choose a President whenever the right of choice shall devolve upon them, before the fourth day of March next following, then the Vice-President shall act as President, as in case of the death or other constitutional disability of the

President.—][9] The person having the greatest number of votes as Vice-President, shall be the Vice President, if such number be a majority of the whole number of Electors appointed, and if no person have a majority, then from the two highest numbers on the list, the Senate shall choose the Vice-President; a quorum for the purpose shall consist of two-thirds of the whole number of Senators, a majority of the whole number shall be necessary to a choice. But no person constitutionally ineligible to the office of President shall be eligible to that of Vice-President of the United States.

AMENDMENT XIII

(Abolition of slavery)

(Proposed January 31, 1865; ratified December 6, 1865)

Section 1. Neither slavery or involuntary servitude, except as a punishment for crime whereof the party shall have been duly convicted, shall exist within the United States, or any place subject to their jurisdiction.

Section 2. Congress shall have power to enforce this article by appropriate legislation.

AMENDMENT XIV

(Proposed June 13, 1866; ratified July 9, 1868)

(Citizenship rights, due process, equal protection of the laws)

Section 1. All persons born or naturalized in the United States, and subject to the jurisdiction thereof, are Citizens of the United States and of the State wherein they reside. No State shall make or enforce any law which shall abridge the privileges or immunities of citizens of the United States; nor shall any State deprive any person of life, liberty, or property, without due process of law; nor deny any person within its jurisdiction the equal protection of the laws.

(Apportionment of representatives)

Section 2. Representatives shall be apportioned among the several States according to their respective numbers, counting the whole number of persons in each State, excluding Indians not taxed. But when the right to vote at any election for the choice of Electors for President and Vice-President of the United States, Representatives in Congress, the Executive and Judicial officers of a State, or the members of the Legislature thereof, is denied to any of the male inhabitants of such State, being twenty-one years of age,[10] and citizens of the United States, or in any way abridged, except for participation in rebellion, or other crime, the basis of representation therein shall be reduced in the proportion which the number of such male citizens shall bear to the whole number of male citizens twenty-one years of age in such State.

(Persons prohibited from holding office)

Section 3. No person shall be a Senator or Representative in Congress, or elector of President and Vice-President, or hold any office, civil or military, under the United States, or under any State, who, having previously taken an oath, as a member of Congress, or as an officer of the United States, or as a member of any State legislature, or as an executive or judicial officer of any State, to support the Constitution of the United States, shall have engaged in insurrection or rebellion against the same, or given aid or comfort to the enemies thereof. But Congress may by a vote of two-thirds of each House, remove such disability.

(Validity of public debts)

Section 4. The validity of the public debt of the United States, authorized by law, including debts incurred for payment of pensions and bounties for services in suppressing insurrection or rebellion, shall not be questioned. But neither the United States nor any State shall assume or pay any debt or obligation incurred in aid of insurrection or rebellion against the United States, or any claim for the loss or emancipation of any slave; but all such debts, obligations and claims shall be held illegal and void.

Section 5. The Congress shall have power to enforce, by appropriate legislation, the provisions of this article.

AMENDMENT XV

(The right to vote)

(Proposed February 26, 1869; ratified February 3, 1870)

Section 1. The right of Citizens of the United States to vote shall not be denied or abridged by the United States or by any State on account of race, color, or previous condition of servitude.

Section 2. The Congress shall have power to enforce this article by appropriate legislation.

---

[9]Superseded by Section 3 of Amendment XX (1933).
[10]Changed by Section 1 of Amendment XXVI (1971).

AMENDMENT XVI

(Income taxes)

(Proposed July 2, 1909; ratified February 3, 1913)

The Congress shall have power to lay and collect taxes on incomes, from whatever source derived, without apportionment among the several States, and without regard to any census or enumeration.

AMENDMENT XVII

(Direct election of senators)

(Proposed May 13, 1912; ratified April 8, 1913)

The Senate of the United States shall be composed of two Senators from each State, elected by the people thereof, for six years; and each Senator shall have one vote. The electors in each State shall have the qualifications requisite for electors of the most numerous branch of the State legislatures.

When vacancies happen in the representation of any State in the Senate, the executive authority of such State shall issue writs of election to fill such vacancies: Provided, That the legislature of any State may empower the executive thereof to make temporary appointments until the people fill the vacancies by election as the legislature may direct.

This amendment shall not be so construed as to affect the election or term of any Senator chosen before it becomes valid as part of the Constitution.

AMENDMENT XVIII

(National prohibition of liquor)

(Proposed December 18, 1917; ratified January 16, 1919)

[Section 1. After one year from the ratification of this article the manufacture, sale, or transportation of intoxicating liquors within, the importation thereof into, or the exportation thereof from the United States and all territory subject to the jurisdiction thereof for beverage purposes is hereby prohibited.

[Section 2. The Congress and the several States shall have concurrent power to enforce this article by appropriate legislation.

[Section 3. This article shall be inoperative unless it shall have been ratified as an amendment to the Constitution by the legislatures of the several States as provided in the Constitution, within seven years of the date of the submission hereof to the States by Congress.][11]

AMENDMENT XIX

(Women's suffrage)

(Proposed June 4, 1919; ratified August 18, 1920)

Section 1. The right of citizens of the United States to vote shall not be denied or abridged by the United States or by any State on account of sex.

Section 2. Congress shall have power to enforce this article by appropriate legislation.

AMENDMENT XX

(Proposed March 2, 1932, ratified January 23, 1933)

Section 1. The terms of the President and Vice-President shall end at noon on the 20th day of January, and the terms of Senators and Representatives at noon on the 3d day of January, of the years in which such terms would have ended if this article had not been ratified; and the terms of their successors shall then begin.

(Terms of office)

Section 2. The Congress shall assemble at least once in every year, and such meeting shall begin at noon on the 3d day of January, unless they shall by law appoint a different day.

(Time of convening Congress)

Section 3. If, at the time fixed for the beginning of the term of the President, the President elect shall have died, the Vice-President elect shall become President. If a President shall not have been chosen before the time fixed for the beginning of his term, or if the President elect shall have failed to qualify, then the Vice-President elect shall act as President until a President shall have qualified; and the Congress may by law provide for the case wherein neither a President elect nor a Vice-President elect shall have qualified, declaring who shall then act as President, or the manner in which one who is to act shall be selected, and such person shall act accordingly until a President or Vice-President shall have qualified.

(Death of president-elect, failure of president-elect or vice-president-elect to qualify for office)

---

[11]Repealed by Section 1 of Amendment XXI (1933).

(Congress and the election of president or vice-president)

Section 4. The Congress may by law provide for the case of the death of any of the persons from whom the House of Representatives may choose a President whenever the right of choice shall have devolved upon them, and for the case of the death of any of the persons from whom the Senate may choose a Vice-President whenever the right of choice shall have devolved upon them.

(Effective dates of sections 1 and 2)

Section 5. Sections 1 and 2 shall take effect on the 15th day of October following the ratification of this article.

(Seven-year limit for ratification)

Section 6. This article shall be inoperative unless it shall have been ratified as an amendment to the Constitution by three-fourths of the several States within seven Years from the date of its submission.

AMENDMENT XXI

(Proposed February 20, 1933; ratified December 5, 1933)

(Repeal of national prohibition of liquor)

Section 1. The eighteenth article of amendment to the Constitution of the United States is hereby repealed.

(Transportation of liquor into "dry" states prohibited)

Section 2. The transportation or importation into any State, Territory, or possession of the United States for delivery or use therein of intoxicating liquors, in violation of the laws thereof, is hereby prohibited.

(Seven-year limit for ratification)

Section 3. This article shall be inoperative unless it shall have been ratified as an amendment to the Constitution by conventions in the several States, as provided in the Constitution, within seven years from the date of submission hereof to the States by the Congress.

AMENDMENT XXII

(Proposed March 21, 1947; ratified February 27, 1951)

(Number of presidential terms)

Section 1. No person shall be elected to the office of the President more than twice, and no person who has held the office of President, or acted as President, for more than two years of a term to which some other person was elected President shall be elected to the office of the President more than once. But this Article shall not prevent any person holding the office of President when this Article was proposed by the Congress, and shall not apply to any person who may be holding the office of President, or acting as President, during the term within which this Article becomes operative from holding the office of President or acting as President during the remainder of such term.

(Seven-year limit for ratification)

Section 2. This article shall be inoperative unless it shall have been ratified as an amendment to the Constitution by the legislatures of three-fourths of the several States within seven years from the date of its submission to the States by the Congress.

AMENDMENT XXIII

(Proposed June 16, 1960; ratified March 29, 1961)

(Presidential electors for the District of Columbia)

Section 1. The District constituting the seat of Government of the United States shall appoint in such manner as the Congress may direct: A number of electors of President and Vice-President equal to the whole number of Senators and Representative in Congress to which the District would be entitled if it were a State, but in no event more than the least populous State; they shall be in addition to those appointed by the States, but they shall be considered, for the purposes of the election of President and Vice-President, to be electors appointed by a State; and they shall meet in the District and perform such duties as provided by the twelfth article of amendment.

Section 2. The Congress shall have power to enforce this article by appropriate legislation.

(Poll tax banned in federal elections)

AMENDMENT XXIV

(Proposed August 27, 1962; ratified January 24, 1964)

Section 1. The right of citizens of the United States to vote in any primary or other election for President or Vice President, for electors for President or Vice President, or for Senator or Representative in Congress, shall not be denied or abridged by the United States or any State by reason of failure to pay any poll tax or other tax.

Section 2. The Congress shall have power to enforce this article by appropriate legislation.

AMENDMENT XXV

(Proposed July 6, 1965; ratified February 10, 1967)

Section 1. In case of the removal of the President from office or of his death or resignation, the Vice-President shall become President.

(Vice-president to succeed president)

Section 2. Whenever there is a vacancy in the office of the Vice-President, the President shall nominate a Vice-President who shall take office upon confirmation by a majority vote of both Houses of Congress.

(Choosing a new vice-president)

Section 3. Whenever the President transmits to the President pro tempore of the Senate and the Speaker of the House of Representatives his written declaration that he is unable to discharge the powers and duties of his office, and until he transmits to them a written declaration to the contrary, such powers and duties shall be discharged by the Vice-President as Acting President.

(Presidential disability)

Section 4. Whenever the Vice-President and a majority of either the principal officers of the executive departments or of such other body as Congress may by law provide, transmit to the President pro tempore of the Senate and the Speaker of the House of Representatives their written declaration that the President is unable to discharge the powers and duties of his office, the Vice-President shall immediately assume the powers and duties of the office as Acting President.

(Presidential disability)

Thereafter, when the President transmits to the President pro tempore of the Senate and the Speaker of the House of Representatives his written declaration that no inability exists, he shall resume the powers and duties of his office unless the Vice-President and a majority of either the principal officers of the executive department or of such other body as Congress may by law provide, transmit within four days to the President pro tempore of the Senate and the Speaker of the House of Representatives their written declaration that the President is unable to discharge the powers and duties of his office. Thereupon Congress shall decide the issue, assembling within forty-eight hours for that purpose if not in session. If the Congress, within twenty-one days after receipt of the latter written declaration, or, if Congress is not in session, within twenty-one days after Congress is required to assemble, determines by two-thirds vote of both Houses that the President is unable to discharge the powers and duties of his office, the Vice-President shall continue to discharge the same as Acting President; otherwise, the President shall resume the powers and duties of his office.

AMENDMENT XXVI

(Proposed March 23, 1971; ratified July 1, 1971)

Section 1. The right of citizens of the United States, who are eighteen years of age or older, to vote shall not be denied or abridged by the United States or by any State on account of age.

(Voting age lowered to 18 years)

Section 2. The Congress shall have the power to enforce this article by appropriate legislation.

AMENDMENT XXVII

(Proposed September 25, 1789; ratified May 7, 1992)

No law varying the compensation for services of the Senators and Representatives, shall take effect, until an election of Representatives shall have intervened.

(Changes in congressional salaries)

The Federalist, No. 10 [1787]

To the People of the State of New York: Among the numerous advantages promised by a well-constructed union, none deserves to be more accurately developed than its tendency to break and control the violence of faction. The friend of popular governments, never finds himself so much alarmed for their character and fate, as when he contemplates their propensity to this dangerous vice. He will not fail, therefore, to set a due value on any plan which, without violating the principles to which he is attached, provides a proper cure for it. The instability, injustice, and confusion introduced into the public councils, have, in truth, been the mortal diseases under which popular governments have everywhere perished; as they continue to be the favourite and fruitful topics from which the adversaries to liberty derive their most specious declamations. The valuable improvements made by the American constitutions on the popular models, both ancient and modern, cannot certainly be too much admired; but it would be an unwarrantable partiality, to contend that they have as effectually obviated the danger on this side, as was wished and expected. Complaints are everywhere heard from our most considerate and virtuous citizens, equally the friends of public and private faith, and of public and personal liberty, that our governments are too unstable; that the public good is disregarded in the conflicts of rival parties; and that measures are too often decided, not according to the rules of justice, and the rights of the minor party, but by the superior force of an interested and overbearing majority. However anxiously we may wish that these complaints had no foundation, the evidence of known facts will not permit us to deny that they are in some degree true. It will be found, indeed, on a candid review of our situation, that some of the distresses under which we labour have been erroneously charged on the operation of our governments; but it will be found, at the same time, that other causes will not alone account for many of our heaviest misfortunes; and, particularly, for that prevailing and increasing distrust of public engagements, and alarm for private rights, which are echoed from one end of the continent to the other. These must be chiefly, if not wholly, effects of the unsteadiness and injustice, with which a factious spirit has tainted our public administrations.

By a faction, I understand a number of citizens, whether amounting to a majority or minority of the whole, who are united and actuated by some common impulse of passion, or of interest, adverse to the rights of other citizens, or to the permanent and aggregate interests of the community.

There are two methods of curing the mischiefs of faction: The one, by removing its causes; the other, by controlling its effects.

There are again two methods of removing the causes of faction: The one, by destroying the liberty which is essential to its existence; the other, by giving to every citizen the same opinions, the same passions, and the same interests.

It could never be more truly said, than of the first remedy, that it was worse than the disease. Liberty is to faction what air is to fire, an ailment without which it instantly expires. But it could not be a less folly to abolish liberty, which is essential to political life, because it nourishes faction, than it would be to wish the annihilation of air, which is essential to animal life, because it imparts to fire its destructive agency.

The second expedient is as impracticable, as the first would be unwise. As long as the reason of man continues fallible, and he is at liberty to exercise it, different opinions will be formed. As long as the connection subsists between his reason and his self-love, his opinions and his passions will have a reciprocal influence on each other; and the former will be objects to which the latter will attach themselves. The diversity in the faculties of men, from which the rights of property originate, is not less an insuperable obstacle to an uniformity of interests. The protection of these faculties is the first object of government. From the protection of different and unequal faculties of acquiring property, the possession of different degrees and kinds of property immediately results; and from the influence of these on the sentiments and views of the respective proprietors, ensues a division of the society into different interests and parties.

The latent causes of action are thus sown in the nature of man; and we see them everywhere brought into different degrees of activity, according to the different circumstances of civil society. A zeal for different opinions concerning religion, concerning government, and many other points, as well as of speculation as of practice; an attachment to different leaders ambitiously contending for preeminence and power; or to persons of other descriptions whose fortunes have been interesting to the human passions, have, in turn, divided mankind into parties, inflamed them with mutual animosity, and rendered them much more disposed to vex and oppress each other, than to cooperate for their common good. So strong is this propensity of mankind, to fall into mutual animosities, that where no substantial occasion presents itself, the most frivolous and fanciful distinctions have been sufficient to kindle their unfriendly passions and excite their most violent conflicts. But the most common and durable source of factions, has been the various and unequal distribution of property. Those who hold, and those who are without property, have ever formed distinct interests in society. Those who are creditors, and those who are debtors, fall under alike discrimination. A landed interest, a manufacturing interest, a mercantile interest, a moneyed interest, with many lesser interests, grow up of necessity in civilized nations, and divide them into different classes, actuated by different sentiments and views. The regulation of these various and interfering interests forms the principal task of modern legislation, and involves the spirit of the party and faction in the necessary and ordinary operations of the government.

No man is allowed to be a judge in his own cause; because his interest will certainly bias his judgment, and, not improbably, corrupt his integrity. With equal, nay, with greater reason, a body of men are unfit to be both judges and parties at the same time; yet what are many of the most important acts of legislation, but so many judicial determinations, not indeed concerning the right of single persons, but concerning the rights of large bodies of citizens? And what are the different classes of legislators, but advocates and parties to the causes which they determine? Is a law proposed concerning private debts? It is a question to which the creditors are parties on one side, and the debtors on the other. Justice ought to hold the balance between them. Yet the parties are, and must be, themselves the judges; and the most numerous party, or, in other words, the most powerful faction, must be expected to prevail. Shall domestic manufactures be encouraged, and in what degree, by restrictions on foreign manufactures? are questions which would be differently decided by the landed and the manufacturing classes; and probably by neither with a sole regard to justice and the public good. The apportionment of taxes, on the various descriptions of property, is an act which seems to require the most exact impartiality; yet there is, perhaps, no legislative act, in which greater opportunity and temptation are given to a predominant party to trample on the rules of justice. Every shilling, with which they overburden the inferior number, is a shilling saved to their own pockets.

It is in vain to say, that enlightened statesmen will be able to adjust these clashing interests, and render them all subservient to the public good. Enlightened statesmen will not always be at the helm: nor, in many cases, can such an adjustment be made at all, without taking into view indirect and remote considerations, which will rarely prevail over the immediate interest which one party may find in disregarding the rights of another, or the good of the whole.

The inference to which we are brought is, that the *causes* of faction cannot be removed; and that relief is only to be sought in the means of controlling its *effects*.

If a faction consists of less than a majority, relief is supplied by the republican principle, which enables the majority to defeat its sinister views, by regular vote. It may clog the administration, it may convulse the society; but it will be unable to execute and mask its violence under the forms of the constitution. When a majority is included in a faction, the form of popular government, on the other hand, enables it to sacrifice to its ruling passion or interest, both the public good and the rights of other citizens. To secure the public good, and private rights, against the danger of such a faction, and at the same time to preserve the spirit and the form of popular government, is then the great object to which our inquiries are directed. Let me add, that it is the great desideratum, by which alone this form of government can be rescued from the opprobrium under which it has so long laboured, and be recommended to the esteem and adoption of mankind.

By what means is this object attainable? Evidently by one of two only. Either the existence of the same passion or interest in a majority, at the same time, must be prevented; or the majority, having such co-existent passion or interest, must be rendered, by their number and local situation, unable to concert and carry into effect schemes of oppression. If the impulse and the opportunity be suffered to coincide, we well know that neither moral nor religious motives can be relied on as an adequate control. They are not found to be such on the injustice and violence of individuals, and lose their efficacy in proportion to the number combined together; that is, in proportion as their efficacy becomes needful.

From this view of the subject, it may be concluded, that a pure democracy, by which I mean a society consisting of a small number of citizens, who assemble and administer the government in person, can admit of no cure for the mischiefs of faction. A common passion or interest will, in almost every case, be felt by a majority of the whole; a communication and concert, results from the form of government itself; and there is nothing to check the inducements to sacrifice the weaker party, or an obnoxious individual. Hence, it is, that such democracies have ever been spectacles of turbulence and contention; have ever been found incompatible with personal security, or the rights of property; and have in general been as short in their lives, as they have been violent in their deaths. Theoretic politicians, who have patronized this species of government, have erroneously supposed, that by reducing mankind to a perfect equality in their political rights, they would, at the same time, be perfectly equalized and assimilated in their possessions, their opinions, and their passions.

A republic, by which I mean a government in which the scheme of representation takes place, opens a different prospect, and promises the cure for which we are seeking. Let us examine the points in which it varies from pure democracy, and we shall comprehend both the nature of the cure and the efficacy which it must derive from the union.

The two great points of difference, between a democracy and a republic, are, first, the delegation of the government, in the latter, to a small number of citizens, elected by the rest; secondly, the greatest number of citizens, and greater sphere of country, over which the latter may be extended.

The effect of the first difference is, on the one hand, to refine and enlarge the public views, by passing them through the medium of a chosen body of citizens, whose wisdom may best discern the true interest of their country, and whose patriotism and love of justice, will be least likely to sacrifice it to temporary or partial considerations. Under such a regulation, it may well happen, that the public voice, pronounced by the representatives of the people, will be more consonant to the public good, than if pronounced by the people themselves, convened for the purpose. On the other hand the effect may be inverted. Men of factious tempers, of local prejudices, or of sinister designs, may by intrigue, by corruption, or by other means, first obtain the suffrages, and then betray the interest of the people. The question resulting is, whether small or extensive republics are most favourable to the election of proper guardians of the public weal; and it is clearly decided in favour of the latter by two obvious considerations.

In the first place, it is to be remarked that, however small the republic may be, the representatives must be raised to a certain number, in order to guard against the cabals of a few; and that however large it may be, they must be limited to a certain number, in order to guard against the confusion of a multitude. Hence, the number of representatives in the two cases not being in proportion to that of the constituents, and being proportionally greatest in the small republic, it follows, that if the proportion of fit characters be not less in the large than in the small republic, the former will present a greater option, and consequently a greater probability of a fit choice.

In the next place, as each representative will be chosen by a greater number of citizens in the large than in the small republic, it will be more difficult for unworthy candidates to practise with success the vicious arts, by which elections are too often carried; and the suffrages of the people being more free, will be more likely to centre in men who possess the most attractive merit, and the most diffusive and established characters.

It must be confessed, that in this, as in most other cases, there is a mean, on both sides of which inconveniences will be found to lie. By enlarging too much the number of electors, you render the representatives too little acquainted with all their local circumstances and lesser interests; as by reducing it too much, you render him unduly attached to these, and too little fit to comprehend and pursue great and national objects. The federal constitution forms a happy combination being referred to the national, the local and particular, to the state legislatures.

The other point of difference is, the greater number of citizens, and extent of territory, which may be brought within the compass of republican, than of democratic government; and it is this circumstance principally which renders factious combinations less to be dreaded in the former, than in the latter. The smaller the society, the fewer probably will be the distinct parties and interests composing it; the fewer the distinct parties and interests, the more frequently will a majority be found of the same party; and the smaller the number of individuals composing a majority, and the smaller the compass within which they are placed, the more easily will they concert and execute their plans of oppression. Extend the sphere, and you take in a greater variety of parties and interests; you make it less probable that a majority of the whole will have a common motive to invade the rights of other citizens; or if such a common motive exists, it will be more difficult for all who feel it to discover their own strength, and to act in unison with each other. Besides other impediments, it may be remarked, that where there is a consciousness of unjust or dishonourable purposes, communication is always checked by distrust, in proportion to the number whose concurrence is necessary.

Hence, it clearly appears, that the same advantage, which a republic has over a democracy, in controlling the effects of faction, is enjoyed by a large over a small republic,—is enjoyed by the union over the states composing it. Does this advantage consist in the substitution of representatives, whose enlightened views and virtuous sentiments render them superior to local prejudices, and to schemes of injustice? It will not be denied that the representation of the union will be most likely to possess these requisite endowments. Does it consist in the greater security afforded by a greater variety of parties, against the event of any one party being able to outnumber and oppress the rest? In an equal degree does the increased variety of parties, comprised within the union, increase the security? Does it, in fine, consist in the greater obstacles opposed to the concert and accomplishment of the secret wishes of an unjust and interested majority? Here, again, the extent of the union gives it the most palpable advantage.

The influence of factious leaders may kindle a flame within their particular states, but will be unable to spread a general conflagration through the other states; a religious sect may degenerate into a political faction in a part of the confederacy; but the variety of sects dispersed over the entire face of it, must secure the national councils against any danger from that source: a rage for paper money, for an abolition of debts, for an equal division of property, or for any other improper or wicked project, will be less apt to pervade the whole body of the union than a particular member of it; in the same proportion as such a malady is more likely to taint a particular county or district, then an entire state.

In the extent and proper structure of the union, therefore, we behold a republican remedy for the diseases most incident to republican government. And according to the degree of pleasure and pride we feel in being republicans, ought to be our zeal in cherishing the spirit, and supporting the character of federalists.

JAMES MADISON

The Federalist, No. 51 [1788]

To the People of the State of New York: To what expedient then shall we finally resort for maintaining in practice the necessary partition of power among the several departments, as laid down in the constitution? The only answer that can be given is, that as all these exterior provisions are found to be inadequate, the defect must be supplied, by so contriving the interior structure of the government, as that its several constituent parts may, by their mutual relations, be the means of keeping each other in their proper places. Without presuming to undertake a full development of this important idea, I will hazard a few general observations, which may perhaps place it in a clearer light, and enable us to form a more correct judgment of the principles and structure of the government planned by the convention.

In order to lay a due foundation for that separate and distinct exercise of the different powers of government, which to a certain extent, is admitted on all hands to be essential to the preservation of liberty, it is evident that each department should have a will of its own; and consequently should be so constituted, that the members of each should have as little agency as possible in the appointment of the members of the others. Were this principle rigorously adhered to, it would require that all the appointments for the supreme executive, legislative, and judiciary magistracies, should be drawn from the same fountain of authority, the people, through channels, having no communication whatever with one another. Perhaps such a plan of constructing the several departments would be less difficult in practice than it may in contemplation appear. Some difficulties however, and some additional expense, would attend the execution of it. Some deviations therefore from the principle must be admitted. In the constitution of the judiciary department in particular, it might be inexpedient to insist rigorously on the principle; first, because peculiar qualifications being essential in the members, the primary consideration ought to be to select that mode of choice, which best secures these qualifications; secondly, because the permanent tenure by which the appointments are held in that department, must soon destroy all sense of dependence on the authority conferring them.

It is equally evident that the members of each department should be as little dependent as possible on those of the others, for the emoluments annexed to their offices. Were the executive magistrate, or the judges, not independent of the legislature in this particular, their independence in every other would be merely nominal.

But the great security against a gradual concentration of the several powers in the same department, consists in giving to those who administer each department, the necessary constitutional means, and personal motives, to resist encroachments of the others. The provision for defense must in this, as in all other cases, be made commensurate to the danger of attack. Ambition must be made to counteract ambition. The interest of the man must be connected with the constitutional rights of the place. It may be a reflection on human nature, that such devices should be necessary to control the abuses of government: But what is government itself but the greatest of all reflections on human nature? If men were angels, no government would be necessary. If angels were to govern men, neither external nor internal controls on government would be necessary. In framing a government which is to be administered by men over men, the great difficulty lies in this: You must first enable the government to control the governed; and in the next place, oblige it to control itself. A dependence on the people is no doubt the primary control on the government; but experience has taught mankind the necessity of auxiliary precautions.

This policy of supplying by opposite and rival interests, the defect of better motives, might be traced through the whole system of human affairs, private as well as public. We see it particularly displayed in all the subordinate distributions of power; where the constant aim is to divide and arrange the several offices in such a manner as that each may be a check on the other; that the private interest of every individual, may be a sentinel over the public rights. These inventions of prudence cannot be less requisite in the distribution of the supreme powers of the state.

But it is not possible to give to each department an equal power of self defense. In republican government the legislative authority, necessarily, predominates. The remedy for this inconveniency is, to divide the legislature into different branches; and to render them by different modes of election, and different principles of action, as little connected with each other, as the nature of their common functions, and their common dependence on the society, will admit. It may even be necessary to guard against dangerous encroachments by still further precautions. As the weight of the legislative authority requires that it should be thus divided, the weakness of the executive may require, on the other hand, that it should be fortified. An absolute negative, on the legislature, appears at first view to be the natural defense with which the executive magistrate should be armed. But perhaps it would be neither altogether safe, nor alone sufficient. On ordinary occasions, it might not be exerted with the requisite firmness; and on extraordinary occasions, it might be perfidiously abused. May not this defect of an absolute negative be supplied, by some qualified connection between this weaker department, and the weaker branch of the stronger department, by which the latter may be led to support the constitutional rights of the former, without being too much detached from the rights of its own department?

If the principles on which these observations are founded be just, as I persuade myself they are, and they be applied as a criterion, to the several state constitutions, and to the federal constitution, it will be found, that if the latter does not perfectly correspond with them, the former are infinitely less able to bear such a test.

There are moreover two considerations particularly applicable to the federal system of America, which place that system in a very interesting point of view.

First. In a single republic, all the power surrendered by the people, is submitted to the administration of a single government; and usurpations are guarded against by a division of the government into distinct and separate departments. In the compound republic of America, the power surrendered by the people, is first divided between two distinct governments, and then the portion allotted to each, subdivided among distinct and separate departments. Hence a double security arises to the rights of the people. The different governments will control each other; at the same time that each will be controlled by itself.

Second. It is of great importance in a republic, not only to guard the society against the oppression of its rulers; but to guard one part of the society against the injustice of the other part. Different interests necessarily exist in different classes of citizens. If a majority be united by a common interest, the rights of the minority will be insecure. There are but two methods of providing against this evil: The one by creating a will in the community independent of the majority, that is, of the society itself; the other by comprehending in the society so many separate descriptions of citizens, as will render an unjust combination of a majority of the whole, very improbable, if not impracticable. The first method prevails in all governments possessing an hereditary or self appointed authority. This at best is but a precarious security; because a power independent of the society may as well espouse the unjust views of the major, as the rightful interests, of the minor party, and may possibly be turned against both parties. The second method will be exemplified in the federal republic of the United States. While all authority in it will be derived from and dependent on the society, the society itself will be broken into so many parts, interests and classes of citizens, that the rights of individuals or of the minority, will be in little danger from interested combinations of the majority. In a free government, the security for civil rights must be the same as for religious rights. It consists in the one case in the multiplicity of sects. The degree of security in both cases will depend on the number of interests and sects; and this may be presumed to depend on the extent of country and number of people comprehended under the same government. This view of the subject must particularly recommend a proper federal system to all the sincere and considerate friends of republican government: Since it shows that in exact proportion as the territory of the union may be formed into more circumscribed confederacies or states, oppressive combinations of a majority will be facilitated; the best security under the republican form, for the rights of every class of citizens, will be diminished; and consequently, the stability and independence of some member of the government, the only other security, must be proportionally increased. Justice is the end of government. It is the end of civil society. It ever has been, and ever will be pursued, until it be obtained, or until liberty be lost in the pursuit. In a society under the forms of which the stronger faction can readily unite and oppress the weaker, anarchy may as truly be said to reign, as in a state of nature where the weaker individual is not secured against the violence of the stronger: And as in the latter state even the stronger individuals are prompted by the uncertainty of their condition, to submit to a government which may protect the weak as well as themselves: So in the former state, will the more powerful factions or parties be gradually induced by alike motives, to wish for a government which will protect all parties, the weaker as well as the more powerful. It can be little doubted, that if the state of Rhode Island was separated from the confederacy, and left to itself, the insecurity of rights under the popular form of government within such narrow limits, would be displayed by such reiterated oppression of factious majorities, that some power altogether independent of the people would soon be called for by the voice of the very factions whose misrule had proved the necessity of it. In the extended republic of the United States, and among the great variety of interests, parties and sects which it embraces, a coalition of a majority of the whole society could seldom take place on any other principles than those of justice and the general good; and there being thus less danger to a minor from the will of the major party, there must be less pretext also, to provide for the security of the former, by introducing into the government a will not dependent on the latter; or in other words, a will independent of the society itself. It is no less certain than it is important, notwithstanding the contrary opinions which have been entertained, that the larger the society, provided it lie within a practicable sphere, the more duly capable it will be of self government. And happily for the *republican cause*, the practicable sphere may be carried to a very great extent, by a judicious modification and mixture of the *federal principle*.

JAMES MADISON

Presidents of the United States

No.	Name	Born–Died	Years in Office	Political Party	Home State	Vice-President
1	George Washington	1732–1799	1789–1797	None	Va.	John Adams
2	John Adams	1735–1826	1797–1801	Federalist	Mass.	Thomas Jefferson
3	Thomas Jefferson	1743–1826	1801–1809	Republican	Va.	Aaron Burr George Clinton
4	James Madison	1751–1836	1809–1817	Republican	Va.	George Clinton Elbridge Gerry
5	James Monroe	1758–1831	1817–1825	Republican	Va.	Daniel D. Tompkins
6	John Quincy Adams	1767–1848	1825–1829	Republican	Mass.	John C. Calhoun
7	Andrew Jackson	1767–1845	1829–1837	Democratic	Tenn.	John C. Calhoun Martin Van Buren
8	Martin Van Buren	1782–1862	1837–1841	Democratic	N.Y.	Richard M. Johnson
9	William Henry Harrison	1773–1841	1841	Whig	Ohio	John Tyler
10	John Tyler	1790–1862	1841–1845	Whig	Va.	———
11	James K. Polk	1795–1849	1845–1849	Democratic	Tenn.	George M. Dallas
12	Zachary Taylor	1784–1850	1849–1850	Whig	La.	Millard Fillmore
13	Millard Fillmore	1800–1874	1850–1853	Whig	N.Y.	———
14	Franklin Pierce	1804–1869	1853–1857	Democratic	N.H.	William R. King
15	James Buchanan	1791–1868	1857–1861	Democratic	Pa.	John C. Breckinridge
16	Abraham Lincoln	1809–1865	1861–1865	Republican	Ill.	Hannibal Hamlin Andrew Johnson
17	Andrew Johnson	1808–1875	1865–1869	Republican	Tenn.	———
18	Ulysses S. Grant	1822–1885	1869–1877	Republican	Ill.	Schuyler Colfax Henry Wilson
19	Rutherford B. Hayes	1822–1893	1877–1881	Republican	Ohio	William A. Wheeler
20	James A. Garfield	1831–1881	1881	Republican	Ohio	Chester A. Arthur
21	Chester A. Arthur	1830–1886	1881–1885	Republican	N.Y.	———
22	Grover Cleveland	1837–1908	1885–1889	Democratic	N.Y.	Thomas A. Hendricks
23	Benjamin Harrison	1833–1901	1889–1893	Republican	Ind.	Levi P. Morton
24	Grover Cleveland		1893–1897	Democratic	N.Y.	Adlai E. Stevenson
25	William McKinley	1843–1901	1897–1901	Republican	Ohio	Garret A. Hobart Theodore Roosevelt
26	Theodore Roosevelt	1858–1919	1901–1909	Republican	N.Y.	——— Charles W. Fairbanks
27	William Howard Taft	1857–1930	1909–1913	Republican	Ohio	James S. Sherman
28	Woodrow Wilson	1856–1924	1913–1921	Democratic	N.J.	Thomas R. Marshall
29	Warren G. Harding	1865–1923	1921–1923	Republican	Ohio	Calvin Coolidge
30	Calvin Coolidge	1872–1933	1923–1929	Republican	Mass.	——— Charles G. Dawes
31	Herbert Hoover	1874–1964	1929–1933	Republican	Calif.	Charles Curtis
32	Franklin D. Roosevelt	1882–1945	1933–1945	Democratic	N.Y.	John Nance Garner Henry Wallace Harry S. Truman
33	Harry S. Truman	1884–1972	1945–1953	Democratic	Mo.	——— Alben W. Barkley
34	Dwight D. Eisenhower	1890–1969	1953–1961	Republican	Kans.	Richard M. Nixon
35	John F. Kennedy	1917–1963	1961–1963	Democratic	Mass.	Lyndon B. Johnson
36	Lyndon B. Johnson	1908–1973	1963–1969	Democratic	Texas	——— Hubert H. Humphrey
37	Richard M. Nixon	1913–1994	1969–1974	Republican	Calif.	Spiro T. Agnew Gerald Ford
38	Gerald Ford	1913–	1974–1977	Republican	Mich.	Nelson A. Rockefeller
39	Jimmy Carter	1924–	1977–1981	Democratic	Ga.	Walter F. Mondale
40	Ronald Reagan	1911–	1981–1989	Republican	Calif.	George Bush
41	George Bush	1924–	1989–1993	Republican	Texas	J. Danforth Quayle
42	Bill Clinton	1946–	1993–	Democratic	Ark.	Albert Gore

A-23

Supreme Court Justices

Name, Home State	Term of Service	Appointed by	Name, Home State	Term of Service	Appointed by
John Jay,* N.Y.	1789–1795	Washington	Joseph McKenna, Cal.	1898–1925	McKinley
James Wilson, Pa.	1789–1798	Washington	Oliver W. Holmes, Mass.	1902–1932	T. Roosevelt
John Rutledge, S.C.	1790–1791	Washington	William R. Day, Ohio	1903–1922	T. Roosevelt
William Cushing, Mass.	1790–1810	Washington	William H. Moody, Mass.	1906–1910	T. Roosevelt
John Blair, Va.	1790–1796	Washington	Horace H. Lurton, Tenn.	1910–1914	Taft
James Iredell, N.C.	1790–1799	Washington	Charles E. Hughes, N.Y.	1910–1916	Taft
Thomas Johnson, Md.	1792–1793	Washington	**Edward D. White**, La.	1910–1921	Taft
William Paterson, N.J.	1793–1806	Washington	Willis Van Devanter, Wy.	1911–1937	Taft
John Rutledge, S.C.	1795	Washington	Joseph R. Lamar, Ga.	1911–1916	Taft
Samuel Chase, Md.	1796–1811	Washington	Mahlon Pitney, N.J.	1912–1922	Taft
Oliver Ellsworth, Conn.	1796–1800	Washington	James C. McReynolds, Tenn.	1914–1941	Wilson
Bushrod Washington, Va.	1799–1829	J. Adams	Louis D. Brandeis, Mass.	1916–1939	Wilson
Alfred Moore, N.C.	1800–1804	J. Adams	John H. Clarke, Ohio	1916–1922	Wilson
John Marshall, Va.	1801–1835	J. Adams	**William H. Taft**, Conn.	1921–1930	Harding
William Johnson, S.C.	1804–1834	Jefferson	George Sutherland, Utah	1922–1938	Harding
Brockholst Livingston, N.Y.	1807–1823	Jefferson	Pierce Butler, Minn.	1923–1939	Harding
Thomas Todd, Ky.	1807–1826	Jefferson	Edward T. Sanford, Tenn.	1923–1930	Harding
Gabriel Duvall, Md.	1811–1835	Madison	Harlan F. Stone, N.Y.	1925–1941	Coolidge
Joseph Story, Mass.	1812–1845	Madison	**Charles E. Hughes**, N.Y.	1930–1941	Hoover
Smith Thompson, N.Y.	1823–1843	Monroe	Owen J. Roberts, Penn.	1930–1945	Hoover
Robert Trimble, Ky.	1826–1828	J. Q. Adams	Benjamin N. Cardozo, N.Y.	1932–1938	Hoover
John McLean, Ohio	1830–1861	Jackson	Hugo L. Black, Ala.	1937–1971	F. Roosevelt
Henry Baldwin, Pa.	1830–1844	Jackson	Stanley F. Reed, Ky.	1938–1957	F. Roosevelt
James M. Wayne, Ga.	1835–1867	Jackson	Felix Frankfurter, Mass.	1939–1962	F. Roosevelt
Roger B. Taney, Md.	1836–1864	Jackson	William O. Douglas, Conn.	1939–1975	F. Roosevelt
Philip P. Barbour, Va.	1836–1841	Jackson	Frank Murphy, Mich.	1940–1949	F. Roosevelt
John Cartron, Tenn.	1837–1865	Van Buren	**Harlan F. Stone**, N.Y.	1941–1946	F. Roosevelt
John McKinley, Ala.	1838–1852	Van Buren	James R. Byrnes, S.C.	1941–1942	F. Roosevelt
Peter V. Daniel, Va.	1842–1860	Van Buren	Robert H. Jackson, N.Y.	1941–1954	F. Roosevelt
Samuel Nelson, N.Y.	1845–1872	Tyler	Wiley B. Rutledge, Iowa	1943–1949	F. Roosevelt
Levi Woodbury, N.H.	1845–1851	Polk	Harold H. Burton, Ohio	1945–1958	Truman
Robert C. Grier, Pa.	1846–1870	Polk	**Frederick M. Vinson**, Ky.	1946–1953	Truman
Benjamin R. Curtis, Mass.	1851–1857	Fillmore	Tom C. Clark, Texas	1949–1967	Truman
John A. Campbell, Ala.	1853–1861	Pierce	Sherman Minton, Ind.	1949–1956	Truman
Nathan Clifford, Me.	1858–1881	Buchanan	**Earl Warren**, Cal.	1953–1969	Eisenhower
Noah H. Swayne, Ohio	1862–1881	Lincoln	John Marshall Harlan, N.Y.	1955–1971	Eisenhower
Samuel F. Miller, Iowa	1862–1890	Lincoln	William J. Brennan, Jr., N.J.	1956–1990	Eisenhower
David Davis, Ill.	1862–1877	Lincoln	Charles E. Whittaker, Mo.	1957–1962	Eisenhower
Stephen J. Field, Cal.	1863–1897	Lincoln	Potter Stewart, Ohio	1958–1981	Eisenhower
Salmon P. Chase, Ohio	1864–1873	Lincoln	Bryon R. White, Colo.	1962–1993	Kennedy
William Strong, Pa.	1870–1880	Grant	Arthur J. Goldberg, Ill.	1962–1965	Kennedy
Joseph P. Bradley, N.J.	1870–1892	Grant	Abe Fortas, Tenn.	1965–1969	Johnson
Ward Hunt, N.Y.	1873–1882	Grant	Thurgood Marshall, Md.	1967–1991	Johnson
Morrison R. Waite, Ohio	1874–1888	Grant	**Warren E. Burger**, Minn.	1969–1986	Nixon
John M. Harlan, Ky.	1877–1911	Hayes	Harry A. Blackmun, Minn.	1970–	Nixon
William B. Woods, Ga.	1881–1887	Hayes	Lewis F. Powell, Jr., Va.	1971–1987	Nixon
Stanley Matthews, Ohio	1881–1889	Garfield	William H. Rehnquist, Ariz.	1971–1986	Nixon
Horace Gray, Mass.	1882–1902	Arthur	John Paul Stevens, Ill.	1975–	Ford
Samuel Blatchford, N.Y.	1882–1893	Arthur	Sandra Day O'Connor, Ariz.	1981–	Reagan
Lucius Q. C. Lamar, Miss.	1888–1893	Cleveland	**William H. Rehnquist**, Ariz.	1986–	Reagan
Melville W. Fuller, Ill.	1888–1910	Cleveland	Antonin Scalia, Va.	1986–	Reagan
David J. Brewer, Kan.	1890–1910	B. Harrison	Anthony M. Kennedy, Cal.	1988–	Reagan
Henry B. Brown, Mich.	1891–1906	B. Harrison	David H. Souter, N.H.	1990–	Bush
George Shiras, Jr., Pa.	1892–1903	B. Harrison	Clarence Thomas, Ga.	1991–	Bush
Howell E. Jackson, Tenn.	1893–1895	B. Harrison	Ruth Bader Ginsburg, N.Y.	1993–	Clinton
Edward D. White, La.	1894–1910	Cleveland	Stephen G. Breyer, Mass.	1994–	Clinton
Rufus W. Peckham, N.Y.	1896–1909	Cleveland			

*Names of Chief Justices are printed in bold type.

Glossary

The number in parentheses at the end of each entry refers to the chapter in which the term is defined and discussed in detail.

A

administrative law Rules created by bureaucrats to control the organizations and activities they regulate. (13)

adversary system A system of justice in which there is a vigorous but controlled debate between a plaintiff and a defendant, both usually represented by lawyers. (14)

affirmative action Aggressive policies to ensure that equal opportunity in employment, college admission, and other areas is implemented in order to overcome the effects of past discrimination. (16)

alternative dispute resolution Negotiation by litigants and the courts to settle a dispute using procedures such as mediation and arbitration instead of a trial. (14)

American dream The pursuit of happiness, whether by acquiring and developing property or by achieving artistic, athletic, intellectual, or spiritual goals. (4)

American legal system The basis for public order, consisting of several types of law which are interpreted and applied by federal, state, and local courts and are enforced by federal, state, and local law officers. (14)

amicus curiae **brief** "Friend of the court" arguments submitted in writing to the Supreme Court to influence administrative policy decisions. (14)

anarchists Those who oppose the idea of government. (4)

Anti-Federalists Those who wanted to amend the Articles of Confederation to make the national government more effective without eroding the power of the states, rather than ratify the U.S. Constitution. (2)

appellate jurisdiction The authority a court has to hear cases on appeal from lower courts that involve legal errors (that is, violations of due process). (14)

apprenticeship system A former practice by which new members of Congress advanced their political careers by attaching themselves to more senior members, who guided their careers, usually by helping them get subcommittee and then committee chair positions. (11)

Articles of Confederation and Perpetual Union The constitutional document drafted by the Second Continental Congress and ratified by the states in an effort to create a national government. (2)

attorney general Head of the Department of Justice and the government's chief lawyer. (14)

authority Recognized or accepted power that obtains obedience without the use of force. (1)

B

baby boomers The children of the World War II generation, born between 1946 and 1964. (4)

backchanneling A mode of bureaucratic resistance in which one circumvents the normal bureaucratic chain of communication by resorting to someone outside the bureaucracy to convey information or exert pressure on key decisionmakers. (13)

bandwagon effect The tendency of people to support the prevailing candidate or issue. (5)

base A group of voters who are likely to remain loyal to a particular candidate unless they become alienated by something the candidate does. (10)

base politics Strategies candidates employ to steal voters from their opponent's base. (10)

beat The particular office, figure, or policy area to which a journalist has been assigned. (9)

Bill of Rights The first ten amendments of the U.S. Constitution. (2)

bill of rights A document that protects individual liberties, or natural rights. (2)

black power movement Black nationalist groups that emerged in the 1960s promoting a positive black identity and encouraging activism. (16)

blanket primary A primary election in which qualified candidates from all parties are listed on a single ballot and voters are allowed to choose among all of them, rather than just the candidates of a single party. (7)

block grants The consolidation of various specific categorical grants into a single sum, giving states and localities more discretion over how to allocate funds within each general area, such as urban development. (3)

brief Legal arguments and precedents that are combined into a document supporting one side of a court case. (14)

bundling The practice by which political action committees pool the contributions of individual members of an organization and distribute these funds to political candidates. (8)

bureaucracy A system of organization that integrates a group of specialized human activities into a hierarchy with legal or rule-based authority to achieve continuous conduct of business. (13)

bureaucratic politicking The perpetual struggle among different bureaucratic agencies for scarce resources and greater responsibilities. (13)

bureaucratic thickening The addition, since 1960, of many levels of officials between the top and the bottom of the bureaucracy. (13)

bureaucratic widening The increase in the size of each level of the bureaucracy since 1960. (13)

busing of students A policy requiring school districts to transport students of one race to a school whose students are primarily of another race. (16)

C

cabinet Presidential advisors consisting of the secretaries, or heads, of all the executive-branch departments and other key officials assigned "cabinet rank." (12)

campaign pollsters Openly partisan pollsters who work for particular candidates, furnishing them with information useful to their campaigns and sometimes "cooked" to improve candidates' images and their messages. (5)

capitalism An economic system in which the means of production (factories, farms, shops) are privately rather than publicly (government) owned. (1)

casework Special work done by the staff of a member of Congress to help a constituent deal with problems, especially those involving the federal bureaucracy. (11)

categorical grant programs Programs that specify the category of activity on which states and cities are to spend federal grant funds and that include detailed regulations about how the program is to be carried out. (3)

charisma A personal magnetism that inspires others to follow a political figure. (1)

charter A grant from the sovereign power of a country conferring certain rights and privileges on a person, a corporation, or the people. (2)

charter schools Experimental schools that operate under a state charter but independently of state authority. (4)

checks and balances The system by which government institutions or branches of government exercise checks on, and balance the activities of, other government institutions and branches. (2)

chief of staff The individual appointed by the president to oversee the White House staff and determine who gets on the president's daily schedule. (12)

circuit courts Federal intermediary appellate courts that do not revisit the facts of a case but determine whether the procedures that led to the decision were fair and followed due process and determine how federal law and the Constitution apply. (14)

civil disobedience Intentional breaking of the law by individuals or groups to call public attention to a law or policy they believe to be unjust, in part by accepting judicial punishment. (6)

civility A respect for social order. (4)

civil law A type of law in which the government acts indirectly as a referee, or adjudicator, of disputes involving private citizens; private law. (14)

civil libertarians Those who rank civil liberties as the highest political value. (15)

civil liberties Freedoms of individuals from the actions of government; freedoms that the constitutions of the nation and the states require those governments to protect. (15)

civil rights Fundamental rights that government acts to protect from the unlawful actions of others, including government. (15, 16)

civil rights movement Collective action of African Americans and their supporters, including legal and political activism, civil disobedience, militancy, and self-help initiatives, to achieve civil rights. (16)

class action suits Cases in which one or more persons sue or are sued as representatives of a larger group in similar circumstances. (14)

classification A practice by which government restricts access to sensitive information for security purposes by categorizing it in terms of its importance. (13)

clear and present danger Doctrine articulated in 1919 by Justice Oliver Wendell Holmes as the test of whether the U.S. government can restrict freedom of speech in the name of national security. (15)

closed primary A primary election in which voters must declare their party affiliation and choose from among the candidates on that party's ballot. (7)

cloture The rule that requires agreement by 60 percent of the senators present and voting to limit debate and move toward a vote. (11)

coattail effect The ability of a popular presidential candidate to carry other candidates on the party's ticket into office "on his or her coattails." (10)

collective deliberation The process by which voters, given accurate information and the opportunity to debate about candidates and issues, reach more informed decisions. (5)

collective goods Goods that, once provided to some members of an actual or potential group, cannot be denied to others in that group. (8)

Committee of the Whole The House of Representatives acting as a committee with less restrictive rules to pass (or on rare occasions amend) a rule drafted by the Rules Committee or to debate legislation before the measure is considered by the whole House. (11)

the common good The good of the public as a whole. (1)

common law Case law generated by judges, generally based on precedent. (14)

communitarianism A political philosophy that values the well-being of the community and seeks to protect it from excessive deference to individualism or individual rights. (4)

communitarians Those who oppose policies that favor the individual to the detriment of the community. (4)

compact A founding document that looks to the people for legitimation. (2)

comparable worth A term for the view that jobs with equal responsibilities should receive equal pay, even though jobs generally held by women command less pay in the economic marketplace. (16)

competitive federalism Active competition among states and cities with differing policy priorities for citizens and businesses and the increased tax base they provide. (3)

computer bulletin board An Internet site that allows computer users worldwide to post messages and request information. (9)

concurrent powers Powers of the federal and state governments that can be exercised concurrently by both levels. (3)

concurring opinion A formal statement written by a Supreme Court justice explaining why he or she agrees with the majority decision on a case but disagrees with the majority's reasoning. (14)

confederation A political alliance based on common interests but allocating very limited powers to the central authority. (2)

conference committee An ad hoc committee consisting of members of the Senate and the House appointed for the sole purpose of negotiating a compromise on a particular piece of legislation passed in a different form by each chamber. (11)

conflict of interest A situation in which an individual benefits personally—usually financially—from something he or she does in an official capacity. (11, 13)

congressional-executive agreement An agreement with another country that requires congressional implementation and the president asks Congress in advance to agree that its approval will require a simple majority of both houses rather than the two-thirds majority of the Senate that a treaty would require. (12)

congressional liaison A representative of the president who lobbies legislators and conveys their concerns to the president. (12)

conscientious objector Someone who objects to military service for reasons of conscience. (15)

conservatives People who tend to support the Republican party, oppose massive governmental intervention in politics and economics, support traditional morals and values, and endorse liberty as their primary political value. (4)

constitutional law Law consisting of the actual text of the U.S. Constitution (including amendments) as well as all the decisions that the Supreme Court has handed down over more than 200 years. (14)

constitutional practice An ongoing commitment by the people in a political society to abide by the rules of their constitution and to accept the enforcement of its guarantees. (1)

context A set of conditions that places an issue in a particular light and that suggests how the issue should be dealt with. (1)

contracts clause Article 1, section 10, of the U.S. Constitution, which states, "No state shall . . . pass any Law impairing the Obligation of contracts." (15)

cooperative federalism The period, beginning in the 1930s, during which the states and the federal government functioned as complementary parts of a single governmental mechanism. (3)

cosmopolitanism The sense that some people have that, because of their education, experience, and tastes, they are citizens of the world rather than of any one country. (4)

covenant A founding document that looks not to the people but to a higher authority, such as God or a king, for legitimation. (2)

creative federalism The term used to describe "Great Society" initiatives of President Lyndon Johnson which increased the number of grant programs and funding to states. (3)

crime A violation of a law or government regulation. (14)

criminal law Statutes specifying crimes against the public or its interest and prescribing punishments for them. (14)

cross-cutting allegiances Beliefs and commitments that bring people together regardless of their race, ethnicity, gender, or class because they cut across those interests. (4)

cue-takers People who rely on sources such as trusted friends, newspaper endorsements, or experts for advice on how to vote. (5, 11)

customary law A body of regulations derived from custom—the practices of social, professional, business, and other communities. (14)

cyberspace federalism The shift of functions that have been performed by central governments, to loose electronic transnational networks and to individuals, rather than to lower-level governments. (3)

D

dealignment A situation that occurs when a significant number of voters no longer wish to identify with a party and become independents. (7)

Declaration of Independence Document drafted primarily by Thomas Jefferson during the Second Continental Congress which declared the colonies free from British rule. (2)

de facto segregation Segregation imposed by social, economic, and political practices. (16)

defendant Someone in a legal proceeding who is accused of having caused harm. (14)

de jure segregation Segregation imposed by law. (16)

delegate A member of Congress who advocates constituents' views rather than his or her own views. (11)

deliberative opinion poll A survey in which individuals are polled twice on particular issues, once before they have been supplied with new information and a chance to deliberate, and again afterward, in order to see how those factors alter their opinions. (5)

democracy A system of government in which political authority rests with the people. (1)

demosclerosis The erosion of government's management ability and limited resource base by hyperpluralism, the excessive competition among interest groups. (8)

description A statement that claims to describe, or say *what is*, about a particular event or issue. (1)

desegregation The removal of racial barriers. (16)

developmental rights The rights a nation has to develop in terms of its own cultural values. (15)

devolution The movement of governing power down from the national level to the states. (3)

Dillon's Rule The principle, formalized in commentaries published by Iowa State Supreme Court Justice John F. Dillon, that local governments must derive their political authority from the states in which they are located. (3)

direct action The attempt by political activists to influence others, including government, by legally obstructing their functions. (6)

direct democracy A form of government in which all citizens have a direct say in what government does by voting on each question. (1)

direct primary An election in which the voters, rather than party bosses, decide which candidates the parties will nominate. (7)

discrimination The making of distinctions that harm a person and are based on the person's membership in a particular class or group. (16)

disinformation The release by the government of false information about policy or government actions to the media in order to deceive the public. (9, 13)

disparate impact Unintended discrimination to older workers as a result of downsizing. (16)

dissenting opinion A formal statement written by a Supreme Court justice explaining why the justices who voted with the minority disagreed entirely or in part with the majority's decision on a case. (14)

docket A court's list of cases to be tried or heard. (14)

double jeopardy The constitutional right not to be tried twice for the same crime. (15)

downshifting The movement of bureaucratic functions from the national to the state or local level. (13)

downsizing Shrinking the size of an organization by eliminating workers who are not needed or are too expensive. (13)

divided government A situation in which the presidency is controlled by one major political party and one or both houses of Congress are controlled by the other major party. (7)

division of powers The distribution of political authority among the national government, the state governments, and the people. (2)

doorstep opinions Opinions given to pollsters in face-to-face interviews that are distorted by respondents' desire to please or make themselves look good. (5)

dual citizenship The notion that people are citizens of their states as well as citizens of the nation. (2, 3)

dual federalism The view of federalism as a system in which the national and the state levels of government remain supreme in their own jurisdictions, as specified in the Constitution. (3)

dual legal system The two distinct legal systems—federal and state—that constitute the American legal system. (14)

dynamic equilibrium A way of keeping the political system in balance by managing pressures for order and change. (1)

E

e-mail Electronic mail that can be written on a computer and sent to anyone with Internet access. (9)

elastic clause The eighteenth clause in Article 1, Section 8, of the U.S. Constitution; grants Congress the power "to make all Laws which shall be necessary and proper" for executing its enumerated powers; also called the necessary and proper clause. (2, 11)

election The process in which citizens cast votes to choose among candidates for public office or to approve a policy position in a referendum or other vote at the local, state, or national level. (10)

Electoral College The collective name for electors from each of the 50 states and the District of Columbia who are chosen by a presidential candidate's campaign to vote for that candidate in the states in which he or she gets a plurality in the popular election. (10)

electoral votes The votes cast by electors in December of a presidential election year to determine who wins the presidency. (10)

electorate All persons permitted by law to vote. (6)

electronic frontier The electronic information revolution, from satellite television to the Internet, giving citizens access to information sources everywhere in the world. (3)

elites Powerful individuals who work inside government as elected or appointed officials or outside government as leaders of business, religious groups, and other important private organizations. (1)

elite theorists Theorists who argue that a small group of privileged insiders—wealthy families, powerful politicians, corporate executives, and military leaders—dominate policymaking at the federal, state, and local levels. (8)

emergency powers The president's inherent power to act without congressional authorization in certain situations. (12)

eminent domain The right of government to confiscate private property for public use so long as it provides just compensation to the owner. (15)

enumerated powers Certain powers explicitly granted in the U.S. Constitution to the central government and the states. (3, 12)

environmental racism The practice by some local governments and private businesses of deliberately concentrating waste-processing plants and other undesirable sites in minority neighborhoods. (6)

equal employment opportunity A personnel policy that guarantees the same opportunities to all individuals. (16)

Equal Rights Amendment A proposed amendment to the U.S. Constitution seeking a guarantee of equal treatment for men and women. (16)

equal time rule A regulation that requires a broadcaster to offer equal access to its airwaves to all candidates for a given office if it sells or grants such access to one candidate anywhere but in its news programs. (9)

equality of results Argument used by conservatives opposing affirmative action, claiming that it illegally exceeds the goal of equality of opportunity. (16)

establishment clause First Amendment clause prohibiting government from sponsoring or supporting any particular religion. (15)

exclusionary rule The rule that evidence obtained in illegal searches must be excluded from a court case. (15)

executive agreement An agreement between the president and another country that need not be submitted to the Senate for approval. (12)

executive branch The branch of government headed by the president and assigned the task of carrying out the laws made by Congress. (2)

Executive Office of the President The various departments and councils that make up the White House staff. (12)

executive order The president's power to require agencies or individuals to take specified actions, bypassing Congress. (12)

executive privilege A policy by which the president is protected from having to disclose information from his own papers and documents on certain matters. (12)

expert Someone with specialized knowledge about a particular area or issue. (1)

expertise Specialized knowledge about a particular field that most people accept as accurate. (1)

evaluation Assigning a value to the evidence produced by a description or an explanation. (1)

explanation An interpretation of or reasoning about a particular state of affairs. (1)

F

fairness doctrine A policy developed by the Federal Radio Commission in 1929 to foster the airing of a wide range of opinions. (9)

faithless electors Presidential electors who could overturn the results of the popular vote by breaking their pledge to vote for a particular candidate. (10)

Federal Communications Commission (FCC) An independent government agency that regulates the broadcast media. (9)

Federal Election Campaign Act (FECA) Enacted in 1971, this first serious attempt at campaign finance reform was modified by the Supreme Court so that it sets limits on an individual's contributions to candidates but not to political parties. (10)

federalism The form of government in which ruling authority over the people is divided between the national and state governments. (1, 3)

The Federalist A collection of 85 letters, most written by James Madison and Alexander Hamilton, containing the major Federalist arguments for ratification of the U.S. Constitution and published in a New York City newspaper between October 1787 and August 1788; also called *The Federalist Papers*. (2)

Federalists Those who favored ratification of the Constitution and wanted a limited central government strong enough to foster a powerful commercial state. (2)

Federalist Papers See *The Federalist*, above.

federal system The system of government consisting of the national or federal government together with the state governments, both levels sharing ruling authority over the people. (3)

feeds Prepackaged electronic press releases in the form of audiotapes and videotapes. (9)

felony A major criminal offense. (14)

filibuster A procedural tactic used by opponents of a bill, who kill the bill by talking it to death, usually by reading irrelevant materials for hours, unless and until 60 percent of the Senate votes for cloture. (11)

focus groups Small groups of people representative of a particular sector of the population whom pollsters use to assess public opinion. (5)

force Power that physically compels a political actor to act against its will. (1)

framing Putting a news item in a particular context, or "frame," that influences readers or viewers to draw certain conclusions about it. (9)

franchise The right to vote. (6)

free exercise clause Clause in the U.S. Constitution prohibiting government from interfering with a person's right to worship or not to worship. (15)

free media News coverage other than paid advertisements sought by political candidates to boost their standing with voters. (10)

free riders People who do not join public interest groups because they know they can enjoy for free the benefits obtained by the group. (8)

G

gender gap The tendency for women voters to be less supportive than men of Republican candidates, and for men to be less supportive than women of Democratic candidates. (6, 7)

general election A vote held in early November in even-numbered years, in which candidates from all parties compete for thousands of federal and state offices nationwide. (7)

gerrymandering The practice of designing unusually shaped voting districts to increase the election chances of candidates from a particular party or ethnic group. (10)

Glorious Revolution The series of events in late seventeenth-century England highlighted by the Declaration of Rights (1688) and Bill of Rights (1689), which expanded the rights of Englishmen. (2)

gotcha journalism Investigative journalism intended to catch public officials in seemingly compromising positions or to unearth claims that they engaged in inappropriate acts at some earlier time. (9)

governing coalition A collection of groups or special interests in the public at large that generally support the president and his program. (12)

government Public laws, public institutions, and public officials that continuously exercise political authority over the members of a political society. (1)

grandfather clause Legal provision by which, in an attempt to bar blacks from voting, certain states exempted voters from property and literacy requirements if they could prove that they, their father, or grandfather had voted before 1867. (6)

grants-in-aid Payments to the states by the federal government to finance such specified state activities as agriculture, vocational education, and highway construction. (3)

Great Compromise Agreement that created a bicameral legislature consisting of two houses of Congress, the Senate and the House of Representatives, at the Constitutional Convention in July 1787. (2)

gridlock Applied to politics, a term suggesting a traffic jam in which competing interests—usually, a president from one political party and a Congress controlled by the other party—block each other so completely that progress is impossible. (7, 11)

H

hard money Contributions made directly to political candidates. (8)

Hatch Act Law intended to protect civil servants from partisan political pressures by declaring it illegal for federal civil servants to participate in political campaigns except for voting and contributing money to candidates. (13)

hate speech Speech that insults and degrades others on the basis of race, religion, gender, or some other characteristic. (15)

home rule Local autonomy in municipal affairs granted to cities by a state. (3)

honeymoon The period at the outset of a presidency when people have high hopes for a new beginning and defeated opponents withhold criticism of the president. (12)

human rights The natural rights people hold simply because they are human. (16)

hyperpluralism The excessive proliferation of interest groups. (8)

I

implied powers Governmental powers consistent with the U.S. Constitution though not expressly enumerated. (3)

impoundment The refusal by the president to spend funds appropriated by Congress for certain specified programs. (12)

impression management Efforts to manage or manipulate the media's image of a candidate so that the media will pass that favorable image on to voters. (10)

incumbency Running for reelection while holding office. (10)

incumbency advantage The tendency for most Senate and House incumbents seeking reelection to win. (10)

incumbency effect Term used to describe the advantages and disadvantages a candidate has by being an incumbent running for reelection. (10)

independent regulatory commissions Government agencies, designed to be free of politics, that regulate a type of commercial activity or a sector of the economy. (13)

individualism The right of each person to think freely and to take initiatives. (4)

information superhighway A national information infrastructure that is being constructed as a web of electronic paths connecting public institutions, workplaces, and homes. (9)

infomercial A paid television program, usually broadcast on cable television stations, used by campaigning politicians. (10)

inherent powers Powers required for the national government to function as a nation-state in a world of nation-states; powers required for an executive branch of government to carry out its duties of implementation. (3, 12)

initiatives Formal petitions for legislative or constitutional changes filed by a designated percentage of the electorate; the legislature or the total electorate must then vote on the proposals. (6)

inquisitorial system A legal system in which judges take the lead role in asking questions of the parties involved and in reaching a decision on the case. (14)

inside strategies Lobbying strategies that include contacting lawmakers and their aides and government bureaucrats directly and getting publicity in the Washington media, where government officials are likely to see it. (8)

integration Bringing the races together with the intention of ending discrimination. (16)

interest group An organization that seeks to convert the interests (the political, economic, social, or moral goals) of its members or supporters into public policies or to influence politics otherwise. (8)

interest group liberalism A term that political scientists use to refer to the positive view that pluralist theorists hold of interest group politics. (8)

intermediate scrutiny test A standard of review falling between the rational basis test and the strict scrutiny test, giving the Supreme Court greater flexibility in reviewing equal protection cases. (16)

Internet A global network connecting many thousands of registered computer networks in countries around the world. (9)

interpretation The act of explaining the meaning of something or translating a complicated matter into understandable terms; a claim about *what is*. (1)

intergovernmental relations Relations among the various levels of government—national, state, and local—to make and implement policy. (3)

iron law of oligarchy The view of elite theorists that all groups, including the most democratically inclined, are ruled by elites. (8)

iron triangle The three "angles" of the policymaking process in a particular policy area, made up of lobbyists, lawmakers or their staffs, and bureaucrats who work together informally on policy issues; subgovernment. (8, 13)

issue network A temporary group made up of various lobbyists, lawmakers, involved bureaucrats, and experts, formed to shape a particular policy. (8, 13)

J

judicial activism The judicial philosophy under which judges play an active policymaking role. (14)

judicial branch The branch of government, composed of the courts, given the task of interpreting and applying the law. (2)

judicial philosophy A set of beliefs about *what is, what's right,* and *what works* that guides legal judgments. (14)

judicial restraint The judicial philosophy under which judges operate strictly within the constitutional limits that constrain the role of the courts. (14)

judicial review The power of both state and federal courts to declare laws, regulations, or acts of the legislative or executive branch, or a decision by a lower court, unconstitutional. (2, 14)

juries Groups of 6, 12, or 23 citizens who are authorized to listen to both sides of a court case and to give a verdict. (14)

jurisdiction The authority to hear and decide a case. (14)

K

kitchen cabinet The president's informal group of advisors. (12)

L

laissez-faire capitalism The theory that government should place no restrictions on economic activity. (2)

lame duck A term applied to officeholders whose power has been curtailed because they must soon leave office as a result of statutory limitation or electoral defeat. (12)

laws Basic rules of conduct passed by a political authority and designed to promote public order. (1, 14)

laws of nature Principles which are claimed to rule all aspects of the universe. (2)

leaks Confidential information about what is happening or what is being considered, passed on secretly to the media by bureaucrats. (9, 13)

learning by doing The practice of learning from experience and using feedback to make corrections and adjustments in the process. (1)

legal standing The right to file suit, determined by the subject matter and the type of law with which a case deals. (14)

legislation The creation of new law by federal, state, or local lawmakers. (14)

legislative branch The branch of the government (at the national level, Congress) assigned the responsibility of lawmaking. (2)

legislative free-lancing Unpredictable voting decisions made by members of Congress when they do not abide by their leader or party line. (11)

legislative intent A record of testimony and conclusions developed by a legislative committee, and the legislature's debate, about a bill's merits and the intentions underlying it. (11)

legislative veto A provision inserted into some bills by Congress stating that once an agency develops a program it must submit the program to Congress, which can then accept or veto the program. (11)

legitimacy The belief that an actor or action is legitimate or legal or right. (1)

***Lemon* test** The Supreme Court's requirement that for a law concerning religion to be constitutional, it must have a primary secular legislative purpose, must not advance or inhibit religion, and must not excessively entangle government with religion. (15)

libel A false written statement that defames a person's personal or professional reputation. (15)

liberals People who support the Democratic party, favor government intervention in politics and economics, endorse equality as a primary goal, and favor a politics of inclusion that seeks representation and participation for all. (4)

libertarians Those who want to shrink the size of government to the bare necessities because they believe big government is wrong and ineffective. (4)

limited government A form of government which has restrictions on the amount of power it has over its people. (2)

line-item veto The president's authority to veto certain items within an appropriations bill without killing the whole bill. (12)

lobbying Efforts by interest groups to win the support of public officials. (8)

log-rolling The practice of vote trading in which members of Congress advise each other on how to vote on issues of interest to each other. (11)

longitudinal studies Studies that examine changes in the opinions of the same people over time. (5)

M

Madisonian dilemma The conflict between the Framers' recognition that individuals have a constitutional right to organize themselves into interest groups and petition government for assistance and their concern that interest groups (factions) would hurt the common good. (8)

Magna Carta Document that established the principles of natural rights and limited government in England in 1215, when King John was forced to grant it to his rebellious barons, thereby submitting himself to the rule of law; these principles were incorporated in the U.S. Constitution and Bill of Rights. (2)

magnet schools Schools specializing in subject areas such as math, science, and the performing arts, designed to attract students of all races and ethnic groups. (16)

major party Political party that has enough political and organizational power to win major elections. (7)

majority decision Agreement by a majority of at least four of the nine Supreme Court justices on a case. (14)

majority leader The majority party's floor leader in the House or Senate. (11)

majority party The party holding the most seats in a legislative body. (7)

mandates Programs that the federal government requires states or cities to undertake, or that a state government requires cities to undertake (3); a claim by a president or party that wins by a large margin that it has voters' approval to implement campaign proposals. (10, 12)

mandatory sentencing Particular punishments that must be imposed for particular categories of crimes. (14)

margin of error The degree of inaccuracy of a poll. (5)

markup The section-by-section examination of proposed legislation by congressional committees and subcommittees. (11)

mass media Massive communications organizations that transmit a standardized message to large audiences. (9)

McGovern Reforms Reforms enacted in 1968 by Democrats (under the leadership of Senator George McGovern) which democratized the selection of national convention delegates and affected party organizations from the national to the local level. (7)

media Newspapers, television, and electronic communication systems, which are the main way the public learns about the political activities of other actors and about the media themselves. (1, 9)

media event An occasion that is staged largely in order to get media coverage. (9)

megabills Comprehensive bills that deal with many facets of general problems such as trade, crime, health care, energy, and environmental protection; also called omnibus bills. (11)

mercantilism The economic policy pursued by sixteenth-century European monarchs to regulate domestic industry, agriculture, and trade, encouraging exports and discouraging imports. (2)

minority leader The minority party's floor leader in the House or Senate. (11)

misdemeanor A minor criminal offense. (14)

multiculturalism Ideology that defends cultural or ethnic diversity and encourages multiple points of view. (4)

multiple referral A situation in which an omnibus bill is sent to two or more congressional committees for consideration at the same time. (11)

N

nation A group of people bound by race, history, or circumstances that lead them to identify themselves as a people. (4)

national primary A proposed national qualifying election in which every voter votes for his or her preferred candidate in his or her party and the winner is that party's candidate in the general election. (10)

nation-state A territory within which political institutions successfully claim the authority to govern and the majority of people in that territory accept it. (4)

national conventions Gatherings in which party activists are brought together from the states in the summer prior to the November presidential election to nominate candidates for the presidency and vice presidency and to write a party platform and rules governing party activities. (7)

natural aristocracy The belief held by many of the Founders that nature gives certain people greater gifts such as education, wealth, and a sense of social responsibility, making them the best political leaders. (2)

necessary and proper clause The eighteenth clause in Article 1, Section 8, of the U.S. Constitution; grants Congress the power "to make all Laws which shall be necessary and proper" for executing its itemized powers; also called the elastic clause. (2, 11)

neoconservatives Those who originally supported liberal policies but abandoned them in favor of more conservative programs. (4)

new news Term used by media critic Jon Katz to describe news coverage that emphasizes the entertainment value of a story, as opposed to the more balanced, moderate, and fact-oriented style of traditional journalism. (9)

news routines Principles that editors use to decide which events and people to cover. (9)

news shapers Experts on particular topics whom reporters interview in order to diversify their information resources. (9)

NIMBY An acronym for "not in my backyard," used in debates over where to locate undesirable facilities. (6)

nonsecret caucuses Open meetings in which voters or party members gather to choose their nominees. (7)

no prior restraint Doctrine stating that, except in rare instances, government may not censor materials before they are published. (15)

nullification The belief that a state convention or legislature can declare a federal law that it finds unacceptable null and void within the state's boundaries and refuse to obey it. (3)

O

omnibus bills   Comprehensive bills that deal with many facets of general problems such as trade, crime, health care, energy, and environmental protection; also called megabills. (11)

open primary   An election that allows voters to choose candidates from any party they wish. (7)

opposition research   Studies of the actions and statements of a political candidate's opponent. (10)

oral argument   Presentations by opposing sides in a case in open court. (14)

original jurisdiction   The authority of a court to be the first to hear a case. (14)

originalism   A judicial philosophy holding that interpreters of the Constitution or other legal document adhere to the words in the text or identify its intended meaning. (14)

outside strategies   Lobbying strategies that stimulate grassroots support for an issue. (8)

outsourcing   Turning government functions over to private companies that become outside sources of work and often can furnish the services more cheaply; privatizing. (13)

oversight   The congressional review of executive branch agencies and the programs and policies they administer in order to determine how well the bureaucracy is doing its job. (11)

P

paid media   Advertisements placed in the media. (10)

pairing of schools   The required combining of predominantly black, white, and brown schools within a school district to achieve greater racial balance. (16)

paper trail   Written documents the bureaucracy uses to communicate information upward to decisionmakers and downward to those who carry out orders; can later serve as a record of decisions and actions. (13)

partisans   Those who are loyal to a particular political party. (7)

party caucus   A private meeting of all members of one chamber of Congress belonging to a party to select its candidates for leadership positions in that chamber. (11)

party loyalists   Committed volunteers who help at party headquarters at election time, donate money and services, distribute political literature and campaign signs, and serve as delegates to their party conventions at the county, state, and national levels. (7)

party loyalty   A promise to a political party to vote for its candidates. (7)

party professionals   Political experts paid to run party organizations at the national, state, or local level. (7)

party system   The system in which political parties compete in the electoral process. (7)

patriotism   The loyalty that one feels for one's country and its heroes, traditions, and governing institutions. (4)

patronage   The practice by which the winner of an election rewards political supporters by giving them government jobs; also called the spoils system. (13)

peak associations   Large umbrella groups that represent a vast array of organizations at a very general level. (8)

Pendleton Act   Officially known as the Civil Service Act of 1883; replaced the spoils system with a merit-based, permanent career civil service. (13)

people's media   Popular media, ranging from talk shows to online computer networks, that enable ordinary citizens to communicate among themselves and, sometimes, with their leaders. (9)

period effects   Conditions and experiences that affect all age groups. (5)

"perks"   Perquisites of office, or special privileges, that an official such as a member of Congress or a president receives in addition to his or her salary. (11)

personal attack rule   The requirement that, if a station broadcasts an attack on the honesty, integrity, or character of a person or group other than in its news or election coverage, it must give the subject of the attack an opportunity to rebut the charge; right of rebuttal rule. (9)

plaintiff   Someone who brings a complaint to court. (14)

plea bargaining   Procedure in which the accused person agrees to plead guilty to a reduced charge in return for a lesser sentence than he or she is likely to receive if convicted in a trial. (14)

pluralist theorist   Political scientist who argues that competing interest groups balance one another in the political arena, thereby contributing to social stability and the common good. (8)

plurality voting   System in which the candidate who gets the most votes, whether or not that is a majority, wins the election. (7)

pocket veto   A tactic by which the president can kill a bill without explicitly vetoing it: if Congress is adjourned and the president does not sign the bill within 10 days, the bill dies. (12)

political action committee (PAC)   An organization set up by an interest group or a political actor that pools individual contributions and distributes them among political candidates or otherwise uses funds to influence political outcomes. (8)

political actors   Individuals, groups, and organizations that participate in politics. (1)

political culture   Beliefs and practices about *what is, what's right,* and *what works* in society and political life that are shared by a large group of people. (4)

political editorializing rule   The requirement that a station that endorses a candidate for public office in an editorial must give other candidates for that office a chance to reply on the air. (9)

political ideology   A cluster of concepts that politicians and parties use to gain authority and legitimacy for their stands on *what is, what's right,* and *what works.* (4)

political participation   Attempts by political actors to advance their beliefs about *what is, what's right,* and *what works* by taking various actions in political life. (6)

political party   A group that organizes to elect candidates to public office under the name of that group. (7)

political question   An issue involving the separation of powers between the legislative and executive branches that the Supreme Court leaves to the normal political process to resolve. (14)

political socialization   The process by which a political culture maintains itself through institutions that transmit its beliefs, values, and practices from one generation to the next. (4)

political society   A group that distributes power to political actors according to some sort of agreement. (1)

political sophistication   The quantity and quality of political information the public possesses about *what is, what's right,* and *what works* in the political process. (5)

political spectrum   A line on which political scientists locate or "plot" various political actors to indicate the extent to which they hold political positions, ranging from liberal to conservative. (7)

political stratification The distribution of political knowledge among the population. (5)

politico A politician concerned primarily with advancing his or her own career. (11)

politics Disputes over claims to the authority to decide *what is, what's right,* or *what works.* (1)

politics of knowledge Strategies of communication that rely on the manipulation of information, logic, and language (rhetoric), often in combination. (1)

polls Surveys that ask a selection of people questions designed to elicit their opinions on some subject. (5)

pollsters Public opinion specialists who conduct opinion polls. (5)

poll tax A fee that a citizen is required to pay before voting. (6)

popular sovereignty The political principle that the authority to rule derives from the consent of the people who are governed. (1)

populism A political movement of the late 1800s that emphasized the concerns of ordinary people; today, any movement with similar objectives. (7)

populists Advocates of popular democracy and defenders of the common people. (4)

"pork" Local special-interests projects, often of questionable value, placed in the budget by members of Congress to benefit their supporters. (11)

pork barrel A term for special-interest spending by the federal treasury; taken from the practice of "going to the pork barrel" for preserved foods in the days before refrigeration. (11)

postindustrial society A term coined by sociologist Daniel Bell in the 1970s to describe the shift in culture and society toward larger, more hierarchical, and more complex institutions; greater specialization; and the displacement of labor by new technologies. (4)

power The capacity to get someone to do something he or she would not otherwise do. (1)

pragmatism A practical approach to problem solving. (4)

precedents Models for making future decisions. (14)

preemption The principle whereby national law automatically takes precedence over state law on the same subject. (3)

preprimary national convention A proposed gathering to be held prior to the national primary at which candidates would be scrutinized by party professionals, who would then select the party's official nominee to be voted on in a subsequent party primary. (10)

prerogative powers Extraordinary powers outside the bounds of the written Constitution that the president can exercise in times of emergency. (12)

prescription Instructions about what should be done to deal with a problem. (1)

presidential electors Representatives from each of the 50 states and the District of Columbia who are chosen by a presidential candidate's campaign to vote for that candidate in the states in which he or she gets a plurality in the popular election. (10)

president pro tempore "President for the time," a designation for the longest-serving member of the Senate. (11)

primary caucus A gathering of party supporters who vote their presidential preferences face-to-face in precinct meetings. (10)

private law A type of law in which the government acts indirectly as a referee, or adjudicator, of disputes involving private citizens; civil law. (14)

privatizing Turning government functions over to private companies that become outside sources of work and often can furnish the services more cheaply; outsourcing. (13)

probable cause A reasonable belief that a crime has been committed and that a search will turn up evidence of it. (15)

procedural due process The fair application of the law in accordance with the rules and customs of the legal system. (15)

procedural law Legal practice intended to ensure that a case is dealt with fairly, according to guidelines specified by the law. (14)

progressivism A reform movement that flourished from the end of the nineteenth century to the First World War and that sought to remedy the problems of industrialization, urbanization, and agrarian poverty through limits on monopolies, the passage of labor laws, and improvements in the way government worked. (7)

proportionality The percentage of minorities in the population as a whole rather than in some lesser group. (16)

proprietary colonies American colonies whose charters were granted by the British monarch to favored individuals, as opposed to corporately owned colonies; they included Maryland, Carolina, New Jersey, New York, and Pennsylvania. (2)

prospective voting Citizens' use of the vote to announce their appraisals of candidates' sincerity, plausibility, and ability to represent voters' interests. (10)

public-access cable A programming arrangement in which a local cable company offers airtime and usually a production studio and equipment free to local government bodies, citizen groups, and interested individuals, without controlling program content. (9)

public campaign financing The proposal to use tax dollars to finance congressional and presidential elections. (8)

public interest group An organization that claims to promote public policies serving the interests of vast segments of the public. (8)

public judgment The willingness of respondents to take responsibility for their opinions. (5)

public law A type of law that deals primarily with the powers and institutions of government, the rights and duties people have with respect to government and one another, and the relations they have with people in other nations. (14)

public opinion The summary of the distribution of expressed attitudes of all or part of the people on some subject at some particular moment. (5)

public policy Laws and government regulations or practices on particular subjects. (1)

pure speech The peaceful expression of ideas to a voluntary audience. (15)

"push" polls Biased surveys that use loaded questions to propel respondents in a particular direction. (5)

Q

quorum A fixed number of members of any body who must be present in order for its transactions to be legitimate. (11)

quota A number in proportion to the percentage or availability of minorities in the population, used to determine some practice such as employment or college admission. (16)

R

racial gerrymandering Redistricting done in a way that increases the likelihood that a racial or ethnic minority such as Latinos or African Americans elect Latino or African-American representatives to Congress. (10)

random sampling A procedure that permits accurate generalizations and predictions about a group on the basis of questions asked of some rather than all of its members. (5)

rational basis test The standard of review the Supreme Court uses to help it decide whether the classification of people into unequally treated groups by a challenged law is rational, in which case the Court defers to the judgment of the state on the matter. (16)

realignment A situation in which voting patterns shift dramatically and there is a change in the balance of power between the two parties for a generation or more. (7)

reapportionment The reassignment of seats in the House of Representatives among the states in accordance with the latest U.S. census data on population growth or decline, obtained every ten years. (10)

reasonable access provision A rule guaranteeing that candidates for federal office will have reasonable access to buy unedited airtime during campaigns. (9)

recall A device used in some cities and a few states that allows citizens to remove a public official from office by petition followed by a vote. (6)

redistricting Redrawing the lines that divide populations into approximately equal, geographically based units. (10)

redlining The denial of mortgages by lending institutions in areas designated as slums. (16)

referendum An electoral procedure in which the legislature refers an issue to the people, asking voters to accept or reject a legislative or constitutional proposal. (6)

regional primaries A series of primary elections held at the same time in different states in order to determine presidential candidates. (10)

registration The practice of making those who intend to vote register, or sign up, ahead of time with a local bureaucrat in charge of voting. (6)

Religious Right Members of ultraconservative, fundamentalist churches and sects, who tend to support the right wing of the Republican party. (4)

representative democracy A political system in which citizens vote for other citizens to represent them and their interests in government. (1)

republic A form of government in which supreme power resides in the people and is exercised by representatives responsible to the general electorate. (1)

republicanism The idea of a representative form of government in which power resides in the people who are entitled to vote and exercise it by electing officials and representatives. (2)

reserved powers Those powers not enumerated in the U.S. Constitution that are delegated to the states. (3)

retrospective voting The practice of deciding whether or not to vote for an incumbent's reelection, depending on one's evaluation of his or her record in office. (10)

revenue sharing A process originated by President Richard Nixon in which the federal government shares tax revenue or borrowed money with the states and localities, primarily by providing block grants. (3)

reverse discrimination The claim that minorities or women receive preferential treatment in employment or other matters at the expense of whites or men who are themselves innocent of discrimination. (16)

revolving door The common practice of ex-lawmakers or former executive branch officials becoming lobbyists. (8)

right The power or privilege an individual claims to possess by nature, tradition, or law. (15)

right of rebuttal rule The requirement that, if a station broadcasts an attack on the honesty, integrity, or character of a person or group other than in its news or election coverage, it must give the subject of the attack an opportunity to rebut the charge; personal attack rule. (9)

right to privacy The right protecting some aspect of a person's private life from government invasion. (15)

royal charter The founding document granted to merchant adventurers seeking to profit commercially from the New World. (2)

rule An operating procedure or regulation that helps shape the way a chamber of Congress operates; in the House, a provision passed by the Rules Committee specifying what debate and amendment will be allowed on a bill during its consideration by the whole House. (11)

rule of four The unwritten rule that any four Supreme Court justices can agree to "grant cert," or order a lower court to certify and send up the record of a case for review. (14)

S

school vouchers A payment from government that can be used to pay for a child's education in a public or private school of the parents' choice. (4)

search warrant A judicial writ specifying the cause of a search, the area to be searched, or the items to be seized for a criminal investigation. (15)

secret party caucus A system in which state and local party machines controlled nominations by meeting privately to pick the candidates they wanted to run for president and for state and local offices before reforms created primaries and open party caucuses. (7)

secret preprimary A fundraising process in which potential candidates for the presidential nomination seek early financial backing before the first primary takes place. (10)

segregation Methods of discrimination that erect arbitrary barriers between individuals or groups. (16)

selective incorporation The case-by-case process by which the Supreme Court has applied provisions in the Bill of Rights to the states. (15)

self-help movement A movement advocating that African Americans cooperate in acquiring the education and economic self-sufficiency needed to overcome poverty and discrimination. (16)

senatorial courtesy Practice by which the president is expected to consult with the senators from the state from which a district or appellate court judge nominee is to be selected. (14)

Senior Executive Service The mechanism that rewards top civil servants with large cash bonuses for good work but transfers or demotes them for bad work; part of the Civil Service Reform Act of 1978. (13)

seniority The principle by which the majority party member who had served the longest on a congressional committee was automatically elected chair of that committee by all party members. (11)

separate but equal The principle that laws providing separate public facilities for black people were constitutional so long as the facilities were equal. (16)

separation of powers The system by which political power is divided among the legislative, executive, and judicial branches. (2)

Shays' Rebellion A 1786 tax revolt by farmers in western Massachusetts, led by Daniel Shays, that influenced the Framers' decision to draft the Constitution of 1787. (2)

silent primary The second stage of a presidential campaign, in which a candidate uses funds raised in the secret preprimary to gain early public recognition and boost perceptions of his or her authority, credibility, and promise in the minds of media people; also called hidden primary (10)

single-issue group An interest group that ardently pursues one goal and resists compromise on its attainment. (8)

single-member districts A district that elects only one candidate to public office. (7)

single referral The referral of a bill to a single committee that has jurisdiction over a particular subject. (11)

slander A false oral statement defaming a person's personal or professional reputation. (15)

socialists Those who want government to own and operate most of the nation's economic enterprises and to ensure that goods and services are distributed fairly. (4)

socioeconomic status (SES) A person's occupation, income, and social class. (6)

soft money Unlimited contributions made to political parties by individuals or groups that can be spent in party-building activities that support their preferred candidate, as long as the funds are not given directly to the candidate's campaign. (8, 10)

solicitor general An appointed official who works under the attorney general and decides which cases in the appellate courts the administration should ask the Supreme Court to hear. (14)

sovereignty The political independence of a ruler or government. (1, 2)

Speaker of the House The presiding officer in the U.S. House of Representatives, selected from the majority party. (11)

special interest group A group that seeks to promote policies that serve the interests of its own members and supporters. (8)

speech plus Verbal expression combined with an action, such as marching or picketing; protected by the First Amendment unless it endangers the public. (15)

split group An interest group that has created both a noncharitable and a charitable group that share the same resources and ideology in order to divert money that would have gone to tax payments for their own means. (8)

split ticket Voting for candidates from both parties for different offices in a single election. (7, 10)

spoils system Practice in which the winner of an election rewards political supporters with government jobs; patronage. (13)

standard operating procedures Rules that bureaucrats are expected to follow in their day-to-day activities in order to increase efficiency and maintain the chain of command. (13)

stare decisis "To stand by that which is decided"; the doctrine that judges must defer to the authority of previous decisions unless they find "good cause" for overturning them. (14)

state constitutions Documents written by colonial assemblies or, later, by state conventions to found and legitimate their individual state governments. (2)

states' rights All rights that the U.S. Constitution does not delegate to the national government or deny to the states; a movement seeking to strengthen the powers of the states as against the national government. (3)

status quo The current condition or state of affairs. (1)

statutory powers Powers granted to the president by Congress that are vital to fulfilling the role of chief administrator, such as reorganizing the executive branch for greater efficiency. (12)

straight ticket Voting for only candidates of one party in a particular election. (7)

strategy of convergence The practice by which Democrats and Republicans move toward the center of the political spectrum in their campaign rhetoric in an attempt to gain more votes. (7)

straw polls Nonscientific surveys that tap the opinions of those who happen to be around or who are easy to contact. (5)

strict scrutiny test The standard of review used by the Supreme Court to decide whether the classification made by a challenged law is suspect, in which case the classification does not fit the purpose of the law or the purpose itself is not legitimate. (16)

subcultures Nondominant cultures nested within the national political culture. (4)

subgovernment The policymaking process made up of lobbyists, lawmakers or their staffs, and bureaucrats who work together informally in a particular policy area; also called an iron triangle. (13)

substantive due process The view that courts have a responsibility to decide whether the substance of a law is reasonable and to use the due process clause to exercise that responsibility. (15)

substantive law Legal practice that concerns the actual content or substance of a law. (14)

suffrage The right to vote. (6)

summary disposition A brief statement rendered by the Supreme Court that affirms a lower court decision, reverses it, or dismisses it for lack of jurisdiction or lack of a substantial federal question. (14)

sunset law The requirement that an existing program or agency be regularly reviewed for effectiveness and either abolished or extended. (13)

sunshine rules Under the Legislative Reorganization Act of 1970, the exposure of lobbyists and the public to the positions that lawmakers take on controversial issues by requiring the recording of votes on amendments; the requirement that an agency conduct its meetings and make its decisions in public, so that the media and interested citizens can observe what happens. (8, 13)

superdelegates Party officers and elected officials who can go to party conventions uncommitted—free to vote for any candidate and to make deals to nominate a candidate who could win the general election. (7)

supremacy clause Article VI of the U.S. Constitution, which declares that federal laws override or replace state laws. (3)

suspect classification When the Supreme Court, in applying the strict scrutiny test, decides not to defer to a state's judgment on classification, it regards that classification as "suspect," and the state must show " a compelling interest" that justifies its use. (16)

symbolic speech Using symbols, such as wearing armbands or burning the American flag to express an opinion; such speech is sometimes protected by the First Amendment and sometimes not. (15)

system A group of elements dynamically related in time, according to some coherent pattern. (1)

T

takings clause Fifth Amendment clause which states, "Nor shall private property be taken for public use, without just compensation." (15)

teledemocracy Proposed interactive electronic networks connecting all citizens to a central databank by telephone or television for the making of electoral or policy decisions. (9)

think tank Research institution that specializes in policy analysis. (8)

third party A minor political party. (7)

three-fifths compromise Added to the Constitution to help settle a North–South population debate by stating that the national census, the basis for calculating the number of seats a state could hold in the House of Representatives and the rate of federal taxation, would count each slave as "three-fifths" of a person. (2)

total incorporation The belief that all the provisions in the Bill of Rights are fundamental and that it was wrong for the Supreme Court to choose among them in nationalizing the Bill of Rights. (15)

tracking polls Nightly telephone calls to carefully selected people who answer questions about their current presidential preference and their reactions to the day's developments in the campaign. (10)

trade association A special interest group that represents business groups in a particular industry—shipping, farming, defense contractors—and offers its members assistance tailored to their needs, often including Washington lobbying. (8)

tradition Inherited, established, or customary patterns of thinking, acting, or behaving that are passed down from generation to generation by word of mouth, writing, or gesture. (1)

trustee A representative who votes for what is best for the district, the state, or the nation, regardless of public opinion or special interests. (11)

turnout The percentage of eligible (registered or not) voters who actually show up, or "turn out," at the polls to vote. (6)

two-party system A party system consisting of two major political parties. (7)

U

unanimous consent agreement A practice whereby all members of the Senate vote to suspend its rules, limiting debate and specifying what amending will be allowed on the floor, in order to facilitate consideration of a bill. (11)

uncivil disobedience Acts of terrorism, such as rioting, arson, assassination, and bombing, that are aimed at subverting the political order. (6)

underdog effect A shift of voters to the candidate who appears to be losing. (5)

unfunded mandates Federal programs that states or cities must undertake and pay for themselves, or state programs that cities must undertake and pay for. (3)

unitary system A political system in which a single national government exercises direct authority over the entire nation and its people. (1)

V

V-chip A computer chip that would allow parents to block televised material rated as offensively violent or sexual. (9)

verdict A ruling or decision on a court case. (14)

vested interest An interest group already receiving benefits from government. (8)

veto The rejection of a proposal or legislative bill, as when the president rejects a bill passed by Congress. (2, 12)

vote A form of political participation that enables people to have a "say" in what happens in the political system. (6)

W

wedge issues Controversial issues that are brought up during a campaign in order to steal voters from an opponent's base. (10)

welfare rights Social, economic, and cultural rights. (16)

whip A party official in the House or Senate who aids the party leader by keeping tabs on voting inclinations and "whipping" members into line to vote "with the party" on important bills. (11)

whistleblower Someone who makes public illegal or inappropriate conduct by some person or agency. (13)

white flight The exodus of whites from the inner cities to the suburbs. (16)

White House Office Staff responsible for coordinating relations between the president and the rest of the government. (12)

white primary A legal practice, common in southern states following Reconstruction, that excluded blacks from voting in the Democratic party's primary elections, thus ensuring that only whites would compete in the general election. (6)

World Wide Web (WWW) The multimedia network made up of hundreds of thousands of Web sites set up by institutions or individuals to offer information to anyone who wants it and has access to the Internet. (9)

writ of *certiorari* A written order to a lower court that signals the Supreme Court's willingness to hear an appeal by ordering it to deliver its record of the case. (14)

Notes

CHAPTER 1

1 Lawrence M. Friedman, "Legal Culture and the Welfare State," in *Dilemmas of Law in the Welfare State*, ed. Gunther Teubner (New York: Walter de Gruyter, 1986), 25; Alexis de Tocqueville, *Democracy in America* (1835), Book 4, Chapter 6.

2 Cecil Andrus, governor of Idaho, quoted in John Daniel, "Dance of Denial," *Sierra*, April 1993, 68.

3 This story is recounted in Norris Hundley, Jr., *The Great Thirst: Californians and Water, 1770s–1990s* (Berkeley: University of California Press, 1992); Donald Worster, *Rivers of Empire: Water, Aridity, and the Growth of the American West* (New York: Pantheon, 1985); Norris Hundley, Jr., *Dividing the Waters: A Century of Controversy Between the U.S. and Mexico* (Berkeley: University of California Press, 1966); Marc Reisner, *Cadillac Desert: The American West and Its Disappearance* (New York: Penguin, 1986).

4 Chris Kelley, "California in Crisis," *Dallas Morning News*, April 16, 1993, 3.

5 Harold Lasswell, *Politics: Who Gets What, When, and How* (New York: McGraw-Hill, 1936).

6 See Robert A. Goldwin and William A. Schambra, eds., *How Capitalistic Is the Constitution?* (Washington, D.C.: American Enterprise Institute, 1982).

7 Quoted in Kurt Eichenwald, "Archer Daniels Agrees to Big Fine for Price Fixing," *New York Times*, October 15, 1996, A1.

8 Hundley, *Great Thirst*, 372.

9 Jane Fritsch, "Friend or Foe? Nature Groups Say Names Lie," *New York Times*, March 25, 1996.

10 *Arizona v. California*, 238 U.S. 423 (1963); Hundley, *Great Thirst*, 301–302.

11 President Bill Clinton, State of the Union Address, 1997.

12 Fritsch, "Friend or Foe?"

13 Peter Passell, "When the Benefits Are Mostly Modest, What Price Clean Air?" *New York Times*, April 3, 1997.

14 See Elman R. Service, "The Law of Evolutionary Potential," in *Evolution and Culture*, ed. Marshall D. Sahlins and Elman R. Service (Ann Arbor: University of Michigan Press, 1960), 97.

15 See Donald Shön, *The Reflective Practitioner: How Professionals Think in Action* (New York: Basic Books, 1983); Henry Petroski, *To Engineer Is Human: The Role of Failure in Successful Design* (New York: St. Martin's Press, 1985); David V. Edwards, "The Theorist as Reflexive Reflective Practitioner," paper presented at the annual meeting of the American Political Science Association, San Francisco, August 1990.

16 S. W. Eisenstadt, *Revolution and the Transformation of Societies: A Comparative Study of Civilizations* (New York: Free Press, 1973).

17 See William Greider, *One World, Ready or Not: The Maniac Logic of Global Capitalism* (New York: Simon & Schuster, 1997); Jeremy Rifkin, *The End of Work: The Decline of the Global Labor Force and the Dawn of the Post-Market Era* (New York: Putnam, 1995); George Soros, "The Capitalist Threat," *Atlantic Monthly*, February 1997, 45–55.

18 Paul Krugman, "We Are Not the World," *New York Times*, February 13, 1997.

CHAPTER 2

1 Thurgood Marshall, speech at the Annual Seminar of the San Francisco Patent and Trademark Association, Maui, Hawaii, May 6, 1987, in Herbert M. Levine, ed., *PointCounterpoint: Readings in American Government*, 3rd ed. (New York: St. Martin's Press, 1989).

2 Donald S. Lutz, *Origins of American Constitutionalism* (Baton Rouge: Louisiana State University Press, 1988), 7.

3 The original text appears in David Pulsifer, ed., *Records of the Colony of New Plymouth in New England*, vol. 1, *The Laws, 1623–1681* (Boston: 1681). A version in standard English appears in W. Keith Kavenagh, ed., *Foundations of Colonial America: A Documentary History* (New York: Chelsea House, 1973), 247–251.

4 Quoted in Lutz, *Origins of American Constitutionalism*, 33.

5 Maurice Ashley, *Magna Carta in the Seventeenth Century* (Charlottesville, Va.: University of Virginia Press, 1965), 48–49.

6 The treatise, entitled "The Rights of the British Colonies Asserted and Proved," is quoted in Page Smith, *The Constitution: A Documentary and Narrative History* (New York: Morrow, 1988), 42–43.

7 James Boyd White, *When Words Lose Their Meaning: Constitutions and Reconstitutions of Language, Character, and Community* (Chicago: University of Chicago Press, 1984).

8 John Adams, "Thoughts on Government (1776)," *The Works of John Adams* (Boston: Little, Brown, 1850–1856), vol. 4.

9 Smith, *Constitution*, 72.

10 Melvin I. Urofsky, *A March of Liberty: A Constitutional History of the United States* (New York: Alfred A. Knopf, 1988), 81.

11 Smith, *Constitution*, 83.

12 Quoted in ibid.

13 Quoted in Eric Cummins, "'Anarchia' and the Emerging State," *Radical History Review*, no. 48 (Fall 1990): 33.

14 See Carl J. Richard, *The Founders and the Classics: Greece, Rome, and the American Enlightenment* (Cambridge: Harvard University Press, 1994); Lutz, *Origins of American Constitutionalism*, 139, 142–143.

15 Joshua Miller, in *The Rise and Fall of Democracy in Early America, 1630–1789* (University Park: Pennsylvania State University Press, 1991), 66, cites the work of historians E. James Ferguson, *The Power of the Purse: A History of American Public Finance, 1776–1790* (Chapel Hill: University of North Carolina Press, 1961), xiv–xv, and Merrill Jensen, "The Idea of a National Government During the American Revolution," in *Essays on the Making of the Constitution*, 2nd ed., ed. Leonard Levy (New York: Oxford University Press, 1987), 6–87.

16 For an analysis of these coalitions, see Calvin C. Jillson, *Constitution-Making: Conflict and Consensus in the Federal Convention of 1787* (New York: Agathon Press, 1988).

17 Historian Forrest McDonald paraphrases their sentiments in an interview with Bill Moyers in the PBS series *In Search of the Constitution* (1987), part 1.

18 See Forrest McDonald's discussion of Hamilton's and Madison's interpretation of Adam Smith's *Wealth of Nations* and their views on shaping the American economy in his *Novus Ordo Seculorum: The Intellectual Origins of the Constitution* (Lawrence: University Press of Kansas, 1985), 128–142.

19 See Michael Kammen, *A Machine That Would Go of Itself: The Constitution in American Culture* (New York: Vintage, 1987), 18.

20 Quoted in Lutz, *Origins of American Constitutionalism*, 165, see also 166.

21 Forrest McDonald, in an interview with Bill Moyers in the PBS series *In Search of the Constitution* (1987), part 1.

22 Franklin's words appear in James Madison's notes, quoted in Smith, *Constitution*, 229–230.

23 H. Jefferson Powell, "James Madison's Theory of Constitutional Interpretation," in *Interpreting Law as Literature*, ed. Sanford Levinson and Steven Mailloux (Evanston, Ill.: Northwestern University Press, 1988), 98.

24 Quoted in ibid., 13, emphasis added.

25 Oliver Ellsworth and John Rutledge, both quoted in Herbert J. Storing, *What the Anti-Federalist Were For: The Political Thought of the Opponents of the Constitution* (Chicago: University of Chicago Press, 1981), 15, 30.

26 Amos Singletary, quoted in Robert E. Shalhope, *The Roots of Democracy: American Thought and Culture, 1760–1800* (Boston: Twayne, 1990), 108.

27 Storing, *What the Anti-Federalists Were For*, 20.

28 John R. Vile, *Rewriting the United States Constitution* (New York: Praeger, 1991), 3.

29 This mechanistic metaphor appears in Chief Justice Joseph Story's *Commentaries on the Constitution of the United States* (Durham: Carolina Academic Press, 1987), 686–687.

30 Alan P. Grimes, *Democracy and the Amendments to the Constitution* (Lexington, Mass.: Lexington Books, 1978), 2.

31 Ibid., 9.

32 Quoted in Kammen, *Machine That Would Go of Itself*, 20.

33 White, *When Words Lose Their Meaning*, 247.

34 See James B. Thayer, "The Origin and Scope of the American Doctrine of Constitutional Law," *Harvard Law Review* 7 (October 25, 1893): 130–131.

35 See Bruce Ackerman, *We the People: Foundations*, vol. 1 (Cambridge: Harvard University Press, 1991). Both Clinton's pollster, Stanley Greenberg, and Republican pollster Frank Luntz accept this view. See Greenberg, *Middle Class Dreams: The Politics of Power of the New American Majority* (New York: Times Books, 1995).

36 George Washington to Bushrod Washington, Nov. 9, 1987, in *George Washington's Writings* (New York: Penguin, 1997), 661; James McHenry, quoted in James Thomas Flexner, *Washington: The Indispensible Man* (Boston: Little, Brown, 1984), 338.

37 Quoted in Roy F. Nichols, *American Leviathan* (New York: Harper & Row, 1966), 278–279.

CHAPTER 3

The chapter epigraphs are from Woodrow Wilson, *Constitutional Government in the United States* (New York: Columbia University Press, 1911), 173; James Bryce, *The American Commonwealth* (London: Macmillan, 1891), quoted in D. W. Meinig, *The Shaping of America*, vol. 1 (New Haven, Conn.: Yale University Press, 1986), 386.

1 See Donald S. Lutz, "The Articles of Confederation as the Background to the Federal Republic," *Publius* (Winter 1990): 55–70.

2 See Carl J. Richard, *The Founders and the Classics: Greece, Rome, and the American Enlightenment* (Cambridge, Mass.: Harvard University Press, 1994), 104–114. Richard points out that contemporary historians question many of the Framers' understandings of history but documents the key role these understandings played in the debates.

3 John M. Murrin, "1787: The Invention of American Federalism," in *Essays on Liberty and Federalism*, ed. David E. Narrett et al. (College Station: Texas A&M University Press, 1988), 37. For a related view, see Samuel Beer, *To Make a Nation: The Rediscovery of American Federalism* (Cambridge, Mass.: Harvard University Press, 1993).

4 Clinton Rossiter, ed., *The Federalist Papers* (New York: New American Library, 1961).

5 Ibid.

6 See Eugene W. Hickok, Jr., "The Original Understanding of the Tenth Amendment," in *The Bill of Rights*, ed. Eugene W. Hickok, Jr. (Charlottesville: University Press of Virginia, 1991), Chapter 30.

7 *McCulloch v. Maryland*, 4 Wheaton 316 (1819).

8 For an interesting analysis of Marshall's argument, see James Boyd White, *When Words Lose Their Meaning: Constitutions and Reconstructions of Language, Character, and Community* (Chicago: University of Chicago Press, 1984), Chapter 9.

9 *Osborne v. Bank of the United States*, 9 Wheaton 738 (1824).

10 John F. Dillon, *Commentaries on the Law of Municipal Corporations*, 5th ed. (Boston: Little, Brown, 1911), 1:448.

11 Doyle W. Buckwalter, "Dillon's Rule in the 1980s: Who's in Charge of Local Affairs?" *National Civic Review* (September 1982): 399–406.

12 Gordon L. Clark, *Judges and the Cities: Interpreting Local Autonomy* (Chicago: University of Chicago Press, 1985).

13 Thomas Jefferson to William Stephens Smith, February 2, 1788, in *Papers of Thomas Jefferson*, ed. Julian P. Boyd et al., vol. 12 (Princeton, N.J.: Princeton University Press, 1956), 558.

14 *Dred Scott v. Sandford*, 19 Howard 353 (1857).

15 *Hammer v. Dagenhart et al.*, 247 U.S. 251 (1918).

16 *United States v. Darby Lumber Co.*, 312 U.S. 100 (1941).

17 See Thomas J. Anton, *American Federalism and Public Policy: How the System Works* (Philadelphia: Temple University Press, 1988), Chapter 7.

18 See *The Federal Role in Local Fire Protection* (Washington, D.C.: Advisory Commission on Intergovernmental Relations, 1980).

19 For a study of both, see Timothy Conlan, *New Federalism: Intergovernmental Reform from Nixon to Reagan* (Washington, D.C.: Brookings Institution, 1988).

20 For an enthusiastic account by Reagan's assistant for intergovernmental affairs, see Richard S. Williamson, *Reagan's Federalism: His Efforts to Decentralize Government* (Lanham, Md.: University Press of America, 1990).

21 For a comprehensive study of preemption, see Joseph F. Zimmerman, *Federal Preemption: The Silent Revolution* (Ames: Iowa State University Press, 1991).

22 Advisory Commission on Intergovernmental Relations, *Federal Preemption of State and Local Authority* (Washington, D.C.: ACIR, 1989).

23 *Garcia v. San Antonio Metropolitan Transit Authority*, 469 U.S. 528 (1985).

24 See Fred Jordan, *Innovating America: Innovations in State and Local Government* (New York: Ford Foundation, 1990), which summarizes outstanding projects awarded prizes in national competitions sponsored by the Ford Foundation.

25 Neal R. Peirce, "The Myth of the Spendthrift States," *National Journal*, August 3, 1991, 1941. See also John Kincaid, "From Cooperative to Coercive Federalism," *Annals of the American Academy of Political and Social Science* 509 (May 1990): 148–152.

26 Timothy J. Conlan, "And the Beat Goes On: Intergovernmental Mandates and Preemption in an Era of Deregulation," *Publius*, 21 (Summer 1991): 43–57.

27 Susan A. MacManus, "'Mad' About Mandates: The Issue of Who Should Pay for What Resurfaces in the 1990s," *Publius* 21 (Summer 1991): 59; David Shribman, "More States, Taking a Leaf from Federal Book, Pass On Their Spending Programs to Localities," *Wall Street Journal*, September 3, 1991.

28 Associated Press, "U.S. to Give Grants to States for Drunken Driving Laws," *New York Times*, January 28, 1992.

29 *Gregory v. Ashcroft*, 59 U.S.L.W. 4717 (1991).

30 *Harmelin v. Michigan*, 501 U.S. 957 (1991); *Barnes v. Glen Theatre*, 501 U.S. 560 (1991).

31 See David Rapp, "Casey Turns Mighty in Court; Outslugs Pesticide Industry, 9-0," *Governing* (September 1991): 69; *Public Intervenor v. Nortier*, 89 U.S. 1905 (1972).

32 See Thomas R. Dye, *American Federalism: Competition Among Governments* (Lexington, Mass.: Lexington Books, 1990).

33 See, for example, William Van Alstyne, "Federalism, Congress, the States and the Tenth Amendment: Adrift in the Cellophane Sea," *Duke Law Journal* (November 1987): 769.

34 Virginia Postrel, "States' Rights, or Dereliction of Duty?" *Washington Post National Weekly Edition*, July 22, 1991, 23.

35 G. Alan Tarr, "The Past and Future of the New Judicial Federalism," *Publius* 14, no. 2 (Spring 1994): 63–79.

36 Quoted in *National Law Journal*, September 29, 1986, special section at S-1.

37 *New York v. United States*, 505 U.S. 144 (1992).

38 *United States v. Lopez*, 63 L.W. 4343 (1995); Michael C. Tolley et al., "Coercive Federalism and the Search for Constitutional Limits," *Publius*, 25, no. 4 (Fall 1995): 73–90.

39 William A. Galston and Geoffrey L. Tibbetts, "Reinventing Federalism: The Clinton/Gore Program for a New Partnership Among the Federal, State, Local, and Tribal Governments," *Publius* 24, no. 3 (Summer 1994): 23–48.

40 Dan Morgan, "Relief from Mandates: What It Does and Doesn't Mean," *Washington Post National Weekly Edition*, February 20, 1995, 7.

41 See Daniel Elazar, "'To Secure the Blessings of Liberty': Liberty and American Federal Democracy," *Publius* 20, no. 2 (Spring 1990): 1–13.

42 For a study of such programs, see Paul Peterson et al., *When Federalism Works* (Washington, D.C.: Brookings Institution, 1986).

43 Lee Christopher Hamilton and Donald T. Wells, *Federalism, Power, and Political Economy* (Englewood Cliffs, N.J.: Prentice Hall, 1990), Chapter 5.

44 For an interesting account, see Daniel J. Elazar, *The American Mosaic* (Boulder, Colo.: Westview Press, 1994).

45 Rosemarie Zagarri, *The Politics of Size: Representation in the United States, 1776–1850* (Ithaca, N.Y.: Cornell University Press, 1987), 7.

46 Clint Bolick, *Grassroots Tyranny: The Limits of Federalism* (Washington, D.C.: Cato Institute, 1993).

47 Dye, *American Federalism*, 184–185.

48 Robert Hawkins, "American Federalism: Again at the Crossroads," in *American Federalism: A New Partnership for the Republic*, ed. Robert Hawkins (San Francisco: Institute for Contemporary Studies, 1982), 10.

CHAPTER **4**

1 Jonathan Swift, *Gulliver's Travels* (London, 1726), is available in numerous modern editions. Kristen Hill Maher, "A Nation of Immigrants: Mapping National Identities in a Post-National

Order," paper presented at the annual meeting of the American Political Science Association, San Francisco, August 29–September 1, 1996, 5.

2 John Taylor, "Are You Politically Correct?" *New York*, January 21, 1991, 33–34.

3 *The Slave's Narrative*, ed. Charles T. David and Henry Louis Gates, Jr. (New York: Oxford University Press, 1985). The earliest accounts of slavery written by slaves and printed in America and England are described in Angelo Costanzo's *Surprising Narrative: Olaudah Equiano and the Beginnings of Black Autobiography* (New York: Greenwood Press, 1987).

4 See David A. Hollinger, *Postethnic America: Beyond Multiculturalism* (New York: Basic Books, 1995), 2.

5 Sara Diamond, "Readin', Writin', and Repressin'," *Z Magazine*, February 1991, 45.

6 Arthur M. Schlesinger, Jr., *The Disuniting of America* (New York: Norton, 1992).

7 See Jeff Spinner-Halev, "Does Multiculturalism Threaten Citizenship?" paper presented at the annual meeting of the American Political Science Association, San Francisco, August 29–September 1, 1996.

8 Quoted in Jonathan Rauch, "The End of Government," *National Journal*, September 7, 1996, 1890.

9 See Francis Fukuyama, *The End of History and the Last Man* (New York: Free Press, 1992).

10 These views are summarized by Rauch, "End of Government," 1890, 1891.

11 Kenneth M. Dolbeare and Janette Kay Hubbell, *USA 2012: After the Middle-Class Revolution* (Chatham, N.J.: Chatham House, 1996), 51.

12 Daniel Bar-Tal and Leonard Saxe, "Acquisition of Political Knowledge: A Social-Psychological Analysis," in *Political Socialization, Citizenship Education, and Democracy,* ed. Orit Ichilov (New York: Teachers College Press, 1990), 128.

13 Urie Bronfenbrenner et al., *The State of Americans* (New York: Free Press, 1996), 201.

14 Bernard N. Dauenhauer, *Citizenship in a Fragile World* (Lanham, Md.: Rowman & Littlefield, 1996), 108.

15 David K. Shipler, "Jefferson Is America—And America Is Jefferson," *New York Times*, April 12, 1993.

16 Christopher Lasch, *The Culture of Narcissism: American Life in an Age of Diminishing Expectations* (New York: W. W. Norton, 1978), 129.

17 Charles Reich, *The Greening of America* (New York: Random House, 1970), 359–369.

18 See, for example, Richard Sennett, *Authority* (New York: Vintage Books, 1981) and Michel Foucault, *Power/Knowledge: Selected Interviews* (New York: Pantheon, 1980).

19 Bertram Gross, *Friendly Fascism: The New Face of Power in America* (New York: M. Evans, 1980), 5.

20 Robert Nisbet, *The Twilight of Authority* (New York: Oxford University Press, 1975).

21 For interesting examinations of the interplay of individualism and community in American culture, see Wilfred M. McClay, *The Masterless: Self and Society in Modern America* (Chapel Hill: University of North Carolina Press, 1994); John P. Hewitt, *Dilemmas of the American Self* (Philadelphia: Temple University Press, 1989).

22 Ruth Lane, "Political Culture and the Concept of Self-Organizing Systems," paper presented at the annual meeting of the American Political Science Association, San Francisco, August 28–September 1, 1996.

23 Spinner-Halev, "Does Multiculturalism Threaten Citizenship?"

24 Martin E. Marty, "Religion in America," in *Making America*, ed. Luther S. Luedtke (Chapel Hill: University of North Carolina Press, 1992), 409.

25 According to one estimate, the United Methodist Church is losing 1,000 to 1,500 members a week. Since 1965 the Episcopal Church has lost one-third of its membership, and Lutheran membership has been declining since 1968. Clark Morphew, "Protestants Must Change Mission in Order to Thrive," *Austin American-Statesman*, September 21, 1996.

26 Marty, "Religion in America," 410.

27 Gallup poll, cited in Richard Morin, "Getting It Right for a Change," *Washington Post Weekly Edition*, August 12–18, 1996.

28 Survey conducted by Tom W. Smith of the National Opinion Research Center at the University of Chicago, cited in ibid.

29 Spinner-Halev, "Does Multiculturalism Threaten Citizenship?" 11.

30 Mark E. Kann, "Individualism, Civic Virtue, and Gender in America," in *Studies in American Political Development* (New Haven, Conn.: Yale University Press, 1990), 46.

31 The precise nature of the Framers' views on individualism and civic virtue has long been debated by scholars. See, for example, C. B. Macpherson, *The Political Theory of Possessive Individualism* (New York: Oxford University Press, 1962); Louis Hartz, *The Liberal Tradition in America: An Interpretation of American Political Thought Since the Revolution* (New York: Harcourt, Brace and World, 1955); and Richard C. Sinopoli, *The Foundations of American Citizenship: Liberalism, the Constitution, and Civic Virtue* (New York: Oxford University Press, 1992).

32 See Amitai Etzioni, *The Spirit of Community: Rights, Responsibilities, and the Communitarian Agenda* (New York: Crown, 1993); Robert Bork, *Slouching Towards Gomorrah: Modern Liberalism and American Decline* (New York: HarperCollins, 1996).

33 Kann, "Individualism, Civic Virtue, and Gender in America," 97.

34 See Garrison Keillor, "The Future of Nostalgia," *New York Times Magazine*, September 29, 1996, 68.

35 See Steven Lukes, "Perspectives on Authority," in *Authority Revisited*, ed. J. Roland Pennock and John W. Chapman (New York: New York University Press, 1987).

36 Mark Warren, "Deliberative Democracy and Authority," *American Political Science Review* 90, no. 1 (March 1996): 54. See also Richard Flathman, *The Practice of Political Authority* (Chicago: University of Chicago Press, 1980).

37 Richard Rorty, "Fraternity Reigns," *New York Times Magazine*, September 29, 1996, 156.

38 James F. Lea, *Political Consciousness and American Democracy* (Jackson: University Press of Mississippi, 1982), 80.

39 Walter Kerr, quoted in *New York Times*, October 10, 1996.

40 For excerpts of this thesis from Aristotle's *Rhetoric*, see Seymour Martin Lipset and Everett Carll Ladd, "The Political Future of Activist Generations," in *The New Pilgrims: Youth Protest in Transition*, ed. Philip G. Altbach and Robert S. Laufer (New York: David McKay, 1972), 63–84, at 66–67.

41 Karl Mannheim, "The Problem of Generations" (1928), reprinted in Altbach and Laufer, *The New Pilgrims*.

42 For a study of the extent to which knowledge crosses generations, see M. Kent Jennings, "Political Knowledge over Time and Across Generations," paper presented at the annual meeting of the American Political Science Association, September 2–3, 1993.

43 Robert S. Laufer, "Sources of Generational Consciousness and Conflict" and Lipset and Ladd, "The Political Future of Activist Generations," 235.

44 James A. Henretta et al., *America's History*, 3rd ed. (New York: Worth, 1997), 969.

45 See William H. Whyte, *The Organization Man* (New York: Simon & Schuster, 1956); David Riesman, *The Lonely Crowd: A Study of the Changing American Character* (New Haven, Conn.: Yale University Press, 1967).

46 The term "Generation X" was coined by Douglas Coupland in *Generation X: Tales for an Accelerated Culture* (New York: St. Martin's Press, 1991).

47 Bronfenbrenner et al., *State of Americans*, 237, 236.

48 A 1993 study by the Family and Work Institute, cited in Steven A. Holmes, "Sitting Pretty: Is This What Women Want?" *New York Times*, December 15, 1996.

49 Gary S. Becker, cited in Samuel H. Preston, "Children Will Pay," *New York Times Magazine*, September 29, 1996, 96, 97.

50 Daniel Bell, *The Coming of Post-Industrial Society* (New York: Basic Books, 1973).

51 Adapted from James F. Lea, *Political Consciousness and American Democracy* (Jackson: University Press of Mississippi, 1982), 60–61.

52 Lasch, *Culture of Narcissism*; Remi Clignet and Richard Harvey Brown, "A Semiotics of the American Self: Personal Identity in the Abstract Society," *American Journal of Semiotics* 8, no. 4 (1991): 17–49, esp. 26.

53 See the *New York Times* poll cited in *New York Times*, March 8, 1996, A13.

54 This thesis was developed by David Osborne and Ted Gaebler in *Reinventing Government: How the Entrepreneurial Spirit Is Transforming the Public Sector* (Reading, Mass.: Addison-Wesley, 1992), and then became a theme of the "reinventing government" program developed by the Clinton administration during its first term in office.

55 Rauch, "End of Government," 1891.

56 Bronfenbrenner et al., *State of Americans*, 52.

57 Elizabeth Kolbert and Adam Clymer, "The Politics of Layoffs," *New York Times*, March 3, 1996.

58 Bronfenbrenner et al., *State of Americans*, 53.

59 See Robyn Meredith, "Executive Defends Downsizing," *New York Times*, March 19, 1996.

60 Steven Rattner, "Downsizing the Downsizing Crisis," *New York Times*, October 16, 1996.

61 Anthony Lewis, "The Fraying of Hope," *New York Times*, March 8, 1996.

62 See Jennifer Hochschild, *Facing Up to the American Dream: Race, Class, and the Soul of the Nation* (Princeton, N.J.: Princeton University Press, 1995).

63 Study conducted by the Annie E. Casey Foundation, reported in Steven A. Holmes, "Children of Working Poor Are Up Sharply, Study Says," *New York Times*, June 4, 1996.

64 Bronfenbrenner et al., *State of Americans*, 148.

65 Robert Weissberg, *Political Learning, Political Choice, and Democratic Citizenship* (Englewood Cliffs, N.J.: Prentice-Hall, 1974), 120.

66 Bronfenbrenner et al., *State of Americans*, 35.

67 Thomas L. Dynneson and Richard E. Gross, "The Educational Perspective: Citizenship Education in American Society," in *Social Science Perspectives on Citizenship Education*, ed. T. L. Dynneson and R. E. Gross (New York: Teachers College Press, 1991), 9.

68 Statistics from the U.S. Department of Education and the Educational Testing Service, published in the National Adult Literacy Survey and cited in Peter A. Waite and Margaret Eisenbeck, "Literacy's Real Meaning," *Austin American-Statesman*, September 7, 1996.

69 Bronfenbrenner et al., *State of Americans*, 176.

70 See Thomas Toch and Missy Daniel, "Schools That Work," *U.S. News & World Report*, October 7, 1996, 58–64.

71 Keillor, "Future of Nostalgia," 68.

72 Charles Bensen, quoted in Jonathan Kozol, *Savage Inequalities* (New York: Crown Publishers, 1991), 200.

73 Census data reported in Shankar Vedantam, "Blacks' Graduation Rates Equal Whites'," *Austin American-Statesman*, September 6, 1996, A9.

74 Former Secretary of Labor Robert Reich, quoted in ibid. See also Peter Drucker, "The Age of Social Transformation," *Atlantic Monthly*, November 1994, 236–274.

75 Jeremy Rifkin, *The End of Work: The Decline of the Global Labor Force and the Dawn of the Post-Market Era* (New York: Putnam, 1995), 240, 241, 245.

76 Maher, "Nation of Immigrants," 8.

77 Ramsey Clark, "What Is Patriotism?" *Nation*, July 15–22, 1991, 81.

78 Michael J. Sandel, "America's Search for a New Public Philosophy," *Atlantic Monthly*, March 1996, 72. See also Mitchell Cohen, "Rooted Cosmopolitanism," *Dissent* (Fall 1992), 487–483; Bruce Ackerman, "Rooted Cosmopolitanism," *Ethics*, no. 104 (1994): 516–535.

CHAPTER 5

1 Walter Lippmann, *Public Opinion* (New York: Macmillan, 1941), 31, emphasis added; George Gallup, *The Pulse of Democracy: The Public Opinion Poll and How It Works* (New York: Simon & Schuster, 1940), 289.

2 Focus group quotations are from Robin Toner, "Word for Word/Advice for Republicans; Attention! All Sales Reps for the Contract with America!" *New York Times*, February 5, 1995.

3 Quoted in David Dahl, "In Washington, They Pick Words Carefully," *St. Petersburg Times*, February 6, 1995.

4 Quoted in Major Garret, "Beyond the Contract; Congressional Republicans," *Mother Jones* 20, no. 2 (March 1995): 54.

5 Quoted in Jacob Weisberg, "The Conformist: Republican Pollster Frank Luntz," *New York Magazine*, January 9, 1995, 16.

6 Quoted in Mark Z. Barabak, "GOP Pollster: Image Maker Takes Language to Cynical New Lows," *San Diego Union-Tribune*, February 11, 1995.

7 Susan Herbst, *Numbered Voices: How Opinion Polling Has Shaped American Politics* (Chicago: University of Chicago Press, 1993), 153.

8 Daniel Yankelovich, *Coming to Public Judgment: Making Democracy Work in a Complex World* (Syracuse, N.Y.: Syracuse University Press, 1991), 61.

9 See Alan D. Monroe, "Consistency Between Public Preferences and National Policy Decisions," *American Politics Quarterly* 7 (1979): 3–19; Robert S. Erickson, Gerald C. Wright, Jr., and John P. McIver, "Political Parties, Public Opinion, and State Policy in the United States," *American Political Science Review* 83 (1989): 729–750.

10 V.O. Key, Jr., made this observation in *Public Opinion and Democracy* (New York: Alfred A. Knopf, 1967).

11 Benjamin Ginsberg, *The Captive Public: How Mass Opinion Promotes State Power* (New York: Basic Books, 1986), 59.

12 See *Newsweek*, August 9, 1994, 19.

13 Quoted in David Van Biema, "A New Generation of Leaders," *Time*, December 5, 1994, 59.

14 Frank Luntz, memo to the Republican Conference, January 9, 1995, quoted in ibid.

15 Daniel Goleman, "Pollsters Enlist Psychologists in Quest for Unbiased Results," *New York Times*, September 7, 1993.

16 See Peter Applebome, "With Education in Rare Political Spotlight, Mainstream Clinton Message Seems to Sell," *New York Times*, October 16, 1996.

17 See Daniel Yankelovich, "How Changes in the Economy Are Reshaping American Values," in *Values and Public Policy*, ed. Henry J. Aron et al. (Washington, D.C.: Brookings Institution, 1994), 29–31.

18 Barry Sussman, *What Americans Really Think and Why Our Politicians Pay No Attention* (New York: Pantheon, 1988), 99.

19 Much of the material in this section comes from Dennis A. Gilbert's helpful introduction to his *Compendium of American Public Opinion* (New York: Facts on File, 1988).

20 Quoted in introduction to "My 'Public Opinion Baths,'" in *Lincoln on Democracy*, ed. Mario Cuomo and Harold Holzner (New York: HarperCollins, 1990), 284–285.

21 Richard G. Niemi et al., *Trends in Public Opinion: A Compendium of Survey Data* (Westport, Conn.: Greenwood, 1989), 7.

22 Ibid., 11.

23 Goleman, "Pollsters Enlist Psychologists."

24 Ibid.

25 Gilbert, *Compendium of American Public Opinion*, 5.

26 Goleman, "Pollsters Enlist Psychologists."

27 Alan F. Kay, "How the Questionnaire Could Have Been Improved," *Public Perspective*, April/May 1996, 20.

28 Niemi et al., *Trends in Public Opinion*, 4.

29 Norman M. Bradburn and Seymour Sudman, *Polls and Surveys: Understanding What They Tell Us* (San Francisco: Jossey-Bass, 1988), 191.

30 David Sears, "Whither Political Socialization Research? The Question of Persistence," in *Political Socialization, Citizenship Education and Democracy*, ed. Orit Ichilov (New York: Teachers College Press, 1990), 83. See also M. Kent Jennings, "Political Knowledge over Time and Across Generations," *Public Opinion Quarterly* 60, no. 2 (1996): 228–252.

31 The information on longitudinal studies comes from Sears, "Whither Political Socialization Research?" 83.

32 See Theodore M. Newcomb et al., *Persistence and Change: Bennington College and Its Students After Twenty-Five Years* (New York: John Wiley, 1967).

33 Duane F. Alwin, Ronald L. Cohen, and Theodore M. Newcomb, *Political Attitudes over the Life Span: The Bennington Women After Fifty Years* (Madison: University of Wisconsin Press, 1991).

34 Michael X. Delli Carpini and Scott Keeter, *What Americans Know About Politics and Why It Matters* (New Haven, Conn.: Yale University Press, 1996), 246–247.

35 Sears describes this 1985 study by D. Ward, "Generations and the Expression of Symbolic Racism," in "Whither Political Socialization," 84.

36 For a more detailed description of this survey, see Niemi et al., *Trends in Public Opinion*, 3–8.

37 Michael W. Traugott, "The Impact of Media Polls on the Public," in *Media Polls in American Politics*, ed. Thomas E. Mann and Gary R. Orren (Washington, D.C.: Brookings Institution, 1992), 137.

38 Yankelovich, *Coming to Public Judgment*, 27–28.

39 Niemi et al., *Trends in Public Opinion*, 2.

40 Delli Carpini and Keeter, *What Americans Know*, 246.

41 David W. Moore, *The Superpollsters: How They Measure and Manipulate Public Opinion in America* (New York: Four Walls Eight Windows, 1992), both quotations on 226.

42 See Robert C. Luskin, "Measuring Political Sophistication," *American Journal of Political Science* (November 1987): 861. Luskin discusses various definitional and technical problems associated with efforts to measure political sophistication.

43 Robert C. Luskin, "Political Psychology, Political Behavior, and Politics: Questions of Aggregation, Causal Distance, and Taste," in *Political Psychology and Political Behavior*, ed. James H. Kuklinski (New York: Cambridge University Press, 1995).

44 Delli Carpini and Keeter, *What Americans Know*.

45 See Philip E. Converse, *Survey Research in the United States: Roots and Emergence, 1890–1960* (Berkeley: University of California Press, 1987).

46 Anthony Downs, *An Economic Theory of Democracy* (New York: Harper, 1972), chaps. 11–13. For a lively debate, see Roderick P. Hart and John D. H. Downing, "Is There an American Public?" *Critical Studies in Mass Communications* 9, no. 2 (1992): 201–215.

47 See Hans Klingemann, "Measuring Ideological Conceptualizations", in *Political Action: Mass Participation in Five Western Democracies*, ed. Samuel H. Barnes and M. Kaase (Beverly Hills, Calif.: Sage, 1979), 215–254.

48 Russell Neuman, *The Paradox of Mass Politics: Knowledge and Opinion in the American Electorate* (Cambridge, Mass.: Harvard University Press, 1986), 185–186.

49 Ibid., 189.

50 Paul M. Sniderman, Richard A. Brody, and Philip E. Tetlock, *Reasoning and Choice: Explorations in Political Psychology* (Cambridge, England: Cambridge University Press, 1991), 21. The information in this section comes from this study.

51 Samuel L. Popkin distinguishes between low-information rationality and high-information rationality in *The Reasoning Voter* (Chicago: University of Chicago Press, 1992).

52 See, for example, James S. Newton, Roger D. Masters, Gregory J. McHugo, and Dennis G. Sullivan, "Making Up Our Minds: Effects of Network Coverage on Viewer Impressions of Leaders," *Polity* 20 (1986): 226–246.

53 Sniderman et al., *Reasoning and Choice*, 87.

54 Delli Carpini and Keeter, *What Americans Know*, 248.

55 Benjamin I. Page and Robert Y. Shapiro, *The Rational Public: Fifty Years of Trends in Americans' Policy Preferences* (Chicago: University of Chicago Press, 1992), 1–2. Most of the information in this section comes from this book.

56 Ibid., 2.

57 This was the conclusion reached by Michel T. Crozier, Samuel P. Huntington, and Taji Watanuki in *The Crisis of Democracy: Report on the Governability of Democracies to the Trilateral Commission* (New York: New York University Press, 1975).

58 Page and Shapiro, Rational Public, 15–16.

59 Yankelovich, *Coming to Public Judgment*, 4–5.

60 Ibid.

61 Ibid., 61.

62 Delli Carpini and Keeter, *What Americans Know*, 278.

63 Page and Shapiro, *Rational Public*, 365.

64 Delli Carpini and Keeter, *What Americans Know*, 227.

65 James L. Gibson, "The Political Consequences of Intolerance: Cultural Conformity and Political Freedom," *American Political Science Review* (1986): 338–356.

66 Delli Carpini and Keeter, *What Americans Know*, 221.

67 Ibid, 250, 290.

CHAPTER 6

1 Commencement Address, St. Lawrence University, 1996, and Commencement Address, Hamilton College, May 1996; both quoted in *New York Times*, May 27, 1996, A8.

2 This case study is based on Michele Wittig's "Electronic Town Hall," *Whole Earth*, no. 71 (Summer 1991), 24–27.

3 Lyndon B. Johnson, "Remarks in the Capitol Rotunda on the Signing of the Voting Rights Act," August 6, 1965, *Public Papers of the Presidents of the United States: Lyndon Johnson*, vol. 2 (Washington, D.C.: U.S. Government Printing Office, 1966), 840–843.

4 John Mack Faragher, Mari Jo Buhle, Daniel Czitrom, and Susan H. Armitage, *Out of Many: A History of the American People* (Upper Saddle River, N.J.: Prentice Hall, 1997), 276–280.

5 Sonia R. Jarvis, "Historical Overview: African Americans and the Evolution of Voting Rights," in *From Exclusion to Inclusion: The Long Struggle for African American Political Power*, ed. Ralph C. Gomes and Linda Faye Williams (Westport, Conn.: Greenwood Press, 1992), 24.

6 *Guinn v. United States*, 238 U.S. 347 (1915) and *Smith v. Allwright*, 321 U.S. 649 (1944).

7 *Harper v. Virginia State Board of Elections*, 383 U.S. 663 (1966).

8 "A Good Law Yields More Voters," *New York Times*, October 19, 1996, A16. On the history of voter registration, see Peter H. Argersinger, *Structure, Process, and Party: Essays in American Political History* (Armonk, N.Y.: M.E. Sharpe, 1992), 46–47.

9 Bill Aleshire, *A Study of Voters and Non-Voters in Travis County* (Austin, Tex.: Travis County Assessor and Collector of Taxes, 1983).

10 Peter Nye, "Will Voter Decline Reverse?" *Public Citizen*, September/October 1992, 12.

11 Jeffrey Lapin of Los Angeles, in *New York Times*, November 8, 1996, A14.

12 Ambroise Tardieu, *La Révolution à refaire, le sourverain captif* (Paris: Flammarion, 1936), 226, quoted in Romain Laufer and Catherine Paradeise, *Marketing Democracy: Public Opinion and Media Formation in Democratic Societies* (New Brunswick, N.J.: Transaction, 1990), 76.

13 Kim Ezra Shienbaum, *Beyond the Electoral Connection: A Reassessment of Voting in Contemporary American Politics* (Philadelphia: University of Pennsylvania Press, 1983), 99.

14 See Lester W. Milbrath and M. L. Goel, *Political Participation*, 2nd ed. (Chicago: Rand McNally, 1977); Shienbaum, *Beyond the Electoral Connection*, Chapter 4.

15 Thomas Dye, *Understanding Public Policy*, 3rd ed. (Englewood Cliffs, N.J.: Prentice Hall, 1972), 301.

16 This concern is raised by Shienbaum in *Beyond the Electoral Connection*, 5.

17 These arguments come from Thomas R. Dye and Harmon Zeigler, *The Irony of Democracy*, 9th ed. (Belmont, Calif.: Wadsworth, 1993), 194–195.

18 Gabriel Almond, "The 1993 James Madison Award Lecture: The Voice of the People," *PS: Political Science and Politics* (December 1993): 684.

19 Benjamin Ginsberg, *The Captive Public: How Mass Opinion Promotes State Power* (New York: Basic Books, 1986), 152–153.

20 Raymond E. Wolfinger and Steven J. Rosenstone, *Who Votes?* (New Haven, Conn.: Yale University Press, 1980), 105.

21 Shienbaum, *Beyond the Electoral Connection*, 84.

22 Wolfinger and Rosenstone, *Who Votes?* Chapter 4.

23 Barry Sussman, *What Americans Really Think and Why Our Politicians Pay No Attention* (New York: Pantheon, 1988), 55. See also E.J. Dionne, Jr., *Why Americans Hate Politics* (Simon & Schuster, 1991).

24 Austin Ranney, "Nonvoting Is Not a Social Disease," *Public Opinion* (October/November 1983): 16–19.

25 See Morris P. Fiorina, *Retrospective Voting in American National Elections* (New Haven, Conn.: Yale University Press, 1981); Paul R. Abramson, John H. Aldrich, and David W. Rohde, *Change and Continuity in the 1980 Elections* (Washington, DC: Congressional Quarterly Press, 1982), esp. Chapter 7; Peter B. Natchez, *Images of Voting/Visions of Democracy* (New York: Basic Books, 1985), 54.

26 Eric M. Uslaner, "Social Capital, Television, and the 'Mean World': A Discourse on Chickens and Eggs," paper presented at the annual meeting of the American Political Science Association, San Francisco, August 28–September 1, 1996, 4.

27 Voter News Service exit poll, 1996.

28 Linda Chavez, "The Hispanic Political Tide," *New York Times*, November 18, 1996.

29 "The Marriage Gap," *Wall Street Journal*, November 15, 1996, A14.

30 Steven Pearlstein, "Their Winter of Discontent: Angry Women Lead the Ranks of Voters Distrustful of Government and the Economy," *Washington Post National Weekly Edition*, February 12–18, 1996, 10, reporting a Post/Kaiser/Harvard poll of 1,500

Americans that attempted to gauge the depth of voter anger going into the election year.

31 U.S. Bureau of Labor Statistics.

32 Kellyanne Fitzpatrick, cited in Pearlstein, "Their Winter of Discontent."

33 Gustav Niebuhr, "Voters of Various Faiths Return to Democrats," *New York Times*, October 9, 1996, 12.

34 Source: Voter research and surveys, cited in *Time*, November 16, 1996, 48.

35 Natchez, *Images of Voting*, 54.

36 Robert Huckfeldt and John Sprague, "Networks in Context: The Social Flow of Information," *American Political Science Review* 81 (December 1987), 1197–1216.

37 Shienbaum, *Beyond the Electoral Connection*, 90–91.

38 Tamar Lewin, "Ignoring 'Right to Die' Directives, Medical Community Is Being Sued," *New York Times*, June 2, 1996, A1.

39 Gwen Pharo, quoted in *Austin American-Statesman*, May 17, 1993, B5.

40 See Sam Howe Verhovek, "Texas Meeting Seeks Rebirth of Populism," *New York Times*, November 25, 1996, A8.

41 "A More Intimate Volunteerism," *New York Times* editorial, April 26, 1997.

42 See James Gleick, *Chaos: Making a New Science* (New York: Viking, 1987).

43 William Grimes, "Heinz Is Donating $450,000 to Children's Arts Programs," *New York Times*, June 6, 1996, B1.

44 Quoted in R.W. Apple, "Voluntarism Campaign: President and Spotlight," *New York Times*, April 25, 1997, A16.

45 Ibid., 25.

46 See Elman R. Service, "The Law of Evolutionary Potential," in *Evolution and Culture*, ed. Marshall D. Sahlins and Elman R. Service (Ann Arbor: University of Michigan Press, 1960), 97.

47 See David M. Eisenberg et al., "Unconventional Medicine in the United States," *New England Journal of Medicine* 328 (February 1993), 246.

48 Dr. Avram Goldstein, professor emeritus of pharmacology at Stanford University, quoted in Natalie Angier, "U.S. Opens the Door Just a Crack to Alternative Forms of Medicine," *New York Times*, January 10, 1993, 1.

49 Howard Rheingold, "Civic Networking: If You Had an Information Highway, Where Would You Want to Go?" *Whole Earth*, no. 82 (Spring 1994): 27.

50 John H. Cushman, Jr., "EPA Innovates at Big Arizona Factory," *New York Times*, November 20, 1996, A10.

51 Tim Weiner, "New Files Prove Vietnam Cover-Up," *New York Times*, June 9, 1996, A1.

52 Murray Edelman, *Politics as Symbolic Action* (Chicago: Markham, 1971), 179.

53 Joseph F. Zimmerman, *Participatory Democracy: Populism Revised* (New York: Praeger, 1986), 3–4.

54 Carol Ford, activist with Save Our Cumberland Mountains, quoted in Frances Moore Lappé and Paul Martin Du Bois, *The Quickening of America* (San Francisco: Jossey-Bass, 1994), 290.

55 Ibid., 21.

CHAPTER 7

1 Madison's note of c. 1821 on a speech at the Constitutional Convention, 1787; Washington's *Farewell Address to the People of the United States*, September 19, 1796.

2 See Marie Brenner, "Perot's Final Days," *Vanity Fair*, October 1992, 74.

3 Ibid., 74–80.

4 James Bryce, *The American Commonwealth*, (New York: Macmillan, 1960). First published in 1900.

5 See Larry J. Sabato, *The Party's Just Begun: Shaping Political Parties for America's Future* (Glenview, Ill.: Scott, Foresman, 1988), 20–21.

6 Austin Ranney, *Curing the Mischiefs of Faction: Party Reform in America* (Berkeley: University of California Press, 1975), 206.

7 James Bennet, *New York Times*, November 6, 1996, A1, A11.

8 Adam Clymer, "Voters Dividing Almost Evenly in House Races, Survey Finds," *New York Times*, November 6, 1996, A15.

9 Robert Huckfeldt and Carol Weitzel Kohfeld, *Race and the Decline of Class in American Politics* (Chicago: University of Illinois Press, 1989), 23.

10 James C. Miller and Larry J. Sabato, both quoted in Alan Greenblatt, "The Struggle for the Soul of a Changing GOP," *Congressional Quarterly Weekly Report*, April 6, 1966, 944, 941. Greenblatt offers many insights into the factions within the Republican party.

11 For views of moderate Republicans going to the 1996 convention, see Steven A. Holmes, "Elbowed Aside in '92, Moderates Expect to Feel Welcome at This GOP Convention," *New York Times*, August 5, 1996, C11.

12 James P. Pinkerton, quoted in Greenblatt, "Struggle for the Soul," 948.

13 R.W. Apple, Jr., "Nation Is Still Locked onto Rightward Path, Leaving Liberals Beside the Road," *New York Times*, November 5, 1996, A14.

14 New York Times/CBS News poll of the delegates, cited in James Bennet, "The Delegates: Where Image Meets Reality," *New York Times*, August 12, 1996, A1.

15 Paul Weyrich, president of the Free Congress Foundation, a conservative research group, "The Republicans Are Fractured by 'Unity,'" *New York Times*, August 17, 1996, A17.

16 Joseph A. Schlesinger, *Political Parties and the Winning of Office* (Ann Arbor: University of Michigan Press, 1991), 189.

17 John Silber, president of Boston University and 1990 Democratic candidate for governor of Massachusetts, made this remark in an op-ed column "How Democrats Can Win," *New York Times*, March 10, 1992.

18 V. O. Key, Jr., *American State Politics* (New York: Alfred A. Knopf, 1956), 133.

19 See Nelson W. Polsby, *Consequences of Party Reform* (New York: Oxford University Press, 1983), 159; Gerald J. Fresia, *There Comes a Time: A Challenge to the Two Party System* (New York: Praeger, 1986), 141–142.

20 Byron E. Shafer, *Bifurcated Politics: Evolution and Reform in the National Party Convention* (Cambridge, Mass.: Harvard University Press, 1988), 343.

21 Thomas Jefferson to James Madison, June 29, 1792, *The Papers of James Madison*, ed. Robert A. Rutland et al. (Charlottesville: University Press of Virginia, 1983), vol. 14, 333.

22 John Hoadley, *Origins of American Political Parties, 1789–1803* (Lexington: University Press of Kentucky, 1986), 189.

23 See Henry Minor, *The Story of the Democratic Party* (New York: Macmillan, 1928), 7.

24 Dean McSweeney and John Zvesper, *American Political Parties: The Formation, Decline, and Reform of the American Party System* (New York: Routledge, 1991), 16.

25 Ronnie Dugger and Jim Hightower, former Texas agriculture commissioner, both quoted in Sam Howe Verhovek, "Texas Meeting Seeks a Rebirth of Populism," *New York Times*, November 25, 1996, A8.

26 For survey data, see Gordon S. Black and Benjamin D. Black, *The Politics of American Discontent* (New York: Wiley, 1994), Chapter 1.

27 Quoted in James Brooke, "Ex-Rivals Give Perot No Sympathy on Debates," *New York Times*, September 21, 1996, A9.

28 Steven J. Rosenstone, Roy L. Behr, and Edward H. Lazarus, *Third Parties in America: Citizen Response to Major Party Failure* (Princeton, N.J.: Princeton University Press, 1984), 41.

29 Lee Epstein and Charles D. Hadley, "On the Treatment of Political Parties in the U.S. Supreme Court, 1900–1986," *Journal of Politics* 52, no. 2 (May 1990): 427–428.

30 Quoted in Linda Greenhouse, "High Court Deals Setback to Minor Parties," *New York Times*, April 29, 1997, A10.

31 See Rosenstone et al., *Third Parties in America*, 4.

32 Ibid., 222; the specialist is historian John Hicks, 8.

33 Schlesinger, *Political Parties and the Winning of Office*, 2. This argument was made in the 1970s by journalist David Broder in *The Party's Over* (New York: Harper & Row, 1971) and by many academics, including Walter Dean Burnham in *Critical Elections and the Mainsprings of American Politics* (New York: Norton, 1975) and Everett Carll Ladd, Jr., and Charles D. Hadley in *Transformation of the American Party System* (New York: Norton, 1975). In the 1980s the argument was made by many others, including William Crotty and Gary C. Jacobson in *American Parties in Decline*, 2nd ed. (Boston: Little, Brown, 1984), and Martin P. Wattenberg in *The Decline of American Political Parties, 1952–1988* (Cambridge, Mass.: Harvard University Press, 1990).

34 Kay Lawson and Peter H. Merkl, "Alternative Organizations: Environmental, Supplementary, Communitarian, and Authoritarian," in *When Parties Fail: Emerging Alternative Organizations*, ed. Kay Lawson and Peter H. Merkl (Princeton, N.J.: Princeton University Press, 1988), 3.

35 William M. Lunch, *The Nationalization of American Politics* (Berkeley: University of California Press, 1987), 225.

36 Sabato makes this argument in *The Party's Just Begun*, and so do Xandra Kayden and Eddie Mahe, Jr., in *The Party Goes On: The Persistence of the Two-Party System in the United States* (New York: Basic Books, 1985).

37 McSweeney and Zvesper makes this argument in *American Political Parties*, 214–215.

38 See Christine Jennett et al., eds., *Politics of the Future: The Role of Social Movements* (London: Macmillan, 1989) and Walter Dean Burnham, "American Politics in the 1970s, Beyond Party?" in *The Future of Political Parties*, ed. Louis Maisel and Paul M. Sachs (Beverely Hills, Calif.: Sage, 1975), 238.

39 Crotty and Jacobson, *American Parties in Decline*.

40 See Joseph Schlesinger, "The New American Party System," *American Political Science Review* 79 (1973): 1152–1169; Sarah McCally Morehouse, *State Politics, Parties, and Policy* (New York: Holt, Rinehart & Winston, 1981); Denise L. Baer and David A. Bositis, *Elite Cadres and Party Coalitions: Representing the Public in Party Politics* (Westport, Conn.: Greenwood, 1988).

41 James L. Gibson, John Frendeis, and Laura Vertz, "Party Dynamics in the 1980s," paper presented at the Midwest Political Science Association annual meeting, Chicago, April 1985, 14.

42 This section is based on M. Kent Jennings, "Women in Party Politics," in *Women, Politics and Change*, ed. Louise A. Tilly and Patricia Gurin (New York: Russell Sage, 1990), 221–248.

43 Quoted in Fresia, *There Comes a Time*, 15.

44 See Harry P. Pachon and Juan Carlos Alegre, "An Overview of Hispanic Elected Officials in 1993," paper prepared for the National Association of Latino Elected and Appointed Officials (NALEO) Educational Fund, Fall 1993. Many of the statistics in this section come from this paper.

45 This section is based on Rodney E. Hero, *Latinos and the U.S. Political System* (Philadelphia: Temple University Press, 1992), 69–71.

46 Ibid., 70.

47 James L. Sundquist asks this question in "A Victim of Divided Government," *American Government, 1992* (Dubuque, Iowa: Brown & Benchmark, 1992). For more such arguments, see Joel L. Fleishman, ed., *The Future of American Parties* (Englewood Cliffs, N.J.: Prentice-Hall, 1982).

48 See, for example, Giovanni Sartori, *Parties and Party Systems* (Cambridge, England: Cambridge University Press, 1976).

49 Frederick Grimke, quoted in Richard Hofstadter, *The Idea of a Party System: The Rise of Legitimate Opposition in the United States, 1780–1840* (Berkeley: University of California Press, 1969), 266.

50 McSweeney and Zvesper, *American Political Parties*, 9–10.

CHAPTER 8

1 Bill Clinton, announcing his economic plan on February 15, 1993; First Amendment, U.S. Constitution.

2 *Cotton Grower Magazine*, quoted in "A Dose of Food Product Damage Control," *National Journal*, September 29, 1990, 2336.

3 Quoted in ibid.

4 Quoted in Dan Morain, "Washington State Apple Growers Fear Huge Losses from Alar Scare," *Los Angeles Times*, March 16, 1989.

5 Quoted in ibid.

6 Michael W. McCann, *Taking Reform Seriously: Perspectives on Public Interest Liberalism* (Ithaca, N.Y.: Cornell University Press, 1986), 17.

7 See Kenneth A. Shepsle and Mark S. Bonchek, *Analyzing Politics: Rationality, Behavior, and Institutions* (New York: Norton, 1997).

8 Mancur Olson, *The Logic of Collective Action* (Cambridge, Mass.: Harvard University Press, 1965). For a critique of Olson's thesis, see Gary Mucciaroni, "Unclogging the Arteries: The Defeat of Client Politics and the Logic of Collective Action," *Policy Studies Journal* 19, no. 3–4 (1991).

9 James Allen Smith, *The Idea Brokers: Think Tanks and the Rise of the New Policy Elite* (New York: Free Press, 1991), 20.

10 Stephen Engelberg and Martin Tolchin, "Foreigners Find New Ally Is U.S. Industry," *New York Times*, November 2, 1993.

11 Robert Salisbury, "Overlapping Memberships, Organizational Interactions, and Interest Group Theory," paper delivered at the annual meeting of the American Political Science Association, 1976, Chicago, 4.

12 *Encyclopedia of Associations*, 32nd ed. (Detroit: Gale, 1997), vii.

13 David Truman, *The Governmental Process* (New York: Alfred A. Knopf, 1951).

14 J. Parton, "Pressure upon Congress," *Atlantic*, February 1870, 145–159.

15 The number 500 comes from E. Pendleton Herring, "Why We Need Lobbies," *Outlook and Independent*, November 21, 1929, 492; the number 6,000 comes from Kenneth Crawford, *The Pressure Boys* (New York: Julian Messner, 1939), 3.

16 See Christopher J. Basso, *Pesticides and Politics: The Life Cycle of a Public Issue* (Pittsburgh: University of Pittsburgh Press, 1987).

17 Washington *Blade's* resource directory, cited in Jonathan Rauch, "The Hyperpluralism Trap," *New Republic*, June 6, 1994, 22.

18 Ibid.

19 See, for example, Leslie Eaton, "Let the Cyberinvestor Beware," *New York Times*, December 5, 1996, C1; James Sterngold, "Virtual Casino Is Coming, but Regulation Is Still a Big Question." *New York Times*, October 28, 1996, C1.

20 See Charles G. Bell, "Legislatures, Interest Groups, and Lobbyists: The Link Beyond the District," *Journal of State Government* 59–60 (Spring, 1986–1987): 12–18.

21 Pat Choate, *Agents of Influence* (New York: Alfred A. Knopf, 1990).

22 Engelberg and Tolchin, "Foreigners Find New Ally Is U.S. Industry."

23 Steve Lohr, "White House Pushing Rules on Repetitive Motion Injury," *New York Times*, December 11, 1996, A19.

24 Bob Edgar, a Democratic representative from Pennsylvania, served from 1974 to 1986. Quoted in Philip M. Stern, *The Best Congress Money Can Buy* (New York: Pantheon, 1988), 119.

25 William P. Browne, *Politics, Programs, and Bureaucrats* (Port Washington, N.Y.: Kennikat Press, 1980), 132.

26 The group Citizens Against Government Waste was founded by J. Peter Grace, who headed President Reagan's "President's Private Survey on Cost Control," also known as the Grace Commission.

27 See Jeffrey H. Birnbaum, *The Lobbyists: How Influence Peddlers Get Their Way in Washington* (New York: Times Books, 1992), 5–6.

28 Quoted in Norman J. Ornstein and Shirley Elder, *Interest Groups, Lobbying, and Public Policy*, 2nd ed. (Washington, D.C.: Congressional Quarterly Press, 1981), 77.

29 Bob Dart, "Box Office Politics: Pairing Stars with a Cause," *Austin American-Statesman*, August 4, 1997.

30 This anonymous legislator is quoted in Ornstein and Elder, *Interest Groups, Lobbying, and Public Policy*.

31 Quoted in W. John Moore, "Knocking the System," *National Journal*, November 23, 1991, 2848.

32 Mark S. Mellman, quoted in Lee Smith, "Trial Lawyers Face a New Charge," *Fortune*, August 26, 1991, 89.

33 An anonymous lobbyist, quoted in Ornstein and Elder, *Interest Groups, Lobbying, and Public Policy*, 72.

34 The legislative counsel for a major hospital association, quoted in Kay Lehman Schlozman and John T. Tierney, "More of the Same: Washington Pressure Activity in a Decade of Change," *Journal of Politics* 45 (May 1983): 370.

35 See Robert E. Norton, "Can Business Win in Washington?" *Fortune*, December 3, 1990, 76–77.

36 Allan J. Cigler and Burdett A. Loomis, "Contemporary Interest Group Politics," in *Interest Group Politics*, 4th ed. Allan J. Cigler and Burdett A. Loomis, ed. (Washington, D.C.: Congressional Quarterly Press, 1995).

37 Van Dongen, of Wholesale Distributors, quoted in Norton, "Can Business Win in Washington?" 76.

38 See Paul Starobin, "On the Square," *National Journal*, May 25, 1996, 1145–1149.

39 Ann Cooper, "Middleman Mail," *National Journal*, September 14, 1985, 2031.

40 Ibid., 2032.

41 Robert H. Salisbury, "The Paradox of Interest Groups in Washington—More Groups, Less Clout," in *The New American Political System*, ed. Anthony King (Washington, D.C.: American Enterprise Institute, 1990), 226–227.

42 Truman, *The Governmental Process*.

43 Robert Dahl, *Who Governs*? (New Haven, Conn.: Yale University Press, 1961).

44 Jeffrey M. Berry, *The Interest Group Society*, 3rd ed. (Reading, Mass.: Addison-Wesley, 1996), 10.

45 Theodore Lowi, *The End of Liberalism* (New York: Norton, 1969).

46 C. Wright Mills, *The Power Elite* (New York: Oxford University Press, 1956). More recent books in the same tradition include Thomas R. Dye, *Who's Running America: The Bush Years* (Englewood Cliffs, N.J.: Prentice Hall, 1991).

47 PBS *Frontline*, "The Best Campaign Money Can Buy," October 27, 1992 (Alexandria, Va.: PBS Video, 1992).

48 See Robert O. Michels, *Political Parties: A Sociological Study of the Oligarchical Tendencies of Modern Democracy*, first written in 1915 (New York: Dover, 1959).

49 Jonathan Rauch, *Demosclerosis: The Silent Killer of American Government* (New York: Times Books, 1994), 239.

50 Rauch, "The Hyperpluralism Trap," 24.

51 Ibid., 25.

52 Thomas R. Dye and Harmon Ziegler, *The Irony of Democracy*, 8th ed. (Pacific Grove, Calif.: Brooks/Cole, 1990), 221.

53 Salisbury, "Overlapping Memberships, Organizational Interactions, and Interest Group Theory," 4.

54 Linda S. Lichter, "Who Speaks for Black America?" *Public Opinion* (August/September 1985): 44.

55 Joyce Gelb and Jennifer L. Disney, "Feminist Organizational 'Success': The State of the Women's Movement in the 1990s," paper presented at the annual meeting of the American Political Science Association, San Francisco, August 29–September 1, 1996, 4.

56 See David Knoke, *Organizing for Collective Action: The Political Economics of Associations* (New York: Aldine de Gruyter, 1990).

57 Jeffrey M. Berry, *Lobbying for the People* (Princeton, N.J.: Princeton University Press, 1977), 71–76.

58 Robert Rabin, "Lawyers for Social Change: Perspectives on Public Interest Law," *Stanford Law Review* 28 (1976): 207–261.

59 Berry, *Lobbying for the People*, 181–182, 186.

60 Clive S. Thomas and Ronald J. Hrebenar, "Regulating Interest Groups in the United States: National, State, and Local Experiences," paper delivered at the annual meeting of the American Political Science Association, San Francisco, August 29–September 1, 1996, 8.

61 See Peter T. Kilbotn, "When Welfare Establishment Gathers, the Topic Is Wrenching Change," *New York Times*, December 11, 1996, A17.

62 Cooper, "Middleman Mail," 2064.

63 Bill Holayter, legislative and political director of the International Association of Machinists and Aerospace Workers, quoted in Stern, *The Best Congress Money Can Buy*, 125–126.

64 Former Senator Charles Mathias, quoted in ibid., 105.

65 Ruth Marcus and Charles R. Babcock, "Feeding the Election Machine," *Washington Post National Weekly Edition*, February 17, 1997, 6.

66 Tim Weiner and David E. Sanger, "Democrats Hoped to Raise $7 Million from Asians in U.S.," *New York Times*, December 28, 1996, A1.

67 Alison Mitchell, "Democrats to Return More Money Received From 'Improper' Sources," *New York Times*, February 22, 1997, A1.

68 Eliza Newlin Carney, "Take Our Donations, Pleeeeeze!" *National Journal*, March 15, 1997, 516.

69 "Senator D'Amato Shuffles the Money," *New York Times*, January 20, 1997, A20.

70 Marcus and Babcock, "Feeding the Election Machine."

71 Stern, *The Best Congress Money Can Buy*, 16.

72 Quoted in ibid., 105.

73 Ibid., 9.

74 Former member of Congress Michael Barnes of Maryland, quoted in ibid., 101.

75 Richard Morin and Mario A. Brossard, "Give and Take: What the Donors Really Want," *Washington Post National Weekly Edition*, February 17, 1997, 10.

76 For arguments in favor of this reform, see Stern, *The Best Congress Money Can Buy*, Chapter 11.

77 Jonathan Cohn, "Reform School," *Mother Jones*, May/June 1997, 62.

78 See Robert H. Salisbury and Paul Johnson et al., "Who You Know Versus What You Know: The Uses of Government Experience for Washington Lobbyists," *American Journal of Political Science* 33 (February 1989): 175.

79 Max Frankel, "The Frauds of April," *New York Times Magazine*, April 13, 1997, 30.

80 Paula Cozzi Goedert, "Lobbying by Charitable Organizations," in *Federal Lobbying*, ed. Jerald A. Jacobs (Washington, D.C.: Bureau of National Affairs, 1989), 148.

81 Ibid., 145.

82 James T. Bennett and Thomas J. DiLorenzo, *Destroying Democracy* (Washington, D.C.: Cato Institute, 1985).

83 David Shenck, "Nonprofiteers: How to Lobby Like a Corporation and Pay Taxes Like a Charity," *Washington Monthly*, December 1991, 35–39.

84 Ibid., 37.

85 *Taxation with Representation of Washington v. Regan, Secretary of the Treasury, et al.*, 461 U.S. 540 (1983).

86 Kurt H. Wolff, ed., *The Sociology of Georg Simmel* (Glencoe, Ill.: Free Press, 1950), 27.

CHAPTER 9

1 Robert Stein, *Media Power: Who Is Shaping Your Picture of the World?* (Boston: Houghton Mifflin, 1972), xii; Michael J. O'Neill, "Who Cares About the Truth? Merger of News and Entertainment and Replacement of Facts with Fiction Are Troubling—and Profitable," *Nieman Reports*, Spring 1994, 14.

2 This side of the story was told by one of the officers; see Stacey C. Koon and Robert Deitz, *Presumed Guilty: The Tragedy of the Rodney King Affair* (Chicago: Regnery, 1992).

3 For a detailed account published a year later, see "The Untold Story of the LA Riot," *U.S. News & World Report*, May 28, 1993, 35–59.

4 See Harold W. Stanley and Richard G. Niemi, *Vital Statistics on American Politics*, 4th ed. (Washington, D.C.: Congressional Quarterly Press, 1994), 74.

5 John Morton, "Chains Swallowing Other Chains," *American Journalism Review*, July/August 1997, 52.

6 See Ben H. Bagdikian, *The Media Monopoly*, 4th ed. (Boston: Beacon Press, 1993).

7 *Broadcast and Cable* magazine, quoted in Jonathan Tasini, "The Dawn of the Tele-Barons: Media Moguls Are Rewriting the Laws and Rewiring the Country," *Washington Post National Weekly Edition*, February 12, 1996, 22.

8 Ben H. Bagdikian, "The Lords of the Global Village," *Nation*, June 12, 1989, 807.

9 See Ken Auletta, *Three Blind Mice: How the TV Networks Lost Their Way* (New York: Random House, 1991); Penn Kimball, *Downsizing the News: Network Cutbacks in the Nation's Capital* (Baltimore: Johns Hopkins University Press, 1994).

10 Jeff Gremillion, "Showdown at Generation Gap," *Columbia Journalism Review*, July 1995, 34–38.

11 David Armstrong, "Alternative, Inc." *In These Times*, August 21, 1995, 14–18.

12 John Herndon, "Talk Radio Fans Defy Expectations," *Austin American-Statesman*, May 19, 1994.

13 See Roderick P. Hart, *Seducing America: How Television Charms the Modern Voter* (New York: Oxford University Press, 1994), 138.

14 Graeme Browning, "Hot-Wiring Washington," *National Journal*, June 26, 1993, 1624–1629; *Internet Index* 18, April 1997, and 16, December 1996.

15 Steve Lohr, "Data Highway Ignoring Poor, Study Charges," *New York Times*, May 24, 1994.

16 See Kelly Anderson and Annie Goldson, "Alternating Currents: Alternative Television Inside and Outside of the Academy," *Social Text* 35 (1993): 56–71.

17 Herbert J. Gans, *Deciding What's News* (New York: Pantheon, 1979).

18 See David H. Weaver and G. Cleveland Wilhoit, "Journalists—Who Are They Really?" *Media Studies Journal*, Fall 1992.

19 Alicia C. Shepard, "Talk Is Expensive," *American Journalism Review*, May 1994, 20–42.

20 Stephen Hess, *The Washington Reporters* (Washington, D.C.: Brookings Institution, 1981), 118.

21 See Graeme Browning, "Too Close for Comfort?" *National Journal*, October 3, 1992, 2243–2247.

22 Gans, *Deciding What's News*.

23 Leon V. Sigal, *Reporters and Officials: The Organization and Politics of Newsmaking* (Lexington, Mass.: Heath, 1973); he studied *Time*, *Newsweek*, CBS, and NBC.

24 Richard V. Ericson et al., *Negotiating Control: A Study of News Sources* (Milton Keynes, England: Open University Press, 1989), 377.

25 Ron Nessen, "The Washington You Can't See on Television," *TV Guide*, September 20, 1980, 10.

26 Quoted in Robert M. Batscha, *Foreign Affairs News and the Broadcast Journalist* (New York: Praeger, 1975), 30–31.

27 William Gamson, "Goffman's Legacy to Political Sociology," *Theory and Society* (1985): 617. See Erving Goffman, *Frame Analysis* (Cambridge, Mass.: Harvard University Press, 1974), for the first use of *framing*.

28 Michael Schudson, *The Power of News* (Cambridge, Mass.: Harvard University Press, 1995), 10.

29 O'Neill, "Who Cares About the Truth?" 12.

30 Nicholas Lemann, "Ordinary People and Extraordinary Journalism," *The IRE Journal*, November–December 1991, 7.

31 Philip Seib, *Who's in Charge: How the Media Shape News and Politicians Win Votes* (Dallas: Taylor, 1987), 5.

32 Daniel Dayan and Elihu Katz, *Media Events: The Live Broadcasting of History* (Cambridge, Mass.: Harvard University Press, 1992), ix.

33 See Howard Kurtz (Washington Post Service), "The Great Exploding Popcorn Exposé of 1994," *Austin American-Statesman*, May 18, 1994; Center for Science in the Public Interest, *Nutrition Action Health Letter*, May 1994.

34 Todd Gitlin, *The Whole World Is Watching: Mass Media in the Making and Unmaking of the New Left* (Berkeley: University of California Press, 1980), 3–4.

35 Denis McQuail, *Mass Communication Theory* (Beverly Hills, Calif.: Sage, 1983), 135.

36 Quoted in Michael Massing, "CBS: Sauterizing the News," *Columbia Journalism Review*, March-April 1986, 30.

37 Shanto Iyengar, *Is Anyone Responsible? How Television Frames Political Issues* (Chicago: University of Chicago Press, 1991), 143.

38 Jon Katz, "The Plugged-In Voter: The New News Has Reconnected People and Politics," *Rolling Stone*, December 10, 1992, 115; see also Jon Katz, "Beyond Broadcast Journalism: Reinventing the Media," *Columbia Journalism Review*, March-April 1992, 19–23.

39 Jean Prescott, "MTV Gives Power to the People Through Their News," *Austin American-Statesman*, January 21, 1996.

40 Jerry Berger, "Damn the Facts—Roll the Presses," *Editor & Publisher*, May 14, 1994, 56.

41 See Chip Rowe, "Watchdog Watch," *American Journalism Review*, April 1993, 32–34; Mark Jurkowitz, "A House of Canards—Critiquing the Media Critics," *Media Studies Journal*, Fall 1992.

42 Marc Cooper and Lawrence C. Soley, "All the Right Sources," *Mother Jones*, March 1990, 21. See also Lawrence C. Soley, *The News Shapers: The Sources Who Explain the News* (New York: Praeger, 1992).

43 The study of media references in 1995 is reported in Michael Dolny, "The Think Tank Spectrum," *EXTRA!* May-June 1996, 21.

44 Quoted in Charles Kenney, "Top of the News," *Boston Globe Magazine*, November 6, 1988, 47.

45 Erwin Knoll, "Becoming a Critical Consumer of News," in *Stenographers to Power*, ed. David Barsamian (Monroe, Me.: Common Courage Press, 1992), 189.

46 Hess, *The Washington Reporters*, Chapter 3. See also journalist Don Campbell's *Inside the Beltway: A Guide to Washington Reporting* (Ames: Iowa State University Press, 1991).

47 Research by Daniel Hallin, cited in Samuel Popkin, *The Reasoning Voter* (Chicago: University of Chicago Press, 1991).

48 Stephen Hess, "White House Press, Revisited," *Nieman Reports*, Spring 1992, 65–70.

49 Wesley G. Pippert, *An Ethics of News: A Reporter's Search for Truth* (Washington, D.C.: Georgetown University Press, 1989), 95.

50 Michael B. Grossman and Martha Joynt Kumar, *Portraying the President: The White House and the News Media* (Baltimore: Johns Hopkins University Press, 1981), 231.

51 See Dan Cogan, "More Champagne, Ms. Mitchell? The Other Side of the Travelgate Story and Why the Media Didn't Tell You About It," *Washington Monthly*, July-August 1993, 17–18.

52 Pippert, *An Ethics of News*, 94. For White House press secretaries' memoirs, see, among others, Ron Nessen, *It Sure Looks Different from the Inside* (Chicago: Playboy, 1978), by Gerald Ford's press secretary; Jody Powell, *The Other Side of the Story* (New York: Morrow, 1984), by Jimmy Carter's; Larry Speakes, *Speaking Out: The Reagan Presidency from Inside the White House* (New York: Scribner, 1988); and Bush's Marlin Fitzwater, *Call the Briefing! Reagan and Bush, Sam and Helen: A Decade with Presidents and the Press* (New York: Times Books, 1996).

53 John Anthony Maltese, *Spin Control: The White House Office of Communications and the Management of Presidential News* (Chapel Hill: University of North Carolina Press, 1992).

54 *RN: The Memoirs of Richard Nixon* (New York: Grosset & Dunlap, 1978), 354.

55 Mark Hertsgaard, *On Bended Knee: The Press and the Reagan Presidency* (New York: Farrar, Straus, & Giroux, 1988), 36.

56 Hedrick Smith, *The Power Game: How Washington Works* (New York: Random House, 1988), 410.

57 James Fallows, "Why Americans Hate the Media," *Atlantic*, February 1996, 45–64.

58 Paul Starobin, "Heeding the Call," *National Journal*, November 30, 1996, 2584–2589.

59 Martin Linsky, *Impact: How the Press Affects Federal Policymaking* (New York: Norton, 1986).

60 Donna A. Demac tells the story of *The Puzzle Palace* (Boston: Houghton Mifflin, 1982) in "Hearts and Minds Revisited: The Information Policies of the Reagan Administration," in *The Political Economy of Information,* ed. Vincent Mosco and Janet Wasko (Madison: University of Wisconsin Press, 1988).

61 See John R. MacArthur, *Second Front: Censorship and Propaganda in the Gulf War* (New York: Hill & Wang, 1992).

62 For an account by a reporter who covered the war for the *Wall Street Journal,* see John J. Fialka, *Hotel Warriors: Covering the Gulf War* (Baltimore: Johns Hopkins University Press, 1992).

63 See Bradley S. Greenberg and Walter Gantz, eds., *Desert Storm and the Mass Media* (Cresskill, N.J.: Hampton Press, 1993).

64 David S. Broder, *Behind the Front Page* (New York: Simon & Schuster, 1987), 208; Lewis W. Wolfson, *The Untapped Power of the Press* (New York: Praeger, 1985), 42.

65 William Rehnquist, *The Supreme Court: How It Was, How It Is* (New York: Morrow, 1987).

66 *Chandler* v. *Florida,* 449 U.S. 560 (1981).

67 "Foreign Bureaus," *American Journalism Review,* April 1994, 29.

68 *Hunger 1994* (Washington: Bread for the World, 1993).

69 See, for example, Hugh Carter Donahue, *The Battle to Control Broadcast News: Who Owns the First Amendment?* (Cambridge, Mass.: MIT Press, 1989), 176.

70 *Reno v. American Civil Liberties Union,* no. 96-511, decided in June 1997.

71 F. Dennis Hale, "Media Rights Prosper Under Influence of States," *Editor & Publisher,* February 10, 1996, 40.

72 W. Russell Neuman, *The Future of the Mass Audience* (Cambridge, England: Cambridge University Press, 1991), 88–89.

73 The term "living room war" was coined by *New Yorker* critic Michael Arlen. See his *Living-Room War* (New York: Viking, 1969).

74 Christopher Lasch, "Journalism, Publicity, and the Lost Art of Argument," *Gannett Center Journal,* Spring 1990, 1.

75 Edmund B. Lambeth, *Committed Journalism: An Ethic for the Profession,* 2nd ed. (Bloomington: Indiana University Press, 1992), 33.

76 Bill Kovach, quoted in Bernard Caughey, "Out of Touch?" *Editor & Publisher,* December 23, 1989, 10–11, quoted in Lambeth, *Committed Journalism,* 195.

77 See Clifford Christians, "Self-Regulation: A Critical Role for Codes of Ethics," in *Media Freedom and Accountability,* ed. Everette E. Dennis et al. (Westport, Conn.: Greenwood Press, 1989), Chapter 4.

78 See A. J. Liebling, *The Press* (New York: Ballantine, 1962).

79 Ralph Nader, "A Citizen's Communication Agenda," *Citizen Participation,* May-June 1980, 3.

80 These and other trends are analyzed in Ithiel de Sola Pool, *Technologies of Freedom* (Cambridge, Mass.: Harvard University Press, 1983), Chapter 9.

81 Quoted in Michael Schudson, "The Limits of Teledemocracy," *The American Prospect,* Fall 1992, 44.

82 Ibid.

83 Majid Tehranian, *Technologies of Power: Information Machines and Democratic Prospects* (Norwood, N.J.: Ablex, 1990), xv.

84 Jeffrey B. Abramson et al., *The Electronic Commonwealth: The Impact of New Media Technologies on Democratic Politics* (New York: Basic Books, 1988), xiii.

85 Richard Saul Wurman, *Information Anxiety* (Garden City, N.Y.: Doubleday, 1989), 32.

86 See, among others, David Burnham, *The Rise of the Computer State: The Threat to Our Freedoms, Our Ethics, and Our Democratic Processes* (New York: Random House, 1983).

CHAPTER **10**

1 Both quotes are from Dave McNeely, "Campaign Strategists Preparing Spin Systems," *Austin American-Statesman,* October 26, 1993.

2 PBS *Frontline,* "The Best Campaign Money Can Buy" (Alexandria, Va.: PBS Video, 1992).

3 See Morris P. Fiorina, *Retrospective Voting in American National Elections* (New Haven, Conn.: Yale University Press, 1981).

4 Brad Lockerbie, "Prospective Voting in Presidential Elections, 1956–1988," *American Politics Quarterly* 20, no. 3 (July 1992): 308–325.

5 See Murray Edelman, *Creating the Political Spectacle* (Chicago: University of Chicago Press, 1988).

6 Kathleen Jamieson, *Dirty Politics: Deception, Distraction, and Democracy* (New York: Oxford University Press, 1994), 3–9.

7 See Michael Nelson, ed., *Congressional Quarterly's Guide to the Presidency* (Washington, D.C.: Congressional Quarterly Press, 1989), 201, for a helpful summary chart comparing the process before and after 1968.

8 Martin P. Wattenberg, *The Rise of Candidate-Centered Politics* (Cambridge, Mass.: Harvard University Press, 1991), 157.

9 Richard Huff, "Political Ads Cost $400 Million in '96," *Austin American-Statesman,* January 27, 1997.

10 James Bennet, "Aftermath of '96 Race: 1,397 Hours of TV Ads," *New York Times,* November 13, 1996.

11 Thomas Patterson and Robert McClure, *The Unseeing Eye: The Myth of Television Power in National Elections* (New York: Putnam, 1976), 22.

12 Thomas Patterson, *The Mass Media Election: How Americans Choose Their President* (New York: Praeger, 1980).

13 See Edwin Diamond and Stephen Bates, *The Spot: The Rise of Political Advertising on Television* (Cambridge, Mass.: MIT Press, 1984).

14 Anthony Corrado, "Financing the 1996 Elections," in Gerald M. Pomper et al., *The Election of 1996: Reports and Interpretations* (Chatham, N.J.: Chatham House, 1997), Chapter 4.

15 *Buckley v. Valeo,* 424 U.S. 1 (1976).

16 David Broder, "Gutless Government," *Washington Post National Weekly Edition,* November 6, 1989, 4.

17 Federal Election Commission, "FEC Finds Congressional Campaign Spending Up $75 Million as 1992 General Election Approaches," press release, October 30, 1992.

18 Jonathan D. Salant, "Million-Dollar Campaigns Proliferate in 105th," *CQ Weekly Report,* December 21, 1996, 3448.

19 Corrado, "Financing the 1996 Election," 155.

20 *Baker v. Carr*, 369 U.S. 186 (1962); *Wesberry v. Sanders*, 376 U.S. 1 (1964); *Reynolds v. Sims*, 377 U.S. 533 (1964).

21 *Shaw v. Reno*, 509 U.S. 630 (1993).

22 See Richard B. Bernstein, *Amending America* (New York: Times Books, 1993), Chapter 4.

23 James A. Barnes, "Greener Acres," *National Journal*, April 23, 1994, 950.

24 Alison Mitchell, "Building a Bulging War Chest: How Clinton Financed His Run," *New York Times*, December 27, 1996.

25 For accounts of candidates' media strategies and the media's role in the 1996 election, see Marion R. Just, "Candidate Strategies and the Media Campaign," in Pomper et al., *The Election of 1996*, Chapter 2; Diana Owen, "The Press' Performance," in *Toward the Millennium: The Elections of 1996*, ed. Larry J. Sabato (Boston: Allyn & Bacon, 1997), Chapter 9.

26 Dick Morris, *Behind the Oval Office: Winning the Presidency in the Nineties* (New York: Random House, 1997), 123.

27 F. Christopher Arterton, "Campaign '92: Strategies and Tactics," 87–88 in Gerald M. Pomper et al., *The Election of 1992* (Chatham, N.J.: Chatham House, 1993).

28 Michael Kelly, "Clinton's Staff Sees Campaign as a Real War," *New York Times*, August 11, 1992.

29 For an inside account of Bush's issue specialist, see James Pinkerton, "Life in Bush Hell," *New Republic*, December 14, 1992, 22–26. See also John Podhoretz, *Hell of a Ride: Backstage at the White House Follies 1989–1993* (New York: Simon & Schuster, 1993), especially Chapter 6.

30 See Walter Berns, ed., *After the People Vote: A Guide to the Electoral College*, rev. ed. (Washington, D.C.: American Enterprise Institute Press, 1992).

31 Jamieson, *Dirty Politics*, 46.

32 Richard Stengel and Eric Pooley, "Masters of the Message," *Time*, November 18, 1996, 87; Susan Paterno, "An Affair to Ignore," *American Journalism Review*, January/February 1997, 31–33.

33 *Campaigns and Elections*, 1835 K Street NW, Suite 403, Washington, DC 20077.

34 The Graduate School of Political Management, 17 Lexington Avenue, Box 510, New York, NY 10010.

35 Bruce Buchanan, *Electing a President: The Markle Commission Research on Campaign '88* (Austin: University of Texas Press, 1991). See also Buchanan's further analysis, *Renewing Presidential Politics: Campaigns, Media, and the Public Interest* (Lanham, Md.: Rowman & Littlefield, 1996).

36 Buchanan, *Electing a President*, Chapter 7.

37 See Curtis Gans, "Yes—Campaign Commercials Should be Regulated," in *Controversial Issues in Presidential Selection*, ed. Gary L. Rose (Albany, N.Y.: State University of New York Press, 1991), 133–142.

38 See Martin P. Wattenberg, "When You Can't Beat Them, Join Them: Shaping the Presidential Nominating Process to the Television Age," *Polity* 21 (Spring 1989): 587–597.

39 Corrado, "Financing the 1996 Elections."

40 Brooks Jackson, *Honest Graft: Big Money and the American Political Process* (New York: Alfred A. Knopf, 1988).

41 See, for example, Curtis Gans, "Campaign Finance Reformers Have Created a 3-D Program—Delusional, Dangerous, and Dumb," *George*, January 1997, 32.

42 Lawrie Mifflin, "Free TV-Time Experiment Wins Support, If Not Viewers," *New York Times*, November 3, 1996.

43 James Bennet, "Political Ad Plan May Test Patience of Broadcasters," *New York Times*, March 13, 1997.

44 Samuel L. Popkin, *The Reasoning Voter: Communication and Persuasion in Presidential Campaigns* (Chicago: University of Chicago Press, 1991), 236.

CHAPTER 11

1 Hubert Humphrey, quoted in Stephen K. Bailey, *Congress in the Seventies* (New York: St. Martin's Press, 1970), 95; James B. Pearson, quoted in *Congressional Quarterly Weekly Report*, September 4, 1982, 2181.

2 The following account relies primarily on Richard E. Cohen, *Washington at Work: Back Rooms and Clean Air* (New York: Macmillan, 1992); Gary C. Bryner, *Blue Skies, Green Politics: The Clean Air Act of 1990*, 2nd ed. (Washington D.C.: Congressional Quarterly Press, 1995).

3 See Richard Morin, "You Think Congress Is Out of Touch? Look in the Mirror, Voters, the Trouble Starts with You," *Washington Post*, October 16, 1994.

4 Quoted by Michael J. Malbin, "House Democrats Are Playing with a Strong Leadership Lineup," *National Journal*, June 18, 1977, 942. For other accounts, see O'Neill's autobiography: *Man of the House: The Life and Political Memoirs of Speaker Tip O'Neill* (New York: Random House, 1987).

5 Richard Bolling, who failed to win a leadership role as a reformer, quoted in Warren Weaver, *Both Your Houses* (New York: Praeger, 1972), 156.

6 Quoted in Rowland Evans and Robert Novak, *Lyndon B. Johnson: The Exercise of Power* (New York: New American Library, 1966), 104–105. One of Johnson's longtime assistants, Robert Parker, later wrote even more candidly of Johnson's approach in his autobiography, *Capitol Hill in Black and White* (New York: Dodd, Mead, 1986); this book, by an African American raised in rural Magnolia, Texas, also offers many insights into the gradual overcoming of racism in Washington.

7 Quoted in Laurence Leamer, "Changing," *Washingtonian*, May 1977, 127.

8 Among recent studies are David R. Mayhew, *Divided We Govern: Party Control, Lawmaking, and Investigations, 1946–1990* (New Haven, Conn.: Yale University Press, 1991); Morris Fiorina, *Divided Government* (New York: Macmillan, 1992); Charles O. Jones, *The Presidency in a Separated System* (Washington, D.C.: Brookings Institution, 1994).

9 John Kingdon, *Congressmen's Voting Decisions*, 2nd ed. (New York: Harper & Row, 1981).

10 Quoted in Lewis A. Dexter, "The Representative and His District," in *New Perspectives on the House of Representatives*, ed. Robert L. Peabody and Nelson W. Polsby (Chicago: Rand McNally, 1963), 6.

11 Edmund Burke, speech to constituents, 1774.

12 See, for example, the classic study by John Wahlke et al., *The Legislative System* (New York: Wiley, 1962).

13 In one study, Roger H. Davidson found that in a group of 87 representatives, 46 percent were "politicos," 28 percent were "trustees," and 23 percent were "delegates." See *The Role of the Congressman* (New York: Pegasus, 1969), 117.

14 Timothy Wirth, "Why I'm Quitting the Senate," *New York Times Magazine,* August 9, 1992, 23.

15 Quoted in J.A. Carroll et al., eds., *George Washington* (New York: Scribner's, 1957) 7:591.

16 Joseph S. Clark, *Congress: The Sapless Branch* (New York: Harper, 1964), 2.

17 See Davidson, *Role of the Congressman*; Bruce Cain, John Ferejohn, and Morris Fiorina, "Constituency Service in the United States and Great Britain," in *Congress Reconsidered,* 3rd ed., ed. Lawrence C. Dodd and Bruce Oppenheimer (Washington, D.C.: Congressional Quarterly Press, 1985), Chapter 5.

18 The study was by *Money* magazine for 1994, reported in Bob Dart, "U.S. Pays $1 Million per Legislator," *Austin American-Statesman,* January 14, 1995.

19 When John Peters and Susan Welch studied congressional roll-call votes and personal financial interests as revealed in the financial disclosure statements that members are now required to file, they found some evidence of conflict-of-interest voting. When they considered the interests of the members' constituencies, however, they found that these usually adequately explained the voting. See their "Private Interests and Public Interests," *Journal of Politics,* 45 (May 1983): 378–396.

20 See Roger H. Davidson and Walter J. Oleszek, *Congress and Its Members,* 4th ed. (Washington, D.C.: Congressional Quarterly Press, 1995), 216.

21 For a detailed analysis of each committee in each house and the changes made by the Republicans in 1995, see the special issue "The Hill People: The New Regime," *National Journal,* June 17, 1995.

22 Quoted in Lawrence J. Haas, "Unauthorized Action," *National Journal,* January 2, 1988, 20. For a study by a onetime legislative aide to former Representative Tony Coelho (D-Calif.), see Stephen D. Van Beek, *Post-Passage Politics: Bicameral Resolution in Congress* (Pittsburgh: University of Pittsburgh Press, 1994).

23 Gary Young and Joseph Cooper, "Multiple Referral and the Transformation of House Decision Making," in *Congress Reconsidered,* 5th ed., ed. Lawrence C. Dodd and Bruce J. Oppenheimer (Washington, D.C.: Congressional Quarterly Press, 1993), Chapter 9.

24 See Roger H. Davidson and Walter J. Oleszek, "From Monopoly to Management: Changing Patterns of Committee Deliberation," in *The Postreform Congress,* ed. Roger H. Davidson (New York: St. Martin's Press, 1992), Chapter 7.

25 Edward Madigan (R-Ill.), quoted in David Maraniss, "Powerful Energy Panel Turns on Big John's Axis," *Washington Post,* May 15, 1983.

26 Quoted anonymously in Cohen, *Washington at Work,* 116.

27 The count was made in 1988 by Sula P. Richardson of the Congressional Research Service. The whole list is reprinted in Roger H. Davidson and Walter J. Oleszek, *Congress and Its Members,* 3rd ed. (Washington, D.C.: Congressional Quarterly Press, 1990), 296–297.

28 For a study, see David Bositis, *The Congressional Black Caucus in the 103rd Congress* (Washington, D.C.,: Joint Center for Political and Economic Studies, 1994).

29 See "The Hill People: The New Regime."

30 Adam Clymer, "Rancor Leaves Its Mark on 103d Congress," *New York Times,* October 9, 1994.

31 Quoted in Ross K. Baker, *House and Senate* (New York: Norton, 1989), 66.

32 Davidson and Oleszek, *Congress and Its Members,* 3rd ed., 308.

33 Quoted in *Congressional Record,* daily ed., 101st Congress, 1st sess., March 3, 1989, S2111.

34 Quoted anonymously in Baker, *House and Senate,* 183.

35 See Eric M. Uslaner, *The Decline of Comity in Congress* (Ann Arbor: University of Michigan Press, 1993).

36 Quoted in Helen Dewar, "The Etiquette of a Revolution," *Washington Post National Weekly Edition,* June 26, 1995, 12.

37 See Uslaner, *Decline of Comity in Congress.*

38. David Broder, "Can Respect Be Restored in House?" *Austin American-Statesman,* July 23, 1996.

39 For a concise summary of the findings of recent congressional voting studies, see Davidson and Oleszek, *Congress and Its Members,* 3rd ed., Chapter 12.

40 Norman Ornstein, quoted in Graeme Browning, "Freelancers," *National Journal,* September 24, 1994, 2203.

41 Quoted anonymously in Thomas O'Donnell, "Managing Legislative Time," in *The House at Work,* ed. Joseph Cooper and G. Calvin Mackenzie (Austin: University of Texas Press, 1981), 128.

42 Quoted in Randall Ripley, *Congress: Process and Policy,* 2nd ed. (New York: Norton, 1978), 125.

43 Quoted in Bernard Asbell, *The Senate Nobody Knows* (Garden City, N.Y.: Doubleday, 1978), 210.

44 See Lawrence D. Longley and Walter J. Oleszek, *Bicameral Politics: Conference Committees in Congress* (New Haven, Conn.: Yale University Press, 1989), 4, Chapter 8; Van Beek, *Post-Passage Politics.*

45. For instances, see Longley and Oleszek, *Bicameral Politics,* 5–9.

46 Both quoted in Francis X. Clines, "President Invites Deal in Congress for Jobs," *New York Times,* December 18, 1982.

47 See James MacGregor Burns, *Presidential Government: The Crucible of Leadership* (Boston: Houghton Mifflin, 1973).

48 This study focused on foreign policy, but its conclusion is equally applicable to domestic policy. See James M. Lindsay, *Congress and the Politics of U.S. Foreign Policy* (Baltimore: Johns Hopkins University Press, 1994), viii.

49 Martha L. Gibson, "Managing Conflict: The Role of the Legislative Veto in American Foreign Policy," *Polity* 26, no. 3 (Spring 1994): 441–472.

50 *Immigration and Naturalization Service v. Chadha,* 468 U.S. 919 (1983).

51 Joel Aberbach, *Keeping a Watchful Eye: The Politics of Congressional Oversight* (Washington, D.C.: Brookings Institution, 1990), 212–213.

52 *Marbury v. Madison,* 1 Cranch 137 (1803).

53 See John Roos, "Thinking About Reform: The World View of Congressional Reformers," *Polity* 15, no. 3 (Spring 1993): 329–354.

54 Gary Orfield, *Congressional Power: Congress and Social Change* (New York: Harcourt Brace Jovanovich, 1975), 325.

55 Quoted anonymously in *A Second Report of the Renewing Congress Project* (Washington, D.C.: American Enterprise Institute and Brookings Institution, 1993), 7.

56 See Daniel Callahan and Bruce Jennings, "Ethics of Legislative Life," *Ethics: Easier Said Than Done*, Spring-Summer 1988, 64–71.

57 For the most comprehensive recent effort, see Dennis F. Thompson, *Ethics in Congress: From Individual to Institutional Corruption* (Washington, D.C.: Brookings Institution, 1995).

58 See John D. Saxon, "The Scope of Legislative Ethics," in *Representation and Responsibility: Exploring Legislative Ethics*, ed. Bruce Jennings and Daniel Callahan (New York: Plenum, 1985), Chapter 10.

59 Lawrence C. Dodd, "Congress and the Politics of Renewal: Redressing the Crisis of Legitimation," in *Congress Reconsidered*, ed. Dodd and Oppenheimer, 418–419.

CHAPTER 12

1 James MacGregor Burns, *Leadership* (New York: Harper & Row, 1978), 397; anonymously quoted in William J. Keefe et al., *American Democracy*, 3rd ed. (New York: Harper & Row, 1990), 449.

2 For a fascinating account on which this case study is based, see Richard E. Cohen, *Changing Course in Washington: Clinton and the New Congress* (New York: Macmillan, 1994).

3 Abraham Lincoln, Message to Congress, December 1, 1862, reprinted in *Documents of American History*, ed. Henry Steele Commager and Milton Cantor, 10th ed. (Englewood Cliffs, N.J.: Prentice Hall, 1988), 1:405.

4 For a more comprehensive account of this transformation, see Roderick A. Bell and David V. Edwards, *American Government: The Facts Reorganized* (Morristown, N.J.: General Learning Press, 1974), esp. Chapters 5, 6.

5 This argument is made by Jeffrey Tulis, "The Two Constitutional Presidencies," in *The Presidency and the Political System*, 3rd ed., Michael Nelson (Washington, D.C. Congressional Quarterly Press, 1990), Chapter 3.

6 See David M. Barrett, *Uncertain Warriors: Lyndon Johnson and His Vietnam Advisers* (Lawrence: University Press of Kansas, 1993).

7 Lyndon Johnson, quoted in Robert K. Murray and Tim H. Blessing, *Greatness in the White House: Rating the Presidents*, 2nd ed. (University Park: Pennsylvania State University Press, 1994), 36.

8 This is the formulation of Bruce Buchanan, *The Citizen's Presidency* (Washington, D.C.: Congressional Quarterly Press, 1987), Chapter 6.

9 Murray and Blessing, *Greatness in the White House*, Chapter 4.

10 Jerald F. terHorst, *Gerald Ford and the Future of the Presidency* (New York: Third Press, 1974), 212.

11 See Bruce Buchanan, *The Presidential Experience* (Englewood Cliffs, N.J.: Prentice-Hall, 1978).

12 Woodrow Wilson, quoted in Forrest McDonald, *The American Presidency: An Intellectual History* (Lawrence: University Press of Kansas, 1994), 471.

13 See Robert H. Ferrell, *Ill-Advised: Presidential Health and Public Trust* (Columbia: University of Missouri Press, 1992); Jerrold M. Post, M.D., and Robert S. Robins, *When Illness Strikes the Leader: The Dilemma of the Captive King* (New Haven, Conn.: Yale University Press, 1993).

14 See Paul J. Quirk, "Presidential Competence," in Nelson, *Presidency and the Political System*, Chapter 7; Marcia Whicker and Raymond Moore, *When Presidents Are Great* (Englewood Cliffs, N.J.: Prentice-Hall, 1988), for interesting examples of recent efforts.

15 Craig A. Rimmerman, *Presidency by Plebiscite: The Reagan-Bush Era in Institutional Perspective* (Boulder, Colo.: Westview, 1993).

16 Roderick P. Hart, *The Sound of Leadership: Presidential Communication in the Modern Age* (Chicago: University of Chicago Press, 1987), 212.

17 This remark, made to ABC's David Brinkley, is quoted in Lou Cannon, *President Reagan: The Role of a Lifetime* (New York: Simon & Schuster, 1991), 38. For a somewhat differing view, see Michael Rogin, *Ronald Reagan: The Movie and Other Episodes in Political Demonology* (Berkeley: University of California Press, 1987).

18 Harry Truman, quoted in Richard Neustadt, *Presidential Power*, 2nd ed. (New York: Wiley, 1976), 77.

19 Harry S. Truman, *Public Papers of the President, 1948* (Washington, D.C.: U.S. Government Printing Office, 1949), 247.

20 Neustadt, *Presidential Power*, 114.

21 Barbara Kellerman, *The Political Presidency: Practice of Leadership from Kennedy through Reagan* (New York: Oxford University Press, 1984), 256.

22 See Lester G. Seligman, "Electoral Governing Coalitions in the Presidency," *Congress and the Presidency*, 10, no. 2 (Autumn 1983): 125–146.

23 Franklin D. Roosevelt, quoted in Burns, *Leadership*, xi. For additional insights into presidential leadership, see p. 4.

24 John F. Kennedy, Inaugural Address, January 20, 1961, in Commager and Cautor, *Documents of American History*, 2:656.

25 Samuel Kernell, *Going Public: New Strategies of Presidential Leadership* (Washington, D.C.: Congressional Quarterly Press, 1986).

26 Quoted in C. Eugene Steverle, *The Tax Decade: How Taxes Came to Dominate the Public Agenda* (Washington, D.C.: Urban Institute Press, 1992), 123.

27 Among the leading studies are Kellerman, *Political Presidency*; Bert A. Rockman, *The Leadership Question: The Presidency and the American System* (New York: Praeger, 1984).

28 See, among many others, Arthur M. Schlesinger, Jr., *The Imperial Presidency* (Boston: Houghton Mifflin, 1973).

29 On the executive order, see Phillip J. Cooper, "By Order of the President: Administration by Executive Order and Proclamation," *Administration and Society* 18 (August 1986): 233–262. On Reagan and the CIA, see Bob Woodward, *Veil: The Secret Wars of the CIA, 1981–1987* (New York: Simon & Schuster, 1987).

30 *Missouri v. Holland*, 252 U.S. 416 (1920).

31 *United States v. Curtiss-Wright Export Corporation*, 299 U.S. 304 (1936).

32 *Ex parte Merryman*, 17 Federal Cases, 144 (1861); *Hirabayashi v. United States*, 320 U.S. 81 (1943); *Korematsu v. United States*, 323 U.S. 214 (1944).

33 In *Youngstown Sheet and Tube Co. v. Sawyer*, 343 U.S. 579 (1952), more commonly known as the Steel Seizure Case, the Court held that the president lacked the power to seize private property under the Constitution.

34 Daniel P. Franklin, *Extraordinary Measures: The Exercise of Prerogative Powers in the United States* (Pittsburgh: University of Pittsburgh Press, 1991).

35 Larry O'Brien, quoted in David Broder, "The Teachings of Larry O'Brien," *Washington Post,* November 24, 1976. See also Larry O'Brien, *No Final Victories* (Garden City, N.Y.: Doubleday, 1974).

36 Lyndon Johnson, quoted in Harry McPherson, *A Political Education* (Boston: Little, Brown, 1972), 268.

37 See James P. Pfiffner, *The Strategic Presidency: Hitting the Ground Running* (Homewood, Ill.: Dorsey, 1988), for a detailed study of presidential transitions.

38 Walter Mondale, quoted in Paul Light, *The President's Agenda* (Baltimore: Johns Hopkins University Press, 1983), 13; see also 36–38 and Chapters 1, 9, where the cycles described in this section are explained.

39 Colin Campbell, *Managing the Presidency: Carter, Reagan, and the Search for Executive Harmony* (Pittsburgh: University of Pittsburgh Press, 1986).

40 See James W. Riddlesperger and James D. King, "Presidential Appointments to the Cabinet, Executive Office and White House Staff," *Presidential Studies Quarterly* 16, no. 4 (1986): 696–697.

41 See Lewis H. Gould, ed., *American First Ladies: Their Lives and Their Legacy* (New York: Garland, 1996).

42 For an interesting account of the evolution of vice presidential responsibilities focusing on Rockefeller and Mondale, see Paul C. Light, *Vice-Presidential Power: Advice and Influence in the White House* (Baltimore: Johns Hopkins University Press, 1984).

43 Richard Nixon, quoted in *New York Times,* November 28, 1972.

44 Stephen Hess, *Organizing the Presidency* (Washington, D.C.: Brookings Institution, 1976), 8.

45 Nelson Polsby, "Some Landmarks in Modern Presidential-Congressional Relations," in *Both Ends of the Avenue: The Presidency, the Executive Branch, and Congress in the 1980s,* ed. Anthony King (Washington, D.C.: American Enterprise Institute, 1983), 20.

46 For a candid description of some policy conflicts, see Alexander Haig, *Caveat: Realism, Reagan, and Foreign Policy* (New York: Macmillan, 1984).

47 See, for example, John Podhoretz, *Hell of a Ride* (New York: Simon & Schuster, 1994); Charles Kolb, *White House Daze: The Unmaking of Domestic Policy in the Bush Years* (New York: Free Press, 1994).

48 See Colin Campbell, "Management in a Sandbox: Why the Clinton White House Failed to Cope with Gridlock," in *The Clinton Presidency,* ed. Colin Campbell and Bert A. Rockman (Chatham, N.J.: Chatham House, 1995), Chapter 2.

49 For his own account, see Donald Regan, *For the Record* (San Diego: Harcourt Brace Jovanovich, 1988).

50 James Pfiffner, *The Modern Presidency* (New York: St. Martin's Press, 1994), 81.

51 For the transcript of a conference that brought together eight former presidential chiefs of staff to talk about their experiences in the job, see Samuel Kernell and Samuel L. Popkin, eds., *Chief of Staff: Twenty-Five Years of Managing the Presidency* (Berkeley: University of California Press, 1986).

52 Gerald Ford, informal talk at the Hinckley Institute of Politics, University of Utah, February 1982, reported in James M. Burns et al., *Government by the People,* 15th ed. (Englewood Cliffs, N.J.: Prentice Hall, 1993), 473–474.

53 See Michael L. Mezey, *Congress, the President, and Public Policy* (Boulder, Colo.: Westview, 1989), 94–96; Kenneth Collier, *Between the Branches: The White House Office of Legislative Affairs* (Pittsburgh: University of Pittsburgh Press, 1997).

54 For a fascinating account of how Johnson used incentives in running and dealing with Congress, see Robert Parker, *Capitol Hill in Black and White* (New York: Dodd, Mead, 1986).

55 Richard P. Nathan, *The Plot That Failed: Nixon and the Administrative Presidency* (New York: Wiley, 1975).

56 Michael Duffy and Dan Goodgame, *Marching in Place: The Status Quo Presidency of George Bush* (New York: Simon & Schuster, 1992), 11–12.

57 For the story, see Bruce W. Jentleson, *With Friends Like These: Reagan, Bush, and Saddam, 1982–1990* (New York: Norton, 1995).

58 Charles Tiefer, *The Semi-Sovereign Presidency: The Bush Administration's Strategy for Governing Without Congress* (Boulder, Colo.: Westview Press, 1994). Tiefer was acting general counsel of the House of Representatives when he wrote the book.

59 Bill Clinton, quoted in Allison Mitchell, "Despite His Reversals, Clinton Stays Centered," *New York Times,* July 28, 1996.

60 *Marbury v. Madison,* 1 Cranch 137 (1803).

61 *Ex Parte Milligan,* 4 Wall. 2, 121 (1866).

62 See Norman C. Thomas, Joseph A. Pika, and Richard A. Watson, *The Politics of the Presidency,* 3rd ed. revised (Washington, D.C.: Congressional Quarterly Press, 1994), Chapter 7.

63 *New York Times v. United States,* 403 U.S. 713 (1971); *United States v. United States District Court for the Eastern District of Michigan,* 407 U.S. 297 (1972); *United States v. Nixon,* 403 U.S. 683 (1974); *Train v. City of New York,* 420 U.S. 35 (1975); *Nixon v. Administrator, General Services Administration,* 443 U.S. 425 (1977).

64 *Morrison v. Olson,* 108 S. Ct. 2597 (1988).

65 See Alexander George, *Presidential Decisionmaking in Foreign Policy: The Effective Use of Information and Advice* (Boulder, Colo.: Westview Press, 1980); Karen M. Hult, "Advising the President," in *Researching the Presidency,* ed. George C. Edwards III et al. (Pittsburgh: University of Pittsburgh Press, 1993), Chapter 3.

66 See Steven A. Shull, ed., *The Two Presidencies* (Chicago: Nelson-Hall, 1991), for various views on this proposal.

67 See James L. Sundquist, "Needed: A Workable Check on the Presidency," *Brookings Bulletin* 10, no. 4 (Spring 1974); Charles Hardin, *Presidential Power and Accountability* (Chicago: University of Chicago Press, 1974); Lloyd Cutler, "To Form a Government: On the Defects of Separation of Powers," *Foreign Affairs* 49 (Fall 1980): 126–143.

68 Thomas E. Cronin, *The State of the Presidency* (Boston: Little, Brown, 1975), 301.

69 Woodrow Wilson, quoted in Arthur M. Schlesinger, Jr., "Against a One-Term, Six-Year President," *New York Times,* January 10, 1986.

70 For a detailed analysis of pros and cons on many of the reforms discussed here, see James L. Sundquist, *Constitutional Reform and Effective Government,* rev. ed. (Washington, D.C.: Brookings Institution, 1992).

CHAPTER 13

1 Harry Truman made this remark to journalist David Brinkley, who quoted it on the public television program "Thirty Minutes with . . .," July 13, 1971; Charles T. Goodsell, *The Case for Bureaucracy*, 2nd ed. (Chatham, N.J.: Chatham House, 1985), 14.

2 John Merline, "Clearing the Air on Pollution," *Investor's Business Daily*, November 14, 1994.

3 The exact figure is not public knowledge, because the government keeps secret the employment figures for its secret intelligence agencies, including the Central Intelligence Agency and the National Security Agency. Current data can be found in the *Statistical Abstract of the United States*, published each year by the U.S. Government Printing Office in Washington.

4 *Budget of the United States, Fiscal Year 1998: Analytical Perspectives* (Washington, D.C.: U.S. Government Printing Office, 1997), 207.

5 *The Federalist Papers* are available in many editions.

6 For a comprehensive history of early federal government administration, see Leonard D. White's four-volume study: *The Federalists* (New York: Macmillan, 1948); *The Jeffersonians* (New York: Macmillan, 1951); *The Jacksonians* (New York: Macmillan, 1954); and *The Republican Era* (New York: Macmillan, 1958).

7 Matthew A. Crenson, *The Federal Machine: Beginnings of a Bureaucracy in Jacksonian America* (Baltimore: Johns Hopkins University Press, 1975).

8 See Michael Nelson, "A Short, Ironic History of American National Bureaucracy," *Journal of Politics* 44 (August 1982): 747–778.

9 *Elrod v. Burns*, 427 U.S. 347 (1976).

10 U.S. Bureau of the Census, *Statistical Abstract of the United States, 1995* (Washington, D.C.: U.S. Government Printing Office, 1995).

11 Paul Light, *Thickening Government: Federal Hierarchy and the Diffusion of Accountability* (Washington, D.C.: Brookings Institution, 1995).

12 Ibid., 9.

13 See Myron P. Glazer and Penina M. Glazer, *The Whistleblowers: Exposing Corruption in Government and Industry* (New York: Basic Books, 1989). The appendix to this collection of case studies lists organizations that assist whistleblowers. See also *The Whistleblower's Survival Guide* (Washington, D.C.: Government Accountability Project, 1997).

14 See Peri E. Arnold, *Making the Managerial Presidency: Comprehensive Reorganization Planning, 1905–1980* (Princeton, N.J.: Princeton University Press, 1986).

15 William E. Pemberton, *Bureaucratic Politics: Executive Reorganization During the Truman Administration* (Columbia: University of Missouri Press, 1979), 176.

16 The premier analyst of bureaucracy was the German sociologist Max Weber. For a helpful summary of his analysis, see Reinhold Bendix, *Max Weber: An Intellectual Portrait* (Garden City, N.Y.: Doubleday Anchor, 1962).

17 The term is used by Karl W. Deutsch in *The Nerves of Government: Models of Political Communication and Control* (New York: Free Press, 1966), 75.

18 For a survey of implementation activities, see Lester Salamon, ed., *Beyond Privatization: The Tools of Government Action* (Washington, D.C.: Urban Institute Press, 1989).

19 This analytical approach was first developed in the study of foreign policy and then extended to domestic policy. See Morton Halperin, *Bureaucratic Politics and Foreign Policy* (Washington, D.C.: Brookings Institution, 1974).

20. See David C. Kozak, "The Bureaucratic Politics Approach: The Evolution of the Paradigm," in *Bureaucratic Politics and National Security*, ed. David Kozak and James M. Keagle (Boulder, Colo.: Lynne Rienner, 1988), Chapter 1.

21. See Anthony Downs, *Inside Bureaucracy* (Boston: Little, Brown, 1967), 88, for distinctions among climbers, conservers, zealots, advocates, and statesmen; Hugh Heclo, *A Government of Strangers* (Washington, D.C.: Brookings Institution, 1977), 148–153, for distinctions among program bureaucrats, staff bureaucrats, reformers, and institutionalists; and James Q. Wilson, "The Politics of Regulation," in *The Politics of Regulation*, ed. James Q. Wilson (New York: Basic Books, 1980), 374–382, for distinctions among careerists, politicians, and professionals.

22 See James Q. Wilson, *Bureaucracy: What Government Agencies Do and Why They Do It* (New York: Basic Books, 1989), Chapter 4.

23 In recent years, as Social Security came under great financial strain and faced unprecedented political struggles, morale and performance suffered. See Martha Derthick, *Agency Under Stress* (Washington, D.C.: Brookings Institution, 1990).

24 Roger Pear, "U.S. Laws Delayed by Complex Rules and Partisanship," *New York Times*, March 31, 1991.

25 Richard Bonnin, "The Knowledge Market," *On Campus*, January 21, 1991, 1, 5. For an interesting account, see Richard Saul Wurman, *Information Anxiety* (New York: Doubleday, 1989).

26 Charles R. McClure et al., eds., *United States Government Information Policies: Views and Perspectives* (Norwood, N.J.: Ablex, 1989); Susan M. Ryan, *Downloading Democracy: Government Information in an Electronic Age* (Creskill, N.J.: Hampton Press, 1996), Chapter 1.

27 See David Sadofsky, *Knowledge as Power: Political and Legal Control of Information* (New York: Praeger, 1990), Chapter 2.

28 See Harold Wilensky, *Organizational Intelligence* (New York: Basic Books, 1967), for a classic analysis of such problems.

29 Sadofsky, *Knowledge as Power*, 23.

30 David L. Altheide and John M. Johnson, *Bureaucratic Propaganda* (Boston: Allyn & Bacon, 1980).

31 Angus A. MacIntyre, "The Multiple Sources of Statutory Ambiguity: Tracing the Legislative Origins to Administrative Discretion," in *Administrative Discretion and Public Policy Implementation*, ed. Douglas H. Shumavon et al. (New York: Praeger, 1986), Chapter 4.

32. Gary C. Bryner, *Bureaucratic Discretion: Law and Policy in Federal Regulatory Agencies* (New York: Pergamon Press, 1987), 1–2.

33. For interesting accounts, see Bob Woodward, *Veil* (New York: Simon & Schuster, 1987); Joseph Persico, *Casey* (New York: Viking, 1990).

34. See Christopher F. Edley, Jr., *Administrative Law: Rethinking Judicial Control of Bureaucracy* (New Haven, Conn.: Yale University Press, 1990).

35. Colin Campbell, S. J., *Managing the Presidency: Carter, Reagan, and the Search for Executive Harmony* (Pittsburgh: University of Pittsburgh Press, 1986), 3–4.

36. Richard W. Waterman, *Presidential Influence and the Administrative State* (Knoxville: University of Tennessee Press, 1989), 193.

37. Dennis D. Riley, *Controlling the Federal Bureaucracy* (Philadelphia: Temple University Press, 1987), Chapter 2.

38. Quoted in Richard Neustadt, *Presidential Power*, 2nd ed. (New York: Wiley, 1976), 77.

39. Quoted in Jonathan Daniels, *Frontiers on the Potomac* (New York: Macmillan, 1946), 31–32.

40. Leslie H. Gelb and Morton H. Halperin, "The Bureaucrat's Ten Commandments," *Harper's*, June 1972, 28–29.

41. For a controversial account, see Kitty Kelley, *Nancy Reagan: The Unauthorized Biography* (New York: Simon & Schuster, 1991). Her own account is presented in *My Turn: The Memoirs of Nancy Reagan* (New York: Random House, 1989). A more balanced account is Lou Cannon, *President Reagan: The Role of a Lifetime* (New York: Simon & Schuster, 1991).

42. Robert Reich, *Locked in the Cabinet* (New York: Knopf, 1997), quoted in "Reich's Kiss-and-Shrug," *Time*, April 7, 1997, 24.

43. Terry M. Moe, "The Politics of Bureaucratic Structure," in *Can the Government Govern?* ed. John E. Chubb and Paul E. Peterson (Washington, D.C.: Brookings Institution, 1989), 276.

44. Wilson, *Bureaucracy*, 275.

45. For a comparison of the perspectives of bureaucrats and judges, see ibid., 290–291.

46. The term was coined by Hugh Heclo in "Issue Networks and the Executive Establishment," in *The New American Political System*, ed. Anthony King (Washington, D.C.: American Enterprise Institute, 1978).

47. For a recent comparison, see Jeffrey M. Berry, "Subgovernments, Issue Networks, and Political Conflict," in *Remaking American Politics*, ed. Richard A. Harris and Sidney M. Milkis (Boulder, Colo.: Westview Press, 1984), 239-260.

48. Riley, *Controlling the Federal Bureaucracy*, 123.

49. See Daniel Gross, "Byting the Hand That Feeds Them," *Washington Monthly*, November 1991, 37–41.

50. For an argument that bureaucracy can and should be made more representative, see Samuel Krislov and David H. Rosenbloom, *Representative Bureaucracy and the American Political System* (New York: Praeger, 1981).

51. Douglas F. Morgan and John A. Rohr, "Traditional Responses to American Administrative Discretion," in *Administrative Discretion and Public Policy Implementation*, ed. S. H. Shumavon et al. (New York: Praeger, 1986), Chapter 13.

52. See John A. Rohr, *Ethics for Bureaucrats: An Essay on Law and Values*, 2nd ed. (New York: Marcel Dekker, 1989).

53. For a comprehensive argument, see John P. Burke, *Bureaucratic Responsibility* (Baltimore: Johns Hopkins University Press, 1986).

54. Donald P. Warwick, "The Ethics of Administrative Discretion," in *Public Duties: The Moral Obligations of Government Officials*, ed. Joel L. Fleishman et al. (Cambridge, Mass.: Harvard University Press, 1981), Chapter 4.

55. David Osborne and Ted Gaebler, *Reinventing Government: How the Entrepreneurial Spirit Is Transforming the Public Sector* (Reading, Mass.: Addison-Wesley, 1992).

56. Al Gore, "The New Job of the Federal Executive," *Public Administration Review* 54 (July/August 1994): 317–331.

57. Jack H. Knott and Gary J. Miller, *Reforming Bureaucracy: The Politics of Institutional Choice* (Englewood Cliffs, N.J.: Prentice Hall, 1987).

58. See James Q. Wilson, "Reinventing Public Administration," *PS: Political Science & Politics* (December 1994): 667–673.

59. Bernard Rosen, *Holding Government Bureaucracies Accountable*, 2nd ed. (New York: Praeger, 1989), 193–194.

60. See Hubert G. Locke, "Ethics in American Government: A Look Backward," *Annals of the American Academy of Political and Social Science*, 537 (January 1995): 14–24.

61. Data for 1993 from U.S. Office of Personnel Management, Central Personnel Data File.

62. Krislov and Rosenbloom, *Representative Bureaucracy and the American Political System*, 196.

63. National Commission on the Public Service, *Leadership for America: Rebuilding the Public Service* (Lexington, Mass.: Lexington Books, 1989), 4–8.

64. Mary G. Kweit and Robert W. Kweit, *Implementing Citizen Participation in a Bureaucratic Society* (New York: Praeger, 1981), 116.

65. See Salamon, *Beyond Privatization*.

66. Donald F. Kettl, *Reinventing Government? Appraising the National Performance Review* (Washington, D.C.: Brookings Institution, 1994), 31.

67. Wilson, *Bureaucracy*, 375.

CHAPTER 14

1. Arthur S. Miller, "The Supreme Court of the United States: A Bibliographical Essay," in *Sources for American Studies*, ed. J. B. Kellogg et al. (Westport, Conn.: Greenwood Press, 1983), 349; Robert H. Bork, *The Tempting of America: The Political Seduction of the Law* (New York: Touchstone, 1990), 177.

2. *San Antonio Independent School District v. Rodriguez*, 411 U.S. 1 (1973).

3. Ibid. Emphasis added.

4. *Edgewood Independent School District v. William Kirby et al.*, no. C-8353, Supreme Court of Texas, October 2, 1989. For a summary of all four *Edgewood* cases, see Janice C. May, *The Texas State Constitution: A Reference Guide* (Westport, Conn.: Greenwood Press, 1996), 246–247.

5. Wolf Heydebrand and Carroll Seron, *Rationalizing Justice: The Political Economy of Federal District Courts* (Albany: State University of New York Press, 1990), 63.

6. These steps are adapted from Edward H. Levi, *An Introduction to Legal Reasoning* (Chicago: University of Chicago Press, 1961), 2.

7. Ibid., 3.

8. Cornelius M. Kerwin, *Rulemaking: How Government Agencies Write Law and Make Policy* (Washington, D.C.: Congressional Quarterly Press, 1994), 61.

9. Christopher F. Edley, Jr., *Administrative Law: Rethinking Judicial Control of Bureaucracy* (New Haven, Conn.: Yale University Press, 1990), 3.

10. Representative of this view is Erwin Chemerinsky, *Interpreting the Constitution* (New York: Praeger, 1987), 2. See also *Marbury v. Madison*, 1 Cranch 138 (1803).

11 *Chisholm v. Georgia,* 2 Dallas 419 (1793); *Dred Scott v. Sandford,* 19 Howard 393 (1857); *Pollock v. Farmers' Loan and Trust Co.,* 157 U.S. 429 (1895); *Oregon v. Mitchell,* 400 U.S. 112 (1970).

12 This estimate comes from Justice Byron White. See Richard L. Williams, "Justices Run 'Nine Little Law Firms,'" *Smithsonian,* January 1977, 90.

13 C. Herman Pritchett, quoted in Tracey E. George and Lee Epstein, "On the Nature of Supreme Court Decisionmaking," *American Political Science Review* 86, no. 2 (June 1992): 323.

14 Douglas Laycock, *Modern American Remedies: Cases and Materials* (Boston: Little, Brown, 1985), 1.

15 Mirjan R. Damaska, *The Faces of Justice and State Authority: A Comparative Approach to the Legal Process* (New Haven, Conn.: Yale University Press, 1986), 237.

16 The Supreme Court did so in *San Antonio Independent School District v. Rodriguez.*

17 Damaska, *Faces of Justice and State Authority,* 1.

18 Carey Goldberg, "Conflicts with Reality in Second Simpson Trial," *New York Times,* November 29, 1996, A12.

19 Ruth Bader Ginsburg, "Confirming Supreme Court Justices: Thoughts on the Second Opinion Rendered by the Senate," *University of Illinois Law Review* 101 (1988): nn. 80, 81.

20 See Lief H. Carter, *Contemporary Constitutional Lawmaking: The Supreme Court and the Art of Politics* (New York: Pergamon Press, 1985), Chapter 2.

21 Burke Shartel, *Our Legal System and How It Operates* (Buffalo, N.Y.: W. S. Hein, 1996), 320.

22 Charles Evans Hughes, speech at Elmira, New York, May 3, 1907.

23 John Marshall, majority opinion in *McCulloch v. Maryland,* 4 Wheaton 518 (1819), discussing the meaning of the necessary and proper clause in Article I, section 8 of the U.S. Constitution.

24 Quoted in Carter, *Contemporary Constitutional Lawmaking,* 161.

25 Quoted in Walter F. Murphy, *Elements of Judicial Strategy* (Chicago: University of Chicago Press, 1964), 13.

26 *Edgewood Independent School District v. William Kirby et al.*

27 Owen M. Fiss, "Objectivity and Interpretation," in *Interpreting Law and Literature,* ed. Sanford Levinson and Steven Mailloux (Evanston, Ill.: Northwestern University Press, 1988), 245.

28 Robert W. Bennett, "The Burger Court and the Poor," in *The Burger Court: The Counter-Revolution That Wasn't,* ed. Vincent Blasi (New Haven, Conn.: Yale University Press, 1983), 55.

29 *San Antonio Independent School District v. Rodriguez.*

30 See H. W. Perry, Jr., *Deciding to Decide: Agenda Setting in the United States Supreme Court* (Cambridge, Mass.: Harvard University Press, 1991), 298.

31 See Cornell W. Clayton, *The Politics of Justice: The Attorney General and the Making of Legal Policy* (Lawrence: University of Kansas Press, 1995), 6–7.

32 Charles Fried, *Order and Law: Arguing the Reagan Revolution—A Firsthand Account* (New York: Simon & Schuster, 1991), 49, 15, 57.

33 Timothy Egan, "Rebuking the U.S., Jury Acquits 2 in Marshall's Killing in Idaho Siege," *New York Times,* July 9, 1993, A1.

34 For critical accounts of J. Edgar Hoover's life, see Anthony Summers, *Official and Confidential: The Secret Life of J. Edgar Hoover* (New York: Putnam, 1993); Curt Gentry, *J. Edgar Hoover: The Man and the Secrets* (New York: Norton, 1991).

35 *Marbury v. Madison; Fletcher v. Peck,* 6 Cranch 87 (1810); *McCulloch v. Maryland.*

36 Historian and diplomat Lord James Bryce (1838–1922), quoted in Jean Edward Smith, *John Marshall: Definer of a Nation* (New York: Henry Holt, 1996), 281.

37 *Fletcher v. Peck; Dartmouth College v. Woodward,* 17 U.S. 518 (1819).

38 *United States v. E. C. Knight Co.,* 156 U.S. 1 (1895).

39 *Lochner v. New York,* 198 U.S. 45 (1905).

40 *Muller v. Oregon,* 208 U.S. 412 (1908).

41 *Adkins v. Children's Hospital,* 261 U.S. 525 (1923).

42 *Schechter v. United States,* 295 U.S. 495 (1935).

43 *West Coast Hotel Co. v. Parris,* 300 U.S. 379 (1937).

44 *Congressional Quarterly Weekly Report,* January 19, 1991, 173 table.

45 Data compiled by Stephan Kline, Alliance for Justice, Washington, D.C., July 1997.

46 Ginsburg, "Confirming Supreme Court Justices," 108.

47 Ibid., n. 57.

48 Mark Silverstein, *Judicious Choices: The New Politics of Supreme Court Nominations* (New York: Norton, 1994), 175–176.

49 Bork, *Tempting of America.*

50 Quoted in Tim O'Brien, "High Court TV," *New York Times,* January 6, 1997, A13.

51 Daniel J. O'Hern, "TV Would Erode Respect for the Supreme Court," *New York Times,* January 19, 1997, 16.

52 Fred M. Vinson, address before the American Bar Association, September 7, 1949, quoted in Perry, *Deciding to Decide,* 36.

53 Quoted in ibid., 53.

54 Ibid.

55 See Robert L. Stern and Eugene Gressman, *Supreme Court Practice* (Washington, D.C.: Bureau of National Affairs, 1978), 320–327.

56 Perry, *Deciding to Decide,* 39.

57 Stern and Gressman, *Supreme Court Practice,* 365.

58 Murphy, *Elements of Judicial Strategy,* 84.

59 Ibid., 53.

60 Bob Woodward and Scott Armstrong, *The Brethren* (New York: Simon & Schuster, 1979).

61 Perry, *Deciding to Decide,* 167.

62 Jeffrey Rosen, "Court Marshall," *New Republic,* June 21, 1993, 14–15.

63 Quoted in Philip J. Cooper, *Battles on the Bench: Conflict Inside the Supreme Court* (Lawrence: University Press of Kansas, 1995), 1.

64 John Brigham, *The Cult of the Court* (Philadelphia: Temple University Press, 1987), 198.

65 Murphy, *Elements of Judicial Strategy,* 204.

66 Robert McCloskey, quoted in ibid.

67 Kenneth Vines, "Southern State Supreme Courts," and Neal Romans, "Role of State Supreme Courts," cited in G. Alan Tarr and Mary Cornelia Aldis Porter, *State Supreme Courts in State and Nation* (New Haven, Conn.: Yale University Press, 1988), 13. This section draws on Chapter 1.

68 *Stanton v. Stanton*, 421 U.S. 7 (1975).

69 Tarr and Porter, *State Supreme Courts in State and Nation*, 14–15; *Mapp v. Ohio*, 367 U.S. 643 (1961).

70 Tarr and Porter, *State Supreme Courts in State and Nation*, 15.

71 *Escobedo v. Illinois*, 378 U.S. 478 (1964); *Miranda v. Arizona*, 384 U.S. 436 (1966).

72 Tarr and Porter, *State Supreme Courts in State and Nation*, 19.

73 *Worcester v. Georgia*, 31 U.S. 515 (1832).

74 *United States v. Nixon*, 418 U.S. 683 (1974).

75 This anecdote appears in Linda Matthews, "Supreme Court: World Inside the 'Marble Temple,'" *Los Angeles Times*, February 2, 1974, 1, cited in Brigham, *Cult of the Court*, 202.

76 For a more detailed look at the politics of compliance, see Charles A. Johnson and Bradley C. Canon, *Judicial Policies: Implementation and Impact* (Washington, D.C.: Congressional Quarterly Press, 1984).

77 See, for example, Stuart Scheingold, *The Politics of Rights: Lawyers, Public Policy and Political Change* (New Haven, Conn.: Yale University Press, 1974).

78 Linda Greenhouse, "How Congress Curtailed the Court's Jurisdiction," *New York Times*, October 27, 1996, E5.

79 Heydebrand and Seron, *Rationalizing Justice*, 53.

80 *Dombrowski v. Pfister*, 380 U.S. 749 (1965).

81 *Younger v. Harris*, 401 U.S. 37 (1971).

82 *Sierra Club v. Morton*, 405 U.S. 727, 755–756 (1972) (Blackmun, J., dissenting). See Mary Ann Glendon, *Rights Talk: The Impoverishment of Political Discourse* (New York: Free Press, 1991), 112–113.

83 Heydebrand and Seron, *Rationalizing Justice*, 33.

84 Ibid., 110.

85 See Judith Resnik, "Managerial Judges," *Harvard Law Review* 96, no. 2 (1982): 324–448.

86 Christopher E. Smith, *Courts and the Poor* (Chicago: Nelson-Hall, 1991), 128.

87 Michael Finger, "A Judge's Sentence May Be, Write One," *New York Times*, February 26, 1993.

88 Smith, *Courts and the Poor*, 35.

CHAPTER **15**

1 *Buckley v. Valeo*, 519 F. 2d 817 (D.C. Cir. 1975); *Buckley v. Valeo*, 424 U.S. 1 (1976). Both quoted in John Gilliom, *Surveillance, Privacy, and the Law: Employee Drug Testing and the Politics of Social Control* (Ann Arbor: University of Michigan Press, 1994), 61, 67.

2 *DeShaney v. Winnebago County Department of Social Services*, 489 U.S. (1989).

3 Ibid.

4 Mary Ann Glendon, *Rights Talk: The Impoverishment of Political Discourse* (New York: Free Press, 1991), 173.

5 See Robert H. Bork, *Slouching Towards Gomorrah: Modern Liberalism and American Decline* (New York: HarperCollins, 1996).

6 *Board of Education v. Barnette*, 319 U.S. 624, 638 (1943).

7 See John Locke, *The Second Treatise of Government* (1690; reprint, Indianapolis: Bobbs-Merrill, 1952), 50; William Blackstone, *Commentaries on the Laws of England* (1765).

8 *Barron v. Baltimore*, 1 Peters 243 (1833).

9 *Slaughter-House Cases*, 16 Wallace 36 (1873).

10 *Gitlow v. New York*, 268 U.S. 652 (1925).

11 *Palko v. Connecticut*, 302 U.S. 319 (1937).

12 *Mapp v. Ohio*, 307 U.S. 643 (1961).

13 *Miranda v. Arizona*, 384 U.S. 486 (1966).

14 *United States v. Harris*, 403 U.S. 924 (1971); *Nix v. Williams*, 104 U.S. 2501 (1984).

15 *United States v. Leon*, 468 U.S. 897 (1984); *New York v. Quarles*, 467 U.S. 649 (1984).

16 *Dred Scott v. Sandford*, 19 Howard 393 (1857).

17 See *Allgeyer v. Louisiana*, 65 U.S. 578 (1897).

18 *Everson v. Board of Education of Ewing Township*, 330 U.S. 1, 15 (1947).

19 *Engel v. Vitale*, 370 U.S. 421 (1962).

20 *Malnak v. Yogi*, 592 F. 2d 197 (3d Cir. 1979).

21 *Grove v. Mead School District*, 753 F. 2d 1528 (9th Cir. 1985).

22 *Everson v. Board of Education*.

23 *Tilton v. Richardson*, 403 U.S. 672, 686 (1971).

24 *Committee for Public Education and Religious Liberty v. Nyquist*, 413 U.S. 756 (1973).

25 *Lemon v. Kurtzman*, 403 U.S. 602 (1971).

26 James E. Leahy, *The First Amendment, 1791–1991* (Jefferson, N.C.: McFarland, 1991), 46–47.

27 *Kiryas Joel Village School District Board of Education v. Grumet*, 62 LW 4665 (1994). See also *Newsday*, November 26, 1994.

28 *Agostino v. Felton*, No. 96-552 (1997).

29 For an overview of the Supreme Court's approach to the establishment clause, see Wayne R. Swanson, *The Christ Child Goes to Court* (Philadelphia: Temple University Press, 1990), Chapter 6.

30 Attorney General William French Smith, quoted from an *amicus curiae* brief in *Lynch v. Donnelly*, 104 S. Ct. 1355 (1984).

31 *County of Allegheny v. American Civil Liberties Union Greater Pittsburgh Chapter*, 109 S. Ct. 3086 (1989).

32 *Cantwell v. Connecticut*, 310 U.S. 296 (1940); *Reynolds v. United States*, 98 U.S. 145 (1879).

33 *Braunfeld v. Brown*, 366 U.S. 599 (1961). The Court majority cited *Reynolds v. United States*. Dissenting were William J. Brennan, Potter Stewart, and William O. Douglas.

34 *Sherbert v. Verner*, 374 U.S. 398 (1963).

35 *Church of Lukumi Babalu Aye v. Hialeah*, 508 U.S. 520 (1993). See also Bob Dart, "Court Hears Case of Animal Sacrifice at Florida Church," *Austin American-Statesman*, November 5, 1992, A21.

36 *Employment Division v. Smith*, 110 S. Ct. 1595 (1990).

37 *City of Boerne v. Flores,* 65 U.S.L.W. 4612 (June 25, 1997), No. 95-2074.

38 Quoted in Geoffrey R. Stone et al., eds., *Constitutional Law* (Boston: Little, Brown, 1986), 1370–1371.

39 *United States v. Seeger* 380 U.S. 163 (1965).

40 *Gillette v. United States,* 401 U.S. 437 (1971).

41 *Schenck v. United States,* 249 U.S. 47 (1919).

42 *Chaplinsky v. New Hampshire,* 315 U.S. 568 (1942).

43 *Tinker v. Des Moines School District,* 393 U.S. 503 (1969).

44 *Village of Skokie v. National Socialist Party,* 431 U.S. 43 (1977).

45 *Texas v. Johnson,* 491 U.S. 397 (1989).

46 *United States v. Eichman,* 496 U.S. 310 (1990).

47 Ira Glasser, "Bush Lowers the Flag," *New York Times,* June 28, 1989.

48 See John M. Broder, "Broadcast Industry Defends TV Rating System," *New York Times,* February 2, 1997, A10.

49 *Roth v. United States,* 354 U.S. 476 (1957).

50 *Miller v. California,* 413 U.S. 15, 24 (1973), quoting ibid.

51 *Stanley v. Georgia,* 394 U.S. 557 (1969).

52 *Reno v. American Civil Liberties Union,* 65 U.S.L.W. 4715 (June 26, 1997), No. 96-511.

53 *New York Times v. Sullivan,* 376 U.S. 254 (1964).

54 *R.A.V. v. St. Paul,* 505 U.S. 377 (1992).

55 *Wisconsin v. Mitchell,* 1135 S. Ct. 2194, 2196 (1993).

56 *Harris v. Forklift Systems, Inc.,* 114 S. Ct. 367 (1993).

57 *Bigelow v. Virginia,* 421 U.S. 809 (1975); *Virginia Pharmacy Board v. Virginia Consumer Council,* 425 U.S. 748 (1976); *Bates v. State Bar of Arizona,* 433 U.S. 350 (1977).

58 *New York Times Company v. United States,* 403 U.S. 713 (1971).

59 *Cohen v. Cowles Media Co.,* 111 S. Ct. 630 (1991).

60 *Cox Broadcasting Corp. v. Cohn,* 420 U.S. 469 (1975).

61 *Nebraska Press Assn. v. Stuart,* 427 U.S. (1976).

62 *Furman v. Georgia,* 408 U.S. 238 (1972).

63 *Gregg v. Georgia,* 428 U.S. 153 (1976).

64 David R. Dow, "Those on Death Row Have Few Options," *New York Times,* January 9, 1997, A14.

65 "Bar Association Leaders Urge Moratorium on Death Penalty," *New York Times,* February 4, 1997, A9; "A Lawyerly Cry of Conscience," *New York Times,* February 4, 1997, A16.

66 See Brennan's dissent in *Glass v. Louisiana,* 471 U.S. 1080 (1985).

67 *Lindh v. Murphy,* 65 U.S.L.W. 4557 (June 23, 1997), No. 96-6298.

68 This figure comes from George Kendall, senior attorney for the NAACP Legal Defense Fund. *FCLN Washington News Letter,* June 1996, 7.

69 Melvin I. Urofsky, *A March of Liberty: A Constitutional History of the United States* (New York: Knopf, 1988), 936.

70 *Richardson v. Ramirez,* 418 U.S. 24, 94 (1974).

71 Quoted in David Rudovsky et al., *The Rights of Prisoners: The Basic ACLU Guide to Prisoners' Rights,* 4th ed. (Carbondale: Southern Illinois University Press, 1988), 87.

72 Alan D. Miller, "Inmates' Loss Is No One's Gain; People Who Meet Eligibility Will Still Get Pell Grants," *Columbus Dispatch,* August 28, 1994.

73 Judge Stephen Reinhardt, U.S. Court of Appeals for the Ninth Circuit, quoted in Lonny Shavelson, "What the Dying Really Need," *New York Times,* March 8, 1996, A19.

74 *Washington v. Glucksberg,* No. 96-110 (1997); *Vacco v. Quill,* 65 U.S.L.W. 4669 (June 26, 1997), No. 95-1858.

75 See *Home Building & Loan Assn. v. Blaisdell,* 290 U.S. 398 (1934); *Penn Central Transportation Co. v. New York City,* 438 U.S. 104 (1978); *Energy Reserves Group, Inc. v. Kansas Power & Light Co.,* 459 U.S. 400 (1983); *Hawaii Housing Authority v. Midkiff,* 407 U.S. 229 (1984).

76 Michael Kammen, *Spheres of Liberty: Changing Perceptions of Liberty in American Culture* (Ithaca, N.Y.: Cornell University Press, 1986), 103.

77 *Home Building & Loan Assn. v. Blaisdell.*

78 *Allgeyer v. Louisiana; Coppage v. Kansas,* 236 U.S. 1 (1915).

79 *Lochner v. New York,* 198 U.S. 45 (1905); *Coppage v. Kansas; Adkins v. Children's Hospital,* 261 U.S. 525 (1923).

80 *Home Building & Loan Assn. v. Blaisdell.*

81 *Hawaii Housing Authority v. Midkiff.*

82 *Metromedia, Inc. v. City of San Diego,* 453 U.S. 490 (1981).

83 *Lucas v. South Carolina Coastal Council,* 112 S. Ct. 2893. For a discussion of the case, see Jane Lehman, "Property Rights Activists Gain in S.C. Case," *Washington Post,* July 17, 1993; Douglas N. Silverstein, "*Lucas v. South Carolina Coastal Council:* Where Has the Supreme Court Taken Us Now?" *Whittier Law Review* 15 (1994): 825.

84 *Olmstead v. United States,* 277 U.S. 438 (1928).

85 *Griswold v. Connecticut,* 381 U.S. 479 (1965).

86 *Roe v. Wade,* 410 U.S. 113 (1973); *Doe v. Bolton,* 410 U.S. 179 (1973).

87 *Planned Parenthood of Missouri v. Danforth,* 428 U.S. 52 (1976).

88 The Hyde Amendment was upheld in *Harris v. McRae,* 448 U.S. 27 (1980).

89 *Webster v. Reproductive Health Services,* 492 U.S. 490 (1989).

90 *Planned Parenthood of Southeastern Pennsylvania v. Casey,* 505 U.S. (1992).

91 K. C. Swanson, "First Shots of Another Grim Battle," *National Journal,* February 15, 1997, 326.

92 *Bowers v. Hardwick* 478 U.S. 186 (1986).

93 *Olmstead v. United States.*

94 *Nardone v. United States,* 302 U.S. 379 (1937).

95 *Katz v. United States,* 389 U.S. 347 (1967).

96 *Tyler v. Berodt,* 493 U.S. 1022 (1990).

97 *United States v. United States District Court for the Eastern District of Michigan,* 407 U.S. 297 (1972).

98 Neil Munro, "How Private Is Your Data?" *Washington Technology,* February 9, 1995, 12, 16.

99 Thomas Weber, "Browsers Beware: The Web Is Watching," *Wall Street Journal,* June 27, 1996.

100 Gilliom, *Surveillance, Privacy, and the Law.*

101 Jeremy Rifkin, "Genetic ID Program Threatens Privacy," *Newsday,* January 8, 1993.

102 John Markoff, "New Communication System Stirs Talk of Privacy vs. Eavesdropping," *New York Times,* April 16, 1993, A1.

CHAPTER 16

1 Kenneth L. Karst, *Belonging to America: Equal Citizenship and the Constitution* (New Haven, Conn.: Yale University Press, 1989), 196; Michael W. McCann, *Rights at Work: Pay Equity and the Politics of Legal Mobilization* (Chicago: University of Chicago Press, 1994), 308, summarizing Antonio Gramsci.

2 *Plyler v. Doe,* 457 U.S. 202 (1982).

3 Ibid. See also *San Antonio Independent School District v. Rodriguez,* 411 U.S. 1 (1973).

4 Frederick Douglass, West India Emancipation Speech, August 1857, quoted in Stokely Carmichael and Charles V. Hamilton, *Black Power: The Politics of Liberation in America* (New York: Vintage, 1967), x.

5 Denise M. Trauth and John L. Huffman, "Heightened Judicial Scrutiny: A Test for the First Amendment Rights of Children," in *Censorship, Secrecy, Access, and Obscenity,* ed. Theodore R. Kupferman (Westport, Conn.: Meckler, 1990), 81.

6 *United States v. Carolene Products Co.,* 304 U.S. 144 (1938).

7 *Loving v. Virginia,* 388 U.S. 1, 9 (1967).

8 *Graham v. Richardson,* 403 U.S. 365 (1971).

9 *Levy v. Louisiana,* 391 U.S. 68 (1968).

10 *Reed v. Reed,* 404 U.S. 71 (1971).

11 Mark V. Tushnet, *Making Civil Rights Law: Thurgood Marshall and the Supreme Court, 1936–1961* (New York: Oxford University Press, 1994), 115.

12 *Plessy v. Ferguson,* 163 U.S. 537 (1896); *Brown v. Board of Education of Topeka,* 347 U.S. 483 (1954).

13 See Tushnet, *Making Civil Rights Law,* 194.

14 *Brown v. Board of Education of Topeka,* 349 U.S. 294 (1955).

15 Ibid.

16 *Alexander v. Holmes County Board of Education,* 396 U.S. 19 (1969).

17 *Morgan v. Commonwealth of Virginia,* 328 U.S. 373 (1946). Segregation on interstate trains was banned in *Henderson v. United States,* 339 U.S. 816 (1950).

18 Gary Nash et al., *The American People: Creating a Nation and a Society,* 2nd ed. (New York: Harper & Row, 1990), 999.

19 Gary T. Marx, *Protest and Prejudice: A Study of Belief in the Black Community* (New York: Harper & Row, 1967), Chapter 5.

20 Robert H. Brisbane, "Black Protest in America," in *The Black American Reference Book,* ed. Mabel M. Smythe (Englewood Cliffs, N.J.: Prentice-Hall, 1976), 569.

21 Robert C. Smith, *Black Leadership: A Survey of Theory and Research* (Washington, D.C.: Institute for Urban Affairs and Research, Howard University, 1982), 69.

22 1984 National Black Election Study, cited in *A Common Destiny: Blacks and American Society,* ed. Gerald D. Jaynes and Robin M. Williams, Jr. (Washington, D.C.: National Academy Press, 1989), 219.

23 Quoted in J. I. Adkins, "Self-Help Should Be the Focus of the 21st Century," *Chicago Tribune,* February 9, 1994.

24 John S. Butler, *Entrepreneurship and Self-Help Among Black Americans* (Albany: State University of New York Press, 1991); W.E.B. Du Bois, *The Negro in Business* (Atlanta: Atlanta University Press, 1899) and *Economic Co-Operation Among Negro Americans* (Atlanta: Atlanta University Press, 1907); Abraham Harris, *The Negro as Capitalist* (1936; reprint, College Park, Md.: McGrath, 1968); Joseph A. Pierce, *Negro Business and Business Education* (New York: Harper, 1947).

25 The printer was Mary Katherine Goddard. See Linda Grant De Pauw and Conover Hunt, *Remember the Ladies: Women in America, 1750–1815* (New York: Viking, 1976), 83.

26 For more information on this period, see Elizabeth Frost and Kathryn Cullen-DuPont, *Women's Suffrage in America* (New York: Facts on File, 1992), Chapter 1.

27 Quoted in Marlene Stein Wortman, ed., *Women in American Law* (New York: Holmes & Meier, 1985), 259.

28 Page Smith, "From Masses to Peoplehood," *Historical Reflections* 1 (1974): 118.

29 Franklin D. Roosevelt, Jr., head of the EEOC in 1966, quoted in John C. Hammerback et al., *A War of Words: Chicano Protest in the 1960s and 1970s* (Westport, Conn.: Greenwood Press, 1985), 20.

30 Benjamin Márques of LULAC, cited in ibid., 32–33.

31 *Hernandez v. State of Texas,* 347 U.S. 475 (1954).

32 See Dee Brown, *Bury My Heart at Wounded Knee* (New York: Holt, Rinehart & Winston, 1970).

33 Curtis E. Jackson and Marcia J. Galli, *A History of the Bureau of Indian Affairs and Its Activities Among Indians* (San Francisco: R & E Research Associates, 1977).

34 See the *Final Report* to the American Indian Policy Review Commission (Washington, D.C.: U.S. Government Printing Office, 1976).

35 Cary Goldberg, "Tiny Tribe in Remote Arctic Is Jolting Alaska," *New York Times,* May 9, 1997, A1.

36 George Judson, "Some Indians See a Gamble with Future in Casinos," *New York Times,* May 15, 1994, E5.

37 Jon Magnuson, "Casino Wars: Ethics and Economics in Indian Country," *Christian Century,* February 16, 1994, 170.

38 Allen R. Bosworth, *America's Concentration Camps* (New York: Norton, 1967).

39 *Korematsu v. United States,* 323 U.S. 214 (1944). For a criticism of this decision, see Roger Daniels, *Concentration Camps in North America* (New York: Holt, Rinehart & Winston, 1981).

40 *Ex parte Endo,* 323 U.S. 283 (1944).

41 Yen Le Espiritu, *Asian American Panethnicity: Bridging Institutions and Identities* (Philadelphia: Temple University Press, 1992), 49. See also Robert W. Gardener et al., "Asian Americans: Growth, Change, and Diversity," *Population Bulletin* 40 (October 1985).

42 *Bowers v. Hardwick,* 478 U.S. 186 (1986).

43 *Romer v. Evans,* 116 U.S. 1620 (1996).

44 See, for example, Jonathan R. Miko and Eric Stoltz in the *New York Times,* May 27, 1996.

45 Quoted in "More Disabled Entering Workplace That's Getting More Accommodating," *Orlando Sentinel,* August 7, 1994.

46 *Hammer v. Dagenhart,* 247 U.S. 251 (1918).

47 *United States v. Darby,* 312 U.S. 100 (1941), reversing *Hammer v. Dagenhart.*

48 See Donald L. Bartlett and James B. Steele, *America: Who Stole the Dream?* (Kansas City, Mo.: Andrews and McMeel, 1996), esp. Chapter 1; and Duncan Lindsey, *The Welfare of Children* (New York: Oxford University Press: 1994).

49 For different views on the subject, see the statement of the Reverend Donald McCarthy in *Hearings Before the Subcommittee on Investigations and Oversights of the House Committee on Science and Technology*, 98th Cong., 2d sess. (1984), 350–359; Charles A. Gardner, "Is an Embryo a Person?" *Nation*, November 13, 1989, 557–558; John Robertson, "Embryos, Families, and Procreative Liberty: The Legal Structure of the New Reproduction," *Southern California Law Review*, 59 (1986): 942–953.

50 Peter P. Kirschenmann, "Justice, Rights, and the Concern for Nature and the Future," in *Morality, Worldview, and Law*, ed. A. W. Musschenga et al. (Assen and Maastricht, the Netherlands: Van Gorcum, 1992), 232.

51 Christopher Stone, *Should Trees Have Standing?* (Los Altos, Calif.: William Kaufmann, 1974).

52 Stephen L. Percy, "Implementing Civil Rights Policy: The Case of Disability," paper presented at the annual meeting of the American Political Science Association, Chicago, September 3–6, 1992, 4.

53 Jess Mowry, "Symposium: Does *Brown* Still Matter?" *Nation*, May 23, 1994, 719.

54 *Bell v. School City of Gary, Indiana* (N.D. Ind. 1963), 213 F. Supp. 819, 324 F. 2d 209 (7th Cir. 1963); *certiorari* denied, 379 U.S. 881 (1964).

55 Jonathan Kozol, "Romance of the Ghetto School," *Nation*, May 23, 1994, 705.

56 For arguments on both sides of the issue, see Barbara R. Bergmann, *In Defense of Affirmative Action* (New York: Basic Books, 1996); Terry Eastland, *Ending Affirmative Action: The Case for Colorblind Justice* (New York: Basic Books, 1996); Clint Bolick, *The Affirmative Action Fraud: Can We Restore the American Civil Rights Vision?* (Washington, D.C.: Cato Institute, 1996).

57 Ronald J. Ficus, *The Constitutional Logic of Affirmative Action* (Durham, N.C.: Duke University Press, 1992), 90.

58 *Regents of the University of California v. Bakke*, 438 U.S. 265 (1978).

59 *Hopwood v. Texas*, 78 F. 3d 932 (5th Cir. Tex. 1996).

60 *Griggs v. Duke Power Company*, 401 U.S. 424, 431 (1971).

61 *United Steelworkers Union v. Weber.*

62 *Fullilove v. Klutznick*, 448 U.S. 448 (1980).

63 *Firefighters Local Union No. 1784 v. Stott et al.*, 467 U.S. 561 (1984).

64 *United States v. Paradise*, 480 U.S. 149 (1987); *Johnson v. Transportation Agency, Santa Clara County*, 490 U.S. 616 (1987).

65 *City of Richmond v. J. A. Croson.*, 109 S. Ct. 706 (1989).

66 *Ward's Cove Packing Co. v. Antonio*, 109 S. Ct. 2115 (1989).

67 *St. Mary's Honor Center v. Hicks*, 113 S. Ct. 2742 (1993).

68 *Adarand Constructors, Inc. v. Peña*, 115 S. Ct 2097 (1995).

69 *Frontiero v. Richardson*, 411 U.S. 677 (1973).

70 For widespread evidence of this claim, see Paula England, *Comparable Worth: Theories and Evidence* (New York: Aldine de Gruyter, 1992); also see Tamar Lewin, "Salary Gap Between Men, Women Grows," *New York Times*, September 15, 1997.

71 Clarence Pendleton, quoted in James W. Singer, "Undervalued Jobs: What's a Woman (and the Government) to Do?" *National Journal*, May 24, 1980, 862.

72 Morris B. Abram, quoted in ibid.

73 Linda M. Blum, *Between Feminism and Labor: The Significance of the Comparable Worth Movement* (Berkeley: University of California Press, 1991), 17.

74. Hans Reinders, "Ethical Universalism and Human Rights," in Musschenga et al., eds., *Morality, Worldview, and Law*, 84.

75. M. Moskowitz, "Implementing Human Rights: Present Status and Future Prospects," in *Human Rights: Thirty Years After the Universal Declaration*, ed. B. G. Ramcharan (The Hague: Martinus Nijhof, 1979), 86.

76 A. J. M. Milne, *Human Rights and Human Diversity: An Essay in the Philosophy of Human Rights* (London: Macmillan, 1986).

77 Moskowitz, "Implementing Human Rights."

Illustration Credits

CHAPTER 1

p. 2 (center) Joseph Van/The Image Bank; (bottom) Calvin Larson/Photo Researchers; p. 6 Jim Edwards/The Press-Enterprise; p. 12 Jim Wilson/NYT Pictures; p. 13 Rob Crandall/Folio, Inc.; p. 19 (right) Andrea Mohin/NYT Pictures; (left) Steve Barrett/Contact Press Images; p. 22 Drawing by D. Fradon; © 1977 The New Yorker Magazine, Inc.; p. 28 Marilyn K. Yee/NYT Pictures; p. 30 Steve Kagan/NYT Pictures.

CHAPTER 2

p. 34 (center) Anthony Suau/Gamma Liaison; (bottom) Sovfoto/Eastfoto; p. 38 Courtesy of Massachusetts Archive; p. 39 (bottom) Corbis-Bettmann; (top) Jim Pickerell/Folio, Inc.; p. 40 The National Gallery of Art, Washington, D.C.; p. 41 The Quaker Collection, Haverford College Library; p. 44 (left) Lafayette College Art Collection, Eastern Pennsylvania; (right) BI/Gamma Liaison; (bottom) Culver Pictures, Inc.; p. 48 Corbis-Bettmann; p. 58 (left) Sandra Baker/Gamma Liaison; (top) Ed Castle/Folio, Inc.; (right) Walter Calahan/Folio, Inc.; p. 60 Corbis-Bettmann; p. 69 Bob Adelman/Magnum Photos, Inc.

CHAPTER 3

p. 72 (center) and (bottom) Bob Daemmrich/Stock, Boston; p. 87 Library of Congress; p. 88 Corbis-Bettmann; p. 89 UPI/Corbis-Bettmann; p. 93 Alon Reininger/Contact Press Images; p. 95 Silvia Dinale; p. 101 AP/Wide World Photos, Inc./Robin Loznak, The Daily Inter Lake.

CHAPTER 4

p. 108 (center) and (bottom) Courtesy *New York* Magazine; p. 112 Steven Rubin/The Image Works; p. 116 Montana Historical Society, Helena; p. 117 (right) Nancy Siesel/NYT Pictures; (bottom) *The Politically Incorrect Cheese Weasel* © 1991 Sideshow Comics; p. 118 Timberline Press, Inc.; p. 119 (bottom) Judy Spencer/AP/Wide World Photos, Inc.; (right) NYT Pictures; p. 120 Courtesy, Winterthur Museum; p. 121 NYT Pictures; p. 124 David R. Frazier/Folio, Inc.; p. 126 (bottom) *The Politically Incorrect Cheese Weasel* © 1993 Sideshow Comics; (top) Culver Pictures, Inc.; p. 131 Lawrence Migdale/Photo Researchers; p. 132 NYT Pictures; p. 134 Bernard Hoffman/Life Magazine © Time Inc.; p. 135 UPI/Corbis-Bettmann; p. 139 M. Wuerker; p. 140 Clay Bennett/North American Syndicate; p. 143 Barney Taxel/NYT Pictures; p. 145 Michael Newman/Photo Edit.

CHAPTER 5

p. 148 (center) Brad Markel/Gamma Liaison; (bottom) David Burnett/Contact Press Images; p. 155 Michael Evans/Sygma; p. 160 Drew Harmon/Folio, Inc.; p. 161 Bob Daemmrich Photo, Inc.; p. 163 Rob Crandall/Folio, Inc.; p. 165 Bennington College; p. 166 ©1997 CNN, Inc.; p. 167 Dennis Brack/Black Star; p. 168 Douglas Cohn, American Publishing; p. 170 (left) Corbis-Bettmann; (right) AP/Wide World Photos, Inc.; p. 175 Brownie Harris.

CHAPTER 6

p. 184 (center) Alon Reininger/Contact Press Images; (bottom) Bruria Finkel; p. 188 Danny Lyon/Magnum Photos, Inc.; p. 189 Corbis-Bettmann; p. 193 Courtesy of Elisabeth M. Edwards; p. 202 Reprinted courtesy of the Seattle Post-Intelligencer; p. 205 Jim Wilson/NYT Pictures; p. 207 Michelle Agins/NYT Pictures; p. 209 Terry Evans/The Land Institute; p. 210 Richard Lord/The Image Works; p. 211 Sygma; p. 212 Wally McNamee/Sygma; p. 213 James Kamp/Silver Image.

CHAPTER 7

p. 218 (center) Stephen Jaffe/Gamma Liaison; (bottom) Charles Barksdale/AP/Wide World Photos, Inc.; p. 225 Michael Dwyer/Stock, Boston; p. 227 (right) Dirck Halstead/Gamma Liaison; (left) Rick Friedman/Black Star; p. 234 Gary Markstein/Milwaukee Journal Sentinel; p. 236 Kenneth Jarecke/Contact Press Images; p. 239 Boston Public Library, Print Department; p. 243 Archives Center, National Museum of American History, Smithsonian Institution, Washington, D.C.; p. 244 Forbes Magazine Collection; p. 248 ©1997 CNN, Inc.; p. 253 Joe Traver/Gamma Liaison; p. 255 Axel Koster/Sygma; p. 259 Arnie Sachs/Sygma.

Illustration Credits

CHAPTER 8

p. 262 (center) Paul F. Gero/Sygma; (bottom) Cindy Charles/Gamma Liaison; p. 266 Majed/Sierra Club; p. 267 L. Stone/Sygma; p. 270 (top) Bob Fitch/Black Star; (bottom) Allan Tannenbaum/Sygma; p. 272 Terry Ashe/Folio, Inc.; p. 274 Alon Reininger/Contact Press Images; p. 276 (top) Cynthia Johnson/Gamma Liaison; (bottom) Amy Toensing/NYT Pictures; p. 279 Michael Ventura/Folio, Inc.; p. 283 R. Ellis/Sygma; p. 286 Patsy Lynch/AP/Wide World Photos, Inc.; p. 292 Uniphoto; p. 295 Tribune Media Services, Inc. All rights reserved. Reprinted with permission; p. 299 Alan Weiner/Gamma Liaison.

CHAPTER 9

p. 302 (center) Sylvie Creiss/Gamma Liaison; (bottom) Kila/Sygma; p. 306 Bob Daemmrich Photo, Inc.; p. 312 C-SPAN; p. 313 Barbara Alper/Stock, Boston; p. 316 (left) Vivian Ronay/Folio, Inc.; (right) Gamma Liaison; p. 319 Patsy Lynch/Gamma Liaison; p. 323 AP/Wide World Photos, Inc.; p. 329 Phoebe Bell/Folio, Inc.; p. 331 Toles/Universal Press Syndicate; p. 334 Venegez/Sipa; p. 337 Cynthia Johnson/Gamma Liaison; p. 339 David Burnett/Contact Press Images.

CHAPTER 10

p. 344 (center) Robert Llewellyn; p. 350 AP/Wide World Photos, Inc.; p. 351 Ted Soqui/Sygma; p. 352 (top) Bob Daemmrich Photo, Inc.; (bottom) ©MacNelly, Tribune Media Services, Inc. All rights reserved. Reprinted with permission; p. 354 Brooks Kraft/Sygma; p. 355 ©Treë; p. 360 AP/Wide World Photos; p. 362 Terry Ashe/Gamma Liaison; p. 366 Jacques M. Chenet/Gamma Liaison; p. 367 (top) L. Stone/Sygma; (bottom) Porter Gifford/Gamma Liaison; p. 374 Gilles Mingasson/Gamma Liaison; p. 375 David E. Kennedy/Austin American-Statesman; p. 377 AP/Wide World Photos, Inc.

CHAPTER 11

p. 388 (center) J. Carl Ganter/Contact Press Images; (bottom) Richard Bloom; p. 393 Samuel F.B. Morse, "The Old House of Representatives," 1822, oil on canvas, in the collection of the Corcoran Gallery of Art, Museum Purchase Gallery Fund; p. 394 Mark Godfrey/The Image Works; p. 396 David Burnett/Contact Press Images; p. 401 Walter P. Calahan; p. 402 Culver Pictures; p. 405 Bill Witmers, DSC-PM, NPS; p. 412 Stephen Jaffe/The Image Works; p. 425 Ira Wyman/Sygma; p. 433 UPI/Corbis-Bettmann.

CHAPTER 12

p. 436 (center) Gary A. Cameron/Reuters/Corbis-Bettmann; (bottom) Reuters/Corbis-Bettmann; p. 443 Library of Congress; p. 444 (top) North Wind Pictures; (bottom) Brown Brothers; p. 446 UPI/Corbis-Bettmann; p. 451 UPI/Corbis-Bettmann; p. 453 (top) and (bottom) Daily News; p. 454 Harry S. Truman Library; p. 458 UPI/Corbis-Bettmann; p. 462 Reagan Library; p. 464 Cliff Owen/UPI/Corbis-Bettmann; p. 466 Mark Richards/Contact Press Images; p. 467 Diana Walker/Gamma Liaison; p. 472 John Ficara/Sygma; p. 475 Darryl Heikes.

CHAPTER 13

p. 480 (center) Glenn Short/Gamma Liaison; (bottom) Robert Trippett/Sipa Press; p. 487 Corbis-Bettmann; p. 488 (left) Library of Congress; (right) Streetwise Maps; p. 494 Joe Marquette/AP/Wide World Photos; p. 499 Bob McNeely/Sipa Press; p. 503 AP/Wide World Photos; p. 508 Joe Marquette/AP/Wide World Photos; p. 514 Robert Trippett/Sipa Press; p. 516 Cynthia Johnson/Gamma Liaison; p. 519 © 1996 by Sidney Harris, "There Goes the Neighborhood," University of Georgia Press.

CHAPTER 14

p. 522 (center) Bob Daemmrich/Stock, Boston; (bottom) *Business Week*, No. 3330, August 2, 1993, p. 62; p. 530 Chase/Collection of the Supreme Court of the United States; p. 533 (left) Paul Hosefros/NYT Pictures; (right) George Tames/NYT Pictures; p. 539 AP /Wide World Photos; p. 542 The Image Works; p. 543 Richard Ellis/Sygma; p. 547 Rollin A. Riggs/NYT Pictures; p. 548 Paul Hosefros/NYT Pictures; p. 550 Ted Soqui/Sygma; p. 559 Drawing by Handelsman; ©1973, The New Yorker Magazine, Inc.; p. 562 Judy Spencer/NYT Pictures.

CHAPTER 15

p. 566 (center) Winnebago County Clerk; (bottom) Steve McCurry/Magnum; p. 571 Frank Dougherty/NYT Pictures; p. 574 Collection of the Supreme Court of the United States; p. 581 Ed Grazda; p. 583 AP/Wide World Photos; p. 584 The Stockhouse; p. 587 Matt Wuerker; p. 588 Jennifer Warburg/Impact Visuals; p. 594 Lloyd DeGrane/NYT Pictures; p. 596 Paul Hosefros/NYT Pictures; p. 597 The Detroit News; p. 600 Cynthia Johnson/Gamma Liaison.

CHAPTER 16

p. 606 Bob Daemmrich; p. 609 Sara Krulwich/NYT Pictures; p. 611 Stephanie Gross/NY Times, 3/23/97, p. A15; p. 612 Robert Trippett/Sipa Press; p. 617 Corbis-Bettmann; p. 618 Bruce Roberts/Rapho/Photo Researchers; p. 619 Alan S. Weiner/NYT Pictures; p. 621 Ira Wyman/Sygma; p. 623 Donna Binder/Impact Visuals; p. 630 AP/Wide World Photos; p. 640 Toles/Universal Press Syndicate ©1995 for US News & World Report; p. 641 David Silverman; p. 644 Richard Shock/Gamma Liaison.

Copyright Notices

CHAPTER 1

Page 9: Adapted from "Nature's Agenda," *New York Times*, February 15, 1997. **Page 19:** President Bill Clinton's State of the Union Address, 1997, and rebuttal by J.C. Watts, quoted in *New York Times*, February 5, 1997, A14.

CHAPTER 3

Page 77: Adapted and updated from Daniel J. Elazar, ed., *Federal Systems of the World* (London: Longman, 1991), app. C.

CHAPTER 4

Page 111: Excerpted from Daniel Yankelovich, "How Changes in the Economy Are Reshaping American Values," in *Values and Public Policy*, ed. Henry J. Aaron et al. (Washington, D.C.: Brookings Institution, 1994), 23–24.

CHAPTER 5

Page 152: Figure 5.1 from *The Public Perspective*, "People, Opinions, and Polls: Men, Women and Politics—All the Data You've Wanted (But Could Never Find)," August/September 1996, p. 24. Reprinted with the permission of The Roper Center for Public Opinion Research, University of Connecticut. **Page 156:** Figure 5.2 from David M. Wiler, "H. Ross Perot Spurs a Polling Experiment (Unintentionally)," *The Public Perspective*, May/June 1993, pp. 28–29. Reprinted with the permission of The Roper Center for Public Opinion Research, University of Connecticut. **Page 157:** Frank Luntz memo quoted in Robin Toner, "Word for Word/Advice for Republicans: Attention! All Sales Reps for the Contract with America!" *New York Times*, February 5, 1995, and "House Republicans Get Talking Points: GOP Pollster's Memo Offers Advice on How to Win with Words," *Washington Post*, February 2, 1995. **Page 158:** Daniel Yankelovich, "How Changes in the Economy Are Reshaping American Values," in *Values and Public Policy*, ed. Henry J. Aaron et al. (Washington, D.C.: Brookings Institution, 1994), p. 22. Reprinted by permission. **Page 159:** Figure 5.3 from Alec Gallup and David W. Moore, "Younger People Today Are More Positive About Polls Than Their Elders," *The Public Perspective*, August/September 1996, pp. 53, 51. Reprinted with permission of The Roper Center for Public Opinion Research, University of Connecticut. **Page 169:** Figure 5.4 from *The Paradox of Mass Politics: Knowledge and Opinion in the American Electorate*, by Russell Neumann. Copyright © 1986 by the President and Fellows of Harvard College. Reprinted by permission of Harvard University Press. **Page 171:** Quotation from *The Paradox of Mass Politics: Knowledge and Opinion in the American Electorate*, by Russell Neumann. Copyright © 1986 by the President and Fellows of Harvard College. Reprinted by permission of Harvard University Press. **Page 177:** Adapted from Daniel Yankelovich, "How Public Opinion Really Works," *Fortune*, October 5, 1992, 102–104, 108.

CHAPTER 6

Pages 198–199: Table 6.2 data provided by the Gallup poll. **Page 201:** Table 6.3 from *New York Times*/CBS News Poll, *New York Times*, October 6, 1996, A14. **Page 208:** Adapted with permission from "How-to-Write a Letter to the Editor," published by the Friends Committee on National Legislation.

CHAPTER 7

Page 229: A. Lawrence Chickering, *Beyond Left and Right: Breaking the Political Stalemate* (San Francisco: ICS Press, 1993), 181, 184–185. Reprinted by permission. **Page 250:** Adapted from J. David Gillespie, *Politics at the Periphery: Third Parties in Two-Party America* (Columbia: University of South Carolina Press, 1993), 26–27.

CHAPTER 8

Page 269: Table 8.1 from Roger H. Davidson and Walter J. Oleszek, *Congress and Its Members*, 4th ed. (Washington, D.C.: Congressional Quarterly Press, 1994), 297. **Page 273:** Adapted from Ronald Facchinetti, "Why Brussels Has 10,000 Lobbyists," *New York Times*, August 21, 1994. **Page 284:** Table 8.2 from Key Lehman Schlozman and John T. Tierney, *Organized Interests and American Democracy* (New York: Harper & Row, 1986), 150. **Page 294:** Table 8.3 from Center for Responsive Politics, cited in *New York Times*, October 18, 1996.

CHAPTER 9

Page 307: Table 9.1 adapted from Harold W. Stanley and Richard G. Niemi, *Vital Statistics on American Politics*, 4th ed.

(Washington, D.C.: Congressional Quarterly Press, 1994), Table 2–12, p. 74. **Page 317**: Excerpted from Michael Kelly, "The Game," *New York Times Magazine*, October 31, 1993, 64–65. **Page 322**: Reprinted by permission from Lawrence K. Grossman, "Regulate the Medium," *Columbia Journalism Review* (November–December 1991), 72.

CHAPTER 10

Page 373: Table 10.2 adapted from *Congressional Quarterly Weekly Report*, January 18, 1997, p. 187. **Page 383**: Table 10.3 adapted from *Washington Post National Weekly Edition*, March 3, 1997, 10.

CHAPTER 11

Page 402: Table 11.1 from *Congressional Quarterly Weekly Report*, January 4, 1997.

CHAPTER 12

Page 450: Chart adapted from James David Barber, *The Presidential Character*, 3rd ed. (Englewood Cliffs, N.J.: Prentice-Hall, 1985).

CHAPTER 13

Page 485: Table 13.1 adapted, expanded, and updated from Charles Adrian and Charles Press, *The American Political Process* (New York: McGraw-Hill, 1965), 528. **Page 491**: Table 13.2 from Paul Light, "How Thick Is Government?" *American Enterprise*, November–December 1994, 60. **Page 507**: Adapted from Leslie H. Gelb and Morton H. Halperin, "Diplomatic Notes: The Ten Commandments of the Foreign-Affairs Bureaucracy," *Harper's*, June 1972, 28–37.

CHAPTER 14

Page 528: Figure 14.1 adapted from Edwin W. Patterson, *Jurisprudence: Men and Ideas of the Law* (Brooklyn: Foundation Press, 1953), 198, 259. **Page 548**: Table 14.1 data compiled by Stephan Kline, Alliance for Justice, Washington, D.C., July 1997. **Page 549**: Table 14.2 data compiled by Stephan Kline, Alliance for Justice, Washington, D.C., July 1997.

CHAPTER 16

Page 633: Figure 16.1 based on *Newsweek* poll published September 14, 1993. **Page 642**: Figure 16.2 from "Social Issues," *Public Perspective*, April/May 1997, 55. **Pages 646–647**: Adapted from Paula England, *Comparable Worth: Theories and Evidence* (New York: Aldine de Gruyter, 1992), 281–283.

Author Index

Aaron, Henry J., 111n, N-6
Aberbach, Joel, 435, N-15
Abram, Morris B., N-24
Abramson, Jeffrey B., N-13
Abramson, Paul R., N-7
Ackerman, Bruce, N-2, N-5
Adams, John, N-2
Adkins, J. I., N-23
Aldrich, John H., N-7
Alegre, Juan Carlos, N-9
Aleshire, Bill, N-7
Almond, Gabriel, N-7
Altbach, Philip G., N-4
Altheide, David L., N-18
Alwin, Duane F., N-6
Anderson, Kelly, N-11
Andrus, Cecil, N-1
Anton, Thomas, 105, N-3
Apple, R.W., N-8
Applebome, Peter, N-6
Argersinger, Peter H., N-7
Arlen, Michael, N-13
Armitage, Susan H., N-7
Armstrong, David, N-11
Armstrong, Scott, N-20
Arnold, Peri E., N-18
Arterton, F. Christopher, N-14
Asbell, Bernard, N-15
Ashley, Maurice, N-1
Auletta, Ken, N-11

Babcock, Charles R., N-11
Bacon, Donald C., 435
Baer, Denise L., 261, N-9
Bagdikian, Ben H., 343, N-11
Bailey, Stephen K., N-14
Baker, Ross K., 435, N-15
Barabak, Mark Z., N-5
Barber, James David, 479
Barnes, James A., N-13
Barnes, Samuel H., N-6
Barrett, David M., N-16
Barsamian, David, N-12
Bar-Tal, Daniel, N-4
Bartlett, Donald L., N-23
Basso, Christopher J., N-10
Bates, Stephen, N-13
Batscha, Robert M., N-12
Becker, Gary S., N-5
Beer, Samuel, 105
Behr, Roy L., 261, N-9
Bell, Charles G., N-10
Bell, Daniel, N-5
Bell, Roderick A., N-16
Bellah, Robert N., 147
Bendix, Reinhold, N-18
Bennet, James, N-8, N-13, N-14
Bennett, James T., N-11
Bennett, Robert W., N-20
Bensen, Charles, N-5
Berger, Jerry, N-12
Bergmann, Barbara R., N-24
Berns, Walter, N-14
Bernstein, Richard B., N-13
Berry, Jeffrey M., 301, N-10, N-19
Birnbaum, Jeffrey H., 301, N-10
Black, Benjamin D., 261, N-9
Black, Gordon S., 261, N-9
Blessing, Tim H., N-16
Blum, Linda M., N-24
Bodenheimer, Edgar, 564

Bolick, Clint, N-3, N-24
Bolling, Richard, N-14
Bonchek, Mark S., N-9
Bonnin, Richard, N-18
Bork, Robert H., 564, N-4, N-19, N-20, N-21
Bositis, David A., 261, N-9, N-15
Bosworth, Allen R., N-23
Bradburn, Norman M., N-6
Brenner, Marie, N-8
Brigham, John, N-20, N-21
Brinkley, David, N-17
Brisbane, Robert H., N-23
Broder, David S., 257n, N-9, N-13, N-15
Broder, John M., N-22
Brody, Richard A., 183, N-6
Bronfenbrenner, Urie, N-4, N-5
Brooke, James, N-9
Brossard, Mario A., N-11
Brown, Dee, N-23
Brown, Richard Harvey, N-5
Brown, Robert E., 53n
Browne, William P., 301, N-10
Browning, Graeme, N-11, N-12
Bryce, James, N-2, N-8, N-20
Bryner, Gary C., N-14, N-18
Buchanan, Bruce, 385, N-14, N-16
Buckwalter, Doyle W., N-3
Buhle, Mari Jo, N-7
Burke, Edmund, N-14
Burke, John P., 521, N-19
Burnham, David, N-13
Burnham, Walter Dean, N-9
Burns, James MacGregor, 652, N-15, N-16, N-17
Burns, Stewart, 652
Butler, John S., N-23

Cain, Bruce, N-14
Callahan, Daniel, N-15
Campbell, Colin, 479, N-17, N-18
Campbell, Don, N-12
Cannon, Lou, N-16, N-19
Canon, Bradley C., N-21
Cantor, Milton, N-16
Carmichael, Stokely, 652, N-23
Carney, Eliza Newlin, N-11
Carroll, J. A., N-14
Carter, Lief H., 564, N-20
Cary, Eve, 605
Caughey, Bernard, N-13
Chapman, John W., N-4
Chavez, Linda, N-7
Chemerinsky, Erwin, 564, N-19
Choate, Pat, N-10
Christians, Clifford, N-13
Chubb, John E., N-19
Cigler, Allan J., 301, N-10
Clark, Gordon L., N-3
Clark, Joseph S., N-14
Clark, Ramsey, N-5
Clayton, Cornell W., N-20
Clignet, Remi, N-5
Clines, Francis X., N-15
Clinton, Bill, N-1, N-9, N-17
Clymer, Adam, N-5, N-8, N-15
Cogan, Dan, N-12
Cohen, Mitchell, N-5
Cohen, Richard E., N-14, N-15, N-16

Cohen, Ronald L., N-6
Cohn, Jonathan, N-11
Collier, Kenneth, N-17
Commager, Henry Steele, N-16
Conlan, Timothy J., N-3
Converse, Philip E., 171n, N-6
Cook, Brian J., 521
Cooper, Ann, N-10
Cooper, Joseph, N-15
Cooper, Marc, N-12
Cooper, Philip J., N-20
Cooper, Phillip J., 564, N-11, N-16
Corrado, Anthony, N-13, N-14
Costanzo, Angelo, N-4
Coupland, Douglas, N-5
Cox, Gary W., 261
Crawford, Kenneth, N-10
Crenson, Matthew A., N-18
Cronin, Thomas E., N-17
Crotty, William, 385, N-9
Crozier, Michel T., 114n, N-7
Cullen-DuPont, Kathryn, N-23
Cummins, Eric, N-2
Cuomo, Mario, N-6
Cushman, John H., Jr., N-8
Cutler, Lloyd, N-17
Czitrom, Daniel, N-7

Dahl, David, N-5
Dahl, Robert, N-10
Damaska, Mirjan R., N-20
Daniel, John, N-1
Daniel, Missy, N-5
Daniels, Jonathan, N-19
Daniels, Roger, N-23
Dart, Bob, N-10, N-15, N-21
Dauenhauer, Bernard N., N-4
David, Charles T., N-4
Davidson, Roger H., 435, N-14, N-15
Dayan, Daniel, N-12
Deitz, Robert, N-11
Delli Carpini, Michael X., 183, N-6, N-7
Deloria, Vine, Jr., 652
Demac, Donna A., N-12
Dennis, Everette E., N-13
De Pauw, Linda Grant, N-23
Derthick, Martha, N-18
Deutsch, Karl W., N-18
Dewar, Helen, N-15
Dexter, Lewis A., N-14
Diamond, Edwin, N-13
Diamond, Sara, N-4
Dillon, John F., N-3
DiLorenzo, Thomas J., N-11
Dimond, Paul R., 564
Dionne, E. J., Jr., N-7
Disney, Jennifer L., N-10
Dodd, Lawrence C., 435, N-15, N-16
Dolbeare, Kenneth M., 147, N-4
Dolny, Michael, N-12
Donahue, Hugh Carter, N-13
Dorn, James A., 605
Douglass, Frederick, N-23
Dow, David R., N-22
Downing, John D. H., N-6
Downs, Anthony, N-6, N-18
Drucker, Peter, N-5
Du Bois, Paul Martin, 343, N-8

Du Bois, W.E.B., N-23
Duffy, Michael, N-17
Dugger, Ronnie, N-9
Dye, Thomas R., N-3, N-7, N-10
Dynneson, Thomas L., N-5

Eastland, Terry, N-24
Eaton, Leslie, N-10
Edelman, Murray, 217, 652, N-8, N-13
Edgar, Bob, N-10
Edley, Christopher F., Jr., 564, N-18, N-19
Edwards, David V., N-1, N-16
Edwards, George C., III, 479, N-17
Egan, Timothy, N-20
Ehrenhalt, Alan, 385
Eichenwald, Kurt, N-1
Eisenbeck, Margaret, N-5
Eisenberg, David M., N-8
Eisenstadt, S. W., N-1
Elazar, Daniel J., 77n, 105, N-3
Elder, Shirley, N-10
Ellsworth, Oliver, N-2
Engelberg, Stephen, N-9, N-10
England, Paula, N-24
Epstein, Lee, N-9, N-20
Epstein, Leon D., 261
Epstein, Richard A., 605
Erickson, Robert S., N-6
Ericson, Richard V., N-12
Espiritu, Yen Le, 652, N-23
Etzioni, Amitai, N-4
Evans, Rowland, N-14

Fallows, James, 343, N-12
Faragher, John Mack, N-7
Faux, Marian, 605
Ferejohn, John, N-14
Ferrell, Robert H., N-16
Fesler, James W., 521
Fialka, John J., N-13
Ficus, Ronald J., N-24
Finger, Michael, N-21
Finkelman, Paul, 605
Fiorina, Morris P., N-7, N-13, N-14
Fiscus, Ronald J., 652
Fiss, Owen M., N-20
Fitzpatrick, Kellyanne, N-8
Fitzwater, Marlin, N-12
Flathman, Richard, N-4
Fleishman, Joel L., N-9, N-19
Flexner, James Thomas, N-2
Ford, Carol, N-8
Ford, Gerald, N-17
Foucault, Michel, N-4
Frankel, Max, N-11
Franklin, Daniel P., N-16
Frendeis, John, N-9
Fresia, Gerald J., N-9
Fried, Charles, N-20
Friedman, Lawrence M., N-1
Fritsch, Jane, N-1
Frost, Elizabeth, N-23
Fukuyama, Francis, N-4

Gaebler, Ted, N-5, N-19
Galli, Marcia J., N-23
Galloway, Russell W., 564
Gallup, George, 183

Author Index

Galston, William A., N-3
Gamson, William, N-12
Gans, Curtis, N-14
Gans, Herbert J., N-11, N-12
Gantz, Walter, N-13
Gardener, Robert W., N-23
Gardner, Charles A., N-24
Garret, Major, N-5
Garson, David G., 301
Gates, Henry Louis, Jr., N-4
Gelb, Joyce, N-10
Gelb, Leslie H., N-19
Gentry, Curt, N-20
George, Alexander, N-17
George, Tracey E., N-20
Gibson, James L., N-7, N-9
Gibson, Martha L., N-15
Gilbert, Dennis A., N-6
Gillespie, J. David, 261
Gilliom, John, N-21, N-22
Gilmour, Robert, 521
Ginsberg, Benjamin, 217, N-6, N-7
Ginsburg, Ruth Bader, N-20
Gitlin, Todd, N-12
Glasser, Ira, N-22
Glazer, Myron P., N-18
Glazer, Penina M., N-18
Gleick, James, N-8
Glendon, Mary Ann, 605, N-21
Goddard, Mary Katherine, N-23
Goedert, Paula Cozzi, N-11
Goel, M. L., N-7
Gold, Martin, 435
Goldberg, Carey, N-20, N-23
Goldin, Claudia, 652
Goldson, Annie, N-11
Goldstein, Avram, N-8
Goldwin, Robert A., N-1
Goleman, Daniel, N-6
Gomes, Ralph C., 217, N-7
Goodgame, Dan, N-17
Goodsell, Charles T., 521, N-17
Gore, Al, N-19
Gormley, William T., 521
Gottlieb, Stephen E., 605
Gould, Lewis H., N-17
Grace, J. Peter, N-10
Graebner, William, 147
Gramsci, Antonio, N-23
Greenberg, Bradley S., N-13
Greenberg, Stanley, N-2
Greenhouse, Linda, N-9, N-21
Greider, William, N-1
Gremillion, Jeff, N-11
Gressman, Eugene, N-20
Grimes, Alan P., 71, N-2
Grimes, William, N-8
Grimke, Frederick, N-9
Gross, Bertram, 435, 652, N-4
Gross, Daniel, N-19
Gross, Richard E., N-5
Grossman, Michael B., N-12
Gurin, Patricia, N-9

Haas, Lawrence J., N-15
Hadley, Charles D., N-9
Haig, Alexander, N-17
Hale, F. Dennis, N-13
Hallin, Daniel, N-12
Halperin, Morton H., N-18, N-19
Hamilton, Alexander, 71
Hamilton, Charles V., 652, N-23
Hamilton, Lee Christopher, 105, N-3

Hammerback, John C., N-23
Hardin, Charles, N-17
Harris, Abraham, N-23
Harris, Richard A., N-19
Hart, Roderick P., N-6, N-11, N-16
Hawkins, Robert, N-3
Heclo, Hugh, N-18, N-19
Henretta, James A., N-5
Herbst, Susan, 183, N-6
Herndon, John, N-11
Hero, Rodney E., N-9
Herring, E. Pendleton, N-10
Hertsgaard, Mark, 343, N-12
Hess, Stephen, 343, 479, N-12, N-17
Hewitt, John P., N-4
Heydebrand, Wolf, 564, N-19, N-21
Hickok, Eugene W., Jr., N-2
Hicks, John, N-9
Hightower, Jim, N-9
Hinckley, Barbara, 435
Hoadley, John F., 261, N-8
Hochschild, Jennifer L., 147, N-5
Hofstadter, Richard, N-9
Holayter, Bill, N-11
Hollinger, David A., N-4
Holmes, Steven A., N-5, N-8
Holzner, Harold, N-6
Hrebenar, Ronald J., N-11
Hubbell, Janette Kay, 147, N-4
Huckfeldt, Robert, 261, N-8
Huff, Richard, N-13
Huffman, John L., N-23
Hughes, Charles Evans, N-20
Hult, Karen M., N-17
Hummel, Ralph P., 521
Humphrey, Hubert, N-14
Hundley, Norris, Jr., N-1
Huntington, Samuel P., 114n, N-7

Ichilov, Orit, 147, N-6
Isaac, Katherine, 215
Iyengar, Shanto, 343, N-12

Jackson, Brooks, 385, N-14
Jackson, Curtis E., N-23
Jacobson, Gary C., 385, N-9
Jamieson, Kathleen, N-13, N-14
Jarvis, Sonia R., N-7
Jay, John, 71
Jaynes, Gerald D., N-23
Jefferson, Thomas, N-3, N-8
Jennett, Christine, N-9
Jennings, Bruce, N-15
Jennings, M. Kent, N-5, N-6, N-9
Jensen, Merrill, N-2
Jentleson, Bruce W., N-17
Jillson, Calvin C., 71, N-2
Johnson, Charles A., N-21
Johnson, John M., N-18
Johnson, Lyndon B., N-7, N-14, N-16
Johnson, Paul, N-11
Jones, Charles O., 479, N-14
Jordan, Fred, N-3
Judson, George, N-23
Jurkowitz, Mark, N-12
Just, Marion R., N-14
Juviler, Peter, 652

Kaase, M., N-6
Kammen, Michael, 53n, 71, N-2, N-22

Kann, Mark E., N-4
Karst, Kenneth L., 653, N-22
Katz, Elihu, N-12
Katz, Jon, N-12
Kavenagh, W. Keith, N-1
Kay, Alan F., N-6
Kayden, Xandra, N-9
Keagle, James M., N-18
Keefe, William J., N-16
Keeter, Scott, 183, N-6, N-7
Keillor, Garrison, N-4, N-5
Keller, Morton, 435
Kellerman, Barbara, N-16
Kelley, Chris, N-1
Kelley, Kitty, N-19
Kelly, Michael, N-14
Kendall, George, N-22
Kennedy, John F., N-16
Kenney, Charles, N-12
Kernell, Samuel, 261, N-16, N-17
Kerr, Walter, N-4
Kerwin, Cornelius M., N-19
Kessel, John H., 479
Kettl, Donald F., 521, N-19
Key, V. O., Jr., 217, N-6, N-8
Kilborn, Peter T., N-11
Kimball, Penn, N-11
Kincaid, John, N-3
Kinder, Donald R., 343
King, Anthony, N-10, N-17, N-19
King, James D., N-17
Kingdon, John, N-14
Kirschenmann, Peter P., N-24
Kline, Stephan, N-20
Klingemann, Hans D., 171n, N-6
Knoke, David, 301, N-10
Knoll, Erwin, N-12
Knott, Jack H., N-19
Kohfeld, Carol Weitzel, 261, N-8
Kolb, Charles, N-17
Kolbert, Elizabeth, N-5
Koon, Stacey C., N-11
Kovach, Bill, N-13
Kozak, David C., N-18
Kozol, Jonathan, N-24
Krislov, Samuel, N-19
Krugman, Paul, N-1
Kuklinski, James H., N-6
Kumar, Martha Joynt, N-12
Kupferman, Theodore R., 605, N-23
Kurtz, Howard, N-12
Kweit, Mary G., N-19
Kweit, Robert W., N-19

Ladd, Everett Carll, Jr., 217, N-4, N-5, N-9
Lambeth, Edmund B., N-13
Lane, Ruth, N-4
Lapin, Jeffrey, N-7
Lappé, Frances Moore, 343, N-8
Lasch, Christopher, 147, N-4, N-5, N-13
Lasswell, Harold, N-1
Laufer, Robert S., N-4, N-5
Laufer, Romain, N-7
Lawson, Kay, N-9
Laycock, Douglas, N-20
Lazarus, Edward H., 261, N-9
Lea, James F., 147, N-4, N-5
Leahy, James E., 605, N-21
Leamer, Laurence, N-14
Lehman, Jane, N-22
Leinberger, Paul, 147

Lemann, Nicholas, N-12
Levi, Edward H., N-19
Levine, Alan H., 605
Levine, Herbert M., N-1
Levinson, Sanford, N-2, N-20
Levy, Leonard, N-2
Lewin, Tamar, N-8, N-24
Lewis, Anthony, N-5
Lichter, Linda S., N-10
Liebling, A. J., N-13
Light, Paul C., N-17, N-18
Lincoln, Abraham, N-16
Lindsay, James M., 435, N-15
Lindsey, Duncan, N-23
Linsky, Martin, N-12
Lippmann, Walter, 183, N-5
Lipset, Seymour Martin, N-4, N-5
Locke, Hubert G., N-19
Locke, John, 605, N-21
Lockerbie, Brad, N-13
Lohr, Steve, N-10, N-11
Longley, Lawrence D., N-15
Loomis, Burdett A., 301, N-10
Love, Jean C., 564
Lowi, Theodore J., 479, N-10
Lukes, Steven, N-4
Lunch, William M., 261, N-9
Luntz, Frank, N-2, N-5, N-6
Luskin, Robert C., 171n, N-6
Lutz, Donald S., 61, 71, N-1, N-2

MacArthur, John R., N-13
MacIntyre, Angus A., N-18
Mack, Charles S., 301
Mackenzie, G. Calvin, N-15
MacLeod, David I., 147
MacManus, Susan A., N-3
Macpherson, C. B., N-4
Madigan, Edward, N-15
Madison, James, 71, N-8
Magnuson, Jon, N-23
Mahe, Eddie, Jr., N-9
Maher, Kristen Hill, N-3, N-5
Mailloux, Steven, N-2, N-20
Maisel, Louis, N-9
Maisel, Sandy L., 261
Malbin, Michael J., N-14
Maltese, John Anthony, 343, N-12
Mann, Thomas E., N-6
Manne, Henry G., 605
Mannheim, Karl, N-5
Maraniss, David, N-15
Marcus, Ruth, N-11
Margolis, Michael, 171n, 183
Markoff, John, N-22
Márques, Benjamin, N-23
Marshall, John, N-20
Marshall, Thurgood, N-1
Marty, Martin E., N-4
Marx, Gary T., N-23
Massing, Michael, N-12
Masters, Roger D., N-7
Mathias, Charles, N-11
Matthews, Linda, N-21
Mauser, Gary A., 171n, 183
May, Janice C., N-19
Mayhew, David R., N-14
McCann, Michael W., N-9, N-23
McCarthy, Donald, N-23
McClay, Wilfred M., N-4
McCloskey, Robert, N-20
McClure, Charles R., N-18
McClure, Robert, N-13

McDonald, Forrest, 53n, 71, 479, N-2
McHenry, James, N-2
McHugo, Gregory J., N-7
McIver, John P., N-6
McNeely, Dave, N-13
McPherson, Harry, N-16
McQuail, Denis, N-12
McSweeney, Dean, 261, N-9
Meinig, D. W., N-2
Mellman, Mark S., N-10
Meredith, Robyn, N-5
Merkl, Peter H., N-9
Merline, John, N-17
Mezey, Michael L., 435, N-17
Michels, Robert O., N-10
Mifflin, Lawrie, N-14
Miko, Jonathan R., N-23
Milbrath, Lester W., N-7
Mileur, Jerome M., 385
Milkis, Sidney M., N-19
Mill, John Stuart, 605
Miller, Alan D., N-22
Miller, Arthur S., N-19
Miller, Gary J., N-19
Miller, James C., N-8
Miller, Joshua, 71, N-2
Mills, C. Wright, N-10
Milne, A. J. M., N-24
Minor, Henry, N-8
Mitchell, Alison, N-11, N-14, N-17
Moe, Terry M., N-19
Mondale, Walter, N-17
Monroe, Alan D., N-6
Moore, David W., 183, N-6
Moore, Raymond, N-16
Moore, W. John, N-10
Morain, Dan, N-9
Morehouse, Sarah McCally, N-9
Morgan, Dan, N-3
Morgan, Douglas F., N-19
Morin, Richard, N-4, N-11, N-14
Morphew, Clark, N-4
Morris, Dick, 385, N-14
Morton, John, N-11
Mosco, Vincent, N-12
Moskowitz, M., N-24
Mowry, Jess, N-24
Mucciaroni, Gary, N-9
Munro, Neil, N-22
Murphy, Walter F., 564, N-20
Murray, Robert K., N-16
Murrin, John M., N-2
Musschenga, A. W., N-24

Nader, Ralph, N-13
Nash, Gary, N-23
Natchez, Peter B., 217, N-7, N-8
Nathan, Richard P., N-17
Nelson, Michael, 479, N-13, N-16, N-18
Nessen, Ron, N-12
Neuman, W. Russell, N-6, N-13
Neustadt, Richard E., 479, N-16, N-18
Newcomb, Theodore M., N-6
Newton, James S., N-7
Nichols, Roy F., N-2
Nie, Norman, 217
Niebuhr, Gustav, N-8
Niemi, Richard G., N-6, N-11
Nisbet, Robert, N-4
Nixon, Richard M., N-12, N-17
Norton, Robert E., N-10

Novak, Robert, N-14
Nye, Peter, N-7

Oakley, John B., 564
O'Brien, Larry, N-16
O'Brien, Tim, N-20
O'Donnell, Thomas, N-15
O'Hern, Daniel J., N-20
Oleszek, Walter J., 435, N-15
Oliver, Michael, 653
Olson, Mancur, N-9
O'Neill, Michael J., N-11, N-12
O'Neill, Thomas P. (Tip), N-14
Oppenheimer, Bruce I., 435, N-15
Orfield, Gary, N-15
Ornstein, Norman J., N-10, N-15
Orren, Gary R., N-6
Osborne, David, N-5, N-19
Owen, Diana, N-14

Pachon, Harry P., N-9
Page, Benjamin I., 183, N-7
Paradeise, Catherine, N-7
Parker, Robert, N-14, N-17
Parton, J., N-10
Passell, Peter, N-1
Paterno, Susan, N-14
Patterson, Thomas, N-13
Peabody, Robert L., N-14
Pear, Roger, N-18
Pearlstein, Steven, N-7
Pearson, James B., N-14
Peirce, Neal R., N-3
Pemberton, William E., N-18
Pendleton, Clarence, N-24
Pennock, J. Roland, N-4
Percy, Stephen L., N-24
Perry, H. W., Jr., 564, N-20
Persico, Joseph, N-18
Peters, John, N-15
Peterson, Paul E., 105, N-3, N-19
Petroski, Henry, N-1
Pfiffner, James P., N-17
Pharo, Gwen, N-8
Pierce, Joseph A., N-23
Pika, Joseph A., N-17
Pinkerton, James P., N-8, N-14
Pippert, Wesley G., N-12
Podhoretz, John, N-14, N-17
Pool, Ithiel de Sols, N-13
Polsby, Nelson W., N-8, N-14, N-17
Pomper, Gerald M., 261, 385, N-13, N-14
Pooley, Eric, N-14
Popkin, Samuel L., 217, N-6, N-12, N-14, N-17
Porter, Mary Cornelia Aldis, 564, N-20, N-21
Post, Gordon C., 564
Post, Jerrold M., N-16
Postrel, Virginia, N-3
Powell, H. Jefferson, N-2
Powell, Jody, N-12
Power, E. James Ferguson-, N-2
Prescott, Jean, N-12
Preston, Samuel H., N-5
Price, David E., 435
Price, Janet, 605
Price, Vincent, 183
Pritchett, C. Herman, N-20
Pulsifer, David, N-1

Quirk, Paul J., N-16

Rabe, Barry, 105
Rabin, Robert, N-10
Rae, Saul Forbes, 171n, 183
Ramcharan, B. G., N-24
Ranney, Austin, N-7, N-8
Rapp, David, N-3
Rattner, Steven, N-5
Rauch, Jonathan, 301, N-4, N-5, N-10
Regan, Donald, N-17
Rehnquist, William, N-13
Reich, Charles, N-4
Reich, Robert, 521, N-5, N-19
Reinders, Hans, N-24
Reinhardt, Stephen, N-22
Reisner, Marc, N-1
Resnik, Judith, N-21
Rheingold, Howard, N-8
Richard, Carl J., N-2
Richard, David A. J., 605
Richardson, Sula P., N-15
Riddlesperger, James W., N-17
Riesman, David, N-5
Rifkin, Jeremy, N-1, N-5, N-22
Riley, Dennis D., N-18, N-19
Rimmerman, Craig A., N-16
Ripley, Randall, N-15
Rivlin, Alice M., 105
Robertson, John, N-24
Robins, Robert S., N-16
Rockman, Bert A., 479, N-16, N-17
Rogin, Michael, N-16
Rohde, David W., N-7
Rohr, John A., N-19
Romans, Neal, N-20
Roos, John, N-15
Roosevelt, Franklin D., N-16
Roosevelt, Franklin D., Jr., N-23
Rorty, Richard, N-4
Rose, Gary L., N-14
Rosen, Bernard, N-19
Rosen, Jeffrey, N-20
Rosenbloom, David H., N-19
Rosenstone, Steven J., 261, N-7, N-9
Rowe, Chip, N-12
Rudovsky, David, 605, N-22
Rutledge, John, N-2
Ryan, Susan M., 521, N-18

Sabato, Larry J., 385, N-8, N-9, N-14
Sachs, Paul M., N-9
Sadofsky, David, N-18
Sahlins, Marshall D., N-1, N-8
Salamon, Lester, N-18, N-19
Salant, Jonathan D., N-13
Salisbury, Robert H., N-9, N-10, N-11
Salomone, Rosemary C., 653
Sandel, Michael J., N-5
Sanger, David E., N-11
Sartori, Giovanni, N-9
Satin, Mark, 215
Saxe, Leonard, N-4
Saxon, John D., N-15
Schambra, William A., N-1
Schattschneider, E. E., 301
Scheingold, Stuart, N-21
Schlesinger, Arthur M., Jr., N-4, N-16, N-17
Schlesinger, Joseph A., N-8, N-9

Schlozman, Kay Lehman, 284n, 301, N-10
Schneier, Edward V., 435
Schudson, Michael, 343, N-12, N-13
Schwartz, Ed, 215
Sears, David, N-6
Seib, Philip, N-12
Seidman, Harold, 521
Seligman, Lester G., N-16
Sennett, Richard, N-4
Seron, Carroll, 564, N-19, N-21
Service, Elman R., N-1, N-8
Shafer, Byron E., 261, N-8
Shalhope, Robert E., N-2
Shapiro, Robert Y., 183, N-7
Sharp, Gene, 217
Shartel, Burke, N-20
Shavelson, Lonny, N-22
Shenck, David, N-11
Shepard, Alicia C., N-11
Shepsle, Kenneth A., N-9
Shienbaum, Kim Ezra, 217, N-7, N-8
Shipler, David K., N-4
Shön, Donald, N-1
Shribman, David, N-3
Shull, Steven A., N-17
Shumavon, Douglas H., N-18
Shumavon, S. H., N-19
Sigal, Leon V., N-12
Silber, John, N-8
Silverstein, Douglas N., N-22
Silverstein, Mark, N-20
Singer, James W., N-24
Singletary, Amos, N-2
Sinopoli, Richard C., 147, N-4
Skerry, Peter, 653
Smedley, Audrey, 653
Smith, Christopher E., N-21
Smith, Hedrick, N-12
Smith, James Allen, 301, N-9
Smith, Jean Edward, N-20
Smith, Lee, N-10
Smith, Page, 53n, 71, N-1, N-2, N-23
Smith, Robert C., N-23
Smith, Tom W., N-4
Smith, William French, N-21
Smythe, Mabel M., N-23
Sniderman, Paul M., 183, N-6, N-7
Soley, Lawrence C., 343, N-12
Sorauf, Frank, 385
Soros, George, N-1
Spinner-Halev, Jeff, N-4
Sprague, N-8
Stanley, Harold W., N-11
Starobin, Paul, N-10, N-12
Steele, Eugene, N-16
Steele, James B., N-23
Stein, Robert, N-11
Stengel, Richard, N-14
Stern, Philip M., N-10, N-11
Stern, Robert L., N-20
Sterngold, James, N-10
Stoltz, Eric, N-23
Stone, Christopher, 653, N-24
Stone, Geoffrey R., N-21
Storing, Herbert J., 50n, 71, N-2
Story, Joseph, N-2
Sudman, Seymour, N-6
Sullivan, Dennis G., N-7
Summers, Anthony, N-20

Sundquist, James L., 261, N-9, N-17
Sussman, Barry, N-6, N-7
Swanson, K. C., N-22
Swanson, Wayne R., N-21
Swift, Jonathan, N-3
Szatmary, David P., 50*n*

Tardieu, Ambroise, N-7
Tarr, G. Alan, 564, N-3, N-20, N-21
Tasini, Jonathan, N-11
Taylor, John, N-4
Tehranian, Majid, N-13
TerHorst, Jerald F., N-16
Tetlock, Philip E., 183, N-6
Thayer, James B., N-2
Thomas, Clive S., N-11
Thomas, Norman C., N-17
Thompson, Dennis F., N-15
Tibbetts, Geoffrey L., N-3
Tiefer, Charles, N-17
Tierney, John T., 284*n*, 301, N-10
Tilly, Louise A., N-9
Toch, Thomas, N-5
Tocqueville, Alexis de, N-1
Tolchin, Martin, N-9, N-10
Tolley, Michael C., N-3
Toner, Robin, N-5
Traugott, Michael W., N-6

Trauth, Denise M., N-23
Truman, David, 301, N-10
Truman, Harry S., N-16, N-17
Tucker, Bruce, 147
Tulis, Jeffrey, N-16
Tushnet, Mark V., 653, N-23

Urofsky, Melvin I., N-2, N-22
Uslaner, Eric M., N-7, N-15

Van Alstyne, William, N-3
Van Beek, Stephen D., N-15
Van Biema, David, N-6
Vedantam, Shankar, N-5
Verba, Sidney, 217
Verhovek, Sam Howe, N-8, N-9
Vertz, Laura, N-9
Vile, John R., N-2
Vines, Kenneth, N-20
Vinson, Fred M., N-20
Vogel, David, 301

Wagman, Robert J., 605
Wahlke, John, N-14
Waite, Peter A., N-5
Ward, D., N-6
Warren, Mark, N-4
Warwick, Donald P., N-19
Washington, George, N-2, N-8
Wasko, Janet, N-12

Watanuki, Toji, 114*n*, N-7
Waterman, Richard W., N-18
Watson, Richard A., N-17
Wattenberg, Martin P., N-9, N-13, N-14
Weaver, David H., N-11
Weaver, Warren, N-14
Weber, Max, N-18
Weber, Thomas, N-22
Weiner, Tim, N-8, N-11
Weisberg, Jacob, N-5
Weissberg, Robert, N-5
Welch, Susan, N-15
Wells, Donald T., 105, N-3
Weyrich, Paul, N-8
Whicker, Marcia, N-16
White, Byron, N-19
White, James Boyd, 68*n*, N-2
White, Leonard D., N-18
White, William Boyd, N-3
Whyte, William H., N-5
Wilensky, Harold, N-18
Wilhoit, G. Cleveland, N-11
Williams, Linda Faye, 217, N-7
Williams, Richard L., N-19
Williams, Robin M., Jr., N-23
Williamson, Richard S., N-3
Willis, Jim, 343
Wilson, James Q., 521, N-18, N-19

Wilson, Woodrow, N-2, N-16, N-17
Wirth, Timothy, N-14
Wittig, Michele, N-7
Wolff, Kurt H., N-11
Wolfinger, Raymond E., N-7
Wolfson, Lewis W., N-13
Wong, Kenneth K., 105
Wood, Gordon S., 71
Wood, James R., 301
Woodward, Bob, N-16, N-18, N-20
Worster, Donald, N-1
Wortman, Marlene Stein, N-23
Wright, Gerald C., Jr., N-6
Wurman, Richard Saul, N-13

Yankelovich, N-7
Yankelovich, Daniel, 111*n*, 158, 183, N-6
Young, Gary, N-15

Zagarri, Rosemarie, N-3
Zeigler, Harmon, N-7
Ziegler, Harmon, N-10
Zimmerman, Joseph F., 217, N-3, N-8
Zimmerman, Richard, 215
Zvesper, John, 261, N-9

Subject Index

Abernathy, Ralph, 254–255, 618
abortion, 206–207, 600–601, 635
absentee voting, 192
access to information
 bureaucracy and, 501–502
 the president and, 461–462
accountability, of the bureaucracy, 512, 517
Accuracy in Media (AIM), 325
activism. *See* political activism
Adams, Abigail, 62
Adams, John, 43, 46, 47, 62, 68, 120, 364, 453
Adams, John Quincy, 238, 239, 375
Adarand Constructors, Inc. v. Peña, 643
ad hoc committees, congressional, 407
Adkins v. Children's Hospital, 546
administrative law, 493, 504, 529
Administrative Procedure Act of 1946, 513
adversary system of justice, 527
advertising
 freedom of speech and, 590
 political, 354, 355
 mass media and, 321
 regulating, 380
affirmative action programs, 201, 639–643
African Americans, 132, 150
 black codes, 612
 black English, 124
 civil rights of, 616–622
 black power movement, 620
 economic activism, 620–622
 legal activism, 616–617
 political activism, 617–620
 Fourteenth Amendment and, 576
 major parties' reaching out to, 254–255
 media of, 311
 public opinion on the treatment of, 642
 redistricting and, 362–363
 self-help movement, 620–621
 slavery and current status of, 610
 use of term, 616
 voting behavior of, 200
 voting rights of, 188–189
age, voting behavior and, 200
Age Discrimination in Employment Act, 93
ageism, 609
agencies, federal. *See* bureaucracy, federal
Agnew, Spiro, 397
Agriculture Council, 264, 265
Agriculture Department, 505, 510
air pollution, 389. *See also* Clean Air Act
Alar, controversy over, 263–266
Alexander, Lamar, 180
Alien and Sedition Acts of 1798, 583
aliens, illegal. *See also* immigrants
 definition of, 11
 education of children of, 607–608
Alinsky, Saul, 210
allegiance(s) of citizens, 132–133, 145
Almond, Gabriel, 195
alternative dispute resolution, 561
alternative sentencing, 561–562
amendments to the Constitution, 65, 394. *See also* Bill of Rights; *and specific amendments*
 overturning of federal or state court decisions with, 530
 procedures for proposing and ratifying, 66, 67
American Bankers Association, 283
American Bar Association (ABA), 551
American Civil Liberties Union (ACLU), 569, 590

American Enterprise Institute (AEI), 267, 298
American exceptionalism, as core value, 111
American Federation of Labor–Congress of Industrial Organizations (AFL-CIO), 280
American Independent party, 247, 250
American Medical Association (AMA), 294
American political culture, 111–115. *See also* political culture
 core values, 111
 current challenges to, 133–141
 decline of public trust, 136–137
 downsizing of the American Dream, 139–140
 growing gap between rich and poor, 141
 heightened expectations of government, 138–139
 intergenerational conflict, 133–136
 diversity, 113–114
 revitalizing, 142–146
 redefining patriotism and citizen allegiance, 145–146
 strengthening community life, 144–145
 upgrading and equalizing education, 142–144
 sources of conflict in, 123–130
 individualism and communitarianism, 126–127
 political ideologies, 127–130
 religion, 124–125
 subcultures, 123–124
 sources of order in, 131–133
Americans with Disabilities Act (ADA), 92, 634, 636–637
amicus curiae briefs, 543, 554
analytical shortcuts, in public opinion, 172–173
anarchists, 130
Anderson, Jill, 118
Andreas, Dwayne, 13, 288
Anglos, 627
animals, rights of, 636
Anti-Federalists, 62, 65
Antitrust Division of the Justice Department, 544
appellate courts, federal, 541
appellate jurisdiction, 538
appointments
 of judges, 547
 presidential, 460, 464
apprenticeship system, for members of Congress, 403
Appropriations Committees, 410
arbitration, 561
Archer Daniels Midland, 13, 288
aristocracy, natural. *See* natural aristocracy
Aristotle, 133
Arizona v. California, 16
armed forces
 gays and lesbians in, 632, 634
 integration of, 637
Armed Services Committees, 410
arms, right to keep and bear, 573
Articles of Confederation, 47–49, 62
 distribution of powers under, 45
 Native Americans and, 85
Ashcroft, John, 210
Asian American Political Alliance (AAPA), 631
Asian Americans, 131, 201
 civil rights of, 630–632
assimilation
 of Latinos, 627–628
 of Native Americans, 629
Association of Trial Lawyers of America (ATLA), 279

attitudes, psychological, voting behavior and, 199–200
attorney general, 543
authority
 definition of, 6
 elections as competing claims to, 349–351
 political socialization and overpromotion of, 121–122
 presidential, 452–458
 public opinion and, 152–153
 sources of, 7–8

baby boomers, 134–135
backchanneling, 507–508
Baker v. Carr, 361–362
Bakke, Allan, 640
Bakke decision, 641
balanced budget amendment, 18, 19, 175
Bamford, James, 331
bandwagon effect, 154, 166
Barber, James David, 449, 450–451
Barron v. Baltimore, 574
bases, candidates', 370, 371
Baucus, Max, 390
Beard, Charles A., 53
beats, journalists', 316–318
 the bureaucracy, 330–332
 Capitol Hill, 332–333
 definition of, 328
 judicial, 333–334
 the White House, 328–330
beliefs. *See also* ideologies; religion
 of journalists, 315–316
 public opinion and changes in, 158
Bell, Daniel, 138
Bellotti v. Baird, 570
bellwether state, 374
Bennett, William, 110
Bentsen, Lloyd, 197
Bernstein, Carl, 456
biases
 in data collection for polls, 162
 of journalists, 315–316
 of mass media, 325–328
bicameral legislature (bicameralism), 52, 61
Bill of Rights, 56, 63, 65. *See also* civil liberties; *and specific amendments*
 additional liberties implied by, 598–599
 children and, 570
 civil liberties in, 571–574
 nationalization of, 574–578
Bill of Rights (England; 1689), 41
bills (draft legislation), 390. *See also* committees of Congress; Congress; legislation
 debate on, 416–418
 markup of, 407
 recommitting, to conference committees, 424
 referral of, 411–412
 voting on, 420–423
bills of rights. *See also* Bill of Rights
 colonial, 40
 state, 63, 95, 573
Black, Hugo L., 546, 552, 558, 599
black codes, 612
black English, 124
Blackmun, Harry A., 552, 600
Black Muslims, 621
Black Panthers, 620
black power movement, 620
blacks. *See* African Americans
Blackstone, William, 572
Blinder, Alan, 638

SI-1

block grants, 90
Bloom, Allan, 110
Body of Liberties (1641), 40
Boerne case, 582, 584–585
Boggs, Hale, 419
Boland Amendment, 470
Bork, Robert, 550
Boston Tea Party, 43
Bowers v. Hardwick, 601, 632
Bowles, Erskine, 472
Bradley, Joseph, 624, 625
Bradwell, Myra, 623, 625
Brady Handgun Control Act, 95
Brandeis, Louis D., 100, 598
Braun, Carol Mosely, 351
Brennan, William J., Jr., 95, 533, 552, 555, 568, 580, 615
Breyer, Stephen G., 548, 553
briefs, legal, 543
Broder, David, 359
Browder v. Gayle, 618
Brown, Jerry, 355
Brown, Tony, 620, 621
Brown v. Board of Education of Topeka, 552, 616, 617, 637
Bryan, William Jennings, 241
Buchanan, Bruce, 449
Buchanan, Pat, 234, 236, 316, 366
Buckley v. Valeo, 293, 357
budget
  congressional, 427
  the president and, 460
  process, 437–438
Budget and Impoundment Control Act, 473
Budget Committee, 410
bulletin boards, computer, 313
bundling, of political contributions, 293
bureaucracies
  criticisms of, 122
  definition of, 483, 495
  federal. *See* federal bureaucracy
  key features of, 495–497
  organizational culture of, 500
  politics of, 499
  public vs. private, 496–497
bureaucratic politicking, 499
bureaucratic thickening, 490
bureaucratic widening, 491–492
Bureau of Indian Affairs (BIA), 629, 630
Burger, Warren E., 533, 552, 580, 600
Burke, Edmund, 402
Burnham, Walter Dean, 170, 171
Bush, Barbara, 369
Bush, George, 89, 114, 138, 201, 203, 206, 222, 230, 236, 244, 346, 355, 366, 367, 373, 390, 447, 449, 467, 515, 553
  coercive federalism, 92–95
  "Iraq-Gate" scandal and, 136–137
  the media and, 330, 331
  personality of, 451
  as president, 455, 470, 474–475, 547
busing of students, 637
Butterfield, Alexander, 456
Byrd, Robert, 398

cabinet, 442, 467. *See also* federal bureaucracy
  kitchen, 443
cable television, public-access, 314
Caddell, Pat, 167
Calendar of General Orders, 416
calendars, in House of Representatives, 416
Calhoun, John C., 239
California, water supply in, 3–5
campaign advertising. *See* advertising, political

campaign contributions (campaign finance), 356–358
  by interest groups, 280
  in other democracies, 383
  Political Action Guide on, 358
  reforming, 381–382
  soft money, 357
campaign finance laws, 292–296, 356–358
  Buckley v. Valeo, 293, 357
  political action committees (PACs) and, 292–293
  proposed reforms of, 294–296
  reforms of, 354
campaign pollsters, 167
Canada, campaign finance in, 383
capitalism
  definition of, 7
  laissez-faire, 7, 55, 128
capital punishment, 593–594
Cardozo, Benjamin, 576
Carswell, Harrold, 548
Carter, Jimmy (Carter administration), 8, 90, 114, 167–168, 197, 207, 236, 243–244, 254, 351, 375, 629–630
  as president, 453, 457–458, 467, 469, 470, 547
Carter, Robert, 45–46
Carville, James, 352
casework, 405
Casey, William, 504
categorical grants, 89, 90
Cato Institute, 13, 268, 296, 298
caucuses, 233
  congressional, 395–396, 414–415
  nonsecret and secret, electoral, 234–236
  presidential nomination and, 366
censorship, 583
  in schools, 118
Center for Media and Public Affairs, 325–326
Center for Science in the Public Interest, 322
central government. *See* federal government
cert pool, 554
chambers, Supreme Court, 554
Chandler v. Florida, 334
character of candidates, 350
  voting decisions and, 197–198
charisma, authority and, 7
Charles River Bridge v. Warren Bridge, 552
charter schools, 143
Chavez, Cesar, 270, 628
checks and balances, 57–59
Cheney, Lynne, 110
Cheney, Richard, 511
Chicago Tribune, 308
Chicanos, 628. *See also* Latinos
Chickering, A. Lawrence, 229
chief of staff, 471–472
child labor, 635
Child Labor Act of 1916, 87
children
  civil liberties of, 570
  civil rights of, 635
  of illegal aliens, right to attend public school of, 607–608
Chinese Exclusion Act (1882), 631
Chinese immigrants, 631
Chisholm v. Georgia, 530
Christian Right. *See* Religious Right
Christian Science Monitor, 308
cities. *See* local governments
Citizens for Excellence in Education, 118
citizenship, dual, 44, 48, 76, 574, 576
City of Boerne v. Flores, 582, 584–585
civil codes, 526

civil disobedience, 210–211
Civil Division of the Justice Department, 544
civility, 112
  and Congress, 28–30
civil law, 525
civil libertarians, 569–570
civil liberties, 65, 567–605. *See also* Bill of Rights
  arms, right to keep and bear, 573
  in the Bill of Rights, 571–574
  civil rights and, 610–612
  death penalty and, 593–594
  definition of, 569
  freedom of expression, 583–592
  freedom of religion. *See* religion, freedom of
  Ninth Amendment and, 599
  origin of, 571
  privacy rights, 598–603
    abortion and, 600–601
    high-tech invasion of privacy and, 602–603
    Ninth Amendment and, 599
    sexual orientation and, 601
    wiretapping and electronic surveillance and, 601–602
  taking of liberty and, 594–596
  taking of property and, 596–598
civil rights, 65, 243, 607–644
  of African Americans, 616–622
  of animals, 636
  of Asian Americans, 630–632
  of children, 635
  civil liberties and, 569–570
  definition of, 569, 608
  of disabled people, 634
  of the environment, 636
  of gays and lesbians, 632–634
  of Latinos, 625–628
  of Native Americans, 628–630
  remedies for discrimination, 636–644
  welfare rights and, 649, 650
  of women, 622–625
Civil Rights Act of 1866, 613
Civil Rights Act of 1875, 613
Civil Rights Act of 1957, 190, 617
Civil Rights Act of 1960, 190
Civil Rights Act of 1964, 619, 641
  Title VII of, 590, 638, 640, 641, 643
Civil Rights Act of 1968, 629
Civil Rights Division of the Justice Department, 544
Civil Rights Restoration Act, 642
civil service. *See* federal bureaucracy
Civil Service Act of 1883 (Pendleton Act), 487
Civil Service Commission, 487
Civil Service Reform Act of 1978, 493
Claims Court, 540
claims to authority, elections and, 349–351
class action suits, 205, 531
  restrictions on, 559
classification, security, 502, 503
classism, 609
Clay, Henry, 239
Clean Air Act, 13, 23, 281, 389, 390
  Amendments to (1990), 92, 390–394, 402–423, 481–482, 495
clear and present danger doctrine, 583
clientelism, 513
Clinton, Bill (Clinton administration), 28, 90, 113–120, 142, 154, 577, 601, 643
  1992 election, 198–203, 230, 244, 346–378
  1996 election, 156, 198, 200–203, 353, 365, 371, 372, 374, 378
  balanced budget amendment and, 18

the bureaucracy and, 515–516, 518
campaign contributions and, 295
education policy, 20, 156
federalism and, 95–96
fiscal policy of, 437–439
gays and lesbians and, 632, 634
Native Americans and, 630
nomination of justices, 547–549
personality of, 451
as president, 453, 455, 463, 471, 474
public opinion and, 153, 154, 156
scandals involving, 137
Clinton, Hillary Rodham, 368, 369–370, 465–466, 508
closed primary, 236
cloture, 395, 418
CNN (Cable News Network), 309, 378
coattail effect, 359
Coke, Sir Edward, 38
Cold War, 20
collective goods, 266
collective rationality, 173–174
colonies, 38–41
commander in chief, the president as, 440, 441, 443
commerce, regulation of
   Articles of Confederation and, 48
   the Constitution and, 52
Commerce Committee, House, 410
Commission on Presidential Debates, 248
Committee of the Whole, 416
Committee on Committees, Republican party's, 398
committees of Congress, 407–414. *See also* specific committees
   assignments to, 410, 411
   conference committees, 423–424
   consideration of bills and deliberation by, 413
   joint, 411
   leadership of, 409, 413–414
   referral of bills to, 411–412
   select, 410–411
   structure of, 410–411
   subcommittees, 412
   substantive or policy, 410
common good, 9
common law, 7, 37, 39, 526–527
Common Sense (Paine), 44
Commonwealth of Independent States (CIS), 36, 44–45
Communications Decency Act of 1996, 336, 588
Communist Party of the U. S. A., 246
communitarians (communitarianism), 126–127, 130, 144
   civil liberties and, 569, 570
compacts, colonial, 40
comparable worth, 644
computers, online political communication and, 312–313
concentration camps, 631
concurrent powers, 79, 82
concurring opinion, 555
confederation, 15, 47
conference committees, congressional, 391, 423–424
confidentiality of news sources, 591–592
confirmation hearings, televised, 549–550
conflicts of interest, 406, 514
Congress, 389–435. *See also* bills; House of Representatives; Senate
   as a bureaucracy, 426–427
   caucuses in, 395–396, 414–415

checks and balances and, 57
committees of. *See* committees of Congress
exemption of Congress from laws passed by, 427
external politics of, 424–431
   the bureaucracy, 427–429, 508–509
   oversight function, 428–429
   the president and the White House, 424–426, 462–464, 472–475
   special interests and, 431
   the Supreme Court and, 430
functions and roles of, 392–407
   members of Congress, 401–407
   political parties in, 395–399
   powers and responsibilities, 393–395
how to communicate with members of, 430
internal politics of, 407–424
   committee systems, 407–414
   conference committees, 423–424
   debate and floor action, 416–418
   informal interest groups, 414–415
   staffers, 415
   style and civility, 418, 420
   voting, 420–423
media coverage of, 332–333
members of, 401
   ambitious politicians (politicos), 403
   effective colleague *versus* loyal party member, 403–404
   policy advocates, 404
   profiteers, 405–406
   representative advocate *versus* responsible deliberator role, 401–402
   service providers, 404–405
powers of, 59, 393–394
presidential support for members of, 461
record of proceedings and debates of, 419
reforming, 432–434
veto power of, 428
Congressional Accountability Act, 427
Congressional Black Caucus, 414
congressional budget, 427
Congressional Budget Office (CBO), 426
congressional campaign committees, 233
congressional elections, 236, 244, 358–363
   incumbency advantage in, 350, 359–360
   media dominance in, 359
   money dominance in, 359
   from party dominance to candidate dominance in, 358–359
   the president and, 463
   reapportionment and redistricting and, 360–363
congressional-executive agreements, 459, 528
congressional liaison, 473
Congressional Record, 419, 421
Congressional Research Service, 426
Congress of Racial Equality (CORE), 616, 618
Connecticut Compromise (Great Compromise), 52
conscientious objectors, 582–583
conscription, 445
consequentialism, in ethics, 24
conservatives (conservatism)
   multiculturalism and, 110
   neoconservatives, 130
   as political ideology, 127, 128
Constitution, U. S., 10, 14, 36–37, 44
   amendments to. *See* amendments to the Constitution
   bureaucracy and, 486
   changing nature of, 64–70
      amendments and, 65–66

interpretation and, 66–69
refoundings, 69–70
distribution of powers under, 45
drafting of, 49, 51–61
   checks and balances, 57–59
   division of powers, 56
   key disputes, 51–54
   limited government, 55
   powers of each branch of government, 59–61
   principles and powers, 56–59
   representation issue, 52
   self-interest of Framers, question of, 53
   separation of powers, 56–58
   slavery issue, 52–54
Indian tribes and, 84
patriotism and respect for, 121
ratification of, 61–64
Constitutional Convention (1787), 51
constitutional law, 527
constitutional practice (constitutionalism), 14–15, 36, 51, 111
civil liberties as, 603
origins of American, 37–42
   colonial founding documents, 38–41
   English rights and colonial rights, 41–42
roles and rules of, 68
constitutions
   Internet resources, 103
   republican (representative), 51
   state, 46, 76
Continental Congress
   First, 43
   Second, 44, 46, 47
contracts clause, 596–597
"Contract with America," 102–103, 113, 149–150, 157
convention delegates, 224, 225, 233–234
conventions of political parties, 233–234
convergence, strategy of, 230–231
cookies, 602
Corporation for Public Broadcasting (CPB), 337
correlation, 203
cosmopolitanism, 133
Council of Economic Advisers (CEA), 469
Council on Competitiveness, 475
courts, 523–564. *See also* judiciary; legal system, American
   federal, 60, 539–542
      appellate courts, 541
      appointment of judges and justices, 547–549
      compliance with Supreme Court decisions by lower courts, 556–558
      district courts, 539–540
      influences on, 545–551
      legal standing in, 538
      media coverage of, 333–334, 549–551
      special, 540
   Native American, 538
   state and local, 60, 538–539
      bills of rights and, 95
      compliance with Supreme Court decisions, 557
Court TV, 550
covenant, 40
Cox, Archibald, 456
crimes, 525–526
Criminal Division of the Justice Department, 544
criminal law, 525
critical elections, 242
critical thinking, 121, 122
Cromwell, Oliver, 41
cross-cutting allegiances, 132–133, 229

C-SPAN, 309, 310, 312, 419, 550
cue-taking, 172, 422–423
cultural diversity, 113–115. *See also* multiculturalism
culture. *See* political culture
culture war, 114
Culver, John, 418
Cuomo, Mario, 227
customary law (case law), 527
cyberspace, 103
Cyberspace Law Institute, 602

Dahl, Robert, 287–288
Dandridge v. Williams, 552
Dartmouth College v. Woodward, 546
Daschle, Tom, 113
data collection, biases in, 162
dealignment, 225, 252
death penalty, 593–595
Declaration of Human Rights, United Nations, 645, 648–649
Declaration of Independence, 44–46, 65, 69, 121
Declaration of Rights and Resolves, 43
de facto segregation, 609
defamation, freedom of speech and, 588–589
Defense of Marriage Act, 98
de jure segregation, 609
delegates to party conventions, 224, 225, 233–234
democracy
    the bureaucracy and, 513
    as core value, 111
    crisis of, 114
    definition of, 5, 16
    direct, 16
    improved political participation and, 214–216
    interest groups and, 287–290
    the media and, 337–338, 341
    presidential campaigns and, 378–384
    representative, 16
Democratic National Committee (DNC), 232, 246, 295
Democratic party. *See also* two-party system
    African Americans and, 254
    base of, 371
    delegates to national convention of, 234
    ideology of, 128, 227–231
    New Deal coalition, 241–243
    origins of, 238, 239
    in the South, 239
Democratic-Republicans, 238, 239
Democratic Study Group, 415
demosclerosis, 288–289
denied powers, 82
deregulation, interest groups and, 275–276
description, 21
desegregation. *See* integration
DeShaney v. Winnebago County Department of Social Services, 567–570
developmental rights, 650–651
devolution, 96
Dewey, Thomas E., 164
Dillon's Rule, 81
Dingell, John, 391, 402, 414
direct action, 210
direct democracy, 16
direct initiative, 205
direct primaries, 234, 237
disabled people, civil rights of, 634
discrimination. *See also* affirmative action; civil rights
    definition of, 609

remedies for, 636–644
    affirmative action, 638–643
    equal pay and comparable worth, 643–644
    integration, 637
    reverse, 640
    social factors and, 609
disinformation, 331, 511
disparate impact, 642–643
dissenting opinion, 556
district courts, federal, 539–540
District of Columbia. *See* Washington, D. C.
diversity, 113–115. *See also* multiculturalism
divided government, 221–222, 243–244, 398
division of powers, 56
docket, Supreme Court's, 553
Doe v. Bolton, 600
Dole, Elizabeth, 370
Dole, Robert, 156, 180, 200–202, 224, 253, 288, 330, 350, 366, 368, 369, 398, 439
doorstep opinions, 164
double jeopardy, protection against, 538, 576
Douglas, William O., 524, 535, 536, 546, 598–599
Douglass, Frederick, 611
Downs, Anthony, 169
downshifting in the bureaucracy, 519
downsizing, 138–139, 140, 519
Dred Scott v. Sandford, 87, 530, 552, 578, 610
drug testing, random, 603
dual citizenship, 44, 48, 76, 574–576
dual federalism, 86–88, 93
dual legal system, 537
due process of law, 538, 572, 593
    procedural *versus* substantive, 577–578
    under Fourteenth Amendment, 38, 40, 87, 526, 566, 568, 574, 576, 592, 599
    writs of *habeas corpus* and, 595
Dukakis, Michael, 255, 350, 377
Dunn v. Blumstein, 190

Eagle Forum, 118, 626
Ebonics, 124
economic globalization, 30–31, 273
economy, president as manager of, 441, 445
Edelman, Murray, 213
Edgewood Independent School District v. Kirby, 524–526, 536, 537
editors, interests of, in media, 321–325
education. *See also* schools
    Clinton policy, 20, 156
    upgrading and equalizing, 142–144
    voting behavior and, 200
    of women, 622
EEOC v. Sears Roebuck, 625
Eighteenth Amendment, 66
Eighth Amendment, 94, 593
Eisenhower, Dwight D., 243, 450, 473, 507, 552
    as president, 446, 454
elastic clause (necessary and proper clause), 59, 394
elections, 347–384. *See also* voting
    claims to authority and, 349–351
        character and life experience of candidates, 350
        expertise of candidates, 351
        gender, ethnicity, and religion, 351
        incumbency *versus* outsider status, 349–350
        maturity *versus* youth and vigor of candidates, 351
    congressional. *See* congressional elections
    definition of, 347

functions of, 347–349
    presidential. *See* presidential campaigns and elections
    primary. *See* primary elections
    recall, 205
    stakes and resources in, 349
Electoral College, 364, 374–376
electoral votes, 374
electorate, 187
electronic frontier, 103
electronic surveillance, 601
Eleventh Amendment, 86, 530
elites, 12–13, 16
    natural aristocracy, 62, 63, 285–286
    public opinion and opinion of, 170–171
elite theorists, on interest groups, 288
Elrod v. Burns, 487
e-mail (electronic mail), 313
emergency powers of the president, 459
eminent domain, power of, 597
End of Liberalism, The (Lowi), 288
Energy, Department of, 212
England. *See* Great Britain
    struggle for rights in (1629–1640), 41
English
    black, 124
    as national language, 124
Enlightenment, the, 54, 76
enumerated powers, 78–79, 82
    of Congress, 393–394
    of the president, 440
environmentalists, 22, 263, 281, 389–391
    preemption doctrine and, 94
Environmental Protection Agency (EPA), 8–9, 12, 23, 212, 263–264, 389, 481, 482, 500–501
environmental racism, 205
equal employment opportunity, 638–639
Equal Employment Opportunity Commission (EEOC), 634
equality
    before the law, 111
    of opportunity, 111, 644
    of results, 638, 644
equal opportunity, 636, 638
equal pay, 643–644
Equal Pay Act, 643
equal protection clause of the Fourteenth Amendment, 614, 640
Equal Rights Amendment (ERA), 66, 625, 626
equal time rule, 336
Ervin, Sam, 422
establishment clause of the First Amendment, 578–581
ethical judgments, 24–25
ethics, 24. *See also various political actors*
    bureaucratic, 514–515
    congressional, 432–433
    interest groups and, 299
Ethics in Government Act, 514
ethnic groups (ethnicity). *See also* immigrants; race; subcultures; *and specific groups*
    Democratic party and, 371
    elections and, 351
    media of, 311
    voting behavior and, 197, 202
European Union, lobbying at, 273
Evers, Medgar, 619
Everson v. Board of Education of Ewing Township, 578, 579
exclusionary rule, 577
executive agreements, 458–459
executive branch. *See also* president
    Constitution and, 56
executive bureaucracy. *See* federal bureaucracy

Executive Calendar, in Senate, 417
Executive Office of the President (EOP), 469, 505
executive orders, 458, 529
executive privilege, 443, 592
expertise
  authority and, 7
  of bureaucrats, 502
  of candidates, 351
experts, 11–12
expression, freedom of, 583–592
  freedom of speech. *See* speech, freedom of
  freedom of the press, 591–592

Fair Credit and Reporting Act, 602
Fair Housing Act of 1968, 619, 637
fairness
  as core value, 111
  FCC guidelines to foster, 336
  as goal of journalists, 320
Fairness and Accuracy in Reporting (FAIR), 325
fairness doctrine, 336
faith in institutions, 137, 141
Families First program, 113
Family Education Rights and Privacy Act of 1974, 14, 592, 602
Family Research Council, 98
Fard, Wallace, 621
Farrakhan, Louis, 160, 621
federal bureaucracy, 481–522. *See also* bureaucracies
  access to information and, 501–502
  administration intent and, 500
  administrative law and, 504
  clientele group support and, 505
  congressional relations with, 427–429
  the Constitution and, 486
  depoliticizing, 492
  discretionary authority of, 502, 504
  evolution of, 486–492
  expertise and, 502
  functions of bureaucrats, 497–498
  growth of, 488–492
  independent agencies, 492–493
  Internet addresses for major agencies, 522
  levels of, 491
  media coverage of, 330–332
  merit system, 487–488
  network of bureaucracies, 483–485
  organizational culture of, 500
  politics of, 499–501
  reforming, 512–520
    accountability, 512, 517
    Clinton's "reinventing government" program, 515–516
    democracy and, 513
    equity and efficiency, 512
    ethics, 514–515
    privatizing and downshifting, 519–520
    Reagan's accountability initiative, 515
    representativeness, increasing, 517–518
    top-down reform, 515–516
  relations with other institutions, 505
    Congress, 508–509
    the media, 510
    the president, 505–508
    the public, 511
    special interests, 509–510
  reorganization of, 493–494
  secrecy of, 502, 503
  spoils system, 443, 487
  Ten Commandments of, 507
  types of bureaucrats and their tasks, 485
Federal Bureau of Investigation (FBI), 543–545

Federal Communications Act, 601
Federal Communications Commission (FCC), 335–336
Federal Election Campaign Act (FECA), 248, 292, 356
Federal Election Commission (FEC), 294, 356
federal government (national or central government), 10, 75. *See also* federalism; federal system
  birth-to-death effects of, 83–84
Federal Insecticide, Fungicide and Rodenticide Act, 94
federalism, 15, 75–78
  advantages and disadvantages of, 97–100
  civil rights and, 612
  competitive, 94
  cyberspace, 103–104
  evolution of, 86–96
    Bush's coercive federalism (1989–1993), 92–95
    Clinton's reinventing federalism (1993–), 95–96
    cooperative federalism (1933–1961), 88–89
    creative federalism (1961–1969), 89
    dual federalism (1836–1933), 86–88
    new federalisms (1969 to the present), 89–96
    Nixon's new fiscal federalism (1969–1977), 90
    Reagan's new regulatory federalism (1981–1989), 91–92
  liberal vision of, 101
  libertarian vision of, 101–102
  participation, innovation and, 99–100
  reform of, 102–103
  states' rights vision of, 101
Federalist, The, 62, 64, 76, 79
  on interest groups, 285–286
Federalists (Federalist party), 62, 68, 238, 239
Federal Register, 513
Federal Regulation of Lobbying Act, 291
federal system, 75. *See also* federal government
  birth-to-death effects of living in a, 83
  Dillon's Rule and, 81
  distribution of powers in, 78–86
    concurrent powers, 79
    denied powers, 82
    enumerated powers, 78
    implied powers, 79–81
    Indian nations and, 84–86
    inherent powers and, 81
    local governments and, 81–82
    reserved powers, 78–79
  expansion of, 77
  in other countries, 77
  parties in, 231–237
Federal Trade Commission, 492
federation, 15
felonies, 525
feminism, 623, 624–625
Ferraro, Geraldine, 351
Fifteenth Amendment, 87, 188, 190, 613
Fifth Amendment, 572, 574
  takings clause of, 596–597
filibuster, 418
Finance Committee, Senate, 410
financial aid for students, 176, 178, 271
Finkel, Bruria, 185–186
First Amendment, 94, 113, 336. *See also* civil liberties
  freedom of expression and, 583
  as fundamental rights, 576
  religious freedom under, 578

  establishment clause, 578–581
  free exercise clause, 581–583
First Continental Congress, 43
first ladies, 465–466
Fishkin, James, 180
flag, American, 119
  burning or desecration of, 229, 585, 587
Flag Protection Act of 1989, 585
flat tax, 367
Fletcher v. Peck, 545, 546
Flowers, Gennifer, 378
Flynt, Larry, 588–589
focus groups, 149, 151, 372
Forbes, Steve, Jr., 180, 367
force, definition of, 6
Ford, Gerald, 89, 167, 197, 243, 397, 466, 472
Foreign Agent Registration Act (FARA), 291
foreign interests (foreign lobbyists), 268
foreign news, 334
foreign policy, president's role in, 440, 441, 443
Foreign Relations Committee, Senate, 410
Forman, Milos, 588–589
founders, 37–70, 75–84, 119–121, *et passim*
founding fathers, use of term, 121
Fourteenth Amendment, 65, 87, 99, 188, 189, 526, 530, 613
  citizenship and, 188, 239
  due process clause of, 38–40, 87, 526, 567, 568, 574, 576, 592, 599
  equal protection clause of, 614, 640
  nationalization of the Bill of Rights and, 574, 576
Fourth Amendment
  nationalization of, 576
  wiretapping and, 601, 602
framing, in the media, 318–319
franchise, 188
Frankfurter, Felix, 532, 534, 546, 547
franking privilege, 406
Franklin, Benjamin, 43, 55
  on the Constitution, 61–62
freedom, as core value, 111
Freedom Americans, 254
Freedom of Access to Clinic Entrances Act, 210
Freedom of Information Act, 592
free-enterprise capitalism (laissez-faire capitalism), 55, 128
  definition of, 7
free exercise clause of the First Amendment, 581–583
free riders, 266
French and Indian War (1755–1763), 42
Fried, Charles, 543
Fruit of Islam, 621
Fuller, Millard, 207
Fullilove v. Klutznick, 641
Fundamental Orders of Connecticut, 40
Furman v. Georgia, 593

Gallup, George, 161, 164, 170, 171
Gallup Organization, 161
Garcia v. San Antonio Metropolitan Transit Authority, 92, 93
Garvey, Marcus, 620
gays and lesbians, 132–133
  civil rights of, 632–634
  right to privacy and, 601
Gelb, Leslie, 507
gender. *See also* women
  elections and, 351
  voting behavior and, 201–202
gender gap, 201, 253
General Accounting Office (GAO), 426, 429

General Social Surveys (GSS), 160
generation(s)
	conflict between, 133–136
	voting behavior and, 200
generation thesis, 133–134
Generation X, 135–136
genetic screening, 603
George, Alexander, 451
Gephardt, Richard, 420
Gergen, David, 316
Germany, 561
	campaign finance in, 383
Gerry, Elbridge, 53
gerrymandering, 362
Gilligan, Carol, 25
Gingrich, Newt, 137, 157, 299, 396, 432, 433
Ginsburg, Ruth Bader, 548, 553
Gitlow v. New York, 576
Glasser, Ira, 587
globalization of the economy, 30–31, 273
Glorious Revolution, 41–42
Goldberg, Arthur, 599
Gonzalez, Rodolfo "Corky," 628
Gorbachev, Mikhail, 35
Gore, Al, 368, 369, 439, 467, 515–516
gotcha journalism, 325
government (government actors)
	definition of, 6
	as a political activist, 211–214
		benefits and costs, 213–214
		resistance, 212–213
		types of government activism, 211–212
	political participation by serving and working in, 204
	resistance by, 212–213
	responsiveness to citizen input, 213–214
government associations, 270
Gramm, Phil, 180
grandfather clause, 189
grants (grants-in-aid), 88
	block, 90
	categorical, 89, 90
	revenue sharing, 90
Great Britain. *See also* Parliament, British
	campaign finance in, 383
	Glorious Revolution, 41
	struggle for rights in, 38–42
Great Compromise (Connecticut Compromise), 52
Great Depression, 69, 242
Great Society programs, 89, 138, 142, 213
Green Parties of North America, 247
Greenspan, Alan, 316
Gregg v. Georgia, 593
gridlock, 222, 398
Griggs v. Duke Power Company, 641–642
Griswold v. Connecticut, 598
Guam, 190
Guinier, Lani, 319
gun control, 573

habeas corpus, writs of, 595
Habitat for Humanity, 207
Hale, Lorraine E., 207
Halperin, Morton, 507
Hamilton, Alexander, 48, 55, 62, 65, 120, 238, 440, 486
Hammer v. Dagenhart, 87
Hancock, John, 43
Hand, Learned, 534
hard money, 293
Harlan, John Marshall, 552, 599
Harper v. Virginia State Board of Elections, 190
Harris, Louis, and Associates, 161, 167

Hart, Gary, 198, 378
Hatch Act, 356, 487
hate speech, 589–590
Hatfield, Mark, 477
Hawaii, same-sex marriages in, 98
Hawthorne effect, 179
Haynsworth, Clement, Jr., 548
Head Start, 635
health care, public judgment on, 177–178
Helms, Jesse, 298
Henry, Patrick, 43, 63
hidden primary, 365
Hispanic, use of term, 627
Hispanic Americans. *See* Latinos
Hofstadter, Richard, 110
holidays, national, patriotism and, 121
Hollings, Ernest, 418, 420
Holmes, Oliver Wendell, 583, 635
home rule, 81–82
homophobia, 609
homosexuality, right to privacy and, 601
honest graft, 381
honeymoon, president's, 462–463
Hoover, J. Edgar, 544–545
Hopwood v. Texas, 641
House of Commons, 38, 61
House of Lords, 38, 61
House of Representatives, 52
	committees, 407–414
	elections to, 100. *See also* congressional elections
	leadership in, 396–397
	powers of, 393, 394
	presidential elections and, 375
	size of, 393
	Speaker of the, 396–397
Housing and Urban Development, Department of, 511
Huang, John, 295
Hughes, Charles Evans, 534
Humane Care for Animals Act, 636
Human Life Centers, 207
human nature, liberal vs. conservative views of, 127, 130
human rights, 645–651
Hume, David, 55
Humphrey, Hubert, 403–404
Hussein, Saddam, 136–137
hyperpluralism, 288

ideologies
	of political parties, 226–231
	as source of conflict, 127–130
	voting decisions and, 196
illegal aliens, 627, 628
immigrants
	Chinese and Japanese, 631–632
	reduction of subcultural differences in, 131
Immigration Act of 1924, 631
Immigration and Naturalization Service (INS), 608
Immigration and Naturalization Service v. Chadha, 428
impeachment, 57, 393–394, 456–457
implied powers, doctrine of, 59, 79–82
impounding of appropriated funds, 425, 473
inalienable rights, 572
incorporation of the Bill of Rights, total vs. selective, 574–576
incrementalism, 113, 513
incumbency advantage, 350, 360
incumbency effect, 360
incumbents (incumbency)
	in congressional elections, 359–360

	in presidential elections, 349–350
independent agencies, 492–493
independent regulatory commissions (IRCs), 492–493
independents (swing voters), 230, 371
Indian Citizenship Act (1924), 84, 190
Indian nations, 84–86. *See also* Native Americans
Indian Removal Act, 628
Indian Reorganization Act, 629
Indians. *See also* Native Americans
	use of term, 628
indirect initiative, 205
individualism, as source of conflict, 126–127
individuals, as political actors, 10
infomercials, 355
information cues, voting decisions and, 196
information shortcuts, voting decisions and, 196
information superhighway, 313
inherent powers, 81, 82
	of the president, 442, 459
initiatives, 205
inquisitorial system, 527, 561
Institute for Global Communications, 21
Institute for Media Analysis, 326
Institutes of the Laws of England, The, 38
integration, 637. *See also* affirmative action
	of the workplace, 638–639
intentionalism, in ethics, 24
intentionalists, in legal interpretation, 534
interest group liberalism, 288
interest groups, 11, 263–301
	common good and, 286–287
	definition of, 265
	democracy and, 287–290
	free-rider problem and, 266–267
	functions and activities of, 277–278
	goals of, 274–276
	indirect lobbying by, 267–268
	informal, in Congress, 414–415
	Madisonian dilemma and, 285–286
	members of, 268–270
	monitoring and regulating, 290–299
		bribery and valuable gifts, laws prohibiting, 292
		campaign finance laws, 292–296
		ethics regulations, 299
		monitoring laws, 291–292
		proposed reforms, 294–299
		"revolving door," closing the, 296–297
		"split groups," outlawing, 298
		tax law loopholes, closing, 297–298
	reasons for formation of, 270–274
	resources of, 278–279
	strategies of, 280–284
		adapting to changing circumstances, 280
		campaign contributions, 280
		cooperation and coalition building, 281–282
		inside strategies, 282
		outside strategies, 282–284
intergovernmental relations, 90
intermediate scrutiny test, 615
International Covenant on Civil and Political Rights (ICCPR), 646, 647
International Covenant on Economic, Social and Cultural Rights (ICESCR), 645–646
International Trade, Court of, 540
Internet, political communication on the, 312–313
Internet resources (Web sites), 21
	on 1996 and 2000 electoral campaigns, 366
	Congress, 431

constitution-related, 103
courts and legal system, 527, 554, 561
federal agencies, 522
financial aid for students, 271
media, 308–310
political activism, 215
privacy and high technology, 602
public opinion and surveys, 160–162, 166
interpretation, politics of knowledge and, 17
interviews, survey, 162–164
Intolerable Acts, 43
intragovernmental strategy, 425
invasion of privacy. *See* privacy, right to
Iran-Contra affair, 136, 470–471, 504, 514
"Iraq-Gate" scandal, 136–137
iron law of oligarchy, 288
iron triangles, 282, 510
Iroquois nations, 85–86
issue networks, 282, 510

Jackson, Andrew, 86–87, 188, 239, 377, 443, 487, 552, 558
Jackson, Brooks, 378
Jackson, Rev. Jesse, 197, 207, 227, 255, 351
Jamestown, 38
Japanese immigrants, 631
jargon, 503
Jaworski, Leon, 456
Jay, John, 62
Jefferson, Thomas, 43, 50, 68, 78, 120, 364, 377, 395, 578, 611
  the Constitution and, 65
  Declaration of Independence and, 44
  Louisiana Purchase and, 79–80
  parties and, 237, 238
  as president, 443
Jennings, Peter, 327
Jews, 202, 580, 581
Jim Crow laws, 612
job discrimination, 643
Johnson, Lyndon, 89, 138, 142, 187, 213, 243, 473, 639
  as president, 446, 448, 462, 473
  as Senate majority leader, 397–398
Joint Committee on the Organization of Congress, 432
joint congressional committees, 411
journalists' role in shaping news, 314–320
  biases, 315–316
  framing, 318–319
  goals of journalists, 320
  sources and beats, 316–318
  values, beliefs, and culture of journalists, 315–316
judicial activism, 532, 533, 599
judicial decisions, 530–537
judicial philosophy, 531–537
judicial restraint, 532, 533
judicial review, 57, 68, 69, 529–530
judiciary (judicial branch). *See also* courts; Supreme Court, U.S.
  the Constitution and, 57
  judicial review and role of, 68, 69
  media coverage of, 333–334
  powers of, 60, 61
Judiciary Act of 1789, 60, 537, 595
juries, 526
jurisdiction, 538
  original, 542
jury, trial by, 38, 39
just compensation, 597
Justice, U. S. Department of, 542–545

Keating, Charles, 275
Kellerman, Barbara, 455
Kemp, Jack, 368, 369
Kennedy, Anthony, 581, 585, 587
Kennedy, John F., 7, 18, 243, 450, 619
  as president, 446, 453, 473
Kevorkian, Jack, 211
King, Rev. Martin Luther, Jr., 69, 617–620
King, Rodney, 303–305, 318
Kirk, William F., 264
kitchen cabinet, 443
Koppel, Ted, 320
Korematsu v. United States, 631
Kozol, Jonathan, 117
Krugman, Paul, 31
Ku Klux Klan, 188
Ku Klux Klan Acts, 613

labor, organized, 280, 294, 371
La Crusada para la Justicia (Crusade for Justice), 628
La Follette, Robert, 241
laissez-faire capitalism (free-enterprise capitalism), 55, 128
  definition of, 7
lame duck, 443
Lamm, Richard, 220, 248
La Raza Unida, 628
Lasch, Christopher, 138, 338
Lasswell, Harold, 5
Latinos, 131, 197
  accommodation, 627
  assimilation, 627
  civil rights of, 625–628
  community activism, 628
  major parties' reaching out to, 255–256
  media of, 311
  protest politics, 628
  use of term, 627
  voting behavior of, 200
law(s). *See also* legal system, American
  administrative, 529
  civil, 525
  civil rights and, 610–612
  common, 526–527
  constitutional, 527
  criminal, 525–526
  customary (case law), 527
  interpreting, 531–537
    judicial review, 57, 68, 69, 529–530
  private, 525
  procedural, 526
  public, 525
  substantive, 526
  types of, 525–526
law enforcement, bias in, 560
lawsuits. *See also* class action suits
  political participation through, 204–205
League of United Latin American Citizens (LULAC), 627, 628
leaks, 317, 326, 507
learning, change and, 26–27
learning by doing, 24–29 *et passim*
Leavitt, Michael, 103
left (left-wingers), 228
legal action. *See also* class action suits
  by government actors, 212
  political participation through, 204–205
legal precedents, 531
Legal Services Corporation (LSC), 508–509, 559–560
legal standing, 537, 538
legal system, American, 525–545. *See also* law(s)
  reform of, 559

alternative and mandatory sentencing, 561–562
  alternatives to trials, 561
  demands for efficiency, 560–561
  social inequality and, 559
  structure of, 537–545
    federal court system, 539–542
    Justice Department, 542–545
    state and local courts, 538–539
  three "legs" of, 526–529
legislation, 527–529. *See also* Congress
  president's role in, 440–442
legislative branch. *See* Congress
legislative free-lancing, 422
legislative intent, 413
Legislative Reorganization Act of 1970, 281
legislative service organizations, 414. *See also* caucuses, congressional
legislative veto, 428
legislature, bicameral, 52, 61
legitimacy (legitimation; legitimate authority)
  definition of, 8
  the media's fostering of, 338
  obedience to the law and, 204
  political socialization and, 122–123
  of the president, 452
  public opinion and, 152–153
  third parties' lack of, 249
Lemon test, 579
Lemon v. Kurtzman, 579
letters to the editor, how to write effective, 208
Lexington, Massachusetts, battle of (1775), 43
libel, 588
liberals (liberalism), 371
  federalism from point of view of, 101
  interest group, 288
  multiculturalism and, 110
  as political ideology, 127
Libertarian party, 246
libertarians (libertarianism), 229, 371
  federalism from point of view of, 101–102
  ideology of, 128, 130
liberty, taking of, 594–596
Library of Congress, 421, 426
Liebling, A. J., 340
Light, Paul, 490, 491
Limbaugh, Rush, 207
limited government, 38, 51, 55
Lincoln, Abraham, 69–70, 160, 239, 377, 475
  as president, 443–444
line-item veto, 459
Lippmann, Walter, 170, 171, 173
Literary Digest, 161
lobby(ing), 265. *See also* interest groups
  definition of, 265
  at the European Union, 273
local governments, 75, 76. *See also* federalism
  birth-to-death effects of, 83–84
  powers of, 81–82
Lochner v. New York, 546
Locke, John, 44, 54, 55, 572, 596
Lockwood, Belva, 623
log-rolling, 422
longitudinal studies, 164–165
Los Angeles Times, 13
Lott, Trent, 398
Louisiana Purchase, 79–81
Loving v. Virginia, 614
Lowi, Theodore, 288
Lugar, Richard, 180
Luntz, Frank, 149, 150, 154, 157
Lutz, Donald, 61
Lynch v. Donnelly, 580

McConnell, Mitch, 279
McCord, James, 456
McCulloch v. Maryland, 55, 80–82, 545
McGovern, George, 224–225
McGovern Reforms (McGovern Rules), 225, 252, 353
McKinley, William, 444
McKinney, Cynthia, 360
Madison, James, 49, 55, 76, 97, 237, 578
   the Constitution and, 49, 50, 52, 61, 62, 64, 65, 79
   on interest groups, 285–286
   on political parties, 257–258
   Republicans and, 238
Madisonian dilemma, 285–286
Magna Carta, 38–40, 44, 65
magnet schools, 637
Magnuson-Moss Warranty Act, 74, 75, 92
majority leader, 397
majority party, 224
major parties, 221, 226. *See also* two-party system
Malcolm X, 621
Managing Trustees, 345–346
mandates
   from the electorate, 348, 462
   federal, to state or local governments, 92–93
mandatory sentencing, 188, 562
Mannheim, Karl, 133
Mapplethorpe, Robert, 587
Mapp v. Ohio, 557, 577
Marbury v. Madison, 68, 430, 475, 545
margin of error, in polls, 161–162
marital privacy, 598–599
"mark up," 407
marriage, same-sex, 98–99
Marshall, John, 68, 80, 81, 430, 534, 545–546, 558, 574
Marshall, Thurgood, 36–37, 524, 535, 536, 552, 555, 612, 616, 617
Marx, Karl, 130
mass media, 303–341. *See also* media, the
Matthews, David, 180–181
Mayflower Compact, 40
mechanistic worldview, of Framers, 54
media, the, 13, 303–343. *See also* press, the, freedom of
   the bureaucracy and, 510–511
   bureaucratic strategies for managing, 331–332
   citizen access to, 340
   definition of, 305
   democracy and, 337–338, 341
   government and political coverage by, 328–334
      the bureaucracy beat, 330–332
      the Capitol Hill beat, 332–333
      foreign coverage, 334
      the judicial beat, 333–334
      the White House beat, 328–330
   government funding of, 337
   government regulation of, 335–337
   language of media insiders, 317
   mass, 306–309
   of minorities and women, 311
   news as shaped by, 314–328
      biases, 325–328
      interests of owners, editors, and producers, 321–325
      journalists' role, 314–320
   people's (individual access), 310, 312–314
   presidential campaigns and, 354–355, 378
   presidential strategies for controlling, 330
   reforms of, 339–341
   self-regulation of, 339
   specialized (alternative), 309–310
   technologies and, 340, 341
media associations, 269
media events, 321–322
Media Research Center, 325
mediation, 561
Meese, Edwin, 470
megabills (omnibus bills), 411, 412
Meinhold, Keith, 632, 634
melting pot, 131
mentally ill persons, civil liberties of, 595
mercantilism, 41
Merit Systems Protection Board, 493
Mexican American Legal Defense and Education Fund (MALDEF), 607, 627
Mexican Americans. *See* Latinos
mid-term elections. *See* congressional elections
Military Appeals, U. S. Court of, 540
military service. *See also* armed forces
   conflicts between conscience and, 582–583
militia, 573
Mill, John Stuart, 598
Million Man March (1995), 160
Mills, C. Wright, 288
minorities. *See* ethnic groups; gays and lesbians; women
minority leader, 397
Miranda v. Arizona, 577
Miranda warning, 577
misdemeanors, 525–526
Missouri v. Holland, 459
Mitchell, Andrea, 315–316
Mitchell, George, 390–391
Molinari, Susan, 253
Mondale, Walter, 351, 463, 467
Monroe, James, 65
Montesquieu, Charles, 49, 54
Montgomery bus boycott, 618
Morris, Dick, 366
Morris, Gouverneur, 60
Most Excellent Privilege of Liberty and Property, The (Penn), 40
Motor Voter Act, 191
MTV, 324
Muhammad, Elijah, 621
multiculturalism, 110, 114, 123
multiparty system, 193, 221, 222, 256–259. *See also* parliamentary system
   appropriateness for America, 257–258
   proportional representation and, 258–259
multiple referral, 411–412
Muskie, Edmund, 423
Myers, Dee Dee, 329

Nader, Ralph, 340
Napoleon Bonaparte, 79
narratives, in media accounts, 323
nation
   definition of, 112
   regulation of order and change and, 112
National Archives, 503
National Association for the Advancement of Colored People (NAACP), 616, 618
National Association of Manufacturers (NAM), 280
national bank, 55
national committees of political parties, 232–233
National Community Network, 314
National Congress of American Indians (NCAI), 629
national conventions of political parties, 233–234, 367–368
   preprimary, proposed, 380

National Federation of Republican Women, 253
National Firearms Act of 1934, 573
National Gay and Lesbian Taskforce, 632
national government. *See* federal government
National Indian Youth Council (NIYC), 629
National Issues Convention (NIC), 180
National Labor Relations Act, 242
National Opinion Research Center (NORC), 160
National Organization for Women (NOW), 253, 624–626
National Park Service, U. S., 9
National Performance Review (NPR), 515–516
national primary, proposed, 237, 380
National Republican party, 239
National Rifle Association, 573
national security
   freedom of speech and, 583, 586
   freedom of the press and, 592
National Security Committee, House, 410
National Security Council (NSC), 469, 475
National Socialist party, 585
National Socialist White People's party, 247
National Women's Political Caucus (NWPC), 624–625
Nation of Islam (NOI), 620, 621
Native American courts, 538
Native Americans, 124, 581–582
   assimilation, 629
   and casino gambling, 630
   civil rights of, 628–630
   federal system and, 84–86
   legal activism by, 629
   media of, 311
   militant activism by, 629
   reservations, 85, 86
   use of term, 628
   voting rights of, 189
natural aristocracy, 62, 63
   interest groups and, 285–286
natural law(s) (laws of nature; natural rights), 40, 42, 44, 624
   the Constitution and, 54–55
Natural Law party, 246
Natural Resources Defense Council (NRDC), 263–264, 266, 277, 280, 289
Nature Conservancy, 207
necessary and proper clause (elastic clause), 59, 394
negative campaigning, 377, 378
neoconservatives, 130
Nessen, Ron, 318
Net Activism: How Citizens Use the Internet (Schwartz), 215
Neuman, Russell, 169, 171–173
Neustadt, Richard, 454
New Alliance party, 246
New Deal, 445–446
   cooperative federalism and, 88
   Democratic coalition and, 241–243
   realignment in party loyalties and, 241
New Democrats, 128, 227
New Jersey Plan, 52
New News, 324
New Options for America (Satin), 215
news. *See also* media, the
   as entertainment, 321–323
   guidelines for interpreting, 326–327
newspapers. *See also* media, the
   Web sites, 308
Newton, Isaac, 54
New York, 40, 48
   Iroquois in, 85–86
   lemon law in, 73–75

New York Times, 308, 316
New York v. United States (1992), 95
nexus theory, 536
NIMBY (not in my back yard), 214
Nineteenth Amendment, 189, 190, 623
Ninth Amendment, 572, 599
Nisbet, Robert, 122
Nixon, Richard M., 89, 90, 136, 243, 292, 330, 425, 451, 548, 629
   as president, 446, 473, 552
   Supreme Court nominees of, 425, 548, 552
   Watergate scandal and, 456–457
nomination
   of presidential candidates. *See also* primary elections (primaries)
     changing the process of, 380–381
     state primaries and caucuses and, 366–367
   of Supreme Court justices, 547–549, 551–553
nonprofit sector (third sector), 144–145, 297–298
nonsecret caucuses, 236
no prior restraint, doctrine of, 591
North, Oliver, 470, 514
North Carolina, redistricting of, 362–363
Northwesterners for More Fish, 20
Northwest Ordinance (1787), 48, 77–78, 84
not-for-profit organizations, 144–145, 297–298
nullification, doctrine of, 87
Nullification Crisis (1832–1833), 443

O'Brien, Larry, 461
obscenity, freedom of speech and, 587
obstructionism, 210
O'Connor, Sandra Day, 548, 553, 556, 580–582, 600
officeholders, political parties and, 224
Office of Communications, White House, 329
Office of Congressional Relations (OCR), 473
Office of Government Ethics, 515
Office of Management and Budget, 515
off-year elections. *See* congressional elections
Olson, Mancur, 266
omnibus bills (megabills), 411, 412
omnibus crime bill (1994), 593–595, 603
Omnibus Crime Control and Safe Streets Act of 1968, 602
O'Neill, Thomas P. (Tip), 396, 420
online political communication, 312–313
open primary, 236
open rule, 416
opinion polls. *See* polls
opposition research, 372
Oregon v. Mitchell, 530
originalism, 534
original jurisdiction, 538, 542
Osborne v. Bank of the United States, 81
Otis, James, 42–43
outside strategies, 282–284
"outside the Beltway," 452
outsourcing, downsizing of the bureaucracy and, 519
Overman Act, 445
oversight, congressional, 428–429

packing, in redistricting, 362
PACs. *See* political action committees
Page, Benjamin, 173–174
Paine, Tom, 44
Palko v. Connecticut, 576
Panetta, Leon, 411, 472
pan-Indianism, 629
paper trail, 496

Parks, Rosa, 618
Parliament, British, 38, 61
parliamentary system, 57, 221, 222
parochial schools, aid to, 579–580
Partial Birth Abortion Act, 601
participation. *See* political participation
parties. *See* political parties
partisans (party loyalists), 224, 228
partisanship, of journalists, 320
party activists, 224
party bosses, 232, 234
party caucuses
   in Congress, 395–396
   nonsecret, 236
   secret, 234
party conventions, delegates to, 224, 225
party identification, 225, 226. *See also* party loyalty
   gender differences in, 201
   voting decisions and, 196–197
party loyalists (partisans), 224, 228
party loyalty, 225
   realignments in, 241, 242
party professionals, 224
party realignment reform, 257
party system, 221. *See also* multiparty system; two-party system
Pataki, George, 191
Patent and Trademark Office, U.S., 540
patriotism
   as core value, 111
   definition of, 119
   political socialization and, 119–121
   redefining, 145–146
patronage, 487
Patterson, William, 52
peak associations, 269
Pendleton Act (Civil Service Act of 1883), 487
Pendleton Civil Service Act, 356
Penn, William, 38, 40–41
Pennsylvania, colonial, 40, 41
Pentagon, the, 330
   smart weaponry, 429
Pentagon Papers, The, 591
People for the American Way, 118, 125
People vs. Larry Flynt, The, 588–589
period effects, in public opinion, 165
perks (perquisites of office), 405–406
Perot, Ross, 200–201, 219–220, 222, 248, 341, 350, 355
Perry, H. W., Jr., 552–553
Persian Gulf War (1991), 20, 331–332, 429, 511
personal attack rule, 336
personal computers, online political communication and, 312–313
Philip Morris Corp., 294
physician-assisted suicide, 595–596
Pilgrim Code of Law, 40
plaintiff, 527
platforms, political party, 226–227, 233
plea bargaining, 561
Plessy v. Ferguson, 616
pluralist theorists, on interest groups and democracy, 287–288
plurality voting, 245
Plyler v. Doe, 533, 607, 608, 615, 627
Plymouth, 40
pocket veto, 459
Poindexter, John, 471, 511, 514
policy. *See also* public policy
   definition of, 8
Policy Committee, in Senate, 398
policy wonk, definition of, 8

political action committees (PACs)
   campaign finance laws and, 292–293, 295–296
   campaign spending by, 357
Political Action Guide
   on accessing political information, 21
   on campaign contributions, 358
   on communicating with members of Congress, 430
   on congressional voting records, 421
   on currently active political parties, 246
   on ethical judgments, 24
   on financial aid for students, 271
   on interpreting news, 326
   on political activism, 215
   on writing effective letters to the editor, 208
political activism. *See also* party activists; political participation
   of government actors, 211–212
   resources for learning, 215
political actors, 5. *See also* government (government actors)
   in American politics, 10–13
   public opinion and responsiveness and effectiveness of, 153–154
political analysis, 20–23
political authority. *See* authority
political candidates. *See* candidates
political correctness (PC), 109–110
political culture, 109–146. *See also* American political culture; political socialization
political editorializing rule, 336
political ideologies. *See* ideologies
political knowledge. *See also* political sophistication; public opinion
   increasing, 176, 178
   participation and, 179, 182
political participation. *See also* political activism
   through government, 204–205
   outside government, 205–210
     doing nothing, 210
     electronic action, 209–210
     pressure activities, 207
     visionary action, 208–209
     voluntary action, 205–207
   political knowledge and, 179, 182
   by resisting, 210–211
   as strengthening democracy, 214–216
   by voting. *See* voting
political parties, 11, 219–261. *See also* multiparty system; two-party system; *entries starting with* "party"; *and specific parties*
   in Congress, 395–399
     creating rules, 395
     legislative leadership, 395–398
     party unity, 398–399
   congressional elections and, 358–359
   definition of, 221
   in federal system, 231–237
     congressional campaign committees, 233
     national committees, 232–233
     national conventions, 233–234
     nominating power lost by parties, 234–237
     primary elections, 234–237
     state and local organizations, 232
   identification with, voting decisions and, 196–197
   ideologies of, 226–231
   interest groups and loss of power by, 273
   major, 221, 226
     reaching out to women and ethnic minorities, 252–256

political parties (*Continued*)
    voter dissatisfaction with, 251–252
  majority, 224
  minor. *See* third parties
  platforms of, 226–227
  the president as leader of, 441
  presidential elections and, 353–354
  public opinion and, 154, 156
  reforming the party system, 256–259
  supporters of, 223–226
  third. *See* third parties
political philosophy. *See also* ideologies
  gender differences in, 201
  "political questions," Supreme Court's use of term, 554
political socialization, 115–123
  overpromotion of authority and, 121–122
  patriotism and, 119–121
  political culture and, 122–123
  primary and secondary, 115–116
political sophistication, 168–169, 172–173
political spectrum, 228
political stratification, 169
politics. *See also throughout*
  definition of, 5
  of knowledge, 17–18
Pollock v. Farmers' Loan and Trust Co., 530
polls (opinion polls). *See also* surveys
  accuracy and reliability of, 159–168
    false answers, 163–164
    interpreting poll results, 166–168
    order in which questions are asked, 163
    reasonable range of answers, 163
    timing of polls, 164–165
    wording of questions, 162
  definition of, 151
  deliberative, 179–181
  presidential campaigns and, 368
  "push," 154
  secret, 155
  straw, 160–161
  tracking, 372
poll tax, 189
polygraphs (lie detectors), 602–603
poor, the
  cutbacks in legal services for, 559
  growing gap between rich and, 141
populism, 241
Populist (People's) party, 250
populists, 130
pork-barrel projects (pork), 404
postindustrial society, 138
Powell, Jody, 329
Powell, Lewis F., Jr., 535, 552, 590
power(s)
  definition of, 6
  federal distribution of, 78–86
    concurrent powers, 79
    denied powers, 82
    enumerated powers, 78
    implied powers, 79–81
    Indian nations, 84–86
    inherent powers, 81
    local governments, 81–82
    reserved powers, 78–79
Power Elite, The (Mills), 288
pragmatism, 127, 133
precedents, legal, 531
preemption, doctrine of, 74, 91–92
  coercive federalism and, 92–94
prerogative powers of the president, 459–460
president, the, 437–479
  access to, 460–461
  appointments by, 460, 464

authority of, 452–458
budget and, 460
the bureaucracy and, 505–508
cabinet and, 467
character of, 449–451
characteristics of, 447–449
congressional relations with, 424–426, 462–464, 472–475
constitutional requirements, 447
the courts and, 475–476
executive agreements, 458–459
executive orders, 458
executive privilege of, 443, 592
governing coalition of, 455
health of, 449–451
information access of, 461–462
lame-duck, 443
life cycle of, 462–464
nomination of Supreme Court justices by, 547–549, 551–553
personality (character) of, 449–451
persuasive power of, 454
previous experience of, 447
reforming the presidency, 476–478
resources available to, 460–461
roles and powers of, 59–60, 440–447
  chief administrator, 440–442
  chief diplomat, 440, 441, 443
  chief legislator, 440–442
  chief of state, 440, 441, 443
  commander in chief, 440, 441, 443
  constitutional roles, 440
  development of, 442–447
  emergency powers, 459
  enumerated powers, 440
  inherent powers, 442
  legal powers, 440–442
  manager of the economy, 441, 445
  mobilizer, 441, 444
  moral leader, 441, 444, 455
  party leader, 441, 443
  prerogative powers, 459–460
  representative of the people, 441, 443
  social reformer, 441, 445
  statutory powers, 442
  veto, 442, 459
  world leader, 444
second term of, 464
skills of, 452
special tools used by, 458–460
spouse of, 465–466
titles and names for, 453
veto, 442, 459
vice president and, 466–467
White House staff and, 468–472
presidential appointments, 460, 464
  of judges, 547
presidential campaigns and elections, 236, 243, 353–358. *See also under names of specific candidates*
  1992
    gender and, 201
    religion and, 202
  from activist dominance to media dominance in, 354–355
  constitutional ground rules for, 364
  critical or realigning, 242
  Internet resources, 366
  negative campaigning, 377, 378
  nomination of candidates
    changing the process of, 380–381
    state primaries and caucuses and, 366–367
  from organization dominance to money dominance in, 356–357

parties and. *See* federal system, parties in
from party dominance to candidate dominance in, 353–354
reform of, 375, 377–384
  campaign finance, 381–382
  democratization of elections, 378–384
  improving the content of campaigns, 379
  increasing voter turnout, 382–383
  media responsibility, 378
  nominating process, 380–381
  regulating campaign advertising, 380
stages of, 364–375
  Electoral College, 374–376
  general election campaign, 368, 370, 372–373
  national convention, 367–368
  popular election, 373–374
  secret preprimary, 365
  silent primary, 365–366
  state primaries and caucuses, 366–367
  vice-presidential candidates and, 369
  votes by groups in (1960–1996), 198
presidential electors, 374, 375
Presidential Succession Act, 397, 466
president pro tempore, Senate, 397
Presidents' Summit for America's Future (1997), 206
press, the. *See* journalists; media, the
  freedom of, 591–592
press secretary, the president's, 329
primary caucus, 366
primary elections (primaries), 234, 366–367
  blanket, 236
  closed, 236
  criticism of, 237
  definition of, 234
  direct, 234, 237
  national, 237, 380
  open, 236
  regional, 381
  silent, 365–366
  white, 189
Printz v. United States, 95
prisoners, civil liberties and rights of, 594–595
privacy, right to, 598–603
  abortion and, 600–601
  high-tech invasion of privacy and, 602–603
  Ninth Amendment and, 599
  sexual orientation and, 601
  wiretapping and electronic surveillance and, 601–602
Privacy Act of 1974, 592, 602
Privacy Protection Act of 1980, 591, 602, 603
private law, 525
privatizing, downsizing of the bureaucracy and, 519
probable cause, 576–577
procedural due process, 577–578
procedural law, 526
Progressive (Bull Moose) party, 241
progressivism, 241
Prohibition party, 247, 250
proportionality, 640
proportional representation, 222
  multiparty system and, 258–259
  in primaries, 236–237
  third parties and, 245
proprietary colonies, 40
prospective voting, 348
protectionism, 31
Protestants (Protestantism), 125
public-access cable, 314
public broadcasting, 337

Public Electronic Network (PEN), 185–186
public goods, 266
public health, conflicts between religion and, 581
public interest groups. *See also* interest groups
    definition of, 265
public judgment, 174–176
    in health care issue, 177–178
public law, 525
public opinion, 149–183. *See also* polls
    changes in beliefs and values and, 158
    competence of, 168–176
        analytical shortcuts, 172–173
        collective rationality, 173–174
        political sophistication, 168–169, 172
        public judgment, 174–176
    definition of, 151
    elections as revealing, 348
    elites' opinions and, 170–171
    importance of, 152–154, 156, 158
    improving, 176–182
        collective deliberation, 179
        increasing political knowledge, 176, 178
        informed participation, 179, 182
    Internet resources, 160–162, 166
    legitimacy of political authority and, 152–153
    responsiveness and effectiveness of political actors and, 153–154
public policy
    the common good and, 9
    judicial decisions and, 531
    media's role in setting agenda for, 338
    pluralist theorists' view of, 287
    public opinion and, 170–171
    voting and, 194, 195
public safety exceptions to freedom of speech, 584
public schools. *See* schools
public trust, decline of, 136
Puerto Rico, 190
pure speech, 584
Puritans, 40, 41
"push" polls, 154

Quayle, Dan, 369, 467
questions, survey
    order of, 163
    wording of, 162
quorum, 416
quotas, 640

race. *See* ethnic groups
racial gerrymandering, 362
racism, 609
    environmental, 205
random sampling, 161
Rather, Dan, 456
rational basis test, 535, 614
Rauch, Jonathan, 288–289
Rayburn, Sam, 397, 404
Reagan, Nancy, 369, 508
Reagan, Ronald, 7, 8, 89, 90, 230, 244, 370, 372, 398, 451
    1980 campaign, 155
    1984 campaign and election, 351
    the bureaucracy and, 506–509, 515
    civil rights and, 641, 644
    Iran-Contra scandal and, 136, 470–471
    the media and, 330, 331
    new federalism, 91–92
    as president, 446–447, 456, 470, 494
realigning elections, 242
realignment, 225

reapportionment, 360–361
reasonable access provision, 336
recall of the president, proposed, 476–477
recall elections, 205
recidivism, 594
reconciliation, 437
Reconstruction, 69, 87, 613
    political parties and, 239
    voting rights and, 188
redistricting, 361–363
redlining, 637
red tape, 512
Reed, Ralph, 125
referendum, 205
referral of bills, 411–412
Reform party, 220, 247, 248, 249
refoundings, 69–70
Regan, Donald, 472
Regents of the University of California v. Bakke, 640
regional primaries, 381
registration of voters, 191–192
regulation by government
    independent regulatory commissions (IRCs) and, 492–493
    interest groups and, 275
rehabilitation of prisoners, 594–595
Rehnquist, William, 249, 333, 550, 552–553, 568, 577, 582, 593, 596, 600, 612
Reich, Robert, 508
reinventing federalism, 95–96
"reinventing government" program, 95–96, 515–516
religion
    conflicts between business and, 581
    conflicts over, 124–125
    as core value, 111
    elections and, 351
    freedom of, 578–585
        aid to parochial schools, 579–580
        conflicts between conscience and military service, 582–583
        conflicts between religion and business, 581
        conflicts between religion and public health, 581–582
        conflicts between religion and the law, 582
        establishment clause of the First Amendment, 578–581
        religious displays on public property, 580–581
    voting behavior and, 202
Religious Freedom Restoration Act, 582, 584–585
Religious Right (Christian Right), 125, 351
    censorship in schools and, 118
    ideology of, 130
reporters. *See* journalists
representation
    definition of, 401
    proportional, 222
    in state legislatures, 100
representative democracy, 16
    the media and, 338
representativeness of the bureaucracy, increasing, 517
republic, 16
republicanism, 51, 127
Republican National Committee (RNC), 232
Republican party (GOP). *See also* two-party system
    ascendancy of (1877–1932), 241
    base of, 371

"Contract with America" and, 149–150
delegates to national convention of, 234, 235
Federalists as ancestors of, 238
ideology of, 227–231
origin of, 239
reforming federalism and, 102–103
reregulation, 276
reservations, Indian, 85–86
reserved powers, 78–79, 82
resistance
    government, 212–213
    as political participation, 210–211
retrospective voting, 348
revenue sharing, 90
reverse discrimination, 640
Revolutionary War, 47
    Native Americans and, 85
"revolving door," closing the, 296–297
Reynolds v. Sims, 362
rich, the, growing gap between poor and, 141
right (right-wingers), 228
right of rebuttal rule, 336
right-to-life movement, 635
Right-to-Life party, 247
rituals, patriotism and, 119
Robertson, Pat, 98, 125
Robinson, Michael, 170–171
Rockefeller, Nelson, 466–467
Rodriguez, Demetrio, 523–524. *See also San Antonio Independent School District v. Rodriguez*
Roe v. Wade, 553, 600, 635
roll-call voting, 420
Roman Catholics, 202
Romer v. Evans, 634
Roosevelt, Franklin D., 4, 7, 26, 88, 161, 241–242, 443, 450, 473, 507, 631
    as president, 445–446, 455, 468, 473
    Supreme Court-packing scheme, 546
Roosevelt, Theodore, 241, 631
    as president, 444–445
Roper Center for Public Opinion Research, 162
royal charters, 38
rule, in House of Representatives, 416
rule of four, Supreme Court and, 542
rule of thumb, 173
Rules and Administration Committee, Senate, 410
Rules Committee, House, 396, 410, 412, 416
Rush, Benjamin, 49
Russert, Tim, 316
Russia, campaign finance in, 383

St. Mary's Honor Center v. Hicks, 642
sampling, random, 161–162
San Antonio Independent School District v. Rodriguez, 524, 526, 531, 534–537, 553, 559, 638
Sanchez, Loretta, 255
Sandel, Michael J., 145–146
San Jose Mercury News, 308
Santería Church, 582
Santorum, Rick, 420
Savio, Mario, 583
Scalia, Antonin, 550, 551, 553, 585
scandals, decline of public trust and, 136–137
Schenck v. United States, 583
Schlafly, Phyllis, 118, 626
Schlesinger, Arthur M., Jr., 110, 397
schools. *See also* education
    censorship in, 118
    charter, 143
    integration of, 637
    language courses in, 124

schools (Continued)
   magnet, 637
   pairing of, 637
   parochial, aid to, 579–580
   political socialization and, 116–117
   right of children of illegal aliens to attend, 607–608
school vouchers, 143
searches and seizures, protection against unreasonable, 576–577
search warrant, 576–577
Sears Roebuck, 624, 625
secession, 87
Second Amendment, 573
Second Continental Congress, 43, 44, 46, 47
secretaries of cabinet departments, 442
secret party caucus, 234
secret preprimary, 365
secular humanism, 118
segregation, 97, 616–617
   de facto, 609
   de jure, 609
select committees, congressional, 410–411
self-help movement, African American, 620–621
Seminole Indians, 86
Senate, 52, 393. *See also* Congress
   leadership in the, 397–398
   powers of, 393–394
senatorial courtesy, 547
Seneca Indians, 85
Senior Executive Service (SES), 493
seniority (seniority system), congressional, 395, 409
sentencing, alternative and mandatory, 561–562
separate but equal doctrine, 616–617
separation of powers, 56–58, 61
   civil rights and, 612
   interest groups and, 285
   origins of, 61
sequential referral, 412
Seventeenth Amendment, 65
Seventh-Day Adventist Church, 581
sex. *See* gender
sex discrimination in pay, 643, 646, 647
sexism, 609
sexist speech, 590
sexual harassment, 590
sexual orientation, right to privacy and, 601
shadow wage, 145
Shapiro, Robert, 173–174
Shaw v. Reno, 363
Shays' Rebellion, 49, 50
shield laws, 591
ship of state, 29
Sierra Club, 560–561
silent majority, 243
silent primary, 365–366
Simpson, O. J., 526, 531–532, 550
single-issue groups, 274
single-member districts, 245
single referral, 411
Sirica, John, 456
Sixteenth Amendment, 65, 445, 530
"60 Minutes," 263–264
slander, 589
SlaughterHouse Cases, 576
slavery, 45–46, 87, 610–611
   the Constitution and, 52–54
   Dred Scott case and, 87, 530, 552, 578, 610
   party system and, 239
Smith, Adam, 7, 55, 596
Smith v. Allwright, 190

social and class factors, voting behavior and, 199–203
social inequality, legal system and, 559
Socialist Labor party, 246
Socialist party, 246, 250
socialists, 130
Socialist Workers party, 247
socialization, political. *See* political socialization
social movements, interest groups triggered by, 272
Social Science Data Collection, 166
social wage, 145
Society of American Indians (SAI), 629
socioeconomic status (SES), voting behavior and, 203
sodomy laws, 601
soft money, 293, 357
solicitor general, 543
Sons of Liberty, 43
Souter, David H., 551, 553
South Carolina, 54
   nullification doctrine in, 87
Southern Christian Leadership Conference (SCLC), 617, 618
southern states
   dual federalism and, 87
   nullification doctrine in, 87
   slavery and, 52–54
sovereign, 15
sovereignty, 15, 45
   federalism and, 76
   popular, 15, 16, 44, 76
Speaker of the House, 396–397
special interest associations, 269
special interest groups. *See also* interest groups
   the bureaucracy and, 509–510
   definition of, 265
speech, freedom of, 576, 583–591
   commercial speech exceptions, 590–591
   defamation exception, 588
   hate speech and sexual harassment exceptions, 589–590
   national security exceptions, 583, 586
   obscenity exceptions, 587–588
speech plus, 584
Spirit of the Laws (Montesquieu), 61
split groups, 298
split referral, 412
split ticket, 252, 359
spoils system, 487
stacking, in redistricting, 362
staffs, congressional, 415
Stamp Act of 1765, 42
standard operating procedures (SOPs), 496
standing committees, 407
Stanton, Elizabeth Cady, 624
stare decisis, 527, 542
state constitutions, 46, 76
state courts. *See* courts, state and local
state legislatures, representation in, 100
State of the Union Address, 425
state party organizations, 232
states (state governments), 10, 75, 76. *See also* federalism; federal system
   birth-to-death effects of, 83–84
   coercive federalism and, 92–95
   dual federalism and, 86–88
   powers of, 78–79
   voting restrictions in, removing, 187–190
states' rights, 87
   competitive federalism and, 94
   federalism from point of view of, 101
States' Rights party (Dixiecrats), 243
statutes, 529

statutory powers, of the president, 442
Steering Committee, Democratic party's, 398
Steinem, Gloria, 588, 589
Stevens, John Paul, 639
Stewart, Potter, 553
Stone, Harlan Fiske, 556, 614
straight ticket voting, 252
strategy of convergence, 230–231
Strauss, Bob, 288
straw polls, 160–161
strict scrutiny test, 535, 614
Student Non-Violent Coordinating Committee (SNCC), 618
subcommittees of Congress, 412
subcultures, 123–124
   reduction of differences among, 131
subgovernments, 510
substantive due process, 577–578
substantive law, 526
suffrage, 189
Sugar Act of 1764, 42
suicide, physician-assisted, 595–596
summary disposition, 555
sunset law, 517
sunshine law, 517
sunshine rules, 281
Sununu, John, 472
superdelegates, 225
Super Tuesday, 381
supremacy clause, 74, 78, 99
Supreme Court, U.S., 7, 60, 542. *See also* specific decisions
   confirmation hearings for nominees to, 549–550
   congressional relations with, 430
   constitutional law and, 527
   dual federalism and, 87–88
   how cases come before the, 541
   media coverage of, 333–334
   nomination and confirmation of justices, 547–549, 551–553
   original jurisdiction of, 542
   policymaking role of, 551–558
      agenda-setting process, 552–554
      compliance with decisions of the Court, 556–558
      hearing and deciding cases, 554–555
      writing opinions and announcing decisions, 555–556
   the president and, 475–476
   rational basis test and strict scrutiny test of, 535
   Roosevelt's attempt to "pack," 546
supreme courts, state, 557
surveys, 151. *See also* polls
   Internet resources, 160–162
   methods of, 160–162
suspect classification, 614
swing votes, 371
symbolic acts
   of government actors, 211–212
   political participation through, 204
symbolic speech, 584
system, concept of, 26, 27

Taft, William Howard, 546, 556
takings clause, 596
talk shows, 310, 312
Taney, Roger B., 87, 552
tax(es)
   Articles of Confederation and, 48
   campaign contributions and, 297–298
   colonies' discontent over, 42–43
   flat, proposed, 367

McCullough v. Maryland and, 80
poll, 189
value added, 145
Tax Court, U. S., 540
Tax Division of the Justice Department, 544
tax expenditures, 297
tax loopholes (exemptions), interest groups and, 297–298
Tea Act of 1773, 43
Team 100, 346
Teamsters Union, 294
technology (technological innovation)
 interest groups triggered by, 272
 invasion of privacy and, 602–603
 the media and, 340, 341
Teeter, Robert, 167
Telecommunications Act of 1996, 336
teledemocracy, 340–341
telephones, wiretapping of, 601
television. *See also* media, the
 alternative, 314
 court proceedings on, 550–551
 judicial system and, 549
television advertising. *See* advertising, political
Tenth Amendment, 56, 78, 79, 82, 88, 93, 95, 572
territories, 77–78
Texas, "no excuse" early voting in, 192
textualists, 534
think tanks, 267–268
third parties, 221, 230, 245–250
 currently active, 246–247
 handicaps of, 245, 248–249
 importance of, 249
 issues adopted by major parties, 250
 multiparty system and, 257, 258
third-party federalism, 89
third sector, 144–145
Thirteenth Amendment, 54, 66, 87, 530, 613
Thomas (congressional Web site), 421
Thomas, Clarence, 550, 553, 639
three-fifths compromise, 54
Tijerina, Reies López, 628
Title VII of the Civil Rights Act of 1964, 590, 638, 640, 641, 643
Tobacco Institute, 298
Tocqueville, Alexis de, 66
tokenism, 213
Tories, 42
Tower, John, 471
town meetings, 16
tracking polls, 372
trade, 31
trade associations, 269
tradition
 authority and, 7
 definition of, 7
transition, presidential, 462
treaties, 528
Treaty of Paris (1783), 85
trial(s)
 alternatives to, 561
 by jury, 38, 39
 pretrial publicity vs. the right to a fair, 592
trial balloon, 326
Trilateral Commission, 114
Truman, David, 270, 287
Truman, Harry, 164, 241, 243, 446, 454, 473
 as president, 494
trust, voting behavior and, 200
trustees, members of Congress as, 402
turnout. *See* voter turnout
Twente, George, 118
Twenty-fifth Amendment, 466

Twenty-first Amendment, 66
Twenty-fourth Amendment, 189, 190
Twenty-second Amendment, 443
Twenty-sixth Amendment, 66, 190, 530
Twenty-third Amendment, 190
two-party system, 193, 221–222
 broader representation and stability promoted by, 259
 evolution of, 237–244
  first national parties, 238–239
  modern party system, 239, 241–244
 multiparty system compared to, 257–259
 today, 251–256
  reaching out to women and ethnic minorities, 252–256
  signs of failure, 251–252

unanimous consent agreement, 418
unborn, civil rights of the, 635
uncivil disobedience, 211
underdog effect, 166
unfunded mandates, 92–93
Union Calendar, 416
Union of Soviet Socialist Republics (USSR), 35–36
unitary system, 15
United Nations
 conventions awaiting U. S. action, 650
 Declaration of Human Rights, 645, 648–649
 developmental rights and, 650–651
United States v. Curtiss-Wright Export Corp., 81, 82, 459
United States v. Darby Lumber Co., 88
United States v. Eichman, 585, 587
United States v. Lopez, 95
United States v. Nixon, 558
United Steelworkers Union v. Weber, 641
United We Stand, America, 220, 250. *See also* Reform party
universities, affirmative action in, 640–641
U. S. Chamber of Commerce, 283
U. S. Taxpayers party, 247

value added tax (VAT), 145
values. *See also* culture; ethics; political socialization
 of journalists, 315–316
 public opinion and changes in, 158
 recent changes in, 158
V-chip, 336
verdict, 526
vested interests, 270, 271
Veterans Administration, 494
veto, 57, 59
 legislative, 428
 presidential, 442, 459
vice president, roles of, 466
vice-presidential candidates, 369
Vietnam War, 243, 338
Viguerie, Richard, 298
Vinson, Fred M., 551, 617
Virginia Plan, 52
Virgin Islands, 190
voluntary action (volunteer organizations), 205–207
voter turnout, 191–194. *See also* elections; voting
 increasing, 382–383
voting, 187–203. *See also* elections; voter turnout
 absentee, 192
 Americans' support for, 193
 in Congress, 420–423
 experts' evaluation of, 195
 explaining voting decisions, 196–203

character issue, 197–198
gender, 201
generation, age, and education, 200
ideologies, shortcuts, and cues, 196
major issues and party identification, 196–197
new information, 203
political factors, 196–198
psychological attitudes, 199–200
religion and ethnicity, 202
social and class factors, 199–203
socioeconomic status, 203
marketing techniques and, 195
origin of the word "vote," 187, 348
party identification and, 225
prospective, 348
registration and voting procedures, 191–192
removing state restrictions on, 187–190
reservations about, 194
retrospective, 348
value of, 193–195
voting age, 189–190, 194
Voting Rights Act of 1965, 187, 619
 amendments to, 189, 190, 362
vouchers, school, 143

wage gap, 643, 646, 647
Wallace, Henry, 243
Wall Street Journal, 308, 319
Wards Cove Packing Co. v. Antonio, 641–642
War on Poverty, 89, 138
War Powers Act, 425, 428
Warren, Earl, 552, 576, 599, 617
Washington, Booker T., 620
Washington, D. C. (District of Columbia), 393
 voting rights of citizens living in, 190
Washington, George, 47, 49, 69, 85, 364, 403
 as national hero, 120
 as president, 442–443, 453, 486
Washington Post, 307, 308, 316
Watergate scandal, 243, 354, 456–457
Watts, J. C., 18
Waxman, Henry, 391
Ways and Means Committee, House, 410
Wealth of Nations, The (Smith), 55
Webster, Daniel, 239
Webster v. Reproductive Health Services, 600
wedge issues, 370–372
Weekly Standard, 207
Welch, Jack, 322
welfare rights, 649, 650
Wesberry v. Sanders, 362
What I Can Do to Make a Difference (Zimmerman), 215
Whig party (U.S.), 239
Whigs (Great Britain), 42
whips, in Congress, 397
whistleblowers, 493
white flight, 637
White House. *See* president
White House beat, 328–330
White House correspondents, 329
White House Office, 469, 505
White House Office of Communications, 329
White House staff, 468–472
white primary, 189
Whitewater affair, 198
Who Governs? (Dahl), 287–288
Whole Earth Review, 215
Wilson, James Q., 509
Wilson, Pete, 191
Wilson, Woodrow, 449–450, 477, 547
 as president, 444, 445
winner-take-all system, in elections, 236

wiretapping, 601
Wirth, Tim, 403
Woman's Christian Temperance Union, 623
women. *See also* gender
   civil rights of, 622–625
   comparable worth issue and, 644
   major parties' reaching out to, 252–253
   media of, 311
   wage gap and, 643, 646, 647

women's suffrage, 189
Woodward, Bob, 456
World War I, 88
World War II, 88–89
World War II generation, 134
World Wide Web (WWW, or the Web), 313. *See also* Internet
writ of *certiorari*, 542

xenophobia, 158

Yankelovich, Daniel, 175–178
Yeltsin, Boris, 36
Yorktown, Battle of (1781), 47
Yosemite National Park, 9